The CIA & the Security Debate: 1971-1975

Editor: Judith F. Buncher

Contributing Editors: Charles Monaghan and Henry H. Schulte, Jr.

Contributing Writers: Joseph Fickes and Stephen Orlofsky

**FACTS ON FILE 119 West 57th Street
New York, New York**

The CIA
& the Security
Debate: 1971-1975

The CIA
& the Security
Debate: 1971-1975

Library of Congress Catalog Card No. 75-18070
ISBN 0-87196-358-2
9 8 7 6 5 4 3 2 1

PRINTED IN THE UNITED STATES OF AMERICA

Preface

The debate on national security currently being conducted in the congressional hearings on intelligence agencies can be viewed as a twentieth century variant of the eighteenth century controversy over the ratification of the Constitution. The larger states were troubled by the powers entrusted to the federal government. Sizeable minorities in Virginia, Pennsylvania, and New York discussed approval only after a bill of rights was added, or withdrawing their ratification if the amendments were not a part of the Constitution by a specified date. Thomas Jefferson wrote in 1788,

> *I wish with all my soul that the first nine conventions may accept the new constitution, because this will secure to us the good it contains, which I think great and important. But I equally wish that the four latest conventions, whichever they may be, may refuse to accede to it till a declaration of rights be annexed. This would probably command the offer of such a declaration and give to the whole fabric, perhaps, as much perfection as one of that kind ever had.*[1]

The responsibility given to the federal government for providing "for the common defense" was modified by the guarantees of free speech and that the "people ... be secure in their persons, houses, papers, and effects, against unreasonable searches and seizures," in the First and Fourth Amendments. Two hundred years later, the problem is still basically the same: where does "common defense" infringe upon the individual's civil liberties? Conversely, where does freedom of speech infringe upon the government's national security role?

In implementing its purpose to provide information for the defense of the United States, the Central Intelligence Agency has been revealed in the past year to have intervened in the domestic affairs of Chile, to have opened the mail and compiled dossiers on American citizens, and to have continued to store toxins in defiance of a presidential order, among other deeds still awaiting the final reports of the congressional committees. The Federal Bureau of Investigation's "dirty tricks" department has harrassed, burglarized, wiretapped, and made use of provocateurs and informers in the name of "national security." Using the same phrase, the Nixon Administration has been shown during the Watergate investigation to have used the CIA, FBI, and the Internal Revenue Service to further its own political purposes, placing dissidents under surveillance and delving into their personal habits.

Individual privacy has been further jeopardized by laws passed by Congress for "perfectly laudable legislative intentions" as President Gerald R. Ford stated recently.[2] Separate from considerations of national security, the sheer size of the federal government has generated massive amounts of easily retrievable data. The President has said, "... We must protect every individual from excessive and unnecessary intrusions by a Big Brother bureaucracy." Many editorials have also been concerned with the possible imminence of a world envisioned by George Orwell's *1984,* in which Thought Police overhear every sound and scrutinize every movement; while "Big Brother Is Watching You" in an ubiquitous threat. President Ford sees "the advancement of individual independence—of specific steps to safeguard the identity of each and every American from the pressures of conformity" to be "the greatest challenge of our next hundred years."

October 1975   Judith F. Buncher

---

[1] Edward Dumbauld, ed., *The Political Writings of Thomas Jefferson,* American Heritage Series (Indianapolis: Bobbs-Merrill Co., Inc., 1955), pp. 137–138.
[2] *Text of Remarks by the President to be Delivered at the Dedication Ceremonies at the Stanford University Law School,* Sept. 21, 1975.

Contents

CIA Disclosures and Investigations: 1974-1975

CIA Intervention in Chile

Kissinger consent reported. A major controversy was touched off in Washington by the disclosure Sept. 8, 1974 that the Nixon Administration had approved covert activities by the Central Intelligence Agency in Chile in 1970–73 in an effort to undermine the government of the late President Salvador Allende Gossens.

To finance these activities, more than $8 million was authorized by the so-called 40 Committee, a high-level intelligence panel chaired by Secretary of State Henry Kissinger in his capacity as national security adviser to former President Nixon, according to testimony by CIA Director William E. Colby to the Subcommittee on Intelligence of the House of Representatives' Armed Services Committee.

Colby's testimony, given in executive session April 22, was revealed in a confidential letter from Rep. Michael J. Harrington (D, Mass.), a critic of U.S. Chilean policy, to Rep. Thomas E. Morgan (D, Pa.), chairman of the House Foreign Affairs Committee. The letter was leaked to the *New York Times* and the *Washington Post.*

Harrington asked Morgan to open a full investigation into the CIA's role in the September 1973 military coup in which Allende died and his elected government was overthrown. He said he had appealed to other legislators including Sen. J. William Fulbright (D, Ark.), chairman of the Senate Foreign Relations Committee, and Rep. Dante Fascell (D, Fla.), chairman of the House Foreign Affairs Subcommittee on Inter-American Affairs, but none had been willing to pursue the matter. Harrington asserted Sept. 8 that Congress avoided an investigation for fear it might turn up facts that would "damage or embarrass Kissinger."

Colby's testimony was made available to Harrington by Rep. Lucien N. Nedzi (D, Mich.), chairman of the intelligence subcommittee. Harrington reported the testimony from memory, having been allowed to read it twice but not to take notes. According to his letter, Colby testified that:

■ In 1969, before Allende's election, the 40 Committee authorized about $500,000 to "fund individuals who could be nurtured to keep the anti-Allende forces alive and intact." (The CIA, Colby testified, had spent $3 million to help Christian Democrat Eduardo Frei defeat Allende in the 1964 presidential election.)

■ During the 1970 election, the committee approved $500,000 to help "opposition party personnel."

■ After the election, which Allende won by a plurality, the committee earmarked $350,000 in an unsuccessful effort "to bribe the Chilean Congress" to choose Allende's opponent in the runoff vote.

■ After Allende's inaugural, the committee authorized $5 million for "more destabilization efforts during the period from 1971 to 1973."

■ About $1.5 million was earmarked by the committee to help opposition parties in Chile's 1973 Congressional elections, in which Allende's coalition improved on its 1970 vote percentage. "Some of these funds were used to support an unnamed but influential anti-Allende newspaper," according to Harrington's account.

■ In August 1973, during the wave of strikes which precipitated Allende's downfall, the committee authorized $1 million for "further political destabilization activities." The program was called off when Allende was overthrown, but the funds were spent after Chile's military government was installed, Colby testified.

The CIA's activities in Chile, Harrington wrote, "were viewed [by the Nixon Administration] as a prototype, or laboratory experiment, to test the techniques of heavy financial investment in efforts to discredit and bring down a government."

Disclosure of Colby's testimony brought immediate protests from a number of sources, including Democratic legislators and newspaper editorials. The *New York Times* said Sept. 8 that Colby's testimony indicated the State Department and the White House had "repeatedly and deliberately misled the public and the Congress about the extent of U.S. involvement in the internal affairs of Chile."

Sen. Edward M. Kennedy (D, Mass.) charged Sept. 9 that CIA funding of Allende's opponents "represents not only a flagrant violation of our alleged policy of non-intervention in Chilean affairs but also an appalling lack of forthrightness with the Congress." He noted that the CIA activities disclosed by Colby had been "denied time and time again by high officials of the Nixon and now the Ford Administrations."

Sen. Frank Church (D, Ida.), chairman of the Senate Foreign Relations Subcommittee on Multinational Corporations, which investigated attempts by International Telephone & Telegraph Corp. (ITT) to subvert Allende's government, said Sept. 11 that he was "incensed" by Colby's testimony. During the ITT hearings, two State Department officials—Charles A. Meyer, former assistant secretary of state for Latin American affairs, and Edward M. Korry, former ambassador to Chile—had testified under oath that the U.S. had maintained a policy of non-intervention toward Chile under Allende. They also refused to answer specific questions about what they said were privileged communications on U.S. policy toward Allende.

The staff of Church's subcommittee, headed by chief counsel Jerome Levinson, issued a report, leaked to the press Sept. 16, recommending that perjury investigations be initiated against Meyer, Korry and former CIA Director Richard Helms, who testified during 1973 hearings on his confirmation as ambassador to Iran, that the CIA had not passed money to Allende's opponents.

The staff report also accused Kissinger of "deceiving" the Senate Foreign Relations Committee in secret testimony Sept. 17, 1973, shortly after the Chilean coup. Kissinger had minimized the role of the CIA in Chile's 1970 election, asserting the agency's objectives were "to strengthen the democratic political parties and give them a basis for winning the election in 1976." The report recommended that the record of hearings for Kissinger's confirmation as secretary of state be reopened and that he be asked to give a "rationale" for covert CIA activities in Chile.

(Kissinger's direct involvement in efforts to undermine Allende was described in *The CIA and the Cult of Intelligence,* a book by two former U.S. intelligence officials which was published in June after being partially censored at the CIA's request. A deleted passage in the book quoted Kissinger as telling the 40 Committee on June 27, 1970: "I don't see why we need to stand by and watch [Chile] go Communist due to the irresponsibility of its own people," the *New York Times* reported Sept. 11.)

The State Department, meanwhile, stood by its previous assertions that the U.S. had not intervened in Chilean internal affairs after Allende's election. State Department spokesman Robert Anderson Sept. 9 backed the testimony of

Korry and Meyer before the Senate multinationals subcommittee. Korry defended his testimony Sept. 15, asserting the U.S. had pursued "an extraordinarily soft line" toward Chile during Allende's first year as president, during which Korry was U.S. ambassador.

Colby refused to comment on his reported testimony, although he did not deny that Harrington's account of it was accurate. He emphasized Sept. 13 that the CIA's covert activities in Chile were approved by the National Security Council, and thus reflected "national policy." He added that "the chairman or various members of" key Congressional committees had been kept informed of these activities.

Colby testified for two hours in an executive session of the Senate Armed Services Intelligence Subcommittee Sept. 12. Sen. Stuart Symington (D, Mo.) said after the session that he had been "surprised" by Colby's revelations.

Ford defends CIA actions—President Ford was asked at his news conference Sept. 16, "Is it the policy of your Administration to attempt to destabilize the governments of other democracies?"

Ford responded that it was "a very important question:"

"Our government, like other governments, does take certain actions in the intelligence field to help implement foreign policy and protect national security. I am informed reliably that Communist nations spend vastly more money than we do for the same kind of purposes. Now, in this particular case, as I understand it and there's no doubt in my mind, our government had no involvement in any way whatsoever in the coup itself. In a period of time, three or four years ago, there was an effort being made by the Allende government to destroy opposition news media, both the writing press as well as the electronic press. And to destroy opposition political parties. And the effort that was made in this case was to help and assist the preservation of opposition newspapers and electronic media and to preserve opposition political parties. I think this is in the best interest of the people in Chile, and certainly in our best interest."

Ford added that a committee had been in existence since 1948 to review covert U.S. operations and the information was relayed to the appropriate Congressional committees. (Ford was referring to the 40 Committee, which had been set up by the late President John F. Kennedy to provide Administration control over CIA activities after Cuban exiles trained and equipped by the agency failed in their 1961 invasion of Cuba.) He said he favored retention of the panel and would meet with the Congressional bodies to see whether they wanted any changes made in the review process.

Congressional probes set—Sen. Fulbright announced Sept. 17, as protests grew over President Ford's defense of CIA activities in Chile, that the Senate Foreign Relations Committee staff had

been authorized to study available evidence that official testimony on these activities had been misleading. Rep. Morgan said the House Foreign Affairs Committee also would take up the issue.

The strongest criticism of Ford's statement on Chile came from Sen. Walter Mondale (D, Minn.), who called the statement "unbelievable" and pledged to introduce legislation to establish a Senate select committee to recommend reforms in the control of foreign intelligence operations.

"If we are so concerned about the existence of opposition elements and the preservation of democracy in Chile," Mondale asked, "do we now have a program to help support the democratic politicians and journalists who have now been muzzled, banned and jailed?"

Senate Majority Leader Mike Mansfield (D, Mont.) said he intended to call for a joint committee to oversee covert CIA operations abroad. His proposal was endorsed by Fulbright.

Ford's statement was criticized by a few Republicans, including Rep. John Anderson (Ill.), chairman of the House Republican Conference, who expressed "surprise" over Ford's willingness to assume responsibility for activities undertaken by the Nixon Administration.

The State Department and White House refused to elaborate on Ford's claim that the Allende government had sought to destroy opposition parties, newspapers and electronic media. Acting White House Press Secretary John W. Hushen said he stood by Ford's statement and any further comment would have to come from the State Department. State Department spokesman Robert Anderson said Ford's statement "speaks for itself."

Kissinger role in aid embargo cited—Secretary of State Kissinger personally directed the Nixon Administration's program to curtail economic aid and credits to Chile during Allende's presidency, according to government sources quoted by the *New York Times* Sept. 15.

The Nixon Administration had repeatedly denied there was any program of economic sanctions against Allende, asserting his government's inability to get loans and credits reflected its poor credit risk.

During Allende's tenure in office, the *Times* sources said, Kissinger, then President Nixon's national security adviser, directed a series of weekly meetings at which Administration officials worked out a policy of economic sanctions. The officials reportedly included assistant secretaries in the State, Defense and Treasury Departments, and national security aides of Kissinger.

"The whole purpose of the meetings in the first couple of months after [Allende's] election was to insure that the various aid agencies and lending agencies were rejiggered to make sure that [Allende] wasn't to get a penny," one source told the *Times*.

CIA linked to anti-Allende strikes. The U.S. Central Intelligence Agency directly

subsidized the strikes by Chilean middle class groups in 1972 and 1973 which helped precipitate the military coup against the late President Salvador Allende, the *New York Times* reported Sept. 20.

Intelligence sources told the *Times* that most of the more than $8 million authorized for covert CIA activities in Chile had been used to provide strike benefits and other means of support for anti-Allende truckers, taxi drivers, shopowners and workers.

This contradicted public and private claims by President Ford and Secretary of State Henry Kissinger that the money had been used solely to protect opposition political parties and news media that were allegedly threatened by Allende's Government, the *Times* noted Sept. 21.

According to the *Times'* sources, the CIA's involvement with anti-Allende labor groups was part of a broad agency effort to infiltrate all areas of Chile's government and politics. By September 1973, when the military seized power, the CIA had agents and informers in every party of Allende's Popular Unity coalition, although it failed to infiltrate the extremist Revolutionary Left Movement, the sources said.

Most of the funds that did go to the opposition news media went to the newspaper *El Mercurio,* according to one source, who called the paper "the only serious political force" in Chilean press and broadcasting. (*El Mercurio* editor Rene Silva denied this in a letter to the Inter-American Press Association, made public Oct. 5. "Although I don't participate in the financial side of the company," Silva said, "I am certain that its incomes have legitimate and normal origins...")

One CIA official who justified the covert activities said he nonetheless considered U.S. policy in Chile a failure because "we were not looking for a military coup," the *Times* reported. However, another source said "people on the far right" who were determined to overthrow Allende "were increasingly seen at the [U.S.] embassy in 1972 and 1973."

A number of sources said CIA director William Colby, contrary to published accounts, had fully briefed two U.S. Congressional subcommittees on CIA financing of labor unions and trade groups during Allende's presidency. The panels were the Senate Foreign Affairs Subcommittee on Western Hemisphere Affairs and the House Armed Services Subcommittee on Intelligence.

The *Times* reported Sept. 21 that Kissinger had not mentioned financing the unions and trade groups in briefings before the Cabinet Sept. 17 and the Senate Foreign Relations Committee Sept. 19. The financing was also neglected in a briefing by Kissinger and Ford for nine Congressional leaders Sept. 19, the *Times* reported.

Kissinger reportedly told Cabinet members Sept. 17 that "all we did was support newspapers and political opponents of Allende who were under siege," and that the total CIA investment in Chile since

1964—some $11 million—was "marginal."

The CIA financing of anti-Allende strikers was part of a "get rougher" policy adopted by the Nixon Administration in mid-October 1971, the *Times* reported Sept. 24. Adoption of the policy followed Allende's announcement that Chile would not compensate nationalized U.S. copper firms; the replacement of U.S. Ambassador Edward M. Korry by career diplomat Nathaniel M. Davis; and U.S. intelligence reports that Cuban arms were being smuggled to Chilean leftists, according to the *Times*.

All CIA activities in Chile from that point were conducted under the direct authority and supervision of Davis, one source told the *Times*.

Foreign firms linked to '73 strikes—Companies based in Mexico, Venezuela and Peru had helped finance the middle-class strikes which helped precipitate the military coup in 1973, according to Chilean businessmen quoted by the *New York Times* Oct. 16.

The businessmen were prominent members of SOFOFA, Chile's most important industrial organization. They said $200,000 donated by the foreign concerns had been channeled to striking truck owners, shopkeepers and professional groups in the weeks preceding the overthrow of the late President Salvador Allende.

Protexa and Grupo Mendoza denied any involvement in the Chilean strikes Oct. 15.

The businessmen quoted by the *Times* said they did not know whether the money donated by the foreign firms had originally come from the U.S. Central Intelligence Agency, which appropriated funds to "destabilize" the Allende government. "We did not ask any questions," one businessman said. "We had a very tough time collecting funds both here and abroad because people were giving up hope that things could change in Chile."

Poll shows 60% opposed—A Harris Poll reported Oct. 28 60% of Americans polled opposed the CIA's intervention in Chilean internal affairs before the coup, while only 18% favored it. The Inter-American Press Association reported Nov. 28 that President Ford had turned down its request for the names of anti-Allende newspapers financed by the CIA.

U.S. envoy stirs protests. The nomination of Harry W. Shlaudeman to be the new U.S. ambassador to Venezuela was denounced by sectors of most political parties, including the rank and file of the ruling Democratic Action Party.

The nomination was announced in the U.S. Jan. 3, 1975. It had become known in Caracas in December 1974, stirring protests over Shlaudeman's alleged links with the U.S. Central Intelligence Agency and the overthrow of Chilean President Salvador Allende. The Venezuelan government had said it would accept Shlaudeman despite the protests, asserting goodwill between Washington and Caracas was more important than the reputation of an ambassador.

Shlaudeman, currently a deputy assistant secretary of state for inter-American affairs, had served in the Dominican Republic in 1962–63 and again in 1965, after U.S. Marines landed there, and had been deputy chief of mission in Chile in 1969–73, leaving shortly before Allende's ouster and death. In June 1974 he denied before a U.S. Congressional committee that the U.S. was in any way connected with the Chilean military coup; it was subsequently revealed that the CIA had illegally intervened in Chilean affairs in an effort to subvert Allende's government.

Because of his presence in Chile before the coup, Shlaudeman was accused by Latin American leftists of being connected with the CIA and the coup. In Washington, he was denounced by Rep. Michael J. Harrington (D, Mass.) as a "major participant in the systematic deception of Congress regarding U.S. policy toward Chile" under Allende, it was reported Jan. 5.

CIA linked to Schneider death. The U.S. Central Intelligence Agency participated in two unsuccessful military plots against the Chilean government in 1970, including one which resulted in the murder of the army commander, Gen. Rene Schneider, the *New York Times* reported July 24, 1975.

The CIA acted under orders from former President Richard Nixon to make "a last-ditch, all-out effort" to prevent Salvador Allende from becoming president of Chile, according to U.S. government sources quoted by the *Times*. Allende had won a plurality of the votes in the presidential election Sept. 4, 1970, and he was named president by the Chilean Congress Oct. 24. He died in a military coup that ousted his leftist government in September 1973.

Nixon reportedly gave his orders at a secret meeting Sept. 15, 1970 with Henry Kissinger, then his national security adviser; Richard Helms, CIA director; and John Mitchell, attorney general. Nixon was described variously as "extremely anxious" and "frantic" over Allende's imminent elevation to the presidency. He told Helms in "strong language" that the CIA must "come up with some ideas" to keep Allende from office, and he authorized an initial expenditure of $10 million in the effort, according to the *Times'* sources.

Following the meeting, the CIA's chief of covert operations, Thomas Karamessines, reportedly visited Chile. Upon his return he reportedly briefed Kissinger Oct. 13 on a plot by retired Gen. Roberto Viaux to kidnap Schneider as a prelude to a military coup. Karamessines told Kissinger the plot was unlikely to succeed, and Kissinger recommended that the CIA try to halt the plot but "keep the pressure up" in other ways, according to the sources.

The Schneider plot went forward despite CIA efforts to end it, the sources said. An attempt was made to kidnap Schneider Oct. 22, but he resisted the abductors and was mortally wounded. Viaux was later imprisoned and exiled to Paraguay.

(Viaux denied any CIA links to the plot, according to the Chilean newspaper *La Tercera de la Hora* July 28. He reportedly said in Paraguay: "I do not accept . . . foreigners' involvement in the affairs of my country. I am nobody's puppet." Viaux said he and Luis Adolfo Gallardo, a businessman who claimed to have participated in the plot, would sue the *New York Times* for false reporting.

The CIA was also involved in a second plot led by Gen. Camilo Valenzuela, commander of the Santiago army garrison, who also planned to kidnap Gen. Schneider, the *Times'* sources reported. The CIA authorized its Santiago station Oct. 24, two days after the Viaux plot was foiled, to give the Valenzuela plotters three machine guns and hand grenades to use in another unexplained kidnapping attempt. The Valenzuela plot was later abandoned and the guns were returned to the CIA unused, according to the sources.

Domestic Spying

CIA spied domestically, report asserts. The *New York Times* reported Dec. 21, 1974 that the Central Intelligence Agency, in violation of its 1947 Congressional charter, conducted "a massive, illegal domestic intelligence operation during the Nixon Administration against the antiwar movement and other dissident groups." (The report was written by Seymour Hersh.)

An extensive investigation, the *Times* said, had established that a special, top secret unit of the CIA had maintained files on 10,000 U.S. citizens. At least one antiwar congressman was among those under CIA surveillance, the *Times* said.

The *Times* also said former CIA Director James Schlesinger had found evidence of dozens of illegal domestic operations by the CIA beginning in the 1950s, including "break-ins, wiretapping and surreptitious interception of mail." These activities, which were also prohibited by the agency's charter,* the *Times* said, had been directed against foreign intelligence operatives in the U.S. and not dissident U.S. citizens.

Richard Helms, director of the CIA during the first term of the Nixon Administration and current ambassador to Iran, issued a statement through the State Department Dec. 24 denying that "illegal domestic operations against antiwar activists or dissidents" had occurred during his stewardship of the CIA.

The newspaper quoted several unnamed sources, who insisted that the CIA had discontinued all domestic operations.

One *Times* source said the domestic spying had been directed during the Nixon Administration by James Angleton, chief of the CIA's counterintelligence department since 1954. Officially, Angleton's job was to insure that foreign agents did not penetrate the CIA.

Along with assembling domestic intelligence dossiers, one *Times* source

---

*According to the 1947 law creating the CIA (Title 50, Section 403 of the United States Code), the agency "shall have no police, subpoena, law enforcement powers, or internal security functions."

said, Angleton's department recruited informants to infiltrate the more militant dissident groups. " 'They recruited plants, informers and doublers [double agents],' " the source said. (It was reported Dec. 24 that Angleton had resigned from his post, effective Dec. 31. He also publicly denied the *Times'* allegations.)

A number of former Federal Bureau of Investigation (FBI) officials, the *Times* said, felt that the CIA's decision to mount domestic counterintelligence operations "reflected, in part, the long-standing mistrust between the two agencies." By the late 1960s, one former FBI official said, "all but token cooperation between the two agencies on counterintelligence and counterespionage had ended." (Under U.S. law, the FBI was empowered to conduct domestic intelligence operations.)

Other unnamed *Times* sources noted that J. Edgar Hoover, director of the FBI, in 1970 had broken off all but formal liaison contact between the CIA and the FBI. This lack of a working relationship, another *Times* source said, might have provided impetus to the CIA's domestic surveillance program.

Ford orders probe of activities—President Ford said Dec. 22 that he had read the *Times'* account. He noted that William Colby, current director of the CIA, had assured him that "nothing comparable" to what was described in the article was happening now. Ford also said that he had told Colby "that under no circumstances would I tolerate any such activities under this administration."

Ford received a report from Colby about the *Times'* allegations Dec. 26. The White House declined to make it public.

Chairmen of Congressional committees responsible for overseeing the CIA said Dec. 23 they would hold hearings when the new Congress convened in January 1975. They were Sen. John J. Sparkman (D, Ala.), new chairman of the Senate Foreign Relations Committee, Sen. John C. Stennis (D, Miss.), chairman of the Senate Armed Services Committee and Rep. Lucien Nedzi (D, Mich.), chairman of the Intelligence Subcommittee of the House Armed Services Committee.

Colby confirms CIA domestic spying role. In a report to President Ford Dec. 26, 1974 William Colby, director of the Central Intelligence Agency, confirmed allegations that the CIA, in violation of its 1947 charter, had engaged in the surveillance of U.S. citizens, the *Los Angeles Times* reported Dec. 31. Colby's report indicated that the CIA had compiled files on at least 9,000 U.S. citizens and had engaged in other illegal clandestine activities. The article said some of the activities, "including at least three illegal entries," had been directed against CIA employes suspected of "slipping over to the other side."

Meanwhile, the *New York Times,* the original source of allegations of domestic spying by the CIA, reported Dec. 29 that an unnamed, undercover CIA agent had said that much of the spying against

domestic radicals had been done by the highly secret Domestic Operations Division of the agency. Previously, the *Times* had implicated the CIA's Counterintelligence Division in the domestic surveillance.

During the late 1960s, the former agent told the *Times,* New York City became a prime target for CIA domestic spying because it was considered a "training ground" for radicals. At the height of antiwar activity at Columbia University and elsewhere, he said, more than 25 CIA operatives were assigned to the city. His own involvement, the former agent said, began with the Black Panther movement in 1967 and increased as antiwar dissent escalated in the last months of the Johnson Administration. "And then it started to snowball from there," he said.

The former agent also admitted participating in wiretaps and break-ins meant to closely monitor activities of radicals in New York City. He added that the CIA supplied him with "more than 40" psychological assessments of radical leaders during his spy career.

(The *Times* said it had been able to verify that its source had worked for the CIA as an undercover agent, but the newspaper said it was unable to check all of his information. A high-ranking, unidentified U.S. intelligence officer familiar with CIA operations said the former agent's description of life as a domestic spy "'seemed a little bit far out.'")

The *New York Times* reported Dec. 31 that convicted Watergate conspirator E. Howard Hunt Jr. had been the first chief of covert actions for the Domestic Intelligence Division. The *Times,* noting that Hunt had revealed his activities in testimony to the Senate Watergate Committee Dec. 18, 1973, said his domestic duties included the secret financing of a Washington news agency as well as underwriting the popular Fodor's travel guides.

In an interview with the *Times,* Hunt said there had been strenuous opposition to the establishment of the Domestic Operations Division in 1962, especially from Richard Helms, later director of the CIA, and from Thomas H. Karamessines, later the agency's head of covert operations.

Continental Press, the Washington news agency, was used mostly to supply news articles or propaganda to foreign clients, Hunt said. Fodor's Modern Guides, Inc., then publisher of the Fodor travel guides, was subsidized by the CIA, Hunt said. He added, "We'd undergo his [Fodor's] losses, and he was on the CIA payroll and may still be for all I know." Fodor's books provided "cover" for CIA agents who posed in foreign countries as travel writers, Hunt explained.

In his testimony before the Watergate committee, the *Times* said, Hunt indicated he had been distressed by the agency's connection to Fodor, because it was an improper extension of CIA activity into the domestic field.

In another development, the *New York Times* reported Dec. 30 that three key

officials of the CIA's Counterintelligence Division had resigned effective Dec. 31, after being informed that none of them was to be named chief of the division. (The post had become vacant due to the resignation of James Angleton, who announced his retirement Dec. 24, two days after the *Times* published its first article about domestic spying.) The retiring officers, whose resignations were accepted without objection by Colby, were Raymond Rocca, Angleton's chief deputy; William J. Hood, executive officer of the division, and Norman S. Miller, chief of operations.

In a separate report, *Time* magazine said Dec. 28 that Associate Supreme Court Justice William O. Douglas, former Rep. Cornelius Gallagher (D, N.J.), Rep. Claude Pepper (D, Fla.) and the late Sen. Edward Long (D, Mo.) were among those under surveillance by the CIA. *Time* said Douglas had visited the Dominican Republic in the mid 1960s; Gallagher had contacts with Dominican Republic officials; Pepper was in touch with many Cuban refugees and Long had contact with representatives of foreign companies in the U.S. Pepper subsequently said he had been personally assured by Colby that he had not been a target of the CIA.

The *Washington Post* reported Dec. 31 that a former CIA official had acknowledged CIA responsibility for a number of burglaries in the U.S. The former official, who doubted break-ins against domestic political groups had occurred, said the CIA had engineered the burglary of the Chilean embassy in Washington in 1972, an earlier break-in at the Israeli embassy, and other entries, particularly in New York City, where foreign governments had embassies for the United Nations.

The CIA was principally interested in foreign codebooks, but on occasion, break-ins were done for "harassment purposes in retaliation for something that had happened overseas," he told the *Post.*

Harrington sues to curb CIA—Rep. Michael J. Harrington (D, Mass.) filed suit in federal district court in Washington Dec. 27 to halt the CIA's covert intervention in foreign countries and the U.S. He stated that his court action was meant to "force the CIA to obey its charter," the National Security Act of 1947. As evidence of violations of the charter, Harrington cited covert actions abroad and allegations concerning domestic spying by the CIA, the agency's "involvement in the Watergate affair and the activities of the White House plumbers."

CIA releases Colby letter. Portions of a 1973 report ordered by James R. Schlesinger, then in charge of the CIA, were released for the first time July 8, 1975 by Director William E. Colby. The materials indicated a major increase in some of the agency's domestic intelligence activities, code-named Operation Chaos, during the time in office of former President Richard Nixon. Publication of the materials was known to be the object of legal action undertaken by Morton Halperin, formerly of the staff of the

National Security Council.

The documents released by Colby were in the form of a letter written by him in Dec. 1974 to President Ford several days after the *New York Times* revealed that the CIA had conducted large-scale domestic intelligence operations. In the letter, Colby gave Ford his "full assurance" that the agency was "not conducting activities comparable to those alleged" in the *Times*. He continued: "Even in the past, I believe the agency essentially conformed to its mission of foreign intelligence. There were occasions over the years in which improper actions were taken as noted above, but I believe these were few, were quite exceptional to the thrust of the agency's activities, and have been fully eliminated."

The letter disclosed that Sen. Stuart Symington (D, Mo.) and Rep. Lucien N. Nedzi (D, Mich.) had been briefed two years earlier on the contents of the Schlesinger report. It said that when the agency built its headquarters in 1961 "paid informants" were recruited among the construction workers in order to prevent the installation of listening devices by foreign intelligence services. Before Nixon's inauguration in January 1969, according to the letter, Operation Chaos had only two full-time professional staff members. By 1971, it had a total of 54.

The *Washington Post* July 10 noted that Colby's letter contradicted one of the findings of the Rockefeller Commission report on the CIA's activities. Colby said the CIA project for intercepting mail "was initialed in 1953" and "from its inception" was "fully coordinated" with the Federal Bureau of Investigation. The Rockefeller report dated the FBI's association with the project from 1958.

CIA began domestic spying in 1950. The *New York Times* reported July 16, 1975 that documents released by the Central Intelligence Agency's Office of Security show that the CIA began to collect information on the Socialist Workers Party in 1950.

The papers, obtained by the party in connection with a lawsuit against the government, indicate that domestic spying antedated "Operation Chaos" by almost 20 years, and became part of the CIA's activities three years after its founding. Infiltration of the party's units in the Washington area continued for at least two years after 1968.

The Socialist Workers Party's suit seeks $27 million in damages, charging that its lawful political activities were "illegally" harassed and disrupted by Federal intelligence agencies.

Rockefeller Commission Named

Blue ribbon panel to probe CIA. President Ford Jan. 5, 1975 named Vice President Nelson A. Rockefeller to head an eight-member commission that was to investigate and report within 90 days on allegations of illegal domestic spying by the Central Intelligence Agency.

In a statement Jan. 4, Ford said he was naming a "blue ribbon" panel to "determine whether the CIA has exceeded its statutory authority, ... to determine whether existing safeguards are adequate to preclude agency activities that might go beyond its authority and to make appropriate recommendations." The commission, the President said, would have the benefit of the report on domestic spying by William Colby, director of the CIA.

Others named to the commission were: John T. Connor, chairman of Allied Chemical Corp. and secretary of commerce in the Johnson Administration; C. Douglas Dillon, managing director of Dillon, Read & Co., a New York City investment banking firm, and secretary of the Treasury in the Kennedy and Johnson Administrations; Erwin N. Griswold, an attorney and solicitor general in the Johnson and Kennedy Administrations; Lane Kirkland, secretary treasurer of the AFL-CIO; Gen. Lyman L. Lemnitzer (ret.), chairman of the Joint Chiefs of Staff in the Kennedy Administration and former supreme commander of the North Atlantic Treaty Organization (NATO); Ronald Reagan, who retired Jan. 6 after eight years as Republican governor of California; and Edgar F. Shannon Jr., who retired in 1974 after 15 years as president of the University of Virginia.

None of the commission members, a White House spokesman said, had former connections with the CIA. Rockefeller was the only member with a direct intelligence background. Since 1969, he had served on the President's Foreign Intelligence Advisory Board, a high-level civilian review board established by President Kennedy in the aftermath of the Bay of Pigs invasion. Rockefeller also had close connections to Secretary of State Henry A. Kissinger, whom the former New York governor had employed as a foreign policy adviser in the 1960s. Kissinger, who was reported to have been instrumental in Ford's decision to set up the blue ribbon commission, was, in his capacity as director of the National Security Council, chairman of the 40 Committee, which oversaw the CIA's covert operations.

Congressional reaction to the commission was mixed. Conservative and moderate Republicans and Democrats generally responded favorably. However, liberal Democrats and Republicans complained that the panel failed to represent a broad cross-section of opinion, that its membership was too favorable to the agency and that its members were not familiar enough with intelligence gathering operations.

Ron Nessen, White House press secretary, said Jan. 6 that all members of the panel had been checked and "would not have been picked if they had any connection with the CIA which would hamper them." He said Rockefeller had some knowledge of how the CIA operated.

Nessen said the Ford Administration would not stop CIA officials from testifying before Congressional committees planning to study charges of domestic spying.

In a separate development, the *New York Times* said Jan. 10 that the Justice Department had confirmed a Jan. 9 report by Jack Anderson, the syndicated columnist, that the department's civil disturbance unit in 1970 had submitted to the CIA a computer printout with the names of U.S. citizens. The source of Anderson's article had been James Devine, in 1970 head of the civil disturbance unit, who suggested that the computer list of 9,000 names was the same list cited in the original *New York Times* account. Anderson called the action a legal effort to coordinate overseas surveillance of these persons.

One of the *Times*' sources in the Justice Department said the computerized list contained 10,000-12,000 names and had been destroyed in 1974. He had good reason to believe, the unidentified official said, that the computerized list from the Justice Department was not the same list being maintained amid great secrecy by the CIA's counterintelligence unit.

The *Times* also reported Jan. 10 that the counterintelligence division had sought authority in 1974 to destroy illegal files on U.S. citizens because it feared the newly liberalized Freedom of Information Act, which provided for judicial review of classified national security information to determine whether the material should be made public. The CIA's legal office reviewed the request, the *Times* said, and concluded that the files should be maintained.

Meanwhile, the *Times* and *Washington Post* reported that the CIA had engaged in other covert, illicit activities. The *Post* Jan. 10 cited an unnamed, former high-ranking intelligence officer, who said he had personally taken part in a CIA mail cover operation. Begun because the CIA was unable to obtain sufficient information from U.S. unions serving as conduits for agency funds to anti-communist trade unions in Europe in the 1950s, the ex-official said, the mail cover operation included interception of the mail of AFL-CIO president George Meany and two of Meany's senior international aides.

The *Times* Jan. 8 cited Melvin Crain, a political science professor at San Diego State University, who said that when he resigned his CIA post in 1959, the Post Office Department was covertly assisting the CIA in intercepting and copying the mail of U.S. citizens. CIA colleagues admitted the "mail tapping" was illegal and an unconstitutional violation of privacy, but justified it as necessary "to achieve our mission" of safeguarding U.S. security against the Soviet Union, Crain said. The alleged screening of letters— mostly correspondence from U.S. citizens to friends and relatives in the USSR—was started in the summer of 1958, the *Times* claimed.

Rockefeller panel begins hearings—The Presidential commission investigating charges of domestic spying by the CIA held its first meeting Jan. 13. The eight-member panel chaired by Vice President Nelson A. Rockefeller heard testimony by Colby, Helms and Secretary of Defense

James R. Schlesinger, who succeeded Helms and preceded Colby as director of the CIA. After testifying in secret, Schlesinger told reporters that "certain things did come to light," but he added that the number of "misdemeanors" in the history of the agency "I think is quite small."

The commission Jan. 20 heard additional testimony from Helms, as well as from John McCone, CIA director from 1961 to 1965, and J. Patrick Coyne, former executive secretary of the President's Foreign Intelligence Advisory Board.

The White House Jan. 15 announced the appointment of David Belin, 46, as executive director of the Rockefeller commission. He was counsel to Warren Commission, which in 1964 investigated the assassination of President Kennedy.

Rockefeller probe extended two months. President Ford March 29 ordered a two-month extension of the Rockefeller Commission's investigation of alleged wrongdoing by the Central Intelligence Agency. The extension of the life of the eight-member commission chaired by Vice President Nelson A. Rockefeller was at least partly due, published reports indicated, to a decision to probe allegations of CIA involvement in foreign assassination plots. The panel, which continued to work behind closed doors, held its 12th weekly session March 31.

Rockefeller panel hears Bundy testimony. The Presidential commission investigating alleged wrongdoing by the Central Intelligence Agency heard closed-door testimony April 7 from McGeorge Bundy, national security affairs adviser to Presidents Kennedy and Johnson. Bundy, who spoke to reporters afterward, refused to discuss his testimony except to say that he had no recollection of plots to assassinate foreign leaders. He could not exclude, however, the possibility that some officials might have had discussions along the lines of "how nice it would be if such and such a leader did not exist," Bundy said.

Rockefeller Panel ends CIA probe. The blue-ribbon Presidential commission investigating charges of illegal domestic activities by the Central Intelligence Agency completed its probe May 12. All that remained for the commission, known as the Rockefeller Commission after its chairman, Vice President Nelson A. Rockefeller, was the writing of its final report to President Ford.

C. Douglas Dillon, vice chairman of the panel, said that "with one or two major exceptions" the CIA's domestic activities were peripheral and connected in one way or another to the legitimate work of the agency. Dillon declined to say what the one or two major exceptions were.

"The allegation is that the agency was devoting a large part of its time on domestic areas when it was supposed to be operating abroad. I don't think that was the case," Dillon said.

Henry A. Kissinger, secretary of state, and James R. Schlesinger, secretary of defense, gave closed-door testimony before the commission May 5. Speaking to reporters afterward, Kissinger said that neither he nor the National Security Council (NSC), which he directed, had been involved in domestic spying. Moreover, Kissinger pointed out that while the NSC was supposed to direct the CIA, the NSC was not alone in having a direct channel to the CIA. Asked about published statements attributing domestic CIA activities to concern by former Presidents Johnson and Nixon about anti-Vietnam war activities, Kissinger replied, "No such Presidential concern was transmitted through me or the NSC" to the CIA.

Schlesinger, who headed the CIA for six months in 1973, supported Kissinger's contention that the CIA had received directions from "senior officials" in the Nixon White House who were not members of the NSC. As an example, he pointed out that John D. Ehrlichman, domestic affairs adviser to Nixon, had approached the CIA about aiding the White House "plumbers unit" in obtaining information on Pentagon Papers trial defendant Daniel Ellsberg.

In his remarks May 12, Dillon confirmed for the first time that the commission had looked into allegations that CIA had been involved in plots to assassinate foreign leaders. Acknowledging that these allegations concerned Cuban Premier Fidel Castro and Rafael Trujillo, the Dominican Republic dictator assassinated in 1961, Dillon declined to discuss any conclusions the commission might have reached. He confirmed that the commission had delved into the allegations at the request of President Ford.

On the matter of the assassination of President Kennedy in 1963, another subject of investigation, Dillon said that he had "no knowledge" that Kennedy had been killed in retaliation for CIA assassination plots against Castro. (Schlesinger May 5 had labeled such theories as "simply preposterous.")

This re-examination of the Kennedy assassination had been prompted by charges by Dick Gregory, the comedian and activist, that a film of the assassination clearly showed Kennedy being shot from the front and not from behind as the Warren Commission had found. The evidence indicated that the assassination was a CIA plot, Gregory said. A news photograph, taken shortly after the killing, purportedly showed Dallas police holding men resembling convicted Watergate burglars E. Howard Hunt Jr. and Frank Sturgis, both of whom were CIA employes at the time. (A Federal Bureau of Investigation [FBI] spokesman said May 11 that the Rockefeller Commission had requested that a photographic expert from the agency study the photograph.)

Other conspiracy theorists suggested that Oswald had acted as an agent for the Soviet Union. However, CBS News reported May 9 that Lt. Col. Yuri I. Nosenko of the Soviet secret police, the KGB, who defected to the U.S. 10 weeks after the assassination, told the CIA that the KGB had considered Lee Harvey Oswald mentally unstable and possibly a U.S. agent.

Another theory was based on Oswald's visit to Havana only a few months before the assassination. According to proponents of the theory, Oswald acted on orders from Cuban Premier Castro, who was retaliating against attempts by the CIA to assassinate him.

Former President Lyndon B. Johnson was said to have believed Castro was connected with the assassination. In her syndicated newspaper column April 24, Marianne Means related a conversation she had with Johnson about a year before his death in 1973. Johnson told her in confidence, Means wrote, that he thought Oswald had acted alone but was under either "the influence or the orders" of Castro. Lee Janos, a former aide to Johnson, also wrote that Johnson had speculated shortly before his death "that Dallas had been in retaliation for the thwarted attempt" to kill Castro, it was reported April 28.

However, Castro May 7 called the theory untrue, and said it would have been "irresponsible" for Cuba to have involved itself in the Kennedy slaying.

Senate, House Create Investigative Committees

Senate votes CIA, FBI inquiry. The Senate Jan. 27, 1975 voted 82–4 to create a bipartisan, select committee to investigate alleged illegal spying on citizens and other abuses of power by the Central Intelligence Agency, the Federal Bureau of Investigation and other government intelligence and law enforcement agencies. (In a related development, a House Democratic task force Jan. 29 unanimously recommended establishment of a separate House select committee to probe intelligence abuses by Federal agencies.)

Under the terms of the resolution approving the investigation, an 11-member panel was authorized to investigate "the extent, if any, to which illegal, improper or unethical activities were engaged in by any agency or by any persons, acting either individually or in combination with others, in carrying out any intelligence or surveillance activities by or on behalf of any agency of the federal government." In addition to the CIA and the FBI, the special committee was to scrutinize the Defense Intelligence Agency (DIA), the National Security Agency (NSA), the Bureau of Intelligence and Research of the State Department, the intelligence arms of the Army, Navy and Air Force, and the Treasury Department's Bureau of Alcohol, Tobacco and Firearms.

Senate majority leader Mike Mansfield (D, Mont.) immediately named Frank Church (Ida.), Philip A. Hart (Mich.), Walter F. Mondale (Minn.), Walter Huddleston (Ky.), Robert B. Morgan (N.C.) and Gary W. Hart (Colo.) as the Democratic members of the committee. In anticipation of the panel's creation, Republican minority leader Sen. Hugh Scott (Pa.) Jan. 22 had named Sens. John G. Tower

(Tex.), Barry Goldwater (Ariz.), Charles McC. Mathias (Md.), Richard Schweiker (Pa.) and Howard H. Baker (Tenn.) as the GOP members of the select committee.

Church was subsequently selected as chairman of the committee, and Tower was named vice chairman. The panel was given a budget of $750,000 and ordered to report within nine months.

In an interview after the Senate vote, Church promised that all efforts would be made to avoid leaks of information from the committee. He added that he would not let the inquiry become a "television extravaganza." "It's too serious to be a sideshow," he said.

Creation of the select committee was initially opposed by Sen. John C. Stennis (D, Miss.), chairman of the Armed Services Central Intelligence subcommittee, who said his own established panel should handle the investigation. However, Stennis voted in favor of the resolution after obtaining passage of a floor amendment requiring the select committee to draft written rules preventing leaks of national security information.

Tower also won voice vote approval of an amendment requiring security clearances for select committee employes having access to classified data. To avoid opposition, Tower agreed that the committee itself, not the executive branch, would grant the clearances.

House creates select intelligence panel. The House Feb. 19, by a vote of 286–120, created a select committee to investigate allegations of "illegal or improper" intelligence activities by U.S. government agencies. Speaker Carl Albert (D, Okla.) named seven Democrats and three Republicans to the Select Committee on Intelligence and appointed Rep. Lucien Nedzi (D, Mich.), chairman of the Armed Services Intelligence Subcommittee, as its head.

The resolution setting up the committee authorized an inquiry into the activities of the following: National Security Council, the U.S. Intelligence Board, the President's Foreign Intelligence Advisory Board, Central Intelligence Agency (CIA), Defense Intelligence Agency, National Security Agency, the intelligence branches of the Army, Navy and Air Force, Intelligence and Research Bureau of the State Department, Federal Bureau of Investigation (FBI), Treasury Department, Justice Department, Energy Research and Development Agency, and "any other instrumentalities" of the federal government engaged in intelligence work in the U.S. and abroad. The resolution also directed the committee to submit a final report by Jan. 31, 1976.

Composition of the committee had been contested by House Republicans, who felt the panel should have five Republicans and five Democrats. However, the House voted down, by a 265–141 margin, an amendment by Rep. John B. Anderson (R, Ill.) giving the Republicans half of the committee's seats.

Democrats named to the committee under Nedzi were Reps. Robert Giaimo (Conn.), Don Edwards (Calif.), James V. Stanton (Ohio), Michael J. Harrington (Mass.), Ronald V. Dellums (Calif.) and Morgan F. Murphy (Ill.). The Republicans, who were chosen by Minority Leader John J. Rhodes (R, Ariz.), were Reps. Robert McClory (Ill.), David C. Treen (La.) and Robert W. Kasten Jr. (Wis.).

While Anderson's amendment on equal party representation failed, two others he proposed passed by voice vote. One limited the committee's budget to $750,000, with no more than $100,000 going to outside consultants. The other required strict security precautions to prevent divulgence of classified material, and barred staff members from profiting from books, articles or speeches about the investigation.

Sens. Frank Church (D, Ida.) and John G. Tower (R, Tex.), respectively chairman and vice chairman of the Senate select intelligence investigations committee, said Feb. 18 they would seek to coordinate their probe with the House select committee's to avoid duplication of effort.

Meanwhile, the Presidential investigative commission chaired by Vice President Nelson A. Rockefeller heard testimony Feb. 17 by Howard J. Osborne, former security chief for the CIA. Raymond G. Rocca and Norman S. Miller, former officials in the CIA's counterintelligence division, also testified at the closed hearing.

Ford qualifies pledge on aid. Sen. Frank Church said that President Ford had declined to offer more than a qualified pledge of cooperation with the investigation of illegal intelligence activities planned by the Senate Select Committee on Intelligence. Church, the committee's chairman, met Ford March 5 together with vice chairman Sen. John G. Tower. Church afterward indicated that Ford said he would not issue a written directive ordering federal agencies to accede to all committee requests for data. Ford preferred instead to deal with committee requests on a case-by-case basis, Church explained, adding that the President had deferred a decision on providing the committee with the December 1974 report by Colby on domestic activities of the CIA.

Church announced Feb. 27 that he had received assurances from Colby that the agency would waive the so-called "contract agreement" signed by all CIA employes. The agreement, a secrecy pledge, bound all employes not to reveal information about the CIA.

Church said Feb. 26 that F. A. O. Schwarz 3rd, a New York lawyer, had been appointed chief counsel to the committee.

President opposes dismantling the CIA—President Ford said April 7 he rejected the view that the nation faced "nothing but a grim future of depression at home and disintegration abroad." His vision, he said, was "one of growth and development worldwide through increasing interdependence of nations of the world. My vision is one of peace. And my vision of Americans is a people who will retain their self-respect and self-discipline so that this vision can emerge."

"America will not give in to self-doubt nor paralysis of willpower," he said. "Americans will not dismantle the defense of the United States. And we certainly will not adopt such a naive vision of this world in which we live that we dismantle our essential intelligence-gathering agencies."

Ford calls intelligence 'a vital national institution'—President Ford cautioned a joint session of Congress April 10 not to cripple "a vital national institution," the country's intelligence system. While he recognized the right of Congress to investigate the intelligence operations, he said current rules "make the protection of vital information very, very difficult" and he hoped to work with Congress to develop new ones.

Senate panel gets secret CIA data. Sen. Frank Church, chairman of the Senate Select Committee on Intelligence, said April 16 that the White House had furnished his committee with a report by Central Intelligence Agency Director William E. Colby concerning allegations that the agency had violated its charter, and all but three of "several hundred" Presidential directives the committee had requested. A method was being worked out to handle portions of the remaining documents to insure that his committee would be fully informed, Church said.

The committee's decision to accept some top-secret material with deletions of certain paragraphs represented a softening of its earlier position that it be given executive branch intelligence documents uncensored and without conditions. According to unnamed Congressional sources cited by the *New York Times* April 17, the Church panel had also acceded to the White House demand that distribution of classified materials be limited to a few persons. Moreover, the sources said, the compromise agreement allowed for the deletion of certain paragraphs or sentences and the paraphrasing of their substance.

Meanwhile, the committee heard testimony April 16 from Clark Clifford, the former secretary of defense and a member of the group that drafted legislation creating the CIA in 1947. Clifford had told reporters the day before that he would recommend that the committee support new legislation to control the U.S. intelligence community, a strong Congressional oversight committee and better White House and Executive branch control of intelligence activities. He also said that the National Security Act of 1974, which instructed the CIA to carry out all operations that the National Security Council might order, contained too broad a mandate for covert operations and needed tightening. Drafters of the 1947 law had not foreseen covert operations by the CIA, nor had the Congress that voted for the law, Clifford said.

While the Senate committee pressed forward with its probe, its counterpart in the House, the select committee on intelligence chaired by Rep. Lucien Nedzi, was moving slowly. As of April 9, seven weeks after its creation, the committee did not have a staff director or a staff.

Senate panel bars monitoring of testimony. The Senate Select Committee on Intelligence May 9 rejected proposals that government attorneys be present to monitor closed-door testimony of employes of the Central Intelligence Agency and the Federal Bureau of Investigation. Chairman Sen. Frank Church said committee members felt that the practice would inhibit witnesses from giving candid testimony.

In another action May 9, the committee authorized Church to subpoena employes of federal intelligence agencies as witnesses before the committee. Church said he would do so only when witnesses refused to appear.

These actions, published reports indicated, were among final committee preparations to insure free flow of information to the committee from the intelligence agencies it was investigating. Church and the panel's vice chairman, Sen. John G. Tower, had complained April 23 that "excessive delays" by the White House and CIA in turning over documents were hampering the probe.

House intelligence panel names director. The House Select Committee on Intelligence May 13 named A. Searle Field, 30, as staff director and chief counsel for its investigation of alleged illegal activities by the Central Intelligence Agency and other government intelligence agencies. Field, whose appointment was approved by a 8–2 committee vote, had formerly been an aide to Sen. Lowell Weicker Jr. (D, Conn.) in the Senate's investigation of the Watergate scandal.

Three committee members—Michael Harrington (D, Mass.), Ronald Dellums (D, Calif.) and Don Edwards (D, Calif.)—sought to have former Attorney General Ramsey Clark named staff director but were unsuccessful because other members felt that Clark, an outspoken antiwar advocate after leaving the Justice Department in 1969, could not instill confidence that the inquiry was bipartisan. In final voting, Edwards switched sides, saying "the votes aren't here for Ramsey."

Nedzi resigns House CIA panel post. Rep. Lucien N. Nedzi (D, Mich.) June 12 resigned as chairman of the House Select Committee on Intelligence Activities amid controversy over his failure to ask for a Congressional investigation of the Central Intelligence Agency after having learned in 1973 of CIA involvement in domestic law violations and assassination plans. Nedzi, also chairman of the House Armed Services intelligence oversight subcommittee, said his resignation had been forced by fellow Democrats on the select committee, who had stripped him of all but a "gavel and a title."

The *New York Times* had reported June 5 that Nedzi had been secretly briefed on the illegal CIA activities but had not informed the general membership of the House or asked for an investigation. Moreover, the *Times* said, Nedzi had maintained his silence after being named

chairman of the select committee in February.

Following the *Times'* disclosure, the other Democrats on the select committee, led by Reps. James V. Stanton (D, Ohio) and Robert Giaimo (D, Conn.), sought Nedzi's resignation as chairman. They said Nedzi's effectiveness had been compromised when he, in Stanton's words, "took no effective oversight responsibilities" on learning of improper CIA activities.

A compromise reached June 9 with the aid of Speaker Carl Albert (D, Okla.) momentarily headed off the rebellion. Under the agreement reached, Nedzi was to appoint a subcommittee, which was to investigate the CIA. Nedzi was to remain chairman of the whole committee and direct its probe of all other intelligence agencies. The compromise subsequently broke down because of a dispute over the composition of the subcommittee. The committee's six other Democrats protested that Nedzi's appointments to the subcommittee had ignored seniority on the full committee. Nedzi had refused to appoint to the subcommittee Reps. Michael Harrington and Ronald V. Dellums, the committee's harshest critics of the CIA.

When Nedzi refused to yield on the issue, the Democrats met and voted 6–1 June 11 to enlarge the subcommittee and to adopt House Democratic caucus rules that would force Nedzi to take seniority into account. Nedzi's resignation soon followed.

Shortly after Nedzi announced his resignation, the newly enlarged subcommittee attempted to hold a committee session as previously planned. The session had to be called off, however, when Republican members of the committee boycotted it because of uncertainty over its legality.

House rejects Nedzi resignation—The House June 16, by a 290–64 vote, rejected Rep. Nedzi's resignation. After the vote, however, Nedzi said he still could not continue as the panel's chairman. Given the current constitution of the committee, Nedzi said, "I frankly don't see how I could make a valuable contribution."

Following the vote, Rep. B. F. Sisk (D, Calif.) introduced a resolution calling for the abolition of the committee, whose investigation of U. S. intelligence operations had been delayed by internal dissension. But it was reported June 18 that House committee action on the resolution had been put off and that Speaker Carl Albert (D, Okla.) was seeking to reconstitute the committee. He was opposed to doing away with the panel, Albert said, because such a move would be seen as a "cover-up."

In a related development, the House Armed Services Committee voted 16–13 June 16 to deny Rep. Michael Harrington (D, Mass.), a former member of the committee, access to its classified files pending a formal ruling by the House Ethics Committee on Harrington's admission that he had made public classified committee transcripts on Central Intelligence Agency involvement in Chilean politics. (Harrington was also a member of the

House Select Committee on Intelligence Activities.)

Heretofore secret transcripts of Harrington's Sept. 25, 1974 testimony before the Armed Services subcommittee on Intelligence, released June 16, indicated that Harrington in June 1974 had inspected secret committee files on CIA testimony on its Chilean operations. Harrington testified that he had sought public hearings on the CIA's activities, and had briefed several of his own aides, an aide to Sen. Frank Church (D, Ida.) and Lawrence Stern, a *Washington Post* reporter. When the *New York Times* subsequently published a story on CIA operations in Chile, based on other sources than him, Harrington said, he told Stern not to feel bound by any confidences. In acknowledging the disclosure, Harrington testified he was concerned about public statements by U. S. officials denying any U. S. involvement in the Sept. 1973 overthrow of Chilean President Salvador Allende.

House replaces spy panel—The House of Representatives July 17 abolished its Select Committee on Intelligence and replaced it with a larger unit having the same authority. Disagreement about two members of the old committee, neither of whom was named to the reconstituted one, had hampered the work of the group in recent weeks.

House Speaker Carl Albert named Rep. Otis G. Pike (D, N.Y.), not previously a member of the intelligence panel, to head the new committee, replacing Rep Lucien N. Nedzi, whose credibility had been challenged after earlier disclosures that he had failed to act on briefings of illegal Central Intelligence Agency activities. Rep. Michael J. Harrington was not reappointed. The size of the committee was enlarged from 10 to 13. The new members named by Albert were Reps. Les Aspin (D, Wis.), Dale Milford (D, Tex.), Philip H. Hayes (D, Ind.) and James P. Johnson (R, Colo.). The *Washington Post* July 23 reported that Rep. Donald Edwards (D, Cal.) had resigned the previous day under pressure of duties as head of a House Judiciary subcommittee and had been replaced by Rep. William Lehman (D, Fla.).

Harrington July 8 defended his publication of secret testimony on CIA activities and branded as "astonishing hypocrisy" the resulting vote by the House Armed Services Committee in June to bar him from further access to its classified materials. He explained that in his view "signing a secrecy pledge does not excuse a Congressman or any other citizen from reporting evidence of a crime. Ordinarily those who sign such agreements expect to see references to secret but legal activities. The enforcement of such an agreement to keep illegal activities secret is itself illegal." He told of a letter to House Speaker Albert, requesting a ruling from the House Democratic Policy and Steering Committee, in which he asked: "What is the responsibility of a member who discovers in classified records a clear indication that his government has broken the law?"

Harrington claimed that the June attack on himself had shifted the controversy "from Lucien Nedzi's shortcomings as an overseer of intelligence operations to Michael Harrington's alleged recklessness in handling official secrets—all on the very day that Nedzi's resignation as select committee chairman was taken up by the House. It does not take a conspiratorial mind to see it as part of a brazen attempt to subvert the select committee investigation."

White House surveillance denied. Administration and CIA officials July 10 denied reports emanating from the House Select Committee on Intelligence, said to have been based on unreleased CIA documents, that the agency had maintained an operative on the staff of the Nixon White House whose function was to secretly provide the agency with information on activities there.

The *New York Times* July 9 had cited a memorandum prepared the previous day by A. Searle Field, the House committee's staff director, indicating the existence of the classified CIA materials. The *Times* reported that an unidentified source close to the House investigation regarded the CIA materials as giving no evidence that President Nixon was aware of this "infiltration of the executive," as Field called it. In its article that day and in subsequent ones, the *Times* said the CIA documents were an unreleased portion of a 1973 study ordered by James R. Schlesinger, then the agency's director, parts of which had been made public July 8 by Director William E. Colby.

CBS television reported July 10 that the CIA document had been made available to it by Rep. Lucien N. Nedzi, chairman of the House committee. The network quoted Nedzi as saying "the issue" was whether the alleged placement of a CIA operative in the White House, or in other branches of the government, had been done "without the knowledge of the office in which the individuals were serving."

CIA Director Colby declared July 10 that the agency had "never done anything with respect to the White House that's not known to the White House" and that reports of infiltration were "outrageous nonsense." Ron Nessen, the presidential press secretary, said there "may be a handful" of CIA agents working at the White House but that their employment "shows up on the payroll . . . they're here quite openly."

The *New York Times* said Rep. Nedzi read a page of the CIA document July 11 which indicated the agency had "detailed" employes to the White House from time to time. However, the paper quoted Nedzi as saying he had heard "nothing" to support claims that a high-level CIA operative had been in the White House when Richard Nixon was in office. Nedzi specifically denied charges by L. Fletcher Prouty, a former Defense Department intelligence officer, that Alexander P. Butterfield, a former Nixon aide in the White House, had been a CIA agent. Col. Prouty, once the Air Force's liaison with the CIA, had told reporters that Butterfield had been the agency's "contact man" in the White House and that Gen. Alexander M. Haig, former chief of staff for Nixon, had been the Army's "contact" with the agency. Prouty said his information came from E. Howard Hunt Jr., a former CIA agent convicted of participating in the Watergate break-in. He said "detailed" CIA personnel went to government jobs "with the knowledge of the department head" but that "if you run that through three or four generations of supervisors" the knowledge "disappeared."

The CIA issued a statement July 11 insisting that Butterfield had "never been an employe" of the agency and had "never been assigned to or worked for" it "in any capacity." It said that "detailing" employes was a "long-established and widespread practice in government."

Butterfield declared July 13 that while on Nixon's staff he "had no contact whatsoever with the CIA" and that he had "never met Howard Hunt in my life." He said Prouty's allegations were "tantamount to a charge of perjury."

In a July 14 telephone interview with the *Springfield (Mass.) Daily News,* Prouty said: "They may have told me the wrong name to cover up the real informer." According to the *New York Times,* however, Prouty denied July 15 that he had made such a statement the previous day. Interviewed July 15 at Eglin Air Force Base in Florida by CBS television, Hunt said the report about Butterfield had been "an unfortunate invention on Mr. Prouty's part." Also interviewed by CBS that day, Prouty declared: "The name that they mentioned was Butterfield. The only name that I heard in the office was Butterfield."

In a related development, the *Washington Post* July 12 reported that Mary M. Wengrzynek, a clerical assistant to Peter G. Peterson when he was commerce secretary, said she had been detailed by the CIA to work at the White House. But the Post quoted Wengrzynek as saying, "I swear to God I didn't report back to the CIA."

Colby, Helms Testify

CIA chief answers domestic spying charges. William E. Colby, director of the Central Intelligence Agency, Jan. 15 told a Senate subcommittee that his agency in the past had engaged in domestic intelligence gathering activities. However, he "flatly" denied that these activities amounted to "a massive, illegal domestic intelligence operation," as alleged in the *New York Times* of Dec. 22, 1974.

Colby's denial was contained in a report he made to the Intelligence Subcommittee of the Senate Appropriations Committee, one of four Congressional panels probing the charges by the *Times.* (These investigations were expected to be superseded by a bipartisan, select Senate committee, whose creation was approved Jan. 20 by a Senate Democratic caucus vote of 45–7.)

In his report, a text of which was released to the press, Colby conceded that CIA agents had infiltrated dissident and antiwar political groups in the U.S., opened the mail of private citizens, tapped the telephone of U.S. residents and participated in a government counterintelligence program that led to the amassment of files on 10,000 U.S. citizens. Colby insisted that such "missteps" in the 27-year history of the CIA were "few and far between and were exceptions to the thrust of the agency's. . . primary mission," the collection and production of foreign intelligence.

Colby's report was essentially an attempted refutation of allegations by the *Times.* As to the assertion that the CIA had accumulated files on dissident groups in the U.S., Colby replied that in 1967, in connection with the investigation of the National Advisory Commission on Civil Disorders, the CIA established a Counterintelligence Office "to look into the possibility of foreign links to American dissident elements." "Periodically, thereafter, various reports were drawn up on the foreign aspects of the antiwar, youth and similar movements and their possible links to American counterparts."

Beginning in 1970, Colby said, the agency participated in the Nixon Administration's interagency intelligence evaluation program, which was instituted after the so-called Huston plan was scrapped. In the course of the program, the CIA sought "to obtain access to foreign circles" and "recruited or inserted about a dozen individuals into American dissident circles in order to establish their credentials for operations abroad," Colby stated. During this time, Colby said, "some individuals submitted reports on the activities" of the dissidents. This information was reported to the Federal Bureau of Investigation and "in the process . . . was also placed in CIA files," he said.

A review of this program in 1973, Colby added, resulted in orders limiting it to collection of data abroad and emphasizing that its targets were foreign connections to U.S. dissidents, not the dissidents themselves. In 1974, even more restrictive guidelines were issued, Colby said.

While this program was in operation, the report stated, "files were established on about 10,000 citizens." About two-thirds were begun because of FBI requests for information on activities of U.S. citizens abroad or by the filing of reports received from the FBI "for possible later use in connection with our [the CIA's] work abroad." The remaining third of the files, he said, "were opened on the basis of CIA foreign intelligence or counterintelligence known to be of interest to the FBI." Colby pointed out that in the "past several months" the files had been cleansed of data not justified by the agency's counterintelligence responsibilities, and that about 1,000 files had been removed from the active index.

Colby also reported that concurrent

with the counterintelligence program, beginning in 1967, the CIA infiltrated 10 agents into dissident organizations operating in the Washington area. The purpose of this program, which he said ended in December 1968, was to gather information "relating to plans for demonstrations, pickets, protests or break-ins that might endanger CIA personnel, facilities and information." As was the case with the rest of Colby's report to the subcommittee, the CIA director did not provide details.

"There have been lists developed at various times in the past, however, which do appear questionable under CIA's authority; for example, caused by an excessive effort to identify possible "'threats'" to the agency's security from dissident elements, or from a belief that such lists could identify later applicants or contacts who might be dangerous to the agency's security. They did not usually result from CIA collection efforts (although as I noted above, they sometimes did), but were compilations of names passed to us from other government agencies such as the FBI, some police forces, and several Congressional committees or developed from news clippings, casual informants, etc. A number of these listings have been eliminated in the past three years, and the agency's current directives clearly require that no such listings be maintained."

Colby denied the *New York Times'* allegation that at least one antiwar congressman had been placed under CIA surveillance. The CIA did have some files on congressmen, Colby admitted, but these fell into "categories" such as ex-employes, routine security clearance and "some whose names were included in reports received from other government agencies or developed in the course of our foreign intelligence operations."

As to the *Times'* charges regarding surreptitious break-ins by CIA agents, Colby responded that there had been three instances involving employes or ex-employes, whose loyalties were in doubt. A fourth attempted entry was unsuccessful, he added. Colby admitted that the CIA between 1951 and 1965 had "employed telephone taps" against 21 U.S. residents.

Each of the taps was initiated to check on leaks of classified information, and all but two of the individuals involved were directly connected with the CIA, Colby said. Two taps against private citizens approved by then-Attorney General Robert Kennedy were placed in 1963 to determine the sources of sensitive intelligence information they were thought to be receiving. In 1965, President Johnson issued an order requiring approval by the attorney general of all national security wiretaps, Colby said.

Colby also said the CIA had conducted "physical surveillance (followed)" in 1971 and 1972 against five U.S. citizens who were not CIA employees. "We had clear indications they were receiving classified information." He also cited an alleged plot in 1971 and 1972 to assassinate the vice president and kidnap the director of the CIA. In this case, Colby said, the CIA alerted the FBI and the Secret Service and

carried out physical surveillance in two U.S. cities.

(The *Washington Post* reported Jan. 16 that it had obtained a private memorandum indicating that Colby had told the appropriations subcommittee that the CIA's physical surveillance of five U.S. citizens involved, among others, Jack Anderson, the syndicated columnist; Michael Getler, a *Post* reporter, and Victor Marchetti, a former CIA employe, who wrote a book critical of the agency.)

Finally, Colby conceded that the CIA between 1953 and 1973 had conducted "several programs to survey and open selected mail between the United States and two Communist countries." (Other published reports identified the countries as the Soviet Union and Communist China.)

Helms denies illegalities occurred— Richard Helms, director of the CIA from 1966 to 1973, testified before the Senate Armed Services Subcommittee on Central Intelligence Jan. 16. Helms, whose testimony was behind closed doors, said in a prepared statement released to the press, "I am indignant at the irresponsible attacks made upon the true ends of the intelligence function."

Helms asserted that the "principal allegations" concerning domestic spying by the CIA remained unsupported and had been "undermined by contrary evidence in the press itself." He did not cite specific evidence, however.

In the past it had been rare that U.S. citizens became involved with foreign intelligence operations, Helms said, but "in the late 1950s and early 1960s came the sudden and quite dramatic upsurge of extreme radicalism in this country and abroad. . . ." In response "to the express concern of the President," the CIA collaborated with the FBI to determine if this unrest was "inspired by, coordinated with, or funded by anti-American subversion mechanisms abroad." Helms, who provided no details, said that an investigation did show that the "agitation here did in fact have some overseas connections."

Helms also gave testimony before the Senate Foreign Relations Committee Jan. 22. Sen. Gale McGee (D, Wyo.), a committee member, quoted Helms as saying that if there had been CIA infiltration of U.S. dissident groups, it had occurred without his knowledge. McGee said questioning of Helms in the closed hearing mostly concerned testimony he had given before the committee in 1973 during confirmation hearings on his appointment as U.S. ambassador to Iran. At that time, Helms denied the CIA had engaged in domestic spying operations. Asked by Sen. Stuart Symington (D, Mo.) if the CIA had tried to overthrow the Allende government or if the agency had passed any money to the regime's opponents, Helms had responded, "No, sir."

However, Helms told the committee Jan. 22 there was "no doubt" in 1970 that former President Nixon wanted the Allende government overthrown. Helms, whose secret testimony was made public

Feb. 9, said the Nixon Administration sought ways to overthrow Allende during the time between Allende's election Sept. 4, 1974 and the ratification of the results by the Chilean Congress Oct. 24, 1970. A "very secret probe . . . just to see if there were any forces to oppose Allende's advent as president . . . quickly established there were not . . . and no further effort was made along these lines," Helms testified. He had erred in his 1973 testimony, Helms said, and should have asked to speak off the record or sought another forum, since the U.S. did not want to create a diplomatic incident.

Regarding the $8 million covertly funneled by the CIA to opposition groups in Chile between 1970 and 1973, Helms stated that it was his understanding at the time that the money had gone not to opposition political parties but to "civic groups, supporting newspapers, radios, and so forth. . . ." "I cannot understand how anyone could interpret [the CIA effort in Chile] as an attempt to overthrow the government or believe that they stood a chance of doing so."

In a related development, the *Washington Post* reported Feb. 12 that the Justice Department was examining Helms' testimony to determine if he had committed perjury.

Other testimony before the House Armed Services Intelligence subcommittee in May 1973—declassified in 1974 and reported by the *New York Times* Feb. 2—indicated that Helms, as director of the CIA, had ordered a high agency official to deny the Justice Department access to letters from James W. McCord Jr., one of the original Watergate burglars. Helms also directed, the *Times* reported, that the FBI not be allowed to interview an agency employe, who had knowledge that John D. Ehrlichman, a key aide to Nixon, had authorized the CIA to establish in July 1971 a working relationship with E. Howard Hunt Jr.

According to the *Times,* Howard J. Osborne, director of agency security until his retirement in 1973, had told the Armed Services subcommittee of letters McCord had sent to Helms between July 29, 1972 and January 1973. Although one of the letters said former Attorney General John N. Mitchell and others at the Committee to Re-elect the President were implicated in the Watergate break-in, Osborne testified, Helms decided not to honor a Justice Department subpoena asking the CIA to forward "all communications" related to Watergate. Osborne said that Lawrence Houston, general counsel to the CIA, had advised Helms that the agency had no legal obligation to turn over the letters.

Osborne also said Helms ordered him not to permit the FBI to interview Karl Wagner, a CIA employe with knowledge of Ehrlichman's connection with Hunt. "You forget about that," Osborne quoted Helms as saying in late June 1972. "I will handle that."

While Helms was not questioned by the subcommittee about Osborne's testimony, the *Times* said, William Colby, current director of the CIA, repeatedly told the panel that Helms had acted out of concern that the agency might become entangled in Watergate.

Colby warns of jeopardy to CIA. In testimony before the House Defense Appropriations Subcommittee Feb. 20, William Colby, director of the CIA, warned that "exaggerated" charges of improper conduct by his agency "had placed American intelligence in danger."

He testified in part:

"Mr. Chairman, these last two months have placed American intelligence in danger. The almost hysterical excitement that surrounds any news story mentioning CIA, or referring even to a perfectly legitimate activity of CIA, has raised the question whether secret intelligence operations can be conducted by the United States.

"A number of the intelligence services abroad with which CIA works have expressed concern over its situation and over the fate of the sensitive information they provide to us. A number of our individual agents abroad are deeply worried that their names might be revealed with resultant danger to their lives as well as their livelihoods.

"A number of Americans who have collaborated with CIA as a patriotic contribution to their country are deeply concerned that their reputations will be besmirched and their businesses ruined by sensational misrepresentation of this association. And our own employees are torn between the sensational allegations of CIA misdeeds and their own knowledge that they served their nation during critical times in the best way they knew how.

Colby says sensationalism endangers CIA. William E. Colby, director of the Central Intelligence Agency, April 7 warned that the CIA was being jeopardized by sensational and unjustified headlines.

Addressing the annual convention of American Newspaper Publishers Association in New Orleans, Colby said the CIA was proud of the U.S.' open society but that "this open society must be protected, and that intelligence,...even secret intelligence, must play a part in that protection."

Because the CIA had become "the nation's number one sensational lead," Colby said, other intelligence agencies were "questioning our ability to keep their work for us secret." U.S. businesses that had aided the CIA were afraid their operations "abroad [will be] destroyed by a revelation of their patriotic assistance to the CIA," Colby said.

Colby argued in his speech that the CIA could not afford to abandon its covert and paramilitary operations. "Some things cannot be learned by the inquiring reporter or even the spy in the sky. Sources within a closed or authoritarian foreign society can let us know its secrets in these days of mutual vulnerability to warfare.... And there are occasions in which some quiet assistance to friends of America in some foreign country can help them withstand hostile internal pressures before they become international pressures against the United States."

CIA Files, Mail Interceptions

Colby admits CIA files on Rep. Abzug. CIA Director William E. Colby acknowledged March 5, 1975 that his agency had maintained files on Rep. Bella S. Abzug (D, N.Y.) since 1953. The files, Colby said, contained copies of two letters Abzug had written on behalf of clients when she was a practicing attorney.

In testimony before House Government Operations Subcommittee on Government Information and Individual Rights, which was headed by Abzug, Colby conceded that Abzug was one of four past and present members of Congress on whom special counterintelligence files had been kept as part of the agency's operation against Vietnam War dissidents. While refusing to name the other three, Colby said the operation, terminated in March 1974, found there had been "no substantial foreign manipulation of or assistance to the antiwar movement."

Among the contents of the CIA's file on Abzug: copies of letters she wrote to the Soviet government in 1958 and 1960 on behalf of clients seeking to locate potential heirs in estate cases; data concerning her representation of a client in 1953 before the now-defunct House Committee on un-American Activities; details of her Paris meeting with the Provisional Revolutionary Government of South Vietnam in 1972; the names of lawyers on the mailing list of the American Peace Council and the minutes of a meeting of the Vietnam Mobilization Committee, once a leading antiwar group.

CIA rifling of senators' files revealed— Agents of the Central Intelligence Agency broke into the offices of the late Sens. Joseph McCarthy (R, Wis.) and Robert Kerr (D, Okla.) during the 1950s, *Penthouse* magazine reported May 6. An article by Tad Szulc, a former *New York Times* reporter, named Kerr, McCarthy and Sen. Hubert H. Humphrey as three additional members of Congress on whom the CIA kept files.

According to Szulc, files of McCarthy and Kerr were photographed during the break-ins and the pictures were retained by the agency. "In McCarthy's case," Szulc wrote, "the CIA was especially interested in the private sources that fed him the information to conduct his witchhunt.... The agency evidently didn't like the idea of Joe McCarthy's knowing something that the CIA's chief didn't know." Of Kerr, who had extensive connections in international oil circles, particularly the Middle East, the article said, "Oil intelligence was as crucial to the CIA 20 years ago as it is today."

Szulc said his sources did not know why the CIA had kept a file on Humphrey or what the file had contained.

Colby explains CIA use of materials, files. CIA Director William Colby acknowledged June 25 in testimony before the House Government Operations Subcommittee on Government Information and Individual Rights that part of the agency's efforts to destroy materials not appropriate for it to retain might have amounted to destroying evidence of criminal activity. He said: "If I had thought of it in those terms, I would not have destroyed it, of course... The idea was not to destroy evidence" but "to destroy substantive information we had no business holding." Colby also sketched in a general way the circumstances in which the agency might keep files on members of Congress. He warned that the CIA continues to keep files on approximately 75 congressmen.

Colby said, "If a Congressman appeared abroad in contact with some group that was a legitimate target of this agency, that name would undoubtedly appear in the files of that group." Rep. Bella Abzug, chairman of the House Subcommittee on Government Information and Individual Rights, countered that "The electorate determines our behaviour and they judge us, not some super-spy organization."

The files on 75 congressmen were defended as legitimate by Colby. He said they contained notes on overseas meetings between congressmen and representatives of potentially hostile foreign governments and information on congressmen who have security clearances.

CIA mail opening detailed. William J. Cotter, chief inspector of the Postal Service, told a House Judiciary subcommittee March 18 that the Central Intelligence Agency had terminated an illegal mail-opening operation Feb. 15, 1973 after he told the agency to "get superior approval for this thing or discontinue it." He said he refused to extend the Feb. 15, 1973 deadline and the CIA suspended the program, which had dated from 1953.

Cotter had submitted to the Courts, Civil Liberties and Administration of Justice Subcommittee March 18 a Postal Service study showing that federal, state and local agencies had conducted more than 8,500 mail surveillances in the previous two years. The surveillance, known as mail cover, did not involve opening of mail, said Cotter, who explained that it entailed making a record of names and addresses from the outside of the envelope.

Cotter said opening of mail required a court order and added that with the exception of the CIA, the rule had not been violated. Four hundred thirty-one such orders were issued the previous year, he said.

Cotter, a CIA agent for 18 years, said the CIA's program had been initiated in 1953 as a "survey" of mail between the U.S. and the Soviet Union. At the time, postal officials understood it to be a simple mail cover operation for monitoring names of senders and addressees on envelopes. However, sometime around 1955, the CIA people "went one step further ... without the concurrence of the postal people and surreptitiously appropriated some letters, opened some letters," Cotter testified. Unlike most mail covers, which postal employes conducted, Cotter said, employes of the CIA were authorized "to shuffle ... and sort mail.... Obviously they ... removed it from the premises, opened it, took pictures of it and got it back in the mainstream the next day."

CIA access to mail barred—Postmaster General Benjamin Franklin Bailar issued an order prohibiting the Central Intelligence Agency from having access "to any kind of mail in the custody of the Postal Service, whether by way of cooperative mail covers or otherwise," it was reported May 21. Bailar's March 5 letter notifying CIA Director William E. Colby of the restrictions had been prompted by earlier disclosures of an unauthorized CIA mail interception program over a 20-year period.

In reply March 13, Colby said he shared Bailar's concern over protecting the integrity of the mails and said the CIA had "no intention of reinstituting" its mail-opening program. Bailar had requested Colby's assurance that "no such operations are presently active or planned, and that in the future the Central Intelligence Agency will refrain from any undertaking that might draw the integrity of the mails into question."

Suit filed against CIA opening of mail— A suit was filed June 13 in San Francisco federal court against the CIA by "John Doe" charging the CIA with opening first class mail addressed to private U.S. citizens between 1955 and 1973. According to the anonymous plaintiff (who used "John Doe" because of "fear of retribution"), the opened mail originated in the Soviet Union. The suit asked for an injunction to stop warrantless opening of mail, and wanted the mail openers and recipients of the mail to be named publicly. Named as defendants were former CIA directors John McCone, Richard Helms, and James Schlesinger (now Secretary of Defense), and present director William Colby.

CIA lost letter to Boston teacher— The CIA microfilmed a letter from a Russian friend to a Boston teacher in 1967, and then lost it, so that it was never received. Bob McElwain told the *Boston Globe* that he had written the CIA in April 1975 to see what was in their files about him, using the Freedom of Information Act as justification. The CIA responded that it had one reference it would have to keep "classified."

McElwain wrote his congressman, Rep. Robert F. Drinan, who urged McElwain that under the appeal process he could demand the information. The CIA Information Review Committee then released photocopies of the letter.

The *Globe* published the letter June 13. In its entirety it read: "Please forgive me my long silence. Now I at home. I am spending this summer preparing teaching materials and notes for publishing. At the end of August I shall go to Black Sea with my family for rest. I hope everything all right with you and Bill's family. Thank you for care about us in the USA."

Director William Colby apologized to McElwain in a letter in which he briefly summarized the history of the mail cover operations. Rep. Drinan found it "outrageous beyond description that the CIA would intercept a letter from Russia—totally innocent in content—and never reveal this interception to the American citi-

zen." Drinan said he was "ashamed of such an agency and I will work with every means available to me to curb an agency that has engaged in such ruthless conduct."

CIA finds mail it opened in '72—Postmaster General Benjamin Franklin Bailar revealed July 17 that the Central Intelligence Agency had written him that 85 postcards and 25 letters intercepted from the Soviet Union in 1972 had just been found.

Bailar said that the Department of Justice and the Postal Inspection Service would investigate. In his reply to CIA Director William E. Colby's letter, Bailar called the mail opening "in clear violation of the sanctity of the mails." He said it would "threaten to shake the public confidence in the integrity of the mail."

Colby's letter to Bailar, dated July 16, reported that the mail had been discovered "on a shelf in a securely vaulted area" during an office rearrangement.

ACLU files suit against CIA—The American Civil Liberties Union filed suit against 30 present and former CIA and other governmental officials in Federal District Court in Providence, R.I. July 22. The class action suit charged that the CIA, FBI, and Post Office had opened the first-class mail from the Soviet Union of Rodney Driver, a University of Rhode Island mathematics professor.

Justice Department reported to find CIA's mail opening illegal. Officials of the Justice Department were quoted in the *New York Times* Aug. 4 as reporting that the department's panel of lawyers found that CIA employes acted illegally in opening and photographing first-class mail between American citizens and communist countries.

Mail opening operations were alleged to have been operated uninterruptedly in New York between 1953 and 1973, and sporadically in San Francisco, New Orleans, and Hawaii. In 1973, the New York operation opened nearly 9,000 letters from the 2 million it had inspected.

Agency opened mail to senators and Nixon. The Senate Select Committee on Intelligence disclosed Sept. 24 that the Central Intelligence Agency, as part of its 20-year mail-intercept program, opened and copied the mail of Richard M. Nixon and Sens. Edward M. Kennedy (D, Mass.) and Hubert H. Humphrey (D, Minn.).

According to committee chairman Sen. Frank Church (D, Ida.), CIA men at a New York post office worked from a "watch list" of at least 1,300 persons targeted for CIA surveillance. These CIA officers, who photographed letters of persons on the list, evidently strayed from the list and opened the mail of many prominent U.S. citizens and institutions that had not been targeted for surveillance, Church said. He added that he even found a letter he wrote to his mother-in-law in the CIA's files.

Besides his own letter and some correspondence to Nixon, Humphrey and Kennedy, Church said the CIA had opened mail to and from the late civil rights

leader Martin Luther King Jr. and his wife, Coretta; John D. Rockefeller 4th; Arthur F. Burns, chairman of the Federal Reserve Board; Rep. Bella Abzug (D, N.Y.); the Rockefeller Foundation; the Ford Foundation and Harvard University. The incident involving Nixon, Church said, occurred in June 1968 when Nixon, who was then a leading candidate for the Republican presidential nomination, received a letter from an aide traveling in the Soviet Union. Among other things, the letter assessed Nixon's chances of obtaining the nomination, Church said.

The committee, operating in open session, heard testimony Sept. 23 from Tom Charles Huston, a former aide to Nixon, who in 1970 drafted a domestic intelligence plan that called for the lifting of "present restrictions" against the use of burglaries and mail openings by intelligence agents. (Nixon approved the so-called Huston plan on June 23, 1970, but rescinded his authorization five days later at the insistence of J. Edgar Hoover, the late director of the Federal Bureau of Intelligence.)

Huston testified that he and, to the best of his knowledge, Nixon were unaware that some of the illegal or improper domestic activities proposed in the Huston plan had been going on for years in the CIA and FBI. "If we had known all these tools were being used and still not getting results, it might have changed the whole approach," he testified.

Huston also said that there had never been any discussion in his presence, in the White House or in the interagency committee that drafted the Huston plan of the questionable constitutionality of the plan. "It was my opinion at the time" that Fourth Amendment prohibitions against search and seizure without judicial warrant "didn't apply to the President" in cases of national security.

Church commented during Huston's testimony that the episode clearly showed that U.S. intelligence agencies had operated as "independent fiefdoms" that told neither the President nor each other of their illicit operations.

The committee took testimony Sept. 24 from James Angleton, former chief of the CIA's counterintelligence section and the official in charge of the mail-intercept program from 1955 to 1973. Angleton acknowledged that the intercept program was illegal but he nevertheless defended it as vital to U.S. security. It was "inconceivable," Angleton said, that a secret intelligence arm of the government should have to comply with all the government's overt orders.

The intercepts of mail to and from Communist countries, particularly the Soviet Union, produced a number of items that were of such intelligence value, Angleton said, that it could only be assumed that the Soviet officials had so decided to communicate with agents and political sympathizers in the U.S. because they believed such communications would not be opened.

Asked by Church who had known of the intercept program, Angleton listed former CIA Director Richard Helms,

Hoover and William C. Sullivan, former head of the FBI's domestic intelligence section. He said he could not refute an assertion by Church that Nixon had not known of the intercept program, although it had been in operation for 15 years before Nixon took office.

CIA photographed more than two million envelopes. The CIA photographed the addresses of 2,705,726 envelopes mailed to and from the Soviet Union during its New York mail interception program. The operation lasted from 1953 to 1973, and opened 215,820 letters. The CIA supplied the Senate Select Committee on Intelligence with the figures which were released Oct. 21. Similar operations were conducted on the West Coast, Hawaii, and New Orleans. Although these were known to have been conducted for a shorter period than the New York operation, no precise figures were given.

Soviet Sub Salvage

CIA sought to salvage sunken Soviet sub. The Central Intelligence Agency financed and operated a $250-million deepsea salvage operation that in the summer of 1974 raised part of a Soviet submarine that sank in 1968 in the Pacific Ocean, 750 miles northwest of Oahu, Hawaii, it was widely reported March 18, 1975.

Official U.S. government sources refused all comment on the subject, but it was widely known that William E. Colby, director of the CIA, had expended considerable effort in trying to convince newspaper and magazine editors and broadcast executives that public disclosure of the top-secret project would harm the national security. The Soviet government, which apparently had been unaware of the salvage operation until February 8 when the *Los Angeles Times* broke the story, declined to even acknowledge that the submarine had gone down.

According to the reports, the Soviet vessel—a class "G" ballistic-missile, diesel-powered submarine constructed in 1958—was racked by explosions of unknown origin, which caused the ship to sink in 16,000 feet of water. The sub went down so fast that the Soviets were unable to pinpoint its location.

The U.S. Navy, using more sophisticated equipment than possessed by the Soviets, found the vessel. But the Navy failed to devise a means for getting at the sub, and the Pentagon sought the advice of the CIA.

That agency subsequently awarded, on a non-competitive bidding basis, a contract to the Summa Corp., a company owned by Howard R. Hughes, the billionaire recluse, who was known for his penchant for secrecy, as well as an interest in deep-sea mining. The salvage vessel, dubbed the Glomar Explorer, was publicly depicted as the world's most advanced deep-sea mining ship. (Despite that the fact that thousands of scientists and workmen had security clearances for the program known as Project Jennifer, the mission was one of the most tightly guarded secrets of the Nixon and Ford Administrations. The *New York Times* March 19 reported that "a number of officials who were interviewed praised repeatedly the CIA 'cover' for the mission."

In addition to the Glomar Explorer, the operation required a deep-diving barge that was constructed in 1971 and 1972 by the National Steel and Shipbuilding Co. and designed by a division of the Lockheed Aircraft Corp. The barge, whose only function to hide the Soviet submarine after it had been brought up from the bottom, was never directly utilized in Project Jennifer.

During the recovery operation in July and August 1974, CIA technicians were successful in grasping and lifting the submarine halfway to the surface—about 8,000 feet—when it broke up and two-thirds of its hull fell back to the ocean floor. Although the operation was only partly complete, it had to be ended at that point because of damage sustained by the Glomar Explorer, and because of rough seas.

The section of the submarine recovered contained the bodies of 70 of the approximately 90-man crew. They were later buried at sea in ceremonies conducted in Russian and English and recorded on color film by CIA technicians.

What else was recovered from the forward section of the ship was not completely clear. The *New York Times* said March 18 the Glomar Explorer had been unsuccessful in recovering any of the ship's nuclear warheads or its coding equipment. However, the *Washington Post* March 20 said one of its sources had implied that at least one nuclear warhead had been salvaged.

The published reports indicated that government officials were divided as to whether the mission's cost—estimated between $250 million and $350 million—could be justified. Some officials said Project Jennifer would have been the biggest intelligence coup in U.S. history had it succeeded. Others, who were more skeptical, doubted that the operation would yield any new information on Soviet weaponry. Still other doubters warned of possible damage to current U.S.-Soviet diplomatic detente.

Panels in Congress to probe sub salvage. Three Congressional committee chairmen March 19 announced plans to investigate the Central Intelligence Agency's effort to salvage a Soviet submarine that sank in the Pacific Ocean in 1968. The chairmen and other members of Congress disagreed over the intelligence value of the operation, which was reported to have cost between $250 million and $350 million.

Sen. Frank Church (D, Ida.) said his Select Committee on Intelligence would incorporate the submarine salvage operation into its general inquiry on U.S. government intelligence activities. Suggesting that the U.S. intelligence community might need "a cost-benefit ratio," Church remarked: "If we are prepared to pay Howard Hughes $350 million for an obsolete Russian submarine, it's little wonder we are broke." (Summa Corp., Hughes' personal holding company, built the vessel, the Glomar Explorer, used in the salvage attempt.)

Rep. Lucien Nedzi (D, Mich.) chairman of the House Select Committee on Intelligence, said it would not be "proper" to ignore a project of that size. He added that he and other members of the House Armed Services Intelligence Subcommittee had been briefed on the operation in the summer of 1974.

Sen. Stuart Symington (D, Mo.) said he would summon William E. Colby, director of the CIA, before the Military Applications Subcommittee of the Joint Atomic Energy Committee. Symington, chairman of the subcommittee, expressed doubt about the operation's value and said he had not been told of the project even though he was a senior member of the Senate Armed Services Intelligence Subcommittee.

In another development, the Securities and Exchange Commission (SEC) released a statement March 31 indicating that its staff had been investigating Global Marine Inc.'s "undisclosed interests" in the project. The SEC was concerned that Global Marine, which operated the Glomar Explorer during the salvage operation, had violated the "full disclosure" requirements of federal securities laws in its reports and filings. The statement also raised the question of whether a company could be partly or fully exempted from the requirements of disclosure laws by reason of classification of material information by another federal agency.

Other developments concerning the salvage operation:

■ A Soviet tugboat believed equipped with sophisticated intelligence gear was reported March 25 to be in the area where the sub had gone down. Three other large, specially outfitted Soviet oceanographic vessels were reported due to dock in Honolulu in April. A harbor official said that Soviet ships usually only docked there once or twice a year. (The site of the sunken submarine had earlier been reported as 750 miles northwest of Oahu.)

■ In Washington, meanwhile, varied reports on the success of the salvage operation circulated. They ranged from an item in the *Washington Post* March 21 suggesting that the Glomar Explorer had in fact retrieved the entire submarine, not just one-third of it, as initial stories had said. If this were true, the *Post* said, then by implication, the CIA had recovered nuclear warheads on the sub's torpedoes, the warheads on three ballistic missiles, and the code machine that unscrambled secret messages the ship would have received. However, the *Post* cited another source who suggested simply that two nuclear warheads from torpedoes had been brought up.

In contrast to the *Post's* reports, the *Los Angeles Times* March 22 quoted unnamed sources as denying nuclear warheads had been recovered. Nuclear torpedoes were not retrieved, the *Times'* source said, but their existence was established through an analysis of residue of recovered fragments.

■ Donald Woolbright, who was sought in connection with the theft of documents reportedly related to the salvage operation, surrendered to St. Louis police March 28. Woolbright allegedly received the documents from four men who burglarized Summa Corp. offices in Los Angeles June 5, 1974.

Assassinations Alleged

Report links CIA to 3 assassinations. Daniel Schorr, Washington correspondent for CBS News, reported Feb. 28, 1975 that an internal Central Intelligence Agency inquiry had developed evidence of agency involvement in assassination plots against at least three foreign leaders. Schorr said that President Ford was concerned that public disclosure of the plots would embarrass the U.S. and damage relations with one foreign nation.

Schorr reported that the assassination plots had been uncovered by James R. Schlesinger, CIA director for part of 1973, when he asked agency employes to report to him any questionable activities with which they were familiar. In August 1973, Schorr said, Schlesinger prohibited such activities.

Ford was reportedly orally informed of the involvement in December 1974 by William E. Colby, current CIA director, who at that time also gave Ford a written report on covert domestic activities of the agency.

The *Washington Post* reported March 6 that the CIA was concerned about the effect of investigations into the agency's alleged involvement in assassination plots against Fidel Castro of Cuba, the late Rafael Trujillo of the Dominican Republic and the late Patrice Lumumba of the Congo (now Zaire).

The CIA refused comment on the report, the *Post* said.

According to an unidentified government source, the *Post* said, the CIA had acknowledged in private that two episodes in Cuba and the Dominican Republic might have been carried forward by persons with close agency connections. The source insisted that the killing of Lumumba in 1961 had been done by individuals not in contact with U.S. intelligence.

The *Post* also identified a former Army captain and CIA operative named Bradley Ayers, who related that he had accidently discovered in 1963 a team of marksmen trained in Miami for "an assassination effort against Castro." Ayers said John Roselli, reputedly a top Mafia figure, was the case officer for the team. Ayers added that the team's captain "made jokes" about the assassination, "quite frankly."

The *Post* also noted that an account of CIA involvement in the 1961 killing of Trujillo was contained in *Inside the Company,* the recently published diary of ex-CIA operative Philip B. Agee. Agee

wrote that the late Ned P. Holman, a CIA station chief in Latin America, had admitted being "deeply involved in planning the assassination, which was done by Cuban exiles from Miami using weapons we [the CIA] sent through a diplomatic pouch."

CIA death plot against Castro claimed. Two aides of the late Robert F. Kennedy claimed that he told them in 1967 that the Central Intelligence Agency had collaborated with the Mafia in a plot to assassinate Fidel Castro, the Cuban premier, the *New York Times* reported March 10. According to Adam Walinsky and Peter B. Edelman, assistants to Kennedy when he was attorney general and a senator, Kennedy told them he had played an active role in aborting the plot.

Kennedy "told us that he had discovered that the CIA had made a contract with the Mafia to hit Castro," Walinsky said. Kennedy had also disclosed to them, Walinsky said, that he had received "assurances in writing" from the CIA that the attempted assassination had been called off. Neither man knew how Kennedy had learned of the alleged plot, although Walinsky noted that Kennedy had learned of CIA-Mafia connections while serving as a member of a Presidential panel reviewing the CIA's planning for the Bay of Pigs invasion of Cuba in 1961.

Meanwhile, *Time* magazine reported March 9 that "credible sources" within the CIA contended "that the CIA enlisted the hired-gun help of U.S. Mafia figures in several unsuccessful attempts to kill Cuban Premier Castro both before and shortly after the CIA-planned Bay of Pigs invasion." *Time* said the CIA received the help of John Roselli and Sam Giancana, reputed members of the Mafia.

Time also cited anonymous sources, who said the CIA had "backed the successful drive to overthrow" Rafael Trujillo, the Dominican Republic dictator assassinated in 1961. According to the sources, the agency thought Trujillo was "getting too friendly with the Communists" and "nobody wanted another Cuba in the Dominican Republic."

In a related development, Jose Figueres said in an interview for Mexican television March 9, "I collaborated with the CIA when we were trying to topple Trujillo." Figueres, the former president of Costa Rica, declined to elaborate.

CIA assassination role opposed—President Ford strongly denounced at the news conference March 17 any involvement by the Central intelligence Agency in any assassination planning or action. "This Administration," he said, "does not condone under any circumstances any assassination attempts" nor would it participate "under any circumstances" in activities of that sort. He said he had followed stories on the matter "with interest and personal attention," had asked his staff for a report, had met with Vice President Nelson A. Rockefeller on it and expected to decide within a few days "the best course of action for the Rockefeller

Commission or any executive branch investigation of such allegations."

As for the material Congress sought for its own intelligence probe, Ford said the Senate committee had asked for "a considerable amount of material" and the request was being analyzed by his staff. He said he could not give a commitment on the degree of his cooperation until the review was completed. "We intend to make as full a disclosure as is possible," he said, "without jeopardizing America's national security."

CIA plot to kill Castro described. L. Fletcher Prouty, a retired Air Force colonel who once served in the Defense Department's Office of Special Operations, said April 27 that in "late 1959 or 1960" he had handled a Central Intelligence Agency request for a small, specially equipped Air Force plane to fly a two-man assassination team into Cuba to kill Premier Castro.

The men, both Cuban exiles, were "equipped with a high-powered rifle and telescopic sights" and "knew how to get to a building in Havana which overlooked a building where Castro passed daily," Prouty said.

The plane, an L-28 "Heliocourier," returned safely to Eglin Air Force Base in Florida, he said, but the "Cuban exiles as far as I know were picked up between where they were left off and town."

Prouty explained that he had come forward now only because of criticism Richard Helms, director of the CIA in 1966–73, had directed at Daniel Schorr, who had reported that President Ford was worried that investigations of the agency would uncover assassination plots against foreign leaders. Helms, who had just emerged from over three hours of testimony before the Rockefeller Commission April 26, angrily said, "I don't know of any foreign leader that was ever assassinated by the CIA." Before his statement, Helms had directed profanities at the CBS-TV newsman and had referred to him as "killer Schorr" for reporting that the "CIA goes around killing people."

Prouty said he was upset because he was "positive" that Helms knew about the mission to kill Castro. At the time of the mission, Prouty said, Helms was in almost total control of clandestine CIA operations against Cuba.

Castro's murder assertedly discussed. According to an Associated Press report May 24, the Rockefeller Commission probing domestic CIA activities had obtained the minutes of a 1962 White House meeting during which the assassination of Cuban Premier Fidel Castro was discussed. Although the idea was immediately dismissed, the AP's unnamed sources said, an assistant to Robert S. McNamara, then secretary of defense, two days later ordered the Central Intelligence Agency to prepare contingency plans for the assassination of Castro. That memo was quickly withdrawn, one AP source indicated, adding, however, that other U.S.-sponsored plots against Castro were subsequently planned.

The sources said the April 10, 1962 meeting had been attended by McNamara, Secretary of State Dean Rusk, CIA Director John A. McCone and McGeorge Bundy, national security adviser to President Kennedy. The McNamara assistant who wrote the memorandum was then-Col. Edward G. Lansdale. The minutes described a meeting of a special group known as Operation Mongoose, which was responsible for all covert activities against Castro.

Time and *Newsweek* magazines reported May 25 that discussions on deposing or eliminating Castro from power were held at the highest levels of the Kennedy Administration. *Time* cited "credible" sources who said that President Kennedy and his brother, then-Attorney General Robert F. Kennedy, angry over the 1961 defeat of CIA-backed Cuban exiles at the Bay of Pigs, ordered U.S. government agencies to find some means to "depose" Castro. Whether the Kennedys authorized assassination attempts against the Cuban leader was still unclear, *Time* said.

Newsweek, which attributed its report to a "highly placed intelligence source," said a major effort had been made by the Kennedy Administration to "get rid" of Castro. "Like several other informants," *Newsweek* said, "this source was careful to say that the intention had been to 'eliminate' Castro; there were at least perfunctory hopes that he could be removed from power without shedding his blood. But this source implied strongly that the decision, made at the highest levels of government, did not preclude outright assassination."

Meanwhile, it was reported by the *New York Times* May 20 that the Rockefeller Commission had learned of the existence of documents supporting charges that the CIA had contracted with Mafia in 1961 to kill Castro. According to sources the *Times* called "authoritative," a former top official of the Justice Department during the Nixon Administration, told the commission that department files contained Federal Bureau of Investigation memorandums confirming that the CIA was in touch with Sam Giancana, a reputed chief of the Chicago rackets, and John Roselli, a soldier of fortune with organized crime connections, concerning a plot to assassinate Castro.

In the 1960s, Giancana and Roselli had been the subjects of federal probes of organized crime. Giancana had spent most of 1964 in jail for refusing to answer questions before a federal grand jury in Chicago. The Justice Department considered bringing Giancana before a second grand jury, but later decided otherwise and prosecution was halted. Giancana subsequently moved to Mexico.

The middle-level Justice Department decision to stop prosecuting Giancana was based on reasoning that another attempt to bring him before a grand jury would be harassment. William Hundley, a Washington attorney formerly in charge of the organized crime section of the department, said he had been unaware of Giancana's connection to the CIA and had not been pressured by his superiors.

Roselli, also under Justice Department scrutiny during the mid-1960s, was convicted of failing to register as an alien and of conspiracy to rig card games at a Los Angeles club. At one point, the *Times* said, Roselli's lawyers sought clemency for their client on the grounds of his cooperation with the CIA. Justice Department files, a *Times* source said, gave no indication that favorable action was taken.

Another version under investigation in Washington involved a story—parts reported as early as 1967 by Jack Anderson, the syndicated columnist—that Giancana and Roselli had been recruited for CIA work by Robert Maheu, the former manager of the Las Vegas, Nevada interests of Howard R. Hughes, the billionaire recluse. According to this scenario, reported by the *Times* May 20, the involvement of the Mafia in the affair was one facet of an "elaborate" cover story for a government assassination plot.

"'If Castro had been killed, it would then be possible to make it appear that the mob did the job because Castro had cut off their gambling interests in Havana,'" said a *Times* source familiar with the scenario. For their part, the source said, gangland leaders would say the assassination had been their work.

Church suggests legal curbs on killing— Sen. Frank Church (D, Ida.), chairman of the Senate select committee investigating U.S. intelligence activities, said May 23 that Congress might have to enact legislation prohibiting the CIA from engaging in assassinations abroad. "It is simply intolerable that any agency of the government of the United States may engage in murder," said Church after emerging from a secret committee session with William E. Colby, current director of the CIA. Colby, making his third appearance before the panel in 10 days, was quizzed solely on his agency's role in assassination plots and attempts, Church said.

Although Church said committee rules barred him from discussing Colby's testimony, he did say that "if the facts were to lead the committee to the conclusion that there have been activities of this kind, . . . [it] will insist that the laws be so written that this will never happen again" in times of peace.

Castro offers death plot documentation. United Press International reported May 17 that Sen. George S. McGovern (D, S.D.), a recent visitor to Cuba, had been offered "documentation" by Castro that the Cuban premier said would prove that the CIA was involved in plots to kill him. McGovern, who said he did not examine the documents during his trip, related being told by Castro of "about 100" attempts on his life and those of other high-ranking Cuban officials. However, Castro quickly added, McGovern said, that the CIA had not been involved in all attempts.

McGovern releases Castro's documents— Cuban Premier Fidel Castro, in a report turned over to the Senate Select Committee on Intelligence July 30, charged that he and other Cuban leaders had been the target of at least 24 Central Intelligence Agency assassination attempts between 1960 and 1971.

The allegations were set down in an 86-page report delivered to Sen. George S. McGovern (D, S.D.) by the Cuban government. McGovern, who had visited Cuba in May, made public a summary of the charges and submitted the full report, along with accompanying photographs, to the Senate committee. He had no way of assessing the charges, McGovern said, but felt they warranted further investigation.

Listing 24 separate plots against Castro, the report repeatedly linked the CIA to the aborted assassination attempts. Some of the plots were attributed without elaboration to groups "with CIA connections," while other efforts were said to involve "CIA agents." On several occasions, the report said, anti-Castro groups used the U.S. Naval base at Guantanamo in eastern Cuba as a haven and supply point for weapons to be used.

Kennedys said to seek Castro removal. Maj. Gen. Edward G. Lansdale (ret.) told the *New York Times* in a telephone interview May 30 that in late 1961 Attorney General Robert F. Kennedy, acting on behalf of President Kennedy, instructed him to prepare contingency plans to depose Cuban Premier Fidel Castro.

Although he said he had never been ordered by either Kennedy brother to plan the assassination of Castro, Lansdale, a retired Air Force general and expert in counter-insurgency warfare, conceded that in later operational planning, assassination as a possible means of removing Castro from power might have been contemplated.

In November or December 1961, Lansdale said, Robert Kennedy asked him to come up with contingency plans to remove Castro. The planning focused on picking a cadre of Cubans from exile groups in the U.S. This politically cohesive group was to be then sent to Cuba, where it would hopefully foment a popular uprising against Castro, Lansdale said. He added that this idea was "never feasible" because he was unable to find the "20 or 30" Cubans necessary.

Lansdale, who indicated the plan had been formulated because of intelligence reports that Castro was negotiating with the Soviet Union, said he could not remember writing a memorandum, mentioned in press reports May 24, concerning the possible assassination of Castro. Nonetheless, he explained, he knew as he prepared the plan that "operationally down the pike, something like this could emerge—not only assassination but other things like defamation of character," which would be in the form of propaganda attacks discrediting Castro in the eyes of his supporters.

Kennedy scores Rockefeller 'innuendos'. Sen. Edward M. Kennedy (D, Mass.) June 16 criticized Vice President Nelson A. Rockefeller for implying that John F. Kennedy and Robert F. Kennedy might have been involved in CIA assassination plots against Cuban Premier Castro. For Rockefeller, chairman of the presidential panel that investigated domestic wrong-doing by the CIA, to indulge in such "innuendos is utterly irresponsible," Kennedy said.

Rockefeller June 15 had suggested that the late president and his brother might have been aware of CIA plots to kill foreign leaders. Stating that the evidence with regard to assassinations was inconclusive, the vice president added, "I think it's fair to say that no major undertakings by the CIA were done without either the knowledge and/or the approval of the White House."

President Ford, who made the Rockefeller commission's findings public June 10, said he would not release a section of the commission's report on assassinations because it was "incomplete and extremely sensitive."

Given Rockefeller's "failure to fulfill his duty on the issue," Kennedy said, "I hope he'll have the decency to maintain his silence ... Such comments come with especially bad grace from the Vice President whose own CIA commission avoided the question of assassination and passed the buck to Congress."

Trujillo plotter denies CIA aid. Dominican Republic Brig. Gen. Antonio Imbert Barreras, one of seven gunmen who assassinated Dominican dictator Rafael Trujillo Molina in 1961, June 20 denied published reports that he and his fellow conspirators had been given "material" aid by the CIA.

The *New York Times* had reported June 12 that authoritative U.S. government sources had said that the CIA had given "material support" to the group of Dominicans who had assassinated Trujillo.

"This report is a cowboy picture without any basis in reality," Imbert said. "The men who participated in that historic act did not need help. We had our own arms ... our own cars ... our own reasons."

"We were living in a situation where nobody trusted anybody," the general continued. "In our group we were convinced that Trujillo was supported by the United States. It would have been madness to talk with the Americans about our plans."

Kennedy reported to have attempted to stop Trujillo's assassination—The *New York Times* reported June 28 that President John F. Kennedy had tried to stop the assassination of General Trujillo. The *Times* quoted former intelligence officers as saying that a cable was sent from the National Security Council to the CIA station chief in the Dominican Republic May 29, 1961, the day before Trujillo was killed.

The cable was alleged to inform the CIA that the U.S. government would not approve the formation of a coup to over-throw Trujillo's government. The cable had no result, according to the *Times*' sources, because the CIA did not "control" the coup against Trujillo. CIA support was only "material", it was reported.

Mafioso linked to Castro plot slain. Sam Giancana, a Chicago crime syndicate boss, who had been linked to Central Intelligence Agency assassination plots against Cuban Premier Fidel Castro, was shot to death June 20 in his suburban Oak Park, Ill. home. Police said they had no leads on the killers of Giancana, 65, who was described by a spokesman for the Chicago Crime Commission as the city's most powerful mobster since Al Capone.

Meanwhile, John Roselli, 69, reputedly Giancana's West Coast lieutenant, testified June 24 before the Senate Select Committee on Intelligence in closed session for more than two hours. (The committee had also planned to question Giancana.)

According to Sen. Frank Church (D, Ida.), the committee's chairman, who spoke to reporters afterward, Roselli's testimony had "filled in, in much greater detail [the plot] and did not depart from what has been published in the press."

The published reports Church referred to said that Robert Maheu, a former Federal Bureau of Investigation agent and later a key aide to billionaire industrialist Howard R. Hughes, recruited Giancana and Roselli on behalf of the CIA to direct an assassination plot against Castro. The racketeers, who established a base of operations in Miami Beach, were asked by the CIA in late 1960 to arrange the poisoning of the Cuban premier, his younger brother, Raul Castro, and Ernesto Che Guevara, the late Argentine revolutionary leader. The plot was subsequently aborted, the reports said, because the assassin inside Cuba entrusted with the mission was never able to get close enough to the Cuban leaders to poison their food as planned. The purpose of the killings was to create a leadership vacuum that would make Cuba ripe for counter-revolution, the reports indicated.

John A. McCone, director of the CIA 1961–1965, also shed light on CIA plots against Castro. Speaking to newsmen after giving secret testimony to the Senate select committee June 6, McCone confirmed that the CIA had planned and undertaken steps to assassinate Castro. McCone, who claimed not to have been told of the attempts on Castro's life even after he became head of the agency, said all of the schemes were "aborted" and that the principal effort was stopped soon after the failed Bay of Pigs invasion in April 1961. He had become aware of the CIA's efforts after reviewing agency files in the previous few months, McCone said.

McCone said the chain of command for the assassination plots against Castro was murky "because the people involved are dead," including Presidents Eisenhower and Kennedy, former Attorney General Robert F. Kennedy, former CIA Director Allen Dulles and former Secretaries of State John Foster Dulles and Christian Herter.

Rockefeller Commission Report Issued

Church disputes Rockefeller on CIA. Sen. Frank Church said June 4, 1975 he felt compelled to protest the "apparent attempt of certain members of the Rockefeller Commission" to characterize the misdeeds of the Central Intelligence Agency as minor transgressions. "I don't regard murder plots as a minor matter," said Church, who asserted that the Senate select committee on intelligence he chaired possessed "hard evidence" of CIA involvement in assassination plots against foreign chiefs of state.

Vice President Nelson A. Rockefeller, chairman of the Presidential commission probing domestic activities of the CIA, had told reporters June 2 that his panel had uncovered CIA violations of the law but no widespread pattern of illegal activity. Stating that he could not agree with the term "massive" that was used in some published reports to describe CIA domestic spying, Rockefeller said, "There are things that have been done ... in contradiction to the statutes, but in comparison to the total effort they are not major."

When Rockefeller was informed of the Idaho Democrat's accusation, he said he had been "misinterpreted" and had only been speaking of the number of the CIA's wrongdoings and not their seriousness. However, Church later responded that he had no intention of making a retraction and would stick by his earlier assertion that remarks by Rockefeller and C. Douglas Dillon, vice chairman of the commission, had clearly conveyed the impression that the CIA's wrongdoings were "not of major importance." "Ours is not a wicked country and we cannot abide a wicked government," Church said.

Rockefeller's disputed statement had come as he was about to enter the commission's last meeting prior to the submission of its final report to President Ford June 6. "We have made extensive recommendations of steps to prevent it in the future," he said with reference to violations of the law linked to the agency. Neither President Ford nor the public, he added, would be shocked by the commission's report and would, he thought, "be surprised and pleased by the comprehensive nature of the material that's in there."

Attorney General to get CIA report. President Ford announced at a news conference June 9 that he was submitting the Rockefeller Commission report on the Central Intelligence Agency to the attorney general for possible prosecution. The President said he would release part of the commission's report, withholding the section on alleged assassination plots against foreign leaders because it was "incomplete and extremely sensitive."

The assassination data, he said, would

be sent in addition to the Justice Department, to the Congressional panels that were conducting their own investigations.

Ford said he believed the credibility of the CIA "can be and will be restored" by the commission's report and the recommendations of the Congressional panels. He said he believed there could be "internal improvement" in the CIA and thought "there can be legislative recommendations that I hope the Congress will enact. And the net result will be that we'll have a strong, effective and proper Central Intelligence Agency."

He asserted that he was "totally opposed to political assassinations." "This Administration," he said, "has not and will not use such means of instruments of national policy." But he said he was reserving judgment on that issue in the report. Ford urged Congress to do the same and use the "utmost prudence" in evaluating the material relating to it. He said the material he had seen on it dated back to "late 1959 and running up to 1967 or 1968," which would span the Administrations of Presidents Eisenhower, Kennedy and Johnson.

Ford indicated that "certain recommendations for some legislation and some administrative action" would be forthcoming to insure that the CIA performed its mission and that the "rights of Americans—domestically—are well protected." It was his understanding that the agency was not chartered for involvement in domestic activities and if any violations were discovered corrective action would be taken. If individuals were involved, he said, "it would be for the attorney general to make a judgment as to whether there should be any prosecution." His decision to make the assassination material available to the attorney general and to Congressional investigators, he said, would show "there's not going to be any possibility of a cover-up" of any CIA wrongdoing.

Why had he had the Rockefeller Commission "stop short in its work and not complete its investigation into alleged political assassinations?" he was asked. Ford said he had not told the commission "that it should not proceed further." The panel decided "on its own" to wind up its operations on the basis of its original responsibilities, which were to probe allegations "concerning domestic violations of its charter." The political assassinations issue came up later and the commission reported its findings on that to him, Ford said.

Did he agree with the panel's decision "to stop without reaching a conclusion in this particular area?"

Ford said he did. The material was being turned over to the attorney general "so that the proper agency of the executive branch of the federal government will be in a position to analyze and to prosecute if there is any need to do so."

A reporter asked why the commission was not the proper agency since it was assigned by Ford to probe the matter. Ford repeated the point that the commission's original assignment was to probe alleged illegal activities "domestically," which he said was "a very major responsibility." The panel concluded its probe "of the basic charges," he continued, and with the submission of the report to him and to the attorney general for any further investigation and prosecution this was "a responsible manner in which to handle this situation."

Most agency activities termed legal. The Rockefeller Commission said in its final report, made public June 10, that the Central Intelligence Agency had engaged in activities that were "plainly unlawful and constituted improper invasions upon the rights of Americans." The report also said, however, that a "great majority" of the CIA's domestic activities during its 28-year history had been in compliance with its statutory authority. [See excerpts below]

According to the commission, an eight-member, blue-ribbon panel chaired by Vice President Nelson A. Rockefeller, the CIA illegally opened mail to and from the Soviet Union and other countries at various times between 1952 and 1974; established in violation of its charter a supersecret Special Operations Group that amassed 13,000 files, 7,200 of them on dissident U.S. citizens, and compiled a computerized index of 300,000 individual names and organizations; infiltrated domestic political groups; and undertook 32 wiretaps, an equal number of room buggings and 12 break-ins, as well as the investigation of the tax records of 16 persons.

In its 299-page report, submitted to President Ford June 6, the commission made 30 recommendations to insure against recurrence of illegal or improper activities. These included strengthened Congressional and executive oversight, internal reorganization of the agency and more precise definition of what the agency should or should not do. In addition, the commission endorsed legislation making it a crime for present or former employes to divulge classified information on foreign intelligence obtained during employment.

President Ford did not make public the section of the commission's report concerning assassination plots against foreign heads of state. Ford, who said he was withholding data on that subject because it was "incomplete and extremely sensitive," indicated he would forward the material to the Justice Department and to Congress for further investigation.

The commission also reported finding "no credible evidence" of CIA involvement in the assassination of President John F. Kennedy.

The commission for the first time disclosed that President Nixon had made use of the CIA for purely political ends. Nixon sought and obtained from the agency, the report said, classified materials on the 1958 U.S. Marine landings in Lebanon, the 1961 Bay of Pigs invasion, the 1962 Cuban missile crisis and the 1963 assassination of South Vietnamese President Ngo Dinh Diem. The report said Nixon had told the CIA he needed the material to set the historical record straight, but concluded that the former president actually intended to use the data against political opponents. In addition, the commission discovered that in 1970 the CIA had, at the White House's request, contributed $38,655 to defray the cost of replying to persons who wrote to Nixon after the U.S. invasion of Cambodia.

Also uncovered, the report said, was a 1954 secret agreement between the Justice Department and the CIA, giving the CIA the right to decide whether to prosecute agency employes for criminal violations. The report, highly critical of the Justice Department because it had "abdicated its statutory duties," asserted that the agreement had directly involved the CIA in "forbidden law enforcement activities" in violation of the agency's 1947 charter. It found "no evidence" that the CIA abused these prosecutorial powers, the commission said, adding that the pact had been ended in January when the department "directed that cases with a potential for criminal prosecution be referred to it for consideration." (A Justice Department spokesman said after the report's release that during the 20-year life of the agreement, most attorneys general had not been aware of its existence.)

Illegal mail surveillance confirmed—According to the commission, the mail interception operation had been begun in 1952 as a program for surveying mail to and from the Soviet Union that passed through a New York City postal facility. Designed to identify persons cooperating with Soviet intelligence and to determine Soviet mail censorship techniques, the interception program's "primary purpose" eventually became participation with the Federal Bureau of Investigation "in internal security functions."

During the year before the termination of the New York mail interception operation in 1973, more than half of 4.35 million pieces of mail intended for the Soviet Union were examined, 33,000 envelopes photographed and 8,700 letters opened, the report stated. Smaller mail intercepts were run in San Francisco in 1969–71, in Hawaii during 1954–55 and in New Orleans for a short period in 1957.

The commission, which noted that the intercept program was in contravention of postal regulations, revealed the existence of a 1962 memorandum indicating the agency was aware that the openings violated federal criminal laws barring obstruction or delay of the mails. Moreover, the intercept operation violated the 1947 National Security Act prohibition against CIA involvement in internal security matters, the commission said.

Operation Chaos—Another section of the Rockefeller Commission's report concerned the Special Operations Group—later known as "Operation Chaos"—established in 1967 at the request of President Lyndon B. Johnson to "collect, coordinate, evaluate and report on the extent of foreign influence on domestic dissidence." Although the stated purpose of the group was to determine if U.S.

dissidents had foreign contacts, the report said, "accumulation of considerable material on domestic dissidents and their activities" occurred. In the six years the operation existed, 13,000 files, 7,200 of them on U.S. citizens, were compiled, and the names of 300,000 persons and organizations found in the files were entered into an agency computer. From the information in these files, the report continued, the group prepared 3,500 memorandums for internal agency use, 3,000 memorandums for dissemination to the FBI and 37 memorandums that went to the White House and high level federal officials. The staff of Operation Chaos, "steadily enlarged in response to repeated presidential requests for more information," reached a maximum of 52 persons in 1971, the commission said.

Beginning in late 1969, Operation Chaos used a number of agents to collect information abroad on connections between U.S. dissidents and foreign groups. To insure proper " 'cover' " for its agents, the commission said, the CIA recruited persons from the dissident groups or sought others who were instructed to join the dissident groups. While these recruits were not generally told to collect domestic information on dissident groups, they nonetheless did so during the time they were developing ties with the dissidents. On three occasions, however, "an agent of the operation was specifically directed to collect domestic intelligence," the commission's report revealed.

"Some domestic activities of Operation Chaos" the report said, "exceeded the CIA's statutory authority.... More significantly the operation became a repository for large quantities of information on the domestic activities of American citizens ... and much of it was not directly related to the question of the existence of foreign connections."

The report also criticized the isolation of the group from supervision by the regular agency chain of command, a situation that made it possible, the report said, for the operation "to stray over the bounds of the agency's authority without the knowledge of senior officials." According to the commission, the operation was so isolated from the rest of the agency that James Angleton, head of the counterintelligence section, of which the operation was nominally a part, was never aware of the Special Operations Group or its successor, Operation Chaos. Testimony by Angleton and the head of Operation Chaos indicated that supervisory responsibility lay with Richard Helms, director of the CIA from 1966–73.

Other chapters of the commission's report dealt with the CIA Office of Security, which was in charge of protecting agency security and sources, besides conducting routine investigations of persons seeking affiliation with the CIA. "Investigation disclosed," the report said, "the domestic use of 32 wiretaps, the last in 1965; 32 instances of bugging, the last in 1968 and 12 break-ins, the last in 1971. None of these activities was conducted under judicial warrant, and only one with the approval of the attorney general." To

determine whether 16 persons were security risks with foreign connections, the report said, the CIA obtained information from the Internal Revenue Service on the income tax records of these individuals. The CIA did not comply with existing statutory and regulatory procedures for obtaining such information, the report stated.

The commission reported learning that the Office of Security, also responsible for the security of persons defecting to the U.S., confined one defector involuntarily at a CIA installation for three years. His credibility in doubt, the defector "was held in solitary confinement under spartan living conditions." However, when a defector was physically abused, the CIA fired the employe involved, the report noted.

Another questionable agency activity revealed in the commission report involved drug testing by the CIA's Directorate of Science and Technology. As part of a research program to determine the effect of drugs on humans, directorate researchers administered LSD to persons unaware they were being tested. In 1953, one subject had a psychotic reaction to the drug, an hallucinogen, and subsequently jumped to his death from a 10th-floor hospital room, the commission disclosed. In 1963 the agency forbade drug testing on unknowing subjects and in 1967 terminated all such programs.

Recommendations—In offering 30 recommendations for change in the CIA, the commission said that the "evidence within the scope of this inquiry does not indicate that the fundamental rewriting of the National Security Act is either necessary or appropriate. The evidence does demonstrate the need for some statutory and administrative clarification of the role and function of the agency."

Amendments to the agency's charter, the National Security Act of 1947, the report stated, should make explicit that all CIA activities must be related to foreign intelligence. The agency's responsibility to protect intelligence sources and methods from unauthorized disclosure should be clarified. (The CIA should also offer guidance and technical assistance to other federal agencies seeking to protect against such unauthorized disclosures, the report said.) With certain exceptions, the report went on, the President should by executive order prohibit CIA collection of data about the domestic activities of U.S. citizens.

Concerning outside supervision of the CIA, the commission recommended the creation of a Congressional joint oversight committee to assume the current roles of the intelligence subcommittees of the House and Senate Armed Services Committees. The functions of the President's Foreign Intelligence Advisory Board should be expanded to include oversight of CIA activities. Congress should consider whether the budget of the CIA, to some extent, should be made public. The Justice Department and the CIA should formulate written guidelines on the prosecution

of CIA employes violating the law; and the CIA should "scrupulously avoid" exercise of the prosecutorial function.

The commission recommended internal reorganization of the CIA. It said that directors of the agency should come from outside CIA career service and be barred for serving more than ten years in that capacity. There should be two deputy directors of the agency instead of the current one. The office of the Inspector General should be upgraded to a status equal to that of the agency's four directorates, and its authority to act against violations of the law by the agency and its employes strengthened. The Office of General Counsel should be invigorated by bringing lawyers from outside the agency and assigning agency lawyers elsewhere in the government to widen their horizons. "To a degree consistent with security," the agency should encourage lateral movement of its personnel between agency directorates, as well as bring into the agency at all levels persons with outside experience. Employes of the agency should be issued detailed guidelines specifying what were legal and proper agency activities.

Other recommendations by the commission included: mail examination should be conducted only in furtherance of legitimate agency activities and should be done in accordance with postal regulations. Presidents should refrain from requesting the agency to involve itself in internal security activities. The agency should resist such attempts to involve it in improper activities and "should guard against allowing any component (like the Special Operations Group) to become so self-contained and isolated from top leadership that regular supervision and review are lost."

The CIA should not infiltrate dissident groups in the U.S. without a written determination by the CIA director that such action was necessary and that adequate coverage by law enforcement agencies was unavailable. The CIA's director should issue guidelines setting forth situations in which the agency would be justified in conducting investigations of persons currently or formerly affiliated with it. The agency should conduct periodic reviews of its files, with a view to declassifying as much of that material as possible. Congress should pass legislation making it a criminal offense for a present or former employe to divulge classified foreign intelligence information obtained in the course of employment at the CIA.

Physical surveillance of persons in the U.S. should be undertaken only after written approval by the CIA's director. The agency should not engage in electronic surveillance in the U.S. that would require a judicial warrant if done by a law enforcement agency. The agency should strictly adhere to established legal procedures governing access to federal income tax information.

To avoid future misuse of the CIA by the White House, "a single and exclusive high-level channel should be established for transmission of all White House staff requests to the CIA."

Excerpts From Summary of Rockefeller Commission's Report on the CIA

The following are excerpts from the official summary of the report to President Ford by the Commission on Central Intelligence Activities Within the United States. It was made public June 10.

The Fundamental Issues

In announcing the formation of this commission, the President noted that an effective intelligence and counterintelligence capability is essential to provide "the safeguards that protect our national interest and help avert armed conflicts."

While it is vital that security requirements be met, the President continued, it is equally important that intelligence activities be conducted without "impairing our democratic institutions and fundamental freedoms."

The commission's assessment of the CIA's activities within the United States reflects the members' deep concern for both individual rights and national security.

A. Individual Rights

The Bill of Rights in the Constitution protects individual liberties against encroachment by government. Many statutes and the common law also reflect this protection.

The First Amendment protects the freedoms of speech and of the press, the right of the people to assemble peaceably, and the right to petition the government for redress of grievances. It has been construed to protect freedom of peaceable political association. In addition, the Fourth Amendment declares:

The right of the people to be secure in their persons, houses, papers, and effects, against unreasonable searches and seizures, shall not be violated. . . .

In accordance with the objectives enunciated in these and other Constitutional amendments, the Supreme Court has outlined the following basic constitutional doctrines:

1. Any intrusive investigation of an American citizen by the government must have a sufficient basis to warrant the invasion caused by the particular investigative practices which are utilized;

2. Government monitoring of a citizen's political activities requires even greater justification;

3. The scope of any resulting intrusion on personal privacy must not exceed the degree reasonably believed necessary;

4. With certain exceptions, the scope of which are not sharply defined, these conditions must be met, at least for significant investigative intrusions, to the satisfaction of an uninvolved governmental body such as a court.

These constitutional standards give content to an accepted principle of our society—the right of each person to a high degree of individual privacy.

In recognition of this right, President Truman and the Congress—in enacting the law creating the CIA in 1947—included a clause providing that the CIA should have no police, subpoena, law-enforcement powers or internal security functions.

Since then, Congress has further outlined citizen rights in statutes limiting electronic surveillance and granting individuals access to certain information in government files, underscoring the general concern of Congress and the executive branch in this area.

B. Government Must Obey the Law

The individual liberties of American citizens depend on government observance of the law.

Under our form of Constitutional government, authority can be exercised only if it has been properly delegated to a particular department or agency by the Constitution or Congress.

Most delegations come from Congress; some are implied from the allocation of responsibility to the President. Wherever the basic authority resides, however, it is fundamental in our scheme of Constitutional government that agencies—including the CIA—shall exercise only those powers properly assigned to them by Congress or the President.

Whenever the activities of a government agency exceed its authority, individual liberty may be impaired.

C. National Security

Individual liberties likewise depend on maintaining public order at home and in protecting the country against infiltration from abroad and armed attack. Ensuring domestic tranquility and providing for a common defense are not only Constitutional goals but necessary pre-conditions for a free, democratic system. The process of orderly and lawful change is the essence of democracy. Violent change, or forcing a change of government by the stealthy action of "enemies, foreign or domestic," is contrary to our Constitutional system.

The government has both the right and the obligation within Constitutional limits to use its available power to protect the people and their established form of government. Nevertheless, the mere invocation of the "national security" does not grant unlimited power to the government. The degree of the danger and the type of action contemplated to meet that danger require careful evaluation, to ensure that the danger is sufficient to justify the action and that fundamental rights are respected.

D. Resolving the Issues

Individual freedoms and privacy are fundamental in our society. Constitutional government must be maintained. An effective and efficient intelligence system is necessary; and to be effective, many of its activities must be conducted in secrecy.

Satisfying these objectives presents considerable opportunity for conflict. The vigorous pursuit of intelligence by certain methods can lead to invasions of individual rights. The preservation of the United States requires an effective intelligence capability, but the preservation of individual liberties within the United States requires limitations or restrictions on gatherings of intelligence. The drawing of reasonable lines—where legitimate intelligence needs end and erosion of Constitutional government begins—is difficult.

In seeking to draw such lines, we have been guided in the first instance by the commands of the Constitution as they have been interpreted by the Supreme Court, the laws as written by Congress, the values we believe are reflected in the democratic process, and the faith we have in a free society. We have also sought to be fully cognizant of the needs of national security, the requirements of a strong national defense against external aggression and internal subversion, and the duty of the government to protect its citizens.

In the final analysis, public safety and individual liberty sustain each other.

FINDINGS AND CONCLUSIONS
Summary of Findings

A detailed analysis of the facts has convinced the commission that the great majority of the CIA's domestic activities comply with its statutory authority.

Nevertheless, over the 28 years of its history, the CIA has engaged in some activities that should be criticized and not permitted to happen again—both in light of the limits imposed on the Agency by law and as a matter of public policy.

Some of these activities were initiated or ordered by Presidents, either directly or indirectly.

Some of them fall within the doubtful area between responsibilities delegated to the CIA by Congress and the National Security Council on the one hand and activities specifically prohibited to the Agency on the other.

Some of them are plainly unlawful and constituted improper invasions upon the rights of Americans.

The agency's own recent actions, undertaken for the most part in 1973 and 1974, have gone far to terminate the activities upon which this investigation has focused. The recommendations of the commission are designed to clarify areas of doubt concerning the Agency's authority, to strengthen the Agency's structure, and to guard against recurrences of these improprieties.

The CIA's Role and Authority
Findings

The Central Intelligence Agency was established by the National Security Act of 1947 as the nation's first comprehensive peacetime foreign intelligence service. The objective was to provide the President with coordinated intelligence, which the country lacked prior to the attack on Pearl Harbor.

The director of central intelligence reports directly to the President. The CIA receives its policy direction and guidance from the National Security Council, composed of the President, the Vice President, and the Secretaries of State and Defense.

The statute directs the CIA to correlate, evaluate, and disseminate intelligence obtained from United States intelligence agencies, and to perform such other functions related to intelligence as the National Security Council directs. Recognizing that the CIA would be dealing with sensitive, secret materials, Congress made the director of central intelligence responsible for protecting intelligence sources and methods from unauthorized disclosure.

At the same time, Congress sought to assure the American public that it was not establishing a secret police which would threaten the civil liberties of Americans. It specifically forbade the CIA from exercising "police, subpoena, or law-enforcement powers or internal security functions." The CIA was not to replace the Federal Bureau of Investigation in conducting domestic activities to investigate crime or internal subversion.

Although Congress contemplated that the focus of the CIA would be on foreign intelligence, it understood that some of its activities would be conducted within the United States. The CIA necessarily maintains its headquarters here, procures logistical support, recruits and trains employees, tests equipment, and conducts other domestic activities in support of its foreign intelligence mission. It makes necessary investigations in the United States to maintain the security of its facilities and personnel.

Additionally, it has been understood from the beginning that the CIA is permitted to collect foreign intelligence—that is, information concerning foreign capabilities, intentions, and activities—from American citizens within this country by overt means.

Determining the legal propriety of domestic activities of the CIA requires the application of the law to the particular facts involved. This task involves consideration of more than the National Security Act and the directives of the National Security Council; constitutional and other statutory provisions also circumscribe the domestic activities of the CIA. Among the applicable constitutional provisions are the First Amendment, protecting freedom of speech, of the press, and of peaceable assembly; and the Fourth Amendment, prohibiting unreasonable searches and seizures. Among the statutory provisions are those which limit such activities as electronic eavesdropping and interception of the mails.

The precise scope of many of these statutory and constitutional provisions is not easily stated. The National Security Act in particular was drafted in broad terms in order to provide flexibility for the CIA to adapt to changing intelligence needs. Such critical phrases as "internal security functions" are left undefined. The meaning of the director's responsibility to protect intelligence sources and methods from unauthorized disclosure has also been a subject of uncertainty.

The word "foreign" appears nowhere in the statutory grant of authority, though it has always been understood that the CIA's mission is limited to matters related to foreign intelligence. This apparent statutory ambiguity, although not posing problems in practice, has troubled members of the public who read the statute without having the benefit of the legislative history and the instructions to the CIA from the National Security Council.

Conclusions

The evidence within the scope of this inquiry does not indicate that fundamental rewriting of the National Security Act is either necessary or appropriate.

The evidence does demonstrate the need for some statutory and administrative clarification of the role and function of the Agency.

Ambiguities have been partially responsible for some, though not all, of the Agency's deviations within the United States from its assigned mission. In some cases, reasonable persons will differ as to the lawfulness of the activity; in others, the absence of clear guidelines as to its authority deprived the Agency of a means of resisting pressures to engage in activities which now appear to us improper.

The CIA's Mail Intercepts
Findings

At the time the CIA came into being, one of the highest national intelligence priorities was to gain an understanding of the Soviet Union and its worldwide activities affecting our national security.

In this context, the CIA began in 1952 a program of surveying mail between the United States and the Soviet Union as it passed through a New York postal facility. In 1953 it began opening some of this mail. This program was expanded over the following two decades and ultimately involved the opening of many letters and the analysis of envelopes, or "covers," of a great many more letters.

The New York mail intercept was designed to attempt to identify persons within the United States who were cooperating with the Soviet Union and its intelligence forces to harm the United States. It was also intended to determine technical communications procedures and mail censorship techniques used by the Soviets.

The director of the Central Intelligence Agency approved commencement of the New York mail intercept in 1952. During the ensuing years so far as the record shows, Postmasters General Arthur E. Summerfield, J. Edward Day, and Winton M. Blount were informed of the program in varying degrees, as was Attorney General John N. Mitchell. Since 1958, the FBI was aware of this program and received 57,000 items from it.

A 1962 CIA memorandum indicates the Agency was aware that the mail openings would be viewed as violating federal criminal laws prohibiting obstruction or delay of the mails.

In the last year before the termination of this program, out of 4,350,000 items of mail sent to and from the Soviet Union, the New York intercept examined the outside of 2,300,000 of these items, photographed 33,000 envelopes, and opened 8,700.

The mail intercept was terminated in 1973 when the chief postal inspector refused to allow its continuation without an up-to-date high-level approval.

The CIA also ran much smaller mail intercepts for brief periods in San Francisco between 1969 and 1971 and in the territory of Hawaii during 1954 and 1955. For a short period in 1957, mail in transit between foreign countries was intercepted in New Orleans.

Conclusions

While in operation, the CIA's domestic mail opening programs were unlawful. United States statutes specifically forbid opening the mail.

The mail openings also raise constitutional questions under the Fourth Amendment guarantees against unreasonable search, and the scope of the New York project poses possible difficulties with the First Amendment rights of speech and press.

Mail cover operations (examining and copying of envelopes only) are legal when carried out in compliance with postal regulations on a limited and selective basis involving matters of national security. The New York mail intercept did not meet these criteria.

The nature and degree of assistance given by the CIA to the FBI in the New York mail project indicate that the CIA's primary purpose eventually became participation with the FBI in internal security functions. Accordingly, the CIA's participation was prohibited under the National Security Act.

Special Operations Group —Operation Chaos

Findings

The late 1960's and early 1970's were marked by widespread violence and civil disorders. Demonstrations, marches and protest assemblies were frequent in a number of cities. Many universities and college campuses became places of disruption and unrest. Government facilities were picketed and sometimes invaded. Threats of bombing and bombing incidents occurred frequently. In Washington and other major cities, special security measures had to be instituted to control the access to public buildings.

Responding to Presidential requests made in the face of growing domestic disorder, the director of central intelligence in August 1967 established a special operations group within the CIA to collect, coordinate, evaluate and report on the extent of foreign influence on domestic dissidence.

The group's activities, which later came to be known as Operation Chaos, led the CIA to collect information on dissident Americans from CIA field stations overseas and from the FBI.

Although the stated purpose of the operation was to determine whether there were any foreign contacts with American dissident groups, it resulted in the accumulation of considerable material on domestic dissidents and their activities.

During six years, the operation compiled some 13,000 different files, including files on 7,200 American citizens. The documents in these files and related ma-

terials included the names of more than 300,000 persons and organizations, which were entered into a computerized index.

This information was kept closely guarded within the CIA. Using this information, personnel of the group prepared 3,500 memoranda for internal use; 3,000 memoranda for dissemination to the FBI; and 37 memoranda for distribution to White House and other top level officials in the government.

The staff assigned to the operation was steadily enlarged in response to repeated Presidential requests for additional information, ultimately reaching a maximum of 52 in 1971. Because of excessive isolation, the operation was substantially insulated from meaningful review within the agency, including review by the Counterintelligence Staff—of which the operation was technically a part.

Commencing in late 1969, Operation Chaos used a number of agents to collect intelligence abroad on any foreign connections with American dissident groups. In order to have sufficient "cover" for these agents, the operation recruited persons from domestic dissident groups or recruited others and instructed them to associate with such groups in this country.

Most of the operation's recruits were not directed to collect information domestically on American dissidents. On a number of occasions, however, such information was reported by the recruits while they were developing dissident credentials in the United States, and the information was retained in the files of the operation. On three occasions, an agent of the operation was specifically directed to collect domestic intelligence.

No evidence was found that any Operation Chaos agent used or was directed by the Agency to use electronic surveillance, wiretaps or break-ins in the United States against any dissident individual or group.

Activity of the operation decreased substantially by mid-1972. The operation was formally terminated in March 1974.

Conclusions

Some domestic activities of Operation Chaos unlawfully exceeded the CIA's statutory authority, even though the declared mission of gathering intelligence abroad as to foreign influence on domestic dissident activities was proper.

Most significantly, the operation became a repository for large quantities of information on the domestic activities of American citizens. This information was derived principally from FBI reports or from overt sources and not from clandestine collection by the CIA, and much of it was not directly related to the question of the existence of foreign connections.

It was probably necessary for the CIA to accumulate an information base on domestic dissident activities in order to assess fairly whether the activities had foreign connections. The FBI would collect information but would not evaluate it. But the accumulation of domestic data in the operation exceeded what was reasonably required to make such an assessment and was thus improper.

The use of agents of the operation on three occasions to gather information within the United States on strictly domestic matters was beyond the CIA's authority. In addition the intelligence disseminations and those portions of a major study prepared by the Agency which dealt with purely domestic matters were improper.

The isolation of Operation Chaos within the CIA and its independence from supervision by the regular chain of command within the clandestine service made it possible for the activities of the operation to stray over the bounds of the Agency's authority without the knowledge of senior officials. The absence of any regular review of these activities prevented timely correction of such missteps as did occur.

Protection of the Agency Against Threats of Violence

Findings

The CIA was not immune from the threats of violence and disruption during the period of domestic unrest between 1967 and 1972. The Office of Security was charged throughout this period with the responsibility of ensuring the continued functioning of the CIA.

The office therefore, from 1967 to 1970, had its field officers collect information from published materials, law enforcement authorities, other agencies and college officials before recruiters were sent to some campuses. Monitoring and communications support was provided to recruiters when trouble was expected.

The office was also responsible, with the approval of

the director of central intelligence, for a program from February 1967 to December 1968, which at first monitored, but later infiltrated, dissident organizations in the Washington, D.C., area to determine if the groups planned any activities against CIA or other government installations.

At no time were more than 12 persons performing these tasks, and they performed them on a part-time basis. The project was terminated when the Washington Metropolitan Police Department developed its own intelligence capability.

In December, 1967, the office began a continuing study of dissident activity in the United States, using information from published and other voluntary knowledgeable sources. The office produced weekly situation information reports analyzing dissident activities and providing calendars of future events. Calendars were given to the Secret Service, but the CIA made no other disseminations outside the agency. About 500 to 800 files were maintained on dissenting organizations and individuals. Thousands of names in the files were indexed. Report publication was ended in late 1972, and the entire project was ended in 1973.

Conclusions

The program under which the Office of Security rendered assistance to agency recruiters on college campuses was justified as an exercise of the Agency's responsibility to protect its own personnel and operations. Such support activities were not undertaken for the purpose of protecting the facilities or operations of other governmental agencies, or to maintain public order or enforce laws.

The agency should not infiltrate a dissident group for security purposes unless there is a clear danger to Agency installations, operations or personnel, and investigative coverage of the threat by the FBI and local law enforcement authorities is inadequate. The agency's infiltration of dissident groups in the Washington area went far beyond steps necessary to protect the agency's own facilities, personnel and operations, and therefore exceeded the CIA's statutory authority.

In addition, the Agency undertook to protect other government departments and agencies—a police function prohibited to it by statute.

Intelligence activity directed toward learning from what sources a domestic dissident group receives its financial support within the United States, and how much income it has, is no part of the authorized security operations of the agency. Neither is it the function of the agency to compile records on who attends peaceful meetings of such dissident groups, or what each speaker has to say (unless it relates to disruptive or violent activity which may be directed against the agency).

The agency's actions in contributing funds, photographing people, activities and cars, and following people home were unreasonable under the circumstances and therefore exceeded the CIA's authority.

With certain exceptions, the program under which the Office of Security (without infiltration) gathered, organized and analyzed information about dissident groups for purposes of security was within the CIA's authority.

The accumulation of reference files on dissident organizations and their leaders was appropriate both to evaluate the risks posed to the agency and to develop an understanding of dissident groups and their differences for security clearance purposes. But the accumulation of information on domestic activities went beyond what was required by the agency's legitimate security needs and therefore exceeded the CIA's authority.

Investigations of Possible Breaches of Security

Findings

The Office of Security has been called upon on a number of occasions to investigate specific allegations that intelligence sources and methods were threatened by unauthorized disclosures. The commission's inquiry concentrated on those investigations which used investigative means intruding on the privacy of the subjects, including physical and electronic surveillance, unauthorized entry, mail covers and intercepts, and reviews of individual federal tax returns.

The large majority of these investigations were directed at persons affiliated with the agency—such as employees, former employees, and defectors and other foreign nationals used by the agency as intelligence sources.

A few investigations involving intrusions on personal privacy were directed at subjects with no relationship to the Agency. The commission has found no evidence that any such investigations were directed against any congressman, judge, or other public official. Five were directed against newsmen, in an effort to determine their sources of leaked classified information, and nine were directed against other United States citizens.

The CIA's investigations of newsmen to determine their sources of classified information stemmed from pressures from the White House and were partly a result of the FBI's unwillingness to undertake such investigations. The FBI refused to proceed without an advance opinion that the Justice Department would prosecute if a case were developed.

Conclusions

Investigations of allegations against agency employees and operatives are a reasonable exercise of the director's statutory duty to protect intelligence sources and methods from unauthorized disclosure if the investigations are lawfully conducted. Such investigations also assist the director in the exercise of his unreviewable authority to terminate the employment of any agency employee. They are proper unless their principal purpose becomes law-enforcement or the maintenance of internal security.

The director's responsibility to protect intelligence sources and methods is not so broad as to permit investigations of persons having no relationship whatever with the agency. The CIA has no authority to investigate newsmen simply because they have published leaked classified information. Investigations by the CIA should be limited to persons presently or formerly affiliated with the agency, directly or indirectly.

Investigative Techniques

Findings

Even an investigation within the CIA's authority must be conducted by lawful means. Some of the past investigations by the Office of Security within the United States were conducted by means which were invalid at the time. Others might have been lawful when conducted, but would be impermissible today.

Some investigations involved physical surveillance of the individuals concerned, possibly in conjunction with other methods of investigations. The last instance of physical surveillance by the Agency within the United States occurred in 1973.

The investigation disclosed the domestic use of 32 wiretaps, the last in 1965; 32 instances of bugging, the last in 1968; and 12 break-ins, the last in 1971. None of these activities was conducted under a judicial warrant, and only one with the written approval of the Attorney General.

Information from the income tax records of 16 persons was obtained from the Internal Revenue Service by the CIA in order to help determine whether the taxpayer was a security risk with possible connections to foreign groups. The CIA did not employ the existing statutory and regulatory procedures for obtaining such records from the IRS.

In 91 instances, mail covers (the photographing of the front and back of an envelope) were employed, and in 12 instances letters were intercepted and opened.

The state of the CIA records on these activities is such that it is often difficult to determine why the investigation occurred in the first place, who authorized the special coverage, and what the results were. Although there was testimony that these activities were frequently known to the director of central intelligence and sometimes to the Attorney General, the files often are insufficient to confirm such information.

Conclusions

The use of physical surveillance is not unlawful unless it reaches the point of harassment. The unauthorized entries described were illegal when conducted and would be illegal if conducted today. Likewise, the review of individuals' federal tax returns and the interception and opening of mail violated specific statutes and regulations prohibiting such conduct.

Since the constitutional and statutory constraints applicable to the use of electronic eavesdropping (bugs and wiretaps) have been evolving over the years, the commission deems it impractical to apply those changing standards on a case-by-case basis. The commission does believe that while some of the instances of electronic eavesdropping were proper when conducted, many were not. To be lawful today, such activities would require at least the written approval of the Attorney General on the basis of a finding that the national security is involved and that the case has significant foreign connections.

Handling of Defectors

Findings

The Office of Security is charged with providing security for persons who have defected to the United States. Generally a defector can be processed and placed into society in a few months, but one defector was involuntarily confined at a CIA installation for three years. He was held in solitary confinement under spartan living conditions. The CIA maintained the long confinement because of doubts about the bona fides of the defector. This confinement was approved by the Director of Central Intelligence; and the FBI, Attorney General, United States Intelligence Board and selected members of Congress were aware to some extent of the confinement. In one other case a defector was physically abused; the Director of Central Intelligence discharged the employee involved.

Conclusions

Such treatment of individuals by an agency of the United States is unlawful. The Director of Central Intelligence and the Inspector General must be alert to prevent repetitions.

Domestic Activities of the Directorate of Science and Technology

Findings and Conclusions

The CIA's Directorate of Science and Technology performs a variety of research and development and operational support functions for the Agency's foreign intelligence mission.

Many of these activities are performed in the United States and involve cooperation with private companies. A few of these activities were improper or questionable.

As part of a program to test the influence of drugs on humans, research included the administration of LSD to persons who were unaware that they were being tested. This was clearly illegal. One person died in 1953, apparently as a result. In 1963, following the Inspector General's discovery of these events, new stringent criteria were issued prohibiting drug testing by the CIA on unknown persons. All drug testing programs were ended in 1967.

In the process of testing monitoring equipment for use overseas, the CIA has overheard conversations between Americans. The names of the speakers were not identified; the contents of the conversations were not disseminated. All recordings were destroyed when testing was concluded. Such testing should not be directed against unsuspecting persons in the United States. Most of the testing undertaken by the Agency could easily have been performed using only Agency personnel and with the full knowledge of those whose conversations were being recorded. This is the present Agency practice.

Funding Requests From Other Federal Agencies

In the spring of 1970, at the request of the White House, the CIA contributed $33,655.68 for payment of stationery and other costs for replies to persons who wrote the President after the invasion of Cambodia.

This use of CIA funds for a purpose unrelated to intelligence is improper. Steps should be taken to ensure against any repetition of such an incident.

Indices and Files on American Citizens

Findings

Biographical information is a major resource of an intelligence agency. The CIA maintains a number of files and indices that include biographical information on Americans.

As a part of its normal process of indexing names and information of foreign intelligence interest, the directorate of operations has indexed some 7 million names of all nationalities. An estimated 115,000 of these are believed to be American citizens.

Where a person is believed to be of possibly continuing intelligence interest, files to collect information as received are opened. An estimated 57,000 out of a total of 750,000 such files concern American citizens. For the most part, the names of Americans appear in indices and files as actual or potential sources of information or assistance to the CIA. In addition to these files, files on some 7,200 American citizens, relating primarily to their domestic activities, were, as already stated, compiled within the Directorate of operations as part of Operation Chaos.

The directorate of administration maintains a number of files on persons who have been associated with the CIA. These files are maintained for security, personnel, training, medical and payroll purposes. Very few are maintained on persons unaware that they have a relationship with the CIA. However, the Office of Security maintained files on American citizens associated with dissident groups who were never affiliated with the agency because they were considered a threat to the physical security of agency facilities and employees. These files were also maintained, in part, for use in future security clearance determinations. Dissemination of security files is restricted to persons with an operational need for them.

The office of legislative counsel maintains files concerning its relationships with congressmen.

Conclusions

Although maintenance of most of the indices, files, and records of the Agency has been necessary and proper, the standards applied by the Agency at some points during its history have permitted the accumulation and indexing of materials not needed for legitimate intelligence or security purposes. Included in this category are many of the files related to Operation Chaos and the activities of the Office of Security concerning dissident groups.

Constant vigilance by the agency is essential to prevent the collection of information on United States citizens which is not needed for proper intelligence activities. The executive order recommended by the commission will ensure purging of nonessential or improper materials from agency files.

Allegations Concerning the Assassination of President Kennedy

Numerous allegations have been made that the CIA participated in the assassination of President John F. Kennedy. The commission staff investigated these allegations. On the basis of the staff's investigation, the commission concludes that there is no credible evidence of CIA involvement.

Drug Experiments

LSD suicide identified. The widow and children of a Central Intelligence Agency employe who killed himself in 1953 after unknowingly taking LSD learned the circumstances of his death only after reading the Rockefeller Commission report on CIA activities, according to July 10 news accounts.

The family of Frank R. Olson—his wife Alice, his sons Nils and Eric and his married daughter Lisa Hayward—decided after weeks of discussion to contact reporters "to get the story out, so our father's friends and colleagues—and also our friends—could know what the CIA has done," the *New York Times* July 10 quoted Eric Olson as saying. The *Times* also said that David W. Belin, director of the Rockefeller panel, had confirmed Olson's death. Belin added: "The staff didn't feel it was necessary to talk to the family. They didn't know what it would add—once we found out what had happened."

In a statement given to reporters at the family home in Frederick, Md., Mrs.

Olson said her husband had been a researcher for the CIA in biological warfare at nearby Fort Detrick, Md., and that two weeks before his death he had attended several days of meetings and been given LSD "without his knowledge or consent." He returned home and "was very quiet, he was an entirely different person," Mrs. Olson said. "I didn't know what had happened. I just knew that something was terribly wrong. The entire weekend he was very melancholy and talked about a mistake he had made. He said he was going to leave his job." During the following week, Olson was taken to New York City to consult Dr. Harold A. Abramson, a psychiatrist, and several days later his family was told he had committed suicide by jumping from the 10th floor of the Statler Hotel in Manhattan. Mrs. Olson declared that a CIA employe, her husband's escort, had told of waking up at 1:30 a.m. and seeing Olson run across the room and jump through both a closed window and a drawn shade.

The *New York Times* July 11 cited a 1953 police report by Detective James W. Ward which gave another version of Olson's visit to New York. It said he had arrived with Col. Vincent Ruwet, also attached to Fort Detrick, and had returned to Washington after two consultations with Dr. Abramson. When Olson came back to New York later that day, according to Ward's report, he was accompanied by a man who called himself Robert Lashbrook. "They again visited the doctor and as a result of this visit Olson was advised to enter a sanitarium as he was suffering from severe psychosis and delusions," Ward said. That night, Lashbrook told Ward, he woke up at about 3:20 a.m. to a "crash of glass," telephoned the hotel operator and, "at this time, learned that Olson had jumped out of the window."

Dr. Dominick Di Maio, acting chief medical examiner for New York City, said July 11 he was reopening the case and that Manhattan District Attorney Robert M. Morgenthau was attempting to determine whether he had jurisdiction and whether the statute of limitations had expired. Dr. Di Maio said Lashbrook "never mentioned the man had taken LSD" or that Olson was "under psychiatric treatment, and he didn't give us the name of the physician."

The *New York Times* July 12 said the Olson family believed Lashbrook and a man they identified as Sidney Gottlieb had given the drug to Frank Olson, but the CIA refused to say whether either Lashbrook or Gottlieb had ever been employed by the agency.

The *Washington Post* July 13 reported a telephone interview the previous day with James Roethe, the attorney in charge of the Rockefeller Commission's study, who said the document did not contain all the panel had learned about CIA drug experiments. Roethe said: "I really don't feel that I'm going to be in a position to make a comment unless something so outrageous comes out that I feel I have to, and at this point I haven't seen anything." The *Post* printed a list of names, furnished by the Olson family, of those present at the 1953 meeting in which Frank Olson and others were given the LSD.

CIA drug spying—The *New York Times* July 10 disclosed that John N. Mitchell, the former attorney general, and former CIA Director Richard Helms had authorized and overseen a project in which CIA agents were placed in the Bureau of Narcotics and Dangerous Drugs. The *Times* said the program, financed by "unvouchered" funds available to Attorney General Mitchell, had not been disturbed by Mitchell's two successors, Richard G. Kleindienst and Elliot L. Richardson, and was ended in 1973 by CIA Director William E. Colby when the Drug Enforcement Administration absorbed the narcotics bureau. The Rockefeller Commission had found the program in violation of the CIA's charter.

Ford apologizes to Olsons. President Ford held a White House meeting July 21 with the family of Frank R. Olson—his widow and three children—and apologized to them for "the wrong that's been done to you."

Presidential Press Secretary Ron Nessen said the initiative for the meeting had come from Ford, who "feels very strongly about this" and had asked Attorney General Edward H. Levi to meet with legal representatives of the family "to discuss the claims they wish to assert against the CIA by reason of Dr. Olson's death." Nessen also said Ford had instructed the White House's counsel to make available all information on the case.

An Olson family statement distributed by the White House at their request July 21 said they were grateful for President Ford's help in trying "to obtain a just resolution of this entire matter." The statement also noted: "We hope this will be part of a continuing effort to insure that the CIA is accountable for its actions and that people in all parts of the world are safe from abuses of power by American intelligence agencies."

David Kairys, one of the family's lawyers, said July 22 that "lots of documents have been destroyed, [See below] but I have the word of the President's counsel that we will be shown everything."

Lashbrook says Olson agreed—Robert V. Lashbrook, a former CIA employe who was with Frank Olson at the time of his suicide in 1953, said July 17 that Olson had agreed in principle beforehand to be the subject of an LSD experiment.

In a telephone interview with the *New York Times*, Lashbrook, now a high school science teacher in Ojai, Cal., declared: "It was my understanding that actually everyone there had agreed in advance that such a test would be conducted, that they were willing to be one of the subjects. The only thing was that the time was not specified." He said it would be "misconstruing things quite a lot to say that any individual or group of individuals were the subject of anyone doing them in." In its account of the interview

with Lashbrook, the *New York Times* July 18 quoted a section of the Rockefeller Commission report that said: "Prior to receiving the LSD, the subject [Olson] had participated in discussions where the testing of such substances on unsuspecting subjects was agreed to in principle. However, this individual was not aware that he had been given LSD until about 20 minutes after it had been administered."

Lashbrook said he himself had been a "guinea pig" several times in LSD tests and "didn't like it." He noted, however, that any "direct relationship" between the drug and Olson's death "would be a little hard to justify" because Olson's body would have eliminated all elements of the drug long before his death, which took place more than a week after the experiment. "Possibly LSD had brought up something in his past that was bothering him," Lashbrook ventured.

The *Washington Post* July 18 reported Lashbrook as saying the reason he didn't mention LSD in his account of Olson's death given to New York police officials in 1953 was that it "was certainly controversial as to what the direct cause and effect might have been." Lashbrook told the *Post* that after Olson's death he had phoned Sidney Gottlieb in Washington to inform him of what had happened. Asked who had decided to administer the drug to Olson and when, Lashbrook replied he was "not too sure" and that "in any case, I don't really want to name them."

Gottlieb destroyed LSD data—The *New York Times* July 18 reported that Dr. Sidney Gottlieb, a biochemist and former head of the CIA's program of testing LSD, had destroyed the program's records in 1973, ten years after the experiments were believed to have been halted.

The *Times*, alluding to sources on the staff of the Rockefeller Commission, said Gottlieb had thrown out a total of 152 separate files and that Richard Helms, then director of the agency, had also destroyed records.

Army LSD tests reported—News sources July 18 reported that the Department of the Army had conducted LSD experiments with some 1,500 persons in the 1950s and the 1960s, some of them at the Edgewood Arsenal in Maryland, the Army's chemical warfare research counterpart to Ft. Detrick, where Frank Olson was a CIA employe at the time of his death.

A total of 585 persons, most of them soldiers, were said to have participated in experiments at the Edgewood Arsenal, at Fort Bragg in North Carolina, Fort McClellan in Alabama, Dugway Proving Ground in Utah and Fort Benning in Georgia.

An additional 900 civilians were tested in Army-sponsored experiments at the University of Maryland Psychiatric Institute, the New York Psychiatric Institute, the University of Wisconsin, the University of Washington Medical School and the Tulane University Department of Neurology and Psychiatry.

The tests were reported to have been conducted between 1956 and 1967.

Army suspends drug test program. The Army said July 28 it was suspending drug and chemical experiments on human subjects in order to "determine all the facts connected with the test programs." The action came 10 days after the Army had acknowledged administering LSD to almost 1,500 military and civilian personnel between 1956 and 1967. It said it planned to find and give all of them physical and mental examinations to determine if they had suffered any ill effects.

The *New York Times* reported July 29, however, that suspension of the testing had occurred partly because of questions raised about the background of the head of the research program, Dr. Van M. Sim, as well as queries from the press, members of Congress and former test subjects.

Sim, at a Pentagon press conference July 23, had defended the test program, which involved 900 civilian and 6,983 military volunteers over a 20-year period. The Army had ended its testing of LSD on humans in 1967, but continued experiments on soldiers with other drugs that produced hallucinations similar to those caused by LSD, said Sim, civilian medical research director at the Army's Edgewood Arsenal in northeastern Maryland.

Sim said none of 585 Army volunteers given LSD was told the name of the drug or that it sometimes produced side effects. To have identified the drug and its possible effects would have prejudiced the experiment, he said. (Sim added that follow-up studies had been done on 10% of the men, but he retracted this statement Aug. 2, saying he had made a mistake and that the Army had done a follow-up on only two test subjects.)

He said he considered the experiments "very important" to national security and did not consider them hazardous because the subjects were carefully supervised. He knew of no deaths or prolonged hospitalizations resulting from the LSD experiments, Sim said. Seven men subsequently showed side effects, but the doctors treating them were sent "full explanations" of the experiments, Sim said.

Sim, who said other test subjects in the Army's program were given drugs ranging from alcohol to barbiturates, claimed he was unfamiliar with the LSD experiments involving 900 civilians. These tests were conducted by universities and private institutions under Army contracts, he said.

Following Sim's news conference, the Army disclosed that 2,940 of the program's military volunteers had been tested with BZ (3-quinuclidinyl benzilate), a hallucinogenic drug more powerful than LSD. BZ, whose effects of disorientation and hallucinations lasted up to 80 hours, was developed for use in situations such as civilian riots, protection of military combat areas and military rescue missions, the Army stated. (No follow-up examinations on volunteers who took BZ were performed, the Army said Aug. 14.)

1953 fatality linked to drug test. The Army disclosed Aug. 12 that a patient in a New York City mental hospital had died in 1953 during an Army-sponsored experiment with a hallucinogenic drug. The patient, Harold Blauer, 42, died shortly after being injected with a derivative of mescaline, said the Army, which had not previously admitted sponsoring the experiment.

According to the Army, Blauer had been given the drug in a series of five tests at the New York State Psychiatric Institute by civilian physicians working under an Army contract with the institute. The first four tests, the Army said, produced mild or no effects. However, Blauer apparently suffered an allergic reaction on the fifth test and his cardiovascular system collapsed.

Army officials indicated they could not say whether Blauer, a tennis pro, had consented to the experiment. One of his daughters, Elizabeth Barrett, 35, said she remembered being told that the drugs were administered on his doctor's orders.

Blauer's widow, who was never told of the Army's involvement, sued the New York State Department of Mental Hygiene and the institute but later settled out of court for $13,000.

The daughter, who said she was only 13 years old at the time of her father's death, recalled being told by her mother (who died in 1974) that her father had received LSD. In addition, she said her mother had said that her father had been given experimental drugs twice before his death and had reacted badly both times. She said her father "absolutely" had not volunteered for the experiment.

Blauer's daughter sues the Army—The daughter of a psychiatric patient who died in 1953 during an Army-sponsored experiment with hallucinogenic drugs filed an $8.5 million lawsuit against the Army for what she said was the wrongful death of her father, it was reported Sept. 4.

The woman, Elizabeth Barrett, also made public a written medical log containing observations of her father for the nine days before his death. The log showed, she said, that her father, Harold Blauer, was "terrified all the way through the experiment" and that he had complained bitterly of his reactions to the test drugs, derivatives of mescaline.

In a related development, the Army disclosed Sept. 10 that less than a year after Blauer's death at the New York State Psychiatric Institute in New York City, it awarded the institute another contract to continue experimenting with hallucinogenic drugs on humans for four more years. Moreover, the Army continued its contract with the institute despite a ruling in 1955 by a state judge that Blauer's death was the result of negligence on the part of the hospital, an Army spokesman said.

Army drug tests ignored guidelines. The Army's surgeon general and its general counsel acknowledged in congressional testimony Sept. 8 that medical "ethics codes and procedural safeguards" had been violated in drug experiments Army

researchers conducted on thousands of volunteers between 1953 and 1969.

Lt. Gen. Richard R. Taylor, surgeon general of the Army, told the House Armed Services Investigations Subcommittee that it had been Defense Department policy since 1953 that human subjects in experiments be completely informed of the nature, purpose and effects of the testing and that they give voluntary, written consent. These same regulations, Taylor testified, required that experiments involving humans be approved by the secretary of the Army.

However, Taylor said he had been unable to find evidence of compliance with the latter requirement until 1958, three years after researchers at Edgewood Arsenal in northeast Maryland had begun giving human test subjects LSD and other drugs. He said he had been able to find only sketchy compliance afterward.

Charles D. Ablard, general counsel to the Army, testified that an internal investigation by the Army had found "some indication" that "some commanders" had "exceeded what they should have done" in attempting to encourage men under their commands to participate in the drug tests. "There are significant unanswered questions as to whether participation in the program was voluntary by today's criteria," he said.

Ablard also testified that the Army had begun experimenting with hallucinogenic drugs partly in the hope of finding an alternative to nuclear war, a concept he said that was openly and enthusiastically discussed in military circles and before Congress in the late 1950s. But the Army had also been interested, he said, in how such drugs might be applied to intelligence operations, particularly as a tool in interrogations or how they might be used by foreign operatives attempting to break down U.S. intelligence agents.

Dr. Van M. Sim, former director of the Edgewood testing program, attempted to rebut Taylor's and Ablard's testimony. Appearing before a joint hearing of the Senate Labor and Public Welfare Subcommittee on Health and the Judiciary Subcommittee on Administrative Practice and Procedure Sept. 12, Sim disputed claims that the surgeon general never had received full reports on the experiments. Sim, who was suspended as head of the program in July amid allegations that he had improperly prescribed the pain-killing drug Demerol for himself before he went to work for the Army in 1954, told the subcommittees that in every experiment a full report averaging 52 pages was made for the Army with copies forwarded to the surgeon general. In addition, Sim said, Edgewood researchers conducted quarterly conferences with staff members from the surgeon general's office.

The subcommittee heard testimony Sept. 10 by Dr. Alexander M. Schmidt, commissioner of the Food and Drug Administration, who said that his office had entered into an agreement with the Pentagon in 1964 whereby the Defense Department agreed to "take full responsibility for the safety of the subjects" in its

A

B

C

D

E

F

G

secret drug tests. Schmidt said a procedure for liaison and review of the experiments had been established, but that in 11 years there had been only four meetings between officials of the Pentagon and FDA to study the classified tests. And only two of the meetings appeared to involve substantive review, he said.

Schmidt said he had "serious questions" about whether the FDA should be involved in areas of national security. Sen. Edward M. Kennedy (D, Mass.), chairman of the subcommittees, countered, however, that he could see no reason for the witness' reservations since Congress had given the FDA responsibility for the supervision of drug experiments with human subjects.

Senate Committee Investigation

Senate panel to receive Nixon data. Former President Richard M. Nixon had agreed to give the Senate Select Committee on Intelligence access to his papers and tape recordings concerning Central Intelligence Agency attempts to block the election of Salvador Allende as president of Chile in 1970, the White House said Sept. 4.

The Senate committee in early August had subpoenaed documents relating to Chile and to domestic intelligence-gathering after lawyers for President Ford insisted they could not produce the records without Nixon's consent.

Sen. Frank Church (D, Ida.), the committee's chairman, said he was satisfied with the arrangement, although Nixon's attorneys would be in charge of deciding which tape recordings and documents were covered by the subpoenas.

The *New York Times* reported Sept. 5 that the Ford Administration's decision to cooperate with the committee had been also forced by secret testimony before the committee Aug. 12 by Secretary of State Henry A. Kissinger. Kissinger had indicated in his testimony that minutes of the meetings of the National Security Council's "40 Committee" on matters involving the Nixon Administration's effort to effect a military takeover of Chile in 1970 might be germane to the information the senators were seeking. The secretary of state said he had no objections to the senators looking at the minutes, the *Times* reported.

The result of Kissinger's statement was to undercut the White House's position that a search of the former president's papers would be an intrusion that would undermine the concept of executive privilege, the *Times* reported. Moreover, the White House had said repeatedly that it would turn over the minutes of the "40 Committee's" meetings only where there was evidence of true abuse by the CIA or other agencies. (Records of the "40 Committee," the National Security Council panel that oversaw U.S. covert intelligence activities, were considered presidential papers.)

CIA kept cache of deadly poisons. Deadly toxins, some of them potent enough to kill thousands of persons, were found in a secret cache maintained by the Central Intelligence Agency, Sen. Frank Church (D, Ida.), chairman of the Senate Select Intelligence Committee, said Sept. 9.

In "direct contravention" of a 1969 order by President Nixon to destroy biological and chemical weapons, Church said, the CIA failed to destroy supplies of an instantly lethal toxin made from shellfish, and smaller amounts of cobra venom. Eight grams of cobra venom and 10.972 grams of the shellfish toxin were kept in a secret vault in a rarely used CIA laboratory in Washington, Church indicated.

CIA Director William E. Colby disclosed in public testimony before the committee Sept. 16 that as part of a secret project, code-named "M. K. Naomi," the poisons had been stockpiled. Colby said the project was so secret that he had only learned of its existence earlier in 1975 when a former agency employe brought it to his attention.

According to one CIA document released by the committee, a standard end-of-year situation report, the purposes of the Naomi project were to "stockpile severely incapacitating and lethal materials for the specific use of TSD" (technical services division of the CIA) and to "maintain in operational readiness special and unique items for the dissemination of biological and chemical weapons." The documents showed that the agency had an array of poisons, many of which caused fatal diseases, and systems for destroying crops.

Another witness before the committee Sept. 16, Dr. Nathan Gordon, a CIA chemist who retired in 1973, testified that it was at his direction the shellfish toxin and cobra venom were not destroyed in 1970. Gordon, who admitted being aware of Nixon's order, testified he received no specific order from the CIA hierarchy to dispose of the material. Moreover, Gordon said he felt that the order was directed at military weapons and that the shellfish toxin did not fall into that category.

When he heard of the presidential order, Gordon said, he approached his superior, Dr. Sidney Gottlieb, director of the technical services division, about transferring the poisons to a private laboratory in Baltimore. However, Gottlieb rejected the suggestion and ordered the poisons sent to an Army laboratory at Ft. Detrick, Md. for destruction, Gordon testified. Instead, Gordon said, he and two staff members decided to store the poisons in the Washington laboratory.

Richard Helms, director of the CIA from 1966 to 1973, informed the Senate committee Sept. 17 that he had issued an oral command to destroy the CIA's biochemical weapons stockpile but that he had not followed through to ensure execution of his order.

Thomas Karamessines, Helms' former deputy for covert operations, told the committee Sept. 17 that he and Helms had discussed the presidential directive with Gottlieb. It was his "understanding with Gottlieb that all toxins in possession of the agency be returned to Ft. Detrick for destruction," Karamessines said.

Testimony before the Senate committee indicated that none of the poisons stockpiled under Project Naomi had actually been used against any persons. Sources cited by the *New York Times* Sept. 17, however, said the panel had heard private testimony that the poisons had been prepared for use in at least two planned political assassinations. In one, the agency contemplated using poison against Patrice Lumumba, a Soviet-backed leader in the Congo (now Zaire), who later died in an unrelated episode. The other instance reportedly involved Cuban Premier Fidel Castro, the *Times* said.

U.S. Health Service aided CIA—Sen. Richard S. Schweiker (R, Pa.) announced Sept. 17 that the United States Public Health Service aided the Central Intelligence Agency in developing a shellfish toxin. Schweiker termed the practice "a perversion of the Public Health Service."

A PHS spokesman, John Blamphin, explained the agency's involvement: "Indeed this would be an improper role for the Public Health service in 1975. But at the time we were involved, national policy recognized the development of chemical and biological weaponry and as a Federal agency we had a role."

Murdock Ritchie, former head of the department of pharmacology at Yale University, testified that the PHS had been originally interested in developing a standard test to determine if shellfish beds were toxic. According to Dr. Ritchie, "The Army knew we wanted to do that and they wanted it for other purposes, obviously. So they, paid us to do it. It is reasonable to assume that under the contract we produced more than would be needed for the Public Health Service."

Army tested gas attack in New York subways. A Department of Defense engineer testified Sept. 18 at a Senate Select Committee hearing that Army scientists spread simulated biological poison on two New York City subway lines in the 1960s. The "attack" was conducted by Charles Senseney and 20 other Army employes who threw bulbs of a simulated poison onto subway tracks. The bulbs burst, and the air created by two passing subway trains carried the chemical from 15th Street to 58th Street.

Mr. Senseney concluded that the subway system "could not be safeguarded against" that type of attack. A New York City Transit Authority spokesman said Sept. 17 that no one in the agency had any knowledge of the test.

House Intelligence Committee Investigation

Intelligence budget data denied. The reconstituted House Select Committee on Intelligence Aug. 4 ended three days of public hearings in which the panel attempted to point out what it felt was the inadequacy of fiscal review of the U.S. intelligence community by the executive branch. According to the committee's chairman, Rep. Otis G. Pike (D, N.Y.), the panel's members were particularly interested in the total size of the U.S. intelligence budget and the amount of discretion intelligence agencies exercised in the expenditure of their funds.

The committee failed to learn the size of the intelligence budget, however. Elmer B. Staats, comptroller general of the General Accounting Office, testified July 31 that his agency did not know how much was spent on intelligence or whether some intelligence functions were being duplicated. The GAO, the accounting arm of Congress, had stopped auditing Central Intelligence Agency expenditures in 1962, Staats said, after being unable to obtain adequate information for a comprehensive review.

James T. Lynn, director of the Office of Management and Budget, who testified Aug. 1, declined to disclose the size of the federal intelligence budget, claiming that for him to do so might be a criminal violation of federal statutes. Under questioning by committee members, Lynn did admit that four of the six budget examiners working in the OMB's national security section had previously worked for intelligence agencies. Nevertheless, Lynn denied that intelligence agencies received special treatment during the annual budget review process.

Lynn also acknowledged under questioning that the CIA was permitted by law to spend large sums of money solely on the authority of its director. It was necessary to rely on the integrity of CIA officials in such matters, Lynn stated.

CIA Director William E. Colby appeared before the committee Aug. 4 as the representative of the U.S. intelligence community. He refused repeatedly to answer questions concerning his agency's financial operations, saying such information would be of aid to adversaries of the U.S.

FBI, IRS intelligence budgets revealed—Although it was unable to elicit budget data about U.S. foreign intelligence, the House panel, in a public hearing Aug. 7, did obtain information on intelligence expenditures by the Federal Bureau of Investigation and the Internal Revenue Service.

Eugene W. Walsh, assistant director of the FBI's administrative division, testified that the agency was spending $82.5 million a year on intelligence gathering and counterespionage. While he declined to offer a breakdown of how the bureau spent the money, he conceded that the funds had never been carefully audited by anyone outside the FBI.

Donald Alexander, director of the IRS, testified that his agency had spent $11.8 million in fiscal 1974 on intelligence gathering, mostly the pursuit of numerous tips about tax cheaters. He said he had found this operation to be generally ineffective and had scaled it down to $4.3 million a year.

U.S. failed on '73 war prediction. U.S. intelligence agencies admitted failure to predict the 1973 Arab-Israeli war despite

information gathered only hours before that such a conflict was a distinct possibility, according to a secret report made public Sept. 11 by the U.S. House Select Committee on Intelligence. The fault was attributed to the inability of the various agencies to properly assess the data they had received rather than a failure to collect intelligence.

Hours before the Arabs launched their all-out attack against Israel Oct. 6, a top-level intelligence agency had issued a statement saying, "We can find no hard evidence of a major, coordinated Egyptian-Syrian offensive across the Suez Canal and in the Golan Heights area," according to the report. The intelligence group had said the Egyptians or Syrians "may have been preparing a raid or other small action."

A Central Intelligence Agency report of Oct. 5 had acknowledged large-scale Egyptian military preparations but said "they do not appear to be preparing for a military offensive against Israel."

According to the House committee's findings, "the information provided ... was sufficient to prompt a warning." Conceding that the data "was not conclusive," the report said it "was plentiful, ominous and often accurate."

In testimony before the House committee Sept. 11, a former director of the State Department's Intelligence Bureau, Dr. Ray Cline, said his analysis one day before the Arab attack had concluded that war was imminent. Cline said he sought to give Secretary of State Henry A. Kissinger a memorandum to that effect, but the secretary's aides refused to trouble him in New York at that late hour, 8 or 9 p.m. "The memorandum was sent by pouch the next morning, but hostilities already had begun," Cline said.

The State Department said Sept. 11 that there was no evidence that Cline had tried to contact other high-ranking officials, who would have transmitted the message to Kissinger.

Tet surprise linked to false data—Samuel A. Adams, a former Vietnam intelligence specialist for the Central Intelligence Agency, charged in congressional testimony Sept. 18 that a deliberate downgrading of enemy strength was the reason the 1968 Tet offensive in South Vietnam caught U.S. officials by surprise.

Adams, who testified before the House Select Committee on Intelligence, backed up his assertions by reading to the committee parts of two "secret eyes only" cablegrams transmitted from Saigon to Washington in last half of 1967.

The first, Adams said, was a cablegram, dated Aug. 20, from the late Gen. Creighton Abrams, then deputy U.S. military commander in Vietnam, to Gen. Earle Wheeler, chairman of the Joint Chiefs of Staff. Abrams told Wheeler that newly documented enemy troop strength figures were in "sharp contrast to the current overall strength figure of about 299,-000 given to the press here." (Adams, told the committee that the new figures cited in the cablegram placed Communist strength at 600,000 troops.)

Abrams "thereupon suggested dropping two categories of VC [Viet Cong] from the strength estimate in order to keep it at its old level," Adams testified. The main reason for this Abrams said in the cable, was "press reaction," Adams told the committee.

The second cablegram, dated Oct. 28, was from Ellsworth Bunker, then U.S. ambassador to South Vietnam, to Walt W. Rostow, national security adviser to President Johnson. Bunker suggested that no public mention be made of the dropping of two Viet Cong force categories from the strength figures, Adams testified. "Given the overriding need to demonstrate progress in grinding down the enemy," Adams quoted Bunker as saying, "it is essential that we do not drag too many red herrings across the trail."

Asked by committee Chairman Otis G. Pike (D, N.Y.) if a fair characterization of his testimony would support the inference that "intelligence was shaped to fit decisions that already had been made," the witness replied, "Yes, sir."

Pike calls security agencies ineffective—Rep. Otis G. Pike, chairman of the House Committee on Intelligence, said Sept. 28 that he doubted if the U.S. intelligence agencies could warn the nation of attack. "If an attack were to be launched on America in the very near future, it is my belief that America would not know that the attack was about to be launched," he commented on CBS' "Face the Nation."

Pike continued, "I think there are thousands of dedicated men risking their lives to get intelligence. I think there are other thousands of brilliant men creating magnificent scientific techniques for gathering intelligence. Above the gathering level, however, it just bogs down every single time. It is not absorbed, it is not delivered. As far as our getting our money's worth out of it, no way we are getting our money's worth out of it."

Because Pike's committee has not yet finished its investigations, he could make no specific recommendations for improving intelligence-gathering. He said that he thought one of the problems was the size of the operation, "We are drowning in information in intelligence, which we are not absorbing."

Portuguese coup surprised intelligence agencies—Officials of three intelligence agencies told the House Intelligence Committee Oct. 7 that the 1974 coup in Portugal came as a surprise to them. William Hyland, director of the State Department's bureau of intelligence and research, testified that U.S. intelligence provided "no specific warning of the coup on April 25, 1974 in Portugal."

House panel refuses Ford offer of data. The House Select Committee on Intelligence Sept. 17 refused to accept a Ford Administration offer of classified intelligence materials, saying that the data was incomplete, had been screened in advance and delivered on the condition that it not be made public.

Rep. Otis Pike (D, N.Y.), the committee's chairman, who refused to accept the packet of documents, which bore on the

A

B

C

D

E

F

G

quality of U.S. intelligence before the 1968 Tet offensive in South Vietnam, charged the White House with attempting to frustrate committee efforts to subpoena such information. However, because of delays that would result, Pike said, the committee would not go to court to obtain compliance with its subpoena of the data.

The dispute between the House panel and the White House stemmed from the committee's publication Sept. 11 of a portion of a top-secret study showing that the U.S. intelligence community had failed to foresee the Arab-Israeli war of 1973. At the request of Central Intelligence Agency Director William E. Colby and other officials, the panel had consented to delete certain segments of the document, but had refused to suppress one four-word phrase Colby had wanted to remain secret. Disclosure of the phrase would jeopardize U.S. intelligence methods and sources, Colby had argued.

(The disputed phrase was in a Defense Intelligence Agency summary of Oct. 6, 1973, which alluded to mobilization of Egyptian troops "and greater communication security" that had been imposed. Intelligence sources said the four words indicated that the U.S. had the ability to intercept Egyptian communications despite precautions by the Egyptian government. Other sources, which the *New York Times* cited Sept. 14, suggested that the phrase referred to the fact that the Egyptian Army on Oct. 1, 1973 had ceased to use radio communication for important military messages and had begun communicating by telephone to avoid eavesdropping. The fact was well known to the Israelis who regularly monitored Egyptian military frequencies, the *Times'* sources said.)

Following the committee's decision to declassify the phrase, President Ford dispatched Assistant Attorney General Rex E. Lee to "request the immediate return" of all classified documents in the panel's possession. Moreover, Ford ordered Lee to inform the committee that no more classified documents would be forthcoming until the committee stopped claiming the right to make them public.

But during Lee's appearance before the committee Sept. 12, Pike argued that the House resolution creating the investigation and rules subsequently adopted by the committee itself made clear the panel's right to declassify documents as it saw fit. Pike protested that effective congressional scrutiny of government operations would be impossible if the executive branch had the sole power to determine what should or should not be made public.

At a closed-door meeting Sept. 17, the committee voted not to return any of the classified documents it already possessed. As a conciliatory gesture, however, the committee members agreed to give the Administration 24-hours notice before they declassified any more secret information. Members of the Administration would thus have time to explain their position and persuade the committee to keep the material secret, committee members said after the session.

House panel accepts Ford's secrecy curbs—The House Select Committee on Intelligence agreed Oct. 1 to accept President Ford's demand that it not unilaterally make public secret documents and testimony provided to it by the executive branch.

The committee's decision to abide by conditions stipulated by Ford came on a 10-3 vote to accept some 50 pages of classified data offered to the panel by William E. Colby, director of the Central Intelligence Agency. The data, which concerned the U.S. intelligence community's foreknowledge of the communists' 1968 Tet offensive in Vietnam, had been subpoenaed as part of the committee's investigation of the intelligence community's contribution to U.S. preparedness in recent international crises.

Under the agreement, President Ford retained the ultimate right to decide if a federal agency could excise portions of secret documents sought by the committee and if the committee could disclose classified or secret material to the public. The committee kept the right to seek a federal court ruling on any dispute between it and Ford.

During the three weeks prior to the agreement, the committee's investigation had been hampered by Ford's Sept. 12 decision to cut off committee access to classified materials until the committee agreed to back down from its insistence on retaining the right to decide on the declassification of secret information.

The panel had voted Sept. 30, by 10-3, to seek a resolution from the full House ordering Colby to comply "forthwith" with its subpoena for data on the Tet offensive. Chairman Otis Pike (D, N.Y.) said the resolution would be the first step in obtaining a contempt of Congress citation against Colby. The request did not come before the full House.

A separate dispute between the committee and Secretary of State Henry A. Kissinger remained unresolved, however. The dispute had arisen Sept. 25 when a State Department spokesman informed the committee that Kissinger had ordered middle-level officials not to testify about alternative diplomatic responses they had recommended to superiors in times of crisis.

Kissinger's order had been disclosed during an appearance before the committee of Thomas D. Boyatt, chief of the department's Cyprus desk at the time of the Turkish invasion of the island in 1974. The committee had sought to question Boyatt about an internal department memorandum he had written criticizing the U.S.'s diplomatic reaction to the invasion.

According to a report in the *New York Times* Oct. 3, Kissinger had two main objections to disclosure of internal memoranda and testimony by middle-level officials. Kissinger and his top aides believed, the *Times* said, that if memoranda reflecting disagreement with policy decisions were made available outside of the executive branch, the candor of such criticisms might diminish in the future. Sec-

ondly, Kissinger opposed the calling of middle level officers to account outside of the department for policy recommendations they had made to superiors.

As a result of Kissinger's refusal to turn over the Boyatt memorandum, the committee Oct. 2 voted, 9-2, to subpoena the document.

Kissinger denies data to Pike Committee—Secretary of State Kissinger Oct. 15 refused to turn over to the House Intelligence Committee a subordinate's report on U.S. policy on Cyprus. Speaking at a press conference in Ottawa, Canada, the secretary said it is "essential to protect the integrity of the Foreign Service." The House committee had subpoenaed a memorandum written by Thomas D. Boyatt, who was director of the Cyprus office in the State Department when Turkish forces invaded. Kissinger proposed "a general summary of all dissenting views" in place of the actual memorandum.

CIA Reforms

CIA aides held liable for crimes. The Justice Department ruled that Central Intelligence Agency employes, who had enjoyed immunity in the past, would henceforth be subject to federal prosecution for criminal offenses, Sen. Charles H. Percy (R, Ill.) said Sept. 11.

Percy, who indicated the new policy was approved by Attorney General Edward H. Levi, said it would put an end to a 1954 agreement between the CIA and the Justice Department whereby the agency handled investigations into and disposition of crimes by its own employes.

Assistant Attorney General Richard L. Thornburg signed a Justice Department letter to Percy which stated: "The Central Intelligence Agency is now, therefore, unquestionably bound by the same requirements as other executive branch departments and agencies with respect to referral of allegations of Title 18, U.S. [criminal] code, on the part of its officers and employes."

Ford may limit CIA's foreign activities. President Ford told the *Chicago Sun-Times* Sept. 15, 1975 that he might strip the Central Intelligence Agency of its authority to conduct secret political operations in foreign countries. Ford said he would include his recommendations on foreign activities in a major package of proposals for reorganizing the secret agency. "It is an issue that people differ on. I have listened to both sides, and I would not want to preempt that we are going to recommend by answering your question because there are strong feelings on both sides," Ford replied to reporters.

The *Sun-Times* claimed that the interview was the first time that the President had contemplated a major overhaul of the CIA. Previously, he strongly defended the agency, both in its intelligence activities and in its covert operations. Ford refused to rule out secret U.S. interventions in other countries in the future. "I don't think, you can say one policy is necessarily good for every situation. Portugal is a unique situation. They had not had democracy in Portugal for almost half a century," Ford said in reference to the CIA's absence in Portugal. He contrasted the Portuguese tradition to the Chilean: "In Chile, they have had, I think they were the first democratic system in Latin America, and in that case there was an alleged takeover through the Allende forces leading to a potential Communist coup." But, Ford continued, "I wasn't President during that period of time so I wouldn't want to pass judgement on the actions of others. I think each situation is a separate one, and you have to treat them differently."

Ford allegedly will retain foreign CIA operations. According to the *New York Times* Oct. 18, the Ford administration will resist any congressional efforts to stop foreign covert intelligence operations. The President would also resist any attempts by Congress to require prior approval before the operation could be mounted, the sources said. The President would refuse any consultations with Congress which "implies approval [in] violation of the doctrine of separation of powers, and we've been fighting this on separate fronts all along."

A

B

C

D

E

F

G

COLBY TELLS OF CIA'S PROGRAM TO UNDERMINE ALLENDE REGIME

The Nixon administration had approved covert activities in Chile by the Central Intelligence Agency in 1970–73 in an effort to undermine the government of the late President Salvador Allende Gossens, it was disclosed in Washington Sept. 8.

To finance these activities, more than $8 million was authorized by the so-called 40 Committee, a high-level intelligence panel chaired by Secretary of State Henry Kissinger in his capacity as national security adviser to former President Nixon, according to testimony by CIA Director William E. Colby to the Subcommittee on Intelligence of the House of Representatives' Armed Services Committee. Colby's testimony, given in executive session April 22, was revealed in a confidential letter from Rep. Michael J. Harrington (D, Mass.), a critic of U.S. Chilean policy, to Rep. Thomas E. Morgan (D, Pa.), chairman of the House Foreign Affairs Committee. The letter was leaked to the *New York Times* and the *Washington Post*.

Harrington asked Morgan to open a full investigation into the CIA's role in the September 1973 military coup in which Allende died and his elected government was overthrown. He said he had appealed to other legislators, but none had been willing to pursue the matter. Harrington asserted Sept. 8 that Congress avoided an investigation for fear it might turn up facts that would "damage or embarrass Kissinger." Colby's testimony was made available to Harrington by Rep. Lucien N. Nedzi (D, Mich.), chairman of the intelligence subcommittee. According to Harrington's letter, Colby testified that:

■ In 1969, before Allende's election, the 40 Committee authorized about $500,000 to "fund individuals who could be nurtured to keep the anti-Allende forces alive and intact."

■ During the 1970 election, the committee approved $500,000 to help "opposition party personnel."

■ After the election, which Allende won by a plurality, the committee earmarked $350,000 in an unsuccessful effort "to bribe the Chilean Congress" to choose Allende's opponent in the runoff vote.

■ After Allende's inaugural, the committee authorized $5 million for "more destabilization efforts during the period from 1971 to 1973."

■ In August 1973, during the wave of strikes which precipitated Allende's downfall, the committee authorized $1 million for "further political destabilization activities." The program was called off when Allende was overthrown, but the funds were spent after Chile's military government was installed, Colby testified.

At his Sept. 16 press conference, President Ford was asked, "Is it the policy of your Administration to attempt to destabilize the governments of other democracies?" Ford responded that "Our government, like other governments, does take certain actions in the intelligence field to help implement foreign policy and protect national security. I am informed reliably that Communist nations spend vastly more money than we do for the same kind of purposes. Now, in this particular case ... our government had no involvement in any way whatsoever in the coup itself ... The effort that was made in this case was to help and assist the preservation of opposition newspapers and electronic media and to preserve opposition political parties. I think this is in the best interest of the people in Chile, and certainly in our best interest."

THE SUN

Baltimore, Md.,
September 11, 1974

Democracy died one year ago today in Chile, once the most democratic of Latin American countries. It died because of an ugly combination of government mismanagement on the left, political disruption by the center, economic sabotage on the right, militarism gone rampant, subversion financed by the CIA and, most important, the endemic burdens imposed by geography and history. For a few misguided days there was hope the military leaders of the coup that toppled Salvador Allende's Marxist government would bring back civilian and democratic rule in short order. This, after all, would have been in the good tradition of the Chilean military, which had consistently supported constitutional government until the tanks moved on Rosada Palace last September 11.

The generals and admirals who seized power, however, turned out to be a frightening new phenomenon for Chile. They engaged in wholesale murder and torture of political opponents. They traduced middle-road democrats who in undercutting Allende little thought the alternative would be a harsh, rightist dictatorship. They defied the Church, saying protesting bishops were the "vehicles of Marxism." And as their regime became a pariah in many quarters they seemed ever more defiant, ever more regressive, ever more convinced that the iron fist was the only way to deal with the double specter of urban guerrilla warfare and hostile Peru.

Indeed, the only important circles even remotely tolerant of the junta have been international bankers and businessmen with interests in Chile. The World Bank, the International Monetary Fund, the Inter-American Development Bank and the so-called Paris Club of creditor nations somehow found the wherewithal to extend the junta the loans and credits that had been denied Allende. Private investments and operations accelerated as industries nationalized by Allende were compensated and induced to resume management functions.

In all this, the United States played a role steeped in hypocrisy and ineptitude. We denied having financed covert subversion against Allende only to have it disclosed last weekend, on the authority of CIA director William Colby himself, that $8 million had been used for this purpose. We engaged in an official wringing of hands over the beastly conduct of General Pinochet and his henchmen but asked Congress to increase military credits to the regime. We found ourselves an easy target for those on the political left who seek to identify the United States with dictatorial rule in Latin America.

This depressing anniversary date thus finds U.S. policy alternatives severely limited. We are properly wary of trying to interfere in the domestic political affairs of a rightist, xenophobic junta having intruded so inexcusably against a leftist regime. We find our belatedly enlightened efforts to help Chile from its economic morass shortcircuited by the sell-cheap, buy-dear squeeze hobbling so many third-world countries unendowed with oil resources. Our only recourse, therefore, is to give quiet yet open and above-board encouragement to a more civilian-oriented government in Santiago, a government that gradually will rediscover the humane and democratic impulses that for so long made Chile the most appealing of Latin nations.

The Charleston Gazette

Charleston, W. Va.,
September 12, 1974

This newspaper owes its readers an apology and the people of America, since one won't be forthcoming from their government owe the people of Chile an apology.

When President Allende either committed suicide or was executed, supporters charged that the United States was responsible for his death and the toppling of his government.

No proof to support such assertions was available, contended the Gazette. Rather President Allende's downfall, we suggested, resulted from his own failings and the inability of his government to govern.

Now an admission by William E. Colby, director of the CIA, to a House committee, strongly supports the charges that President Allende was the victim of U.S. interference.

The Nixon government, said Colby, authorized $11 million be spent on covert activities to "destabilize" Chile's Marxist government.

Colby's testimony is massive evidence that the United States did have a great deal to do with the death of both President Allende and his government. Eleven million dollars spent on subversion in a country, whose population is only 10 million, was certain to have a profound impact. In addition, President Allende's commonplace problems were severe enough without his being required to blunt dirty tricks operations financed by a supposed ally.

What right did the United States have determining that Chileans shouldn't be governed by the government they elected to power democratically in accordance with their constitution?

The answer is no right. None whatsoever.

Chileans surely have as much right to elect a Marxist president as Americans have to elect a crooked president.

What our government did in Chile was vile, vicious, contemptible, dishonorable — an action not apt to be forgotten either in South America or throughout the third world.

It is absurd to imagine that such arrogance, treachery, and unwarranted intrusion into the affairs of another nation — an ally at that — won't produce repercussions and retaliation.

No wonder most South Americans despise the gringo to the north. They have ample justification for their hatred: The CIA and America's ruthless rule-or-ruin good neighbor policy

The Philadelphia Inquirer

Philadelphia, Pa., September 18, 1974

It is bad enough to learn that the United States meddled extensively and officially in the internal affairs of Chile because Washington didn't approve of the government the people there had elected; it is worse to find such action defended by our President as sound and acceptable policy.

Yes, said President Ford at his press conference Monday evening, our government "does take certain actions in the intelligence field to help implement foreign policy and protect national security." But, he added, the Communists spend "vastly more money than we do for the same kind of purposes." And besides, what we did in Chile was not only in our best interest but "in the best interest of the people of Chile."

About that, two observations.

First, the fact that the Communist nations try to subvert other governments is no excuse or justification for our doing the same. Subversion is part of their tradition; it is alien to ours.

Second, it is not the manifest destiny of the United States to decide what is in the best interest of the people of Chile. That's for the people of Chile to decide, and they chose the government we set out to "destabilize," to use a word that has turned up in previously secret congressional testimony.

President Ford insists that the United States had "no involvement in any way whatsoever in the coup" which toppled the government of the Marxist Allende and led to his death.

But that is drawing a fine line in view of our acknowledged involvement and heavy spending in the period preceding the coup.

Even if our role had been nothing more than Mr. Ford mentioned — an attempt to help preserve opposition parties and opposition news media — it would have been improper. The indications from that congressional testimony by CIA Director William Colby, however, are that our "destabilization" campaign was substantially more aggressive than Mr. Ford's remarks suggest.

President Ford cannot be held responsible for what the CIA did in Chile before he was in the White House. In fact, as a member of Congress when all this was going on he was among those deceived by State Department testimony that the U. S. government was not intervening.

He is responsible now, however, and in defending our meddling in Chile he is getting off to a bad start with the Latin nations which have always been suspicious and fearful of an overbearing Uncle Sam. Instead of trying to justify subversion as a national policy, Mr. Ford should reject it and move to see that the Chilean experience is not repeated.

The Virginian-Pilot

Norfolk, Va., September 15, 1974

Rulers have intrigued against each other since before the dawn of recorded history. And spying upon foreign countries and subverting their governments is among the most ancient of diplomatic black arts. By intervening in the internal affairs of other nations, the United States has been obedient to a long and not altogether dishonorable tradition, however unhappy.

Moreover, U.S. shaping of the destinies of Latin Americans is hardly new. A House of Representatives report in 1962 listed more than a hundred instances in which Washington intervened militarily in Latin America between 1798 and 1945. The list being limited to overt employment of the armed forces, it was clearly an incomplete record of U.S. intervention in the Western Hemisphere, much of it in support of the Monroe Doctrine, of course—that is, President Monroe's 1823 warning to Europeans to not meddle on this side of the Atlantic and his promise that the U.S. would not meddle on the other side. (With the end of the Napoleonic Wars, it was feared that the Holy Alliance might assist in the reestablishment of the Spanish colonial empire through the subjugation of the newly independent Latin American republics.)

Washington's hand in Latin America is still apparent. Sometimes it is heavy and highly visible, at other times veiled. The U.S. Central Intelligence Agency's successful June 1954 coup d'etat in Guatemala toppled from power the Communist-dominated regime of President Jacob Arbenz Guzman. CIA agents were involved in attempts to unseat Costa Rica's moderate socialist President, Jose Figueres, in the mid-1950s, because Figueres had given haven to both Communist and non-Communist political exiles. The CIA was in charge of the ill-fated Bay of Pigs invasion by Cuban exiles in April 1961. And President Johnson dispatched the U.S. Marines to the strife-torn Dominican Republic in April 1965, fearing a Communist takeover.

So Washington's throwing its weight around in Latin America is a well-established custom. But it enrages many, if not most, Latin Americans. Thus Washington has taken more and more to pretending that it is aloof from power scrambles South of the Border. And when key members of the Nixon Administration were asked publicly as well as privately by appropriate members of Congress whether U.S. agents were secretly aiding and comforting foes of Salvador Allende, the late Marxist President of Chile who died in a bloody coup d'etat, they "misled" their questioners.

But, then, wilful deception long has been standard operating procedure at the highest levels of government in such matters. President Eisenhower's Secretary of State, John Foster Dulles, once assured everyone with a straight face regarding the revolt in Guatemala that the "situation is . . . being cured by the Guatemalans themselves." And Secretary of State Dean Rusk, who served both Presidents Kennedy and Johnson, said during the Bay of Pigs battle: "The American people are entitled to know whether we are intervening in Cuba or intend to do so in the future. The answer to that question is no. What happens in Cuba is for the Cuban people themselves to decide."

Well. There is growing sentiment following CIA Director William E. Colby's candid acknowledgement that the U.S. Government spent millions to "destabilize" the Allende Government for a tighter rein on clandestine operations by the CIA, and some fervor for abolishing such activities altogether. The latter may not be possible. But Washington has seen fit to ally itself with too many repressive regimes around the globe in behalf of the "national interest"—and to poke its nose into the business of others when standing aside probably would have produced no worse results.

It is well that several members of Congress and many other Americans are wondering to what degree, if at all. Washington should engage in secret campaigns against governments it deems odious or wicked. An independent panel of retired citizens—judges, academics, industrialists, scientists, ambassadors, and military brass—perhaps should be assembled to review intelligence-community operations and recommend reforms. Of course, we ought to know what our friends and enemies are doing and to judiciously aid the former and frustrate the latter. But we ought to restrict those enterprises that require us to lie to ourselves and the world.

THE PLAIN DEALER
Cleveland, Ohio, September 16, 1974

If indeed $11 million in U.S. funds were used for secret political action against the late Chilean president, Salvador Allende, that would have been an improper and ugly intervention. So far the issue is still in controversy. The State Department still denies it.

One year has passed since Allende was killed and a military junta led by Gen. Augusto Pinochet, now chief of state, took over from the Marxist government Allende ran. Chile is under a hard-knuckled dictatorship. There is no free press. Chile's Congress is closed. No political parties are allowed. Civil liberties are replaced by tight surveillance.

Allende's government failed. Its need for foreign credit was squandered early in the game. But the successor government is a nasty militarism which United States manipulators should be ashamed to have helped bring to their Chilean neighbors.

THE CHRISTIAN SCIENCE MONITOR
Boston, Mass., September 11, 1974

Now the facts are coming to light. The Central Intelligence Agency was not the innocent bystander in Chile that the United States Government tried to imply it was at the time of the overthrow of Salvador Allende.

The CIA, it turns out, engaged for years in clandestine activities against the late Chilean President. CIA director William Colby acknowledged in secret testimony to the Congress that some $8 million had been authorized by a high-level intelligence committee headed by Henry Kissinger to "destabilize" Allende's Marxist government and bring about its downfall after 1970.

The disclosures are shocking and dictate the urgent need for a public scrutiny of national security policies, a reform of CIA functions, and a system of strict accountability for CIA actions. They also point again to the deception practiced by previous administrations.

The State Department sticks by its guns. It stated this week it backs the testimony of high officials who previously told Congress that the U.S. had not intervened in the domestic affairs of Chile after Allende's election.

Clearly the full story has yet to be told. In light of the developing dispute we favor full-scale public hearings into the CIA's role in Chile, as called for by Congressman Michael Harrington.

This is not the first time the CIA has been involved in questionable covert operations against foreign states. Its record includes the aborted Bay of Pigs invasion, the secret war in Laos, and efforts to overthrow governments in Iran and Guatemala. More recently, on the domestic front, it furnished the White House "plumbers" with technical aid and a psychiatric profile of Daniel Ellsberg — acts that violated its mandate.

The record is disturbing.

However distasteful, clandestine operations sometimes are necessary. If a foreign power, for instance, is engaged in activities in a country that could impair American interests, it stands to reason the U.S. must know what it is up to. But gathering information and exposing Communist subversion, say, are one thing. Attempts to undermine or overthrow legitimate governments are quite another.

A distressing aspect of all this is the double standard which the U.S. has set for its international conduct. It apparently is permissible for the CIA to maneuver against local governments which Washington does not like — this is deemed in the national interest. But when the U.S. declines to use its influence to dissuade repressive regimes from antidemocratic excesses — as in South Korea or Greece — this is justified as "noninterference" in another country's internal affairs.

If the CIA is permitted to abet the disintegration of constitutionally elected governments — however unpalatable their ideology — does not the U.S. lose its moral authority to condemn similar subversive action by a Communist power?

The Allende regime was hardly a model for Latin America. But the late President did carry on his Marxist experiment within the constitutional framework. If Washington chose not to render help — except to the Chilean military — that at least was an overt, if debatable, position.

But by colluding in the effort to undermine the Chilean Government by covert means, Washington has only helped destroy the credibility of the argument that Communists should participate in the democratic process rather than seek power through violent means.

THE CALGARY HERALD
Calgary, Alta., September 23, 1974

Henry Kissinger's hollow sophistry in defence of the CIA's recently-discovered political meddling in Chile during the Allende regime can do nothing but reinforce Canadian fears that the U.S. secretary of state would just as cheerfully meddle in Canada's affairs.

On Thursday, Mr. Kissinger testified before the foreign relations committee of the Senate.

He was talking about expenditures by the CIA during 1972 and 1973 (Allende was overthrown as president of Chile in the latter year). An estimated $7 million was spent. It went to subsidize strikes and other social disruptions.

★ ★ ★

Mr. Kissinger's defence, incredibly, was that Allende had been elected by only a 37 per cent popular vote in the 1970 elections (there were several candidates in the election) and that he was trying to lead the South American country to a one-party state.

This nonsense insults the intelligence. Canada, for instance has frequently been governed by prime ministers whose parties obtained less than 40 per cent of the popular vote. Only once or twice in its history has this country been governed by parties which won more than 50 per cent of the vote. The same thing is true of most parliamentary democracies and, indeed of most presidential systems; except where the two-party system is virtually immutable as in the United States, or where there are run-off elimination, votes, as in France. Even in the two-party U.S., there have been minority presidents.

The arrogance of justifying internal provocation on the basis of the popular vote of a country's leader is breathtaking. It was during Mr. Kissinger's tenure that the United States supported the dictatorship in Greece. Where was the electoral justification for that? It was a one-party government that savagely persecuted political opponents. Why did Mr. Kissinger do nothing there? Would it, perhaps, have something to do with the fact that in Chile, Allende was nationalizing American copper interests, but in Greece Papodopolous was faithfully supporting U.S. military interests? And doesn't the same apply to Spain, Portugal, and a host of other one-party countries that have historically enjoyed almost devout U.S. support?

The United States obviously interfered in Chile, partly because of its ideological fears about Allende's Marxism, but mainly because of his interference w i t h American economic interests as defined by Americans. This should be instructive for Canada. Mr. Kissinger's mendacious diversions do not alter the fact that he is obviously perfectly willing to tamper with any country whose own definition of nationalism threatens American economic self-interest.

★ ★ ★

American investments are more prominently entrenched in Canada than in any other place on earth. Canadian nationalism is rising. Various recent legislative enactments seek to control and potentially limit further American economic penetration. A vocal segment of the population calls for even sterner measures. Not all Canadians agree with that point of view, but is it a question to be resolved by Canadians, or are Mr. Kissinger and the CIA to occupy a role of interventionist partnership?

One fact is plain. First President Ford, and now his super-influential secretary of state, clearly support a doctrine of interference in the internal affairs of other nations. That they do so on the basis of contradictory, transparently hypocritical justifications just adds to what ought to be widespread Canadian concern.

The Globe and Mail

Toronto, Ont., September 18, 1974

There are times when a national leader cannot sit on the fence. That if he refuses to condemn a practice, his silence condones it.

That is the situation facing United States President Gerald Ford regarding the clandestine operations of the Central Intelligence Agency which are designed to influence the domestic affairs of other countries.

In his press conference on Monday, President Ford acknowledged that the CIA had intervened in the domestic affairs of Chile. "In a period of time, three or four years ago, there was an effort being made by the Allende Government to destroy opposition news media, both the writing press as well as the electronic press," he said. "And to destroy opposition parties.

"And the effort that was made in this case was to help and assist the preservation of opposition newspapers and electronic media and to preserve opposition political parties. I think this is in the best interests of the people of Chile and certainly in our best interest."

Unquestionably, the CIA was wrong to intervene in this way. But Mr. Ford refused to criticize it. When asked if such action contravened international law he replied, "I'm not going to pass judgment on whether or not it is authorized under international law. It is a recognized fact that, historically as well as presently, such actions are taken in the best interests of the countries involved."

His response, to echo the words of former Prime Minister Lester Pearson, is unacceptable.

If the President will not chastise the CIA, then CIA officials know they can continue meddling in the affairs of other countries without hindrance.

Canadians have had more than their quota of interference. It was the cry of "Vive le Quebec libre" by former French President Charles de Gaulle during a visit to Montreal in 1967 that prompted Mr. Pearson to have a diplomatic note delivered to Gen. de Gaulle telling him that his interference was unacceptable.

A decade earlier, it was U.S. policy standing in the way of the Ford Motor Company of Canada delivering cars to Communist China that prompted Mr. Pearson, then opposition leader, to urge that the United States should be told, in no uncertain terms, not to try to force its national policies on Canadian companies.

The cars never did get shipped. This year, a similar situation faced MLW Worthington Ltd. of Montreal, also an American subsidiary, that wanted to ship locomotives to Cuba. This time Canadian protests were successful and the deal will go through.

And, lest Canadians begin to feel holier than thou, there is also the case of Canadian aid to liberation movements in Africa which was to be channelled through the Canadian International Development Agency. When the plan came to light early this year there was an uproar which resulted in External Affairs Minister Mitchell Sharp ordering the program shelved until Parliament could debate CIDA's budget. The budget has not yet been debated.

These examples of interference are the ones that are easiest to cope with because they are not clandestine. The more scandalous, the more noxious, are those that are carried out secretly and subversively.

Mr. Ford's refusal to condemn can be read only one way: that no nation on earth can feel itself secure from CIA meddling, Canada included. And that is simply intolerable.

The Boston Globe

Boston, Mass., September 18, 1974

Even if there were a factual foundation for President Ford's defense of Central Intelligence Agency meddling in Chilean domestic affairs, it is alarming that the United States pursued a policy of bribery and subversion, first to rig free elections, then to stack the deck against a democratically elected government in Chile.

In his news conference on Monday, Mr. Ford acknowledged that the Nixon Administration between 1970 and 1973 had directed the CIA to intervene in the internal politics in Chile. By implication, the President seemed to confirm newspaper disclosures that the CIA had dispensed at least $8 million, including $350,000 in bribes for Chilean legislators and $500,000 in subsidies for opponents to Marxist President Salvador Gossens Allende, to create stumbling blocks for Allende.

Mr. Ford sought to justify the covert CIA largesse as a counter to "an effort being made by the Allende government to destroy opposition news media . . . and . . . opposition political parties." In fact, during Dr. Allende's three years in office Chile stood, a notable exception in Latin America, as a nation tolerating a wide spectrum of political viewpoints among its press and broadcast media.

Mr. Ford denied that the CIA had any part in the bloody coup d'etat in which President Allende died a year ago. But it is likely that the CIA dollars for "destabilization" of the Allende regime benefited the military junta that now rules Chile in seizing power.

The junta, while more favorable to United States corporations with heavy investments in Chile, nonetheless has defeated the purposes of US policy, as defined by President Ford. The military leaders have imposed on Chile a repressive police state, closed the Congress, banned political party activity and muzzled newspapers.

It is a further irony that the clandestine CIA operations may have been unnecessary for the ultimate demise of the Allende government. His administration was besieged by galloping inflation, widespread shortages, and labor strife. Allende might have foundered on an impression of his own ineptitude. But now it seems clear that the CIA helped to create that impression.

The United States, in staging the CIA exploits, has lost considerable face, and to no avail. It is evident that this country has encroached on the domestic political sovereignty of Chile, in violation of the spirit and perhaps the letter of the United Nations Charter. In Article Two it constrains all member states to refrain from any threat to the "political independence" of another state.

Other nations are unlikely to abide gunboat—or sinister bankroll—diplomacy in the 20th century, as Indian Ambassador Daniel P. Moynihan suggested in a dispatch to the State Department disclosed last week. Moynihan predicted that the CIA's exploits in Chile would reinforce Indian Prime Minister Indira Gandhi's conviction that the United States has become a "profoundly selfish and cynical counterrevolutionary power."

The cynicism both at home and abroad stems partly from the numerous deceptions and untruths that American officials have disseminated about US operations in Chile, Vietnam, Cambodia and elsewhere. Even the US Congress has been a victim of the falsehoods.

Congressional committees rightfully are considering contempt citations and perjury actions against those Nixon Administration officials who may have lied in their sworn testimony that the CIA had done nothing to undercut the Allende regime. And if the United States is to return to constitutional government, Congress must reassert effective scrutiny over the CIA, apparently embarking on ever more questionable ventures. Information on such serious matters should not be secretly confided only to a few committee chairmen who wink and say nothing.

President Ford takes a shortsighted view of American interest when he predicates it on a need for cloak-and-dagger subversion of other democracies. Nor is it a defense to such shenanigans that the other side indulges in it as well. Such means will frustrate achievement of the ends that this country established in its own revolution nearly 200 years ago.

Twin City Sentinel

Winston-Salem, N.C., September 18, 1974

When the voters of Chile, the oldest democracy in Latin America, elected Salvador Allende as their president four years ago, the United States had no cause to rejoice. What is at issue now is whether the U.S. government had cause to do what it did.

Allende was a socialist who admired Fidel Castro. He campaigned against the American corporations that had invested in his country. His program was Marxist. He vowed to move Chile's mixed economy further to the left by democratic means, and bring social justice to Chile's impoverished lower class.

But what threat did Allende represent to the United States? As Henry Kissinger then joked, Chile under Allende was "a dagger aimed straight at the heart of Antarctica."

But Kissinger's joke did not reflect the true U.S. policy toward the Allende government. The purpose of that policy was to bring about Allende's fall. Immediately after the 1970 election, Kissinger began directing a campaign of economic retaliation against Chile. The World Bank was forbidden to extend him credit. U.S. loans were cancelled. All this figured prominently in the collapse of the Chilean economy, which brought on the 1973 military coup and Allende's death (by suicide, according to those who overthrew him).

Along with the economic blows, the Central Intelligence Agency began a secret, $8 million campaign of "political destabilization" against the Chilean government.

Asked about that covert program, President Ford claimed Monday night that the money went to preserve a free press and opposition parties in Chile. What he ignored is that Allende had neither shackled the press nor outlawed his opposition. In the Communist world, in fact, he is scorned today for being too democratic. And it was U.S. officials, in fact, who conspired to bribe the Chilean congress against him, even before he took office.

The policy that Kissinger directed toward Chile assures that "Yankee, go home" will be a rallying cry in Latin America for decades. Allende's economic mismanagement and middle-class opposition did far more harm to him than the agents of the CIA. But the now-public details of our policy link the United States to the repressive military dictatorship in control today.

In the past year, U.S. economic and military aid for Chile has resumed. It goes to a government that has no respect for civil liberties, that has condoned torture, closed the Chilean congress, banned political activity, and has shown no inclination to restore free elections. In Chile now, as in Greece under the late, unlamented regime of the colonels, opposition to communism makes strange bedfellows of democracy and dictatorship.

The Chilean revelations raise new questions about the secretive foreign policy that former President Nixon and Secretary Kissinger instituted. Throughout the policy toward Allende, Congress was kept uninformed — and given false testimony by Kissinger's underlings.

The foreign affairs committees should demand that Kissinger explain what the United States has gained from the Chilean policy that he directed.

The Washington Post

Washington, D.C., September 11, 1974

THE UNITED STATES has consistently denied using the CIA to fight leftist Salvador Allende in Chile. Yet, it now turns out, CIA director William E. Colby told a House committee last April that: The CIA gave $3 million to the Allende political opposition in 1964 and $500,000 more to "anti-Allende forces" in 1969. It authorized $350,000 to bribe the Chilean congress against him in 1970, the year he won. It contributed $5 million for "more destabilization efforts" in 1971-73 and $1.5 million in by-elections in 1973. In August of that year, it authorized $1 million for "further political destabilization activities." A coup ousted him, and he was killed, a year ago today.

The Colby revelations do not answer once and for all the question of whether, as the Latin left already believes, the United States destroyed Allende; some part of his difficulties were of his own making. Nor do the revelations demonstrate that the CIA had a direct hand in the coup. They prove beyond dispute, however, that the United States acted in a way to aggravate Mr. Allende's problems, and played into the hands of those who made the coup. We did so, moreover, deliberately: According to Mr. Colby, the anti-Allende acts were not the work of a mindless uncontrolled agency but of a CIA operating at the instructions of the appropriate White House review panel, the "Forty Committee," headed by Henry Kissinger.

Dr. Kissinger and President Nixon, one gathers, had decided there were to be "no more Cubas": no more Marxist states in the western hemisphere. Any means, apparently, would do. Would it not be better, Dr. Kissinger was asked at his confirmation hearing as Secretary of State a year ago, to take the CIA out of such clandestine efforts as overturning Latin governments? "There are certain types of these activities, difficult to describe here," the Secretary-designate replied, "that it would be dangerous to abolish."

This information comes to light now through the surfacing of a confidential letter from Rep. Michael Harrington (D-Mass.) to House Foreign Affairs Committee Chairman Thomas E. Morgan (D-Pa.), in which Mr. Harrington asks for a deeper investigation. Dr. Morgan, like his Senate counterpart, J. William Fulbright (D-Ark.), has been reluctant to press such a probe. But it is laughable for Congress to assert a larger foreign-policy role if it is to shy away from this outrageous instance of hemispheric realpolitik. Last year, for instance, the Senate Foreign Relations Committee's subcommittee on multinational corporations investigated charges that in 1970 ITT had sought to induce the CIA to block Allende. The subcommittee found that the CIA had not followed ITT's bidding. But now it turns out that—before, during and after the ITT episode—the CIA was intervening in Chilean politics.

Since the 1960s, the United States has used its influence to keep Cuba a hemispheric pariah. And why? A principal stated reason has been Cuba's ostensible support of subversion in Latin America: putting guerrillas ashore here and there, sounding the revolutionary trumpet, and the like. But whatever Cuba has allegedly done in the past is peanuts next to what the United States has admittedly done in Chile. To bar Cuba from hemispheric society on the basis of a test we fail ourselves is absurd.

AKRON BEACON JOURNAL
*Akron, Ohio,
September 19, 1974*

BLAMING THE Central Intelligence Agency for the recently disclosed interference with the duly elected government of the late Salvador Allende in Chile is a little like blaming the bulldog when your neighbor sics it on you.

The CIA is an instrument of the U. S. government, answerable to the executive department's "Forty Committee" and to the Congress. If the CIA bulldog has gotten out of hand, then the blame belongs with its handlers in the White House and on Capitol Hill.

The CIA has admitted that it tried to prevent Allende from coming to power, then tried to "destabilize" his government after he took office. President Ford, Secretary of State Kissinger and CIA Director William E. Colby have all denied involvement in the coup in which Allende was overthrown and killed.

In his press conference Monday night, President Ford acknowledged that it was common practice for governments to involve themselves in other countries' domestic affairs. He indicated he approved.

Questions of CIA involvement in the internal affairs of other countries should not even come up. Neither the CIA nor any other U. S. government agency has any business "destabilizing" governments or trying to prevent particular parties or men from assuming office.

Such practices are in violation of international agreements and, in the case of Chile, in violation of our own Monroe Doctrine.

There is, of course, a legitimate function for the CIA, and, as far as we can see, just one: the gathering and evaluating of information. It is important work.

J. William Fulbright, chairman of the Senate Foreign Relations Committee, agrees: "In my view, it's very questionable practice to go beyond the collection of intelligence. I personally have always thought they should be confined to intelligence gathering."

There does not seem to us to be any great need to investigate past practices of the CIA in Chile or Indochina or the countries of Central America. But there does seem to be a great need to curb future CIA activities.

The Congress has the power to bring the CIA under control through the agency's budget. The CIA spent millions of dollars in Chile and it got that money from the Congress.

If the Congress were on the ball, it would demand to know from the intelligence agency what it was spending, where it was spending it and for what purposes. And if the CIA declined to answer fully, the Congress should then decline to fund fully.

There is, of course, a need for some secrecy even in innocent intelligence work. It would be unwise to publish the identity of agents, for example, even if they were doing no more than listening to gossip in foreign capitals.

But the need for secrecy must not be allowed to extend to the Congress. Anyone elected from a constituency of nearly half a million American citizens must be presumed to be a good security risk. And, frankly, we doubt that congressmen would be very interested in knowing the identity of individual agents.

They should, though, be interested in knowing the kinds of activities those agents are involved in. They have the power to find out. And, as the recent disclosure of past practices in Chile demonstrates, they must use that power.

BUFFALO EVENING NEWS
Buffalo, N.Y., September 18, 1974

The revelations concerning intervention by the U. S. Central Intelligence Agency in Chile raise searching questions about the role of the CIA generally in this era of the fading cold war. The CIA grew originally out of the wartime Office of Strategic Services, and in the tense days of the cold war carried on many similar cloak-and-dagger functions. Today, with relations between countries becoming m o r e normal, t h e CIA's emphasis is changing from clandestine "dirty tricks" to ordinary surveillance.

That is why the Chilean revelations were startling. President Ford said in his news conference that the CIA had attempted "three or four years ago" to help opposition news media and parties in Chile which the Allende government was trying to "destroy," adding that he thought this was "in the best interest of the people of Chile, and certainly in our best interest." As events turned out later in Chile, of course, with a harsh military regime in control and with the CIA's earlier role n o w revealed, the U. S. intervention is proving to be embarrassing elsewhere in the world.

By definition, it is only the CIA's failures to keep its covert operations covert, where the cover is finally blown as in Chile or the Bay of Pigs, that we hear much about. But merely on the basis of the harmful effect such revelations have on the U. S. image abroad, we have to question the advisability of engaging in such clandestine intervention in other countries' internal affairs, except in the most unusual circumstances.

Some poisonous effects of the Chilean operation have been revealed in a cable to Washington from Daniel P. Moynihan, ambassador to India.

He noted that when rumors of CIA intervention in Chile circulated last year, he had formally reassured Indian Prime Minister Indira Gandhi that the charges were false. Now, he said, Mrs. Gandhi feels **her** suspicions are confirmed and h e r concern is "whether the United States accepts the Indian regime. She is not sure but that we would be content to see others like her overthrown."

Obviously, in the present state of the world, it would be unwise to rule out all secret operations. That, as CIA Director William E. Colby said recently, would "leave us with nothing between a diplomatic protest and sending in the Marines." But it is also obvious that in this era of detente, when it is U. S. policy to foster good relations with both the Soviet Union and Communist China, it would be harmful to undercut that policy with boat-rocking "dirty tricks" operations that go beyond the necessities of international surveillance.

The CIA's very reputation as an agency engaged in far-flung covert operations all over the world makes faces at the American policy of keeping a "low profile" wherever it is felt that our interests require an American presence abroad.

President Ford said that the procedures for supervision of the CIA by Congress will be reviewed. This is the important thing, since too often there has been either a l a c k of proper supervisory procedures or even a lack of interest by congressmen in knowing about some of the clandestine operations. And there has also been a history of supervisory inertia allowing covert CIA missions to continue long after the original need had passed, until at last their cover is embarrassingly blown. Sen. Humphrey (D., Minn.) says the CIA is "not under any meaningful supervision whatsoever" — and he should know at least how it used to be because, when he was vice president, he sat on the National Security Council which supposedly controls the CIA. Sen. Fulbright, outgoing chairman of the Foreign Relations Committee, has proposed setting up a joint congressional supervisory committee, a n d President Ford promises to meet with the responsible congressional committees "to see whether they want any changes in the review process."

As we see it, the role of the CIA today should be mainly what the name implies, a central agency for the coordinating of America's worldwide intelligence operations, and Congress should assume responsibility to keep it so.

Long Island Press
Jamaica, N.Y., September 19, 1974

Earlier denials are now inoperative: Officials of the Central Intelligence Agency admit that the CIA was involved in events that led to the overthrow of the Allende government in Chile. This is scary news for Americans who believe the agency should stick to spying.

Gathering intelligence in other countries is a distasteful but necessary business. But helping overthrow other governments is not a proper function for an agency whose operations are so secret even Congress doesn't know what has been going on.

In spite of President Ford's defense of such covert activities and his insistence that this government was not involved in the actual coup against Allende, Sen. J. William Fulbright, chairman of the Senate Foreign Relations Committee wants Congress to clamp down on the CIA, and he is right. Congress should insist on being fully informed and on having a say about what the agency can — and cannot — do.

San Jose Mercury
San Jose, Calif.,
September 10, 1974

Any doubt that the U.S. Central Intelligence Agency played an active role in the internal affairs of Chile has been erased by disclosure of secret testimony by CIA Director William F. Colby. The result must be a crackdown on all such CIA activities.

It has been almost exactly a year since Chilean President Salvador Allende was killed in a military coup that toppled his leftist government. The CIA continues to insist that it played no active role in the coup, but there is no longer any real doubt that the CIA spent large sums in an unsuccessful effort to prevent Allende's election and then for "political destabilization activities."

These disclosures will hamper U.S. r e l a t i o n s with other Latin American nations. Equally disturbing is the fact that such CIA activities occurred without prior consultation with any congressional leadership. What emerges is another deplorable example of non-accountability. A democratic society cannot tolerate such clandestine interference in the internal affairs of other nations.

THE SACRAMENTO BEE
Sacramento, Calif., September 20, 1974

The US government has an important responsibility to reappraise the role of the Central Intelligence Agency and to put strict limitations on its operations in various parts of the world.

This clandestine agency, operating with what seems a blank check to interfere in the activities of foreign governments, requires stricter watchdog control by the appropriate congressional and executive authorities.

It was disappointing to hear President Ford recently defend the CIA operations in Chile as simply attempting to maintain a free press and a counterbalance to the powerful Marxist political factions. The President did admit the CIA involvement, but his picture of its actions was, to give him the benefit of the doubt, naive.

Congressional inquiries had previously determined that over the past several years the CIA spent millions of dollars, first to prevent the election of Marxist Salvadore Allende, and then to bribe Chilean legislators to tip the 1970 election, in which neither Allende nor his opponent, Christian Democrat Eduardo Frei received a clear majority, in favor of Frei. More-

over, CIA officials testified additional millions have been spent since then to "destabilize' Allende's democratically-elected government, contributing to its takeover by the military coup.

These practices by the CIA are intolerable in a nation which professes to support the self-determination of other governments. It is one thing to conduct intelligence-gathering. It is another to directly interere in the internal affairs of other nations.

Equally disturbing was Ford's likening of CIA operations to those of the Soviet Union's clandestine apparatus, with the direct rationale that if they do it, we must do it too.

How is the rest of the world to regard the US as being any different from the authoritarian Kremlin regime if this nation follows the same subversive practices?

Congress must determine whether the improper CIA activities are the result of specific direction from the executive branch or the result of a free-wheeling intelligence operation that has too much money and not enough supervision.

CHICAGO Sun-Times
Chicago, Ill., September 17, 1974

The latest disclosures concerning the role played by Sec. of State Henry A. Kissinger and the Central Intelligence Agency in the internal affairs of Chile demonstrate anew that Congress must take a more effective part in making foreign policy.

Our Washington Bureau chief, Thomas B. Ross, reported Sunday that he learned from key intelligence officials that Kissinger played an active, aggressive and personal role in ordering secret CIA activities in Chile. Some $11 million was spent in efforts to destabilize the government of then President Salvador Allende. This meddling was organized by the 40 Committee, a supersecret intelligence organization that officials said became a one-man operation headed by Kissinger in his role as chairman of the National Security Council.

CIA operations are supposed to be monitored by the Appropriations and Armed Services committees of both houses of Congress. But over the years, the committees have failed to do their jobs, in spite of the fact that Congress and the electorate have repeatedly been misled and possibly even lied to about the CIA's various activities. And the 40 Committee has never been monitored by Congress at all. Kissinger himself has been treated with kid gloves. His diplomatic triumphs have endowed him with such awe that some members of Congress are simply too timid to treat him the way are too timid to treat him the way they treat other Cabinet members.

We have long believed that the CIA should be compelled by law to restrict its foreign activities to the collection of intelligence. Congress also needs to revise the administrative setup under which the State Department and the NSC are headed by the same person. The potential for abuse is simply too great when these two agencies are headed by the same man.

THE MILWAUKEE JOURNAL
Milwaukee, Wisc., September 22, 1974

As more and more information on CIA activities in Chile comes bubbling out of the cracks in Washington's bureaucracy, it seems increasingly clear that high Nixon administration officials were not exactly candid with Congress about US involvement in that South American country. Included in that category is Secretary of State Kissinger himself. Some officials even might have lied under oath.

Beyond the problem of deception, there is the basic question whether the US has any right to intervene as actively in the internal affairs of Chile, as it now appears the CIA did during the regime of Marxist President Allende. Kissinger, in his latest statements to Congress justifying the American role in Chile, was not reassuring that he had any great overriding concern about the moral or ethical implications of such a policy and its implications for how the US is viewed throughout the world.

There have been disturbing reports that the Senate Foreign Relations Committee may be reluctant to take an exhaustive look at this situation, as it should. This would be a grave error, especially since the committee's chairman, Sen. Fulbright, has been a leading proponent of the reassertion of congressional prerogatives in foreign policy. Here is an area where Congress should reclaim its authority.

Chicago Tribune
Chicago, Ill., September 30, 1974

To judge from his comments to the press this week about the Central Intelligence Agency, President Ford has decided on a new policy of candor and plain speaking. He frankly said the CIA will go right on being as deceptive and underhanded as ever. That's letting it all hang out.

Mr. Ford had to say something, of course, and his choices were rather limited. He couldn't very well denounce the CIA, particularly now when congressmen are queuing up on all sides to investigate its role in bringing down the Allende government in Chile. On the other hand, he couldn't come out foursquare for unlimited undercover meddling by one nation in the internal politics of another.

So he took a middle course, explaining that everybody engages in this sort of meddling and suggesting that it is very bad except when we do it. The explanation is not, let us say, perfect.

After seeing one President destroyed by Watergate, it is not comforting to hear from the new President that there's something to be said for lawbreaking—after all, it does help us get what we want. That, we hope, is a minority view right now. Beyond that, Mr. Ford seems convinced that the cold war is still on and still justifies any tactics we may care to use against governments we don't trust. Former President Nixon's optimism about an "era of cooperation instead of confrontation" evidently left the scene with him.

Obviously this country must have an efficient worldwide intelligence system. The rub comes when the system starts making other governments' decisions for them, and enforcing the decisions by criminal means. Whatever this approach may do for other countries [not much, we suspect], for us it succeeds mainly in setting off riots outside United States embassies and discrediting American intentions and policies everywhere.

The time may have come to change our approach to the whole business. We might, for instance, deemphasize the cloak-and-dagger scene—which is getting a bit old-fashioned and counterproductive anyway—and try something really new: A public-spirited CIA. A force of frank, manly, plainspoken intelligence agents may be just what the world is waiting for.

CIA agents could be clearly identified by lapel badges. These should carry the agent's full name and say something engaging, like "Hi, there!" Operatives should be friendly but frank with the people they're spying on; interviewees should be asked to speak up and talk directly into the agent's martini olive. Any secret drawers around should be plainly labeled "Secret Drawer."

It would be a wholly new, thoroly American approach to spying, and it would completely paralyze enemy agents. They'd spend all their time trying to figure out what we were really up to.

THE DAILY OKLAHOMAN
Oklahoma City, Okla., September 23, 1974

ONCE AGAIN, as on a dozen prior occasions, the Central Intelligence Agency is being dissected in public—in large part by critics who have only a colorful but inaccurate idea of its functions and operations. The agency cannot function under the glare of publicity. And the speculation about its operations and methods has already jeopardized the security of this country.

That is no exaggeration. The decisions of American leaders, from the President down, are based in many cases on information supplied by the CIA. There is an old saw that a man's judgment is no better than the information on which it is based. If the CIA supplies misinformation, or bad evaluations of correct information, the nation—perhaps the world —suffers.

Its overriding importance makes the CIA of interest to all Americans. But because it must operate in secrecy, suspicions flourish, and feed on each other. Demagogues and foreign propagandists use it as a whipping boy.

Despite its secret nature, there are some facts about the CIA everyone ought to know. It is concerned, by law, only with foreign intelligence; the FBI has sole internal intelligence responsibility. Most of the CIA's work is in processing, collating, evaluating, and reporting on data procured quite openly and legally. (Russian intelligence subscribes to most American journals, including scientific and industrial periodicals. The secrecy is concerned with what data our government considers important enough for detailed study, and what evaluations are made.

Electronic intelligence collection, data transmission, and satellite photography are areas in which the agency's operation are secret for technical reasons. And all modern nations do get leads, at least, from spies, although they represent little of the total operation. So CIA is the agency of government most protected by secrecy, for good reasons.

That has led, from the outset, to its problems. Because Congress understood that its budget must be hidden from foreign powers, it was given special status. And because Congress has never had the nerve to create a separate department to carry out "dirty tricks" in other countries but wanted that work available at least as an option to the president, a division which has nothing to do with providing accurate, evaluated information to our leadership has been a part of the CIA since 1947.

The Bay of Pigs, the alleged interference in Chile, the operations in Laoes, Central America, and other far corners of the world that have earned the CIA a bad name were the work of this "stepbrother" agency. Those who have studied what went wrong in such cases, and what went right in others, agree that this should not be CIA activity. But they have no solution because the CIA has the only legal way to hide such operations in the massive federal budget.

Until this lingering problem is faced squarely, the CIA will suffer from a bad name and the country will risk its vital functions being crippled by Congress.

Washington Star-News
Washington, D.C., *September 19, 1974*

In the best of all possible worlds, nations would not intervene in the domestic affairs of other nations. Unfortunately, we do not live in such a world, our ancestors did not and it is highly unlikely that our descendants will.

Indeed, in the interdependent world in which we live the distinction between domestic affairs and foreign policy is blurred. And it can be argued that there is no such thing as non-intervention, since the failure to intervene is itself a form of intervention with its own probable consequences.

Intervention has two faces, positive and negative. Did we not intervene in the domestic affairs of India, to the detriment of the opposition parties, when we poured billions of dollars worth of aid into the governments controlled by the ruling Congress Party? Is not West Germany intervening in the domestic affairs of Italy by granting a $2-billion loan that is perhaps the last chance of preserving democracy in Italy?

In the Chilean affair, there has been a leak of secret testimony from CIA Director William Colby to the effect that the agency poured $11 million into Chile to prevent the election of Marxist President Salvador Allende and to "destabilize" his government after he became president.

One does not have to approve of the military regime that seized power in Santiago last year — and we do not— to recognize that Allende was a friend neither of this country nor of democracy. Nor has much been said by congressional or other foes of the CIA about the arms and money Cuba was pouring into Chile with the apparent intention of ultimately subverting that country's democratic institutions.

Nor was there any obligation on the United States to provide a regime inimical to its interests with soft loans from the World Bank, the Inter-American Development Bank and the Export-Import Bank. The fall of the Allende government was due as much to its narrow political base, incompetence and excesses as to any covert American political action taken against it.

This does not mean that the procedures for congressional oversight of the CIA do not require overhauling and strengthening. It does not mean that agency officials have a right to lie to or mislead congressional committees, although the leaking of secret testimony by congressmen can only encourage such officials to be something less than candid.

But we have to recognize that we live in a tough neighborhood and that the gang down the street is not exactly squeamish in the means it uses to attain its ends and to frustrate ours.

The present regime in Chile is an authoritarian one. But it is not totalitarian in the sense that Castro's Cuba is: The possibility and the means of a return to democracy still exists in Chile. Had Allende and his foreign backers had their way, that option might have been foreclosed. Over the long term, that $11 million may turn out to have been a good investment, not for the copper companies or even for the United States but for the Chilean people and the cause of democracy.

Herald News
Fall River, Mass., September 19, 1974

The admission by President Ford that this country was engaged in trying to influence the political situation in Chile, although he claimed it was not involved in President Allende's overthrow, has created a fresh controversy over the CIA. The Senate Foreign Relations Committee has even considered perjury proceedings against State Department personnel who denied knowledge of U.S. activities in Chile during the Allende regime.

There is a fundamental inconsistency in the attitude of Congress and some of the press toward the CIA. It is supposed to be an organization to gather information about other countries, in other words, espionage. It is obvious that its spying cannot be conducted with perfect candor, and once candor is insisted on in or out of Congress, then its usefulness diminishes to the vanishing point.

This country dislikes being engaged in espionage, but how it can function as a world power without it remains unexplained. Furthermore, after our experience with Cuba, could the United States be expected to assist Allende to turn Chile into a Marxist country with all that implies in terms of hostility toward the North American colossus? The ideological struggle between Marxist and non-Marxist states is real, even when many Americans wish to pretend it does not exist. The CIA was presumably acting as an agent of the U.S. Government in obstructing Allende.

Perhaps the administration's policy toward Chile was wrong. Certainly no one can be happy about the dictatorship that succeeded him. But it is transparently silly to argue that somehow the CIA should operate as a non-secret organization, and that its activities must be approved, say, by Congress in advance.

THE RICHMOND NEWS LEADER
Richmond, Va., September 18, 1974

Dr. Johnson said that patriotism is the last refuge of the scoundrel. Sometimes the Central Intelligence Agency is the scoundrel's first refuge. When things go wrong, foreign leaders often find the CIA an object of convenient blame. And because secrecy is necessary to the success of its operations, the CIA usually must remain silent in the face of such charges. A case in point is the stir over alleged dirty tricks in Chile, where the CIA spent about $10 million to disrupt the government of Salvador Allende.

Now, the suggestion that an outside force was needed to disrupt — the fashionable word is "de-stabilize" — the Allende regime is a bad joke. Allende did a fine job of de-stabilizing things on his own. He gained power with only 36 per cent of the votes — not unusual in Chilean politics. But Allende's plurality was hardly a mandate for the wrenching, Marxist reforms that he tried to impose on the Chilean people. A certain amount of turmoil, and the political involvement of an army that had long avoided such entanglements, was inevitable.

Specifically, the charge is that the Nixon administration, through the CIA, hastened that inevitability along. The three complaints: (1) that the United States used its influence to cut off lines of credit and foreign aid; (2) that the U.S. used its dollars to finance Allende's opponents; (3) that the Nixon administration lied about what it was doing.

These are grave charges. But the U.S. cannot be expected to bankroll real or potential enemies. Nor can the U.S. control grants-in-aid or lines of credit that other nations, including non-Communist nations, might wish to make. Nor, finally, is there any pressing need for aid to Chile compared with, say, aid to Bangladesh. As with the funding of left-wing student groups, it is unlikely that the CIA received much value for its money in Chile — the money having been used primarily to subsidize opposition newspapers and political parties, according to President Ford. Alleged invasion plans, if there were any, stayed on the drawing board.

The charges also are largely irrelevant. President Ford has pointed out that Communist nations "spend vastly more than we do for the same kind of purposes." The Communists act, moreover, with none of the democratic checks that mark the operation of the CIA. It is unfortunate that we live in a world where a Central Intelligence Agency — and a bagful of dirty tricks — are sometimes necessary. But the problem is that we do live in the real world.

It is a world where the moral niceties to which we Americans would like to subscribe possess little allure for others. Allende, after all, was close to establishing a Soviet colony in Chile. And the interventions of Fidel Castro were far grosser than anything the CIA accomplished in Chile. Communists tell us that they still are determined to spread their doctrine — an armed doctrine — throughout the world. Subversion is one of Communism's weapons. As long as Communists continue to use that weapon, the CIA will remain a regrettable necessity.

COLBY CONFIRMS ALLEGATIONS OF CIA'S DOMESTIC ACTIVITIES

In a report to President Ford Dec. 26, William Colby, director of the Central Intelligence Agency (CIA), confirmed allegations that the CIA, in violation of its 1947 charter, had engaged in the surveillance of U.S. citizens, *The Los Angeles Times* reported Dec. 31. Colby's report indicated that the CIA had compiled files on at least 9,000 U.S. citizens and had engaged in other illegal clandestine activities.

According to the 1947 law creating the CIA (Title 50, Section 403 of the United States Code), the agency "shall have no police, subpoena, law enforcement powers or internal security functions."

Seymour Harsh had written in *The New York Times* Dec. 21 of the CIA's "massive, illegal domestic intelligence operation during the Nixon Administration against the antiwar movement and other dissident groups." The *Times* also reported that former CIA director James Schlesinger had found evidence of dozens of illegal domestic operations by the CIA beginning in the 1950s, including "break-ins, wire-tapping and surreptitious interception of mail."

The newspaper quoted several unnamed sources, who insisted that the CIA had discontinued all domestic operations. One *Times* source charged that the domestic spying had been directed during the Nixon Administration by James Angleton, chief of the CIA's counterintelligence department since 1954. Officially, Angleton's job was to insure that foreign agents did not penetrate the CIA. Along with assembling domestic intelligence dossiers, one *Times* source said, Angleton's department recruited informants to infiltrate the more militant dissident groups. "They recruited plants, informers and doublers [double agents]," according to the source. (It was reported Dec. 24 that Angleton had resigned from his post, effective Dec. 31. He also publicly denied the *Times'* allegations.)

A number of former Federal Bureau of Investigation (FBI) officials, the *Times* said, felt that the CIA's decision to mount domestic counterintelligence operations "reflected, in part, the long-standing mistrust between the two agencies." By the late 1960s, one former FBI official noted, "all but token cooperation between the two agencies on counterintelligence and counterespionage had ended." (Under U.S. law, the FBI was empowered to conduct domestic intelligence operations. Recent reports have disclosed domestic counterintelligence operations of the FBI. [See pp. 1457–1463])

Other unnamed *Times* sources noted that J. Edgar Hoover, director of the FBI, in 1970 had broken off all but formal liaison contact between the CIA and the FBI. This lack of a working relationship, another *Times* source commented, might have provided impetus to the CIA's domestic surveillance program.

Richard Helms, director of the CIA during the first term of the Nixon Administration and current ambassador to Iran, issued a statement through the State Department Dec. 24 denying that "illegal domestic operations against antiwar activists or dissidents" had occurred during his stewardship of the CIA.

ARKANSAS DEMOCRAT
Little Rock, Ark., December 30, 1974

We find it hard to get too worked up over reports that the Central Intelligence Agency has "spied on Americans." We have two reasons — one, we remember too well what kind of "Americans" it was that CIA reportedly spied on around 1968-70. And, two, we know it's just an accident of history that the CIA's spying is restricted to foreign parts.

To amplify the second reason: We don't see much difference between a spy in the streets of Paris or a Marxist bomber at, say, Stanford. What this means is that it isn't extra devilish by definition if the CIA treats the Marxist as a legitimate blip on its screen: It's a violation of the law which, 27 years ago, gave the FBI the domestic job and the CIA the foreign job of protecting American security.

In any case, all that's ever needed is a renewal of the charge that the CIA is up to its old trick of "muscling in" on U.S. territory. When the New York Times the other day offered a detailed accusation of domestic spying, the anti-CIA camp was under full arms in a matter of hours. There will indeed be investigations, probably several — not the least by Congress.

Perhaps it will be established that CIA actually did maintain a list of 10,000 "unfriendlies" back around 1968-70 and that Nixon did suborn the agency to do the unlawful surveillance then and perhaps even later in the Watergate. Watergate is going to be dragged into it and may even dominate the inquiry.

But keep in mind the Times story — that it was against the domestic violence of the late 1960s and early 1970s that Nixon is supposed to have employed the CIA. Then go back and read the history of those times. The bombings, the killings, the assaults on police, on property (public and private) the revolutionary acts and declarations of such groups as the Weathermen — the marches of thousands on campus and off.

It amounted to a serious attempt at revolution by the New Left — a class struggle, as the revolutionaries themselves phrased it, against imperialism. Violence was their weapon. Nixon feared it. So did the New York Times.

Here is part of a Times editorial of March 13, 1970: "The actual and threatened bombings of the past few days must not be glossed over as the actions of idealistic if misguided revolutionaries; they are the criminal acts of potential murderers . . . the mad criminals who threaten and bomb must be recognized for what they are and prosecuted with the full force not only of law but of the community they would rule and ruin."

Plain enough. Four months later, Nixon announced and then supposedly rescinded the so-called Huston plan to increase surveillance of the revolutionaries. Perhaps he did not rescind it after all. In any case, the "intelligence community" was to intensify surveillance of those — foreign or American — who posed a threat to national security. That threat was real. So maybe the CIA was used after all.

Three years later (after the scare was over) the New York Times got and printed details of the Huston plan and called it an approach to a police state.

None of this is to defend CIA's breaking of the law if it did break the law. But it is well that some intelligence agency — or all of them — was on the job in 1968-70. All you have to do is go back and read the record.

The Birmingham News

Birmingham, Ala., December 25, 1974

If the Central Intelligence Agency spied on U. S. civilians during the period of anti-war protest, it should have been ashamed of itself. The CIA charter specifically said that such activities are out of bounds for that agency.

President Ford, while acknowledging that he has had information about past improper investigations by the CIA, has given assurances that such wrongdoing won't be tolerated by his administration.

However, the full-scale investigation that Sen. William Proxmire wants, under the circumstances, simply to be warranted. The abuse has been corrected, so what is to be gained by a rehash, a-la-Watergate, of the episode? The fact that the abuse has been corrected demonstrates that wrong can be corrected without the involvement of Congress—a thought which should offer some comfort to those who observed the glacial speed of Congress' investigation of Watergate.

What does Proxmire intend that Congress find out about the episode? Which agents were involved? Upon whom the agency spied? What kinds of techniques were used? These would be details of interest only to the sort of cultists who read the published Watergate transcripts all the way through.

Congress has urgent business to which it should attend. It does not need to disinter the corpse of this long-buried affair and perform an autopsy in full public view.

Under the law, the Federal Bureau of Investigation is the proper agency to carry out domestic intelligence work. But there are those, of course, who would like to see all domestic intelligence work abolished.

The often used phrases are that "dissident individuals" and "dissident groups" are the targets of such investigations. The connotation is that anyone who disagrees with government policy is liable to be spied upon—shades of the Soviet Union! But anyone who remembers the unrest of the Vietnam war knows that the people under surveillance frequently went far beyond simple dissent. On some occasions they made bombs which they exploded in public buildings.

Clearly the CIA shouldn't have been in the spying business within the United States. But this usurpation of the FBI's function is not the horror that some depict it to be. It was illegal and deplorable, but no more threatening to the average non-bomb-making citizen than if the police of one city wrongly began to patrol streets within another city's jurisdiction. To the innocent, what difference would it make?

The furor over the CIA may be a prelude to a sweeping curtailment of all domestic intelligence operations. If that proves to be the case, the average citizen will have less protection from fanatic groups ranging from the Ku Klux Klan to the Black Panthers.

The right of privacy is important, but not so important that it should be a shield against the efforts of the proper authorities to prevent violence-prone weirdos from making war against the rest of society.

MANCHESTER NEW HAMPSHIRE UNION LEADER

Manchester, N.H., December 27, 1974

Over last weekend the Sunday New York Times, whose naive publisher and owners don't seem to understand that their paper is being used by certain very clever people to destroy the free enterprise system and the safety and security of the nation, came out with what this editor would call a news story played all out of proportion as the lead story of the day. It was to the effect that—horror of horrors—the CIA had been engaging in espionage and intelligence work regarding the various domestic revolutionary organziations which the Times refers to politely as "dissidents."

Actually, of course, the correct description of many of these people in the United States would be revolutionists — cold-blooded, bomb-throwing killers without remorse.

President Ford, reacting like a puppet on a string to any nonsense the liberal news media comes up with, immediately and excitedly called the head of the CIA from his plane as he was going West to a ski vacation, and demanded that all such investigative work of subversive groups in this country be stopped by the CIA. Ford then piously announced that no such action would be allowed during his administration!

The question this newspaper would like to ask the New York Times is, "Whose side are they on?" We would like to ask President Ford why he doesn't understand reality and what's going on in the world today.

What President Ford and the Times have said really amounts to informing the bomb throwers and the revolutionary murderers in this country that we certainly will never violate "your civil rights" by investigating "your dissident activities," so go right ahead. If you do throw a bomb and kill people, **after that** we will look into the matter — but not beforehand. It would be just very nasty, unpleasant and evil of us to possibly keep track of your plans to throw the bombs and to stop you from doing so ahead of time. That just wouldn't be nice!

It is the function of every security organization, CIA, FBI or any other which can possibly do so, to keep track of the revolutionaries in this country and, by penetrating their organizations and gaining as much intelligence as possible about them ahead of time, to prevent their doing irreparable damage to the United States and killing hundreds and thousands of people by their activities.

IF THERE IS OBJECTION TO THE FACT THAT THE CIA IS SUPPOSED TO CONCENTRATE ON FOREIGN INTELLIGENCE ACTIVITIES AND NOT ANYTHING INSIDE THE UNITED STATES, IT MUST BE REMEMBERED THAT MOST OF THESE REVOLUTIONARY ORGANIZATIONS INSIDE THE UNITED STATES ARE NOT HOME GROWN VARIETIES BUT ARE SUPPORTED AND FINANCED FROM ABROAD. THEREFORE, IT IS VERY NATURAL FOR THE CIA TO FOLLOW THE TRAIL FROM ABROAD TO WHERE THE REVOLUTIONARY CANCER ERUPTS INSIDE THE UNITED STATES.

There is something tragically simpleminded about the New York Times and other liberals in this country who do not seem to understand that freedom is up against a world-wide conspiracy to destroy it through revolutionary groups which have their home bases in Soviet Russia, Red China and other Communist satellites.

It would be a great mistake, for instance, to regard the Irish Republican Army revolutionists who are now bombing London and Birmingham and killing hundreds of people in Ireland as well as England, as simply local, patriotic folk. The same applies to the Arab terrorists who have been murdering at random now for years.

None of these organizations could exist or survive if it were not for support by the Communist nations of the world, which are deliberately supplying and encouraging the terrorists as a method of bringing the Free World to its knees.

The question remains, do some of these revolutionaries have to kill some of the leading liberals or members of their families before the liberals recognize reality? Of course, they are not apt to be the victims of the terrorists, because as far as the terrorists are concerned, these well-meaning but completely confused and misguided liberals are doing exactly what the revolutionaries want, which is to insist that freedom demands that we allow terrorists to destroy freedom.

The logic or common sense of this theory certainly escapes any sensible individual.

MR. FORD'S KNEE-JERK REACTION IN THIS SITUATION, OF COURSE, ILLUSTRATES WHAT THIS NEWSPAPER HAS SAID FROM THE VERY BEGINNING, (NOT TO MAKE A BAD PUN) GERRY IS INDEED A JERK. AND MR. SULZBERGER IS A NICE GENTLEMAN WHO DOESN'T UNDERSTAND WHICH END IS UP IN THIS WORLD.

William Loeb

William Loeb, Publisher

ARGUS-LEADER
Sioux Falls, S.D., December 29, 1974

There may well be some comparatively few abuses by the Central Intelligence Agency (CIA) that included domestic spying in this country as the New York Times has alleged in some news stories.

The congressional reaction is typical. There are many calls for investigation of the CIA as to whether or not it exceeded its charter in its worldwide operations. Domestic spying is not part of that charter. The Times claims the CIA had files on 10,000 American citizens and performed break-ins and surveillance in the United States during the administration of former President Richard Nixon.

What the country does not need in 1975 is another fullblown investigation or inquiry, a la Watergate. If the CIA has indeed abused its power, there are some existing congressional committees that can look into it. President Gerald Ford has called for a complete report and can take appropriate action. He apparently has given strict orders circumscribing the CIA to its assigned duties in developing intelligence.

The country needs an intelligence apparatus to tell its government what is going on in the real world. The activities that American spies, Russian agents, Chinese intelligence operatives and proper British types are engaged in around the world, from Santiago to Cairo, are not "fun and games." Their purposes are to advise their own governments about what is happening, so those governments may act in their own national interest.

Let Solons Use Restraint

Congressmen should be restrained in their approach to investigating the CIA. There is linen in its closet that should not be washed in public. To do so would destroy the effectiveness of the country's intelligence system. Congress can and should find out what the abuses are—and take discreet steps to prevent recurrence if there really has been a misuse of the CIA by interference in domestic matters.

At present, four subcommittees of Congress have been delegated the job of overseeing the CIA. These are intelligence subcommittees made up of most senior members of the House and Senate Armed Services committees, and also appropriations subcommittees in both chambers.

It could be that the four committees and the leadership of the House and Senate in both parties should give closer scrutiny to the CIA in the future. Congress has been somewhat derelict in the past in looking after some of the agencies it has created. But any move to have 535 members of Congress supervise the CIA would be ridiculous.

The country can't afford to have every Tom, Dick and Harry in Congress (1) spouting off about the CIA's secrets or (2) running a Watergate-type investigation on the CIA.

This Isn't Kiss And Tell

Much has been made about the CIA's mistakes: the Bay of Pigs fiasco, its misreading of the so-called missile gap, financing of college students during the period of campus unrest in this country and its cloak and dagger actions in Chile. There have also been occasions when the CIA failed to note signs of impending military action in the Mideast or elsewhere. But nothing can be said of the CIA's successes. These incidents must remain hush-hush. Governments which kiss and tell aren't very successful in espionage.

It's in the nature of the CIA's business that mistakes are headlined, but successes must remain secrets.

The British, in their proper ways, know how much to tell and what to say about their covert operations. They don't spill the beans when there's a crisis or a flub. The United States should take a lesson from the British, and show some maturity about spies, intelligence networks and the sometimes nasty business in which they are engaged.

This country has had the CIA for 25 years. We still need it. Some changes may be warranted. If so, make them.

Ford and Congress should not let 1975 become the year of the CIA inquiry. They have other things to do.

TULSA DAILY WORLD
Tulsa, Okla., December 24, 1974

WATERGATE has eased over the hill as a target for Congress, but we can look for the next session to keep one of its related "villains" handy: The Central Intelligence Agency.

Watergate inquiries in the past year have brought out revelations about CIA activities that will make the agency suspect in some minds until its role is narrowed and tightly policed.

A weekend report in the Sunday NEW YORK TIMES related that at least 10,000 Americans were put on file by the CIA during the NIXON Administration—in a period of antiwar agitation and growth of such groups as the Black Panthers.

The allegations a l r e a d y have brought from PRESIDENT FORD a statement that he will not tolerate illegal domestic spying by the CIA in his Administration. And Sen. WILLIAM PROXMIRE, a leading opponent of the agency's domestic operations, is calling for an investigation by the JUSTICE DEPARTMENT.

PROXMIRE also wants the resignation of RICHARD HELMS as Ambassador to Iran. HELMS was CIA Director during much of the domestic surveillance period.

The CIA orders to conduct secret investigations of American citizens clearly were an overreaction by the NIXON Administration, even though there was good reason at the time for concern about the extent and danger of antiwar and guerrilla-type organizations. The FBI continues to be the nation's main resource against internal danger, and it seems fully capable of doing the job.

Perhaps it was the interconnection of protest organizations with foreign agents that led the CIA to become involved. But if the condition has been corrected, one wonders what service will be performed by having an all-out public unfolding of our Government's intelligence activities. Can't we agree to keep domestic and foreign security operations separated—without exposing for all the world to see just how we go about them? After all, both the FBI and CIA need some protection from all-out public exposure if they are to do their jobs effectively.

THE KNICKERBOCKER NEWS
··· UNION-STAR ···
Albany, N.Y., December 26, 1974

Our heritage from the Nixon administration is being revealed as more noisome even than had first been thought.

We are now presented with strong indications that the Central Intelligence Agency, in violation of the law which created it, engaged in domestic surveillance of citizens and in many other illegal ways invaded their privacy. All was done surreptitiously, all was concealed from Congress and the people and all it would appear, was winked at or tacitly approved by the White House which was obsessed, at that time with an inordinate fear of "enemies."

In testimony before the Senate Watergate committee more than a year ago, Richard Helms, then head of the CIA told how the President's Foreign Intelligence Advisory Board had suggested that the CIA "make a contribution" to domestic intelligence operations. Mr. Helms said there was no way his agency could do so but that he kept receiving "feelers" on the matter.

And the White House tapes show former President Nixon as once saying, " Well, we protected Helms from one hell of a lot of things."

There is no indication that the illegal surveillance of citizens has been continued under William Colby, present head of the intelligence agency.

Congress is preparing to look into the entire matter, as it should. The evidence is strong that it will find a nest of vipers—a can of worms.

Arkansas Gazette.

Little Rock, Ark., December 26, 1974

We have been convinced for too many years that if this country finally succeeds in doing itself in through its own devices it will be in the name of "national security" and the exaggerated, indeed, limitless, definition given to the expression by the people to whom we entrust that amorphous commodity.

Pre-eminent among the many overlapping agencies engaged in this field is the CIA, which, we now have seen, finally succeeded in extending its brief to the domestic Intelligence field, though it was specifically enjoined from doing so by the congressional language that created this inbred band of super-sleuths. Could it possibly have turned out otherwise, considering?

If it *had* been possible for the CIA to stick to its overseas knitting, Richard Nixon would have seen to it that it didn't, as in fact he did see to it. Nixon distrusted everybody and everything, J. Edgar Hoover included, and, in the end, wound up distrusting the CIA, too, for all its extra-legal striving, moving finally to set up his own *private* band of political spies, made up in considerable measure of old CIA hands such as E. Howard Hunt. There is a certain CIA mystique surrounding people who have ever served in the body, a CIA *mentality,* if you please, as exemplified by the present director, William E. Colby.

And while we are on the subject of Mr. Colby, will everybody who accepts this cold-eyed man's (and President Ford's) assurances that the CIA now has fully extricated itself from domestic Intelligence gathering please stand on his left forefinger? There, that makes a pretty spectacular solo scene, whoever you are.

The reason for our own doubts is that agencies such as the CIA generate their own momentum, once they slip their leash in any direction.

What the CIA really represents, of course, was the first fruit of our national determination to defeat "Communism" — Russian Communism, most especially — by becoming as much like Russia and the other Communist states as we could be, given certain archaic restraints embedded in the national Constitution.

The Constitution still lives, but there are ways of getting around anything, as the CIA knows full well, and as Richard Nixon knew from the beginning of his public life. Other foolish excesses, too, many, had been perpetrated by the CIA before — the Bay of Pigs being at least the *best-known* example, but it was Nixon who put it all together, corrupting, one by one, every unit of government with even the remotest claim to a place in the "national security" picture.

The results are well-known, and for those who say that the Watergate, the attempt to impose gag rule on the New York Times in the Pentagon Papers case, all the rest of it, was really nothing in the perspective of history, we will say that our contrary opinion is that what it all added to was a kind of domestic Pearl Harbor that didn't come off, quite.

Up until the Times's new, detailed allegations about the CIA's domestic spying,

the prevailing belief had been that the agency, under former director Richard Helms, went along with Nixon for awhile, as in the assistance it gave Hunt in the Ellsberg break-in, but that it then withdrew into its prescribed shell. We have reason to believe now that this wasn't so, but we know also that, *even then,* Nixon wasn't satisfied. Enter the "Plumbers."

The CIA was born out of the Cold War, and of course — and vice-versa — though there were subsidiary reasons for its creation in the form that it was, one of them being to pinch off J. Edgar Hoover and "his" FBI from any activities in the area of foreign Intelligence-gathering. But to make Hoover a little happier in his disappointment, it was necessary to try to insure that the CIA, in its turn, not impinge on "Edgar's" turf at home, which was fair enough, at that.

★ ★ ★

THERE HAVE BEEN SPIES since the Peloponnesian Wars and earlier, and always will be. The fact that rival spies frequently cancel each other out is neither here nor there, for that is part of the idea. What is to the point here is that the CIA was moving toward the beginning of an American police state without any real let or license from the people charged with overseeing its activities insofar as anyone *has* overseen them, meaning by the national Congress.

There are a number of things that we have never quite understood about the CIA, and perhaps the first one is why, necessarily, the size of its operating budget should be kept secret from the American people and from all but a tiny handful of their representatives in the Congress. We mean, just knowing what the boys are spending isn't going to blow anybody's cover overseas and so compromise an informer.

We also would like to have some vague idea of the agency's scorecard in terms of wins and losses. Some losses are inevitable, *many* are inevitable, but what we are talking about is the balance of error. This particular set of statistics, unlike the size of the CIA budget, is basically unknowable, anybody's guess.

But just as it is dangerous for the good health of the Republic to allow *any* agent of government to have *carte-blanche* at the Treasury pot, so it is dangerous for any agency to be, for all practical purposes, beyond any accountability in non-money areas either. This is why we not only have no confidence in Mr. Colby's and Mr. Ford's promise that the CIA now has recognized the error of its ways in getting into domestic spying and is determined to mend those ways, neither do we have any real confidence in those congressional committees that now are riding off in all directions talking of "investigations." Not at least in most of the spokesmen who have come forward so far, men such as Senate Armed Services Chairman John C. Stennis of Mississippi. People like Stennis have too long a history of rolling over on their back with all four legs in the air when someone tickles their stomach and mumbles something vague about "the national security."

The New York Times

New York, N.Y., December 24, 1974

Yet another conspiracy under the Nixon Administration to defy the law and infringe upon the constitutional rights of American citizens has now sprung into the open. The domestic intelligence-gathering operation of the Central Intelligence Agency, the maintenance of secret files on several thousand American citizens suspected of political dissidence were flatly illegal activities; there is no alternative now to invoking appropriate legal procedures against the officials responsible.

The basic rationale for the C.I.A. as an independent intelligence organization is not at issue; it is unfortunate that a valuable, even essential, institution has been cast under a cloud by the misguided zeal of those inside and outside the agency who thought nothing of twisting and misusing an important national asset.

It is reassuring to hear from President Ford and the present director of Central Intelligence, William E. Colby, that all such domestic surveillance activities have been terminated; more to the point is how they could have been permitted in the first place when Federal statutes so clearly bar the C.I.A. from internal security functions.

In defending the C.I.A. against recent months of criticism arising from unwise but not illegal covert activities abroad, Mr. Colby has persuasively argued that the agency was simply carrying out the duly issued policy directives of the National Security Council. It will be important now to learn whether this domestic surveillance program—unwise *and* illegal—was also initiated by the N.S.C. or the Nixon White House or, alternatively, grew up from the independent unchecked initiative of the agency's own Counterintelligence Department, most secret and impenetrable branch of a sheltered bureaucracy.

Defenders of the intelligence community argue that domestic surveillance is permissible when clearly related to foreign intelligence purposes. A more concrete attempt at justification arises from the decision in 1970 of J. Edgar Hoover, late director of the Federal Bureau of Investigation, to cut off working relations with the C.I.A. Since the agency could no longer rely on the F.B.I., the body legally charged with internal security, it was pushed into its own domestic surveillance, so the argument goes. Professional rivalries are endemic among secret services, but this particular feud, stretching back even to the predecessor organization of C.I.A., has had deplorable implications for national security.

This illegal surveillance operation and the failure to institute legal proceedings until after its public disclosure suggest an intolerable breakdown of institutional checks and balances. For many years this newspaper—among others—has urged closer oversight by Congress of the intelligence system. But the first responsibility for preventing any further misuse of power must rest with the C.I.A. and other elements of the intelligence community, if they wish to continue receiving the trust absolutely required for the conduct of their mission.

DAYTON DAILY NEWS
Dayton, Ohio, December 24, 1974

The New York Times report of extensive CIA domestic spying, now partially confirmed by President Ford, calls for considerably more in the way of official response than Mr. Ford's assurance that he, at least, won't let such a thing happen again.

The law against the CIA carrying on spook activities within the United States is clearer than CIA officials suggest when they say there are gray areas in the prohibition. The law flatly forbids the CIA from any domestic projects. Never mind that the CIA-at-home program apparently evolved as counterintelligence. That, by law, is the FBI's charge.

According to the Times report, the CIA moved on a request from the Nixon White House to find out whether U.S. antiwar activists were being run or funded from abroad. That led to an eventually major program of spying on, and keeping records about, American political dissidents—including even some congressmen.

There are claims in the Times story that the program also included occasional "covert" activities on the Watergate-break-in sort, though the report is vague about those.

These are not matters merely to be deplored in retrospect and poulticed with warm promises that it won't happen again. More than an impropriety, CIA misbehavior at home can be—and was, if Watergate in any way proceeded from it—the beginning of rot in the nation's political fabric.

First, a complete, open investigation ought to be conducted by a select committee of the type Sen. Sam Ervin chaired in the Watergate probe. Perhaps special legislation should be enacted making it clear to present and former CIA officials who are called as witnesses that their higher obligation in the circumstances is to candor with the committee rather than to the preservation of CIA secrecy.

Second, the Justice department must be instructed not to quail at prosecuting criminal charges against any CIA official who appears to have violated the law barring CIA activity within the United States.

Third, serious attention must be given to the structure, operation and control of the CIA. That the United States needs an agency that is deft and thorough in gathering intelligence and sophisticated in analyzing it is not in doubt. This the CIA is, and the capacities should not be lost.

But Congress ought to pull the CIA—which is to say, the United States—out of the foreign "dirty tricks" business, an involvement that, first, is plain wrong and one that creates more trouble for this country than it solves, that invites foreign policy short-cuts, disposes the presidency to presumptuousness about its privileges in foreign dealings and outfits the CIA with too-dangerous abilities for domestic mischief, whether by its current or its former agents.

Not until that is done can Congress then hope to accomplish, reliably, what it must—the secure reassertion of the limited mandate what was the CIA's originally and the development of complementary congressional and presidential mechanisms for guaranteeing that the CIA will stay within bounds.

San Jose Mercury
San Jose, Calif., December 24, 1974

The latest allegation of misconduct against the Central Intelligence Agency, that it engaged in massive, illegal domestic spying during the Nixon administration, demands more than another perfunctory congressional investigation.

The CIA has been in and out of hot water for most of its comparatively short life; this is not the first time it has been accused of violating its basic charter, the National Security Act of 1947. That law specifically assigns the responsibility for all domestic intelligence work, that is spying and counter-spying in the United States, to the Federal Bureau of Investigation.

There was a sound reason for giving the FBI this responsibility and not the CIA. The FBI is far more amenable to congressional review than the CIA, whose overseas activities frequently justify silence on genuine "national security" grounds. The FBI is — and should be—more visible, if for no other reason than that every citizen's Fourth Amendment rights demand it.

Thus, the American people have every right to demand of Congress and President Ford that the CIA be brought up sharply this time, that its organization be reshaped so that no further episodes of this sort can occur and that Congress devise the means for effectively keeping this agency accountable for its actions.

Lack of accountability is the real problem, as Sen. Stuart Symington (D-Mo), a ranking member of the Senate Armed Services Committee, pointed out over the weekend.

Commenting on charges that the CIA had spied on Vietnam war dissenters and others at odds with the Nixon foreign policy, Sen. Symington said in part:

"If the story is true, and I am speaking as a member for many years of the subcommittee that is supposed to review the operations of the Central Intelligence Agency, it simply verifies the point that I've been making for many years, namely that this agency does not have good supervision or review by the Congress. It actually has no real review at all..."

That is stating the case as simply and as directly as possible.

Congress can move to get this review in one of two ways. It can persuade President Ford to ride personal herd on the CIA and keep the leaders of Congress informed unofficially of all pertinent activities. This is a variation of the system that was supposed to be in effect during the Nixon years and even before that.

The system has flaws, the biggest being the human element. Everything depends on the willingness—or the ability — of the man in the White House to cooperate.

The second way to ensure adequate congressional oversight of the CIA is to open its budget requests to public scrutiny. This procedure, coupled with a pinch-penny approach to CIA appropriations, would ensure professional rectitude.

The problem with this approach is that what it gains in accountability it stands to lose in flexibility. Some intelligence simply cannot be gathered without a certain amount of hush-hush.

The problem is real and it is sticky, but it can no longer be ignored by Congress and the President.

Chicago Tribune
Chicago, Ill., December 27, 1974

Charges that the Central Intelligence Agency carried out illegal spying operations against American citizens may be a shock. They cannot exactly be called a surprise. This has always been the recognized, built-in risk of having government agencies like the CIA, where power is necessarily combined with secrecy. The combination does not easily conform with laws or rules, not even its own.

There is no choice now but to establish the facts, in full and without cosmetics, about the CIA's past domestic operations. We believe the best way to do that is to set up a special congressional committee to investigate them—one that will include, but will not be limited to, members of the House and Senate Armed Services committees who have regularly dealt with the CIA in the past. Those committees have pretty well demonstrated their inability to act as efficient watchdogs over its operations.

No doubt there will be strong objections to such an inquiry. We will be told that our counterintelligence system will be compromised and the United States left virtually defenseless if the American public finds out too much about what the CIA has been doing. Two things, we think, need to be said.

First, we've heard it before. It seemed to a guiding principle of the Nixon administration—almost its only one—that the public is better off not knowing what its leaders are doing; that patriotism means not asking too many questions. The last two years have been a massive disproof of that doctrine, and it cannot be made to sound convincing now. If Watergate proved anything, it proved that the more we know about our government the safer we—and it—are.

Second, the charges concern CIA operations during the Nixon administration and before. Investigating them does not mean that every detail of the agency's present workings must be exposed. [They have been greatly changed under the two men who succeeded Richard Helms as director of Central Intelligence.] The point is not to cripple the CIA but to keep it from crippling us; and to do that, the American public will have to know exactly what happened to this agency—why the seemingly iron-clad rules against spying on U. S. citizens turned so soft and porous that they could be set aside almost at will.

After that, we'll have to face a still tougher question: Whether any rules will be permanently binding on an agency whose specialty, after all, is to operate beyond them.

The New York Times started the uproar Sunday by printing allegations that the CIA, in flat violation of its own charter, had conducted massive surveillance against members of antiwar and other dissident groups during the Nixon administration. It said that a special counterintelligence unit, reporting directly to Mr. Helms, had compiled files on at least 10,000 American citizens. It appears that the spying did not begin with Mr. Nixon: Documents in the CIA's files indicate that hundreds of other illegal operations were carried out in the United States beginning in the 1950s.

There has been a commendable hurry to investigate these findings. President Ford requested and got a detailed report from CIA Director William E. Colby. The chairmen of four congressional panels, including the armed services committees of both chambers, announced plans for full inquiries when the new Congress convenes.

A flurry of activity, however, is not enough. Nor is it sufficient to launch more investigations by panels that failed to turn up anything in the past. The task now is not only to find out how that happened, but how to make absolutely certain it can never happen again.

THE SUN
Baltimore, Md., December 24, 1974

Senator William Proxmire is certainly correct to call for a prompt investigation of the latest charges against the Central Intelligence Agency. Those charges are serious and disturbing in the extreme. The CIA is accused (apparently by present and former CIA officials and by Federal Bureau of Investigation officials) of gathering information on private United States citizens. This intelligence gathering often involved violating the constitutional rights of citizens. Even if it had not, it is wrong and illegal for the CIA to engage in such activity. That is secret police stuff. When the CIA was created in 1947 Congress took great pains to circumscribe the agency. It was authorized to gather intelligence in foreign countries only. "We don't want a Gestapo," a congressman warned during the 1947 debate.

Have we ended up with one? According to the allegations, the CIA compiled dossiers on thousands of citizens, including members of Congress, that agents deemed to be "dissidents." These were for the most part members of anti-war groups, but some others who expressed political objections to one or another Nixon administration policy also seem to have been put under surveillance. All of this activity involving America citizens is said to have started in 1969, under Nixon, but there are also charges that the CIA operated illegally in this country prior to that by doing counter-intelligence work involving foreign nationals.

Senator Proxmire wants the Justice Department to investigate these charges. It should begin at once. If illegal acts have been committed by officials, those officials should be charged and prosecuted to the limit of the law. That would clearly demonstrate to the CIA, to other U.S. intelligence agencies that might believe they are somehow beyond the law, and to the American public that there is not going to be a Gestapo here, that it can't happen here. In addition to a Justice Department investigation, there also ought to be a thorough airing of these charges by the Congress. And we don't mean by the Senate Armed Services Committee's CIA Oversight subcommittee, either. That "watchdog" has been sleeping in the sun for 20 years, as one member, Senator Stuart Symington, has complained. A broader based investigating committee is called for, perhaps a special, short term committee like the Ervin panel of Watergate fame.

Whether or not such a committee is decided on, and whether or not the charges now before the public prove true, there is still a need for a permanent real congressional watchdog for the CIA and other intelligence gathering operations. The potential for abuse—the potential for a Gestapo—is too great to leave oversight to the sort of coziness that, to Congress' shame, has prevailed. If Congress won't protect the rights of citizens from arrogant bureaucracies, who will?

THE KANSAS CITY STAR
Kansas City, Mo.,
December 26, 1974

Finding itself in hot water has become almost a permanent condition for the Central Intelligence Agency. This time it is not one of the CIA's dubious covert actions overseas, such as attempting to overthrow an unfriendly government, that has thrust the supersecret agency into the spotlight it abhors. The question is whether the CIA, in direct violation of its charter, conducted a massive, illegal domestic spying operation during the Nixon administration against the antiwar movement and other dissident groups in the United States.

The New York Times has made such a charge after an extensive investigation of CIA activities in the late 1960s and early 1970s. The Times also claimed that evidence exists of earlier illicit CIA activities that included break-ins, wiretapping and the surreptitious inspection of mail. But these efforts were said to have been directed at suspected foreign intelligence agents. The main concern now is whether American citizens have been subjected to unlawful—and outrageously improper—surveillance for whatever reason.

The charge has rolled up an immediate public furor and strong official reactions. President Ford has ordered Henry A. Kissinger, secretary of state, to get a report from the CIA on the allegation and that study is now completed. The chairmen of four congressional committees or subcommittees have announced that they would begin extensive hearings on the matter soon after the new Congress convenes next month. The head of the CIA's counterintelligence operations has resigned. Richard Helms, former chief of the agency, has denied that the CIA spied on antiwar activists in the United States during his tenure. Yet the New York Times charge seems to be directly related to the period of Helms's authority.

Now it is up to the President and Congress to establish the facts. Either the officials who ran the CIA a few years ago were or were not guilty as charged by the New York Times. Sworn testimony should be able to bring out the truth one way or the other.

Special oversight subcommittees in both the Senate and the House are supposed to protect against any abuses of authority by the CIA. But members of the subcommittees have not always been well informed on the agency's most secretive programs in the past and Congress has recently shown interest in strengthening this monitoring system.

Tightening these checks is a subject for urgent attention for the new Congress. The oversight groups should in fact concern themselves with the whole field of government intelligence efforts. There are still scars from the disclosure a few years ago that the Army—under a directive that was never pinned down by Senate investigators—had actually spied on dissident civilians much in the manner that the CIA is now accused of having done.

In a nuclear-armed world, intelligence efforts properly and legally carried out can be of life-and-death importance to the nation. But there is infringement on our civil liberties if this function is distorted for misuse against suspected critics of official policies.

If the CIA has actually veered from its legitimate mission as charged, then President Ford and Congress must act to make certain that it will be the last such outrage.

The Toronto Star

Toronto, Ont., December 28, 1974

There are few countries in the world which haven't felt the ubiquitous tentacles of the Central Intelligence Agency (CIA) probing their sensitive regions, and the latest is none other than the United States itself.

There were reports this week that during the administration of former president Richard Nixon, the CIA conducted massive illegal spying on members of the anti-war movement and other dissidents and compiled dossiers on some 10,000 Americans.

Although prohibited by law from operating within the U.S., the spy force acted as secret police. So secret, in fact, that the Federal Bureau of Investigation, the authorized agency for domestic intelligence, apparently wasn't aware of the activity.

Americans have never been much troubled by the most arrogant and atrocious behavior of the CIA in other countries. But now the wiretappings, break-ins, mail interceptions, planting of informants and general surveillance is taking place at home, the reaction may be different.

President Gerald Ford has demanded an explanation from the agency. While that doesn't amount to much in the way of an independent investigation, it's better than his reaction to the news that the CIA sunk $11 million into Chile in an attempt to oust democratically-elected Salvador Allende.

He wasn't about to pass judgment on the morality or legality of such actions, he said. "It is a recognized fact that, historically and presently, such actions are taken in the best interests of the country involved."

It will be interesting to see if the president adopts such a patronizing attitude in his homeland.

Few people would question the importance of keeping the U.S. government up to date on significant world-wide activity. Canada and other western alliance countries obviously benefit from the CIA's vigilance.

But there is cause for concern when the agency steps beyond the job of collecting foreign information to interfere and disrupt in other countries or secretly spy on its own citizens.

The existence of such a powerful and super-secret agency—its annual budget is thought to be almost $1 billion—within an open, democratic society must be considered extraordinary and treated with extraordinary care and control.

If the current excesses of the agency lead to a review by Congress and the application of additional controls, Americans and free people everywhere will feel more secure in their freedom.

The first thing is to bring back former director Richard Helms to explain the agency's activities. He is now serving as ambassador to Iran.

The parting may be sorrowful to both Helms and the Shah. The CIA is generally credited with engineering the 1953 coup that installed the Shah after Premier Mohammed Mossadegh had nationalized foreign oil companies. The Shah immediately returned 40 per cent ownership to the U.S. firms.

EVENING EXPRESS

Portland, Me., December 30, 1974

As much as anything, what distinguishes the community of free men from the dictatorship state is absence of covert spying on the individual's activities, and the associated perils of blackmail and intimidation.

Yet while this protection is written into the constitution of this country, the prohibition on spying is not self-enforcing. For free men to be truly free they must work at it, and they will be indifferent at the risk of losing this most precious form of liberty.

In the case of the Central Intelligence Agency, which was established to protect the security of the United States through surveillance and other means of gathering information, it is clearly written into law that the CIA shall conduct no spying within this country.

But last week the New York Times, on the basis of a good deal of probing, alleged that the CIA had been spying on as many as 10,000 Americans citizens, among them Jack Anderson, who writes for this newspaper, with the consent and knowledge of former President Nixon.

President Ford does not flatly deny that internal spying has not been carried out in the past, and even the present director of the CIA, William E. Colby, is said to have given partial off-the-record confirmation.

This is an alarming situation that demands a thorough investigation by a strong congressional probe panel, on the pattern of the Erwin committee, and later a powerful prosecutor who cannot be sidetracked or short-circuited.

If the Times is right, no American citizen is wholly free, and while other forms of all too prevalent business espionage can sometimes be halted by court action, the CIA is much more powerful, and it will require all of the resources of the U.S. Government at the highest levels to get at the truth. But we must have it, no matter what the cost.

St. Petersburg Times

St. Petersburg, Fla., December 24, 1974

Outraged, we are. Surprised, we are not. And we doubt that it comes out of the blue to any old CIA-watcher that our government's spooks have been up to their dirty tricks not just abroad but at home.

Sure, it is against the law for the Central Intelligence Agency to deal in any way with the "internal security" of the United States. That's the FBI's job.

BUT WITH a blank check from Congress to hire, spend, travel, bribe, lie, eavesdrop, wiretap, house-break, and by inference, even to kill without any public accounting — so long as it's all done in some other country — CIA couldn't help getting in trouble here too.

It previously had been caught, anyway, secretly using tax funds to subsidize student groups, foundations, labor unions and schools. It helped bungle the Pentagon Papers affair. It was up to its false eyebrows in various aspects of the Watergate mess, supplying red wigs, cameras, and finally five of its ex?-operatives to burgle and bug in support of four more years for President Nixon.

So how surprised can official Washington be to learn from The New York Times that CIA during the first Nixon term conducted a massive counterintelligence operation against dissident groups in the United States?

Actually, any number of highly placed officials had to know about this, including key members of Congress (especially considering that some lesser members of Congress reportedly were on CIA's list of suspected subversives).

The difference now is that they know that the public knows too. So they all are issuing appropriate cries of alarm. President Ford, for one, has assured us that nothing like that is going on now, and that it won't as long as he is in office.

That's a correct position. It is good also to hear, once again, that Congress may call everybody in for a hearing, and, for the first time, that the Justice Department may be thinking about bringing criminal charges.

BUT WE AREN'T highly optimistic about any of that. Spying by nature is a dirty business, and by nature it has to be conducted in secret. So don't hold your breath waiting for congressional or other action against past CIA criminal acts.

What you do have a right to expect and to demand, however, is that Congress and the President (it will take both) jerk a knot in the necessary number of necks at CIA headquarters at Langley, Va.

It is long past time to bring CIA under control, not only as to some of its offensive actions abroad, but also, now more than ever, as to its illegal assumption of secret police powers at home.

After all, this isn't Russia.

The Dallas Morning News
Dallas, Texas, December 24, 1974

THE CHARGE that the Central Intelligence Agency has engaged in massive domestic spying operations sends shudders of apprehension through all Americans who revere this country's constitutional freedoms.

These freedoms are the very basis for our prosperity today, our ability to live life as we choose, 185 years after the framers of the Constitution fashioned the Bill of Rights.

Here is what they envisioned in the Fourth Amendment: "The right of the people to be secure in their persons, houses, papers and effects, against all unreasonable searches and seizures, shall not be violated, and no warrants shall issue, but upon probable cause, supported by oath or affirmation . . ."

What justification can there be for the domestic operations of the CIA, if even one half of what was reported Sunday by the New York Times is true?

There is none.

This newspaper has always considered the guarantees of the Constitution to be paramount, and we cannot condone abuses by government agencies that cut deep against the grain of our freedoms. We have seen the Constitution battered in this decade. A president and a vice-president ignored their constitutional duties, and resigned in ignominy. The men entrusted to enforce our laws on the highest levels failed us.

Now it is charged that an agency that is strictly limited by law to intelligence activities abroad has turned its reach inward.

Despite a charter which specifically forbids domestic operations, the CIA has allegedly carried out broad, unreasonable and illegal surveillance against as many as 10,000 American citizens.

The agency's supposed activities since the 1950s include break-ins, wiretapping and the surreptitious inspection of the United States mail. Most of the surveillance was conducted in the 1960s against persons whose most suspicious activity was the exercise of the right to dissent in connection with the Vietnam War.

It is not a political question of how to respond to the allegations against the CIA. There is no politics to the law of the land, or to the rights of Americans to lead their lives unfettered and unworried.

The right response is to peel back the top and see what's in this can of worms. That's the Congress' job—and we ask only that the committee appointed to investigate the CIA's activities not be headed by a presidential aspirant.

Indeed, this is no time for political posturing. It's time to get back on line with the letter and spirit of the law and the Constitution, and live with assurance as free Americans—just as our forebears intended.

THE ATLANTA CONSTITUTION
Atlanta, Ga., December 26, 1974

Eternal vigilance is the price of liberty.

The United States Central Intelligence Agency is supposed to guard our liberties by eternal vigilance against threats from foreign foes.

One of our liberties is the right to dissent, publicly, when we disagree with a policy of our government. Like, say, the undeclared war in Vietnam. Now what would happen if the CIA, which by law is forbidden to police or spy on American citizens in this country, should nevertheless start doing exactly that?

One possibility was foreseen way back in the 1940s when Congress was debating the formation and powers of the CIA. Some legislators expressed fears that such an agency, if not properly controlled, could become a gestapo. And the nation itself might begin to take on some of the features of those totalitarian police states we have so long opposed.

There are now strong and seemingly well-supported allegations that the CIA, in violation of its charter — in violation of the law — has been spying on American citizens in the free exercise of their rights. It is alleged that 10,000 or more dossiers were compiled on anti-Vietnam war activists, well-known and unknown. The CIA official in charge of counterintelligence operations has already resigned under fire.

We have an agency, the Federal Bureau of Investigation, whose duty it is to deal with internal subversion. The CIA is unique in that it is practically answerable to nobody. Members of Congressional "overseer" committees are as much in the dark on some of its operations, particularly this internal spying, as the rest of us. So long as the CIA did its job within the limits set by law nobody was worried. But now that it appears some top officials have abused their powers, whether on their own or at the request of still higher officials, a halt has to be called right now. President Ford has publicly said the CIA must strictly observe its limits and must not spy on citizens in this country. But that's not enough. Those officials who abused power and who violated the law ought to be held accountable.

Congress has a duty to the nation to find out what was happening during the late 1960s and early 1970s as far as CIA involvement in internal spying is concerned, and it has a duty to make sure that our liberties are safe from the threats of those who abuse their power. This is of concern to every American, not just those who express themself themselves in street demonstrations and other public activity. If an uncontrolled government agency can tap your phone, burglarize your home, steal your records, and otherwise operate outside the law, you can say goodbye to freedom.

Los Angeles Times
Los Angeles, Calif., December 27, 1974

Defenders of the Central Intelligence Agency have developed a two-point rebuttal of allegations that the CIA conducted a widespread and illegal domestic intelligence operation against antiwar activists. They argue, first, that domestic spying by the agency is permissible when related to foreign intelligence purposes, and second, that the Federal Bureau of Investigation pushed the CIA into domestic intelligence when the bureau stopped cooperation with the CIA in 1970.

President Ford, relying on the assurances of William E. Colby, the present director of Central Intelligence, says the CIA is not now conducting domestic surveillance.

Richard M. Helms, former director of the CIA, "categorically denied" that the CIA under his tenure conducted any illegal spying in the United States.

Secretary of State Kissinger, the President's chief national security adviser, is reported to have informed Mr. Ford of Helms' denial and the secretary of state is said to feel the matter closed.

Rep. Lucien N. Nedzi (D-Mich.), chairman of the House armed services subcommittee on intelligence, said that "information was conveyed to me (by Director Colby) which suggested the overstepping of bounds, but it certainly wasn't of a dimension . . . of what has appeared in the newspapers."

All this is not good enough. There is no basis to doubt President Ford's sincerity, but how does he know the information submitted to him is accurate? How does Rep. Nedzi know?

James Angleton, the recently resigned counterintelligence chief, said he quit because the agency had become involved in domestic "police state" activities, but Angleton's disjointed elaboration of that remark, as reported in a telephone interview, seemed to indicate a troubled man.

It is reported that the current CIA director, Colby, revealed in an off-the-record talk that an investigation he ordered into CIA domestic activities had disclosed improprieties, but Colby is said to have added, "I think family skeletons are best left where they are—in the closet."

He is mistaken. The CIA, with an annual budget of $750 million and 16,000 employes, is not a "family." It is a profoundly important agency with authority to carry out secret operations that affect the security of this nation.

As this newspaper documented nearly a year ago, congressional oversight of the CIA has been almost totally lacking since Congress created the agency 27 years ago. What is needed now is a special inquiry by a select committee of the Congress.

COLBY, HELMS TESTIFY ON CIA; FBI ALSO TO BE INVESTIGATED

William E. Colby, director of the Central Intelligence Agency (CIA), Jan. 15 told a Senate subcommittee that his agency in the past had engaged in domestic intelligence gathering activities. However, he "flatly" denied that these activities amounted to "a massive, illegal domestic intelligence operation," as alleged in the *New York Times* of Dec. 22, 1974. Colby's denial was contained in a report he made to the Intelligence Subcommittee of the Senate Appropriations Committee, one of four Congressional panels probing the charges by the *Times*. Colby conceded that CIA agents had infiltrated dissident and antiwar political groups in the U.S., opened the mail of private citizens, tapped the telephone of U.S. residents and participated in a government counterintelligence program that led to the amassment of files on 10,000 U.S. citizens. Colby insisted that such "missteps" in the 27-year history of the CIA were "few and far between and were exceptions to the thrust of the agency's ... primary mission," the collection and production of foreign intelligence.

Richard Helms, director of the CIA from 1966 to 1973, testified before the Senate Armed Services Subcommittee on Central Intelligence Jan. 16. Helms, whose testimony was behind closed doors, said in a prepared statement released to the press, "I am indignant at the irresponsible attacks made upon the true ends of the intelligence function." Helms asserted that the "principal allegations" concerning domestic spying by the CIA remained unsupported and had been "undermined by contrary evidence in the press itself." He did not cite specific evidence, however.

The Presidential commission investigating charges of domestic spying by the CIA held its first meeting Jan. 13. The eight-member panel chaired by Vice President Nelson A. Rockefeller heard testimony by Colby, Helms and Secretary of Defense James R. Schlesinger, who succeeded Helms and preceded Colby as director of the CIA. After testifying in secret, Schlesinger told reporters that "certain things did come to light," but he added that the number of "misdemeanors" in the history of the agency "I think is quite small."

Clarence M. Kelley, director of the Federal Bureau of Investigation (FBI), Jan. 21 confirmed newspaper reports that the bureau kept files on members of Congress. However, he asserted that such information had not been actively sought by the FBI and was mostly the byproduct of unrelated FBI investigations.

The Senate Jan. 27 voted 82–4 to create a bipartisan, select committee to investigate alleged illegal spying on citizens and other abuses of power by the CIA, FBI and other government intelligence and law enforcement agencies. (In a related development, a House task force Jan. 29 unanimously recommended establishment of a separate House select committee to probe intelligence abuses by Federal agencies.) Sen. Frank Church (D, Ida.) was selected as chairman of the 11-member committee, which was given a budget of $750,000 and ordered to report within nine months.

The Providence Journal

Providence, R.I., January 25, 1975

The vote of the Senate Democratic caucus for a single select committee to investigate charges of illegal CIA spying on Americans at home and also stories of unethical FBI files on members of Congress, is the sensible way to avoid a rash of duplicate probes. The House would be well advised to use the same method—even better would be a single joint committee of both houses. As things stand, there will be at least two full-scale investigations, since the group appointed by President Ford already is at work hearing testimony on the CIA.

What must be kept in mind throughout the investigations—however many there may be—is that both the CIA and the FBI have given invaluable service to the country. Both have been organizations of high professional standards and achievement. And if they have developed defects that threaten the health of a democratic country, then the defects must be eradicated, so that the valuable work of protecting the United States from outside enemies and of fighting crime within the country may continue unimpeded and without being unfairly besmirched.

The CIA has been accused of breaching the prohibition against domestic operations, to the extent of investigating and keeping files on up to 10,000 dissidents and others during the sometimes violent protests and demonstrations against the Vietnam War. The FBI has been accused of compiling and filing derogatory information on a number of public figures, including some senators and congressmen. There have always been rumors that the late J. Edgar Hoover used such information as a subtle form of blackmail to win support for his agency, its budget and activities from Congress. Now, there seems to be corroboration from two former high-ranking subordinates of his.

The most serious aspects of these charges, of course, is the temptation for political interests to co-opt a legitimate police or intelligence operation for political purposes. Therein begins the drift toward a police state. If such misuse has indeed taken place, the concern of Congress must be to uncover that fact and correct it — immediately. This is necessary not only to preserve democratic freedoms, but also to save the CIA and FBI so they can continue their legitimate and necessary functions.

Sen. John O. Pastore put his finger on the matter when he insisted to his fellow senators that "we must cleanse whatever abuses there have been so that we can put these agencies on the right track." Recognizing the tendency of congressional oversight committees to become overprotective of the agencies over which they are supposed to act as watchdog, the Rhode Island senator called for "fresh faces ... who have not settled their minds or prejudiced themselves one way or the other," to conduct the investigations. It was a brave speech, for Senator Pastore is by his own admission "a little prejudiced ... in favor of the CIA, of military intelligence, and of the FBI."

THE CINCINNATI ENQUIRER
Cincinnati, Ohio, January 29, 1975

INITIAL RESPONSE by officials of the Central Intelligence Agency (CIA) to inquiries by the Senate Appropriations Intelligence Subcommittee and the President's commission looking into the agency's domestic intelligence activities reveals both a pattern of possibly illegal domestic surveillance and the difficulty of effectively limiting the scope of the agency.

CIA Director William Colby has disclosed that "files were established on about 10,000 citizens" in the agency's counterintelligence unit, which he admitted was a "questionable" use of the agency's authority to engage in foreign intelligence activities.

Much of that surveillance was apparently undertaken in response to demands by Presidents Johnson and Nixon that the agency investigate domestic antiwar dissidents for the source of their foreign support. It is both ironic and reassuring that, according to the CIA, American dissidents provided their own inspiration and their own financing, with few exceptions.

The healthy skepticism Americans have for secret agencies whose knowledge of their lives is a source of power is forcing the agency to reveal information about the nature and scope of its responsibilities it would rather keep secret. Because this nation has learned anew the lesson that power is abused, we believe it is in the public interest that the agency disclose as fully as possible its activities in domestic surveillance. Because such activities are illegal anyway, those disclosures will hardly weaken the national security of the United States.

As much as these disclosures will tell us of the extent of the agency's illegalities, it will tell us more of how difficult it will be to frame legislation to prevent such abuse in the future.

• If the agency deems its facilities here are endangered by domestic subversives, should it be forced to report such fears to the Federal Bureau of Investigation (FBI), rather than investigate for itself those who would plot to destroy the agency's capability to gather foreign intelligence?

• Should the CIA director be so independent of a President that he can refuse his order to investigate domestic dissidents who take to the streets to oppose a President's foreign policy?

• Should the CIA director, who is appointed by the President and serves at his pleasure, be politically strong enough in his own right that he can refuse a presidential order he believes would require the agency to violate its charter?

• Can an agency limited to foreign intelligence-gathering conduct its affairs without investigating applicants for jobs with the agency, or their references or even the credibility and competence of domestic sources who provide it information essential to the agency's role in foreign intelligence?

The disclosures by the New York Times of the agency's activities as well as the disclosures made by Mr. Colby and his predecessors reconfirm the view we have expressed on other issues, that in the absence of a keen desire on the part of public officials to obey the spirit as well as the letter of the law in difficult situations, there is a limit to what legislation alone can accomplish in forcing men to obey laws.

These disclosures provide further evidence that in the absence of the desire to follow the letter of the law, only surveillance by the press, the Congress and the presidency will serve the cause of restraint. And even that does not always suffice.

Sentinel Star
Orlando, Fla., January 23, 1975

THE DAY when the Central Intelligence Agency will be legally confined to sorting through clippings from the world press seems to be drawing nigh. One American newspaper, the New York Times, can take much of the credit for popularizing the game of 'catch the CIA out' — its riposte to the Washington Post's star role throughout the Watergate affair. The whole business may be good for providing sensational headlines (based increasingly on a suspension of disbelief that allows serious papers to print less and less plausible stories on the authority of anonymous 'inside sources') but it could also have a damaging effect on the CIA's capacity to mount defensive operations against its Communist counterparts, on its ability to protect the identity of its sources and so, potentially, on the future course of American foreign policy. — **London Economist Foreign Report.**

The San Diego Union
San Diego, Calif., January 18, 1975

CIA Director William Colby's public testimony has removed any doubt that the Central Intelligence Agency overstepped its bounds in conducting surveillance of American citizens in their own country. It did. The problem now is to set matters right without damaging the agency any more than it has already damaged itself.

Both Mr. Colby's testimony and the defense of the domestic CIA activities by former director Richard Helms leave the impression that the agency made the familiar mistake of letting the ends justify the means.

We would expect our government to find any links between radical organizations in this country and foreign powers, and we would expect the CIA to be concerned about the security of its own agents and facilities. However, we also would expect that the separation of authority between the CIA and the Federal Bureau of Investigation in the fields of foreign intelligence and internal security would be respected even under the conditions that prevailed during the wave of radical protest in the 1960s. Responsible people in both the Administration and Congress should have been close enough to the situation to see that the CIA was bending, if not breaking, the law defining its powers.

Congress should pause at this point until the Rockefeller Commission can complete its investigation of the CIA and make its recommendations. The proposal in the Senate to appoint a special prosecutor to look into all government intelligence activities threatens a damaging witch hunt.

An overriding fact that Congress must face is that the threat of subversion is very real and the government must have some means of dealing with it—legitimate means, to be sure. Washing the dirty linen of the CIA in public and fixing responsibility for its mistakes does not bring us any closer to assuring that suspected threats to our security can be investigated in the future without leading as powerful an agency as the CIA into illegal activities.

Washington Star-News

Washington, D.C., January 22, 1975

The director of the Central Intelligence Agency, William E. Colby, has made a persuasive rebuttal to charges that the agency engaged in "massive illegal domestic intelligence operations." Unless Colby is hiding something — and there is no reason to believe he is — the most the CIA can be accused of is that it strayed somewhat beyond the bounds of its charter.

The heart of the so-called expose of "massive illegal" operations involves the compilation of files on 10,000 citizens involved in or somehow connected with dissident activities and civil disorders that swept the country during the years of protest against the war in Vietnam. Colby's explanation as to how and why these files were kept is too detailed to set forth here, but reasonable people reading his Thursday statement to the Senate Appropriations Committee could hardly draw the conclusion that the CIA is some kind of an internal gestapo.

It is evident that the CIA activity in regard to the dissidents was carried out with full knowledge, even at the instigation, of the White House and the Federal Bureau of Investigation, which has responsibility for domestic intelligence gathering relating to the national security. The purpose, according to Colby, was to determine whether foreign stimulus or support was being provided to the dissident activity.

Colby flatly denied the charge that an anti-war congressman, or any other congressman for that matter, was placed under surveillance. As to "break-ins" in this country, Colby listed three and said they involved premises related to agency employes or former employes whose activities involved questions of national security.

On wiretapping charges, the director listed 21 taps between 1951 and 1965, involving 19 agency employes or former employes and two other citizens thought to be receiving sensitive intelligence information. One CIA employe was wiretapped after 1965 and that was done with approval of the attorney general.

Physical surveillance of citizens within the United States was rare, Colby said, and was done only when there was reason to believe those being shadowed might be passing information to hostile intelligence services. Colby acknowledged several instances when mail was inspected but said the primary purpose was to identify persons in correspondence with Communist countries for presumed counterintelligence purposes.

Aside from providing some equipment to one of the Watergate figures —Howard Hunt — and preparing a psychological assessment on Daniel Ellsberg, Colby denied any CIA involvement in Watergate.

The activities outlined by Colby do not add up to "massive illegal domestic intelligence operations" to us. It does appear that CIA was involved to some extent in domestic intelligence gathering that should have been left to the FBI. It also is evident, as Colby

suggested, that the legislation establishing the CIA needs to be amended to make it more clear where foreign intelligence gathering ends and domestic intelligence begins.

But if there is nothing more to the "expose" than has been detailed by Colby, it seems to us that the CIA has been dealt an unjust blow. Further investigation by appropriate authorities certainly is not out of order, but the investigators ought to be careful that the CIA's ability to carry on its vital national security functions is not further impaired.

There is nothing particularly wrong

with the Senate's decision to appoint a special committee to look into the CIA, as well as into the intelligence gathering operations of other government agencies. President Ford's overloading of his "blue-ribbon" panel with persons friendly to the CIA made it inevitable that Congress would make its own probe. The House probably won't want to be left out, so it is likely that another investigation will be started on that side of Capitol Hill. The danger is that the whole thing could turn into a three-ring circus more damaging than enlightening.

The Des Moines Register

Des Moines, Iowa, January 23, 1975

Committees investigating the Central Intelligence Agency (CIA) have heard testimony from the present CIA director and his two immediate predecessors. In each case the men denied the allegation published in the New York Times that the CIA had engaged in a "massive, illegal domestic intelligence operation."

The denials, however, were keyed to the word "massive." The testimony adds up to admission that the CIA did conduct surveillance of domestic groups despite the law barring it from internal security functions.

William Colby, the present director, acknowledged the infiltration by CIA agents into dissident groups, but he pooh-poohed the extent of the spying. James Schlesinger, a former CIA director, described the number of "misdemeanors" by the agency as "quite small." Richard Helms, another former director, said the checks conducted by the CIA on antiwar groups have been distorted out of all proportion.

The 1947 law creating the CIA did not prohibit the agency from engaging only in "massive" domestic spying. Laws are intended to be obeyed — not just part of the time or even most of the time.

Law violations by a super-secret agency are especially dangerous, because

the usual restraints on government conduct are missing. Once an agency stretches or breaks a law and gets into a forbidden area, the practice could become commonplace.

The testimony by Helms demonstrates the risk. He told senators on the Armed Services Committee that the CIA became concerned during the late 1950s and early 1960s about the "upsurge of extreme radicalism in this country." He declared:

"By and in itself, this dissent, this radicalism was of no direct concern to the Central Intelligence Agency. It became so only in the degree that the trouble was inspired by, or coordinated with, or funded by, anti-American subversion mechanisms abroad."

If the CIA believed it could keep tab on groups "inspired by" foreign elements, there is no limit to its involvement in internal security. The Communist Party and all of its front groups could be regarded as "inspired by" the Soviet Union and be proper targets of CIA surveillance.

The testimony by Helms is not reassuring. It makes it all the more urgent that the precise nature and extent of CIA activities be brought to light.

THE SAGINAW NEWS

Saginaw, Mich., January 20, 1975

On the basis of admissions last week by William E. Colby, director of the Central Intelligence Agency, there is ample reason to go ahead with a probe of the agency's alleged domestic activities.

Colby admitted the CIA kept files on about 10,000 U.S. citizens in operations which started, in some cases, as long ago as the Truman administration, shortly after the CIA was set up.

It's too soon to tell how seriously the CIA may have violated its ban on internal security functions. It

should be noted that had the FBI performed precisely the same actions, there would have been no doubt of legality, and that many apparent CIA intrusions into the domestic arena seem to have been at FBI request. Few can quarrel with the need for coordination between the agencies.

But Colby conceded the CIA may have "strayed over the edge" of its authority. It's for Congress and President Ford's blue-ribbon panel to find out where that edge is and how far the CIA went beyond it.

CHICAGO DAILY NEWS

Chicago, Ill., January 23, 1975

Former director Richard Helms of the Central Intelligence Agency told the Senate Armed Services Committee that the press was irresponsible and seriously out of line in what he described as "the attack on the agency." He said there is a need "for educating the press and through the press the American people" in the practices, precepts and distinctions that exist in the intelligence community.

Such an education, seriously undertaken, could indeed prove enlightening to the public and beneficial to the CIA. But there is at least an equivalent need to educate the CIA, from its directors down through all the ranks, in the practices, precepts and values of democracy that are vulnerable to attack or erosion.

The point on which Helms centers his criticism of the press is the charge, which appeared first in the New York Times, that the CIA in violation of its charter spied and maintained files on 10,000 private American citizens. The agency's present director, William E. Colby, concedes that this was done, but denies the activities were as "massive" as charged. Helms, who in 1973 denied to the Senate Foreign Relations Committee that the CIA had engaged in surveillance of anti-war students, appeared last week to draw back from that denial.

Helms told the Armed Services Committee that the CIA "in collaboration with the Federal Bureau of Investigation" performed "a real, a clear and proper function" during the "upsurge of violence against authority and institutions" in the late 1950s and 1960s. It was proper, he explained, because in some cases the trouble "was inspired by, or co-ordinated with, or funded by, anti-American subversion mechanisms abroad."

Now, there is no disputing the fact that the appropriate governmental agencies must do what is necessary to detect and counter subversive efforts at home and abroad.

We also would agree with Helms that the intelligence community on the basis of the over-all quality of its work and its character recently has been put in an unfair light before the public.

But what Helms and his successors must come to understand is that the public has reason to fear that something has gone off the track, and needs fixing. Helms said he operated under the assumption that "the needs of the President were paramount." But the public has lately seen that the needs of the President do not necessarily coincide with the needs of the democracy, and that a President can turn the FBI or CIA to police-state purposes. And that is another form of subversion.

As Helms acknowledges, the law draws a clear line between the functions of the CIA and the FBI, precisely because of these hazards. If a single secret police force held the total responsibility at home and abroad, its oversight and control would be extremely complicated and difficult, with State and Defense and Justice Departments all holding different stakes and different viewpoints.

There must certainly be collaboration between CIA and FBI for the reasons Helms cites. Just as certainly there must be stern supervision by a Congress charged with reconciling all aspects of the public interest. And there must also be, in our judgment, an alert and inquisitive press keeping an eye on both the agencies and the Congress, in the public's behalf.

THE NASHVILLE TENNESSEAN

Nashville, Tenn., January 21, 1975

THE Central Intelligence Agency has admitted that it has infiltrated so-called dissident groups in the United States and established files on about 10,000 U.S. citizens.

In testimony to a Senate committee, CIA director William Colby attempted to justify the agency's actions by pointing to the possibility of foreign influence on these groups and the spied-upon citizens. He also said that many of the CIA's activities of this nature were the result of the late President Lyndon Johnson's concern about civil disorders in 1967.

Mr. Colby's testimony is helpful insofar as it places the CIA's domestic operations in a historical context. But it is no justification. It is a warning about how the paranoia of the government and of the people was twisted and ultimately used against the government and the people.

The Nixon administration, with its contempt for the constitutional rights of opponents, may very well have been the logical result of the fears in the final years of the 1960s. But again, to understand the history is not to justify the events.

And perhaps more dangerous than these domestic activities of the CIA (which if they are not violations of the letter of the agency's charter are certainly violations of the law's intent) is the admission that the information gathered was made available to the Federal Bureau of Investigation, the Secret Service and local police departments.

This entire intelligence operation begins to look like a witch-hunt. Persons who exercise their constitutional right of protest are to be suspect; they are somehow different. The various agencies will feed information to one another and create their own paper reality of scheming anarchists and dissidents.

But Mr. Colby protests: these were not "massive illegal domestic operations" although "on a few occasions" the CIA may have stepped over its bounds. One instance was, and is, one too many.

The Boston Globe

Boston, Mass., January 19, 1975

Once upon a time the government decreed a war, and said it was good.

But some of the people thought the war was bad, and they said so in private conversation, in public meetings and in writing.

The government ascribed this disagreement to a kind of innate wickedness. People who didn't believe what the government believed were considered evil. It wasn't that they actually did anything wrong. They just thought wrong, and that was worse.

So the government, secretly, sent out hordes of agents to spy on all those who refused to think right. They snapped their pictures, they listened in on their telephone conversations, they opened their mail and sometimes they entered and searched their houses. Whatever they found out, by such means, they recorded on paper and filed away in yards and yards of cabinets. All this was done illegally, to be sure, but the government's view was that anybody who refused to think right was a menace and needed to be checked up on.

But lo! Time passed and the government, which had thought the war was good, came to see that it was bad, and with ill grace made peace.

Thus it was perceived that the dissenters, who had been considered bad, had been in fact good.

Nevertheless, their names remained on the secret list of suspected wrong thinkers and probable criminals. Not until years had passed did the people even know that the snooping had occurred.

Moral: The CIA should be ashamed of itself, and so should the government which employed it in such a shabby way.

Arkansas Gazette.

Little Rock, Ark., January 19, 1975

Where are the snowjobs of yesteryear? Right here swirling again, awash in a sea of euphemism, outright non-language and attempts to down-play developments dangerous to the continued life and health of the Republic in a manner reminiscent of the other dead days of Nixon and the slow-to-emerge unfolding of the Watergate Story, as well as of what might be called the peak low of the Vietnam War, which, for shorthand's sake, we will refer to as "My Lai." The subject now—not really all that new a subject to the *cognoscenti*— is the degree to which the Central Intelligence Agency has engaged in spying here at home, an area that the Congress thought it was putting off limits at the time that it authorized legislation to create the new overseas sleuthing agency.

"No big thing," the immortal Lt. William Calley said of My Lai. Only a third-rate "caper," Ron Ziegler first said of the burglarizing of Democratic National Headquarters in Washington's Watergate complex, thus unknowingly providing us with a working title for what could be a really bang-on horror movie, "The Caper That Devoured A President."

Today, Mr. Nixon continues to tell Rabbi Korff that the only thing he was guilty of was errors in judgment; that is, unless you wanted to count in an excess of "compassion." The mental image of the remorseless Nixon oozing compassion from every pore, like Uriah Heep oozing unction, is an intriguing one and no farther from the truth than anything else Nixon has ever told us—or told to Korff either. From the sidelines the present President still professes to believe, and would have us believe, that Nixon's eager acceptance of the all-inclusive Pardon was *prima facie* evidence of criminal guilt, not just of the possession of a possibly criminal concentration of fluid in the compassion ducts.

AND SO, with all this plausible background in mind, we now hear Defense Secretary James R. Schlesinger, himself a former Director of the CIA, say of the agency's ventures into domestic spying that the media have "overblown" news accounts of these acts, just as Ziegler and the Nixon White House generally — those who were left — continued to insist that news accounts of the third-rate caper, had been overblown almost to bag-packing time. Put another way, domestic spying by the CIA was — is? — no big thing."

The Euphemism Department. Schlesinger, having first used the word "misdemeanors" to describe the little peccadilloes that the CIA has been part of, switched his explanation around to make it "inappropriate" activities on the ground that "misdemeanor" was a legal term that would carry an inference of guilt beyond what actually had occurred. We are surprised that he didn't go all the way and say that the CIA — like Nixon — had been guilty only of errors in judgment. Actually this deficiency was to be remedied a couple of days later by Richard Helms, another former director of the CIA, who out-Nixoned Nixon by refusing to own up to any errors in judgment even: Neither he nor the agency had done anything wrong, so he was wholly "without apology." We would have been a little ashamed of lending E. Howard Hunt

that red fright wig for the Dita Beard Caper, as was done under Helms's incumbency, but, then, we are not Richard Helms.

The present Director of the CIA—William E. Colby—has emerged from the *maquis* to complement Schlesinger's delicate language with a little of his own: "Various things happened that *maybe* [our italics] shouldn't have happened, but they're exceptionally few and far between, that kind of thing."

Because it is Colby talking and the CIA we are talking about, we can't help getting the feeling that the most heartfelt word in that sentence was the "maybe." "Maybe, we did wrong, but * * *." It is hard for the spooks to think that they are *ever* doing wrong for sure, no maybes, because they see their work as the be-all of government.

Just so did E. Howard Hunt, we are sure, see Watergate, not as a blot on the record he made before retiring as a CIA agent, but as a kind of after-the-fact culmination of that formal career. We must say here in defense of William E. Colby that, for all his strained, restraned, language elsewhere, he came directly to the point in an interview with Newsweek, in which he said that what *he* would like to see would be for the CIA to become more, rather than less, secret. This of a secret police agency so secret already that only a few congressmen have knowledge even of the agency's own official explanation of what is going on.

Colby meanwhile, along with his predecessor, Helms, is making the rounds of the congressional committees that are leapfrogging over each other to get into the act, the super-sleuths appearing much like guests making the rounds of the late night talk shows. If, that is, the compeers of the talk show could somehow be persuaded to carry on their activities in secret, too, as do

most of the congressional committees used to hearing from self-serving witnesses from the CIA.

Although Senator Mike Mansfield, the Democratic Leader in the Senate, had called for a new all-Congress investigating committee on the pattern of the Watergate Committee, the kind of Senate committee chairmen who did so much to let the military have its head in Vietnam and the sometimes irrelevant authorities here at home have their heads in dealing with protesters against the war — in short, men like John L. McClellan of Arkansas and John C. Stennis — were there fustest with the leastest with what we fear will turn out to be pinch-off investigations of their very own.

Both men have been known to fool you on rare occasion, and here is what McClellan says his committee will be trying to do:

> We wish to make certain that the Intelligence function has been adequately exercised not only to defend the national security of the United States but also in a manner fully consistent with the individual freedoms guaranteed by the Constitution.

We will have to say that John McClellan has not been known to us as a man primarily interested in preserving individual rights, but even when he has tried or let others try — as in the specific court authorizations required for wiretaps spelled out in his Omnibus Crime Act of 1968 — the mania for "security" that has provided so much of our national momentum since World War II saw to it that Richard Nixon and John Mitchell would airily proceed with their unauthorized wiretaps anyway, claiming absolute executive authority in the matter.

This is what we have been talking about for more years than we like to think of.

The Evening Bulletin

Philadelphia, Pa., January 20, 1975

The remarkable public admissions by Central Intelligence Agency Director William E. Colby have confirmed initial New York Times disclosures that the CIA had engaged in domestic spying.

As a defense, Mr. Colby contended that the CIA's "steps over the line" were "few and far between." He cited some investigations in this country involving checks on the agency's own people, including some wiretapping that ceased 10 years ago.

But other activities he conceded appear to conform more closely to the Times' description as "massive illegal domestic intelligence" than to the director's own characterization as taking "a few wrong steps."

Of the 22 agents planted by the CIA in protest groups, for example, 12 were spying as recently as 10 months ago — hardly the distant past in which his statement attempted to place all these activities.

The compiling and keeping of files on 10,000 members of the antiwar movement similarly bespeaks a major, if not "massive" effort. And Mr.

Colby's explanation that two-thirds of these names came from the Federal Bureau of Investigation raises the question of whether the CIA cooperated with the FBI's campaign to discredit the antiwar movement through its own use of infiltrators.

Mr. Colby's dramatic, but incomplete statement left other questions unanswered such as the identity of organizations and individuals spied upon. Evidence exists that some Washington reporters were targets of CIA surveillance. Why was the CIA used and how were the results of its surveillance used?

The answers will probably be elicited by one of the six investigations currently scheduled. However, the chief business at hand still remains for Congress to impose the kind of tight legislative oversight whose absence permitted abuses to occur in the first place.

The creation of a single, select congressional committee on intelligence seems the best way not only to exercise this control but also to conduct an efficient investigation.

OREGON Journal
AN INDEPENDENT NEWSPAPER

Portland, Ore., January 30, 1975

Some congressmen have waxed indignant lately over the FBI's practice of filing information on them.

Implied, somehow, in their indignation is the idea that an FBI file is OK for the ordinary citizen but not for congressmen who, after all, are important functionaries of the Republic.

There is a certain appeal in this line of reasoning.

On the other hand, it could also be claimed that the FBI ought to keep a closer eye on congressmen than on most people.

Regardless of the philosophical side of the argument, the FBI is very largely a victim of circumstances when it comes to filing information on people, including elected officials. When the night clerk at the FBI office receives a tip that Congressman Joe Doaks is taking bribes, evading taxes, or is being set up for blackmail by hoodlums, his only alternative is to write down the information and pass it along to the agent in charge.

So, what does the chief agent do? A former Portland FBI agent who spent 31 years on the job explained it this way:

"If the tip comes into the local office, they try to screen it first. If the story seems highly unlikely and if the informant refused to identify himself, or herself, the tip usually goes into File 13 — the wastebasket.

"If the informant is identified, and isn't on the 'nut' list of crank callers, the information is handled discreetly in whatever way is appropriate. I know of cases back in Washington where a congressman has become involved with a girl who was mixed up with hoodlums.

"There was the possibility that the congressman was being opened for blackmail, so he was contacted by the FBI in a confidential manner and informed of the circumstances."

In other cases, said the agent, tips by informants resulted in indictments for bribery and various other crimes.

It is a philosophical question as to whether one views the intelligence activities of the FBI as too inclusive. Is it the FBI's business to warn a congressman about his girl friend? And what about tipping a military committee chairman on the drinking habits of a colleague who tends to tell all he knows when he hits the bottom of the bottle?

Certainly there can be no objection to keeping close check on the FBI and its activities. But it would be extraordinary if the public, or Congress, insisted on a free romp through files that may contain evidence of criminality, names of good-faith informants, and, quite certainly, a lot more about some public officials than we really want to know.

The State

Columbia, S.C., January 27, 1975

WHAT is there, we wonder, about members of Congress which should set them apart from ordinary Americans in terms of immunity from the Federal Bureau of Investigation?

This is not to suggest that the FBI maintain surveillance over the deeds (or misdeeds) of congressmen as a standard practice. For that matter, FBI agents should not concern themselves with the activities of any citizens until those individuals run afoul the law. But there is nothing sacred about congressmen, nothing to warrant their present agitation over news that FBI files contain certain information about them which surfaced in the course of normal FBI procedures.

Unhappily, election (or appointment) to public office does not automatically insure that officeholders become paragons of virtue. And while public officials, as a class, should not be subjected to special attention by the FBI or other law enforcement agencies, by the same token they should not be excluded from such attention when circumstances warrant.

A certain hysteria prevails in Washington just now as a consequence of disclosures that the CIA may have conducted domestic intelligence operations beyond those authorized by its charter. If the CIA has been guilty of excesses, the agency should be brought back into line. And if (as has been speculated but not proved) the FBI has moved out of its proper sphere of action, that agency likewise should be put back on the track.

But if we correctly judge the temper of the American people, they repose enough confidence in the Bureau not to want it hamstrung by insulating any category of persons — be they congressmen or not — from proper FBI routines and record-keeping.

TULSA DAILY WORLD

Tulsa, Okla., January 21, 1975

THE WAVE of disclosure and disillusionment that is washing over Washington is now lapping at that once impregnable wall, the Federal Bureau of Investigation.

First the CIA came under criticism in the wake of Watergate, for its alleged surveillance of civilians during antiwar-demonstration days. And now two former top FBI men are quoted as saying the "Bureau" kept files on the personal lives of Congressmen during the reign of the late Director, J. EDGAR HOOVER.

The former FBI men, CARTHA D. DE-LOACH and LOUIS NICHOLS, insist that the files on members of Congress were not compiled in order to give HOOVER a lever over the legislators; nor were Senators or Representatives under surveillance at the time.

The files, we are told, came from incidental information given by various sources who either sent it in voluntarily or told it in interviews with FBI agents.

The indication is that at least some of the material dealt with personal indiscretions of Congressmen—excessive drinking, for example, or other potentially embarrassing conduct.

It will not be necessary to disclose the contents of these files to know that Congressmen aren't going to like the idea of the FBI keeping dossiers on them—for whatever reason. Some of the more outspoken lawmakers already have expressed their shock and anger. Coming on top of the CIA allegations, this new disclosure could shake our national security and intelligence forces to their foundations.

That is truly unfortunate. Both the FBI and CIA have been supported on the grounds they were needed to protect the nation against crime and subversion and in the case of the CIA, against foreign spies.

Certainly the FBI has been made into an institutional hero for its exploits, many of them truly important to our national security. J. EDGAR HOOVER himself is considered by many an almost sainted figure.

But when individuals or agencies are given almost unlimited power, great restraint is needed to keep from using it improperly. Human nature doesn't protect most of us against such temptation.

The Senate Democratic Caucus voted yesterday to create a special committee to investigate the conduct of the FBI, CIA and other U.S. intelligence agencies.

The danger in the present situation is that reaction against the FBI—and possibly the CIA—may cripple their valuable security functions. The nation would be as poorly served by that kind of over-reaction as it has been by the agencies' excesses now being revealed.

The Kansas City Times

Kansas City, Mo., January 23, 1975

Clarence M. Kelley, director of the Federal Bureau of Investigation, has been about as straightforward as anyone could be in the matter of FBI files kept on members of Congress.

Kelley said that the FBI does have files on individual members of Congress, but only in the sense that files are kept on other citizens. Information comes in unsolicited and it is put away. The FBI does not actively seek out information unless it is in line with prescribed duties. Checking on the background of an individual who has been named to the federal court would be an example.

Like other citizens, members of Congress occasionally are charged with crimes, prosecuted, convicted and sent to prison. Members of Congress are not above the law or outside the routine investigatory procedures of law enforcement agencies.

Yet there *is* a difference. The FBI files are under the jurisdiction of the Justice Department which is headed by a cabinet officer—often a political appointee who has been closely associated with the election of the President. Recent history shows that the misuse of powerful government agencies can be tempting to certain types of politicians. If the name of a prominent congressional leader of the opposition party is connected with a nasty bit of gossip, obviously this is going to stir the interest of such politicians.

Whether information of this type ever has been used in the past to intimidate members of Congress has been debated. Perhaps the knowledge that such files exist has been sufficient to quicken guilty consciences. Presumably the FBI has had much experience with unprocessed rumors and the sort of vicious, hate-inspired reports that must come to it in large volume.

Members of Congress and other persons in public life are vulnerable to damage from such reports far more than is the private citizen. The consequences of political extortion or blackmail could affect the nation. The extent to which sensitive agencies of government have been used to harass or frighten political foes and citizens in the past is the subject of current investigations.

The only really satisfactory way out of the dilemma, of course, is to attract to public service individuals of such character that the misuse of files would be out of the question. But this is an imperfect world. So long as the files exist there will be temptation. That is why they must be maintained under the closest scrutiny and with the most limited access. In the long run, the removal of the Department of Justice from politics could be a large part of a better answer.

The Washington Post

Washington, D.C., January 14, 1975

It is the Majority Leader's view and my view that there is a need to examine in depth to what extent, if any, covert activities are required by the United States. There is a need to understand not only the requirements of the United States for these activities, but what systems or procedures or oversight and accountability are required to assure that constitutional guarantees and processes are not abused in the future, as they have on occasion been in the past . . .

The history of the past twenty-five years has shown that the creations authorized by the National Security Act have severely strained our constitutional system. As a consequence, there is clearly a requirement to revise the basic authorities for our intelligence agencies. But to what extent and in what ways, neither Senator Mansfield nor I can assert at this time. Nor do we believe that anyone is in an informed position to do so. From a statement by Senator Mathias, urging creation of a Select Senate Committee to study government intelligence activities.

ACCORDING TO SENATOR MATHIAS, in the 28 years since the creation of the Central Intelligence Agency there have been more than 200 separate resolutions and legislative proposals urging the reform one way or another of the agency itself. And the amount of reform that has been achieved by this ad hoc approach has been almost nonexistent. Now the reformers are having another go; fresh resolutions are being prepared and several different congressional committee hearings are under way on various aspects of the latest crisis in CIA's affairs. We think Senators Mansfield and Mathias, and Rep. Michael J. Harrington, have a better idea. The two senators are supporting a resolution to set up a select Senate committee, equally divided between Democrats and Republicans, to study not just CIA but all domestic and foreign intelligence activities of the United States government. It would review the past, report on the present and make some proposals for the future. Mr. Harrington would establish a new House Select Committee on Intelligence, which would also take a broad view of the intelligence problem, while addressing itself to the particular allegations which have recently been made against the CIA.

The point of all this, as we understand it, is by no means to pre-empt or postpone an urgent examination of the ways in which the CIA appears to have gone beyond its legislative charter over the years. On the contrary, we think that this matter cannot be left solely to President Ford's "blue ribbon" commission and that standing committees of both houses have some responsibility to make immediate inquiries into charges which have raised serious questions in the public mind about whether assorted intelligence agencies of the federal government are even now under effective control. But none of these committees has a sufficiently broad area of interest to undertake the sort of full-scale investigation that is sorely needed.

For what is sorely needed is not only to know whether on this or that occasion, or in this or that particular fashion, the CIA or the FBI or other intelligence operations have violated regulations or the laws in ways that impinge on the rights of private citizens. Rather, it also seems necessary at this point to go back to the drawing board and re-examine in the most searching and painstaking way what this country's current requirements are in terms of an intelligence capability and how that capability can best be accomplished without undermining constitutional rights of individuals or putting at risk our legitimate national security interests. There is no use pretending that these two objectives are not by their nature in conflict much of the time. Just as there are risks to rights of privacy in any domestic intelligence operations so there would be a risk to our national security in ending secret intelligence activities by the government. Unless you are prepared to accept extreme solutions, one way or the other, it comes down to a balancing of risks and some very hard choices.

And it also comes down to the question of who does the balancing and to what extent the decisions are subject to effective supervision and control by both the Congress and the Executive Branch. Clearly some of the intelligence machinery and some of the practices have outlived their usefulness. But this is not necessarily to say that a wholesale dismantling is indicated. The point is to decide, first, what the real requirements are. That is why the proposals for broad and searching congressional inquiries by select committees strike us as a good idea.

The Virginian-Pilot

Norfolk, Va., January 22, 1975

A broad-based inquiry into the government's intelligence operations by a bipartisan select committee of the Senate is welcome.

Such an investigation was mandated by the Senate Democratic caucus Monday, 45 to 7. The members of the select committee will be chosen by the leadership once the resolution is ratified by the full Senate. The one-sided vote within the caucus suggests that approval will be a formality.

The resolution calls for the leadership to name seven to eleven Senators to the select committee, which will have a budget initially of $750,000 and nine months to report to the full Senate.

The action of the caucus was a setback for Senator John C. Stennis, chairman of the Armed Services Committee. His committee had initiated an investigation into the allegations of domestic spying by the Central Intelligence Agency, an area that the conservative and powerful Senator Stennis saw as his turf.

He bitterly opposed the creation of a special committee, and it is a measure of the new Senate's temper that he was snowed under.

The action of the Senate caucus is as significant as the bumping of a brace of committee chairmen by the Democrats in the House of Representatives. The new boys on Capitol Hill aren't showing their elders much respect. As one of the grandees of the Senate, Mr. Stennis is accustomed to having his way. But a bare half-dozen of his fellows (including Harry F. Byrd Jr. of Virginia, who is designated an Independent but sits with the Democrats in the Senate) were willing to stand with him.

"What happened today was a kind of revolution," said Senator Frank Church of Idaho, who is emerging as one of the leaders among the younger Democratic Senators. If the rebuke to Senator Stennis was gentler than that administered by the House Democratic caucus to Representative F. Edward Hebert, who was booted from the chairmanship of the House Armed Services Committee, it is nonetheless telling.

The 94th Congress is not going to put up with the palsy-walsy relationship that has existed between the Heberts and the Stennises and the armed services. But that is not to suggest that the special committee is going to go off headline-hunting and housewrecking. A constructive investigation is what's needed at this time.

A Senate select committee will have a broader mandate and more public support than the Presidential commission to investigate the CIA, headed by Vice President Rockefeller.

What appears to be involved in the stories about the CIA's domestic spying and the activities of the Federal Bureau of Investigation, which reportedly had derogatory data about Congressmen in its files, is not police-state subversion of our system, but something a good deal less sinister: the conventional excesses, foul-ups, and jealousies of bureaucracies in Washington.

The special committee is to be empowered to investigate not only the CIA and the FBI, but the rest of the government's intelligence undergrowth. According to a recent study, "The CIA and the Cult of Intelligence," the agencies comprising the intelligence community have an estimated 153,350 employes and a budget of $6.2 billion per year.

It is clear that the CIA transgressed when it got involved in antiwar counterspying, and it is equally evident that the FBI was guilty of hanky-panky in the aging J. Edgar Hoover's last years. A retired admiral charged only this week that the Navy's passion for security is unwarranted. About 95 per cent of its secrets, he said, are meant to be hidden from Congress, the public, and rival services.

Where there are many agencies at work, where they are working out of the public view, where their budgets as well as their day-to-day operations are protected from public scrutiny or critical supervision, it is natural to assume that Parkinson's Law probably is working. It is doubtful that there is any invisible network threatening to strangle us. But it is highly likely that "the cult of intelligence" has gotten out of hand and needs to be pruned and watched more closely. An intelligent investigation of the government's intelligence operations is the first step to take.

Pittsburgh Post-Gazette

Pittsburgh, Pa., January 22, 1975

IN VOTING overwhelmingly to establish a bipartisan select committee to investigate government surveillance of American citizens, the Democratic caucus in the U.S. Senate has responded sensibly to serious allegations against the Central Intelligence Agency and the Federal Bureau of Investigation.

It has become increasingly clear that the commission named by President Ford to weigh charges of CIA domestic spying is not likely to produce a verdict that will be respected by the agency's critics or by the public.

* * *

Already the commission headed by Vice President Rockefeller, has become bogged down in the semantics rather than the substance of a New York Times report that the CIA had engaged in "massive" domestic surveillance "in direct violation of its charter," leading to speculation that its members are bent on putting the best possible interpretation on CIA activities in the U.S. Even if that speculation is unfounded, the conservative, "establishment" cast of the commission's members and the fact that its hearings are being conducted in secret make it unlikely that its eventual findings will win public confidence.

The same might easily be said of a congressional investigation of the CIA conducted by those committees in both houses traditionally charged with "oversight" of the secret agency. For such committees to find that the CIA had violated its charter, which prohibits domestic spying, would be to confess lax monitoring in the past.

Moreover, like the Rockefeller commission, congressmen who have had jurisdiction over the CIA have been identified in the public mind with an overindulgence of any and all policies justified in the name of "national security." For example, Sen. John Stennis, D-Miss., who as chairman of the Armed Services Committee would ordinarily be responsible for a probe of the CIA, has already indicated that he feels present operations of the CIA will be jeopardized by a thorough ventilation of the agency's past misdeeds — a view which places him in a small minority.

Mr. Stennis did not favor the creation of a special select committee to investigate domestic spying. In overruling him, 45 out of 52 members of his party's caucus wisely recognized that the public demands a single investigation conducted by senators not associated with either the CIA or its habitual critics. That investigation should also probe charges made this week that the FBI compiled potentially embarrassing information about congressmen, including a prominent critic of the late J. Edgar Hoover.

* * *

Two of the less happy legacies of Watergate are widespread cynicism about the integrity of government agencies and a new receptiveness to conspiracy theories. Both attitudes will be irreversibly abetted if charges against the CIA and the FBI are not investigated publicly and objectively. The best hopes for such an investigation are offered by the special Senate committee proposed by the Democratic caucus.

Chicago Tribune

Chicago, Ill., January 30, 1975

The Senate is setting up a special committee to investigate the Central Intelligence Agency and the FBI—specifically, to find out how far these agencies may have strayed into illegal spying activities against American citizens, and to determine how to keep them from doing it again. And that's fine. What may make it less than fine is any attempt to abuse this obviously needed inquiry—to work it for self-serving drama rather than facts. The temptation to do that will be great, but we hope the senators resist it.

The Senate panel clearly will not err on the side of reticence. Of its 11 members, only two—conservative Republicans John Tower of Texas and Barry Goldwater of Arizona—rank as defenders of the CIA. The rest, three other Republicans and six Democrats, range from moderate to strongly liberal; they include two newcomers to Congress with no stake in the status quo. Any fears of a coverup can safely be laid away.

What's needed from this committee is a straightforward job of housecleaning—getting rid of the dirt accumulated in hidden corners and letting in fresh air. There is no government agency that does not need such a sweeping out every so often. None needs it more urgently than these two, where a valid need for secrecy, in its place, seems to have mushroomed into a kind of institutional paranoia.

The job will involve some careful organizational rethinking. Closer overall supervision is needed; so are more clearly defined relationships among the different intelligence agencies. As it is, their mutual rivalries and suspicions have intensified their secrecy mania while blurring the boundaries between their fields of action.

Committee members have taken on a complicated, demanding job. It is also one likely to be highly gratifying to the ego, and that is what concerns us. The urge to pin down a witness, to show oneself as a relentless defender of liberty, may make it easy for panel members to forget that some secrets really are important and that lives may depend on keeping them. It would be futile to ask the senators to pass up completely the chance for a little grandstanding; all we ask is that they do it prudently.

Los Angeles Times

Los Angeles, Calif., January 28, 1975

Congress must first establish the facts about the charges against the Central Intelligence Agency and the Federal Bureau of Investigation; second, Congress must set new and clear limits on their powers, and, third, Congress must devise a new system of oversight and control to enforce those limits.

The task is easily defined; its execution will be a formidable one, but it is not beyond the capability of Congress. The Senate Democratic Caucus took a sensible step by voting to create a special committee to look into all U.S. intelligence agencies. A joint committee of House and Senate would be more appropriate still.

New disclosures over the weekend should lend impetus to the inquiry. A Senate Watergate committee memorandum says the FBI conducted political spying for the late President Lyndon B. Johnson at the Democratic National Convention in 1964. A Senate subcommittee reports that the Internal Revenue Service investigated thousands of American citizens whose names were on the secret domestic CIA list of radicals and war protesters.

The issue before an investigating body is not only one of alleged improprieties of the CIA, FBI, the IRS or any other federal agency. The broader issue is the danger of uncontrolled government surveillance of American citizens.

There have been periodic warnings of this danger over the years. In 1967, Alan Westin, professor of public law and government at Columbia University, said, "At least 50 different federal agencies have substantial investigative and enforcement functions, providing a corps of more than 20,000 investigators working for agencies such as the FBI, naval intelligence, the Post Office, the Narcotics Bureau of the Treasury, the Securities and Exchange Commission, the Internal Revenue Service, the Food and Drug Administration, the State Department and the Civil Service Commission. While all executive agencies are under federal law and executive regulation, the factual reality is that each agency and department has wide day-to-day discretion over the investigative practices of its officials."

The most recent disclosures fit into a long-established pattern of excesses:

—A Senate subcommittee in 1973 reported that the U.S. Army engaged in surveillance of private citizens.

—Between 1956 and 1971, the FBI conducted a "cointelpro" program that consisted of surveillance and disruption of organizations that the FBI considered suspect, among them the Urban League and the Congress of Racial Equality. Atty. Gen. William B. Saxbe described some of the FBI actions as "abhorrent to a free society."

—The IRS, acting at the direction of the White House, monitored the tax reports and political activities of thousands of individuals and groups between 1969 and 1973, including organizations like the National Council of Churches.

During its long life, a House committee, principally known as the House Committee on Un-American Activities, compiled a list of 750,000 allegedly subversive Americans.

The U.S. Passport Office once maintained a list of 240,000 names of Americans of "questionable citizenship" until a U.S. Supreme Court decision put a stop to the practice.

Such surveillance becomes contagious. A news report from Houston last week suggested that political spying by government on all levels may be more widespread than has ever been suspected. The Houston Police Department compiled a list containing personal data on more than 1,000 persons in "all walks of life" in Houston, including clergymen, judges, businessmen, and state and federal officials.

After the revelation that the FBI under J. Edgar Hoover kept dossiers on senators and representatives with information on their private lives, some congressmen complained of the threat of blackmail implicit in such files. A former aide to Hoover asked, "What are they afraid of? What the hell separates them from the American people?"

The answer is that all Americans should be equally secure in their rights against unwarranted invasion of privacy. Neither a member of Congress nor the least citizen should be the target of this kind of probe. A congressman's independence can be threatened, and personal information in secret files can have a chilling effect on the participation of citizens in public affairs. This sabotages democracy.

The police power is a potent power that must always be watched. Some 20 years ago, Supreme Court Justice Felix Frankfurter warned:

"The accretion of dangerous power does not come in a day. It does come, however slowly, from the generative force of unchecked disregard of the restrictions that fence in even the most disinterested assertion of authority."

THE PLAIN DEALER

Cleveland, Ohio,
January 30, 1975

Selection of Sen. Frank Church, D-Idaho, to chair the Senate select committee investigating U.S. intelligence agencies, appears to be a good choice. Church has been critical in the past of the Central Intelligence Agency but he has assured he will not be prejudiced in the examination.

The committee itself has been forewarned by the Senate against leaks, misuse of television and destruction of the CIA's program abroad.

However, we agree with Church's reply when he was asked if the investigation might be harmful to the CIA. "Nothing can be more injurious to these (intelligence) agencies in the long run than lack of public confidence that occurs when charges of wrongdoing are leveled against them."

Thus the committee will look into allegations of domestic spying by the CIA, a subject that has become confused because of conflicting testimony apparently offered by its former director, Richard Helms, at various congressional hearings.

The public also has been shaken by disclosures that the Federal Bureau of Investigation kept files on congressmen, among other people, and tried to have a college professor fired because of his political bent — and sent an anonymous letter in an attempt to "get" the professor.

Church has excellent credentials. He has voted on the liberal side for the most part. He was an early critic of U.S. meddling in Vietnam. He was cosponsor of the amendment which placed the first congressional restrictions on U.S. military involvement in Indochina. He has said the inquiry is much too serious to be dealt with in a frivolous way and that is the correct approach to a delicate investigation.

THE KNICKERBOCKER NEWS
··· UNION-STAR ···
Albany, N.Y., January 29, 1975

The Senate has created a special committee to inquire into operation of the Central Intelligence Agency, the Federal Bureau of Investigation, the Defense Intelligence Agency, the intelligence branches of the armed forces and other snoop and spy agencies.

Crucial element in the inquiry is whether, in carrying out their legal and necessary duties, the agencies have become lawless themselves and invaded the fundamental rights of citizens to privacy.

Vice President Rockefeller, heading a special commission inquiring into charges of CIA domestic spying, has expressed the belief the CIA did "stray" into illegal domestic surveillance and says the commission wants to find out who it spied on, to what extent, why and at whose orders. His attitude gives no indication that he thinks whatever sins the CIA committed were grievous.

The FBI has admitted it has dossiers on members of Congress and others, but maintains they were incidental to other inquiries. It can be remember, however, that J. Edgar Hoover, former director of the agency, dearly loved to collect inside stories on the peccadillos of the powerful.

The presence around the fringes of the CIA of such as Howard Hunt, the Watergate conspirator, can be taken as an indication of the attraction of secret agencies to the lunatic fringe.

The history of Vietnam indicates there is blood on the CIA's hands and the indications from other countries indicate CIA money flowed even more copiously.

The accomplishment of all of these agencies cannot be belittled. The unpublicized accomplishment cannot be evaluated by the public.

The evidence is overwhelming, however, that the Senate committee is necessary. Prudence indicates, also, that many areas of that inquiry must be discreet. Member of that committee must avoid the temptation to seek the limelight by "revelations" or seek to win friends by leaking its findings.

It is a highly serious and highly sensitive area into which that committee will be probing.

It must reveal the character those agencies have come to adopt and the power they have come to seize, without destroying their value to the nation.

But it is not an impossible task. And above all those watchdogs of the government must come to know that the public, too, has watchdogs over them and that there is a morality governing even the land of undercover.

THE CHRISTIAN SCIENCE MONITOR
Boston, Mass., January 22, 1975

The Senate Democratic caucus is going in the right direction by voting for investigation of the whole system of American foreign and domestic intelligence by a bipartisan select committee similar to the Watergate committee.

So many of the charges and explanations of alleged illegal activity involve the relations between agencies and their jurisdictions that piecemeal efforts are inadequate. Various congressional committees have their proper concerns in following up on the charges. But, in the absence of a joint congressional committee as previously suggested here, a Senate select committee can provide the thoroughgoing synthesis of information that is required for considering whatever further legislation or controls may be necessary.

Part of the committee's mandate would be to examine the extent to which intelligence units are governed by secret orders from the executive branch. Such facts are important in the light of such testimony as that by former CIA director Helms, suggesting that domestic operations were presidentially initiated.

What must not be omitted from the investigation is the responsibility of congressional and administration bodies charged with oversight of the intelligence agencies. CIA director Colby asserted that "there are no secrets" from congressional oversight committees — which would mean that they share responsibility for keeping the agency within its legal mandate. Similarly the presidential foreign intelligence advisory board, on which Mr. Rockefeller served, ought to be evaluated on its effectiveness as a top reviewing body for secret intelligence work.

These are among the reasons in favor of the Democratic caucus's vote for having the Senate leadership choose members of the select committee in a stated effort to avoid bias. Senator Stennis reportedly favored drawing them from committees that already have CIA oversight responsibilities. His defeat on this is interpreted as an example of Senate Democrats beginning to defy seniority traditions as House Democrats have done.

Senator Stennis ought to be heeded, however, when he sounds a warning about the possibility of hampering the legitimate activities of the CIA through thoughtless investigation. This is one of the dangers to be guarded against as intelligence investigations proliferate. Another is the possible politicization of them either for self-promotion by headline-hunting politicians or to affect the findings of the investigations themselves.

Such dangers must be avoided if a major purpose of the investigations is to be achieved — maintaining public confidence in key institutions.

THE ATLANTA CONSTITUTION
Atlanta, Ga., January 29, 1975
Now, wait a minute, fellas...

We've lost count of how many committees are now investigating or preparing to investigate the Central Intelligence Agency. There's the Rockefeller Committee set up by President Ford and headed by Vice President Nelson Rockefeller; there's a committee or two in the House and now the Senate is gearing up for a special Watergate-type panel to be headed, probably, by Sen. Frank Church.

There are so many snoops snooping around the CIA's super snoops that Washington is going to look like a Keystone Kop Komedy ere long. And it occurs to us that the nation has some other pressing matters that need attending to.

This investigative orgy was set off by a news story saying the CIA had violated its mandate by spying on people in this country. A fairly broad spectrum of opinion holds that the reports were exaggerated, though it does appear that the CIA has fudged a bit.

Whatever the truth of the matter, we trust that Vice President Rockefeller, a man of force and integrity, will seek it out and let us know about it. He made that very clear in a weekend interview. Rocky seems to feel his integrity is at stake, and he's determined to do an honest job of work.

The over-all makeup of the Rockefeller panel has been criticized as being too heavily loaded with people who would be inclined to give the CIA the benefit of every doubt. Perhaps that is why the Senate and other congressional groups feel it is necessary that they get into the act.

But we've said it before and we'll say it again. There is no reason to doubt the Rockefeller committee will do an honest and conscientious job. Its report is due in a couple of months — not too long a period for us all to wait and see. If there is reason then to think the panel didn't do its job, maybe Congress would have good cause to go forward. But until then, Congress should cool it.

THE LINCOLN STAR
Lincoln, Neb.,
January 28, 1975

Vice President Rockefeller at first inspires confidence when he talks about his panel's effort to get to the bottom of alleged CIA spying in domestic political dissidents.

The investigation, Rocky said, will go "wherever the facts lead us."

"We'll go as far as any action leads us, to a Republican president, to a Democratic president or anybody else. We are there to get the facts, to get them out, to get them to the public and the reasons for whatever happened and then to make recommendations. And we'll put the whole report out. We'll make a report to the President and we'll release it to the public."

In our opinion, Rockefeller is one of those people in public life in whom you can believe. He has a record of integrity and besides, he is one of those politicians who sounds as if he even believes himself. He obviously is filled with good intentions about getting the truth out. He wants to play fair with both the CIA and the public and he understands that there are certain elements of the CIA mission that can't be compromised just as there are certain alleged practices which must be exposed if there is substance to the charges.

But an American vice president, one of the least powerful of citizens, leading an investigating commission unquestionably stacked with a right-wing, pro-national security bias which would allow most of the members to wink at just about any domestic surveillance scheme, can't be expected to come up with too much.

We'll put our money on Congress to uncover illegal and unconstitutional activity, through secret hearings or otherwise. It is in that forum that the penetrating questions will be asked and where answers given will be subject to the proper skepticism.

If the Rockefeller panel comes up with something other than a whitewash, it will be a surprising bonus.

COLBY DISCLOSES CIA KEPT FILES, OPENED MAIL OF REP. BELLA ABZUG

William E. Colby, Director of the CIA, acknowledged March 5 that his agency had maintained files on Rep. Bella S. Abzug (D, N.Y.) since 1953. The files, Colby said, contained copies of two letters Abzug had written on behalf of clients when she was a practicing attorney, among other papers.

In testimony before House Government Operations Subcommittee on Government Information and Individual Rights, which was headed by Abzug, Colby conceded that Abzug was one of four past and present members of Congress on whom special counterintelligence files had been kept as part of the agency's operation against Vietnam War dissidents. While refusing to name the other three, Colby said the operation, terminated in March 1974, found there had been "no substantial foreign manipulation of or assistance to the antiwar movement."

EVENING EXPRESS
Portland, Me., March 8, 1975

We share with U.S. Rep. Bella Abzug of New York a sense of outrage that the Central Intelligence Agency would stoop to steaming open the mail of private American citizens.

And we find it contemptible that the files of the Federal Bureau of Investigation would contain personal information on the sex life and drinking habits of citizens of the United States.

United States Attorney General Edward H. Levi has confirmed that the late director of the FBI, J. Edgar Hoover collected such personal information on prominent Americans.

And CIA Director William Colby has testified that the agency had spied on the activities of American citizens to the extent to apparently opening Mrs. Abzug's personal mail when she was in the private practice of law. Colby agrees that some of the information in the CIA file on Mrs. Abzug should never have been collected.

There is a frightening, Kafkalike quality to Colby's assertion that the information compiled and filed on Mrs. Abzug came as a by-product of CIA investigations into other unnamed organizations. "We were not following your activities," Colby blandly assures U.S. Rep. Abzug, even as he concedes that she was spied upon, her mail opened and her rights violated.

Where is the sense of responsibility when gutter gossip can find its way into the personal files of the director of the Federal Bureau of Investigation and into the hands of presidents of the United States?

When can spying on innocent Americans be defended on the grounds that "others" were actually the target of the investigation?

The Chattanooga Times
Chattanooga, Tenn., March 13, 1975

The future collapse of the United States — in terms of personal freedom — is more likely to result we are frequently told from subversion within than from an external attack This subversion it is said is being carried out by Communists and by US citizens working to implement communism's aims

No one, of course can safely discount the extent of communism s influence in world affairs But if the fall of the US is preceded by a neutralization of the institutions that have protected our rights for some 200 years, it is necessary that we rebuff the forces, foreign or domestic who attack those institutions

We have seen in recent weeks a cavalier disregard for the importance of individual liberty guaranteed by the Constitution Atty Gen Edward Levi revealed that the FBI had maintained dossiers of derogatory information on a variety of individuals, including congressmen, at the insistence of the late J Edgar Hoover

Last week we learned that the CIA has kept a file on Rep Bella Abzug dating back to 1953, many years before she was elected to Congress The CIA's denial that it has kept dossiers on 100,000 other Americans is suddenly suspect.

Ms. Abzug doesn't fit everyone's idea of the best example of a U.S representative, personally or ideologically. But her personality or political philosophy are not what is at issue here.

It is a dangerous undermining of our institutions when a secret agency, with little or no effective oversight, undertakes surveillance of legislators and their staffs, collects dossiers based mainly on hearsay or trivia that, taken alone, appear damaging, labels legitimate dissenters as "conspirators," or infiltrates government spies into legal organizations. Such activities are blatant violations of our right to privacy, freedom of association and freedom of expression explicitly guaranteed by the Constitution.

There is an obvious need for a government to engage in intelligence activities for self-preservation; just as obviously, many of those activities cannot be made public. But there is a fragile dividing line between legitimate activities and those which in their excess quickly become counter-productive. The danger is that such counter-productivity jeopardizes the freedoms of millions.

A mania for accumlation of information on individuals must always be strictly controlled lest it be horribly misused and we become an "open society" in the worst sense of the term.

THE BLADE

Toledo, Ohio, March 9, 1975

BELLICOSE Bella Abzug, who can work up a good head of steam under nearly any circumstances, is justified in storming at the Central Intelligence Agency as she did last week.

Representative Abzug got her hackles up when William E. Colby, CIA director, acknowledged that the agency had maintained a dossier on her for more than 20 years, including contents of letters she had written on behalf of clients when she was a practicing lawyer.

"To find myself in your files is outrageous," the New York Democrat and ERA and anti-Vietnam war activist stormed at Mr. Colby who nervously drummed his fingers on the table as he testified at a House individual rights subcommittee hearing. Her raspy voice rising in anger, Ms. Abzug added, "Let's get one thing clear right away. Opening mail of a lawyer representing a client is illegal."

Mr. Colby conceded that a considerable amount of the material in the Abzug file should not be there. Moreover, he said, he did not know how or why some of it got there. Nor did he make clear what would happen to that file or similar ones the CIA admits having kept on 10,000 other Americans. If the CIA continues to be as obscure as investigations into its activities go deeper, even more and angrier outbursts may be expected from Capitol Hill.

THE COMMERCIAL APPEAL

Memphis, Tenn., March 7, 1975

REP. BELLA S. ABZUG is a brassy, garish sort of person. She attracts "lightning" like a century-old oak.

Consequently few people probably were surprised when it was revealed at a congressional investigation Wednesday that she had been one of the four present or former members of Congress on whom the Central Intelligence Agency had collected files.

But the question is not whether Mrs. Abzug is lovable. The question is whether what the CIA was up to violated the constitutional rights of all citizens of this nation.

And the answer which emerged from the hearing of the House subcommittee which Mrs. Abzug was chairing was that the CIA probably had overstepped its bounds.

CIA Director William E. Colby admitted that "a considerable amount of the material in your file should not be in there." Some of the material collected by the CIA over the last 27 years "may not be appropriate today," he added.

In explaining how the material got there, Colby said the collection was undertaken "under the belief that it fell within the charge of the director of central intelligence to protect intelligence sources and methods or under the belief that it was included within our charge to collect foreign intelligence or counterintelligence."

In short, the CIA was sincere in its belief that it was doing what it was authorized to do, but in fact it was not.

This indicates what seems to be the basic problem before both the presidential commission investigating the intelligence agencies and the congressional investigators of the same area.

There is bound to be a gray area between what is known to be wrong and what is known to be right. Just where does this gray area begin and end? And who really should determine when the CIA or the FBI or the military is allowed to enter that gray area? And, further, what is to happen to the material that is gathered when that gray area has been entered by the investigators?

Perhaps that area never can be defined precisely. But surely oversight of the agencies delving into it must be better than it has been in the past if the rights of individuals to privacy are to be given full constitutional protection.

COLBY SAYS some of the practices of the CIA to which Mrs. Abzug now is objecting have been ended. That is good. But unless the functions of the CIA and the FBI and other investigating agencies are more clearly defined and supervised, the fear will persist that the old practices may at any time be reinstituted and rights again abused.

THE CHRISTIAN SCIENCE MONITOR

Boston, Mass., March 7, 1975

The United States intelligence hierarchy continues to make promises. The degree to which they are kept will determine just how much confidence will be restored to agencies whose legitimate activities are vital to informed and effective government.

"I said we're not going to do the questionable things," asserted director Colby of the Central Intelligence Agency, after acknowledging that a CIA file on Rep. Bella Abzug contained "a considerable amount of material" that "should not be in there."

The disclosure of the CIA file on Representative Abzug came shortly after Representative Drinan had discovered a Federal Bureau of Investigation file on himself. Mr. Colby promised all U.S. citizens that the CIA would honor requests to see any files on them (with the exception of sensitive material) to which they are entitled under the Freedom of Information Act.

Mr. Colby also said that the CIA had been destroying portions of files that were no longer "appropriate" but was suspending the process at the request of congressional committees until investigations are complete.

It is through continued cooperation with the investigators that the CIA and other agencies will best serve not only the public interest but their own. It is to be hoped that President Ford also will follow through on cooperating with the congressional committees, though some doubts about his wholehearted participation were raised when he did not commit himself to fulfilling some requests by the Senate committee this week.

Meanwhile, Americans received a reassuring piece of information from Mr. Colby in the midst of his testimony that Mrs. Abzug was among four present or past members of Congress included in counterintelligence files on Americans against the Vietnam war. He said the CIA had come to the conclusion that there was "no substantial foreign manipulation of or assistance to the antiwar movement."

Needless to say, it was important for the government to know whether improper foreign influence was involved. How to obtain such information without invading individual rights is the complex problem that should be clarified during the current investigation.

The Providence Journal

Providence, R.I., March 9, 1975

Rep. Bella Abzug of New York was justifiably outraged the other day when it was disclosed that the Central Intelligence Agency had been keeping a file on her activities for more than 20 years and had intercepted and opened letters she had written, in the course of her law practice, to the Soviet Union.

CIA Director William E. Colby admitted to Mrs. Abzug that "a considerable amount of the material in your file should not be in there." This is only stating the obvious, and Mr. Colby's awkward acknowledgement does not begin to explain what other unwarranted files may be locked up in the CIA's data bank, or what the agency may be doing to prevent such excesses of zeal in the future. The CIA's charter specifically prohibits it from getting involved in domestic matters, and we trust that Mr. Colby means what he says when he assures Congress that such "questionable" activities will not recur.

Mrs. Abzug has no complaint, however, about the agency's surveillance of meetings she held in Paris in 1972 with the representatives of the Provisional Revolutionary Government of South Vietnam. This was a meeting on foreign soil between an American and representatives of a then-hostile force, and CIA scrutiny was understandable and justified. Yet in the main she has made a telling point, and Congress should insist that the CIA's domestic excursions outside its authority be assuredly stopped.

BUFFALO EVENING NEWS
Buffalo, N.Y. March 7, 1975

The "outrage" voiced by Rep. Bella Abzug.(D., N. Y.) over finding herself in the CIA's files consists, as we read what's in those files, of about equal parts legitimate anger and overblown political hysteria. We think it is important for congressional investigators of this country's intelligence operations to distinguish the one from the other.

The main point on which Rep. Abzug, or any other American citizen similarly treated, is entitled to feel that her privacy has been outraged is the CIA's red-faced admission that it had surreptitiously opened her mail. This was during a period when she, as a lawyer, had represented clients involved abroad in anti-war movements; and when the CIA was engaged in what is delicately referred to as "mail surveillance" between the U. S. and Communist countries. That probably illegal program h a d been disclosed previously and was discontinued in 1973, according to C I A Director William Colby.

Mr. Colby concedes that Rep. Abzug's anger is justified not only as to that operation but as to "a considerable amount of the material in your file," which he admits "should n o t be in there." It will be destroyed, along with much other outdated or improperly gathered material, he promised, as soon as the many current investigations of the CIA are over. For the moment, he wryly noted, everything is being preserved so that the investigators can learn just what kinds of material the CIA used to think was relevant.

As for Rep. Abzug's general outrage at even finding herself listed in CIA files, however, Director Colby stood h i s ground and spelled out some reasons — perfectly valid, in our view — as to why she should be there. For, as a vocal anti-war figure, she had a lot of connections abroad with individuals and groups in which the CIA had a valid "intelligence interest"; in fact, it would be derelict if it did not keep an eye on them.

Among the "entirely proper" reasons for the CIA to have gotten the names of Rep. Abzug and countless other Americans into its files, said Mr. Colby, were (1) its interest in finding possible foreign intelligence l i n k s w i t h American dissident groups; (2) its cross-filed biographical collections of information on millions of foreign personalities, many of them with American connections; (3) its separate "foreign counter-intelligence index" of Americans "of intelligence interest" because of some often tenuous connection with foreign espionage or security services; (4) data containing texts of intelligence documents that may contain references to U. S. individuals or groups, and (5) personal records of CIA employes or prospects and their contacts.

The point for serious public concern here is not how many names of U. S. citizens may have turned up in the various files which it is the CIA's primary intelligence business to collect, index and maintain. It is when such intelligence data is misused or gathered illegally, that U. S. citizens are entitled to feel outraged by its presence in the files.

The Morning Star
Rockford, Ill., March 7, 1975

U.S. Rep. Bella Abzug of New York has a good case against the CIA, which spied on her for 10 years or more, and built up a file on her activities.

The fiery Democrat from New York drew an admission from CIA Director William E. Colby that the agency not only spied on her, but opened some of her mail.

Colby admitted before a House subcommittee that some of the material in CIA files may not be appropriate.

An understatement, at best, from Mr. Colby, who also is in the process of answering to a special Senate committee investigating U.S. intelligence operations.

These investigations, and the disclosures concerning Mrs. Abzug, will be helpful in bringing to an end the supersnoop complex that seems to afflict the more clandestine of government agencies.

Proper activities of investigative agencies do not extend into such areas as individuals' personal lives, except as they may have bearing on foreign spy operations.

Certainly, a citizen's mail ought to be secure from the prying eyes of any police agency, federal or otherwise.

Colby has refused to say how many individual citizen files are on hand in the CIA, but estimates have run from thousands to a million or more.

Somewhere in the bowels of government an extremely important idea has been lost: A prime purpose of government is to ensure and protect individual rights.

THE LINCOLN STAR
Lincoln, Neb., March 8, 1975

Bella Abzug, the fiery, floppy-hatted Democratic congresswoman from New York, might not win any popularity contests in Nebraska, but we've long admired her gadfly instincts, her irritating habit of bursting establishment balloons, her preference to lead sacred cows to the slaughterhouse.

Mrs. Abzug lately has taken aim at the Central Intelligence Agency (CIA), which has kept a file on her activities for over 20 years, since the time she was a young lawyer who represented a client brought before the House UnAmerican Activities Committee. The CIA opened Mrs. Abzug's mail and it made her mad. It should make anybody mad.

The congresswoman has wrung from CIA Director William Colby a promise not to open her mail or keep a dossier on her any longer (although he defends such practices and sees nothing particularly wrong with it, which is somewhat contradictory) and he has so much as pledged that domestic espionage efforts will be curtailed.

This of course does not bring an end to the controversy surrounding the nation's many intelligence gathering operations. A number of investigations will continue as presidential and congressional panels look into the scope of intelligence and surveillance activities which are directed at private American citizens for questionable purposes. Investigators will attempt to sort out various practices of such as the CIA and the FBI and a determination will be made as to what was done legitimately to further the ends of national security and what was done illegally or unethically on behalf of power abusers who sought to stay in power. The debate carries over into the foreign policy arena as well and a policy may well be enunciated which says that Americans as a people do not condone murder and assassination as a means of bringing about governmental change in nations where American interests are at stake.

For whatever good may come of the investigations, and we suspect that a great deal of good will come of them without jeopardizing the critical legitimate missions of our intelligence-gathering and law enforcement agencies at the national level, people like Mrs. Abzug, or Sen. Lowell Weicker, for example — those obnoxious people who ask obnoxious questions — must be given much credit.

During the recent testimony, and sort of as an afterthought to the point of this piece, we take note of Colby's observation that the CIA concluded there was no substantial foreign manipulation of the U.S. anti-war movement in the late 1960s and early 1970s.

We hope that admission by Colby did not slip past people. That is a real balloon-buster for those who saw red money behind every street demonstrator and campus speaker. But it comes straight from the horse's mouth, so to speak, that resistance to the war in Vietnam was a genuine, home-grown product, not something made in Moscow, Peking or any place else. Shocking, isn't it?

THE MILWAUKEE JOURNAL
Milwaukee, Wisc., March 26, 1975

Two startling disclosures have put the problems of the Central Intelligence Agency in clearer perspective. First came revelation of the CIA's fantastic attempt to recover a Soviet submarine lost on the ocean floor. Then came exposure of 20 years of CIA snooping into the mail of American citizens. Each tells something important.

The wisdom of the sub recovery venture is, of course, debatable. Some argue that potential intelligence gains were never great enough to offset heavy financial cost — or the diplomatic damage if the cover story about "deep seabed mining" blew. That's hard to judge, even now.

Apparently partial recovery was achieved — itself a remarkable feat and a useful technical development. Perhaps worthwhile information also was gained, even though the sub was obsolete. On the basis of available facts, however, a layman cannot accurately determine whether intelligence benefits justified the financial outlay. Similarly, it's too early to assess the diplomatic impact of exposure — either on Soviet-US detente or on international efforts to write rules for scientific inquiry in the oceans. US deception could hurt in both cases, but perhaps not much.

But one key point is plain. The sub project was a legitimate CIA caper, in keeping with its mandate to gather intelligence data abroad. Perhaps the congressional committees that are supposed to oversee CIA activity should know more about such a Buck Rogers operation before it begins. Here a sticky question of appropriate secrecy is raised. But the CIA was doing its basic job. It was not overthrowing governments, getting tangled in assassination plots, tracking US dissidents. It was out in international water, imaginatively trying to raise a sunken hulk, hoping to learn about Soviet weapons and codes.

In contrast, the mail snoopery — reportedly terminated in 1973 — was a disgusting abuse of power. It's probably the most jarring example so far of how the CIA has run out of control on the homefront. After all, there is a federal law against opening first class mail without a court order.

One answer may be prosecution of the guilty, to set a stern example. What is most appalling, however, is the breakdown of congressional oversight. This is at the heart of the CIA matter. If Americans are ever again to feel halfway comfortable about the CIA, this secret enterprise must be brought under stricter congressional accountability — not just when the lid on misconduct blows, but routinely, week in and week out.

THE ARIZONA REPUBLIC
Phoenix, Ariz., March 8, 1975

Rep. Bella ("Give 'Em Hella") Abzug, the noisy New York Democrat, is outraged.

This is not a new emotion for her. Mrs. Abzug lives in a perpetual state of outrage.

Right now, she's erupting because the Central Intelligence Agency for many years, until quite recently, kept a file on her.

"To find myself in your files is most outrageous," she told CIA Director William E. Colby when she learned this. "It is most repugnant to me."

Offhand, we can't think of anyone more deserving of the CIA's attentions than Mrs. Abzug. Her association with the Communist Party and Communist causes, not merely in the United States but overseas as well, goes as far back as 1939.

During the Hitler-Stalin pact, she was a militant isolationist, who saw no material difference between the Nazis and the allies. For a Jew, this was an unusual attitude to say the least, but not for a Jew who followed the Communist Party line.

Predictably, as soon as Germany invaded Soviet Russia, she became a militant interventionist.

In 1948, as a member of the National Lawyers Guild, a Communist front, she attended the Third Congress of the International Association of Democratic Lawyers, another Communist front, in Prague. There she cosponsored a resolution denouncing "persecutions directed against the leaders of the American Communist Party by the government of the U.S.A."

She first attracted the attention of the CIA in 1953, when she was a lawyer representing clients before the House Un-American Activities Committee. The agency started intercepting mail she was receiving from Soviet Russia.

Mrs. Abzug says these letters were in response to inquiries for next-of-kin information she needed to settle several estate cases.

Maybe so, but, given her background, the CIA can hardly be blamed for being curious.

In 1967, at a New Politics Conference in Chicago, she supported Black Caucus resolutions, which, among other things, condemned Israel as "an imperialist aggressor." Again, this was an unusual attitude for a Jew, but not for one who follows the Communist Party line.

At a convention of the New Democratic Coalition, she opposed offering sanctuary to anti-Communist Vietnamese in the event of a Communist victory. They deserve "the punishment that awaits them," she declared.

The CIA ran onto her trail again in 1972, when she and Rep. Patsy Mink, D-Hawaii, met in Paris with representatives of the People's Provisional Revolutionary Government of South Vietnam. As Colby has explained, the CIA wasn't following her, but it had been keeping tabs on the Vietnamese Reds.

The right to privacy is a precious right and the U.S. mails should be inviolate. As a member of Congress, however, Mrs. Abzug is a public official, with access to a great deal of confidential information.

Apparently, the CIA found no evidence of treasonable conduct on her part, but the agency had every reason to suspect the worst.

The outraged Mrs. Abzug has been outraging the nation for the past 35 years.

MANCHESTER UNION LEADER
Manchester, N.H., March 29, 1975

Congresswoman Bella Abzug, whose election to Congress illustrates the insanity of the voting population in the United States, has been screaming bloody murder because she has discovered that the C.I.A. has been keeping a file on her for more than 20 years.

That's the best news about the C.I.A. we have heard in a long time. If this writer were heading up the C.I.A., Bella Abzug would be one of the first people we would want to keep track of in the United States!

The fact that Bella Abzug is a congresswoman is merely incidental. There is nothing sacred about congressmen or senators. They are perfectly capable of going astray and doing something that would endanger the safety of the United States, probably more so than other citizens. The fact that they are congressmen and senators may build up their egos, but it doesn't change facts.

Miss Abzug has a record of radical affiliations a yard long. She has even met in Paris with the Communist provisional government of South Vietnam.

This newspaper has very serious doubts as to where Congresswoman Abzug's real loyalties lie—whether to this country or to the Communist cause.

The C.I.A.'s and the F.B.I.'s job is to protect the citizens of the United States from those members of our nation who, unfortunately, because of confused loyalties, are apt to adhere to the enemy rather than to the United States. Under that duty the C.I.A. and the F.B.I. have every obligation to watch any citizen in the United States who they suspect is engaged in any activity harmful to this country. There is nothing improper about this. In fact, it is exactly what their duty is.

The pious screeching of certain members of Congress, such as Miss Abzug, who have been among those citizens watched by the C.I.A. and F.B.I., is in the opinion of this newspaper, merely a smokescreen designed to try to frighten off the C.I.A. and the F.B.I.—something we sincerely hope will not happen.

CIA ATTEMPTS TO SALVAGE SUNKEN SOVIET SUBMARINE

The Central Intelligence Agency (CIA) financed and operated a $250-million deepsea salvage operation that in the summer of 1974 raised part of a Soviet submarine sunk in the Pacific Ocean, it was reported March 18. Official U.S. government sources refused all comment on the subject, but it was known that William E. Colby, director of the CIA, had expended considerable effort in trying to convince the press that public disclosure of the top-secret project would harm the national security. The Soviet government declined to even acknowledge that the submarine had gone down.

According to the reports, the Soviet vessel—a class "G" ballistic-missile, diesel-powered submarine constructed in 1958—was racked by explosions of unknown origin, which caused the ship to sink in 1968 in 16,000 feet of water 750 miles northwest of Oahu, Hawaii. The sub sank so quickly that the Soviets were unable to pinpoint its location. The U.S. Navy, using more sophisticated equipment, found the vessel. But the Navy failed to reach the sub, and the Pentagon sought the advice of the CIA.

That agency subsequently awarded, without competitive bidding, a contract to the Summa Corp., owned by Howard R. Hughes. The salvage vessel, the *Glomar Explorer,* was publicly depicted as the world's most advanced deep-sea mining ship. (Despite the fact that thousands of scientists and workmen had security clearances for the program known as Project Jennifer, the mission was one of the most tightly guarded secrets of the Nixon and Ford Administrations. *The New York Times* March 19 reported that "a number of officials who were interviewed praised the CIA 'cover' for the mission.")

During the recovery operation in July and August 1974, CIA technicians were successful in grasping and lifting the submarine halfway to the surface—about 8,000 feet—when it broke up and two-thirds of its hull fell back to the ocean floor. Although the operation was only partly complete, it had to be ended at that point because of damage sustained by the *Glomar Explorer* and because of rough seas.

THE ATLANTA CONSTITUTION
Atlanta, Ga., March 22, 1975

Bravo for the Central Intelligence Agency!

Bravo for that remarkable CIA effort in recovering most parts of a sunken Soviet submarine from deep on the ocean floor!

The achievement was an incredible technical one. Special equipment and a special ship were required. The CIA planned the recovery operation of a Soviet sub that sank northwest of Hawaii. The recovery reportedly included at least two nuclear warheads from torpedoes, coding and decoding equipment, and perhaps significant information about the state of Soviet technology.

The CIA's success was a splendid technical accomplishment and by any measure a major intelligence victory for the United States.

How do we know about the achievement? Only by an offshoot of the current investigations going on about the CIA, critical investigations, fueled by accusations that the CIA became involved in domestic spying beyond its permitted mandate.

Some of the questions raised about CIA operations are entirely proper; the criticisms need to be examined and explored and corrected in terms of future activity where necessary.

But at the same time some of the things being said and reported about the CIA, in almost breathless tones, are silly. Did the CIA wiretap and open mail secretly? Of course they did. That was part of their job.

Moreover, it is an old axiom of intelligence work that your failures immediately become public knowled,: in many instances; yet, your greatest successes must often be closely guarded secrets. The recovery of that Soviet submarine rates as a major intelligence success; there are undoubtedly many other such CIA successes, some of which will become publicly known, some of which will not. That is worth remembering as the current investigations of the CIA continue.

Long Island Press
Jamaica, N.Y., March 22, 1975

Under international law, deep sea salvage operations in search of another nation's sunken vessels are acceptable once the ship is given up for lost. Maritime law, moreover, makes no distinction between commercial and military vessels.

The Central Intelligence Agency's partial recovery of a Soviet submarine that exploded and sank in three miles of water in the North Pacific in 1968, therefore, met these criteria. The Russians made no effort to recover the sub, even though it had nuclear missiles, its torpedoes had atomic warheads, and there may have been other secrets aboard, certainly the Soviet navy's communications code.

This remarkable recovery of a portion of the submarine set no precedent beyond the great obstacles that were overcome. In the past, espionage-salvage, American and British forces recovered electronic gear from a Soviet aircraft which crashed in the North Sea. Americans salvaged similar equipment from a sunken Soviet ship, plus a nuclear weapon from a Russian plane, both in the Sea of Japan.

No doubt, similar efforts to recover lost American planes and ships have been made by the Russians and others. Indeed, espionage-salvage projects are as old as warfare itself.

* * *

It is obvious why Russia did not try to salvage the submarine: It did not have the technical equipment to undertake such a mission. We did, however, and the $300 million or more that was spent on the operation — while it sounds excessive — may pay handsome dividends in the future.

The CIA project was a legitimate act that has opened the door to future exploration of deep ocean floors for such peaceful purposes as the harvesting of food and essential minerals.

However, there is good reason for Congress to question the cost and the excessive secrecy that surrounded the project for so long. The veil of secrecy was so thick that even members of Congress who serve as legislative watchdogs of the CIA were not told.

This angered Sen. Stuart Symington, D-Mo., a veteran member of both the Senate Armed Services Committee and the CIA oversight panel, who complained that he was never informed. Indeed, it's strange that the CIA would brief the news media in a long-successful attempt to clamp a lid on the story, plus a few favored members of Congress, but not lawmakers like Sen. Symington who has every right to the information.

* * *

Congress should correct this fault at once, just as it should stop other CIA excesses that have been disclosed in recent months. This includes the agency's illegal spying on American citizens at home, properly the function of the Federal Bureau of Investigation. The lawmakers should also make sure that the CIA's future activities abroad do not include plots to depose leaders of other nations or otherwise interfere with their internal affairs.

But correcting faults must not detract from the real importance of the deep sea operation known as Project Jennifer — the opening of new horizons for mankind in the unexplored depths of seas that cover 70 per cent of the earth's surface.

Los Angeles Times
Los Angeles, Calif., March 20, 1975

The plot was Jules Verne, with an update from Ian Fleming. The feat must rank with the greatest exploits in the history of espionage:

Part of a Soviet submarine was plucked from the depths of the North Pacific under the very noses of Soviet operatives, and the United States thereby could acquire invaluable information with which to plan its national security and negotiate for international arms control.

There, for all the world to see, was a rare glimpse of the new kind of spy—a scientist, scholar and technologist. Perhaps few other espionage missions have required such elaborate preparation, such costly investment. Hundreds of millions of dollars went into the ship, the great grappling hook, the barge bigger than the Rose Bowl turf.

Some people are already arguing that it was money wasted. We doubt it. In the cold war competition, which persists in spite of detente, there is no alternative to trying to penetrate the secrecy that is so much easier for dictatorships than democracies to rig. The project was intrinsically worthwile. The potential of this technological breakthrough to harvest the ocean floor for a more universal good is extraordinary.

Some people are already using this story as another stick to beat the Central Intelligence Agency with. But they are missing the point. The CIA is under attack, and it should be, for it has erred. But it is not under attack for its intelligence-gathering, for the way it has harnessed scholarship and technology to provide national leaders with a basis for strategic planning and, beyond strategic planning, for detente. New arms agreements must be based on facts, not faith alone.

This great adventure of the Glomar Explorer is a sobering and salutary reminder of the importance of the intelligence operation. It is a timely reminder, too, because some people, shocked by the abuse of trust and by the violation of law that has characterized some of the things the CIA has done, would do away with spies altogether.

It is well to keep in mind that the transgressions and excesses of the CIA have been in two areas: in operations, the so-called "dirty tricks," which include assassination and covert intervention, and in domestic operations, where the CIA was in violation of the law that created the agency for overseas operations. The Rockefeller commission and congressional investigations will make clearer what needs to be done to discourage these abuses. The investigators should also take a thorough look at the relationship between the CIA and private business.

It would be a mistake, however, to let the national outrage over these mistakes divert resources from the vital task of maintaining an excellent intelligence apparatus—an apparatus competent to sort out the global surveillance from satellites, to interpret distant foreign broadcasts, to unscramble obscure political events or to implement one of the most astonishing salvage operations in marine history.

The Toronto Star
Toronto, Ont., March 22, 1975

There are already angry rumblings in Washington over the salvage of a sunken Soviet submarine by a super salvage ship designed for the purpose by the Central Intelligence Agency (CIA).

Some U.S. congressmen are talking about a public inquiry into the feat. Others complain that it was too much money to spend. Still others mutter about the effect the venture might have on the, well, almost, brotherly relations developing between the two super-powers. "What will the Russians say?"

To us it seems that it does not much matter what the Russians will say. One might recall the U.S. spy ship Pueblo, seized by the North Koreans in January, 1968. The vessel, in fact, was eavesdropping on the military communications in North Korea and probably, the Soviet maritimes, and it was full of the best electronic gadgetry the American intelligence community had been able to devise.

No one at the time heard Moscow say a word about the seizure—even though it might have well started a dangerous war on the Soviet threshold. Instead, there were reports of top spies in Moscow and Peking rushing post-haste to Pyongyang to learn America's secrets.

The truth is that, for all the pious talk of detente, the two super-powers remain rivals, and in many key areas even foes. And if we have relative peace today, it is based on these professions but on the balance of nuclear deterrents. This balance can be credible only if each of the rivals knows, with a reasonable sureness, what the other one is up to.

For many years, Moscow has opposed mutual on-site inspection of nuclear missiles. Indeed, it has branded the idea as ignoble: "They want to spy on us." The problem was solved when satellites, with their sensors and cameras, began to crisscross the skies over both America and Russia. It was this, and not Moscow's love for peace, that permitted the present agreements on limiting nuclear arms. Each rival has become reasonably sure of what big guns the other fellow was building.

But the satellites are not enough. Each side wants to know how advanced is the rival's rocketry, where it is deficient, what kind of carpentry and materials it employs. It was for this reason that the U.S. leaders and the CIA decided to recover the sub the Soviets had lost somewhere in the Pacific.

Indeed, the CIA would have been dreadfully remiss if it had foregone this chance to look at the Soviet weapons. Knowing something about your rival in this age of nuclear horror is essential to policy-making. And it is irrelevant whether the spies talk of world peace while they go about their business—or simply of the urgent need to know.

Detente is a wondrous creature. It enables Moscow to pour weapons into Indo-China and Syria while denouncing Washington for its war-mongering. It permits Moscow to provide all help possible to the Communists now driving toward power in Portugal—even as it speaks of a summit conference to sign a European security pact.

Moscow's actions—as distinct from its pieties—are hardly conducive to international brotherhood. And the Kremlin could hardly complain when the other side does some rummaging on the sea bottom to learn what it can about some of the Soviet secrets. We do not hail espionage as a path to peace. But we do believe that without intelligence there can be no peace.

The Times-Picayune
New Orleans, La., March 20, 1975

The latest disclosure about the Central Intelligence Agency's activities in the underwater world of the Pacific Ocean has caused quite a stir atop Capitol Hill.

Gist of the newest flap involves the CIA's multi-million dollar plan to pluck a sunken Russian submarine out of the Pacific and snare for U. S. intelligence purposes all of the confidential data aboard the vessel. The project was partially successful. Only one-third of the submarine was brought to the surface, a portion containing bodies of the Soviet crewmen who died in the 1968 sinking. From the parts of the sub recovered, analysts were able to unravel some Soviet secrets

There is genuine concern that widespread dissemination of the operation might harm the currently harmonious, though tenuous, relationship between Washington and Moscow. Some are likening the American quest for the Soviet submarine to the U-2 spy plane incident of 1960 which scuttled a summit meeting between then President Dwight Eisenhower and Soviet leader Nikita Khrushchev. Revelation of the highly secret salvage operation comes at a time when Soviet chieftain Leonid Brezhnev is readying for a trip to the United States.

Though there may be diplomatic repercussions, it seems that much more is being made of the Pacific affair than is warranted. In the first place, it has already been revealed that the Soviets were aware of the American operation The Soviets had been unsuccessful in their own sea hunt for the lost sub; the Americans simply were more successful. Salvaging sunken vessels has been the established law of the high seas for centuries.

Secondly, the decision by the CIA to go ahead on the salvage operation may have been prompted by a highly-charged event that took place earlier in the seizure of the American vessel Pueblo by the North Koreans. It is generally assumed that the daring capture of the Pueblo had the beforehand approval of the Soviet Union. That incident resulted in the death of one American seaman and the capture of 82 others, who were held prisoners for more than 11 months.

Tragic as the sinking of the Soviet sub was in loss of life, it was an opportune moment to gather important intelligence data. The CIA rightly seized the opportunity for our advantage.

Anchorage Daily Times
Anchorage, Alaska, March 21, 1975

LET'S HEAR ONE for the good, old CIA.

From what has been published so far, it sounds to us as though the Central Intelligence Agency deserves a round of applause and a hearty cheer for recovering part of a sunken Russian nuclear submarine from the bottom of the Pacific Ocean.

But as the story has been told in bits and pieces and leaks out of Washington, there are overtones that the CIA — a favorite whipping boy these days — was engaged in some kind of nefarious scheme that might upset our warm and friendly relations with that lovable bear, the Soviet Union.

No matter, of course, that the submarine in question was stalking the waters off Hawaii armed with three missiles capable of making Pearl Harbor Day look like a fizzled firecracker.

THE IMPLICATIONS, however, seem to be that the CIA operation was bad and the secrecy surrounding the whole thing was sinister.

Of course it was sinister. What the submarine was doing for the Soviet government was sinister, too.

But that doesn't bother some of the liberal thinkers in Congress.

Among those to be heard from, predictably, was Sen. Frank Church, D-Idaho, who is disturbed that a contract to build the recovery vessels involved went to Howard Hughes and may have cost $350 million. "The disclosure suggests that the intelligence community may need a cost-benefit ratio." He scoffed at what he described as merely "an obsolete submarine."

Sen. Jacob Javits, R-N.Y., said disclosure of the CIA operation proves to him that "we have got to fashion means to supervise and monitor everything it does and see that it's authorized by Congress."

Isn't that wonderful? How safe would you feel with having Congress — which has a hard enough time monitoring its own free mailing privileges — in charge of the country's international intelligence missions?

THANK HEAVEN there were at least a few congressional voices heard in favor of the CIA action.

Sen. John Tower, R-Tex., said it appeared to him that there might well have been "some extremely valuable intelligence" collected as a result of the operation. "If the roles were reversed," he added, "I'm sure the Soviets would not have any inhibitions about it."

And Sen. Robert Byrd, D-W.Va., called it a "perfectly legitimate operation to attempt to retrieve that submarine and to determine any facts that might be useful to our own security."

Even Senate Democratic Majority Leader Mike Mansfield of Montana, hardly a hawk, admitted that findings in the wrecked submarine "may have been of some value."

THE TRUTH may well be that the salvage of the sub was a fantastic technical accomplishment — one that may have significant importance to America's national security.

But if any Soviet secrets were discovered, you can count on Congress to blab about it so that Moscow won't have to wonder just how much of its own military plans, codes and weaponry were pulled from the bottom of the deep.

HOUSTON CHRONICLE
Houston, Texas, March 24, 1975

The Central Intelligence Agency is coming under heavy criticism for its project which recovered part of a Russian submarine from the floor of the Pacific Ocean.

We disagree with the critics. The CIA's job is to develop intelligence, and getting our hands on a sunken Soviet submarine seems to be a proper exercise in that goal.

The opportunity existed, our technology proved capable of meeting the challenge and we gained important information.

Was the project worth $350 million? That is difficult to judge. There will be those who point out how much food $350 million would have bought, or how many hospitals that much money could have built. The same comparison can be made for any military or intelligence agency expenditure.

Then the question is asked in turn how much freedom and security are worth and whether we could have reached so high a standard of living if we were not capable of defending ourselves. At some point, the decision to proceed was made, and it is a supportable one.

The CIA is wide open to criticism for some of its operations that have come to light lately. It went beyond its jurisdiction domestically and deserved to be brought up short. Better oversight and better decision-making within the agency itself is necessary.

The CIA is a prime target now. For an agency that supposedly operates in secret, it has lately developed a gift for grabbing news space that a circus advance man would envy.

No sensible person, however, can favor abolishing or crippling the CIA, for it plays an essential role in national defense. While the great hue and cry tends to confuse issues, we must not lose sight of the essential function of the agency.

The Courier-Journal
Louisville, Ky., March 23, 1975

OF ALL the Central Intelligence Agency activities that have come to the surface in the past year, the aims of the attempt to recover a sunken Soviet submarine are surely the most legitimate. In fact, since the operation is incomplete, there must be serious misgivings about the fact that the details have been publicized.

The value of salvaging the vessel, lying on the bottom of the Pacific Ocean northwest of Hawaii, was thoroughly discussed before the operation was approved. Leading congressmen were properly informed. And the aim, to recover the nuclear missiles and code machines the submarine was carrying, was certainly a legitimate intelligence function.

Moreover, despite off-the-cuff criticisms from some members of Congress, valuable information might well have been gleaned from inspection of the weapons and equipment. The fact that some of the gear would be obsolete by now wouldn't detract from its usefulness. The United States would stand to learn how accurate its information from intelligence sources had been about Russian nuclear submarine equipment in 1968, the year this ship sank.

The CIA may continue its efforts to raise the submarine. But, though the Soviet Union has been slow to react, and administration officials hope that disclosure of the operation will not interfere with the process of detente, the Russians now are almost forced to register at least a strong protest. The old rule in espionage, that a government can get away with a lot so long as it doesn't publicly admit anything, has been broken.

In this instance, the press doesn't show up in a good light. Many newspapers had known of the story. Though they were responsible enough to defer to CIA requests to withhold publication, they felt compelled to jump in as soon as a less scrupulous journalist opened the door. Once columnist Jack Anderson broadcast an account, there was no reason to hold back.

First Amendment guarantees forbid government censorship of the news in peacetime. Secrecy in matters affecting national security has always depended on precautions against damaging leaks from government departments and the sense of responsibility of editors. The CIA has been fair game for journalistic investigation in recent months, most of the time for good reason. But this was one occasion where the agency was not abusing its power and where more consideration of the national interest would have been appropriate.

The Detroit News
Detroit, Mich., March 20, 1975

How the CIA salvaged part of a sunken Soviet submarine—a vessel carrying nuclear missiles and torpedoes and secret codes—ranks as the most bizarre cloak-and-dagger tale of the century. It makes good reading—but should it have been told at all?

As pieced together by various reporters, the story contains an amazing wealth of detail about CIA methods, the conduct of the salvaging operation and what the salvagers found and did not find—all very sensitive information.

After the Los Angeles Times published some information last year, the New York Times pursued the story and was warned by the CIA that publication would jeopardize national security. The New York Times and other elements of the press withheld publication but kept right on building the story.

This week, tired of exercising responsible self-restraint, the New York Times splashed the story across Page One, thus opening the floodgates of national publicity and blowing the CIA's cover irretrievably.

The nation pays a heavy price for those nine columns of type in the Times. Such disclosures do irreparable harm to the intelligence and security systems while creating embarrassment for the government in its relations with other nations.

Whether Project Jennifer justified the money and effort expended on it is not the immediate question, although we can certainly understand the value of trying to see what a Soviet submarine contains. That information might help this nation survive on better terms than it might otherwise enjoy 10 or 20 years from now.

Nor do we question, as some do, the legality and propriety of such an operation. After all, this was a sunken vessel abandoned by its owners in international waters and containing information that could prove valuable to U.S. security and the conduct of arms negotiations with the Soviet Union.

If the situation were reversed, you can bet your eye teeth the Soviets would try to salvage the vessel—assuming they have the technical ability to do so, which apparently they don't.

The main questions raised by this fantastic episode concern the integrity of secret information and the responsibility of the press. The officials who leaked secret information or failed to guard it were wrong, as were the newsmen who shrugged aside national security for the sake of headlines.

Such conduct can destroy the CIA entirely, which could only help the Soviet Union in its continuing struggle for power and influence, and may produce a strict law of secrecy that will destroy many of the gains made by the American press in its fight for unfettered expression.

DAILY NEWS
New York, N.Y., March 20, 1975

STRANGER THAN FICTION

—is the intriguing story of how the Central Intelligence Agency salvaged part of a sunken Russian submarine in the Pacific Ocean and thereby acquired data of immense value for U.S. strategic arms-limitation negotiators.

The absorbing tale shows the CIA at its best throughout—alert, imaginative, energetic and ingenious in devising a cover for the operations that kept the Soviet Union wholly ignorant of what was going on.

The "good press" is not much consolation, however, for CIA Director William Colby. Premature publicity has jeopardized plans for a renewed effort to raise the rest of the sub, with

William Colby

its nuclear weapons and code equipment. Furthermore, the "research vessel" which the CIA had built for the job is now a marked ship as far as Soviet spymasters are concerned.

Detailed disclosures about the CIA coup—in spite of Colby's earnest pleas for silence—raised anew a nagging and perplexing question: How can the U.S. reconcile the public's right to know and the press' duty to inform with the CIA's legitimate need for secrecy?

Colby has been deeply concerned that CIA secrets imparted to the various commissions and committees probing the agency's affairs would leak to the media, and be exploited in ways damaging to our espionage efforts.

The tell-all treatment accorded the sub-salvage effort shows that there are ample grounds for worry.

The San Diego Union
San Diego, Calif., March 22, 1975

Disclosure that the United States of America, through the Central Intelligence Agency, mounted a $350 million project to retrieve a sunken Soviet submarine from the ocean floor raises questions going beyond the obvious one of whether a piece of a Soviet submarine was worth it. Questions that are far more important involve the role of Congress and the news media in relation to this and other CIA activities.

The value of the submarine project is best known to our military strategists and weapons specialists. What we do know is that harnessing the technology to undertake a heavy salvage operation at a depth of more than 17,000 feet adds a new dimension to the deep-sea capability of the United States of America — a fact of continuing significance quite beyond any knowledge we have gained about Soviet submarines or their weapons.

While it is fascinating to contemplate this engineering feat, we are sure that most Americans also feel uneasy when they read or hear about it. It is obvious to them why such an undertaking had to be planned and carried out in secret. It is obvious that the current publicity can benefit no one but the Russians—that it can do irreparable harm to U.S. foreign policy. We cannot estimate how much our national security would have benefited — how many lives might have been saved —if the salvage operation had been completed in secrecy.

We treasure our free press, realizing that freedom of expression and our constitutional system are inseparable. The news media, however, must never see their position as more favored than that of a private citizen. The Constitution gives us all obligations as well as protections.

If a citizen were to disclose a state secret and in so doing adversely affect the welfare of his country, he could expect to suffer serious consequences. We should expect some repudiation of the indefensible action of a radio commentator and a major newspaper who "broke" the submarine story when the reasons for not doing so were irrefutable.

Neither the CIA nor any other government agency owes accountability to the news media. Government accountability is to the people, and information about CIA operations should be transmitted to the people's chosen representatives—responsible members of Congress who can satisfy the public interest in the scope and purpose of the agency's activities.

Congress as a whole now appears unable to assure that such information will not sometimes become public through negligent leaks or deliberate revelations. In its probing into the affairs of the CIA, Congress already has unnecessarily diminished the contribution the Agency makes to national security.

Congress should consider its own security problem as it helps rebuild the CIA on a new basis of legitimate public accountability for its activities. And the media should give deep thoughts to their obligation as well as their privileges in a free society.

The Cincinnati Post
TIMES STAR
Cincinnati, Ohio, March 22, 1975

The Central Intelligence Agency, which has been taking some well-deserved lumps lately, in fairness now should be credited with an astonishing feat.

We refer to the disclosure that a CIA-designed and operated salvage vessel recovered part of a Soviet missile-firing submarine from the seabed 17,000 feet under the Pacific Ocean last summer. Unfortunately, two-thirds of the submarine broke away as it was being lifted and the CIA may not have gained access to its main targets: the Soviet codes and missiles tipped with hydrogen-bomb warheads aboard the sunken craft.

THE SALVAGE OPERATION is said to have produced valuable intelligence data from the submarine, which mysteriously exploded and sank in 1968. Time obviously had eroded the code books of any operational value—Senator Frank Church questions the cost-benefit of the whole adventure—but the possible strategic payoff in an age of undersea nuclear fleets was tempting.

The CIA had been planning to return to the spot this summer and attempt to recover the rest of the submarine, but that is now doubtful because of all the publicity. While the wreckage is in international waters and salvage work is legal, the Soviet navy might try to interfere with the CIA operation. And the salvage attempt itself could put unwanted strain on Soviet-American detente. The Russians have canceled a visit by 12 U.S. senators in what some think is a reaction to disclosure of the salvage effort.

IF THE CIA had been able to go back and recover the whole submarine, it might have been, as CIA Director William Colby claims, the biggest single intelligence coup in history—bigger for certain than the prize the Soviet Union won when it netted Francis Gary Powers' U-2 spy plane, unless the CIA has recovered more than it is admitting.

In any event, it's reassuring to learn that the CIA is up to more useful and legal things than opening Bella Abzug's mail.

THE RICHMOND NEWS LEADER
Richmond, Va., March 21, 1975

The temptation is to dismiss as another example of science-fiction foolishness the Central Intelligence Agency's plan to recover a sunken Soviet submarine resting 17,000 feet below the surface of the Northern Pacific.

Surely, this entire episode smacks of our best fantasy imagination:

A reclusive millionaire clandestinely constructing a contraption looking like something out of Jules Verne; the device snaking three miles under the sea to have its huge claw grasp a Soviet submarine whose location only our Navy knew; the oddly touching burials-at-sea conducted for the Soviet seamen by the U.S. Navy; the breaking of the Soviet sub's hull, and the consequent loss of its section most important to the United States; the decision to make a second effort to retrieve the lost section; the burglarizing of a safe in the millionaire's company — a safe containing information about the entire operation; and — over the objections of the director of the CIA — public disclosure of the operation by the nation's leading yellow journalist, who thereby blew the second attempt right out of the water.

Yet it all apparently happened. And about it, two essential thoughts:

(1) *Regarding the way the public learned of the operation.* Over the radio, Columnist Jack Anderson related details of the operation. Justifications for his having done so — justifications based on "the public's right to know" — are beside the point. Given the magnitude of such a story, and given the degree to which disclosure of it can enhance one's reputation as a diligent journalist, a man such as Jack Anderson will opt for disclosure, and to hell with the damage that disclosure can do to the United States.

Both *The New York Times* and *The Los Angeles Times* deserve credit for not disclosing the operation when they first heard about it several months ago. Perhaps they have learned something from their mistaken decisions some years back to publish the stolen Pentagon Papers. *The New York Times* did not disclose it evidently because the newspaper believed that the value of the information gleaned from the operation did not justify disclosing it, and thus jeopardizing U.S.-Soviet *détente.* But *The Los Angeles Times* did not disclose the operation precisely because that newspaper did understand the profound value of the information that the first retrieval had brought to the U.S. — and the even more valuable information that the U.S. might obtain through the planned second retrieval effort. Wrote *The Los Angeles Times'* Jerry Cohen and George Reasons about the information derived from the retrieval:

What the analysts discovered was of critical importance and it was this: The Russians had modified the 1958-model sub to fire not only nuclear-tipped torpedoes but Polaris-type missiles as well.

The experts also were able to project the current state of Soviet nuclear submarine technology. What the CIA crews recovered led them to believe the remaining section of the sub would yield even more valuable data, possibly including the key to the Russian code. As a result, the CIA won the approval of President Ford about two months ago to undertake a second mission to recover the critical section still on the ocean floor.

According to subsequent reports in *The Washington Post,* some code information and some Soviet missiles may have been obtained in the retrieval that did succeed.

(2) *Regarding the damage caused by public disclosure of the operation.* The Soviet reaction to the retrieval is not yet known, but the degree of expressed Soviet wrath will be calculated to accrue to the benefit of the Soviet Union. Yet the greatest benefit to the Soviet Union — and make no mistake, Jack Anderson has done the Soviets a considerable service — will derive from the damage that disclosure has done, and will do, to the CIA.

Four investigations of the CIA are underway. The CIA currently is this nation's suppositional Enemy No. 1. In the words of Ray S. Cline — deputy director of the CIA from 1962 to 1966 — writing in the February 27 *New York Times:* "A great many critics of United States policy in the 1950s and 1960s, especially the young ones who grew up in the era of retreat from Vietnam and of worldwide *détente,* have applauded United States withdrawal from the clandestine international political arena. They consider covert activities incompatible with international law, morality, and the fundamental principles of our open society." Yet, he continues, given the intentions of the Soviet Union, it is doubtful that the U.S. should "be too high-minded" about clandestine operations by the CIA.

Public disclosure of the CIA's submarine retrieval provides further ammunition to those who have the CIA under attack. And that attack is related closely to America's new — and growing — isolationism. If it can be successfully argued that the U.S. should withdraw its support from long-time allies around the world because the Communists no longer have designs on us, it can be argued with equal success that the U.S. should draw in its intelligence-gathering forces as well. The inescapable conclusion of such arguments is that the CIA is a relic of the past — a relic that, as seen in the submarine retrieval, can only get us into trouble.

The truth remains, however, that as Communists on the battlefield rush in when America withdraws support of its allies, so the Soviets will rush in to fill the vacuum left by the withdrawal of the CIA from useful intelligence operations. The dispiriting disclosure of the CIA's submarine retrieval has removed yet another of the CIA's underpinnings, hence weakening it, and — by necessary extension — weakening the United States.

The Washington Star
Washington, D.C., March 21, 1975

There are two major points to make in the case of the sunken Russian submarine that the Central Intelligence Agency tried to recover: First, the CIA was doing its job; second, the chances of keeping anything secret in the interests of national security are getting more remote every day.

It has become fashionable to kick the CIA around; and investigations into it and other intelligence-gathering agencies have sprouted thicker than spring crocuses. We have no quarrel with attempts to determine whether the CIA has over-stepped its bounds on domestic spying, nor with reining it in if it has—so long as the matter is handled in such a way as not to destroy the agency and its vitally needed functions in the process.

This is not a marshmallow world. Anyone who thinks the United States can lower its guard and dismantle its intelligence-gathering apparatus is living in dreamland. Soviet leaders and the KGB no doubt are rubbing their hands in glee over the public fix the CIA has gotten into.

The sunken sub case has given the CIA's critics some more ammunition. Boys playing at cops and robbers; it was a waste of money; whatever information that might have been gleaned from the Russian submarine would have been of minimal value, they say. All of a sudden everyone has become an intelligence expert.

We regard "Project Jennifer," as the submarine operation was known in official circles, as a tremendous feat. It was an extraordinary accomplishment for U.S. intelligence forces to pinpoint the location of the sub that even its owners couldn't find, and then to devise and have built a vessel with the capability of raising the sunken hulk out of 17,000 feet of water — and to pull it off apparently without the Russians knowing what was going on. That the submarine broke up and the important section sank back to the bottom certainly was a disappointment but it doesn't detract from the value of the project.

The significant thing that ought to be remembered is that the CIA was doing exactly what it was supposed to be doing: gathering foreign intelligence. It wasn't shadowing U.S. dissidents around Washington or New York; it was out on the high seas performing a function that was legitimate and potentially of high intelligence value.

Fear has been expressed in some quarters that it will harm the move toward detente with the Soviet Union and queer efforts to reach agreement on strategic arms limitations. That is absurd. Who believes for a minute that the Soviet Union would not do the same thing if it had the opportunity? If detente is so shaky as to be thrown off course by this, it was never going anywhere in the first place.

This brings us to our second point. If there are diplomatic repercussions, they can be put down to the publicity about the operation, not to the operation itself. The Soviets understand espionage and the need to keep it from public view. If they complain in this case, it will be because they feel that public exposure of the sub-raising operation somehow has made them appear inept or has challenged their national manhood.

If secrecy on this kind of operation is not in the national interest, what is? CIA officials are reported to have made strenuous efforts to keep the operation from being printed or broadcast by the U.S. news media, but to no avail.

What has been gained by spreading this over the airwaves and across the front pages of the nation's newspapers? Sure, it was interesting reading. Sure, someone gets to claim he was first to blab it to the public. Well, first is not always best — and especially it is not best when the national interest is involved.

The Boston Globe
Boston, Mass., March 20, 1975

First the good news. There does not seem to be much question that the Central Intelligence Agency acted within the letter and maybe even the spirit of international and US law in attempting to recover a Soviet submarine sunk off Hawaii. That's a change from other recent stories about the supersecret group.

Now the bad news. The effort may have represented something less than the most intelligent use of manpower and resources. At worst it has cast a shadow on the spirit of detente and especially on intellectual and scientific exchanges between Soviet and American groups.

As a purely technical achievement, the bringing up of even part of the Soviet submarine from more than three miles deep was truly remarkable The creation of two special vessels, one for lifting the submarine and the other for concealing the submarine, is a tribute to the power to act once minds have been made up. Using the reputation of millionaire eccentric Howard Hughes as a blind for the operation suggests a flair for inventiveness that one expects from spy thrillers. For that matter, those who have wondered whether there really is a Howard Hughes may now be forgiven if they suspect that he is just a fiction created to suit the convenience of the CIA. It would explain why Hughes is such a successful recluse.

There are destructive elements in the whole transaction. In addition to Hughes, the CIA operation used the infant sea bed mining industry as a blind for its creation of the two vessels and to explain their presence 750 miles northwest of Hawaii in a region where there are significant amounts of minerals lying on the sea floor.

The specially designed vessel, Glomar Explorer, was supposedly testing the practicality of the recovery process. Its purpose, now unmasked, raises a question in everyone's mind about each peaceful operation conducted by American or foreign enterprises in areas where the Soviet Union may feel it has legitimate interests. And, as discussions of detente proceed, one can imagine Soviet hawks telling their comrades today that "we told you so."

The question of secrecy is also troublesome. Hundreds of people were involved in the project and even though some of them, especially those who built the two vessels, may not have known what they were working on, it i highly improbable that the project could have been kept secret. As it was, at least two newspapers and a columnist got wind of it and developed a good deal of information before the story got too big to contain.

The CIA may argue that secrecy was important only for the period of the salvage effort, to keep the Soviet Union from interfering physically with the project. Maybe. But that would imply there was no sense of embarrassment about the affront to Soviet sensibilities.

If the CIA thought the project could be kept forever secret it is guilty of foolishness. If, on the other hand, it thought it could later reveal the information because it no longer cared, it is guilty of rascality.

Congress ought to look closely at another aspect of the project. Its exact cost is not yet clear. The Los Angeles Times reports it as $200 million for the vessels, which may or may not have some future usefulness. The New York Times says it may be as much as $350 million.

As entertainment, it may be worthwhile. But as a means of collecting intelligence, we're not so sure. Congress has every reason at least to look at the way the decision was reached. Perhaps, on balance, it can be defended. But we have a right to know.

ST. LOUIS POST-DISPATCH
St. Louis, Mo., March 21, 1975

Disclosures that the CIA spent $250,000,000 to try to raise an old Russian submarine do not so far seem to have outraged the Russians as much as spokesmen for the Central Intelligence Agency. Congressmen are questioning the practicality of the venture; Senator Church of Idaho says that "the intelligence community may need a cost-benefit ratio."

Perhaps so. There may be endless, sometimes amusing and possibly unprofitable debate on whether the $250,000,000 was well spent. What the CIA got for that sum was perhaps one third of the Soviet submarine, but no missiles or codes. The agency did determine that Russia was arming older subs (this one was built between 1958 and 1962 and sank in 1968) with nuclear missiles, and may have obtained two warheads. In some respects this was a remarkable venture, but did it represent that brilliant stroke of intelligence as claimed, more costly even than the Ford Administration's proposed aid to Cambodia?

Under the circumstances it is not surprising that the CIA tried to get the media to suppress the story. But the CIA's case for prior censorship here is as weak as it usually is. What harm is there in letting the public know about the venture and, for that matter, why should Congress itself have to find out about a large public expenditure by reading of it in the press?

The incident illustrates, not the need for more secrecy, but for less, and certainly the need for the kind of congressional oversight that obviously did not exist. For the submarine affair is only the latest in a series of major developments that Congress was not told about or did not find out about for itself: the Bay of Pigs, the intervention in Chile, the secret bombing of Cambodia, even the truth of the Tonkin incident that led to the whole Southeast Asia involvement.

The American Government should not, cannot, operate in such a way. The whole principle of checks and balances is lost when the legislative branch provides money for secret acts of the executive branch, and does not even ask questions. Senator Church says his special committee on intelligence will review the submarine salvage project. That investigation can do an immeasurable public service by returning Congress to its duty of scrutinizing how intelligence uses the money legislated for it.

THE SUN
Baltimore, Md., March 20, 1975

A report by the Comptroller General on United States ocean interests and the Law of the Sea Conference, out last week, contains this gem: "Accurate information on the current investment in undersea mining is not available because of the competition among the corporations involved. It is estimated, however, that one corporation has spent about $100 million on research and owns a vessel built for nodule recovery, but the extent of its operations is not known." The question of whether art imitates life, or life art, is much older than its present form, which is whether James Bond movies are based on the big spy agencies or vice versa. But now we know, at least, that the Comptroller General's report really refers to "Project Jennifer" and a vessel, the Glomar Explorer, designed by Howard Hughes's Summa Corporation for the CIA to mine not manganese nodules but a Soviet submarine that sank in 1968 with three nuclear missiles and coding equipment intact.

Just picture it as a Bond film: The floating derrick releases a giant claw, which submerges three miles to grab the submarine, lifting it gently toward the submerged barge, until, half way up, the sub breaks apart and the H-bombs and coding gear tumble a mile and a half to the bottom. American taxpayers pay a quarter billion dollars or so for a Soviet sub and get the wrong end. The CIA, finding itself with Russian bodies instead of secrets, gives them a proper sea burial.

And it was all legal. We have as much right to salvage a sunken Soviet sub with its secrets as a Spanish galleon with its gold. What this failed operation will do to detente and the SALT talks is anybody's guess. Or how it will feel to stockholders of corporations that plunged into deepsea mining development because they feared Hughes's lead.

Where this is bound to be felt is at the resumed Law of the Sea Conference at Geneva. The United States is in disagreement with most smaller nations there over oceanic research in coastal waters and mining in the deep seabed. The American position is that science requires that research vessels operate freely; poor coastal nations want to control or prohibit research vessels in their "economic zone," between 12 and 200 miles out. The United States wants an international agency to license international mining of the seabed; poor nations want the international agency to do the mining. The suspicious small nations already knew that the U.S. called the Pueblo a research vessel. Now they know that the mining ship was really a spy ship. Their position will harden.

And what of the Glomar Explorer's sister ship, Glomar Challenger, which has been drilling beneath the high seas for years, lately with Soviet scientists aboard? Will other nations let it within 200 miles of their coast? What of the remains of that Soviet sub lying 750 miles from Oahu? Will Tonga or Nauru beat the superpowers to it? How many other hydrogen bombs are resting on the ocean floor? Just what is the relationship between the Hughes empire and the CIA? Who burgled the Summa Corporation to learn the secret of Project Jennifer, anyway? Would Soviet missiles, coding equipment and a sub, all possibly obsolete, be worth a quarter billion dollars so that they might be compared with previous intelligence about them? And why do CIA operations produce more questions than answers?

THE NASHVILLE TENNESSEAN
Nashville, Tenn., March 20, 1975

DISCLOSURE of the Central Intelligence Agency's project to raise a sunken Russian submarine from the floor of the Pacific Ocean has touched off a new round of controversy about the already troubled agency.

The project is being attacked by some as outrageously expensive for the benefit it produced and as an unnecessary risk to the improving relations between the U. S. and Russia.

However, the project's defenders contend the project proved to be of much value. If the effort had accomplished all that was expected of it, the benefits would have been even greater, it was said.

Whatever the truth may be, the project raises many questions and should be investigated along with the C.I.A.'s other activities now under study by Congress and the President's special commission.

Some of the most important questions are the cost of the project — estimated to be between $250 million and $350 million — and the part the Howard Hughes industrial empire, through its Summa Corp., played in the attempt to raise the submarine.

The Hughes connection becomes even more interesting in view of the fact that Mr. Hughes's name has often been linked to large campaign contributions for ex-President Nixon, whose administration authorized the search.

High government officials insist that Mr. Hughes made very little money in the construction of the salvage vessel which attempted to raise the sub and that he was selected for participation in the highly-secret project because of "his patriotism."

The taxpayers are likely to gag on this explanation. Mr. Hughes's patriotism is not questioned. But many taxpayers will find it hard to believe that a businessman with his reputation for turning a profit did not have some incentive in addition to his patriotism.

If the cost of this project was $350 million, or even $250 million, just who did get all this money if not the ones who carried out the operation of locating the submarine and attempting to raise it?

The C.I.A.'s determination to keep the project secret, even after it had become known to thousands of persons, is also difficult to understand. The agency has put pressure on numerous reporters who had come into possession of the facts not to publish the story on grounds that it would damage the national security.

This appears to be another example of the C.I.A.'s readiness to invoke the national security when it wants to cover up facts that may prove embarrassing to the C.I.A.

How the disclosure of the submarine salvage attempt could damage the national security has not been explained. How it might embarrass the C.I.A. is easy to see. For despite what the C.I.A.'s defenders say about the value of what it learned, the submarine recovery attempt is beginning to look like a major operational blunder with overtones of political boondoggling.

The expedition was largely a failure. It did not recover any nuclear warheads, although it was said there were indications the submarine was armed with three missiles that normally would carry nuclear warheads.

The searchers also failed to recover an old code book they were looking for which some C.I.A. spokesmen say would have been helpful in evaluating all prior Soviet submarine communications but which critics of the program say would have been of little benefit, certainly not enough to justify the cost of the program.

It seems that all the mission did accomplish was to learn that the old submarine may at one time have carried some type of nuclear device. If the C.I.A. had to spend $350 million to find this out, it seems that the business of intelligence gathering may eventually bankrupt the nation.

DAYTON DAILY NEWS
Dayton, Ohio, March 21, 1975

Although rewarded by only limited success, the CIA's attempt to snatch a Soviet submarine from the Pacific ocean floor was a clever and appropriate undertaking. It is among the types of intelligence gathering that the CIA should be busy at.

The troublesome aspect of the exercise is the CIA's involvement with one of Howard Hughes' corporations. The Hughes company built the ship that dredged up part of the sub, and the company provided the legitimate-seeming cover for the operation.

How deeply, in what subtle ways, do such complex interweavings of governmental and private interests compromise the government's ability to police corporate interests on behalf of the public interest? There is no question that Mr. Hughes profited unfairly from this deal. The CIA insists he took a smaller cut than he would have in ordinary corporation-to-corporation dealings, and there is no reason to doubt that.

But the federal government sought out Mr. Hughes' firm, was granted its good offices and itself benefited substantially from the arrangement. How could it not be grateful? Would a government that had used a private interest in such a delicate matter not be more inclined thereafter to give the corporation the benefit of the doubt in the firm's other dealings with the myriad of federal regulatory and contracting agencies?

The worry here is not of overt corruption, in the ordinary payoff sense. The worry is that such arrangements of mutual convenience, especially when they are necessarily secret, can be deeply corrosive to the independence of judgment the government is supposed to exercise in its watchdog role. That could be more undermining of the public interest in the long run than plain (and prosecutable) bribes.

The Virginian-Pilot
Norfolk, Va., March 20, 1975

Project Jennifer—the multimillion-dollar operation to recover from Pacific Ocean depths a sunken Soviet Navy ballistic-missile submarine—was controversial even as a secret contained within the innermost councils of the Nixon and Ford Administrations. The questions raised about it then are being asked again now that the enterprise's cover has blown.

Was the game worth the candle? Expenditures for construction of the submarine-recovery vessel Glomar Explorer and an extraordinary barge, plus attendant operating expenses, reportedly topped a quarter-billion dollars and purchased mixed results. Nonetheless, the venture had proceeded with the blessing of the Forty Committee, the secret panel—headed by Secretary of State Kissinger—that reviews and finances all national intelligence operations. Clearly it was the sober judgment of leaders at the highest levels in Washington that Project Jennifer would yield priceless information about Soviet missilery, submarine technology, and cryptography. Presumably the development of machinery that could be used to raise other sunken vessels in deep waters and scoop minerals from the seabed was counted as a probable residual benefit of immense value.

But Senator Frank Church (D-Idaho), chairman of the new special committee probing the CIA, was aghast this week: "If we are willing to pay Howard Hughes $350 million for an obsolete 18-year-old Russian submarine, no wonder we're broke," Mr. Church said. On the other hand, Senators John Tower (R-Texas) and Robert C. Byrd (D-West Virginia) were approving of the salvage effort. Bystanders are ill-prepared to umpire the quarrel.

Meanwhile, the CIA is on the defensive, its purposes and conduct undergoing unprecedented criticism and scrutiny to an uncertain end. Its embarrassments multiply. Details of its activities read like Cold War spy novels. A sunken ballistic-missile submarine, Project Jennifer. Summa Corporation. Howard Hughes. The Glomar Explorer "sea-mining" ship. Filmed burials at sea of the bodies of Soviet submariners brought up from the depths. These are the stuff of escape fiction.

So, too, are they the stuff of the surreal world of intelligence gathering, as were the U-2, Colonel Penkovksy, the Gehlen Organization, Burgess and Mac-Lean, the Bay of Pigs, the Ultra secret (the cracking of the Nazis' toughest codes), and Magic (the cracking of the Japanese naval code) . . .

The list of intelligence triumphs and debacles is extensive, most of it hidden, much of it unsavory. Yet there is no assurance that the spotlight on the CIA, however necessary and appropriate, will improve U.S. intelligence o tions. Indeed, the consequences well be harmful for years to con

Be that as it may, it is notable some U.S. Navy officials had stron servations about the Jennifer o tion. The submarine to be salva they pointed out, was old, th "reconfigured"; they doubted much would be gained from bring up. They cited, too, the project's p tial for heightening tensions betw the superpowers and provoking a seas incident. They were relucta the circumstances to disturb the marine's grisly cargo.

These were sensible misgivings. difficult to shake a suspicion that ject Jennifer, like so much that W ington has undertaken, came into primarily because the U.S. had money and the resources and the whow to carry it off.

ROCKEFELLER COMMISSION ON CIA ISSUES REPORT, URGES 30 REFORMS

The Rockefeller Commission said in its final report, made public June 10, that the Central Intelligence Agency had engaged in activities that were "plainly unlawful and constituted improper invasions upon the rights of Americans." The report also said, however, that a "great majority" of the CIA's domestic activities during its 28-year history had been in compliance with its statutory authority.

According to the commission, an eight-member, blue-ribbon panel chaired by Vice President Nelson A. Rockefeller [see pp. 104–106], the CIA illegally opened mail to and from the Soviet Union and other countries at various times between 1952 and 1974; established in violation of its charter a super-secret Special Operations Group ("Operation Chaos") that amassed 13,000 files, 7,200 of them on dissident U.S. citizens, and compiled a computerized index of 300,000 individual names and organizations; infiltrated domestic political groups; and undertook 32 wiretaps, an equal number of room buggings and 12 break-ins, as well as the investigation of the tax records of 16 persons.

In its 299-page report, submitted to President Ford June 6, the commission made 30 recommendations to insure against recurrence of illegal or improper activites. These included strengthened Congressional and executive oversight, internal reorganization of the agency and more precise definition of what the agency should or should not do.

President Ford did not make public the section of the commission's report concerning assassination plots against foreign heads of state. Ford, who said he was withholding data on that subject because it was "incomplete and extremely sensitive," indicated he would forward the material to the Justice Department and to Congress for further investigation. The commission also reported finding "no credible evidence" of CIA involvement in the assassination of President John F. Kennedy.

The commission for the first time disclosed that President Nixon had made use of the CIA for purely political ends. Nixon sought and obtained from the agency, the report said, classified materials on the 1958 U.S. Marine landings in Lebanon, the 1962 Bay of Pigs invasion, the 1962 Cuban missile crisis and the 1963 assassination of South Vietnamese President Ngo Dinh Diem. The report said Nixon had told the CIA he needed the material to set the historical record straight, but concluded that the former president actually intended to use the data against political opponents. In addition, the commission discovered that in 1970 the CIA had, at the White House's request, contributed $38,655 to defray the cost of replying to persons who wrote to Nixon after the U.S. invasion of Cambodia.

Also uncovered, the report said, was a 1954 secret agreement between the Justice Department and the CIA, giving the CIA the right to decide whether to prosecute agency employes for criminal violations. The report, highly critical of the Justice Department because it had "abdicated its statutory duties," asserted that the agreement had directly involved the CIA in "forbidden law enforcement activities" in violation of the agency's 1947 charter. It found "no evidence" that the CIA abused these prosecutorial powers, the commission said, adding that the pact had been ended in January.

The New York Times

New York, N.Y., June 15, 1975

In the aftermath of Vietnam and Watergate, this nation's public institutions are being profoundly reexamined and reappraised. It is now the Central Intelligence Agency that is the focus of attention. The Rockefeller Commission's report released last week and the House and Senate investigations now under way make it certain that the inquiry will proceed for many months.

Although the revelations are disturbing, the fact that they are aired is reassuring and uniquely American. Other nations, even those that are free and self-governing, do not open wide so many closet doors of their foreign intelligence services. These controversies and investigations are a testament to the inherent vigor of this nation's freedom.

Under the chairmanship of Vice President Rockefeller, a panel composed mostly of former high-ranking Government officials has looked into the activities of the C.I.A. within the United States and submitted a notably candid and critical report. Some of the illegal excesses engaged in by the agency such as the interception of mail between this country and the Soviet Union and the occasional ventures into wiretapping and electronic "bugging" might have been guessed at. They cannot be condoned but their motivation is at least comprehensible, involving as it does potential foreign intelligence.

Much harder to understand was the willingness of the C.I.A. to delve into the activities of antiwar demonstrators, student radicals and dissident blacks. Since the law creating the C.I.A. clearly forbids the exercise of any "police, subpoena, or law-enforcement powers or internal security functions," Operation CHAOS—as the agency dubbed this venture—was wholly illegal from the outset.

The rationale pressed upon the agency first by President Johnson and even more insistently by President Nixon was to discover possible links between domestic dissidents and foreign, especially Communist, countries. Plausible though it was, this was unquestionably an assignment for the Federal Bureau of Investigation. The only acceptable role for the C.I.A. was to supply to the F.B.I. such information on the foreign relationships of domestic radicals as came to the attention of its overseas offices. Instead, the C.I.A. embarked in 1967 on an ambitious and steadily proliferating investigation of American citizens and organizations.

President Ford originally extended the life of the Rockefeller Commission by two months to permit it to investigate the C.I.A.'s alleged involvement in assassination plots against certain foreign leaders. For reasons that remain obscure, Mr. Ford abruptly suppressed this section of the Rockefeller report and handed the painfully embarrassing topic to the House and Senate committees to explore further.

The Rockefeller Commission urges strengthening the Foreign Intelligence Advisory Board and establishing in Congress a Joint Committee on Intelligence, a reform proposed by Senator Mansfield twenty years ago and supported then and since by this newspaper. The commission also proposes budgetary, auditing, and legal reforms that would make it easier for Congress and the President to control all aspects of the C.I.A.'s work. Essentially, however, the commission recommends naming good people to run the C.I.A. and then watching them closely.

Simplistic as this sounds, there is probably no better answer. Even in this era of détente, an alert intelligence-gathering agency is a necessary instrument in the making of foreign policy. If perilous world conditions compel a measure of secrecy and if the records of recent Presidents show that they cannot be trusted to prevent abuse of authority by the C.I.A., the circle of responsibility has to be widened to include a joint committee of Congress; and the C.I.A.'s internal checks and balances have to be strengthened. However, in a democracy as in all other forms of government, there is no foolproof system against human folly.

The Globe and Mail

Toronto, Ont., June 12, 1975

Illegal bugging and wiretaps, burglary, systematic interference with personal mail, preparation of dossiers on thousands of American citizens who had committed no crimes, dangerous drug experiments performed without the subject's knowledge or consent, protection against Justice Department prosecution for criminal activities—the findings of the Rockefeller Commission inquiry into the activities of the Central Intelligence Agency would, in any age but the jaded post-Watergate era, have come to public attention with shattering impact.

It is of course doubtful that any of this would have been brought to public attention had it not been for the impact of Watergate on the confidence of Americans in the integrity of their national institutions and establishments. Yet the numbing effect of the long series of revelations that preceded it is evident in the restrained manner in which The New York Times, the newspaper mainly responsible for the inquiry being made, reports its findings as an important story but far from an earth-shaking one. Revelations that government officials, or agencies, felt they were above the law, have become almost routine. That is how far the impact of the "third-rate burglary" has gone.

What the commission makes clear is that there was no ultimate line of authority to call the CIA to account for its activities. Not even the President of the United States had the effective power to get from the agency what he wanted or to have it do what he wanted done. Now that we know what we do of the presidency of Richard Nixon that may not seem altogether a bad thing. But what is bad, what is frightening, is the evidence that the CIA was a police force that was ultimately responsible to no one but itself—an autonomous police state within the state.

How autonomous it has been was demonstrated by the revelation that for 20 years, until January, 1975, the agency had a secret agreement with the Justice Department—allegedly unknown even to a series of Attorneys-General—that gave CIA agents and employees effective immunity to normal prosecution for criminal activities. It is small comfort that the commission concluded that this power had not been abused. What is frightening is that it existed, to be used at the discretion of an agency that enjoyed enormous latitude to ignore all rules but its own.

As the commission found "The CIA has not as a general rule received detailed scrutiny by the Congress." It does receive some limited supervision from the National Security Council, the Office of Management and Budget, and the President's Foreign Intelligence Advisory Board (of which Vice-President Nelson Rockefeller was himself a member for several years). But "none of these agencies has the specific responsibility of overseeing the CIA to determine whether its activities are proper." The Justice Department, the one body that did have a role of this kind, was neutralized by the covert agreement.

Such a permissive framework could hardly, by design, have been made more conducive to the perversion of a police agency, from the service of the public good to the pursuit of its own interests

as defined by itself. The CIA revelations are not an indictment of American society which—more than most societies—expects its public policies to be guided by moral ideals. It is a frightening warning of the folly of allowing any agency—and the more vital its role the greater the danger—to interpret for itself and by itself the laws and the national interest it is assigned to service.

The Chattanooga Times

Chattanooga, Tenn., June 13, 1975

The CIA's Blight . . .

Intelligence operations — spying is the blunter term — are a necessary adjunct to the normal, aboveboard gathering of information by a government that wants to survive in a world of open hostilities and suspected subversion.

What the Rockefeller Commission proves in a 300-page report on the Central Intelligence Agency is not that we have no need for it. The major point, which must not be lost, is that the agency departed from its legitimate role, evaded a clear mandate of authority, engaged in large scale illegal domestic operations, trespassed upon the rights of numberless citizens, and thus endangered needlessly its own credibility as a useful arm of a free society.

President Ford says he is certain the CIA can regain its place of acceptance. The proof of what he believes lies in the swiftness and certainty of corrective measures.

Blame for the CIA's fall is diffused. Over-financed and under-watched, it developed its own kind of arrogant power which feeds so greedily upon itself that corruption no longer is a taint.

From the outside, high officials, even presidents, pressured the agency to undertake programs clearly beyond the guidelines set by law. The cumulative effect of the repeated violations was to make the transgressions of the Nixon Administration appear more numerous and more despicable than any of the others. There can

be no excuse, however, for its predecessors who used the CIA for their own purposes if for varying ends. Orders wrongfully issued by one set of officials assume no rightfulness when they flow from another.

Finally, there was never a public demand for an honest accounting of the scope of the CIA's operations. The great majority of citizens did not know enough to complain; their elected representatives in Washington rarely like to rock the ship of state by prying into matters their superiors by seniority say are being tended.

The result is an ugly record of the compilation of secret files on nearly half a million Americans, mail openings, wiretapping, room bugging, secret drug testing, and infiltration of domestic political groups.

The question of the agency's possible participation in "destabilizing" certain foreign governments by the assassination of unfriendly heads of states has yet to be dealt with in congressional probes.

The truth is that, as a part of the trauma of Watergate, the country almost accidentally stumbled onto evidence of the growing deadliness of covert direction over American life, constantly strengthened by CIA-like operations.

They cannot be forgotten, forgiven, or allowed to persist, if we are to remain a free people.

. . . Suggested Cures . . .

The Rockefeller Commission has not condemned the CIA to an early death despite its feverish intrusions into forbidden areas of operation. Instead, there are 30 recommendations for corrective action by which the agency can hope to rebuild a solid base for public trust and official usefulness.

Some of the proposals are so simple as to seem unnecessary. The limitation of the agency to foreign intelligence operations, for instance, is to be explicitly spelled out, as is its authority to gather information in this country only from willing citizens. The idea is to strengthen by public confirmation the heretofore presumed restrictions on CIA activities.

Potentially the most powerful restraint on the agency is the proposed creation of a joint congressional committee to oversee the CIA's conduct of its assigned mission. This sort of watch-dog responsibility has rested in the Senate Armed Services Committee, but increasing both the scope of the congressional supervision and the weight given its evaluation would add greatly to the degree of public control.

A number of internal changes, de-

signed to sharpen the agency's own ability to judge its own performance, would be helpful from a standpoint of management. Limiting the director to a maximum of ten years' service dilutes the possibility of a clique being formed to keep the agency on any one given path.

Although it should not have to be spelled out, there is a recommendation that "presidents should refrain from directing the CIA to perform what are essentially internal security tasks."

None of the recommendations can undo what has been done (although one does suggest that all information gathered in one internal project should be destroyed if it has no foreign intelligence value) but they provide the framework for effective performance of what should have been the CIA's sole task all along.

There has to be the accompanying realization, of course, that no mere procedural changes will accomplish the desired reforms. The men who are granted the power of the CIA's secretive operations — and the men whose orders they follow — will be the determinative factors.

The Washington Post

Washington, D.C., June 11, 1975

THE VALUE of the Rockefeller commission report on the CIA is that it puts on record what appears at first reading to be a full and reliable account of the agency's "activities within the United States"—otherwise known as "illegal domestic spying." All previous accounts have been either journalistic and therefore impressionistic, or official and therefore suspect. This one had the twin advantages of being written with good access to official sources *and* with a saving awareness that congressional investigators would shortly be pounding down the same path. Not much of the serious detail is new but it becomes now more authentic for having been set in a comprehensive frame.

To those who believe that any CIA venture into improper or illegal domestic activity is permanently defiling, this report's listing of surveillance of domestic dissidents, mail intercepts and the like will confirm the conviction that the United States came close, and might again come close, to being devoured by the security apparatus it had devised to ward off external threat. Others will be appalled that a great nation's security agency had been subjected to this sort of humiliating and possibly crippling scrutiny at a moment when external dangers remain very great.

The Rockefeller commission's view, reflected both in its revelations and judgments of past acts and in its prescriptions for future policy, is quite different. The commission recognizes that national security and individual rights can tug in opposite directions. It makes plain that the CIA, sometimes in response to presidential pushing and sometimes out of its own carelessness or zeal, has time and again in the past engaged in improper or illegal conduct. The commission accepts, however, that the perceptions of external threat which guided the CIA in earlier years are no longer so relevant and that it has now become possible from a security viewpoint, just as it is necessary in relation to citizens' rights, to impose more effective oversight and stricter controls over the CIA.

So, far from being a "whitewash," the Rockefeller commission report is a clear summons to professionalism in intelligence and to respect for Americans' rights. This is the thrust of its several dozen recommendations, most of them calling for adjustments in legislation or in administrative or congressional procedure. While we are hardly prepared to endorse every single one of them, we do endorse the positive and mature way in which the commission went about its work.

President Ford's decision to keep secret the commission's uncompleted study of allegations of foreign assassinations, and to pass those materials on to congressional investigators, is reasonable. Mr. Rockefeller did him no favor by his clumsy juggling of the assassination materials over the weekend. But the important consideration is that the allegations are rigorously pursued. The Rockefeller commission's original mission did not include an investigation of alleged assassination plots; that was an afterthought. For that Commission to release its "incomplete" study of the matter now would risk raising more questions that it would answer. It now falls to the select Senate committee on the CIA to run down the allegations as far as possible. Just how far that may be we are not prepared to say. Any president who may have contemplated the murder of a foreign leader would no doubt have taken pains to keep his own fingerprints off the enterprise. The assassination story inquiry needs more time. The public has the Rockefeller Commission's report to consider while it waits.

LEDGER-STAR

Norfolk, Va., June 12, 1975

The Rockefeller Commission's report on abuses within the Central Intelligence Agency does not make a pretty picture. Even if it is acknowledged that the CIA is legitimately an undercover operation, some of the activities which have been revealed will be difficult for most Americans to accept.

But if the findings and the conclusions in the 300-page package are ultimately to benefit the national interest, then the basic, chartered function of the CIA must be acknowledged and respected. For the danger in the continuous, critical scrutiny we are witnessing in the U.S. today is that proper, vital intelligence-gathering capacity will be destroyed with inevitable damage to the United States' security.

So, first off, any response to the Rockefeller Commission disclosures ought to concede not only the CIA's right to exist but its need to exist. If this basic premise can be agreed and held to, then perhaps appropriate safeguards against excesses and abuses can emerge while leaving the function itself intact.

The temptation to go beyond these sensible bounds will be large indeed. For one thing, many people who quite properly will be outraged by specific events—illegal events—which occurred can easily lose sight of the legitimate CIA functions. For another, these same unfortunate and in some cases inexcusable activities can offer the politician just too easy a target not to take potshots. For still another, many Americans, including some in the Congress, remain naive about today's international challenges and dangers.

★ ★ ★ ★

Cooler heads, however, should prevail. Just prior to the release of the report, President Ford commented at some length on his own views and also tried to establish the national atmosphere in which he thought the commission findings ought to be received. He helped greatly to encourage national calm in assessing both what has gone on before that was wrong and what ought to be done to prevent recurrences.

Assuming that in general the Rockefeller Commission recommendations are followed, the CIA will not in the future have the free rein it has held since its inception after World War II. And, of course, some of the things which have occurred under that free rein suggest plainly that greater conventional oversight by government is not only appropriate, but necessary. Hence the commission has contributed toward a balance between intelligence-gathering and civil rights by suggesting both congressional and White House apparatus for keeping tabs on the agency.

★ ★ ★ ★

The commission has made helpful suggestions, too, to remove ambiguities. It would have the law state explicitly what the CIA can do and what it cannot. Numerous other specific proposals also were included as the commission sought to provide solutions to the defects which it uncovered or confirmed.

The published report is an outgrowth of the commission's initial charge to look into domestic spying. The allegations of plots to assassinate foreign leaders are not treated, this sensitive material being turned over to others in government for further study and possible action.

In this regard especially, public judgment ought to await a fuller accounting. There must be distinctions made between the suggestion or the consideration of such a plan and an order to carry one out. But here, too, the central requirement is for the kind of safeguards that will prevent this sort of thing, not the dismantling of effective intelligence-gathering.

The Rockefeller Commission has been able to take exhaustive evidence and frame wide-ranging recommendations without indicting or opposing the basic mission of the Central Intelligence Agency. If the American people and their representatives in the Congress can maintain a like balance of thought, then there should be little question that protection of Americans from domestic spying can be achieved without destroying that larger protection which depends on our foreign spying.

NEW ORLEANS STATES-ITEM

New Orleans, La., June 12, 1975

The Rockefeller Commission's report on what it describes as "plainly unlawful" domestic activities of the Central Intelligence Agency (CIA) emphasizes the need for closer congressional supervision of the agency.

It is obvious from the report, and from earlier disclosures, that Congress, which was assigned this responsibility, has acted more like a CIA auxiliary than a deterrent against irresponsible behavior.

The commission has recommended the creation of a joint congressional committee to oversee all CIA operations. Such a committee would presumably prevent the kind of inexcusable violence to individual constitutional rights perpetrated against U.S. citizens by the agency in the past.

The function of the CIA is information gathering for purposes of national security. It is in the business of spying. Americans should not be shocked that spying sometimes calls for unorthodox methods.

They should be shocked, and rightfully so, by the CIA's penchant for breaking the law at the expense of their constitutional rights.

The CIA, by its charter, is barred from internal security functions.

Yet the agency conducted a "clearly illegal" (the commission's words) program to test the influence of drugs on humans, resulting in one death.

The CIA infiltrated the campaign of a congressional candidate in the 1970s and contributed its own funds to Richard Nixon's White House to pay postage costs for replies to persons who wrote letters following the invasion of Cambodia. The agency opened domestic mail and collected information for dossiers on Americans whose political views did not coincide with those of the government.

Much of what the commission made public Tuesday, including the possible existence of plots to assassinate foreign leaders, is not new.

What is new is an apparent determination by all branches of government to see that the contempt for the rights of American citizens, so prevalent in government during the past decade, gives way to fairness and reason.

Wisconsin ▲ State Journal

Madison, Wisc., June 13, 1975

The Rockefeller Commission recommendations to curb abuses by the Central Intelligence Agency are valid but the ultimate answer is selection of Presidents and top officials who believe in the Bill of Rights.

It is shocking that the commission placed much of the blame for the CIA's illegal domestic spying on Presidents Johnson and Nixon, stating they and their staffs made "continuing and insistent requests of the CIA for detailed evaluation of possible foreign involvement in the domestic dissident scene."

The commission said the CIA's repeated conclusion that it could find "no significant foreign connection" led only to further White House demands for continued investigation known as "Operation Chaos."

It led to the CIA developing files on some 300,000 persons and groups suspected of varying degrees of dissent against U.S. foreign policy, a much higher figure than revealed by The New York Times in breaking open the case last fall.

The domestic spying—expressly forbidden in the CIA charter—involved telephone taps, surreptitious opening of mail and infiltration of anti-war groups.

It is difficult for any governmental agency to resist presidential pressure, particularly so for one so hidden from public view as the CIA.

Unfortunately, an intelligence apparatus is

a necessity in an imperfect world. The CIA was created with public support in 1947 to avoid another intelligence lapse such as the one that made possible the surprise attack on Pearl Harbor.

Intelligence activities and reports cannot be effective unless hidden from the public view. Too much secrecy, however, led to twisted activities that subverted American principles at home.

What now?

The Rockefeller Commission has recommended a permanent watchdog panel in the executive branch and a joint congressional oversight committee to keep the CIA from abusing its authority.

It also was recommended that Congress should consider revealing the CIA budget, now hidden in a variety of appropriation bills.

It will take more than that.

Once again the value of a free and aggressive press is underscored. The CIA abuses, as were the Watergate scandals, were disclosed in large part by newspaper reports.

Finally, it takes election of people of character and integrity in the highest elective offices of this nation if the principles of individual freedom upon which this nation was founded are to remain secure. The kind of arrogance demonstrated by Johnson and Nixon no longer can be tolerated.

Rocky Mountain News

Denver, Colo., June 12, 1975

THE ROCKEFELLER Commission's 299-page report clearly demonstrates the need for more independent leadership and tighter supervision of the Central Intelligence Agency (CIA).

The commission found numerous instances over the past 20 years in which the CIA violated its own charter by gathering domestic (rather than foreign) intelligence and by engaging in mail-opening, wiretapping and other shady activities in violation of federal law.

"Some of these activities were initiated or ordered by presidents," the report said. "Some of them were plainly unlawful and constituted improper invasions upon the rights of Americans."

It's true that fear and suspicion of communism in the early 1950s and violent war protests in the late 1960s created a climate in which tough security tactics were condoned.

BUT THE CIA was set up in 1947 primarily to conduct foreign intelligence activities—not to meddle in internal security matters which supposedly were to be left to the FBI.

To prevent future abuse of authority, the Rockefeller Commission rightly recommends that a joint committee of Congress be formed to monitor CIA activities, that all or parts of the CIA budget be made public and that no director should serve for more than 10 years.

Among the excesses uncovered by the commission were a 20-year period in which private mail was opened by the CIA in direct violation of federal law, files were compiled on 7,200 Americans and index cards were kept on 300,000 individuals and organizations.

Overall, while more charitable to the CIA than some other investigative commissions might have been, the Rockefeller group came up with a report that in no way can be considered a "whitewash." It found plenty wrong with CIA activities in recent years and was especially critical of former President Nixon for attempting to use the CIA and its secret files for "personal political ends."

The assessment will be incomplete, however, until full disclosure is made of the CIA's alleged involvement in assassinations of foreign political leaders. President Ford, who says he's "totally opposed" to assassinations, has turned over the evidence collected by the Rockefeller Commission to the Justice Department (for possible prosecution) and to congressional committees now studying the CIA.

Sen. Frank Church, D-Idaho, says his committee will make all the facts public — a promise we hope he sticks to regardless of which political party may be embarrassed.

The purpose of all this probing and soul-searching should not be to destroy the CIA, but to mold it into a sounder organization. Presidents and responsible members of Congress are — or should be — well aware that espionage and counterespionage are absolutely essential to the survival of the United States.

The basic need, as the Rockefeller Commission aptly points out, is to maintain an effective intelligence system without sacrificing the freedom or privacy of individual citizens along the way.

St. Louis Globe-Democrat
St. Louis, Mo., June 12, 1975

To put the charges against the CIA in proper focus, it must be appreciated there has been no procession of individuals claiming they have suffered from any of the alleged "crimes" committed in the name of national security.

If, for example, someone's mail was opened by the CIA without the individual's knowledge 10 years ago, and no action followed, how can the "victim" prove he was harmed?

Short of any truly grievous violation of an individual's civil rights, the security of the nation must outweigh other considerations.

It is preposterous to lump all the excesses and indiscretions of the CIA together as "crimes" without distinction. In the normal course of events a violation of the law can range from a parking ticket to mass murder.

To call every mistaken deed by the CIA a "crime" is to overstate the situation to the point of absurdity.

Americans whose lives have been made safer in the course of the occasional CIA blunder or intrusion are not likely to complain about the invasion of privacy.

SEN. WILLIAM PROXMIRE, Wisconsin Democrat who in many ways distinguishes himself as the thinking man's liberal, gave a fair appraisal of the Rockefeller Commission's report. "This is not a whitewash. . . it's a better report than I thought it would be," Proxmire commented.

More significantly, Proxmire called the report's recommendations for the prevention of abuses "excellent." And he emphasized that CIA secrecy must be maintained for its rightful mission.

Secrecy is at the very heart of intelligence gathering. That is why it is wise and sound to separate the domestic doings from the rumors of conspiracies involving alleged foreign assassination plots.

Sen. John G. Tower, vice chairman of the Senate intelligence committee, correctly praised President Ford for not allowing the report to contain information on any CIA involvement in alleged assassination attempts.

"There is a lot of highly sensitive material there," Tower said. "There isn't any evidence that any assassination plots were successful."

The key word in Tower's appraisal is "evidence." Now is not the time for a rash of unsubstantiated, wild tales about fanciful murder plots that never occurred.

THE REAL SUBSTANCE of the Rockefeller report is its finding that "the great majority of the CIA's domestic activities comply with its statutory authority," the National Security Act of 1947.

Moreover, the commission makes proper distinctions on domestic intelligence operations:

"The commission finds that whether agency domestic activity is prohibited depends principally on the purpose for which it is conducted. If the principal purpose of the activity is the prosecution of crimes or protection against civil disorders or domestic insurrection, then the activity is prohibited. On the other hand, if the principal purpose relates to foreign intelligence or to protection of the security of the agency, then activity is permissible, within limits, even though it might also be performed by a law enforcement agency."

Thus the Rockefeller Commission disabused critics of the notion that the CIA's maintenance of files which contain the names of thousands of individuals and organizations is in itself a violation of laws prohibiting the agency's involvement in domestic spying.

"The test is always the purpose for which the files were accumulated and the use made of them thereafter," the commission observed.

While recommending that the President should, by executive order, generally prohibit the CIA from collecting information about domestic activities of citizens, the commission again made important exceptions.

The prohibition, the report said, need not apply to:

√"Persons or activities that pose a clear threat to CIA facilities or personnel;

√"Persons suspected of espionage or other illegal activities relating to foreign intelligence;

√"Information which is received incidental to appropriate CIA activities;

√"Investigations of persons presently or formerly affiliated, or being considered for affiliation, with the CIA, directly or indirectly."

In general the Rockefeller report should satisfy reasonable people. It is neither a whitewash nor a witch hunt license.

The greatest mistake Congress could make in pursuing its own investigations would be overkill.

DAILY NEWS
New York, N.Y., June 11, 1975

The supposedly mountainous "domestic surveillance" program which some media folk and politicians ascribed to the Central Intelligence Agency turns out to have been overblown considerably in the telling.

That is the conclusion drawn by the presidential commission which delved into the allegations. And it has facts and figures to back its assessment.

The CIA does not emerge with a clear bill of health. The probers headed by Vice President Nelson Rockefeller found that the cloak-and-dagger boys did indulge in some illegal or dubious capers.

Sen. Church

But their transgressions—such as bugging, wire-tapping, and opening letters—hardly were on a massive scale.

A number of the illicit or questionable activities occurred many years ago and have long since been discontinued.

Nonetheless, Rockefeller & Co. did recommend some reforms—in the shape of new legislation, executive orders or administrative improvements — to better define the agency's area of operations and see that it sticks to it.

But it also emphasized—as President Gerald R. Ford did in his Monday night press conference—that the CIA remains a vital organ in the nation's defense, and that it must have sufficient scope and freedom from prying eyes to permit it to carry out its function effectively. Let's never lose sight of that overriding necessity. As for the—

'MURDER PLOT' CHARGES

that have been flung at the CIA, the Rockefeller commission looked into them, but its investigation was incomplete and inconclusive. At Mr. Ford's direction, the material it gathered will be given to the Justice Department and two Congressional committees, including the Senate group headed by Frank Church (D-Idaho).

Exactly where that trail will lead, or what will develop, no one can safely predict at this time.

In the circumstances, most Americans would be well advised to heed another bit of advice Mr. Ford gave: Don't leap to conclusions or make hasty judgments on the basis of rumors, leaks and speculation.

BUFFALO EVENING NEWS
Buffalo, N.Y., June 12, 1975

"The preservation of the United States requires an effective intelligence capability, but the preservation of individual liberties within the United States requires limitations on gatherings of intelligence. The drawing of reasonable lines . . . is difficult."
—Rockefeller Commission Report on CIA.

Those CIA critics who feared a whitewash when President Ford appointed the Rockefeller Commission early last winter have been proved wrong. In its final report to the President, the commission has unsparingly documented instances of serious abuse by the Central Intelligence Agency in what should be the forbidden area of domestic spying on Americans. It plainly defined the major difficulty to be resolved, and recommended constructive steps to prevent future abuses.

Part of the commission's assigned task was to determine with certainty whether the CIA, created in 1947 to fulfill functions related to foreign intelligence, had exceeded its statutory authority with respect to domestic spying.

The Rockefeller panel's answer is yes.

* * *

However one wishes to characterize the degree of CIA meddling, the report dispels any doubt that certain activities did occur repeatedly and were "plainly unlawful." From 1952 to 1973 the CIA unlawfully opened and observed mail. It monitored long-distance phone calls and illegally collected data on dissident Americans by the thousands between 1967 and 1973. It conducted experiments with drugs on unsuspecting subjects before 1963. It infiltrated one campaign for Congress.

Some of these activities, the commission said, "were initiated or ordered by presidents, either directly or indirectly." Improper pressures especially took place in the Johnson and Nixon administrations during the crest of the anti-war protests at home.

Without in any way minimizing the irresponsibility of these two presidents, this defines a classic example of extremist excesses triggering extremist responses.

In any event, those are the facts laid out by the commission in posing the delicate problem cited by the commission in the italic paragraph quoted above. The drawing of reasonable lines, between preserving an effective intelligence capability in today's world and preserving the individual liberties of American citizens, is indeed difficult. But it is certainly not impossible, and that remains the urgent task of the Congress and the Ford administration.

* * *

In line with that responsibility, the two most fundamental recommendations of the commission are: (1) that the federal statute governing the CIA should be amended to "explicitly" limit its operations to foreign intelligence matters so there will be no inviting ambiguities; and (2) that a Joint Congressional Committee be established to monitor the CIA in order to consistently assure that it functions only within its assigned sphere of legitimate duties.

Just as the Rockefeller report makes clear that presidents have misused the agency, and that the agency has exceeded its statutory authority, so it also by implication shows that the oversight function supposedly exercised in the past by Congress has been perilously inadequate and demands major reform.

The commission includes other sound recommendations, such as destroying the illegally collected data about Americans once all the pending probes by Congress end, limiting the tenure of any CIA director to 10 years, and looking outside as well as inside the agency when considering new directors.

But the clarification of function and strengthened supervision by Congress, as well as future administrations, deserve priority now. It is imperative that the United States find an effective arrangement that balances our values as a free and open society protecting citizen liberties with the important, continuing need for viable intelligence operations in a dangerous world. First and foremost, those demands must involve precise definitions of bureaucratic roles with responsibilities pinpointed to elected officials assigned to supervise those functions and accountable to the public.

The Salt Lake Tribune

Salt Lake City, Utah, June 4, 1975

To those people who "saw" an agent of the Central Intelligence Agency behind every bush in the United States, the Rockefeller Commission's report is going to be a bitter disappointment. The eight-member commission, headed by Vice President Nelson A. Rockefeller, has found no widespread pattern of illegal activity by the CIA.

In a press conference Monday, Mr. Rockefeller told reporters, "There are things that have been done which are in contradiction to the statutes, but in comparison to the total effect they are not major." He said the agency was guilty of some illegal acts, but there was no evidence to support contentions of large-scale domestic spying by the agency, a practice clearly prohibited to the CIA by law.

The vice president in response to a question as to whether the report supported claims there had been "massive" instances of CIA domestic spying said he could not agree with the use of massive, but "that does not mean there haven't been things done that were wrong."

Despite Mr. Rockefeller's enthusiasm for and confidence in the report, his assessment of its contents does nothing to diminish a need for closer surveillance of the nation's top intelligence gathering agency, along with the rest of the intelligence community.

The American public can find reassurance in the Rockefeller Commission report, in the fact that those running the clandestine agency have, at least to date, been reasonably scrupulous in observing the letter and intent of the statutory restrictions placed on the CIA. Nevertheless, there have been enough violations, albeit they were "not major," to justify establishing some non-agency surveillance mechanism. And it must be a process by which the inspectors are not likely to become the apologists and handmaidens of the CIA, or any other agencies of the intelligence community in the armed services or civilian branches of government.

The congressional oversight committees, which for the most part were just as secretive as the agency they were overseeing, have been little more than rubber stamp operators. So often, it is apparent, what the CIA wanted the CIA got, with the clear and unquestioned approval of the scant dozen or so members of Congress privy to the request.

An intelligence agency must, by the very nature of the work assigned it, do much in the dark, nevertheless it is as true as when John Philpot Curran said it in 1790, the price of liberty remains eternal vigilance. And without some public and continued scrutiny of the CIA liberty in America runs a grave risk of being short-changed.

ST. LOUIS POST-DISPATCH

St. Louis, Mo., June 11, 1975

The Rockefeller Commission's report on the Central Intelligence Agency is not the whitewash that might have been expected from its establishment composition and preliminary statements. It is, instead, a strong indictment of many CIA actions that makes the conclusion that most CIA activities were legal seem almost irrelevant. Yet, largely because of the nature of its charter and circumscriptions by President Ford, the commission report may touch only on the periphery of what is wrong with the CIA.

Mr. Ford ordered the commission to report only on domestic misdeeds. Of these the commission lists hundreds, many of them discovered earlier by the press but some new and shocking. The CIA did keep secret files on thousands of Americans and a computer index on 300,000 other citizens and groups. It did in one year open some 8700 pieces of mail. It did engage in scores of wire taps and electronic eavesdropping, it did commit 12 burglaries and did obtain federal income tax returns. And all of these endeavors broke the law.

The CIA also tried to serve the Johnson and Nixon Administrations through "Operation Chaos," which became massive espionage against the political activities of citizens, particularly antiwar dissidents. That operation failed totally to prove that the antiwar movement had foreign sources, but it violated the CIA's charter and was an outrage against the First Amendment.

Then the CIA was used or misused by the Nixon Administration for its own political purposes in the Watergate and Ellsberg cases and others, as is well known, but in many of these matters the agency itself was ignorant of its own abuse.

The bill of particulars against the CIA on the domestic scene is enough to justify the Rockefeller Commission's recommendations for putting such an agency on a tighter leash. Many of these deal with internal reforms, which would let the agency control itself. One would strengthen the President's Foreign Intelligence Advisory Board whose supervision of the CIA has so far been wanting.

Three proposals, however, go closer to the heart of the problem. One is to create a joint congressional committee on intelligence to perform the kind of strict oversight of the CIA that Congress has not performed. Another is to make the CIA's budget public "at least to some extent." Why only to an extent? The Constitution requires that a regular account of all federal expenditures be published.

Then there is the recommendation for rewriting the National Security Act of 1947 which created the CIA to state explicitly that the agency's activities "must be related to foreign intelligence." The 1947 law is supposed to say that, but it should be said again, and not only to keep the CIA's hands off domestic affairs.

At its inception the agency was never intended to indulge in the kind of dirty tricks abroad that start wars, subvert governments and even contemplate assassinations — a part of the Rockefeller Commission report that Mr. Ford is not making public. Do the American people really want the agency to operate in a way that violates the nation's principles and corrupts its foreign policy?

If the immorality of such operations is not enough, if it is not yet sufficient to question the Cold War assumption that the ends justify the means, then it still may be asked whether the means do not become the ends, and whether they do not in the end promote the distortion of the CIA's basic purpose, which is intelligence-gathering. And that purpose has become far more important in a technological world.

Since the Rockefeller Commission was not told to ask such questions and was probably ill-prepared to answer them, they remain for Congress and particularly Senator Church's committee, to which the President fortunately has referred secret commission findings.

What the CIA requires is a more thorough and broader inspection now, and in the future a continuing and intensive review of its operations by a responsible joint committee. The CIA needs that for its own efficiency and protection from executive misrule, and the public needs it for its protection from the CIA. The American people must regain control over an agency created to serve them.

Los Angeles Times

Los Angeles, Calif., June 12, 1975

The Rockefeller commission report is a remarkable document in the studied restraint of its revelations about the Central Intelligence Agency. Because of this, it is, in fact, doubly convincing.

What comes through the low-keyed, measured report is the CIA's record of widespread illegal domestic activities that violated the constitutional rights of American citizens for many years.

The report raises a central problem of democracy in a dangerous world, a problem easily stated but difficult to resolve: How can a democracy manage a large intelligence agency, which must operate in secret but which also must be kept under sufficient control so that it does not become a threat to the liberties of a nation it was established to protect?

The commission found that "the great majority of the CIA's domestic activities comply with its statutory authority," the National Security Act of 1947. This pronouncement is not as reassuring as it was intended to be; the same can be said about all departments of government. The danger lies in the exceptions and their significance.

In connection with the CIA, the exceptions were numerous and significant.

From the most casual reading of the report, it becomes obvious that the CIA must be brought under more effective control. The commission proposes a 10-year limit on the term of the CIA director, Senate confirmation of the director and his principal assistants, and a joint committee of Congress to supervise the agency.

Yet, though these and other reforms are necessary, a restructuring of the agency will not supply two final and essential elements: the character of the director of the CIA, and the integrity of his subordinates. Indeed, the problem goes even further—to the character of the President of the United States, and the resolve of the American people to maintain democratic government.

It is especially significant that two Presidents, Lyndon B. Johnson and Richard M. Nixon, both well aware of the legal limits of the CIA, brought undue and heavy pressure on the agency to gather improper intelligence on American citizens.

Democratic institutions, structured to prevent the misuse of great power, are of fundamental importance, but they must be infused from the leadership down with a democratic spirit. If that is lacking, we have only the form of democratic government, not its substance.

The Oregonian

Portland, Ore., June 12, 1975

The Rockefeller Commission report on the Central Intelligence Agency is a beginning toward the goal of bringing the CIA under responsible federal controls. The commission concluded that "the great majority of the CIA's domestic activities comply with its statutory authority." But this is not good enough. There is a variety of revelations that the agency illegally and wrongly used its privileged position in violation of the privacy of U. S. citizens.

The Department of Justice should deal with those aspects of the report in which there are questions of violation of the law. Congress should undertake amendment of the statutes governing the operation of the CIA to ensure that forbidden activities are specified and penalties defined. There is a need for a tighter oversight arrangement, both in the Congress and in the executive branch of the government.

A Senate committee has been holding secret sessions in an independent investigation of the CIA. A House subcommittee is preparing to launch a similar scrutiny of the agency. The commission's recommendation that Congress create a joint oversight committee is for the long range. The current investigative committees should be allowed to complete their work, so that the Congress will have the information on which to base amendments to statutes governing CIA operations.

The commission's 299-page report includes a distillation of testimony of more than 50 witnesses filling almost 3,000 pages of the record of the hearings. It relates such CIA transgressions as illegal wire taps and opening of mail, surveillance of private citizens somewhat indiscriminately classed as "dissidents," and drug experiments on unsuspecting persons resulting in one suicide. But the report leaves plenty of questions to be answered by other investigations.

The commission deliberately withheld such information as it uncovered about alleged CIA involvement in assassination plots against foreign political leaders. It explained that it did not have enough time to complete this aspect of the investigation. It is a question that must have responsible answers eventually. Left as a rumor it could grow out of proportion to its real importance.

The commission performed a useful and timely service in supporting the findings of the Warren Commission in the matter of the assassination of President John F. Kennedy. It impaneled a team of doctors and scientists who were unanimous in the view that Kennedy was struck by only two bullets, both fired from the rear in the direction of the individual charged with the assault, Lee Harvey Oswald.

Investigations of the CIA must be undertaken in a manner that will not permanently harm the agency. A sophisticated intelligence agency is essential in today's world. But there must be safeguards better than the ones heretofore employed to ensure that the agency does not violate the rights of those it is supposed to protect against dangers from abroad.

WORCESTER TELEGRAM.

Worcester, Mass., June 12, 1975

It is going to be difficult for Americans to keep a proper perspective on the CIA and the function of intelligence agencies in general.

The Rockefeller Commission Report has uncovered a deplorable series of illegal wiretaps, buggings and burglaries committed by the CIA from 1965 to 1971. It has concluded that the CIA illegally gathered files on 3,000 American citizens, and that these files were fed into computers. As many as 300,000 names may be on file. Further, the Rockefeller Commission has found that the CIA for years illegally opened mail from and to American citizens. Finally, the commission says that the CIA knuckled under to White House pressure and allowed itself and its records to be misused for domestic political purposes, which is as far from its legal responsibilities as anything that can be imagined.

This makes for scary reading. The thought of a secret and powerful spy agency acting on its own without proper controls is disturbing to any democracy. These violations must be rectified, as the commission points out.

But it will be well if the public reads all of the Rockefeller commission comments and recommendations and not just those that deal with the CIA's transgressions. For all its faults and misadventures, the CIA or something like it is a necessity in the real world. It has, in general, performed well, and the American people owe it a great deal. Without a top-flight intelligence gathering agency, we would be naked in a world of dangerous wolves.

To take one point made by the report: Communist bloc intelligence forces are thought to number over 500,000 worldwide. "The number of Communist government officials in the United States has tripled since 1960 and is still increasing. Nearly 2,000 of them are in this country — and a significant percentage of them have been identified as members of intelligence or security agencies."

The commission says that thousands of private American telephones are probably tapped by foreign governments. "This raises the real specter that selected American users of telephones are potentially subject to blackmail that can seriously affect their actions, or even lead in some cases to recruitment as espionage agents."

That is the other side of the picture. It is essential that it not be lost sight of. In getting rid of the abuses that have been found by the Rockefeller Commission, we must not cripple this nation's ability to find out what is going on. The commission's recommendations — particularly for tighter supervision of the CIA by a special executive agency — makes a lot of sense. The Senate select panel looking into the assassination rumors may come up with more findings and suggestions.

But Americans cannot indulge themselves in the wishful thought that they don't need an intelligence agency in an era of "detente" or that it need not operate in secret. The main danger to the American people comes not from the CIA but from those powers that are fundamentally hostile to all we stand for.

The Des Moines Register

Des Moines, Iowa, June 12, 1975

The American people have long needed the kind of review and analysis of the Central Intelligence Agency which the Rockefeller commission has now delivered. The CIA was formed in the panicky atmosphere of the cold war and the early days of nuclear weapons. Congress and the public were so fearful of Communists and spies they were inclined to give free rein to anti-subversive and counter-spy and political and military intelligence activity.

CIA had little real surveillance from presidents who were themselves caught up in the national paranoia. Indeed, many abuses committed by CIA against the rights of U.S. citizens and in violation of its charter were instigated by presidents, especially Johnson and Nixon.

The commission recommends stronger oversight by means of a new executive branch agency and the President's Foreign Intelligence Advisory Board. It also proposes a new joint congressional committee, similar to the Atomic Energy Committee, to assume the oversight role instead of the armed services committees. The commission also suggests that Congress consider whether the CIA budget "at least to some extent" should be made public.

These are good proposals. But the excesses of the past brought out by the commission make us wonder whether tighter oversight is enough. The secrecy passion is intense in all branches of government, and, in any agency whose business is secrecy, it is especially difficult to achieve public control.

We conclude, therefore, that the secret functions of intelligence and counter-intelligence must be kept to a minimum in a free society. This means slashing the budget for such work in CIA and in the other (military) intelligence agencies. It would require careful oversight of the Defense Department budget, as well as CIA, to find out whether funds were being diverted from other purposes to spy work.

CIA often states that most of its intelligence gathering is overt, that is, review of foreign publications, interviewing travelers, studying foreign military and scientific reports, etc. Why not break down the intelligence function, then, into an open agency doing such things and another, much smaller, secret agency?

The centralization of intelligence in 1947 was thought to be vital to national security. One result, however, has been to place a large part of the federal government out of reach of the citizens. The overt part of CIA is hidden from the public and from public control by its connection with the secret part.

We learn from the Rockefeller report what has been widely suspected, that CIA was working with the FBI in spying on the American people — opening mail (illegally), keeping files on thousands of U.S. citizens suspected of dissenting activities, carrying out assignments from presidents that were essentially political.

The commission recommends that such files be destroyed. It recommends that CIA quit taking part in domestic police operations and work out a detailed agreement with FBI on their separate jurisdictions and for sharing information on matters of mutual concern.

All this, if followed up, may help. But Congress ought not to stop with CIA. We recall that the Army also kept dossiers on American citizens thought to be engaged in anti-war activities. The last we heard those files still had not been destroyed, though that was ordered.

In order to protect Americans against police-state abuses by over-paid and under-supervised intelligence agencies, Congress needs to examine the military, FBI and other secret organizations.

The Rockefeller investigation of foreign CIA activity was confined to political assassinations. The facts uncovered in this probe are to be turned over to congressional committees. Ultimately, we assume, the public will be given the full story.

Congress is obligated to carry this study further. CIA has been doing lots of things overseas besides engineering assassinations, we assume. These activities need to be reviewed, both the covert and overt functions.

There is ground for suspicion that CIA actions have had major impact on the nation's foreign policy, including almost getting the country into war — this by an agency which has been "going it alone" with a secret budget.

The Rockefeller report is only a beginning.

Minneapolis **Tribune**

Minneapolis, Minn., June 12, 1975

Unlike many government studies, the Rockefeller Commission report on CIA activities in the United States makes good reading. It addresses, philosophically but succinctly, the issue of what role an intelligence agency plays in a free society and affirms that "the individual liberties of American citizens depend on government observance of the law." It describes the ways in which the CIA failed to do so; while concluding that the "great majority" of the agency's activities were legitimate, the report points to a number "that should be criticized and not be permitted to happen again." To that end, it offers recommendations for improving the agency's internal controls and external supervision.

In one respect the report stopped short—whether by White House directive or the commission's own decision is not clear. An 80-page summary of an investigation into allegations of CIA involvement in assassination attempts was not made public because, President Ford said Monday night, it is "incomplete and involves extremely sensitive matters." But that material, along with other data from White House files, is being sent to the Justice Department and to congressional committees conducting their own investigations. The argument about whether that information should have been made public is interesting, but not central; the issue isn't being dropped and is already one focus of the congressional inquiries.

More to the point now, we believe, is what the Rockefeller Commission report discloses and what use can be made of it.

News accounts of last year are shown to have been essentially accurate in portraying large-scale, illegal domestic spying by an agency charged with foreign intelligence-gathering. That was only one category of activity described by the report as plainly unlawful or in a doubtful area.

There were mail intercepts, in clear violation of federal statutes. There was a bizarre program of drug testing on unknowing individuals during the Eisenhower and Kennedy administrations. Infiltration of dissident domestic groups began under the Johnson administration and grew during the Nixon administration. For two decades the CIA, through an ostensibly private firm, provided training for foreign police under an Agency for International Development program. That was technically legal; but the firm's sale of firearms to foreign trainees was, according to the commission report, an activity that should not be repeated. There was complicity in pettiness—for example, the use of $33,000 in secret CIA funds for White House replies to citizens who wrote to President Nixon after the invasion of Cambodia. And the list of wrong or questionable practices goes on.

But disclosure for its own sake would be sterile, and the Rockefeller Commission was demonstrably aware of that. Throughout the report, findings of improper activities are a c c o m p a n i e d by thoughtful suggestions on how to prevent their recurrence while preserving an effective intelligence apparatus.

Among the report's noteworthy recommendations are these:

The agency's governing directives, statutory and administrative, need clarification, with emphasis on its foreign-intelligence responsibility. There should be less isolation of functions within the CIA (by increasing "lateral movement" of employees among CIA departments) and less isolation of the agency itself (by bringing in outside specialists at all levels). Consideration should be given to making the CIA budget public. A single channel for White House directives to the agency is necessary. A new executive body to oversee the agency should be established, and the present civilian advisory board should be greatly strengthened, with "access to all information in the CIA." Congres-

sional supervision, which by all accounts has been desultory in the past, should be invigorated by a joint committee established for that purpose.

Although we might question some of the details in those recommendations, their main theme makes eminent good sense and dismisses any question that the generally conservative commission was engaged in a whitewash. The CIA has not suffered from a lack of zeal, but from a lack of the checks and balances essential to a democratic society. In its report, the commission has made careful suggestions on how to redress the balance and restore the checks on one powerful agency. The congressional investigations will undoubtedly produce proposals that are different in specific aspects, but not, we hope, in purpose—to prevent abuses while maintaining a strong national intelligence establishment.

The Detroit News

Detroit, Mich., June 12, 1975

The Rockefeller Commission's report confirms charges that the Central Intelligence Agency has been guilty of violating the law and invading the civil rights of many American citizens.

The list of such violations is long and shocking, even though President Ford withheld the commission's findings on possible CIA assassination plots against foreign leaders.

Fortunately, most if not all of the violations already have been stopped. That is no guarantee some will not be resumed in the future but publicizing the nature of the illegal acts ought to make it possible to draft new controls to prevent any repetition without seriously damaging the CIA.

The CIA's designated major function is foreign intelligence gathering but it also is empowered to conduct some domestic activities in support of its foreign intelligence mission. This is where it most frequently went astray. But it often exceeded its legal authority for domestic operations on direct orders of the president of the United States.

Thus in 1967, on President Johnson's order, the CIA set up a Special Operations Group within the CIA to collect, coordinate, evaluate and report on the extent of foreign influence on domestic dissidents.

But the CIA group—whose activities later were dubbed Operation CHAOS—obviously went beyond that broad purpose when it compiled 13,000 files, which with the related materials contained the names of more than 300,-000 U.S. citizens.

The trouble here is not that a government should avoid investigating possible plots against its existence but that the CIA lacked authority for domestic intelligence gathering. That is supposed to be the jurisdiction of the FBI.

However, because President Johnson, and later President Nixon, had their troubles with the crusty FBI chief, the late J. Edgar Hoover, they apparently turned to the CIA to obtain intelligence about the dissidents and their organizations.

Here, too, the illegal operations are at an end. Operation CHAOS was formally terminated in March, 1974, and the commission properly warned both

the CIA and presidents against any such operations in the future.

In this instance and others, the commission recommended a series of controls, by legislative action and presidential order, that would provide better guarantees against any illegal acts by the CIA in the future. Some stricter controls obviously are in order.

In addition, it may be useful for Congress to set up a joint CIA oversight committee like that which kept an eye on development of the U.S. atomic energy program. But its success would depend on the quality of the overseers appointed because many congressmen become sieves when given secrets. Yet secrecy is required if the CIA is to serve its purpose—and get cooperation from other friendly foreign agencies..

Congress will make its own recommendations after it completes its investigations into CIA practices. Unfortunately, Chairman Frank Church, D-Idaho, of the Senate committee and Chairman James V. Stanton, D-Ohio, of the House subcommittee are CIA critics and their investigations are already suspect in some quarters.

Intelligence gathering at home and abroad appears to run counter to democratic traditions. Americans believe in an open government and suspect that secrecy serves as a cloak for unfair deals. After World War I, Woodrow Wilson called for open convenants openly arrived at—but learned to his sorrow that wasn't the way peace was made.

Yet the fact is that operations like those the CIA conducted are carried out by other national intelligence agencies all over the world. Some democratic nations, including Great Britain, have highly effective—but little publicized—intelligence agencies and still protect individual liberties.

Thus, in fashioning new controls to prevent further CIA violations of the law, Congress and the executive department will have to reconcile the nation's need for intelligence gathering with the necessity for protection of individual rights. It will not be an easy task to do so without further damage to the usefulness and credibility of the CIA.

New York Post

New York, N.Y., June 11, 1975

In a sense both President Ford and Vice President Rockefeller did an injustice to the Rockefeller commission's CIA report when they depicted it in advance as a document that would reassure and relieve the country. Their comments inevitably created the impression that the findings would disclose only minor malfeasance and, in Ford's words, reestablish the "credibility" of the agency.

In fact, with all its inadequacies, unfinished lines of inquiry and evasions of some harsh conclusions, the report dramatically fortifies the case for more extensive, tough-minded investigation by the committee headed by Sen. Church (D-Idaho).

The presidential commission was created as a direct result of allegations that the CIA had engaged in mass violations of the rights of American citizens and flagrantly flouted its own charter in the process. Those charges are grimly confirmed by the study.

Plainly the CIA long ago moved far beyond its original mission of foreign intelligence and became a strong arm of an incipient domestic police-state operation.

In view of the pending Congressional inquiries, perhaps the commission realized that any lesser degree of revelation would have been a national scandal. Certainly, however, even its limited disclosures cannot be viewed as "minor" infractions. A computerized index of 300,000 citizens chiefly identified with antiwar dissent — rather than any machinations of a foreign power—can hardly be dismissed as a deplorable excess of zeal.

The close links between many commission members and the CIA structure inevitably invite speculation that what has been released represents only the tip of the iceberg. Such skepticism is intensified, of course, by the decision to withhold those sections of the report dealing with political assassination.

The mandate to the Church committee becomes infinitely more urgent as a result of this development. While the Rockefeller commission valiantly insisted that "the great majority" of the CIA's domestic works complied with the law, that is a rhetorical irrelevance. The magnitude of the crimes committed cannot be blurred by arithmetical evidence that they were outnumbered by the lawful deeds performed. Nor does a perfunctory proposal for more vigilant Congressional "oversight" clear the air.

We have been permitted to glimpse isolated fragments of the CIA story. The Church committee's responsibility is to uncover the whole truth, or as much of it as diligent, fearless investigation can find.

Chicago Sun-Times

Chicago, Ill., June 12, 1975

One of the more sinister revelations of the Rockefeller Commission's report on the Central Intelligence Agency was a 20-year secret agreement with the Justice Department that gave the agency discretion in the prosecution of criminal actions by its employes. The Rockefeller Commission said that, by granting the CIA such law-enforcement power, the Justice Department had "abdicated its statutory duties." In fact it did more than that. It made the CIA immune from the law.

The Rockefeller Commission contradicted itself when it said that it had found no instance of CIA abuse of this agreement, which was terminated last January. The commission's documentation of numerous CIA violations of its charter and of U.S. law is proof that agency employes carried out criminal actions. And since, to the best recollection of Justice Department officials, no CIA employe ever was prosecuted during the two decades of the agreement, it is obvious that the agency did abuse the secret and illegal pact.

It is astonishing that numerous attorneys general reportedly were unaware of the agreement that gave the CIA the power of decision whether prosecution involving its employes would reveal matters detrimental to national security. Such power, in effect, made the CIA "extraterritorial," or outside the jurisdiction of the law if it chose to be. And it clearly did. That a series of chief legal officers were not even told of this gross contradiction of the American legal system is frightening.

It is no solace that the agreement has ended. Crimes were committed, many of them having little to do with U.S. security or the functions of the CIA, according to the Rockefeller Commission. We urge a thorough investigation, by Congress and by Atty. Gen. Edward H. Levi, of this shameful abrogation of the law.

Pittsburgh Post-Gazette

Pittsburgh, Pa., June 11, 1975

THE RELEASE of the Rockefeller commission's report on illegal domestic spying by the CIA is overshadowed by commission findings not made known to the public — those concerning allegations that the intelligence agency plotted the murder of foreign leaders.

The eclipse of the domestic-spying issue, so sensational a scandal a few months ago, was inescapable at the news conference Monday night at which President Ford rightly promised to supply the commission's assassination-plot data to the Justice Department and two congressional committees.

The shift in public concern has an obvious explanation: Reports of a CIA plot to murder Fidel Castro—in connivance with the Mafia—are infinitely more dramatic (and disturbing) than allegations that the agency trespassed the statutory line separating foreign and domestic intelligence-gathering. This is especially true now that President Ford's counsel, Roderick Hills, has admitted that there is a "sound basis" for further investigation of the rumors.

There is, however, another explanation for the public and congressional reaction to the assassination-plot reports, and the current demands for full disclosure of past "dirty tricks" and prosecution of the officials allegedly involved. What might be called the post-Watergate ethic, which had its origins in revulsion at an election-year burglary at Democratic headquarters and a subsequent White House cover-up, has gradually been extended to an area, secret "national security" operations, at one time considered by citizens and congressmen alike a special case, exempt from the usual rules governing public policy.

This is to a large extent a salutary development Americans who — witness the success of the television program "Mission Impossible"—felt no moral qualms about secret "dirty tricks" in the cause of national security had their faith shaken by the revelation that Howard Hunt and Gordon Liddy passed naturally from dirty tricks abroad to dirty tricks at home.

More disturbing still, the White House plumbers — and their fellow countersubversives in the FBI—were exposed in Watergate revelations as not only sinister but also foolish. The FBI attempted, through a phony letter-writing campaign, to pit the Mafia against the Communist party. The CIA, according to current reports, planned to enlist the same Mafia in an anti-Castro plot. Such covert activities recall not "Mission: Impossible" but the Keystone Cops.

Against such a background, it is no surprise that reports of assassination contingency plans in the CIA do not evoke the image of agonized patriots resorting to brutal, but necessary, measures in the cause of national security. If the reports currently circulating are true, moreover, no such image is appropriate. The would-be long-distance assassins of Fidel Castro sinned most spectacularly not against the Sixth Commandment but against political reality. Assassinating leaders of foreign governments is an inefficient, as well as an immoral, way to deal with a perceived political threat.

The necessary investigation of the assassination reports should result in a Central Intelligence Agency strictly accountable to the President (it has been suggested that some assassination planning went on without presidential knowledge) and to a manageable number of congressmen. When President Ford properly announced Monday night that he is "totally opposed to political assassinations," he equally properly did not add the obvious qualification: that his or any other president's opposition would crumble in the highly unlikely, but still possible, case of a genuine threat to the national security of the United States.

Such cases are no doubt few. But when they occur the responsibility must belong to the President, not to the sort of rash operatives whose sins are now being visited upon the CIA.

The Charlotte Observer

Charlotte, N.C., June 11, 1975

Whatever is contained in the Rockefeller Commission's report on alleged illegal activities by the Central Intelligence Agency, the responsibility for getting to the heart of the matter remains where it was all along: in Congress.

From the beginning, it seemed unlikely that the Rockefeller findings would be definitive. The commission's decision not to pursue allegations of CIA plots against foreign leaders makes its report little more than another document to be considered by congressional investigators.

President Ford's decision to turn reports of CIA wrongdoing over to the Justice Department for investigation and possible prosecution is welcome, however. It should be made clear that murder is not an instrument of this country's foreign policy. Agents of the United States government must be expected to obey our laws, just as other Americans are.

If President Ford cooperates fully with the congressional investigation as he says he will, he can both absolve himself of any charges of a cover-up and rid himself of a serious political problem. Much of the alleged CIA wrongdoing may have occurred with the tacit approval — if not at the urging — of Democratic presidents. If that is the case, it is far better for Mr. Ford to have a committee led by congressional Democrats reveal that information than to do so himself.

So now it is up to Congress, a body that has been slipshod in its supervision of the intelligence community in the past. If new laws are needed to insure that our intelligence activities truly serve our national interests, Congress must enact them. But before doing so, Congress must find out how existing laws are inadequate and what new ones must cover. Only a thorough investigation can accomplish that.

St. Petersburg Times

St. Petersburg, Fla., June 11, 1975

A government agency run in almost total secrecy comes to believe about itself that: It is its own law; it need not obey other laws; it need not respect moral or legal rights; it need not feel restrained by the Constitution, by the Bill of Rights, by the courts.

Those are among the self-perceptions of the CIA revealed by the Rockefeller Commission report, made public Tuesday, which said the agency engaged in "plainly unlawful" and "clearly illegal" acts in this country. The report turned up little that was new, but it confirmed the danger of CIA abuses to the principles upon which this country depends.

THE CIA WAS established in 1947 to collect information and to help protect the United States. But it has become a faithless protector, turning against the precepts of the country it serves. Thus the need for better safeguards against CIA abuses, as recommended by the Rockefeller group. Thus the need for President Ford's call for steps to ensure the "proper functioning" of the intelligence community. Thus the need for the Select Senate Committee's further investigation of the CIA.

Some of the agency's acts have exceeded its "proper functioning." It used drugs on unsuspecting humans, resulting in at least one death. It spied on Americans, opened mail, tapped phones, and even used secret CIA funds to buy stationery and pay postage for former President Nixon at one point. The amount, $33,000 is less important than the arrogance of power behind such an illegal act.

That such activities as reported by the Rockefeller Commission could occur underscores the points that (1) the CIA has not had adequate supervision by Congress and (2) that any agency set up to operate in effect outside the Constitution will likely, in the end, undermine constitutional principles and constitutional government.

WHAT'S MORE, there is more. The Rockefeller group probed only the CIA's domestic activities. Information on its suspected foreign misdeeds will come from the Senate committee headed by Sen. Frank Church, D-Idaho, who said last week that his panel has "hard evidence" of CIA involvement in assassination plots. "Murder is murder," said Church.

Norman Cousins, the distinguished editor of Saturday Review World magazine, has asked of the CIA, "Who gave Americans the authority to set aside the political and human rights of other people whenever we thought it might be in our national interest to do so?" The answer, clearly, is no one.

Mr. Ford, the Rockefeller Commission, the Church committee — all agree new restraints are needed on the CIA. They can't come too soon on an agency which sets aside "the political and human rights" of people in our countries and here at home.

DAYTON DAILY NEWS

Dayton, Ohio, June 11, 1975

The challenge to public policy posed by the Rockefeller commission report is twofold. It is to set up safeguards to keep the CIA from lapsing or being pushed into illegal domestic operations in the future and to rescue the CIA's excellent and vital intelligence gathering and analysis abilities from the shambles that this and the coming congressional investigations have made of the agency.

For all the commission's pleas that the CIA's trespasses be understood in the context that, overwhelmingly, the agency's acts have been lawful, it is clear the CIA overstepped its authority or allowed itself to be pushed over the line too often, too far.

Not only did the CIA—as had already been virtually confirmed—collect data on American political dissidents (if you can also call such a bland outfit as the Urban league dissident) and not only did it snoop into Americans' mail, but there were other "horrors," to revive former Attorney General John Mitchell's word from the Watergate hearings.

The misuse of agency funds to aid one of President Nixon's political operations, the infiltration of a congressional candidate's campaign, the wiretapping and shadowing of journalists who reported leaks, the eavesdropping on phone calls of suspected criminals (not the CIA's field), the aid to local police departments—even all these do not, as the commission insists, add up to a picture of an intelligence agency amok.

They do, however, reveal an agency vulnerable to misuse by presidential authority, one which, once its ethical compass had been disoriented, drifted farther off course, each new slip being measured only from the most recent one, not by the growing distance from shore.

What to do? The Rockefeller commission's recommendation that both a joint congressional and an executive branch committee be set up is all right as far as it goes, though there is no reason why either or both couldn't be co-opted or deceived eventually.

Very likely some criminal prosecutions will be necessary. No bloodbath in the criminal courts is in order, but in cases in which the authority was high, the responsibility clear and the transgression serious, accountings in law could have important deterrent effect.

Most important, the agency must be thoroughly cleansed of its covert action, its "dirty tricks," capacity. It seems clear that most of the CIA's mistakes were the result of that handy, at-the-ready capacity and of the mystique that goes with it, not of abuses of its ordinary intelligence functions.

If the United States sometimes must undertake "dirty tricks" as the lesser of evils in a world not always congenial to its vital interests—and the case for that has by no means been proved—then the function should be quartered in a separate agency, one publicly budgeted with its general purposes if not its specific actions freely admitted.

The legal restraints on such an agency, and the presidential responsibility for all its actions should be severe.

St. Louis ⚜ Review

St. Louis, Mo., June 13, 1975

Perhaps the most frightening aspect of disclosures that the Central Intelligence Agency has been involved in assassination plots against leaders of other countries is that it does not appear to horrify the American people. The very thought that an agency of our government could view murder as a tool of its trade, or that it could be debased enough to enlist the assistance of criminals and murderers to carry out its designs, ought to make us sick to our stomachs. Have we as a nation become so inured to violence as a solution that we are willing to condone the transfer of agents licensed to kill from the pages of cloak and dagger fiction into the real world? To date, only Senator Frank Church has voiced the moral indignation that should be felt by every decent American.

The question of the morality of political assassinations was widely discussed centuries ago, and the church's response was invariably that it is a grave moral evil. No one is permitted to do evil so that a good result might be achieved. Medieval theologians posed the question in its most extreme form: Would it be morally justifiable to kill a tyrant? The response of Catholic morality has been consistent: No matter how convinced one might be that a regime is unlawful from its very inception or has lost its right to authority by abuse, no private person has the right to sentence anyone to death. And if the killing of a tyrant on private decision is seen as gravely unjust, immoral and unlawful, the murder of politically obnoxious opponents is even less defensible. Murder is always murder.

The church's teaching that tyrannicide is gravely sinful does not mean that one cannot engage in active resistance against civil authority which has grossly abused its prerogatives. The late Pope Pius XI in his encyclical letter of March 28, 1937, "Firmissimam Constantiam" spoke approvingly of the right of active resistance to a tyrannical regime, while stressing the necessary moral restrictions on this resistance. The resistance itself can only be offered against a regime which has suppressed the citizens' most essential freedoms, which has completely substituted might for justice and right and which has subverted the economy to the advantage of parties or groups instead of for the common good.

The United States does not have a divine right to overturn other governments or murder the leaders of other nations. Any agency of our government which carries on such activities shames us before the world. In at least two of the cases about which there has been publicity, the CIA allegedly became involved in plots against the lives of Prime Minister Diem in South Vietnam and Dictator Trujillo in the Dominican Republic, neither of whom was even antagonistic to the U.S.

We must insist that our Senators and Representatives enact federal legislation barring any agency of our government from participation in plots to assassinate foreign leaders or to overthrow the governments of other nations.

THE DAILY HERALD

Biloxi, Miss., June 12, 1975

If the Rockefeller Commission findings —at least, the portion that has been released — tell us one thing, it says that the Central Intelligence Agency is above the law.

And if that phrase is reminiscent of the attitudes associated with former President Nixon and his White House staff during the time between the Watergate burglary and their fall from power, it should.

The Rockefeller Commission found that the CIA engaged in "plainly unlawful and improper" domestic operatons; its report is liberally sprinkled with descriptive phrases such as "doubtful propriety", "poor judgment" and valid necessity."

It is not sufficient that the commission complete its task with a few chastising remarks, a slap on the wrist, and an admonition "Don't do it again."

The same bugaboo that was bandied about by Mr. Nixon and his cohorts—national security—has been bandied, about during the CIA's tribulations. And in the CIA instance, not without justification. But the national security justification is not without limitation and the CIA seems clearly to have exceeded that limitation, not in one instance. or even several but over an extended period of time, as a matter of policy.

The nature of the agency is spying — intelligence, if the euphemism is preferred — and that is of prime importance to national seurity. It must be secretive, clandestine, even deceitful. But it need not be unlawful and cannot be allowed to be above the law.

If one agency of the government can be allowed to trample wantonly upon the rights of American citizens within the United States, then those rights do not exist for any citizen and the U.S. Constitution and Bill of Rights are a sham. The CIA will have become a Gestapo.

The challenge has been given to Attorney General Edward Levi to study the report, along with the still secret portions that have been labeled "extremely sensitive" for a determination of possible prosecution. Levi should have no difficulty determining that prosecution is indeed justified in the instances of the CIA's unlawful domestic operatons.

The Rockefeller Commission said its investigation "yielded no evidence of disloyalty" and that is good news. But memory recalls that there was no disloyalty among Mr. Nixon's men, but rather an intense loyalty that was misdirected.

OREGON Journal
AN INDEPENDENT NEWSPAPER

Portland, Ore., June 12, 1975

The public cannot be expected to be content with those portions of the Rockefeller report on the CIA made public, nor with the investigation conducted by the committee.

An initial reaction to the public report is that we have been allowed to see the tip of the iceberg.

For this, the Rockefeller committee probably is only partly at fault.

In the first place, the initial assignment given the committee by President Ford was narrow. It was confined to investigations of allegations of domestic spying and surveillance of U. S. citizens in violation of the CIA's charter.

Only as something of an afterthought was the committee told to look into charges of CIA involvement in foreign assassination plots, and this part of the report has not been made public.

On the basis of information which has been made public, the CIA does not come out too badly. True, there was domestic spying, but much of this was a result of presidential goading.

But even without outside influence, the CIA cannot be condemned too strongly for following foreign leads into this country.

The idea of having two spy organizations, one for foreign work and one for domestic, may be fine in theory, but the practical difficulties of changing horses at the border are many.

This is particularly true, when, if CIA claims are correct, the FBI frequently did not have the manpower to meet CIA requests.

As to CIA involvement in assassination plots or in direct intervention in foreign governmental operation, the public still knows little, if anything. This part of the report is in the hands of the attorney general and congressional committees.

However, even on the basis of what the public now knows, it seems obvious that the CIA needs a tighter rein and greater surveillance.

Like any bureaucracy, an investigative or spy organization, if given a completely free hand, will not only expand but will begin to operate as if it were a law unto itself.

Also, there appears to be a need for much clearer guidelines for intervention in foreign governmental operations, as distinguished from spying or information gathering.

Certainly, assassination should not be on our list of tools for dealing with international problems. President Ford strongly disapproves any such tactics.

It is conceivable that if there was involvement in assassination plots in the Cold War climate of the distant past, it should not be publicized, because of potential damage to international relations.

An initial appraisal is that we need more inquiry and a great deal of clarification of the guidelines for investigative organizations both at home and abroad, plus a greater degree of congressional surveillance.

The Virginian-Pilot

Norfolk, Va., June 12, 1975

In 1939 Secretary of State Henry L. Stimson shut down the "black chamber," the State Department's primitive code-breaking section, saying, "Gentlemen do not read each other's mail."

Those were happier times.

The Central Intelligence Agency routinely surveyed some 4 million pieces per year in the course of its 20-year surveillance of mail between the Soviet Union and the United States, according to the Rockefeller Commission's report on domestic political spying. Some 13,000 letters were opened in the process.

The mail cover is only one item in 299-page report that details the assembling of dossiers on activists and dissident groups, the monitoring of overseas telephone calls, buggings and burglaries and wiretaps, contacts with local police, an agreement with the Justice Department to permit the CIA to investigate itself, and a bizarre program of drug-testing that led to the death of an Army employe who was administered a dose of LSD without his permission. (He jumped to his death from a 10th floor window several days later.) While the "great majority" of the activities of the CIA complied with the law, the Rockefeller Commission said, a number of its operations "were plainly unlawful and constituted improper invasions upon the rights of Americans."

That is something of an understatement. The Rockefeller Commission's findings, maintains The New York Times, serve to confirm its original newspaper report, written by Seymour M. Hersh, saying that the CIA had conducted "massive illegal domestic operations." There is not much profit in debating whether the CIA's dirty work was "massive" or not.

For it is clear enough that the Rockefeller Commission is engaged in slamming barn doors after an entire stable of horses has been stolen. The CIA's involvement in domestic intrigues and knavery in the name of national security is the product of the attitudes of the Cold War, which were compounded and intensified by the protests of the Sixties and ended in Watergate. But indignation may be redundant today.

The country is disillusioned with foreign involvements and the idea of saving the world from the Communist menace — or anything else. Detente is appealing to a people who are born war-weary and world-weary. If the CIA's effectiveness is impaired by the Rockefeller report, that may not be as bad a thing as it might have seemed once upon a time.

For the obsession with Red threats is what got us into the Indochina quagmire, where we had no genuine national interests to involve us. So we invented enemies and theories to justify what might be better understood as the tragic version of Parkinson's Law in the field of foreign policy: war expands infinitely to fill the time allotted for it.

We have learned our lesson the hard way, and the CIA inquiry is only part of the undoing of the ideas that a generation swore by. We are beginning a process of rethinking that is already changing our concept of our role in the world and may radically revise "the American way of life" and its familiar institutions, such as the two-party political system. The end of the revisionism is not in sight yet. But a good place to begin the national rethinking is the notion that Americans are the enemies of the United States that is implicit in the CIA's domestic hanky-panky.

THE SAGINAW NEWS
Saginaw, Mich., June 12, 1975

The contents of the Rockefeller Commission's report on the Central Intelligence Agency belies its conclusion that the CIA's overall record of staying within the law is good.

It has not been good. It has been terrible. It has been 20 years of violation of the law by misguided zealots urged on by misguided presidents and encouraged by a careless Congress.

Even in a bobtailed summary of findings on CIA activities which hardly touches upon assassination, the public bears witness to a glossary of domestic spying that is terrifying in its scope, criminal in its purest intent.

Not just thousands but hundreds of thousands of Americans have had their Constitutional rights violated in the grossest of ways. If they didn't agree with the way their government was doing things — or if somebody simply considered them suspect — they have had their mail opened. They have had their phones tapped, their offices broken into and bugged and their daily lives laid open to invasions of privacy — all details minutely cataloged and computerized.

Even this does not touch the limits to which the agency went in prostituting the law and its own integrity.

There is hard evidence in the commission report that the CIA infiltrated domestic politics in a covert attempt to smear reputations. It tailed and trailed people and paid police for information. And in at least one instance it literally wasted a human life conducting its own tests on the effects of the use of LSD — the drug administered to a subject without his knowledge or consent.

We submit that these kinds of subversions have no place in a free democratic society. Least of all do they suggest that the CIA's record of staying within the law is "good."

They suggest, rather, that we have come within a step of a police state run in Gestapo fashion. As the Rockefeller Commission itself acknowledges, the CIA has done things "that were illegal then and that would be illegal now."

In sum, the report becomes devastating testimony on just how badly the Central Intelligence Agency has abused its authority. And just how badly things can get off the track when there is little or no check-and-balance on a spy organization and even less insistence on accountability.

Clearly the first of three reports says there is nothing frivolous or counter-productive in the investigation into where the CIA has been over the past two decades. Its leadership, its direction, its thinking, its activities now become matters of prime importance.

Where, then, do we go from here? Nothing is gained by attempting to soft-soap what has gone on. Neither is anything gained by flying into hysteria over the grave mistakes of the past.

What the nation does not need is an irrational attempt to dismantle the CIA or blatant exposes that might give away information vitally important to national security in the area of foreign intelligence gathering.

Though the Rockefeller Commission has left the gorier details of murder plots and Mafia connections to Senate and House select committees, it has made some contribution. It has shown the extent to which the CIA broke the law domestically. And it has sent forward recommendations aimed at putting Central Intelligence under much tighter scrutiny in the future.

The President ought to act on these quickly as he says he intends to.

Mr. Ford will also be helpful to the congressional committees by sending to them and to the Justice Department all information contained in the commission report as well as other material he says has been gathered by administrative agencies.

Thereafter the nation will await the findings of the congressional panels and the decisions of the Justice Department on possible prosecutions.

Beyond question, however, the need for a properly directed CIA, thoroughly conversant with and aware of its legitimate areas of operation, has been demonstrated. It has for years patently fractured the limits of its charter authority.

What it says is we never again want to look at how close we have come to a police state abjuring all legal and constitutional safeguards on the right of assembly, free speech and personal privacy.

SENATE COMMITTEE DISCLOSES TOXIN CACHE, MAIL INTERCEPTS

Deadly toxins, some of them potent enough to kill thousands of persons, were found in a secret cache maintained by the Central Intelligence Agency, Sen. Frank Church (D, Ida.), chairman of the Senate Select Intelligence Committee, said Sept. 9. In "direct contravention" of a 1969 order by President Nixon to destroy biological and chemical weapons, Church said, the CIA failed to destroy supplies of an instantly lethal toxin made from shellfish, and smaller amounts of cobra venom. Eight grams of cobra venom and 10.972 grams of the shellfish toxin were kept in a secret vault in a rarely used CIA laboratory in Washington, Church indicated.

CIA Director William E. Colby disclosed in public testimony before the committee Sept. 16 that the poisons had been stockpiled as part of a secret project, code-named "M. K. Naomi." Colby said the project was so secret that he had only learned of its existence earlier in 1975 when a former agency employe brought it to his attention. Another witness before the committee, Dr. Nathan Gordon, a CIA chemist who retired in 1973, testified that it was at his direction that the shellfish toxin and cobra venom were not destroyed in 1970. Gordon, who admitted being aware of Nixon's order, said he received no specific order from the CIA hierarchy to dispose of the material. He felt that the order was directed at military weapons, and that the shellfish toxin did not fall into that category. Richard Helms, director of the CIA from 1966 to 1973, informed the Senate committee Sept. 17 that he had issued an oral command to destroy the CIA's biochemical weapons stockpile but that he had not followed through to ensure execution of his order.

The Senate committee disclosed Sept. 24 that the CIA, as part of its 20-year mail-intercept program, opened and copied the mail of Richard M. Nixon and Sens. Edward M. Kennedy (D, Mass.) and Hubert H. Humphrey (D, Minn.). According to Sen. Church, CIA men at a New York post office worked from a "watch list" of at least 1,300 persons targeted for CIA surveillance. These CIA officers, who photographed letters of persons on the list, evidently strayed from the list and opened the mail of many prominent U.S. citizens and institutions that had not been targeted for surveillance, Church said. He added that he even found a letter he wrote to his mother-in-law in the CIA's files. Besides his own letter and some correspondence to Nixon, Humphrey and Kennedy, Church said the CIA had opened mail to and from the late civil rights leader Martin Luther King Jr. and his wife, Coretta; John D. Rockefeller 4th; Arthur F. Burns, chairman of the Federal Reserve Board; Rep. Bella Abzug (D, N.Y.); the Rockefeller Foundation; the Ford Foundation and Harvard University.

THE SUN
Baltimore, Md., September 28, 1975

When Senator Frank Church predicted in an interview with Muriel Dobbin of *The Sun* some time ago that the Central Intelligence Agency would be revealed as "a rogue elephant rampaging out of control," a number of knowledgeable officials responded that the spy agency had never done anything without presidential approval. Now, after two weeks of public hearings by the select Senate committee studying intelligence operations, the Church prediction looks right on the nose.

Present and former high-level CIA officials have testified to the effect that various agency operations were carried on illegally and without orders from higher authority. Indeed, in two cases, the CIA did things expressly forbidden by Presidents. In one case it opened mail after President Richard Nixon ordered it to, then changed his mind and ordered it not to. The CIA was already doing that when Mr. Nixon considered ordering it to. His order to do it and his subsequent order not to do it were something of a joke to the CIA. As Senator Church, chairman of the select committee, put it, the President is not the commander in chief to the CIA, just "a problem."

In another case President Nixon ordered the agency to destroy some poisons so toxic as to sound like science fiction potions rather than something from the real world. The then director of the CIA, Richard Helms, said under oath he relayed the order only orally and didn't check up because he "read in the newspaper" that the poisons had been destroyed. If that doesn't make Mr. Helms a perjurer, it makes him a singularly incompetent chief spy. The CIA official directly responsible for destroying the poison says he didn't do it because he considered the presidential order "unwise." That is the hallmark of a bureaucracy out of control.

Each revelation creates a new picture of the formerly hush-hush agency. Not only have its top officials casually and routinely broken the law by opening mail (and breaking into homes and offices, wiretapping and planting bugs, combing through income tax returns, etc.); not only has it ignored presidential directives. It has also bungled its principal function of gathering and assessing foreign intelligence. The House select committee demonstrated that in 1967-8 the CIA totally misjudged or, what may be worse, deliberately misreported, Communist strength in Vietnam. In 1973 the agency believed no war was likely in the Middle East—even as hostilities were about to begin.

The congressional investigations have already developed facts far beyond anything found by the Rockefeller Commission, many of whose cautious recommendations now seem inadequate to the task. It is easy to understand why many critics want to disband the agency, but that is too drastic a remedy. The Ford administration's current attempts to shore up the CIA during the remainder of the investigation may be necessary but should not be confused with real reform. A start toward the basic changes that are needed could be made now by dusting off one Rockefeller recommendation that does deal with one of the underlying problems. It proposed that an "individual of stature, independence and integrity" from outside the intelligence community be brought in to head the CIA. The time has definitely come for that. If ever an organization needed a tough manager, it is the CIA. Many of its top and middle leaders developed their ideas of their mission in World War II and the worst days of the early Cold War, when anything went. A complete shakeup at the top may be needed, and possibly extensive reorganization of the middle levels, too. Only a new director, from outside the agency, can be expected to do the extensive work that is needed. Even that is likely to be only a beginning. But it is not too soon to start, even while the congressional committees probe deeper into the rot.

CHICAGO DAILY NEWS
Chicago, Ill., September 29, 1975

A spy-fiction writer might have written the scenario the Central Intelligence Agency has been following in these past few years.

Imagine a sedate, self-respecting government intelligence agency getting mixed up in plots to "eliminate" foreign chiefs of state. Imagine such an agency dabbling in shellfish toxin and cobra venom, and a dozen kinds of exotic poisons. Imagine such an agency stealthily opening the mail of members of the U.S. Senate. Imagine such an agency steaming open the mail of a candidate for President of the United States.

These acts may burden the imagination, but the CIA did 'em — each and every one, and it did a lot more that has come to light and who-knows-what-all that hasn't. In the process its agents have blithely countermanded the orders of practically everybody in a position to issue them, including the director of the CIA and *his* boss, the President of the United States. And not only that, but when it came to a perfectly legitimate intelligence operation such as warning the nation on the impending outbreak of the **Yom Kippur War** in the Middle East, the CIA fell on its sternum with a dull

thud. Could it have been too busy playing 007 to bother with the humdrum business of ordinary intelligence?

By now, enough really seems to be enough — it's time for a drastic airing, housecleaning, and restructuring, to the end that at least somebody will be in charge and somebody will know what's going on.

This is the unmistakable upshot of all that Sen. Frank Church and his Senate Select Committee have uncovered in the hearings, and what Church meant when he said the agency at times behaved like "a rogue elephant on a rampage."

President Ford has now finally indicated his own concern, and is considering recommending legislation to reorganize the CIA and especially to take it out of the business of secret overseas political operations. In view of all the evidence, it strikes us that no time should be lost. Intelligence is an imperative governmental function, but in the case of the CIA it appears that the responsible men in government were the last to know what these free-wheeling, free-booting, to-hell-with-everybody characters were up to. It's time somebody took charge and put them back on the track.

The Ottawa Citizen
Ottawa, Ont., September 27, 1975

It looks as though the U.S. Central Intelligence Agency, while it didn't drag away people in the middle of the night as its counterparts did in totalitarian countries, did just about everything else.

Between 1952 and 1972, for example, it opened the mail of such individuals as Richard Nixon, Hubert Humphrey and Edward Kennedy and such organizations as the Ford Foundation, Rockefeller Foundation and Harvard University.

Former CIA director Richard Helms has said that though he gave orders to destroy stockpiles of deadly poisons, the orders were ignored.

The CIA also defied an order from then president Richard Nixon to destroy poison it had developed and stockpiled.

The CIA, over the years, had developed both deadly poisons and assassination weapons. These included 10 lethal substances, including a toxin made in laboratories from shellfish and cobra venom, 26 substances which could incapacitate temporarily, and four different kinds of assassination devices.

As Senator Frank Church's select committee on intelligence continues its probe, more revelations are likely. Already, it appears that the CIA's reputation — or notoriety — is well-earned.

Pittsburgh Post-Gazette
Pittsburgh, Pa., September 19, 1975

"The President has further directed the destruction of all existing stocks of toxins which are not required for a research program for defensive purposes only." From a White House press release, datelined Key Biscayne, Fla., of Feb. 14, 1970, which was a clarification of then-President Richard M. Nixon's directive of Nov. 25, 1969.

THIS democracy cannot survive with two separate governments, one that's duly elected and answerable to the public and another one that's covert, unelected and answerable only to itself. It's utterly intolerable for the CIA or any other agency to defy, for example, a legal, constitutional presidential order.

Yet Nathan Gordon has admitted to a Senate committee that at his direction two deadly poisons were stockpiled by the CIA in 1970. That, according to CIA Director Colby, was in violation of President Nixon's directive. Mr. Gordon, who retired from the CIA in 1973, should be prosecuted—if it's possible within in the present laws—for the insubordination that he's apparently admitted

to. If there's no law covering ex-CIA agents, Congress should enact one.

None dare, at this too-early moment, to call it treason, but stories have too often appeared about the CIA's apparently conducting, as if it were a separate government, foreign policy operations at variance with the publicly enunciated policies of U.S. presidents and secretaries of state.

In August of last year, for example, State Department leaks revealed that the Athens CIA station chief subsidized Greek politicians, including ex-dictator Papadopoulos, and helped King Constantine buy Center Union deputies in order to topple the democratically elected government of George Papandreou.

In the case of the stockpiled poisons, Mr. Gordon may have been acting in what he believed to be the best interests of the U.S.

* * *

We're not even sure that it was wise for then-President Nixon to extend his laudable 1969 ban on the development and deployment of germ-warfare agents to the storage of military toxins.

We are sure that he was the pres-

ident and that the CIA or any other agency cannot be allowed to disobey the legal, constitutional order by him or any other president. We also know that the way to deal with foreign leaders of whom the U.S. disapproves is not to shoot them with silent toxin guns that leave no trace; as a nation we're strong enough and smart enough to compete on a higher level than that. But that's a matter of policy to be determined by our elected officials, not by middle-level officials in a supersecretive agency answerable to no one.

Nor should that mean that we must dispense with research into— but not production of—chemical and biological warfare agents in order to learn what others may do to us and how to protect ourselves.

Nor does it mean that a secret intelligence agency like the CIA or some successor isn't necessary to the nation's security. It does mean, however, that such an agency cannot be allowed to work at odds with the President and the Congress. Two central governments into one democracy won't go.

THE MILWAUKEE JOURNAL
Milwaukee, Wisc., September 18, 1975

President Ford has given a broad hint that he may end covert political operations from the CIA. Certainly the bizarre stories (of deadly poison caches, dart guns that kill silently at 100 yards and contemplated assassinations) now coming out of the CIA ought to reinforce those inclinations in the president.

It has been questionable from the beginning whether the CIA should ever have been involved in such James Bond nonsense. But more disturbing is the revelation that when President Nixon had ordered certain poisons destroyed, they weren't, only the records noting their existence were.

The whole command and control system involving extremely dangerous products showed a looseness beyond belief. The fact that a middle echelon CIA administrator could effectively squirrel these poisons and weapons away, for whatever reasons, without the knowledge or accountability to top CIA management underscores the need for internal CIA reform

— if it has not been undertaken already.

These incidents also point out again the continuing need for better outside, independent oversight of the intelligence agency. The Rockefeller commission's recommendation calling for something on the order of the joint congressional committee on atomic energy to oversee the CIA is an idea worth pursuing.

At the same time, the kind of impasse that has occurred between the White House and the House Intelligence Committee over the release of CIA information to the committee needs solution. The executive should be concerned with the confidentiality of national security information. But it serves no good purpose when the White House, out of pique or exaggerated caution, refuses to co-operate with the congressional panel. If the president wants the kind of joint oversight that the CIA needs, Congress must have access to information. Some compromise must be reached.

THE STATES-ITEM
New Orleans, La., September 18, 1975

It is time for the United States government to bring the Central Intelligence Agency under close administrative and congressional controls.

It is imperative that this be done, whether the CIA is reorganized from top to bottom or not.

To protect its interests in the hard world of international politics, the U.S. must have covert intelligence operations at home and abroad. But the agencies that carry out those functions must be accountable to the nation's highest authority.

It is now clear that the CIA has been operating outside normal governmental controls, beyond the system of checks and balances designed to guarantee that government will be responsible to the people.

The testimony of William E. Colby, CIA director, that the espionage agency has stockpiled poisons and the means to use them in defiance of a presidential order is a shocking revelation that the agency has pursued its own edicts.

It already had been established that the CIA was involved in plots to assassinate foreign leaders. Richard Bissell, a former chief of the CIA's secret operations, has confirmed that the agency ordered the preparation of plans to assassinate Fidel Castro. The CIA also considered assassination as a means of getting rid of former Congo leader Patrice Lumumba. Whether these and other CIA assassination plans were known to presidents or other high government officials is a matter the Senate Select Committee on Intelligence has been delving into.

Whatever the outcome of the committee's investigation, already there is enough evidence to warrant full administrative control and congressional supervision of the CIA.

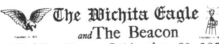

The Wichita Eagle
and The Beacon
Wichita, Kans., September 20, 1975

The admission by Director William Colby that the CIA had retained a secret cache of deadly poisons and forbidden weapons despite presidential orders in 1970 to destroy them pinpoints perhaps the basic fear the public has of the agency.

And that is the suspicion that America's intelligence community considers itself not only above the law but beyond the reach of orders from the chief executive as well.

Exposure during the past two years of CIA involvements and procedures justifies the apprehension many Americans feel for the operation.

In The CIA and the Cult of Intelligence, authors Victor Marchetti and John D. Marke, had this to say:

"Nurtured in the adversary setting of the Cold War, shielded by secrecy, and spurred on by patriotism that views dissent as a threat to the national security, the clandestine operatives of the CIA

have the capability, the resources, the experience — and the inclination — to ply their skills increasingly on the domestic scene."

The CIA's capacity to defend itself against such attacks, which may be overblown, is limited by its overriding need to operate in secret. To provide a detailed rebuttal might expose sensitive matters of national security.

Still, such admissions as this latest that a presidential order

was ignored, gives force to the move for greater congressional oversight of the CIA.

And they certainly give credibility to the idea, now being considered by President Ford, that administrative changes be made within the CIA concerning its direction, authority and operations, both at home and in foreign lands.

Many Americans agree these changes are needed desperately.

Boston Herald American
Combining the best features of the Herald Traveler and Record American
Boston, Mass., September 18, 1975

CIA Director William E. Colby told the Senate Intelligence Committee this week that for five years — the agency kept a secret cache of deadly poisons and assassination weapons — in direct violation of orders from former President Nixon in 1970 to destroy them.

Colby said the poisons, which cost $3 million, were to have been used for assassination purposes only once, to his knowledge, but the plan was cancelled.

Who was behind that plan? Who was to have been the victim? Who was responsible for defying the President's order? Who ordered the destruction — not of the poisons, but of CIA records concerning their existence? Colby didn't say.

There is only one word to describe this incredible affair and the CIA director's attempt to explain it. The word was supplied by the committee's chairman, Sen. Frank Church, who told Colby that he found his testimony "astonishing."

San Jose Mercury
San Jose, Calif., September 19, 1975

Congressional hearings into the sub-rosa activities of the Central Intelligence Agency have produced so many sensational revelations that the main thrust of the hearings has all but been obscured.

What Congress is trying to find out—and what the American people have the obligation to consider carefully—is whether there is any legitimate "action" role for the CIA. To date, the evidence produced suggests there is not.

Nobody in his right mind would suggest the CIA be disbanded and that ingelligence gathering be fragmented anew among the military services. The world is too untidy for that.

At the same time, there is a growing doubt that the national interest is served by an intelligence apparatus that can engage—and perhaps has engaged—in political assassinations or less deadly forms of coups—such as "destabilizing" the Allende regime in Chile and returning the Shah to power in Iran.

The problem, apart from any moral considerations, is lack of accountability—as the matter of the shellfish toxins and other deadly poisons illustrates so clearly.

The CIA—or more precisely a party or parties unknown within the CIA—decided to ignore a presidential directive issued in 1970 and retain the poisons in inventory. Their presence was discovered more or less by accident in the course of the present CIA investigations.

Richard Helms, now the United States Ambassador to Iran and director of the CIA at the time the poisons were ordered destroyed, has testified he told subordinates to carry our the presidential directive. He never issued a written order, however, and he obviously never checked to see if his orders were carried out.

The matter was never discovered in the normal course of congressional oversight of the CIA; nor is it likely it ever would have been discovered. Congress makes a point of not inquiring too closely into what the CIA does with the money appropriated to it.

When the cash is used to pay secret agents or to buy information in any one of a number of less than savory ways, secrecy is both understandable and justifiable. The same cannot be said of subversion and murder. They have no place in the activities of any decent government save in wartime.

Such activities are wrong, judged by almost any moral code. They can be counter-productive even when they succeed; the Shah of Iran is a case in point; and they circumvent the normal system of checks and balances that keep the American government reasonably responsive to the needs and desires of the American people.

On balance, it would seem the CIA should be restricted to gathering intelligence, analyzing it and—perhaps—suggesting courses of action to the President. The CIA should have no "action" capability of its own.

Chicago Sun-Times
Chicago, Ill., September 19, 1975

Congressional testimony concerning the Central Intelligence Agency's development and storage of dart guns, cobra venom, shellfish toxin, lethal bacteria and other lurid weapons is useful. It shows something about the slipshod fashion in which the CIA has been run.

Former CIA Director Richard M. Helms told the Senate Intelligence Committee of Sen. Frank Church (D-Ida.) on Wednesday that he issued oral instructions to halt the CIA's biochemical weapons program and to destroy its stockpiles. But he never followed up to make sure the order was carried out.

It wasn't. The committee had already learned that poisons and bacteria had been kept in a CIA vault for five years after they were supposed to have been destroyed.

The original order was not a routine administrative directive. It was a presidential command issued as a result of international treaty obligations. It dealt with weapons with a potential for killing thousands of persons. It had important legal, military and diplomatic overtones. That an order of that kind was not put in writing by Helms and painstakingly followed through reveals a laziness or apathy that borders on dereliction of duty.

Helms also testified that he was surprised to learn of the presence of the outlawed weapons in the CIA's vault. It was, he remarked, one of the few instances in which an order had been disobeyed.

The remark suggests several important questions that the Church committee has a duty to start asking of Helms and others. What were those other orders? And were there only a few of them? We already know that the CIA targeted $11 million to destabilize an elected government in Chile. We already know similar actions were taken in Guatemala, Iran and elsewhere. Where else, if anywhere, has the CIA been violating international law and its charter?

These are the issues that need to be promptly and thoroughly explored by the Church committee. Only through such an exploration can there be assurances that the CIA will be the lawful servant of a democracy, not the creature of reckless outlaws.

The Charleston Gazette
Charleston, W.Va., September 29, 1975

One outrageous CIA assault upon the personal freedom of American citizens is scarcely absorbed before the next one is disclosed.

We are no longer certain that the CIA requires reformation rather than extinction. Its free-wheeling existence, without accountability to anyone, may have produced the crazed belief that it is an agency of God.

The latest revelation of the CIA's police state conduct was the disclosure by the Senate Intelligence Committee (Whatever happened to Vice President Rockefeller's investigating committee, which was going to put the facts on the table?) that the CIA had opened the mail of such stalwart capitalists as John D. Rockefeller IV in the apprent assumption that he poses a threat to the American system.

Others whose mail has been opened and scrutinized are Hubert Humphrey, Edward Kennedy, Bella Abzug, Martin Luther King Jr., Harvard University, the Ford Foundation, and, for heaven's sake, Federal Reserve Chairman Arthur Burns, whose political conservativism glows like an Olympic torch.

It is becoming increasingly clear that the CIA, given carte blanche by the most reactionary elements of Congress and assumed by others to be doing its work responsibly, has been running completely out of control. The signs are there to show that it has placed itself above the people, above the people's representatives, and above even the President. Richard Nixon's mail was read by the CIA. So was that of Sen. Frank Church, D-Idaho, chairman of the Senate Intelligence Committee. Church saw a copy of one of his letters admittedly read by the CIA. It was a letter to his mother.

Is your mail read? Who knows? The CIA obviously has taken it upon itself to question the loyalty of many Americans. If the loyalty of Jay Rockefeller is open to question, so may be yours.

If the nation needs an espionage agency, it might by wise to dismantle the CIA altogether and start anew with an organization containing no remnants of an agency which, while opening the mail of decent, law-abiding citizens, was conferring with dope-peddling mobsters on prospective assassinations. Enough is enough.

The Des Moines Register

Des Moines, Iowa, September 27, 1975

When it was disclosed that the Central Intelligence Agency (CIA) illegally had opened mail between this country and the Soviet Union, it was assumed that the agency was keeping track of dissidents and "subversives." But the persons and groups subjected to the CIA's mail surveillance turn out to include some of the most prominent names in American life.

The list released by the Senate Intelligence Committee reads like an excerpt from Who's Who: Richard Nixon, Edward Kennedy, Hubert Humphrey, Frank Church, Martin Luther King, jr., Jay Rockefeller, Arthur Burns. Mail addressed to the Ford Foundation, Harvard University and the Rockefeller Foundation also was scrutinized.

The 1968 letter to Nixon opened by the CIA was from a Nixon speechwriter traveling in the Soviet Union. Nixon was seeking the Republican presidential nomination at the time. What was the CIA doing reading the private correspondence of a presidential candidate who was a former vice-president of the United States?

The CIA ran amok with its mail surveillance in all likelihood because there was no accountability. As an illegal operation, it was subject to no governing standards. The top CIA officials who knew about the illegal mail surveillance seemed content to permit mail to be opened indiscriminately.

The Justice Department has been investigating to determine whether to bring criminal charges against those responsible for the mail operation. The chief justification advanced for the mail surveillance is that it was necessary to protect national security. The Senate committee's disclosures will make it hard to explain how knowledge of the contents of a letter from a speechwriter to a presidential candidate furthered national security.

Equally hard to explain is how Richard Helms is still on the U.S. payroll as ambassador to Iran. Helms was director of the CIA when the Nixon and other letters were opened. He knew about the law-breaking throughout most of the 20-year life of the mail project. Helms also was responsible for having a CIA man named chief U.S. postal inspector, a position from which the official could assist the agency in gaining access to the mails.

The CIA's involvement in mail surveillance was shameful, and the U.S. shames itself by having a man so intimately associated with it as its representative abroad.

THE NASHVILLE TENNESSEAN

Nashville, Tenn., September 26, 1975

THE BILL of Rights protects individual liberties against encroachment by government, and this is buttressed by statutes and common law. The Supreme Court has defined the parameters of such encroachment.

In short, any intrusive investigation by government must have a strong enough basis to warrant it and its scope cannot exceed a reasonable degree.

With this in mind, the Congress of the United States, in setting up the Central Intelligence Agency, included a provision saying that the agency should have no police, subpoena, law-enforcement power, or any internal functions. In short, the CIA has no domestic powers.

Nevertheless, the Senate Select Committee on Intelligence has discovered that the CIA had a 20-year program of opening and reading the mail of such Americans as Messrs. Richard Nixon, John D. Rockefeller IV, Federal Reserve Board Chairman Arthur Burns and Sens. Hubert Humphrey and Edward Kennedy.

Mr. James Angleton, a former CIA executive, told the committee that the mail-opening program was an "indispensable" espionage tool, but said that he knew all along that it was illegal.

Sen. Frank Church, the committee chairman, said the program's value must be balanced against the harm it did to the constitutional rights of American citizens.

Assuredly that is a point of concern, since individual freedoms and privacy are fundamental to our society. But those liberties set forth in the Constitution, in the law and in the spirit of this nation must depend on government observance of the law.

When government itself is the lawbreaker, when its employes and leaders knowingly pursue a course of illegality, how under heaven can there be a public respect for law?

How is it to be possible to inculcate in the young of the nation a respect for lawful authority, a confidence in institutions, and a trust in the process of democratic government when that government violates the law, ignores the Constitution and acts as if it is superior to both?

The Salt Lake Tribune

Salt Lake City, Utah, September 27, 1975

One of the more contemptible utterances of recent years before a Congressional committee was that of John Angleton, the former chief of Central Intelligence Agency counter-intelligence work. He said:

"Certain individual rights have to be sacrificed for the sake of national security."

This came as he acknowledged it is illegal to open other peoples' mail. The former CIA executive was testifying about the agency's mail surveillance campaign during which, for 21 years, agents opened, read and photographed the mail prominent Americans sent or received from the Soviet Union.

Mr. Angleton's concept of the rights of Americans is very reminiscent of those held in Nazi Germany.

Earlier this month, in a deposition, Mr. Angleton said, "It's inconceivable that a secret intelligence agency had to comply with all the overt orders of the government." This guy would like to have been a government all to himself.

When Sen. Richard Schweiker, R-Pa., called the remark to Mr. Angleton's attention he asked that it be withdrawn because it was "imprudent." Sen. Schweiker, however, said the statement was "indicative of the problem this committee has to deal with" in learning the truth.

Increasingly, it is becoming apparent that the Central Intelligence Agency, at one time at least, enrolled a number of people at relatively high levels, who believed it is permissible to lie, cheat, steal or kill in the pursuit of their jobs and it made little difference to them whether doing so was legal or illegal.

If such is the case, and worriedly the amassing evidence points that it is, then it is time to start wondering if the United States can any longer afford the Central Intelligence Agency. It is time to start questioning whether the agency isn't a greater liability to the safety, security and freedom of every American than it is an asset.

THE COMMERCIAL APPEAL
Memphis, Tenn., September 26, 1975

THE FACT that the Central Intelligence Agency over the years has been intercepting mail to and from American citizens has been reported and investigated by congressional committees and even by President Ford's own commission on domestic CIA activities.

But it was not until Wednesday when the Senate Select Committee on Intelligence brought the CIA's chief of mail interception into a public hearing that the nation learned how far this sort of operation had gone.

The hearing brought out the fact that the CIA not only was watching the mail of known or suspected radicals but also had seized and read letters sent or received by Sen. Frank Church (D-Idaho), who is chairman of this select Senate committee; Sen. Hubert Humphrey (D-Minn.), who is a former vice president of the United States; Sen. Edward Kennedy (D-Mass.); Richard Nixon, who was a former vice president cranking up to become the Republican nominee for the presidency in 1968; John D. Rockefeller IV, and Dr. Arthur F. Burns, chairman of the Federal Reserve Board and former chief economist for President Eisenhower.

Arthur F. Burns! Now who in this world would think there was reason for intercepting a letter to or from him, even if it came from or went to the Soviet Union?

If anybody in the "establishment" of the United States represents the straight-laced, free-enterprise, conservative elements, it certainly would be Burns. There are some avowedly radical economists in the U.S. whose correspondence might under certain circumstances reveal something of interest, but hardly Dr. Burns.

The inclusion of such names on its list of intercepts of mail indicates how ridiculous this whole business became.

But it is not just the ridiculous aspect of it that merits attention.

There is a fundamental question here of just what right the CIA had to intercept anybody's mail.

James J. Angleton, the retired chief of CIA counterintelligence who admits responsibility for the mail snooping over 20 years, acknowledges that the program was undertaken in direct violation of federal statutes that specifically prohibit any tampering with first-class mail.

He offered no good explanation of his actions in having undertaken the program in the first place. He had nothing to say about why the program went on even after President Nixon had first approved and then disapproved the so-called Huston plan which called for mail intercepts, or why then-President Nixon never had been informed that the intercept program had been in effect all those years before the Huston plan was conceived.

THERE ARE TIMES when mail censorship is necessary. Such a program was in effect during World War II, for what should be quite obvious reasons.

But even when a true national security reason exists, as it does during such a war, the program is carried out with the full knowledge and consent of the government and people of this nation.

THE SENATE committee has decided that it must now have testimony from President Nixon to determine what he knew and when he knew it about such CIA snooping into the affairs of American citizens.

Nixon's testimony should be sought, and the former president should consent to give it.

But it is obvious already that the investigation of this affair needs to dig even deeper, since the program of mail interception predates his administration.

Who was responsible for initiation of such an illegal, unconstitutional program? And why were the letters of prominent and highly responsible officials in government opened, read and photocopied by the CIA? What were they really looking for, and why?

What has been revealed is disturbing. But what it suggests about what has been going on in the intelligence community is somewhat frightening. It implies at least that we have had a kind of Big Brotherism which no one would have believed possible.

Post-Tribune
Gary, Ind., September 28, 1975

The Central Intelligence Agency has blown its cover.

It has been revealed as a self-perpetuating agency of snoops who have read too many spy tales. As a protector of the country and the guardian of our free way of life, it has worked its wonders in mysterious ways. Illegal ways.

The revelation that for more than 20 years the CIA has been opening private and public citizens' mail is more evidence that the agency has gotten too big for its britches. It has been running loose too long without a leash.

Sen. Frank Church said that a letter he wrote to his mother-in-law while on a trip to Russia was opened. Hubert Humphrey and Edward Kennedy are among other senators whose mail was pried open.

Former President Richard Nixon, Martin Luther King and Linus Pauling are just some of the prominent Americans whose mail was read by the great spies who say they are on our side. Pauling and King were Nobel Peace Prize winners, hardly dangerous to our national security.

James Angleton, a former CIA counterintelligence chief, testified before a Senate committee that the mail-opening program was an "indispensable" espionage tool aimed primarily at getting information from Soviet-bloc nations.

Come on, now Jim, you took your job too seriously.

Angleton said something else that reveals the mentality of the mail-opening operations. He knew it was illegal all along.

So the CIA is above the law. Breaking the law in the name of espionage is espionage on the American people. Do we need that?

Invasion of privacy is insidious. If it happens to somebody else, it can happen to all of us. It is a slimy business and none of it has been proved essential to anything except the perpetuation of a secret operation that itself appears to be dangerous to our liberties.

One "talking paper" given to Nixon for use at a 1970 meeting with top intelligence officials showed a deep "distrust of the American people," according to Sen. Walter Mondale of Minnesota. The paper said that "hundreds or perhaps thousands of Americans — mostly under 30 — are determined to destroy our society" and that their elders were unwilling to believe it.

Mondale said the document showed "an enormous unrestricted paranoid fear of the American people."

Paranoia is the right word and it is a frightening, sick kind of word. If Congress, or the President, or someone doesn't grab the CIA by its ears and shake it into a semblance of sanity, we all will become paranoid. Not in fear of each other, but of this super-agency — the Central Intelligence Agency — that isn't living up to its middle name.

The Courier-Journal
Louisville, Ky., September 28, 1975

THE NIGHTMARISH world of citizens under constant governmental surveillance that George Orwell created in 1984 may not yet be upon us. But continuing revelations from the congressional investigations into governmental intelligence operations indicate that this fantasy has come closer to fact in the United States than most Americans realized.

For over 20 years, from 1952 to 1973, the Central Intelligence Agency intercepted mail to and from Americans on a massive scale. The original aim was to keep a Cold War watch on communications between individual Americans and people or groups in the Soviet Union, Communist China and Cuba. But the screening went far beyond the initial list of suspect persons, so that letters to or from such prominent people as Richard Nixon (shortly before he was elected President), Senators Edward Kennedy and Hubert Humphrey and the late Dr. Martin Luther King, as well as such institutions as Harvard University, were among those opened and copied.

The Federal Bureau of Investigation was guilty of similar abuses of federal authority. From 1942 to 1968, it reportedly conducted an average of close to 10 illegal break-ins a year. Again, the purported aim was to check on foreign agents and domestic subversives, as well as ordinary criminals. But the fact that these operations were conducted without judicial authority and in elaborate secrecy suggest that J. Edgar Hoover and his aides knew full well that what they were doing was illegal.

Both these agencies have had a long tradition of independence from either executive or legislative control. During Mr. Hoover's long reign, the FBI was virtually a personal fiefdom that even Presidents were reluctant to challenge. The CIA, largely protected from outside interference by the convenient cloak of "national security," became so corrupted by the need for secrecy that a former top official, James Angleton, could shock even the hardened members of the Senate Select Committee on Intelligence last week. He said he found it "inconceivable that a secret intelligence arm of the government was to comply with all the overt orders of the government."

This congressional probing should do much to restrain over-zealous CIA officials and FBI agents in the future. Admittedly, it won't be easy to find a way of supervising the operations of these two agencies without destroying their effectiveness in legitimate areas of activity. Yet the attempt must be made.

Americans are entitled to assurances that in the normal business of their private lives — writing letters, talking on the telephone, meeting people — they are guaranteed what Supreme Court Justice Louis Brandeis once called "the right to be left alone — the most comprehensive of rights, and the right most valued by civilized men."

The 1974 Privacy Act, which coincidentally became law yesterday, affords some extra measure of protection against unnecessary governmental intrusion. Citizens are now able to inspect information about themselves in government data banks and to challenge inaccuracies. But some agencies have been exempt from such scrutiny, among them the CIA and the law enforcement agencies, including the FBI.

Congress must therefore establish clear boundaries so that the CIA and the FBI are left in no doubt about the kinds of intrusions into private lives that are not permissible. New attitudes also must be fostered within these agencies, so that a healthier respect can develop for the individual's right to privacy. It's a challenging task, but it must be attempted or 1984 will be more than just a fictional nightmare.

The Cincinnati Post

Cincinnati, Ohio,
September 30, 1975

First off, let there be no doubt that we believe the United States requires the services of a Central Intelligence Agency.

International espionage on the scale practiced by the CIA is a relatively new concept in American life. During the generations when this country's security was based on its geographic isolation, such activities would have been shunned as contrary to our philosophy of an open society.

HOWEVER, IT'S TRUE as it is sad that without the CIA's eyes and ears we would be stripped of our first defenses in today's intricate and dangerous world

For that reason, it is especially disturbing that in past months it has become plain that individuals within the labyrinths of the CIA have engaged in undeniably illegal activities in the name of national security to an extent that the integrity of the agency may be endangered.

One recently exposed example of these activities is the practice, routinely followed for 20 years, of photographing the contents of mail posted in Iron Curtain countries and addressed to Americans. The fact that some of the addressees have been members of Congress— not to mention Richard M. Nixon when he was campaigning for president in 1968 —makes this sort of surveillance neither more nor less evil. It's just plain illegal.

Perhaps even more disturbing was the statement by a veteran former CIA official before a Senate committee that he found it "inconceivable that a secret intelligence arm of the government has to comply with all the overt orders of the government."

This concept of an agency above government is chilling, and brings up a crucial question:

Should a secret intelligence agency, serving a democratic society, be permitted to make its own laws?

Our own deep conviction is that no such concept can be tolerated within the framework of American society.

Those members of the CIA who have grossly overstepped their mandate have, no doubt, done so from the purest of patriotic motives. They have been convinced that the danger from militant communism is glaringly and immediately real.

We, no less than they, have reservations about the durability of today's tenuous detente. However, we also believe that what the CIA is called upon to defend is the basic concept of American personal liberties, and among these is the right to privacy.

CERTAINLY IT ISN'T easy to run an intelligence service according to strictly American rules—especially when the potential enemy observes no rules at all.

No one is suggesting that the CIA should conduct itself like a den of Cub Scouts. But neither should it accept as a model Russia's KGB or Hitler's Gestapo.

To do so would put us on the way toward losing the liberties that the CIA, like all American institutions, should be dedicated to defend.

The Virginian-Pilot

Norfolk, Va., September 26, 1975

For some 20 years the Central Intelligence Agency opened mail sent to American citizens from Communist countries.

A number of prominent politicians are among the correspondents whose letters were purloined by the CIA snoops. One was Richard M. Nixon. A copy of a letter written to Mr. Nixon in June 1968 by Ray Price, one of his speechwriters who was visiting the Soviet Union, was discovered in the CIA files. So was a letter that Senator Frank Church, the chairman of the Senate select committee investigating the government's intelligence operations, wrote to his mother-in-law in Boise, Idaho when he was visiting the Soviet Union in 1971.

Other public figures whose correspondence was intercepted included Senators Hubert Humphrey and Edward M. Kennedy, Representative Bella Abzug, Dr. Martin Luther King Jr. and his wife, and Dr. Arthur Burns, the chairman of the Federal Reserve Board.

The details of the mail intercept program — which was against the law — were revealed in testimony to the Church committee this week.

James Angleton, who directed the program from 1955 to 1973, acknowledged that it was illegal, but defended it as necessary to national security. "From a counterintelligence point of view," he testified, "it was vitally important to know everything possible about contacts between U. S. citizens and Communist countries."

Compared to the assassination attempts, drug experiments that killed people, and disastrous meddling in politics previously revealed, the intercepting of mail is not the worst in the catalogue of horrors attributed to the CIA.

But the gratuitous invasion of privacy is further proof that the agency habitually operated outside the law and beyond the control and effective review of the Congress and — perhaps the President of the United States. The Angleton attitude that the CIA ought to be above the law is the stuff of tyranny.

The CIA did not grow into an American Gestapo — though there were some in Mr. Nixon's White House who wanted to create a political secret police. But nurtured by the Cold War, and abetted by a certain popular paranoia, the CIA did grow into a bloated bureaucracy careless of the law, free to spend unchecked and unwisely, and prone to confuse its own vested interests with the national interest.

The lurid revelations about the activities of the CIA are certain to result in its restructuring. The exact nature of the reform awaits the completion of the investigations and the action of Congress on the forthcoming recommendations. Congress must be careful not to cripple the government's intelligence operations — those that are necessary and proper — as the country's diplomatic intelligence was crippled by the excesses of McCarthyism in the Fifties. But it is clear that the CIA must be curbed and leashed. And perhaps it would be wise to abolish the agency, in name if not in fact and function, since "the CIA" has now become a club for the country's enemies to beat us with.

Anchorage Daily Times

Anchorage, Alaska, September 22, 1975

NOTHING IN the current probe of CIA operations has captured headline attention as much as the display at Senate hearings of a hand gun capable of firing a dart carrying an instantaneously lethal dose of poison over a distance of 100 meters.

This is James Bond stuff. But it's not from spy thriller fiction. It's the real McCoy.

As a sign of the bureaucratic syndrome, however, it's worth noting that the pistol-like dart gun was officially described in Central Intelligence Agency lingo as a "nondiscernable microbionoculator."

In other words, once "inoculated" with the poison — a shellfish toxin — the victim is kaput, without a trace of what caused the death.

Furthermore, testimony by CIA Director William E. Colby disclosed that, contrary to specific presidential orders that this type of deadly toxin should be destroyed, two teaspoons of the material were hidden and preserved in the innards of the agency's secret storage bins.

Those two teaspoons, he said, would be sufficient to kill several thousand people.

THE SENATE inquiry will undoubtedly dig much deeper into this story and may well focus on an attempt to identify the CIA man or men who took it upon themselves to disobey the directive.

This disclosure adds to the black marks that have been scored against the CIA in recent weeks and follows indications that the agency, in violation of its legal scope of responsibility, participated in domestic intelligence activities.

Such actions are to be condemned, of course. As a result of the current probes, it is expected that some stringent new controls will be placed on the CIA's operations.

BUT THE whole sensational business about dart guns and deadly poisons points up the realities of the dark world in which spies are required to function and provides startling reminders that this sort of activity is part of life today — not something out of the pages of the latest best-seller.

If this kind of thing, as unsavory as it may seem when exposed to the glaring lights of a Senate hearing room, is part of the American intelligence operations, we can be assured that it is part of the modus operandi of America's enemies as well.

Pretending that these things don't exist is no way to make them go away. And as much as Americans might like to think there should be no covert intelligence gathering missions either for or against the United States, the truth is they exist.

Maybe some day there will be no need for such things. But the world, unfortunately, isn't yet at that time and place.

HOUSE COMMITTEE, FORD AGREE ON DOCUMENTS' CONFIDENTIALITY

The House Select Committee on Intelligence agreed Oct. 1 to accept President Ford's demand that it not unilaterally make public secret documents and testimony provided to it by the executive branch. The committee's decision to abide by conditions stipulated by Ford came on a 10–3 vote to accept some 50 pages of classified data offered to the panel by William E. Colby, director of the Central Intelligence Agency. The data, which concerned the U.S. intelligence community's foreknowledge of the communists' 1968 Tet offensive in Vietnam, had been subpoenaed as part of the committee's investigation of the intelligence community's contribution to U.S. preparedness in recent international crises.

Under the agreement, President Ford retained the ultimate right to decide if a federal agency could excise portions of secret documents sought by the committee and if the committee could disclose classified or secret material to the public. The committee kept the right to seek a federal court ruling on any dispute between it and Ford.

During the three weeks prior to the agreement, the committee's investigation had been hampered by Ford's Sept. 12 decision to cut off committee access to classified materials until the committee agreed to back down from its insistence on retaining the right to decide on the declassification of secret information. The dispute between the House panel and the White House stemmed from the committee's publication Sept. 11 of a portion of a top-secret study showing that the U.S. intelligence community had failed to foresee the Arab-Israeli war of 1973. At the request of Colby and other officials, the panel had consented to delete certain segments of the document, but had refused to suppress one four-word phrase.

(The disputed phrase was in a Defense Intelligence Agency summary of Oct. 6, 1973, which alluded to mobilization of Egyptian troops "and greater communication security" that had been imposed. Intelligence sources said the four words indicated that the U.S. had the ability to intercept Egyptian communications despite precautions by the Egyptian government. Other sources, cited by the *New York Times* Sept. 14, suggested the phrase referred to the fact that the Egyptian Army on Oct. 1, 1973 had ceased to use radio communication for important military messages and had begun communicating by telephone to avoid eavesdropping. The fact was well known to the Israelis who regularly monitored Egyptian military frequencies, the *Times'* sources said.)

Following the committee's decision to declassify the phrase, President Ford dispatched Assistant Attorney General Rex E. Lee to "request the immediate return" of all classified documents in the panel's possession. Moreover, Ford ordered Lee to inform the committee that no more classified documents would be forthcoming until the committee stopped claiming the right to make them public. Committee Chairman Otis Pike (D, N.Y.) argued that the House resolution creating the investigation and rules subsequently adopted by the committee itself made clear the panel's right to declassify documents as it saw fit. Pike protested that effective congressional scrutiny of government operations would be impossible if the executive branch had the sole power to determine what should or should not be made public.

BUFFALO EVENING NEWS
Buffalo, N.Y., October 2, 1975

The potentially explosive confrontation between the Ford administration and the special House committee probing the CIA has apparently been settled, as most people undoubtedly hoped it would be, by negotiation rather than by the courts.

Under the agreement, the House committee gets all but fragments of the secret material it asked for from the CIA. But the legislators agree not to release to the public any secret data without first hearing objections from the intelligence committee. Any unresolved dispute would go to the President in a "final appeal."

If that means what it seems to, that President Ford retains the ultimate authority to veto any committee declassification of information so confidential that it would damage the country's intelligence capacity, then this arrangement makes sense. If it doesn't mean that, then it had better be further clarified until it does. This entire controversy, after all, flared early last month when the erratic House committee unilaterally, and irresponsibly in our judgment, blabbed material the administration contended could tip friend and foe alike to information not otherwise known.

Perhaps the elements of this compromise reached by the committee and White House could provide a basis for long-term agreements on similar situations in the future.

The two fundamental considerations here concern the secret information itself and its disclosure to the public. We believe responsible committees of Congress should get whatever information they need from any administration in order to fulfill their responsibility to monitor and oversee agency performance. This is particularly necessary in the sensitive areas of military, intelligence and foreign policy, because the extra requirements of secrecy there place a correspondingly heavier burden on the public's elected representatives to check performance.

While Congress retains a legitimate area of jurisdiction, however, the President, charged with carrying out intelligence functions and protecting the security of these complex systems, must retain the authority to disclose or not disclose specific details of intelligence work to the public. Once a piece of top-secret information is released beyond the narrow circle of those especially cleared to see it, its release, no matter how damaging, is beyond recall.

Thus, what the House committee and President Ford have worked out in this ad-hoc situation might sensibly be refined and formalized to cover future problems of a similar nature. And one key ingredient should be that leaders in Congress assume the demanding responsibility for disciplining breaches of that arrangement by legislators or their staff.

ST. LOUIS POST-DISPATCH
St. Louis, Mo., October 4, 1975

The House Select Committee on Intelligence has forced some minor concessions from the Ford Administration on the committee's right to obtain CIA information from the Executive Branch. But as a result of Executive Branch intransigence, the committee has approved a subpena to force Secretary of State Kissinger to surrender a secret memorandum detailing a subordinate's view of State Department mismanagement of the Cyprus crisis last year. Even the compromise between the committee and the White House on CIA information falls short of assuring the congressional investigating group of full access to information or of assuring the public that material revealing misconduct or shortcomings of intelligence agencies will be published.

Under the agreed-on arrangement, Central Intelligence Agency Director William Colby avoided the prospect of a House contempt citation by promising to surrender material the committee wanted on U.S. intelligence in connection with the 1968 Vietnam Tet offensive.

On its side, the committee agreed not to release information or testimony about such information without giving Mr. Colby a chance to object, which seems fair enough. But the committee also agreed not to release information at all if President Ford certifies that its disclosure "would be detrimental to the national security."

By agreeing to let the President be the final judge of what information the public should have, the committee accepted again the customary cozy arrangement under which members of Congress have often kept silent about information embarrassing to the Government as long as they were permitted the ego-boosting satisfaction of sharing the executive's secrets behind a screen of "national security." So-called "national security" has been used frivolously on countless occasions to conceal information which would merely harm some agency's or official's reputation.

To their credit, three committee members — Representatives Giaimo of Connecticut, Aspin of Wisconsin and Dellums of California — voted against accepting various executive conditions attached to delivery of the Tet documents. And Chairman Otis Pike, while going along with the compromise, properly insisted on forcing the issue with the State Department, where Mr. Kissinger has not only barred the release of documents relevant to the committee's investigation but has also forbidden lower level officials to testify on recommendations they may have made in developing policy decisions.

In its contest with the State Department, the committee may yet vindicate its right to receive necessary information from the Executive Branch. But in its contest, the committee will need the backing of the full House. And if that support is not provided, the House will not have faced up to its obligation as a part of a co-equal branch of government to insist on access for itself and the public to information — under rules that prevent arbitrary concealment for suspect purposes.

Long Island Press
Jamaica, N.Y., October 2, 1975

By standing his ground against the White House and the Central Intelligence Agency, Rep. Otis Pike has won a significant victory for Congress and for the public.

After Mr. Pike's House Intelligence Committee had released a document, including a few words the CIA considered vital to security, President Ford ordered CIA Director William Colby and others in authority not to give the committee any more documents.

But the White House began backing away when Rep. Pike, supported by his entire committee, Republicans and Democrats, threatened to go to the full House to seek contempt action.

Mr. Ford offered a compromise which had serious limitations on the committee's access to material it might want. That wasn't good enough for Rep. Pike's belief, who said "it's time the Congress took a stand and said 'we want this information.'" Faced with a confrontation reminiscent of those between former President Nixon and the House Judiciary Committee, Mr. Ford backed away some more. Mr. Colby, turned over to Rep. Pike the material he sought.

Rep. Pike is still leery of reported presidential assurances that other secret material will be given on request, and we can't blame him. We hope Mr. Ford continues to cooperate; in the meantime, the committee should keep its contempt threat as a lever over the White House, as Rep. Pike suggests.

The committee has every right to all the material it needs as it pursues its investigation.

Newsday
Garden City, N.Y., September 23, 1975

For at least three years, Americans have been beset by leaks, innuendoes and suspicions concerning the quality of the U.S. intelligence effort. Whatever your feeling about that catalog of alleged shortcomings, it shouldn't be confused with the entirely different sort of information now emerging from Congress' parallel inquiries into the CIA. Today the information comes from officials or former officials, not faceless "sources." It is sworn testimony, not surmise. And what's called for is hard decisions, not evasive action.

The public hearings of the Senate and House committees on intelligence have barely begun, but three conclusions have already emerged:

• By its own admission, the CIA has been involved in projects that have only the remotest, if any, connection with its charter to gather information on potential enemies and where necessary to protect the U.S. from their dirty tricks. There's no better example of this than the dry run on spreading poison gas (simulated) through the New York City subway system.

• As for the CIA's proper mission, we now have testimony that the agency botched two of its most significant assignments in the past decade. Documents released by Representative Otis Pike's House committee indicate that the CIA was caught unaware when war broke out in the Middle East two years ago. That's unfortunate but not inconceivable; no one expects intelligence estimates to be 100 per cent correct. But according to a second revelation before Pike's committee, the inconceivable did happen: An accurate analysis of Viet Cong strength was surpressed by the CIA to preserve the fiction of U.S. invincibility in Vietnam—with the result that the U.S. was caught with its pants down by the Tet offensive and President Lyndon Johnson felt unable to seek reelection in the aftermath.

• Even so, the present managers of the CIA and the White House still believe they hold a warrant for suppressing bad news. There's no other realistic interpretation of President Ford's attempt to withhold classified documents from the Pike committee unless it blindly agrees to stand by the secrecy classifications imposed by the executive branch. On the present evidence, Pike's judgment is surely as trustworthy as that of bureaucrats who more than once have shown a strong urge to keep the American public from passing judgment on their work.

In short, the CIA not only wandered away from its appointed work, but failed demonstrably even at its primary task. And yet the Ford administration, ignoring the lesson of the Nixon debacle, is opposing rather than assisting Congress' legitimate and indeed restrained effort to share responsibility for one of government's toughest jobs. Unless the President quickly alters course, the CIA's failure will become his as well.

St. Petersburg Times

St. Petersburg, Fla., September 20, 1975

The U.S. government, which must hold every world record for volume in daily production of prose, currently is in its biggest flap of the year over four insignificant words.

President Ford complains those words were supposed to be secret. But a House committee investigating the CIA's recurring abuses and failures saw fit to disclose them.

So Mr. Ford says the committee can't have any more information from the executive branch. And Chairman Otis Pike says if that's the way Mr. Ford wants to play he'll see him with a subpoena in court.

Of course, we don't qualify for the kind of clairvoyant interpretation expected of spies. But it beats us why those words — "and greater communications security," for whatever help it may be — were deemed so important.

TAKEN IN CONTEXT with the sentence from which CIA wanted them censored, they do disclose that despite its eavesdropping and gumshoeing around the Mideast, the CIA goofed something awful in not foreseeing the 1973 Arab-Israeli war. But that was already a matter of record.

The CIA seems to think more than that can be read into the words. It told the committee about that, beforehand and in executive session. But the committee (which agreed to some other deletions) wasn't convinced.

We're willing to take the committee's judgment on that. Especially in light of Pike's explanation that a lot more is at stake here than four insignificant words.

PIKE SAYS the government for years has been covering up its mistakes (and worse) by stamping them secret. And Congress usually has gone along meekly. Not for him, Pike says, not anymore.

He notes that his committee comprises reasonable, responsible, elected members of Congress. They are entitled to see whatever government records they want.

And after hearing whatever claims to secrecy the government may want to offer, they will make their own judgments on what to make public.

To demand anything more, in Pike's view, is to deny the fundamentals of our form of government. We agree, and we doubt that Mr. Ford, after thinking it over, will want to do that.

MEANWHILE, Pike's committee, calling an ex-CIA witness not subject to the President's whim, has turned up fresh evidence of why the CIA would rather keep the whole story — not just the four challenged words — under cover of official secrecy labels.

Samuel A. Adams, a former CIA analyst, explained Thursday why the U.S. was caught off guard by the 1968 Tet offensive in South Vietnam. He said the CIA's estimates of Viet Cong strength were cut in half for public consumption, to help sustain support for the war.

"Although our aim was to fool the American press, the public and the Congress," he told the committee, "we in intelligence succeeded best in fooling ourselves."

The Evening Bulletin

Philadelphia, Pa., September 25, 1975

The dispute between President Ford and the House Intelligence Committee over access to secret data constitutes one of the most important confrontations between Congress and the executive since Watergate—and the solution appears almost as clear.

Appropriate congressmen must have access to classified documents in order to oversee U.S. intelligence operations. And Congress must exercise this function to maintain its powers intact and separate from the executive's.

This clash began when President Ford, angered by the committee's release of secret information, refused to provide more unless the committee promised confidentiality. Committee Chairman Otis G. Pike (D-NY) rejected such a condition.

Then, in recognition of the responsibility all congressional units have to maintain valid confidentiality and to protect national security, the House committee agreed that before declassifying any information, it would give the Administration 24 hours notice to defend existing secrecy.

The White House's choice of an essentially bland document to make its stand on suggests more concern with the general issue of control rather than the sensitivity of this specific piece of information.

The President maintained that part of a summary of the Arab buildup during the 1973 Middle East War, publicized by the committee, could have revealed the extent of U.S. knowledge of Arab communications. But surely the Arabs cannot be so naive nor so ignorant of American intelligence capabilities.

The chief reason for giving the committee access to these documents is to enable it to control the country's virtually uncontrolled intelligence agencies. The names alone of some of their past operations such as Bay of Pigs, "destabilizing" Chile and Operation Phoenix indicate the necessity for congressional supervision.

While most of the recent disclosures about intelligence agencies have centered on possible abuses of their authority, the information the committee now seeks relates to whether the Central Intelligence Agency actually performed its acknowledged responsibilities. For example, the fact that the Arab attack in the 1973 Middle East War took the U.S. as much by surprise as it apparently did the Israelis brings into question the quality of American intelligence.

Only by Congress conducting a complete investigation now can this country provide an accountable, and hopefully more efficient, intelligence operation in the future. And such an investigation requires full White House cooperation.

The Oregonian

Portland, Ore., September 21, 1975

The intelligence records dispute between Rep. Otis Pike's House Intelligence Committee and the Ford administration is neither trivial nor transitory. The disagreements — centering on whether the legislative branch can get classified intelligence data only on conditions imposed by the executive branch — reflect separation of powers issues that have not been confronted fully since passage of the National Security Act of 1947, and possibly since the birth of the republic. They should be resolved now.

Without discussing details of the current dispute, which erupted over alleged or actual congressional disclosure of intelligence information that could work to the disadvantage of U. S. interests, the paramount policy question in the debate is: Can Congress effectively exercise oversight of the intelligence community if it must beg, plead and cajole to gain access to agency records and then receive them only if it agrees in advance how it will use the information?

Unequivocally, the answer is no.

No constitutional directive makes Congress a second-class branch in funding and evaluating use of funds by intelligence agencies. Common sense, sharpened by an instinct for national safety and personal political survival, dictates that lawmakers use sensitive security data with discretion, and Congress has the means — and should have the will — to discipline those among its members who deliberately or negligently violate this trust.

Those who would reserve complete control, including oversight, of intelligence operations to the executive branch place too much trust in any one branch of government — as intelligence foul-ups from the U-2 flights of Francis Gary Powers, to the Bay of Pigs fiasco, to the cobra venom-shellfish toxin assassination caches attest.

Our form of government is healthiest and our freedoms safest when there is push and pull between Congress and the administration, a democratic exercise that requires a full exchange of information.

There will be times when Congress will decide to release information that the executive believes should be suppressed. It must be remembered that Congress has a responsibility, as does any administration, to help shape a national consensus for support of its policies. It may decide that security risks absorbed by releasing certain information are less burdensome than possible consequences of lack of public support for congressional actions in intelligence and defense if cogent data are not disclosed.

Appropriate congressional committees must gain an overview of activities of the multi-billion-dollar intelligence community. The executive branch should not be allowed to make that a myopic view by simply classifying and withholding anything its members — all too many of whom seem accountable to nobody — choose to sequester. If necessary, the Supreme Court may have to be asked to affirm the role and rights of Congress in reviewing intelligence activities.

Wisconsin ▲ State Journal

Madison, Wisc., September 22, 1975

The dispute between the Ford Administration and the House Intelligence Committee over the committee's disclosure of classified material seems a bit preposterous to innocent onlookers.

Ford has cut off the committee's access to secret intelligence documents because the committee released four words in a report which he maintains damaged the nation's intelligence apparatus.

The words are, "and greater communication security . . ."

On the surface at least, it is difficult to comprehend how release of those words could do that much harm.

There are indications that they serve more to point up an intelligence failure to correctly analyze events leading up to the 1973 Arab-Israeli war.

All too often, government classification of documents is used to cover up agency failures rather than protect American interests.

Certainly, congressional committees should not recklessly disclose questionable material without consulting with the agencies involved.

But Congress is charged with investigating the CIA and other agencies which have had serious charges raised against them. And if the investigators are to do their job they cannot continue to play the coverup game.

If, after consultation, Congress is convinced that the public interest would be better served by disclosing certain material it should be disclosed. There is too much tendency for the CIA and other agencies to equate their own well being with that of the country.

The Birmingham News

Birmingham, Ala., October 1, 1975

It is too early to predict the denouement of the drama on Capitol Hill which pits President Ford against the House Intelligence Committee. But one devastating result is already obvious: The Central Intelligence Agency, the Federal Bureau of Investigation and various sections of the State Department will be a long time recovering desperately needed confidence and effectiveness.

It appears that Chairman Otis G. Pike, D-N.Y., and most of the members of the Intelligence Committee are mesmerized by a compulsion to commit the nation to a kind of suicide in their demand that traditionally secret intelligence material be flaunted in the face of America's enemies.

Little question remains that the CIA and the FBI indulged in some illegal practices over the past 20 years. This has been admitted by senior officials in both agencies.

Instead of dissecting every move the agencies have made over the past 20 years or so, and engaging in primitive infighting with the administration, the committee should be concerning itself with exploring how intelligence agencies should operate in a decade which demands that government servants operate in a fish bowl.

It must be clear to millions of Americans that the Intelligence Committee by its insistence on its right to declassify official secrets is abdicating its obligations toward the national security for what is beginning to smell of partisan politics. While Mr. Ford cannot possibly be damaged politically by events in other administrations, committee

members recognize, however, that he can be hurt by maintaining secrecy regarding those events. The committee's apparent goal is to make Ford's defense of the secrets come through to the public as an endorsement of illegal acts.

As the world is now constituted the nation cannot operate safely and effectively without some secrecy. If the Intelligence Committee continues with its efforts to force CIA Director William E. Colby to surrender documents regarding cooperative intelligence operations with other nations the results will be tragic. No reasonable government, however friendly toward the United States, is going to engage in intelligence operations that may be plastered on TV screens and in newspapers around the world.

Obviously the Congress presently feels that the American people want the CIA and the FBI crippled, and congressmen with intelligence activity oversight feel they are playing to the galleries and winning popular support by castigating these agencies.

But the opposite is true. Americans are wise enough to know that the CIA and the FBI and other intelligence agencies are vital to the welfare and security of this nation. They do not want to see these agencies weakened and disbilitated by unreasoning attacks from the Congress.

Americans know that their right to know must be balanced by their right to survive in a world that still operates by the law of the jungle.

THE LOUISVILLE TIMES

Louisville, Ky., September 17, 1975

President Ford looks absurd in threatening Congress over a security dispute involving four words.

By now the entire world knows the four words were: ". . . and greater communications security." In context, they simply said that Egypt, in October 1973, was trying to guard its communications against spying.

The House Select Committee on Intelligence released the four words in making public an Oct. 6, 1973, summary of the Mideast situation prepared by the Defense Intelligence Agency. President Ford retaliated by ordering that the committee get no more classified material and that no administration officials testify before the committee. This order could lead to a constitutional confrontation between the President and Congress.

If U. S. national security were indeed at stake, the President's action might be justified. It is not the United States, however, but the inept U. S. intelligence agencies that the President is actually protecting.

For the first time ever, a congressional committee is asking hard questions about the quality of the work of our intelligence forces, including the Central Intelligence Agency. Spearheading the tough-minded House investigating committee is U. S. Rep. Otis Pike, D-N. Y., a World War II Marine Corps dive-bomber pilot and a veteran member of the House Armed Services Committee.

Rep. Pike is *not* a naive dove about national security. He has long been a strong advocate of the armed services. However, he is not taken in by the old mumbo-jumbo of "don't talk about this embarrassing situation because it will hurt our national security."

The emerging record of the House investigating committee shows that the CIA and other intelligence agencies have been doing a shockingly bad job of intelligence gathering.

The four "secret" words in question, for instance, come from a larger report that was grossly in error. That report, made on the day that Egypt and Syria launched their 1973 war against Israel, said, ". . . There are still no military or political indicators of Egyptian intentions or preparations to resume hostilities with Israel." That was roughly equivalent to saying that the Japanese attack on Pearl Harbor did not really indicate a war-like situation.

The 1973 Mideast war, about which the United States got such poor ad-

vance warning from the intelligence community, resulted in the Arab oil boycott and a worldwide energy crisis. The impact of that war will be felt for decades.

Tragically, the congressional committee was told by the former director of the State Department's Bureau of Intelligence and Research that the war and the oil boycott could have been avoided by diplomatic efforts if U. S. intelligence had recognized the danger signals.

That assessment could be regarded as merely 20/20 hindsight if the 1973 miscalculation had been an isolated incident. But the CIA has a long record of bobbles.

In 1960, without telling the State Department, it foolishly sent a U2 flight over Russia just two weeks before President Eisenhower was to go to Europe for a summit meeting. The summit meeting crashed along with the U2 when the plane was shot down.

A year later the CIA turned the attempted invasion of Cuba into one of the most embarrassing episodes in American history. In the shambles of the Bay of Pigs, President Kennedy attempted to make tighter checks on the agency. He failed, however, by not demanding its complete overhaul.

Four years after that, the CIA was a source of bad information and bad advice for President Johnson about the Dominican Republic. President Johnson was so confused and irritated that he ordered the FBI to look into the extent and nature of alleged Communist influence in the Dominican civil war.

In the 1970s, the CIA dabbled in domestic intelligence operations — something strictly prohibited by its congressional charter. The Watergate-related crimes of President Nixon's administration had tentacles into the CIA. It was those excesses, in fact, that triggered the current probe, the first serious congressional scrutiny of the agency since it was created.

That Congress is unearthing unpleasant facts about the CIA and other intelligence agencies, including the fact that they have incompetents on their payrolls, should not be surprising. What is surprising is Mr. Ford's seeming effort to keep the lid on. Mr. Ford should not be allowed to get away with that. For if our secret billions cannot purchase competence, then what are they buying?

The Detroit News
Detroit, Mich., October 4, 1975

The House Intelligence Committee has agreed to a sensible compromise with President Ford regarding secret papers and testimony obtained from the executive branch by the committee in its probe of federal intelligence agencies.

Hoping to have a field day with such materials, Rep. Otis Pike, D-N.Y., chairman of the committee, had insisted that the committee obtain and dispose of classified information in any way it chose. If allowed that latitude, the committee could have done irreparable harm to the process of intelligence gathering and to foreign policy.

Naturally, President Ford halted access to secret information until the committee agreed that it must not decide on its own to make secret materials public. By a decisive 10-3 margin, the committee voted this week to accept the President's principal terms.

The committee recognizes Mr. Ford's right to delete parts of classified documents and decide what can be released. If it disagrees with the President's decisions, the committee has the right to carry the dispute to court.

This agreement will prevent Rep. Pike from making a complete shambles of U.S. intelligence operations. However, a lot still depends on the committee's integrity. Does it have the discipline to prevent leakage of material entrusted in its hands?

Unfortunately, promises don't seem to mean much on Capitol Hill these days. In recent times, congressional committees have leaked classified information in torrents. Lawmakers and staff members involved in the Watergate investigations raced one another out of committee rooms to spill their guts to selected reporters in the hall.

The Pike committee and any others dealing with sensitive information could take a page from the late Sen. Richard Russell's book. Following the firing of Gen. Douglas MacArthur by President Harry Truman, the Georgia senator headed an inquiry touching on military security and delicate matters of foreign policy.

He found it necessary to conduct some of the sessions behind closed doors and to screen the transcript before releasing it to the press. Sen. Russell and the members of his committee strictly observed the rules of security they had adopted for themselves. They kept secret information secret. They were honorable men who performed impartially, placing national interest above their own petty political desires.

Congress could use some of that honor and impartiality today in its investigations. We've come a long way since the Russell era — and the path has not led entirely upward.

WORCESTER TELEGRAM.
Worcester, Mass., October 3, 1975

In their attempt to uncover mistakes that may have been made by the Central Intelligence Agency and the State Department, various congressional investigators are treading a narrow line. If they are not careful, they may create a political climate in which the agencies would find it difficult to function.

The threat of bringing contempt of Congress charges against CIA director William E. Colby for not delivering all the secret material demanded by the House Intelligence Committee is one example. Committee chairman Otis Pike's assertion that U.S. intelligence has become so ineffective that it could not warn the country of an impending enemy attack is another. Another worrisome point is the Pike committee's method of secretly interviewing junior staff members of the State Department — instead of senior policy makers — on controversial intelligence issues.

Colby got himself into hot water with the committee after President Ford cut off access to secret documents, following a committee release of certain phrases indicating American ability to monitor communications in the Middle East. The issue may have been resolved when the CIA agreed to supply all but 50 words of a new batch of material subpoenaed by the committee, this time about matters relating to the 1968 Tet offensive.

There are some conditions attached, with the President being the final arbitrator on what may be publicized.

Pike's investigation of the Cyprus crisis and the State Department's role in it created another furor. Although Secretary of State Kissinger offered to testify before the committee and sent two of his senior assistants to do the same, the intelligence committee summoned a junior officer, Thomas D. Boyatt, who had sharply disagreed with the policies of his superiors. By seeking out dissenters instead of those responsible for policy-making, the congressmen followed an approach made infamous during the McCarthy era.

In the wake of the Vietnam-Watergate period, it is understandable that Congress is trying to rebuild its authority. Perhaps not all is well with intelligence gathering and foreign policy-making in this country. And if agencies like the CIA have been guilty of transgressions or undue secrecy — particularly in the domestic area where they do not belong in the first place — a congressional investigation may be useful in correcting the mistakes.

But if the investigators, motivated by honest concern, political ambition, or both, manage to cripple the effectiveness of the CIA — or discourage foreign service officers from making policy recommendations freely — the country will be taking a risk.

The Houston Post
Houston, Tex., September 24, 1975

Decapitation is scarcely the most effective form of brain surgery. But in attempting to excise malignant growths in the CIA, some congressmen are using an ax where a scalpel is needed.

Distressing charges are being leveled at the CIA these days, some of them horrendous. The covert action division discussed assassination of government leaders in other countries. Assassination has no part in any activity of any agency of the United States. The covert action division intruded in the elections of other countries to an unjustifiable degree. The time has certainly come for the public to know and for the administration to revise the leadership of the covert action section.

But the CIA employs some 15,000 men and women. Of these, fewer than 5 per cent are connected with covert operations. The rest collect information from newspapers, books, maps, government reports in countries around the world, for filing and digesting in Washington. Thousands of tiny pieces of data gradually come together making a mosaic that gives a picture or a warning. Do we as a people want to strip ourselves of intelligence? Do we want not to know what is going on in the world? Are we willing to junk our entire intelligence agency and blunder unaided and uninformed through foreign affairs and future dangers?

Rep. Otis Pike, D-N.Y., says there is no question about congressional rights to declassify documents. But does the right require a congressman to blurt on national television documentary details having no public interest, details which telegraph significant information to foreign countries? The irresponsible comments of some congressmen have done more damage to the intelligence agency of the United States than any foreign counter-intelligence agency could hope to do. Congress can safeguard the public's right to know without shouting every small phrase to the world.

The CIA supplies the White House with briefs. Rep. Pike demanded to see them. The White House complied with one provision: That four words be kept secret because they would have meaning to the country about which the report had been written. Within 48 hours those precise words had been tossed to the media. They meant nothing to Pike because he is not versed in the language of intelligence. To the country under scrutiny, they meant that the CIA had deciphered its messages. Five years of intelligence work was blown off. But what had the public gained?

Sen. Frank Church, D-Idaho, is using a blunderbuss on the incident of the CIA poisons. He refers to 10 grams of shellfish toxin and 10 milligrams of cobra venom — less than a handful — — as a "stockpile" of poisons..

Most parents know the experience of being unable to silence a child who insists on blurting a fact or a comment which is embarrassing or detrimental to the family interest. The inability of some congressmen to hold their tongues, to be discreet on matters important to the nation, is reminiscent of such a child. Whether the congressmen are irresponsible or seeking publicity for political purposes, they must be blamed for a continuing indiscretion that does disservice to the nation. A statesman should be able to correct abuses in one branch of a large agency without destroying the whole.

THE SPRINGFIELD UNION
Springfield, Mass.,
September 19, 1975

The House Intelligence committee can't be faulted for its general performance in the probe of intelligence operations, but it slipped in its release of four words from a secret report. That was enough to disclose U.S. monitoring of Egyptian communications before the 1973 Middle East war.

Perhaps the "secret" classification was unwarranted from the standpoint of national security, but that's not a conclusion to be jumped at. Certainly the judgment should not be spread all over federal officialdom. Confidentiality must be respected even while classifying procedure is under challenge.

White House refusal, after the committee's faux pas, to release any more classified material resulted in a committee subpoena of more secret documents. The administration tried to extract a promise no more public disclosures would be made, but the committee refused.

Instead, the committee said it would give the administration 24 hours' notice before publicly disclosing secret material in the future. The committee, whose proper function is oversight of intelligence operations, seems to be on a high-and-mighty binge.

Somebody — perhaps the House majority leadership — should pull the reins before the intelligence committee, as self-appointed changer of classifications, really fractures the national security.

The Washington Star
Washington, D.C., September 29, 1975

Representative Otis G. Pike of New York is not known as the most patient of the legislators on Capitol Hill. As chairman of the House Select Committee on Intelligence, he has strong views about the dignity of his position and the prerogatives of the Congress in general. When these prerogatives, in his view, are defied by another branch of the government, Pike's indignation knows no bounds.

Thus it is that the whole Ford administration is today threatened with a contempt of Congress action if it continues to "obstruct and delay" the House committee's investigation of federal intelligence agencies. Pike has not yet decided exactly what officials may be cited in the contempt action. Possibly President Ford himself will be named as the culprit. But Secretary of State Henry Kissinger and Central Intelligence Agency Director William E. Colby are more likely targets. Pike, for his part, has no doubt that the administration as a whole "is in contempt of Congress." His recommendation is that "we should move carefully and deliberately but steadily to determine that issue."

There are two chief causes for the congressman's ire. To begin with, Pike's committee voted on September 11 to declassify some intelligence data on the 1973 Middle East war which, in the view of the CIA, compromised American intelligence operations. The next day, by presidential order, the committee was barred from access to further classified information until some agreement on release of such information could be worked out. Chairman Pike angrily rejected any restrictions. Congress, he proclaimed, was not bound by any classification rules of the executive. The legislative branch, in his view, had an absolute right to any secret material that it wanted. Furthermore, it had an absolute right to make any such information public on its own discretion.

But the dispute didn't stop there. A few days later, Chairman Pike exploded again, this time on being informed of certain restrictions placed on the testimony before his committee by lower-echelon members of the State Department. As explained by Lawrence S. Eagleburger, undersecretary of state for management, these officials could testify as to facts and their own interpretation of them. But, in order to protect the confidentiality of the decision-making process in the executive branch, they could not testify as to the advice on policy matters passed up to senior officials in the State Department. Only these relatively few top officials who make policy could discuss options before the committee, Eagleburger said.

The committee which, for starters, is looking into intelligence failures in Vietnam, the Middle East, Cyprus and Portugal, has been outraged by these examples of what it considers to be executive effrontery. Pike is reported to be preparing a resolution to take to the floor of the House asking for a vote of confidence in his efforts to get information. If the vote is favorable, says Pike, "I would then ask for the House of Representatives to state that someone was in contempt."

The issue is not likely to be settled in Congress. For us, at least, it is hard to visualize a vote which would empower the House sergeant at arms to sally forth and arrest President Ford or Henry Kissinger or Bill Colby — or all of them — and haul them off for detention in the basement of the Capitol. Although this is apparently the prescribed procedure for this sort of thing, it has never been tried in the 200 years of this republic's history. As an alternative, a battle in the courts over the constitutional issues involved seems far more probable.

That is, a court test is probable if Rep. Pike really means to go through with his threat of a contempt action. The issues which he has raised have arisen many times in the past and they have always been resolved by compromise without any definitive ruling by the courts which might drastically change the relationship between the executive and legislative branches for all time. The courts themselves have been commendably reluctant to tip the balance in any definitive way. It may be that some members of Congress believe that the time is ripe today for a showdown of historic implications. For our part, we believe that if the courts — or the people — were forced to decide who really governs the nation, the verdict would not be in favor of the House of Representatives.

The News and Courier
Charleston, S.C., October 2, 1975

Debate between President Ford and Congress over access to material of vast significance to the U.S. in information-gathering operations around the world is being handled with a degree of restraint by both sides. That is important. If such a debate ever gets out of hand, a collision could ensue which might wreck operations essential to national security and well-being. Mr. Ford presumably can be counted on to exercise common sense in withholding extra-sensitive items from congressmen who are demanding them more on grounds of principle than anything else but the more fervently the matter is discussed the more uncertainty is implanted in the minds of observers about the safety of secrets about whose security there should be no uncertainty.

Congressional demands for lists of agents, for example, cannot help but implant the notion in the minds of intelligence operatives that their "cover" — if not, indeed, their lives — is at risk. No agent can operate effectively if he is looking over his shoulder for fear of his own side. If Congress does not really need those lists, and we can't imagine why it should, it should be careful about asking for them.

Unfortunately for the credibility of the Select House Intelligence Committee, which may be thoroughly justified in a general desire to break down excessive government preoccupation with secret-keeping, deliberations are tending more and more to traverse party lines. One gets the impression, inevitably, that a Democratic majority is more interested in belaboring President Ford than it might be if the President were their man.

There can be hardly any explanation, except that it is the desire of the committee to embarrass President Ford, for stubborn insistence on making disputed secret material available to the whole House. That demand puts Mr. Ford in an absolutely untenable position when it comes both to pleasing Congress and protecting the country. It is hard enough to keep secrets when they are shared among a few people. A secret broadcast to 435 people is no secret at all.

Minneapolis Tribune

Minneapolis, Minn., September 18, 1975

The potential for sensationalism has been high from the start in congressional investigations of U.S. intelligence activities. Revelations such as CIA plots of past years to assassinate foreign leaders have been shocking, but that is because the facts themselves are shocking, not because the investigators overdramatized them. For the most part, there's been a high degree of cooperation between the administration and Congress, and judicious use by the congressional committees of highly sensitive material furnished by the administration.

An exception that threatens to become a constitutional confrontation is President Ford's refusal to comply with subpoenas by the House Intelligence Committee for certain material. That step last Thursday was supplemented by a directive to all executive agencies to provide no further information to the committee and a demand that the committee return all classified documents. The reason for such abrupt and all-encompassing actions was the committee's inclusion last week of the four-word phrase "and greater communications security" in its release of intelligence reports for the period just before the 1973 Middle East war. Committee members and intelligence officials had agreed on most of what was to be released. Publishing the phrase would, according to the officials, jeopardize current intelligence sources and methods, but the committee included it anyway.

That is why the president at his news conference Tuesday expressed great concern over the effects on national security that further disclosures of that kind could have. "Until I find from the committee what their procedure is going to be," he said, "I will not give them the information." Committee chairman Otis Pike sounded equally adamant. He would oppose a compromise, he said, on the right of Congress to declassify material or to subpoena presidential documents.

But a compromise would surely be preferable to a time-consuming and probably rancorous constitutional test. Without trying to guess what the outcome of such a test would be (for example, does the Signal Intelligence Act apply to Congress?), we do think that on the narrow issue at hand, Ford's position is stronger than Pike's. Access to executive documents is not really in question, since up until last week the administration had given the committee what it requested. The issue is who decides what intelligence material can be declassified. Although the committee yesterday voted to give 24 hours' notice before making such information public, that leaves the basic issue unresolved.

The phrase whose publication alarmed intelligence experts was not essential to public understanding of American intelligence and the 1973 war — or, for that matter, essential to congressional understanding. If the executive branch were engaged in a cover-up or capriciously preventing large amounts of intelligence-related material from becoming known, Pike would be on firmer ground. But that has not been the case, and under these circumstances it seems reasonable for the administration to retain a final say on declassification.

Sentinel Star

Orlando, Fla., September 25, 1975

U.S. REP. OTIS Pike's ideas on declassifying secret papers are at best simplistic and unworkable, at worst stupid.

The New York Democrat, chairman of the House Intelligence Committee, says Congress has the right and duty to declassify documents at will. Otherwise, he argues, the executive branch of government can cover up all kinds of crookedness and incompetence simply by using a secret rubber stamp on the papers that prove such goings on.

☆ ☆ ☆

WE DON'T dispute Pike's contention that many documents are improperly classified and kept that way too long, and to that end Congress should be watchful in its function as overseer.

Surely, however, Pike understands that there are legitimate state secrets in the function of any government on earth, especially a major power with complex and delicate foreign commitments.

Administration officials say, with justification, that Pike's committee is jeopardizing U.S. foreign policy by quoting directly from secret documents without permission.

Pike says he's only trying to prove that President Ford is covering up what a bad job U.S. intelligence agencies are doing. If the congressman wants to make that point, we'll listen, but we'd prefer that he and other committee chairman not usurp the final say over what is and isn't properly secret. That isn't freedom of information; it's a flirtation with chaos.

THE ROANOKE TIMES
Roanoke, Va., September 21, 1975

Revelations during the past several months about the operations of U.S. intelligence services—especially the Central Intelligence Agency—are broad and disturbing. Congress and the White House need to rein in these agencies and keep them from reckless, unmonitored meddling overseas or from tampering with civil liberties of Americans at home.

Congress and the executive branch obviously have not found a way to cooperate on this. Both mood and method favor confrontation. The White House is in a swivet over four revealing words in classified material made public by the House Intelligence Committee; President Ford says the panel should not be given any more material. The committee has refused to return to Mr. Ford secret documents previously subpoenaed, although it will give the administration 24 hours' notice before letting out any more secrets. "There is no question," said Committee Chairman Otis G. Pike, D-N.Y., "about our (Congress') right to keep documents or declassify them. The only question is how we will exercise that right."

Legally, the Congressman may well be correct; and doubtless there is, and has been, too much secrecy within government. Official secrecy customarily is used to cloak misdeeds as well as mistakes, and when an intelligence agency is involved, the hidden blunders are likely to be all the more outrageous and the cries about perils to national security all the louder.

Nonetheless, we are not panting to see the CIA paraded naked through the square. To make the essential reforms in its structure and its operations, it is not necessary to uncover every last one of its wrongs, embarrass or endanger some of its agents, and further discredit U.S. policies abroad. Momentum already is strong, in Congress and in the thrust of public opinion, for an overhaul.

To accomplish this, Congress will need more, not less, secret information, obtained in cooperation with the White House and handled with prudence. Both sides should back off from the lines they have drawn in the dust. What's important is not to establish somebody's manhood, but to get U.S. intelligence activities under accountable, responsible control.

CIA Foreign Covert Operations

Marchetti, Agee Books

Suit filed over censorship. Alfred A. Knopf, Inc., publisher of *The CIA and the Cult of Intelligence*, and the authors, Victor L. Marchetti and John D. Marks, filed suit in New York federal court Oct. 30, 1973 to enjoin the Central Intelligence Agency from censoring one-tenth of the material in the book. Marchetti and Marks, who had been employed by the CIA and the State Department respectively, had signed secrecy agreements. But the suit contended that the agreements constituted "prior restraint upon freedom of the press" and violated the First and Fifth Amendments to the Constitution.

Authors win round in CIA secrecy fight. Victor L. Marchetti and John D. Marks, authors of a forthcoming book on the Central Intelligence Agency, won the latest round in their court battle against CIA attempts to exercise prior censorship on sections of their book considered by the CIA to be harmful to national security if revealed.

In a ruling announced April 1, 1974, U.S. District Court Judge Albert V. Bryan Jr. ruled that the CIA had exceeded its authority in ordering the deletion of 168 passages from the book *The CIA and the Cult of Intelligence*. After reviewing the excisions by the CIA, Bryan reduced the number to 15.

Bryan said the CIA could not classify a fact simply because an official of the agency declared it to be so. Decisions on what was classified, Bryan said, seemed to have been made by each deputy director of the CIA "on an ad hoc basis as he viewed the manuscript, founded on his belief, at that time, that a particular item contained classified information which ought to be classified." Calling such a basis "not sufficient" if the 1st Amendment rights of the plaintiffs were to survive, Bryan held that the CIA should have been able to produce documents or other evidence to demonstrate that the material in the book was classified.

Before issuing his ruling, Bryan had heard secret testimony March 1 from CIA Director William E. Colby, and the day before from the four deputy CIA directors. At that time, Colby said publicly that this case was crucial to his statutory role as protector of national security sources and secrets. If this case were lost,

Colby said, he would ask Congress to pass legislation imposing criminal penalties on former CIA employes who divulged what the CIA deemed to be classified information.

In 1972, when the book was only in outline form, the CIA had obtained a court order requiring Marchetti and Marks to submit their manuscript, when completed, to the CIA for review. Subsequently, the CIA ordered over 300 passages deleted. Taking advantage of the part of the original court order which allowed them to appeal the deletions by the CIA, the authors won a ruling by Judge Bryan Dec. 21, 1973 that the CIA had to supply evidence, justifying the deletions, to the court and other co-plaintiffs in the suit.

Marks expelled from South Vietnam— John D. Marks, co-author with Victor Marchetti of *The CIA and the Cult of Intelligence*, was arrested in Saigon Dec. 26, 1974 and expelled from the country the next day. He had arrived in South Vietnam undetected Dec. 21 to do research for a magazine article. No official reason was given for his expulsion, but police said Marks was on the blacklist of persons whose presence was considered undesirable.

Court finds undue pressure on CIA book. The U.S. 4th Circuit Court of Appeals ruled Feb. 11, 1975 that a lower court judge had unduly pressured the Central Intelligence Agency to prove information contained in a book about the agency was classified. The appeals panel returned the case to U.S. District Court Judge Albert V. Bryan Jr. for further action.

The case involved the book, *The CIA and the Cult of Intelligence* by Victor L. Marchetti, a former CIA agent, and John D. Marks, a former State Department intelligence officer. Backed by a court order, the CIA had initially sought deletion of 339 items from the book for reasons of national security. Subsequently, negotiations between the agency and Marchetti's lawyers resulted in the reduction of the number of deletions to 168. Bryan later reduced the number to 15 deletions, but stayed his ruling pending appeal by the CIA.

Supreme Court declines hearing—The Supreme Court announced without comment May 27, 1975 that it would allow to stand a 4th U.S. Circuit Court of Appeals ruling sustaining the right of the Central Intelligence Agency to censor the writings of former employes who signed

contracts in which they agreed not to divulge information they learned about the agency while working for it.

In so ruling, the court rejected First Amendment freedom of press claims on behalf of the book, *The CIA and the Cult of Intelligence*, by Victor L. Marchetti and John D. Marks. The appellate court had upheld the CIA's deletion, for reasons of national security, of 170 passages from the authors' original manuscript and concluded that security classifications had to be presumed correct because the government would be overburdened if private citizens could force it to prove otherwise.

Only Associate Justice William O. Douglas dissented. In his dissent, he declared: "No official, no matter how high or majestic his or her office, who is within the reach of judicial process, may invoke immunity for his actions for which wrongdoers normally suffer."

The defense had sought to prove that this was the first case in which a writer was required to submit his work to a government agency for advance clearance. Melvin L. Wulf, legal director of the American Civil Liberties Union and counsel for Marchetti in the case, noted that only four Justices constituted the minimum required to hear a case. Wulf said, "The inevitable inference is that their minds are closed to any argument which would dare question the awesome power now vested in the CIA in direct derogation of the First Amendment. A Supreme Court which declines to consider a question of that magnitude puts its reputation in serious jeopardy."

Book details CIA activities. A book describing day-to-day operations by the U.S. Central Intelligence Agency in three Latin American countries was published in London by Penguin Books, it was reported Jan. 14, 1975.

The book, *Inside the Company: CIA Diary*, was written by Philip Agee, who worked for the agency in Ecuador, Uruguay and Mexico in 1960–68.

Agee described the CIA as an instrument to frustrate revolution and protect capitalism.

The book listed nearly 250 persons whom Agee called officers, local agents, informers or collaborators of the CIA. They included businessmen, labor and student leaders, and politicians in the countries where Agee served; in Mexico, Agee named as collaborators two former presidents, Gustavo Diaz Ordaz and

Adolfo Lopez Mateos, and the current president, Luis Echeverria Alvarez. He said Echeverria cooperated with the CIA only in his capacity as interior minister, before he was elected president.

Agee said that during his years in Latin America, the CIA's main objective was to counteract Cuban influence in the hemisphere. He described CIA infiltration of local political parties, cooperation with local police forces to eliminate leftist subversives, tampering with local mail services, and wiretapping embassies of Communist countries.

The truth of Agee's account was not questioned, according to press reports. Miles Copeland, a former high-ranking CIA official, said in a review of the book in the British magazine *The Spectator:* "The book is. . . an authentic account of how an ordinary American or British 'case officer' operates. . . All of it. . . is presented with deadly accuracy."

CIA, Venezuela Exxon subsidiary linked—Agee testified before the second Bertrand Russell Tribunal in Brussels Jan. 12 that his work as a CIA agent had included carrying out personal name checks of Venezuelan employes of Creole Petroleum Corp., the Venezuelan subsidiary of the U.S. Exxon Corp.

In 1960, Agee said, Creole was "letting the CIA assist in employment decisions, and my guess is that those name checks. . . are continuing to this day." The CIA customarily performed this service for subsidiaries of large U.S. corporations in Latin America, Agee wrote.

An Exxon spokesman in Washington denied Agee's claim Jan. 13.

CIA officer retires to defend agency. David A. Phillips, 52, chief of Latin American operations for the Central Intelligence Agency, resigned effective May 9 to organize an association of former agency employes for the purpose of defending the organization against outside attack, it was reported March 22, 1975.

An open letter Phillips sent to 25C former agency officers said in part:

"As chief of Latin American operations, I have been deeply concerned about the decline of morale at Langley [CIA headquarters outside Washington] and abroad. Snowballing innuendo, egregious stories and even honest concerns have presented us with the basic dilemma of issuing either a general statement which reassures few but preserves security or a comprehensive accounting which satisfies some but at the expense of operations and agents.

"Under the circumstances, there is little doubt that a thorough Congressional review is the best, if not only, solution even though some leakage of sensitive details on foreign operations seems almost inevitable . . . our capabilities abroad are being damaged. More of our agents and friends . . . are saying thanks but no thanks. Friendly liaison services are beginning to back away from us. The Marchettis and the Agees have the stage and only a few challenge them."

Indochina War

Laos refugee aid diverted. Sen. Edward M. Kennedy (D, Mass.) charged Feb. 6, 1971 that American aid for war refugees in Laos was being supplied to guerrilla forces directed by the Central Intelligence Agency. "Until recent times," he said, "The U.S. AID [Agency for International Development] refugee program was simply a euphemism to cover American assistance to persons who agreed to take up arms against the [Communist] Pathet Lao."

"A very significant measure of this assistance apparently continues," Kennedy said. Such activity had been disclosed in 1970.

The information was based on reports from the General Accounting Office which were released by Kennedy's Senate Refugees and Escapees Subcommittee. The reports said "substantial amounts" of medical supplies were being furnished "Lao military" by AID.

Laos aid diversion continues—Sen. Edward M. Kennedy made public March 18, 1972 a General Accounting Office report that the diversion of funds intended for relief of civilian victims of war in Laos was continuing despite Nixon Administration assurances in 1971 the practice would be ended. The report said almost half the relief funds were being diverted to the clandestine guerrilla force in Laos.

Kennedy, chairman of a Senate Refugees and Escapees Subcommittee, released another GAO report April 22 that aid funds were being diverted to feed and otherwise assist paramilitary forces and their dependents in Laos, including Meo tribesmen serving in the clandestine army operated by the Central Intelligence Agency.

Sen. Stuart Symington (D, Mo.), chairman of a Senate subcommittee on U.S. overseas commitments, issued a subcommittee report May 7 that the U.S. had pledged to provide up to $100 million a year to support a Thai irregular army of 10,000 men in Laos.

The report, prepared by staff members James G. Lowenstein and Richard M. Moose, also reported that U.S. helicopter gunships, under U.S. Army command but apparently flown by Thai pilots, were being used in Northern Laos to support medical evacuation missions. The report also said the Thai Air Force was flying combat support missions in Laos with equipment and ammunition supplied by the U.S.

Ex-Green Beret admits 1969 slaying. Robert F. Marasco, a former captain in the U.S. Special Forces who was charged but never tried in the 1969 slaying of a suspected South Vietnamese double agent, said April 2, 1971 that he had shot and killed him on orders from the Central Intelligence Agency.

Marasco said he was admitting his complicity in the death of the agent out of a sense of anger over the conviction of 1st Lt. William L. Calley Jr. on charges of murdering 22 civilians at Mylai.

Marasco, now a life insurance salesman, was one of eight Green Berets charged with killing Thai Khac Chuyen, whose body was dropped from a boat into the South China Sea and never found.

(There were no trials as CIA Director Richard Helms decided not to permit any CIA personnel to appear as witnesses. President Nixon was also involved in the CIA decision to drop the case against the Green Berets.)

Marasco, 29, said Chuyen was killed on "oblique yet very, very clear orders" from the CIA. He described Chuyen as "my agent" and said it was "my responsibility to eliminate him with extreme prejudice."

According to Marasco, Chuyen's death was approved "up and down our chain of command."

For the most part, Marasco's story corroborated earlier reports on how the agent was murdered. He said Chuyen, whose identity as a double agent was discovered when he was seen in a Vietcong photograph, was drugged with morphine on a boat before he was shot. Marasco said he killed Chuyen with two shots to the head. His body was then tossed overboard in a weighted mail sack by three officers in the boat.

Because Marasco was no longer in the Army, he was not subject to court-martial. He had never before admitted direct participation in the killing.

Senate reviews U.S. role in Laos. The Senate met in secret session June 7, 1971 to review the extent of U.S. involvement in the war in northern Laos.

The unusual session had been requested by Sen. Stuart Symington, who said May 28 the public and Congress had "little or no knowledge" of the Laotian situation and the Senate should ascertain the facts of the U.S. role before more funds were appropriated "for this clandestine war."

Symington said June 6 the U.S. was spending "hundreds of millions" of dollars on the war in Laos, much more than the $52 million acknowledged by the Administration as its economic aid for the area. In the secret session, Symington had said such spending was amounting to at least $350 million annually.

The use of B-52s for raids over northern Laos in support of the Laotian government troops was acknowledged May 3 by Undersecretary of State John N. Irwin 2nd, who told the Senate Foreign Relations Committee the B-52s were used on a regular basis to attack enemy troop formations and supply lines. Previously, the Administration had admitted use of the B-52s for such purpose on only one occasion in February 1970—during a battle for the Plaine de Jarres.

Committee Chairman J. W. Fulbright (D, Ark.) said May 21 that 4,800 Thai troops financed by the U.S., through the Central Intelligence Agency, were fighting in Laos in support of the Royal Laotian government. Fulbright charged that the U.S. role was "inconsistent with the spirit" of the "antimercenary" amendment enacted in 1970.

Sen. Edward M. Kennedy, joining Symington June 6 in attacking American policies in Laos, protested Administration "whitewashes" concerning its efforts in Laos and said the policy grounds for involvement there would justify "new military adventures by the President anywhere in Southern Asia." In a letter to Kennedy, the State Department had justified the Laotian role on the President's constitutional authority to "take reasonable measures" in northern Laos as part of his program to protect American forces withdrawing from South Vietnam. Kennedy had asked for the grounds of the U.S. military involvement.

In a statement issued just prior to the Senate's secret session June 7, the State Department said U.S. financial and material support of Thai "volunteers" fighting in Laos for the Laotian government was "fully consistent with all pertinent legislation." One of its arguments was that the program of using "volunteers" in Laos predated enactment of the "anti-mercenary" amendment.

Covert war policy indicated. The *New York Times* halted publication June 15 of a series of Vietnam war articles drawn from a secret Pentagon study after the Justice Department obtained a temporary court order barring publication of the articles.

The Pentagon study traced increasing U.S. involvement in the Vietnam war and covering a period ending in 1968. The study contained some startling developments, such as Johnson Administration plans for major American military action against North Vietnam almost five months before the 1964 Tonkin Gulf incident, a covert commitment of U.S. ground combat troops to the war and an anxiety lest the escalation become publicized.

The *Times* printed three installments of the series June 13–15 covering 18 pages of newsprint with documents and analysis drawn from the Pentagon study. The study itself consisted of 3,000 pages of analysis and 4,000 pages of official documents on the policy decisions which led to U.S. involvement in the war. The Pentagon papers did not include Presidential papers and included only those State Department documents that turned up in the Defense Department files.

The Laos bombing phase of the covert war included strikes by T-28 fighter-bombers carrying the markings of the Laotian Air Force. The report said, however, that some of the planes were manned by pilots of Air America, described as a private operation run by the Central Intelligence Agency, and by Thai pilots. In addition, reconnaissance flights over Laos were conducted by regular U.S. Air Force and Navy jets. After two Navy jets were shot down by enemy ground fire June 6 and 7, 1964, Washington added armed escort jets.

Geneva accords undermined—The *New York Times* reported July 5 that the Pentagon study concluded that the U.S. had "a direct role in the ultimate breakdown of the Geneva settlement" of the Indochina conflict in 1954. The study indicated that in August, immediately after the Geneva convention, the Eisenhower Administration decided to replace French advisers and supply direct aid to the South Vietnamese government of Ngo Dinh Diem.

The *Times* report also said that Col.

Edward G. Lansdale of the Central Intelligence Agency, who had been sent to Saigon in June, headed a team of agents that began covert sabotage operations against North Vietnam soon after the close of the Geneva conventions. Included in the Pentagon papers was a lengthy report in the form of a diary describing the operations of Lansdale's Saigon Military Mission (SMM) from June 1954 through August 1955.

The study described Lansdale's SMM team and its "paramilitary operations" and "political-psychological warfare" against North Vietnam. The French were scheduled under the Geneva agreement to evacuate Hanoi Oct. 9, 1954. The Lansdale report included the following description of the team's activities immediately before:

> The northern team had spent the last days of Hanoi in contaminating the oil supply of the bus company for a gradual wreckage of engines in the buses, in taking the first actions for delayed sabotage of the railroad (which required teamwork with a CIA special technical team in Japan who performed their part brilliantly), and in writing detailed notes of potential targets for future paramilitary operations (U.S. adherence to the Geneva Agreement prevented SMM from carrying out the active sabotage it desired to do against the power plant, water facilities, harbor, and bridge). The team had a bad moment when contaminating the oil. They had to work quickly at night, in an enclosed storage room. Fumes from the contaminant came close to knocking them out. Dizzy and weak-kneed, they masked their faces with handkerchiefs and completed the job.

One of the team's operations in South Vietnam, described in the report, was to hire Vietnamese astrologers to predict doom for the Communists and publicize good omens for Diem. According to the Pentagon study, Lansdale also had a hand in rallying Diem's prospects in April 1955 when Secretary of State John Foster Dulles had decided to stop supporting his regime.

Laotian tribesmen seize plain. Laotian Meo tribesmen were reported July 13 to have seized complete control of the Plaine des Jarres in northern Laos in a drive begun July 7. No significant resistance was met in the recapture of the strategic heights formerly held by North Vietnamese, Viet Cong and Pathet Lao forces, the Laotian Defense Ministry reported.

Laotian officers said the Meo offensive was coordinated by the U.S. Central Intelligence Agency and that some of the tribal commandos were led by American advisers. The U.S. State Department July 9 denied that any U.S. advisers were accompanying Laotian forces.

A Laotian Defense Ministry spokesman, Gen. Thongphanh Knoksy, July 8 had confirmed the Plaine des Jarres drive, but said his government "is not responsible for this operation." He added: "You should ask the American embassy. This is their affair."

U.S. officials in Vientiane July 9 acknowledged the sweep was under way, but declined comment on American involvement.

CIA force in Laos acknowledged. The Nixon Administration officially confirmed for the first time Aug. 2, 1971 that

the U.S. Central Intelligency Agency was maintaining an "irregular" force of 30,000 fighting men now engaged in battle throughout most of Laos.

The acknowledgment was made in a staff report prepared for the Senate Foreign Relations subcommittee on foreign commitments.

The report was written by two former foreign service officers who made a trip to Laos in April. Their report, once classified top secret, was released Aug. 2 after clearance by the CIA as well as the Defense and State Departments.

According to the report, the CIA-backed force had become "the main cutting edge" of the Royal Laotian army. Thai "volunteers" recruited and paid by the CIA were among those in the 30,000-man force. The report indicated that the use of the "irregulars" was more widespread than had been generally reported in news accounts.

The report was made public by Sen. Stuart Symington, subcommittee chairman. Symington said of the Administration's acknowledgment: "It is an encouraging sign that the executive branch has finally agreed that much of what the United States government has been doing in Laos may now be made public."

The report also gave the first detailed description of the cost of U.S. involvement in the Laos war theater. In fiscal 1970 a "partial total" of U.S. expenditures in Laos was $284.2 million, of which $162.2 million was for military aid, $52 million for economic aid and $70 million was spent by the CIA exclusive of the amount spent on the Thai forces.

In fiscal 1972, the report said, the cost of military assistance had already "risen rapidly." The cost of military and economic aid plus the CIA expenses was expected to reach $374 million.

The report also noted increased Chinese Communist activity in northern Laos. The Chinese, the report said, had increased their defenses along a road they were building from Muong Sai in northern Laos sweeping towards Dienbienphu in North Vietnam. The road area, according to the report, was now "one of the most heavily defended in the world." New radar-directed anti-aircraft guns had been placed along the road, the report noted. Some of the guns were said to have a range of 68,000 feet.

More Chinese Communists were also said to be in the road-building area. In the last two years, the report said, the size of the Chinese contingent had increased from 6,000 to between 14,000 and 20,000.

House upholds secrecy on Laos—A proposal that the House be informed by the State Department about covert military operations in Laos was rejected by the House July 7 by a 261-118 vote. The proposal was offered by Rep. Paul N. McCloskey Jr. (R, Calif.), who also offered three other resolutions requesting information on Laos and Vietnam. They were rejected by voice votes.

Pentagon Papers trial reconvenes. The second Pentagon Papers trial began Jan. 18, 1973 in Los Angeles. The first had been declared a mistrial by Federal District Court Judge William M. Byrne Jr., Dec. 8, 1972. Brig. Gen. Paul Gorman, in testimony Jan. 24, said the revelations contained in the Pentagon Papers "could have damaged the national defense." He cited specifically a volume entitled *The Overthrow of Ngo Dinh Diem,* which detailed the part that U.S. Ambassador Henry Cabot Lodge played in the overthrow of Diem. According to the volume, Lodge told the plotters that the U.S. would not interfere and would offer the aid of the Central Intelligence Agency for tactical planning.

U.S. pilot captured in Laos. The downing and capture of a U.S. pilot in Laos May 7, 1973 was claimed by the Pathet Lao guerrilla forces June 1. Also taken with the American, identified as a major, were six members of the U.S.-trained Meo special forces.

A Pathet Lao broadcast June 13 said the 'copter was downed by guerrilla riflemen in the village of Nam Poung in Xieng Khouang Province in north central Laos.

The State Department reported June 15 that the captured pilot was a civilian, identified as Emmet Kay. It said the plane he was flying was a small transport downed while ferrying Laotians behind Communist lines. Kay was an employe of Continental Air Services, which operated under a contract with the U.S. Central Intelligence Agency. He was the only known American captured in Laos since the Jan. 28 Vietnam truce.

U.S. cuts Laos flights. Sharply decreased military activity in Laos had prompted a reduction in the number of charter pilots flying for the Central Intelligence Agency and other U.S. government agencies in the country, it was reported in Vientiane July 2, 1973. The flight cutback was further attributed to the American disengagement from Indochina and a $500 million slash in American military assistance to Laos and South Vietnam in the new fiscal year, begun July 1.

Seventy-five pilots of Air America and Continental Air Service had received notices of dismissal, it was reported June 30. The two airlines had contracts with the CIA, the U.S. Information Service and the U.S. Agency for International Development (AID).

In one of the few military engagements reported in Laos, military sources said July 21 that Pathet Lao and North Vietnamese troops had captured the Phra Hom valley, 115 miles southeast of Vientiane, killing several government soldiers and gaining control of thousands of refugees who had settled there. A total of six government positions or refugee settlements had been taken by the Communist forces in an offensive in central and southern Laos in the past week.

U.S. admits aides in Cambodia. In response to a *Washington Star-News* report July 24 that American civilians operating under the Central Intelligence Agency had been recruited from Laos to advise on paramilitary operations in Cambodia, the State Department admitted July 25 that civilians were operating in Cambodia to provide information on the military situation there, but denied they were engaged in paramilitary activities.

Department spokesman Charles W. Bray 3rd said that 10 U.S. civilian officers were assigned to provincial Cambodian towns "because of the need for better information on conditions in the provinces." Bray said that "none of personnel in Cambodia are performing tasks in contravention of existing legislation."

False CIA note stirs Thai dispute. The U.S. embassy in Bangkok, Thailand confirmed Jan. 5, 1974 that an agent of the U.S. Central Intelligence Agency had sent a false cease-fire offer to the Thai government in November 1973 in the name of the Thai Communist insurgents.

The embassy acknowledged the incident after three Bangkok newspapers reported on the matter. It said Ambassador William N. Kintner had apologized to Thai Premier Sanya Dharmasakti and King Phumiphol Aduldet, disavowed embassy involvement in the affair and ordered that no "American official be involved in any activity which could be interpreted as interference in Thai internal affairs."

The Nation, an English language newspaper in Bangkok, said the CIA had apologized to Thai authorities.

The CIA letter was said to have been sent by a U.S. agent to Premier Sanya from the provincial capital of Sakon Nakhon, in an area where 1,600–2,000 rebels were believed to be operating. The message, signed on behalf of the Communist Party of Thailand in the northeast, proposed a cease-fire in exchange for local autonomy in "liberated areas" near the Laotian border. The agent was said to have sent the letter in the belief that it would increase defections of the rebels to the government side.

Thailand scores U.S. over CIA note— Thailand formally complained to the U.S. Jan. 17 over the note the Central Intelligence Agency had sent to the government, purporting to be from a Thai rebel leader seeking peace with Bangkok.

A Foreign Ministry statement said U.S. Ambassador William N. Kintner had met with Premier Sanya Dharmasakti and was told of "the dissatisfaction of the students and people" with the CIA's "interference in the internal affairs of Thailand."

Kintner apologized and assured Sanya that the agent responsible for the letter had been returned to the U.S.

U.S. officials in Washington announced Jan. 18 plans to reduce the 150-man CIA force in Thailand and to limit its operations in the country. Most of the CIA agents were involved in counter-insurgency and the rest in combatting drug smuggling from Burma.

Rallies were directed Jan. 9 against the U.S. for its alleged interference in Thai-

land's internal affairs. More than 4,000 students and professors gathered in front of the U.S. embassy, demanding the ouster of Ambassador William N. Kintner and the Central Intelligence Agency.

CIA doubles Air America use. Rep. Les Aspin (D, Wis.) said Jan. 8, 1974 that the Central Intelligence Agency had more than doubled the work it had contracted to Air America, a charter airline long reputed to be an arm of the CIA. Aspin said Air America's contracts had increased to $41.4 million last year compared to $17.7 million for the prior year.

"Apparently unknown to the American public, the CIA has taken up the slack created by our military withdrawal" from Indochina, Aspin said. "Without a doubt the contracts reflect substantial U.S. involvement in the Southeast Asia war . . . ," he asserted.

Aspin noted that almost all Air America contracts were for operations out of Thailand.

Laotians free prisoners. The first exchange in Laos of war prisoners since the Laotian cease-fire began Feb. 22, 1973 was carried out Sept. 19, 1974 as the Vientiane and Pathet Lao factions traded 350 North Vietnamese, Thai and Laotian captives in a ceremony in the village of Phong Savan. The POWs included 150 Thai irregulars recruited by the U.S. Central Intelligence Agency to fight for the Laotian government, 173 North Vietnamese, who were on the side of the Pathet Lao, 20 Royal Lao troops and seven Pathet Lao.

Laos army troops rebel. About 100 Laotian army troops mutinied Dec. 24, 1974 and seized the provincial capital of Ban Houei Sai, 230 miles northwest of Vientiane. The rebels ended their uprising after talks with government negotiators, it was announced Dec. 29.

The soldiers, members of the Lao Theung tribe, shot their way into Ban Houei Sai, wounded several pro-government troops and held 19 American civilians, most of whom worked for the Agency for International Development, under house detention. The rebels demanded the repeal of a 1971 law banning the growing of opium, immediate dissolution of the Laotian National Assembly, neutralization of Ban Houei Sai and the implementation of a Communist-backed political program.

Government officials who participated in the negotiations said Dec. 29 that the insurgents had been assured that their demands would be satisfied. The agreement, not yet implemented, also provided for the release of the American hostages. The Americans, however, fled Ban Houei Sai Dec. 30 for the Thai border town of Chiang Khong and were then flown to Vientiane.

The Lao Theung tribesmen had been sponsored as a "clandestine army" by the U.S. Central Intelligence Agency to fight the Pathet Lao rebels during the war. The same troops that seized Ban Houei Sai had occupied the town in October after the tribal force was disbanded and many of its members were not transferred to the regular Laotian army.

Nationalist China

U.S. aides linked to dissidents. The U.S. was reported May 31, 1971 to have transferred from Taiwan at least five aides following Nationalist Chinese government charges that they had assisted the outlawed Taiwanese independence movement.

The Defense Ministry was said to have filed a protest in April with U.S. military and diplomatic authorities. The ousted men were said to have given the Taiwanese dissidents advice on the use of explosives and on means of promoting international support for their cause. The Americans also were accused of using their military postal privileges to assist the Taiwanese in contacting their countrymen abroad. These alleged activities were uncovered during interrogation of antigovernment Chinese and Taiwanese arrested in February and March, it was reported.

Newsmen confirmed the transferred aides were two Army men, two Navy officers and a civilian employe of the U.S. Army Technical Group, the cover name for the Central Intelligence Agency.

Communist China

U.S. halts spy flights over China. The U.S. government announced July 28, 1971 a suspension of American intelligence-gathering missions over Communist China by manned SR-71 reconnaissance planes and unmanned drones. The decision was aimed at preventing any incident that might mar President Nixon's scheduled trip to Peking. U.S. earth satellite missions were to continue over China, however. They were considered less provocative since they were well above China's airspace.

It was presumed that Nationalist China would continue to fly U-2 spy planes over China. A Washington informant was quoted as saying that "the mainland Chinese have good enough radar to distinguish between an overflight by the kind of aircraft we possess and the kind flown by the Chinese Nationalists."

The decision to stop the espionage flights over China was in accord with a July 16 White House statement commenting on the meeting between Chinese Premier Chou En-lai and Henry A. Kissinger, President Nixon's national security affairs adviser, arranging Nixon's visit to Peking. The statement said that neither the U.S. nor China would "knowingly do something that would undermine the prospects of something that it took so long to prepare and that it took such painful decisions to reach."

The SR-71 had replaced the U-2 in the array of American espionage aircraft. The twin-jet plane flies at an altitude of 80,000 feet and its cameras were said to be capable of taking pictures of small details from that height. A small number of SR-71s were said to be piloted by the Air Force and were normally based in Okinawa. Additional SR-71s reportedly were in other parts of the Far East and were said to be flown by civilians under contract with the Central Intelligence Agency. The plane was capable of flying at 2,000 miles an hour, making it the fastest American aircraft in service.

Chinese free two Americans. Two Americans released Dec. 12, 1971 from prisons in Communist China arrived in the U.S. Dec. 13.

A dispatch Dec. 13 from the official Communist Chinese press agency Hsinhua identified the former prisoners as Richard G. Fecteau and Mary Ann Harbert.

Hsinhua said Fecteau of Lynn, Mass., and John T. Downey of New Britain, Conn. had been shot down in a military aircraft over China in 1952 after dropping espionage agents trained in Japan into Manchuria. Downey's life sentence was being reduced to five more years because "both men had admitted their crimes during the trial and their behavior was not bad while serving their terms."

Miss Harbert had strayed into Chinese waters off southern Kwangtung Province in 1968 while sailing from Hong Kong in a yacht with Gerald R. McLaughlin, a family friend. Hsinhua declared that McLaughlin had "behaved badly" during detention, "resisted investigation and, taking the warders unawares, committed suicide on March 7, 1969."

White House Press Secretary Ronald L. Ziegler released a statement Dec. 13 saying that President Nixon "welcomes the act of clemency of the People's Republic of China" in commuting Downey's sentence and releasing Fecteau and Miss Harbert. Ziegler revealed that Nixon had been given "advance knowledge" that these actions were forthcoming. He also said that on two visits to China, Henry A. Kissinger, Nixon's adviser for national security, had discussed the prisoners with Premier Chou En-lai.

Fecteau, who had been given a physical examination along with Miss Harbert Dec. 14 at Valley Forge Army Hospital in Pennsylvania, said at a news conference the following day that he "never gave up hope" during his 19 years of confinement but that he had been "in solitary for so much time that I'm not used to conversation." He said he had been in a prison camp in or near Peking with Downey, Air Force Capt. Philip E. Smith and Naval Cmdr. Robert J. Flynn. Fecteau replied with "No comment" when asked by newsmen if he and Downey had worked for the Central Intelligence Agency. (His divorced wife Margaret said at a news conference Dec. 13: "It's very involved and I'm not supposed to get into it. He was a civilian working for the U.S. government. I know what he was doing, but I can't say. Let me put it this way—the Chinese haven't been lying." Mrs. Fecteau retracted her statement Dec. 14.)

Nixon admits Downey was CIA agent. President Nixon said Jan. 31, 1973 that he anticipated no immediate release for another China captive, John T. Downey, who, for the first time, was officially acknowledged to be a Central Intelligence Agency operative.

China releases Downey, Flynn, Smith— Downey, a CIA agent shot down over China in 1952, arrived in New Britain, Conn. March 12, 1973 after he had been released by Chinese authorities that day.

Three days later, two U.S. airmen imprisoned in China after being shot down during missions in the Indochina war were released. They were Lt. Cmdr. Robert J. Flynn, 35, of Colorado Springs, Colo., shot down Aug. 21, 1967 aboard an A-6 in southern China and Maj. Philip E. Smith, 38, of Roodhouse, Ill., shot down Sept. 20, 1965 over Hainan Island near the Gulf of Tonkin when his F-104 veered off course. Flynn and Smith crossed the border into Hong Kong and were flown to Clark Air Force Base.

Downey had been flown via Clark Air Force Base in the Philippines and Elmendorf Air Force Base in Alaska in order to be with his mother, who was suffering from a stroke in a New Britain hospital. His impending release had been announced March 9 by Ronald L. Ziegler, White House press secretary, who said Premier Chou En-lai had agreed to free Downey earlier than planned after being informed by the U.S. of his mother's illness. Ziegler said also China would release Flynn and Smith March 15.

At a March 13 news conference in New Britain, Downey said he looked on his 20-year imprisonment as "to a large extent wasted," adding: "I don't see that it benefited anybody."

Downey noted that during his first eight or nine months in jail he was questioned closely by his captors and that he "revealed about every bit of information I had."

Asked about the Chinese people, he said he felt "sympathy for them in some respects" and they were "more behind their government than I dreamed would be possible."

India

CIA activity charged. Student riots broke out in northeastern Bihar State Sept. 7 and 9, 1972. One student was reportedly shot to death by police in a demonstration at the state capital at Patna Sept. 7. To protest the police action, mobs of students Sept. 9 burned railway stations, stormed police outposts and stoned policemen in various parts of the state. Similar riots occurred in five other states —Kerala, Tamil Nadu, Orissa, Gujarat and Rajasthan, it was reported Sept. 13.

New Congress President Shandar Dayal Sharma had accused the U.S. Central Intelligence Agency of being involved in India's civil disturbances in an attempt "to sour relations between India and Bangla Desh." The U.S. embassy in New Delhi denied the charges Sept. 21, saying they were "outrageous and have absolutely no basis in fact."

Another Indian charge that the U.S. Central Intelligence Agency was active in India was leveled by Prime Minister Indira

Gandhi Oct. 2. Mrs. Gandhi did not specify what the CIA was doing in the country, but she urged Congress party workers to be on the alert and counteract the agency's role. Mrs. Gandhi said: "It is not for us to prove that this agency is working in our country. It is for the CIA to prove that it is not active in India." A U.S. State Department spokesman in Washington denied the charge.

Australia

U.S. denies CIA election role. U.S. Ambassador Marshall Green Sept. 23, 1974 denied reports that the Central Intelligence Agency had offered funds to Australian opposition parties in an attempt to defeat the Labor government in the May 18 general elections.

The allegations were contained in a book, *Looking at the Liberals,* whose advance copies appeared Sept. 23. The author, Ray Aitcheson, former Canberra bureau chief of the Australia Broadcasting Commission, disclosed that during a visit to Washington before the elections, he had received information about the reported offer, but did not state that the CIA funds were actually spent in Australia.

Guinea

U.S. newsman accused. Two former Guinean officials accused William Attwood, publisher of the U.S. newspaper *Newsday* and former U.S. ambassador to Guinea, of paying them to help the Central Intelligence Agency and U.S. mining firms to gain access to bauxite and iron ore deposits in the country.

The charges, made by Bangoura Karim and Fadiala Keita, successive Guinean ambassadors to the U.S., had been included in confessions made by the two men at trials beginning July 29, 1971 to determine local responsibility for the 1970 invasion of Guinea.

According to the *Washington Post* Nov. 29, Karim said he was approached in 1964 by Attwood, who made final arrangements in a deal that resulted in payment of $657,000 to Karim to promote U.S.-Guinean economic exchanges. Karim also named Thomas H. Wright Jr. of the Ford Foundation as having helped carry out the payoffs.

Both men denied the charges, the *Post* said, with Attwood describing them as "so fantastic" that they could only have been "obtained under duress" and adding that he had in any case been U.S. ambassador to Kenya in 1964.

The *Post* quoted an unnamed Guinean government official as saying that his country "did not accuse the U.S. government because we don't know if they [the confessions] are true or false. This will not affect our relations with the American government and people."

Malagasy Republic

Partial amnesty declared. The new military government in Tananarive announced May 17, 1975 an amnesty for approximately 270 of the 297 persons charged in connection with the assassination of President Richard Ratsimandrava in February. Interior Minister Richard Andriamaholison said the amnesty would make it easier for the authorities to find the "big people" behind the anti-government plots.

U.S. role in assassination intimated—In an article published in the June issue of *Penthouse* magazine, former *New York Times* correspondent Tad Szulc revealed that the Central Intelligence Agency had ties to the Mobile Police Group which was allegedly responsible for the assassination of President Ratsimandrava. Szulc said U.S. and CIA interest in the Malagasy Republic lay in getting military facilities at a former French base on the Indian Ocean near the entrance to the Persian Gulf.

Radio Free Europe

Radio Free Europe funding. Sen. Clifford P. Case (R, N.J.) charged Jan. 23, 1971 that the Central Intelligence Agency had expended several hundred million dollars "from secret" budgets during the last 20 years to support Radio Free Europe and Radio Liberty broadcasts to Eastern Europe.

While both stations "claim to be nongovernmental organizations sponsored by private contributions," Case said, "available sources indicate direct CIA subsidies pay nearly all their costs."

Case made the disclosure in announcing plans to introduce legislation to fund the stations by direct appropriations.

Pole accuses Radio Free Europe. A Polish intelligence officer claimed March 10 in Warsaw that during six years of employment at Radio Free Europe's (RFE) headquarters in Munich he had unmasked "a whole lot" of informers in Poland.

The officer, Capt. Andrezj Czechowicz, asserted that RFE was "engaged in detailed activity in the service of the American intelligence, not only in Socialist countries but also Western countries, for example in Austria, France, Sweden and other countries. A lively exchange of espionage information and services is thus blossoming in the Munich center."

Czechowicz also declared that "only about 20%–30% of the materials gathered by Radio Free Europe were used as a basis for broadcasts . . . The rest of them constituted valuable intelligence material."

The *New York Times* reported March 14 that RFE had an annual budget of $21 million, most of it coming from the CIA, and that its Munich director, identified as Ralph Walter, was a CIA employe. The *Times* also said newspaper correspondents were paid by RFE to enter East European countries and bring back specific information.

Administration approves RFE open funding. Sen. Clifford P. Case Jr. announced May 22 that the Nixon Administration had endorsed his proposal for open, public funding of Radio Free Europe and Radio Liberty. Case had proposed in January that the covert Central Intelligence Agency financing of the stations, which broadcast to Eastern Europe, be ended. He maintained that CIA funding was running at $30 million annually.

Senate panel keeps CIA control of RFE. The Senate Foreign Relations Committee turned down July 21 a Nixon Administration proposal to create a tax-exempt corporation chartered by Congress to run Radio Free Europe and Radio Liberty.

Later at the same closed-door session, the committee approved a proposal to give the stations $35 million to operate for another year and leave them under the control of the Central Intelligence Agency. The proposed legislation would end any pretense that the stations were controlled by private groups. The CIA reportedly had run the stations since the first was opened in 1950.

The proposal approved by the panel was sponsored by Sen. Clifford P. Case. (R, N.J.). Case had touched off a controversy over the stations by charging the CIA had spent several hundred million dollars to keep them operating.

According to published reports, Sen. J. William Fulbright, committee chairman, won majority support for Case's measure. Fulbright was reported to have questioned the continuing needs for the stations during the closed-door meeting.

House authorizes funding for RFE. The House, by a 271–12 vote Nov. 19, passed a bill to authorize funds for Radio Free Europe and Radio Liberty for two years and establish a commission to evaluate international radio broadcasting activities of the two stations. The Nixon Administration supported the measure, although it differed from its own proposal for creation of a nonprofit organization to administer the stations.

The House bill was returned to the Senate, which had passed by voice vote Aug. 2 a bill to provide $35 million to fund the stations for fiscal 1972. The House bill called for a fiscal 1972 funding of $36 million and a fiscal 1973 funding of $38.5 million.

CIA funding of RFE is stopped. President Nixon signed into law Oct. 20, 1973 a bill authorizing $50.2 million for operation of Radio Free Europe and Radio Liberty for fiscal 1974. Under the bill, the two radio stations would no longer be financed by the Central Intelligence Agency. They would be publicly financed by an International Broadcasting Board created by the bill.

Europe

Ashland took CIA money, acted as cover for spy. Ashland Oil Inc. secretly accepted nearly $100,000 from the Central Intelligence Agency and acted as a cover for covert CIA activities for five years, the *Wall Street Journal* reported July 9, 1975. The disclosure was made in the report filed with the SEC and federal court by the special committee of Ashland's board charged with investigating illegal corporate payments to politicians.

The CIA confirmed Ashland's admission and said other U.S. firms had been used as secret conduits for the funding of intelligence operations abroad. The Ashland case was "not an isolated practice," a CIA spokesman said, refusing to elaborate.

According to the *Journal*, Ashland's independent auditors, Coopers and Lybrand, informed the board on June 18 that the CIA had paid the firm $50,468 in cash from 1958 through 1971 and $48,500 in two checks, the last in March 1973. Ashland officials placed the money in an office safe and did not record it on corporate books until October 1973 when $58,600 was deposited in a corporate bank account.

The accountants did not specify why the CIA money was paid or how it was spent, but officials of Ashland and the CIA claimed that the money was not used for illegal political payments made in the U.S. or abroad. (Other sources, however, said the CIA cash was mingled with Ashland's secret political fund and disbursed as illegal corporate contributions.) An anonymous government official told the *Journal* that the money probably was used to reimburse Ashland for salaries of CIA agents whose initial payments had come from the oil firm.

The official said Ashland, probably unwittingly, had purchased an unidentified small firm around 1968 that was a front for the CIA. When Ashland discovered that the firm was a cover for the agency, the oil firm agreed to pay the salaries of secret CIA employes and accept secret reimbursement from the agency.

An authoritative source told the *New York Times* July 9 that Ashland was paid by the CIA for allowing a secret agent to operate in Western Europe for five years, posing as one of its officials. The agent was not infiltrated into the oil company, but employed by the small firm acquired by Ashland, according to the source.

After Ashland bought the firm (in 1967), the CIA informed officials of the oil company that one of the executives in the newly-purchased firm was a secret operative and asked Ashland to continue the relationship.

After five years, the agent decided to leave the CIA, but remained in Ashland's employ. A spokesman for the oil company said no "arrangement" with the CIA currently existed.

Greece

Papadopoulos deposed by military coup. President George Papadopoulos was ousted Nov. 25, 1973 in a bloodless military coup.

In a communique the military leaders who staged the coup said the president had been overthrown because he was moving too quickly toward parliamentary elections, threatening "chaos and catastrophe," and because he had not achieved the goals of the 1967 colonels' coup. Athens radio later confirmed that the elections scheduled for 1974 had been called off.

Papadopoulos was replaced by Lt. Gen.

Phaedon Gizikis, 56, chief of the First Army, whom Papadopoulos had tried to oust in October. The recently named civilian Cabinet headed by Spyros Markezinis was immediately replaced by a new 17-man civilian Cabinet, with Adamantios Androutsopoulos, 54, a former Cabinet member under Papadopoulos, as premier. The ousted president was placed under house arrest.

The coup was supported by elements of all three branches of the military, which staged shows of force in and around Athens. But the new rulers immediately retired the armed forces chief and the commanders of the army, air force and central intelligence service, presumed to be Papadopoulos allies. Military police chief Brig. Gen. Dimitrios Ioannidis, whom Papadoupoulos had earlier tried to remove, was reported to have led the coup.

Opposition to Papadopoulos among some military leaders had been reported for some time. Opponents charged the former president with monopolizing power, tolerating corruption and mismanaging the economy. The recent student-worker riots, suppressed at the cost of 13 lives as of Nov. 21 by official count and more by opposition estimates, reportedly convinced the plotters that Greece was not ready for moves toward democracy. Ioannides reportedly opposed the regime's delay in suppressing the initial demonstrations.

Exiled opposition figure Andreas Papandreou said in Stockholm Nov. 25 that the coup had been engineered by the U.S. Central Intelligence Agency, and that Androutsopoulos, who had worked as a lawyer in the U.S. for 12 years, was a paid CIA agent. Nevertheless, he welcomed the overthrow of "the hated President Papadopoulos," calling it a victory for the Greek people, a view shared by other exiles.

A U.S. State Department spokesman denied Nov. 26 that the U.S. had any role in the coup. U.S. officials in Washington said Nov. 25 they had had strong indications of an imminent coup before it occurred, but no "specific prior information." The U.S. had publicly pressured the former regime to move toward democratic reforms.

CIA ordered to halt interference. Top Washington officials ordered the Central Intelligence Agency not to interfere in the internal affairs of Greece, the *New York Times* reported Aug. 2, 1974. The instructions were said to reflect the views of Secretary of State Henry A. Kissinger and CIA Director William E. Colby.

One Washington official said the CIA had halted its subsidies of Greek political figures only in 1972 and many State Department officers noted that the CIA had actively assisted King Constantine's efforts to undermine the liberal Center Union Party in the years preceding the 1967 coup.

According to the *New York Times* Aug. 6, all U.S. contacts with Brig. Gen. Demetrios Ioannides, the military junta's leader since November 1973, had been

made through the CIA's Athens station chief; Ambassador Tasca had not met the dictatorship's strongman until July 20, the day Turkey invaded Cyprus.

Cyprus

Makarios denounces invasion. Archbishop Makarios, the deposed Cypriot president, issued a statement from New York July 20, 1974 charging that the Turkish invasion of Cyprus was "not at all justifiable since all diplomatic means for a peaceful settlement ... had not been exhausted." He expressed hope that "the Security Council and especially the great powers will find a way to put an end to this tragic and most dangerous situation."

Makarios, who had flown to New York to plead his case at the United Nations, also sent cables to the chiefs of state of all countries except Greece and Turkey charging that "Turkey has committed an act of aggression" and appealing for assistance to safeguard the independence of Cyprus.

Makarios had told the U.N. Security Council July 19 that the "Greek junta has extended its dictatorship to Cyprus." He appealed to the Council to "use all ways and means at its disposal" to restore constitutional order and democratic rights on Cyprus "without delay." The Council had decided July 18 that it would hear Makarios as head of state of Cyprus, even though his government had been overthrown.

Makarios had landed in New York from London July 18. On arrival, he had denounced Greece for organizing the coup and rejected suggestions that the U.S. Central Intelligence Agency was implicated as well. "The U.S. government is not involved at all," he said.

Ambush of Makarios backer fails—Unknown gunmen failed in an assassination attempt against Vassos Lyssarides, a leading Greek Cypriot politician and supporter of Archbishop Makarios, in Nicosia Aug. 30.

Later Aug. 30, Lyssarides expressed his belief that the assassination attempt was the work of EOKA B, the guerrilla group fighting for enosis (union of Cyprus with Greece) and instrumental in the overthrow of Makarios as president of Cyprus in mid-July. He added he was "almost certain" that the U.S. Central Intelligence Agency was involved in the murder attempt. He asked his Greek Cypriot supporters to refrain from retaliation.

Italy

Ex-U.S. envoy said to have urged political funds. Graham A. Martin, nominated to be the U. S. ambassador to South Vietnam, had tried as ambassador to Italy to persuade the U.S. Central Intelligence Agency to resume its secret financing of the Christian Democratic party in 1970, the *New York Times* reported May 13, 1973. Unidentified sources cited in the report said that Martin had sought a $1 million subsidy for the conservative wing of the Christian

Democrats, led by former Premier Amintore Fanfani, to head off Communist participation in the then shaky coalition under Mariano Rumor.

President Nixon, according to the sources, had rejected Martin's request with the scribbled note, "No, we want to stay out of this kind of thing."

Fanfani, currently presiding officer of the Senate, May 14 denied the *Times* report that he had asked Martin for the funds during a series of covert meetings in Rome beginning in 1969. The Christian Democratic party denied the same day that it had ever received any "foreign subsidies."

Former intelligence officers had revealed in the *Times* report that the CIA secretly subsidized the Christian Democrats from the end of World War II until 1967. The subsidies were said to have averaged about $3 million annually in the late 1950s.

The issue had emerged when U. S. Senator J. W. Fulbright (D, Ark.), chairman of the Senate Foreign Relations Committee, had asked Martin, during a confirmation hearing May 9 on his pending appointment as ambassador to South Vietnam, whether he had recommended the CIA funds. Martin refused to answer the question in public.

Switzerland

CIA agent worked on Vesco's release from Swiss prison. The Associated Press reported Feb. 22, 1975 that an agent for the Central Intelligence Agency was used to win Robert Vesco's release from prison in 1971. According to a confidential memo written by the CIA agent to an official of the U.S. embassy in Switzerland, the agent told the chief of Swiss intelligence "that there was unusual interest in higher U.S. government circles, including Attorney General Mitchell, in this case and that we hoped that Vesco would be released on his own recognizance today." The CIA confirmed that the conversation occurred but said the agent did not act "in his CIA capacity." The conversation was regarded as a "routine cover mission," a CIA spokesman said.

Vesco had been imprisoned on charges stemming from a Swiss shareholder's suit alleging Vesco tried to remove from a Swiss bank assets of an investment fund he controlled. The Securities and Exchange Commission later filed suit against Vesco charging he had masterminded a multimillion-dollar mutual fund swindle.

France

***Canard* says Mitterrand home tapped.** The satirical weekly *Le Canard Enchaine*, in an article published Jan. 16, 1974, charged that the government had placed wiretapping devices in the Paris home of Socialist Party leader Francois Mitterrand and in the homes or offices of 15 high civil servants, including the prefect of Paris and the head of the French narcotics squad. Mitterrand's home had reportedly been tapped for a year.

Le Canard also quoted Premier Pierre Messmer as suggesting recently that the U.S. Central Intelligence Agency might have been involved in the abortive attempt to place wiretap devices in *Le Canard's* office in December 1973. This referred to the fact that the wiretap cables found in the *Canard* offices led to an unused chimney in a building occupied by what Messmer reportedly said was a U.S. company "known to be a cover for the CIA."

The director of the French internal counter-espionage agency DST denied Jan. 4 that his staff had participated in the wiretapping of *Le Canard*. A DST inspector filed a libel suit against the weekly magazine *Le Point* and a French radio station Jan. 8 for reporting that a concierge had identified him as one of the participants in the attempt.

Germany

Spy probe report issued. An independent investigating commission issued a report Nov. 18, 1974 blaming structural weaknesses and a breakdown in communication among West Germany's three security services for employment of the East German spy, Gunter Guillaume, in the Chancellery. The commission absolved former Chancellor Willy Brandt of direct blame for the spy scandal, which led to his resignation, but criticized his chief of staff, Horst Ehmke, and the security services for giving "speed precedence over caution" in granting secret clearance to Guillaume.

A parliamentary commission also investigating the case had opened its public hearings Aug. 27. Brandt testified Sept. 20 that the security forces had informed him in May 1973 of their suspicions of Guillaume, but then said nothing more about the matter. He said he concluded it "rather unlikely" that Guillaume was a spy. Foreign Minister Hans-Dietrich Genscher, former interior minister, also testified Sept. 20, charging that Gunther Nollau, head of the Federal Office for the Protection of the Constitution (counterintelligence), had failed to give him an adequate report on security.

In other evidence given to the committee Oct. 9, Ehmke had disclosed that the Federal Information Service, whose mandate was to collect only foreign intelligence, had kept illegal dossiers on 54 of the nation's leading public figures, including prominent persons in politics, universities and the armed forces. The agency, created by the U.S. Central Intelligence Agency during the postwar occupation period and initially financed by the U.S., had kept files on Brandt and former Chancellors Ludwig Erhard and Kurt Georg Kiesinger, among others.

(The government had complained to Washington about unwarranted interference in West German affairs by a CIA agent who had monitored the activities of Soviet officials in West Germany, it was reported Nov. 30. The agent had compiled a list of six Soviet officials who had met with 11 members of the West German Parliament and sent the list to a member of the Bundestag. The 11 were members of a Soviet-German parliamentary group.)

Canada

CIA activities probed. Solicitor General Warren Allmand May 28, 1975 directed the Royal Canadian Mounted Police to undertake an investigation concerning possible U.S. Central Intelligence Agency activities in Canada. He also said he was concerned about U.S. Federal Bureau of Investigation operations in Canada and wanted additional safeguards against U.S. agents crossing the border without permission.

A spokesman for the External Affairs Department warned that covert CIA operations in Canada would be "clearly unacceptable conduct." Allmand warned of diplomatic repercussions if the CIA were found to be operating illegally in Canada.

Latin America

CIA, government links cited. The interior ministers of nearly all Latin American governments "collaborated" with the U.S. Central Intelligence Agency, according to David A. Phillips, former chief of CIA operations in Latin America.

Phillips told a press conference in New York May 10, 1975 that although the Latin officials worked with the agency, they did not know "everything that the agency does" in their countries. The CIA's major preoccupation in Latin America was uncovering "the activities being prepared" by the Soviet and Cuban intelligence services, he added.

Phillips denied that the agency had organized the overthrow of any Latin American head of state—notably, the late Chilean President Salvador Allende—but he conceded that "this type of operation might have been discussed as a possibility."

Former President Jose Figueres of Costa Rica had said in an interview March 9 that most Latin American presidents collaborated with the CIA, and that he personally had worked "in 20,000 ways" for the agency. Figueres praised the CIA for its "excellent work in espionage and counterespionage," but he expressed regret that the agency had frustrated several plots against Latin American military dictators on which he had worked during the past three decades.

Harrison Salisbury, a former correspondent and editor for the *New York Times,* asserted in an article in the U.S. magazine *Penthouse,* reported by the Mexican newspaper *Excelsior* April 17, that the CIA maintained links with the secret police and armed forces of "all Latin American governments." Salisbury said Latin American police chiefs and their top aides were brought to the U.S. for CIA training.

Salisbury said the CIA had participated in the overthrows of Guatemalan President Jacobo Arbenz in 1954 and Allende in 1973. Allende's ouster and death were the "culmination" of a 10-year CIA effort which began with opposition to Allende's presidential candidacy in Chile's 1964 elections, Salisbury said.

Chile

Allende imposes state food control. In an address before a national congress of the Communist-controlled Central Labor Union Dec. 8, 1971, President Salvador Allende announced that the government would take over full control of food distribution as part of an "offensive against fascist sedition."

He also called for the organization of "neighborhood vigilance committees" to fight food hoarders and black marketers.

The government had assumed control of three major wholesale distributors and ordered 22 cattle auction markets under state management Dec. 7.

The action came a week after a shortage of some foodstuffs brought a protest march Dec. 1 by 5,000 women. The Communist party newspaper *El Siglo* charged in an editorial Dec. 8 that the women's march had been organized and financed by the U.S. Central Intelligence Agency.

ITT and U.S. policy in Chile. Columnist Jack Anderson made public March 20–22, 1972 material purporting an effort by the International Telephone and Telegraph Corp. to influence U.S. policy in Chile and in Latin America generally. The conglomerate had six affiliates with 7,900 employes in Chile. Anderson used allegedly private ITT documents.

March 21 column (made public March 20)—William R. Merriam, head of ITT's Washington office, in a memo to John A. McCone, an ITT director and former CIA director, said that a CIA source he had met with was "very pessimistic about defeating Allende," that "approaches continue to be made to select members of the armed forces in an attempt to have them lead some sort of uprising" and that "practically no progress has been made in trying to get American business to cooperate in some way so as to bring on economic chaos."

March 22 column—J. D. Neal, ITT's director of international relations, telephoned an aide to Henry A. Kissinger, President Nixon's adviser on national security affairs, talked of ITT President Harold S. Geneen's "deep concern about the Chile situation" and asked the aide to tell Kissinger that Geneen was ready to discuss ITT's interest and ITT was "prepared to assist financially in sums up to seven figures."

Anderson said his material revealed ITT efforts and "fervent hopes for a military coup" in Chile and the "generally polite but cool reception" it got from the White House and the State Department. A "more friendly" reception was attributed to the CIA's William V. Broe, who was reported to have visited ITT Vice President E. J. Gerrity Jr. to "urge ITT to join in a scheme to plunge the Chilean economy into chaos and thus bring about a military uprising that would keep Allende out of power."

In the material released March 22:

■ Neal wrote Merriam "we should hope the Nixon Administration will be prepared to move quickly to exert pressure on Allende" but that "because of our weak policy in the hemisphere during the last two years, we cannot count on such immediate and effective action."

■ Merriam wrote Kissinger about ITT's concern over the "serious exposure" of foreign private enterprise in Latin America and the need to "reappraise and strengthen U.S. policy in Latin America." He enclosed ITT's proposals for reaction to expropriation of private U.S. holdings. One of the proposals was to inform Allende that if compensation was not forthcoming "there will be immediate repercussions in official and private circles" and "this could mean a stoppage of all loans by international banks and U.S. private banks." An apparent reply from Kissinger said it was "helpful to have your thoughts and recommendations, and we shall certainly take them into account." Merriam considered the reply "more than perfunctory."

■ Neal reported having been told by U.S. Ambassador to Chile Edward M. Korry that if Geneen "had any ideas about U.S. policy toward Allende's government he hoped this would be relayed to the White House immediately."

ITT received a report from its representatives in Santiago that the State Department had given a "green light" to Korry "for maximum authority to do all possible, short of a Dominican Republic-type action" (a reference to U.S. military intervention) to "keep Allende from taking power."

Administration denial—State Department press officer Charles W. Bray 3rd said March 23 that the Nixon Administration had "firmly rejected" any ideas of "thwarting the Chilean constitutional processes following the elections of 1970." Bray added that the disclaimer applied to the period before the elections as well, and to actions attributed by the documents to the CIA.

Labor rallies attack U.S.—Four marches organized by the Central Labor Confederation (CUT) converged on the center of Santiago March 23 to express massive support for the Popular Unity government in its struggle with the opposition-dominated Congress.

According to the *Washington Post* March 24, U.S. columnist Jack Anderson's recent report on the International Telephone and Telegraph Corp.'s encouragement of a 1970 plot against President Allende was a major issue during the rally. In his speech to the marchers, Luis Figueroa, a Communist and secretary general of the CUT, quoted extensively from ITT documents released by Anderson, frequently attacking "the North American imperialists."

(The *New York Times* reported March 24 that the government press and television system were devoting most of their space and time to the documents, asserting that they not only confirmed leftwing charges of an anti-Allende plot in 1970, but also showed there was a present campaign, backed by the U.S. Central Intelligence Agency, to overthrow Allende).

Anderson disclosures investigated—The Chilean Congress voted March 28 to appoint a 13-member commission to investigate activities by ITT aimed at keeping Allende from taking office in 1970.

According to the magazine *Business Week* April 1, John McCone, a director of ITT and former director of the U.S. Central Intelligence Agency, admitted in an interview that the Anderson documents were authentic. McCone said the company had let the CIA know that it would help with any plan to prevent Allende's inauguration, but denied that ITT had proposed measures of "economic repression" in Chile.

The Chilean government April 4 put on sale a book called *The Secret Documents of the ITT*, containing English- and Spanish-language versions of the Anderson documents.

Opposition implicated—The heated debate in Chile over the Anderson disclosures was fueled by government attempts to implicate opposition forces in an alleged CIA-directed plot to bring down the Allende government through economic crisis, scare tactics influencing consumers to hoard scarce supplies, and exaggerated accounts of rural violence over land disputes, the *New York Times* reported April 1.

According to the *Times*, the government campaign was directed against the Fatherland and Liberty party, the right-wing National party, and Christian Democratic former President Eduardo Frei Montalva.

Opposition leaders, who angrily denied any dealings with the CIA, demanded that a commission also investigate recent allegations by Anderson that the Cuban embassy in Santiago was a center for fomenting armed revolution in South America, *Le Monde* reported April 1.

New ITT plot revealed. The International Telephone and Telegraph Corp. had submitted to the Nixon Administration in October 1971 an 18-point plan to assure that the Allende government would not "get through the crucial next six months," the *New York Times* reported July 3, 1972.

The most recent plan, contained in a letter and "action" memorandum from William R. Merriam, ITT's vice president for Washington relations, to Peter G. Peterson, then assistant to President Nixon for international economic affairs, was submitted to the White House Oct. 1, 1971, two days after Chile placed the ITT-controlled Chilean Telephone

Co. under provisional state administration.

In the documents, Merriam called for extensive economic warfare against Chile to be directed by a special White House task force, assisted by the Central Intelligence Agency. ITT further recommended subversion of the Chilean armed forces, consultations with foreign governments on ways to put pressure on Allende, and diplomatic sabotage.

Merriam proposed putting an "economic squeeze" on Chile through denial of international credit, a ban on imports of copper and other Chilean products, and a similar ban on vital exports to Chile. The measures, Merriam said, should cause sufficient "economic chaos" to convince the armed forces to "step in and restore order."

Merriam suggested that the CIA could help in the squeeze, and urged a deliberate interruption of fuel supplies to the Chilean air force and navy to precipitate the crisis. He also urged that other potential anti-Allende forces, including "the judiciary, civil service, crippled news media [and a] fragment of the legislative branch," be "utilized to every advantage" during "the crucial period."

ITT's plans in Chile revealed. A special Senate Foreign Relations Committee subcommittee on multinational corporations began a two-year investigation into the effects of those firms on the U.S. economy and conduct of foreign policy. Opening testimony was given by officials of the International Telephone and Telegraph Corp.

John McCone, former CIA director, told the subcommittee March 21, 1973 that he had met with Henry A. Kissinger, President Nixon's national security adviser, and Richard Helms, then director of the CIA and a "close friend," in mid-1970 to offer the U.S. government $1 million in financial aid from ITT. The money would be used to block the runoff election of Salvador Allende Gossens as president of Chile.

McCone made the $1 million offer in his capacity as a director of ITT. The money had been authorized by ITT President and Chairman Harold S. Geneen. McCone denied that the money was intended for "surreptitious" purposes or would be used to create "economic chaos."

"What he [Geneen] had in mind was not chaos but what could be done constructively. The money was to be channeled to people who support the principles and programs the U.S. stands for against the programs of the Allende-Marxists," McCone testified.

The money would be used in Chile, McCone said, for programs such as housing projects and technical agricultural assistance.

"International communism has said time and again that its objective is the destruction of the free world, economically, politically, militarily. . . . That was what Mr. Geneen was thinking of," according to McCone.

The ITT plan proposed to Kissinger and Helms was termed the "Alessandri Formula." It called for financial support to be given to a coalition of the conservative National party, headed by Jorge Alessandri Rodriguez, and the Christian Democratic party, led by Radomiro Tomic. It was planned that they would oppose Allende in the expected runoff election and that Allesandri would be elected. He would then resign and call for new elections, permitting former President Eduardo Frei Montalva to challenge Allende in the subsequent two-man race.

"A number of people were trying to explore alternatives about what might be done. The Chilean military was discussing the Alessandri Plan. Mr. [William V.] Broe [director of clandestine operations in Latin America for the CIA] had a shopping list and the staff of the CIA had a shopping list," McCone told the subcommittee.

The plan was abandoned when Alessandri withdrew from the runoff race because of his lack of support in the Chilean Congress where the final decision would be made.

McCone testified that Helms had told him "the matter was considered by an interdepartmental committee of senior representatives of the Defense and State Departments as well as the CIA, and the decision was reached that nothing should be done."

Although the ITT plan was rejected, McCone said that at his request, Helms put Geneen in contact with Broe. This corresponded with testimony given the previous day.

William R. Merriam, vice president of ITT and former director of its Washington office, had testified March 20 that ITT President Geneen had arranged to establish a working relationship between the corporation and the CIA in order to prevent the election of Allende as president of Chile, and, failing that, to bring about the "economic collapse" of Chile.

Merriam said his association with the CIA's Broe began at a Washington meeting held July 16, 1970 which was arranged and attended by Geneen. Geneen instructed him to "stay in touch" with Broe, Merriam testified, and subsequent phone conversations and meetings with the CIA agent occurred "many times."

Merriam told the subcommittee that Broe was impressed with the quality of information gathered by ITT operatives in Latin America. When shown a Sept. 17, 1970 cable from ITT officials Bob Berrellez and Hal Hendrix, Broe "approved" the recommendation, Merriam declared.

The cable urged ITT "and other U.S. firms in Chile" to head off Allende's election by contributing advertising funds to a conservative Chilean newspaper in financial difficulties. The report also recommended that ITT "bring what pressure we can" on the U.S. Information Agency to circulate the Chilean newspaper's editorial in Latin America and Europe. (In testimony given March 21,

Hendrix claimed the plan was never carried out because its intent was too obvious.)

According to an ITT memo dated late September 1970 when the Chilean election results were still in doubt, ITT Senior Vice President Edward Gerrity told Geneen that Broe had suggested the company "apply economic pressures" to influence the voting.

Broe "indicated that certain steps were being taken, but that he was looking for additional help aimed at inducing economic collapse," Gerrity told Geneen, "Realistically I don't see how we can induce others involved to follow the plan suggested," Gerrity concluded.

As part of this plan, Merriam said the CIA made "repeated calls to firms such as General Motors, Ford Motor Co. and banks in California and New York." All refused to cease or reduce operations in Chile, according to ITT documents submitted to the subcommittee.

Other CIA recommendations called for cessation of U.S. aid to Chile, under the guise of a policy review, and government intervention with the World Bank group and the International Monetary Fund to halt their loans to Chile.

Broe testifies—Broe testified before a closed session of the subcommittee March 27. Portions of the proceedings were made public March 28 after the CIA reviewed the transcript.

Broe described Geneen's offer made at a July 16, 1970 meeting in Washington to provide a "substantial fund" for the support of Alessandri's candidacy. The money was rejected, Broe testified, because the CIA refused to "serve as a funding channel."

"I also told him that the United States government was not supporting any candidate in the Chilean election," Broe said. He added that Geneen never suggested at that time that the money be used for social assistance programs.

According to Broe, Geneen told him that ITT and other American companies had raised money to influence the 1964 Chilean election of Eduardo Frei but that CIA Director John A. McCone had refused the offer.

After the Sept. 4, 1970 election in Chile when Allende won a small plurality of the vote, the CIA altered its policy of neutrality and met with ITT officials to devise anti-Allende plans, Broe testified.

During the same period in 1970, ITT held a board of directors meeting Sept. 8–9 when Geneen asked McCone to repeat the offer of financial assistance to the government with the new aim of funding an anti-Allende coalition before the second presidential vote. This plan, detailed by McCone at the hearings March 21, was termed the "Alessandri Formula."

Broe admitted devising a series of secondary proposals in September 1970 for Gerrity which would create economic chaos in Chile, also with the aim of preventing Allende's presidential victory.

Broe claimed he had acted with the full

knowledge of CIA Director Richard Helms and that Geneen had initiated the company's first contact with the CIA in 1970.

Broe met with Geneen Sept. 29, 1970 to discuss plans for accelerating Chile's economic deterioration in order to "influence a number of Christian Democratic [party] congressmen who were planning to vote for Allende." Among the proposals Broe presented were delays in bank credits and delivery of spare part shipments, and withdrawal of technical assistance.

Broe also confirmed the testimony of another top ITT official, William M. Merriam, who had said Broe gave his approval Sept. 29, 1970 to a plan supporting an anti-Allende newspaper and "propagandists."

Other portions of the Broe testimony were released March 29 relating to the September 1970 conversations with Gerrity. Broe insisted that the CIA plan for the disruption of the Chilean economy had been approved by superiors in the intelligence gathering agency.

Charles A. Meyer, former assistant secretary of state for inter-American affairs and currently with Sears, Roebuck & Co., told the subcommittee March 29 that he saw no inconsistency between Broe's disclosures and his own testimony that the Nixon Administration had steadfastly maintained a policy of nonintervention in Chile.

Geneen admits ITT offers—Harold S. Geneen, International Telephone and Telegraph Corp. chairman, April 2 admitted to a Senate Foreign Relations subcommittee probing the political role of multinational corporations that he had twice offered the U.S. government money to prevent the 1970 election of Chilean President Salvador Allende.

Geneen's admission regarding the first offer of funds was cautious. Having "no recollection to the contrary," Geneen told the subcommittee he would accept the testimony of William V. Broe that the money was offered at a July 1970 meeting and was intended to finance a CIA effort to stop Allende.

Geneen justified the gesture as an "emotional reaction" resulting from his conversations with Broe in which the CIA representative said the U.S. planned no efforts to circumvent the Chilean election of Allende, who was running on a Socialist-Communist platform.

According to Geneen, this policy of nonintervention represented the reversal of a 14-year U.S. "policy to maintain a democratic government in Chile." Geneen said he had been particularly disturbed by the talks with Broe because ITT had invested in Chile as part of the U.S. government's economic assistance policy to develop the country. In contrast to its past encouragement, the Nixon Administration appeared unwilling to aid ITT when the company anticipated the expropriation of its Chilean properties.

The matter "died right there," Geneen claimed, although he admitted making a second offer to the government in Sep-

tember 1970 when Allende had won his first election test and required ratification by the Chilean Congress in an October vote.

'64 anti-Allende U.S. aid reported. The U.S. contributed considerable money and manpower to help elect Eduardo Frei president of Chile in 1964, the *Washington Post* reported April 6, 1973. Frei's Christian Democratic party disputed the report April 11.

The report, written by *Post* staff reporter Laurence Stern, said "knowledgeable officials" in Washington asserted the U.S. had dispatched up to $20 million and 100 agents of the Central Intelligence Agency and State Department to help Frei defeat the current president, Salvador Allende.

"U.S. government intervention in Chile in 1964 was blatant and almost obscene," an intelligence officer told the *Post*. "We were shipping people off right and left, mainly State Department but also CIA with all sorts of covers," the officer asserted.

The *Post* said Cord Meyer Jr., whom it called a "Cold War liberal," directed the CIA's covert programs to neutralize Communist influence in important opinion-molding sectors such as trade unions, farmer and peasant organizations, student activist groups and communications media before the elections.

One conduit for CIA money, the International Development Foundation, was employed in the 1964 campaign to subsidize Chilean peasant organizations, according to a former official responsible for monitoring assistance to Chile from the State Department's Agency for International Development (AID), the *Post* reported.

Covert financing reportedly was also arranged for a newspaper friendly to the interests of the Christian Democrats. "The layout was magnificent. The photographs were superb. It was a Madison Avenue product far above the standards of Chilean publications," another State Department veteran of the campaign recalled.

Among State Department personnel, another source told the *Post*, "individual officers . . . would look for opportunities. And where it was a question of passing money, forming a newspaper or community development program, the operational people would do the work. AID found itself suddenly overstaffed, looking around for peasant groups or projects for slum dwellers. Once you established a policy of building support among peasant groups, government workers and trade unions, the strategies fell into place."

A former U.S. ambassador to Chile privately estimated the covert program on Frei's behalf had cost about $20 million, the *Post* reported. In contrast, the figure that emerged in U.S. Senate hearings as the amount ITT was willing to spend to defeat Allende in 1970 was $1 million. AID funds alone were substantially increased for 1964, the *Post* reported.

The number of "special agents" dis-

patched to Chile at various stages of the campaign was estimated by one official at about 100.

The *Post* story was given extensive coverage in Chile by the official Communist newspaper *El Siglo,* which charged the story proved Frei guilty of treason, it was reported April 14.

Christian Democratic denial—The Christian Democratic party president, Renan Fuentealba, denied at a press conference April 11 that the U.S. had contributed $20 million to Frei's 1964 campaign. He also called for an investigation of the *Post's* charges and asked the *Post* to examine the financing of campaigns by Chile's Marxist parties.

Fuentealba asserted that Christian Democratic races in Chile were "fundamentally" funded by the monthly dues of some 70,000 paying party members. Party sources acknowledged some income from abroad, such as Chileans living outside the country and from companies doing business in Chile.

Allende suicide reported. The armed forces and national police ousted the Popular Unity government Sept. 11, 1973, in the first successful military coup against a Chilean civilian administration since 1927.

Police officials in Santiago said President Salvador Allende Gossens had committed suicide rather than surrender power. A newspaper photographer allowed to see the body, and a military communique Sept. 12 confirmed that the president was dead, but there was some confusion over whether he had taken his own life.

A four-man military junta seized control of the government and declared a state of siege, imposing censorship and a round-the-clock curfew. The junta members were the army commander, Gen. Augusto Pinochet Ugarte; the air force chief, Gen. Gustavo Leigh Guzman; the acting navy commander, Adm. Jose Toribio Merino Castro, and the national police chief, Gen. Cesar Mendoza. Pinochet was sworn in as president of Chile Sept. 13.

U.S. denies coup complicity—The U.S. State Department and White House Sept. 11-12 declined to comment on Allende's overthrow, asserting it was an internal Chilean matter, and denied charges from Communist and other countries that the U.S. had a hand in the military coup.

However, a State Department official admitted to senators Sept. 12 that the U.S. had advance knowledge of the coup. Jack Kubisch, an assistant secretary of state, told members of the Western Hemisphere Subcommittee of the Senate Foreign Relations Committee that a Chilean officer had told a U.S. official in Chile of the coup some 10-16 hours before it occurred, but officials at "the highest level" in Washington had decided not to intervene in any way.

(State Department and White House spokesmen subsequently denied the U.S. had known of the coup beforehand. Paul

J. Hare, State Department spokesman, admitted the U.S. embassy "did receive reports that Sept. 11 was to be the date," but said it had previously been advised of coups planned for Sept. 8 and Sept. 10, and thus considered the last prediction a rumor likely to be false. "There was absolutely no way of knowing beforehand that on any of these dates, including the Sept. 11 date, a coup attempt would be made," Hare asserted.)

The U.S. reluctance to comment on the coup was attributed to sensitivity over charges that the Central Intelligence Agency and the International Telephone and Telegraph Corp. had previously conspired against Allende.

U.S. critics of the Nixon Administration's policies in Latin America blamed the U.S. Sept. 12 for helping create the conditions in which military intervention in Chile became likely, according to the *Washington Post* Sept. 13. One critic, Joseph Collins of the Institute for Policy Studies, a Washington research organization, charged U.S. "tactics" in Chile under Allende were aimed at causing "economic chaos."

Charges of CIA involvement in the coup were made in the capitals of several Communist countries and by supporters of Allende in South American and Western European nations.

Some 30,000 leftists marched past the Chilean embassy in Paris Sept. 11, denouncing the CIA for allegedly overthrowing Allende. In Rome, thousands of demonstrators held similar rallies.

U.S. policies linked to coup. U.S. Rep. Michael J. Harrington (D, Mass.) said in Santiago Oct. 27 that U.S. economic policies of "deprivation" had set in motion the events that led to the Chilean military coup.

Harrington asserted that three days of intensive contacts in Chile, including a two-hour meeting with three of the four military junta members, had reinforced his view that "United States economic policy was the really damaging part of our relationship" with the deposed government of President Salvador Allende.

He stressed "the enormous pressures [the U.S.] brought to bear" on the late President by curbing credits, expressing "chilling interest" in the private sector, and failing to continue economic programs. "We lost a major opportunity in not trying to deal with the freely elected government," Harrington declared, asserting the U.S. could have demonstrated pluralism by cooperating with Allende's Marxist experiment.

Harrington said the junta members had "tried to convey" to him "a strong sense of legitimacy for what they had done," but had been evasive when he expressed "concern over the suppression of the rights of expression and political parties."

Harrington was a member of the House of Representatives' Subcommittee on Inter-American Affairs, which received secret testimony Oct. 11 on Central Intelligence Agency operations in Chile during Allende's presidency. The testimony,

by CIA Director William E. Colby and agency official Frederick D. Davis, was obtained by journalist Tad Szulc, who reviewed it in an article in the *Miami Herald* Oct. 22.

Testimony by Colby and Davis, at times unclear and contradictory, touched on "the CIA's own very extensive role in Chilean politics, but it also helps in understanding and reconstructing the [Nixon] Administration's basic policy of bringing about Allende's fall one way or another," according to Szulc.

"The [CIA] activities described range from the 'penetration' of all the major Chilean political parties, support for anti-regime demonstrations and financing of the opposition press and other groups to heretofore unsuspected agency involvement in financial negotiations between Washington and Santiago in late 1972 and early 1973 when Chileans were desperately seeking an accommodation," Szulc wrote.

"There are indications that the CIA, acting on the basis of its own reports on the 'deterioration' of the Chilean economic situation, was among the agencies counseling the White House to rebuff Allende's attempts to work out a settlement on the compensations to be paid for nationalized American property and a renegotiation of Chile's $1.7 billion debt to the United States," he continued.

"The Nixon Administration's firm refusal to help Chile, even on humanitarian grounds, was emphasized about a week before the military coup when it turned down Santiago's request for credits to buy 300,000 tons of wheat [in the U.S.] at a time when the Chileans had run out of foreign currency and bread shortages were developing," Szulc noted. "On Oct. 5, however, the new military junta was granted $24.5 million in wheat credits after the White House overruled State Department objections. The department's Bureau of Inter-American Affairs reportedly believed such a gesture was premature and could be politically embarrassing."

Colby reportedly told the subcommittee that the CIA and the National Security Council had felt it was "not in the United States' interest" for Allende's government to be overthrown. He made the comment in response to a question about a similar statement reportedly made by Jack Kubisch, assistant secretary of state for inter-American affairs.

A letter Oct. 8 from Richard A. Fagen, professor of political science at Stanford University, to Sen. J. William Fulbright, chairman of the Senate Foreign Relations Committee, reported that Kubisch had told a group of U.S. scholars, "It would have been better had Allende served his entire term, taking the nation and the Chilean people into complete and total ruin. Only then would the full discrediting of socialism have taken place. Only then would people have gotten the message that socialism doesn't work. What has happened has confused this lesson."

Argentina

U.S. envoy called CIA agent. The left-wing Peronist weekly *El Descamisado* charged Jan. 8, 1974 that the new U.S. ambassador to Argentina, Robert C. Hill, was a member of the Central Intelligence Agency. Hill's appointment had been approved by President Juan D. Peron, but the envoy had not yet arrived in Buenos Aires.

Hill was a former vice president of W.R. Grace & Co. and a former director of the United Fruit Co.—whose operations had been bitterly criticized by Latin American nationalists—and had been directly linked, in testimony before the U.S. Senate, to the CIA-planned coup which overthrew Guatemalan President Jacobo Arbenz in 1954.

Argentina and the U.S. were nevertheless enjoying warm relations, as shown by the signing in late 1973 of a $756 million loan pact with the Inter-American Development Bank, which would have been impossible without U.S. support, the newsletter *Latin America* noted Jan. 4.

Rightist violence increases. Political violence continued in Buenos Aires and other cities Sept. 19–30, 1974 as a right-wing group, the Argentine Anticommunist Alliance (AAA), stepped up its campaign to murder several dozen prominent leftists.

Former presidential candidate Oscar Alende, leader of the small Popular Revolutionary Alliance, demanded Sept. 22 that the government "identify" the AAA's members and investigate their "connections," particularly any possible links to the U.S. Central Intelligence Agency, which was recently shown to have intervened in the internal affairs of Chile.

The independent daily newspaper *La Opinion* wondered in an editorial Sept. 25 what the objectives of the CIA in Argentina might be. Hector Sandler, the congressman on the AAA's death list, asked the government Sept. 25 to call in U.S. Ambassador Robert Hill and question him on local CIA activities. Hill had been called a "CIA agent" by left-wing Peronist publications before he arrived in Argentina early in 1974.

Prats killed—Retired Gen. Carlos Prats Gonzalez, the former Chilean army commander, and his wife were killed early Sept. 30 when a bomb exploded in or under their car as they drove to their Buenos Aires home.

The Prats' assassins were unknown. Initial speculation centered on either the AAA or rightists from Chile. Prats, who had lived in Argentina since Chile's Sept. 1973 military coup, had a reputation as a leftist because he had served in the Cabinet of the late Chilean President Salvador Allende.

A close friend of Prats, quoted by the *Washington Post* Oct. 1, said Prats had said recently that he had received information of a plan to kill him. Prats had said the assassination would be made to look like the work of the AAA, but would

A

be staged by Chilean or U.S. rightists who knew he was writing his memoirs and could divulge much information about the preparations for the Chilean coup.

Bolivia

Military rule declared. The armed forces officially took control of the country Nov. 9, 1974 after President Hugo Banzer Suarez personally led loyalist troops in crushing a military revolt in the southeastern city of Santa Cruz.

The opposition to Banzer stemmed partly from his refusal to declare an amnesty for political prisoners and his apparent intention to run for the presidency in 1975. Political leaders were reported stunned by Banzer's assertion Sept. 21 that he would run "if the people ask me," and by his nomination for the presidency by the National Peasants Confederation, reported Oct. 4. Banzer said Oct. 9 that he would not be a candidate in 1975, but his opponents were not reassured.

Opponents were also outraged by the formation Sept. 2 of the National Action Committee (CAN), a right-wing paramilitary force pledged to eradicate leftist extremism. The Christian Democratic Party charged Oct. 16 that the CAN was created by Banzer and, like the terrorist Argentine Anticommunist Alliance, was funded by the U.S. Central Intelligence Agency.

Bolivian former minister charges CIA. Former Interior Minister Antonio Arguedas, asserted at his exile home in Cuba that Bolivia had received illegal payments from the U.S. Central Intelligence Agency, the *Washington Post* reported May 17, 1975. Arguedas said he had been present at a meeting in 1966 at which the CIA station chief in La Paz had agreed to give Rene Barrientos $600,000 for his presidential campaign that year. The CIA also made contributions to other rightist parties in the elections, asserting it could not "place all our bets on one horse," according to an unnamed agent quoted by Arguedas.

Peru

Peace Corps ousted. The military government asked the U.S. to withdraw its 137 Peace Corps workers from Peru within 90 days, a U.S. State Department spokesman announced Nov. 14, 1974.

The government said Peruvians could do the Peace Corps' work, which was

mostly in agricultural development projects. However, government-controlled newspapers charged Nov. 15 that the Peace Corps was linked to the U.S. Central Intelligence Agency.

President Velasco had said Nov. 14 that in the late 1960's he had asked the U.S. to remove two alleged CIA agents from Peru, whom he identified as Ernest V. Siracusa and Frank Ortiz. The State Department asserted the two men were not intelligence agents but career diplomatic officers.

Velasco charged the CIA was connected with protests against his government and with the smuggling of food out of Peru. "Everything is possible, since the CIA is like God—it's everywhere," Velasco said.

State of emergency extended. The government extended the state of emergency and suspension of guarantees for another 30 days March 6, 1975. These had been imposed Feb. 5 during the rioting and looting which followed the crushing of the police strike in Lima. A night curfew imposed Feb. 5 was lifted Feb. 24.

Government officials estimated that more than 100 persons were killed in Lima during the disturbances, according to press reports Feb. 8. Other sources said the death toll rose to 500 counting disturbances in other cities, the *Miami Herald* reported Feb. 9. Hundreds of persons were wounded in Lima, and 1,000–2,000 were arrested, according to varying press reports.

Meanwhile, the government and its press continued to blame the disturbances on the opposition left-of-center APRA party, on local "oligarchs" and on the U.S. Central Intelligence Agency. President Velasco implicated the CIA and APRA leader Victor Raul Haya de la Torre in a nationwide address Feb. 17, although he did not name either directly. Complicity was denied by the U.S. State Department (on behalf of the CIA) Feb. 18 and by Haya de la Torre Feb. 24.

The newsletter *Latin America* reported Feb. 28 that there seemed "little doubt" that APRA "shock troops" were active in the Lima rioting under the direction of Armando Villanueva, the party's former secretary general and leader of hardline opposition to the government.

Paraguay

Widespread political arrests. Interior Minister Sabino Montanaro admitted at a

press conference that "more than 1,000" political arrests had been made since the discovery in November 1974 of an alleged plot against President Alfredo Stroessner, the Paris newspaper *Le Monde* reported Feb. 21, 1975.

Reports that several detainees had been tortured to death were cited by both *Latin America* and *Le Monde*. Teruco Papalardo, Stroessner's chief of protocol, said the U.S. Central Intelligence Agency had sent an interrogation team to help question the detainees, *Latin America* reported.

Costa Rica

U.S. CIA official recalled. The U.S. State Department confirmed Feb. 10, 1971 that it was recalling Earl J. Williamson, chief of the Central Intelligence Agency office in Costa Rica. Williamson's withdrawal followed rumors and charges in Costa Rica that he was involved in an attempt to overthrow President Jose Figueres Ferrer.

The State Department, however, denied the rumors that the U.S. was involved in a plot to overthrow the Costa Rican government. In addition, Rep. John S. Monagan (D, Conn.) of the House Foreign Affairs Subcommittee on InterAmerican Affairs, said Feb. 10 after the subcommittee had been privately briefed by U.S. Assistant Secretary of State Charles Meyer, that the affair was probably due to "personality conflicts" between U.S. Ambassador to Costa Rica Walter C. Ploeser and his staff and also to "over-zealous actions" by unnamed U.S. officials.

President Figueres had said Feb. 9 that the coup rumors stemmed from people "who never could prove it." He said that he and Ploeser "are on very good terms." Figueres added that Williamson and his wife held political views "distinct from that of the [Costa Rican] government, but that's their privilege."

Reports had indicated that Williamson was upset over Costa Rica's plans to renew diplomatic relations with the Soviet Union, but Figueres said: "This diplomatic recognition in no way shakes our loyalty to the United States or to the democratic cause. People everywhere are tired of the cold war. Russia controls half of Europe and we want to make the Russians drink coffee instead of tea." (The Soviet Union had purchased about $10 million worth of coffee from Costa Rica over the past two years.)

B

C

D

E

F

G

SUPREME COURT DECLINES HEARING ON CIA BOOK BY MARCHETTI, MARKS

The Supreme Court announced without comment May 27 that it would allow to stand a 4th U.S. Circuit Court of Appeals ruling sustaining the right of the Central Intelligence Agency to censor the writings of former employes who signed contracts in which they agreed not to divulge information they learned about the agency while working for it.

In so ruling, the court rejected First Amendment freedom of press claims on behalf of the book, *The CIA and the Cult of Intelligence,* by Victor L. Marchetti and John D. Marks. The appellate court had upheld the CIA's deletion, for reasons of national security, of 170 passages from the authors' original manuscript and concluded that security classifications had to be presumed correct because the government would be over-burdened if private citizens could force it to prove otherwise. Justice Douglas dissented.

The Philadelphia Inquirer

Philadelphia, Pa., June 2, 1975

The U. S. Supreme Court's ruling in the case of "The CIA and the Cult of Intelligence" is inexplicable—for one thing, because the court did not explain it.

In deciding not to decide, over the dissent of Justice William O. Douglas, the court followed its usual procedure of not issuing a formal opinion, which upheld the CIA's power to compel former employes to submit anything they wrote about the agency to the CIA for censorship.

The lower court based its ruling on the theory that anything public officials classify for security reasons must be presumed correctly classified and that the burden of proof is upon the citizen to prove otherwise.

It is a strange theory, in our own view of the wording of the Constitution and the intent of the framers. And it is an impossible presumption to make, in view of all we have learned over the past few years about how and why government officials keep information from the public.

As just one example, let us cite one of the approximately 339 passages which the CIA censored out of the book, which was co-authored by former agent Victor L. Marchetti. The censored passage (restored in negotiations between the agency and the authors and publisher) is in boldface type:

"The NSC meeting had officially **begun,** and, as was customary, Helms set the scene by giving a detailed briefing on the political and economic background of the countries under discussion. Using charts and maps carried by an aide, he described recent developments in **southern Africa. (His otherwise flawless performance was marred only by his mispronunciation of 'Malagasy' [formerly Madagascar], when referring to the young republic.)"**

The government argued successfully that the case involved a contract which Mr. Marchetti had signed in which, like other CIA employes, he had agreed not to disclose information he learned while working for the agency. On this, it seems to us that the court should have ruled on the question of whether the CIA has the legislative authority to enforce such an agreement, since even CIA Director William E. Colby has conceded that there is nothing in the statute setting up the agency giving it such authorization. Beyond that, though, there is the question of whether any citizen can be required to sign away his constitutional rights as a condition of government employment.

There are unique features in the case and fine legal questions, but fundamentally it comes down to the right of a free people to know what their government is doing. It is a pity that the Supreme Court seems itself to have succumbed to the "cult of intelligence" and come out on the wrong side.

ST. LOUIS POST-DISPATCH

St. Louis, Mo., March 7, 1975

An astonishing insensitivity to the First Amendment was registered by the U. S. Court of Appeals for the Fourth Circuit in a recent decision upholding the right of the United States Government, acting through the Central Intelligence Agency, to censor a book before its publication. For the first time in the history of the nation a book was published last year with blank spaces on its pages.

This ominous development for a free press arose as a result of the efforts of Victor Marchetti, a former CIA executive, and John Marks, a former State Department employe, to write a book exposing some of the CIA's operations, including the agency's blunders. The CIA in 1972 sought and got a federal court injunction against the authors, the only case of prior restraint of the press in U.S. history, except for the Pentagon Papers case, in which the Supreme Court lifted the restriction.

Under a court order to do so, Messrs. Marchetti and Marks in 1973 submitted their completed manuscript to the CIA for censorship. As a result of objections from the authors, the CIA finally reduced its demanded deletions from 339 to 168. After a trial in which the agency sought to justify its deletions, U. S. District Judge Albert V. Bryan Jr. of Virginia ruled that only 26 items were excludable from the manuscript as properly classified. But with the district judge's decision subject to a long process of appeal, the publisher, Alfred A. Knopf, brought out the book, "The CIA and the Cult of Intelligence," with 168 blank spaces.

Despite the unwillingness of the conservative trial judge to permit the CIA to censor more than 26 items, the Court of Appeals has now upset his decision. It ruled that the case must be heard anew under a presumption of truth for the Government's claim that an item was properly classified and may not be published even though some of the material had already leaked and even though new amendments to the Freedom of Information Act put the burden on official agencies to sustain their classification actions and authorized judges to review classified material in private and decide for themselves. The court said that judges were not equipped to decide.

Such deference toward government censors is astounding in the light of congressional testimony by experts (former classifiers themselves) that 99 per cent of millions of classified documents ought not to be classified at all and in the light of newly published material revealing the lawless activities of the CIA. Still more astounding is the court's reaffirmation of the doctrine that the Government may restrain publication on the strength of the oath of secrecy taken by government employes who work in fields related to national security. Such secrecy agreements are routinely made by thousands of government employes and just as routinely broken by official and unofficial leaks. The absurdity of the system of flagrant over-classification is illustrated by the fact that officials and former officials must breach their agreements in order to get legitimate information to the public. Former cabinet officers and generals have done so when they wrote their memoirs, and have never been subject to injunctions based on nondisclosure "contracts." Yet now the Government has set an appalling precedent for using such contracts to restrain publication.

The prospect for avoiding a system of censorship totally antithetical to the American system lies with the Supreme Court. That court should hark back to its 1971 Pentagon Papers decision in which it said any attempt at prior restraint must come to court "bearing a heavy presumption against its constitutional validity" and should require proof by the Government that disclosure would "surely result in direct, immediate and irreparable injury to the Nation or its people."

Herald ⚛ News

Fall River, Mass., May 30, 1975

The Supreme Court has refused to reverse a court order requiring former CIA employes to submit future writings about the CIA to the agency before publication. The case arose over a book by Victor Marchetti, who sued for the right to restore material deleted as classified.

The issue raised by Marchetti is the basic one of free speech, and the Supreme Court's ruling, from which only Justice Douglas dissented, amounts to asserting the inalienable right of the CIA to secrecy. The conflict between the two principles is self-evident, and in recent months the CIA has been repeatedly and bitterly criticized for some of its hitherto secret activities.

The critics seem not to realize that a non-secret service will be totally useless to perform the functions for which it was organized. Yet it is hard to believe that former employes of the CIA are similarly naive. They must have known what they were doing when they joined it, and, in effect, gave the organization the right to censor any future disclosures they might wish to make about it.

The issue must have been a difficult one for the Supreme Court to decide, but on the whole, its ruling seems justified. The alternative would be to dismantle the CIA altogether, as some of its critics seem bound on doing. Given the present state of the world, this would be a disaster, and the Supreme Court was surely justified in refusing to permit the Marchetti case to become an excuse for accomplishing just that.

Pittsburgh Post-Gazette

Pittsburgh, Pa., June 4, 1975

ALMOST casually, a near-unanimous U.S. Supreme Court has compromised freedom of the press and free speech by allowing the Central Intelligence Agency to censor a critical book by a former CIA employe.

The former CIA agent is Victor Marchetti, who with John D. Marks wrote a book, "The CIA and the Cult of Intelligence," which was published without some sections stricken by agency officials. The Supreme Court refused to review a lower-court decision, denying Mr. Marchetti's suit to have the censored portions reinstated.

The court thus sanctioned — blithely, and in a relatively obscure case — the prior restraint long considered anathema to the Bill of Rights. The effect of the decision is to encourage government agencies unhappy about proposed books by former employes to suppress such writings — on the pretext of their choice.

* * *

Unlike other nations, including Great Britain, the United States has no "official secrets" act to allow the government to censor newspapers in the name of national security. Nor are there laws, such as also exist in Britain, prohibiting the press from discussing matters under litigation.

The reason for the absence of such opportunities for censorship is a strict and literal construction of the First Amendment to the Constitution, which prefers the risk of license to the risk of thought-control.

This tradition does not release American citizens — or publishers — from the responsibility to be law-abiding. Libel laws exist for the prosecution of those who abuse freedom of the press by malicious distortion of the facts. Treason and espionage laws provide a similar punishment for the publication of troop movements or other truly vital defense secrets.

What makes the Supreme Court action in the Marchetti case doubly disturbing is that the court allowed prior restraint not for reasons of national security but to enforce a contract between private parties — a secrecy agreement signed by Mr. Marchetti when he joined the agency. The court upheld the CIA's argument that in signing the agreement Mr. Marchetti effectively forfeited the First Amendment rights that would have protected his right to publish.

* * *

The CIA is not the only government agency which could suffer embarrassment from published criticism by former employes. The encouragement offered by the Supreme Court's action will make prior restraint, no matter how repugnant to our constitutional traditions, increasingly attractive.

Our hope is that the next time this issue reaches the court, the justices will insist on hearing the case themselves, rather than rely on the record of proceedings at a lower level. And we further hope that that, after hearing those arguments, the court will change its position.

The Providence Journal

Providence, R.I., June 1, 1975

The United States Supreme Court, by upholding a lower court's open-ended censorship order against an author who is a former intelligence agent, has set an unhealthy precedent that nibbles away at the First Amendment.

The author is Victor Marchetti, a Central Intelligence Agency agent from 1955 to 1969 who, with John D. Marks, has written a controversial study of the agency — *The CIA and the Cult of Intelligence.* Mr. Marchetti twice, while with the CIA, signed secrecy agreements pledging not to divulge information he had learned while he was an agency employe. The CIA, seeking to uphold those agreements, fought successfully in court to have selected passages excised from the book on security grounds.

By refusing to review the Marchetti case, the Supreme Court upheld the lower court's censorship of sections of the book. Also left untouched, however, was a more significant court order, requiring Mr. Marchetti to submit all his future writing about the CIA to the agency for pre-publication censorship.

This order, which amounts to a lifetime injunction, represents a disturbing departure from the constitutional prohibition on pre-publication restraint that the Court reaffirmed in the Pentagon Papers cases in 1971. The order is uniquely selective, and thereby unfair, because it applies restraints on a single former agency employe not known to have been imposed on any others.

Such a blanket restriction, furthermore, will tend to reverse the recent trend away from excessive government secrecy and over-classification of documents. In Mr. Marchetti's case, it will give the CIA the legal right to eradicate whole passages, whole articles or whole books — before they ever see publication. Acting under the court order, the agency apparently will have this power even over material that never should have been classified in the first place, or that Mr. Marchetti obtained outside his former employment. The order thus seems to exceed the limits of Mr. Marchetti's secrecy pledge to the agency and to reinforce the widespread government penchant for secrecy. It opens the way, in Mr. Marchetti's case and perhaps others, for the government without judicial review to invoke secrecy on the grounds of national "security." This term, as the late Justice Hugo L. Black wrote in the Pentagon Papers opinion, "is a broad, vague generality whose contours should not be invoked to abrogate the fundamental law embodied in the First Amendment."

To argue that the court's permanent censorship order against this writer is excessive is neither to defend his own actions nor to assail the CIA for the secrecy pledge it exacts from employes. To do its job effectively, the agency must shield its operations and its information from prying eyes: this demands that its employes keep quiet about the agency, even after they leave. The secrecy agreement was valid; Mr. Marchetti should have observed it.

Beyond this, however, the lower court, with its permanent censorship order against Mr. Marchetti, has stretched the boundaries of prior restraint to new limits. If such orders can be upheld for the CIA, then in time they may be upheld to gag other former government employes. Even though the government cannot possibly prove that this restraint would be justified in all future writings of Mr. Marchetti, the courts have censored him for good.

It's not a bright omen.

U.S. ACTIVITIES IN LAOS REVIEWED; FULBRIGHT ATTACKS CIA FINANCING

The Senate met in secret session June 7 to review the extent of U.S. involvement in the war in northern Laos. The unusual session had been requested by Sen. Stuart Symington (D, Mo.), who said May 28 the public and Congress had "little or no knowledge" of the Laotian situation and the Senate should ascertain the facts of the U.S. role before more funds were appropriated "for this clandestine war."

Symington said June 6 the U.S. was spending "hundreds of millions" of dollars on the war in Laos, much more than the $52 million acknowledged by the Administration as its economic aid for the area. In the secret session, Symington had said such spending was amounting to at least $350 million annually.

The use of B-52s for raids over northern Laos in support of the Laotian government troops was acknowledged May 3 by Undersecretary of State John N. Irwin 2nd, who told the Senate Foreign Relations Committee the B-52s were used on a regular basis to attack enemy troop formations and supply lines. Previously, the Administration had admitted use of the B-52s for such purpose on only one occasion in February 1970—during a battle for the Plaine de Jarres.

Committee Chairman J. W. Fulbright (D, Ark.) said May 21 that 4,800 Thai troops financed by the U.S., through the Central Intelligence Agency, were fighting in Laos in support of the Royal Laotian government. Fulbright charged that the U.S. role was "inconsistent with the spirit" of the "antimercenary" amendment enacted in 1970.

DESERET NEWS
Salt Lake City, Utah, July 10, 1971

If the United States isn't careful, it can let itself get dragged into Laos the same way it got dragged into Vietnam.

So it's understandable that the Senate wants to set a ceiling — $200 million has been proposed— on U.S. spending in Laos.

And it's hard to swallow the Pentagon's story that such a ceiling won't work because nobody knows exactly how much American money is being spent there.

Granted that precise figures are hard to come by because much of the money going into Laos is being funneled through the Central Intelligence Agency — and CIA spending is properly kept secret as a security matter. But the CIA ought to know how much of its funds is going into Laos, and lumping that amount in with overall spending in Laos could be no breach of security.

Granted that keeping track of U.S. spending in Laos could involve complicated accounting procedures that may not be inexpensive. But the Pentagon ought to know for its own purposes how much the support of Laos is costing in American dollars as well as possibly in American lives.

Granted, too, that as more U.S. troops are brought home from Southeast Asia, more U.S. funds will have to be sent there to help replace them. But this can't be an open-ended arrangement, since America's treasure is not inexhaustible.

There's room for quarreling with the specific level of the proposed ceiling. Already the U.S. is said to be spending some $174 million a year more than the proposed limit of $200 million.

But the Pentagon can't be handed a blank check on Laos. If the Defense Department really doesn't know how much it is spending in Laos or any other individual country in Southeast Asia, that's sufficient reason for setting a ceiling to find out.

The Charleston Gazette
Charleston, W.Va., June 10, 1971

The State Department, in a rather roundabout way, has finally come out with an admission that it is paying Thai "volunteers" to fight in Laos on behalf of the Laotian government.

There was no accounting for the number of Thai mercenaries under contract to the State Department at the expense of U. S. taxpayers, although Sen. J. William Fulbright earlier had indicated that 4,800 Thai troops were so employed in Laos.

The cat was let out of the bag by way of a State Department defense of its clandestine activities as being "fully consistent with all pertinent legislation." This question was debated Monday in an unusual secret session of the Senate to review the extent of American military involvement in northern Laos, and the State Department's defense of its action is highly questionable.

The fact is that, in approving defense appropriations for the current fiscal year, the Congress adopted a Fulbright amendment barring the use of mercenaries. But the State Department takes the incredible position that its continued employment of mercenaries is "fully consistent" with the law because the program of using "volunteers" in Laos predated enactment of the Fulbright amendment.

This is a position that defies reason, for it is to say that Congress lacks the power to outlaw any practice. The use of mercenaries may have been legal last year, but certainly it became illegal with adoption of the Fulbright amendment— and no amount of squirming can make it otherwise. The Fulbright amendment clearly was intended to stop the employment of mercenaries, and stop it must.

What is most distressing about the State Department admission, however, is that it exposes the utter despondency of American diplomacy in Southeast Asia. Instead of trying to inspire a defense of democracy by example and gifts of food and education, we permit the CIA to go on playing cloak and dagger games that would be laughable if they were not so tragic.

Certainly the State Department practice of employing troops of one country to fight in another kills off the domino theory, for if the Laotians are not interested in defending themselves no amount of propping up with U.S. dollars is going to make them more interested.

We should know by now that we can't buy allegiance, and if the Laotians show no inclination to put down the pro-Communist Pathet Lao in northern Laos, it is obviously futile for the United States to pay Thai troops to do so.

THE STATES-ITEM

New Orleans, La., June 8, 1971

Is the United States deepening its involvement in Laos, while "winding down" the war in Vietnam. At least two leading Democrats think so.

Sen. Stuart Symington of Missouri, one of the Senate's top military authorities, says that instead of the $52 million publicly acknowledged by the Nixon Administration, the United States actually is spending "hundreds of millions of dollars" in a clandestine war in Northern Laos.

At the same time, Sen. Edward M. Kennedy has charged the Nixon Administration with a whitewash on the question of American involvement in the war in Northern Laos.

Sen. Symington's statement is based on a still-to-be-released report prepared by two members of a Senate Foreign Relations Committee subcommittee—James G. Lowenstein and Richard M. Moose —who recently visited Laos.

Among the developments which the administration is alleged to have covered "with a mantle of secrecy" are an increasing Chinese presence in Laos, the introduction of Thai troops into the war and B-52 bombing raids into Northern Laos.

Much of the current American aid is said to go for support by the Central Intelligence Agency of a semi-autonomous force of mountain tribesmen who, according to the Lowenstein-Moose report, have been supplemented by almost 5,000 Thai troops who also are being paid by the United States.

In addition, according to the report, as the U.S. involvement in Laos has deepened, Air Force planes based in Thailand have been providing regular combat support for ground forces.

Scarcely more than a month ago, William H. Sullivan, former ambassador to Laos, and now deputy assistant secretary of state for East Asian and Pacific Affairs, testified before a Senate subcommittee that the war in Northern Laos has "nothing to do with military operations in South Vietnam or Cambodia."

Why, then, are we there?

The credibility gap that now surrounds administration policy on Southeast Asia is strangely reminiscent of the one that helped force President Lyndon B. Johnson from office.

The Des Moines Register

Des Moines, Iowa, June 9, 1971

The secret session of the United States Senate to discuss the secret war in Laos turned out not to be very secret. The war isn't very secret, either.

Senator Stuart Symington (Dem., Mo.) asked for the session to make sure the senators got a full picture of the secret war before voting another $34 million for military and economic assistance to Laos.

Symington was chairman of a subcommittee which in 1969 and 1970 investigated U.S. commitments around the world in the interest of "the people's right to know" — but it took the subcommittee five months of negotiating with the Administration to get it to release a drastically censored version of the subcommittee hearings on Laos.

The release came in April, 1970, a few weeks after President Nixon was goaded into a 3,000-word statement on Laos. News accounts had made public the exploits and plight of the secret army of Meo tribesmen financed and trained by the U.S. Central Intelligence Agency. The country was shocked by that story and by the "incursion" into Cambodia that same April.

As a result, Congress wrote into law a ban on sending U.S. ground combat troops into Cambodia (there already was such a ban for Laos) and a ban on U.S. financing of foreign troops in support of the Laotian or Cambodian governments, except to promote safe withdrawal of American troops from Southeast Asia or to aid in the release of prisoners of war.

The secret army is still operating, and the U.S. is now also financing 4,800 Thai troops operating in Laos. Symington considers that a violation of the law. The Administration says no. If North Vietnam conquered all Laos, it argues, it would be in better position to attack American troops in South Vietnam.

This is stretching a point pretty far. The Administration spokesman contradicted the testimony of another spokesman to the subcommittee that the operations in northern Laos had nothing to do with the operations in Cambodia or South Vietnam.

But every Administration since Dwight Eisenhower's has slithered into the war in Laos, and tried to get out again. The Nixon Administration slipped in more deeply than its predecessors, in spite of congressional efforts to stop it.

Subcommittee members figure the cost of the war in Laos to America at a billion or more a year, including the heavy bombing. Symington plans to try to set a new limit of $200 million — and to hold the Administration's nose to the grindstone of the 1970 law. Three wars are three too many.

The Philadelphia Inquirer

Philadelphia, Pa., June 9, 1971

The U. S. Senate rarely goes into secret session. The time before last was in December, 1969, on the subject of Laos and charges of an escalating secret war in that landlocked semi-country bordering—moving counterclockwise—on North Vietnam, China, Burma, Thailand, Cambodia and South Vietnam.

That session produced a heavily censored transcript and congressional action to bar the introduction of American ground troops in Laos and the expenditure of defense appropriations to finance foreign mercenaries in Laos as well as Cambodia.

This week, the Senate went into another secret session and on the same subject.

Two Senate Foreign Relations Committee staff members, after an inspection trip to Laos, reported that the U. S. is financing some 4800 Thai troops to defend the beleaguered Laotian government. Other charges have been made that the U. S. is financing mountain tribesmen for further fighting and is conducting heavy air support of government forces in the northern part of the country, where they are contending with the North Vietnamese.

So far, no transcript, censored or otherwise, has emerged from the Senate's secret proceeding. Presumably, one eventually will be issued. Meanwhile, more confusion than facts about our involvement has been brought to—we started to say "light" but that is definitely not the word—public attention.

The State Department has at long last conceded publicly that those 4800 Thai troops are fighting in Laos. But the State Department insists that they are legitimately being financed by the U. S under a provision in the law permitting the President to take needed actions "to insure the safe and orderly withdrawal or disengagement of U. S. forces from Southeast Asia, or to aid in the release of Americans held as prisoners of war."

Is this a matter of semantics or substance? Impossible to tell, because like the rest of the press we weren't in the Senate galleries to hear the evidence which Sen. Stuart Symington, who had called for the secret session, submitted to his colleagues and the attending debate in which Sen. Clifford Case reportedly made an effective and "emotional plea to bring this thing out in the open."

How much bombing is going on, and where? Rep. Paul N. McCloskey, who spent three days in Laos recently, has charged that the government has deliberately concealed the extent to which American bombers have plastered villages in northern Laos, and the figures on cost range as high as $2 billion a year.

Senator Symington, who comes from Missouri, says he intends to introduce an amendment to limit the amount that the U. S. can spend on its sundry operations in Laos to $200 million—for economic, military and CIA assistance. Well, we come from Missouri too, in the figurative sense, and we would raise a couple of further questions.

If, as charged, the administration is flouting the will of Congress where its amendments of two years ago are concerned, what makes the senator think that it would not do the same again? But if, as the administration holds, it is acting "fully consistent with all pertinent legislation," the place to make its case is not in a secret session but in public.

We agree with Sen. Case. This thing should be brought out in the open. Our adversaries may be presumed to know what's going on in Laos. The people in Laos may also be presumed to know. The senators have informed themselves, more or less. But what about the America people's right to know?

The Senate ought to forget about secret sessions and open its doors to the public and the press.

THE TENNESSEAN
Nashville, Tenn., June 9, 1971

BACK IN MARCH of 1970, President Nixon promised to give the American people the "fullest possible" information on the U.S. role in Laos. But the public still does not know how deeply the nation is involved, or what it is costing the taxpayers.

★ ★ ★

After a secret session of the U.S. Senate, Sen. Stuart Symington of Missouri said he will propose a $200 million ceiling on American spending there. Even if Senator Symington got such a ceiling, it is rather obvious there are ways and means to get around it.

About all that emerged from the Senate session was public acknowledgement that the U.S. is financing volunteers from Thailand fighting in Laos in behalf of the Lao government. But the numbers are secret and so is the expense.

Both the U.S. mission in Laos and Washington are, and have been, deliberately hiding the extent of American involvement. U.S. newsmen are given the shuttlecock treatment in that they are told in Saigon they must go to Vientiane for information, and in Vientiane they are told they must go back to Saigon for answers.

U.S. air missions over Laos are kept secret. There is simply no information given out on the number of missions, the targets, the results, or even the planes that don't return.

The U.S. is obviously running a ground war in Laos under the auspices of the Central Intelligence Agency. Its use of Thai troops and Meo tribesmen is common gossip in Indochina. Lao troops talk frequently about American "commando leaders" based at Pakkao, who apparently train and accompany Meo tribesmen and other ethnic units to battle against the Pathet Lao and North Vietnamese forces.

But U.S. newsmen have no way of getting into the areas where these forces operate since both military planes and those of the CIA-run airline decline to take them, and the only other way in is through guerrilla-infested areas too rugged for Jeeps and too dangerous to try on foot.

Adding up bits and pieces of information only leads to the conclusion that the U.S. is fighting a covert war and spending immense sums in doing so.

★ ★ ★

One estimate is that the U.S. is pouring in about $2 billion annually, which is interesting if one compares it to the $5 million proposed for "general" revenue sharing to help states and localities at home. The only figure that has ever been given by the Nixon administration is $52 million in economic aid for the current fiscal year. Congress reportedly has appropriated some $100 million in military aid. But these figures are only a drop in the bucket, and Mr. Symington's proposal to limit spending to $200 million would really put the administration in a bind, if it didn't have several ways to channel in funds and still hide the amounts from Congress and the people.

If Americans had all the facts of the Laos operations, they would be astonished, if not horrified. But "all the facts" are precisely what the Nixon administration isn't going to give them.

HOUSTON CHRONICLE
Houston, Tex., June 10, 1971

"What we are doing in Laos is totally inconsistent with our kind of society." This is what a U.S. diplomat in Vientiane, Laos, recently told a correspondent.

The official, who did not want to be quoted by name, added: "We are fighting a war by covert means and an open society cannot tolerate that."

If this is correct, the administration has much to answer for to the American public. The disclosures made so far raise more questions than they answer.

For example: Officially the public has been told that the United States is contributing $52 million a year to the Laotians in economic aid. Unofficially, it has been reported that $100 million has been approved for military assistance.

Tuesday, following a rare closed session of the United States Senate to discuss our activity in Laos, different senators put total expenditures at $200 million, $250 million, and one went as high as $350 million.

Sen. Stuart Symington, D-Mo., a former secretary of the air force, said he told his Senate colleagues that "what was actually going on in Laos was quite different in some details than we have been told."

One reported activity in Laos is the financing of 4800 Thailand troops in Laos by the U.S. Central Intelligence Agency. Another is financial support for Royal Laotian troops and irregulars.

The Republican leader in the Senate, Hugh Scott of Pennsylvania, claimed that nothing new had been disclosed in the secret session of the Senate; that the Thai troops are not mercenaries; and the activity is justified because, "If Laos were to fall it would greatly decrease the already slim chances of successful negotiations with the Communists who would then have completely outflanked the rest of Indochina."

He could be right on all counts, but why should the facts be kept from the American people? The Communists are certainly aware of much of what we are doing in Laos. The American public should know at least as much.

The secrecy on the part of the administration raises the fear that the United States may be enlarging operations in Laos when a majority of Americans favor a withdrawal from Indochina; that in winding down the war in Vietnam, the administration is at the same time increasing our involvement in other Indochina nations which would be contrary to laws passed by Congress. Specifically a law forbidding the use of U.S. funds to support foreign forces fighting for the governments of Cambodia and Laos.

Sen. Symington has urged the administration to approve release of the transcript of the secret session as well as a report on financing of Thai troops in Laos. If our society is open and, as administration supporter Scott said, nothing new was disclosed, there should be no hesitancy to let the people know.

The Courier-Journal
Louisville, Ky., June 12, 1971

LET US MAKE one thing perfectly clear about those Thais who are fighting in that clandestine war in northern Laos: They're perfectly all right.

True, we have a law against hiring mercenaries to fight on our side in the Indochina war. True, the CIA is paying the Thai government for the use of 4,800 soldiers. But the CIA was paying for the troops before Congress passed that law last year, so the law doesn't apply to the Thais, see? And besides, they're not mercenaries, they're volunteers.

Now, the Thai volunteers shouldn't be confused with the North Vietnamese "volunteers" who North Vietnam says it isn't sending to South Vietnam. Nor should they be confused with the Red Chinese "volunteers" who fought in Korea. They weren't really volunteers. They were forced by their government to lay down their lives in behalf of the North Korean cause.

But the freedom-loving Thais really *want* to lay down their lives for the freedom-loving Laotian government, which is fighting a war against Communist Laotians and North Vietnamese, who are in Laos because their Communist government forced them to go. That is, the North Vietnamese in Laos aren't really volunteers.

That is, the CIA isn't paying the North Vietnamese who are fighting in Laos, only the Thais, who aren't mercenaries, but volunteers. But even if they are mercenaries, we were paying them before we decided it was illegal to pay mercenaries, so it's all right.

NIXON THREATENS TO CUTOFF AID TO PROTECTORS OF DRUG TRAFFIC

President Nixon Sept. 18 pledged to cut off aid to any foreign government whose leaders protected international drug traffickers, an authority granted but never invoked under the 1971 foreign aid act. Appearing before an international narcotics control conference at the State Department, Nixon defended his Administration's record on narcotics control and responded to Democratic presidential nominee George McGovern's charge the day before that the President's war on drugs had failed. McGovern had charged that Southeast Asia had become "a major source of heroin supply" where the Administration would never crack down because it "needs air bases in Thailand, Laos mercenaries and Vietnamese soldiers to fight its war." Nixon cited specific progress in Laos, Thailand, Turkey, France and Paraguay where, he said, "important breakthroughs" had been achieved in the war on drugs by U.S. officials "in partnership" with local authorities.

The Miami Herald
Miami, Fla., September 20, 1972

"THERE must be something we can do to stop it," President Nixon said angrily early this year when the chief of the narcotics bureau in the Justice Department reported that all sorts of dangerous drugs were being smuggled into the United States at faster and faster rates.

Something was done. More agents and more money were thrown into the battle against international traffickers in heroin and cocaine. Mr. Nixon can feel better about the increasing number of arrests at Miami International Airport and other; major entry points.

But the battle goes on. This week the President felt compelled to reply to Sen. McGovern's accusation that the administration is going easy on opium and heroin racketeers in Southeast Asia because of the need for air bases and official cooperation to maintain the air war against Hanoi. The President's reply was a promise to cut off all aid to any foreign government whose leaders protect those who traffic in narcotics.

Coincidentally, on the day Mr. Nixon made that promise, the House Appropriations Committee made only a $50 million cut in the White House's request for $780 million in outright military assistance for Thailand, Cambodia, Turkey and Korea. There is no heroin problem with Korea, and Turkey appears to be making an effort to reduce planting of opium poppies. But Cambodia and Thailand are up to their necks in the production, processing and export of heroin that reaches the street in the United States through Saigon, Hong Kong and Latin America.

At least that is the story told by American officials who have been assigned to Southeast Asia to cut off the export of heroin, but who are frustrated by the practicalities of U.S. strategy in the Vietnam war.

It is also the story told by a Yale scholar who spent 18 months tracing the sources of heroin and is the author of a sensational book titled, The Politics of Heroin in Southeast Asia. Alfred W. McCoy draws on a vast store of documentation to make one strong point: that the men in power in Southeast Asia are totally corrupted by the traffic in heroin and that the production of the drug would not be possible without the knowledge and involvement of every political leader in Thailand, Laos, Cambodia and South Vietnam.

This, then, is the President's dilemma. And it is recognized by top Foreign Service officers who doubt that any foreign aid will be denied to any country in Southeast Aisa because of narcotics until the war can be settled.

The Washington Post
Washington, D.C., September 23, 1972

Mr. Nixon can point with pride to considerable achievements in his worldwide battle against drugs. In funding, organization, law enforcement at home and abroad—especially in cooperation with Turkey—and in addict treatment programs and research, he has a record fit for valid use in his re-election campaign. In truth, no president has ever done more.

His is, however, a record deeply flawed in one major respect. His dedication to fighting Communists in Indochina has kept him from exploiting his full resources in the war against drugs there. The connivance of high officials in the region has been established repeatedly by American intelligence and by more public sources. These officials serve governments supported by the United States. No doubt President Nixon has vigorously impressed on Saigon how harmful to American boys, and how damaging to American public support of the war, would be any less-than-complete effort by it in combating drugs. Yet the patron-client relationship simply does not permit unlimited pressure to be applied, or full results to flow therefrom. One does not have to share George McGovern's views on the war to recognize that no all-out assault on the narcotics traffic in Southeast Asia can be made while Washington continues to use South Vietnamese soldiers, Laotian mercenaries and Thai air bases for purposes of the Vietnam war.

In fact, Mr. Nixon has not declared "total war on drug abuse," as he suggested last Monday. He has declared limited war. Implicit in his restraint is a judgment that, however terrible the effects on young Americans would be from pressing with less than full vigor on drug traffickers in Indochina, these effects are less terrible than would be the political consequences of ending the American role in the Vietnam war on terms available now. Perhaps Mr. Nixon is right in this judgment, although frankly we do not believe so. It would be interesting to hear him explain it publicly.

But is the President changing his own views? We have in mind his categorical unqualified pledge of last Monday: "Any government whose leaders participate in or protect the activities of those who contribute to our drug problem should know that the President of the United States is required by statute to suspend all American economic and military assistance to such a regime. I shall not hesitate to comply fully and promptly with that statute."

This statement should be taken literally and hailed by all who agree with Mr. Nixon that he bears "no more solemn trust" than eradicating drug abuse. If it is acted upon, to the letter, not only would a major crimp be put in the world drug traffic but the American role in the Vietnam war would be entirely over. If it is not, then the President should be held to account for failing to take every step he could to protect Americans from the heroin plague, and for dismissing yet another solid argument for ending our entanglement in the fate of Southeast Asian nations which either no longer need, or have forfeited their entitlement to, continued American military support.

Arkansas Gazette.

Little Rock, Ark., September 21, 1972

RICHARD NIXON is a sly one, all right. If he really wants a face-saving excuse, not only to end American participation in the Indochina War, but to cut off any further American aid to our corrupt "allies" in Southeast Asia, he now has a perfect one, conveniently self-provided.

Sensitive to campaign charges that his celebrated "war" against the drug traffic has been no more successful than, let us say, his "Vietnamization" of the real shooting war, Mr. Nixon now has threatened to cut off aid to "any government whose leaders participate in or protect the activities of those who contribute to our drug problem * * *."

Since there is no one of the countries in which we are operating in Indochina either overtly or clandestinely, where the drug operators themselves do not operate with the overt or covert co-operation of local authorities, the Nixon threat, if ever implemented, would constitute a wipe-out of the whole lot of them.

In a major take-out on this subject last year, the *New Republic's* Eliot Marshall wrote in advance of passage of the legislation that Mr. Nixon claims he will use if pressed:

The countries most likely to be affected by such a bill—Laos, Thailand, and South Vietnam—probably would be unable to stop [the] drug traffic *even* [our italics] if they wanted to. Poppy farms [the source of opium and its derivative, heroin] usually operate in remote border areas where governments have little control; and when government forces are present, corrupt officials use men and equipment in their command to protect their own investment in the drug market. Laos is notorious for corruption. The official, U.S.-subsidized airline is known locally as "Air Opium." Representative Robert Steele (Rep., Ct.), testifying before a House Foreign Affairs subcommittee on July 8 [1971], named the chief of staff of the Laotian Army and the South Vietnamese commanding general of II Corps as "chief traffickers" in narcotics. They both have political connections * * *.

Elsewhere—which in this case is South Vietnam, the Big One—charges of involvement in the lucrative hard drug pipeline have run all the way up to the estimable Thieu himself. As for our own official *apparat*, the familiar reference here to the American-supported chartered airline, Air America, as "Air Opium" was a reminder of the CIA's at least oblique involvement in the opium growing that seems to be one of Laos's principal reasons for being.

It was all for the best of purposes—"winning the war against Communism", as all of the CIA's most dubious undertakings are self-justifying by definition —but there is something pretty unsettling about such things as the General Accounting Office's recent charge that American tax dollars appropriated for refugee relief in Laos were being diverted to support of paramilitary operations by "our" Meos in the North in contravention of the will of Congress, which tribe doubles as one of the principal regional producers of raw opium.

* * *

A WHOLE BOOK has in fact just been published on this subject—"The Politics Of Heroin In Asia," by Alfred W. McCoy —and the September 21 issue of *The New York Review* has an instructive account by the author of the CIA's unsuccessful effort to exert prior restraint against publication, complete with an exchange of correspondence between the counsel for the cloak-and-dagger agency and Mr. McCoy's publishers, Harper and Row.

There can exist no drug traffic without a source of original supply or without a pipeline for distribution, but, first of all, there can exist no drug traffic without a body of consumers for the end product. Demand comes first. It is in this area that the exchange in the *New York Review* may be most instructive of all.

Mr. McCoy, concluding his case there, says:

In 1969, before significant numbers of GIs started using heroin in Vietnam, this country had an estimated 315,000 heroin addicts. Three years later that estimate has nearly doubled. Early this year the government estimated that there were almost 600,000 addicts.

This increase in demand is confirmed by the CIA as part of its larger attempted defense against Mr. McCoy's accusations—though, to be sure, from a different standpoint and with some understandable qualifying shading of emphasis and tone:

The opium trade has existed in Southeast Asia for generations. This trade depended upon the market, *and until recently* the market for Southeast Asian opium was in Southeast Asia. The increase in the opium trade and the appearance of heroin were a result of the increased market, *in part* due to the presence of large American military forces in Vietnam. [Our italics.]

"In part," indeed! Euphemism will get you nowhere, for what "until recently" really means in the above context is that "until the massive American involvement there" the market for Southeast Asian opium had been confined to Southeast Asia.

N i x o n—"M r. Thimblerigg"—presently is engaged in the most important pea-under-the-shell game of his career lifetime. He must (1) convince large numbers of otherwise sane Americans to vote against their own best economic interests out of some accumulated store of vague hobbies and prejudices. He must at the same time (2) convince people who have always prided themselves on having a sense of what is an[d] is not real that American participatio[n] in the war in Indochina is just abo[ut] over when, in fact, there has been a n[ew] increase in American strength the[re] since the punitive bombing was resume[d] at the highest forces level ever.

Mr. Nixon's Indochina "pea" now is Thailand, then, instead of in Vietnam, [as] far as ground-based force levels a[re] concerned, and so how goes it with o[ur] augmented forces in Thailand, "narc[ot]ics-wise?" Here is an appraisal by Ste[ve] Cramer, a recently returned Arm[y] medic, as related to the Chicago Su[n] Times:

"I saved a few lives." In what way[?] he was asked. "Taking care of OD[s] (overdoses), rushing them to the hos[s]pital, he replied. * * *
"Drugs were everywhere, A brick o[f] marijuana — a pound-and-a-half — coul[d] be bought for 50 cents." * * * Hard drug[s] also were easily accessible, Cramer re[lated. "Opium was very cheap," he said "either in liquid, powder or red rock[s] which was hard granules * * *."

When we hear Richard Nixon talki[ng] now, more than three years later, [of] "cutting off aid" to Southeast Asian ho[st] nations that aid and abet further narc[ot]ics addiction among young American[s,] let us remember that when Alfr[ed] McCoy writes that there has been an a[l]most 100 per cent increase in heroin a[d]diction among young Americans "sin[ce] 1969" what he is saying is that this h[as] all happened since Mr. Nixon first ca[me] to office pledged both to stamp out t[he] narcotics traffic and to end the war th[at] by the CIA's own admission, cited he has done so much to nourish and expa[nd] the market for "hard" narcotics subs[e]quently.

DAYTON DAILY NEWS

Dayton, Ohio, September 20, 1972

President Nixon's statement on the international heroin trade was possibly a useful thing to say, as long as he doesn't really mean it.

Mr. Nixon swore that the United States will cut off military and development aid to any government whose officials either are involved in heroin dealing or refuse to take conscientious action against heroin routes that pass through their countries toward the United States.

If that alleged policy has the effect of intimidating some of the few Asian, Latin and Middle Eastern nations that participate in or shrug at the traffic, then Mr. Nixon's bombast may have been worth the small amount of energy and credibility it cost him.

Otherwise, the policy will come a cropper, both at home and abroad.

As Mr. Nixon presumably knows and as the State department knows for sure, the United States cannot let its foreign policy be controlled by the issue of state-side heroin addiction, serious and tragic as is the problem.

The United States can afford to stand showily aloof from implicated nations whose positions are irrelevant to major f o r e i g n policy considerations, but it would be an act of folly bordering on nuttiness to abuse any nation whose position might be i m p o r t a n t to the scheme of major U.S. national interests.

All Mr. Nixon really is saying, then, is that the United States will be tough on any drug-dealing nation that is unimportant to us.

As such, the policy turns out to be only a posture, domestically an act of campaign demagoguery promising the American public a toughness that Mr. Nixon can indulge only when it is convenient. If he gets caught in a geopolitical bind, the President either will have to cover up for the offending nation or concede that the rule exists merely to the degree it is comfortable.

These risks the President must have weighed and judged to be smaller than the political gains to be made with an electorate that he obviously believes is gullible. It will be good luck, and nothing more, if some of the i n t e r n a t i o n a l connections also are gulled.

The Honolulu Advertiser

Honolulu, Hawaii, September 27, 1972

There is much pseudo-glamor associated with the world heroin trade. Shadowy French-Corsican gangsters, international smuggling trips, mysterious Chinese war lords in the outreaches of Burma and stalwart undercover agents.

The glamor stops on the streets, however, with the misery and fear of the addict. While it is said Hawaii does not have that many addicts on the street yet, Honolulu stands to be very much a part of the heroin story for another reason.

WORLD HEROIN TRADE is shifting from Turkey and France to the "Golden Triangle" area of Southeast Asia. In this region — northern Thailand, western Laos and eastern Burma — some 700 tons of opium is produced yearly.

As the U.S. effort against heroin smuggling from Europe continues on the East Coast, more traffic is bound to flow through Hawaii. Myles J. Ambrose, U.S. Customs Commissioner, said here last year he expects "serious attempts" to bring heroin through Honolulu as the Turkey supply dries up. The arrest of eight Malaysians charged with smuggling $8 million worth of heroin recently at Honolulu Airport shows it is happening.

THE NIXON Administration is aware of the problem. It has greatly increased the number of customs inspectors, narcotics agents and amount of antinarcotics spending. The effects of the drive are beginning to show, say Washington officials, particularly on the East Coast.

Customs efforts have been stepped up in Honolulu as well.

Where the antiheroin efforts seem less realistic is when the U.S. attempts to stop the production and export flow of opium and heroin from Southeast Asia. Burma, the "real source of production" in that part of the world, according to the U.S. Cabinet Committee on International Narcotics Control, produces around seven times the total amount of opium needed to serve America's heroin needs each year.

The Burmese government refuses U.S. help against opium producers in that country. In fact, the Burmese permit independent Chinese "armies" which dominate the opium trade to operate freely as a means of developing strength against antigovernment rebel groups.

THERE IS EVEN evidence that the United States may have aided opium traffickers through the CIA or other agencies. Alfred W. McCoy, in his recent book "The Politics of Heroin in Southeast Asia," makes the claim that the U.S. has directly or indirectly allied itself with and supported shaky anti-Communist governments in Southeast Asia who have long been in the opium business.

The CIA attempted to deny McCoy's charges, but were unable to convince Harper & Row (the book's publishers). In fact, several CIA or State Department officials have been quoted as independently admitting some smuggling and "looking the other way" has gone on in Southeast Asia. But they say the situation has changed in recent years.

IT WOULD HARDLY seem that the answer to the heroin problem is glamorous adventures against remote hill tribesmen of Burma or Laos. The answer is at home. Tough and efficient measures to prevent the entry of heroin into the country are part of it. The government must continue its efforts in that direction.

And while the controls are being strengthened, more effort and money should be spent on the less-easily tackled but inherently more important question of why people need to use such drugs in the first place.

The Des Moines Register

Des Moines, Iowa
September 22, 1972

President Nixon said he would comply fully and promptly with the statute which requires him to suspend aid to "any government whose leaders participate in or protect the activities of those who contribute to our drug problem."

Taken literally, the statute would require him to suspend aid to South Vietnam, Laos and Thailand, all of which have leaders deeply involved in the drug trade.

Formerly nearly all the heroin for Americans came from Turkish poppy fields via French processors and smugglers. In recent years the United States has been paying Turkey to cut off opium production and catching the French smugglers. So the traditional Southeast Asia opium trade has greatly expanded, begun manufacture of heroin and gone after customers among American soldiers in South Vietnam and in the world market. Burma is part of the chain, too, but Burma scorns U.S. aid.

If the U.S. Central Intelligence Agency were a foreign power (sometimes it acts like one), the President would have to cut off support for it, too. For years the C.I.A. has tolerated the opium and heroin trade of Southeast Asia in its search for "freedom fighters." The opium-growing Meos of Laos are C.I.A. proteges, and so, earlier, were the opium-growing Chinese Nationalist exiled guerrillas in Burma. The chain of smugglers who brought the opium from the interior highlands to processing and distribution points as heroin included Laotian and South Vietnamese generals and officials.

Unfortunately, all this is hard to prove in any individual case, though the general outlines are well-known.

The C.I.A. denies everything, and the Thai, Laotian and South Vietnamese governments do the same — and occasionally co-operate in crackdowns to keep the White House satisfied.

Still, the President would be wise to keep his pledge on file and consider actually carrying out the threat. America's "honor" and "face" have been hopelessly smirched by the long, cruel Indochina war, but he could still salvage a little honor by ending the whole war (not just for Americans on the ground) out of refusal any longer to co-operate with those who are corrupting American troops with heroin.

St. Louis Review

St. Louis, Mo., August 25, 1972

We have all heard frightening stories about China and other enemy nations supplying narcotics to demoralize our troops in Southeast Asia and to likewise sap the spirit of Americans here at home. Now President Nixon's Committee on International Narcotics has found that "there is no reliable evidence that China has either engaged in or sanctioned the illicit export of opium and its derivatives." Furthermore, it found that the Soviet Union "is neither a source nor a transit point for illicit opiates."

Instead of coming from our enemies, the Presidential Commission finds that the vast majority of the illegal drugs that enter America comes from nations that are our friends, especially Turkey, Mexico, and the countries of Southeast Asia. Coupled with the charges made last week that the C.I.A. was directly involved in encouraging the production and distribution of narcotics in return for the fidelity and fighting qualities of Vietnamese tribesmen, we might well ask just who our friends are.

As long as a demand for narcotics can be fostered in the United States, the task of controlling the importing of narcotics is going to be a complex one. The United States is doing everything possible to help foreign governments control their own drug producers, even to the extent of subsidizing foreign growers for not growing opium poppies. Now the time has come to apply the stick as well as the carrot. We have invaded foreign nations, deposed foreign rulers and spent millions to influence foreign legislators when we felt our national interests were at stake. Surely our national interest in opposing the imposition of the drug tyranny on our citizens demands the strongest possible economic and diplomatic sanctions to dry up the sources of illicit drugs.

And the charge that the C.I.A. has itself been directly involved in the drug market deserves full investigation. Those who made the accusation do not charge that the C.I.A. decision was based on greedy or ignoble motives but simply because winning the war has become the only priority. We must know whether this is true.

HOUSTON CHRONICLE

Houston, Tex., June 3, 1971

President Richard Nixon is correct when he says that drug addiction is a national problem and not only a question of U.S. troops in Vietnam becoming hooked on heroin.

However, the problem of drugs in Vietnam and throughout the services should not be minimized in any way. The mounting drug usage there is alarming.

Reps. Robert Steele, R-Conn., and Morgan Murphy, D-Ill., reported after a three-week investigative tour that best estimates are that 25,000 to 40,000 U.S. troops in Vietnam are now heroin addicts.

This a horrible, unwanted result of a war that the majority of Americans now want to disown. As in most areas where addiction is rife, heroin is easy to come by in Vietnam. It is also strong and cheap.

Why is heroin so available? Charges have been made that the Central Intelligence Agency indirectly helps provide the funds for some drug production and transport by payments to Laotian guerrillas. There have been hints, too, that high South Vietnamese officials, members of the government we are protecting, are profiting from the drug traffic.

In too many cases, the services have done little more than ignore the drug problem in Vietnam. The result is a shocking addiction rate. Similar neglect has been shown when servicemen are released: There has been no regular program of testing for addiction or of treatment for the soldier victims.

Presidential aide Robert H. Finch has said that addicts are being released from the services at the rate of 20,000 a year. In most cases, these men must turn to crime to get the money needed to support their habit in the United States.

They will join tens of thousands — possibly more — civilian addicts who are shoplifting, burglarizing, robbing and cheating to pay for the illict drugs which keep them in a living hell.

The President is calling for a national offensive on the drug problem but it appears that some branches of the executive department are going in another direction. For example, the hesitancy of the Food and Drug Administration to approve methadone use on a broad basis.

This drug is addictive, but it blocks the craving for heroin in addicts and enables them to hold a job and lead a productive life.

Methadone is cheap and if dispensed under supervision could prevent disease among addicts caused by dirty needles and impure illicit drugs, as well as eliminate much criminal activity.

Another administration contradiction is to close the clinical research center in Fort Worth to addicts. The Department of Health, Education and Welfare is proceeding with plans to turn the drug treatment facility over to the Justice Department for use as a prison hospital.

The President's offensive would cut off overseas drug sources, prosecute drug pushers, treat addicts and institute an information program on drug abuse.

All of these are necessary elements but the closing of the Fort Worth facility, one of two federal addict centers in the nation, and the failure to make a decision on methadone which has been tested in some areas for eight years or more, seem to hinder such an offensive.

Minneapolis Tribune

Minneapolis, Minn., June 6, 1971

"The U.S. went on a holy war to stamp out communism," said Ramparts Magazine, ". . . and it brought home heroin." The truth in that assertion is bad enough. The irony is even worse. To think that the "noble" cause has come to this.

The additional irony is that deadly drugs are being made available to American troops not by the enemy, but by the Asian allies we are fighting to protect. Military personnel and even high-ranking officials of South Vietnam, Laos and Thailand apparently have been involved in the opium traffic from jungle areas of Southeast Asia. Reports indicate that opium is being grown even by Meo tribesmen who were selected by the CIA for counterinsurgency efforts against the Pathet Lao in Laos. In addition, former Nationalist Chinese troops are buying and reselling the opium to maintain themselves in Thailand.

The Nixon administration may be able to limit the problem by placing pressure on our allies to stop the drug traffic. We have our doubts, however, about how effective that undertaking will be. Those making a profit from the opium business will not give up easily. Beyond that, U.S. Narcotics Chief John E. Ingersoll pointed out the other day that many farmers in these countries rely on opium crops for their subsistence. They will not be any more inclined to give up their livelihood than are the farmers in this country who grow tobacco, another crop harmful to users.

Still, efforts to get at the source of opium supply are important. So are the efforts by the armed services to treat addiction once it has developed. But they miss the real cause of the problem. An American psychiatrist in Vietnam said recently that the soldiers there are reacting to Vietnam much as deprived persons react to life in a ghetto, where narcotics addiction has long been a serious problem. They take drugs and try to forget.

Society has treated the ghetto drug victims harshly over the years, putting them in prisons, giving them felony records that make it difficult for them to obtain jobs, doing little to change the conditions that lead to drug use. The armed services acted much the same in handling their drug problem at first. Countless servicemen were punished or given dishonorable discharges that deprived them of veterans' benefits and impaired their employment status. The Marines have been the most arbitrary, and are said to have the biggest problem.

At the very least, it would seem that the drug victims in Vietnam or in America who suffered from the punitive approach before laws and policies were liberalized should be cleared of damaging records. A dishonorable discharge can be changed. A felony record—for a crime later defined as minor—can be erased. But the country must also get at the real causes of drug addiction, whether the despair born of a war that must be ended, or the despair of ghetto conditions that can be alleviated.

CASE DISCLOSES CIA FUNDING OF RFE, PROPOSES PUBLIC, PRIVATE FINANCING

Sen. Clifford P. Case (R, N.J.) charged Jan. 23 that the Central Intelligence Agency had expended several hundred million dollars "from secret" budgets during the last 20 years to support Radio Free Europe and Radio Liberty broadcasts to Eastern Europe. While both stations "claim to be non-governmental organizations sponsored by private contributions," Case said, "reliable sources indicate direct CIA subsidies pay nearly all their costs."

The Nixon administration endorsed Case's plan for open, public funding of RFE, Case announced May 22. The Senate Foreign Relations Committee turned down July 21 the bill introduced by Sen. Case May 24 to create a tax-exempt corporation chartered by Congress to run Radio Free Europe and Radio Liberty.

The Detroit News

Detroit, Mich., July 25, 1971

The doves on the Senate Foreign Relations Committee have given the American public another demonstration of their belief that the United States can unilaterally turn the world into a dovecote.

They did so by defeating a Nixon administration plan to finance and operate Radio Free Europe and Radio Liberty under a tax-exempt corporation chartered by Congress and by voting, instead, to permit the stations to operate for another year under CIA auspices with a limited appropriation.

Chairman J. W. Fulbright, however, thinks the stations are remnants of the cold war and questioned the continuing need for them. He has asked that studies of their feasibility be made before the committee decides whether to terminate the stations or continue them under annual congressional scrutiny, authorization and appropriations.

Whatever the recommendations, however, most observers feel that both Radio Free Europe and Radio Liberty perform useful functions. Radio Free Europe broadcasts to Eastern Europe and Radio Liberty broadcasts to the Soviet Union provide citizens of those countries with balanced news reports which they seldom get from their own government-controlled radio, press and television.

The fact that Radio Free Europe and Radio Liberty have been financed by the Central Intelligence Agency was one of the world's poorest-kept secrets. In view of the criticism of the CIA and this type of supposedly secret financing, the administration was wise to propose an alternative. But the time certainly is not yet ripe to discontinue the excellent service the stations provided to the people behind what is still in many respects an Iron Curtain.

ST. LOUIS POST-DISPATCH

St. Louis, Mo., May 12, 1971

With the laudable intention of getting CIA spooks out of the operation of Radio Free Europe and Radio Liberty, the Nixon Administration reportedly is preparing to ask Congress to create a "public-private" corporation through which annual federal appropriations of $36,000,000 would be channeled to the two "unofficial" U. S. radio voices in Europe.

Commendable as the change in financing may be, however, it seems to us doomed to failure. Ever since the disclosure some four years ago that the CIA was financing what had been presumed to be the voice of freedom for listeners in Eastern Europe and the Soviet Union, that voice has had a suspicious accent. Now that the new financing plan is said to have been prepared with the aid of the CIA and with the approval of a subcommittee of the National Security Council, what listener can hear the broadcasts without seeing agents in disguise manipulating the transmitters?

We are afraid Radio Free Europe and Radio Liberty have been irreparably corrupted.

San Francisco Chronicle

San Francisco, Calif., July 14, 1971

IT IS ONLY RESPECTABLE that the Government, under the prod of Senator Case of New Jersey, should give up the subterfuge of pretending that Radio Free Europe and Radio Liberty, which have been operated on CIA funds, are a privately owned and financed outlet for the Free World's truth.

For years, bus and subway patrons in this country have idly gazed at car cards advertising the courageous and selfless role of Radio Free Europe in bringing the truth to the mind-shackled Communists. This has been a public service activity of the Advertising Council, providing free media space for messages that urge the bus rider to send a contribution to an address in Mount Vernon, New York, for the support of the radio stations.

Though they have been palmed off to the public as privately financed by corporations, foundations and individual gifts, these stations, Case has shown, are actually operated on hidden appropriations from the CIA at around $30 million a year. The campaigns carried on in free media space, he has shown, have run to "less than $100,000" a year.

Radio Free Europe and Radio Liberty are both doing a good job of sending news to Eastern European and Russian audiences, respectively. But there is no excuse for maintaining the shattered pretense of their being anything but what they are, Government run. If a Nixon Administration proposal goes through, a tax-exempt, non-profit corporation will be set up to finance and supervise the two stations. This is as it should be.

The Pittsburgh Press

Pittsburgh, Pa., March 4, 1971

It's too bad that U. S. Sen. Clifford P. Case has spilled the beans about Radio Free Europe and Radio Liberty. For he may have seriously undermined their effectiveness.

Both stations are based in Munich, Germany, and broadcast to the Soviet Union, Poland, Hungary, Czechoslovakia, Romania and Bulgaria.

For many millions behind the Iron Curtain, they are the only reliable source of news about the outside world and the listener's own country.

Naturally, the Communist regimes of East Europe fear and dislike such holes in their public-information monopoly.

So they are leaping with great propagandistic glee on Sen. Case's disclosure that some $30 million of the stations' $34 million annual cost comes from the Central Intelligence Agency (CIA).

Unfortunately, the issue is embarrassing West German Chancellor Willy Brandt.

Brandt is struggling to improve relations with Russia and its satellites. Now they are pressing him to evict the "CIA stations" from German soil as a step toward normal relations.

★ ★ ★

For years the CIA has been strongly suspect of having ties with Radio Free Europe and Radio Liberty. But nobody could state that as a fact.

Now, thanks to Sen. Case's blabbing, propagandists in the Communist-bloc countries have been supplied with some made-in-the-U. S. ammunition. They can, without fear of contradiction, label these two useful stations as CIA subsidiaries.

One result may be to reduce the stations' credibility in East Europe. Over the years, the governments there have labored to turn the CIA into a dirty word (while playing down their own more vicious intelligence organizations).

Sen. Case is not trying to halt broadcasting to the Soviet bloc.

He just wants to bring it out in the open and has introduced a bill to appropriate $30 million to Radio Free Europe and Radio Liberty.

The stations' activities would then come under the scrutiny of Congress.

Such a move now seems unavoidable. Cutting the CIA ties will not only make the stations less vulnerable to attack but also will improve their chances of staying on in Munich.

★ ★ ★

President Nixon should consider turning the stations into a public corporation with a board of directors of businessmen, diplomats, broadcasters and scholars specializing in East Europe. The corporation could be openly funded by Congress and be responsible to it for its activities.

However the problem is solved, one thing should be stressed: We must continue broadcasting news, commentary and entertainment to the subjects of Communist regimes until their rulers give them more than just one slanted side of every story.

The Washington Post

Times Herald

Washington, D.C., June 26, 1971

Radio Free Europe, which undertakes to tell East Europeans the news about themselves that their own controlled media withhold, is under harsh political attack for that reason from governments of some of the East European countries it broadcasts to. It may face an even greater peril, however, from the confusion of efforts underway in Washington to end its covert financing by the C.I.A. and to finance and operate it on a new open basis. The situation has got to be taken into hand quickly, for as matters stand, funds will run out for RFE—and for Radio Liberty, which broadcasts to the Soviet Union—quite soon. The two stations are much too valuable to be lost in a summer haze.

East European governments resentful of RFE's broad appeal to their populations have long stewed and fulminated about it—along with pulling such dirty tricks as putting poison in the salt shakers of its Munich headquarters. They could do little more, until Willy Brandt opened his policy of reconciliation with the East. Then, sensing an opportunity for leverage, they said that his *Ostpolitik* and RFE are incompatible. In fact, they are not, but Germany was embarrassed. Once Mr. Nixon made clear his position that American troops and American radios in Germany are part of a package, however, Bonn diplomatically told the protesting East Europeans to cool down.

Some East European governments bored in harder when Senator Clifford Case stated publicly what almost everybody had known for years—that the C.I.A. finances RFE (and Radio Liberty). Poland, for instance, called upon the United States last month to put RFE off the air.

Senator Case's point was to get RFE out in the open and so he offered a bill to finance it by direct appropriations, through the State Department. The administration, correctly contending that much of RFE's audience appeal lies in its appearance of independence from the American government, countered with a bill to set up a publicly funded "private" corporation to run both RFE and RL.

(West Germany, for its own reasons, favors the latter approach.) In the meanwhile, there arose on Capitol Hill legitimate questions about the cost of the stations, their research functions, their relationship to other American propaganda and cultural programs, and their coordination with political efforts for detente. The administration did not allow enough time for Congress to cope adequately with these questions and, as a result, the stations are now hanging by the thread of a continuing resolution which provides funds only until August.

We do not have dogmatic views on the kind of organizational home the stations ought to have or on the size of their budgets or the scope of their non-broadcasting activities. We would like to make the emphatic point, however, that RFE and RL do an extremely important job and, in our judgment, do it well.

RFE still carries an image of irresponsibility dating from its indeed-irresponsible words of encouragement to Hungarian rebels in 1956. Together, RFE and RL have the reputation of being the voices of bitter emigres and primitive anti-Communists. The two stations, however, have considerably changed and they can no longer be fairly accused of the sins of their past. What they do now is to communicate directly with the people of East Europe who want to listen to them in order to learn what they cannot learn from their own captive press and radio. The stations do not incite to revolution or preach anti-Communism; they say what is going on in East Europe. It would be an unpardonable breach of faith with the stations' millions of listeners to deny them their choice of radio fare.

Detente, if it means anything, means widening the West's contacts with the East, not helping the East to seal off its people from the West. It means the exchange of people, goods, words and ideas. This is the essential business of RFE and RL. The Congress, in its rightminded determination to shake the stations free of the CIA, should not lose sight of the reason for letting them continue it.

ANDERSON REVEALS ITT'S DOCUMENTS ON DISRUPTING ELECTION IN CHILE

Columnist Jack Anderson made public documents he said came from ITT's files March 20–22 which disclosed attempts by the company to prevent the election of Salvador Allende Gossens, the marxist president of Chile, in 1970.

In one memo from an ITT official to John A. McCone, a former director of the Central Intelligence Agency, the possibilities of encouraging a military *coup d'etat* or of disrupting Chile's economy were mentioned. In another incident, Anderson said J. D. Neal, ITT's director of international relations, had offered a White House aide ITT's financial backing "up to seven figures" to prevent Allende's inaugural.

According to Anderson, ITT's proposals received a "polite but cool reception" from the White House and the State Department. He said, however, that one CIA official had proposed that ITT aid in a scheme "to plunge the Chilean economy into chaos and thus bring about a military uprising."

ITT's representative in Chile had reported at one point, according to Anderson, that the U.S. ambassador had received the "green light" from the State Department "for maximum authority to do all possible, short of a Dominican Republic-type action" to "keep Allende from taking power."

A State Department spokesman said March 23 that the administration had "firmly rejected" any ideas of "thwarting the Chilean constitutional process following the elections of 1970."

ST. LOUIS POST-DISPATCH
St. Louis, Mo., March 23, 1972

Perhaps the International Telephone & Telegraph Corp. was not satisfied to assist the Nixon Administration with political arrangements and advise it on antitrust policy. For ITT now appears to have pursued its own foreign policy.

New documents published by Columnist Jack Anderson include accounts of meetings of ITT officials with contacts at the White House, State Department, Central Intelligence Agency (whose former chief, John McCone, is now an ITT director) and the Chilean military. The documents speak of trying to bring about economic chaos or a military revolt in Chile, to prevent Marxist Salvador Allende from being elected or becoming president.

Mr. Allende became president, of course. He nationalized ITT holdings valued in the millions. Meanwhile the Nixon Administration attempted to rebuff the new Chilean government by word and denial of credit. Chile

formally protested against a statement by a White House staff member that the Allende government would not last long. The one thing the White House has not done so far is to invoke the Hickenlooper amendment denying aid to countries that nationalize private American property without "adequate" compensation. ITT lobbied that amendment to passage.

ITT has, of course, issued a denial that it was involved in Chilean politics. The White House says the Government does not act in concert with private companies on foreign policy. That hardly answers the question of whether it tried. In view of the companionship of ITT and the Administration, and the CIA's lamentable interventions in other countries, Latin America is bound to wonder whether the new reports do not spell a vast commitment to dollar diplomacy. Instead of weakening the Allende government, meddling with Chile will only strengthen it.

The New York Times
New York, N.Y., March 26, 1972

Already mired in political controversy at home, the International Telephone & Telegraph Corporation has now been plunged into Chile's politics in a time of crisis. Whatever the truth about I.T.T. activities, columnist Jack Anderson's charges will inevitably make life more difficult for it and other American firms hoping to survive in Chile or at least to obtain fair compensation if nationalized by the Marxist-dominated Government.

The charges are certain to damage as well the "cool but correct" relations Washington has tried to maintain with Chile. Perhaps most important, they may have the ironic effect of bailing out President Allende just when internal difficulties had forced him to suspend Congress for a week. He was trying, through secret talks, to revive a working relationship with the opposition Christian Democrats and to investigate a Supreme Court report that illegal land seizures by revolutionary leftists have brought anarchy to a southern province. Some observers report civil war already under way in Cautín, with small landholders banding together to retake their properties from left-wing guerrillas.

The alleged I.T.T. memos, purporting to implicate not only the State Department and C.I.A. but even President Nixon himself in plans to prevent Dr. Allende from taking office, can be exploited by the Government in a country ever sensitive to charges of Yankee interference. There is danger that Dr. Allende might seize upon them to end his talks with the opposition and go ahead with his projected plebiscite aimed at replacing Congress with a People's Assembly.

To point these things out is not to suggest either that Mr. Anderson should have withheld the memos or that their contents—allegedly the work of two ex-journalists now in I.T.T. public relations—accurately mirror the behavior of the American ambassador in Chile at the time or of his Washington superiors. On the public record, Ambassador Edward M. Korry behaved impeccably and Assistant Secretary of State Charles A. Meyer exercised good judgment in the Chilean election.

If the memos are authentic they furnish a classic example of how a giant international corporation should never behave, particularly in a democratic country with every right to work out its political destiny without outside interference.

The inquiry to be conducted by the Senate Foreign Relations Committee, both into the I.T.T. affair and more broadly into the influence of corporations on foreign policy, could cut this country's losses with the Chilean people if not with the Marxists in their Government. More important, the inquiry should aim at assuring Americans that special interests will not be allowed to meddle secretly in this nation's relations with other countries.

© 1972 by The New York Times Company. Reprinted by permission

The Washington Post
Times Herald

Washington, D.C., March 22, 1972

Jack Anderson, in his column yesterday, quoted from purported ITT documents which state that ITT dealt with the Central Intelligence Agency over Chile and that the company tried (and failed) in 1970 to generate enough economic chaos there to trigger a military coup that would bring down the elected Marxist president, Salvador Allende. In his column today, Mr. Anderson goes on to show, from the purported ITT documents, that ITT pressed its anti-Allende campaign at the White House and State Department and with the Attorney General as well. On Sept. 15, 1970, one document says, the American ambassador in Santiago "finally received a message from the State Department giving him the green light to move in the name of President Nixon. The message gave him maximum authority to do all possible—short of a Dominican Republic-type action—to keep Allende from taking power." But, an ITT report of Oct. 16 said, "it is a fact that word was passed to Viaux [General Roberto Viaux, identified as ITT's choice of coup maker] from Washington to hold back last week . . ."

These allegations are astonishing. It is perhaps one matter that ITT—whose Chilean telephone property, valued by it some $108 million, was nationalized last September—might seek to intervene in a foreign election, dealing with a CIA activist in Washington and seeking out in Santiago a general (Viaux) who is now in jail facing court-martial on charges of participating in the 1970 slaying of the army chief of staff. If true, this is outrageous enough. In any event, publication of the charge is likely to make it politically impossible for any Chilean government to consider ITT's compensation claim for a long time to come. In view of reports that Chile was about to make an important compromise on that claim, in order to break the political logjam in its foreign loan and debt renegotiation situations, this is a particularly inopportune time for the story to break.

It is quite another matter, however, and a far graver one, that President Nixon stands charged, in what is purported to be an authentic ITT document, of personally approving an attempt "to do all possible—short of a Dominican Republic-type action—to keep Allende from taking power." This is a charge so serious that it is hard to see how anything short of a major congressional investigation can dispose of it. Hardly less pressing is the question of why, if a "green light" had been given on Sept. 15, it had turned red by Oct. 16. Could there have been a threat of exposure of a CIA

hand, possibly in the Senate? We do not know. So much of an open secret is the CIA's support of the victorious Christian Democrat Eduardo Frei in Chile's 1964 elections, however, that suggestions of a CIA role in 1970 cannot be easily dismissed.

That the latest Anderson columns will let President Allende play the aggrieved nationalist, and thereby gain him months' reprieve from his own deep political troubles, goes without saying. The resultant surge of anti-American propaganda can be all to well predicted. What must concern Americans more, however, is the revealed troubles of our own. ITT is now accused of manipulating not only key aspects of domestic policy but of foreign policy as well. What kind of system is it that permits a powerful corporation to wander through the corridors of official power as though they were its own? How can it be—if it is so—that in 1970 an American President could consider the possibility of acting to prevent the democratically elected president of a supposedly friendly country from taking office? The Dismisal Swamp we have been talking of in connection with the affairs of ITT for some days is becoming ever more dismal.

The Boston Globe

Boston, Mass., March 21, 1972

Columnist Jack Anderson's allegation that the International Telephone & Telegraph Corporation conspired with officials of the Central Intelligence Agency in an attempt to trigger a military coup in Chile, with which the United States maintains diplomatic relations, verges on the incredible.

And not the least chilling aspect of it is that the Justice Department, in casually dropping three antitrust suits against ITT, added to the power and influence of a corporation already so big and so powerful that it functions virtually as an independent government, ignoring Washington foreign policy makers if it does not, indeed, draw them along in its own wake.

In the alleged plot to trigger a military uprising that would have prevented the election of Chilean President Salvador Allende in 1970, ITT president Harold S. Geneen, others of the corporation's top personnel as well as members of the CIA (unless they were acting with

the consent of the Federal government) have acted in what State Department spokesmen tentatively view as a clear violation of several sections of the neutrality laws as enumerated in Title 18 of the US Code.

What the Department of Justice may elect to do about it has not been disclosed. But plainly the ITT case now goes considerably beyond the initial charges, now being heard by the Senate Judiciary Committee, that ITT and the Justice Department colluded in the dropping of antitrust charges against the corporation and the corporation's agreement to help finance the Republican National Convention in San Diego in August. The confirmation of Acting Atty. Gen. Richard Kleindienst to succeed John N. Mitchell, President Nixon's campaign manager, as Attorney General has been hanging in the balance and now obviously will have to wait the fullest possible exploration of the new charges against the corporation

with which both the White House and the Justice Department have had such friendly relations.

The Globe on prior occasions has suggested that the Senate Judiciary Committee, which about a month ago unanimously recommended Mr. Kleindienst's confirmation, may not be the proper committee to handle the allegations that the out-of-court settlement of the antitrust cases was a trade-off for ITT's agreement to help finance the GOP convention. Certainly the Judiciary Committee, with all respect for the diligence with which it has pursued the trade-off charges, does not seem the proper committee for the larger investigation. Yet, the Justice Department cannot be expected to investigate itself. This puts the whole nasty and larger affair squarely up to the congressional leadership, which may not yet have had sufficient time to weigh the full import of Mr. Anderson's astounding allegations.

In the case of ITT's contribution

to the GOP convention and the agreement not to prosecute the antitrust cases against it, it has been established that at least one of President Nixon's aides, Peter Flanigan, knew what was going on and even participated. In the new case, to which the then director of the CIA's Latin American Division, William V. Broe, and former CIA Director John McCone are alleged to have been privy, either White House indifference or White House ignorance verging on incompetence seems indicated.

The specifics of the anti-Allende plot, as spelled out in the ITT documents which have come into Mr. Anderson's possession, are chilling. Even more chilling are the consequences that could so easily have been the result if the plot had not been aborted. Foreign policy resulting in American expeditionary forces and the deaths of American youths are bad enough when set by the American government. The concept of such policy being set by American corporate giants is intolerable.

THE MILWAUKEE JOURNAL
Milwaukee, Wis., April 3, 1972

If one wonders why the expression "dollar diplomacy" brings Latin Americans' blood quickly to a boil, the shenanigans of International Telephone & Telegraph in Chile should serve as a prime example.

The revelations of columnist Jack Anderson and others indicate that if ITT did not overtly try to block Chilean President Allende's assumption of office, it talked about such moves and would have been willing to co-operate in any US supported effort. Business Week quotes John McCone, former CIA chief and member of the ITT executive committee, as saying the company was willing to aid any administration plan.

Allende, a Marxist, has made political hay out of this, claiming that it again proves America's imperialistic tendencies. It strengthens Allende's hand at a time when.

he is particularly plagued by domestic troubles and opposition. US-Chilean relations are no better for it.

But Chileans legitimately can fear actions similar to those contemplated by ITT. A firm of ITT's size looms much larger on the Chilean economic landscape than it does in the US. A simple statistical comparison will illustrate this. In 1970 Chile had a total economic output of $6.7 billion. That same year ITT's sales amounted to almost $6.4 billion. In 1971 they totaled $7.3 billion. When the Chilean government deals with an ITT it is dealing with at least an equal.

If such firms act in unison with the US government, it is easy for a foreign country to feel put upon. And because of its implications for American foreign policy, the Senate is justified in taking a good look at this relationship.

THE ANN ARBOR NEWS
Ann Arbor, Mich., April 12, 1972

PERHAPS the most damaging (and the most believable) of the Jack Anderson documents relating to International Telephone and Telegraph's alleged behind-the-scenes activity in Chile was the one which had ITT "doing what it could to help out" if the CIA or U.S. interests tried to block Salvador Allende from taking over the presidency of Chile.

To our knowledge, ITT has not specifically denied that charge. It makes a certain kind of sense, too, that ITT would not choose to stand idly by in an American-engineered attempt to freeze out Allende.

The CIA pulled off a similar caper in Guatemala during the Eisenhower adminstration. Our interest in keeping in power governments which are favorable to the U.S. has led to certain chummy relationships with some of the worst dictators the southern continent has raised up.

* * *

COLUMNIST Anderson's disclosures, whether accurate, partially accurate or unfounded (which doesn't seem likely) have played into President Allende's hands. They were a boost to a weakened government.

Now, according to United Press International, "The Secret Documents of the ITT" has become a best seller in Chile. The street

corner Chilean is reading this material and having his old impressions of Uncle Sam reinforced. He thinks Uncle Sam has interfered in his country's affairs, whether he is an Allende sympathizer or not.

The ITT dustup may force Allende's hand. His leftist supporters will want to get on with the process of nationalizing ITT's holdings. If Allende succeeds in this, he will have done on an accelerated basis exactly what ITT feared most at the impending takeover of a Marxist President: nationalization. And it may have been this fear which allegedly led ITT to promise "to do what it could."

* * *

SEPARATE congressional committees, Chilean and American, have launched investigations into ITT's activities in Chile. What these two bodies find may well determine ITT's standing in Chile, and whether it goes the way of the big copper companies.

But wherever the full truth lies, the damage has been done. In the minds of most Chileans, the flag once again has followed United Fruit, or in this case, I Tel and Tel. And all the while ITT has been getting most of the bad publicity, very little has been said about just who it was the ITT was supposed to be aiding in 1970 — the U.S. government.

THE PLAIN DEALER
Cleveland, Ohio, April 14, 1972

Ten days after copies of the compromising memos attributed to officials of the International Telephone & Telegraph Corp. arrived in Chile the government printing house put a bound version of them in Spanish and English on the newsstands.

President Salvador Allende, who is in a constitutional fight to the finish with the Chilean Congress, had discovered a propaganda weapon and he was using it. Ultimately there may be danger in this not merely for capitalism but for democracy.

The memos, dug up by columnist Jack Anderson, indicate that ITT tried to keep Marxist Allende out of office because he planned to nationalize ITT-owned enterprises, among others. If the documents are accepted as authentic — and there seems no reason not to — one must also admit that ITT failed in efforts to enlist the U.S. government in its plot.

But that is not the way Allende will treat it. The scheme was allegedly hatched by a CIA official. It did involve interference by a U.S. corporation in a Latin American country's politics. The memos do suggest, at least, that the U.S. government tolerates this kind of behavior. The possibility of other interference is raised.

So now Allende and his followers can assert with conviction that Chile's integrity is identical with maintenance of the Allende government. Thus, as the Organization of American States opens its general assembly meeting, Chile charges that the United States interfered in Allende's election. How? Why, there's nothing in the memos to show that the U.S. government warned ITT it was violating the OAS charter, that's how.

Allende was elected president by the Congress because he was the leading candidate in popular election that gave him 36% of the vote. Until ITT stumbled onto the political stage in San Diego and Santiago, his position seemed to be weakening.

Now, as Allende's government fights to broaden its economic powers, the Chilean Congress is going to investigate ITT and the CIA, and Allende's opponents are demanding that Russian and other influences be investigated, too.

Thus, the ITT affair may help bring an already heated situation to a boil. The conflict in Chile becomes increasingly bitter. Words such as "treason" are readily used. Plots are charged and arrests made. Anti-Marxist demonstrations are forbidden, and a big one is held. Armed peasants seize farms, and armed landholders organize against them. The government is clearly moving to control production of the paper on which newspapers are printed. It harbors Castroite Bolivians who are reportedly planning another guerrilla campaign in Bolivia.

There is growing talk of a plebiscite to dissolve Congress or (on the other hand) to declare no-confidence in Allende's government. There is also talk of civil war.

The danger in all this is that the extremists in Allende's leftwing coalition will abandon parliamentary democracy and resort to force. There is a Marxist-Leninist disposition to regard disagreement as wicked, unreasonable, crazy, something to be crushed. From Santiago a Los Angeles Times reporter wrote: "Except for the so-called Allende wing, a minority within the party, the Socialists here have never really believed the revolution they want can be achieved without the 'armed struggle' of classic Leninism."

It may be starting in the farm fights. Speaking of those, an opposition Chilean newspaper asked: "Can democracy exist under such conditions or is democracy dying?"

ITT OFFERED U.S. $1 MILLION TO DEFEAT ALLENDE IN CHILE

John A. McCone, former director of the Central Intelligence Agency (CIA) and a consultant to the agency since his retirement in 1965, told a Senate Foreign Relations Committee subcommittee on multinational corporations March 21 that in 1970 he had met with presidential adviser Henry Kissinger and CIA directory Richard Helms in his capacity as a director of the International Telephone & Telegraph Corp. (ITT) to offer the U.S. government $1 million for use in blocking the election of Salvador Allende Gossens as president of Chile. The ITT plan called for financial support to be given to parties opposing the Marxist Allende in an election runoff. When the ITT plan was subsequently rejected, McCone testified that at his request, Helms put ITT President Harold Geneen, who had authorized the expenditure, in contact with William Broe, director of clandestine operations in Latin America for the CIA.

McCone's testimony corresponded with that given by ITT vice president William Merriam one day earlier. Merriam had testified that Geneen had arranged to establish a working relationship between the corporation and the CIA in order to prevent the election of Allende, and, failing that, to bring about the "economic collapse" of Chile. An ITT memo and documents made public at the hearings revealed that Broe "approved" ITT's plans to "apply economic pressures" to influence the voting and that the CIA itself had made "repeated calls to firms such as General Motors, Ford Motor Co. and banks in California and New York" in an effort to get them to cease or reduce their Chilean operations.

THE CALGARY HERALD

Calgary, Alta., March 27, 1973

Since he was first elected president of Chile in 1970, Salvador Allende has labored long and hard to expose the techniques of the U.S. Central Intelligence Agency and large U.S.-headquartered multi-national firms such as International Telephone and Telegraph Co.

He is probably extreme with his warning that the wars of the future will be fought between nations and multi-national corporations, but he serves a useful function in pointing out how entwined and how influential the tentacles of large corporations can become in the economies of small nations.

Evidence is now coming out in a U.S. senate investigation to support Allende's charge that the CIA and ITT combined efforts to oppose his Socialist regime in Chilean elections. There is something particularly sinister about the CIA since it seems to be independent of political and administrative controls in its home country.

Aside from the traditional friendly relations between the U.S. and Canada, it would be naive for Canadians to think the CIA wasn't active in its interest in this country. There are substantial U.S. investments in Canada and the investors can be depended upon to keep themselves posted with the most sophisticated analyses of the political climate and the course it might take.

The New York Times

New York, N.Y., March 22, 1973

Sordid, even against the dreary backdrop of earlier revelations, are the latest disclosures about the effort of the International Telephone and Telegraph Corporation to block the democratic election of a President of Chile and to enlist United States Government help for that abortive project. On I.T.T.'s own testimony, it offered the White House and the Central Intelligence Agency a million-dollar contribution to underwrite a plan for preventing the election of Dr. Salvador Allende in 1970.

And who carried that offer to Henry A. Kissinger in the White House and to Richard Helms, then director of the C.I.A.? None other than Mr. Helms' distinguished predecessor as head of the intelligence organization, John A. McCone, still a consultant to the C.I.A. as well as a director of I.T.T. According to Mr. McCone, Mr. Helms had earlier promised "some minimal effort" by the C.I.A. to try to bring about Dr. Allende's defeat.

Mr. McCone says, and there is no reason to doubt him, that I.T.T. did not originate the plan for which the contribution was offered. But a year after the offer, after Chile had expropriated the I.T.T.-controlled Chilean Telephone Company, the American conglomerate did submit to the White House an eighteen-point plan designed to insure "that Allende does not get through the crucial next six months."

William R. Merriam, an I.T.T. vice president, explained to a Senate subcommittee that Dr. Allende "had stolen our property without compensation," and that the company was simply trying to get help from the Government to force Chile "to pay us off. That's all we wanted." How can that statement be reconciled with the revelation that Mr. McCone's million-dollar offer was made even before Dr. Allende had been elected and a year before his Government moved against I.T.T.?

Here is exactly the kind of brazen behavior on the international scene that has given a bad name to giant American business firms and that prompted Senator Frank Church of Idaho to launch his investigation into their conduct. No Marxist critics, whether at home, in Chile or elsewhere, could inflict half as much damage on the standing of American international corporations or half as much discredit on the free enterprise system as has I.T.T.'s own behavior. Ironically, its antics have helped Dr. Allende enormously rather than hurting him.

While the record is still far from complete, there is no evidence yet that the Nixon Administration ever seriously considered the more extreme shenanigans which the corporation advocated to bring down Dr. Allende. Unfortunately, however, as a working paper of the Securities and Exchange Commission has disclosed, the Administration did come in force to the aid of I.T.T. in its successful effort to retain the Hartford Fire Insurance Company in a controversial 1971 antitrust settlement.

Thus if I.T.T. has furnished ample material for a book on how a giant corporation should not behave in the last half of the twentieth century, the Administration has supplied the stuff for a chapter on the pitfalls of a close relationship between such a firm and the Government.

THE LOUISVILLE TIMES
Louisville, Ky.
March 26, 1973

The International Telephone and Telegraph Corp. (ITT) should certainly be awarded the first annual Gen. William Westmoreland Prize in recognition of its efforts to save our friends the Chileans from themselves.

As John McCone, former director of the Central Intelligence Agency (CIA) and now a member of the board of directors of ITT, explained to a U.S. Senate subcommittee on multinational corporations, the company offered to contribute $1 million to the CIA to stop the spread of "international communism" in the South American nation.

The money was to be used to help the Chileans grasp the folly of electing Marxist candidate Salvador Allende to be their president. Allende's opponents were to receive financial support. The rest of the money was to be spent on housing, agricultural and technical programs, apparently to demonstrate the true nature of ITT's interest in Latin America.

The contumelious concocters of calumny on the campuses and in the peace movement will inevitably suggest that ITT was really trying to protect its multimillion dollar investment in its Chilean telephone monopoly. And they will whine that ITT and CIA had no business even considering a proposal for interfering in a free election in a friendly nation.

On the contrary, the ITT plan, had it been accepted by the interdepartmental council that determines CIA policies, would have been in the finest tradition of American altruism. McCone hit the nail right smack on the head when he compared it with such splendid examples of enlightened self-interest as the post-World War II economic aid we gave to Greece and Turkey, the Marshall Plan, and the Berlin airlift.

Some liberal senators who are oversensitive to complaints about neocolonialism and imperialism undoubtedly winced at the revelation that the CIA and ITT discussed a plan to create economic chaos in Chile in order to undermine Allende's candidacy. They may also be offended by McCone's statement that other private firms have offered the CIA money, presumably in return for assistance in dealing with thorny problems abroad. Yet, in the final analysis, the CIA is well equipped to steer other nations away from dangerous foreign ideologies. Some of the agency's methods may be hard. But over the years, the peoples of Chile and other underdeveloped lands, like little children that must be spanked from time to time, will love us the more for our efforts to reveal to them the error of their ways.

The disclosure of ITT's generous offer should lay to rest any silly notions any senator might have about establishing an international regulatory body to assure that multinational corporations don't ignore the public interest as they pursue profit around the globe. Let it never be said again that these vast, seemingly impersonal enterprises don't care about people.

ST. LOUIS POST-DISPATCH
St. Louis, Mo., March 21, 1973

A Senate Foreign Relations subcommittee has opened an inquiry into whether the giant International Telephone & Telegraph Corp. worked with the Nixon Administration as a kind of conglomerate in foreign policy—this being apart from a House investigation of ITT's influence on domestic antitrust policy.

Senator Church of Idaho, the subcommittee chairman, says he wants to find out whether ITT and the Central Intelligence Agency cooperated to try to prevent the election of President Allende of Chile in 1970. The first witness was William R. Merriam, head of ITT's Washington office. He testified that the ITT president, Harold S. Geneen, met privately in July, 1970 with William V. Broe, chief of clandestine services (the "department of dirty tricks") for the CIA in the Western hemisphere.

The witness did not know what Mr. Geneen and Mr. Broe talked about, but acknowledged that the CIA officer said he supported recommendations of ITT representatives in Chile. Published documents indicate that these representatives wanted to foment economic chaos and possibly a military coup to stop Dr. Allende, a Marxist. Mr. Merriam conceded that the ITT leadership had pressured the White House to threaten Chile with economic collapse, to force Chile to "pay us off." That was all the company wanted, he said.

Questions: Did ITT seek to use the Government for its private interest in Chile, or did the Government seek to use ITT, or did they simply have a community of interest? Or did ITT, as it insists, do no more than petition the Government to protect its rights in a Chilean telephone company which the Allende government later expropriated?

These are the points of the Senate inquiry, and not only the public generally, but American taxpayers and the people of Chile have a stake in the answers.

The Overseas Private Investment Corp. faces an April 1 deadline for a decision on whether to pay ITT $92,600,000 as compensation for its property taken by Chile. If it is shown that Chile was properly provoked to nationalization by ITT domestic interference, then the compensation might be reduced or eliminated. But, in an irony of law, if ITT can show that its Chilean activities were carried out at Government request, then it could claim full reimbursement.

While ITT naturally wants the money, and the Administration may want to pay it, neither could possibly want to demonstrate collaboration in intervention in Chile. Therefore their logical defense is to show that nobody intervened.

American taxpayers, of course, would hardly want to subsidize a company that suffered partly from its own dubious operations in a foreign country. Chileans are already highly suspicious that the United States supported its companies against their elected government in an example of what Latins call Yankee imperialism.

Beyond that, there is likely to be world-wide interest in whether the Subcommittee on Multinational Corporations finds that any multinational corporation has grown so powerful that it can prosecute foreign policy, with government assistance and, perhaps, a public subsidy.

The Washington Post
Washington, D.C., March 24, 1973

The first thing to be said of the Senate's investigation of the ITT affair in Chile is that, so far, no charge has been made and no proof offered that the Central Intelligence Agency actually conspired to prevent Marxist Salvador Allende from being elected president and taking office in 1970. In testimony before a Foreign Relations subcommittee, one ITT official, former CIA Director John McCone, said he transmitted ITT president Harold Geneen's block-Allende proposal to McCone's "close personal friend," then CIA Director Richard Helms, and to Henry Kissinger as well. Another ITT official, vice president Edward Gerrity added that some such proposal was made by the CIA's own William Broe, who has yet to testify publicly himself. A pattern of frequent and easy ITT-government contacts has been established, including "25 visits" to the State Department.

But all witnesses so far have agreed that the United States did not act on the block-Allende proposals. He did take office. So on the basis of this testimony it would be wrong and unfair to accuse the Nixon administration, whose disputes with Chile *over expropriation issues* are a matter of record, of having tried to keep Mr. Allende from taking power. We emphasize the point with the hope of not making the situation seem any worse than it actually is.

For the situation—without embellishment—is in fact pretty bad. Whether out of common and reflexive cold-war tradition, a custom peculiar to Chile, or ITT's own special style, when the giant company felt it had a problem in Chile in 1970, it went promptly and repeatedly to the innermost corridors of official power. Its problem was its fear that the Allende government might nationalize its telephone company; Santiago later did nationalize, on grounds (among others) of "rotten service." To save this $150 million property, ITT—by Mr. McCone's word—concocted the extraordinary notion of giving the CIA up to $1 million to implement an ITT plan to create enough economic and political disorder to prevent Mr. Allende from taking office.

Note well: any citizen or corporation has a right, within certain limits, to petition his government. But have you ever heard of any citizen or corporation offering the government an *extra* sum to provide a special service: flouting a foreign government's electoral process at that? It's as though ITT considered the U.S. government to be, well, a multinational corporation, with varied services to sell to various customers. A concept more defiant of democratic government is hard to imagine.

Mr. McCone said he conceived of the $1 million project as being in the same anti-Communist spirit as the Marshall Plan and the Berlin Airlift. His ITT colleague, Mr. Gerrity, expressing surprise at the McCone testimony, said *he* conceived of the $1 million as "seed money" for a housing project—to sweeten Mr. Allende. The difference is intriguing and, we trust, will be thoroughly explored. ITT has its honor to defend, to say nothing of its $92 million expropriation insurance claim pending before the U.S. government's tax-supported corporate insurance agency.

The ITT hearings, the first conducted by Senator Church's new multinational corporations subcommittee, are to continue next week. Subsequent hearings planned over the next three years are to address other aspects of multinational corporate activity. Already, however, enough material has emerged to indicate that the public is woefully ignorant of both the ways in which American corporate power is employed in Washington and its effects not only on the corporate position but on the American national standing abroad. We do not assume that the ITT role in Chile, whatever further inquiry shows that role to have been, is typical of multinational performance everywhere. We trust, moreover, that the Church subcommittee will be as diligent in laying out the corporations' benefits to Americans and foreigners as it is in indicating the pitfalls in their path. Meanwhile, the rest of the ITT story in Chile needs to be told.

Detroit Free Press

Detroit, Mich., March 24, 1973

THE INTERNATIONAL Telephone and Telegraph Corp. may be a master at communication, but it would be putting it mildly to say it does not always communicate with perfect credibility.

Testimony Thursday by ITT senior Vice President Edward J. Gerrity left senators shaking their heads in disbelief. "It just doesn't make any sense to reasonable, rational men," said Sen. Charles Percy of Illinois, who, incidentally, is a Republican. Another GOP senator, Clifford Case of New Jersey, called Gerrity's statement "a cover story."

The doubtful story was that ITT tried to funnel $1 million into Chile in 1970 to help with the social reconstruction of the country, not to keep Marxist Salvador Allende out of power.

Gerrity's fairy tale about low-cost housing and farm programs contradicts testimony by John McCone, former director of the CIA and presently a director of ITT. It also contradicts three volumes of the giant corporation's internal correspondence.

ITT clearly wanted to keep Allende from power and made a massive effort to do so in Santiago, Washington and other world capitals.

The corporation has recently had its public relations firm distribute a press kit asking, "What did ITT really do in Chile?" On the inside, it says, "Nothing," in bold letters, then lists a few good deeds. If it didn't do anything, it wasn't because it didn't try.

The kit includes a booklet of secret documents, and the first, written by J. D. Neil, director of international relations for the firm, is particularly interesting. It tells of a conversation between Neal and a "Pete" Vaky of the State department.

"I told Mr. Vaky to tell Mr. Kissinger Mr. Geneen (ITT's chief executive officer) is willing to come to Washington to discuss ITT's interest and that we are prepared to assist financially in sums up to seven figures. I said Mr. Geneen's concern is not one of 'after the barn door has been locked,' but that all along we have feared the Allende victory and have been trying unsuccessfully to get other American companies aroused over the fate of their investments, and join us in pre-election efforts."

That does not sound to us like low-cost housing or farm programs. Mr. Kissinger wisely refused the offer.

ITT tries to defend its involvement on the ground that it was a corporate citizen of Chile. In a strictly legal sense, that may be true. But citizens do not lobby with foreign governments to influence internal affairs in their country. Neither do they plot—even though they eventually reject the idea—the economic collapse of their country.

ITT is an American company with multi-national operations. It is a citizen of the U.S. and its actions in other countries reflect on the U.S. Needless to say, ITT has done nothing to help the U.S. image in Chile or elsewhere in Latin America.

When a company begins to think it can conduct its own foreign policy, it is simply too big. Whatever the backroom arrangements might have been, the Hartford Fire Insurance Co. merger should never have been allowed by the Justice Department.

The evidence may be circumstantial, but it is mounting from Santiago to San Diego that ITT is more than willing to buy governmental favors.

In its international operations, ITT represents a menace to U.S. foreign policy. The corporation needs to be cut down a few notches. The Senate Foreign Relations subcommittee on multinationals could start by determining whether Mr. McCone or Mr. Gerrity is telling the truth about ITT's role in Chile. And Justice should seriously consider reopening ITT's merger cases.

PORTLAND EVENING EXPRESS

Portland, Me., March 26, 1973

There is a federal law, in Section 953 of Title 18 of the U.S. statutes which says, in brief, that no citizen of this country, without its authority, may carry on any correspondence or intercourse with any foreign government with intent to influence its conduct "in relation to any disputes or controversies with the United States . . . ."

But now we have the disclosure that the International Telephone & Telegraph Company, which has a habit of getting into hot water of one kind or another, offered the White House and the CIA a million dollars to finance a plan to block the election of Dr. Salvador Allende three years ago.

This goes far beyond the intent of the statute quoted from above; it is close to subversion of a friendly state. And after the election of Dr. Allende, a year or more later, ITT submitted to the White House an 18-point plan designed to insure "that Allende does not get through the crucial next six months.

By this time the Marxist government of Dr. Allende had expropriated the Chilean Telegraph Co., which ITT controlled, and an official of the firm complained to a Senate subcommittee that Chile had stolen its property "without compensation." So ITT was merely, in its defense, trying to force Chile to pay for the property.

To its credit in this case, the Nixon Administration did not buy the wild plans of the huge conglomerate. Maybe it backed away because it had been burned badly in the prosecution of ITT for gobbling up too many companies. In that instance, the White House helped ITT hang onto the Hartford Fire Insurance Company in a settlement very lucrative to ITT.

Needless to say, the Chilean affair has hurt us badly in countries who need very little evidence to fear and hate us as economic exploiters. And they have long memories.

The Toronto Star

Toronto, Ont., March 27, 1973

When the people of Chile democratically elected a Marxist, Salvadore Allende, as president in 1970 it was almost too much for the giant American-owned International Telephone and Telegraph Corp. (ITT).

ITT had extensive holdings in Chile and Allende had made no bones about the fact that he proposed to take them over as quickly as possible.

Under the circumstances, it was understandable that the corporation would go to Washington for help. But what ITT had in mind was more than a government-backed protest. If the word of one of ITT's top executives is to be believed, the corporation wanted help from the White House and the Central Intelligence Agency (CIA) to overthrow the Allende government.

A sub-committee of the Senate Foreign Relations Committee in Washington last week was told the CIA was offered $1 million to subvert the Chilean economy, start riots leading to a military takeover or do whatever was necessary to prevent Allende's election.

According to the testimony, plans were developed at lower levels in the CIA to approach select members of the Chilean armed forces "in an attempt to have them lead some sort of uprising." The subversion program included trying to get American banks in Chile to suspend operations and thus create economic problems that could bring about Allende's downfall. Nothing actually happened; both the CIA's plans and those of ITT were rejected at the top.

This is pretty disturbing stuff, nonetheless. Particularly for Canadians who have more American investment than any other country in the world. We've already seen evidence, in the case of Time magazine and Citibank, of U.S. companies seeking help from their government in getting concessions from Canada by methods that seemed to go beyond conventional exchanges. These may have been small potatoes beside the overthrow of governments.

But one cannot help wondering what would happen if Canada decided to restrict the operation of American corporations transporting needed raw materials—oil, for instance—to the U.S.

Would American corporations be on the doorstep of the CIA offering money for help in influencing political decisions so that American rather than Canadian interests got top priority?

Perhaps the ITT testimony is a warning to Canada of the dangers in allowing foreign-owned firms to become involved in strategic resource areas.

Chicago Tribune

Chicago, Ill., March 29, 1973

Officials of International Telephone and Telegraph Corp., a large conglomerate, have stated in testimony before a Senate subcommittee that the corporation proposed thru the Central Intelligence Agency that $1 million of its funds be used to head off the ascension of Marxist Salvador Allende as president of Chile in 1970.

The corporation had assets of $165 million in the country, consisting mainly of a 70 per cent ownership in the Chilean telephone system. One of its vice presidents, William R. Merriam, said that I. T. T. feared that an Allende regime would "steal" its properties. The fear was warranted. President Allende subsequently nationalized I. T. T. holdings and the properties of American copper companies without compensation.

John A. McCone, former director of the CIA, now a director of I. T. T., discussed with CIA officials a plan to unite the two opposition parties against Allende's assumption of power. The CIA failed to act and Mr. McCone said that Dr. Henry Kissinger, Presidential adviser on foreign relations, whom he also approached, did not reply to his proposals.

I. T. T. has been a favorite whipping boy for Senate Democratic "liberals" ever since the Justice Department, before last year's Presidential election, settled an antitrust action against the corporation. I. T. T. at the time proposed making a substantial contribution to the Republican National Convention when it was originally scheduled for San Diego, where the corporation owned a hotel.

An I. T. T. Washington lobbyist, Dita Beard, in a memorandum which came into possession of the Senate, made sweeping claims about her agency in reaching the settlement which put her employer in a questionable light and sought to imply that the Nixon administration had been bought off.

If it were not for this checkered background, the Senate critics would have had less reason to indulge in the present field day over the attempted intervention in Chile. After all, it has traditionally been regarded as a responsibility of the federal government to protect American lives and property abroad. In the past, stern measures have been taken to carry out that responsibility.

Businessmen therefore have a proper right to make approaches to the government in defense of their interests. We wouldn't say I. T. T. has taken the most intelligent approach in asserting this right; but it is only fair to remember that I. T. T. and the government might not have been led to invite the present suspicion of secret conspiracy if earlier governments had not conditioned the world to think that American business interests can be kicked around with impunity. And the same people who encouraged this attitude in the past are in general the ones who now think they can tar I. T. T. and the administration and make political hay all at the same time.

THE INDIANAPOLIS STAR

Indianapolis, Ind., March 30, 1973

Liberals in the Senate have been investigating the International Telephone and Telegraph Corporation's attempt in 1970 to prevent a Communist-Socialist takeover of Chile.

Information thus far revealed indicates that representatives of ITT in Chile attempted, ineffectively, to forestall the anticipated vote by the Chilean Congress to elect as president Salvadore Allende, who had won a plurality but not a majority in a popular election. It is also indicated that ITT officials tried without success to interest the White House and the State Department in trying to head off Allende, offering up to seven figures in dollars toward the cost of such a venture.

The ITT has been put on the defensive by liberal senators whose line of probing seems to imply something unusual and perhaps even wicked in a United States corporation's effort to try to defend its property holdings abroad. Company officials foresaw that the election of Allende would lead to seizure of ITT properties in Chile, and they were right.

It is worth noting that in its action to try to protect its property holdings ITT was also working in behalf of preserving democracy in Chile from being destroyed by a Marxist revolutionary gang.

Doing just that kind of thing is supposed to have been a U.S. foreign policy objective for the last quarter-century. It's also supposed to be U.S. policy to defend the interests of U.S. property-holders abroad.

Two-thirds of Chile's voters originally voted against the Marxist regime, which having seized property of great value from ITT and other U.S. companies and thrown the economy into chaos is now busily wiping out Chile's once-vigorous democracy.

The great majority of Chileans whose freedom and other interests are being trampled by the Marxists through political manipulation find the only choice open to them now, if they wish to regain control of their country, may be revolution.

Do the senators who are badgering ITT truly believe that American corporations have no right to protect the interests of their stockholders abroad? Do they truly think that U.S. citizens have no legitimate stake in helping a majority of citizens of a foreign country to stave off Marxist domination?

Do they think the U.S. government should look the other way when democracy in an American state is being raped?

Does not the tenor of the ITT probe on the Chile matter reflect more of the liberal disastrous policy of defeat and retreat in the face of Marxist advancement?

To yield piecemeal the freedoms of the countries that still have them will spell the ultimate defeat of freedom everywhere on earth.

St. Petersburg Times

St. Petersburg, Fla., March 25, 1973

Gathering intelligence (and that includes spying) is one thing. Meddling in foreign elections is something else again.

THE UNFOLDING story of clumsy, high-handed efforts by CIA and ITT to block installation of Chilean President Salvador Allende shows that CIA has not learned the difference.

The International Telephone and Telegraph Corp. is a U.S. conglomerate known for its offer to help Republicans finance their convention at a time when it had antitrust problems. It operated a telephone system in Chile.

Allende, a Marxist, campaigned on a promise to grab the telephone system (and when elected made good on that promise).

ITT officials were understandably upset at this threat to their investment. On the scene and in Washington they connived with the CIA to block Allende's election and, when that didn't work, to disrupt his government by wrecking the Chilean economy.

AS FAR as the record shows, cooler heads prevailed. Henry Kissinger among others said no to the plot. The dirty tricks were not played. The fact they were planned and seriously discussed by CIA operatives feeds ugly suspicions about an agency that rarely reflects credit on the United States.

The Central Intelligence Agency was set up by Congress after World War II to consolidate intelligence work. It got a blank check to hire, spend, travel, bribe, lie, and according to some evidence from the Vietnam War, even kill, without any public accounting.

Its appropriations are hidden. Its payroll is secret. As for the consolidation of intelligence work, that never came off.

Meantime, agents like William P. Broe, chief of CIA's "clandestine operations" in Latin America and ITT's fellow-conspirator in Chile, have plenty of time to get us in trouble.

PRESIDENT NIXON now seems determined to accomplish what other presidents have attempted without much success — to bring CIA under proper control. For starters, about 1,000 of its employes are being lopped off by Nixon's new agency boss.

"Nobody feels safe," complained one CIA bureaucrat about the current housecleaning.

If nobody at CIA feels safe, at least the rest of us can feel not so uneasy, knowing that somebody there is looking out for our interests.

The Des Moines Register
Des Moines, Iowa, March 27, 1973

THE TENNESSEAN

Nashville, Tenn., March 24, 1973

IT WAS just a year ago when Columnist Jack Anderson made public documents which disclosed attempts by the International Telephone & Telegraph Corp. to prevent the election of Salvador Allende Gossens, the Marxist president of Chile.

In one memo from an ITT official to Mr. John McCone, a former director of the Central Intelligence Agency and an ITT director, it was suggested there were possibilities of encouraging a coup d'etat, or of disrupting Chile's economy. In another incident, Mr. Anderson said an ITT official offered a White House aide financial backing "up to seven figures" to prevent Allende's inaugural.

ITT issued a denial that it was involved in Chilean politics. It sought to leave the idea that Mr. Anderson's revelations were without foundation.

Now, a year later, Mr. McCone has testified before a Senate foreign relations subcommittee that he offered the White House a million dollars for government intervention in Chile. And Mr. Robert Berrellez, ITT's public relations chief for South America, told the subcommittee he offered financial aid to associates of Jorge Alessandri, the conservative candidate whom Mr. Allende narrowly defeated in 1970.

Mr. McCone denied suggestions that the plan was to use the money to bribe Chilean legislators to prevent Allende's election approval by congress and insisted there was nothing "covert" about the idea.

Mr. McCone met both with his successor at the CIA, Mr. Richard Helms, and apparently with Dr. Henry Kissinger, who turned down the offer.

The documents Mr. Anderson made public were astonishing enough. It is even more astonishing to hear ITT officials admit the incidents he previously made public. The ITT has grown so huge and powerful that the idea of assisting a Republican administration in making political arrangements and setting anti-trust policy as well as dealing in foreign policy must have seemed a matter of course.

One wonders what might have been the consequences had the government agreed to go along with ITT in Chile. The political fall-out has been bad enough in the wake of the Anderson columns. It will doubtless be worse in the wake of the Senate hearings, but one shudders to think what might have happened had the foreign policy of the U.S. been set in Chile by this corporate giant.

Newspaper readers are gaining a more detailed picture of the maneuvers of the International Telephone and Telegraph Corp. in the inner sanctums of the federal government.

John A. McCone, former head of the Central Intelligence Agency, told a Senate committee that he had transmitted an offer by ITT to help finance an effort to block the election of Chilean President Salvador Allende in 1970. McCone said he carried the offer personally to Richard Helms, then head of CIA, and to Henry Kissinger, presidential foreign affairs adviser.

ITT was afraid that its telephone company and other property in Chile would be confiscated by the left wing Allende regime. McCone, former head of the CIA and still very influential in both the government and the Republican party, was a logical choice to make the appeal to the government—especially since he is also a director of ITT.

Meddling in the Chilean election by financing opposition to Allende could have backfired on the U.S. throughout Latin America. It is revealing that ITT officers thought they could drag the government into such an imperialistic operation.

The enormous pressure exerted by ITT on high officials of government to get approval of a merger it wanted with a cash-loaded insurance company has also been exposed by the Senate committee. (The pressure was successful.)

You could get the impression that ITT moves in to get its way with the U.S. government in much the same way that big international companies long have operated with governments in undeveloped areas. There is a certain disdain for officialdom and a ruthlessness that ignores laws and codes of ethical behavior.

★ ★ ★

ITT is not different, we suspect, from many other multinational companies which have been growing so rapidly in recent years. These companies, whe their headquarters are in London, P or New York, operate about the sa Their managers are the true inte tionalists, with little or no allegiance any country.

The big Japanese companies may an exception, so far, since they seem follow directions of their governmen ligiously. Or is it the other way aroun

One of the clearest illustrations of non-national attitudes of the internat al companies is shown in their shif of funds around during the disruptio monetary markets. In the recent against the dollar, a Frankfurt ban estimated that 60 per cent of the sale dollars were by IBM, ITT, Volkswa Nestle and such firms. The so-ca American companies do not hesitat shift cash balances in ways that h icap the U.S. government efforts to bilize the dollar.

There is no loyalty to U.S. polic Latin America, either—only to U.S. ernment action that will help the con nies.

The French and some other E peans have worried about U.S. con nies coming in and dominating their nomy—economic imperialism, they it. But the biggest firms do not seer operate with bias toward any cour Contrary to Marxist theory, they d act as partners with imperialist gov ments. They simply go out to mak buck for themselves.

The international companies c worry about the political system o country they operate in. Just so it is ble and can keep order. Even s Communist countries may fill the bill

It would be ironical if large, capit tic business corporations should turn to be the most powerful instruments creating "one world." Some people t so. They are becoming more influen certainly, in world economic affairs many governments.

The Philadelphia Inquirer

Philadelphia, Pa., March 23, 1973

The International Telephone and Telegraph Corporation is not running for public office, so we can only hope at the moment that the latest and cumulative evidence of its tinkering with the public process will serve to alert and armor public servants against the dangers that tinkering represents.

Nonetheless, the sanguine testimony by former Central Intelligence Agency director John A. McCone about a frustrated ITT escapade in banana-republic-era dollar diplomacy is sufficiently appalling to suggest need for a substantial Federal reform:

American business enterprises should be prohibited, under criminal sanctions, from interfering in the political processes of foreign nations.

★ ★ ★

Mr. McCone, an appointee of President Kennedy, testified Wednesday to the Senate Foreign Relations Committee's panel on multinational corporations. He spoke of approaches through him to Richard M. Helms, a successor to Mr. McCone as CIA chief, and to the White House's Henry Kissinger by Harold S. Geneen, board chairman of ITT.

The subject was Chilean politics, in 1970. The concern was over ITT's subsidiary, the $150 million telephone system in Chile, which Mr. Geneen feared would be nationalized or otherwise disturbed by the election of Salvador Allende Gossens, a Marxist, who is now President.

"Mr. McCone testified that Mr. Geneen "told me he was prepared to put up as much as $1 million in support of any government plan for the purpose of bringing about a coalition of opposition to Allende . . . to deprive Allende of his position. It would not be a plan generated by ITT or Mr. Geneen. I was asked if I supported it. I did, and I came to Washington several days later and told Mr. Helms of the availability of the funds and then met with Mr. Kissinger and told him the same thing Mr. Kissinger thanked me very much and said I'd hear from him. I didn't hear from him and assumed it was national policy not to do so."

To that we say three cheers for good ol' Henry the K, and for all else who had hands in turning down the plan.

But the facts that Mr. Geneen came forward with the proposal, and that Mr. McCone, with his vast experience with the top levels of American government, endorsed it, leave deep doubt that the idea is dead.

We have some deep philosophical misgivings about the ideology and programs of President Allende, as clearly do many Chileans. But we are delighted to leave the problem of resolving those misgivings to Chileans. For it has been demonstrated, we believe beyond rebuttal, that American tinkering in domestic politics of foreign lands produces, beyond all else, perilous mischief — whether it be in behalf of commercial pelf or well-intentioned and underinformed abstract sentimentalities.

★ ★ ★

We are all for American business, or anybody else's, competing for profits anywhere. We believe the prospect of profit and the threat of loss generally comprise the most productive and humane economic force man has conceived.

But if the force and the diplomatic and covert-intelligence machinery of the U. S. is marshalled behind the interests of such enterprises, they can soon become ferocious power monopolies and intolerable intrusions in the public process at home and abroad.

Governmental Security and Individual Privacy

Data Banks and Subversive Lists

Passport Office admits keeping data bank. Sen. Sam J. Ervin Jr. (D, N.C.) reported during a four-day symposium on data banks at Dickinson College (Carlisle, Pa.) Feb. 9, 1971 that the U.S. Passport Office kept a secret computerized file of 243,135 Americans. He said the computer was programmed to report to various law enforcement and intelligence agencies—without the subjects' knowledge—the passport applications of persons suspected of being subversive."

Miss Frances Knight, Passport Office director since 1955, admitted the existence of the file Feb. 10 but claimed that "a vast majority" of the subjects were persons of "questionable citizenship." A spokesman for Ervin, however, said Feb. 10 that the State Department had reported to the senator that the largest group on the list were "known or suspected Communists or subversives."

■ Four individuals and the Socialist Workers party filed suit Feb. 24 in federal court in New York City demanding destruction of the Passport Office file. The suit denounced the file as potential "political blacklisting" and said it threatened "freedoms of speech, association, belief and travel."

■ Health, Education and Welfare Secretary Elliot Richardson said Feb. 7 that the government had begun to investigate the growing practice of using Social Security numbers as identification by private firms. Richardson said he was "concerned that if the Social Security numbers were used too broadly, such widespread use and dependence upon the number might lend itself to abuses of individual privacy."

Ervin hearings open. Sen. Ervin opened nine days of hearings by his Subcommittee on Constitutional Rights Feb. 23 on the effect of government and private surveillance and computer data banks on individual privacy in the U.S. The subcommittee was also considering the Army's activity in gathering domestic intelligence information.

In opening the Feb. 23 session, Ervin said: "When people fear surveillance, whether it exists or not, when they grow afraid to speak their minds freely to their government or anyone else, . . . then we shall cease to be a free society." Ervin

said people were concerned about information being fed into government or commercial data banks without screening or control over who would see it.

The first witness, Arthur R. Miller, University of Michigan law professor and author of "Assault on Privacy," said, "each time a citizen files a tax return, applies for life insurance or credit card, seeks government benefits, or interviews for a job, a dossier is opened under his name and an informational profile on him is sketched." He said the information gathering activities, "by and large . . . are well-intended efforts to achieve socially desirable objectives" but warned that "it is simply unrealistic to assume that the managers or proprietors of computer systems—government or private—will take it upon themselves to protect the public against misuse." He said that with "no effective restraints" on the data gatherers and disseminators, the nation was being led toward a "dossier dictatorship."

Rep. Edward I. Koch (D, N.Y.) urged support for a federal privacy bill he introduced Jan. 22 with the support of 20 other congressmen of both parties. The bill would require government agencies who keep records on individuals to notify the individual of the record and to inform him when information was transferred to another agency. Another bill introduced the same day by Koch would require the same procedure by the House Internal Security Committee.

Sen. Birch Bayh (D, Ind.) had introduced a bill Feb. 25 that would compel government agencies to inform citizens of files kept on them and allow subjects of such files to correct information in them.

Administration upholds intelligence gathering activities—U.S. Assistant Attorney General William Rehnquist told a Senate subcommittee March 9 that the Nixon Administration would oppose legislation that would hamper the government's domestic intelligence gathering activity.

Rehnquist said, "Self-discipline on the part of the executive branch will provide an answer to virtually all of the legitimate complaints against excesses of information gathering." He said such activity was essential in crime control and that the Administration "will vigorously oppose

any legislation which, whether by opening the door to unnecessary and unmanageable judicial supervision of such activities or otherwise, would effectively impair this extraordinarily important function of the federal government."

However, another Administration spokesman, Health, Education and Welfare Secretary Elliot L. Richardson, told the subcommittee March 15 that the nation "must develop the means of controlling the potential for harm inherent" in the government's computer banks of information on citizens. Richardson said if present safeguards were inadequate, "statutes designed to define and protect an individual's rights in computerized information storage and exchange can be enacted."

Explaining the apparent divergence of views between Richardson and Rehnquist, spokesmen for HEW and the Justice Department said March 15 that the two officials spoke only for their respective departments.

Ervin questioned Richardson March 15 on the increased use of Social Security numbers for identification purposes by both government and private agencies. Richardson said, "It is not illegal for a non-federal organization to use the Social Security number in its record keeping system." He said the "potential for invasion of privacy or breach of confidentiality" did not lie in the use of the number itself, "but rather in how the organization uses computerized collections of data which are indexed by the number" and "the existence of a universal identifier."

The Justice Department's position on the government's right to collect information was questioned when Rehnquist again appeared before the subcommittee March 17 along with Assistant Attorney General Robert Mardian, in charge of the Internal Security Division. Ervin told Rehnquist, "There is not a syllable in there [the Constitution] that gives the federal government the right to spy on civilians."

Mardian said "we do not have specific, published documents" to regulate surveillance activities of the Federal Bureau of Investigation. He said internal memorandums provided operating instructions to the FBI. Sen. Edward M. Kennedy (D,

Mass.), who had asked Mardian about Justice Department guidelines, said, "you haven't been terribly reassuring." He added, "It appears that on behalf of the attorney general you have washed your hands of any responsibility for surveillance."

Rehnquist was also questioned March 17 by Sen. John V. Tunney (D, Calif.), who accused the Justice Department of failing to fully investigate charges that San Francisco Mayor Joseph L. Alioto made before the subcommittee March 3. Alioto had accused six federal agencies and two California police departments of supplying confidential information to writers from *Look* magazine in connection with a 1969 article linking Alioto to the Mafia.

Accusing the government of having "not only a big ear, but a big mouth as well," Alioto had said the information given to the writers was "characteristic of what finds its way into investigatory files." He said it was "raw, unverified, unedited, unevaluated, hearsay information."

In answer to Tunney's challenge March 17, Rehnquist said only one San Francisco FBI agent had been involved in the Alioto leakage and that agent had been disciplined and retired. Rehnquist said the Bureau of Narcotics and Dangerous Drugs was continuing to investigate another possible illegal disclosure.

Ervin cites data bank dangers. Sen. Ervin said May 20 that computers and data banks had been used to feed "the insatiable curiosity of government to know everything about those it governs." Ervin made his remarks at an Atlantic City, N.J. meeting of the American Federation of Information Processing Societies.

Ervin said, "if the attitude of the present Administration is any indication," computer technology would become increasingly central in the government's "pursuit of its current claim to an inherent power to investigate lawful activities and to label people on the basis of their thoughts." He said he had learned from Federal Communications Commission Chairman Dean Burch that the FCC checked all license applications against a computerized list of about 11,000 persons considered suspicious by such agencies as the Justice Department, the Internal Revenue Service, the Central Intelligence Agency, and the House Internal Security Committee.

ABA scores 'repressive' climate in U.S. A committee of the young lawyers section of the American Bar Association (ABA) said in a report issued July 8 that "there is currently an anti-libertarian climate in the United States which properly can be labeled 'repressive.' " The Committee on Protection of Civil Liberties and Civil Rights said in its 28-page report that the "national stress" caused by "a highly unpopular war in Southeast Asia" underlay the crisis. The group also blamed government agencies and officials for "unprecedented" surveillance and rhetorical attacks on dissenters.

Plans to link computer banks criticized. Separate proposals by the Federal Bureau of Investigation and the Department of Agriculture (USDA) to expand their computer information systems were criticized as unnecessary and dangerous by members of Congress and agencies within the executive branch, it was reported June 4, 1975.

The FBI's proposal to establish a computerized criminal-history system linking up police department records across the nation came under fire in a report by the Law Enforcement Assistance Administration, the Justice Department agency disbursing federal crime-fighting grants to state and local governments. The LEAA report, which voiced support for the principle of computerized criminal histories, questioned the advisibility of centralizing such information under federal control.

The bureau's proposal, the LEAA report said, raised concern over "(a) the development of the Big Brother system; (b) reduced state input and control over security, confidentiality and use of state-originated data and (c) increased dangers resulting from the use of non-updated, and hence, inaccurate, centrally maintained 'rap sheets.' "

"It is critical to recognize that decisions in these areas raise basic questions re: federal/state relations and the concept of federalism," the report said, adding that "in this connection it is significant to note that the importance of preserving state and local control over law enforcement responsibility has been specifically recognized within the executive branch by Presidents Johnson, Nixon and Ford."

Rep. John E. Moss (D, Calif.), a member of the Government Operations subcommittee on Government Information and Individual Rights, who had made the LEAA report public, also released a copy of a letter, dated May 12, from John Eger, acting director of the White House Office of Telecommunications Policy, to Harold R. Tyler, Jr., deputy attorney general. The FBI proposal, Eger wrote, could evolve into "a potentially abusive, centralized, federally controlled communications and computer information system. Our basic concern is the threat posed by a system which could be used by a federal law enforcement agency to monitor in detail the day-to-day operations of state and local law enforcement authorities."

Moss, who noted that the LEAA report and an FBI response to it had been given to him only after four months of repeated demands, said he would oppose the FBI plan. Sen. John Tunney (D, Calif.), chairman of the Judiciary Subcommittee on Constitutional Rights, expressed similar misgivings over the computer link-up proposal.

A General Accounting Office study, requested and made public by Moss, recommended that the Agriculture Department be prohibited from going ahead with its eight-year, $398 million plan to centralize department records. Asserting that USDA officials had begun acquisition of a new computer system before accurately determining their needs, the GAO report said that Congress should be concerned that it had not been fully informed of the plans for the project and because the USDA's computer bank "could pose a serious threat to the privacy of individuals, particularly since such a network might be expanded to link all government computers."

Party platforms oppose data banks. The Democratic Party platform, announced July 12, 1972, contained the following sections on privacy:

Free Expression and Privacy. The new Democratic Administration should bring an end to the pattern of political persecution and investigation, the use of high office as a pulpit for unfair attack and intimidation and the blatant efforts to control the poor and to keep them from acquiring additional economic security or political power.

The epidemic of wiretapping and electronic surveillance engaged in by the Nixon Administration and the use of grand juries for purposes of political intimidation must be ended. The rule of law and the supremacy of the Constitution, as these concepts have traditionally been understood, must be restored.

We strongly object to secret computer data banks on individuals. Citizens should have access to their own files that are maintained by private commercial firms and the right to insert corrective material. Except in limited cases, the same should apply to government files. Collection and maintenance by federal agencies of dossiers on law-abiding citizens, because of their political views and statements, must be stopped, and files which never should have been opened should be destroyed. We firmly reject the idea of a National Computer Data Bank.

The Nixon policy of intimidation of the media and Administration efforts to use government power to block access to media by dissenters must end, if free speech is to be preserved. A Democratic Administration must be an open one, with the fullest possible disclosure of information, with an end to abuses of security classifications and executive privilege, and with regular top-level press conferences.

The Republican Party platform, announced August 22, contained the following:

We will continue to defend the citizen's right to privacy in our increasingly interdependent society. We oppose computerized national data banks and all other "Big Brother" schemes which endanger individual rights.

Nixon calls privacy a 'cardinal principle.' President Nixon delivered a State of the Union Message in person before a joint session of Congress Jan. 30, 1974. He included a section on individual liberties:

One measure of a truly free society is the vigor with which it protects the liberties of its individual citizens. As technology has advanced in America, it has increasingly encroached on one of those liberties what I term the right of personal privacy. Modern information systems, data banks, credit records, mailing list abuses, electronic snooping, the collection of personal data for one purpose that may be used for another—all these have left millions of Americans deeply concerned by the privacy they cherish.

And the time has come, therefore, for a major initiative to define the nature and extent of the basic rights of privacy and to erect new safeguards to insure that those rights are respected.

I shall launch such an effort this year at the highest levels of the Administration, and I look forward again to working with this Congress and establishing a new set of standards that respect the legitimate needs of society but that also recognize personal privacy as a cardinal principle of American liberty.

Privacy panel announced. President Nixon announced in a radio address Feb. 23 that he was creating a "top-priority" Cabinet-level committee to recommend measures to protect individual privacy against computerized data banks and other developments of "advanced technology" used by both government and private institutions.

Calling the right to privacy "the most basic of all individual rights," Nixon said "a system that fails to respect its citizens' right to privacy, fails to respect the citizens themselves." With the names of "more than 150 million Americans" in "computer banks scattered across the country," Nixon said, there was always the possibility that a citizen's rights could be "seriously damaged . . . sometimes beyond the point of repair. Careers have been ruined, marriages have been wrecked, reputations built up over a lifetime have been destroyed by the misuse or abuse of data technology in both private and public hands."

Nixon said "well-intentioned" government bureaucracies "seem to thrive" on collecting information," which "is now stored in over 7,000 government computers." The same process had been at work in the private sector, placing "vast quantities of personal information in the hands of bankers, employers, charitable organizations and credit agencies."

Nixon said the problems had grown despite a number of steps "in the right direction," including the Fair Credit Reporting Act of 1970. To meet the added "challenge of these dimensions," Nixon said he was creating the "blue-ribbon" Domestic Council Committee on the Right of Privacy, to be chaired by Vice President Gerald R. Ford and composed of six Cabinet members and four other Administration officials. Nixon directed the panel "within four months to begin providing a series of direct, enforceable measures . . . all of which we can immediately begin to put into effect."

Nixon did not refer directly to wiretapping or other forms of electronic surveillance in his speech, but a "fact sheet" issued by the White House said the President had asked the new committee "to defer recommendations" on wiretapping pending receipt of a report by the Congressionally-created National Commission for Review of Federal and State Wiretapping Laws.

The review commission was to have been composed of seven members appointed by the White House and four each by the two houses of Congress. According to the fact sheet, the commission's status was still uncertain; the Senate and White House had named their 11 prospective members, but the House—whose previous appointments had lapsed—had not named new ones.

(Nixon was asked in his news conference Feb. 25 to explain, in light of the Feb. 23 privacy speech, the issuance in 1973 of an executive order allowing the Agricultural Department to examine farmers' individual income tax returns and a subsequent Justice Department advisory opinion calling the order a model for all government departments. Nixon replied that while he "did not raise this question specifically," he wanted "that question along with others con-

sidered" by the new White House committee, "because in the full area of privacy it isn't just a question of those who run credit bureaus and banks and others with their huge computers, but the federal government itself . . . can very much impinge on the privacy of individuals." A department official said March 6 that while the executive order was still in effect, the plan to use tax returns as a source of mailing lists for statistical surveys was currently "inoperative.")

Hart scores 'political spying'—The Democrats' "equal time" reply to Nixon's address was delivered March 2 by Sen. Philip A. Hart (Mich.), who called on the President to "immediately" ban any wiretapping or electronic surveillance not authorized by court order and to "state without equivocation that the label of 'national security' will not be used again to hide or excuse illegal acts." Instead of "the naming of a new committee," Hart said, Nixon should have ordered "everyone in his Administration to refrain from political spying of any kind."

"Perhaps understandably in the light of Watergate," Hart said, "the President chose to paint the primary threat as one of technology. We have learned to our regret that, with or without sophisticated technology, unprincipled men can find ways to invade our privacy."

Hart noted that in addition to the acts of the Watergate burglars and the White House "plumbers" unit, the government had used Army personnel "to spy on peaceful political meetings" and had used the confidential files of the Internal Revenue Service "to harass persons on a White House enemies list."

Hart charged the Administration with a long record of opposing or failing to support legislation to prevent invasions of privacy, including bills prohibiting government employes from being asked about religious beliefs, politics and social activities, and prohibiting military spying on civilians.

Saxbe orders study of subversive list. Attorney General William B. Saxbe said April 3 that he had ordered the Justice Department to make a new study of the controversial attorney general's list of subversive organizations.

It was the duty of the Justice Department to protect the people from "subversive activities, terrorism and so on," Saxbe said, adding that the duty included knowing the organizations posing threats. The investigation he was ordering, Saxbe said, would seek to determine whether there should be such a list and whether the present list, last revised in 1955, was "realistic."

Citing a shift from the 1950s, Saxbe noted that "worldwide trends are more toward terrorism" and said "we're dealing with a different type of person." "There was [during the McCarthy era] a great distrust of the intellectual," he said, adding that "one of the changes that's come about is because of the Jewish intellectual, who was in those days very enamored of the Communist Party." He added, "Communism has in many ways"

lost its attractiveness to Jewish intellectuals.

Saxbe was strongly criticized April 3 by Benjamin R. Epstein of the Anti-Defamation League (ADL) of the B'nai B'rith for his remarks. Epstein called Saxbe's linking of the Jewish intellectual and communism "incredible" and said "Mr. Saxbe's comment confirms the ADL's newest findings about the insensitivity of otherwise responsible Americans to the harmful impact of false anti-Jewish stereotyping." Jacob Sheinkman, president of the American Jewish Congress, questioned Saxbe's fitness for office. He said Saxbe's "aspersions of the loyalty of American Jews is incompatible with his responsibilities as head of the Justice Department."

Saxbe, an Episcopalian, issued a clarification April 4, saying he had "long felt that there was a great deal of anti-Semitism in the Communist witch-hunts of the late 1940s and 1950s." "Much of it was directed at some highly visible Jewish intellectuals who were considered sympathetic to Russia." "Because of the Soviet posture toward issues of importance to Jews, this is no longer the case today and I believe this change can best be seen by the totally different type of individual involved in terrorist groups now operating."

Saxbe's clarification did not satisfy Howard M. Squadron, chairman of the American Jewish Council, who April 4 demanded that Saxbe resign or that President Nixon dismiss him.

Subversives list abolished—The attorney general's controversial list of subversive organizations—27 years old and not updated since 1955—was abolished by presidential order June 4. Attorney General William B. Saxbe said it was "now very apparent that it serves no useful purpose."

According to the Justice Department, all but about 30 of the 300 organizations still on the list had been out of existence for five years or more. A spokesman said a recent survey of government agencies had found only the Defense Department still using the list as an "investigative device in background checks."

President Nixon had attempted to have the Subversive Activities Control Board update the list in 1971, but the board was later eliminated from the budget.

SACB, HISC

Senate disputes funding SACB. The fiscal 1972 appropriation bill for the Departments of State, Justice and Commerce, the judiciary and some related agencies, was approved by 337–35 House vote Aug. 2, 1971, 46–44 Senate vote Aug. 3, and signed by President Nixon Aug. 10. The close Senate vote reflected disputes over funds for the Subversive Activities Control Board (SACB).

SACB's scope broadened. By executive order issued July 2, President Nixon broadened the SACB's scope by authorizing it to keep a list of subversive groups and to determine, after hearings, whether a group was "totalitarian, fascist,

Communist, subversive, or whether it has adopted a policy of unlawfully advocating the commission of acts of force or violence to deny others their rights under the Constitution."

Sen. Sam J. Ervin Jr. (D, N.C.), chairman of the Subcommittee on Constitutional Rights and Separation of Powers, proposed an amendment to prohibit the SACB from using any of its $450,000 funds provided by the bill to carry out the new duties called for in the executive order. The Senate adopted the amendment by a 51–37 vote July 19. The House, however, upheld the President's position, rejecting by a 246–141 vote July 27 a proposal to accept the Senate amendment.

The Ervin amendment was dropped from the bill by the House-Senate conferees, whose decision, despite objection in both houses, was approved for the final version of the bill. In the House, the objection was raised Aug. 2 by Rep. Don Edwards (D, Calif.), chairman of a Judiciary subcommittee handling civil rights bills, who said the executive order was a "usurpation of legislative authority by the executive branch."

In the Senate, Ervin Aug. 3 urged rejection of the conference bill because the executive order was "unwise," reflected "the spirit of McCarthyism," and was unconstitutional two ways—impinging on freedom of speech and association and on the legislative powers of Congress. "I hate to say this," Ervin said, "but there are some people in high positions in the executive branch of the government who indicate by their recommendations that they do not like the Bill of Rights." The reference was interpreted as pointing to Attorney General John N. Mitchell, whose department had the responsibility shifted to the SACB for maintaining the subversive-group listing.

Mitchell sent to Congress July 7 proposed legislation to rename the SACB the Federal Internal Security Board and give it the expanded role outlined under the executive order.

The successful defense for deletion of the Ervin amendment was made on the grounds that the courts could decide the constitutional issues involved.

Suit attacks SACB order—The American Civil Liberties Union filed suit in federal court in Washington Sept. 1 attacking a July 2 order by President Nixon granting new powers to the Subversive Activities Control Board (SACB). The suit asked that the attorney general's list of allegedly subversive groups be banned as unconstitutional and that the SACB be barred from conducting hearings to update the list.

Plaintiffs in the suit included antiwar groups that contended SACB proceedings would subject their members to "irreparable injury solely because of their political beliefs and associations." The plaintiffs also included three groups already on the subversives list, the Communist party of the United States, the Industrial Workers of the World (IWW) and the Socialist Workers

party.

A Senate amendment prohibiting funding for expansion of SACB powers had been eliminated from an appropriations bill by a House-Senate conference committee. However, Congress still had to vote on the conference report.

House approves funds for SACB. A $4.6 billion fiscal 1973 appropriation bill for the State, Justice and Commerce Departments was approved by the House May 18, 1972 by voice vote. The House rejected proposals May 18 to delete the bill's $450,000 for the Subversive Activities Control Board and to prohibit payment for federal employes refusing to testify before Congressional committees. The vote on the latter was 180–132.

SACB name change—The House approved legislation by a 226–106 vote May 30 to change the name of the Subversive Activities Control Board to the Federal Internal Security Board and to expand its activities. The board would be authorized to investigate the character of organizations if the President considered the probe relevant to federal employe loyalty.

Senate votes against SACB funds—The Senate voted 42–25 June 15 against funding the Subversive Activities Control Board (SACB).

House Internal Security Committee ends. The House allowed Jan. 14, 1975 the demise of its Internal Security Committee (HISC), formerly known as the House Un-American Activities Committee. The panel was abolished, its pertinent jurisdiction and files transferred to the Judiciary Committee, when the House adopted a set of rules, formulated by the Democratic majority, by a 259–150 vote. There was no direct vote on abolition of the committee, which had a 1974 budget of $725,000 and a staff of 39 persons. A vote on a motion to open the resolution on rules to amendment, which would have permitted an attempt to retain the panel, or attempts on other points in the rules, was rejected 247–172, with all 143 Republicans present in the minority.

Loyalty Oaths, Probes, and Detention Camps

Bar loyalty oath rulings. In three 5–4 decisions Feb. 23, 1971 the Supreme Court held that a state may require applicants for licenses to practice law to take an affirmative loyalty oath. But the court banned wide-ranging questions on membership in organizations or requirements that the applicant disclose membership in alleged subversive organizations. Justice Potter Stewart cast the deciding vote in all three rulings.

The court rejected an Arizona test for bar applicants that asked a law school graduate if he had ever joined a subversive organization. The ruling reversed the Arizona Supreme Court in the case of Sara Baird of Phoenix, who had been denied a license because she refused to say whether she belonged to any organization "that advocates over-

throw of the United States by force and violence."

The justices also said that Ohio illegally asked bar applicant Martin R. Stolar to list all organizations to which he had ever belonged. Dissenters in both the Arizona and Ohio cases were Chief Justice Warren E. Burger and Justices John M. Harlan, Byron R. White and Harry A. Blackmun.

Stewart joined the dissenters in the Arizona and Ohio cases to form the majority in the third ruling, whereby the court allowed an affirmative New York State loyalty oath for prospective members of the bar. Unlike the Arizona test, New York asked bar applicants whether they belonged to a subversive group and whether they had "the specific intent to further the aims of such organization." Writing for the majority, Stewart emphasized that no known applicant had ever been denied a license to practice law in New York because of his beliefs.

Dissenting Justices Black, Douglas, Marshall and Brennan argued that the New York procedure examined too deeply an applicant's political beliefs.

Judge bars passport oath. U.S. District Court Judge Thomas A. Flannery ordered the State Department in Washington June 26, 1972 to remove the loyalty oath from passport applications, and to cease denying passports to citizens who refuse to swear or affirm an oath of allegiance.

Flannery ruled that the Fifth Amendment to the Constitution guaranteed the right to travel abroad, and "no serious national purpose" was served by the oath, since it would not likely be effective against those "intent upon committing acts contrary to the country's interests." Only "those persons who find a public affirmation of loyalty repugnant to their integrity and conscience" were harmed by the oath requirement, Flannery said.

The decision was made in a case brought by the American Civil Liberties Union on behalf of Beverly A. Woodward and Allan Fletcher, who were denied passports after refusing the oath.

The loyalty oath, required for passports since 1861, had been made optional in 1966, but restored in November 1971 after a federal district court judge ruled that the option "unfairly discriminates against U.S. citizens."

FBI probe at State Department. A State Department spokesman, in response to questions at a press briefing Sept. 2, 1971 confirmed that Federal Bureau of Investigation (FBI) agents had questioned State Department personnel recently in a probe of unauthorized news leaks. Sources established that "three or four" officials had voluntarily submitted to lie detector tests concerning a July 23 *New York Times* story on U.S. negotiating positions at the American-Soviet strategic arms limitation talks (SALT).

Secretary of State William P. Rogers said Sept. 3 that the investigation had been launched because "it looked on the surface as if there might be" a crime. He added, "I don't believe there was a crime." Rogers said it "was an investigation of a violation of law, and it wasn't directed at the State Department. In fact, it wasn't even started here."

A Justice Department official had said Sept. 2 that the questioning had extended to Defense Department officials. The *Times* story was written by William Beecher, the newspaper's Pentagon reporter.

The investigation reportedly caused distress among some personnel at the State Department, where, officials said, the FBI had not been involved since the wholesale loyalty-security investigations of the 1950s on charges of Communist infiltration raised by the late Sen. Joseph R. McCarthy. The department had its own division empowered to investigate security leaks. An internal study by the State Department in 1970 had dealt with lingering bitterness and inhibitions at the department because of the McCarthy experience.

Rogers said Sept. 3, "I think it is a fact that the State Department had suffered from the scars of those [McCarthy] days." He said he had met "with my top assistants" to insure that a "policy of openness, which is so essential to a free nation, will be continued." But he said such an investigation could not be curtailed "because it might reawaken those fears." Rogers said he had reservations about lie detector tests "in terms of proof," but he said they could help establish innocence.

At the press briefing Sept. 2, State Department spokesman Robert J. McCloskey admitted that some topics had been placed temporarily off limits for discussion with reporters, such as the President's proposed China trip and the South Vietnamese presidential elections. But he said there had been no attempt to limit contacts with the press and that department personnel had only been asked to "use their common sense in dealing with the journalists."

Detention Act repealed. The bill repealing the Emergency Detention Act (Title 2 of the 1950 Internal Security Act) had been approved by 356–49 House vote Sept. 14, 1971 and Senate voice vote Sept. 16. The act had provided for detention of persons suspected of possible espionage or sabotage in periods of invasion or insurrection. It had never been used and six camps established under it had never been used for detention. There was concern among minority groups, especially Negroes, that the law could be used against them. Japanese-Americans also were wary of the legislation in light of the detention after Pearl Harbor in 1941 of more than 110,000 American citizens of Japanese origin in relocation centers.

In his speech at the Portland airport Sept. 25, Nixon deplored the World War II detention camps. In a later statement,

he referred to the "concern among many Americans that the act might someday be used to apprehend and detain citizens who hold unpopular views." He signed the repeal, he said, "to put an end to such suspicions."

Secret Documents

Secrecy role to be weighed. The Supreme Court said March 6, 1972 it would rule on the extent of the government's authority to classify military and other government documents as secret, keeping them from Congress and the public.

At issue in the case were nine government reports and letters prepared for President Nixon in advance of an underground nuclear test blast on the Alaskan island of Amchitka.

(The reports, prepared by a committee headed by Undersecretary of State John N. Irwin 2nd, brought together information on the test's potential effects on the environment, national defense and foreign relations.)

When existence of the letters was leaked, 33 members of Congress led by Rep. Patsy Mink (D, Hawaii) sued for release of portions of the Irwin file after the White House refused to make them available.

Their suit was initially dismissed by a federal district court, but a U.S. appeals court reversed the decision. The appeals court sent the case back to the district court with instructions that it inspect the letters and decide whether any of them should be revealed.

The Justice Department brought the case to the Supreme Court after the appeals court ordered the release of any "nonsecret" portions of the Irwin reports, "if the nonsecret components are separable from the secret remainder and may be read separately without distortion of meaning."

Document classification curbed. President Nixon signed an executive order March 8 to limit the practice of classifying government documents as secret, and to speed the process of declassification. Meanwhile, two House committees considered measures to assert a Congressional role in secrecy control.

While the President's order would limit the number of agencies and individuals with classification powers, punish abuses for non-security purposes and require routine disclosure of most secret papers within six to ten years, Nixon admitted that any improvement in information flow would depend "upon the good judgment of individuals throughout the government," and remain strictly under executive control.

Under the order, no document could be restrictively classified unless its release "could reasonably be expected" to damage the national interest. The number of agencies in possession of a "top secret" stamp would be reduced from 24 to 12, and only 13 others could use the "secret" stamp. Only 1,860 officials would have "top secret" clas-

sification power compared with about 5,100 in the past. "Repeated abuse" of such power, such as "to conceal inefficiency or administrative error," could result in "administrative action."

In general, "top secret" papers would automatically drop to "secret" status after two years; "secret" documents would be downgraded to the "confidential" category after two years, and all "confidential" material would be released after six years.

Exceptions, which would undergo automatic review after 10 years, included documents supplied in confidence by foreign sovereignties, lawfully protected information such as atomic energy data, information damaging to spies, and information "the continuing protection of which is essential to the national security." An agency withholding such data would have to explain its action to anyone requesting a specific paper.

After 30 years, all documents would be declassified unless countermanded in writing by the head of the originating agency. Presidential papers, however, would remain undisclosed unless released by the individual president.

The entire procedure would be supervised by an interagency review committee under the National Security Council.

Nixon also announced March 8 that he had ordered Secretary of State William P. Rogers to speed publication of the department's document series, "Foreign Relations of the United States," which currently lagged 26 years behind events, with a goal of six years of data to be published in the next three years.

House hearings. A House Armed Services subcommittee began hearings March 8 on a proposal by Committee Chairman F. Edward Hebert (D, La.) and ranking Republican Leslie Arends (Ill.) to set up an executive-legislative-judicial secrecy review commission.

The Government Information Subcommittee of the House Government Operations Committee began hearings March 6 on secrecy practices. George Reedy, former press secretary to President Lyndon Johnson, advised Congress to probe the centralization of executive activities at the White House, where they were protected from Congressional scrutiny by Presidential privilege.

Report on classification changes. The White House announced Aug. 3 that a government report had shown that the number of federal employes authorized to classify U.S. documents "top secret," "secret" or "confidential" had been reduced by 63% in the past 60 days.

The cutback was one part of the Nixon Administration's program to streamline the government's security classification system.

The report was presented by John Eisenhower, chairman of the new Interagency Classification Review Committee.

According to the report, the number

of government employes authorized to classify national security information had been reduced from 43,586 to 16,238 since May 17.

According to the report, there was a 53% reduction in the number of officials who could classify materials "top secret," the highest security classification. There was a 39% drop in the number of officials who could classify documents as "secret," and a 76% drop in those who could label materials "confidential," the lowest security classification.

The report showed that the biggest reduction was at the Pentagon, where the number of employes who could classify materials dropped from 30,542 to 8,809.

End to secrecy proposed. Sen. Lawton Chiles (D, Fla.) proposed a bill Aug. 4 that would virtually end all secret meetings in Congress and at the executive level. Chiles described his proposal as a "government in the sunshine" law.

Chiles's bill would require an open-door policy for all Congressional commitee meetings and government agencies except in matters relating to national security and defense, matters required by law to be kept confidential, matters relating to the internal management of agencies and disciplinary actions that would adversely affect a person's reputation.

Old documents still unavailable. Despite a presidential directive to ease the public's access to once-secret data, problems remained for those interested in seeing that information, according to a *New York Times* report Nov. 21, 1972.

In June, President Nixon had pledged to "lift the veil of secrecy" from needlessly classified official papers. To that end, he ordered that access to secret and confidential papers more than 10 years old be made easier. But despite his order, the output of such information was still no more than a trickle, according to historians, other scholars and newsmen. More requests for documents had been denied or labeled "pending" than had been granted.

Prohibitive costs, bureaucratic red tape and general confusion over Nixon's directive were said to be behind the apparent slowness in making the documents more available.

Document secrecy backed. In a 5–3 decision, the court ruled Jan. 22, 1973 that the government need not submit classified documents to a court to determine whether portions of the documents could be released to citizens seeking information.

Reversing a ruling by the U.S. Court of Appeals in the District of Columbia, the court rejected a suit by Rep. Patsy Mink (D, Hawaii) and 32 other House members who tried to obtain nine documents submitted to President Nixon in 1971 by various government agencies and officials about the underground nuclear test at Amchitka Island, Alaska.

The representatives had argued that the 1966 Freedom of Information Act entitled them to the information, and said a secret or top secret classification stamp

did not automatically protect information not vital to the national security that was included in a classified document. They said federal judges should review the documents and release any nonsensitive information.

But Justice White, writing for the court, said the Freedom of Information Act specifically excluded documents "required by executive order to be kept secret" for national security purposes. He said it would be "wholly untenable" to subject "the soundness of executive security classifications to judicial review at the insistence of any objecting citizen."

In a concurring opinion, Justice Potter Stewart blamed Congress for including in the act "an exemption that provides no means to question an executive decision to stamp a document secret, however cynical, myopic or even corrupt that decision might have been."

The court ruled that three of the memoranda might be subject to judicial scrutiny. The act exempted from public release interagency memoranda that would not be subject to subpoena in an ordinary civil case. The court upheld the exemption, but left the burden of proving its applicability to the agencies in question.

Justices William O. Douglas, William J. Brennan Jr. and Thurgood Marshall dissented regarding the classified documents, but only Douglas dissented in upholding the exemption for interagency memoranda. Rehnquist did not take part in the case.

Supreme Court affirms data access. The Supreme Court in a decision announced March 18, 1974 affirmed lower court decisions establishing procedures under which citizens could obtain access to government documents under the Freedom of Information Act. Lower court guidelines required the government to meet the burden of proving that documents in question should not be divulged.

Freedom of Information Act. The House approved and sent to the Senate March 14, 1974 a bill to revise the Freedom of Information Act of 1966 and strengthen public access to government information and records. The vote was 383–8.

The bill would require federal agencies to respond to public requests for data within certain time periods and would require annual reports to Congress from the agencies on the subject. Coverage of the 1966 law would be extended to such agencies within the executive branch as the Office of Management and Budget and the National Security Council.

Federal courts would have the option under the bill of examining classified documents to determine if they had been legitimately withheld from the public and could award court costs to successful plaintiffs.

Bill to ease access to data vetoed—President Ford vetoed a bill Oct. 17 amending the 1966 Freedom of Information Act to give freer public access to government data. Ford said the bill was "unconstitutional and unworkable" and a threat to

U.S. "military or intelligence secrets and diplomatic relations." But he praised the bill's goals and hoped new legislation would be enacted from his own proposals in the next session.

Ford objected to the bill's authority to the courts to declassify secret documents "in sensitive and complex areas where they have no expertise." He had no objection for courts "to inspect classified documents and review the justification for their classification," he said, but the law should read that the courts would have to uphold the classification "if there is a reasonable basis to support it." In the bill, the burden of proof was on the government to justify a secrecy classification.

The President also objected to a provision that agency investigatory files, including those of the Federal Bureau of Investigation, be made public on request unless the agency could prove that disclosure would be harmful to the national interest. Such a provision would be excessively burdensome to the agencies, he said, as well as the bill's requirements for a 10-day time limit for response to requests for data and a 20-day limit for rulings on appeals.

Other provisions of the bill authorized (a) procedure for penalty in the event data were withheld "arbitrarily or capriciously," (b) recovery of legal fees by successful petitioners, (c) publication of indexes of agency decisions, and (d) access to data if it were "reasonably" described.

The Senate had approved the final version of the bill by voice vote Oct. 1, the House by 349–2 vote Oct. 7.

Ford's veto overriden. The amendments to the Freedom of Information Act vetoed by President Ford were enacted into law when the House Nov. 20 and Senate Nov. 21 voted to overturn the vetoes. A two-thirds vote of both houses was required to override. The House vote to override was 371–31. In the Senate, it was 65–27 (three more than the required two-thirds majority).

Privacy Act proposed. A bill to restrict federal collection and use of data on individuals was approved by the Senate Dec. 17 and House Dec. 18. The bill required public disclosure by agencies of any computer data bank operation by them or collection of data on individuals. The individuals would have the right to inspect such files and correct misinformation.

Exchange of the data between agencies was barred without the individual's permission except for "routine" exchanges, such as for paycheck information. There was an exemption in the bill for data on individuals kept by federal law enforcement agencies.

The bill barred the sale or rental of mailing lists maintained by federal agencies and prohibited, beginning in 1975, state and local governments from requiring Social Security numbers as a condition for voting or registering a car or obtaining a driver's license. A special commission was to be established to study the problems of protection of individual privacy in this area.

Privacy Act guidelines published—
The Office of Management and Budget has established guidelines for the implementation of the Privacy Act of 1974. The act becomes effective Sept. 27, 1975, and by that date all departments and agencies must publish a list of records systems they are maintaining. It has been estimated that at least 850 systems exist. The OMB guidelines, released July 7, state: "A key objective of the act is to reduce the amount of personal information collected by Federal agencies to reduce the risk of intentionally or inadvertently improper use of personal data. In simplest terms, information not collected about an individual cannot be misused."

Hiss given access to 'pumpkin papers.'
Alger Hiss will be given access to the "pumpkin papers", microfilms regarded as crucial evidence in Hiss' 1950 conviction for perjury. The microfilm will be made available as a result of the requests filed by Hiss and three scholars under the Freedom of Information Act.

Attorney General Edward H. Levi said June 25, 1975 that Hiss would be able to see the five rolls of microfilm, subject only to national security or other "compelling" reasons. Hiss has consistently denied that he had given Whittaker Chambers government documents when he was a State Department official. Chambers admitted that he was a communist agent, and claimed that the microfilms of the documents were evidence of his charge against Hiss. The microfilms were alleged by Chambers to have been stored in a pumpkin on his farm.

Hiss, now 70, was convicted of perjury and imprisoned for 44 months. His recent appeal of the conviction failed. With the new access to the microfilms, Hiss' contention that he did not give documents to Chambers may be validated by age tests on the film. A Kodak spokesman had said the film was not manufactured before 1938 (the alleged year of the transfer of the documents), but later retracted the statement.

Army Surveillance

Army surveillance suit dismissed. Judge Richard B. Austin of the U.S. district court in Chicago dismissed a suit Jan. 5, 1971 brought by the American Civil Liberties Union, which sought an injunction to halt Army domestic surveillance operations and an order to destroy files collected during the alleged spying. After nearly two weeks of hearings, Austin dismissed the Army intelligence activity as "typical Washington bureaucratic boon-doggling."

Referring to testimony that much of the Army activity was in clipping and filing newspaper stories about their "targets," Austin said "the chief beneficiary of Army intelligence has been newspaper circulation. The only detriment... appears to have been an increase in air pollution from burning the newspapers after they were read." Although he referred to the intelligence unit that was the subject of the hearings as an "assemblage of

Keystone Cops," Austin said the federal government was "well within its rights" to use any available facilities to prepare for civil disturbance emergencies.

In a related development, Oliver A. Pierce, a former Army undercover agent stationed at Fort Carson, Colo., said Jan. 4 that he had spent six months spying on a Colorado Springs youth group. Pierce said the head of G2, the intelligence unit, feared that the leader of the group "would get GIs into his youth group and then would indoctrinate them with antiwar beliefs." Pierce said the Army's method of identifying targets for surveillance was decentralized. He said: "It depends on the attitude of the commanding officer or, in this case, the G2."

Civilian panel to check Army investigations. Defense Secretary Melvin Laird announced Feb. 18 formation of a civilian-dominated board to directly control military intelligence investigations in the U.S. He said tighter civilian control "protects the national security interest while insuring the constitutional, civil and private rights" of individuals and organizations.

Laird established a five-man Defense Investigative Review Council, to be headed by Assistant Secretary of Defense Robert F. Froehlke. Three other civilian members were Undersecretaries of the Army, Thaddeus R. Beal; Navy, John W. Warner; and Air Force, John L. McLucas. The only military man appointed was director of the Defense Intelligence Agency, Lt. Gen. Donald V. Bennett.

In a Dec. 23, 1970 action, Laird had ordered the Defense Intelligence Agency to direct all domestic and foreign military intelligence activity and to report directly to him rather than through the Joint Chiefs of Staff. Froehlke said that after study, Laird had decided the civilian-controlled board would be preferable for overseeing domestic intelligence. Froehlke also said Laird's decision to bypass the Joint Chiefs in control of foreign intelligence activity "has been reversed" at least for the time being.

At the Pentagon news conference to announce the new panel, Froehlke said he believed abuses by military domestic spy operations had occurred and that the blame belonged to both military and civilian leaders. He said the biggest "culprit" was the political climate that followed the 1967 Detroit riots leading to alarm about potential riots all over the country. Froehlke said he believed civilian officials ordered a "reluctant" military to conduct probes in specific areas. He said "the military over-reacted" once it became involved but added, "I have found no grand conspiracy."

Among related developments:

■ Rep. Ogden R. Reid (R, N.Y.) released a letter from Army Secretary Stanley R. Resor Feb. 17 in which Resor acknowledged that "some reports" filed by Illinois Army intelligence agents "could have contained the names" of Sen. Adlai E. Stevenson III, Rep. Abner Mikva, former Illinois Gov. Otto Kerner and other Illinois political figures. How-

ever, Resor said these names would be in the form of newspaper clippings or reports of speeches rather than representing an effort to develop detailed dossiers on political figures.

■ With Army permission, Reid also disclosed Feb. 17 part of a May 2, 1968 intelligence collection plan that led to the surveillance of persons active in the civil rights and antiwar movements. Reid said the plan had been distributed to 319 federal and state government officials, but that "no one had the sense or the courage to question what they were doing." Reid added, "To me, it's almost as disturbing that so many remained silent as that this [plan] was conceived in the first place."

■ In a protest against Army surveillance of peace groups, 11 members of SANE lurked outside the Bethesda, Md. home of Defense Secretary Laird Feb. 15. The demonstrators questioned bystanders, took notes and carried tape recorders, cameras and toy telescopes. Sanford Gottlieb, executive director of the Citizens Organization for a Sane World, said Ralph Stein, a former Army intelligence agent, had admitted putting himself on the organization's mailing list under an alias as part of surveillance activity.

Ervin opens hearings on surveillance.
Sen. Sam J. Ervin Jr. (D, N.C.) opened hearings on government surveillance policies Feb. 23. Ervin was chairman of the Subcommittee on Constitutional Rights.

John M. O'Brien, a former Army intelligence agent whose letter to Ervin prompted the hearings, told the senators Feb. 24 that despite Army denials, agents had spied on Sen. Adlai E. Stevenson III (D, Ill.) during 1969–70 when he was Illinois state treasurer. He said he had complained to superiors about the files on Stevenson and on the American Civil Liberties Union, which he said had been described in the files as a Socialist-Communist organization.

Rep. Abner J. Mikva (D, Ill.), mentioned by O'Brien as one the persons kept under Army surveillance in the Illinois operation, appeared before the subcommittee to demand a complete Congressional ban on domestic spying by the military and "a complete purging of every command official who was responsible for establishing and operating this spy network." Mikva said he believed that much of the activity was unknown to top civilian officials in the Defense Department.

Christopher H. Pyle, a former captain of military intelligence, said a Justice Department unit had become "the government's headquarters for civil disturbance and political protest information." Pyle also claimed that some military intelligence units, particularly the 113th Military Intelligence Group at Fort Sheridan, Ill., continued to collect political information months after orders to stop the activity were issued in June 1970. He said information on individuals, forbidden under the Army directives, was being hidden in files on organizations, which were permitted in some instances.

Military domestic spying—During the Feb. 25 hearing, Ervin said "the Army was not alone in keeping tabs on civilians." He said the Navy was active in domestic surveillance as late as December 1970 and "had the Episcopal bishop of California, Bishop [C. Kilmer] Myers, under surveillance for his antiwar activities" in 1969. He said the Air Force Office of Special Investigations "has collected and does maintain information" on student and minority organizations.

Lawrence F. Lane, a former intelligence sergeant with the 5th Infantry Division at Ft. Carson, Colo., described the overlap of domestic intelligence efforts Feb. 25. Lane said rumors of a large antiwar demonstration outside Ft. Carson in September 1969 had drawn agents from his division and from the 113th military intelligence unit as well as Air Force and law enforcement agents and "even two Navy intelligence officers from somewhere on the West Coast." Lane said the group of 119 demonstrators included 53 "intelligence gathering personnel or representatives of the press."

Assistant Defense Secretary Robert J. Froehlke testified March 2 that the department had cards on 25 million "personalities" and on 760,000 organizations and incidents in the Defense Central Index of Investigation (DCII), established in 1965. Froehlke said, "On an average day, 12,000 [information] requests are processed and 20,000 additions, deletions and changes are made." He said the DCII had grown at a rate of about 2,500,000 additions annually but was expected to level off in 1971.

Froehlke also announced a new Defense Department directive, effective March 1, which banned "physical or electronic surveillance of federal, state or local officials or of candidates for such offices."

During the March 11 hearing, Ervin said he planned to call new Army witnesses to "tell us what they have in their computers" on political activities and personal habits of American citizens. In a letter to Defense Secretary Melvin Laird released March 14, Ervin asked Laird to allow testimony by three Army generals who directed intelligence activity from 1967 to the present. The Army had declined to allow the officers to testify earlier, claiming that the generals could be material witnesses in the Army's own investigation.

(Sen. Bayh made public Feb. 27 the Army's "civil disturbance information collection plan" of May 2, 1968, part of which had been disclosed earlier. The plan, which had been rescinded Dec. 14, 1970, contained a directive to gather information on the "aims and activities of groups attempting to create, prolong or aggravate racial tensions," listing among such groups the National Association for the Advancement of Colored People [NAACP] and the Southern Christian Leadership Conference [SCLC]. Bayh called the inclusions "absolutely incredible.")

Other testimony and developments—During the March 4 hearing, Ervin disclosed an Army file of cards that apparently indexed dossiers on persons or organizations under surveillance at the University of Minnesota and in the St. Paul-Minneapolis area. Included in the file were Harry Davis, the Democratic-Farmer-Labor party candidate for mayor of Minneapolis in 1970; members of the university faculty; the elected student government group; and the St. Paul Department of Human Rights, an official arm of the city government.

Private 'subversives' file. The Associated Press reported July 8 that extensive private files of alleged Communists and subversives had been turned over in March to Sen. James O. Eastland (D, Miss.) by the Defense Department. The files had been compiled by Maj. Gen. Ralph H. Van Deman, a former Army chief of intelligence, between his retirement in 1929 and 1952, the year of his death.

J. Fred Buzhardt, Defense Department general counsel, told about the transfer of the Van Deman files to Eastland, chairman of the Senate Internal Security Subcommittee, in a June 10 letter to Sen. Sam J. Ervin Jr. which was made available to reporters. Buzhardt said July 8 that the current policy of the Defense Department prohibited keeping such files. He said giving them to the Eastland subcommittee "was as good a way to get rid of them as any."

The New York Times reported Sept. 7 that the files contained information on politicians, labor leaders, civil rights leaders and entertainers, all suspected by Van Deman of being subversives. Among those reportedly listed in the files were Rep. Emanuel Celler (D, N.Y.), author Pearl Buck, actresses Joan Crawford and Helen Hayes, former Rep. Adam Clayton Powell (D, N.Y.) and Nobel Prize chemist Linus Pauling.

The *Times* reported an Army memorandum written in 1970 after investigation of the files said, "There may be some embarrassment to the Army because of the information contained on labor and civil rights movements. The question of the Army's relationship to Van Deman could also be embarrassing." There was reportedly evidence of a give-and-take of information between Van Deman, with his network of volunteer agents, and Army and Navy intelligence, the Federal Bureau of Investigation and agencies in California, Van Deman's home state.

Court to decide on Army spy role. The court agreed Nov. 16 to decide whether citizens could take the Army into court to curtail the use of Army surveillance agents in monitoring civilian political activity.

The court said it would hear an appeal by the Justice Department of a lower court ruling that citizens and civilian groups that claim to have been spied upon by Army surveillance agents were entitled to a trial if there had been a "chilling effect" upon their free expression.

Ervin enters amicus curiae brief—Sen. Sam J. Ervin Jr. wrote that Army surveillance of domestic political activity had been more widespread than previously reported, in a brief entered in a Supreme Court case Feb. 28, 1972.

According to information supplied by the Army to the Senate Constitutional Rights Subcommittee from reports and intelligence data bank printouts, the Army's 1967-70 program of surveillance had extended to the political activities of a Supreme Court justice (whom the *New York Times* had identified as Thurgood Marshall), leading Democratic senators, and representatives and governors of both parties.

A spokesman for Ervin said the objects of surveillance included Sens. Edmund Muskie, George McGovern, Edward Kennedy, Harold Hughes and Fred Harris, and former Sens. Ralph Yarborough and Eugene McCarthy; also Reps. Philip M. Crane (R, Ill.) and John Rarick (D, La.), both outspoken conservatives, and former Reps. Adam Clayton Powell and Allard Lowenstein, both New York Democrats.

Governors included were Francis W. Sargent (R, Mass.) and Kenneth Curtis (D, Me.), and former Gov. Philip Hoff (D, Vt.).

In filing his brief, Ervin entered as amicus curiae the case of Arlo Tatum, head of the Central Committee for Conscientious Objectors, who had obtained an appeals court injunction against Army surveillance.

Supreme Court dismisses Army surveillance case—The Supreme Court ruled June 26 that the Army could not be brought into court to defend the mere existence of its surveillance of civilian political activities against charges that the surveillance discouraged freedom of speech.

The justices held 5-4 that surveillance by the Army could be challenged in court only if and when individuals could demonstrate "actual or threatened injury" by having been watched by Army agents. In other instances, the court said, control of such surveillance must be left in the hands of Congress and the executive branch.

Chief Justice Warren E. Burger wrote the majority opinion. Joining him were Justices Harry A. Blackmun, Lewis F. Powell Jr., William Rehnquist and Byron White.

Justices William J. Brennan Jr., William O. Douglas, Thurgood Marshall and Potter Stewart dissented.

Burger said that to permit such a trial of the Army for the mere existence of its surveillance apparatus would make federal courts "virtually continuing monitors of the wisdom and soundess of executive judgment."

At issue in the case was a lawsuit filed by Arlo Tatum, executive director of the Central Committee for Conscientious Objectors, and 12 other individuals and groups who said they were targets of the Army's surveillance.

The plaintiffs had sought an injunction seeking to prevent further surveillance and a court order to require the Army to destroy the dossiers compiled by its agents.

The four dissenting justices held that Tatum and the other plaintiffs had judicial precedents to take the Army to court over the surveillance issue.

Following the court's decision, Aryeh Neier, executive director of the American Civil Liberties Union (ACLU), which represented the plaintiffs, said he would seek a rehearing because of the participation in the decision by Rehnquist, a former assistant attorney general.

Neier said the ACLU would contend that Rehnquist should be disqualified from the case because he had "appeared as an advocate for the Justice Department" before a Senate subcommittee in March 1971 on the Army surveillance issue.

Rehnquist defends role in Army case—In an unusual move, Justice William H. Rehnquist issued a detailed memorandum Oct. 10 defending his participation in a case in which he had earlier expressed an opinion as a government advocate.

Rehnquist issued his 15-page memorandum as he rejected the plaintiffs' demand that he disqualify himself from a plea to the court for a rehearing of the case.

Rehnquist wrote that all judges begin their Supreme Court careers with views on some issues that would later arise in cases before them. He said the mere fact that justices had expressed those views should not disqualify them from participating in a case.

He wrote: "Proof that a justice's mind at the time he joined the court was a complete tabula rasa [clean slate] in the area of constitutional adjudication would be evidence of a lack of qualification, not lack of bias."

Rehnquist denied the American Civil Liberties Union (ACLU) motion to have him step aside on the question of a rehearing of the activists' case. The full court also denied the ACLU motion for a rehearing.

Presbyterians oppose DOD surveillance. The General Assembly of the United Presbyterian Church in the U.S.A., May 23 approved a statement calling for "maximun protection of privacy" in affairs ranging from welfare investigations to matters of national security. The statement urged government regulations that would "prohibit any branch of the Department of Defense from engaging in surveillance of or data collection on domestic political activity" as well as the destruction of "political surveillance file accumulated by the military."

Army drops 'anti-dissident' program. The U.S. Army in Heidelberg, West Germany, Aug. 9, 1973 rescinded a new program of "counter-dissidence" by the

8th Infantry Division after the directive was leaked to the press.

An Army statement said the plan, dated July 23 and disclosed in the *New York Times* Aug. 7, "was determined to be inappropriate, as guidance on dissent contained in Army regulations is considered sufficient and soldier dissent within the command is presently at a very low level." The statement also denied reports that the U.S. Army, Europe was "directing an intensified military counter-intelligence program against underground activities" among soldiers in Germany.

It said the Army's major concern was with "unlawful acts, such as espionage and sabotage, including bombing, arson and damage to equipment." It noted that bomb attacks against Army headquarters in May 1972 had killed three men and that there had been recent reports of equipment damage.

The Army anti-dissident directive had been leaked to the press by Spec. 4 Wayne Sparks, 21, of the division's adjutant general's office. He had said he believed the plan violated the soldiers' constitutional right of free speech.

The directive had ordered the Army's intelligence section to note the name, rank, unit and race of participants in such acts as sabotage, vandalism, anti-U.S. demonstrations, teach-ins, unauthorized meetings with controversial topics and writing complaint letters to congressmen.

The New York Times had first reported July 28 a concerted "summer counterintelligence offensive" by the Army in Germany, including surveillance of German university organizations and a civilian Protestant mission in Mainz suspected of inducing U.S. soldiers to desert or defect and tapping of civilian telephones. Transcripts of conversations on the phone of Tomi Schwaetzer, an Austrian-born journalist writing for an underground news service, were leaked to the press by U.S. intelligence agents.

One of the American agents, Spec. 4 John M. McDougal, charged at a news conference Aug. 7 that "Army intelligence is out of control" and accused the headquarters intelligence chief, Maj. Gen. Harold R. Aaron, of ordering an intensified "offensive counterintelligence" program. McDougal identified himself as one of the agents who originally disclosed the intelligence activities to the press.

Bonn admits wiretaps for U.S.—The West German government admitted Aug. 2 it had tapped phones at the request of U.S. Army intelligence as well as British and French military officials. The tapping was legal, the government said, under a 1968 German law permitting the three Western former occupation powers to ask West German authorities to tap local telephones in cases of suspected security breaches. However, the government's chief spokesman, Rudiger von Wechmar, denied that U.S. Army agents had illegally tapped phones themselves.

An unidentified German source said German authorities had been notified of the U.S. military surveillance of the Protestant mission, in accordance with

laws, although U.S. agents had told the *New York Times* that original plans for the operations had instructed them not to do so.

Weicker charges on spying—U.S. Sen. Lowell P. Weicker Jr. (R, Conn.) charged Aug. 3 that U.S. Army intelligence units in West Germany had spied on an American organization supporting Democratic Presidential nominee George S. McGovern in 1972. He said he had turned over documentary evidence of his charges, obtained by one of his staff members during a recent visit to West Germany, to three Senate committees.

Army curbs spying on civilians. Secretary of the Army Howard H. Callaway, issued an order, effective Oct. 1, 1974 that would curtail surveillance by Army intelligence of most U.S. citizens. Under the terms of the order, the Army would still be empowered to investigate U.S. civilians working for the Defense Department abroad. Surveillance of civilians not affiliated with the Defense Department would not be permitted unless there was "substantial evidence" of illegal activities that threatened Army troops, property or functions.

In a related development, the Army's highest-ranking intelligence officer stationed in West Germany admitted in a sworn statement filed in Washington federal district court Oct. 28 that the Army, in the course of its "countersubversion" operations in West Berlin and West Germany, had penetrated civilian organizations, had civilian phones tapped and had intercepted mail, at least until September. The affidavit was filed in connection with a suit against the Army by a group of U.S. civilian and political organizations in West Germany. They charged the Army with illegally spying on their activities and tapping their telephones.

Army admits use of subversive list—The Army admitted Nov. 12 that it still used the attorney general's list of subversive organizations to discharge suspect military personnel, despite a June 4 presidential order abolishing use of the list for "any purpose." Continuing Army use of the list came to light when Steven Wattenmaker, a leader of the Young Socialist Alliance, challenged his involuntary dismissal from the Army Reserve because he belonged to an organization on the subversive list. The notice of discharge received by Wattenmaker said his retention was not in the interests of national security since he was a member of the Young Socialist Alliance, which was "controlled and dominated by the Socialist Workers Party, which has been designated as a subversive organization by the attorney general."

Army, Chicago police linked to terrorism. The *Chicago Daily News* reported April 12, 1975 that an Army intelligence unit, working with Chicago police, aided the terrorist activities of a right-wing group that preyed on anti-Vietnam war groups from 1969 to 1971. The terrorists, "who were members of a now-defunct organization known as the Legion of Justice, beat, gassed and wreaked general havoc on members of groups opposed to the Vietnam War," the *Daily News* said. The paper asserted that Army's 113th Military Intelligence Group headquartered in suburban Evanston supplied the legion with tear gas, mace, and electronic equipment in addition to money.

Army finds files on citizens. Howard H. Callaway, secretary of the Army, in a memorandum to Congress made public June 13, said that a survey of Army intelligence files had found 9,200 documents on the activities of U.S. civilians. Callaway, who said the documents should have been destroyed in accordance with a 1971 Pentagon order to purge Army files on political dissidents, indicated that an action to eliminate all such documents had been recently begun but later suspended until the completion of congressional investigations of U.S. intelligence activities.

In a related development, David O. Cooke, a deputy assistant secretary of defense, told the House Government Operations Subcommittee on Government Information and Individual Rights June 8 that the Army's files on political dissenters might exist in U.S. intelligence agencies that exchanged information with the Pentagon in the late 1960s. Although the Army had destroyed its own files, Cooke said, it did not know what the CIA, the FBI and other agencies had done with the data from the Army. "I assume the files are retrievable, but not by us," Cooke said.

Army denies existence of computer files on citizens—Cooke told a Senate subcommittee hearing June 23 that although the Department of Defense used many computers, none held files on American citizens. Referring to the biggest Pentagon computer network, ARPANET, Cooke said, "Let me emphasize that it is not a 'secret' network, that it is used for scientific research purposes, that it contains no sociological or intelligence data on personalities, and that it is a marvel in many ways. But it simply does not fit the Orwellian mold attributed to it."

National Security Agency

NSA denies wiretapping. The National Security Agency "at the present time" was not eavesdropping on telephone calls in the United States, the *New York Times* reported Aug. 9, 1975. Representative Otis G. Pike (D, N.Y.) told the press that officials had testified for four hours before his House Select Committee on Intelligence, but that "a great many members" of the committee still had "doubts" that the agency did not wiretap telephone calls.

Air Force Gen. Lew C.O. Allen Jr., director of the NSA, told the House panel Aug. 8 that "no director of the National Security Agency has ever before been required to come before a Congressional committee in open session." President Ford had informed the committee through his counselor, John O. Marsh Jr., that he wanted NSA testimony treated as "top national security."

Central Intelligence Agency Director William E. Colby had told the House committee Aug. 6 that the NSA eavesdropped on American calls.

Ron Nessen, presidential press secretary, told reporters Aug. 7 that "the intelligence agencies, including NSA, have vital national security responsibilities and the President in no way will preclude these intelligence agencies from carrying out legitimate foreign intelligence responsibilities." He added that the President had "stated all intelligence agencies will operate within the Constitution and applicable law."

NSA said to spy on cables and calls. Almost all overseas telephone calls from and to the U.S. and most international cable and nontelephonic communications were being monitored by the National Security Agency, it was reported Aug. 31. The NSA, an intelligence arm of the Defense Department chartered in 1952, was charged with coordinating U.S. electronic intelligence gathering and with the developing and breaking of codes.

According to the reports on NSA eavesdropping, the ultra-secret agency used computers that were programmed to look for "trigger words." The computers scanned the message traffic and automatically recorded any message containing words they were programmed to look for.

Newsweek said in its Sept. 8 issue that its intelligence sources insisted "that the agency regularly scans most if not all overseas cables and telephone traffic and a large volume of written domestic communications. Some of the intercepted messages, moreover, have dealt with such civilian concerns as antiwar activism and, reportedly, grain sales to Russia." The magazine added, "there are indications that the NSA has begun to cut back on the monitoring program, perhaps because of the attention it has attracted."

NSA reports on Americans abroad revealed. The *New York Times* revealed Oct. 11 that Presidents Nixon and Johnson had received reports from the National Security Agency on prominent Americans' activities abroad. An agency spokesman refused comment on the information received by the *Times* from "former Government officials."

The NSA's alleged reports had been made known earlier at a closed meeting of the House Intelligence Committee. When questioned on how the material was obtained, NSA officials indicated that eavesdropping on foreign governments' communications and embassies in Washington could supply information on what Americans had said to foreign governments. Foreign telephone and cable traffic is also monitored by the NSA.

Ford administration seeks to modify NSA. The *New York Times* reported Oct. 14 that the Ford administration has become convinced that the NSA's intelligence gathering may be of "questionable legality". Administration sources told the *Times* that the President was considering an Executive order to empower Attorney General Edward H. Levi to rule on specific electronic intrusions by the NSA. When the NSA records something it believes important to the national security, the agency would then notify the attorney general. Levi would either authorize the recording, or the recording would be destroyed.

IRS

IRS secret unit ordered disbanded. The Philadelphia *Evening Bulletin* revealed Jan. 27, 1975 that a secret unit of the Internal Revenue Service had been collecting personal information on thousands of U.S. citizens. According to high government sources, the unit was ordered disbanded Jan. 23 or 24 because of fear that the congressional investigations of the Central Intelligence Agency might reach the IRS.

The *Bulletin*'s sources said that the unit was known as the Intelligence Gathering and Research Unit (IGR). It was reported to have been established during the first Nixon Administration. One of the IGR's first leaders was Tom Lopez, head of the IGR Miami office. Lopez was said to have been in regular contact with John W. Dean 3rd, White House counsel, throughout 1971 and 1972.

The IRS attempted to hide the IGR's existence and members from even the IRS intelligence community. The IRS classified directory was alleged to list home address and telephone numbers of IRS intelligence chiefs, but only "IGRU" for members of the secret unit.

The IGR was reported to have investigated drinking and sexual habits, friends, and political leanings. According to the *Bulletin*, "files more often than not were filled with strictly personal information, with nothing included on tax violations, narcotics dealings, or any other illegal activity."

A confidential memo from IRS director of intelligence John J. Olszewski reported on the IGR in 1973: "The intelligence gathering and retrieval system has been fully developed and is now operational. The system provides an effective, uniform means to gather, evaluate, cross-index, retrieve, and coordinate intelligence data on individuals and entities involved in illegal activities on a district and national basis."

IRS had data file on 466,442 names—Hearings of House Government Operations Subcommittee revealed a master list of 466,442 names kept in the IRS computer in Detroit, the *New York Times* reported June 20. IRS officials said that the subcommittee's document appeared to be a genuine copy of the index to the IRS' Intelligence Gathering and Retrieval System begun in 1973 and disbanded early in 1975.

The *Times*' analysis of the document found that "like most of the Governmental lists of persons to be watched that were made during the Nixon Administration, [the] list is dominated by liberals, radicals, antiwar activists and blacks." Among the groups on the list were the American Civil Liberties Union, the Black

Panther party, the Gay Liberation Front and the Medical Committee for Human Rights. They were indexed under a "subversive activities" code.

IRS Commissioner Donald C. Alexander testified that he believed it was wrong to collect information not related to tax collection. Rep. Benjamin S. Rosenthal (D, N.Y.) told Alexander, "I don't think you are sensitive to the problem we perceive of the invasion of civil rights and civil liberties in the United States."

IRS confirms gossip files—The Internal Revenue Service confirmed June 23 that it had maintained a nationwide computer file until Jan. 23, 1975. The data bank contained personal information on taxpayers. Included were sex and drinking habits.

The IRS conducted an internal investigation after newspaper reports alleged the agency was delving into gossip. The report on the investigation was released by Rep. Al Ullman (D, Ore.), chairman of the Joint Committee on Internal Revenue Taxation. Since the committee had not read the report, it "therefore, of course, is not endorsing it," Ullman said.

The report concentrated on Florida citizens. Nearly one-quarter of the Miami information dealt with sex and drinking habits. The IRS claimed that the data could establish income levels. "Operation Leprechaun" investigated 70 Miami-area residents, not the 30 originally reported. In 63 of the cases, the information "was of little or no value," the report stated. The IRS expects eventually to receive tax penalties of more than $1 million from one case uncovered by the operation.

IRS alleged to have sent personal information to White House. The *Miami News* reported Feb. 1, 1975 that the Internal Revenue Service had compiled dossiers on the personal habits of several Miami residents and sent the data to the Nixon White House. The files had been largely destroyed, the *News* stated.

Among those under surveillance by the IRS were football player Joe Namath, entertainer Danny Thomas, Mayor Maurice Ferre, Dade County Mayor Steve Clark, and Miami Dolphins owner Joe Robbie.

'Operation Leprechaun' disclosed—Elsa Suarez told reporters March 14 that she was recruited in 1972 by the IRS "to get dirt" on 30 Miami-area officials. She said her contacts were most interested in "sexual hangups." She was instructed to "Get Gerstein in particular because he's making trouble with his Watergate investigation." Richard Gerstein was the state attorney for Dade County. Three federal judges were also included on her list of subjects.

Mrs. Suarez said she had been recruited because of her earlier experience with the Drug Enforcement Administration and because she volunteered information to the IRS about tax violations. She showed several supporting documents to prove the existence of "Operation Leprechaun." One was a photocopy of a letter which she alleged concerned a check for $2,960 paid

her by the IRS. She claimed that the IRS gave her a car, membership in four exclusive Miami clubs, and promised her $20,000 a year for life and a home abroad if she could find compromising information. "I never did sleep with anybody or get any good dirt during the three months I was on the job," she said.

Donald C. Alexander, IRS Commissioner, said April 14 that he was investigating the 1972 charges, noting that he was not then the commissioner. "I do know this, that the IRS has no business engaging in any activities of the type that have been described, and the IRS is not going to engage in any such activities while I am commissioner. If anyone engages in these types of activities, I am going to do my best to cause his or her dismissal."

More Florida undercover work revealed—In Testimony before a House Government Operations subcommittee July 8, Internal Revenue Service Commissioner Donald C. Alexander revealed that an undercover IRS agent had been paid $54,961 over a year-and-a-half period during which he eavesdropped on conversations in bars in Miami and Fort Lauderdale, Florida and gathered allegations against 913 persons, none of which were substantiated.

The project, in which the agent attempted to draw out persons frequenting the bars and obtain from them evidence of financial irregularities, was known as Operation Sunshine. Also discussed before the subcommittee but not elaborated on in news accounts were two similar IRS activities in the Miami area, Operation W and Operation Rosebud. After testifying that he had learned of Operations W and Rosebud only the previous day, Commissioner Alexander remarked: "We don't need money, in my judgment, for such things as Operation Sunshine, Operation W and Operation Leprechaun."

One of the subcommittee members, Rep. Robert F. Drinan (D, Mass.), expressed himself in favor of banning all IRS undercover work and said the service's report on Operation Sunshine "is not complete, is not candid, it's not even comprehensible."

Suit alleges IRS political harassment. The New York Civil Liberties Union (NYCLU) filed a class-action civil rights suit in Washington federal court March 25, 1975, charging that the Internal Revenue Service had subjected over 11,000 individuals and organizations to special tax investigations "due to their political beliefs and activities." The suit was brought by Walter Teague 3rd, an antiwar activist, and the Indochina Solidarity Committee, an antiwar group.

An NYCLU spokesman indicated the suit was the first court test of the legality of the Special Service Staff (SSS), an IRS intelligence unit created in 1969 to gather tax data on political dissidents. The SSS was abolished in 1973 by Donald C. Alexander, who, shortly before, had become IRS commissioner.

Former Sen. Sam J. Ervin Jr. (D, N.C.) said in December 1974 in the introduction

to a staff report of the Judiciary Constitutional Rights Subcommittee that the operations of the SSS represented "a dangerous abuse of the enormous powers Americans have given to the tax collection arm of government." Ervin found the SSS involved in political surveillance "unauthorized by law, unnecessary to the administration of tax laws, and in the very least, a waste of the taxpayers' money." "The purpose of the IRS is to enforce the tax laws, not ... political orthodoxy," he said.

IRS chief asks outside inquiry. Donald Alexander, commissioner of the Internal Revenue Service (IRS), said April 7 that he saw a need for an outside investigation of alleged corruption and improper activities within his agency. While Alexander did not indicate whether he believed wrongdoing had occurred, he said a probe was needed because "we have an obligation" to assure "the public that the IRS is not corrupt."

Alexander said he favored strengthening the Congressional Joint Committee on Internal Revenue Taxation rather than creating a new oversight agency.

In a related development, Alexander told a Senate Appropriations subcommittee April 16 that in fiscal 1974 the IRS had made available to a dozen other federal agencies the tax returns of 8,210 individuals. The bulk of the returns, Alexander and other IRS officials testified, was given to the Justice Department and the Federal Bureau of Investigation.

The IRS officials said the agency had not usually checked on the legitimacy of requests by federal agencies. However, they stated that the IRS no longer provided tax returns of prospective Presidential appointees to the White House and instead was informing the President as to whether the individuals had outstanding tax obligations or were under IRS investigation. The officials conceded that present system for distribution of tax returns could result in abuses.

Former chiefs back IRS data access limit. Five former commissioners of the Internal Revenue Service told a Senate Finance subcommittee April 28 that they favored some sort of Congressional action to limit disclosure of tax information to other federal agencies. In their testimony before the Subcommittee on the Administration of the Internal Revenue Code, four of the former officials warned against going too far, however, stating that an overly strict disclosure law would hamper prosecutions not involving tax laws.

Harold R. Tyler, deputy attorney general, who testified before the subcommittee April 21, also had cautioned against unduly restricting Justice Department attorneys in their prosecution of non-tax cases. Other Justice Department officials had expressed similar concerns, saying that narrowed access to tax information might have a disastrous impact on investigations and prosecutions involving white collar crime and corrupt politicians.

Rep. Jerry Litton (D, Mo.), sponsor of a bill to curb dissemination of tax data, said in subcommittee testimony April 28 that the measure he proposed would not stop the Justice Department from going to court and obtaining a court order when it needed tax information for non-tax related probes or prosecutions.

Alexander testifies on IRS data policies. Donald C. Alexander, commissioner of the Internal Revenue Service, told the House Select Committee on Intelligence Aug. 7, 1975 that the IRS gave 30,000 tax returns of 8,000 Americans to 12 other governmental agencies. He said the Justice Department used 500 returns.

The IRS' computer in Martinsburg, W.Va. could be tapped electronically, Alexander testified, but the facility was surrounded by a high metal fence to keep the eavesdroppers from approaching it.

The IRS' school for teaching agents to wiretap and make surreptitious entries was ended in 1965, Alexander said. He claimed that a program to test IRS agents' ability to withstand large amounts of liquor and the advances of women was also abolished then.

IRS data link with CIA investigated— An Internal Revenue Service spokesman told the *New York Times* Aug. 23, 1975 that an "intensive internal investigation" was being conducted by the IRS to probe the legality of sharing tax return information with the Central Intelligence Agency.

The Rockefeller Commission report had revealed that at least 14 occasions occurred when the CIA was given tax return information out of the prescribed method. The commission had reported, "Formal procedures for obtaining the necessary authorization have been in effect for some time. They require the applicant to make formal application to the Commissioner of Internal Revenue for each tax return desired, setting forth the reason why the return is needed. The commission has found no evidence that this procedure was ever followed by CIA personnel."

A *Times* source commented, "The CIA, like most government agencies is entitled to tax return information under certain conditions. All the CIA director had to do was to write a letter of request to the commissioner."

IRS head defends halt of tax probes. Donald C. Alexander, commissioner of the Internal Revenue Service, Sept. 30 defended his decision in August to suspend largescale undercover investigations of trust accounts established in the Bahamas and on some Caribbean islands by U.S. citizens to avoid paying taxes.

Alexander said that as a result of his decision, some "former and a few present IRS employes," had begun a concerted effort to discredit him because they disagreed with his policies. These individuals, Alexander said, "have reacted by criticizing me personally, attempting to block efforts to uncover and eliminate inappropriate activities by IRS employes and informers, and by circulating scurrilous rumors about my personal character."

Published allegations in the weeks following the suspension of the investigations said that Alexander had halted an intelligence-gathering operation to protect businessmen, that he once arranged to meet a convicted swindler in connection with a tax problem and that, as a lawyer before entering government service, he gave a client improper advice. Other subsequent reports said that the Justice Department was investigating the allegations.

Much of the criticism directed at Alexander concerned his decision to curtail dissemination of information from two previously top-secret operations intended to identify U.S. citizens trying to evade income taxes by means of illegal overseas tax shelters. The first of the operations designed to penetrate the secrecy of these foreign trusts was begun in 1965. Dubbed "Operation Tradewinds," the operation was put together by an IRS agent who assembled network of

confidential informants in the Bahamas to obtain information about secret U.S. investments, particularly those by organized crime.

In 1973, an informant in Miami obtained a list of 300 Americans with secret trust investments in the Castle Bank and Trust Co. Ltd. of the Bahamas.

The list became the basis for "Operation Haven," a nationwide investigation based in New York. According to IRS officials, Operation Haven resulted in recommendations for prosecutions in five criminal cases, in seven criminal cases still under investigation and in the processing of 63 civil cases with recommended taxes and penalties of $33 million.

However, when the IRS's investigative methods came under criticism earlier in 1975, Alexander ordered a halt to payments to informers, and Operation Tradewinds stopped. When the incident involving the photographing of the briefcase's contents came under investigation in August, Alexander halted dissemination of information already obtained through Operation Haven.

Intelligence agencies' use of IRS reported. The CIA and the FBI used the Internal Revenue Service to harass political groups, Sen. Frank Church (D, Ida.) reported Oct. 2. The FBI had obtained a list of contributors to the Southern Christian Leadership Conference in order to disrupt its fund raising. The CIA had urged the IRS to begin investigating *Ramparts* magazine to avoid publication of a series of articles on CIA infiltration of the National Student Association.

Church also disclosed that the Special Services Staff operation had collected 11,000 names of individuals and agencies kept under surveillance because they "were promoting extremist views and philosophies," according to an IRS memo. IRS Commissioner Donald C. Alexander abolished the program in August 1973. His staff had withheld details of the SSS program from him for nearly four months after he took office in May 1973, he testified.

SEN. ERVIN WARNS OF DATA BANKS, OPENS HEARINGS ON SURVEILLANCE

Sen. Sam J. Ervin Jr. (D, N.C.) said Feb. 9 that the U.S. Passport Office kept a secret computerized file of 243,135 Americans. He appeared at a four-day symposium on data banks at Carlisle, Pa. Ervin explained that the computer was programmed to report to various law enforcement and intelligence agencies—without the subjects' knowledge—the passport applications of persons suspected of being "subversive" or who might fail to "reflect credit" upon the U.S. abroad.

The Senate Subcommittee on Constitutional Rights, chaired by Sen. Ervin, opened hearings Feb. 23 on the effect of government and private surveillance and computer data banks on individual privacy in the U.S. Opening the session, Ervin said, "When people fear surveillance, whether it exists or not, when they grow afraid to speak their minds freely to their government or anyone else . . . then we shall cease to be a free society."

The Providence Journal

Providence, R.I., March 1, 1971

"Dossier dictatorship" is spreading its tentacles across the United States because most Americans have no overall picture of its insidious character nor its mushrooming size.

"Dossier dictatorship" is the label applied to the electronic storage system of all kinds of data about individuals that is being used by a growing number of organizations, public and private. It was coined by a Michigan Law School professor to describe the invasion of privacy that threatens all Americans, law-abiding as well as law-breakers, those who shun the spotlight as well as those who seek public acclaim, those who merely want to maintain a few charge accounts as well as those who borrow millions, those who want to express their opinions as well as those who want to overthrow the government.

The "dossiers" that can be assembled and maintained easily through electronic data banks may some day be interchangeably used by a whole range of agencies, public and private. They may be used legally or illegally; human ingenuity and corruption always can find ways of getting around whatever rules are devised to protect the confidential nature of many files.

Meanwhile, millions of Americans, feeling they have nothing to hide or simply unaware of the capabilities of the new machines, cooperate with the collection of personal information. These data, in the bits and pieces by which it is gathered, have little harmful effect but lumped all together, can give a complete profile of a man that could be used detrimentally by unscrupulous persons or by a vindictive government. Nor does that possibility include the damage to individuals that can be done by incorrect data perpetuated in the machines, unknown to the subject, or derogatory information derived, say, from a false accusation or criminal charges dropped without prosecution.

Many Americans who shudder at the implications of the cybernetic monsters, especially when they are tied to the kind of pervasive spying and snooping that has involved as many as 1,500 military investigators, are at a loss to find ways of combatting the inroads that even George Orwell, in his famous book *1984*, did not entirely foresee. One means of control has been suggested in a bill filed by Rep. Edward I. Koch, New York Democrat. Designed to preserve as much privacy as possible for the individual, it would require each government agency keeping records on him to notify him that the record exists, to notify him when information is transferred to another agency, to disclose information only with his written consent or when legally required. It would require maintenance of a file of all persons with access to the file and permit the individual to inspect his records, copy them, and to put supplementary or explanatory information in them. It ought also to permit him to challenge clearly false or erroneous information.

Even if the envelopment of the individual in the "dossier dictatorship" cannot be stopped, it can at least be regulated; the persons directly affected can at least have some chance to fight back against the dissemination of false, derogatory, or just plain confidential information on a nationwide and life-long basis.

THE DENVER POST

Denver, Colo., February 16, 1971

THE U.S. SENATE subcommittee on constitutional rights is about to start extensive hearings on the use by various federal agencies of computers to amass vast data banks of information on American citizens who have never been convicted of any crime.

Such a hearing was originally scheduled for last fall but had to be postponed because of the press of other business. Now Sen. Sam J. Ervin Jr., D-N.C., has set aside nine days for a careful investigation of this troublesome question.

Computerized records on millions of persons have been gathered and stored away in recent years by a wide variety of agencies.

The Civil Service Commission, for example, has what has been called a computerized "blacklist" of more than 1.5 million persons, compiled to a large extent from references to individuals contained in radical student publications.

Thus a person favorably mentioned in a left wing publication may turn up in the commission's "subversive activities" file and find years later, when his ideas and beliefs may have changed, that he is barred from possible government employment.

The Secret Service, a branch of the Treasury Department, keeps extensive files not only on persons believed to be potential assassins but also on persons who make abusive statements about high government officials, and on persons who insist on contacting high government officials for the purpose of getting redress for imaginary grievances.

Other agencies have similar computerized data banks and often exchange information with one another.

No law authorizes the keeping of information of this kind on law-abiding citizens. The agencies that keep such records generally justify their actions on the ground that such information is necessary to prevent crimes and subversion.

This network of surveillance of citizen activities has disturbed many people who see it as the start of a "big brother" system for thought control. Senator Ervin, an expert on the constitution, has said that the very existence of government files on how people think, speak, assemble and act in lawful pursuits is a form of "official psychological coercion" by the government agencies.

He says no one objects to the government keeping criminal records on individuals but he is worried by a system which may label a person as a "radical" or a "subversive" based on the say-so of some faceless data collector who may or may not possess the ability to make judgments of that kind.

SENATOR ERVIN'S REVIEW should lead to the setting of reasonable rules for establishing and keeping government records on non-criminals.

The purposes for which surveillance data may be assembled and kept need to be spelled out. Criteria for deciding whether a person's name and activities should be listed should be established. Some provision should be made to allow persons whose files contain derogatory information to furnish rebuttal and prove any inaccuracies.

It probably is not realistic to try to keep government from amassing files on suspect individuals. But firm guidelines, based on constitutional rights of freedom to speak and dissent, are essential.

Los Angeles Times

Los Angeles, Calif., February 21, 1971

It is the fashion to blame computers for just about everything that has gone wrong in our society, and more often than not it turns out that the electronic brains are taking a bum rap.

But this does not seem to be true in the case of charges that computers, by their very efficiency, may one day turn America into a "dossier" society where no man will have many secrets from some public, or private, Big Brother.

Sen. Sam Ervin (D-N.C.), chairman of the Senate subcommittee on constitutional rights, is worried by the trend and hopes to come up with legislation to do something about it. The hearings which begin Tuesday are the first step in that effort.

The original impetus for the hearings came from the revelation last year that the military services, especially Army intelligence, had been engaged in building computerized dossiers on the activities, associations and public statements of many thousands of civilians in this country.

There is a strong case for the right of the services to carry out limited surveillance of radicals of the left or right who may pose a direct danger to military personnel or installations.

★

As Ervin put it, however, the Army gumshoes also seem to have concerned themselves with the political activities of elected public officials and others "against whom no charge of extremism can possibly be made."

Pentagon officials have ordered the computerized dossiers destroyed, the more questionable type of domestic spying ended, and civilian control established over domestic military intelligence.

Obviously the American people are entitled to assurance that this threat to basic American liberties does not recur, and the Ervin hearings are aimed in part at nailing the Administration down on this point.

Fortunately, though, the subcommittee will not limit its inquiry to domestic spying by the military. It will look into the whole range of perils which computerized information technology pose to individual liberties—particularly the right to privacy.

The average citizen has no idea of how many government and private agencies have material relating to his character, life-style and behavior stored away in their files.

The Social Security Administration, for example, has earnings records on just about everybody. The Department of Transportation keeps on tap the names of 2.6 million citizens whose drivers licenses have been suspended or revoked.

The U.S. Passport Office keeps a secret, computerized file on more than 243,000 Americans—many of them "known or suspected subversives"—whose names will be turned over to the FBI, the CIA or other interested agencies if they apply for a passport. Persons listed may never be aware of it.

Details from the tax returns of 75 million citizens are kept on computer tapes at the Internal Revenue Service—and are available to other government agencies and even to governors.

There is movement, too, toward creation of a nationwide, computerized data bank of criminal records.

An Ervin aide tells of a plan considered by the Department of Housing and Urban Development to combine its computer files on thousands of builders and businessmen with the Justice Department's file on organized crime. This kind of computer tie-up could cause a businessman to be blackballed out of a government contract without ever knowing why—and as the result of information which may even be incorrect.

Then, outside government, there are the credit rating bureaus which hold personal information on an estimated 110 million Americans, much of it computerized.

There is nothing new about creditors and government agencies keeping files on people, and for that matter there is nothing necessarily wrong with it. But a new situation has been created by the computer, with its massive memory, its capacity for instant total recall—and its ability to exchange data with other computers.

In short, the computer brings a disturbing and possibly perilous efficiency to the keeping and exchanging of dossiers.

Ervin has ideas about some safeguards which might be imposed on this new "information power," and other theories are bound to arise from the hearings.

★

One proposal is to enact a law that information collected for one purpose cannot be used for another without the knowledge of the individual concerned. Another, even more basic, is to legally empower any citizen to examine the records and clear them of false information which may be entered against his name.

Objections undoubtedly will be raised to such proposals—particularly by law enforcement agencies. And indeed there may be two sides to the question.

We believe, though, that Ervin is justified in fearing the evolution of a "dossier society"—a society in which government knows "all about the individual citizen—his habits, his livelihood, his hopes and aspirations, even his thoughts and fears."

Such a society, as the North Carolinian points out, "would not be free." If some sacrifice in governmental efficiency is necessary to safeguard the substance as well as the letter of our constitutional liberties, it is worth it.

Minneapolis Tribune

Minneapolis, Minn., March 5, 1971

BIG BROTHER, Americans have been discovering to an increasing degree, hasn't waited until 1984 to begin watching them. As Prof. Arthur Miller of the University of Michigan Law School told Sen. Ervin's Constitutional Rights Subcommittee last week, there are probably 10 to 20 dossiers, on the average, held by private firms and government agencies on every person in the country. The federal government, according to another estimate, has card files containing information on one out of every eight Americans.

Much of this information is stored in computers. It's instantly available and quickly transmitted. This ease of accessibility is one of the reasons behind the recent massive invasion of Americans' rights to privacy: An individual knows that dossiers on him were compiled when he attended school, served in the armed forces, applied for a job or an insurance policy or a loan, registered an automobile—but he has no way of knowing what other private organizations or public agencies might also be dipping into these data banks to make use of the information they contain. Nor does he know whether the information is accurate or not. And if it's inaccurate, he has no way of refuting it even if he does learn about it.

Two solutions to these problems were proposed Wednesday by Robert Henderson, associate group vice-president of Honeywell Information Systems. Henderson told Sen. Ervin's subcommittee that an individual should be given the right, by law, to examine files on himself and to challenge the contents if he feels they are inaccurate. He further urged that the firms, organizations and government agencies that have computerized data make use—as too few of them are doing now—of the security devices computer manufacturers have developed to guard against access by unauthorized persons.

We would go one step further than Henderson, however. Security devices will do little to stop the proliferation of data on Americans if the owners of existing records continue to make them available to virtually anyone who asks for them. A security device, after all, can only keep information out of the hands of an unauthorized person—and the problem, apparently, has been that authorization to examine records is being given too freely. Some hard questions about the need for the information—and how it is to be used, and by whom, and for what purposes—should be answered before a firm or organization opens its files to anyone.

THE ROANOKE TIMES
Roanoke, Va., March 2, 1971

It is hard not to feel a bit paranoid when one reads about the testimony recently given in Washington on the extent of the personal files, both public and private, that have been built up on people in this country in the computer age.

To be sure, not a great deal of it has a really sinister touch to it. Even the spying and the compiling of dossiers by the military on all manner of civilians seems largely innocent of intent to suppress free thought. It is more a matter of large information-gathering bureaucracies, given a vaguely worded mission from above, getting out of effective control and going mindlessly on toward the goal of finding out everything about everybody.

Those agencies are a long way from that goal, and recent publicity about such activities has slowed them down, but has not stopped them. They continue. Meanwhile, legions of law enforcement bureaus, government offices, private credit-checking companies and the like are compiling data on people and, for efficiency's sake, storing it in computers.

These mountains of information, so readily accessible, constitute a clear threat to freedom in the hands of anyone inclined to use them in that way—the more so as, with technical developments, computers can be made to communicate with one another and exchange data in a matter of minutes at most.

To repeat: The intent so far is not sinister. And the complexities of modern society actually make it imperative that we use efficient methods of record-keeping. Similarly, technology should be brought to bear against crime, and quick retrieval of information on enemies to society can be most helpful in apprehending and convicting them.

But this is a two-edged sword. The computer, of itself, can make no distinctions among people. If told to spew out a list of individuals who hold "subversive" views, it will do so to the limit of its data, just as it will if directed to print out a rundown on convicted felons. We cannot afford to shrug off the possibility that dossiers, however innocently compiled, can be used in repressive fashion.

Sen. Sam Ervin, D-N.C., who has been holding the hearings on intrusions into privacy, has noted that, on the basis of some of his expressed views, he himself might be considered by some to be an undesirable trouble-maker. So, fellow citizen, might you or I.

Herald News
Fall River, Mass., February 26, 1971

The difficulty in maintaining privacy is increasing all the time. A Senate subcommittee on Constitutional rights has heard testimony disclosing that the government has between 10 to 20 dossiers of private information about every citizen locked away in computer data banks. It is probably true that the purpose for which the information was collected is harmless. Much of it is needed for the steadily growing number of government services to which every citizen has a right.

But it is also true that this immense stockpile of information could be used to the disadvantage of individuals if at any time the government were controlled by persons interested in setting up a totalitarian state. One witness at the subcommittee hearing said the country is in danger of a "dossier dictatorship."

The phrase may be an exaggeration, but there is some truth in the claim that, even if the reasons for collecting it are innocent, the stockpiling of personal information about all of us is distasteful to most people. It is, in fact, an invasion of privacy.

The problem created by the data banks is more complicated than it seems on the surface. There is a real conflict, although a peaceful one, between the kinds of services Americans need and want in the age of technology and the traditional rights which they expect and demand. Men of good will in and out of government are trying to reconcile the conflict without the loss of services on the one hand or liberty on the other.

The disclosures to the Senate subcommittee about the individual dossiers on file illustrates how difficult that reconciliation will be.

The San Diego Union
San Diego, Calif., February 28, 1971

When George Orwell's book, "1984," was published 22 years ago, his chilling portrayal of an omniscient big-brother government keeping constant watch over every citizen seemed remote. Now, however, there are growing fears that such an Orwellian nightmare is indeed possible. Computers and electronic devices have given the federal government detailed knowledge about the private lives of millions of citizens and an almost frightening surveillance over their activities.

The hazard to individual rights from the misuse of information stored in data banks has prompted hearings by the Senate Judiciary Subcommittee on Constitutional Rights, under the chairmanship of Sen. Sam J. Ervin, a constitutional authority in the Senate.

Senator Ervin plans to take an exhaustive look at how an "overzealous, computer-ridden bureaucracy" could compromise constitutional guarantees of personal freedom and privacy.

Various branches of the federal government have continued to expand, at a staggering rate, their files of detailed information on nearly every living American. More than 10,000 computers within the executive branch are busy at this task. For example, dossiers in the Federal Housing Administration contain intimate information on the personal habits, the marriage stability, and credit rating of large numbers of Americans. The Department of Transportation keeps data on 2.6 million citizens who were deprived of a driving license.

The Justice Department computers remember the misdeeds of nearly everyone ever convicted of a crime. And the Department of Health, Education and Welfare, like the Internal Revenue Service, adds mountains of additional statistics about the private lives of Americans. Washington computers now even "talk" to each other to exchange information.

Senator Ervin recognizes the requirement for this new technology. He does not quarrel with the government's need to acquire and store the basic essential information that is needed for administrative purposes. It is the abuse of this information that alarms the senator.

He is, of course, also concerned with the constant pressure by many businesses to gain access to these data, particularly through use of Social Security information.

To the extent that the collection and use of these data increase the efficiency of our republican form of government, without infringing on either privacy or liberty, they are acceptable.

It is wholly unacceptable, however, to countenance the ungoverned use of this information in any way that abridges the freedoms of the citizens of the United States of America.

The danger that this might be occurring makes it important that the investigative efforts of Senator Ervin be given wholehearted support by all of the branches of the federal government that are involved in the gathering of statistics pertaining to our private lives.

The Miami Herald

Miami, Fla., February 25, 1971

SEN. SAM J. Ervin Jr. has taken on the formidable task of taming the computer. He would throw a saddle over it and keep man in charge — if he can.

Trouble is, the computer can think faster, remember more and spit it out in more orderly fashion than man can. So he is outmatched from the start, and that is what worries the senator from North Carolina.

Neither the man putting information into the computer nor the man receiving the computations fully comprehends what the machine has done. Thus awed, he therefore tends to accept and act on its testimony on blind faith.

That puts in motion some rather terrible propects.

First, there is the matter of simple error and malice. Thus fed, the computer thus issues — within a magnificent web of fact. The difference is that when error and malice come out of the mouth of a computer it takes on the aura of 1984 holy writ.

Then, there is the man who receives these cowing analyses and projections and summations out of that blinking, whirring machine. He, too, is subject to error and malice and this frailty again is magnified by the authority of the computer.

And, finally, because the computer so outstrips the human mind, a man or his issue gets no individual judgment. Human factors do not compute.

As one witness before Sen. Ervin's subcommittee testified, man now leaves "electronic tracks" of which he often is not aware. Enter Big Brother.

The effect of it all is an immense pressure to conform. When a man does not, he leaves electronic tracks. The data are fed, computed: he is a non-conformer, stamped and certified and ready to be acted upon. He is not like everybody else; he is different; he doesn't go along. Add an error; add a distorted judgment.

The pluralistic society feels a gravity pull to be singular. As someone once said, there must be order on the anthill. But must it be achieved through lockstep?

Sen. Ervin does not think so, and we applaud his efforts to explore the dangers and prove his point.

The Boston Globe

Boston, Mass., February 22, 1971

The right of the people to be secure in their persons, houses, papers, and effects, against unreasonable searches and seizures, shall not be violated, and no warrants shall issue, but upon probable cause, supported by oath or affirmation, and particularly describing the place to be searched, and the person or things to be seized.

—Art. IV of the Bill of Rights, US Constitution.

How far this nation has come along the road that George Orwell predicted in "1984," with Big Brother watching and listening, will presumably be described in some detail starting tomorrow when the Senate subcommittee on Constitutional Rights, headed by Sen. Sam J. Erwin (D-N.C.), begins hearings on the question of whether the military and other Federal agencies have violated individual rights in computerizing unevaluated information about American citizens.

But even before the hearings, it is already clear enough, to judge from last-minute moves by the Pentagon, that their results are both expected and feared by the nation's snoopers.

In a move intended to be reassuring but which is hardly that, Secretary of Defense Melvin Laird on Feb. 19 announced that henceforth a high-level, civilian-dominated board would control investigations in this country by military intelligence operatives. For the last several years the armed services have conducted such activities independently.

Last December, when Sec. Laird ordered a review of the matter, he had said that all intelligence gathering by the military should be directly under civilian control. His Feb. 19 announcement still leaves the Joint Chiefs of Staff directly in charge of foreign intelligence, and competing in that field with other agencies, including the Central Intelligence Agency.

That announcement was accompanied by admissions from the Pentagon that the military has at times been overzealous in its domestic spying and "overreacted," and that another "culprit was that civilian officials ordered the military in." This came from Robert F. Froelke, an Assistant Secretary of Defense, who will head the new control board.

The new development should fool no one. Technically, but only technically, the whole Pentagon has been under civilian control all along anyway, and it is hard to see how another board will change things. The Army as well as other Federal agencies will still be spying on civilians in this country.

Nor is this the only threat to the basic freedom of Americans. The American Bar Assn. departed so far from its fine traditions at its recent winter meetings in Chicago that it approved, to all intents and purposes, wiretapping and bugging in foreign intelligence cases even without a court warrant. And the ABA ignored completely US Atty. Gen. John Mitchell's current proposal, filed recently with two US Appellate Courts, to allow electronic eavesdropping, without any form of warrant or disclosure, when ever the Executive Branch deems there is a threat to the national security.

Why this departure from the judicial process? Why is it necessary to eavesdrop without even telling a judge the reason for it and getting a warrant?

Such warrants or court orders are authorized specifically under the Omnibus Crime Control and Safe Streets Act of 1968. Time and again the US Supreme Court has ruled that such snooping requires prior judicial approval. To snoop without it is to give the Executive the very power that has made Communist dictatorships anathema to every lover of freedom.

We wish Sen. Ervin's committee hearings good hunting.

San Francisco Chronicle

San Francisco, Calif., February 25, 1971

NOTHING COULD BE MORE IMPORTANT for the future pursuit of happiness by the citizens of this country than Senator Sam J. Ervin Jr.'s hearings on the threat to privacy and individual civil rights which is found in Government dossiers and computer data banks.

The North Carolina Senator's inquiry began Tuesday and will run on for nine days. Already the shocking outlines and implications of this vast "dossier dictatorship," as one witness called it, are clearly visible.

For example, the hearing opened with the melancholy revelation that the private life of the average American is the subject of 10 to 20 dossiers in the files of government and private agencies. It continued with the observation that everywhere a person goes, he leaves electronic tracks: each time he files a tax return, applies for life insurance or a credit card, seeks Government benefits, or interviews for a job, a profile of him begins to take shape.

ONCE ALL THESE DETAILS have gone into a computer, from which they are recallable at the pressing of a button, the free-born American becomes a quantifiable statistic, the helpless prey of malignant Government snoopers and witchburners with his privacy assaulted and his thoughts as well as his acts subject to intimidation.

The story that Senator Ervin is developing is not entirely new, of course. Last December he had caught the Army out in an election-time spying operation that involved the military in gathering "intelligence" on Adlai E. Stevenson III, now a Senator; on Governor Otto Kerner, on Representative Abner Mikva (Dem-Ill.) and on 800 other Illinoisans, not all of them young, long-haired or rebellious.

Yesterday Representative Mikva expressed his shock and outrage over this performance by the military, and he denounced the officers responsible for it as "true subversives of our society."

THAT'S JUST WHAT THEY ARE, for as one witness eloquently testified: "The tone of spontaneity of spirit which characterizes a free society cannot survive in an atmosphere where all deviation from the norm are immediately noted by the state and stored for future reference."

Much more will be heard from the Ervin tribunal, but as a starter, we like the suggestion for an Act of Congress that would guarantee the citizen an opportunity at least to review any files kept on him and to challenge and dispute errors in them and set the record right.

ERVIN PANEL'S HEARINGS CONTINUE; ADMINISTRATION CRITICIZES LIMITS

Assistant Attorney General William Rehnquist told a Senate subcommittee March 9 that the Nixon Administration would oppose legislation that would hamper the government's domestic intelligence gathering activity. He said, "Self-discipline on the part of the executive branch will provide an answer to virtually all of the legitimate complaints against excesses of information gathering." Rehnquist's testimony came during the hearings on government surveillance and information gathering which Sen. Sam Ervin of North Carolina has been holding since December 1970.

Sen. Birch Bayh (D, Ind.) had introduced a bill Feb. 25 that would compel government agencies to inform citizens of files kept on them and allow subjects of such files to correct information in them. Similar legislation had been introduced in the House by Rep. Edward I. Koch (D, N.Y.).

Detroit Free Press

Detroit, Mich., March 14, 1971

THE GLIB assistant attorney general who testified last Tuesday on government data banks may have revealed more than he intended about the world as seen through the eyes of the Justice Department.

William H. Rehnquist told the Senate subcommittee on constitutional rights that surveillance of civilians is an "extraordinarily important function of the federal government," and does not invade private rights. Though people frequently complain that others are intimidated by surveillance, he argued, they never seem to feel the need of complaining for themselves.

Rehnquist insisted that "self-discipline on the part of the executive branch" would be a sufficient safeguard against abuses. And he promised that the Justice Department would "vigorously oppose any legislation" that might mpar the government's ability to gather information on citizens.

It seems fair to guess that people seldom complain about being watched because most have no way of knowing whether they are among the millions now recorded in government files. Any who might wish to complain, moreover, have no way of doing so with effect. Established procedures offer no means of reviewing the contents of government data banks, no means of purging erroneous or unauthorized information—no guarantee, in fact, that the very act of complaint will not earn the protestor a place in someone's file on malcontents.

Rehnquist's paean to "self-discipline" likewise affronts common sense. The very reason for the Senate hearings is that the federal bureaucracy has shown neither the will nor the ability to restrain itself in data-gathering.

And even by the bureaucracy's own standards, abuses and improper leaks have been impossible to prevent. Rehnquist himself conceded the essential truth of allegations that leaked FBI files fueled Look magazine's charges of links between the Mafia and San Francisco Mayor Joseph Alioto.

Indeed, it now is said that Time-Life Inc. possesses an entire file cabinet of FBI documents. Reportedly the Justice Department has written to ask if Time-Life does have such files and, if so, to plead for their return.

Taken together, Rehnquist's assertions paint a telling picture. Justice Department spokesmen are claiming an ever broader right to peek on citizens not only as an aid in prosecuting crime, but as a means of preventing it. They hold that the citizen has no paramount right to the dignity of a private life, and that the Congress is not entitled to affirm that right for him.

Fortunately, there are others in government who do not believe that this view can be squared with any rudimentary understanding of constitutional and statue law. We can imagine no better way of settling the issue than for Congress to accept Rehnquist's challenge, and begin drawing stern legislation.

WORCESTER TELEGRAM.

Worcester, Mass., March 11, 1971

Few responsible Americans would disagree that keeping records on the activities of certain individuals is necessary to protect society and our institutions.

It is the degree and extent of that surveillance that has generated concern in Congress and the general public.

Current hearings by Sen. Sam Ervin's Subcommittee on Constitutional Rights revealed that government data banks keep detailed, computerized files on a vast number of citizens who have not violated any laws. In addition to the Federal Bureau of Investigation and the Secret Service, federal bodies with extensive dossier systems include the Departments of State; Health, Education and Welfare; Transportation; Housing and Urban Development; Justice and Defense — not to mention the Census Bureau, Civil Service Commission and the Internal Revenue Service. The practice by Army intelligence of spying on the activities of politicians and private individuals has also been discovered recently.

The Justice Department served notice that it "will vigorously oppose any legislation" to curtail the government's ability to gather information about American citizens. The department claims that "self-discipline" by the executive branch is sufficient to weed out "isolated imperfections" in the data-gathering process.

Some members of Congress, including Sen. Charles Mathias Jr., a Maryland Republican, believe that "we need far more reliable and consistent controls" and that "it is not only proper but essential for Congress to enact controls" over the criminal data systems maintained by federal agencies. Earlier, Sen. Ervin warned that unless computerized snooping is curtailed, "some day we may well discover that the machines stand above the laws."

That may be overstating the case. Some concern, however, is understandable.

In our highly sophisticated electronic age, computers can "interface" — talk to each other — thus making information gathered by one agency for one specific purpose available to all other federal bodies. The unthinking computers are unable to change their "picture" of a person even if the individual changes. For example, the Bureau of Narcotics and Dangerous Drugs maintains computerized files on more than 64,000 persons, including three boys under three years old. Will those three be pursued for life due by the tragedy that exposed them to drugs before they were able to go to school?

Congress has the responsibility to review and, if necessary, tighten the procedures before the Big Brother syndrome gets out of hand.

THE MILWAUKEE JOURNAL

Milwaukee, Wis., March 12, 1971

The Nixon administration opposes any legislative restraint on its ability to snoop on Americans on the ground that "self-discipline on the part of the executive branch" will protect against excess. This assumption not only is naive and dangerous but flies in the face of history.

One need only look at the Alien and Sedition Acts of 1798, the Espionage and Sedition Acts of 1917 and 1918, the red baiting campaign of Atty. Gen. A. Mitchell Palmer after World War I and the witch hunts of Wisconsin's own Joe McCarthy in the '50s to wonder where self-discipline disappeared to. In periods of passion it is nonexistent.

Spying—gathering information is the government's "nice" term for it — is an invasion of privacy and of the basic rights of American citizens. Surveillance capabilities with today's electronic gadgetry are awesome and indiscriminate. There should be more than governmental promises to protect the individual. If the founding fathers believed in self-discipline there would have been no need for the Bill of Rights.

Richmond Times-Dispatch

Richmond, Va., March 15, 1971

A distressingly simplistic and short-sighted attitude toward the potential abuse by the federal bureaucracy of its enormous power to collect, store, and disseminate information about private citizens was displayed last week by a Justice Department official.

Appearing before the Senate Judiciary Subcommittee on Constitutional Rights headed by Sen. Sam J. Ervin Jr. (D-N.C.), Assistant Attorney General William H. Rehnquist put the department on record in opposition to legislative restraints on the government's freedom to monitor the lives of its subjects. "Self-discipline on the part of the executive branch," he said, will prevent "virtually all" excesses.

Posh! Are we to believe that the 113th Military Intelligence Group exercised self-restraint when, according to testimony that has not been disproved, it spied in the Chicago area on state and local officials, political contributors, lawyers, clergymen, newspaper reporters — everyone, in fact, from liberal Sen. Adlai E. Stevenson III to Father Francis Lawlor, a Catholic priest who opposes forced integration of Chicago's schools?

Too many disquieting signs exist of an uncoordinated burgeoning of the governmental record-keeping function, made all the more pervasive by computerization, to be lulled into apathy by cooing sounds from the Justice Department. While Mr. Rehnquist would have us sleep, Sen. Charles McC. Mathias (R-Md.) warns that the officialdom is "hurtling" in the direction of a single, nationwide, federal-state-local system for collecting and transmitting personal histories. The interface of machines already makes this feasible. Are citizens to have any say-so in this development? What are the implications? Consider one: The Bureau of Narcotics and Dangerous Drugs, Mathias reports, has a computerized drug users' file of 64,000 individuals, including three boys under *three years old!* Are these boys forever to be stigmatized by something that happened to them almost before they were old enough to say "mama?"

A certain amount of governmental surveillance for the public safety and welfare makes sense. Wiretapping, for example, can nail elusive criminals and upset subversive schemes. But there are legislative restraints on wiretaps. Law enforcers are required by a 1968 law to obtain a court warrant before tapping a wire, except where national security is involved. By contrast, there are no restrictions on the keeping of dossiers or computerized files — and the exchanging of same for whatever high purpose may be claimed. An individual's right to privacy does not currently permit him to see or correct any malicious or untrue statements on his personal histories.

Don't worry, Mr. Rehnquist says, just trust Big Brother. We'd rather trust the constitutional-democratic system, thanks, and we hope his is not the final word from the Nixon Administration.

The Washington Post

Washington, D.C., March 12, 1971

We thought we had heard about the ultimate in official snooping when Attorney General Mitchell proclaimed that the Executive Branch has an unlimited right to eavesdrop on anyone it considers a threat to national security. But now Assistant Attorney General Rehnquist has outdone him. Appearing before the Ervin subcommittee the other day, Mr. Rehnquist said the Executive Branch has and must continue to have the right to collect and store data on the affairs of any citizen so long as those affairs are relevant to a subject in which the federal government has a legitimate interest.

Mr. Rehnquist, of course, didn't quite put his position so starkly. He talked first of the Executive Branch's right to investigate, resting that right on the constitutional responsibility of the President to enforce the law and on the promise to the states in the Constitution that the federal government will assure that they continue to have a republican form of government and will help them put down domestic violence if need be. Then he talked about the federal government's role in preventing as well as prosecuting violations of the law. And he concluded by arguing that this vital investigative function must remain unimpaired although it could be confined to matters in which the government has a legitimate interest. He also conceded that some restrictions might properly be placed on the way the government handles and makes public what its files contain.

When you examine this position, the question that leaps to mind is what—if any—subjects the government may be said not to have a legitimate interest in. It has a legitimate interest in every penny of your income and, maybe, of your spending; the income tax law touches directly on income and tax evasion cases are sometimes based on showing that the taxpayer spent more than he reported receiving. The government contends it has a legitimate interest in the political views of citizens; the loyalty-security program is deeply concerned about those views and so, apparently, are those government officials who worry about protecting the states against domestic violence. That takes care of the fiscal and political affairs of every citizen. Now for the family and social affairs. Some of these matters are considered relevant in security investigations and others are considered relevant to such things as the sentencing of persons convicted of crime or the granting of welfare and social security benefits.

When you add up these interests and apply to them Mr. Rehnquist's argument, it appears that the government has a right to investigate, and collect and store data on, just about everything you do, except, perhaps, your religious affairs. As Senator Mathias points out elsewhere on this page, such an approach to the investigatory function of government raises fantastic possibilities. That is particularly true since Mr. Rehnquist was not merely talking about information the government acquires after it suspects a person of wrongdoing: he was also talking about information collected by the government in its effort to prevent violations of law. How many people have led such perfect lives that they would be willing to have them immortalized inside a government computer?

There is no doubt that the tools of modern technology can be a great aid to the government in its fight against crime. Computers and data storage banks may be able to produce many of the linkages —particularly in the area of organized crime—that old-fashioned methods of intelligence gathering cannot. But it simply cannot be that the government has a right to rummage around in the affairs of any citizen as it chooses, whether or not it has cause to suspect him of committing crime. That, it is worth remembering, was the nightmare in the telescreen of which George Orwell wrote in 1984:

> There was of course no way of knowing whether you were being watched at any given moment. How often, or on what system, the Thought Police plugged in on any individual wire was guesswork. It was even conceivable that they watched everybody all the time . . . You had to live—did live, from habit that became instinct—on the assumption that every sound you made was overheard, and, except in darkness, every moment scrutinized.

The alleged power of government to collect and store data on anyone's affairs, anytime it wants to, is not *that* far from the telescreen.

ST. LOUIS POST-DISPATCH
St. Louis, Mo., March 19, 1971

Assistant Attorney General William H. Rehnquist has been the selected defender of the Government's powers of domestic surveillance, in hearings before the Ervin Subcommittee on Constitutional Rights. While Mr. Rehnquist says the Administration might accept some congressional restrictions on spying and data-gathering, his whole case is for untrammeled government liberty to pry into the people's liberties.

Mr. Rehnquist s u g g e s t s that government should be able to investigate and collect information on anything in which government has a "legitimate interest." As an editorial in today's Mirror of Public Opinion says, this could touch anything; personal income, spending, family relations, welfare needs and, of course, politics. Indeed, Mr. Rehnquist defended surveillance of political protesters, saying this does not violate constitutional rights.

The question is, of course, what kind of government and what kind of nation the people want. Have we come so far in 1971 that the people are ready to accept a government that can investigate them on anything at any time, a government that is public master instead of public servant? We do not think so, and we do not think the people will accept the Rehnquist idea that "self-discipline on the part of the Executive branch will provide an answer to virtually all legitimate complaints." What is clearly needed is congressional law protecting the people from excesses.

The New York Times
New York, N.Y. March 12, 1971

American democracy rests on faith in government by laws, and not by men. From time to time, arrogant or frightened men have deviated from that principle, in the mistaken belief that only their wisdom could keep the nation protected from its enemies.

An occasional Attorney General, though appointed as guardian of the law, has sometimes succumbed to that dangerous and foolish temptation. But rarely has this un-American ideology been more crassly propounded than when Assistant Attorney General William H. Rehnquist, defending the Government's growing domestic intelligence operations, said: "Self-discipline on the part of the executive branch will provide an answer to virtually all of the legitimate complaints against excesses of information gathering."

Mr. Rehnquist's statement that he would "vigorously oppose" any legislation that might limit the Government's ability to gather information on the activities of American citizens places a special responsibility on Congress and the courts to prevent the Justice Department from arrogating to itself powers which pose a threat to the privacy and freedom of every American. Mr. Rehnquist expressed the Justice Department's opposition to "opening the door to unnecessary and unmanageable judicial supervision" of domestic intelligence. This view bespeaks a low opinion of the courts' capacity and functions; it also ignores the fact that, far from merely fighting against the opening of the door, Justice Department and Pentagon have already broken down that door, without knocking or court orders.

The Justice Department has been trying to pacify its critics by describing as minimal the excesses and abuses of its extra-legal activities. Even if this could be believed, it would in no way diminish the greater risk—the stifling of free speech through intimidation.

BUFFALO EVENING NEWS
Buffalo, N.Y., March 17, 1971

The U. S. Justice Department has unwisely decided to oppose any new federal legislation that would limit the government's present capacity to collect information about American citizens. An assistant attorney general, William Rehnquist, contends that "self-discipline on the part of the executive branch will provide an answer to virtually all of the legitimate complaints against excesses of information-gathering."

He should tell that to the Founding Fathers. Such a trusting notion would have been laughed out of the Constitutional Convention of 1787, which spent much of its time devising secure checks and balances against governmental tyranny. They didn't rely on future self-discipline. Thomas Jefferson wasn't at the convention, but his idea that "the natural progress of things is for liberty to yield and government to gain ground" definitely was.

Even more pointedly, the Bill of Rights, which came along three or four years later and shielded individual rights from government abuse, demonstrated a supreme distrust of "self-discipline" on the part of future national officials.

Congress, like the realists of 1787, can best guarantee "self-discipline" with precise legal curbs vigilantly enforced.

The Philadelphia Inquirer
Phiadelphia, Pa., March 6, 1971

If somebody can dial into a competitor's computer and steal information by telephone, as a California man has been charged with doing, how secure are those Federal data banks a Senate subcommittee is investigating?

That is another question for Senator Ervin and his colleagues to look into as they probe snoopery by the Army and others.

But some recent testimony before them suggests that technological trickery is not really necessary to get at the information the government is busily storing away.

San Francisco Mayor Joseph L. Alioto charges that six Federal agencies and two California police departments engaged in "wholesale disclosure of confidential government documents" to the two Look Magazine writers who, in an article in September 1969, accused him of having Mafia connections.

"The government," Alioto told the Senate Subcommittee on Constitutional Rights, "has not only a big ear but a big mouth as well."

Anyone who doubts that should recall the recklessness with which the House Internal Security Committee (formerly the House Un-American Activities Committee) has leaked or openly distributed rumors, accusations, innuendoes and gossip from its voluminous files.

Nor is it any great comfort when Assistant Attorney General William H. Rehnquist denies that the Look authors got an official peek but admits that an FBI agent confirmed their information and was cashiered for doing so.

The snoopery invites more snoopery, and the files invite disclosure, officially or unofficially.

★ ★ ★

The other day a Defense Department official testified that the Army keeps 7,138,181 personality dossiers on aliens, employes and ex-employes of industrial security contractors, members and ex-members of the Armed Services and persons "considered to constitute a threat to security and defense."

Other witnesses have testified to the vast congeries of files which sundry Federal agencies are methodically building up on American citizens—and not just Federal but state and local agencies have gotten into the act as well.

As Prof. Arthur Miller of the Michigan Law School declared, "Americans are scrutinized, measured, watched, counted and interrogated by more government agencies, law-enforcement officials, social scientists, and poll-takers than at any time in our history."

★ ★ ★

The Justice Department's position, as stated by Mr. Rehnquist to the Ervin subcommittee, is that "self-discipline on the part of the Executive Branch will provide an answer to virtually all of the legitimate complaints against excesses of information gathering."

The men who wrote the charter of our liberties took a more skeptical view of executive "self-discipline," which is another way of saying unrestrained executive power.

That is why they wrote a Constitution with a Bill of Rights to go with it, with specific prohibitions on what the government could do and a system of checks and balances to sustain our liberties.

Freedom of speech and of the press, the right to assemble peaceably and to petition the government for a redress of grievances, "the right of the people to be secure in their persons, houses, papers, and effects, against unreasonable searches and seizures"—none of these are safe if we must rely upon the "self-discipline" of a government which has amply demonstrated itself to be without it.

Mr. Rehnquist informs the subcommittee that the Justice Department "will vigorously oppose any legislation which, whether by opening the door to unnecessary and unmanageable judicial supervision of such activities or otherwise, would effectively impair this extraordinarily important function of the Federal Government."

Exactly. It is the judiciary which imposes discipline upon the Executive Branch and upon Congress as well and places restraints upon those who, in the name of national security, would surrender individual liberty. The men in charge of the Justice Department may mean well, but as Justice Brandeis observed, "The greatest dangers to liberty lurk in insidious encroachment by men of zeal, well-meaning but without understanding."

Portland, Ore., March 23, 1971

The most disturbing thing turned up by Sen. Sam Ervin's investigation into bureaucratic snooping is that there seems to be so little sense of propriety about what is the government's business and what isn't.

As the people's instrument, the government unquestionably needs to have considerable information about people, just for sound planning if nothing else.

Secretary of Health, Education and Welfare Elliott L. Richardson observed correctly, "A balance must be struck between society's need for information and the individual's right of privacy."

But then Richardson went on to defend widespread public and private use (misuse, according to Ervin) of Social Security numbers by declaring there is no law against it.

It is that attitude that is bothersome. The bureaucratic assumption seems to be that, if a specific kind of federal snooping is not illegal, then it is okay.

The Social Security matter is but a minor item in the North Carolina senator's investigation of governmental meddling into private lives of American citizens. Other cases of outright spying where there is no apparent justification are worse.

But the point is that the very balance to which Secretary Richardson referred seems to be missing. At least it has been inconspicuous among the various functionaries who have appeared before Ervin's Constitutional Rights subcommittee so far.

The cold, machine-like approach that seems to view the people of a country as so many numbered automatons is the picture that is emerging from the subcommittee hearings.

Of course there needs to be a balance. Some information is vital to plan for the needs of people. Intelligence is needed to guard against violence.

But the individual is still the basic strength of the country and his privacy needs to be considered, too. The balance can hardly be written into law. It depends on the judgment of officials given the governmental responsibility. If that judgment becomes a matter of how much they can get away with, within the law, then there is no balance.

Perhaps Sen. Ervin can get the point across. If so, his investigation will have been well worthwhile.

The Salt Lake Tribune

Salt Lake City, Utah, March 22, 1971

Hearings of the Senate subcommittee on constitutional rights have documented a growing threat to individual freedom. The hearings suggested that the government, armed with computers and increasingly security minded, is in no mood to reverse the dossier-oriented drift.

The Constitution is not clear on some major issues raised. This was brought out when Assistant Attorney General William H. Rehnquist told committee Chairman Sen. Sam J. Ervin, D-N.C., that the government could put any citizen, even a senator, under surveillance without violating his constitutional rights.

It was noted that citizens who feel their privacy or freedom of association have been curtailed by government surveillance can appeal to the courts for relief. That they can, but the process is lengthy, it is expensive and may subject the appellant to publicity and even personal abuse he is not willing to bear.

Mr. Rehnquist, in an earlier appearance before the committee, said government "self restraint" was sufficient to prevent abuse. In light of recent incidents that demonstrated lack of self restraint, that suggestion evoked more derision than delight.

Laws placing strict curbs on collection and use of data appear to be the solution presently favored. But "passing a law" is only part of the process. Enforcing that law is more important and enforcement would be entrusted to some of the same agencies whose eager surveillance activities have brought on the current complaints. The Department of Justice, for instance, has adamantly opposed legislation and insisted that its own data gathering must be exempt from such laws in any event.

When Mr. Rehnquist first proposed self-restraint as the best answer, we questioned his judgment. We observed then that government efforts in that direction would be enhanced by enactment of legal restrictions. In view of apparent reluctance of enforcement agencies to submit to new legal curbs, we are moved to reconsider. Self restraint may not be the best way to prevent abuse, but it could prove to be the only way.

The Kansas City Times

Kansas City, Mo., March 18, 1971

"Is your neighbor married, divorced or something? Are the children little devils? Does the family fight loudly? Any drunks? Strange guests? How about it now, maybe there is something a little funny about those people next door. Maybe?"

These are the questions people sometimes get nowadays from investigators checking out a routine insurance application. Questions that come from the government about somebody who is thinking about serving the country through the Peace corps or Vista may be a little more circumspect. But the process is pretty much the same. The central impression is that the applicant for insurance or public service is guilty until his neighbors are willing to prove him innocent and even then, who is really sure. You can't trust anybody these days, least of all somebody who wants to buy insurance or join the Peace corps.

The federal government recently has given nefarious activity of this type a boost by engaging in it at unprecedented lengths. The Army which is—don't forget—a part of the federal government, has said that it will spy on civilians no more. But once started, the habit is hard to stop.

The Federal Bureau of Investigation has decided that special precautions are needed to make certain that a national crime information system would respect privacy. The word—by no means official—is that a network of intelligence on criminal data, computerized and available to all law enforcement agencies, would be limited to material that is a matter of public record and would contain no confidential or unverified reports. Moreover, right of access would be guaranteed to anyone who has a record in the files. If this is so, the FBI is showing a proper concern for the rights of citizens.

The same guarantees should be extended to individuals whose names are in the files of credit rating bureaus and companies that extend and withdraw credit cards.

It is the ordinary citizen who pays for the existence of insurance companies, credit-card operations and, of course, the military, the FBI and any other governmental department. The taxpayer is not sending his dollars to Washington to be used against him in a surveillance plot as if he were a foreign power. And while credit checking may be a part of the cost of doing business, it is not the sort of thing that needs to be extended beyond whether an individual can pay his bills.

Both government and industry sometimes seem to fall for the Keystone Kop mentality that is willing to fill dossiers with nonsense at a high price, paid for by the taxpayer or consumer who is being investigated. If extreme abuses become the norm, a strong reaction by the besieged taxpayer-consumer will be in order.

HERALD EXAMINER

Los Angeles, Calif., March 26, 1971

Sen. Sam Ervin's subcommittee on constitutional rights has completed several weeks of hearings on governmental infringement of the personal privacy rights of American citizens.

Testimony presented before the committee indicates that many government agencies, and the Army also, are involved in calculated data processing of information about individuals without their explicit consent.

Legislation is presently being drafted by the subcommittee staff to put congressional curbs on federal data banks. Hopefully they will be enacted swiftly.

Restraint in the government's use of computerized collections of information about the private lives of individual citizens should be guaranteed by law.

Every citizen has the right to know what is written or alleged about him in government files and to have the power to refute inaccuracies and rebut false testimony.

FBI, USDA DATA BANK PROPOSALS SCORED BY CONGRESS, LEAA, GAO

Separate proposals by the Federal Bureau of Investigation and the Department of Agriculture (USDA) to expand their computer information systems were criticized as unnecessary and dangerous by members of Congress and agencies within the executive branch, it was reported June 4.

The FBI's proposal to establish a computerized criminal-history system linking up police department records across the nation came under fire in a report by the Law Enforcement Assistance Administration, the Justice Department agency disbursing federal crime-fighting grants to state and local governments. The LEAA report, which voiced support for the principle of computerized criminal histories, questioned the advisibility of centralizing such information under federal control. The bureau's proposal, the LEAA report said, raised concern over "(a) the development of the Big Brother system; (b) reduced state input and control over security, confidentiality and use of state-originated data and (c) increased dangers resulting from the use of non-updated, and hence, inaccurate, centrally maintained 'rap sheets.'"

A General Accounting Office study, requested and made public by Rep. John E. Moss, recommended that the Agriculture Department be prohibited from going ahead with its eight-year, $398 million plan to centralize department records. Asserting that USDA officials had begun acquisition of a new computer system before accurately determining their needs, the GAO report said that Congress should be concerned that it had not been fully informed of the plans for the project and because the USDA's computer bank "could pose a serious threat to the privacy of individuals, particularly since such a network might be expanded to link all government computers."

THE ROANOKE TIMES
Roanoke, Va., June 17, 1975

Revelations by Atty. Gen. Edward Levi about the FBI's secret-police activities under J. Edgar Hoover indicate that he intends to keep the bureau out of many areas where it has previously infringed on civil liberties. But it seems he has made no decision about the FBI's proposed expansion of computerized communications and record-keeping.

The Law Enforcement Assistance Administration (LEAA)—which, like the FBI, comes under Mr. Levi's direction in the Justice Department—has denounced the FBI plan. LEAA says such a system could lead to federal control of police around the country, a criticism also made by the White House Office of Telecommunications Policy, the Domestic Council's committee on privacy, and chairmen of both the House and Senate Constitutional Rights subcommittees.

LEAA's report said that the FBI's proposal raises concerns over "(a) the development of the 'Big Brother' system; (b) reduced state input and control over security, confidentiality and use of state-originated data and (c) increased dangers resulting from use of non-updated, and hence inaccurate, centrally maintained 'rap sheets'."

What the FBI wants is to acquire equipment that would automatically switch local police messages through the bureau's existing information center. To the LEAA and others, this looks like an end run around present arrangements controlled by the states in the National Law Enforcement Telecommunications System.

The FBI is said to be pushing hard for this change. In a way, this is understandable; modern technology should be put to use in combatting crime, and instant communications along with quick data retrieval have many potential advantages. But it could be a big mistake to plug a federal law enforcement agency into local police messages, enabling the FBI to store mountains of data in computerized systems that know all and understand nothing.

As Attorney General, Mr. Levi so far has shown a commendable concern for civil liberties; his sole lapse seems to have been in embracing a search-without-warrant policy in supposed espionage cases. One hopes that he will advert again to the Bill of Rights and step hard on this latest FBI foray.

The Houston Post
Houston, Tex., June 18, 1975

Despite opposition from other federal agencies, the FBI is pressing for approval of a plan that would enable it to monitor exchanges of information between local and state law enforcement agencies and keep computerized records of them. The bureau's proposal to expand its communications and record-keeping role would require the addition of equipment that would automatically switch messages between various police agencies through its National Crime Information Center. The center now transmits information and requests for information from police departments in one part of the country to those in another part.

Critics of the FBI plan complain that the message-switching capacity would give the bureau the ability to surreptitiously gather intelligence. A report by the Law Enforcement Assistance Administration, which, like the FBI, is an arm of the Justice Department, raises the possibility that the proposed computerized system could lead to federal control of police agencies.

Opposition to the proposal has also been registered by the White House Office of Telecommunications Policy, the Domestic Council's Committee on Privacy and the chairmen of the House and Senate constitutional rights subcommittees. The LEAA report outlines some of the plan's potential dangers—abuse of the confidentiality of information produced by state and local police departments, the use of "rap sheets" that had not been updated and contained inaccurate information, a reduction of the amount of data supplied by local law enforcement agencies, and the possibility of creeping federal big brotherism.

Once stored in a government computer, information, however erroneous, is hard to correct or eradicate. A Defense Department spokesman recently told a House subcommittee that material gathered by Army intelligence agents on Vietnam war protesters and other dissidents may still be in the files of other federal intelligence agencies with which the Defense Department exchanged information.

Regrettably, the FBI's record for respecting individuals' rights of privacy is not unblemished, as revelations of the past few years clearly show. But even if it were, the bureau should not have the authority it is seeking in its message-switching plan without strong safeguards against misuse of the information.

St. Petersburg Times

St. Petersburg, Fla., June 9, 1975

If you ever were nabbed for robbing a bank, stealing a car or striking an officer, your name is in a computer. Your name also is in a computer if you joined the Army, subscribed to a magazine, bought a car, charged a dress, paid taxes, flew to Europe or applied for insurance.

And in most cases a lot of information about you goes right in there with your name. Let's face it. This is the computer era.

Without computers to keep track of bank robbers, car thieves, cop sluggers, veterans, readers, drivers, shoppers, taxpayers, passport applicants and policy holders — in other words, everybody — neither government nor business any longer could stay abreast of its work.

For a people raised on the notion of individual privacy, this can get to be a worrisome thing. It is especially worrisome when the various compu-

ters with their various lists and their various tidbits of intelligence start learning to talk to each other. And if ever they're all fully linked, Uncle Sam will be known as Big Brother.

TO MAKE SURE that doesn't happen, Congress last year passed, and President Ford signed, a "privacy act" putting definite limits on what uses the government can make of computerized files. But despite the new law, many congressmen again are concerned at the whirring of the official list-keepers, especially those operated by the FBI and other agencies dealing with security matters.

The computer's memory bank is a marvel. And it can dredge up on command all it knows. It knows everything humans put in it. These things sometimes are untrue, half true, or wrong. Everybody has had his own battle with a fouled-up computer.

That can be ludicrous when it involves a mixed-up mailing address. It can be frustrating when it involves a bad credit rating based on rumor or misinformation. It can be tragic when it involves an erroneous or cleared criminal charge.

No wonder a House subcommittee is worried about the FBI's latest computer proposal. This is to tie its electronic list-keepers and data retrievers directly to those of state and local police agencies.

An interstate police link of this kind already exists, under control of the states. The FBI, members were told, wants to route this police data flow through an "automated switching system" that it would control.

Looking into these electronic marvels, the subcommittee turned up a fresh piece of evidence in support of

its new concern about computer abuses.

Members recalled the flap that arose in 1970 when it was disclosed that Army Intelligence illegally had spied on war protesters and other suspected civilians. The Defense Department at that time ordered the destruction of lists and files that grew out of this. The lawmakers inquired if those records had in fact been destroyed.

A defense official said most of them had. But was it true, members asked, that copies of all the destroyed dossiers had been fed into computers of other agencies, like the FBI, and thus were still in existence?

The official said he was "relatively certain" that was the case.

SO IF YOU thought 1984 was at least nine years away, maybe you've been kidding yourself.

The San Diego Union

San Diego, Calif., June 9, 1975

Science fiction writers have spun tales about a future in which computers take control of the world. That's not quite what is happening in the current quandary about the use of computerized data banks by the federal government, but we detect at least a drift in that direction.

Computers do not have to think for us in order to influence our thinking. It is now possible for computer systems to store data about every man, woman and child in America and to spew it out on command. We suspect that it is because this capability exists, and not because such a capability is desirable, that some people in government are finding reasons to create huge federalized data banks.

That computers can increase efficiency in storing and retrieving information is unquestionable. The Federal Bureau of Investigation can see greater efficiency in law enforcement if there were a centralized Washington data bank containing the criminal history of everyone who has had a run-in with the law anywhere in America. The Department of Agriculture could eliminate a lot of paperwork by putting its files on individual farmers, including information on their income and financial position gathered in connection with crop and commodity programs, into a centralized computer system.

It would be easier to buy the argument that efficiency dictates these steps if there had been a visible impact on the size of government payrolls from the extensive use of computers and data processing systems already in the hands of public

agencies. The real issue, however, is more basic. It starts with the question of whether it is really necessary for the government to demand as much personal information about us as it does. And if we are going to submit to those interrogations that take place every time we fill out a government form, are government agencies justified in keeping this information in electronic banks where it is as easy to use it for questionable purposes as for any legitimate purpose?

The threat to individual privacy is so obvious that any federal agency that wants to create a nationwide data bank will have a hard time arguing that its potential for increased efficiency outweighs its potential for abuse.

We should not let computer technology interfere with our judgment about the value or significance of certain kinds of information. Because it is now much easier to store and retrieve personal data about Americans does not change the fact that there are limits to what a government needs to know about citizens in a free society, and much of what it does know deserves to be kept under lock and key. Some information deserves to be thrown away, a fact that escapes many custodians of data banks.

Privacy is inseparable from personal freedom. Our governmental Big Brother does not need even bigger files on us simply because technology is making it easier to keep them.

The Dispatch

Columbus, Ohio., June 10, 1975

THAT UBIQUITOUS and necessary tool of modern business and industry, the computer, can become a freedom-robbing monster, witness revelations about the federal government's use of it.

Recent testimony before a U.S. House subcommittee on government operations reveals how federal agencies can twist interpretation of statutes and continue practices which constituted law has banned.

THE HOUSE group was told by an undersecretary in the Defense Department that domestic military intelligence files, ordered destroyed in 1970, had not been expunged after all. Instead, the data had been transferred to a computer network, thus making that information available to myriad agencies at the touch of a computer recall button.

In addition, it has been revealed the federal government has developed technology which translates information from any computer, of whatever make, into a common language instantaneously.

IT IS CALLED the Interface Message Processor (IMP). Webster has another definition for imp — a small demon.

Millions upon millions of American citizens have all kinds of data about themselves in this massive computer brain storage arrangement.

Possible interlocks are the White House, National Security Council, Central Intelligence Agency, Federal Bureau of Investigation plus the Justice and Treasury Departments.

ABOUT the time the House subcommittee was hearing that domestic military intelligence material had been diverted to this network, two federal departments were revealed to be planning new computerized data banks containing millions of more names.

One, by the FBI, would link it with every police department in the country and enable the federal agency to monitor day-to-day operations of state and local law enforcement authorities.

The other, by the Department of Agriculture, would enable the Washington-based agency to keep personal information on this nation's farmers including incomes and financial positions.

NO AMERICAN can question the need for responsible agencies to be alert against subversive elements which would destroy the government.

However, a dossier society is not needed to either assure security or to maintain fundamental liberties. On the contrary, Washington's "IMP" well could be the thief of liberty.

The Dispatch has consistently maintained that not only is there need for balance in surveillance procedures, there must be eternal vigilance against establishing a watchman over whom there is no responsible watchman.

BACK IN 1928, a distinguished member of the Supreme Court of the United States sounded a pertinent warning. Justice Louis Brandeis declared:

"The makers of our Constitution conferred, as against the government, the right to be let alone. To protect that right, every unjustifiable intrusion by the government upon the privacy of the individual, whatever the means employed, must be deemed a violation of the Constitution."

We hold unequivocally with Mr. Justice Brandeis.

AUTHORITIES as far back as Sir William Blackstone say the greatest single safeguard to freedom has been the writ of habeas corpus.

With the development of such procedures as "IMP", the time may have come for American citizens to demand protection for their data being as well as their physical being. Perhaps we need a constitutional "writ of habeas data" so citizens could at least have the right to know what "IMP" knows about them and is bandying about from one federal bureau to another.

The unsuspecting and unprotected citizen is in danger.

BATTLING OVER SUBVERSION: CONGRESS VS. THE PRESIDENT

The Nixon Administration won the decisive battle in the see-saw war waged over a plan to give the Subversive Activities Control Board expanded powers. Under fire for some time, the board had had its investigative powers reduced by the Supreme Court to such an extent that its five members did little more than collect their $36,000 yearly salaries, according to board chairman John W. Mahan. But on July 2, President Nixon issued an executive order granting the SACB new authority to investigate protest groups and add to the list of subversive organizations maintained by the attorney general. The move was countered in the Senate July 19 when Sen. William Proxmire attached an amendment to an appropriations bill which would have eliminated the $450,000 authorization for the board altogether. It was defeated 40–47. Soon thereafter, however, the Senate endorsed an amendment by Sen. Sam J. Ervin Jr. prohibiting the use of any SACB funds to carry out Nixon's order. Ervin said that the executive order overstepped presidential authority and, more importantly, that it violated constitutional guarantees of free speech and free assembly. The Senate vote was 51–37.

When the appropriations bill went to the House, it was adopted 246–141 on July 27, but without the restrictive Ervin amendment. The bill was then sent back to the Senate conference committee, where it was decided to delete the Ervin amendment so that the major $4 billion appropriation legislation could be passed before Congress recessed. On August 3, the Senate passed the bill—with the $450,000 SACB grant intact—by two votes, 46–44.

The Philadelphia Inquirer
Philadelphia, Pa., July 22, 1971

Under the axiom that half a loaf is better than none, the Senate did well in rejecting an administration proposal to broaden the powers of the Subversive Activities Control Board.

Even better news would have been a whole loaf: doing away with that outmoded, discredited and inherently dangerous vestige of the age of the late Sen. Joseph McCarthy.

The SACB is taken seriously today by few people; its chairman, John W. Mahan, recently testified that there is not enough work around to keep him, the four other board members and their staff of 10 busy.

The total annual budget is $450,000. Board members are paid $36,000 a year. Their task is to investigate and publicly expose the activities of fewer than 300 subversive groups on a list which has remained unchanged since 1955. In addition, under present powers, the board can investigate Communist action groups controlled by the Soviet Union.

In an executive order issued on July 2, President Nixon sought to give the board very substantial new powers. The order and other legislative proposals would have allowed the SACB to hold hearings, under subpena and contempt sanctions, and to decide what new groups should be added to the attorney general's list of un-American organizations.

Membership in a listed group can be used to bar a person from federal employment. But since sources on the board itself say that some 80 percent of the organizations on the list are out of date, it is largely useless.

The July 2 directive sought to allow the SACB to "determine whether any organization is totalitarian, Fascist, Communist, or subversive." The standards set by the administration included groups which obstructed, or advocated obstruction of, such things as "the recruiting and enlistment service of the United States," and organizations connected with damage to property or with civil disorders.

The dangers inherent in these proposals are obvious. With the awesome powers of subpena and contempt, the board could have unleashed public witch hunts involving almost anyone in the country who took exception to administration policy or engaged in a protest demonstration.

This threat was dealt a heavy blow by the Senate, in voting 51 to 37 to prohibit the board from carrying out Mr. Nixon's directive. But, by a preceding vote of 47 to 40, the Senate failed to kill it outright. Attorney General John Mitchell has given every indication that the matter will be pressed further by the administration, and the Senate action still faces the test of conference committee approval.

In a time when increasing numbers of Americans are feeling the hot breath of arbitrary government power, this country does not need a nostalgic return to the worst devices of the repressive and anti-democratic McCarthy era.

The Charleston Gazette
Charleston, W.Va.
July 21, 1971

The United States Senate has exercised its wisdom by increasing the allocation of money to the Subversive Activities Control Board and then making certain the Subversive Activities Control Board continues to have nothing to do.

Senators, including West Virginia's Byrd and Randolph, voted against an amendment which would have stricken from an appropriations bill the $450,000 already approved by the House for the board.

Then they adopted Sen. Sam J. Ervin's amendment to bar the board from using the money to carry out an executive order issued by President Nixon. The President, perhaps embarrassed by the fact that board members do nothing to earn their salaries of $36,000 a year, had proposed some modest duties for them.

Since its conception, the board hasn't turned up a single subversive activity or exposed a single subversive person. Some early forays against communism, in the form of restrictions and penalties, ran afoul of a Constitution which stubbornly persists in providing equal protection to all citizens.

In recent months, board members have filled in the time by lobbying Congress for action which would insure the continuation of the board and its $36,000-a-year salaries. Specifically, they lobbied for approval of the President's proposal that they be charged with identifying and listing organizations that seek the violent overthrow of the government or which violently interfere with the rights of others.

The Constitution has no greater defender than North Carolina's Sen. Ervin, who immediately perceived the danger inherent in such a proposition. Sen. Ervin said quite properly that such activity on the part of the board wouldn't only constitute usurpation of legislative power but also would infringe upon the constitutional right of free speech and assembly.

A Senate majority agreed with him and cut out the President's proposal, voting only for the $450,000 appropriation. This is $49,000 more than was appropriated last year.

There was a day in the not too distant past when senators would eagerly permit a committee of five men to determine what constitutes a subversive organization. Such was the power of the McCarthyism which produced the board in the first place.

Therefore, the Senate is due some credit for refusing to go along with a Nixon order that clearly would violate basic rights. On the other hand, one is left to wonder why the Senate simply didn't vote to abolish a useless agency by declining to allocate money to it.

To understand the inconsistency it is necessary to understand the tenacious influence of McCarthyism which continues to hold congressmen in thrall. The plain truth is that congressmen are afraid to vote to abolish an agency which purports to combat communism, even though they know the agency to be a wasteful fake.

Perhaps we should adopt a mood of leniency toward a Senate which at least exhibited a kind of half-courage last Monday in Washington. The day may come when senators will take a deep breath, close their eyes, and heed the advice of Sen. Edward Kennedy. He urged his colleagues Monday to "end the witch hunt" once and for all. To this we say amen.

New York Post

New York, N.Y., July 19, 1971

It may have been one of those ludicrous accidents of history that President Nixon's executive order drastically broadening the powers of the Subversive Activities Control Board was made public on the day when Dr. Kissinger was secretly slipping into Peking.

Alternatively, the coincidence may suggest something about the nature of the complex political double-game the President is now undertaking. Thus NBC Nixon-watcher Herb Kaplow remarked last night that the President, still mindful of the conservative "sitdown" that contributed to his defeat in the California gubernatorial race in 1962, is resolved to offer numerous gestures of reassurance to his right-wing constituency on the home front while he pursues the affirmative quest for accommodation with Peking.

Specifically, the executive order, quietly signed on July 2 and publicly revealed a week later, gives Attorney General Mitchell new, significantly enlarged criteria for asking the SACB to place organizations on the notorious Justice Department list of subversive organizations. Numerous peace groups as well as black militant organizations would appear to fall within the loose definitions now presented as the basis for black (or red) listing.

In fact, under the vague characterizations of political activism embraced by the new order, a Committee for Closer Relations with the People's Republic of China might well find itself the target of an SACB inquiry sponsored by Mr. Mitchell.

Thus the domestic price we may be asked to pay for the President's audacious fraternization with the Chinese Communists—and perhaps other sectors of the Communist world—could be the unleashing of Mitchell and Agnew on even more repressive expeditions.

We must assume that the wit and wisdom of the American people will rebel against such double-think.

The Des Moines Register

Des Moines, Iowa, July 23, 1971

The U.S. Senate came within a few votes Monday of voting to abolish the Subversive Activities Control Board. The Senate then voted to bar use of any of the board's $450,000 appropriation to carry out President Nixon's new plans for the agency.

The Administration had sought to breathe life into the moribund board by assigning it the task of classifying organizations as "totalitarian," "fascist," "communist" or "subversive." The board also was directed to classify groups which would deny persons their rights under the Constitution or which seek overthrow of the government.

The Subversive Activities Control Board was established by Congress in 1950. Its statutory duty is to investigate and classify groups as "Communist-action," "Communist-front" and "Communist-infiltrated" organizations. The courts have so restricted the board in this activity that it has had nothing to do.

A July 2 executive order by President Nixon sought to empower the board to check into a flock of new enumerated groups. Suspected "totalitarian" and other groups would be referred to the board by the attorney general. If the board found that a group fit one of the new definitions contained in the executive order, the organization would appear on the attorney general's list. The list is used to determine the fitness of applicants for government jobs.

The Subversive Activities Control Board was given specific duties by Congress. The President's executive order attempts to enlarge the authority of the agency. The President tried, in effect, to "pass" a law giving the board sweeping authority to conduct political inquiries, complete with definitions of "totalitarian," "subversive," etc.

This is a questionable extension of executive power into legislative territory.

What is worse, it would make possible placing organizations on the attorney general's list because of what they advocate rather than for what they had done — a clear subversion of free speech and thought.

A "totalitarian" organization, for example, is defined as one that "engages in activities which seek by unlawful means the establishment of a system of government in the United States which is autocratic and in which control is centered in a single individual, group or political party, allowing no effective representation to opposing individuals, groups, or parties and providing no practical opportunity for dissent."

An organization that advocated in an abstract way establishing such a system by forcible overthrow of the existing order could be cited by the Subversive Activities Control Board. An organization which sought the same end but not by forcible overthrow of the government could be cited if its advocacy was at a park meeting unlawfully held with permit.

The U.S. Supreme Court has that, except in the event of clear immediate danger to the nation, ac cy of revolution or of any radical i protected under the free speech a ment to the Constitution.

Membership in an organization nothing about an individual's suppo the purposes of the group or his edge or understanding of them. persons have joined groups without knowing or approving their aim joined when their beliefs were different. Attempting to divide into various shades of subversiven an exercise in futility anyway.

The Senate is wise to refuse to the Administration to enlarge the of the Subversive Activities C Board. It would have been wiser the government out of the politica sifying business by abolishing the

The Dispatch

Columbus, Ohio, July 26, 1971

AMERICANS have every right to expect their federal government to be alert to any criminal effort to thwart enemies who would engage in espionage or sabotage of this nation.

They therefore have cause to wonder about recent actions by United States senators in this sector. They seem to be having difficulty in getting to the nub of such questions as "security indexes" and "concentration camps."

THE WHOLE problem dates back to 1950 when Congress passed a measure called the Internal Security Act. What has been bothering the senators are two of the act's provisions—a Subversive Activities Control Board and powers for "emergency detention."

The Nixon administration in 1969 recommended abolition of the detention camp plan partly because the camps do not exist and partly to "allay fears and suspicions, unfounded as they may be, of many of our citizens" the government planned to use the detention areas as herding quarters for dissident minorities.

THE SENATE Judiciary Committee recently approved a bill, already concurred in by a similar panel in the House, to revoke authority for operating the camps.

The senators obviously recalled such ugly chapters in history as the Third Reich's concentration camps and America's own World War II practice of gathering up more than 110,000 citizens who had Japanese ancestry.

SENATORS were far less decisive with regard to the Subversive Activities Control Board whose original mandate was to identify and require registration of Communists and Communist-front organizations.

The board is made up of five members, each receiving salaries of $36,000-a-year, and a staff of 10 assistants.

But it has been virtually inactive and useless for federal courts have ruled the functions for which it was created to be unconstitutional. It has registered no Communists in all of its 20 years. For 2½ years, it held no hearings. In the last six months, it has heard only three witnesses but still has a subversive list which ha been revised since 1955.

ON JULY 2, President N directed the board to wide scope and determine wh any organization in the U Communist, Fascist, tota ian or subversive based on lent utterances as well as of violence.

The Senate denied fun implement the Nixon dire but voted $450,000 for co uance of this hands-tied b

The mystery of it all is our senators are ready to detention of subversives, refuses to empower a boa identify such culprits. F nately, the nation has the eral Bureau of Investigati rely upon for such dete work.

Arkansas Democrat

Little Rock, Ark., July 29, 1971

Previous Presidents have hesitated to act friendly to China mainly because they feared the reaction of the anti-Communist fear mongers. Mr. Nixon has shown that he does not share that fear. But, oddly enough, he has attempted to expand the activities of the Subversive Activities Control Board, a useless agency that continues to exist because of fear of anti-Communist reaction.

Ironically, the Senate voted to block the expansion but to continue the existence of the board. Leading the fight against expansion was that tough old conservative, Sam Ervin of North Carolina, who labeled it an unconstitutional usurpation of legislative authority.

The board should be abolished. It is wasting $450,000 a year, including $36,000 apiece for the five political appointees who comprise it. One member admitted they heard only three witnesses last year and did nothing else. Everyone in Congress knows it is useless. Its members know it is useless. President Nixon knows it is useless. And now, with the President openly trying to get on good terms with Communists all over the world, why should he be timid about incurring the wrath of the professional anti-Communists by abolishing this board?

The only function the board ever had was to label organizations and individuals as subversive without the due process guaranteed in the Constitution. That's why the courts stripped it of its functions. Mr. Nixon's move would merely have restored some of those functions, at least until ruled unconstitutional again. It was an irresponsible act, trying to expand it.

It also is ironic that the administration would be trying to extend the board's function at the same time it is prosecuting Daniel Ellsberg for leaking Pentagon secrets. The administration just got Otto Otepka appointed to the board, as a reward for his leaking State Department secrets to congressional committees.

The SACB is a useless, expensive board that should be abolished and probably can be without alienating many voters — certainly fewer than will be alienated by Mr. Nixon's China trip. The Senate came close to doing it — the vote was 47-40 on the appropriation. Maybe next time, after another half-million dollars has been squandered, this board will go the way of earlier witch-hunting tribunals.

St. Louis Globe-Democrat

St. Louis, Mo., July 19, 1971

The federal Subversive Activities Control Board was intended to serve as a federal watchdog against the Communist party and other groups that have advocated the overthrow of our government.

It was largely defeated in its purpose by a series of Supreme Court decisions in the mid-1960's, such as the ruling it was unconstitutional to declare individuals members of Communist-front organizations.

To give the agency a new lease on life and allow it to function, Attorney General John N. Mitchell has prepared and sent to Congress legislation that would rename the board and give it work to perform.

Mitchell proposes that the agency be renamed the Federal Internal Security Board. The bill also would authorize the attorney general to ask the new agency to determine whether a particular organization sought to overthrow the government or had unlawfully advocated violent acts to deny others their constitutional rights.

The board then would hold public hearings to make a determination and report its findings. It would have the powers of subpoena and of finding recalcitrant witnesses in contempt.

Exposing the activities of subversive groups is the best way to nullify their efforts. For when their real purpose—subversion—is known to the public, their acceptance is largely gone, and with it their effectiveness.

Congress should pass the Mitchell bill. Subversives in the country have been having a field day ever since the Subversive Activities Control Board has been restrained.

The Courier-Journal

Louisville, Ky., July 22, 1971

CONGRESS often works in strange and wonderous ways. Take the Subversive Activities Control Board, for example. A miserable relic of the McCarthy witch-hunt days, the SACB has nothing to do and nobody can think of much of anything constitutional it can do. The Board never has controlled a subversive activity, and it's a safe bet that it never will.

Yet Congress continues to prolong the agency's life. Over the past 20 years more than $6 million has been tossed down the SACB rabbit hole, although it never has made a single worthwhile contribution to national security.

From the time it was established in the early 1950s under the McCarran Internal Security Act, the SACB has existed in a twilight zone of constitutionality. Over the years successive court decisions have struck down most of its legislatively prescribed duties as being in violation of the First and Fifth Amendments to the Constitution.

Even so, the Justice Department and Congress have been unwilling to let the SACB expire quietly, as it should. In 1967, for example, the Senate said the SACB would have to do something or be voted out of existence. The Justice Department quickly stepped in and asked the SACB to declare 10 persons as "known Communists," a silly act in itself since the Justice Department provided the evidence that the persons named were indeed Communists, and since there's nothing illegal about being a Communist in the first place.

Finally, after the SACB chairman conceded to a Senate committee recently that he and his colleagues didn't have enough work "to fill our time," President Nixon intervened and transferred certain minor Justice Department functions to the Board. But even this makework arrangement was prohibited this week by the Senate, which voted to bar the Board from performing the duties authorized by President Nixon in his executive order.

So it passes understanding why the Senate, at the same time it voted to restrict the almost nonexistent duties of the SACB, approved a new $450,000 annual appropriation for the Board—almost 50 per cent more than it was getting four years ago.

Maybe the question is too obvious and has been asked so often that no one listens, but what possible justification is there now for maintaining the Subversive Activities Control Board? Perhaps Kentucky's Senator Marlow W. Cook, the only member of the Kentucky and Indiana delegations in the Senate to support continuing the appropriation, could provide an answer. Certainly, it's time someone explained why the public's money continues to be wasted on an agency that was, is and will be not only useless but insulting to the Constitution.

156—SACB

Newsday

Garden City, N.Y., July 19, 1971

Until President Nixon decided to pump new life into it, the Subversive Activities Control Board, an overstaffed, underworked vestige of McCarthyism, was about to die an unlamented death, conceivably from boredom. The chairman of this five-member board, with a 10-man staff and $450,000 annual budget, conceded during a Senate hearing that "we do not have enough to fill our time" and reported having heard only three witnesses last year.

But rather than allow this unfortunate reminder of Cold War political thought-control to expire quietly, the President signed an executive order strengthening the board and broadening its constitutionally questionable powers. Under the order, the board can brand organizations "totalitarian," "fascist," "Communist" or "subversive" on the basis of what they *advocate* rather than what they *do*.

According to such standards, contends Melvin L. Wulf, legal director of the American Civil Liberties Union, "support of some 'allies' as well as some 'enemies' of the United States could be grounds for being included on the [attorney general's subversive] list." Wulf, who said that the ACLU will seek to have the order declared unconstitutional as a violation of the First Amendment, put it properly: "It is one of the fundamental principles of our form of government that society is served by permitting, indeed encouraging, as wide a variety of political ideas as the human mind can grasp. Some of them may strike us as evil, trivial or foolish; but so long as they do not constitute an integral part of an illegal act, they are protected by the First Amendment."

This week Sens. Philip Hart (D-Mich.) and William Proxmire (D-Wis.) plan to kill the board's $450,000 appropriation, thus killing the board. We wish them good hunting.

Minneapolis Tribune

Minneapolis, Minn., July 21, 1971

For all of President Nixon's opposition to what he calls dead-end, make-work jobs, he seems to have no reservations about not only keeping the Subversive Activities Control Board alive, but expanding its role as well. Yet if anything is the white-collar equivalent of leaning on a shovel, it is the non-activities of the five-member board, which now costs the taxpayers $450,000 a year.

What does the board do to earn its money? Well, nothing — which is a good thing for the democratic traditions of the country, but a bad thing so far as economy in government is concerned. The board was established under provisions of the Internal Security Act in 1950 and charged with ferreting out Communist organizations. Courts, however, have ruled its activities to be unconstitutional, and the board has been forced into inactivity.

Mr. Nixon's proposal was to make work for the board by giving it authority to hold hearings on which groups — Communist or not — should be listed as subversive by the attorney general. The likely targets would be the radical pacifist and civil rights groups that have been demonstrating against Nixon policies. The plan, it seems to us, overlooks the obvious — that a quasi-judicial hearing that brands a group as subversive, making it and its members guilty in the public mind, would be just as much an assault on constitutional rights and freedoms as would a proceeding that labels a group as Communist.

The Senate was right in rejecting Mr. Nixon's plan this week. Unfortunately, however, it first defeated Sen. Proxmire's attempt to eliminate funding for the board in the new fiscal year. The Senate's logic is curious: It knows that the board does nothing to justify receiving a $450,000 appropriation; it apparently recognizes that it would be improper to go along with Mr. Nixon's plan for giving the board something to do, but it refuses to allow the board to go out of existence.

Sen. Proxmire has tried before to persuade the Senate to take that last, logical step. He's sure to try again. We hope he's successful next time.

THE ROANOKE TIMES

Roanoke, Va., July 26, 1971

The Senate did a service to American freedoms last Monday when it rejected President Nixon's attempt to add to the powers of the Subversive Activities Control Board (SACB).

The SACB was set up in 1950 by the Internal Security Act, a law passed at the threshold of the Joe McCarthy era. The law gave the board investigative power and the authority to officially designate groups as Communist or Communist-related, and require them and their members to register with the government—in a word, to blacklist them. Court decisions since then have greatly narrowed the board's enforcement powers and left it with almost nothing to do for the past few years.

Recently President Nixon issued an executive order to broaden the board's powers—that is, give it duties the 1950 Congress did not choose to do. Although he sought congressional ratification after the fact, the President in effect, seemed to be trying in his executive order to bypass the legislative branch. The attempt was unconstitutional, in the opinion of Sen. Sam Ervin, Jr., D.-N.C., a conservative who is sturdy in defense of liberties.

The duties the President sought to add to the SACB were to investigate and list organizations as totalitarian, Fascist, Communist or subversive, or as "unlawfully advocating the commission of acts of force or violence to deny others their rights under the Constitution or laws . . . or seeking to overthrow the government . . . by unlawful means."

Opponents of the action said this was clearly aimed at peace demonstrators, militant blacks and other dissenters, and infringed upon individual rights to free speech and association.

Sen. Ervin also cited that as a second unconstitutional effort. The Senate, by 51-37 vote, declined to underwrite the powers that the President seeks to add to the board.

It acted rightly, for crimes are committed by individuals, and should be prosecuted as such. There is no justice in blacklisting groups, a method that imputes guilt by association and discourages dissent of any kind.

The past several months have been trying times, but events have shown that the FBI and other agencies are able to protect the government. There is no need for the country to lose its nerve and slip back into the hysteria of another era. The Senate did a good job. The job would have been even better had it voted to save $450,000 by eliminating a do-nothing agency and the sinecure jobs that go with it.

HOUSE VOTES 247-172 TO CURTAIL HISC'S SECURITY INVESTIGATIONS

The House virtually abolished its Internal Security Committee Jan. 14 by transferring its jurisdiction and files to the Judiciary Committee. The House Democratic Caucus had included the recommendation that the HISC be disbanded in a resolution changing several House rules. The resulting vote was on a motion to open the resolution to amendments (which would have permitted an attempt to retain the panel.) All the 143 Republicans present for the voting sided with the minority in the motion's defeat 247-172.

The House had voted Oct. 2, 1974 246-164 to retain the committee. In mid-December, the Democratic Steering and Policy Committee assigned only one member, Rep. Richard H. Ichord (D, Mo.) to the HISC. Rep. James W. Symington (D, Mo.) said after the caucus vote that "Ichord was really a captain without a crew," and that "we were just formalizing something that had already become a fact." The committee's 1974 budget was $725,000, and its staff numbered 39.

The HISC was known until 1969 as the House Committee on Un-American Activities (HUAC). The House had established a Special Committee on Un-American Activities to investigate subversion in 1938, with its mandate renewable every two years. The special committee was called the Dies Committee after its chairman, Rep. Martin Dies (D, Tex.) The HUAC became the permanent successor to the Dies Committee in 1945, and was most frequently in the news in 1945-50. It investigated the motion picture industry in 1947 and State Department official Alger Hiss in 1948.

The Houston Post
Houston, Texas, January 28, 1975

It had to reach up to touch bottom. Its proceedings recalled Halloween in a madhouse. It was peopled some by zanies and some by zealots and some by opportunists. Often it refuted what it purported to defend — America. Its targets included the then dimpled innocent of the screen, Shirley Temple, not to mention someone said to be Mussolini's mistress but who, like quicksilver, could never be pinned down in the flesh.

The House Committee on Un-American Activities, later retitled the House Internal Security Committee, died the other day, unmourned by few, after a 40-year farrago of absurdity. It made a celebrity of J. Parnell Thomas, for just one. Chairman of the committee when it caused 10 Hollywood figures to be jailed for contempt, Thomas went to jail himself a little later when he was convicted of taking kickbacks from his congressional secretaries.

Those were the days when the committee was feted with an event called "Cocktails Against Communism"; when a staff member proposed that Kreml hair tonic be investigated because the Russian word for Kremlin was Kreml; and when Ring Lardner Jr., testifying before the committee, was asked if he could name any Communists. "I could," he replied, "but I'd hate myself in the morning."

The committee also brought fame to a young California congressman, Richard M. Nixon. The future President persistently pursued the Alger Hiss-Whittaker Chambers case, which he recalled often in the White House tapes. It was Nixon Chambers conducted to a pumpkin on his Maryland farm to produce microfilm he said came from Hiss.

Perhaps we learned something from the committee's long four decades. Perhaps we learned that dissent can be sounded by patriots, that to corner our friends is no way to reveal our enemies.

Arkansas Gazette.
Little Rock, Ark., January 26, 1975

Some obituaries are a positive pleasure to write and one of the most satisfying in recent years involves the demise, finally, of the House Un-American Activities Committee, a war baby bequeathed to us by World War II.

HUAC managed to add a few years to its life by changing its name to the "House Internal Security Committee," though nobody was fooled by it who did not want to be. The Committee had not done anything much for many years, which was all right, since it has already done so much before — almost all of it bad. Even at the end the last chairman of HISC, Richard H. Ichord (Dem., Mo.) was able to unload the patronage boondoggle that was the committee's staff upon the already burdened shoulders of Chairman Peter W. Rodino of the House Judiciary Committee, who, while he would just as soon have passed up the honor, we think will know what to do with this latest barnacle or carbuncle, or whatever it is, when the time comes. At least, as Mary McGrory has pointed out, we can rest more comfortably in the knowledge that so does the reliable Rodino have custody now over the almost three-quarter-million names that HUAC's catch-as-catch-can "investigators" — members and staff — accumulated over the years.

The Story of HUAC is one more proof of the truism that good intentions are not enough. It was the brainchild of a private citizen, himself a Jew, who envisaged it as a wartime vehicle for combatting Nazi sympathizers and anti-Semitism in general. HUAC actually did a little of that, too, under its first chairman, the unforgettable Martin Dies of Texas, but its principal reason for being was always the fanning to life and perpetuating of the anti-"Red" scare that then Attorney General A. Mitchell Palmer had flogged so vigorously in the period after the first World War in the hope of thereby possibly winning the Democratic nomination for President, a hope that, mercifully, was never realized.

It is fairly safe to say that almost never in the course of human history was so much noxious done to so many by so few, though, come to think of it, quite a few people had served on the Committee at one time or another before the end finally came. It attracted bad apples like the flies that are attracted by bad apples, the most transparent grifters, grafters, mountebanks and common crooks, such as Richard M. Nixon, the Republican, and J. Parnell Thomas, the Democrat.

The Committee's general intellectual level was indicated by the famous occasion when actor Gary Cooper was given a standing ovation when he "testified" that he didn't know what Communism was, but that he was ag'in it.

Before it was finally "terminated" as they used to say during "Operation Phoenix" in 'Nam, HUAC had spawned a whole passel of imitators and sometime competitors, such as the Senate Internal Security Committee (it was actually there first with the more innocuous name), the Subversive Activities Control Board, another one that ran out of anything to even pretend to do but was kept in being anyway as a patronage boondoggle.

It was only in recent years that HUAC began to attract a type of member who would not instantly arouse the suspicions of a bail bondsman, men such as the Jesuit priest from Massachusetts, Robert Drinan, and the liberal California Democrat, Philip Burton of California, who infiltrated the Committee for the principal purpose of doing it in from within, thus of course confirming the worst fears of the people who professed to think that HUAC itself still had, or had ever had, a purpose.

Long Island Press

Jamaica, N.Y., January 17, 1975

The House has finally abolished its Internal Security Committee, the long-dormant successor to the discredited Un-American Activities Committee. From now on, investigations of subversive activities will be the function of a special panel of the Judiciary Committee.

For years, the original committee flaunted the Constitution in a political witch hunt for people considered dangerous to the nation's security. Guarantees of freedom of speech, assembly, the press, and of personal associations were disregarded. Many innocent people lost their jobs and/or reputations in quasi-judicial proceedings which denied the accused of such a fundamental right as the identification and cross-examination of their accusers.

Five years ago, the committee's name was changed, and so was its direction. Most Americans had enough of legislative tar-brushing that not only injured the innocent, but also didn't produce any subversives unknown to the Federal Bureau of Investigation. Since then, the House Internal Security Committee has been inactive.

Its demise is welcome. However, this does not mean that those few people who want to overthrow the government by force or violence—revolutionaries at both extremes of the political spectrum—will escape proper legislative attention. In the future, thanks in part to the infusion of new blood in Congress, the work of the old committees will be carried out under the direction of the Judiciary Committee. Its fairness in conducting impeachment proceedings against former President Nixon suggests that future investigations will not be done at the cost of anyone's civil liberties.

The Courier-Journal

Louisville, Ky., January 18, 1975

BECAUSE the House Internal Security Committee had been so long on its death bed, its demise this week at age 37 was anticlimactic. But Congress still deserves censure for waiting so many years before scuttling such a costly, useless and unsavory reminder of the McCarthyite days when witch-hunting was in flower.

Even a cosmetic name change couldn't erase memories of the way the old Un-American Activities Committee pursued and harried the innocent and guilty alike. That was the heyday of anti-communism (ironically, the committee originally was established in 1938 to probe right-wing, fascist influences), when to speak or write liberal thoughts was to risk persecution.

The committee's character was aptly summed up by Massachusetts Representative Robert Drinan, the liberal Catholic priest who deliberately joined the committee in order to work from within for its abolition. In the committee's 1973 report he wrote: "The history of this committee is replete with baseless attacks on individuals and groups, executive sessions which are no more than third-party, hearsay name-calling and endless pages of self-serving testimony from some citizens whose chief concern is the patriotism of others."

On a more practical level, the committee spent a lot of money — $475,000 was authorized for 1974 — to produce considerable Cold War posturing but few legislative proposals. Even as an investigatory body, its effect was limited. Many contempt citations were issued against reluctant witnesses, but few survived challenge in the courts. And the committee cast little light on some of the recent organizations which could legitimately be categorized as "subversive" — such groups as the Weathermen and the Symbionese Liberation Army.

For many Americans, the committee was little more than material for rueful jokes, perhaps about such headline-seeking chairmen as Martin Dies and J. Parnell Thomas. For those who roused its wrath, however, the committee's activities often resulted in marred careers and ruined lives. But this peculiar blend of tragi-comedy has now run its course. The house has found an excellent way to begin its Bicentennial session, by finally ringing down the curtain on this most un-American saga.

THE ROANOKE TIMES

Roanoke, Va., January 21, 1975

The House Democratic Caucus has voted to abolish the House Internal Security Committee which was the old House Un-American Activities Committee. Such internal security functions as are proper for the House will be transferred to the House Judiciary Committee. The House approved the caucus decision.

The idea that such a decision could be made would have been unthinkable even a decade ago and outrageous in the 1940s in and in the 1950s. The Un-American Activities committee—the Dies committee, Thomas committee and Joe Pool committee, to name some of its illustrious names of the past—was a sacred cow even when its output was bull. To reduce its appropriations was enough to make a Congressman himself open to a charge of being friendly to communism.

What has happened to the American mind? Watergate is part of the answer. No longer are the people so pure in heart and so naive as to be taken in by the pretensions of politicians who play on their patriotism. If those who cry law and order are revealed to be cynical phonies, so could those who pretend that their Americanism is superior to other Americans'.

The movement towards *detente*, a practical agreement with the Soviets and the Chinese Communists, also has had an effect. There is not one international red menace that the old committee and its hired turncoats used to talk about; there are two, possibly three, and a practical agreement might be worth obtaining. One of the ironies of the day is that former President Nixon is credited with achieving what he once denounced Democrat Adlai Stevenson for advocating: a practical understanding with Chinese Communists.

If the nation now is a little more weary and a little less enthusiastic, it is also a little more mature; it doesn't want to be fooled, anymore. The old HUAC has its tiny reason for being; and it wrote some important footnotes. But it got terribly out of hand, needlessly wrecked and damaged the careers of thousands. The country is safer without it than with it.

The Boston Globe

Boston, Mass., January 16, 1975

The US House, post-Watergate soul-searching coursing through its veins, Tuesday inaugurated its 1975 session on an appropriate note. It consigned to infamy the House Internal Security Committee, a catapult in the late 1940s and early 1950s for a politically ambitious and conspiratorially minded young congressman named Richard M. Nixon.

A precursor of Watergate, the committee for three decades ran roughshod over civil liberties in the name of national security. Mr. Nixon, as a member, beat a demagogic drum in his anticommunist crusade. Although a conspicuous example, the former President was by no means the only offender.

The committee—known until six years ago as the House Un-American Activities Committee—issued 174 contempt citations, 10 times as many as the other House committees combined, but mostly to no avail. The courts found most of the citations unwarranted, and few of the defendants ever went to jail.

Yet only six of the bills originating in the committee since 1945 ever became law. The committee activities, invading the privacy of countless individuals for dubious legislative advantage. In a 1971 suit, three persons subpoenaed to testify before the committee challenged its authority, charging with some justification that it merely sought the "exposure of witnesses . . . to public scorn, obloqy and harassment and intimidation . . . without any legislative purpose."

In recent years, the power of the committee has withered, as anticommunist hysteria has subsided. Its $725,000 budget of a few years ago has been shaved by more than $100,000 and its staff of 39 persons diminished by 15. It has tended to avoid the raucus confrontations, a staple of the committee in the past, between members and witnesses.

Indeed, the committee had become a shadow of its former self. Many of its members had resigned. No freshmen in the House sought membership this year.

The House thus recognized the inevitable in abolishing the committee. It has assigned its functions to the House Judiciary Committee, steeled from Watergate and equipped to inquire into internal subversion, where necessary. Ironically, it was the Judiciary Committee which had this jurisdiction before the advent of House Un-American Activities Committee.

The demise of the committee represents a personal victory for Rep. Robert F. Drinan of Massachusetts, who joined it four years ago to challenge it from within. In one of his trenchant critiques of the committee, Drinan said in 1971: "Men and women old enough to recall the use of the US Congress as a vehicle for systematically wrecking the careers and reputations of individuals whose associations did not meet with the approval of their accusers will always look back upon the episode with embarrassment and discomfort." The words stand as a fitting epitaph for the Internal Security Committee.

Chicago Tribune

Chicago, Ill.,
January 25, 1975

The disappearance of the House Internal Security Committee—successor to the once-famed House Committee on Un-American Activities—has impelled a great many commentators to murmur about "the end of an era." Actually the era ended quite a while ago. The committee outlasted it so long because it is the way of congressional committees to outlast practically everything, including usefulness.

For many years after World War II, the committee's nationwide hunt for subversives and Communist sympathizers kept the press and public in an uproar. Its sensational hearings fed on publicity and spread into virtually every corner of American life: government, labor, the academic community, Hollywood, the arts. Its investigations made some reputations—including that of a formerly obscure California congressman, Richard M. Nixon — and wrecked many others. It has been generally [tho inaccurately and sometimes derisively] known as HUAC, and its activities were denounced and defended with equal fury.

From the vantage point of 1975, it is easy to sneer at this panel. What we see most plainly in retrospect are its abuses. During the 1950s, tho, fears of Communist penetration were quite real and reasonable. We had seen Communist agents score substantial successes here and abroad—including the theft of atomic bomb secrets—and the nation was uncertain of its own power to block them. Not to have been alarmed, not to have taken steps against the threat, would have been insanity. The Tribune supported HUAC's goals [if not all its techniques] on that basis.

Since then Americans have found out a great deal about themselves and their enemies. We know that we and they both have strengths and weaknesses, that neither the U. S. nor the Soviet government is composed of supermen. We know that the Communist movement, evil as it is, is not the only threat to freedom—that those who seem most eager to protect us may be dangerous too.

We have seen Soviet-style Communism, which once seemed a nightmarish threat to this country, come to look rather stodgy and old fashioned compared with other brands of Communism and with our own "new Left" revolutionary crazies; and we have seen even the latter fall prey to disillusionment. [It seems that even Weathermen eventually grow up.]

The threat of Communist subversion is still there and we must be alert to it. It's just that we no longer need to get hysterical about it. Communism has discredited itself among Americans and especially among the laboring class upon which it is supposed to thrive. We are better able to protect ourselves at home without the help of a special House committee—or even of the CIA.

So the 94th Congress has quietly abolished the Internal Security Committee by transferring its functions to the Judiciary Committee. And it was time to close its books. Whatever virtues HUAC's successor may have claimed, it had one fatal drawback: The nation had outgrown it.

Chicago Sun-Times

Chicago, Ill., January 18, 1975

A panel snooping on Americans by any other name is still a panel snooping on Americans — and that's why the notorious Committee on Un-American Activities, renamed the House Internal Security Committee, has been scrapped.

The committee never had and never would have justification for being. During the irrational Communist witch-hunting days of the 1950s, it became a powerful body that found a Communist under every rug. It fed on fears and ruined reputations, all in the name of preserving national security.

It survived, partly because residual fears of a Communist or left-wing takeover in this country kept it alive, and partly because it's easy to create a bureaucracy, but tough to kill one. Previous congressional efforts to do so have failed.

But now the House has voted for abolishment, with the concurrence of the chairman of the ISC, Rep. Richard Ichord (D-Mo.). Jurisdiction will go to the Judiciary Committee.

When the head of a committee as unneeded as this one wanted it axed, the message was clear: it was time to bury one of this country's major contradictions of the democratic process.

The Hartford Courant

Hartford, Conn., January 16, 1975

Congressional reformers are only getting their own House in order by eliminating the House Internal Security Committee. They can hardly criticize domestic spying by such agencies as the CIA while retaining this leftover bit of McCarthyism.

Internal Security is the gentler name bestowed five years ago on the old Committee on Un-American Activities. This committee was formed in 1930 to specifically investigate Communist propaganda.

It won its greatest attention, naturally enough, in the immediate postwar years with its highly-publicized investigations and accusations of Communist subversion. The climax came in the case of Alger Hiss, a former State Department official. Committee hearings led to a perjury conviction for Mr. Hiss and national prominence for Congressman Richard M. Nixon.

In later years, the committee concentrated on radical groups, most recently the Symbionese Liberation Army. But the people's perspective has changed sharply. Red-hunting may have been "in" in 1950, but today we look with suspicion on government spying for any purpose.

Even in matters such as the terrorist SLA, investigation is best left to law enforcement agencies. The object should be arrest and conviction, not mere accusation.

The committee's functions, its $725,000 annual budget, and its 750,000 files on individual Americans will be transferred to the Judiciary Committee. The best thing Judiciary could do would be finally to dispose of the whole works.

THE CINCINNATI ENQUIRER

Cincinnati, Ohio, January 25, 1975

GIVEN THE COMPLEXION of the vastly expanded liberal contingent in the 94th Congress, nothing is less surprising than that the House, as one of its first official acts, abolished the House Internal Security Committee.

The Internal Security Committee (formerly known as the House Committee on Un-American Activities, which critics insisted on calling the "House Un-American Activities Committee") has inspired an almost irrational fury among the nation's left-wing demonologists. Hence, every Congress for a decade or more has begun with a ritualistic attempt either to abolish it outright or to deny it realistic funding.

The left wing's animosity to the committee has not been diminished by anything that has transpired in the United States in the last dozen years. Neither the assassination of a President by an avowed Marxist nor the murder of his brother by an Arab under Marxist influence occasioned any second thoughts. The bombing of university buildings by the chanters of Marxist slogans made no greater impression. The emergence of such insanities as the Symbionese Liberation Front produced not a ripple of concern.

Beyond our own frontiers, terrorism has become institutionalized as an instrument of protest, and no society can count itself permanently immune.

These factors make it an extraordinary moment to proclaim that Congress has no further need of a committee to monitor threats to the nation's internal security.

Under the measure proposed by Rep. Robert F. Drinan (D-Mass.), the committee's jurisdiction is being transferred to the House Judiciary Committee, which no less respected an observer than Joseph Alsop once characterized as "a kind of dumping ground for left-wing Democrats of the more far-out type."

Nothing would please most Americans more than sharing the optimism of Representative Drinan and the House majority. But most must wonder what it would take to convince the Drinans in Congress that they have allowed their emotions to run away with their judgment.

St. Louis Globe-Democrat
St. Louis, Mo.,
January 20, 1975

The House Internal Security Committee, which for 45 years has been Congress' major investigative unit probing subversive activities, has been abolished. Technically, a few records and staff will be transferred to the super-liberal House Judiciary Committee, but chairman Peter W. Rodino Jr. plans to halt further investigations. The Internal Security Committee is deader than a doornail in all respects, and everyone knows it.

The abolition, voted by the caucus of House Democrats, is the culmination of many years of effort by House liberals and radical and revolutionary groups throughout the country. The relentless drive included two votes last year alone, plus a crude scheme which involved the refusal of liberal leaders to assign any representatives to the committee (except chairman Richard Ichord of Missouri, who in effect had to be assigned by House rules). Now, in caucus, Democrats have done what the full House repeatedly declined to do. But this year they probably have the votes to win full House approval, so Ichord is planning no appeal.

There is a nominal investigating committee on internal security in the Senate, but it is so feckless that it is of no consequence. The abolition of the House Internal Security Committee is the end of any significant congressional supervision over national security. This is quite strange, considering how exercised Congress was over presidential uses and abuses of such internal security matters as wiretaps, invasion of privacy, surveillance, etc., during the Watergate fray, or over alleged improper activities by federal agencies such as the FBI and CIA. Who is better equipped to make intelligent recommendations on such matters than a congressional committee assigned to look after the requirements of internal security?

While Congress is taking a Pollyanna view that subversives either don't exist or shouldn't be investigated, liberals have succeeded in wiping away other government investigations or monitoring of Communists and other revolutionaries. The Subversive Activities Control Board has been abolished, as has the Attorney General's Subversive List. Last year the FBI was castigated for its work against subversives, and this year's target is the CIA. In between the two have been new restrictions on wiretaps.

The grand plan seems to be to outlaw any interference or checking whatsoever on anyone or any group. The usual justification is that "today it's so-and-so, but tomorrow it could be you," or simply, "these are witch hunts abhorrent to a democracy." But the instances of abuses are infinitesimal. And just as the government has a clear duty to investigate possible tax cheats, illegitimate business, phony charities, or organized crime, so too should Americans be investigated when they acknowledge or advocate security-oriented lawbreaking. What can be more important than the security of the American form of government against those who would forcibly destroy it, or at least destroy some of its protections?

The United States is not seriously threatened by the demise of a committee which probed subversive activity. But the action in the House makes it that much easier for subversives to operate openly, often in seeming innocence that is totally deceptive. No longer will a warning be sounded.

THE RICHMOND NEWS LEADER
Richmond, Va., January 30, 1975

For lo, these past 37 years, the House Committee on Un-American Activities — known widely as HUAC — has been a target of polemical opportunists. An outgrowth of the Select Committee to Investigate Communist Propaganda, established in 1930, HUAC was made a permanent committee of the House of Representatives in 1938. It was mandated to investigate — and to inform the public about — subversives and subversive activities, alleged and real; and to recommend legislation to combat subversive activities. So from 1938 forward, HUAC investigated such things as the German-American Bund, the Ku Klux Klan, the American Nazi Party, the Symbionese Liberation Army, assorted extremist groups of the Left, and — of course — the Communists.

Now HUAC is dead. Two weeks ago, the House affirmed an earlier vote by the Democratic caucus to transfer HUAC's files and most of its staff to the House Committee on the Judiciary. In effect, those votes mean that Congress has withdrawn from the field of investigating the activities of subversives in the United States.

For its probings into far Leftism and Communism, the Committee drew its heaviest fire; indeed, it drew practically no sustained fire for its probings of the kook Right. HUAC was most conspicuously in the news during the late forties, (a) when it investigated Communist influence in Hollywood, culminating in contempt of Congress citations against the Hollywood Ten, and (b) when — through the testimony of Whittaker Chambers — it informed the public about the activities of Alger Hiss. Hiss subsequently served 44 months in prison for perjury.

Since that time, one could not lay claim to the credentials of impeccable Liberalism without mouthing routine denunciations of HUAC — to the effect that its very existence was a profane violation of American rights. Yet there can be little doubt that the relegation of HUAC to one of the nation's most defamatory categories was less the result of the Committee's conduct than the result of the conduct of Committee witnesses and the conduct of the press. On this latter point, hear — for instance — Irving Ferman, at one time the Washington, D.C., director of the American Civil Liberties Union, writing in *The Committee and Its Critics* [Putnam, 1962]:

The press in the broadest sense — newspapers, radio, and TV combined —

[does] more to coercively inhibit [free] expression than is realized. The reporting of a Committee hearing by these media normally seems designed to excite a public fever of recrimination, and it is this that also tends to penalize the witness.... Such distorted emphasis of the record of a legislative inquiry helps not a little to create an atmosphere that tends to make of the whole investigation a penalty for past thought and action.

The courts repeatedly have upheld the investigatory power of Congress. Practically no one has denied the legitimacy of that power, except as it relates to the investigation of Communism. No one objected to it in connection with the various malignancies and ineptitudes subsumed under the heading "Watergate." Few object to it now in connection with the impending investigation of the CIA and the nation's clandestine security network. No one seriously suggested that Congress was trampling on individual rights when it subpoenaed members of Richard Nixon's staff; nor does anyone suggest now that Congress is trampling on anyone's rights with its subpoenas of members of the CIA.

Yet the cry went up almost whenever HUAC subpoenaed an alleged Communist. And now, for its many supposed transgressions, HUAC has been killed. Which is to say, perhaps, that today we regard Communism as a less serious potential domestic malignancy than we regard those things, say, that H.R. Haldeman and the CIA allegedly sought to do to us. Which, in turn, speaks reams about the illusions on which we feed.

Lincoln told us that a nation's first obligation is to itself. By that he meant that if a nation does not seek to preserve itself, it has little business seeking to preserve anything else. Yet today we have Heaven-knows-how-many congressional committees investigating our own intelligence-gathering agencies, and Congress has abolished the one committee it had established to investigate the activities carried out in the United States by the Soviet secret police. A nation that will not protect itself from others clearly needs to be protected from itself. In the words of Whittaker Chambers, "It is a law of history that no one can save those who will not save themselves, whose plight is the proof that they have lost the instinct of self-preservation." As his words were an anticipatory epitaph for the House Committee on Un-American Activities, so they might also prove to be an anticipatory epitaph for ourselves.

EMERGENCY DETENTION ACT REPEALED BY CONGRESS

By an overwhelming 356–49 tally, the House of Representatives Sept. 14 voted to repeal the Emergency Detention Act of 1950. The McCarthy-era legislation authorized the federal government to establish detention camps for the purpose of holding "each person as to whom there is reasonable ground to believe . . . probably will engage in . . . or conspire to engage in . . . acts of espionage" in time of war or of invasion or "insurrection in aid of a foreign enemy." The law had aroused concern among minority political and ethnic groups, especially blacks, who feared it could be used against them. Critics of the act, led by Rep. Spark M. Matsunaga (D, Hawaii), pointed to the detention of 110,000 Japanese-Americans in camps at the outbreak of World War II as evidence of the inherent danger of the law.

The Nixon Administration had given its endorsement to the repeal of the law. The House, however, went beyond rescinding it. It also voted to ban the establishment of detention camps by executive order, as had been done during World War II. The Senate was quick to approve the repeal and the legislation was sent to the President for signature.

AKRON BEACON JOURNAL
Akron, Ohio, September 17, 1971

The House vote to repeal the 1950 detention camp law brought back memories—

Of Sen. Joseph McCarthy of Wisconsin, who made a career of persecuting liberals as "Communist sympathizers" in the early Fifties.

And of the "relocation centers" where 112,000 Japanese-Americans were detained during World War II because they were deemed to be security risks. (A vivid memory to the writer of this editorial; as a soldier in the Pacific he was closely associated with Nisei GIs—interpreters and translators —whose parents were locked up in these camps.)

★

The 1950 act provided that in time of war, invasion or insurrection, the government could detain any persons who, there was "reasonable ground" to believe, "probably" would engage in sabotage.

Though the authority thus created has never been used, its existence has given rise to rumors that the government planned to round up black militants and throw them into concentration camps.

The Nixon administration favored repeal of the detention camp provision. Encouraged by leaders of both parties, the House went even further. Attempting to prevent a repetition of what was done in 1942 by executive order, the House added to the repealer a stipulation that no American citizen could be detained or imprisoned by the federal government except by an act of Congress.

As was to be expected, repeal was opposed by the House Internal Security Committee, successor to the House Un-American Activities Committee which sponsored the 1950 law. But the vote for repeal was overwhelming, 356 to 49. (Two Ohioans, we note with regret, voted to retain this ugly reminder of the McCarthy era. They were John M. Ashbrook and Samuel L. Devine.)

Appropriately, the chief sponsor of the repeal measure was Rep. Spark Matsunaga (D-Hawaii), who fought for his country with the all-Nisei 442nd Regimental Combat Team while some of his relatives were held in detention camps.

With Senate concurrence yesterday, the concentration camp threat is gone —and good riddance.

ST. LOUIS POST-DISPATCH
St. Louis, Mo., September 25, 1971

The House voted 68 to 22 to reject an Internal Security Committee substitute for the Emergency Detention Act, and then went on to repeal that outrageous law. America never had a rightful place for detention—or concentration—camps, and that was as true in the days of McCarthyism when the law was passed as it is today. The Nixon Administration itself has backed repeal.

But not Representative Ichord of Missouri and his Internal Security Committee. He proposed a substitute, requiring Congress to declare the existence of an insurrection before the Executive branch could round up political suspects without trial and lock them away.

President Harry Truman had the right idea about all this 20 years ago; he vetoed the measure. It has taken a while for the House to catch up with his ideas about elementary democracy and justice, but now that it has done so the Senate should quickly follow suit.

Record American
Boston, Mass., September 23, 1971

One of the most gratifying signs of maturity in a government, a group or an individual is a demonstrated willingness to abandon a position on the basis of new information, experience or after due reflection.

The House of Representatives and the Senate have just provided us a salutary example of this sound judgment by their overwhelming votes to repeal the 1950 Emergency Detention Act.

This insidious act, enacted in the period of uncertainty caused by the cold war, would permit the government to operate camps in time of war, invasion or insurrection for the detention — without due process of law — of anyone suspected of espionage or sabotage.

Although the law was never invoked, its continued presence on the books has been a stain on our image as a free, democratic and high-principled nation. It is a credit to President Nixon that he asked for the law's repeal. The House and Senate are to be commended for their speedy compliance.

The Providence Journal
Providence, R.I., September 22, 1971

For more than 20 years Americans have tolerated a law that should not have been enacted — the detention provision of the Internal Security Act of 1950. Each attempt at repeal has stirred fiery controversy and met ultimate defeat. "Subversion, infiltration, attack from within"—all the emotional terms of the McCarthy era were employed to keep alive a statute that sends chills down the spine of anyone who can recall Nazi Germany and World War II.

At last Congress has come to its senses. At last it has dissociated this country from anything that smacks of Hitlerian brutality. And it has done so in a way that leaves no room for doubt.

Said the congressman who led the fight for repeal, Rep. Spark M. Matsunaga, D-Hawaii, "There is no place for concentration camps in the American scheme."

The authority to detain suspected spies or saboteurs in time of war or insurrection has never been invoked although the government created six detention camps in Arizona, California, Florida, Oklahoma and Pennsylvania. But merely the existence of such a law and the knowledge that there were centers prepared and ready for the mass systematic suspension of individual rights without due process of law has weighed heavily on the conscience of many Americans.

Small wonder that some civil rights groups and many black Americans harbored strong suspicions that — given the continuing escalation of dissent over poverty, war and social injustice in this country and a government that has backed preventive detention of criminal suspects, forced entry in drug abuse cases, mass arrests in Washington demonstrations and other tactics of questionable constitutionality— they might be the victims of some future human roundup.

The House rightly blocked an attempt by Rep. Richard H. Ichord, chairman of the internal security committee, to leave such power in the hands of the President. Only by act of Congress can such authority now be revived.

Congress has ended this ugly chapter in American history. What cannot be erased is the memory of herding 112,000 Japanese-Americans, most of them born in this country, into "relocation centers" soon after the attack on Pearl Harbor in 1941. What can be done is to make certain it does not happen again.

THE SACRAMENTO BEE
Sacramento, Calif., September 21, 1971

Americans are a freedom-loving people and the Congress staunchly supported that tradition by the overwhelming vote to repeal the onerous, albeit never-used, detention camp law. The House of Representatives voted 356 to 49 and no dissent was heard in the Senate voice vote.

This act, passed during the hysterical days of 1950, allows the executive branch of government, without prior approval of the legislative or the judiciary, to herd suspected spies or saboteurs into detention camps during times of national emergency.

The law's existence has given rise to widespread fears, particularly among Negroes, that it might be used to establish concentration camps for black militants.

There is substance to the fears because in 1942, during World War II, 112,000 citizens of Japanese ancestry were put into such camps under presidential executive authority.

It is a tribute to the Congress that it included in the repeal measure language to prevent recurrence of even that kind of episode. Under the bill no citizen can be arrested or detained by the federal government in such camps except with express approval of the Congress.

The California congressional delegation is to be commended for its vote of 35 to 1 in favor of the repeal measure. Many individuals rate credit for pushing this bill through the House, particularly Rep. Chet Holifield, D-Los Angeles County, dean of the state's delegation and one of the few public figures in the state who opposed the Japanese-American relocation program from the first.

The victory represents an accolade for Chief Justice of the United States Earl Warren, retired, who as state attorney general and candidate for governor backed the internment program.

After he retired from the Supreme Court he joined the move to repeal the detention law and said:

"Action by the Congress would prove to the world that we learn some useful things even from war."

The action removes this stain once and for all from democracy's fabric. It is as Rep. Robert L. Leggett, D-Vallejo, said, there is no place for concentration camps in the United States.

The New York Times
New York, N.Y., September 18, 1971

Fired by the anti-Communist hysteria that followed the outbreak of the Korean war, Congress in 1950 overrode a veto by President Truman and enacted a law authorizing the Federal Government to put suspected spies or saboteurs into detention camps in time of war or insurrection. In 1952, the Government established six detention camps in Arizona, California, Florida, Oklahoma and Pennsylvania.

The law was never invoked and the detention camps were later abandoned, except for one which became a Federal prison. But the survival of the statute, despite efforts at repeal in the last Congress, has engendered fears of "concentration camps" among black militants and other dissenters. And it has stood as a betrayal of the spirit, if not the letter, of American constitutional freedom, repugnant to all who cherish the Bill of Rights.

This repugnance has now been overwhelmingly expressed by swift votes in both houses of Congress to repeal the act and also to stipulate that no citizen can be detained or imprisoned by the Federal Government except pursuant to an act of Congress. President Nixon's signature is needed to complete burial of this un-American legislation.

The Philadelphia Inquirer
Philadelphia, Pa., September 21, 1971

If liberty under law means anything, it means no citizen can be locked up, under order of any government official, without due process of law.

Yet for 21 years this country has had on the books a law which would permit precisely that.

Title II of the 1950 Internal Security Act authorizes the U. S. Attorney General, after the President has declared an internal security emergency, to put into "detention centers" any person whom he considers to be a potential spy or saboteur, and to act without bothering with the troublesome inconveniences of due process.

True enough, the law, enacted at the height of hysteria over domestic subversion in the McCarthy years, had never been put into effect. But who could say for certain that it never would be?

In World War II, some 110,000 Americans of Japanese ancestry were herded into "relocation centers" — without a law. Two years ago, the House Internal Security Committee, then known as the Un-American Activities Committee, suggested that the problems posed by "mixed Communist and black nationalist elements" might be met by utilizing the detention centers for "temporary imprisonment of warring guerillas."

So fears of minority groups that the law might be invoked against them were not entirely without foundation, and when Congress voted—the House, 356 to 49, the Senate, by voice vote—to wipe the law off the books, its action was more than a symbolic gesture of reassurance.

But it is that, and something more. One after another, provisions of that infamous Internal Security Act of 1950 have been struck down over the years—but always by the courts. This time, Congress itself took action. We commend it for so doing and urge it to follow up by getting rid of that other useless hangover of the McCarthy years, the Subversive Activities Control Board.

THE MILWAUKEE JOURNAL
Milwaukee, Wis., September 16, 1971

Public Law 81-831, Title II, is a blot on the nation and the concept of rule of law. It allows the government to put Americans in a concentration camp in so-called times of emergency on little more than the pretext of their danger to national security. The House of Representatives has overwhelmingly voted to repeal the law. The Senate immediately approved the House bill and it has gone to the White House for final action.

The fact that the detention camp law has never been used since its passage in the witch hunting days of the 1950s is little assurance that it wouldn't be. In May the government arrested and confined some 12,000 persons in Washington in what the courts have found was largely an illegal procedure. And the district government is now seeking anticrime money "to plan our role in detaining people" in future demonstrations.

President Nixon's attempt to revitalize the inactive Subversive Activities Control Board to probe "totalitarian, Fascist, Communist, subversive" or violent groups is, in view of past experience, an invitation to witch hunting that could lead to mass arrests in emergency, without due process. And we have the recent examples of Great Britain and Canada: The first making mass arrests and detaining persons without warrants in Northern Ireland and the latter having detained 450 persons in last October's Quebec kidnaping crisis.

The United States and its basic guarantees of civil rights depend upon due process of law. The detention camp concept and mass arrests violate the rule of law. The shameful concentration camp law must be wiped from the books.

HOUSTON CHRONICLE

Houston, Tex., September 25, 1971

Congress has wisely repealed a law that could have been the source of great injustice.

The law gave the federal government the authority to put suspected spies or saboteurs into detention camps during time of war or insurrection. It was passed by Congress over President Harry S. Truman's veto in 1950, during the Korean War. Six detention camps were established; all but one, now a federal prison, have been abandoned.

Even though the measure was never used, its presense gave rise to fears that it could be used against minority groups. The Nixon administration urged repeal as a gesture of assurance.

In the House, the move for repeal was led by Rep. Spark M. Matsunaga, D-Hawaii, who served as a captain in a U.S. Nisei regiment during World War II while relatives and friends were in detention camps set up by executive order.

In addition to repealing the 1950 law, the new measure prohibits establishment of detention camps except by affirmative action of Congress.

Rep. Matsunaga expressed our sentiments when he said: "There is no place for concentration camps in the American scheme."

Wisconsin ⚖ State Journal

Madison, Wis., September 24, 1971

Wisconsin should be proud that all of its senators and representatives voted with the majority to erase the nation's 1950 law which permits the use of detention camps.

The very existence of that law to permit the wholesale arrest of persons even on the basis of race, color, or ancestry is repugnant to this nation's constitutional protection of individual liberty.

Rep. Robert Kastenmeier (D-Wis.), chairman of the Judiciary subcommittee which handled the bill, deserves special credit for steering the legislation through the lower house.

The original detention camp law was an outgrowth of World War II when more than 110,000 Americans of Japanese origin were evacuated from the Pacific Coast on the grounds of "military necessity." More than two-thirds were native-born Americans.

Understandably, Hawaii with its large population of citizens of Japanese descent has been particularly concerned about repealing the act. Members of other minority groups, especially Negroes, have felt threatened by the provision.

There is no reason to believe that existing criminal laws would not be sufficient to meet any threat from individuals or groups, following normal due process.

The Nixon Administration has supported the repeal of the law. The House added a declaration, moreover, that "no citizen shall be imprisoned or otherwise detained by the United States except pursuant to an act of Congress."

Good bipartisan cooperation has gone into the effort to do away with a law that is an anathema to our democracy.

CHICAGO DAILY NEWS

Chicago, Ill., September 17, 1971

Congress has belatedly come around to agreeing that concentration camps have no place in the American scheme of things. It voted this week to repeal the 1950 law permitting the government to set up such camps in time of emergency.

Repeal of this law has been the particular concern of Rep. Abner J. Mikva since he first went to Washington. The South Side Chicago congressman learned early that its presence on the books was a sore point with blacks, who considered it made to order for suppressing minority groups any time the majority so chose. His crusade has now paid off. The House voted 356 to 49 for repeal Tuesday, and the Senate gave its approval on Thursday.

The bark of this law is much worse than its bite, for it has never been used, and there is little likelihood it would be. It was enacted during the McCarthy aberrations, and although six sites for detention camps were at one time designated, that was as far as it went.

But as long as the law remained, it was an irritant to blacks and the source of a continuing mythology that a vast conspiracy exists to herd black people into concentration camps. Wiping the law off the books was the best way to set such fears to rest.

THE NASHVILLE TENNESSEAN

Nashville, Tenn., September 17, 1971

BOTH THE House and Senate have wisely voted to repeal a 1950 law which permits the government to operate detention camps for suspected spies and saboteurs.

While the act has never been invoked, the government did establish six detention camps in the U.S. in 1952. They have never been used, but the law has created real fears among minority groups in recent years that they might be.

In debate on repeal, backers frequently harked back to World War II when 112,000 Japanese-Americans were rounded up and sent to West Coast and Arkansas detention camps where they lived under armed guard.

Now, the Congress has not only repealed what some have termed a "concentration camp" law, but included language that would prohibit the government from imprisoning anyone except under existing laws with an act of Congress.

It is a sad commentary on the times that minorities are so suspicious of their own government. But repeal of the act ought to allay the fears and suspicions about the detention camp law and that is of benefit.

The Chattanooga Times

Chattanooga, Tenn., September 22, 1971

Without much fanfare and on an almost deserted Senate floor, another vestige of the Joe McCarthy era came to an end last Thursday with the repeal of the Emergency Detention Act of 1950. It was passed during the height of American hysteria over the alleged infiltration of Communists into high offices in the United States and allowed for the detention of "anyone who may or probably might commit sabotage." The arrest was to be based only on the judgment of law enforcement officials and required neither evidence nor constitutional judicial practices.

Sen. Richard Nixon was a member of the House committee which wrote the legislation in 1950, but President Richard Nixon is expected to sign the legislation promptly. President Harry Truman had vetoed the measure when it came to his desk, but Congress overrode him.

Actually the act has never been used although underground newspapers and radical leftist leaders have been known to spread the rumor that the government was preparing detention camps for a roundup of political dissidents.

The Justice Department favored repeal and said that there are sufficient laws on the books now to handle saboteurs and radicals who commit criminal acts. It's a law we're glad to see stricken from the books, even though it took far too long to do it.

ARKANSAS DEMOCRAT
Little Rock, Ark., September 17, 1971

Congress, with the Arkansas delegation voting yes, repealed the law that allowed the U. S. government to operate detention camps.

The hero of this week's victory — the first time in history that the House Internal Security Committee (the old unAmerican activities committee) has had a recommendation overturned — was Rep. Spark M. Matsunaga, D-Hawaii. He had a sort of a personal bias. While he was in the U.S. Army fighting the Nazis in Europe in World War II, the U.S. government rounded up his relatives and put them in detention centers in places like Rohwer, Ark. Their only crime was that they were Japanese. To them, the only major difference between the Nazi centers and theirs was that the Nazis' were equipped with full-length gas ovens.

After that bitter experience, no American President would ever again order Americans to be penned up in wholesale lots. But that's not the point. To minority-group Americans like Congressman Matsunaga, the fact that their country would keep such a law on the books was an affront — and a fright, because they know that if it were ever used, it would be against them.

Now that this relic is out of the way, maybe someone with Congressman Matsunaga's energy will go to work and get the Congress finally to approve the 25-year-old international treaty against genocide.

The Hartford Courant
Hartford, Conn., September 18, 1971

Federal detention camps that were set up under a law adopted during the hysteria of the early 1950s have never been used, but their continued existence has reflected on the judgment of the government. Now that the House has voted to abolish them by a vote of 356 to 49 and the Senate has agreed by a voice vote, the uneasiness they have caused among minority racial and political groups may be near an end.

The Nixon administration had suggested the step, but Congress went further with the adoption of a restriction of the setting up of new resettlement camps, detention centers or concentration camps, whatever they may be called, by the President except by affirmative action of Congress. This will prevent the rounding up of militants and imprisoning them in camps by executive order.

It could have saved American Japanese in World War II, although a strong plea to Congress might have caught its members off guard and resulted in the same injustice, one that has put a permanent blot on the record. Congress probably remembers that it was responsible for the detention camp law, but it is right in considering that it is more difficult to infect many then one with unreasoning fears.

It was appropriate that the repeal action was led by Representative Spark M. Matsunaga of Hawaii, many of whose friends were detained in camps in this country while he was fighting with a Nisei regiment in the Pacific during World War II. At the outbreak of the war 112,000 Japanese-Americans were rounded up and placed in 10 relocation centers. Mr. Matsunaga has earned the right to remind Congress, which passed the law over President Truman's veto, that "there is no place for concentration camps in the American scheme."

The wording of the law is responsible for fears that it could be used to punish almost anyone whose views the government disliked. All officials had to do was to say they believed a person might engage in or conspire to commit acts of espionage or sabotage in times of war or insurrection in aid of a foreign enemy.

The six camps established under the law have never been used for the designated purpose and were abandoned. One is now used as a federal prison. Sabotage can be dealt with by existing laws or those that may be adopted to meet specific conditions. New mistakes may be made in irrational times. But the dangers of the concentration camp mentality have been demonstrated, in this country and abroad, and this knowledge ought to help avoid them in the future.

THE  SUN
Baltimore, Md., September 18, 1971

The two branches of Congress have voted, sensibly and decisively, to repeal the so-called Emergency Detention Act which has been on the books since 1950. The law has not been used but so long as it is in being it is an ugly reminder of the concentration camps of the Nazi era and of the wartime arrests and detention in the United States of some 112,000 Japanese-Americans. For good measure in its repealer the House put in a provision forbidding any executive action to detain citizens in the absence of direct legislative authority, and this was agreed to by the Senate.

In 1969 the Senate passed a repeal bill which was not acted upon by the House. The Senate Judiciary Committee had approved a bill repealing the detention camp authority, and the Senate thus was ready to act without delay. There was no good reason for passing the law in the first place; it was a product of the old House Un-American Activities Committee and the McCarthy era and, without much doubt, could not have survived a constitutional challenge if it had ever been tested.

THE BLADE
Toledo, Ohio, September 19, 1971

SOMETIMES there is substance in symbolism, and a commendable example is the repeal of the 1950 federal law permitting the establishment of detention camps for suspected spies and subversives. The act never had been used and quite probably never would have been, so its removal from the code books was — as nearly all who pushed the repeal measure readily conceded — largely a gesture. But not an empty one.

For one thing, the move to abolish the law was prompted a couple of years ago by widespread rumors among Negroes that the provision might be used against them, particularly black militants. The Nixon administration vigorously denies there was any foundation to the notion but — probably because it had been fostered in part by some unfortunate remarks by a key official — recognized that the mere persistence of the reports represented a reality to be concerned about. The Administration itself, therefore, recommended the repeal as a means of putting the rumors to rest.

But beyond that precipitating factor, the old statute is properly done away with merely because it was so offensive in other respects. The very concept of concentration camps is alien to fundamental American precepts of liberty and the law, and one of the infamous stains on the nation's record was the internment of more than 100,000 citizens of Japanese descent shortly after Pearl Harbor. The bitterness left from that deed — done on the mere executive order of President Franklin Roosevelt — was very much in evidence as the House debated the repeal measure before approving it. Wisely, the majority added a provision barring any future establishment of detention camps even in time of national emergency without express affirmative action by Congress.

That is not an absolute guarantee against future abuse, of course — Congress, after all, passed the 1950 act over the veto of President Truman. Nevertheless, its repeal at long last is a welcome erasure of one more vestige of Joe McCarthy hysteria — and an implicit reminder that this nation should have enough faith in the strength of its principles to protect itself through the proper processes of law without resorting to the tactics of totalitarianism.

PRESIDENT VETOES BILL INCREASING PUBLIC ACCESS TO GOVERNMENT DATA

President Ford vetoed a bill Oct. 17 amending the 1966 Freedom of Information Act to give freer public access to government data. Ford said the bill was "unconstitutional and unworkable" and a threat to U.S. "military or intelligence secrets and diplomatic relations." But he praised the bill's goals and hoped new legislation would be enacted from his own proposals in the next session.

Ford objected to the bill's authority to the courts to declassify secret documents "in sensitive and complex areas where they have no expertise." He agreed that the courts could "inspect classified documents and review the justification for their classification," he said, but the law should read that the courts would have to uphold the classification "if there is a reasonable basis to support it." In the bill, the burden of proof was on the government to justify a secrecy classification.

The President also objected to a provision that agency investigatory files, including those of the Federal Bureau of Investigation, be made public on request unless the agency could prove that disclosure would be harmful to the national interest. Such a provision would be excessively burdensome to the agencies, he said, as would the bill's requirements for a 10-day time limit for response to requests for data and a 20-day limit for rulings on appeals.

Other provisions of the bill authorized (a) procedure for penalty in the event data were withheld "arbitrarily or capriciously," (b) recovery of legal fees by successful petitioners, (c) publication of indexes of agency decisions, and (d) access to data if it were "reasonably" described.

The Senate had approved the final version of the bill by voice vote Oct. 1, the House by 349–2 vote Oct. 7.

The Washington Post

Washington, D.C., October 21, 1974

PRESIDENT FORD'S assurances of openness in government were dealt a serious blow by his decision Thursday night to veto the amendments to the Freedom of Information Act. Those amendments, intended to make it easier for citizens and the press to learn what is going on within government, could have played an important role in bringing about that promised openness. Congress was willing; the amendments passed both houses by substantial margins. But Mr. Ford chose instead to accept the counsel of the bureaucracy that these changes in the law somehow menaced the operation of government.

The section that caused the President to bring down the weight of his veto power provides that documents that are stamped "secret" must be proved to contain valid secrets if a citizen or a reporter seeks to inspect them. An orderly mechanism was provided for seeing this purpose through. The legislation required that, when a dispute arose over such a document, a federal district court judge would inspect the document in private and determine whether it was in the public interest for the document to be released.

There were other provisions of the act, all of them of paramount importance in the effort to make the government more accountable to those it seeks to serve. The new legislation would have reduced the number of days within which an agency would be required to say whether it intended to provide the public with a previously withheld document. The FBI and other investigative agencies would no longer have been able to withhold material unless they could justify doing so on the grounds that a current investigation or a defendant's rights would be compromised. And, perhaps most important of all from the bureaucrat's vantagepoint, if an official withheld a document and the court decided the document should not have been withheld, the official might be required by the Civil Service Commission to give an account of his actions.

All of these provisions were in the spirit of the kind of relationship between government and the public that Mr. Ford assured the Congress he wanted when he made his first appearance before a joint session only days after taking office. Now he has vetoed a piece of legislation that sought to overhaul a well-intentioned law that has languished ineffectively for nearly a decade. In so doing, the President has put it up to both houses of Congress to muster the votes to make the Freedom of Information Act a more effective servant of the public's right to know.

THE INDIANAPOLIS NEWS
Indianapolis, Ind., October 23, 1974

President Ford's veto last week of amendments to the Freedom of Information Act is based on a legitimate objection.

The Supreme Court ruled last year that under the act, as currently written, Federal judges do not have the authority to inspect classified government documents to determine if they contain defense or foreign policy material that should be kept secret. In response to the ruling, the new bill specifically gives Federal judges this power and puts the burden of proof on the Executive branch.

The effect, as seen by President Ford, could be to lay bare all manner of government documents relating to the conduct of diplomacy and defense policy. Ford questioned the ability of judges with no background in military or diplomatic matters to make such decisions, and he declared: "I simply cannot accept a provision that would risk exposure of our military and intelligence secrets and diplomatic relations because of a judicially perceived failure to satisfy a burden of proof."

The President's position is rooted in legitimate constitutional powers. He is the commander-in-chief of the armed forces, and he is given primary responsibility for the conduct of foreign affairs, with limited review by the Senate. To interject the judiciary into these areas of clear, historic presidential responsibility would be a radical departure from constitutional principle and a severe handicap to the President. No government in the world opens its intelligence and diplomatic files for inspection, and it is naive to suppose that the United States can do so and continue to perform in a major world role.

In this light, the proposed amendment is less of an information reform than a rather peculiar and dangerous expression of the nation's isolationist mood.

Aside from this provision, however, the vetoed bill contains several important changes that would assist the press and the public in obtaining information. One requires government officials to respond to information requests within a specified period of time, thus preventing officials from defeating the purposes of the Freedom of Information Act with endless delays. Another provides for suspension or other punishment for bureaucrats who withhold information "arbitrarily or capriciously." Others assist citizens in knowing what to ask for or in obtaining information when they may not know what specific documents to request.

The need now is for Congress to write legislation that will assist Americans in their day-to-day dealings with the government while respecting the President's right to conduct external affairs without judicial interference.

THE CINCINNATI ENQUIRER
Cincinnati, Ohio, October 27, 1974

PRESIDENT FORD'S veto of the Freedom of Information Act amendments raises serious questions about that important legislation which Congress ought to think about before an effort is made to override the President's eighth veto of his new administration.

The 17 amendments to the 1966 Freedom of Information Act are important weapons in the struggle against government secrecy. When The Enquirer endorsed the act on September 4, we suggested the amendments "would make it a little easier for the public to learn what its government is doing." The principle we supported then remains just as important now as before the President's veto.

It is clear that federal agencies have abused their privilege of keeping intraoffice memoranda confidential in that some agencies commingle those memoranda with information the law says should be part of the public record when someone seeks it. The new legislation would help correct that abuse.

But the President apparently vetoed the new amendments for two reasons. First, one of the amendments would give federal judges the authority to reject a decision by the secretary of defense or the secretary of state that a document originally marked "classified" should instead be made public. The President's objection—and it is a valid one—is that the courts will be making "the initial classification decision in sensitive and complex areas where they have no expertise."

It is clear that there are matters of foreign policy and national security which must, for a time, remain classified. To give a plaintiff's view that a classified matter should be made public the same weight as the judgment of a Cabinet officer charged with national security affairs may well be inimical to the national interest.

The President suggested an alternative solution which merits examination.

Instead of allowing the courts to decide the merits of a decision to classify some matter involving national security before the material can be withheld, the President suggested that the courts "inspect classified documents and review the justification for their classification."

This is a reasonable alternative since it would subject a decision to classify a document to judicial review without running the risk that a matter which should remain secret will automatically be made public.

Beyond his objection to the amendments on national-security grounds, the President also vetoed the bill because it would require that files of the Federal Bureau of Investigation and other agencies would have to be made public unless the government could prove that such disclosures would harm the national interest. The President's veto apparently reflected a concern expressed earlier by the Justice Department that "informers and other confidential sources in criminal investigations" be protected.

It would be well for Congress to reconsider this amendment to the act, as well, before a vote to override the veto is taken.

In an atmosphere in which secrecy in government fostered wrongs by the Nixon administration against individuals and the Constitution, it is understandable that the House passed the original amendments by a vote of 349-2. The Senate approved the measure by a voice vote.

In an atmosphere in which openness has quite properly become a virtue, many in Congress may be anxious to let the White House know any effort at secrecy in government will be resisted. We applaud this attitude, but at the same time we recognize the validity of the President's concern and hope Congress will, too.

As we wrote on September 4, "It is difficult to frame legislation to correct" the abuses of excessive secrecy in government "in the absence of an eagerness on the part of government agencies to comply with a law that has been in force since 1967."

This is the heart of the matter. Aggressive legislation *is* needed to ferret out unwarranted secrecy. But it should not be done at the expense of national security.

The risk in this position is apparent to us. Where secrecy is legitimized it will be abused. And where it is abused, we will oppose it. But protecting national security has priority.

The Chattanooga Times
Chattanooga, Tenn., October 23, 1974

President Ford's veto of legislation containing 17 amendments to the 1966 Freedom of Information Act is depressing news, coming as it does in the wake of two national tragedies—Watergate and the Vietnam war—which might have been ended sooner had not the leaders involved been able to hide their actions in secrecy.

The FOI Act required the federal government and its agencies to make available to citizens, upon request, all documents and records. There were exceptions—national security or foreign policy information, internal personnel practices, trade secrets, personal information, law enforcement investigatory information, and the like.

But difficulties soon developed. Citizens complained about bureaucratic delay, the cost of bringing suit to force disclosure and excessive charges levied by agencies for finding and providing the requested information. Then, in 1973, the Supreme Court ruled that Congress had not given the courts the power to go behind a "classified" stamp on information sought by a citizen under the law. In short, classification meant exemption.

The amendments to the law sought to clarify the matter, especially the Court's

decision. One amendment gave federal courts the power to obtain improperly withheld documents and examine them privately to determine if they had been properly exempted.

It was to this point that Mr. Ford explicitly referred in his veto message, objecting to the courts' being permitted to make what amounts to 'the initial classification decision in sensitive and

complex areas where they have no expertise.'

This is nonsense. Such a sentiment presupposes that federal judges lack sufficient common sense or integrity to enable them to rule against the release of national security information.

This means that citizens will continue to have difficulty obtaining information improperly withheld because some bureaucrat who has made a mistake has hidden it behind a "classified" label.

Mr. Ford has promised his own proposals for broadening the FOI legislation. But can we be sure that he will come forth with anything other than that which seeks to protect, first of all, the interests of the federal agencies who would be affected by the bill? The best answer appears to be: Not likely.

The Charlotte Observer
Charlotte, N.C., October 23, 1974

Take away Linus's blanket and this usually mild-mannered inhabitant of the Peanuts comic strip becomes a tiger. Bureaucrats sometimes react similarly when someone threatens to take away their precious "top secret" classification stamps. In their efforts to keep information from the people, they now have received a boost from President Ford.

Aware when he assumed office that people were sick and tired of secrecy, of being lied to, and of finding that Washington was a Byzantium on the Potomac, President Ford promised to make candor and openness the touchstones of his Administration. But now he is buying the tired arguments that have been invoked so many times to defend secrecy.

In his veto of a bill to strengthen the Freedom of Information Act, he said it was a threat to American "military intelligence secrets and diplomatic relations." He also said it would give the courts power in an area they were unfamiliar with and complained that it would require too much bureaucratic work would be required to go through those mountains of classified documents in complying with requests for information.

The intent of the amendments was to strengthen the bill, particularly by putting the burden not on the citizen seeking information but the bureaucrat withholding it. When the act passed in 1966, it was hailed as a breakthrough for citizens and newsmen anxious to know what their government was up to. But the act has not lived up to its billing, and part of the reason is that bureaucrats are able to frustrate requests for information through administrative hurdles and the courts.

The bill would have changed this by cutting the time limit for agency responses to requests for information, setting administrative penalties for arbitrary refusal and permitting recovery of legal fees by successful petitioners. The courts would have been allowed to review classified documents and classification procedures. And a bureaucrat would have been criminally liable if the court found he "arbitrarily or capriciously" withheld desired information. In short, the act would have some teeth.

Attorney General William Saxbe also recently moved to put shrouds around government information. He in effect has reversed a 15-month old decision by his predecessor, Elliot Richardson, which gave authorized scholars access to investigatory files more than 15 years old. A scholar writing a book on the Alger Hiss case obtained FBI files that had numerous deletions, apparently made because of the scholar's request. Mr. Saxbe backed up the FBI on this, thereby violating the spirit if not the letter of Mr. Richardson's policy.

For weeks now, we have been hearing about the "lessons of Watergate," and we will undoubtedly hear more as moralists of every type look for Watergate lessons like shamans examining entrails for signs. But there is one lesson that must be obvious to all: Secrecy creates the environment for a Watergate, a Vietnam, a Bay of Pigs. The power of a bureaucrat or Administration official to cover his mistakes with a classification stamp is inherently anti-democratic. President Ford could not see that. Congress should override his veto of the Freedom of Information bill when it returns in November.

BUFFALO EVENING NEWS
Buffalo, N.Y., October 23, 1974

President Ford acted on bad advice, in our view, when he vetoed changes in the law that would provide Americans with greater access to information maintained by the federal government.

The enlightened changes, overwhelmingly approved by Congress, apply to the Freedom of Information Act originally adopted in 1966. Among other things, they would discipline departments that withheld public information illegally, surely an incentive to more bureaucratic openness. To prevent unending and unnecessary delays, requests by the public and press for information would have to be decided within 20 working days.

President Ford objected principally to a change that would authorize federal judges to review whether a "secret" or "top secret" classification on a piece of military or diplomatic information was justified. If it was, the information would not be released; if it was not, then it would be made public. The President contended that the courts shouldn't be involved in what amounted to the "initial classification decision in sensitive and complex areas where t h e y have no expertise."

More persuasive arguments lie on the other side of the issue. The court review would be made in private. The Supreme Court ruled last year that the courts could, constitutionally, have such authority. The traditional problem in this area has been far too much rather than too little secret classification, reflecting the bureaucratic tendency to play it safe w i t h p o t e n t i a l l y embarrassing information.

But the public in a democracy needs timely, accurate information in order to reach informed judgments about policy and the performance of its elected representatives. And judges, secure with lifetime appointments and independent of the executive branch, can generally be counted on — in weighing all the pros and cons bearing on a specific classification dispute — to balance national security needs against the public's right to know, while fairly checking excesses of secrecy fostered by self-serving federal agencies and bureaucrats.

For all these reasons, Congress ought to override the Ford veto, thus ensuring a fair trial for statutory changes designed to provide the American people with wider and more timely access to public information about their own government.

SAN JOSE NEWS
San Jose, Calif., October 21, 1974

President Ford's veto of a measure to improve the 1966 Freedom of Information Act means the public will continue to encounter unwarranted difficulties and delays in obtaining information about their government and its operations.

The President objected to empowering federal d i s t r i c t courts to examine documents withheld from public release in order to determine if they had been properly classified.

The Freedom of Information Act exempts documents and records involving secret national security or foreign policy information, personal information, trade secrets and other critical material, such as law enforcement investigative reports.

The President argued that to give civilian judges authority to overrule government security classification would jeopardize diplomatic relations and military or intelligence secrets.

There is this danger. But it is perhaps exaggerated. Congress, alerted to this concern, already had modified its measure to d e c l a r e that federal judges should give "substantial weight" to the arguments of federal agencies where d o c u m e n t s concerning such critical matters are involved.

Federal agencies have grossly abused the "classified" stamp, as virtually every study of g o v e r n m e n t documents and records has shown. R e d u c t i o n of these abuses could be expected if judicial review were readily possible, in contrast to an administrative review within the i n f o r m a-tion-withholding agency itself.

How many federal agencies can be expected to admit that they have been guilty of misclassifying documents and records? The public, seeking access to information about its government, could expect a more impartial ruling from a third party — in this case, the courts.

The President has pledged to submit his own plan to improve public access to government records without the risks he sees in the congressional amendments to the Freedom of Information Act. As an advocate of candor and open g o v e r n m e n t, Ford must approach this task as a compelling obligation.

Other features of the vetoed Freedom of Information Act amendment p a c k a g e definitely s h o u l d be implemented. These include time limits on providing requested information, reasonable fees for f i n d i n g and copying materials, and preparation of indexes to agency records and documents.

Honolulu Star-Bulletin

Honolulu, Hawaii, October 19, 1974

During the fight to prevent an underground nuclear test in the Aleutian Islands, Rep. Patsy T. Mink of Hawaii filed a citizen's court suit to gain access to secret advance evaluations of the test made for the Environmental Protection Agency.

This led to a 1973 Supreme Court decision that the courts had no right to go behind a "classified" stamp placed on information sought by a citizen under the 1966 Freedom of Information Act — even though such stamps automatically exempted the data from the act's disclosure provisions.

Congress responded to this court ruling, with a bill plugging a number of loopholes by which bureaucrats had circumvented the Freedom of Information Act.

A centerpiece dealt with the issue in the Mink suit. It provided that in the future, federal district courts will be able to compel the production of contested material so that the judge can decide in chambers whether it is properly exempted from disclosure.

On Thursday President Ford vetoed the bill, claiming that it would allow federal judges to make "the initial classification decision in sensitive and complex areas where they have no expertise."

Congressman John Moss, D-Calif., the leader of the fight for a strong Freedom of Information Act, will lead a fight to override the veto. In such matters, he said, the Watergate experience is enough to convince him "I would rather trust the courts."

Our vote goes with Congressman Moss and Mrs. Mink Federal courts deal with the most sensitive matters in America. If they aren't qualified to judge the validity of a "secret" stamp, we're in real trouble.

The Dispatch

Columbus, Ohio, October 23, 1974

IN LARGE measure the preservation of a free and responsive government depends on its openness with the people and in its reliance upon their judgment in the end.

We believe President Ford basically adheres to that principle and that he chose the wrong alternative to improve its workability when he vetoed the 17 amendments adopted by Congress to the Freedom of Information Act of 1966.

THE ACT has not worked particularly well since it went into effect due to the inherent tendencies of federal bureaucracies to overclassify their documents or otherwise obstruct legitimate efforts by citizens and news agencies seeking information.

The President fears the new amendments jeopardize military and diplomatic secrets. He objects, particularly, to a provision which would allow judicial review of government contested efforts to gain governmental information.

WITHOUT judicial review, a decision to release or withhold government information would continue to rest with bureaucrats who have themselves and their respective agencies, as well as legitimate government secrets, to protect.

In preparing the amendments, responsible legal, legislative and news media leaders considered their national security implications for three years.

They rightfully exempted criminal investigative records from the amendments.

THE MARGINS by which each house of Congress passed the amendments—349 to 2 in the House and a voice vote in the Senate—reflect the Legislative Branch's broad confidence in the checks and balances provided by judicial review.

It is difficult to see any justifiable fears about the amendments' adequacy to protect authentic national secrets.

One should keep in mind, too, that no law is sacred once enacted. If it does not fulfill its intended purpose, it can be amended to do so or be abolished, as need be.

THE AMENDMENTS should be given a chance and for that reason the Congress should override Mr. Ford's veto.

There is a good chance that may happen. But if there is any doubt it may not, it should be done.

Any citizen who believes the government should conduct its business as openly as possible — even including risks which may not be foreseeable—can readily wish the same.

THE DAILY OKLAHOMAN
Oklahoma City,
October 23, 1974

ALTHOUGH legitimate arguments exist on both sides, President Ford's announced reasons for vetoing an improved version of the Freedom of Information Act clash with the people's right of access to knowledge about the operation of their government.

Ford tempered his veto statement by commenting on the "laudable goals" of the legislation and expressing the hope that Congress will pass a new bill incorporating the changes he wants. Considering the margins by which the vetoed bill was passed —366 to 8 in the House and 64-17 in the Senate—Congress is more likely to override Ford's objections.

The bill was designed to achieve more faithful compliance with the basic 1966 FOI Act, which many federal agencies have continued to resist. Lengthy hearings before the Senate Judiciary Committee last year documented numerous abuses in which the clear intent of the law was being subverted by bureaucrats unwilling to respond to public requests for information.

At every turn many departments and agencies were erecting roadblocks against the flow of information to which the public is entitled. Inordinate delays in fulfilling valid requests; excessive charges for search and copy fees; cumbersome and costly court procedures to force compliance—these were among the loopholes plugged by the vetoed bill.

For example, the bill required government payment of legal fees and court costs when a citizen had to resort to litigation to gain information. It also provided for penalties against government employees who refused to comply with the law.

Ford's main hangup over the bill was its provision that subjected the government's classification authority to review by federal courts. The President argued in effect that judges were not always competent to rule on whether military or diplomatic secrets might be compromised by public disclosure.

There is some merit in this contention, but the fact remains that the great majority of disputes over government's failure to comply with the law have involved documents not even remotely connected with national security or U.S. relations with other countries. One arrogant agency at first refused and then delayed for months before releasing a copy of its own regulations.

Even former President Nixon conceded "the many abuses" of the document classification system in urging reforms two years ago. People cannot respect or trust their government, he said, if information which properly belongs to them "is systematically withheld by those in power. . ."

Regardless of whether Ford's veto is sustained or overridden, there is no reason why a good faith effort by the White House and Congress cannot resolve the national security issue and still make the Freedom of Information Act work the way it should for the American people.

BOTH HOUSES OF CONGRESS OVERRIDE FREEDOM OF INFORMATION ACT VETO

President Ford's Oct. 17 veto of the amendments to the Freedom of Information Act was overturned by the House Nov. 20 and the Senate Nov. 21. A two-thirds vote of both houses was required to override. The House vote was 371–31. In the Senate it was 65–27 (three more than the required two-thirds majority.) The amendments would give citizens freer access to government information.

FORT WORTH STAR-TELEGRAM
Fort Worth, Tex., October 22, 1974

President Ford acted contrary to his own preachments for openness in government with his veto of the new Freedom of Information Act.

The measure was designed to eliminate some strategies government officials have used to get around the intent of the first freedom of information act, passed in 1966, which in turn was designed to stop the widespread flouting by government officials of the people's right to know as guaranteed in the Constitution.

The first act laid down the general rule that the people have the right to know all that goes on in their government, but it listed some exceptions. The most important of these were defense secrets, investigatory files, business and trade secrets in government hands and government memos circulated in the executive branch.

These exceptions have been flagrantly abused by government officials to hide their own incompetence or for other reasons to deny the public access to information it ought to have.

The chief strategies used have been applying the secrecy stamp to material that has no business being so classified and delaying release of unclassified material until its content is no longer of any significance.

Under the new act, deadlines would be set for release of unclassified information requested to be made public and federal judges would be given the job of reviewing materials with questioned secrecy classifications to determine whether they should indeed be secret.

Mr. Ford objected to the judicial review provision. This would permit courts to make "the initial classification decision in sensitive and complex areas where they have no expertise," he said.

However, some third party must be brought into the decision process. Otherwise, the government is left with the final say on what the people have a right to know about the government—a flagrant flouting of the principles on which our free society is based. And, since there must be a third party, the judiciary seems the logical agency for the role.

Mr. Ford, it seems to us, has violated the spirit of his own public dedication to openness in government with the veto of this measure, and it's to be hoped that Congress will lose no time in overriding his decision when it returns to business.

CHICAGO DAILY NEWS
Chicago, Ill., November 23, 1974

Congress did well to override President Ford's veto of a measure amending the Freedom of Information Act. The law as now revised provides fewer opportunities for the government to withhold information the public is entitled to have.

Contrary to Ford's veto message, the new provisions still protect government secrets where secrecy is a valid concern, as in national security and diplomatic relations. What they strive to do is remove the cover from documents that might be withheld for fear they would be embarrassing or politically damaging.

Ford's veto of the bill overwhelmingly passed by Congress was inexplicable in light of his pledge to conduct an open and candid administration. Both houses have now held him to that pledge, and the country should be the better for it.

ARGUS-LEADER
Sioux Falls, S.D., November 25, 1974

Congress was correct in overriding President Gerald Ford's veto of the Freedom of Information bill. Enactment of the measure should lead to more openness by the federal government when citizens and the press deal with the bureaucracy.

The question of releasing secret national security or foreign policy information, internal personnel practices, trade secrets and other information exempt by law and law enforcement investigatory reports is not involved. Those categories were exempted from the Freedom of Information Act passed in 1966 which requires the federal government and its agencies to make available, upon request all government documents and records. The 1974 change amends the wording of the national defense and national security exemption to make it clear that it applies only to properly classified information.

President Ford asked the House-Senate Conference committee in August to delay action so that he could propose changes in the committee's bill amending the 1966 law. He got four of the five changes he proposed, but vetoed the final bill anyway, demanding that Congress grant all five of his original proposals and add a new one.

President Ford has emphasized that he wants his administration to be an open one, within pragmatic limits. It seems apparent that his advisers did not give him an accurate reflection of congressional feelings about the importance of the 1974 amendments to the 1966 Freedom of Information act. These were the first changes in the 1966 legislation approved by Congress.

The House vote to over-ride Ford's veto was 371-31 and the Senate vote, 65-27. Two-thirds is required in each House. South Dakota's U.S. Sen. James Abourezk, D-S.D., and the two representatives, Frank Denholm, D, and James Abdnor, R, voted with the majority to override the veto. Their votes were in the public interest.

Herald ☰ News

Fall River, Mass., November 27, 1974

When Congress overrode President Ford's veto of HR 12471 it served the people of this nation splendidly.

HR 12471 comprised a series of amendments to the Freedom of Information Act which, in effect, gave the people greater access to government information and documents. The amendments were to a bill passed in 1966 which had been meant to attain true freedom for the public to get information which the government had been concealing. The act only was partly successful. Bureaucrats in Washington opened a few records. They reclassified others to make them secret from the people.

The veto by President Ford of the amended bill was a surprise for he had made a commitment to open government upon taking office. That the Congress could not be hoodwinked by his contention that the amended bill required too little time for agencies to make available data sought by senators, representatives, newsmen and citizens, was a plus for the nation.

What the amendments do is end bureaucratic delay by requiring agencies to respond within 10 working days to a request. If an agency refuses such a request and an appeal is entered it must answer within 20 days why it has taken a negative stand, restricts what have been regarded as exorbitant fees asked by federal units for data, and creates civil service and court proceedings to ascertain whether any federal official or employe has acted capriciously or arbitrarily in withholding information.

President Ford and his advisors protested that foreign policy and military matters might become available when they should be classified. Nowhere in the original act nor in the amended act is such permitted. Specifically exempted from its provisions are secret national security or foreign policy information, and other data of similar nature.

What the new law does is speed up the informational process, close the loopholes in the old act, provide disciplinary action for those who would disregard the law, and permit judicial review of contested cases.

Congress has struck a blow for open government — something that the events of the past few years have proved is needed in this country now more than ever.

The Miami Herald

Miami, Fla., November 24, 1974

THE PRESIDENT will find broad support in the Congress and throughout the country for his efforts to whittle the federal budget and amputate large chunks of the bureaucracy that feeds on tax dollars. Presidential vetoes of outlandish spending programs are not likely to be overturned by a Congress mindful of its members' solemn campaign promises of government frugality and mindful also of the belt-tightening being done by the voters back home.

But Gerald Ford was in a different ball park when he vetoed an improved version of the 1966 Freedom of Information Act. The legislation broadens the right of citizens to find out what their government is doing. It narrows the bureaucrat's power to shield public business from the public that is paying salaries of those handling public business. Yet President Ford vetoed the bill on hazy grounds of national security.

As one congressman put it, the White House veto indicated that the same federal bureaucrats who opposed the original measure in 1966 have not learned the lesson of Watergate. Rep. Bill Alexander (D., Ark.) made a good point when he asked rhetorically during the House debate on overriding, "Hasn't the White House learned that government secrecy is the real enemy of democracy?"

Which is why the House and Senate wasted no time in overriding Mr. Ford's veto when they came back into session last week.

An important new provision of the information act compels the government to respond to requests within 10 days. Agencies had been taking months. Mr. Ford in his veto message said he preferred giving federal agencies up to 65 working days to answer a request, plus the right to seek unlimited extensions of time through appeals to federal courts.

The revised act allows for federal judges to review the decision of bureaucrats who classify documents as secret in the interest of national defense or foreign policy. Under previous law, there was no judicial review of such classification no matter how stupid or corrupt it might be. The Watergate coverup is perhaps only the tip of an immense iceberg of bureaucratic conspiracy to hide the extent of influence peddling and bribery.

The cost of supplying requested information is limited by the amended act. Agencies will now be able to charge for copying and search time, but nothing more. The advice Mr. Ford got from the bureaucrats was to insist on payment for review and examination of requested records when such costs ran beyond $100. The potential abuse here is obvious. The citizen seeking information would find himself billed for the salaries of whole staffs of agency executives and lawyers for as much as three months and with no guarantee that the information would be released.

In the Nixon years, that was the method used to block investigation by consumers. When one group sought records from the Agriculture Department on meat inspections, it was told the file might be made available on payment of $89,000 for review and examination within the executive branch.

Last week The Herald was named winner of the 1974 Public Service Award of the Associated Press Managing Editors Association for uncovering corruption in the Federal Housing Administration. The investigation by reporters Mike Baxter and James Savage took three years. The same careful and documented work would not have taken that long if public employes within the executive branch of the federal government had not been able to hide the corruption behind the veil of administrative authority.

The public treasury was looted by the FHA scheme. It could not have happened so easily and been hidden for so long under the broader provisions of the amended Freedom of Information Act.

Los Angeles Times

Los Angeles, Calif., November 25, 1974

Congress has taken action in support of two compatible goals: more disclosure by government of its affairs, and less invasion by government of individual privacy.

Both the House and the Senate overturned President Ford's veto of a bill to strengthen the Freedom of Information Act.

Designed to provide easier access to government information, the measure sets a 10-day limit for agency decisions on information requests, a 20-day limit on determination of administrative appeals, and a 30-day limit for the government to reply to lawsuits.

In addition, the bill limits the power of agencies to withhold law enforcement investigatory files, requires the maintenance of an index of documents available to the public and, finally, authorizes federal judges to examine classified documents to decide whether they should be made public.

Mr. Ford, in vetoing the legislation, expressed fear that federal judges, without any expertise in national security matters, might order the release of information that would endanger the nation. That is a legitimate concern, but it is not warranted by history. The courts always have been cautious, as they should be, in this area.

With the intent of safeguarding individual privacy, both branches of Congress have adopted legislation to restrict an increasing government demand for more personal information on Americans.

The Senate bill would require federal agencies to disclose their use of personal data, set standards for handling such information and create a Privacy Protection Commission to investigate violations. And beginning next Jan. 1, the measure would bar federal, state and local government agencies from denying any benefit or right to a citizen because of refusal to disclose his Social Security number. This provision would block the trend toward use of Social Security numbers as part of a universal identification system. The House version is essentially the same.

Significantly, the legislation developed overwhelming support for a simple but vital principle: government should collect no personal information for which it cannot show a legitimate need.

The Evening Bulletin
Philadelphia, Pa., November 22, 1974

Congress acted wisely yesterday in voting to override President Ford's veto of the 17 amendments to the 1966 Freedom of Information Act, which had been overwhelmingly approved by both chambers last month.

At a recent press conference in Phoenix, Mr. Ford defended the veto, citing concern for national security and individual privacy, and expressed hope that Congress would "make a few small but significant changes" in the legislation rather than override the veto.

The changes Mr. Ford suggested, however, were not small. They would have substantially weakened the amendments and permitted governmental agencies that have no reason to conduct business under the cloak of secrecy to continue doing so.

For far too long public officials and government bureaucrats have felt free to abuse their authority, withhold vital information from the public and sweep embarrassing blunders under the rug, knowing they were effectively shielded from public scrutiny.

DAYTON DAILY NEWS
Dayton, Ohio., November 24, 1974

Congress acted in the public's interest, but in its own as well, when it overrode President Ford's veto of a bill to expand the Freedom of Information act. The revision will, among other features, make some currently classified military information subject to court suits seeking its release.

The Freedom of Information act has been working well. It has forced the bureaucracy to release large amounts of information that the public clearly has a right to know —most recently, the report of FBI operations against political groups and the list of organizations the Nixon administration marked for harassment by the Internal Revenue service.

Itself often frustrated trying to get data from the executive branch, Congress no doubt sees the expansion of the act particularly as a means to airing the military issues that increasingly concern many congressmen. Even the armed services concede that much of what they too-routinely classify as secret is not data vital to national security.

The new provisions of the act will permit an impartial, judicial decision when someone chooses to dispute a "secret" stamp on information. President Ford hedged on his promise of an open administration when he vetoed the proposal.

ST. LOUIS POST-DISPATCH
St. Louis, Mo., November 21, 1974

By voting by 371 to 31 to override President Ford's veto of legislation strengthening the Freedom of Information Act, the House has made a further commitment to an open government that Mr. Ford himself once promised the nation.

Both houses of Congress earlier adopted the legislation, by overwhelming votes, because in eight years the Freedom of Information Act has not done what it was supposed to do. It was supposed to make it easier for individuals and the public to learn what their government was doing about them, for them and to them. After all, a responsible citizenry is supposed to be an informed citizenry.

Despite the 1936 law, officials from top to bottom found one means after another to ignore and obstruct the purpose of the law. The Nixon Administration sought to keep secret a history of the Vietnam war. The DBI kept under lock and key records on two long-past cases so that individuals had to go to court to try to get a look at them. Bureaucrats tried to put the burden for obtaining information on citizens who presumably had a right to it: the Tennessee Valley Authority charged citizens for clerical time spent in divulging data.

To prevent such blatant obstructionism Congress decided to amend the law in three fundamental ways. Where national security was advanced as the reason for secrecy, as it so often is, the new legislation would provide for court determination. Where officials withheld matters improperly, they would be subject to penalty. Moreover, officials would have 10 days to consider a request for information and 20 days to consider an appeal — and 30 days is surely time enough to find some good reason for secrecy if there is one. In general, the new bill would put the burden for executing the law on the Government.

It is remarkable enough that Mr. Ford would veto such a bill, but in doing so he repeated many of the excuses long advanced for secret government. He said the 30-day time limit was too short, and he argued that the measure would jeopardize national security. That, he said, should be left to the officials concerned, not to judicial determination.

And that, of course, is where the issue of secrecy has always been left, which is why the nation is overburdened with secrecy about its government. Secrecy was carried too far in the Watergate scandals, and it should never be carried so far again. The Congress was right to bring government closer to the people. Like the House, the Senate should override the veto.

THE KANSAS CITY STAR
Kansas City, Mo., November 25, 1974

President Ford's veto of amendments to the Freedom of Information Act last month seemed strange then, and in view of the dispatch with which the veto was overridden, it seems stranger now.

In October it was assumed that the President got bad advice from transitory White House employees—some of the old gang still left over holding tightly to Nixonian concepts of rule by those who know best.

Now it seems likely that this was not the case. The President was getting advice, instead, from the same old fossil mentality that characterizes the worst side of entrenched bureaucratic custom and convenience.

Congressional observers who have followed the situation closely say that some White House aides were stunned by the veto. They had, in fact, been planning a presidential signature ceremony with numerous pens and onlookers for this step in the interests of an informed public. Instead, came the veto.

The President, it is said, got pressure from four sources, and they were the same sources that had opposed the original Freedom of Information Act of 1966 when Lyndon Johnson had enough savvy to ignore them. These were elements in the Department of Justice, the Federal Bureau of Investigation, the Central Intelligence Agency and spokesmen for the Army, Navy and Air Force, although not the Pentagon, itself.

Part of the resistance came from the ingrained bureaucratic belief that the bureaucrats could do a better job for the people if the people would only leave them alone. It is an attitude in which government is seen as a personal possession of its operatives, not of the people, who are an annoyance. This attitude probably always will be with us. There were numerous discussions among administration and House and Senate staff people, and it was thought by congressional staff that FBI and CIA fears over investigations and precious secrets were allayed after some rewriting. The Republican and Democratic sponsors of the amendments went down to the White House and had the impression that the President understood. But then came the intervention and the President changed his mind.

The whole purpose of the Freedom of Information Act is to let the people know what its government does in their behalf—or to them— and to keep government from hiding ineptitude or worse in classified pigeonholes. The amendments will strengthen the concept of open government at a time when the people badly need reassuring. Such reassurance will serve the interest of politicians and professionals in government no less than the public.

The veto, coming as it did, and the prompt overriding, may have been fortunate for Mr. Ford. John Kennedy, new in the White House and eager to do the right thing, listened to the wrong voices on the Bay of Pigs and paid a frightful price. Mr. Ford listened to the wrong voices on the Freedom of Information veto but the cost to him and to the country was much less.

The Evening Gazette

Worcester, Mass., November 26, 1974

Congress has strengthened the the people's right to information about what their government is doing. The new law closes loopholes in the 1966 Freedom of Information Act.

These revisions have been three years in the making. In general, they are sound.

The basic principle is that whatever government does is public business. The exceptions come only when there is clear and general agreement that the public interest is best served by withholding information for a period of time. Such exceptions should be relatively few and relate mainly to national security and particularly to military information.

Unfortunately, the shoe has been on the other foot. The thousands upon thousands of bureaucrats in federal service have, in too many cases, built a wall around their operations. They have thrown press releases over that wall. But they haven't allowed the public its easy, natural and required access to public records.

In the first six years of the 1966 law, interested persons had to make 254,637 formal requests of federal departments to get information that should have been available, in most cases, without formal request. In 80 per cent of the cases, the requests were eventually granted. But the press and others are still fighting to get the rest of that information.

The new law makes it clearer than ever to the bureaucrats where their responsibilities lie. It is a fresh reminder that they, in an old and too-often forgotten term, are public servants.

The new law had to be passed over a veto by President Ford. He was concerned about four sections. He thought the courts would have too much power to rule on classification of documents. He wanted the law changed so that a court might not make public a document that it found improperly classified, if the bureaucrat's decision to classify it had been "reasonable." Such limitations on the courts seem unnecessary.

The President also was concerned that agencies would be forced to respond more promptly than they could reasonably be expected to. Perhaps so, but the act permits agencies to seek additional time.

President Ford also suggested opening the way to stiff fees for examining material. That has plausibility, but it could have been used to force individuals to -hire lawyers or other experts at substantial cost to review material that ought to be readily available to any citizen.

Another of the President's concerns was that investigatory files might be a little too open under the language approved by Congress. He suggested a weakening amendment.

It was clear that Congress, in the wake of Watergate, was in no mood to endorse anything that could be regarded as a cover-up. If history holds, federal agencies will work diligently at ways to circumvent the clear intent and language of this new law. However, it does arm the citizen with greater power to inquire into federal affairs with some hope of getting a straight answer.

If the new law creates really serious problems, President Ford can go back to Congress for tighter limits. In his veto, he was showing his sympathy for the concerns of certain federal agencies. They cannot accuse him of failing to stand with them, but Congress was not to be moved at this point.

The new law should have a positive effect. It should make government cleaner and more open. If it does not, then Congress and the President will have more work to do. If the public is to be expected to support so vast a structure as the federal government, it is elementary that the public should know what that structure, in all its parts, is doing.

Minneapolis Tribune

Minneapolis, Minn., November 30, 1974

The entire Minnesota congressional delegation (eight representatives and two senators) is to be congratulated for joining an overwhelming majority of their colleagues in overriding President Ford's veto of needed amendments to the Freedom of Information Act. The size of the votes (371 to 31 in the House and 65 to 27 in the Senate) and the high number of Republicans participating were a sharp rebuke to Mr. Ford who, after entering the White House with a promise of "open government," vetoed a bill aimed at opening up government.

The purposes of the original 1966 act have been undercut by bureaucratic pettifogging, often based on spurious claims of "national security" — a claim, incidentally, Mr. Ford used in his veto. The changes will do much to breach the wall of official secrecy and allow bona fide information seekers to get at the facts. The new provisions call for *in-camera* judicial review of national-security claims, place restrictions on investigatory agencies claiming exceptions, make agencies pay attorneys' fees under certain conditions and require government officials to reply to requests within 10 working days.

The amendments got through Congress easily the first time round — hastened on their way by the lessons of Vietnam and Watergate. But federal officials, leery of their effects on "classified" matters, persuaded Mr. Ford to veto them. This was bad advice, and we are pleased to see that Congress has corrected it.

ALBUQUERQUE JOURNAL

Albuquerque, N.M., November 26, 1974

The House and Senate have moved overwhelmingly to strip the secrecy shroud from operation of many facets of their government.

The House voted 371-31 and the Senate 65-27 to override President Ford's veto of a bill designed to plug loopholes bureaucrats used to withhold information from the public.

Both New Mexico senators, Joseph M. Montoya and Pete V. Domenici, voted with the Senate majority. Congressman Harold Runnels voted against the veto override while Congressman Manuel Lujan Jr. was recorded in favor.

The legislation extensively amends the 1966 Freedom of Information Act to make documents and information held by federal agencies more readily available to the public. The 1966 law provided exceptions which were subverted by government officials to thwart legitimate requests for information. A 1973 U.S. Supreme Court decision had weakened the act and made changes necessary.

The 1974 amendments still protect confidential and secret documents involving national security or foreign policy from unwarranted exposure but the courts rather than government underlings will have the final determination of confidentiality based on evidence presented by both sides.

ERVIN COMMITTEE HEARINGS REVEAL 25 MILLION LISTED IN ARMY FILES

During an earlier session of the Ervin hearings, Assistant Defense Secretary Robert J. Froehlke testified March 2 that the Pentagon had cards on 25 million "personalities" and on 760,000 organizations and incidents in the Defense Central Index of Investigation. Froehlke said, "On an average day, 12,000 [information] requests are processed and 20,000 additions, deletions and changes are made." He said the Index had grown at a rate of about 2,500,000 additions annually but was expected to level off in 1971. He also announced a new Defense Department directive, effective March 1, which banned "physical or electronic surveillance of federal, state or local officials, or of candidates for such offices."

HOUSTON CHRONICLE

Houston, Tex., March 8, 1971

Sen. Sam J. Ervin of North Carolina is performing a great service to the nation in ferreting out the extent and the nature of the Army's covert program of spying on civilians.

This whole operation smacks of Hitlerism or communism — the concept of the Army, which is supposed to defend the nation against foreign forces — snooping around, gathering information on American citizens. It is particularly frightening in view of the fact that some of the Army's targets have been distinguished Americans whose integrity or patriotism should not be open to question.

There may be instances, of course, when police or other government investigative agencies such as the F.B.I. should keep an eye on civilians, for certainly there are some groups in America which give evidence of wanting to destroy our society.

If this is true, however, it is work for civilian agencies under the tight supervision of civilian officials. It is not work for the military. We have seen in far too many countries how easy it is for the armed forces, since they have military power and a ready-made organization, to take control of a country. That is why our nation is dedicated to the principle of civilian control of our armed forces.

Sen. Ervin is an old-fashioned conservative, and the country needs more of his kind. He is repelled by the idea of Army snoopers checking on the activities of private individuals. Indeed, he is opposed to the whole concept of Big-Brother government in which an American can never be quite sure that somebody's not watching him, or listening in on his conversations, or surreptitiously checking on his private affairs.

He has challenged the Pentagon's assertions that its massive surveillance of civilians is legal. Ervin is a former North Carolina Supreme Court judge and he is an authority on the U.S. Constitution. He says he finds nothing in the articles cited by the Pentagon "that says the Army has the power to convert itself into a detective agency."

A Defense Department official has acknowledged that the Pentagon maintains a centralized intelligence card index, begun in 1965, with some 25 million names, plus another 760,000 cards on organizations or incidents involving counter-intelligence activities or criminal investigations.

The official, Asst. Secretary of Defense Robert F. Froehlke, acknowledged that the Army's civil disturbance information collection plan was so broad and uninhibited that it opened the door to spying on virtually anyone. And worse, Froehlke said little civilian direction or guidance was given the Army program.

Big Brother — in uniform — may be watching you!

The New York Times

New York, N.Y., March 8, 1971

Privacy, said the late Prof. Clinton Rossiter, "is an unbreakable wall of dignity...against the entire world." Today, that wall is crumbling. It is being undermined by government snooping and by persistent manipulation through public relations posing as public information. Independence of thought and action is subverted through secret intrusion and subtle indoctrination.

While outright repression always remains the ultimate danger, freedom now faces the more sophisticated threat of electronic surveillance and governmental hucksterism.

"Electronic surveillance," Justice William Brennan Jr. has warned, "destroys all anonymity and all privacy; it makes the government privy to everything...."

The Pentagon has admitted that it has dossiers on 25 million American "personalities." These include persons loosely described as "considered to constitute a threat to security and defense" as well as such public figures as Senator Adlai Stevenson 3d. According to testimony, the data bank, which keeps files on 760,000 organizations and incidents, processes 12,000 requests on an average day. Requests by whom and for what purpose?

Other agencies in the business of keeping tabs on Americans are proliferating. They include the Federal Bureau of Investigation, the Central Intelligence Agency, the Congressional committees dealing with "security," and the Passport Office. An airline has been asked to aid official surveillance by feeding into a computer information on where and in whose company its passengers travel.

Attorneys General, defying the courts, in recent years have stretched their customary privilege of tapping the telephones of potential foreign spies to aim similar surveillance at suspected domestic subversives. Reluctance on the part of Justice Department officials to try to obtain court orders for such purposes — readily granted in any plausible case — is tantamount to admission that these invasions of privacy would be difficult to justify.

* * *

Symbolic of the pernicious trend toward secret incursions into privacy and high-powered manipulation of public attitudes is the Pentagon's deep involvement in both activities. The Defense Department's massive data banks have been exposed in the hearings before the Senate Constitutional Rights Subcommittee; its equally massive propaganda machine was portrayed in the Columbia Broadcasting System's documentary, "The Selling of the Pentagon."

Democratic freedoms are in jeopardy when the military simultaneously arrogates to itself the power to act as watchdog over civilians and, under the cover-all of public information, the right to advocate its own views on war and peace. When high-ranking officers — in violation of all military regulations — are allowed to blame domestic dissenters for the failures of American action in Vietnam, the dangers become acute from Army-operated data banks on dissent.

Powerful governmental public relations efforts today try to make war mean "pacification." Opposition to the war thus subtly implies disloyalty. Such manipulations diminish the capacity of individuals to reach political decisions rationally and unafraid.

The Fourth Amendment upholds "the right of the people to be secure in their persons, houses, papers and effects, against unreasonable searches and seizures...." Modern computer technology and public relations techniques, in the hands of powerful government agencies, are capable of extending such searches and seizures into men's minds. When that happens, privacy and freedom are the victims.

Arkansas Gazette.

Little Rock, Ark., March 12, 1971

Assistant Attorney General William H. Rehnquist says there is no need for legislative controls on electronic snooping and computerized criminal dossiers on private citizens who have never been convicted of so much as a traffic violation, because the problem — which he clearly thinks is exaggerated anyway — can be easily and safely handled by "self-discipline on the part of the executive branch."

We will say only that a society that depends for very long in such matters on "self-discipline on the part of the executive branch" is already dead. It is just that nobody has bothered to wake it up and tell it.

Why, we wonder, did we bother to go through with the Magna Charta and its often bloody *sequelae*? Why did we in this country keep on petitioning George III, and then finally quit petitioning him?

Please note that Mr. Rehnquist in the context necessarily was speaking for the generals and the admirals as well as for his own Department, through the connecting link formed by the Janus faces of Richard M. Nixon, who, as he keeps reminding us so insistently, is both President and Commander-in-Chief? This is so because it was surveillance of private citizens by the Armed Services — sometimes vying with each other in the best tradition of inter-service rivalry — that was the principal catalyzing agent for the Ervin Committee's investigation of the whole larger subject.

Personal freedoms can be destroyed by civilian-clad spyers, fabricators and combination all-purpose prosecutors and judges just as surely and finally as by uniformed ones. However, it is the Army that has been the traditional enemy of private freedom in almost every country in the world save our own, which we used to claim was "different." At what precise instant in history did it cease to be? Sam J. Ervin and some like-minded citizens in and out of Congress are attempting mouth-to-mouth resuscitation, but it might already be nothing more than a goodbye kiss.

AKRON BEACON JOURNAL

Akron, Ohio, March 11, 1971

When constitutional rights are at issue, we don't often find ourselves in disagreement with Sen. Sam J. Ervin, the North Carolina Democrat who has long been an authority on the subject.

When Ervin revealed last December that the Army had "conducted political surveillance" of several elected officials in Illinois, we reacted as he apparently had. By what strange line of reasoning were these individuals — Adlai Stevenson III and former Gov. Otto Kerner, among others — deemed to be appropriate subjects for surveillance? And why was the Army doing this kind of spying?

Since then, it is said, the Army has given up this role — turning it over to the Internal Security Division of the Justice Department.

And this week a spokesman for the Justice Department told Ervin's subcommittee on constitutional rights that the department would "vigorously oppose" any move by Congress to limit the government's surveillance powers.

This statement, from Asst. Atty. Gen. William H. Rehnquist, came in response to Ervin's comment that the Constitution gives the people certain rights and that putting them under surveillance "stifles those rights."

We're not sure we agree with the senator on this point.

Suppose the civilians under surveillance had not been liberal Democrats like Stevenson and Kerner but suspected Communists or anarchists of the Weatherman variety. Would disclosure that a government agency was keeping track of these persons' activities have caused a stir? Of course not.

It wasn't the fact of surveillance that caused a stir. It was (1) the stupidity shown by whoever put the likes of Stevenson and Kerner on the list and (2) the fact that the Army, rather than a civilian law enforcement agency, was doing the snooping.

We can see that unrestricted surveillance, even by the Justice Department, could LEAD to abuses, but we're not sure that the surveillance itself amounts to infringement of anybody's rights. In any event, we don't think Congress can outlaw bureaucratic stupidity. It can't pass a law which says that certain types of persons are subject to snooping and all others are immune.

THE NASHVILLE TENNESSEAN

Nashville, Tenn., March 4, 1971

A SPOKESMAN for the Defense Department told a Senate subcommittee Tuesday that the Pentagon keeps records on 25 million Americans as part of the military's plans to keep down civil disorder in the nation.

Mr. Robert F. Froehlke, assistant defense secretary, attempted to soften the impact of this disclosure by saying the Pentagon had ended the surveillance of civilians. "The Army is out of it," he said.

However, the reasons given for halting the surveillance and the Pentagon's continuing defense of its right to snoop on American citizens offers little assurance that this hateful practice will be ended for long.

Mr. Froehlke said the surveillance was ended—not because the Pentagon thought it was wrong or illegal—but because it was "inappropriate" and bad management.

The chairman of the subcommittee on constitutional rights, Sen. Sam Ervin, D-N.C., questioned Mr. Froehlke closely on the constitutional aspect. Senator Ervin himself contends the snooping is without legal authority and that it violates the constitutional right of free speech, free association and free petition of grievances against the government. He said there was no legal authority for the Defense Department to spy even when civil disturbances were imminent.

Mr. Froehlke refused to concede under Senator Ervin's questioning that military spying on civilians was illegal or unconstitutional. He did acknowledge that it was an open question, but said the Pentagon maintains "right now" that the action is legal.

Thus, it seems the military wants to keep its options open in case it wants to resume its surveillance of civilians. As long as there are high officials in the Pentagon who believe the military has the legal right to pry into every aspect of the private lives of citizens, the practice is likely to be resumed as soon as the military thinks there is a need for it.

But whether the spying is done by the military, the civilian police or a private insurance company, most people object to having the innermost details of their lives put down by electronic devices and filed away in some government computer—perhaps to be used to embarrass and coerce them later.

Senator Ervin is right. The formers of the Constitution never intended anything like this. If there is any doubt—and there seems to be quite a bit—about the constitutional right of a citizen to be secure from violations of privacy by the military and other agencies of government, Congress should take steps to put the question beyond all doubt.

ST. LOUIS POST-DISPATCH
St. Louis, Mo., March 14, 1971

Senator Ervin doubts he will be able to find out how far up the scale in the Executive Branch or Pentagon goes responsibility for military domestic espionage. He does not think it likely that such an extensive watch could be kept on the American people without the consent of the White House.

The evidence supports that suspicion. The Army began its sweeping spy program at home after the urban riots of 1967, 1968 and 1969. Robert F. Froehlke, an Assistant Secretary of Defense, has already told the Ervin subcommittee that White House and Justice Department personnel participated in the planning and direction of programs, including intelligence,

dealing with civil disturbances. The President's Foreign Intelligence Advisory Board and the National Security Council, along with other Executive agencies, received copies of the Army's intelligence plan.

If they were willing to testify, White House officials and generals would no doubt deny responsibility for the way the program developed in all directions, and yet it was their final responsibility because they approved the program. This was true of the Johnson Administration that initiated the program and it is true of the Nixon Administration that has continued it, and even implicitly defended it by sending an Assistant Attorney General to tell the Ervin

committee the Administration would fight congressional efforts to restrain executive surveillance activities.

It is a commentary on the growth of the military organism that Congress cannot exercise a power of review over it, and a sorrier commentary on what is happening to civilian control of the military. The other, and more immediate, repository for civilian control is in the office of Commander-in-Chief. If President Nixon does not end military spying on the people he should be held accountable by the people for resulting intrusions on their rights and privacy.

BUFFALO EVENING NEWS
Buffalo, N.Y., March 5, 1971

Testimony from a Defense spokesman before the Senate subcommittee investigating serious encroachments on traditional American privacy confirms our belief that the military should be barred from conducting domestic surveillance of civilians.

Such intelligence-gathering by the military is neither proper nor necessary. On the contrary, it poses continuous perils to democratic freedoms infinitely greater than any dangers it tends to thwart.

In fairness, it should be noted that the military came to the new assignment fairly recently. Assistant Secretary of Defense Robert Froehlke told the Senate subcommittee that military snooping mushroomed quickly after the tumultuous urban riot summer of 1967. And it evolved because, in Mr. Froehlke's words, "civilian agencies — federal, state and local — had demonstrated a lack of capability to provide the quantity and types of in-

formation believed to be necessary effectively to cope in a timely fashion with the emergency then prevailing."

So there it is: Instead of continuing to locate the surveillance responsibility where it belonged and had traditionally been — with civilian agencies — and then improving them as seemed necessary, high officials in the Johnson administration unwisely brought the military into the picture. To compound the error, when the emergency subsided nobody bothered to get them out of it again.

Consequently, we now have an invidious system that spies on the legitimate political activities of civilians, keeps dossiers on leading candidates for high public office, infiltrates classrooms, impersonates newsmen, and, according to Mr. Froehlke, maintains files on 25 million Americans — an index that grows by 2.5 million a year. The demonstrated "lack of capacity" evident in mid-1967 no longer exists. But a worse threat, all the more ominous because it is largely invisible and unfelt, does.

The assistant secretary went on to assure the senators that a revised, more limited and less abusive military intelligence-gathering network took effect this week.

But this should reassure no one. If the snooping got out of hand before, it could again. And refinement begs the more trenchant question whether the Pentagon should be involved in domestic intelligence networks at all.

Plainly, in our view, it shouldn't be. The mere existence of such a network can numb the vitals of a democracy. It undermines and threatens to overturn the sound doctrine of civilian control of the military. And why take such unnecessary gambles anyway? Just get the Pentagon out of the practice of intelligence-gathering inside the United States altogether, and let civilian agencies, local and state police and the FBI, maintain whatever far-more-circumscribed surveillance over shady characters may be deemed necessary.

St. Petersburg Times
St. Petersburg, Fla., March 4, 1971

One year ago this week the House Invasion of Privacy subcommittee chairman said the Army had promised to destroy computer data collected over a three-year period on 7-million persons it considered threats to internal security.

AS EVERYONE now knows, the promise was not kept. This week's Senate testimony revealed that all 7,890,630 dossiers are still on file at Ft. Holabird, Md.

Moreover, the Defense Department reported it keeps records on 25-million persons. That's one of every eight Americans.

Defense Secretary Melvin Laird no longer denies unjust snooping took place. He has admitted "inappropriate" files were kept, that

"abuses" took place, and that wire-tapping and electronic surveillance occurred.

It appears the Pentagon felt justified in endangering basic American freedoms in the name of defending them.

THE ARMY has been the worst offender against liberty. Without written guidelines to go by, it went beyond constitutional limits, and when told to destroy illegally gathered information, the Army saved it by subterfuge.

"The tendency was to keep the information while obeying the order," said a former Army spy. "The order didn't say destroy the information, just destroy the compendium." So the information was microfilmed.

Other government responses have been dismayingly weak. Though the order to gather civil disturbance information has been rescinded and token reforms ordered by Laird, there still exist uncounted files which the Pentagon says cannot be purged of illegally gathered or erroneous data.

THE POTENTIAL for further violations still exists.

Explaining how the Army ranged so far afield of basic liberties, a Pentagon spokesman said the Army was given no written orders on how to proceed.

Explaining how the Army got the job in the first place, the Pentagon says the Army was the only American institution with enough money and men to do the job.

Those "explanations" speak volumes about misplaced spending priorities, about too many Army men with nothing to do, and about the possibilities for a recurrence of spying.

No one is safe. A letter to the President or a congressman, participation in anti-war or civil rights activities, membership in a certain church or organization may have already put you in a government computer as a potential troublemaker.

To get to the source of these abuses, current Senate hearings should subpoena Johnson Administration officials who started it, and root out the chances of it happening again.

Democrat 🦅 and Chronicle

Rochester, N.Y., March 4, 1971

Is your name in a computerized file maintained by the FBI, the Secret Service, Army Intelligence, or any one of many government agencies? You may not have committed a crime. You may have done nothing more than "bark" at a high government official or demonstrated against a public agency. That would be enough to do it.

Sen. Sam Ervin Jr. started his subcommittee hearings a few days ago by warning that present laws do not prevent unnecessary and improper snooping.

The fact that a citizen need not break a law to get his name into a data bank raises disturbing constitutional questions. Is recording this information a violation of the Fourth Amendment guaranteeing the right of Americans to be secure in their persons, houses, papers and effects against unreasonable searches?

Secret Service guidelines require gathering data on persons who personally insist upon seeing high government officials for grievances. This is considered a protective measure. But the Constitution permits petitions to government for redress of grievances. Where does one draw the line?

"The basic question," explains Ervin, "is the power of the Executive Branch to monitor activities of individuals when there is no probable cause to believe they have committed a crime. Unless we take command now of the new technology, with all that it means in terms of substantive due process for the person who is computerized, we may well discover some day that the machines stand above the law."

There are now so many spying agencies, one witness said, that some agents found they were trailing each other.

The most insidious spying apparently is done by the Army. Howland Pyle, former counter intelligence-agent, left his Army job realizing military intelligence had created the apparatus of a police state. One witness said that Army Intelligence spied on every possible aspect of a subject's life, from his sex life to family quarrels. Army files and black lists, said another witness, included names of many nationally known citizens. Small wonder that the American Civil Liberties Union and others are pushing legislation to keep the Army out of political surveillance. Small wonder some fear a dictatorship by dossier. Small wonder that President Nixon has called for a study of the nation's colossal network of intelligence for the purpose of an organizational shakeup.

Surveillance and computerization may start with a worthy purpose but like a virus spread out of control. Not every citizen is disturbed but many who suspect they're "in the bank" cannot be blamed for wondering if the data will sometime be used against them.

As the hearing attests, information gathering is misused. Why, for example, should Army Intelligence spy on 800 civilians in Illinois? Why must Selective Service collect computerized information on registrants across the nation? The potentials for mischief are heightened by the ability of computers to "interface"—talk to each other. What happens to your right of privacy when government agency computers start exchanging information about you? Giving facts about yourself to one agency does not mean you have given up your right of privacy.

The worst danger is that the computerized version doesn't change, even though you may have improved and have valid reason to disown your past. In the data bank everyone's past is an inescapable part of his present and future, and all without the citizen's being able to do a thing about it.

The Pittsburgh Press

Pittsburgh, Pa., March 10, 1971

It all apparently started in July, 1967, when President Johnson sent federal troops to Detroit to help quell the disastrous riots then raging in that city.

On the assumption that other cities might need troops, the Army was told to get itself ready.

And if the Army was to be used to curb such civil disturbances, the Army figured it had better gather up all the intelligence it could find so it would know who was involved, or might be involved, where trouble might start, and so on.

One thing led to another, and pretty soon the Army's agents were off on a snooping binge across the country.

It turns out now, according to testimony before a Senate subcommittee, that much of the collected information was trivial, went far afield from the original intent and wasn't of much use.

In short, according to 1971 official testimony about what happened in 1968, the job more or less got botched.

"It was not a good plan," Assistant Defense Secretary Robert F. Froehlke has testified.

From all that has been said up to now, at least, it's hard to see any ogres amidst this confusion, or any great military conspiracy to stomp on free speech—just a blunderbuss operation.

By now, the Army has destroyed its massive files of miscellaneous information and more or less put an end to this boondoggle.

But if any such critical uprisings should break out again, the Army very well might be essential to restoring order—or preventing the trouble by timely appearance. In that case, it certainly would need all the essential information it could command.

So defense officials won't promise, and ought not promise, that they never, never again will undertake surveillance of civilians.

As Mr. Froehlke says, in extreme circumstances, it might have to.

In which case let's hope that the mistakes now being recorded will not be repeated.

The San Diego Union

San Diego, Calif., March 5, 1971

Disclosure that intelligence officers of the U.S. Army have kept civilian organizations and individuals under surveillance has aroused justifiable concern among the American people. This is certainly an uncommon role for any branch of our military service.

The fact must not be overlooked, however, that the Army was carrying out this intelligence assignment on orders from the executive branch of the government. Nor should we forget that at the time this activity was begun, in 1967, the nation was facing a period of grave civil disorders.

It emerges that former President Johnson, through a National Security Council directive, ordered the Army to gather information that would assist in efforts to control disorders in our cities. The President issued his directive in conformity with the policy that the Army has always been at the disposal of the government to augment civilian law enforcement agencies when disorder of major dimensions threatens.

The Senate Judiciary Committee does not need to address the question of whether the Army should or should not have executed this intelligence-gathering function. The Army was simply carrying out its orders. The only question remaining is whether good judgment and discretion were used in the process.

ARMY FILES ON CIVILIANS UPHELD BY SUPREME COURT

The Supreme Court ruled June 26 that the Army could not be brought into court to defend the mere existence of its surveillance of civilian political activities against charges that it discouraged freedom of speech. The justices held 5–4 that such surveillance could be challenged only if and when individuals could demonstrate "actual or threatened injury" by having been watched by Army agents. In other instances, the court said, control of these activities must be left in the hands of Congress and the executive branch. Chief Justice Burger wrote the majority opinion. He was joined by Justices Blackmun, Powell, Rehnquist and Byron White. Voting in the minority were Justices William J. Brennan Jr., William O. Douglas, Thurgood Marshall and Potter Stewart.

Chicago Sun-Times

Chicago, Ill., June 28, 1972

Last week the Supreme Court stood firm for the right to political dissent and said that it must not be inhibited by fear of officials eavesdropping through electronic bugging. Monday, the court refused to give judicial relief to a group of citizens who had been spied on by the Army and who said this had an inhibiting effect on their rights of free speech and assembly.

How could the court change in one week? The answer: application of the "strict constructionist" view held by President Nixon's four appointees. This holds that judicial power cannot be invoked without a showing of direct injury. In the first case, defendants in a bombing case stood to be damaged by evidence on what the court found to be illegal government wiretapping. In the second case, no injury was shown.

The Army program can be challenged in the courts, Chief Justice Burger wrote, only when and if particular civilians can demonstrate "actual or threatened injury by reason of unlawful activities of the military." That is, it is all right for the Army to gather data secretly on civilians — what are termed "potential trouble makers" — and store it in a computer bank, but the civilians can't object, even if this surveillance is unlawful, unless or until the Army uses the information to hurt them. And if the Army did, then there could be remedies available.

This decision may square with "strict constructionist" philosophy, but to our layman's concept it is a cop-out by the court, enabling it to avoid ruling on what it concedes may be an unlawful activity of the military. The petitioners wanted to prove at a trial that the Army program had an inhibiting effect on their rights of free speech and assembly. They could have quoted the court's own one-week-earlier statement in the bugging case: "The price of public dissent must not be a dread of subjection to an unchecked surveillance power."

Is not putting a chilling effect on a citizen's free speech an injury?

Four justices — a minority — thought so. Justice Douglas charged "surveillance of citizens is none of the Army's business and Congress has not undertaken to entrust it with any such function. This case is a cancer in our body politic."

Congress in fact objected to the practice some time ago. The Army said it had stopped surveillance of purely civilian matters and had destroyed many dossiers. But the petitioners wanted more than the Army's word and wanted judicial relief from the spying Big Brother tactics, reminiscent of the novel "1984."

If the Court and the Chief Executive will not obliterate such tactics Congress should act to outlaw them and to erase the computer banks.

Long Island Press

New York, N.Y., June 29, 1972

The U.S. Supreme Court, by a 5-to-4 margin, has taken the strange position that Congress, not the judiciary, should decide the propriety of Army spying on civilians.

Chief Justice Warren Burger, who wrote the majority opinion, said courts should not sit "as virtually continuing monitors of the wisdom and soundness of executive actions." This is Congress' job, he said.

But, then how does the Supreme Court explain why it monitors the executive's enforcement — or lack of it — of civil rights laws or any other constitutional process? By the same reasoning, it should protect a citizen's First Amendment rights against unreasonable surveillance — such as the military spy system. As the Newhouse News Service disclosed, that snooping produced dossiers on three million people, including civil rights, antiwar and poverty movement leaders.

That the Pentagon claims to have destroyed many of the computer tapes is not important. Most of the information was probably cross-computerized with the FBI or CIA files, anyway.

What is more disturbing is the abrogation of the judicial department's responsibilities by Justice Burger and those who voted with him. Does his premise that the legislative branch should be the chief — or perhaps only — bulwark against executive excesses mean that the courts should be limited to policing themselves? What does that do to the Constitution's carefully-framed balance of powers doctrine?

Justice William O. Douglas said in dissent that Congress has never authorized Pentagon surveillance of civilians. "One can search the Constitution in vain for any such authority," he said. Without a declaration of martial law or authority from Congress, he contends, the military has no right spying on civilians — but it is up to the courts to keep it in line. We agree.

* * *

The court's ruling is questionable for another reason. Justice William R. Rehnquist, who joined in the majority opinion, testified in the suit against Army surveillance of civilians before a Senate subcommittee in March, 1971. At that time, as a Justice Department official, he told the subcommittee that the suit was not properly before the courts. Under the circumstances, the American Civil Liberties Union is justified in arguing that Justice Rehnquist should have disqualified himself in this week's decision.

The Rehnquist vote is crucial because the Supreme Court decision overturned a Court of Appeals ruling. If Justice Rehnquist had not voted, the 4-4 tie would have forced the Pentagon to detail its spying methods.

We hope the Supreme Court reconsiders its action. But if the 5-4 vote stands, we agree with Sen. Sam J. Ervin Jr., D-N.C., that Congress must step into the breach.

He promises to introduce legislation putting strict limits on military spying. Civilians could be shadowed by the military only on direct orders from the President and only when necessary to guard against invasion and domestic violence or to investigate civilians looking for work with the military.

That's not the best way to attack the problem, but until the courts are willing to accept their responsibility, it may be the only way.

BUFFALO EVENING NEWS

Buffalo, N.Y., June 28, 1972

The U. S. Supreme Court, in its 5-4 decision rejecting a legal suit brought against the Army over its alarming military surveillance of civilians, confined itself to procedural considerations. But the majority opinion's pointed reminder that passing judgment on the Army's intelligence gathering operations is up to Congress ought to spur Congress to tackle the substance of the issue and pass a law to curb this kind of military snooping.

A vehicle for such action could be Sen. Sam Ervin Jr.'s promised proposal to strictly limit such surveillance. Certain exceptions may be needed, but the central thrust of appropriate legislation on the subject should reflect the spirit of a dissenting opinion by Justice Douglas: "Surveillance of civilians is none of the Army's constitutional business."

The real point here is the imperative to safeguard individual liberties. The Army says it has discontinued its civilian surveillance activities of the 1967-1969 period. But if this happened once, it could happen again and, indeed, might be easier next time, in the absence of either judicial or statutory restraint.

The democratic tradition of this nation is for civilians to watch the military, not the military to watch the civilians. We should conserve that tradition. Leaving this up to the self-restraint of the executive or the military, as some have suggested, is demonstrably not enough. A statute outlawing improper military snooping is plainly necessary.

The Evening News

Newark, N.J., June 27, 1972

It is regrettable that the U.S. Supreme Court did not see fit to permit a full-scale judicial inquiry into the Army's over-zealous snooping in the civilian sector. Only a margin of one vote on the nine-member court sustained the dismissal of a suit brought by nine organizations and four individuals seeking a declaration that the surveillance of suspected domestic subversives, radicals, activists and others much less likely to cause trouble was an unconstitutional enlargement of military authority.

The court chose to dispose of the issue on very narrow procedural grounds — a finding that the plaintiffs had no standing to bring the suit, for they could not show that the Army's action put them in the immediate danger of "sustaining a direct injury."

Public hearings by a Senate subcommittee early last year helped spread on the record some details of how 1,000 Army agents went about the nasty business of gathering dossiers, but a judicial ruling might have helped delineate further, for the Army's enlightenment, its constitutional — and traditional — role in the life of these United States. We have no doubt that a trial court would have been persuaded to the view that Army surveillance of civilians is a piece of overreach that cannot be countenanced in a society that has always emphasized the non-role of the military in civilian affairs.

Even the Supreme Court majority, as it dismissed the case, was constrained to note that the suit reflected the "traditional and strong resistance of Americans to any intrusion into civilian affairs." We hope that it will always stay that way.

New York Post

New York, N.Y., June 28, 1972

When is a man harmed? This was the deeper issue in the Army surveillance case—Laird v. Tatum—which is one of the whoppers that came out of the Supreme Court delivery basket this week. (One more delivery is due on Thursday before the Court recesses.)

The outward thrust of the case was on the question of whether the famous —or infamous—Army surveillance of people who might be politically dangerous put a damper on freedom of political expression. A federal Circuit Court of Appeals said it did. But now the Supreme Court says it can't crack down on the high brass and order them to destroy all those dossiers. It's up to Congress, say five of the nine judges, and they add that they can't step in unless there is a suit by someone who has been personally harmed, not just as an ordinary citizen.

Which brings us to the question behind the surveillance question: when is a man harmed? Are you harmed only when your direct property, income, employment, or reputation are hurt? Or are you harmed when you are a political activist, and the whole atmosphere around you becomes chilly and repressive, even if you can't prove that your own freedom was concretely impaired?

We think the Court majority's definition of harm is too narrow, and that a political climate can hurt a man in his First Amendment rights even if a direct personal gag isn't applied to him. If the Court's current narrow view had been used in the apportionment cases, and it had all been left to Congress, we wouldn't have had the "one-man one-vote" decisions.

* * *

We can sympathize with the Chief Justice Burger majority (the four Nixon appointments plus Kennedy-appointed Justice White) in their feeling that they don't want to open the floodgates to a spate of "political climate" cases. But we feel more strongly that the Court has a duty to say no to something as monstrous as the build-up of Army surveillance dossiers in 1968. It could have said no carefully enough to slap at the Army and still place limits on the flood of later cases.

TWIN CITY SENTINEL

Winston-Salem, N.C., June 29, 1972

RULES are made to be broken, but Supreme Court justices break them at the risk of being singled out for special criticism. Those who uphold the sanctity of the law are expected to abide by the house rules as well — particularly if a rule is just and reasonable.

Mr. Justice Rehnquist, one of the two most recent Nixon appointments to the Supreme Court, joined a 4-5 majority this week in rejecting the argument that the continuing military surveillance of civilians tramples on the U.S. Constitution. Had Justice Rehnquist not voted, the ensuing 4-4 deadlock would have affirmed the lower-court decision permitting a test case on the question.

While serving as U.S. assistant attorney general last year, Justice Rehnquist was the chief government spokesman for the Army's right to spy on civilians. When he appeared before Sen. Ervin's subcommittee hearings to defend this right, he argued that anti-war protesters could not legitimately seek protection from Army surveillance through the courts. The case he was commenting on at that time is the same case he helped decide on Monday.

As a rule, justices and judges do not hear cases in which they have been personally involved. The rule becomes even more binding when a judge or justice has actually taken sides in a case — as Justice Rehnquist did in this case.

Now Mr. Rehnquist may have felt that the precedent was too important to be lost because of an obscure disqualification rule. But it occurs to us that the associate justice who sat in judgment this week on his own case is the same man who drafted such proposals as pre-trial detention for the Nixon administration. The only difference is the black robe — which in itself confers neither wisdom nor tolerance.

There is a popular belief that elevation to the high court changes a man. Conservatives become liberal, liberals become conservative, and all become more deliberate, less certain in their own biases, more open to persuasion.

But this rule of thumb is no more binding than the house rule Justice Rehnquist airily ignored. For some justices, it is business as usual.

ARMY INTELLIGENCE FILES CONTAIN 9,200 DOCUMENTS ON U.S. CIVILIANS

Howard H. Callaway, secretary of the Army, in a memorandum to Congress made public June 13, said that a survey of Army intelligence files had found 9,200 documents on the activities of U.S. civilians. Callaway, who said the documents should have been destroyed in accordance with a 1971 Pentagon order to purge Army files on political dissidents, indicated that an action to eliminate all such documents had been recently begun but later suspended until the completion of congressional investigations of U.S. intelligence activities.

In a related development, David O. Cooke, a deputy assistant secretary of defense, told the House Government Operations Subcommittee on Government Information and Individual Rights June 8 that the Army's files on political dissenters might exist in U.S. intelligence agencies that exchanged information with the Pentagon in the late 1960s. Although the Army had destroyed its own files, Cooke said, it did not know what the CIA, the FBI and other agencies had done with the data from the Army. "I assume the files are retrievable, but not by us," Cooke said.

The Des Moines Register

Des Moines, Iowa., June 23, 1975

The Army has admitted keeping 9,200 documents about the activities of American civilians four years after such data were supposed to have been destroyed. Some of the files relate to the activities of anti-war groups, but the Army did not say how many persons have been subjected to illegal surveillance.

Army Secretary Howard Callaway disclosed existence of the data to Congress and said he is considering disciplinary action against officers who failed to obey orders. He added that "it is not the Army's business to know what American citizens are doing except when their activities appear to pose a criminal threat to the security of our armed forces or when the President has ordered out the Army to deal with a civil disturbance. . . ."

Callaway's attitude is a welcome change from that of some generals who regarded the American people (whose taxes maintain the military establishment) with the suspicion usually reserved for foreign enemies.

That may not be the end of the matter, though. Deputy Defense Secretary David O. Cooke conceded to a House Government Operations subcommittee recently that some of the dossiers gathered in the 1960s probably were given to other federal agencies and may be stored in the files of the FBI, CIA, National Security Agency and possibly other agencies.

BUFFALO EVENING NEWS

Buffalo, N.Y., June 17, 1975

Somebody in Washington ought to see to it that the Army promptly and completely destroys the more than 9000 documents on American civilians still stored in its microfilm library four years after they were supposedly eliminated.

In a report, Army Secretary Howard Callaway said they had been held at the request of Congress while investigations were continuing. He said consideration was now being given as "to whether any administrative action should be taken against any of the officials whose oversight or misunderstanding" might have contributed to the problem.

Maybe it should be, but it probably won't be. And Congress long ago moved on to other investigations. In the meantime these documents, collected by Army snoopers in flagrant disregard of civil liberties, could still damage innocent reputations. The best solution under the circumstances is surely the simplest. Insist the Army do what it originally pledged to do—destroy the documents before nine more years roll by and we suddenly find ourselves in the middle of 1984.

DESERET NEWS

Salt Lake City, Utah, June 7, 1975

Despite orders to destroy the records in 1971, the Pentagon still maintains files on the political activities of American civilians.

Despite the administration's repeated pledges to preserve each citizen's right to privacy, the federal government is proceeding with plans to centralize computer files on millions of Americans.

These disclosures this week provide more ammunition to those critics who insist that America is well on the road to becoming a police state.

It's bad enough that the Pentagon never had any business snooping on civilians, that it was doing a job properly reserved only for civilian agencies. Now the failure to follow through on orders to destroy those records raises questions about whether or not the military establishment has become a law unto itself and is no longer amenable to civilian control.

As for plans to centralize in Washington the computer files that some federal agencies such as the FBI and the Agriculture department maintain on American citizens, there's a point at which this is no longer good administration but a danger to liberty.

The more various files are consolidated, the greater becomes the danger of law enforcement information becoming available to agencies not involved in police work. Likewise, the greater becomes the opportunity for blackmail. And the greater becomes the reluctance of citizens to exercise their right to dissent from governmental decrees.

As one lawyer has noted, "The tone of spontaneity of spirit that characterizes a free society cannot survive in an atmosphere where all deviations from the norm are immediately noted by the state and stored for future reference. The existence of the file itself is chilling, even if it is never used."

If this is to remain a free society, it must do a more conscientious job of safeguarding the privacy of its citizens.

The Providence Journal

Providence, R.I., June 7, 1974

Every new disclosure about the government's domestic snooping ans surreptitious record-keeping works to deepen concern for the future of this country. Despite the alarms raised in Congress and the academies about Washington's surveillance over the doings of American citizens, the practice appears to be growing without letup.

The latest such development involves the Army's massive files on civilian dissenters, compiled at the order of President Lyndon B. Johnson during the late 1960s. Despite the Army's assurances to Congress in 1970 that these files would be destroyed, NBC News reports, at least some of them still exist. Compounding the matter, says NBC, is the transfer of some of this computerized data from the Army to the FBI and the Central Intelligence Agency. Instead of destroying the files, the network reports, the Army continued to conduct domestic surveillance to the point when, as of last January, it held 600,000 entries on Americans who had been involved in antiwar protests and other forms of dissent.

The Army's surveillance plan seems to have begun in 1967, when President Johnson was determined to track down the forces behind antiwar protests. As many as 1,000 Army intelligence agents were sent out in 1968, 1969 and 1970, according to testimony from several former agents to Congress in 1970. They spied on radical groups, college students, welfare mothers, black militants and others, In some cases, said one former agent to a congressional subcommittee in 1970. they posed as journalists and infiltrated civilian organzations.

Their raw data, covering untold thousands of civilians, was compiled on Army computers. Now, according to NBC and at least partly confirmed in congressional testimony on Tuesday by Deputy Defense Secretary David O. Cooke, some of this information has been exchanged with the FBI, the CIA and perhaps the National Security Agency.

This stealthy, secret accumulation in the Army computers of data on private citizens is the stuff of nightmares; it is precisely this kind of surreptitious government activity that presents the deadliest sort of threat to individual freedom and the right to privacy.

The military has no business at all conducting intelligence surveillance on private American citizens. And, lest we forget the protection of the First Amendment, no governmental arm has the freedom, under the Constitution, to impose limits on peaceable expressions of dissent; yet the continuing collection of data on protestors would surely work as a limiting (and, hence, illegal) action.

Former Sen. Sam. J. Ervin Jr., who helped bring the Army's domestic surveillance plan to light five years ago, was unflinching in his criticism. The motivations behind the plan, he said, "were directly counter to the principle that the Army is controlled by civilian authority." And the dangers are real, as Malcolm Moos, then president of the University of Minnesota, warned Congress in 1971: "Information can be mishandled or misused or it can be deliberately collected and employed for purposes that debase the principles of free speech and inquiry."

The new disclosures about the Army's durable domestic intelligence data should evoke the strongest response from President Ford and Congress. Clearly, the Army, by transferring data in its files to other agencies, has evaded its commitment, formally made to Mr. Ervin's subcommittee in 1970, to destroy the files. Congress cannot rely on executive orders to guard against these excesses, or to insure that these files from the 1960s are completely wiped out. Some firm legislative action — including, if need be, a freeze on appropriations — is needed for Congress to make plain that this dangerous precedent must not recur.

THE SACRAMENTO BEE

Sacramento, Calif., April 27, 1975

Less than a year ago, then-Atty. Gen. William B. Saxbe testified before joint hearings of three Senate subcommittees that the FBI was the only government agency engaged in electronic surveillance of American citizens.

His statement, repeated under close questioning, differs with evidence unearthed by the American Civil Liberties Union and disclosed last week that at least 22 other agencies engaged in wiretapping.

The ACLU based its charges on government affidavits produced in connection with a military court-martial in West Germany. It is not clear whether the wiretaps were conducted with or without a warrant. It is clear enough, however, that Congress has yet to fully curtail unwarranted snooping into the lives of Americans.

Sen. Gaylord Nelson, D-Wisc., who has sought legislation to control government prying, told Congress shortly after Saxbe's testimony that a 1973 Senate subcommittee report showed both the extent and dangers of covert bugging operations.

The report detailed surveillance secretly conducted by 1,500 agents of the U.S. Army on more than 100.000 civilians in the late 1960s. It was directed principally at those suspected of engaging in political dissent.

The Nixon administration assured the public the military no longer would spy on civilians, but Sen. Nelson said the Army had kept on doing it all the same. The affidavits obtained by the ALCU indicate snooping was not confined to either the Army or the FBI.

There is a place in our society for spying in the interests of genuine national security. What worries people who defend civil liberties is that Democratic as well as Republican administrations since the 1930s have been known to use taps on law-abiding individuals in the name of national security.

Warrantless wiretaps confer an unchecked power on the executive branch which we know only too well can lead to arbitrary invasion of privacy and abuses of fundamental rights.

Oliver Wendell Holmes, an associate justice of the U.S. Supreme Court from 1902 to 1931, called such taps "dirty business." He said so not being able to know just how widespread and sophisticated that shadowy business would become in the electronics age of today.

IRS INFORMER DISCLOSES DETAILS OF MIAMI 'OPERATION LEPRECHAUN'

The Internal Revenue Service was alleged to have used a female informant to gather information of the sex lives and drinking habits of prominent Miami residents in "Operation Leprechaun." The woman, Elsa Suarez, told reporters March 14 she was recruited in 1972 "to get dirt" on 30 Miami-area public officials, including three federal judges and Richard Gerstein, state attorney for Dade County. She claimed to have been offered $20,000 a year for life and a home abroad if she came up with information that would "get" Gerstein. "I never did sleep with anybody or get any good dirt during the three months I was on the job," she said.

The San Diego Union

San Diego, Cailf., June 25, 1975

Disclosure that the Internal Revenue Service has been engaged in spying on the affairs of private citizens in the United States of America may be a blessing in disguise.

Thousands of Americans who have hang-ups about the methods and conducts of the IRS now have something to get their teeth into. Telephone taps, clandestine bugging and undetected recording of conversations all are clearly outside the legal purview of the federal tax-collecting agency. The IRS should be obliged to answer for all these repugnant acts, not just because they represent an invasion of the privacy which is the right of every citizen, but because they also constitute a misapplication of public funds.

The country was understandably outraged by news that the Central Intelligence Agency had spied on private citizens. There has been a rash of investigations of the CIA, some of which have departed widely from their original purpose. They undoubtedly have damaged our capability to amass the international intelligence we need for survival in a dog-eat-dog world.

As wicked and unpalatable as the CIA conduct was, however, it can at least be said that its illegal prying into domestic affairs was aimed at helping preserve our national security. The motive had something to do with the welfare and safety of the very people whose privacy was being invaded.

Not so with the IRS. Its spying was not aimed at protecting the national security in any remote sense. It was simply checking surreptitiously to see if taxpayers were telling all on their income tax returns.

The IRS has the authority to require taxpayers to document every statement they make on a tax return. Indeed, as many taxpayers know, the agency can be meticulous to the point of harassment in this auditing process. The agency has just assigned a formidable corps of auditors, economists and other experts to examine the books of 50 large corporations simply on the suspicion that they may have concealed illegal political contributions or pay-offs in foreign countries.

The purpose of the IRS investigative bureaucracy is to examine tax returns against the requirements of tax laws which often are so complex that the taxpayer cannot be sure whether he is obeying them or not. There is no basis in law, custom or equity for the IRS to be resorting to the tactics of espionage against citizens.

Congress is responsible for creating both the burden of intricate tax requirements which lies heavily on individuals and businesses, and the burden on the public purse of supporting the big agency that collects taxes. If congressional committees are looking for some way to defend the taxpayer for a change, they should determine who was responsible for assigning IRS employes to illegal activities, who authorized public funds to be expended on them and how they were concealed from the light of day for so long.

The Miami Herald

Miami, Fla., March 21, 1975

TAKING it from the top slowly, let us assume that paid informants and spies employed by the Internal Revenue Service managed to secure movie film and tape recordings that established proof of sexual activity and immoderate drinking by certain public officials and judges in Miami.

What would the IRS have done with the information? As we read the federal tax code, there is no penalty assessed against those who maintain a mistress. Unless you are selling and buying untaxed whisky, there is no reason for the IRS to be interested in your getting sloshed regularly. And if you suffer from a special type of sexual hangup, what business is it of the federal tax agents so long as you are not padding a bill for psychiatric counseling? Was blackmail to be the objective?

This is not to make light of the revelations of IRS snooping under the exotic code name of "Operation Leprechaun." We think it serious business that the government that is of, by and for the people has been employing such disreputable types for illegal spying on citizens, public officials or not. And we are not encouraged by reports from Washington that highest officers of the Internal Revenue Service were not aware of the spy ring in Miami.

We ask the classic question: "Who's in charge here?"

Coming on the heels of admitted illegal acts by agents of the Federal Bureau of Investigation and the Central Intelligence Agency, it seems apparent that what we have in this IRS scandal is another case of "Big Brotherism" by some third-rank bureaucratic clerks. We suspect that if there is any evidence of kinky sex, it rests with those who plotted to install recorders under mattresses and on the intimate person of their apprentice spy.

The Ford administration has a tough problem on its hands with this Miami case. It smells like Watergate but cannot be sloughed off on the crew of the sunken Nixon ship. If the tax clerks in the Miami office were out playing Dick Tracy and Mata Hari, there is reason to believe personnel in other IRS offices felt they had the same authority for illegal activity. President Ford must deliver a clear verdict on this point.

As for what to do now with those who conceived and carried out the Leprechaun snooping in Miami, we suggest that headquarters break up the office and ship the players off to other locations. That is what is done customarily in federal agencies when hanky-panky is indicated. Nome might be the very place to cool off some of the hot blood of the snoop directors. Or maybe a remote station in Montana or Idaho.

But get them out of this town.

THE MILWAUKEE JOURNAL
Milwaukee, Wisc., April 18, 1975

If you've always pictured Internal Revenue Service people as the sort who would fit right in at a chess tournament but wouldn't be much fun at a party, you've probably had to revise your thinking.

It turns out that some of them in the Washington area participated in undercover training programs that must be among the most popular devised. Others were mixed up in a Florida spying operation called "Leprechaun," which involved snooping into the sex lives and drinking habits of public figures.

A leprechaun is a wizened little fellow who must tell you where to find a crock of gold if you catch him. That makes him a proper subject for IRS interest, all right, although it's hard to picture the agency as a place that believes in leprechauns instead of taxpayers as a source of wealth.

Those IRS training programs in motels near the Potomac must have been at least as interesting as hunting for crocks of bullion. Agents destined for investigative work were encouraged to prove they could hold their liquor and their tongues simultaneously.

To make the evening even more memorable, once enough drinks had been dispatched in the line of duty a bevy of lovely young women arrived to ask questions like, "what do you do for a living, honey?" The record does not show what answers they got, but presumably they were more interesting than the ones required on Form 1040.

There's always one man in any crowd who spoils a good thing and the training program ended after an agent was picked up by police outside the motel, mumbling incoherently.

Such revelations of a hitherto hidden side of IRS make the agents seem more human. But the agency's commissioner, Donald C. Alexander, is right in suggesting that an outside agency or committee ought to investigate what's going on. At the very least, requiring the IRS to answer embarrassing questions instead of ask them would improve taxpayer morale, invariably at a low ebb this time of year.

Chicago Tribune
Chicago, Ill., April 15, 1975

Internal Revenue Commissioner Donald C. Alexander seems determined to make the IRS not only a law-enforcing body but a law-obeying one. On top of a series of orders restricting intelligence-gathering activities by tax men, Mr. Alexander last week came up with the most controversial idea yet: a suggestion that charges of abuses and corruption within the service be investigated by an outside agency.

He proposed giving the assignment to the investigative staff of the joint congressional Committee on Internal Revenue, rather than setting up a new agency for the purpose. But he added that the staff would have to be strengthened, because "it looks as tho investigating the IRS may be a permanent or semipermanent part of their job."

This suggestion is likely to heat up the IRS' domestic quarrels well past the boiling point. Mr. Alexander, who took office in 1973, has been drawing in-house criticism and resentment by pruning IRS powers. He has ordered a halt to some long-established practices—for instance, soliciting and paying for confidential information on citizens' tax returns—and has let some investigative tasks be transferred to other agencies. [The retirement of John Olszewski, national director of the IRS intelligence division, appears to be one result of this policy crunch.] A move to open up the IRS' own books to outside investigators is likely to be taken by many tax officials as an outright betrayal by their own boss.

It isn't. In our view, an independent scrutiny like this is the best way—perhaps the only way—to reassure the public that its taxes are being fairly collected. And reassurance is needed. Stories of harsh, arbitrary, or plain wrong decisions by IRS collectors are becoming common currency; in fact they've been the subject of several recent news documentaries on network TV. Faith in the IRS has also been shaken by the disclosure of dirty tricks like "Operation Leprechaun," a surreptitious checkup by federal agencies in 1972 that included spying on the sex and drinking habits of prominent Miami residents.

Mr. Alexander said 30 IRS agents are now investigating the agency's involvement in the spying, which is welcome news. Still, as he told the Public Citizen Forum in Washington, "there is a real problem in investigating ourselves." Said the commissioner: "We have an obligation to ensure to the public that the IRS is not corrupt."

We couldn't agree more. The point is not that IRS intelligence activities should be stopped—that would be a wide-open invitation to the cheaters. It is that this agency, like any other, needs checks and balances, and the ones now provided for by law [such as the General Accounting Office or the Freedom of Information Act] have not been effective. Without some outside, enforceable limitations on its activities, a government body can only go on increasing its power—with the natural result that it loses public trust, and must claim still more power to compensate for the loss.

Trading trust for power is a particularly bad bargain for the agency that collects our taxes. We welcome Mr. Alexander's proposal.

The Houston Post
Houston, Tex., May 13, 1975

The Internal Revenue Service is concerned about what its spies and paid informants may have been investigating besides legitimate tax cases and how they perform their duties. The IRS is conducting its own probe to determine if its intelligence agents used questionable, even illegal, tactics to gather information on private citizens for reasons other than suspected income tax violations.

IRS Commissioner Donald Alexander has already admitted that Internal Revenue agents went too far in an investigation of 30 Miami residents. The participants in the Miami cases say they involved burglary and attempts to pry into the private lives of several people. Earlier this year, the IRS ordered discontinuance of its Intelligence Gathering and Retrieval System, a nationwide data-gathering program. Whether it was involved in excesses like those claimed in Miami is not known, but IRS officials say they want to find out.

It is encouraging to see the nation's tax-collecting agency show some concern about the propriety of its agents' investigative practices. It is an indication that the federal bureaucracy is becoming more sensitive to post-Watergate public opinion, which clearly disapproves of unjustified snooping into citizens' private lives. But it is regrettable that the current investigation was necessary at all.

One gets the disturbing impression that part of the vast bureaucracy apparently got out of control. That is not quite as bad as the head of an agency directing such unwarranted activities, but it is serious enough. The IRS has effectively used its police powers over the years to snare kingpins of organized crime and other lawbreakers who were impervious to prosecution except for violations of federal income tax laws. But it is one thing to gather evidence on shady operators and people whom the IRS suspects of tax law violations and quite another to spy on citizens for reasons that may have nothing to do with their tax returns. Presumably, if IRS officials find that their intelligence agents have committed excesses, they will take steps to prevent future recurrences. That's fine. But the public would be more reassured if Congress established an oversight committee for the tax collection agency. Such a panel could act on complaints from citizens who felt the IRS was overstepping its investigative authority. This would give the IRS two watchdogs, one inside, one outside.

ST. LOUIS POST-DISPATCH
St. Louis, Mo., March 30, 1975

If there is something ominous about the initials SSS, let it be said at once that if SSS operations were potentially ominous, they were sometimes ridiculous. SSS stands for the Special Service Staff of the Internal Revenue Service. A Florida state's attorney has demanded an investigation of reports that the SSS spied on the drinking and sexual habits of prominent Miami citizens and officials. Beyond that, an ABC television documentary discloses that the SSS kept a list of 3000 names, including actors, comedians and basketball players, several conservative columnists and organizations ranging from conservative to liberal.

An IRS spokesman said the list covered some groups with questionable tax exemptions, but one group was the United States Civil Rights Commission, an official government agency, which of course pays no taxes. In short, the SSS list makes no sense, it should never have been compiled and the agency, which has been abolished, should never have been created. Somehow, though, the governmental penchant for spying on citizens seems to reach epidemic proportions before it can be cured by a generous application of public disclosure.

Los Angeles Times

Los Angeles, Calif., April 17, 1975

How can the immense government bureaucracies, which have power over the lives of 210 million Americans, be brought under rational control and required to stay within the limits of their designated functions?

The question has come to the fore repeatedly in recent years, and it is raised again with the latest revelations about surveillance conducted by the Internal Revenue Service.

In August, 1973, IRS Commissioner Donald C. Alexander announced the abolition of the secret intelligence-gathering Special Services Staff (SSS). This action followed the disclosure that the IRS had gathered data on some 8,000 individuals and 3,000 organizations defined as extremist.

In the intervening 20 months since Alexander's order, the IRS has continued to conduct surveillance of individuals and groups in violation of the directive and far afield from the agency's legal function. These clandestine activities continued at least through last January.

For example, an IRS memorandum of Jan. 18, 1975, produced by court order, identified seven persons who attended a meeting of Americans for Constitutional Action and described a film shown at the session. Other documents revealed that IRS agents followed protesters to a church and reported on the content of the sermon. On other occasions, agents recorded the names and car license numbers of persons attending meetings of the Los Angeles Tax Rebellion Committee and other anti-income tax groups.

An IRS spokesman said Alexander on Jan. 21 ordered an indefinite halt to all intelligence gathering by the IRS pending a review. But if his order of August, 1973, was ignored, how can the IRS commissioner be certain that his Jan. 21 directive will be followed?

In announcing the discontinuation of the SSS nearly two years ago, the IRS issued a statement asserting, "It is neither our intention nor desire to suppress dissent or to persecute individuals because they are critical of, or identified with groups critical of, the tax system or government politics."

Yet a Jan. 13, 1974, IRS memorandum contained a report on tax protesters who attended a church meeting, and described in detail the gist of the sermon they heard. How does this kind of surveillance correspond to the policy statement of the IRS?

Bringing law-abiding citizens under surveillance and collecting information on them unrelated to any illegal activity constitutes an attempt to do what the IRS said it was not trying to do. It is no less than an attempt to interfere with the right of Americans to assemble freely and to speak freely without fear of reprisal by their own government.

THE ANN ARBOR NEWS

Ann Arbor, Mich., May 2, 1975

THE LONG BRUSH of Watergate has tarred many an individual and a few institutions as well, including the FBI. Time was when the FBI was wholly thought of as a crack crime-busting agency and of course, to a lesser extent it still enjoys that reputation.

But let's face it, the FBI isn't held in as high regard any more. It became a politicized agency and its cherished independence from the White House was shown to be a myth. The secret and highly personal files on certain members of Congress and other top Americans that were alleged to have amused and fascinated Presidents Kennedy and Johnson were not flattering to the agency when their existence came to light.

On a parallel tract is the Internal Revenue Service. The IRS is quite a system really more or less efficiently separating the masses from its hard earned money while trusting to the public's sense of honesty and obligation.

But if Americans are tax honest, they also want to be assured that the IRS is honest. And that assurance has been shaken of late. Television documentaries have cited some IRS activities as of questionable ethical value. IRS too fell afoul of Watergate; there were allegations that IRS was used for political purposes, contrary to its charter, and there were stories of IRS spying on the private lives of some citizens.

And all the time, the citizen was under the impression that his tax return was a matter between him and the government, and that the role of the IRS was that of tax-gatherer rather than some political adjunct.

It is Congress' duty to see that the IRS stays free of politics and chicanery. People need to be assured that institutions like the IRS are working honestly and efficiently FOR them. The careful going-over that the CIA is getting might profitably be extended to the IRS, too, if further abuses are revealed.

THE INDIANAPOLIS NEWS

Indianapolis, Ind., June 26, 1975

Like the U.S. Census Bureau, the Internal Revenue Service is privileged to extract highly personal data from American citizens against their will.

Unlike the Census Bureau, the IRS is not required to protect the identity of the individuals about whom it gathers information, nor is it insulated from the law-enforcement function of government. The Internal Revenue Service is among the Federal agencies making up the "Organized Crime Strike Force."

While basically a Justice Department project, this "strike force" also makes use of the Customs Bureau, the IRS and other U.S. agencies. It was reportedly at the urging of the strike force head that IRS initiated its "Operation Leprechaun" which snooped and pried on citizens in order to gather information on their sex and drinking habits.

We are not reassured by the IRS report on this now-halted operation. The report blandly declares that the compiling of data on the drinking and sex habits of taxpayers was abandoned after two years because it was "of no value to tax administration." Which leads, naturally, to the question: What if it were of value in administering the tax agency? Are the private lives of Americans so totally at the disposal of Federal officials that the criterion for snooping is whether or not it helps the bureaucrats?

Nor do we find much candor in the claim that the program was dropped because it had "major defects." The IRS report says the spying was begun in five districts early in 1972 and expanded to cover the entire nation in May 1973.

IRS did not discover the "major defects" until a couple of enterprising newspaper reporters discovered the program. Those inclined to be skeptical of official explanations may suspect that public disclosure, not official dissatisfaction, put an end to the snooping.

The IRS, in recent years, has suffered serious blows to its reputation for fairness and integrity. The running of political errands, rewarding of agents who harass taxpayers and invasions of privacy are among the charges that have been leveled.

A loss of confidence and respect could be crippling for the agency, as the collection of the Federal income tax depends to a great extent on voluntary compliance by the bulk of Americans.

Such abuses as Operation Leprechaun do not encourage co-operation by the citizenry.

The Washington Post

Washington, D.C., April 28, 1975

THE INTERNAL REVENUE Service has become a popular subject for congressional scrutiny. At least half a dozen panels are now looking into various aspects of IRS operations, from the treatment of ordinary taxpayers to recent political intelligence-gathering. But it is not yet clear to what extent Congress will follow through by considering the broad, basic issue of the role of IRS.

A good example of fastening firmly on a corner of the problem is the widespread interest in restricting access to income-tax returns. The need for tough new rules was amply shown during the Nixon years. Indeed, there are few more sensitive records systems in the government, since IRS is the only agency that collects detailed annual reports on the finances of most citizens. Yet that is just one aspect of IRS's extraordinary power over people's fortunes and lives. The agency also has exceptional authority to investigate citizens' activities, to collect private information by administrative summons —often, as with bank records, without the taxpayer's knowledge or consent—and to seize property in the most peremptory ways. Thus the basic question is how the whole panoply of IRS powers ought to be used.

Some answers are obvious. IRS should be scrupulously apolitical; its awesome powers should not be misused to help political friends, to harass those regarded as "enemies," or to collect information unrelated to the enforcement of the laws. But the answers are not so simple when one proceeds to the problem of how IRS's records and investigative strengths should be used in legitimate federal law-enforcement efforts.

At present, IRS does share its resources with other agencies. Last year, for instance, 8,210 returns—out of a total of 81.5 million—were made available to other federal offices; 7,676 of those, or 93 per cent, went to the Justice Department and U.S. Attorneys. Even more significant, IRS agents, with their specialized investigative skills, have been invaluable in recent probes of organized crime, fraud, and corruption in many states.

Many people, including IRS Commissioner Donald C. Alexander, believe that such general law-enforcement activities should be cut back, that the sharing of tax returns should be tightly curbed, and that IRS should function almost exclusively as a revenue-collecting agency. This, of course, has great surface appeal and some real advantages. It would greatly reduce the possibility that tax returns might be misused by other agencies, or that IRS might become entangled in improper surveillance projects again. It could enhance public confidence and might even produce more revenue. For instance, if taxpayers could be sure that their returns would not go to U.S. Attorneys or the FBI, corrupt officials, drug dealers and the like might even report and pay tax on all their illegal gains.

But the isolation of IRS along those lines has all the defects of its merits. As Deputy Attorney General Harold R. Taylor Jr. testified before a Senate panel last week, such strict curbs on the sharing of resources would greatly hamper the Justice Department's ability to prosecute white-collar crime, corruption and other offenses. The enforcement of tax laws might also be hurt. Moreover, if denied access to IRS files and specialists, other federal agencies might be driven to create or enlarge their own financial intelligence units thus opening up new problems.

All this is not to say that the present system is perfect. The sharing of tax returns for non-tax law-enforcement purposes does raise privacy problems and no doubt limits some citizens' compliance with tax laws. The demands on IRS's limited manpower can be too great. Finally, if IRS is to continue to serve as an arm of general law enforcement, the agency's special powers to search and seize ought to be re-examined. Congress authorized such shortcuts of due process for tax-collection purposes, not so the agency could function as a proxy for other offices whose authority is more circumscribed.

The point is that, when one moves beyond the areas of obvious abuses, the choices involving IRS are more complex and consequential than they may seem. Tighter standards and more consistent oversight could reduce many problems, especially in regard to tax returns. But overall, defining the role of IRS is not a simple matter of balancing claims of privacy against those of law enforcement, for there are interests of citizens' rights and governmental effectiveness on every side. This is the kind of problem Congress often ducks. But if the current flurry of studies are to be very meaningful, such questions will have to be seriously addressed.

ALBUQUERQUE JOURNAL

Albuquerque, N.M., April 22, 1975

Congress should force the Internal Revenue Service to change its practice of sharing with other federal agencies the tax returns of citizens and corporations.

IRS officials recently admitted to Sen. Joseph M. Montoya, D-N.M., that it gave partial or complete tax returns of 8210 citizens or corporations to other federal agencies last year.

IRS Commissioner Donald C. Alexander said the returns were shared under federal regulations which permit federal department heads to obtain the information by certifying it is needed for investigative purposes.

The official suggested that federal policy should be turned around to keep the returns confidential except for clearly defined cases in which they might be examined outside the IRS.

It would be even more meaningful if federal agencies were required to follow due process through the courts before the IRS could be forced to surrender information contained in income tax reports. Only that would provide adequate safeguards against the invasion of an individual's right to privacy.

The Evening Bulletin

Philadelphia, Pa., April 30, 1975

The Internal Revenue Service has joined the expanding list of federal agencies which have abused their intelligence gathering powers to invade the privacy of U.S. citizens.

The IRS has confirmed a disclosure by The Bulletin's Washington bureau chief Lawrence O'Rourke that it closed down a secret unit which compiled general information. In other words, until only last week the IRS was in the business of snooping into the drinking and sexual habits of individuals, including politicians, as well as their friends and families.

The unit was formed on orders from the Nixon Administration during the 1972 reelection campaign which suggests it may have been used to identify and harass enemies similar to Watergate's infamous list. With offices throughout the country, including Philadelphia, the unit apparently used wiretaps and microphones planted on agents to do its dirty work.

Because the Internal Revenue code specifically limits IRS investigations to tax violations, these activities either violate that code or exploit a loophole to circumvent its intent. As with similar excesses of bureaucratic power on the part of the Central Intelligence Agency and the Federal Bureau of Investigation, the effect is to shatter public confidence in agencies which perform functions crucial to this country's well-being.

Such abuses could only occur in the absence of adequate oversight by Congress. If, for example, the congressional appropriations committees had been closely scrutinizing how the IRS spent its budget, the agency could never have kept this 700-man operation secret for over two years.

Many questions must still be answered: who was investigated? why? on whose orders? and how was the personal information used?

These answers can best be obtained by the Senate Select Committee recently formed to investigate all government intelligence operations. While aimed primarily at the CIA and the FBI, this committee's mandate is clearly broad enough to encompass the IRS.

Once its investigation is completed, Congress will face the problem of improving its oversight over these agencies. One way would be to include some of the new wave of younger, enthusiastic congressmen among the watchdogs.

PRIVACY ACT REQUIRES U.S. AGENCIES LIST DATA BANKS, MEANS OF ACCESS

The Privacy Act of 1974 went into effect Sept. 27. Federal agencies are required to publish annually the names of their record systems and procedures for an individual to follow to obtain information on any record system covered by the act. Exempt are data concerning police intelligence and investigation, federal employment and contracts. A citizen can also discover if anyone has been looking at any particular government file. The names of more than 8,000 record systems of 79 agencies have already been announced. Former Sen. Sam Ervin (D, N.C.) and Sen. Charles H. Percy (R, Ill.) sponsored the law.

The San Diego Union

San Diego, Calif., September 28, 1975

Americans awoke today with some new assurance that they still live in a free country. The Privacy Act of 1974 which went into effect yesterday promises to tilt the scale back toward the individual in what has become a running battle to keep the government from prying unnecessarily into his affairs.

There is a touch of irony in the fact that new protections of individual privacy are coming into force as the Central Intelligence Agency is on the griddle for spying illegally on American citizens in their own country. As President Ford pointed out in Palo Alto last week, the Privacy Act which he helped draft as vice president was not inspired by any illegal activities by government agencies. It is aimed at controlling the use and abuse of information which government agencies gather quite legally and with good intentions.

No American needs to be reminded of how many forms he has filled out during his lifetime at the behest of some agency of federal, state or local government, or how many questions about his personal affairs he has answered while a government clerk took down the data. In addition to the information we are required to give the government, there are cases where the government gathers information about us behind our backs.

The Privacy Act imposes some clear restraints on what a federal agency can ask and what it can do with the answers. It can henceforth collect no personal information that is not relevant to the job the agency is doing. The exchange of such information between agencies will be curtailed. The government will have to curb its mania to use Social Security numbers as a universal identifier. A citizen can now demand to see his file — with some exceptions dealing with law enforcement — and demand that anything untrue or extraneous be removed.

The new law is certainly welcome, but it raises the question of how the American people got into the situation where such a law became necessary. Those files and computers now gorged with personal information about us are the by-product of countless programs that made aspects of our private lives the government's business.

A citizen who is now worried about how much the government knows about him must shoulder some of the blame. The Big Brother bureaucracy which has computerized our personal affairs was created, after all, by elected representatives promising to solve one problem or another. Whether the problems have been solved or not, government data banks are a price we have paid in the process.

Under the Privacy Act the citizen can slap the wrist of Big Brother when he gets too inquisitive, is loose with his tongue or makes mistakes. That is some measure of comfort, but we would feel better if he were not sending us so many questionnaires in the first place.

The Washington Post

Washington, D.C., September 19, 1975

A NEW ERA in federal record-keeping will officially begin Sept. 27 when the Privacy Act of 1974 goes into effect. The law gives citizens the right to inspect many kinds of government files about themselves, and sets down strict rules for the collection, use and exchange of information about individuals. The principles involved — accuracy, relevance, fairness and need-to-know—are elementary. But applying them to the great volume and variety of federal records has proved to be, as expected, quite a monumental task.

The part of the law that has generated the most work and grumbling in many agencies is the requirement for full disclosure of the nature of all files involving individuals. This provision, in effect an annual public inventory of the government's information stock, was enacted because Congress found that nobody knew the full extent of federal record-keeping about citizens. Some agencies were maintaining secret files and concealing some abusive practices from Congress and the public. The broader difficulty, however, was simply that the government's data demands had grown so fast, and had been answered in so many uncoordinated ways, that not even the agencies themselves had a firm grasp of all their information practices.

The inventory is now nearing completion. The results are staggering, to put it mildly, even to those who have long suspected that the government has a file on everything. So far, over 8,000 records systems have been summarized in fat volumes of the Federal Register totaling 3,100 pages and more. The entries range from the controversial to the commonplace. There are listings for the sensitive files of the Defense Investigative Service; for records of the participants in National Security Council meetings since Jan. 20, 1969 (classified "SECRET"); for HEW's roster of licensed dental hygienists; for the Agriculture Department's list of people interested in forestry news, and for the Export-Import Bank's roster of employees who want parking spaces. There are outlines of huge computerized networks such as the Air Force's Advanced Personnel Data System, summarized in 11 columns of small print; there are earnest entries for little lists such as the key personnel telephone directory of the Administrative Office, Assistant Secretary of Defense (Intelligence)—a roster kept, according to the Aug. 18 Federal Register (Part II, section 1, page 35379), on "8 x 10½ Xerox plain bond sheets."

The huge pile of records of records and lists of lists may seem to reach new heights of regulatory overkill. Indeed, there are bound to be jokes and complaints about the agencies that keep so many files—and about the Congress that required such detailed, indiscriminate reports. But such an inventory, however tedious to prepare—and however trivial parts of it may be—is a useful and necessary step. For the first time, the awesome range of government records has been catalogued. For the first time, all agencies have been compelled to define what they collect on individuals, how the materials are used, who has responsibility for what, and which records, primarily in law enforcement fields, are so sensitive that they should be withheld from inspection by the citizens involved.

The catalogs and related agency regulations merit scrutiny on a number of grounds. Many citizens will no doubt want to inspect various records on themselves. Congressional committees and interested groups in many fields may wish to challenge some uses of data and some exceptions from disclosure, notably the extensive withholding proposed by the Justice Department on law enforcement grounds. Congress may now be able to sharpen the focus of the Privacy Act and modify the reporting requirements for mundane records systems such as internal telephone lists. And federal administrators, given some time to review their reports, may well start questioning some of their offices' data-collecting practices and weeding out their files. Indeed, it is quite possible that some bureaucrats, faced with the chore of cataloguing marginal or redundant files, may have already employed a very unbureaucratic strategy: throwing some records out. If that has happened even in one agency, the Privacy Act has already done some good.

THE ATLANTA CONSTITUTION
Atlanta, Ga., September 29, 1975

The trauma of Watergate has been therapeutic for the American democratic system in several ways. For one thing it reversed the drift toward a secret police state. Government is becoming more open. As a result, we are able to see more of the flaws in our system and move to erase them. And we are able to find out more about ourselves.

For instance, the new federal Privacy Act went into effect Saturday. Under its provisions, U.S. citizens can find what information the government has recorded about them and correct any erroneous facts on their records.

The law requires the bureaucrats to pitch in and help the searching citizen find the particular records system where his name might be stored. It also allows him to discover who else may have been looking at his file.

Nearly 80 agencies have already publicly listed the names of more than 8,000 record systems that may be searched—ranging from the highly sensitive lists of persons who come to the attention of the Justice Department's criminal division, to files kept by the Postal Service on who maintains substandard mail boxes.

The new Privacy Act augments the Freedom of Information Act which also allows people to discover whether such agencies as the FBI, CIA and IRS are keeping dossiers on them and what those dossiers contain. Some legal observers suggest there are technical conflicts in the two laws which must eventually be ironed out by the courts.

Some federal law enforcement agencies also have complained that most of the people inquiring about their records are suspected criminals.

Be that as it may, the feds are moving in the right direction. The free and open flow of information is necessary to maintaining a responsive government. Besides, the new Privacy Act also should serve to keep the keepers of the records on their toes and be a little more careful about what they put into those folders about the people who pay their salaries.

THE SAGINAW NEWS
Saginaw, Mich., September 28, 1975

Starting this weekend, the rights of the ordinary American citizen will be a little less folded, stapled and mutilated by the federal bureaucracy's enormous stores of information.

The Privacy Act of 1974 went into effect Saturday. It permits citizens to find out what information about them the government has stored away and to correct that data if it is erroneous, with appropriate rights to sue the government in case of violations.

As might be expected, the Privacy Act does little to restrain the government's ability to maintain those files in the first place. But it does help reaffirm what Supreme Court Justice Louis Brandeis once called the "right to be let alone — the most comprehensive of rights, and the right most valued by civilized man."

Several types of data are exempt from the law, including CIA and Secret Service files and Civil Service test data. Some of the exemptions are clearly reasonable. The importance of efficient and comprehensive Secret Service records, for instance, has been re-emphasized by the near-tragic events involving President Ford in the last three weeks.

But enough government files have been opened up to significantly reduce the dangers to personal privacy. Many might be startled by the range of knowledge maintained on them in government computers.

Dozens of agencies have disclosed existence of more than 8,000 record systems. A Senate study found that in June, 1974, the government kept 858 data banks with more than 1.2 billion records.

The information ranges from lists of persons who have applied for government parking space to lists of people keeping pets on military bases, yielding visions that the U.S. may turn into one big "Animal Farm" by "1984."

The pet peeking presumably is in the case of rabies outbreaks. Many other strange records similarly may have a reasonable purpose. But the new law at least allows citizens to find out if the government thinks they have a poodle when they have a Pekingese, and thus doggedly delay 1984 a little.

One aspect of the law may pose some problems. Since it attempts to limit access to files dealing with individuals, it may clash with the Freedom of Information Act, which seeks to open government data to the public. If there are disputes, a legal resolution will have to be sought.

Still, the Privacy Act is an encouraging step toward President Ford's goal to "protect every individual from excessive and unnecessary intrusions by a Big Brother bureaucracy."

THE KANSAS CITY STAR
Kansas City, Mo., September 26, 1975

The Privacy Act of 1974, just now becoming law, is a start on dealing with a great and growing dilemma: How to reconcile individual rights of privacy with the massive file systems kept on millions of Americans by government, business and various institutions.

The new law concerns only records held by the federal government, and it does not go as far as many would like. Individuals will be permitted access to personal information in federal agency files in order to correct or amend the information *with the exception* of records maintained by the Central Intelligence Agency; law enforcement agencies (the FBI, for example); the Secret Service and a few other obvious categories.

These, of course, are the very files a great many people are most curious about as they might relate to themselves. Yet there is no way the information could be laid open without wrecking law enforcement and national security systems. One safeguard in this area would prohibit agencies from making information available to others for a second purpose without the individual's consent.

Imperfect as the statute is, it will have an effect. More than a year ago a Senate subcommittee determined that there were 858 data banks in 54 federal agencies containing more than 1.2 billion records on various individuals. At least 29 of the data banks were set up to gather derogatory information, and more than half of these had no statutory authority for existing. In recent weeks the Federal Register has printed page after page of documents from the agencies relating to the Privacy Act. Such publication is required by the law. Those who want to know what records exist have only to look in the Register's table of contents.

The urgency of it all was brought on by the computerization of the world and, ironically, the events of Watergate, for the idea of a privacy investigation got its impetus in the Nixon administration.

Government, of course, must maintain files on its activities and on the citizens it is supposed to serve and protect. The nature of the bureaucracy is such that probably 10 times more information than is needed is preserved in triplicate in several bureaus. But it was always thus. And there probably has always been the hidden file in some corner of the office, not available to the public. The danger in the computer is not in hiding information, but in making it easy to store more information and to transfer it with lightning speed from one agency to another.

The federal law is experimental. Elements of it will be discarded and expanded, and sections will come to apply at other levels of government and in the private sector. It is in the latter area that the greatest abuses to individual privacy may presently lie. But now a small counterattack is being mounted, and well before 1984. Big Brother may not have the last word yet.

The Providence Journal
Providence, R.I., October 3, 1975

Somewhere in more than 8,000 record systems maintained by more than 80 government agencies, your name and assorted information about you is tucked away. Under the new Privacy Act of 1974, which went into effect this week, you can ask to see what they have on you—if you know what agency to ask and where.

But the aim of this act isn't to make the information public. Rather, it is to keep the data away from snoopers and spies and others who don't have a legitimate reason for knowing it. The Freedom of Information Act was designed to pry information out of the federal bureaucracy; and to some extent, the privacy act clashes with the "sunshine" act.

If a federal agency has some investigative intelligence on you, other people aren't supposed to be able to get it. But, then, neither are you. Criminal records are available, so a person can check on whether they are accurate and, presumably, do something about the matter if they aren't.

But the most discouraging part of the whole business is the enormous amount of information about individuals the government has in its files. Just to list the systems of information kept by all the agencies has taken up 3,000 pages in the Federal Register.

Everybody is concerned these days about the huge amount of paperwork spawned by all the bureaucratic machines. What the government needs is a genius who can go through the agencies tossing out all the questionnaires and forms and their myriad duplicate copies. And in the process, he ought to scale down not only the amount but the number of persons about whom information is kept on file.

That would be a real protection of privacy. And it would also be a real protection against government being swamped by oceans of paper records and computerized information not needed.

THE ANN ARBOR NEWS
Ann Arbor, Mich., September 25, 1975

SPEAKING at Stanford University, President Ford noted that a law taking effect this week requires that government files on individuals be accurate and relevant and gives everyone a right to check the data.

Ford said the right of privacy must be protected, and he pointed to the federal bureaucracy, with its computers, as one of the chief threats.

Well, we couldn't agree more. If the CIA can open even the President's mail with impunity, how much more is the average citizen's privacy endangered? It is scant comfort for us to have the right to check on government-gathered data on ourselves, allowing that these files are necessary in the first place.

When it comes right down to it, citizens' privacy is assailed in many ways. The odd thing about it is that people complain so little about these affronts to the quality of life, to use a term much in vogue these days.

* * *

SPEAKING of the law to which President Ford alluded, how do Americans know where to begin to check material on themselves? A four-year study by the Senate Judiciary Subcommittee on Constitutional Rights found 858 data banks with more than 1.2 billion records in 54 federal agencies.

These data banks, the study noted, "are by no means all of the government files on individuals.

Rather, they are the systems which the 54 agencies polled by the subcommittee were willing to admit they maintained."

In addition, there is much which is exempted from the disclosure requirement of the Privacy Act of 1974. Records maintained by the CIA and by law enforcement agencies; statistical information; federal testing material; Secret Service records and other material are still kept under lock and key.

Like the nuclear genie which can't be pushed back into the bottle, it may be too late to cut Big Brother down to size. A monster has been created which is aided, rather than checked, by technology. High-speed computers store and retrieve data of all kinds; previously such material was the preserve of error-prone (and often inefficient) bureaucrats.

Computer technology also has made it more difficult to distinguish between the legitimate needs of government and private agencies for information on an individual and the right of the individual to keep information private. Most of the time, the individual is unaware of what information about him is on file, and where.

Justice Brandeis once called the right to be let alone "the most comprehensive of rights." The Privacy Act is a small step toward regaining a right which has suffered from erosion.

THE CHRISTIAN SCIENCE MONITOR
Boston, Mass., September 26, 1975

A landmark in the protection of privacy in the United States should not be overlooked in the midst of media preoccupation with the past's spectacular invasions of privacy.

Tomorrow the United States Privacy Act of 1974 goes into effect. It does not address the privacy problems presented by this week's Washington disclosures of FBI break-ins and of CIA mail openings now identified as having reached to institutions such as the Ford Foundation and to prominent individuals including Richard Nixon when he was running for the Republican nomination in 1968. Control of such activities will have to be part of the future legislation toward which current congressional investigations are directed. There are encouraging reports that President Ford may take administrative steps of reform to bolster the credibility of U.S. intelligence even before offering his own legislative proposals.

Meanwhile, Mr. Ford has given a firm send-off to the Privacy Act of 1974, in which he played a role as Vice-President. If the law is carried out as ordered, it will control the federal government's impact on the privacy of far more ordinary citizens than were ever likely to have their homes burgled or mail opened in the name of domestic or national security.

Now individuals will have access to personal information in the proliferating files of all federal agencies (with such exceptions as the CIA and Secret Service), and they will be able to correct or amend it. They will be allowed to recover actual damages if an agency has acted with "willful or intentional" negligence. And each agency is not only prohibited from selling or renting names for mailing lists but from passing material on an individual to another agency for another purpose unless it has the individual's consent.

The magnitude of the problem attacked by these and the act's other controls on federal data gathering is suggested by the first federal files inventory prepared as required by the new law. More than 8,000 file systems have been described in more than 3,000 pages of the Federal Register. They range from huge computerized military files to listings for parking places.

What has escalated the threat to privacy is the technology to bring together personal information from many sources, not necessarily accurate, and make whole personal profiles much more easily available than in the past. Certainly the federal government, with all its cradle-to-grave inputs on citizens, must get its own house in order, as the 1974 act seeks to do.

Unfortunately the final compromise legislation omits the Senate's proposal for an independent privacy protection commission to police the implementation of controls, a commission which Mr. Ford opposed. And the law does not deal with the whole remaining question of the massive personal data network in the hands of the private sector. Congress finally dropped even the proposed regulation prohibiting private businesses from withholding services from customers who refuse to supply their social security numbers.

Minor as this may sound, the trend toward making the social security number a kind of "standard universal identifier," in informational jargon, has to be resisted. It raises the specter of credit agencies, insurance companies, and other inquirers being able to press the button for one number and get everything on an individual. Some psychiatrists have said they give insurance companies less than full facts on patients because they doubt confidentiality is protected — just one indication of how misleading items could become perpetuated and exchanged.

What is encouraging is that Reps. Barry Goldwater Jr. and Edward Koch have already introduced legislation against any organization's development of a standard universal identifier. And both these congressmen are on the seven-man privacy study commission established by the 1974 act. Its chairman, David Linowes, has made statements unfortunately appearing less concerned about threats to privacy than privacy advocates would like — but he also sees the need for safeguards on consumer credit files, for example.

It is to be hoped that, during its two-year term, the commission will come up with strong recommendations for privacy protection in the private as well as governmental sector. Then another privacy landmark will be reached.

THE SACRAMENTO BEE
Sacramento, Calif., October 11, 1975

The Privacy Act of 1974 which has just gone into effect is another link in the fence Congress has been urged to erect to protect law-abiding Americans from governmental snoopers.

There can be no question of the need for such legislation. Consider this: The U.S. government alone has more than 1 billion dossiers, or five files for every man, woman and child in the nation.

The new statute provides greater access to personal files on individuals maintained by some 100 federal agencies. Persons will be able to find out what records, if any, various federal offices have stored about them and what the agencies may be doing with the data.

Theoretically and hopefully, such access will discourage if not prevent the accumulation of erroneous information which is fed into a computer and which can follow an individual all through his life.

If the act succeeds, it will be a major achievement but far from completely halting the erosion of privacy in both the public and private domains.

Great gaps still exist in the protective fence envisioned by lawmakers like former Sen. Sam Ervin, D-N.C., who pushed through the Privacy Act of 1974 before he retired.

Some of the measures pending in Congress seek to restrain the power of government to spy on average Americans — a growing threat with the development of all-too-efficient surveillance gadgetry.

Others recognize that, with the exception of the limited rights of access to credit reports under the Fair Credit Reporting Act, there is little or no law to secure banking, telephone, employe, medical, law enforcement and other personal records.

The excesses in snooping which have been disclosed in recent years and the inherent dangers in data banks have written a compelling case for strengthening the basic civil rights of privacy.

The legal barriers will not be complete, however, unless and until more is done to extend guarantees those rights will be preserved within the private sector as well as the government bureaucracies.

Los Angeles Times

Los Angeles, Calif., September 28, 1975

As a new federal privacy law goes into effect, Congress is considering another privacy bill that already has stirred serious dispute and is certain to arouse even more.

The difference between the new law, which became operative Saturday, and the proposed statute is significant, although the goal of both is ostensibly the same.

The new law, acclaimed a week ago in California by President Ford, has four essential features:

—It requires the federal government to reveal the location of all federal data systems containing identifiable personal information.

—It gives an individual access to his own file and the right to make corrections.

—It requires the government to use information only for the purpose for which it was collected.

—It mandates that the files be accurate, complete and relevant to their stated purpose.

In addition, and equally important, the law generally forbids the collection of information that involves a person's exercise of First Amendment rights.

The purpose of the new legislation, as set forth in the language of S 2008, is also to "protect the constitutional rights and privacy of individuals," but it would accomplish this by placing severe restrictions on the release of information by the criminal-justice system.

One provision of the proposed act calls for "the prompt sealing or purging of criminal-justice information relating to an offense by an individual who has been free from jurisdiction or supervision of any criminal-justice agency for a period of seven years, if the individual has previously been convicted and such an offense is not specifically exempted from sealing by a federal or state statute."

The censorship implicit in this section is hardly lessened by another provision that says the act does **not** prevent a criminal-justice agency from disclosing factual information about an individual. But the choice, significantly, is left to the agency and, furthermore, the bill would permit an agency to adopt regulations even more stringent than those contained in the federal legislation.

Regardless of the intent of its supporters, this legislation, under the laudable goal of protecting privacy, would increase the power of government to withhold from the public information the public has a right to have.

Ford, in hailing the new privacy law, was talking about the need to protect the law-abiding citizen from "excessive and unnecessary intrusions by a Big Brother bureaucracy."

But the kind of privacy he emphasized is not involved in S 2008. This bill would place Big Brother firmly in control of the data in the criminal-justice system by largely converting the public record into a private record.

Serious crime is not a private matter between the offender and the state, although some supporters of the legislation seem to believe that it should be. One witness at a hearing on the legislation said he felt that such information should be kept within "the law-enforcement family."

Sen. John V. Tunney (D-Calif.), chairman of the Senate subcommittee on constitutional rights and the introducer of the bill, remarked on the same occasion that "people shouldn't have (criminal-record) information . . ." and that criminal-justice agencies "need a law to allow them to deny information." This misguided view of criminal information as private information led a representative of the American Civil Liberties Union to urge the barring of press access to a record of criminal convictions without the consent of the person convicted.

Press access means public access, and the public, without access to information, would have no means of judging some areas of government that are of critical importance: the police, the prosecutorial agencies and the courts.

The philosophy of this legislation already is reflected in the regulations adopted by the Law Enforcement and Assistance Administration last June on the control and release of criminal information. Here again the purpose is clear, and the purpose is to restrict the flow of criminal information to the public. At the same time, the Department of Justice adopted a rule that prohibits the release of information concerning a defendant's prior criminal record. This reverses the former procedure of confirming a prior criminal record on inquiry.

California legislation, similar to the Tunney bill, went into effect nine months ago; State Atty. Gen. Evelle J. Younger has called it "overly restrictive," and has proposed substantial revision of the law. Passed to stop what was regarded as abuse in the dissemination of criminal records, the California law prevents school districts from checking for criminal records of prospective employes, prevents utilities from access to criminal records of persons applying for jobs as security guards or repairmen who enter private homes, and bars police from disclosing criminal records of arrested persons or suspects being sought. This is a classic illustration of a law that creates more abuses than it was intended to prevent.

Some proposals in S 2008 have merit. One would give an individual the right to review his criminal record and challenge its accuracy or completeness. Others are at least debatable. One would seal an arrest record if no prosecution was pending after two years. Another would purge the record if a law-enforcement agency did not refer a case to the prosecutor or the prosecutor decided not to file criminal charges. Records of persons wrongly arrested or wrongly convicted and whose convictions were set aside should be expunged for their protection.

But the vice of the legislation, a similar bill in the House, and the LEAA regulations, is their emphasis on secrecy. Together they represent a repudiation of the concept of open government, and they assert a proprietary claim by government officials to information that should be available to the public. Moreover, by restricting information, the legislation would help screen the operation of the criminal-justice system and make it less accountable to the public.

Individual privacy is fundamental to any civilized society, but it is the criminal offender himself who breaches the wall.

The Hartford Courant

Hartford, Conn.,
September 26, 1975

As of September 27, private citizens are legally entitled to know everything—well, nearly everything—the government knows about them. A new federal privacy act has been described on one hand as landmark legislation and on the other as a modest attempt to cut Big Brother down to size.

The object is to protect privacy by allowing citizens to see and to challenge the personal information kept in federal government files. It is also hoped that the new law will discourage unnecessary record-keeping.

President Ford recently criticized the widespread collection of personal information and called the federal government "one of the worst offenders." He mentioned government social programs and their interest in human behavior. He did not mention the excessive zeal of some intelligence and law enforcement agencies.

It is in this latter area that the average citizen will find the law least useful. Law enforcement files are exempt from disclosure. Such agencies as the CIA, FBI and Secret Service may determine for themselves whether to open a personal file. There are other exceptions in such areas as pending court cases and evaluations of federal employes.

But the greatest barrier may be that the average citizen does not know where to look. A Senate subcommittee last year found 858 data banks with more than 1.2 million records in 54 federal agencies—and feels it only scratched the surface.

The law does require that agencies list all the files they maintain, and the government will compile these lists into a booklet. It will go on sale in December.

Even so, the thorough file-searcher will face a difficult task, with no guarantee that any incorrect or unneeded information will be corrected or removed. If the agency does not agree to do so, the citizen can only file his own rebuttal along with the challenged information.

Since finding and correcting all one's personal files would still be a monumental task, the law must be ranked as a modest attempt rather than a landmark. But the government also expects major problems of its own, dealing with public requests for disclosure. In that way the law might well serve this valid purpose: More information would go into the familiar round file, and less into government computer banks.

The FBI's 'Dirty Tricks'

Media, Pa. Files Stolen

Stolen FBI files disseminated. Stolen Federal Bureau of Investigation (FBI) intelligence files were received March 22, 1971 by Sen. George McGovern (D, S.D.) and Rep. Parren J. Mitchell (D, Md.). The documents, most of them relating to peace and black activist groups, were sent by the Citizens Commission to Investigate the FBI, which admitted stealing the files after breaking into the FBI office at Media, Pa. March 8.

Both McGovern and Mitchell returned the documents immediately. McGovern said he refused to be associated with "this illegal action by a private group" and said he favored Congressional investigation of the bureau. Mitchell said in a speech March 23 that burglary was a crime and should be dealt with as such. However, he added that "the investigation and surveillance of individuals, peace groups and black student groups," as indicated by the files, was also criminal.

Attorney General John N. Mitchell said March 23 that copies of the stolen records had also been distributed to the press. He urged that the information be withheld so as not to "endanger the lives or cause other serious harm to persons engaged in investigative activities on behalf of the United States." He also said disclosure of national defense information "could endanger the United States and give aid to foreign governments whose interests might be inimical to those of the United States."

The *Washington Post,* which received the documents March 23, published a description of the files in its March 24 editions but omitted most names and specific locations. Copies were also received by the *New York Times* and the *Los Angeles Times.*

According to a Justice Department source, the 14 documents distributed were among nearly 800 stolen. Most of them were marked "United States Government Memorandum."

One was a Nov. 4, 1970 memorandum by FBI Director J. Edgar Hoover ordering investigations of all groups "organized to project the demands of black students." The memo said, "Increased campus disorders involving black students pose a definite treat to the nation's stability and security and indicate need for increase in both the quality and quantity of intelligence information on Black Student Unions and similar groups which are targets for influence and control by violence-prone Black Panther party and other extremists."

Another document, a newsletter from the Philadelphia FBI office, encouraged agents to increase interviews with dissenters "for plenty of reasons, chief of which are it will enhance the paranoia endemic in these circles and will further serve to get the point across there is an FBI agent behind every mailbox." The document, dated Sept. 16, 1970, added, "some will be overcome by the overwhelming personalities of the contacting agent and volunteer to tell all—perhaps on a continuing basis."

One of the documents related to a philosophy professor at a Philadelphia-area college evidently suspected of harboring fugitives. The file indicated that a college switchboard operator had agreed to report on long distance calls received by the professor and that the agent had the cooperation of a campus security guard. Another reported attempts to infiltrate a 1969 war-resisters' conference at Haverford (Pa.) College and a 1970 convention of the National Association of Black Students at Wayne State University (Detroit). The documents contained a report from the Swarthmore (Pa.) police department on black militant activities at Swarthmore College.

Other groups under surveillance included the Philadelphia Black Panthers and the National Black Economic Development Conference. Muhammad Kenyatta, 27, who headed the conference in Philadelphia and was mentioned prominently in three of the documents, said March 24 he had received the documents concerning him before they were made public. Asked how he came into possession of the files, he replied, "Let it suffice to say that revolutionary information networks are growing all across America.... Both sides can play the 'I Spy' game," a reference to a popular TV series.

More stolen documents distributed. The *Washington Post* received a new quantity of Federal Bureau of Investigation documents April 5. The 11 documents, sent to the *Post* and other newspapers, brought to 25 the number of FBI memos made public by a group called the Citizens' Commission to Investigate the FBI, which claimed responsibility for the March 8 raid.

One of the documents, reported by the *Post* April 6, noted a "few instances where security informants in the New Left [movement] got carried away during a demonstration, assaulted police, etc." The document said agents should advise informants that "they should not become the person who carries the gun, throws the bomb, does the robbery or by some specific violative, overt act becomes a deeply involved participant."

Another document related to the sending of anonymous radical material to college educators who "have shown reluctance to take decisive action against the 'New Left.'" Another described efforts to set up a network of informers in black neighborhoods in Philadelphia by recruiting "men honorably discharged from the armed services, . . . employes and owners of businesses in ghetto areas, . . . persons who frequent ghetto areas on a regular basis such as taxi drivers, salesmen. . . . Installment collectors might also be considered [as sources] in this regard." Among related developments:

■ In the March 30 Harvard *Crimson*

C

D

E

F

G

(Cambridge, Mass.), the first group of 14 documents were printed in their entirety "except for the removal of the names and numbers in cases which might be harmful to those who have been spied upon." The paper received copies of the memos from Resist, a draft resistance organization.

■ The board of trustees of Swarthmore College, according to an Associated Press report April 4, passed a resolution criticizing the FBI's alleged surveillance of a philosophy professor, Daniel Bennett, 40. Bennett had told reporters March 26 that the file relating to him was an example of "the incompetence of the FBI."

He denied that he knew Katherine Power, 21, or Susan E. Saxe, 20, two suspects sought for the murder of a Boston policeman and on the FBI's "most wanted" list. The memo indicated the FBI thought the two women might contact Bennett. Bennett also said the FBI information was in error about the number of children and cars he had.

File on Reuss' daughter disclosed. A memorandum containing biographical information about the daughter of Rep. Henry S. Reuss (D, Wis.) was contained in a new packet of stolen Federal Bureau of Investigation documents distributed April 10 by the Citizens Commission to Investigate the FBI. The latest release brought to 31 the total number of documents sent to newsmen, politicians and radical organizations by the group.

The document on Jacqueline Reuss, 21, a senior at Swarthmore (Pa.) College, was written Nov. 19, 1970 and contained routine educational background based on information obtained from a secretary in the college registrar's office. The memo did not indicate why the information had been collected.

Reuss, a critic of the Vietnam war, said in an April 12 statement the FBI's "mission is not to compile dossiers on millions of Americans, congressmen's daughters or not, who are accused of no wrongdoing." Miss Reuss said April 10 that she thought the reason for the FBI investigation was "the typical sort of thing—leftist activity."

In distributing the new packet of documents April 10, the Citizens Commission also released the text of a letter it had mailed March 30 to persons identified as informers in the stolen FBI memos. The letter stated that persons or organizations against whom they had informed would be notified, and copies of the pertinent documents were sent to the subjects of the FBI investigations April 3. The commission's letter to the informers said, "We regret that this action was necessary" but that "the struggle for freedom and justice in this society can never succeed if people continue to betray their brothers and sisters."

Among related developments:

■ Haverford College President Dr. John R. Coleman, in a memo March 29, and Swarthmore College president Dr. Robert D. Cross, in statements March 29 and April 9, warned that it was against the policies of the colleges to supply unauthorized information about colleagues to the government. Activities at both of the Philadelphia area institutions were the subject of FBI documents stolen from the Media office. Cross announced April 9 the appointment of a committee to recommend ways to safeguard confidential information. He said some persons on the campus may have gone "beyond the limits of reasonable cooperation" with the FBI and warned that those who divulged confidential information risked dismissal.

Thieves analyze stolen FBI files. The Citizens Commission to Investigate the FBI sent out an analysis of the subjects of the files in a mailing received by the *Washington Post* May 8. The group said 40% of the documents revealed political surveillance while only 1% concerned organized crime.

Included in the packet, sent to the *Washington Post* and other newspapers and radical groups, were several copies of FBI documents. They brought to more than 60 the number of stolen files made public. The analysis was made of all the stolen documents, estimated to number 800–1,000.

Included in the 40% listed by the Citizens Commission as evidence of political surveillance were two documents concerning what the group defined as right-wing groups, 10 concerning immigrants and more than 200 about "left or liberal groups."

The right-wing files, both included among the documents made public that day, included one on the militant Jewish Defense League (JDL) and one on plans for a Ku Klux Klan meeting in Darby, Pa.

Besides the 40% dealing with political groups and the 1% which the commission said concerned organized crime, mostly gambling, the breakdown on the remaining documents was reported as follows: 25% involved bank robberies; 20% involved murder, rape and interstate theft; 7% on draft resistance; and 7% on military desertion or AWOL cases. The group said the analysis did not include about 30% of the documents dealing with procedural matters.

Besides the files on the JDL and the KKK, the latest release contained a document on a rally protesting chemical and biological warfare and one indicating an arrangement with the Philadelphia office of the Bell Telephone Co. whereby the company would supply the FBI with names and addresses of all its customers, including those with unlisted numbers.

Earlier releases, received by the press April 23–27, included documents on draft resisters in the U.S. and Canada, files on plans for a Black Panther convention and on a black student group at Pennsylvania Military College (Chester) and reports on U.S. citizens who traveled in Communist countries or had dealings with Communist visitors to the U.S.

Quaker group releases FBI memos. A Philadelphia project of the American Friends Service Committee released a series of Federal Bureau of Investigation documents May 17 about police community activity and riot control. The Quaker group said it had received the papers from the Citizens Commission to Investigate the FBI.

Among the memos released by the group, called National Action-Research on the Military-Industrial Complex (NARMIC), was a document praising a Rochester, N.Y. program through which Boy Scouts were recruited as 20,000 "extra eyes and ears for the police department." The program involved distribution of cards to Boy Scouts with police, FBI and other emergency numbers and instructions to report unusual activity, criminal acts and "suspicious acts—persons loitering . . . around schools, neighborhoods and parks."

(A statement by the Boy Scouts of America, issued from its national headquarters in New Brunswick, N.J. May 18, said the Rochester program only asked the scouts to exercise the same surveillance demanded of any citizen. The statement said it was a "positive program" to reduce crime and there was no "follow-up" beyond distribution of a pamphlet prepared by the Rochester Emergency Services Committee.)

Another document distributed by NARMIC described a Pontiac, Mich. program where police worked in schools and summer programs for children to "exert a positive influence upon the individual's values and attitudes." The memo advocated "pre-prevention" of "pre-offenders."

Also included were a "police instructor's bulletin" listing four types of riot control gases available to police departments and a "riot control information bulletin" dated 1967 that said "officers in Philadelphia have orders to shoot anyone who either fires at police or throws missiles of any type." A document on the organization of police anti-sniper patrols advised the use of "former members of the military or avid hunters" and said squads should have "high-powered rifles and machine-guns" for use from helicopters.

NARMIC was consolidating several of the documents into a booklet, *Police on the Homefront.* Anne H. Flitcraft, an employe of the American Friends Service Committee who was working on the booklet, said FBI agents had raided her apartment May 16, armed with a warrant, and had confiscated her notes, books and typewriter along with copies of the stolen documents.

Residents of Powelton Village, the Philadelphia community near the University of Pennsylvania where Miss Flitcraft lived, organized a "Know Your FBI Street Fair" June 5. Photographs of alleged FBI agents and copies of stolen documents were displayed to about 1,000 persons who attended the fair. Members of the community charged harassment by FBI agents in connection with the Media theft investigation. The night after the raid on Miss Flitcraft's apartment, Powelton residents set up an alarm system designed to organize legal and community support in the event of other FBI raids.

(Copies of other FBI documents, received by the *Washington Post* May 15 from the Citizens Commission to Investigate the FBI, involved a prominent Philadelphia civil rights leader. A letter from the commission accompanying the documents said the black leader, unnamed in the report, had been an FBI agent for several years.)

Stolen FBI papers printed. "A virtually complete collection" of 271 documents on political surveillance stolen from the FBI's Media, Pa. office in March 1971 was printed in the March 1972 issue of *Win,* an antiwar magazine. The documents were received from the Citizens' Commission to Investigate the FBI.

The documents, some of which had been released earlier, further detailed FBI surveillance of peace, student and black groups. According to a statement by the commission included in the *Win* article, over 200 documents concerned "left or liberal" groups, while only two referred to "right-wing" groups, the Philadelphia branches of the Ku Klux Klan and the Jewish Defense League.

Responding to Justice Department charges that the documents previously released overemphasized the proportion of FBI activity devoted to political surveillance, the commission said that about half the substantive documents from among the 800 stolen pertained to this area, equal to the attention paid all criminal activities and military desertion together.

Other documents told of a program of regular "liaison contact" with 10 Philadelphia area hotels, 8 colleges, 15 newspapers and broadcast stations, 16 banks, and various other businesses, in order "to create goodwill and develop sources of new cases."

Muskie, Boggs Charge FBI

Muskie charges FBI Earth Day spying. Sen. Edmund S. Muskie (D, Me.), in a Senate speech April 14, 1971 charged that the Federal Bureau of Investigation spied on 40–60 Earth Day conservation rallies April 22, 1970, including the Washington gathering where he was a speaker. Muskie called the surveillance a "fishing expedition" that represented "a threat to our privacy and freedom."

In support of his charge, Muskie made public an FBI intelligence report on the Washington rally. He said he had obtained the report, which mentioned his speech, from "a third party" and that it was in no way connected with a Media, Pa. theft of FBI documents.

Muskie said he knew of at least one other senator, "and probably others," whose Earth Day speeches and actions were "subject to surveillance." He said, "If there was widespread surveillance

over Earth Day last year, is there any political acitivity in the country which the FBI does not consider a legitimate subject for watching? If antipollution rallies are a subject of intelligence concern, is anything immune? Is there any citizen involved in politics who is not a potential subject for an FBI dossier?"

Presidential Press Secretary Ronald L. Ziegler said he was "exercised" over Muskie's speech as well as recent charges by Rep. Hale Boggs, House majority leader, that the FBI tapped the telephones of some congressmen. Ziegler said such statements were "aimed at getting big headlines" and gave "a totally misleading impression" about Administration policy. He said the "President's attitude is that snooping or surveillance of private citizens is quite repugnant to this administration."

Muskie proposed establishment of a domestic intelligence review board to oversee the surveillance activities of the FBI and other agencies. He said the board, to be composed of members of government intelligence agencies, Congress, the judiciary and the bar, could recommend actions and legislation "required to curb the unnecessary use of surveillance in our society."

The document Muskie released was a June 10, 1970 memorandum bearing the Justice Department-FBI seal, which was evidently distributed among other government agencies. The report included a chronology of preparations for the Washington rally, a list of individuals involved and a detailed description of speeches made and songs sung at the rally. Muskie said two appendixes attached to the report—describing the Students for a Democratic Society and the Progressive Labor party—"underscores my concerns" since it could be inferred that the Earth Day activity was "somehow related" to the radical groups.

Muskie charges answered—Attorney General John N. Mitchell, in a statement released by the Justice Department April 15, said FBI agents had attended the 1970 Washington Earth Day rally, as charged by Muskie. He said they were there because of "advance information" indicating that individuals with records of violence would attend the rally.

Mitchell said, "The FBI has no interest with an Earth Day meeting as such, but it does have a most legitimate interest in the activities of persons whose known records reveal a likelihood of violence, incitement to riot or other criminal behavior." Mitchell mentioned no names, but Sen. Robert P. Griffin (R, Mich.) said April 15 that FBI agents had been at the meeting to watch "such individuals as Rennie Davis," one of the Chicago Seven defendants convicted of inciting a riot at the 1968 Democratic National Convention.

White House Press Secretary Ronald L. Ziegler called Muskie's charges "blatantly political" April 16 and accused the senator and others of trying to create "a feeling of fear and intimidation among the people."

Muskie said April 16 the Administration's "reluctance to come to grips with the facts is of considerable interest." He called on Mitchell to make public all FBI reports concerning Earth Day and "Let us judge for ourselves."

Nixon calls criticism 'malicious'—President Nixon said April 16 that much of the recent criticism of Federal Bureau of Investigation Director J. Edgar Hoover was "unfair and malicious." Responding to questions from a panel of newspapermen during a Washington convention of the American Society of Newspaper Editors, Nixon said Hoover was "taking a bad rap on a lot of things, and he doesn't deserve it."

Nixon defended the FBI as the "best law enforcement agency in the world." He said he would not comment on Hoover's tenure in office since he had not discussed the matter with the FBI director, but he added, "I believe it would be most unfortunate to allow a man who has given 50 years, over 50 years, of dedicated service to this country to go out under a cloud, maligned unfairly by many critics." Nixon said he thought such criticism would cause Hoover to "dig in" rather than hasten his retirement.

Dole objects to Muskie's remarks—GOP National Chairman Robert J. Dole said to the Republican governors conference in Williamsburg, Va. April 20 that Muskie's attacks on the FBI made the McCarthyism of the 1950s pale by comparison. Gov. William G. Milliken (R, Mich.) took objection to Dole's remarks the next day, saying "the days of McCarthyism were frightening days" and he saw "no relationship to those days" now.

Agnew scores FBI critics. Vice President Spiro T. Agnew, in a New Orleans speech April 26, denounced critics of J. Edgar Hoover and the Federal Bureau of Investigation as political "opportunists" and said they were trying to win the favor of the radical left. Agnew devoted his half-hour speech, before the Southern Gas Association convention, to a defense of the FBI and its director.

Agnew said persons trying to drive Hoover out of office used the issue of his age—76 years—but that "a more likely explanation" of the opposition to Hoover "is the fact that he is anathema to the New Left and extremists of every stripe." He added, "Personally, I have complete confidence in this dedicated, steel-willed public servant with the 20-20 vision into our national security and crime control problems and the institution that he has made the beacon of law enforcement in America."

Agnew referred specifically to two Democratic Presidential aspirants, Sens. George McGovern (D, S.D.) and Edmund S. Muskie (D, Me.), and their criticism of Hoover. He said, "These opportunists are being aided and abetted by certain of their friends in the liberal news media who automatically shout 'Right on!' every time someone claims his civil liberties have been threatened, regardless of the transparency of such charges." While not mentioning him by name, Agnew also dismissed charges by Rep. Hale Boggs (D, La.), the House majority leader, that the FBI had tapped the telephones of congressmen.

Boggs had attempted to back up his case against the FBI in an hour-long House speech April 22. He denounced the "secret police spying and prying" of the FBI and asked President Nixon to appoint an investigatory commission "to go to the core of this cancer and remove it before the poisons spread further."

Hoover's Role Debated

Youth conference calls for Hoover's resignation. About 900 youths, ages 14–24, and 500 adults gathered in Estes Park, Colo. April 18, 1971 for a four-day White House Conference on Youth. One recommendation of the study groups was the resignation of Federal Bureau of Investigation Director J. Edgar Hoover and a review board to oversee FBI surveillance.

FBI aide resigns. William C. Sullivan, a top administrative official in the FBI, resigned Oct. 2 after a series of policy disputes with bureau director J. Edgar Hoover. His resignation was effective Oct. 11.

The *Washington Post* reported that while Sullivan, an assistant director, was on sick leave, his name was removed from his office door and the locks changed. According to the Post, FBI officials said Sullivan, 59, had voluntarily retired.

FBI spokesman refused to deny or confirm reports that Hoover had been putting pressure on Sullivan for months to step down.

Sullivan, who was with the FBI for 30 years, was to be replaced by Alec Rosen, head of the bureau's General Investigation Division.

According to one report, tensions between Hoover and Sullivan became strained after Sullivan told a group of newspaper editors and publishers in a speech in Virginia in October 1970 that the Communist party "is not in any way causing or directing or controlling the unrest we suffer today in the racial field and in the academic community."

The FBI was said to have been deluged with mail critical of Sullivan's remarks. The mail, some said, angered Hoover, who had long held that Communists posed a major threat to America's security.

Ex-official urges curb on FBI powers—William C. Sullivan, third ranking official of the FBI before his retirement in 1971, warned that the agency represented a threat to U.S. civil liberties and urged that its power and budget be reduced. He also called for a three-year moratorium on electronic surveillance by all federal agencies, during which time a study would be undertaken to assess the effect on criminal justice and internal security operations. An independent commission would determine the need for an internal

security apparatus, he said. If such activity were necessary, Sullivan said, it should be conducted by an independent board chosen by Congress, not the FBI.

Sullivan, whose recommendations were in a paper presented to the annual Earl Warren Conference of the Roscoe Pound-American Trial Lawyers Association and made public Nov. 24, 1974 said, "FBI headquarters was wrong in releasing to the American people propaganda that pictured us as an elite corps far superior to any other government organization.... The gulf between public relations and our actual performance was indeed very great."

Beginning in 1939, when the agency first took on internal security duties, Sullivan said, "To be candid, the 'right to privacy' was not at issue nor was it an impediment to solving cases. . . . The primacy of civil liberties on occasions gave way to expediency."

TV report stirs debate. A report prepared by National Education Television (NET), charging that FBI agents had hired "provacateurs" to encourage and participate in radical violence, was deleted by the Public Broadcasting System (PBS) shortly before its scheduled showing Oct. 6 as part of the "Great American Dream Machine" program. It was broadcast two days later amid charges of censorship and reports of FBI displeasure.

The report, put together by Paul Jacobs, a California radical political activist, presented interviews with three youths, two in Seattle and one at the University of Alabama in Tuscaloosa, who said they had been paid by the FBI to infiltrate radical groups and encourage illegal acts that could lead to prosecutions. The program included denials by the FBI agents named by the alleged infiltrators.

FBI Director J. Edgar Hoover, in a letter sent after press screenings of the show, called the charges "totally and absolutely false." He added that the Bureau had "referred this matter to the Department of Justice."

After New York's Channel 13 announced it would broadcast the deleted report Oct. 8, PBS officials offered it for broadcast to all its stations. According to the *New York Times* Oct. 9, the program was broadcast in most major areas.

Responding to charges by NET officials that PBS had exercised "censorship" in its cancellation decision, Hartford N. Gunn Jr., PBS president, said the report had lacked on-screen "documentation" and that PBS had wanted the subject presented in greater depth as a separate program.

Hoover defends FBI. J. Edgar Hoover, director of the Federal Bureau of Investigation, defended the FBI as efficient and fair in a September letter to a group of lawyers, scholars and journalists planning a conference on the bureau.

News of the existence of Hoover's letter was made known Oct. 16. But the

group which was planning the public conference on the FBI said it would not release the contents of the letter.

Hoover sent the 10-page letter to Dr. Duane Lockard, chairman of the politics department at Princeton (N.J.) University, where the conference was to take place Oct. 29–30.

According to published reports, Hoover turned down Lockard's invitation to attend the conference, which was to be sponsored by the Woodrow Wilson School at Princeton and the Committee for Public Justice. Hoover also reportedly declined to send a representative of the FBI to the conference.

Most of the letter was devoted to a defense of the FBI. According to one report, Hoover closed his letter by saying that if information such as he had provided was taken into account at the Princeton conference, he believed that, while some criticism of the agency's operations and procedures might be justified, any "verdict" pronounced on it would have to be an "acquittal."

Conference asks probe of FBI—A two-day conference of lawyers, academics, journalists and former government aides on the Federal Bureau of Investigation ended Oct. 30 with a call for Congress to investigate the bureau's aims and practices.

The three co-chairmen called for a "national commission of inquiry" to probe charges made at the conference that the agency had violated civil liberties and discouraged dissent while failing to fight organized crime. The chairmen were Burke Marshall, a former assistant attorney general, and Professors Norman Dorsen of New York University and W. Duane Lockard of Princeton University.

Much of the criticism centered on alleged intimidation of peaceful dissent. Yale Professor Thomas I. Emerson Oct. 29 asked that the FBI, which he said "conceives of itself as an instrument to prevent radical change," be prevented from photographing peaceful protests or gathering files on "people not charged with a crime or reasonably suspected of a violation of the law."

But Richard Wright, one of two representatives of Americans for Effective Law Enforcement at the conference, responded that "the FBI has a basic duty to make sure the radicals don't get away with intimidating the rest of us." He suggested that surveillance might be justified to prevent violence.

Newsman Victor Navasky Oct. 29 criticized FBI wiretap practices, but placed major responsibility for abuses on past presidents and attorneys general. He warned that no reform would be possible without an "external overseeing body."

Congressional funding of the FBI was criticized Oct. 29 by Walter Pincus, former Senate Foreign Relations Committee aide. He charged that the House Appropriations Subcommittee avoided the usual line item review of budget requests in the FBI's case because some subcommittee investigators were on loan from the bureau. In 21 years, he said, Congress had always appropriated at least as much as the bureau requested.

Two former FBI agents were among its detractors Oct. 29. William Turner, who had been asked to resign in 1961, charged that the bureau had regularly put pressure on local authorities to protect agents accused of petty crimes. Robert Wall, who resigned in 1970, said individuals had been put under FBI surveillance merely for opposing the Vietnam War.

William Hundley, chief of the Justice Department organized crime division in 1958-66, charged Oct. 30 that the FBI had not been diligent in probing organized crime in order to remain on good terms with congressmen who had criminal connections. An FBI spokesman denied the charge and challenged Hundley to produce specific evidence.

The bureau was defended Oct. 30 by John Doar, former assistant attorney general in the civil rights division. Doar defended the use of informers and electronic surveillance to combat organized crime and probe violations of civil rights.

Pro-FBI group sets study—Responding to recent criticisms of the FBI, a group called Friends of the FBI announced Nov. 10 that it was commissioning a $70,000 study of the Bureau "as an institution protecting the public from militant, radical aims."

J. A. Parker, president of the Friends and Virginia chairman of the conservative Young Americans for Freedom, said the study would be conducted by Americans for Effective Law Enforcement, a Chicago group established as a counterweight to the American Civil Liberties Union (ACLU) and endorsed by Attorney General John Mitchell.

The study was to be directed by Richard O. Wright, who warned of a "concerted effort" to limit the FBI, citing an ACLU lawsuit filed in Philadelphia to curb the agency's surveillance of radical groups. (The ACLU suit charged that the FBI had "engaged in gathering information which relates exclusively to lawful and peaceful activities protected by the First Amendment," in order to "harass and intimidate" people from exercising their rights.)

Hoover defends informers. In an annual report to Attorney General John Mitchell, FBI Director J. Edgar Hoover Oct. 26 defended the use of "confidential informants." Hoover said they had led to over 14,000 arrests by the FBI and other law enforcement agencies in the year ending June 30.

The informants had not only solved and prevented crimes, he said, but helped clear innocent persons of false charges.

CIA ties strained. The *New York Times* reported Oct. 10 that Director Hoover had prohibited all personal contact between agents of the FBI and the Central Intelligence Agency (CIA) early in 1970. (The FBI was responsible for counter-

espionage work within U.S. borders, while the CIA handled foreign activities.)

Hoover's order reportedly came after the CIA backed one of its agents who had refused to divulge the identity of an FBI agent who had passed confidential information to him. The information had concerned the disappearance of a Czecho-slovak-born Russian history professor at the University of Colorado. The CIA agent had informed the university that no foul play had been involved after the FBI, which had made the investigation, refused to reveal the information.

According to the *Times*, all regular contact between the intelligence agencies was conducted by mail or telephone, which some critics said limited the counter-espionage effort.

Ex-FBI agent sues Hoover. John F. Shaw, a former agent of the Federal Bureau of Investigation, filed a suit Jan. 27, 1971, charging Director J. Edgar Hoover with a "capricious and vindictive act of personal retribution" that forced his involuntary resignation. In the suit, Shaw said he was forced out of the FBI over a letter in which he criticized some of its inner workings.

Shaw asked for reinstatement, back pay dating from September 1970 and a court declaration barring the bureau from imposing sanctions against him. The suit was filed in his behalf by the American Civil Liberties Union in federal district court in New York.

Shaw's criticism of the FBI and Hoover was made in a 16-page letter written Sept. 15, 1970 to a professor at the John Jay College of Criminal Justice in New York. At that time, Shaw was enrolled at the college at FBI expense preparing for a teaching assignment at the National Police Academy. The letter, however, never reached the professor. It was called to the attention of Shaw's FBI superiors who ordered him "to surrender the letter for examination." He refused.

According to Shaw, his letter defended the FBI against criticism by the professor, but it also criticized some FBI operating procedures.

Shaw said he received notice from Hoover Sept. 22 that he had been suspended for 30 days, placed on probation and transferred to the FBI's Butte, Mont. field office. Shaw resigned from the FBI Sept. 24, and Hoover accepted his resignation "with prejudice."

Shaw charged in the suit that his criticism of the FBI was legitimate and that he had "been all but fired" for his letter. Shaw said the fact that his resignation had been accepted "with prejudice" had prevented him from obtaining employment with other law enforcement agencies.

FBI officers criticize McGovern—Sen. George S. McGovern published in the *Congressional Record* March 9 letters from 21 senior FBI officers who denounced him as an opportunist and defended J. Edgar Hoover.

McGovern had called for a Senate and

Justice Department investigation of the Shaw incident Jan. 31. He said of Hoover's actions, "such vindictiveness is intolerable on the part of an important federal official." McGovern published March 1 a letter from 10 FBI agents criticizing Hoover for "stifling" initiative and promoting personal publicity through the FBI.

In a speech March 25, McGovern said the nation could not afford another "sacred cow" when Hoover was eventually replaced. He said Hoover's successor must be "someone who can be held accountable." McGovern said he thought the FBI currently was a "separate law unto itself, and beyond the reach of the attorney general or even the President." McGovern's remarks came in an address at the John Jay College of Criminal Justice, where Shaw had been enrolled at the time when he wrote a letter partially critical of Hoover.

New charges by McGovern—Sen. George S. McGovern said April 19 that Hoover had tried "to destroy the career" of a Trans World Airlines pilot who had criticized FBI handling of a hijacking in 1969. The pilot, Capt. Donald J. Cook, had said FBI agents had jeopardized the lives of his crew in attempting to stop the hijacking from California to Rome.

In an address at Lewis College (Lockport, Ill.), McGovern said Hoover had tried to prevent FBI agents from acting as sky marshals on TWA flights after Cook's criticism. McGovern said Hoover had sought the pilot's dismissal by informing TWA that Cook had "experienced some personal difficulty" in the Air Force before his employment with TWA.

Challenge of FBI dismissals planned—Two women who said they had been forced to resign from the FBI because of off-duty antiwar activity said April 7 they would sue Director J. Edgar Hoover to get their jobs back. Linda Janca, 21, and Christine Hoomes, 18, both clerical workers, said their suit was being handled by the American Civil Liberties Union.

The two said they would seek to prohibit Hoover from interfering with outside activities of FBI employes in the future. A third woman, Janice Bush, 19, was also asked to resign. The three women, none of whom had security clearances, were reportedly told by their supervisor that the FBI knew they had been working evenings for the National Peace Action Coalition, which was organizing April 24 peace marches in Washington and San Francisco.

Gallagher charges FBI 'blackmail.' Rep. Cornelius E. Gallagher (D, N.J.), pleaded not guilty to a multi-count indictment for conspiracy, perjury and income tax evasion April 21 in federal court in Newark, N.J. Gallagher, 51, had been indicted April 11, 1972.

Two days before he was arraigned, Gallagher charged that the Federal

A

B

C

D

E

F

G

Bureau of Investigation had sought to "blackmail" him into quitting after he refused to help FBI Director J. Edgar Hoover in a feud with the late Robert F. Kennedy, then attorney general.

Gallagher made the charges in an emotional speech on the floor of the House. He asserted there was "corruption at the highest level" of the FBI, and he called on Hoover to resign.

J. Edgar Hoover dies. J. Edgar Hoover, the first and only director of the Federal Bureau of Investigation, died in his Washington home May 2, 1972. He was 77. His death was attributed to the effects of high blood pressure.

President Nixon named L. Patrick Gray 3rd, an assistant attorney general, to be the bureau's acting director May 3.

At the time of his death, Hoover was in his 48th year as director of the FBI. Under his aegis, the bureau had become one of the most efficient and controversial organizations in America's law enforcement history. During his tenure Hoover served eight Presidents and 16 attorneys general.

Among the more recent incidents embroiling the FBI and Hoover were his announcement to a Congressional committee about an alleged plot to kidnap Henry A. Kissinger, his personnel shifts within the FBI that led to the apparent forced resignation of William C. Sullivan, assistant to the director, and charges by congressmen that their telephones were being tapped by the bureau.

Hoover's body lay in state in the Capitol Rotunda May 3, marking the first time a civil servant had been honored in such a way virtually reserved for presidents, military heroes and congressmen.

In all, only 21 persons had lain in state at the Capitol before Hoover. Eight of those were presidents or former presidents.

Chief Justice Warren E. Burger delivered the eulogy at the Capitol ceremony. Burger eulogized Hoover as "this splendid man who dedicated his life to his country in a half-century of unparalleled service."

Hoover's body was removed May 4 to the National Presbyterian Church, where he was a lifelong member.

President Nixon headed a long list of government officials who attended the funeral service.

At the church services, Nixon called Hoover a "legend" during much of his life and an American institution.

Speaking to an overflow crowd of Washington dignitaries and private citizens, Nixon said that the real memorial to Hoover would be the "bureau he built to last" during the 48 years he was its director.

Following the funeral service, Hoover's body was taken to the Congressional Cemetery, one of Washington's oldest, for burial.

Gray named interim director—L. Patrick Gray 3rd, the No. 2 man in the Justice Department, was named by President Nixon May 3 to serve as acting director of the FBI until after the November presidential election.

White House Press Secretary Ronald L. Ziegler attributed Nixon's decision to the President's desire to keep the appointment apart from partisan politics in an election year.

Gray, who was also a long-time Nixon friend, was to serve until Nov. 7.

But the President's decision evoked expressions of displeasure from some Senate Democrats, who had expected to have a chance to confirm a new FBI director. As an interim director, Gray needed no such confirmation.

Gray had been nominated to replace Richard G. Kleindienst as deputy attorney general when the latter was selected to be attorney general. But with his new assignment, Gray's nomination to be deputy attorney general would be withdrawn.

According to Ziegler, Gray would function in two roles—as acting FBI director and as assistant attorney general in charge of civil division.

Out of the announcement of Gray's selection grew a story reported by the *New York Times'* Robert M. Smith May 3 that several of Nixon's chief policy advisers had urged him to dismiss Hoover as FBI director in 1971. According to Smith, an Administration source said Nixon had been asked by those advisers to relieve Hoover, in a dignified fashion, on at least three occasions in 1971. Nixon refused.

The identity of the President's advisers involved in the alleged disagreement was not disclosed.

Gray discusses new post—One day after he was named the FBI's acting director, Gray discussed with newsmen some of the actions he had already taken and some of his views on the new assignment.

Gray disclosed that when President Nixon told him about his appointment, Nixon stressed the need to have the FBI operate in a totally nonpolitical way. In fact, Gray said, Nixon told his wife, Beatrice, that she would have to stop working for the Committee to Re-elect the President.

Gray also revealed that he had met with 15 of the bureau's top officials May 3, only two hours after the White House had announced his appointment.

Among those at the meeting was Mark Felt, an assistant FBI director who had told Gray earlier that some of the officials were thinking of resigning. According to Gray, Felt told him after the conference that the meeting dissuaded them.

At that meeting, Gray assured the officials that the Nixon Administration intended to "maintain the FBI as an institution." Gray also said he told the men about his background: "I tried to tell them what makes up the man Pat Gray."

Gray said that one of the first actions he took as director was to insure that the bureau's files were safeguarded. "My main concern," Gray said, "is the integrity of the FBI as an institution." Gray

added that there "are no dossiers or secret files." He said there "are just general files, and I took steps to insure their integrity. Asked to describe those steps, Gray said "I personally asked the questions, and was satisfied with the procedures required right now."

In another official action, Gray accepted the resignation of Clyde A. Tolson, 71, the bureau's associate director. Tolson who submitted his resignation May 3, said he was quitting for reasons of ill health.

COINTELPRO

FBI campaign against left disclosed. J. Edgar Hoover, the late director of the Federal Bureau of Investigation, ordered a campaign in May 1968 to "expose, disrupt and otherwise neutralize" the "New Left" movement, according to internal FBI memoranda released Dec. 6, 1973 by the Justice Department.

Hoover ordered all bureau offices to take advantage "of all opportunities for counter-intelligence and also inspire action in instances where circumstances may warrant." The "organizations and activists who spout revolution and unlawfully challenge society to obtain their demands must not only be contained, but must be neutralized," Hoover said.

A second memo, issued April 28, 1971, ordered that the campaign be discontinued immediately.

The memos were released after the Justice Department decided not to appeal a federal district court decision ordering that they be turned over to National Broadcasting Co. newsman Carl Stern, who had sued for their release under the Freedom of Information Act.

FBI anti-radical activities revealed. Attorney General William B. Saxbe and Clarence M. Kelley, director of the Federal Bureau of Investigation, Nov. 18, 1974 released some details of a Justice Department report on certain FBI counterintelligence operations conducted from 1956 to 1971 under the designation COINTELPRO. Part of COINTELPRO—counterintelligence efforts against the New Left—had been disclosed late in 1973.

The Justice Department report revealed that COINTELPRO had been composed of seven different programs, with five directed at domestic organizations and individuals and two aimed at foreign intelligence services, foreign organizations and individuals connected with them. Among the domestic targets of COINTELPRO were two black civil rights groups not considered radical by many observers: the Southern Christian Leadership Conference (SCLC) and the Congress of Racial Equality (CORE). All the programs were abruptly terminated in mid-1971 by J. Edgar Hoover, the late FBI director.

The Justice Department committee, headed by Assistant Attorney General Henry E. Petersen, said in its draft report that some of the operations could "only be considered abhorrent in a free society." But the report added that such "improper activities were not the major purpose or indeed the major characteristic of the FBI's COINTELPRO efforts."

The first COINTELPRO operation, which was against the Communist Party USA, was an outgrowth of the "Red Scare" of the mid-1950's, the report said. Begun in 1956 on Hoover's orders, CO-INTELPRO—Communist Party USA was the FBI's response to the then-prevailing "view in Congress and the American people" that the federal government should act against domestic subversion. Moreover, the report noted, later activities were based on the CO-INTELPRO—Communist Party USA model, but reflected "changing threats to the domestic order" during the 1960s.

Other COINTELPRO operations and their effective dates were: Socialist Workers Party (1961–1971), White Hate Groups (1964–1971), Black Extremists (1967–1971) and New Left (1968–1971). The other two COINTELPRO efforts were Espionage or Soviet Satellite Intelligence (1964–1971) and Special Operations (1967–1971). According to the Petersen committee, which for national security reasons declined to provide any details, the overall objectives of the latter two programs were to encourage and stimulate counterintelligence efforts against hostile foreign intelligence sources and foreign communist organizations. In all, various FBI field offices submitted 3,247 proposals for domestic counterintelligence; 2,370 were approved and implemented. More than half the proposals concerned the Communist Party USA, the report said.

The COINTELPRO activities were characterized in the report as sending anonymous or fictitious materials to groups to create internal dissension; leaking of informant-based or non-public information to friendly media sources; use of informants to disrupt a group's activities; informing employers, credit bureaus and creditors of members' activities; informing or contacting businesses and persons with whom members had economic dealings of members' activities; attempting to use religious and civil leaders and organizations in disruptive activities; and informing family or others of radical or immoral activities.

The report also singled out over 20 instances that it called "most troubling" or "egregious" examples of COINTEL-PRO actions. Among them: investigating the love life of a group leader for dissemination to the press; obtaining income tax returns of members of a group; mailing an anonymous letter to a member of a group who was a mayoralty candidate in order to create distrust toward his comrades; sending an anonymous letter, purported to be from a concerned parent, to a local school board official alerting him that candidates for the school board were members of a group; and making an anonymous phone call to a defense attorney, after a federal prosecution had resulted in a mistrial, "advising him (apparently falsely) that one of the defendants and another well known group individual were FBI informants."

According to the report, COINTEL-PRO programs were reported to at least three attorneys general, as well as key White House personnel between 1958 and 1969, although none of the activities was revealed during the period in which it was implemented. No activity involving improper conduct was so reported nor did Hoover ever allow use of the term COINTELPRO outside of the FBI, the report added.

Saxbe and Kelley said the New Left groups targeted by the FBI were Students for a Democratic Society (SDS), the Progressive Labor Party, the Weathermen and the Young Socialist Alliance. Black groups subject to FBI operations were CORE, the SCLC, the Student Nonviolent Coordinating Committee (SNCC), the Black Panther Party, the Revolutionary Action Movement and the Nation of Islam. So-called White Hate groups that were objects of FBI counterintelligence efforts were various Ku Klux Klan organizations, the Minutemen, the American Nazi Party and the National States Rights Party.

U.S. bars charges against FBI—The Justice Department said Jan. 3, 1975 it would not prosecute anyone in connection with the Federal Bureau of Investigation's domestic surveillance program known as COINTELPRO. It had been determined, the department said, that there was "no basis for criminal charges against any particular individual involving particular incidents."

Antiwar professor harassed. As a part of its domestic counterintelligence program, COINTELPRO, the FBI sent an anonymous, accusatory letter to an Arizona State University faculty committee deciding whether to dismiss an antiwar professor, the *New York Times* reported Jan. 29, 1975. The information was contained in documents released to the *Times* by the Professor, Morris Starsky, who had obtained the data by invoking his rights enumerated in the Freedom of Information Act.

Starsky, an associate professor at Arizona State from 1964 to 1970, had organized antiwar teach-ins and had won campus rights for various radical organizations.

According to the documents, J. Edgar Hoover, the late director of the FBI, approved a suggestion by a senior agent in Phoenix that a derogatory letter be sent to each of the faculty members of the university committee reviewing Starsky's case. Another FBI memorandum obtained by Starsky said that "various charges ... and other anonymous charges ... greatly tarnished Starsky's reputation and standing in the academic community."

The chairman of the university committee, Dr. Ross R. Rice, told the *Times* Jan. 28 that he didn't believe the letter had any direct effect on the committee's final decision, but he added, "I don't think it helped him."

The committee did not recommend the termination of Starsky's contract, but the university, under pressure from the state legislature, eventually put him on a year's terminal leave.

FBI harassed King, ex-agent says. The Federal Bureau of Investigation attempted to end criticism of the agency by civil rights leader Martin Luther King Jr. by mailing to his wife, Coretta King, a tape recording considered "unsavory" by some agents of the bureau, the *New York Times* reported March 9, 1975. The recording, picked up by an electronic bug placed in a room of the Willard Hotel in Washington in 1963, was apparently of a party held by King and other officials of the Southern Christian Leadership Conference, which King headed.

An unidentified, former key FBI official said the incident stemmed from a statement by King in 1964 that criticized the agency for having assigned agents with southern backgrounds to handle civil rights cases. J. Edgar Hoover, the late FBI director, then arranged for a copy of the tape to be sent to Mrs. King in such a way that it could not be traced. Bureau officials felt at the time, the *Times* said, that the contents of the tape were detrimental to King and some of his associates, and indicated conduct not consistent with King's position as a religious leader.

Mrs. King told the *Times* that she remembered receiving in January 1965 "a tape that was rather curious, unlabeled." "As a matter of fact," she said, "Martin and I listened to the tape and we found much of it unintelligible. We concluded there was nothing in the tape to discredit him." She and her husband immediately "presumed" that the FBI had been the source of the tape, Mrs. King added.

One retired FBI agent, Arthur Murtagh, who was then attached to the bureau's Atlanta office, characterized the agency's activities against the late civil rights leader as second "only to the way they went after Jimmy Hoffa," former president of the Teamsters Union. The *Times* noted that the Justice Department previously had confirmed that King had been a target of the FBI's counterintelligence program, COINTELPRO. In admitting the existence of COINTELPRO, the FBI had said that one of the techniques of COINTELPRO involved "investigating the love life of a group leader for dissemination to the press."

Other incidents of harassment, the *Times* said, included:

The bureau sought to disrupt a banquet in Atlanta honoring the awarding of the Nobel Peace Prize to King in 1964.

Two former FBI officers said a "monograph" on King's personal life was circulated among government officials during the Kennedy Administration. When Kennedy learned of the "monograph," he ordered Hoover to retrieve every copy.

Murtagh and other former officials recounted the FBI practice of telephone calls—sometimes false fire alarms—to places where King was to speak and to King's associates to cause discord among them.

FBI threat against activist charged. The American Civil Liberties Union (ACLU) March 17 made public documents indicating that the Federal Bureau of Investigation had fabricated a threatening letter to persuade a black civil rights worker to leave Mississippi in 1969. Within a month of receiving the letter, the civil rights worker, Muhammad Kenyatta, returned to Pennsylvania with his family.

The ACLU said it had obtained the documents in connection with a suit Kenyatta had filed against the FBI charging violations of his constitutional rights. They showed that Kenyatta, then known as Donald W. Jackson, had been a target of the FBI's counterintelligence program, COINTELPRO.

The letter, purportedly written by a committee of Tougaloo (Miss.) College students, was actually prepared and sent by the FBI's office in Jackson, the documents showed. It warned Kenyatta that if he did not leave, "we shall consider contacting local authorities regarding some of your activities or take other measures available to us which would have a more direct effect and which would not be as cordial as this note."

A year before the letter was sent, the FBI documents showed, Kenyatta had been placed in its COINTELPRO "agitation list." The FBI said Kenyatta had tried to organize black power groups and start racist publications.

The documents said that the Jackson office of the FBI, acting on a tip that Kenyatta had stolen a television set from the Tougaloo campus, encouraged college officials to file a complaint against Kenyatta. (Kenyatta said the charge was dropped after he agreed to pay a fine for disturbing the peace. He denied both charges.)

Levi reveals more FBI harassment. Attorney General Edward H. Levi revealed May 23 that the Federal Bureau of Investigation had conducted five previously undisclosed counter-intelligence programs from 1960 to 1971. Two of these programs—part of the FBI's anti-radical effort known collectively as COINTELPRO—were designed to pit organized crime against the Communist Party USA and to disrupt the activities of unidentified Puerto Rican independence groups. Levi, who made the disclosures in a letter May 23 to House Judiciary Committee Chairman Peter W. Rodino Jr. (D, N.J.), did not provide details on the other three programs, which he said "were in the area of foreign intelligence and ... classified secret."

According to Levi, the program to turn organized crime against the Communist Party was dubbed "Operation Hoodwink" and in operation between October 1966 and July 1968. It revolved around four bogus letters prepared and mailed by FBI agents, Levi said. The letters contained, among other things, accusations of unfair labor practices against one organized crime figure, as well as charges that organized crime had been behind the

bombing of the Communist Party USA headquarters in New York City.

Asked about the purpose of Operation Hoodwink, a Justice Department spokesman said it was "just to have them sort of disrupt each other." To his knowledge, he said, it was not the FBI's intention for the groups to commit violent acts against each other.

The activities against the Puerto Rican independence groups, Levi stated, involved 37 separate actions between August 1960 and April 1970, including mailings by FBI agents to individuals and groups. Among the examples cited by Levi was a letter to two members of an independence group saying that the group leader and a member were having a "love affair." Another instance, involved the mailing of 300 copies of a flier alleging that an independence group had misused its funds.

ACLU reports on FBI's 'secret army.' The American Civil Liberties Union released a report June 26 describing the FBI's alleged sponsorship of a San Diego, Calif. rightist group called "the Secret Army Organization." A FBI spokesman told the New York Times that the bureau had "nothing to do" with a secret army, "nor did we have anything to do with the direction of its activities."

The ACLU alleged that the paramilitary group was established "on instructions of FBI officials" to carry out terrorism, espionage, vandalism, mail theft, and assassination in southern California. One example cited was an assassination attempt against Peter G. Bohmer, a former economics professor at San Diego State University. Shots were fired into his Ocean Beach home, reportedly from an automobile carrying Secret Army members. Bohmer had organized the San Diego coalition in 1971, designed to bring demonstrators to San Diego to disrupt the 1972 Republican National Convention. The ACLU report contains a statement from John Rasperry, an FBI informer, that he was instructed to assassinate Bohmer in the winter of 1971–72.

FBI fears publication of COINTELPRO operatives. Sen. Frank Church (D, Idaho), the chairman of the Senate committee investigating the intelligence community, told reporters July 11 that his group might be forced to subpoena FBI agents to get information about the agency's activities. Church declared: "It seems that the more serious the inquiry, that is to say, the more it has to do or may have to do with improprieties, the more obstacles are put up by the Justice Department to the committee. This we can't really tolerate ... Now, if it becomes necessary to subpoena FBI agents in order to obtain their testimony, then clearly the committee is prepared to do this." The threat followed news reports, persisting since May, that the committee and the agency were unable to agree on a method for examining classified FBI documents. The agency was said to fear publication of the names of operatives and informants in the COINTEL-

PRO undercover project.

Justice Department provides more FBI data—Attorney General Edward H. Levi met July 11 with K. William O'Connor, who has been the liaison between the congressional investigating committees and the Justice Department. After the meeting, O'Connor gave the Church committee staff access to the "full, unexpurgated file on COINTELPRO," according to the New York Times. Justice Department officials said July 13 that they were "very concerned" over the possibility of congressional leaks of informers' names.

FBI admits opening mail. The New York Times said August 6 that an FBI source revealed that from 1958 until possibly 1970 the bureau had opened and photographed letters to communist embassies and consulates in New York, Washington, San Francisco and other cities.

A spokesman for the FBI issued a statement: "In connection with its foreign counterintelligence responsibilities, the FBI did engage in opening of mail until 1966, when former Director J. Edgar Hoover ordered the activity to be discontinued. The motive behind it was solely to carry out FBI counterintelligence responsibilities in order to thwart espionage efforts directed against the United States by foreign powers."

COINTELPRO disrupted Ku Klux Klan. Reporters obtained FBI documents under the Freedom of Information Act which disclosed the FBI had infiltrated the Ku Klux Klan with approximately 2,000 informers. The documents were released Aug. 15.

Former Director J. Edgar Hoover wrote Sept. 2, 1965 that the bureau's infiltration of the Klan had helped to solve the murders of civil rights activists and reduced southern violence. Hoover reported that the Klan leader in a southern state was "our informant, and we have had him warn every member of his organization that we will not tolerate violence in any form." Of the 14 different Klan groups, Hoover claimed, "we have penetrated every one of them through informants and currently are operating informants in top-level position of leadership in seven of them."

A fictitious organization was begun by the FBI, called "The National Committee for Domestic Tranquility," which mailed thousands of letters to Klansmen. Klan leaders were called communist agents: "By placing themselves above the law of the land through the invocation of the Fifth Amendment, these irresponsible Klan leaders have joined hands with Communists who also always hide behind the Fifth Amendment."

COINTELPRO curb planned. Attorney General Edward H. Levi said Aug. 13, 1975 that he would curtail domestic intelligence operations of the Federal Bureau of Investigation. In a speech before the American Bar Association in Montreal, Levi sketched the background of the COINTELPRO operation:

"Before 1972, and for a number of prior years, the bureau engaged in special programs directed at domestic groups; for example, it improperly disseminated information from its files to discredit individuals, or arranged for the sending of anonymous letters, or the publication of material intended to create opposition."

Levi proposed guidelines for FBI operations, which the attorney general called "sometimes outrageous." "Interests of individuals in privacy" and possible effects on "legitimate domestic political activity" were included in some of the tentative guidelines.

GAO audit finds few FBI convictions. The Federal Bureau of Investigation's domestic intelligence operation produced few warnings of extremist or subversive activities and even fewer convictions, the General Accounting Office said in a report to Congress Sept. 24.

The GAO study, undertaken for the House Judiciary Subcommittee on Civil and Constitutional Rights, said that a survey of 676 FBI domestic intelligence investigations in 10 cities indicated that only 12 produced advance warning of extremist or subversive activities. Of the 676 investigations, 16 were referred for prosecution and four resulted in conviction.

Use of 'Provocateurs' and Informers

FBI charged in Camden raid. Robert W. Hardy, the informer who aided the Federal Bureau of Investigation in the August 1971 Camden, N.J. draft office raids, said in an affidavit filed March 15, 1972 in U.S. district court in Camden that he had been used by the bureau as a "provocateur" without whom the raid could never have taken place.

Hardy's affidavit was filed in support of a pretrial motion to dismiss charges against 20 defendants for breaking and entering federal property and stealing and destroying federal records, and against eight others charged with conspiring and abetting the crimes.

Hardy's affidavit said the plot had been abandoned before he first reported it to the FBI, which paid him about $60 a day plus expenses thereafter to keep the agency posted, to help plan the raid, to provide tools, instructions and supplies, including groceries and the van and gasoline used in the raid. He said he "provided 90% of the tools necessary for the action. They couldn't afford them, so I paid and the FBI reimbursed me. It included hammers, ropes, drills, bits, etc. They couldn't use some of the tools without hurting themselves, so I taught them." He also provided the defendants with diagrams of the draft office and the entire building.

In explaining why he was filing the affidavit, Hardy said the FBI had first told him arrests would take place before the building was actually entered, limiting the charges to conspiracy and ruling out jail terms. He was later told by the FBI that "the higher-ups, someone at the Little White House in California, they said, which I took to mean someone high in the FBI or Justice Department,

then in California, wanted it to actually happen."

Defense attorney David Kairys said in his motion that his clients had been "as a matter of law, entrapped" by the government. He called the incident "a case of manufacturing crimes to support repressive policies and the political futures of persons in power," and cited as a similar case the role of FBI informer Boyd Douglas in the Harrisburg 7 conspiracy trial.

In a reply reported April 18 the government argued that the "defense of entrapment is available only to a person who is otherwise innocent, i.e., one who had no predisposition to commit the crime," and that the predisposition should be determined in a jury trial.

Draft raiders acquitted—Seventeen of the 28 accused in the August 1971 Camden, N.J. draft office raid were acquitted in federal district court May 20, 1973 after Judge Clarkson S. Fisher told the jury it could acquit if it found that the government had exceeded permissible limits in using a "provocateur" in setting up the crime.

Defense and prosecuting attorneys concurred in seeking dismissal of all charges against the 10 remaining defendants whose cases had been severed from the current trial. One had pleaded guilty to a misdemeanor.

The verdict marked the first total legal victory for the antiwar movement after a long series of draft records incidents. Judge Fisher's charge to the jury was also seen as a legal breakthrough.

In his instructions May 17, Fisher said although the defendants admitted breaking into the office and destroying draft files and were predisposed to do so, the jury need not consider the "predisposition of any defendant" if it found the actions of government agents "so fundamentally unfair as to be offensive to the basic standards of decency and shocking to the universal sense of justice." His position ran counter to an earlier Supreme Court decision in a related case.

Fisher told the jurors, however, they did not have the power to acquit, as the defense contended they did, by "nullifying" the law against breaking and entering because they might approve of the defendants' antiwar protest.

The key to the case was Robert W. Hardy, a Camden contractor who said the Federal Bureau of Investigation had paid him to provide the means to carry out the raid. Testifying for the defense, he said that one of the two FBI agents to whom he had regularly reported told him that "someone in the little White House" in San Clemente, Calif., wanted the FBI to let the crime happen before making arrests, rather than arrest the 28 for conspiracy before the break-in.

The defense contended that the reason for waiting was to "create" additional crimes to generate enough publicity to discredit the antiwar movement. Hardy and other defense witnesses said the

group had abandoned plans for the raid because of a lack of expertise, but Hardy's intervention with instructions and equipment resurrected the scheme.

Some jurors told the *New York Times* May 21 that, although Hardy's actions had been the principal consideration in their deliberations, their own reservations about U.S. participation in the Indochina war led them to "join the defendants in taking a stand against the war."

Two of the defendants, the Rev. Edward J. Murphy and the Rev. Edward J. McGowan of New York City, had been charged only with conspiracy. The other 15, charged with breaking and entering, stealing and destroying government records, interfering with Selective Service, possession of burglary tools and conspiracy, faced maximum terms of 47

Six antiwar vets indicted. Six members of the Vietnam Veterans Against the War (VVAW) were indicted in Tallahassee, Fla. July 14, 1972 on charges of conspiring to disrupt the Republican National Convention in Miami Beach in August with bombings and shootings.

The six were John W. Kniffen of Austin, Tex., William J. Patterson of El Paso, Tex., Peter P. Mahoney of New York, Alton C. Foss of Hialeah, Fla., Donald P. Perdue of Gainesville, Fla. and Scott Camil of Gainesville, who was also indicted for manufacture and possession of a firebomb and with instructing others in the use of explosives. Perdue and Mahoney were still at large July 16.

The conspiracy charges were based on provisions in the 1968 civil rights bill against crossing state lines to stir disorder, used to convict the Chicago Seven after the 1968 Democratic National Convention. According to the indictment, at least four meetings were held April 1–June 24 to plan the disorders, and a variety of weapons were assembled.

VVAW leaders charged July 15 that the indictments were based on false evidence given by William Lemmer, a former VVAW official who they said had been an informer for the Federal Bureau of Investigation and provocateur. The group claimed to have tape recordings in which Lemmer admitted the charges.

Vietnam vets' trial set—Six members of Vietnam Veterans Against the War pleaded innocent Aug. 24 in Gainesville, Fla. to charges of planning to disrupt by violence proceedings at the Miami Beach Republican National Convention.

U.S. District Court Judge David L. Middlebrooks set an Oct. 10 trial date for the six, who would remain free under $25,000 bail each.

The U.S. 5th Circuit Court of Appeals in New Orleans dismissed contempt of court charges against four members of the antiwar group Sept. 26, ruling that the government had not adequately denied charges that it had used illegal wiretaps at the group's Gainesville headquarters and at defense attorneys' Tallahassee, Fla. homes. The four had been freed on their own recognizance Sept. 7 by Middlebrooks, after Supreme

Court Justice William O. Douglas ordered their release. They had been held in contempt for refusing to testify before the grand jury that handed down the six indictments, after being granted immunity.

Douglas acted Sept. 5, after Justice Lewis F. Powell refused to accept the defense plea. Douglas gave as reasons the possibility that illegal wiretapping had been used to obtain evidence leading to the subpoena of the four veterans, and that the grand jury might have abused its powers in questioning the men after indictments had already been handed down. The four had been freed once before, only to be jailed again Aug. 9 after a contempt hearing, that had been ordered by the 5th U.S. Circuit Court of Appeals, was held.

Antiwar vets' trial opens. Testimony began Aug. 3, 1973 in Gainesville, Fla. in the trial of seven members of Vietnam Veterans Against the War and one of their supporters, all charged with conspiring to disrupt the 1972 Republican National Convention in Miami Beach.

In his opening statement Aug. 3, chief prosecutor Stewart J. (Jack) Carrouth portrayed the defendants as a well-organized group of radicals who plotted to cause riots and attack buildings with bombs, automatic weapons, crossbows and slingshots.

The defense countered with charges that the government had built up the conspiracy with provocateurs in order to discredit the VVAW and justify political "dirty tricks" such as the Watergate break-in.

U.S. District Court Judge Winston E. Arnow, saying that "the government is not on trial here," halted defense attempts to link the case to the Watergate scandal, but allowed a defense attorney to tell the jury that one of the reported government informers, Pablo Fernandez, was on the payroll of the Committee to Re-Elect the President.

The prosecution's key informer in the case, William W. Lemmer, testified Aug. 6 that Camil had told him of training "political assassination squads" armed by trading drugs for weapons. Defense attorneys called for a mistrial, contending that the testimony was "inflammatory and prejudicial" and that no such charges were covered by the indictment. Judge Arnow denied the motion.

Lemmer, a former VVAW leader from Arkansas, then described a meeting in Camil's Gainesville house in May 1972, during which various weapons were demonstrated and plans for disrupting the convention were discussed. During the meeting, Lemmer said, he was unmasked as an informer for the Federal Bureau of Investigation.

After the discovery, Lemmer continued, he offered to become a double agent and assured the group that he had only been a "political monitor" for the FBI and was not interested in criminal acts planned by the group. He said he continued to be treated as an insider and was later given more details of plans for the Miami Beach operation.

Lemmer concluded his direct testimony Aug. 7 with further descriptions of secret meetings and discussions of ways of obtaining weapons. The prosecution then disclosed the existence of 10 hours of tape recordings of statements by Lemmer on the case, as well as two written statements.

Judge Arnow, reportedly angry with the late disclosure of the material, ordered it turned over to the defense and called a one-day recess before cross-examination.

Wiretap clash precedes testimony— Defense attorneys charged July 31—the first day of jury selection—that two FBI agents who had been found in a closet adjacent to the office of the defense in the federal court building could have been attempting to monitor the defense's conversations.

The agents, who possessed telephone receiving devices and other electronic equipment, maintained they were only "checking FBI lines" in the building.

Judge Arnow at first denied a defense motion for a hearing on the wiretap issue, saying the FBI agents had been "perfectly candid and honest" in answering the charges.

After a jury had been selected Aug. 2, Arnow ordered a separate hearing on the wiretap question. After three sessions of inconclusive testimony ending Aug. 7, Arnow ordered a recess to coincide with the break in the main trial. Defense attorneys had contended that the FBI action was further evidence of the government's improper investigation and prosecution of the case, while prosecutors maintained they needed to "sweep" government lines to detect possible taps.

Antiwar protesters acquitted— After deliberating less than four hours, a federal jury in Gainesville, Fla. Aug. 31 acquitted seven members of the Vietnam Veterans Against the War and one of their supporters of conspiring to violently disrupt the 1972 Republican National Convention in Miami Beach.

The verdict concluded a bizarre trial during which several defendants acted as their own counsel and were often chastised by Judge Winston E. Arnow for their courtroom conduct.

Fears of wiretapping were expressed by the defense and some jurors. Arnow had ruled Aug. 9 that there was "no basis for belief" that defense office phones were being tampered with by Federal Bureau of Investigation agents. Arnow disclosed Aug. 13 that five jurors had complained their home phones "had been acting strangely;" a check of the lines, Arnow said, revealed no indications of wiretapping.

The defense called only one witness, chemistry professor Steven Stellman, who testified Aug. 28 that an "incendiary" device allegedly possessed by defendant Scott Camil was an often harmless concoction of drugstore chemicals and not legally a "bomb." The prosecution's key witness, former VVAW member William W. Lemmer, had testified that Camil suggested putting the devices in police car gasoline tanks.

Lemmer had been cross-examined Aug. 9-13 on his allegations that Camil, described as the leader of the group, and other defendants had told him of plans to attack police, incite riots and bomb buildings in Miami Beach. Throughout the cross-examination the defense sought to discredit Lemmer as a witness, portraying him as a provocateur hired by the FBI and citing indications of mental instability.

Under intense questioning Aug. 10-11, Lemmer repeatedly denied that he had "set up" arrests of radicals in other cases during his year as an FBI informer, but conceded that he had been involved in other cases, including a firebombing at the University of Arkansas and a marijuana "harvest" in Kansas.

Lemmer conceded Aug. 11 that plans for concealment of weapons had not been suggested to him by the defendants, as prosecutor Stewart J. Carrouth had alleged in his opening statement. A transcript of a conversation between Lemmer and his FBI supervisor (which had been turned over to the defense) indicated that the concealment ideas had originated with the FBI agent.

Although the prosecution called 28 witnesses, it relied chiefly on the testimony of Lemmer and four other informers. One of them, Emerson L. Poe, had been described by Camil as his "best friend" until his appearance in court Aug. 17. Government statements given to the defense showed that Poe had been an FBI informer since January 1972, when he first met Camil.

Poe said Aug. 17 he had reported to the FBI "every conversation" with Camil since the July 1972 indictment of the group. The defense immediately objected that it had been improperly infiltrated, since Poe had been represented by the same attorneys as the defendants during the grand jury proceedings. Defense attorneys Aug. 17 cited a list of their clients during the 1972 proceedings, including Poe, which Guy L. Goodwin (the Justice Department official supervising the prosecution) had sworn contained no informers or agents. After Poe testified that he had not been involved in defense strategy planning, Judge Arnow denied a defense motion to dismiss the charges.

Under cross-examination Aug. 21, Poe said the only plans he knew of by the Camil group were to urge peaceful demonstrations, with some provisions for "self-defense" in case of attacks by police. The "self-defense" plans were corroborated in cross-examination Aug. 22 by another former VVAW member, Aaron P. Simonton, who had said in direct testimony that Camil had discussed firebombing buildings.

The prosecution rested its case Aug. 24 with the testimony of an undercover police officer, Harrison Crenshaw, who said some of the defendants had mentioned the possible use of powerful weapons and the severing of telephone and power lines. On cross-examination, Crenshaw said the only weapons he had been shown were slingshots.

Those acquitted, in addition to Camil, were Alton C. Foss, John W. Kniffen, Peter P. Mahoney, William J. Patterson, Donald P. Perdue, Stanley K. Michelson and John K. Briggs.

'Gainesville 8' sue U.S.—Seven members of the Vietnam Veterans Against the War and one of their supporters filed a $1.2 million lawsuit in U.S. district court in Washington May 28, 1974, charging that the government had illegally infiltrated the defense camp during their 1973 trial.

The suit alleged that Emerson L. Poe, a paid informer for the Federal Bureau of Investigation, had reported regularly to the prosecutors on defense tactics during the trial, depriving the defendants of constitutional rights of due process. The suit also charged that other, unnamed informers had infiltrated the defense throughout the trial.

Sham Red reveals FBI work. Joseph A. Burton, a Tampa, Fla. resident, told the *New York Times* that he had made about 10 trips to Canada at the FBI's direction, while posing as a member of a Marxist revolutionary group, the newspaper reported Feb. 16, 1975. Burton said that for two years, beginning in May 1972, he had headed a sham revolutionary organization in Tampa called the Red Star Cadre, which had been set up with FBI financing. The purpose of his trips to Canada, Burton said, was to develop contacts with the pro-Chinese wing of the Canadian Communist party and to report to the FBI on its activities, including signs that funds were being passed from China to pro-Chinese groups in the U.S.

An official statement by the FBI said Burton had been a paid informant and denied he had done anything illegal.

Warren Almond, soliciter general of Canada, said Feb. 18 that Burton's trips to Canada had been approved by the Canadian government and monitored by Royal Canadian Mounted Police.

AIM security chief was FBI informant. Douglas Durham, chief security officer for the American Indian Movement (AIM) during the trial of the leaders of the Wounded Knee occupation, admitted March 12, 1975 he had been a paid informant for the Federal Bureau of Investigation.

Ken Tilsen, chief counsel for AIM, said the infiltration had constituted an "illegal invasion of the defense." AIM would file motions to have charges dropped against 30 remaining Wounded Knee defendants and to have convictions of nine others set aside, he said.

In an affidavit at the 1974 trial, Justice Department prosecutors had indicated they had no informers in the defense camp. Durham stated, however, "I exercised so much control that you couldn't see Dennis or Russell without going through me. You couldn't contact any other [AIM] chapter without going through me, and if you wanted money you had to see me." (Dennis Banks and Russell Means, leaders of AIM, had been

indicted on federal charges of conspiracy, larceny and assault in connection with the 71-day occupation of the village of Wounded Knee on the Oglala Sioux reservation of Pine Ridge in South Dakota in 1973. The charges were dropped Sept. 17, 1974 by presiding U.S. District Court Judge Frederick J. Nichol, who cited government misconduct and the refusal of the prosecution to proceed with an 11-person jury after a juror became ill, eight and a half months into the trial.)

Judge Nichol March 13 said he was shocked by Durham's revelation. He stated his belief that the government knew of Durham's relationship. "I believe I was deliberately misled by R. D. Hurd and Joseph Trimbach," Nichol said. (Hurd was chief prosecutor at the trial and Trimbach was director of the FBI's regional office in Minneapolis.)

Durham, who was paid as much as $1,100 a month by the FBI, said his cover had been broken March 7, when suspicious AIM members confronted him with law enforcement documents establishing his role as an informer.

His first contact with the AIM leadership was as an undercover police operative working as a photographer for an underground newspaper, which assigned him to take pictures of the Indian take-over, Durham said. On returning from Wounded Knee, he was asked by the FBI to infiltrate AIM. A skilled pilot, he was quickly able to get close to Banks, whom he later flew around the country on speaking trips. Subsequently, he became AIM's security office at the trial, Durham said. He told AIM members he was one-fourth Chippewa.

Durham said the FBI told him not to report on defense tactics, but to look for signs of foreign involvement, arms caches or plans for other take-overs.

Harassment

Socialists sue government. The Socialist Workers party (SWP) and the Young Socialist Alliance filed a $27 million damage suit in federal court in New York City July 18, 1973 charging President Nixon and other past and present government officials with a "systematic campaign of excessive interrogation, employment discrimination and other harassment" which impaired the groups' participation in elections.

The suit asked that the government be permanently prohibited from wiretapping, monitoring mail and breaking into party offices. The suit also sought an order striking the SWP from the attorney general's list of subversive organizations.

Supreme Court declines hearing—The Supreme Court Oct. 9, 1973 refused to consider an effort by the Socialists Workers Party to have the attorney general's subversive list declared unconstitutional. The decision was made over the dissents of Justices William O. Douglas, William J. Brenann Jr. and Byron R. White.

'Subversive' file ordered destroyed—The

Federal Bureau of Investigation was ordered Aug. 29, 1974 to destroy its file on Lori Paton, a Chester, N.J. girl who had sought information from an allegedly subversive group as part of a high school classroom project.

U.S. District Court Judge James A. Coolahan refused, however, to grant a class-action request that the FBI be generally prohibited from conducting the type of mail cover surveillance that had led to the existence of a "subversive" file on Miss Paton. Coolahan also denied her claim for $65,000 in damages.

In early 1973, Miss Paton had sent a letter to the Young Socialist Alliance, an affiliate of the Socialist Workers Party. The party was on the then-active subversive list maintained by the U.S. attorney general and subject to an FBI mail cover.

The FBI received Miss Paton's name from a postal inspector and began an investigation, which included a check on her family and a visit to her high school. The agent who investigated was reportedly surprised to learn the reason for her letter to the party, and recommended that "the case be closed administratively." The FBI, however, maintained a file under her name, with a notation signifying "subversive matter—Socialist Workers Party."

In his ruling, Coolahan said there was no legal justification for her file, which could become an unfair detriment in later life.

FBI allowed to watch Socialist meeting—Thurgood Marshall, associate justice of the Supreme Court, Dec. 27, 1974 refused to set aside an appellate court ruling allowing the Federal Bureau of Investigation to send agents and informants to the convention of the Young Socialist Alliance, which opened in St. Louis Dec. 28.

The 2nd U.S. Circuit Court of Appeals Dec. 24 had reversed an injunction issued Dec. 16 by U.S. District Court Judge Thomas P. Griesa that prohibited the FBI from conducting surveillance of the Young Socialist Alliance, the youth affiliate of the Socialist Workers Party.

Griesa had acted on a complaint that FBI surveillance of the Trotskyite political group inhibited people from attending meetings and exercising their freedom of speech. Ordering the FBI to keep its informants and agents away from the convention, Griesa said, "You've been looking at this group for 35 years and you haven't produced one single solitary crime or incitement to violence in the U.S. by anyone in this organization."

The three-judge appellate court panel ruled that Griesa's injunction had been based on inadequate information and represented an "abuse of discretion." In vacating Griesa's injunction, the panel said that the FBI could watch the convention on the condition it did not transmit the names of those attending to the U.S. Civil Service Commission or other government agencies that might use the information against persons seeking employment.

Judges Henry J. Friendly, William H. Timbers and Murray Gurfein comprised the appellate panel.

FBI harassed Socialist Workers Party—The Federal Bureau of Investigation made public over 3,000 pages of internal documents March 18, 1975 detailing agency efforts to harass the Socialist Workers Party, a splinter communist party loyal to the ideology of the Leon Trotsky, the Soviet revolutionary. (A civil suit filed under the amended Freedom of Information Act resulted in a federal court order compelling the FBI to release 3,138 pages of documents to the party and its youth affiliate, the Young Socialist Alliance.)

The documents showed that the party had been an object of FBI surveillance since 1944, as well as a target of the agency's counterintelligence program, COINTELPRO, whose purpose was to disrupt party activities and harass party members and their families. According to the documents, COINTELPRO had involved 41 separate operations against the party between 1961 and 1971.

Among the activities described by the documents:

■The arrest and conviction record of the party's candidate for a New York City political office was sent anonymously to the *New York Daily News,* which later published the information in one of its columns.

■In 1963 an anonymous letter was sent to a black candidate for mayor of San Francisco, telling him of the presence of party members in his campaign staff.

■J. Edgar Hoover, director of the FBI until his death in 1972, personally approved dissemination of anonymous leaflets designed to cause dissension among various political factions and parties of the far left.

■An anonymous phone call alleged that a party-operated print shop was attempting to defraud the State of New York by creating bogus unemployment insurance claims for party members. (A state audit of the print shop's records in 1966 or 1967 produced one violation, a party spokesman said).

Spokesmen for the party said neither the parent organization nor its youth affiliate had been the subject of a federal prosecution since 1945.

Socialist Workers Party obtains COINTELPRO documents. The Socialist Workers Party released June 24 FBI documents it had obtained under the Freedom of Information Act. The 256 pages from the FBI files, as summarized in the *New York Times* June 25, reveal attempts to cause the firing of politically active teachers, among other anonymous harassments.

A Texas teacher was fired after FBI agents had informed school authorities that she had been a Socialist Workers candidate. Although she was fired in 1970, as late as 1972 FBI agents visited her succeeding employers and told them about her political background. The agents would ask if she were "still working here."

The FBI in Detroit and Washington also sent letters signed "a concerned citizen" and "a fed-up taxpayer!" detailing the political activities of two other teachers.

The released documents contained a memorandum dated April 27, 1971 which seemed to end COINTELPRO campaigns against the Socialist Workers, the New Left, "white hate groups," the American Communist Party and others.

Secret Files

Kelley: FBI kept files on congressmen. Clarence M. Kelley, director of the Federal Bureau of Investigation, Jan. 21, 1975 confirmed newspaper reports that the bureau kept files on members of Congress. However, he asserted that such information had not been actively sought by the FBI and was mostly the byproduct of unrelated FBI investigations.

Ron Nessen, White House press secretary, said Jan. 22 that the FBI had assured President Ford that it had not spied on members of Congress.

The *Washington Post* Jan. 18 had cited two former top officials of the FBI, who said the agency had compiled files containing information on the personal lives of members of Congress. Cartha D. DeLoach and Louis B. Nichols said the files contained data on "girl friends and drinking problems...," as well as other personal information," which DeLoach characterized as "junk," the *Post* said.

While the two former officials claimed that the information had been placed in the files after persons interviewed by the FBI on unrelated matters had volunteered it, the *Post* cited an informed source who said that J. Edgar Hoover, the late director of the bureau, had ordered derogatory material gathered on former Rep. William R. Anderson (D, Tenn.). Anderson had criticized Hoover for his statements about Philip and Daniel Berrigan, Catholic priests named by Hoover as having plotted to kidnap a high government official, later identified as Henry A. Kissinger, then director of the National Security Council.

In a written statement Jan. 21, Kelley said, "Such files exist because they relate to an investigation or a background check, correspondence with the member of Congress, or information not solicited by the FBI, but volunteered by the public." In the case of unsolicited allegations, Kelley said, the FBI investigated only when the charges fell under bureau jurisdiction.

Hoover's secret files confirmed by Levi— J. Edgar Hoover, director of the Federal Bureau of Investigation until his death in 1972, kept secret files with derogatory information on presidents, congressmen and other prominent persons, Attorney General Edward H. Levi disclosed to a House subcommittee Feb. 27. His testimony—Levi's first as attorney general—also indicated that the FBI had been misused by at least three presidents for political purposes.

Hoover's files, which dated to 1920, contained 164 file folders and jackets, 48 of which concerned "public figures or prominent persons," Levi told the Judiciary Committee's Subcommittee on Civil Rights and Constitutional Rights. Included in the 48 files, Levi said, was information on "presidents, executive branch employes and 17 individuals who were members of Congress." (Two of the men named in the files were still in Congress, Levi added.) One document suggested that derogatory material on a congressman who had attacked Hoover "was improperly disseminated," Levi said without elaboration.

Levi described five instances of "misuse of the resources" of the FBI. He did not name the Presidents who allegedly misused the agency, but Deputy Attorney General Laurence H. Silberman supplied the names to newsman after the hearing.

Levi said one instance involved "a check of FBI files on the staff of a campaign opponent." According to Silberman, President Johnson made the request through an aide, Bill Moyers, about Sen. Barry Goldwater, the 1964 Republican candidate.

One president, Levi testified, "caused the FBI to gather intelligence relating to a political convention under circumstances that ... could ... have been suspected of being politically motivated." Silberman confirmed that it was Johnson and the incident was the bugging of the hotel suite of Martin Luther King Jr., the late civil rights leader, at the 1964 Democratic national convention in Atlantic City, N.J. Silberman said a similar incident had occurred in 1968 but did not elaborate. The *New York Times* reported Feb. 28 that the 1968 case concerned the FBI's obtaining telephone records of members of the staff of Spiro T. Agnew.

In a "few instances," Levi testified, the FBI was ordered to report on "certain activities" of congressmen who opposed presidential policies. A Justice Department spokesman said that President Johnson on two occasions, President Nixon once and President Kennedy once had ordered data gathered on representatives and senators critical of their policies.

"In a very small number of instances ...," Levi said, "derogatory information legitimately obtained by the bureau was disseminated to other members of the executive branch to enable them to discredit their critics." Silberman declined to cite examples.

Levi said the FBI was used to conduct an investigation of another federal law enforcement agency. Justice Department officials said that President Johnson in 1967 asked the FBI to look into the involvement of the Treasury Department's Narcotics Bureau in the 1965 investigation of Robert G. (Bobby) Baker, a Johnson protege later convicted of income tax evasion. According to one Justice Department source, Johnson demanded to know if any of the persons involved were close to Robert Kennedy, then the attorney general.

In his subcommittee testimony, Levi

urged that an executive order be issued restricting to a few officials the authority of the White House to ask the FBI for information. He said it was "inappropriate" for a president to ask the FBI for information on congressmen.

Levi and FBI Director Clarence M. Kelley, who also testified, said that present law and procedures did not allow the FBI to destroy the existing files on congressmen.

Ford objects to FBI files—President Ford said Jan. 23 that "under no circumstances" should the Federal Bureau of Investigation spy on members of Congress or other U.S. citizens. Noting that "mistakes were made going back to 1964 or 1965," he said: "It has stopped now."

Burglaries

FBI admits burglaries. Clarence M. Kelley, director of the Federal Bureau of Investigation, admitted July 14, 1975 that the agency had conducted a number of burglaries and break-ins since World War II in order to get "information relative to the security of the nation." Speaking at a news conference to mark the start of his third year in office, Kelley said the break-ins had continued beyond 1966, previously given as the year they had been terminated, but that he himself had not been asked to approve any while serving as FBI director.

He described the number of break-ins he knew about as "not many" and said he did "not note in these activities any gross abuse of authority." They were not, he said, "a corruption of the trust that was placed in us." Kelley indicated that at the request of the Senate Select Committee on Intelligence agency was compiling materials on past break-ins and would hand them over to Attorney General Edward H. Levi to decide the form and manner in which they should be given to the committee. Regarding the prospect of future FBI break-ins, Kelley added: "If ever anything of this type comes up—and I can't foresee this need—but if ever it did come up and it became a matter of grave concern, a matter that is to be solved only through such activity, I would present it to the attorney general and would be guided by his opinion as to such activity."

In answer to another question, Kelley said the FBI would go on collating whatever material it received about the lives and habits of famous people, including members of Congress, because the "abuse" of such information was in its "publication" rather than its collection.

The *Washington Post* July 16, citing an unnamed former FBI agent, said that until 1966 the agency had committed as many as 100 burglaries a year, mostly in "security cases" but also in ordinary criminal proceedings. The *Post* said the break-ins had been stopped by former Attorney General Ramsey Clark.

According to the *New York Times* July 22, FBI agents in 1959 entered the Washington, D.C. hotel room of a *New York Post* reporter at the request of J. Edgar Hoover, then agency director, who was concerned about an investigation of the bureau being conducted by the newsman.

The *Times* said its source, who asked not to be identified, had come forward to discredit remarks made in his July 14 news conference by Kelley, who had asserted the break-ins had all been carried out for reasons either of foreign intelligence or national security. The paper quoted its source as declaring the purpose of the Washington break-in had been to find signs that the reporter "might have had a female in the room or was drinking heavily." However, the "fellow was clean as a whistle" and the agents didn't find "anything that was worthwhile."

FBI committed 238 burglaries. The Federal Bureau of Investigation committed at least 238 illegal break-ins against dissident U.S. groups and individuals, according to data made public Sept. 25 by the Senate Select Committee on Intelligence.

Sen. Frank Church, chairman of the committee, said an FBI report showed 238 "entries" by FBI agents in connection with the investigation of 14 "domestic subversive targets" had been made between 1942 and 1968, and "numerous" but uncounted entries involving three other "domestic subversion targets" had been carried out between 1952 and 1966. (According to sources outside the committee, the *New York Times* reported Sept. 26, the FBI's statistics did not include break-ins involving espionage and organized crime investigations.)

The committee also made public a top-level bureau memorandum acknowledging the unlawful nature of such break-ins. The memorandum, dated July 19, 1966, was sent by Assistant FBI Director William C. Sullivan to Cartha D. DeLoach, a high ranking aide to J. Edgar Hoover, then the bureau's director. It said:

"We do not obtain authorization for 'black bag' jobs outside the bureau. Such technique involves trespass and is clearly illegal; therefore, it would be impossible to obtain any legal sanction for it. Despite this, 'black bag' jobs have been used because they represent an invaluable technique in combatting subversive activities of a clandestine nature aimed directly at undermining and destroying our nation." (The break-ins were designated "black bag" jobs because of the small black bag often used to carry burglar's tools.)

Detailed memoranda giving approval for the burglaries were signed by Hoover or his long-time aide, the late Clyde Tolson, and placed in a safe in the office of the assistant director under a "Do Not File" procedure, the Sullivan memorandum said. At the same time, "in the field, the special agent in charge prepares an informal memorandum showing that he obtained bureau authority and this memorandum is filed in his safe until the next inspection by bureau inspectors, at which time it is destroyed."

Sen. Richard Schweiker (R, Pa.), a member of the committee, said headquarters memoranda signed by Hoover or Tolson were kept out of regular bureau files, which carried serial numbers and could not be destroyed without leaving a gap in the numbering.

The Sullivan memorandum ended with an order in Hoover's handwriting: "no

more such techniques must be used. H."

Charles Brennan, a retired FBI official who succeeded Sullivan as chief of the bureau's domestic intelligence division, testified before the committee Sept. 25. He said that Presidents Johnson and Nixon put "tremendous pressure" on the FBI in the late 1960s and early 1970s to determine whether the antiwar movement in the U.S. was obtaining financial support from abroad. In response, Brennan testified, the bureau compiled a report showing that antiwar leaders had met with Communist leaders abroad but that they had not received financial assistance.

Future Roles of the FBI

Curbs on some FBI tactics to be set. Attorney General Edward H. Levi said Aug. 13 that he had tentatively approved Justice Department guidelines designed to curtail some of the Federal Bureau of Investigation's domestic intelligence operations. The proposed guidelines, which Levi outlined before the American Bar Association's annual convention in Montreal, were part of the results of a comprehensive review of FBI investigative practices ordered by the attorney general.

Among the details of the guidelines:

All FBI files containing unsolicited charges about individuals would have to be thrown out after 90 days if the charges could not be proved.

Electronic surveillance would be used in "full-scale investigations" only and would be subject to periodic review by the attorney general. (Levi did not define "full-scale.")

Infiltration of domestic groups would be prohibited except in cases when intrusions by FBI agents were intended to prevent violence.

The decades-old practice of conducting open-ended, unsupervised probes of domestic groups suspected of subversive activities would be ended.

The FBI would be barred from using informants as agents provocateurs, who incited others to commit criminal acts.

To end use of the FBI by the White House for political purposes, all White House orders would have to be in writing and signed by a high-level authority.

Kelley's view of FBI's responsibilities— FBI Director Clarence M. Kelley had told the ABA Aug. 9 that the rights of individuals must not be allowed "to transcend the safety and security of others." "We must surrender a small measure of our liberties to preserve the great bulk of them," Kelley said. He recommended no further restrictions on wiretapping because the nation's security demanded special "latitude" to gather foreign intelligence data: "If an individual's rights are violated by a law enforcement officer, remedies are available. But there is no appeal, no remedy for a terrorist's bomb." The FBI director argued that it was a "commendable philosophy" to "present ourselves as sterling examples of people who know no limits in the recognition of human rights," but "what if one of [a foreign nation's] top priorities is the destruction of our democracy?"

FBI FILES STOLEN IN MEDIA, PA.; PAPER CITES ANTIWAR 'PARANOIA'

A group called the Citizens Commission to Investigate the FBI stole almost 800 documents from the Federal Bureau of Investigation office in Media, Pa. March 8. Most of the documents related to peace and black activist groups. Copies were sent to Sens. George McGovern (D, S.D.) and Parren J. Mitchell (D, Md.), to the *Washington Post, New York Times,* and *Los Angeles Times.*

One of the stolen documents, a newsletter from the Philadelphia FBI office, encouraged agents to increase interviews with dissenters "for plenty of reasons, chief of which are it will enhance the paranoia epidemic in these circles and will further serve to get the point across there is an FBI agent behind every mailbox." The newsletter, dated Sept. 16, 1970, added, "some will be overcome by the overwhelming personalities of the contacting agent and volunteer to tell all—perhaps on a continuing basis."

THE LOUISVILLE TIMES
Louisville, Ky., April 24, 1971

It comes as no surprise to learn that FBI agents were ordered to step up interviews of suspected radicals "for plenty of reasons, chief of which is that it will enhance the paranoia endemic in these circles." Such tactics were a weapon in political intelligence long before even J. Edgar Hoover became an institution.

The irony is that in refining and adapting this procedure to the American political scene, the FBI has done irreparable damage to its own image and reputation. It has been over-zealous in its surveillance.

As a result, the paranoia is not confined to the political fringes. It is present among the loyal opposition where it feeds upon revelations of surveillance on Capitol Hill by a "bugged" informer and the presence of an FBI branch office near the House office buildings. It is reinforced when Sen. Edmund Muskie produces a report that takes note of his speech at an Earth Day rally last year.

Documents stolen from the FBI office in Media, Pa., point to a pre-occupation with blacks, campus radicals and undercover agents that leads one to wonder if the agency still is in the business of catching bank robbers and kidnappers.

The debate has toppled J. Edgar Hoover, about whom many metaphors have been cast, from the pedestal where he so long stood into a frankly political arena. His peccadillos, while neither new nor unusual, now are broadcast in prime network time or garner front-page headlines. Ten years ago, those same stories found their way into print only in "little" magazines or books published to languish on library shelves.

So it is not because he is 76 years old that Mr. Hoover is being labeled a vain, inflexible autocrat. The available evidence indicates that he has always operated the bureau in such a manner.

But of late he has been pushing his vindictiveness beyond the limits a tolerant American public is willing to accept. He wins no sympathy by firing an agent (whose wife was dying of cancer) for writing a letter exploring the strengths and weaknesses of the FBI. He perpetuates racial stereotypes by alleging that Puerto Ricans and Mexicans "don't shoot straight, but if they come at you with a knife, watch out."

Forbidding three young girl clerks from working in the peace movement is an unwarranted infringement upon their personal rights. Casting slurs at Dr. Martin Luther King Jr., showing open contempt for Robert F. Kennedy and characterizing Ramsey Clark as a "jellyfish" are activities demeaning to a man in such a high position.

Frank Donner, of the Yale Law School who has spent years researching political surveillance in America, estimates that the FBI is only the principal agency among at least 20 federal agencies engaged in the field. Of these activities, he writes:

Before it is too late we must take a cold look at our political intelligence system: not to determine whether one aspect or another is repressive . . . but to decide whether internal political intelligence as an institution, divorced from law enforcement, is consistent with the way we have agreed to govern ourselves and to live politically.

The question is one almost impossible to divorce from an evaluation of Mr. Hoover's stewardship, so tangled has his personal image become within the web of questions about our national security.

Yet now that his days are drawing short—and it is plain that neither Mr. Nixon nor the Congress can allow him to continue unchecked—it would be a good time to sort them out. For only by establishing firm ground rules that will curb the "big brother is watching" syndrome can the FBI and all domestic intelligence agencies be channeled into proper roles.

Then a new director—nonpolitical and fiercely independent—could set about restoring the FBI to the pinnacle of public esteem that it once earned.

ARKANSAS DEMOCRAT
Little Rock, Ark., May 5, 1971

People who are supposed to know J. Edgar Hoover best say that nothing has ever upset him as much as the robbery of the Media, Pa., FBI office by radicals who cleaned out the secret files. The information in them was spread all over the country and even printed in newspapers, revealing surveillance techniques, results of investigations, the names of informers, etc.

Hoover's first reaction, so we are told, was to order agents to guard every office 24 hours a day, but he backed off when it was pointed out to him that this would require more agents than most of the small offices had. (Only two men were assigned to the Media office, for instance.) At last report, Hoover was considering closing some of the smaller offices in order to lessen the chances of more robberies.

For some reason there was more laughter and even joy (on the part of the New Left) than there was alarm about this ransacking of the FBI files. Undoubtedly this is because of the unpopularity of J. Edgar Hoover. But like him or not, he and his men are in the important job of catching criminals, and how can they do it when the criminals know their secrets? All Americans ought to be concerned about this — the left and the right.

Consider informers, for example. Those files contained the names not only of those spying on the Weathermen and the National Peace Action Coalition but also those keeping up with the Ku Klux Klan and the Minutemen. Not much has been heard from the Klan lately, and it is generally acknowledged that undercover men in its ranks are responsible for holding down its terrorism.

People who will blow up either office buildings or synagogues don't mind playing rough. So you can imagine the reaction of undercover men and informers when they read about the robbery of the FBI files. They quit and got out of town.

It was law-abiding citizens who were hurt by the breach of the FBI files. Not J. Edgar Hoover.

St. Petersburg Times

St. Petersburg, Fla., March 25, 1971

Evidence from Federal Bureau of Investigation files indicates the FBI may pose a threat to the nation's security.

Copies of stolen FBI records sent to members of Congress and The Washington Post, plus public utterances by FBI head J. Edgar Hoover, show how far the bureau has departed from its founding function.

ONE FBI document, stolen by unknown persons from a Media, Pa., office early this month, encourages more FBI interviews with campus dissenters ". . . for plenty of reasons, chief of which are it will enhance the paranoia endemic in these circles and will further serve to get the point across there is an FBI agent behind every mailbox."

The "interviews" then, are not to gather information, or to investigate, they are to instill fear, to leave the impression that Big Brother is everywhere, waiting, watching, ready to deal with those who disagree with their government.

That is, coincidentally, an effect of Soviet KGB surveillance, and is hauntingly reminiscent of the fears stirred by Nazi Gestapo among Germans who opposed their government's policy toward Jews.

That is decidedly not the function of the FBI.

The FBI was established in 1908 as the investigative arm of the Justice Department. It is a fact-finding agency with two primary areas of responsibility — general investigations and security operations.

Evaluation of the results of investigations, or recommendations for prosecutive action, are not with in its founding scope, and the bureau certainly was not intended to be politically oriented.

But Hoover has gone out of his investigative way to evaluate his agency's findings, most particularly where he judges communism to be at work, and has even become embroiled in prosecutive matters, as with his testimony before Congress on the Rev. Daniel Berrigan case.

He has become a highly political figure, amassing a public following with attacks on lawyers, parole systems, courts, Communists, civil rights leaders, educators and "fair weather patriots," and has even branched into foreign policy matters.

Discovery of the contents of secret FBI documents, like the news of widespread Army spying, lead to strong suspicion the FBI's paranoia aims may themselves contribute to civil unrest and national insecurity — the precise opposite of the bureau's function.

Perhaps it is time for Congress to take a hard look at what the FBI has become, determine just how much it has become derailed, and put it back on the track of founding duties.

The Providence Journal

Providence, R.I., March 30, 1971

What does a newspaper, a radio station, or a television station do when it receives by mail a bundle of material purportedly filched from the files of the Federal Bureau of Investigation? Does it go ahead and publish the material, as presented, or does it wait until FBI authenticates the material as genuinely taken from its files?

The problem was posed recently when several newspapers and other news outlets received copies of material reportedly stolen from FBI files in Media, Pennsylvania. The records indicated that the agency is engaged in active surveillance of student, Negro, and peace groups. About 14 of 800 stolen documents were offered through the back door for publication.

At least one major newspaper elected to publish the material but without the names of individuals. Others, it would appear, took advantage of the surreptitious gift and published whatever they thought newsworthy. A reasonable question: Why were only a selected 14 documents passed along? But there is a far more basic question about such material.

How can any newspaper or other news outlet be sure of the authenticity of filched material without first checking with the FBI or whatever agency suffered theft? In this instance, the FBI moved quickly to authenticate the reports, but a Justice Department spokesman urged caution in publication to prevent harm to persons engaged in investigative activities.

Shadowing the issue is the simple fact that the forgery of documents is as old and familiar a business as spying itself. A group intent on discrediting the FBI might be angry enough to arrange for the forging of material, to be released by mail in the hope that publication would precede any effort to authenticate.

Even if the FBI has established the authenticity of the material stolen in Media, there is no guarantee that similar material, delivered in the future by anonymous sources, will be equally authentic. In fact, groups antagonistic to the FBI may be inspired by the recent events to try to arrange a repeat, offering fabrication as the real thing.

Tulsa Daily World

Tulsa, Okla., April 15, 1971

NOBODY could have foreseen the unseemly aftermath of the burglary a week ago of the Federal Bureau of Investigation office in Media, Pa.

If FBI offices are to be victimized by hoodlums and subversives for the purpose of weakening the nation's internal defenses, it may be necessary to close many of them, according to the Bureau.

The Media burglary exposed a flaw in FBI security. It has neither the manpower nor the time and money to devote to complete self-protection. Its duties are more required in other areas of criminal activity. Yet, if its own offices are going to become the targets of dissidents interested in destroying private files, it is going to have to centralize and guard them.

This is precisely what Director J. EDGAR HOOVER is considering in the wake of the Media robbery. To do so, however, would weaken the agency's ability to act quickly and efficiently when called upon . . . which we fear may be the goal of the Media burglars. If they can cripple the FBI's efficiency, and place a doubt in the public mind of its worthiness, they will have wrought as much mischief as a Molotov cocktail or a pipe-bomb in a public building.

Clearly, the Federal Bureau of Investigation is under frontal attack. Recent criticisms against HOOVER are indicative of the anti-law bent of a growing segment of the nation's people. The theme seems to be, HOOVER must go!, and ostensibly responsible citizens who should know better are numbered among the chanters. The Media burglary, whether directly connected or not, seems to fit this peculiar and dangerous pattern.

The FBI has traditionally worked out in the open. But such forays as that in Media could conceivably force it "underground." If it is required to shut down its offices and station its men in hotel rooms away from public access, it will lose much of the moral and security justification for its being. It will become more and more a "secret" organization with little fraternity with the citizen taxpayer.

This would be disastrous, and those who nip at the FBI know it. Which is by far the best reason yet why the nation must preserve the organization and resist efforts to dismantle it.

Honolulu Star-Bulletin

Honolulu, Hawaii, March 31, 1971

Recently members of Congress and newsmen have been supplied with information stolen from files of the Federal Bureau of Investigation. These files demonstrated activity on the part of the FBI in political surveillance of individuals and groups who, in some cases, were doing no more than raising a placard in protest against the Vietnam war.

The Justice Department has been most frank in explaining these tactics. It wants to dissuade, by example, any who might be tempted to take part in a demonstration. A recent FBI newsletter came right to the point. It wants left-wing dissenters to believe "there is an FBI agent behind every mailbox."

The Army, which recently was revealed to be conducting a mass surveillance program of civilians, appears to have recanted, now that influential members of Congress, which supplies the money that the Army spends on these and other activities, took umbrage at the idea that the military should build up a mass file on civilians. If there has been a similar relaxation on Mr. Hoover's wing of the Justice Department, however, it has not been announced.

If neither the Executive Department nor Congress has the power or the will to restrain these zealous exponents of law and order, it seems that we civilians bound for the master file might be allowed one simple request. Could not the F.B.I., if it is going to place us, unbeknownst or not, in the master file, at least keep the master file secure? With a better lock, or more security guards? Otherwise the wrong people might get their hands on the record of our personal lives some day.

The Washington Post
Times Herald

Washington, D.C., March 25, 1971

With due deliberation and with considerate regard for the Attorney General's objections, this newspaper yesterday published the substance of some FBI records—stolen by unknown persons from the FBI's office in Media, Pa. and sent to The Washington Post anonymously by mail. The Attorney General, naturally, would have preferred no account at all of the records and, indeed, no mention of the theft. Because he asserted that "these records include information which would disclose the identity of confidential investigative sources and information relating to the national defense," this newspaper carefully refrained from any facsimile reproduction of the documents sent to it and from any disclosure of the various FBI codes on the records, including identification numbers and names of agents and of persons under surveillance. We reported the substance of the records, however, because we were convinced that it served the public interest to do so.

The records afford a glimpse, not often granted to the general public or even to committees of Congress, of some of the ways in which the FBI works and of some part of its concept of internal security. They indicate that the bureau focused a good deal of attention on college campuses and particularly on black student groups which, according to a memorandum issued by FBI Director J. Edgar Hoover "pose a definite threat to the nation's stability and security" and that on one college campus in the Philadelphia area the bureau enlisted the services of the local police chief, the local postmaster, a campus security officer and a college switchboard operator to maintain surveillance on a professor regarded as a "radical." Other documents indicated that students were used, sometimes on a paid basis, as informers.

This lifting of a corner of the curtain on FBI activity in the name of internal security seems to us extremely disquieting. Granted that it by no means presents a complete picture, it nevertheless suggests strongly that an appropriate committee of the United States Congress ought to look much more thoroughly at what the bureau is doing. Disorder on college campuses undoubtedly presents a problem to the colleges concerned and perhaps to the communities where they are situated as well. But it does not rise to the level of a threat to the internal security of the United States.

Moreover, the intrusion of undercover operatives and student informers into the life of an institution which has the interchange of ideas and the conflict of opinion as its very *raison d'etre* introduces a disruptive element more deadly than disorder. The FBI has never shown much sensitivity to the poisonous effect which its surveillance, and especially its reliance on faceless informers, has upon the democratic process and upon the practice of free speech. But it must be self-evident that discussion and controversy respecting governmental policies and programs are bound to be inhibited if it is known that Big Brother, under disguise, is listening to them and reporting them.

The FBI is not only insensitive on this score; it is shown by these records to be callous and, indeed, deliberately corrupting. One of the documents encourages agents to step up interviews with dissenters "for plenty of reasons, chief of which are it will enhance the paranoia endemic in these circles and will further serve to get the point across there is an FBI agent behind every mailbox. In addition, some will be overcome by the overwhelming personalities of the contacting agent and volunteer to tell all—perhaps on a continuing basis."

That is a concept of internal security appropriate, perhaps, for the secret police of the Soviet Union but wholly inconsonant with the idea of a Federal Bureau of Investigation in the United States. A government of snoopers in a nation of informers was hardly the vision in the minds of those who established the American Republic.

We believe the American public needs to know what the FBI is doing. We believe the American public needs to think long and hard about whether internal security rests essentially upon official surveillance and the suppression of dissent or upon the traditional freedom of every citizen to speak his mind on any subject, whether others consider what he says wise or foolish, patriotic or subversive, conservative or radical. That is why we published the substance of the stolen FBI records.

New York Post

New York, N.Y., March 25, 1971

It might be easier to accept Attorney General Mitchell's anxious pleas to the press not to publish any details about some stolen FBI records—he suggested that hostile "foreign governments" might possibly benefit—if it were not quite so apparent that the least friendly government involved seems to be the one in Washington.

For example, among the documents snatched from the files of an FBI office in Pennsylvania and sent to the Washington Post was a memorandum proposing that agents make more contacts with campus and black militant groups "for plenty of reasons, chief of which are it will enhance the paranoia endemic in these circles and will further serve to get the point across there is an FBI agent behind every mailbox."

Some of the sources, it was suggested, "will be overcome by the overwhelming personalities of the contact agent and volunteer to tell all." It is not clear from this whether split personality is now required of agents; more importantly, the FBI has yet to convince anyone that promoting "paranoia" strengthens national security.

It has been known for years that the FBI files are chocked with "raw" data—some of it approximately as appealing as raw sewage. Surely Sen. Ervin (D-N.C.) and the Senate Subcommittee on Constitutional Rights might pursue some new inquiries in this direction. We hold no brief for those who stole the documents; but the contents are not rendered inconsequential by the way they came to light.

The Salt Lake Tribune

Salt Lake City, Utah, March 28, 1971

Coming on the heels of a Senate investigation of government surveillance, disclosure that the Federal Bureau of Investigation is engaged in widespread snooping on college campuses is chilling news indeed.

It has been widely speculated that government agents had infiltrated chapters of Students for a Democratic Society (SDS) and maybe other militant or left-leaning organizations. But records stolen from the agency's Media, Pa., office show that agents were — and presumably still are — busier than previously believed.

News accounts of the stolen records indicate that in its zeal to keep tabs on the political left, the FBI also assembled dossiers on obscure persons such as an Idaho Boy Scout leader who plans to take his troop camping in the Soviet Union.

There are instances where the FBI would be well within its jurisdiction in sending its operatives on campus. In cases of violation of federal law the campus cannot claim immunity from federal police action. But the documents stolen at Media reveal that the bulk of the FBI's activity on college and university campuses is directed toward spying on and frustrating student dissent which the agency considers "a threat to the nation's stability and security." Campus disturbances are upsetting and some constitute temporary threats to the stability of their community, but we don't recall any that seriously threatened national security.

There is nothing wrong in maintaining order, it is how order is maintained that is important. Sending teams of undercover investigators and faceless informers to infiltrate an institution whose very heart is the exchange of ideas and expression of differing opinions will cause more serious damage than a few broken windows or even a burned ROTC building.

Secret government surveillance which attempts to ferret out and neutralize those who hold and express unpopular opinion will mean slow death to free expression even if no arrests are made. It can kill a university even quicker.

If FBI activities in this field are as widespread as the stolen documents indicate — a charge the Justice Department denies — then the time has come for a public airing of the FBI and what it is supposed to be doing.

The New York Times

New York, N.Y., March 29, 1971

Without in any way condoning the theft of documents from an office of the Federal Bureau of Investigation, one is tempted to ask: who watches the watchman? Little confidence is inspired by the security measures of a security agency whose files can be so easily burglarized.

More disquieting than the bureau's internal security is the evidence, provided via the stolen files, of F.B.I. incursions into political surveillance which far exceed legitimate efforts to protect the national interest. One need not minimize the seriousness of certain violent and lawless episodes in the recent history of student unrest to be disturbed by the F.B.I.'s measures of campus infiltration; especially its apparent stress on surveillance of black students and their organizations. Such procedures assume undertones of latent racial prejudice. With rare exceptions, the protests by Negro students have been concerned with their personal place in the academic community rather than with the revolutionary excesses of the white (or black) radical fringe.

The Justice Department replies that the main thrust of F.B.I. activities has been distorted by the disclosure of only fourteen documents out of a total of 800 taken from the files. This argument offers small comfort to those whose right to privacy is improperly invaded. But even more dangerous are the consequences — clearly intended — that flow from the widespread use of informers. These tactics, said an F.B.I. newsletter, "will enhance the paranoia" among left-wing dissenters and "get the point across there is an F.B.I. agent behind every mailbox."

The dictionary definition of paranoia is "a mental disorder marked by delusions or irrational suspicions." It is difficult to be paranoid over police surveillance which, far from being a delusion, is carried out with such plainly stated intent.

Assistant Attorney General William H. Rehnquist recently denied that political surveillance as currently practiced has a "chilling effect" on free expression of dissent. Apparently the F.B.I., the Justice Department's investigatory arm, disagrees. Could anything be more chilling than the knowledge that the Federal Government allows law enforcement to be perverted into a deliberate process of spreading fear and suspicion, on the campuses or anywhere else in a society that wants to remain free?

Amsterdam News

New York, N.Y., April 3, 1971

It is fact that today we are living in a police state. The military keeps records and an eye on black leaders, the FBI watches closely black activist groups and black students on campuses who merely ask for inclusion of black studies and teachers.

And if you are against the never-ending war in Vietnam, and are for peace, you automatically fall under the surveillance of these national zealous-protectors of the flag.

This ever-growing practice of snooping and prying into the lives of private citizens is reprehensible and to the extent that it has grown nauseating.

Big Brother has now reached the point of no return. Anyone who dissents from what is put down as right by the powers-that-be is thereby subject to suspicion and thus falls under the eye of the military of FBI complex. And one's name and his family's and his associates' and his everyday activities then become numbers in the ever-growing files that are kept on us.

The FBI files that were stolen and mailed to several newspapers and individuals last week showed that the agency is actively engaged in watching student, Black, and peace groups.

There have been warnings before of the possibility of detention camps for Blacks in this country who dare shout out too loud against the status quo.

Is this the beginning?

ST. LOUIS POST-DISPATCH

St. Louis, Mo., May 25, 1971

That mysterious group known as the Citizens Committee to Investigate the FBI, now engaged in making public files taken from the FBI office in Media, Pa., has broken down the purloined material by subject matter. Apart from routine manuals and forms, 40 per cent of the material involved political surveillance, 25 per cent bank robberies, 20 per cent such crimes as murder, rape and interstate theft, 7 per cent draft resistance and another 7 per cent military desertions—and 1 per cent organized crime.

The investigation of organized crime is, of course, supposed to be one of the FBI's main functions. Indeed, the Nixon Administration used organized crime as a principal excuse for the legislation authorizing electronic eavesdropping by court order, though it rejects even the need for court orders in some of its political surveillance. In any case, the Media office evidently did not regard organized crime as all that important. Or isn't there any in the Philadelphia area?

The Charleston Gazette

Charleston, W. Va., April 6, 1971

When FBI files were stolen from a Media, Pa., office, Atty. Gen. John Mitchell asked the press not to publish the information the files contained. (Copies had been mailed anonymously to several papers.)

It was, we believe, a valid request, insofar as revelation might hamper criminal investigations or, possibly, endanger the lives of FBI agents. But one is compelled to wonder, in view of what some of the stolen papers revealed, if these were the principal reasons for Mitchell's request.

It might be argued that embarrassment might have something to do with it. One of the files was on a Boy Scout leader who had inquired about Russian youth camps because he proposed to take a small group of Scouts abroad.

It is difficult to believe there was anything sinister in the scoutmaster's request, for it was mailed directly to the Soviet Embassy. The information the scoutmaster sought was routine information which is sought daily from the embassy by many Americans contemplating overseas travel.

The Boy Scout file lends credence to the frequent accusation that the FBI wastes thousands of hours in petty snooping on subjects highly unlikely to overthrow the government or mount any kind of offensive against law and order.

Although the Boy Scout file is funny, the implications of it are far from humorous. It is obvious now that many perfectly innocent citizens are under federal surveillance and that FBI cabinets are bulging with dossiers on persons whose political views don't jibe with those of J. Edgar Hoover.

We, here in Charleston, aren't excluded from this un-American Big Brotherism. Agents of the FBI were watching carefully at a peace demonstration and at a "prayer vigil" conducted by clergymen on the State Capitol steps.

The stolen files have established that advocacy of peace is considered by the FBI to be a suspicious activity, almost as questionable as having black skin.

We can hardly recommend the theft of property from the FBI. But we cannot recommend, either, the FBI's totalitarian concept of society.

The Des Moines Register

Des Moines, Iowa, March 30, 1971

The persons who broke into an FBI office in Pennsylvania and stole records are guilty of criminal conduct and they should be prosecuted. The records they have brought to light also deserve attention.

The records, which the Justice Department concedes are authentic, show that FBI agents were advised to step up interviews with dissenters to "enhance the paranoia endemic in these circles and . . . further serve to get the point across there is an agent behind every mailbox." They show extensive FBI surveillance of black organizations and peace groups. The surveillance of one college professor included an arrangement with the college's switchboard operator to report on his long distance telephone calls.

The FBI is charged with responsibility for protecting the country against espionage, sabotage and other subversion. Unlike the recently-exposed Army intelligence operation, which included spying on civilians and ranged far beyond its assigned mission, the FBI's jurisdiction clearly encompasses internal security.

But how does the FBI define "internal security?" Who are regarded as proper surveillance targets? Does the FBI maintain dossiers? Are they political dossiers? How reliable is the information? Who has access to it?

The recent Senate hearings on invasion of privacy dealt largely with Army spying. It is evident that investigative activities of the FBI can pose just as great a threat to privacy if there is inadequate control. The fact that the FBI is performing a mission it is assigned to perform is no guarantee against abuse. One has only to recall that the FBI eavesdropped for years on Dr. Martin Luther King to realize the potential for abuse.

William H. Rehnquist, assistant U.S. attorney general, told the Senate investigating committee:

"I think it quite likely that self-discipline on the part of the executive branch will provide an answer to virtually all of the legitimate complaints against excesses of information gathering."

Rehnquist's assurance is less than reassuring. He later told the committee he believed the Constitution places practically no limits on surveillance of citizens by government.

The FBI's secrecy requirements present problems in checking on the agency, but it should be possible for Congress to subject it to review without compromising security. The long-standing practice by Congress of treating this agency as beyond reproach is a failure to meet its responsibility. Under the checks and balances of the Constitution, Congress is supposed to serve as a check on the executive branch of government.

The Justice Department's bid to be free of outside surveillance while claiming an unlimited right of surveillance of others is frightening. The time has come for Congress to assert its intention of holding the FBI and other federal information-gathering agencies accountable to it.

The Birmingham News
Birmingham, Ala., April 16, 1971

A group calling itself "The Citizens Commission to Investigate the FBI" continues to try to embarrass the Federal Bureau of Investigation by releasing documents stolen from one of the FBI's offices.

Critics of the FBI no doubt are gleeful at the prospects of some harm being done to the esteem in which the FBI is held by the public.

It should be remembered, however, that these persons seeking to discredit the FBI engaged in a criminal act when they broke into the office and made off with the documents. Tactics of this nature are a reflection on the individuals involved. It is a sad thing for criminals seeking to undermine the chief law enforcement agency in the country to be given such widespread public attention.

Americans should not lose sight of the necessity for such an organization as the FBI. At a time when extremists go so far as to bomb the nation's Capitol, a national investigative agency is needed more than ever.

The theft of the documents has made the FBI more conscious of security—the agency reportedly plans to close a large number of its small offices.

But if judged on face value, the information revealed in the stolen documents made public is really not damaging to the integrity of the FBI. The documents indicate that school and credit records are used as sources of information, but there seems to be no particular threat in this. It is difficult to see how persons could wrongly incur suspicion of criminal activity on the basis of these records alone.

As far as the investigation of the daughter of Rep. Henry S. Reuss, D-Wis., is concerned, the FBI, in our opinion, was within its rights to investigate her background in the radical-activist Students for a Democratic Society. Nothing came of the agency's check, and it would have remained confidential if the documents had not been stolen and released.

Due consideration must be given to the individual's right to privacy, surely. But the country also has to consider the right of individuals and institutions to be protected against criminal and violent acts.

The FBI has the responsibility for providing that protection, and we hope that it will continue vigorously to meet that responsibility.

The Philadelphia Inquirer
Philidelphia, Pa., March 28, 1971

All two hundred million of us in this country are in a bad way—and our freedoms may be in jeopardy—if we are dependent upon information from burglars to find out what the Federal Bureau of Investigation is doing.

Files stolen from the FBI office at Media, in Delaware County, and subsequently circulated among members of Congress and news media, are revealing not so much of the FBI as the massive public ignorance about this super-secret national investigative organization.

Some of the information distributed by the anonymous thieves, who hardly could be called a reliable source, seems to indicate that FBI agents have engaged in systematic invasions of privacy going beyond reasonable procedures for criminal investigation. The purloined records suggest the FBI routinely carries out surveillance assignments —prying into the lives of civil rights leaders. for example—that may exceed the notorious espionage activities of Army Intelligence brought to light in the hearings conducted by Senator Ervin of North Carolina.

★ ★ ★

Why is the FBI investigating these people? What have they done? Are citizens placed under surveillance for capricious reasons, at the whim of someone in authority, and what use is made of the information compiled on the private lives of persons who are accused of no crime and have no reason to suspect they are being shadowed by government agents? These are questions too fundamental in a free society, with implications too suggestive of police state tactics, to be brushed lightly aside.

It would be unfair and rather naive to make a judgment of the FBI on the basis of documents no doubt selected by the burglars for the purpose of making the FBI look bad. But the harsh truth is that we know too little about the FBI to make an informed judgment on the credibility of its explanations either.

In nearly a half-century under the leadership of one man, who is somewhat of an enigma himself, the Federal Bureau of Investigation has become a legend in its own time—surrounded by an aura of romantic mysticism reminiscent of the best fiction that has been written about Scotland Yard and the Royal Mounted Police.

There is no denying that the FBI very often gets its man—and sometimes in rather dramatic fashion, as people old enough to remember the Dillinger era will testify—but exactly what else the FBI does isn't so clear.

★ ★ ★

Giving Director J. Edgar Hoover the full benefit of the doubt, which is something many of his critics would be reluctant to do, the fact remains that he is not immortal. Someday his far-ranging investigative apparatus—the closest thing to a national police force this country has—will pass to other leadership.

It is in the national interest for Congress and the people to know more about the FBI —its assignments, its objectives, its methods of operation. The light of public exposure could be directed with discretion to prevent violations of security and to avoid compromising the effectiveness of FBI investigators and informants.

If the FBI is doing a good job, let credit be given where credit is due. And if it isn't, let's find out about that, too. Most important of all, we ought to know more than we do about the nature of the job itself.

A committee of Congress should conduct a public inquiry into these matters, not for vindictive purposes but to be sure there are adequate safeguards to insure that the FBI will always act in the national interest, with due regard for the constitutional rights and freedoms of all.

The Detroit News
Detroit, Mich., May 22, 1971

The inability of the FBI to protect its own files against thieves is absurd. But even more absurd is the attitude of righteous indignation assumed by the so-called Citizens Commission to Investigate the FBI upon examining the contents of those stolen files.

Apparently suffering no pangs of conscience at possessing and distributing stolen documents, this anonymous group darkly announces that most of the documents involved "political surveillance" — from which we are supposed to conclude that the FBI has been hacking away at our cherished liberties.

"Political surveillance" means either surveillance conducted for political reasons or surveillance directed at organizations essentially political in character. There is no evidence of the former kind of surveillance. As for the latter, why shouldn't the FBI keep its eye on extremist groups—white or black, reactionary or radical—known for their propensity for subversive and violent action? The FBI would be derelict not to do so.

Unfortunately, t h e m y t h has sprung up that an activity which can be described as "political" becomes automatically sacrosanct. The term has grown to be a semantical sanctuary for people who dynamite buildings and incite riots.

Those now making public the files they stole from the FBI may accurately be described as a political group, but surely no one would argue that their activities should remain free of FBI surveillance— assuming, of course, the FBI's ability to identify them.

Crime or potential crime arising from political motives deserves the same attention given any other crime. An extremist who plots the bombing of a federal building — or steals government documents — does not become an exception in the eyes of the law merely by calling himself a political activist.

MUSKIE CHARGES FBI SURVEILLANCE OF 40-60 1970 EARTH DAY RALLIES

Sen. Edmund S. Muskie (D, Me.), in a Senate speech April 14, charged that the Federal Bureau of Investigation spied on 40–60 Earth Day conservation rallies April 22, 1970, including the Washington gathering where he was a speaker. Muskie called the surveillance a "fishing expedition" that represented "a threat to our privacy and freedom." Muskie asked, "If there was widespread surveillance over Earth Day last year, is there any political activity in our country which the FBI does not consider a legitimate subject for watching? If antipollution rallies are a subject of intelligence concern, is anything immune? Is there any citizen involved in politics who is not a potential subject for an FBI dossier?"

The San Diego Union

San Diego, Calif., April 20, 1971

Inasmuch as challenging of the Federal Bureau of Investigation has become popular among liberals, it is not surprising that Sen. Edmund S. Muskie, a presidential aspirant, should add his voice to the hue and cry. The senator seeks the limelight. Thus he is expressing outrage because the FBI maintained a surveillance over an Earth-Day rally in the nation's capital last year which he addressed.

Unlike House Democratic Leader Hale Boggs, who has failed to produce any evidence to support his charge that the FBI had tapped the telephones of congressmen, Senator Muskie has possession of an FBI report that proves his point. The first issue then is whether the FBI surveillance at this and other rallies was justified or "a threat to freedom" as he asserts.

Sen. Robert P. Griffin has come forward with what should be the final word on this question: "It is obvious to anyone who reads the FBI memorandum," he said, "that FBI agents were there not because of Senator Muskie's presence but because of the presence on the same platform of such persons as Sammy Abbott, a leader of the American Communist Party, and Rennie Davis, one of the convicted defendants in the Chicago Seven trial."

The FBI would be derelict in its duty if it did not keep track of revolutionary agitators or persons with records of criminal violence.

If Senator Muskie dislikes being under the watchful eye of the FBI, he should be more careful about the company he keeps.

EVENING EXPRESS

Portland, Me., April 23, 1971

We think he does protest too much.

Sen. Edmund S. Muskie, with the competition growing stronger, seems too eager to grab any cudgel with which he may take a swipe at the administration. Of course, if anyone swings often enough he's bound to land a few blows. But the percentage of misses increases too. It strikes us that the Senator has missed with his big swing against the FBI for what he calls clandestine surveillance at last year's Earth Day rallies.

The Senator is not alleging, as are some of his colleagues, that his telephone has been tapped. He is condemning as "intolerable" and a "threat to our freedom," what he terms "general political surveillance." The FBI report the Senator introduced into the Congressional Record was little more than a chronology of speakers at the rally where Sen. Muskie spoke.

That report, along with White House comment, insists that the monitoring of the rally was focused on anti - administration speakers whose militance might bear reporting. Particularly singled out was Rennie Davis, one of the convicted Chicago conspiracy defendants who, incidentally, is among the leaders of the scheduled peace march this month — a march already endorsed by Senator Muskie.

Keeping an eye on Davis and others of his record is not a bad idea at all. And we suspect many others in Senator Muskie's constituency share that view. The "threat to our freedom" may be contained far better by this type of surveillance.

We agree that J. Edgar Hoover should have stepped down long ago. We agree that indiscriminate spying on citizens is intolerable. But we also grow weary of indiscriminate allegations which, if not motivated by politics, at least serve political ambition.

Maine is proud of Senator Muskie. Only last Fall it expressed emphatically its willingness for him to take such time from his senatorial duties as he might deem necessary to further his prospects for a presidential nomination. He may or may not make it. But we'd hate to see him blow it by intemperate, hasty, superficial or ill-considered arguments.

It was Senator Muskie's capacity for statemanship, his reasoned approach, his image of solidity and sound, unhurried judgment that carried him to his present position of eminence. That's what the nation seeks in leadership. It has more than enough of the every-day sort of politics and politicians.

Senator Muskie, the tall man from Maine, cut a more impressive and sincere figure than Senator Muskie, the big Democrat from Washington. People here understand as Senator Muskie outgrows Maine. They will, however, be disappointed if Senator Muskie outgrows Senator Muskie.

The Courier-Journal
Louisville, Ky., April 16, 1971

WHEN A MASTER lives in fear of his servant, the servant has become master. So when honorable, law-abiding, patriotic citizens have reason to fear the men hired to protect their liberties, it must be assumed that those liberties are in peril. This is the pass to which J. Edgar Hoover, the FBI and too many years of congressional timidity have brought us.

In recent days, a scoutmaster has learned to his surprise that the FBI was in possession of a letter he wrote to someone else; a mother has learned that an FBI agent tricked her into informing on her own daughter; an anti-war Congressman, Henry S. Reuss, has discovered that the FBI has been watching his daughter. None of these citizens has been accused of a crime, and had it not been for the burglary of an FBI office in Pennsylvania, they would still be unaware of the Justice Department's interest in them.

Another Congressman, Hale Boggs, says the FBI tapped his telephone. He has not yet furnished any evidence, and Mr. Hoover and Attorney General Mitchell have denied it. Mr. Hoover—parroted by Mr. Mitchell, who could not possibly know—has declared that the FBI has tapped no congressional telephones at all since he became director in 1925, "nor has any member of the Congress or the Senate been under surveillance by the FBI."

Spying on Earth Day

Nevertheless, the House of Representatives has deemed it prudent to hire an independent electronics firm to make periodic checks for hidden microphones in the Congressmen's offices. And now Senator Edmund S. Muskie, a man whose verbal circumspection is cited as a political liability by many of his colleagues, has called FBI snooping "a threat to our freedom" and has urged Congress "to legislate precise limits over the scope of domestic surveillance and over the use of collected information."

Why? Because the FBI, apparently sniffing subversion in the wind, sent spies to between 40 and 60 Earth Day rallies on April 22, 1970, took notes on the speeches and filed official reports. At one of the rallies, an agent carefully noted, Senator Muskie "gave a short anti-pollution speech." So the Senator, while not under surveillance himself, inadvertently stepped into Mr. Hoover's field of vision by consorting with people who were under surveillance—people who don't like pollution.

How about other groups?

"If there was widespread surveillance over Earth Day last year, is there any political activity in this country which the FBI doesn't consider a legitimate subject for watching?" the outraged Senator Muskie asked. "Is there any citizen involved in politics who is not a potential subject for an FBI dossier?"

Good questions. Does the FBI's loving care extend, for instance, to the DAR, the American Legion, the VFW and other flag-waving groups who make political statements, or is it restricted to those groups that call attention to the warts on Uncle Sam's face? Are the industries which foul our water and air being infiltrated by agents looking for un-American activity, or does the danger to America lurk only in the conclaves of the opponents of dirty water and dirty air? Just what is "orthodox" and what is "heretic" in the FBI's interpretation of the national faith? When a person has violated no law, how does the FBI determine that he is dangerous and should be watched? Senator Sam Ervin and his subcommittee on constitutional rights have tried to find out, but Mr.

Hoover has permitted no spokesman for his bureau to participate in the hearings. Deputy Attorney General Richard G. Kleindienst, in an apparently unsanctioned attempt to allay public and congressional fears, said he would "welcome an investigation by the responsible members of Congress" of "the whole operation of the FBI." But the word came down and the suggestion was withdrawn.

Dossiers of suspicion

So Mr. Hoover's bureau remains responsible only to him, and he remains responsible to no one. Of course, no investigative agency can operate entirely in the public view, but the continual growth of FBI manpower and the development of electronic surveillance has made Mr. Hoover the virtual dictator of a huge and very powerful federal police establishment. When such an agency, operating in a democracy, extends its investigations beyond those who have committed crimes to anyone it suspects *might* commit a crime *someday*, some regulation becomes necessary.

A computer, fed enough raw and unchallenged data from secret dossiers and guided by a "correct" ideology, can make a *potential* criminal of anybody. And when the mere exercise of free speech merits notations in those dossiers, the master had better take his servant in hand, and quickly, for some very "orthodox" American liberties are at stake.

THE DAILY OKLAHOMAN
Oklahoma City, Okla., April 20, 1971

SHRILL and insistent complaints come from Sen. Edmund Muskie, D-Maine, and other "liberal" lawmakers about the surveillance they say the FBI is exercising over their Earth Day activities.

The FBI's concern rests not so much with the "liberal" lawmakers as with the known subversive tendencies of other speakers who often occupy the same platforms.

Some of these other rabble rousers are Trotskyite Communists, Maoist Communists and representatives of other far-left front organizations which openly advocate violent overthrow.

The FBI would be derelict if it didn't keep them under surveillance. If the "liberal" lawmakers are offended, they can avoid surveillance by refraining from appearing on the same platforms with known revolutionaries.

Herald News
Fall River, Mass., April 15, 1971

Senator Muskie's remarks on the controversial issue of the invasion of congressional privacy by the FBI are illuminating. The Maine senator says that he finds himself being very careful about what he says unless he is certain he is not being overheard through electronic devices. This, finally, is the main point involved. It is possible that no senator or representative's phone is tapped or his office bugged, but the chances are that they may be. With that in mind, a man like Muskie whose integrity is unquestioned finds himself exercising a voluntary censorship in terms of what he says.

This is precisely what Americans for the past several decades have been most critical of in Soviet Russia, Communist China or Nazi Germany: the surveillance by government agents and the consequent impairment of free speech and free thought. Unless Senator Muskie is not to be believed, this is what is happening here and now. It may be that he is mistaken. Perhaps he has no reason to suspect his remarks are being monitored. But he is a most responsible person. If he thinks the possibility he is being spied on is real, it is reasonable to think that most of us in the same position would also think so.

In other words, a climate of suspicion and fear, as well as a climate favoring the repression of free speech even in private, has been fostered in Washington by what has been made known about wire-tapping and bugging. The whole practice is antithetical to the basic principles of American life and should be stopped at once. Otherwise, the damage to the democratic process may be very serious indeed.

The Virginian-Pilot

Norfolk, Va., April 20, 1971

McCarthyism — a political attitude of the mid-Twentieth Century closely allied to know-nothingism and characterized chiefly by opposition to elements held to be subversive and by the use of tactics involving personal attacks on individuals by means of widely publicized indiscriminate allegations esp. on the basis of unsubstantiated charges.
—Webster's Third New International Dictionary

Senator Robert Dole says that it is his responsibility as Republican National Chairman to mix it up with the Democrats at every opportunity, and particularly to cut down Democratic Presidential pretenders whenever he has a shot at them.

That is why he was chosen as Republican spokesman, succeeding the affable and softspoken Rogers Morton—who is much too nice a guy for that sort of thing. Mr. Dole's gutfighter's instincts are surely what appealed to President Nixon, who was often called upon to do his party's political street-fighting in the Eisenhower years.

And it is easier to understand Mr. Dole's remarks in Williamsburg when they are considered only as a partisan reflex. For that is all that can explain Mr. Dole's style.

In a speech he made to the GOP governors yesterday, but pre-released to the Monday morning papers, Mr. Dole defended the Federal Bureau of Investigation and lambasted Senator Muskie, the Democrats' front-running prospect for '72.

Mr. Dole said that Mr. Muskie was trying to turn Americans against the FBI and contended that the Nation is threatened with what he called a "concentrated effort to destroy public confidence in law enforcement." (Echoes of the familiar "law 'n' order" pitch.) He disputed Mr. Muskie's statement that the FBI had kept watch upon a number of Earth Day rallies last spring, saying that he had been informed that agents attended only four of the rallies.

"What we have here," continued Mr. Dole, "whether or not those who are leading the attack will admit it, is a concerted and deliberate effort to turn the FBI in the eyes of the American people into an American version of the Gestapo.

"It has been well said in recent days that the McCarthyism of the Fifties pales by comparison with the Muskieism of the Seventies."

Well. One is supposed to think that Mr. Muskie is against the FBI and against national security, and that he is for "professed revolutionists, anarchists, and advocates of violence." (Mr. Dole dragged in a few old subversives too. He garnished one of the rhetorical questions that he put to Mr. Muskie with a phrase that evokes the Nixon of yesterday. "If the answer to that is yes," Mr. Dole orated, "then let us pardon Alger Hiss and repent the executions of the Rosenbergs.")

And certainly Mr. Dole is fostering the suggestion that Mr. Muskie compared the FBI to the Gestapo. After all, that was in the news recently, wasn't it?

Let's look at the record. What did Mr. Muskie say in his Senate speech of last Wednesday?

He charged that the FBI had conducted surveillance on Earth Day rallies and he made public an FBI intelligence report on the Earth Day rally in Washington, which said that Mr. Muskie arrived at the rally shortly after 8 p.m. and "gave a short anti-antipollution speech."

Mr. Muskie also said that he understood there were 40 to 60 FBI reports on other Earth Day rallies around the country and that at least one other Senator had been under FBI surveillance for participation in the rallies. He characterized such surveillance as "intolerable in a free society" and asked the Senate:

"If there was widespread surveillance over Earth Day last year, is there any political activity in the country which the FBI does not consider a legitimate subject for watching? If antipollution rallies are a subject of intelligence concern, is anything immune? Is there any citizen involved in politics who is not a potential subject for an FBI dossier?"

That is what Mr. Muskie really said. And Mr. Dole does not dispute that the FBI kept watch upon the Earth Day rally at which Mr. Muskie spoke.

It was Representative Hale Boggs of Louisiana, not Mr. Muskie, who said that the FBI is adopting "the tactics of the Soviet Union and Hitler's Gestapo." Mr. Dole would have been justified in attacking "Boggsism" perhaps—but Mr. Boggs is not a potential rival in '72.

And it is Mr. Dole himself who dragged Alger Hiss, the Rosenbergs, and assorted subversives into the act in order to give "Muskieism" a little zing.

So who is guilty of McCarthyism? Consult the dictionary definition and judge for yourself.

HOUSTON CHRONICLE

Houston, Texas, April 16, 1971

Civilian law enforcement agencies need certain information on American citizens to maintain law and order, to preserve this nation's internal security. But there is a fine line between legitimate intelligence gathering and overt violations of an American's right of privacy and free expression. This line can be crossed by unrestricted surveillance.

A case in point is the Federal Bureau of Investigation's heavy surveillance of Earth Day rallies last April lance of certain Earth Day rallies last April 22.

With Maine's Democratic Sen. Edmund Muskie, we are curious as to why the FBI needed to know who attended and what was said at Earth Day rallies across the nation. Can it be that an interest in trying to save our endangered environment from destruction is somehow regarded as subversive by the powers-that-be in the FBI? On another tack, this ludicrous waste of highly paid and highly trained FBI manpower happened during a nine-month period when serious crime in the United States increased 10 percent.

Sen. Muskie, one of the persons mentioned briefly in the Earth Day surveillance reports, asked another rhetorical question which should trouble every American who values freedom:

"If there was surveillance over Earth Day last year, is there any political activity in the country which the FBI doesn't consider a legitimate subject for watching?"

Obviously, nothing and no one appears to be above the purview of the FBI. No one, regardless of the innocence of actions or motives, is above being filmed and recorded and reported on, with the accumulated information filed away in a data bank for possible coercion or intimidation at the pleasure of Big Brother. This is frightening. As a modern phenomenon it most definitely is a serious threat to our freedoms

No agency of the federal, state or local government should have the unconstitutional, unrestricted right to spy on the legal activities of American citizens. This is a violation of many tenets of the Constitution. Yet the FBI appears to have assumed this role of political watchdog.

To counter this trend toward totalitarianism through federal snooping into political, social and civic activities, Sen. Muskie suggests that Congress take steps to curb the spying. He proposes Congress set up a "domestic intelligence review board" to supervise operations of the FBI and other agencies engaged in surveillance in the United States. The board would be answerable to both the President and Congress. Once each year it would be required to make a public report to the citizens of this nation.

Certainly some responsible group must take the lead in limiting the scope of all domestic surveillance and supervising the use of whatever information is collected. The Congress, a representative body standing for election by the people, is the logical agency to undertake this responsibility.

The Dallas Morning News

Dallas, Texas, April 20, 1971

IT IS CLEAR that the cause-of-the-month crowd have made J. Edgar Hoover and the FBI the fashionable targets this season.

The progressives' rush to get in a few kicks at this mainstay of law enforcement has quickly become a stampede. That's not surprising. The FBI is dedicated to the protection of this Republic and its people—in some circles, that seems to be enough to earn it suspicion and hostility.

The federal agency made many enemies years ago when it led in tracking down communist agents in the U.S. More recently it has played a part in making life difficult for radical terrorists who had planned a nationwide campaign of violence against Americans and American institutions. Its insistence on regarding these criminals primarily as criminals, rather than as overenthusiastic idealists, has brought new outcries that the FBI is repressive, an American gestapo.

To gain perspective on these charges, it should be noted that the Senate's fiery champion of civil liberties, Sen. Sam Ervin, has not been one of those caught up in the stampede. Sen. Ervin said Sunday that he will not call for an investigation of the FBI until he sees some evidence that the bureau has acted illegally.

As for the charges by Sen. Ed Muskie that the FBI had "spied" on the 1970 Earth Day ceremonies, Ervin agreed with the administration's explanation that among the thousands present were individuals with records of political violence.

"Surveillance of people of the character of Rennie Davis is probably the duty of the FBI," he said.

That's just the point. The FBI does its duty and leaves politics alone. Under the leadership of J. Edgar Hoover the agency has concentrated on its assigned role as a law-enforcement agency, resisting all efforts to turn it into a political police force or force it to serve partisan causes.

As Sen. Ervin says, before taking these latest charges against the FBI too seriously, it would be wise to await some supporting evidence. The evidence so far indicates that the charge of playing politics fits the FBI's critics, not the FBI.

The Morning Star

Rockford, Ill., April 21, 1971

● **THE ISSUE: Self-serving politics in criticism of J. Edgar Hoover and the Federal Bureau of Investigation.**

★ ★ ★

Much of the criticism that has been unleashed against the Federal Bureau of Investigation and its director, J. Edgar Hoover, in recent weeks can be attributed to self-serving politics.

Heading the hounds is Sen. Edmund S. Muskie, the Maine Democrat and presidential aspirant, who sees "a dangerous threat to constitutional rights" in the presence of FBI agents at last year's anti-pollution rallies on Earth Day.

Then there is Rep. Hale Boggs, D-La., House majority leader, who has charged that the FBI has tapped the telephones of congressmen and senators and used tactics of "the Soviet Union and Hitler's Gestapo."

To date he has produced no proof for his accusations, and the administration has said it would welcome a congressional investigation of Boggs' charges.

And this week at Northern Illinois University in DeKalb, Sen. George S. McGovern, D-S.D., another presidency seeker, called on President Nixon to fire Hoover. McGovern called Hoover "irresponsible," but the tag better fit the South Dakota senator, who failed to substantiate his vague charges against the FBI director.

The grand design appears to have many prongs of attack — get rid of J. Edgar Hoover, discredit the role of the FBI and embarrass the administration.

In this republic, a federation of states, it is absolutely necessary to have a federal investigative agency with responsibility both for domestic crime and espionage.

When there are self-styled revolutionaries loudly proclaiming their intent to bring the downfall of government and society as it has existed, increased FBI surveillance is necessarily mandated.

For nearly five decades, under J. Edgar Hoover's direction, the FBI has managed to operate within a framework carefully and delicately protected from both criminal and political corruption.

Hoover, now 76, is near retirement. His critics seek to put both Hoover and the FBI on the spot by trying to give him the bum's rush under fire. Such tactics should be repudiated by all responsible Americans.

If the critics have some facts to back up their fantasies that the FBI somehow is lurking behind every bush indiscriminately spying on innocent citizens, let them bring the facts out for Americans to judge.

Otherwise, they'll be branded for playing a despicable, paranoic, hysterical game of political opportunism.

The Burlington Free Press

Burlington, Vt., April 20, 1971

THE RECKLESS, CHILDISH, unfounded and plainly political attack on the Federal Bureau of Investigation is backfiring in a big way.

The anti-FBI campaign first gained headlines when House Majority Leader Hale Boggs charged that the Bureau had tapped the telephones of members of Congress. Then the campaign gained more headlines when Senator Edmund Muskie charged that the FBI had spied on Earth Day rallies last year. Few observers took Boggs' charges very seriously, perhaps because he has a history of instability, but Muskie's charges — also unproven — were quickly branded as blatantly political. There simply was no other rational reason for them.

Senator Sam J. Ervin, who is chairman of the Senate Constitutional Rights Subcommittee, said yesterday he has yet to find any evidence whatsoever of any illegal actions by the FBI. As for FBI Director J. Edgar Hoover, Ervin said: "I think he has done a very good job in a difficult post."

Nobody can accuse Ervin, a Democrat as are Boggs and Muskie, of being insensitive to the issue of federal surveillance. Ervin recently conducted hearings on the Army's domestic intelligence operations and the information gathering activities of other federal agencies, and he won flowery editorial praise from even the "liberal" New York Times.

The charges of Boggs and Muskie are so patently phony, and potentially destructive, that Senate Democratic Leader Mike Mansfield has directly challenged his fellow Democratic worriers to put up or shut up. If any member of Congress has any evidence — "not just words" — of any wrongdoing by the FBI, he should produce it, said Mansfield. And he added: "I am for the FBI. And as far as Mr. Hoover is concerned, I expect him to stay in office."

As for the Earth Day "spying," Ervin noted that "surveillance of people of the character of Rennie Davis is probably the duty of the FBI."

Muskie's witch-hunting has been compared with the tactics of McCarthyism, and correctly so. We lived through the McCarthy period in Washington, and we don't want to see it repeated by Muskie or anybody else.

In New Hampshire on Saturday, for example, Muskie said he is "careful how I use my phone" for fear it is bugged. Reflections of the "Reds under beds" hysteria; no doubt Muskie also fears there are FBI agents under his bed!

As always, the nation can count on Senator George McGovern to stretch any issue to its ultimate absurdity. McGovern charged yesterday, apparently in a state of sobriety, that Hoover keeps a record of agents "who fail to remember the Director at Christmastime and his birthday with appropriate gratitude."

This anti-FBI hysteria reflects most damagingly on the character and motives of those who promoted and participated in it. They are receiving the public's displeasure and they deserve it!

It should be noted that this editorial is not a flag-waving defense of the FBI or Hoover. It is simply a statement of essential facts about which all Vermonters should be aware. — F.B.S.

NIXON, AGNEW SUPPORT HOOVER AS CRITICS DEMAND HE RESIGN

Controversy centered upon J. Edgar Hoover, FBI director, during April and May. Critics of the FBI, led by Sen. Edmund S. Muskie (D, Me.) and Rep. Hale Boggs (D, La.), demanded his resignation for alleged wiretapping of congressmen and surveillance at 1970 Earth Day rallies. Hoover was defended by President Nixon April 16 who called charges against Hoover "unfair and malicious." Nixon defended the FBI as the "best law enforcement agency in the world." Vice President Agnew denounced Hoover's critics as political "opportunists" because they were using his age—76 years—to drive him from office. Agnew said, "Personally, I have complete confidence in this dedicated, steel-willed public servant with the 20-20 vision into our national security and crime control problems and the institution that he has made the beacon of law enforcement in America."

THE STATES-ITEM

New Orleans, La., April 19, 1971

The national debate over whether J. Edgar Hoover should retire obscures the fundamental issue, it seems to us.

The practices which the Federal Bureau of Investigation uses to spy on American citizens is the immediate issue. The long-term issue is the institutional immunity of the nation's top police agency to periodic review and criticism.

Serious charges have been made in recent days about the extent and manner of the FBI's surveillance methods.

Congressman Hale Boggs, Sen. Edmund S. Muskie and House Whip Thomas J. O'Neill have questioned FBI practices and suggested that Mr. Hoover should step down and let a younger man take over the directorship.

Mr. Hoover, now 76, has been at the helm of the FBI for 47 years and could retire with national gratitude for his extraordinary service to this country. We would guess that, at his age, retirement is not exactly a foreign thought to Mr. Hoover.

It is not hard to appreciate President Nixon's unwillingness to retire a man of Mr. Hoover's stature who has served his country with fierce dedication.

But the bureaucracy of the top police agency and how it works is another matter.

U. S. Sen. Henry "Scoop" Jackson of Washington has the right approach to the controversy, it seems to us.

In a discussion with the editorial board of The States-Item last Friday, Sen. Jackson suggested the FBI should get the same sort of review which Congress routinely gives to the Central Intelligence Agency.

A standing congressional watchdog committee might emerge from such a review, the senator suggested.

No government agency in this country should be entirely immune from periodic scrutiny and re-evaluation. Left entirely alone, there is always the danger that any bureaucracy will eventually overreach its original purpose. We do not know whether the FBI has reached that point. But some of the nation's leading congressmen indicate they believe it has in certain c a t e g o r i e s. Their charges alone are sufficient to warrant a thorough congressional review of the bureau's methods of operation.

Detroit Free Press

Detroit, Mich., April 7, 1971

THE ADMINISTRATION is hard put to ignore any longer calls that FBI Director J. Edgar Hoover show why he should not be removed from office.

The latest call comes from House Democratic Leader Hale Boggs, who charges that the FBI's wiretapping abuses extend to the telephones of senators and congressmen themselves. Sen. Joseph Montoya of New Mexico made the same charge last month.

The astounding fear shown by these two lawmakers is only part of a greater storm of debate over surveillance and invasions of privacy, a storm increasingly focused on the FBI. Not long ago, stolen FBI documents revealed signs of wide surveillance on citizens thought politically unsavory. More recently has come evidence that portions of the Army's domestic spy apparatus have not in fact been dismantled, but only abandoned to the Justice Department.

Reports say that much domestic surveillance is being carried on by what the Justice Department calls its Interdivisional Information Unit. Set up in 1967 by former Attorney General Ramsey Clark, its function was to help the government make "adequate, measured response to the civil disorders that may arise."

Since the Army quit the field under fire the IDIU has greatly increased its size and activity, with considerable assistance from the FBI. Reports say the unit now has nearly 14,000 computerized dossiers on Americans considered notably dissident—rightists, leftists, even elected officials and moderates who are thought to condone or encourage civil disobedience.

The pattern is sadly familiar. An information-gathering project begins with unremarkable goals: Better preparation for civil upheaval; more efficient administration in law enforcement; better understanding of social patterns and problems.

But somewhere along the line the project develops its own self-serving momentum. The line is crossed between information-gathering and outright snooping. Privacy means little. Reputations are casually handled, and may be casually ruined.

Where surveillance is done to enforce law and keep order, politics seems inevitably to enter. Even among the varied forms of legal peaceful expression, bureaucrats judge what is proper and what is not proper. In an important sense, political expression within the law is not free, but is subject to review, and is reviewed.

No one would argue that keeping society is an easy job, that departures need not be made from the habits of simpler days, that the distinctions here involved are simple to draw and maintain. But surely it is worth arguing that society should be jealous of the distinctions, and insistent that cherished rights of privacy and personal freedom not be abandoned without ironclad reason.

This is the heart of the outcry against Mr. Hoover and his agency. There was a time when it could be said that the animus against him rose from a narrow segment of political opinion, and should not overshadow his agency's good record and his own good service. But the time has come when even members of Congress fear his actions, and when the FBI's reputation is being needlessly tarnished by his Olympian refusal to be challenged.

THE SACRAMENTO BEE

Sacramento, Calif., May 7, 1971

The mounting controversy over J. Edgar Hoover's seemingly endless tenure as director of the FBI ought to be focused now on devising mechanisms to insure his successor does not assume the same inordinate power.

Undoubtedly Hoover will retire soon. A groundswell of public opinion favors it. A recent Gallup survey put the number at 51 per cent. Erstwhile supporters, such as the moderate Los Angeles Times, have called outright for his resignation.

What appears to be delaying the retirement is Hoover's understandable reluctance to leave under a cloud of criticism.

———

This does not diminish the case for his departure. Although long a respected and intrepid agency protecting Americans from criminal racketeers, the FBI has become embroiled in political ideology stemming from Hoover's long-standing militancy. He has put the agency to questionable work of surveillance of private citizens in the name of fighting subversion.

Deservedly or not, the agency has become identified in the public mind as part of a big brother snooping apparatus. One consequence has been a grievous erosion of public confidence in government. At the same time the FBI is thought by many to have shifted its main attention from the appalling crime rate.

———

Hoover, in his person, has become the target for these criticisms. As long as he heads the agency, they are sure to become worse, not better. Hoover would give his final public service by bowing out gracefully.

Assuming this will happen in the near future, attention should turn to insuring his successor will not hold such absolute dominance. As the Los Angeles Times says: "What has to be devised is a new mechanism for handling the FBI, for bringing it under the scrutiny of the people without opening it to the control of any president or any political party."

The New York Times

New York, N.Y., April 21, 1971

Recent disclosures concerning the Federal Bureau of Investigation make clear that a Congressional review of the agency's numerous and far-ranging activities is necessary. Appropriations subcommittees perform some of this Congressional function. With regard to the F.B.I., however, these subcommittees have long since reduced themselves to the role of claques dutifully applauding for J. Edgar Hoover.

It is disappointing that Senator Ervin of North Carolina, chairman of the subcommittee on constitutional rights, has shown himself reluctant to look into the F.B.I.'s work. This subcommittee is the logical group to conduct an inquiry into issues of F.B.I. policy that have aroused public uneasiness because they relate to grey areas where legality is not clearly defined. It may well be that a Congressional inquiry would show the need for revising the law.

There is also concern about Mr. Hoover. This concern is heightened by the growing public awareness that for decades, most Attorneys General have feared Mr. Hoover's political influence and have negotiated with him as a sovereign entity, instead of supervising him as a subordinate. The effusive endorsements of Mr. Hoover in recent days by President Nixon and Attorney General Mitchell suggest that top-level supervision within the executive is no firmer under this Administration.

The revelation that F.B.I. agents monitored last year's Earth Day rallies implies that undercover work against violent conspirators has been widened into a wasteful, inefficient dragnet covering all kinds of peaceful politics.

These problems as well as the belief by several Congressmen that the F.B.I. taps telephones on Capitol Hill are deserving of sober evaluation. Senators Edward Kennedy of Massachusetts and John V. Tunney of California, members of the Ervin subcommittee, have proposed that it undertake an inquiry. As Senator Ervin recognizes, such an inquiry would be controversial. But who supposed that the defense of individual liberty could ever be non-controversial?

THE WALL STREET JOURNAL.

New York, N.Y., May 11, 1971

The campaign against J. Edgar Hoover has been one of those heady mixtures of fact and fancy that makes rational conclusions all but impossible. If in the end it inhibits rather than promotes Mr. Hoover's retirement it will be unfortunate but not without a certain rough justice. That kind of outcome is what this kind of campaign deserves.

In the abstract, we would certainly agree that the FBI director would be well advised to retire, though we just as certainly don't see any urgency about it. At 76, Mr. Hoover is past the age when even the best public official ought to retain an important executive post. While in general his agency seems to retain its traditional efficiency, his administrative touch was scarcely deft recently in the summary treatment of a mildly critical FBI agent and the premature disclosure of the kidnap-Kissinger charges.

In the real world, at any rate, the question the nation is faced with is not whether Mr. Hoover ought to retire but whether he ought to be forced out of office by the actual campaign being waged against him. That is quite another matter, for the campaign is by no means based merely or even primarily on Mr. Hoover's age. It seems to be fed by emotional springs that flow up regardless of fact or evidence.

The current anti-Hoover drive, after all, hit the headlines when Rep. Hale Boggs said the FBI had tapped his telephone and its director must go. As everyone knows by now, Rep. Boggs was laughed out of court when the time came to present his promised evidence. But the anti-Hoover drive he started rolled on with scarcely a bump.

When Mr. Boggs came up empty-handed, it seems to us the question ought to have become, "What then is behind his attack?" Instead, newsmagazine cover stories and television controversy shows continue to address the question, "Should J. Edgar Hoover resign?" Indeed, The Washington Post ran a perfectly delightful editorial specifically arguing that the paucity of Rep. Boggs' evidence of wrongdoing should not be allowed to detract from the truth of his charges, for instance that the FBI is "a vine of tyranny."

Even more amusing is the "blue-ribbon citizens inquiry" into the FBI being led by Ramsey Clark and Burke Marshall. Here you have two gentlemen with 12 years' combined service in the highest offices of the Justice Department, which has official jurisdiction over the FBI. Thanks mostly to the Republican victory in 1968, they now qualify as "blue-ribbon citizens." *Now* they decide the FBI needs investigating.

These attacks are taken with a straight face by exactly the same people who believed that 28 Black Panthers were killed by a police conspiracy, and that the kidnap-Kissinger episode could not possibly be anything but a figment of the FBI's imagination. In the latter case we pity the jury that has to decide whether what seems to have happened was a serious conspiracy or a fit of radical delirium, but the recent disclosure of alleged correspondence certainly suggests it was not Mr. Hoover's mind that was addled.

The emotional component that keeps the anti-Hoover drive rolling regardless of the evidence for any given charge also creates an atmosphere in which it's exceedingly difficult to sort out legitimate issues concerning how best to supervise the FBI, which unquestionably has vast powers subject to potential abuse. In all the talk so far, however, we find no evidence of actual abuse. Until we do, we will continue to think that while Mr. Hoover's retirement may be advisable it is scarcely a burning issue.

We do not find it as important, in fact, as another range of issues the anti-Hoover drive raises: whether public officials will be vulnerable to assaults as unfounded as the one Rep. Boggs launched; whether ex-officials should embark on publicity drives for resignations they would not have requested when they were in power; whether, that is, the public discourse of this Republic can regain a little responsibility and decency.

The Virginian-Pilot

Norfolk, Va., April 7, 1971

J. Edgar Hoover is becoming an embarrassment. It is bad enough to be criticized, but deadly for a public man to become the butt of jokes. For Mr. Hoover, once upon a time that was unthinkable. But it is commonplace nowadays, suggesting that his days in office are numbered.

Those are hard things to say about the man who has served as director of the Federal Bureau of Investigation for 47 years—the man who invented the FBI, really.

The judgment is, in a sense, unfair. It discounts Mr. Hoover's success in building the FBI and jealously protecting its reputation. It is not an accident that the FBI has been free from scandal and suspicion for most of Mr. Hoover's long tenure. ("Given the general, and sometimes idolatrous, popularity of the FBI," Joseph Kraft once noted, "it is especially illuminating to compare FBI agents with the astronauts in the matter of vulgar commercialization. Hoover has simply not allowed it to happen.") Indeed, it is not the FBI agent who is being criticized even now—it is Mr. Hoover personally.

That is ironic, and tragic. For the career of Mr. Hoover has been marked by a flair—genius is hardly too strong a word—for public relations. Mr. Hoover not only survived in the bureaucratic, budgetary, and political strife of Washington, he triumphed. He had but to ask, and it was given to him. Appropriations, commendations, the favor of Presidents, whatever he wanted—nothing was too good for J. Edgar Hoover.

For a generation he was a kind of monument, a patriotic symbol. Now, so to speak, the monument is being defaced with all sorts of obscene slogans and J. Edgar Hoover has turned into a symbol of what's ugly and un-American in the United States. The gods make sport of us.

Still, there can be no doubt of the decline of J. Edgar Hoover when, in one week, he is caricatured on the cover of *Life* m a g a z i n e as "E m p e r o r of the FBI" and denounced by the Majority Leader, Hale Boggs of Louisiana, on the floor of the House of Representatives. Mr. Boggs charged that the FBI has tapped the telephones of Congressmen and is using "the tactics of the Soviet Union and Hitler's Gestapo." He called for the firing of Mr. Hoover. Attorney General Mitchell responded by "categorically" denying that the FBI has ever tapped Congressional telephones, and defended Mr. Hoover. Others also came to the defense of Mr. Hoover yesterday. But Mr. Boggs' criticism of Mr. Hoover is the harshest yet, and it is difficult to think that he is just making things up. We are sure to hear more of the matter.

Mr. Hoover is 76 and long past the time when he might have retired to the applause of a grateful Nation. He evokes ridicule today, and worse. (It is Mr. Hoover's misfortune, like Chicago's Mayor Daley, to look the part that his critics contend he plays.) He has become identified in the minds of many with the Indochina War and is one more casualty, in an obscure way, of that wretched war. (Caesar has his Brutus, Charles I his Cromwell, and Lyndon Johnson his McCarthy; J. Edgar Hoover, one suspects, has the Berrigan brothers.) It is a pity that Mr. Hoover will not resign with what grace he can muster yet.

Portland Press Herald

Portland, Me., May 11, 1971

It was easier a year or so ago than it is today to state with conviction that J. Edgar Hoover should step down as head of the Federal Bureau of Investigation.

He should have retired even earlier than that. But at the time he reached retirement age, public opinion might have been against any presidential pressure applied toward that end. Now, probably less because of what Mr. Hoover has actually done but more because of what a few politicians have attempted to make of it, he cannot stand aside without some impression of quitting under fire.

If Mr. Hoover had retired at 65 or even 70 he could have done so among almost unanimous plaudits of a grateful nation. His service certainly has been unique. There can never be a greater monument to his dedication and zeal than the FBI itself. It is significant that two recent polls revealed a continuing high degree of public confidence in that organization although opinion was very evenly divided about the director himself.

A Louis Harris poll showed 43 per cent believing Mr. Hoover should quit with exactly the same percentage in favor of his remaining.

A Gallup check reported 51 in favor of retirement for the director.

In the Harris poll, 71 per cent approved of Hoover's record. In the Gallup poll, 70 per cent.

Harris reported 81 per cent approval of the FBI's work, Gallup had 80 per cent.

It is not disillusion with Mr. Hoover. It is not suspicion, at least we don't believe there is a significant degree of doubt about his integrity. It is simply the belief that he is beyond his prime.

Mr. Hoover's image does not suggest a man who might continue in some sort of advisory capacity. He has been the take charge type too long. And he has been uncommonly successful in that role.

It would have been so much better had he ended it voluntarily a few years ago. But the longer he remains now the stronger the doubts about his leadership, in a key post, will become if for no other reason than that he continues to grow older.

It is an unpleasant conclusion after so many years of such devoted and constructive effort, but the single greatest service he can now perform for the agency he has molded so skillfully is to leave it.

OREGON Journal
AN INDEPENDENT NEWSPAPER

Portland, Ore., April 21, 1971

It can happen to some of the best of men that they overstay their time and by so doing diminish both their stature and their effectiveness.

A classic case in point is J. Edgar Hoover.

His country owes much to Mr. Hoover. He dedicated his career to the service of his nation, he designed an outstanding Federal Bureau of Investigation, and he personally deserves much of the credit for its successful development.

But there comes a time in most endeavors when a man should look back upon his work, accept his achievements and turn his duties over to the next generation to carry on. The FBI director could have done so with a great deal of satisfaction and with the plaudits of his countrymen adding strength and contentment to his retirement years.

That time, however, has passed for Mr. Hoover. With all of his strengths, he succumbed to a couple of weaknesses — his vanity and his refusal to yield the reins of bureaucratic power. Consequently, an illustrous career will close in a climate of controversy and doubt.

The image he worked so hard to create as a symbol of strength and righteousness of the FBI has been tarnished.

It is true, as President Nixon said, that some of the criticism is narrowly political.

But can anyone imagine the J. Edgar Hoover of 65 or even 70 being in a position where he or his bureau could be kicked around as a political football? The J. Edgar Hoover of 76 is in that unlikely situation.

As the distinguished Hoover career aproaches its close, a couple of questions linger on.

Should any head of a government agency acquire so much personal power that he is beyond the control of his superiors?

Should any agency, for that matter, become so sacrosanct that its policies or practices are beyond challenge?

Neither of these qualities is befitting a democratic system. The exercise of power must especially be subject to scrutiny in a law enforcement operation, because the potential for abuse poses a threat too great to ignore in an open society.

TWIN CITY SENTINEL
Winston-Salem, N.C., April 15, 1971

IT IS NO SECRET that the administrative staff of the Federal Bureau of Investigation is split into two unhappy factions. This internal friction has not noticeably impaired the bureau's efficiency, but it does suggest that each group has found its own candidate for J. Edgar Hoover's job, when the Director retires. This situation, in fact, is considered one reason Mr. Hoover has stayed on beyond retirement age. He—and he alone, apparently — prevents the feud from exploding into the news.

Now, it seems, these internal differences have taken an uglier turn. Sen. Edmund Muskie charged this week that the FBI "spied" on last year's Earth Day activities. In support of his charge, the Senator released an official FBI letter detailing Earth Day activities in Washington. Sen. Muskie did not say how he came by the document; but it is a fair assumption that someone in the bureau—someone with his own axe to grind—made the document available for publication.

Muskie can hardly be faulted for using the document. A good many of the charges made in recent years about improprieties in government agencies have been based on confidential information or documents that somehow got into the hands of members of Congress. Sen. Sam Ervin, to mention one, received much of his initial information about the Army's snooping activities from former employes of the department.

But in the case of the FBI, the situation is aggravated by all the other charges now being thrown at the bureau and its top man. And as these charges accumulate—with or without evidence to substantiate them—the morale and efficiency of the bureau is bound to be impaired.

Mr. Hoover is approaching the end of a long and controversial career. Nothing can hurt him now. He is beyond all that. But so long as he puts off his retirement, so long as the President is loathe to think about Hoover's successor, the bureau infighting and the outside criticism will continue to mount. Sooner or later, Mr. Hoover must retire; and the sooner he retires, the sooner the bureau he shaped can resolve its internal problems and get on with the real business at hand.

THE ANN ARBOR NEWS
Ann Arbor, Mich., May 3, 1971

LAST December, before the current wave of criticism of J. Edgar Hoover and the Federal Bureau of Investigation, The News suggested that Mr. Hoover retire "while he still has a firm grasp of the reins."

We spoke as one who has "high admiration for the way Hoover has conducted the affairs of the Bureau over the years" and said "we would hate to see the director close such an illustrious career on anything but a high note."

It was pointed out then that "the not too numerous critics of the FBI are relatively quiet."

That isn't true today, and Mr. Hoover may have missed his chance to retire gracefully at an advanced age and with the well deserved tributes of the nation showered upon him.

For the critics are out in full force now, and a committee including former Attorney General Ramsey Clark announced this week that it would investigate the FBI's role in American life. The study will be "a clear, dispassionate review," the committee said, but an agency like the FBI, which has to operate in sensitive areas and maintain secrecy over much of its operations, can't really come out ahead in such an inquiry.

* * *

THE BUREAU is already suffering because of the attacks on its director. Most Americans associate Mr. Hoover so closely with the FBI that criticism of him becomes criticism of the agency he heads. And that agency has for so long been the model for local police administration.

This is particularly unfortunate for the man who is chosen to succeed J. Edgar Hoover and expected to institute any reforms suggested by the criticism or the current inquiries into the department's operations. He has big shoes to fill. He doesn't need additional problems.

The Detroit News
Detroit, Mich., May 8, 1971

J. Edgar Hoover must be asking why he needs friends when he has enemies such as Ramsey Clark and Hale Boggs.

Clark, the former attorney general and confirmed "liberal," has engaged for years in a running battle with the FBI director. Last year, Clark wrote a book in which he scolded Hoover for wasting FBI time and tinkering with "the foundations of personal integrity" in the "dirty business" of wiretapping.

Recently an enterprising reporter for Time magazine dredged up a 1967 memorandum in which Clark had urged FBI investigators to "use the maximum available resources, investigative and intelligence," to find out whether riots in urban ghettos had been caused by conspirators.

Liberal Clark's memo said: "As a part of the broad investigation which must necessarily be conducted . . . sources or informants in Black Nationalist organizations, S.N.C.C. and other less publicized groups should be developed and expanded to determine the size and purpose of these groups and their relationship to other groups, and also to determine the whereabouts of persons who might be involved in instigating riot activity in violation of federal law."

Not a bad memorandum, at that, but a rather surprising one coming from a man who now calls surveillance dirty business and who jeers the "conspiracy theory" of riots as a pursuit of "phantoms."

As for Boggs, the house majority leader recently accused the FBI of tapping his telephone, demanded the resignation of Hoover and asked rhetorically: "Has the power of one man become so great that the American system is in paralysis before him?"

Whereupon Rep. Durward Hall inserted in the record a quotation of remarks made when Hoover celebrated his 40th anniversary as FBI director:

"His work in behalf of our national security in exposing the Communist threat, his unceasing battle against crime all over the country, his works in reference to juvenile delinquency, his great interest in the young people of our country, his dedication to intelligent police research all have made for him a place in history unequaled by any similar official in the history of mankind."

Author of those words? Hale Boggs.

TWO WHO CRITICIZED FBI THREATENED BY JOB LOSS

John F. Shaw, a former agent of the Federal Bureau of Investigation, filed a suit Jan 27, charging Director J. Edgar Hoover with a "capricious and vindictive act of personal retribution" that forced his involuntary resignation. In the suit, Shaw said he was forced out of the FBI over a letter in which he criticized some of its inner workings. He said that his criticism of the FBI was legitimate and that he had "been all but fired" for his letter.

Sen. George S. McGovern (D, S.D.) called for a Senate and Justice Department investigation of the Shaw incident Jan. 31. On April 19 he disclosed that Hoover had tried to "destroy the career" of a Trans World Airlines pilot who had criticized FBI handling of a hijacking in 1969. The pilot, Capt. Donald J. Cook, had said FBI agents had jeopardized the lives of his crew in attempting to stop the hijacking. McGovern alleged that Hoover informed TWA that Cook had "experienced some personal difficulty" in the Air Force before his employment with TWA in an attempt to have Cook fired.

THE ROANOKE TIMES

Roanoke, Va., May 17, 1971

At the risk of being labeled New Left wild-eyes for again mentioning possible FBI abuses, we think our readers ought to know about J. Edgar Hoover's latest caper.

A TWA pilot, Captain Donald J. Cook Jr., recently emerged as a hero when he devised a way to get his jetliner, his crew and his passengers safely through a harrowing hijack attempt. It involved a mentally disturbed AWOL Marine corporal armed with a carbine, a knife and a pistol.

Cook made only one mistake: He criticized the FBI. And, as a string of recent incidents reveals, Mr. Hoover doesn't like criticism. Referring to FBI efforts to keep his plane from taking off at the hijacker's direction, Cook had said: "The FBI plan was damned near a prescription for getting the entire crew killed and the plane destroyed."

That may or may not be true; but even if it wasn't, there's really no excuse for what Hoover did in retaliation. According to TWA's board chairman, Hoover wrote him a letter "touching, among other things, on Captain Cook's 'difficulties in the Air Force' prior to his employment with TWA."

What those "difficulties" were, we don't know; obviously, however, Mr. Hoover had no business snooping through Air Force and FBI files to rake up s o m e t h i n g he could use against a non-criminal.

A l t h o u g h neither Hoover nor Atty. Gen. John Mitchell seems yet to understand, it's incidents like this (Hoover told his men to boycott TWA) that play directly into the hands of F B I-h a t i n g radicals. Mitchell no doubt will go on insisting in public speeches that criticism of Hoover is politically inspired—and that people have to take it on faith alone that agencies like the FBI and the CIA will always act properly, and thus ought not to be made to answer even to the courts, for example, for their eavesdropping a n d under-the-bed snooping.

Before he makes more of those speeches, though, Mr. Mitchell perhaps ought to examine this latest misuse of FBI files by a once-respected G -m a n —o n e who clearly has stayed on too long, has become much too powerful and is now absurdly thin-skinned.

The New York Times

New York, N.Y., March 19, 1971

The Federal Bureau of Investigation has responded with predictable denials to charges of vindictive treatment of its employes and obsolescence of its own bureaucracy. But the central question remains: is the F.B.I. as efficient as its mission requires and its own publicity proclaims? Senator George McGovern's call for an investigation of the F.B.I. is very much in order. It is in no way undermined by the blatantly political attack on the Senator by Clyde Tolson, the bureau's second-ranking official, who merely illustrates by his impertinent and thoroughly improper comments the kind of problem such an inquiry ought to examine.

Criticism of the bureau has gained in credibility because it comes increasingly not from political opponents, but from concerned insiders. A detailed letter by former agent John F. Shaw, for example, was written not for public disclosure but as an analytical and confidential exchange of views among law-enforcement experts. The document reached the public only because it impelled F.B.I. director J. Edgar Hoover to force Mr. Shaw's resignation under conditions that only do credit to Mr. Shaw and discredit to the F.B.I.

Another letter received by Senator McGovern, purporting to represent the views of ten F.B.I. agents, suffers the limitation of its authors' anonymity. But doubts that surround unsigned exposures must be tempered by the understandable reluctance on the part of any F.B.I. employe, following Mr. Shaw's experience, to put his career on the line. A major obstacle to F.B.I. efficiency according to these inside critics, is the F.B.I.'s obsession with protecting and enhancing Mr. Hoover's image.

Quite apart from these internal criticisms, questions concerning the bureau's effectiveness are raised by specific incidents related to the duties of a Federal law-enforcement and investigatory agency. For example, repeated failure to obtain easily verifiable background information on appointees to important and sensitive positions has embarrassed President Nixon and should have embarrassed the F.B.I.

At the very least, all this adds up to the need to ask hard questions about the efficiency and orientation of the bureau. Beyond the issues raised about Mr. Hoover's personality, there is legitimate concern whether the F.B.I. has outgrown its televised gang-busting image and its preoccupation with spy-thriller intrigues of domestic and international Communism sufficiently to focus attention on the real problems of crime, regardless of politics. Clearly, this is one investigation that cannot be left to Mr. Hoover himself.

The Charleston Gazette

Charleston, W.Va., July 3, 1971

Justice has triumphed in John F. Shaw vs. J. Edgar Hoover.

Shaw is the New York City FBI agent who resigned rather than be banished to Butte, Mont., after committing the unpardonable. In a letter to a professor conducting a course in which he was enrolled, Shaw criticized agency and its aging director. Although on the whole laudatory, the appraisal wasn't a paean of unabashed adoration. To paraphrase James Thurber's remark about U.S. senators, Shaw made it plain he didn't believe in the immaculate conception of his boss.

The breaches of gallantry inspired the order for Shaw's exile, which was insisted upon despite a wife suffering from terminal cancer and their four children farmed out to two sets of grandparents living in the East. Understandably, Shaw resisted the new assignment.

Hoover was adamant. Shaw must relocate or quit. He had to be punished. Shaw reluctantly surrendered his badge. Hoover still wasn't satisfied. He wanted one last dram of bloody revenge. To establish just how mortal he is, Hoover inserted in the Shaw personnel file that the departing agent was forced out "with prejudice." This additional retaliatory blow reduced to zero Shaw's chances of securing employment in the field for which he is most qualified.

But Shaw, unlike many colleagues who over the years have been victimized by Hoover's petty tyrannies, fought b a c k. With assistance from the American Civil Liberties Union he filed a civil suit against Hoover, demanding retroactive pay and elimination of the damaging, unfair statements appended to his service record.

Now Shaw has been cleared — totally. The Justice Department has consented to remove the "with prejudice" slur. It has agreed further that Shaw receive $13,000 in payments for the months he unsuccessfully sought a job.

Shaw's persecutor remains silent. Yet it's a cinch Hoover is inwardly seething. Among the accusations brought against him was "an arbitrary, capricious and vindictive act of personal retribution." The Justice Department's compact with Shaw not only substantiates this harsh charge but is powerful evidence that Atty. Gen. Mitchell, Hoover's immediate superior, also isn't convinced that the Hoover birth date is celebrated in holy writ.

Post-Tribune
Guarding Your Interests Daily

Gary, Ind., April 22, 1971

J. Edgar Hoover's immunity to high-level criticism is crumbling, a turn that could benefit the whole country.

Most of the recent attacks, it is true, have come from representatives and senators who probably see some political advantage in joining the snowballing assaults on the FBI chief's aura of infallibility.

But their criticisms add up to about the same thing: Hoover has outstayed his usefulness. The times and the challenge call for a new approach and less hero worship.

The latest blast, by Sen. George McGovern, alleges that Hoover persecuted the pilot of a hijacked plane who criticized the FBI's performance in the incident. The pilot, Capt. Donald Cook, was pilot of the TWA plane that was hijacked from California to Rome in November, 1969. He described the FBI plan as ". . . damned near a prescription for getting the entire crew killed and the plane destroyed."

McGovern charged that former agents told him Hoover began an investigation into the private life of the pilot "and it is clear he was trying to destroy the career of Capt. Cook." He also charged that Hoover harassed the airline and tried to block service by FBI personnel as air marshals on TWA flights.

McGovern's allegations may be exaggerated. But following attacks by Sen. Edmund Muskie, Rep. Hale Boggs and others, they should arouse skepticism about Hoover's continued effective service as head of the Federal Bureau of Investigation. He is 76, and has served the country ably. But he is not indispensable and should not be untouchable.

There is no reason to doubt that under new leadership and under a reorganization the FBI can more vigorously and skillfully attack the problems that are waiting to be solved.

Hoover is a unique figure — his bosses don't boss him, nor do they tolerate criticism. It is t i m e for that to change. The future of the FBI is much more important than top-level deference to a public figure who reached the pinnacle years ago.

Des Moines Tribune

Des Moines, Iowa, June 19, 1971

The Federal Bureau of Investigation (FBI) has agreed to an out-of-court settlement with a former agent who made the mistake of criticizing J. Edgar Hoover.

John F. Shaw became something of a conversation piece last summer after he was disciplined for comments about Hoover and FBI methods. Actually, Shaw set out to defend his superiors against an attack by a professor at Manhattan's John Jay College of Criminal Justice.

Shaw was taking a course at the school. He prepared a 16-page response in which he expressed confidence in Hoover's integrity and defended the FBI as an important national institution. He conceded, though, that Hoover at times used antiquated procedures and maintained a "cult of personality" within the agency.

That did it. Hoover ordered Shaw transferred from New York City to Butte, Mont., which has acquired a reputation as the place of punishment for agents who fall into disfavor with the top G-man. Shaw refused to go, resigning from the FBI in September. Hoover accepted the resignation "with prejudice," making it difficult for Shaw to find another job.

In January, Shaw filed suit against the investigative agency, charging Hoover with "an arbitrary, capricious and vindictive act of personal retribution." The agency has now agreed to give Shaw $13,000 in back pay and to remove and destroy all prejudicial material about him in his personnel file.

Shaw viewed the settlement as a "total vindication" of his position. It will be hard for the FBI to disagree.

Meanwhle, various groups inside and outside the government are making strenuous efforts to marshal public support for Hoover. One of these efforts is led by Efrem Zimbalist, jr., who portrays an FBI agent in a television series. Zimbalist is trying to raise funds for the "Friends of the FBI," a group which plans "an effective educational campaign", to combat the "vicious smear campaign" against Hoover.

These contrived attempts to make Hoover look bigger than life tend to confirm Shaw's reference to the personality cult surrounding him.

ST. LOUIS POST-DISPATCH

St. Louis, Mo., June 21, 1971

Former FBI agent John Shaw and the American Civil Liberties Union have won a clear-cut victory over J. Edgar Hoover and the FBI, but perhaps it is more significant that Mr. Hoover suffered a personal defeat. He has not had many.

Mr. Shaw was an FBI agent for nearly seven years. While taking a college c o u r s e authorized by the agency, he answered a professor's comments by defending the FBI and Mr. Hoover's integrity, but he included mild comments on Mr. Hoover's "cult of personality." Mr. Hoover then criticized Mr. Shaw for "atrocious judgment," meaning criticism of the FBI, and had him transferred. Whereupon Mr. Shaw resigned from the bureau, Mr. Hoover accepted the resignation "with prejudice," and Mr. Shaw found it difficult to get another job.

The ACLU sued the FBI chief accusing him of a vindictive act of personal retribution. A few days ago the Government agreed to a settlement, providing Mr. Shaw with $13,000 in back pay and promising to destroy all prejudicial records about him. Aside from the clear defeat for J. Edgar Hoover and his way of running things, the result means that the taxpayers will pay for Mr. Hoover's m i s t a k e. There goes $13,000 for the cult of personality.

J. EDGAR HOOVER DIES AT 77; GRAY NAMED INTERIM FBI CHIEF

J. Edgar Hoover, the first and only director of the Federal Bureau of Investigation, died in his Washington home May 2. Hoover, 77, was in his 48th year as director of the FBI. His death was attributed to the effects of high blood pressure.

Hoover had served eight presidents while molding the FBI into one of the most efficient and controversial organizations in the history of American law enforcement. In recent years Hoover had come under increasing criticism from Congress and the press for his attacks on war and civil rights protestors and his opposition to court decisions extending the rights of defendants and limiting wire-tapping.

Hoover's body lay in state in the Capitol Rotunda May 3; it was the first time this honor, usually reserved for presidents, congressional leaders, and military heroes, had been accorded to a civil servant. At a ceremony in the Capitol, Chief Justice Warren E. Burger eulogized Hoover as "this splendid man who dedicated his life to his country in a half-century of unparalleled service." President Nixon said at Hoover's funeral service that his real memorial would be the "bureau he built to last."

President Nixon May 3 named L. Patrick Gray III, an assistant attorney general, to be the bureau's acting director until after the November election. White House Press Secretary Ronald L. Ziegler said the decision to make an interim appointment had been made to keep the nomination out of partisan pre-election politics.

The Wichita Eagle

Wichita, Kans., May 6, 1972

No offense intended to J. Edgar Hoover or his memory, but there was something about the manner in which news of the FBI director's death was handled that disturbed us. It smacked too much of the doings of a secret police in some other country.

The death, you will recall, was discovered around 7:30 a.m. Tuesday and it was some three hours later that a public announcement was made. From what happened in between one might have thought someone feared an insurrection.

Around 10 a.m. news of the director's death was told as a secret to Lynda Johnson Robb, who happened to be in his office for an interview. Ten minutes later she "got the go-ahead to telephone her parents in Texas . . ." and when she placed the call through a phone in the hall agents hustled people away so they could not overhear the conversation.

It was midday before agents started telling those they were conducting on tours through the building that Mr. Hoover had died.

We fully appreciate the propriety of first informing certain government officials and FBI employes of the director's death. But such a long delay in informing the public and handling the matter in such a secretive fashion had a bad ring in it to us.

It could set a pattern of secrecy for the handling of government business.

THE SACRAMENTO BEE

Sacramento, Calif., May 3, 1972

In a public career which spanned nearly five decades, J. Edgar Hoover, director of the Federal Bureau of Investigation, had the unusual distinction of wielding great power under eight presidents and 16 attorneys general.

Because of his relentless pursuit and capture of such outlaws as John Dillinger, Baby Face Nelson, Ma Barker and Alvin Karpis and eliminating what in the 1930s and 1940s came to be called "public enemies," Hoover and his G-men became folk heroes.

He expanded on that reputation with his brilliant direction of anti-espionage programs during World War II; there was no more vigilant a servant in government against the subversive activity. It is true that in recent years Hoover had become increasingly controversial because of his clashes with public figures, his conduct of investigations and his public statements. Nonetheless Hoover will be remembered as the man who built the FBI almost from scratch into a crime-fighting agency without peer.

To his credit he steadfastly refused to use his power to make the FBI a national police force. He staunchly resisted the pressure to make the bureau a tool of any political party.

Withal, he was a remarkable man and a devoted public servant.

The Dispatch

Columbus, Ohio, May 3, 1972

AMERICAN flags are flying at half staff today in memory of J. Edgar Hoover, a deserved tribute to a man who served his country 48 years with dedication and devotion to duty.

Mr. Hoover, director of the Federal Bureau of Investigation, built the agency from a force of 500 men to its present complement of some 15,000.

MUCH AS he loved the FBI, he hated subversive elements more. He reduced the Communist Party USA to a shell and constantly hounded those who sought to destroy the fabric of this country.

President Nixon said it well when he declared Mr. Hoover's "magnificent contribution to making this a great and good nation will be remembered by the American people long after the petty criticisms of his detractors are forgotten."

THAT CONTRIBUTION included more than a constant vigilance against enemies of the nation. For Mr. Hoover had a high standard of everyday morality and this was reflected in his stern supervision of the agency. The ranks of the FBI have been scandal-free.

Too, state and local law enforcement agencies benefitted from expertise amassed by the FBI for it would go out of its way to work in partnership with lower level authorities.

J. Edgar Hoover's record long will stand as his monument.

The New York Times

New York, N.Y., May 4, 1972

For nearly a half century J. Edgar Hoover and the Federal Bureau of Investigation were indistinguishable. That was at once his strength and its weakness. The extraordinary—and extraordinarily valuable—institution that he created became so identified with his personality and his character that, long before the end, Mr. Hoover had become an institution in himself, increasingly and unfortunately remote from the mainstream of American life and thought.

Appointed 48 years ago by Calvin Coolidge's Attorney General, Harlan F. Stone, the youthful Hoover was entrusted initially with the task of cleaning up one of the shadier agencies in what was then known as the "Department of Easy Virtue." Mr. Hoover built, by sheer personal strength, a clean and highly effective agency, with trained and devoted personnel and some of the finest crime detection facilities in the world. Along with the rest of the country, the gangsters and kidnappers of the thirties acquired a healthy respect for the G-Men, and so did scores of Nazi agents and saboteurs in the decade that followed.

Inevitably an agency that was so quickly clothed with glamor and was so soon established as a model for the young took on a sanctity that seemed to place it above criticism—and sometimes above the law itself. As it reached this position of untouchability by the fifties, the country's (and therefore the Bureau's) focus of fear had moved from gangsters and Nazis to real or alleged Communists in government, to atomic spies and to leftist political dissidents—with civil rights proponents, peace demonstrators and campus radicals soon to follow. A force handpicked for crime detection and for its devotion to the ultra-conservative personal philosophy of J. Edgar Hoover was not necessarily the agency best able to cope with the subtleties of racial disaffection or radical politics.

While the F.B.I.'s anti-crime work continued with distinction, Mr. Hoover himself became identified behind the scenes with many political leaders of the right. His great mistake was to allow his own political and philosophical tendencies to be projected in public, thus doing violence to the basic requirement of his office: total and absolute political neutrality.

During all this time, Mr. Hoover and his men were wrapped in an increasingly protective immunity from criticism by Congressmen, Attorneys General, Presidents and public. Not one to suffer silently the rare adverse comment that came his way, Mr. Hoover lashed out fiercely at even his mildest critics; and those within the Bureau courageous enough to voice criticism suffered harsh reprisal.

The moral of Mr. Hoover's astonishing career is that any public servant, no matter how able or how devoted, can be spoiled by exemption from the normal workings of democratic government. Through the autocratic exercise of concentrated power and the failure of his superiors in Congress and successive administrations to exercise effective checks, Mr. Hoover became especially in his later years a symbol of domestic illiberalism. Yet the fact that he was allowed to remain in office far too long and was permitted to become almost a separate and independent arm of government cannot obscure wholehearted recognition of his unique service to his country in the field of law enforcement for nearly five decades.

The Sun Reporter

San Francisco, Calif., May 6, 1972

The sudden death of J. Edgar Hoover, FBI director, was a shock to the nation. However, for many Americans his passing was a relief. Never before in the history of the nation -- and we should hope never again -- has one man become so powerful. While Hoover was the protector of the law, in the last two decades of his reign his behavior indicated his belief that he was either above the law or the personificaton of the law itself.

To millions, Hoover was a great American. We do not quarrel with this designation, because he served the status quo and the Establishment well.

Any adulation which we might have held for J. Edgar Hoover was quickly dissipated when he called Martin Luther King, Jr. "the most notorious liar in the country," and indicated that King was "the last one in the world who should ever have received the Nobel Peace Prize."

Hoover was a myopic man, who bragged of his commitment to Law and Order while shunning any connection of the FBI's mission, to uphold the role of Justice as a cornerstone of the American nation. Hoover should have been retired as FBI director three presidential administrations ago. We have never believed any man so indispensible to the nation that special dispensation must be made for him to continue his authoritarian role in the FBI.

If we would guard our freedom and individual liberties well, never again must the nation permit such accumulation of power and authoritarianism as ultimately resided in the person of J. Edgar Hoover.

TWIN CITY SENTINEL

Winston-Salem, N.C., May 5, 1972

THOUGH the eulogies suggest otherwise, J. Edgar Hoover was always a sophisticated city boy, born and raised and educated in Washington, D.C., and much more at ease in the gourmet restaurants of New York than in the government canteens of the federal city.

He counted among his closest friends, for example, the late French-born chef, Henri Soule, who came to the United States in 1939 for the New York World's Fair and remained to become a celebrated New York restaurateur. Once, when asked what this unusual friendship between a high government official and a French emigre was based on, M. Soule shot back: "I would think . . . my *Langoustes a la Parisienne, Sauce Mayonnaise.*"

A voracious reader and something of a stylish writer before his later books came to be composed by committee, the Director "read everything" he could lay hands on. Fond of horse racing and considered a prudent and thoughtful betting man by the experts, he could often be seen in his salad days at Bowie and other tracks near Washington, resplendent in silk gabardine suit and elegant tie.

Mr. Hoover dressed to ´please himself, but he also understood the negative uses of sartorial vanity. He was among the first to apply a policy of "mussing up" richly attired gangsters taken into custody, just to make certain they weren't taken for heroes by the nation's clothes-conscious young people. One pudgy racketeer fond of silk shirts and rainbow-hued suits was once deprived of belt and suspenders following his arrest, forcing him to hold up his trousers with his hands. The Director was not only aware of the psychological appeal of get-rich-quick gangsters, he also knew how to cope with the problem in a dramatic way.

There were many great moments in his long career, but J. Edgar Hoover's finest hour had nothing to do with gangsters and racketeers.

In December, 1941, after the Japanese attack on Pearl Harbor. officials in California, Oregon and Washington appealed to federal officials to arrest and isolate Japanese-Americans living on the west coast. Such reform liberals as Earl Warren of California, far from condemning such blatantly unconstitutional acts, joined in the cry for federal action.

Those who defend President Roosevelt's support of these xenophobic fears argue that his advisers, in the dark days of 1941-42, unanimously favored deportation of Japanese citizens to the interior, if only to calm western anxieties over a Japanese invasion.

But one of his advisers did not go along with such drastic measures. J. Edgar Hoover — a man who stood to gain a great deal from a federal detention policy aimed at Japanese-Americans — argued that such detention was unconstitutional and wrong.

These are loyal Americans, he pointed out, and Pearl Harbor will only serve to enhance their loyalty. Strip them of their personal rights, strip them of their wealth and property and pride, and you leave an indelible black mark on the pages of American history.

And he was right, down the line. The most decorated unit in World War II was a regimental combat team made up of young Japanese-Americans who were finally allowed to fight for their country. Its casualty rate in the Italian campaigns of 1944-45 was close to 60 per cent.

As for the policy of detention, it stands as a shameful blot on our nation's good name, as Mr. Hoover said it would.

So the man we pay final tribute to this week was not a simple-minded, straight-ahead, unimaginative bureaucrat. Rather, he was a paradox of a man, immensely complex, as sharp as a razor and perfectly attuned to the nuances and subtleties of human behavior.

This, in fact, partly explains the size and variety of his accomplishments. For no self-serving Gray Eminence, hunkered down in the rabbit warrens of big government, could have lived life with such enjoyment while achieving so much for his country and his people.

Mr. Hoover was quite a man.

THE MILWAUKEE JOURNAL
Milwaukee, Wis., May 7, 1972

President Nixon had a wise, right instinct when he moved, even before J. Edgar Hoover was buried, to keep the FBI above the battle in this political year. By naming an interim director to fill in until a new presidential term begins next January — whosoever it is—he served the best interests of the FBI and the country, as well as his own.

As for his own, he is in enough appointment trouble with the Senate already through the implication of his attorney general nominee in the ITT scandal. Nor are his own re-election odds so great that he can afford needlessly to hand his foes another issue to chew on. Inescapably, a nomination to succeed Hoover now would be controverted, because Hoover was controversial and the agency that he created in his own image touches the most sensitive nerves in the body politic.

The postponement serves the general pubic interest as well as Nixon's personally. For the FBI most of all must be free of suspicion that it can be touched by political motivations and manipulations. The president unfortunately has not shown this same delicate concern for the institutional integrity of the United States Supreme Court.

Hoover's death, furthermore, abruptly ended an era that bore his unique stamp and cannot simply be carried on by others — nor should it be. The interim directorship gives opportunity to ponder what the new era should be like, where the FBI and its director should fit into the establishment in the future.

The president could follow one wise step with another, by now appointing a blue ribbon, nonpolitical task force to counsel about that future. Should future directors serve fixed terms, instead of the lifetime t e n u r e that was granted to Hoover? Should professional qualifications be specified by law? Should the FBI be spun off from the Department of Justice, to assure against its coming under the thumb of a partisan attorney general? Should the FBI jurisdiction be more carefully defined and limited, to keep it always in spiritual harmony with the Bill of Rights?

Arkansas Gazette.
Little Rock, Ark., May 5, 1972

THERE WERE at least two John Edgar Hoovers. It was the increasingly political Hoover, as opposed to the professional Hoover, who brought increasingly heavy criticism down upon both the FBI and upon himself during the last third or so of his long public career. Mr. Hoover would deny that he was "political" at all, and with rather more sincerity than Mr. Nixon when he says that his presentation before a bipartisan group of Texas moneybags at the Connally ranch last week end was designed to be above politics. But the facts are to the contrary, and this, mainly, was what all the static was about.

It is true that there were always some critics of Mr. Hoover's personal capacities as a cop, too, by no means all of them crooks or Communists, but there is no question that he made a great contribution to the "professionalization" of police work in America at every level, at least in a technical sense, and to some extent even in an attitudinal sense.

So it was the gradual (and, lately, not so gradual) politicization, less of the Bureau as such than of the role of The Director himself, that led to the great majority of the criticism of the man and the Bureau.

Mr. Hoover was a confidant of a long succession of Presidents, and he would "intimidate" them, too (in the football expression) if he could, but in a sense he was anybody's dog who would hunt with him when it came to presidents, not above using blandishment in concert with a little intimidation, such as providing light bedtime reading for Lyndon Johnson out of the *curiosa* section of the FBI's files.

Mr. Hoover was human, and, as a citizen, had his right to have his preferences among other humans, including presidents, but it was when material that could only have come from the FBI's "raw" files started turning up in the hands of Joe McCarthy and his imitators for the purpose of trying to embarrass one of the two major parties and a particular sitting President that the myth of a scrupulously apolitical Federal Bureau of Investigation began to weaken at the seams. It was symptomatic of the gingerly approach that even presidents felt they had to take toward J. Edgar Hoover that even the testy Truman continued to treat him with public deference during this period, or at least tried to avoid coming into open conflict with him. How many of us still remember that the first presidential act of the resident architect of Camelot was to announce that he was keeping Mr. Hoover on as Director of the FBI?

*   *   *

WHAT HOOVER really was, we suppose, was simply a consummate administrator and builder of empires, an empire in which he acted as his own grand vizier and his own caliph. He was the best natural PR man of his times, perhaps the best ever, since Barnum. His budget presentations were masterpieces, every bit worthy of Lockheed's Board chairman making his case for loan support from the federal government, though made easier for the fact that the FBI had a rather better performance record. The spectacle of J. Edgar Hoover arguing for a still higher annual appropriation was made all the more magnificent for the fact that the congressmen personally would have brought the money to him unasked if they had been able to fully anticipate his wishes, stacking it up on the table in unmarked bills if that was the way he wanted it. Mr. Hoover himself, though, would not have missed these little performances of his for anything in the world, these friendly meetings that were rarely without a few "inside" revelations to the committee members of some real or imagined new threat to the Republic, such as the supposed plot to kidnap Henry Kissinger.

That was the way it was, and now there is the problem of "the succession," in a more royalist sense than this Republic may have ever known it. The situation now is rich with irony. For example, the Nixon administration had scarcely bothered to deny generally accepted reports that it was planning to replace Mr. Hoover as FBI director—as many even of its own adherents were urging—though not of course unless and until it was safely returned to office. Instead, the White House has been left with the necessity of doing something — or not doing something — now.

The supreme irony, however, is that the Senate now has the right of confirmation over Mr. Hoover's eventual successor, thanks to the late Everett McK. Dirksen of Illinois, who was afraid that some unworthy future administration, probably Democratic, someday might try to slip through a successor "unworthy" of the Hoover heritage.

Our first recommendation in the whole larger matter is that the directorship of the Federal Bureau of Investigation never again be made a lifetime job, that is, not unless we are prepared to write it into the Constitution, as we did with Supreme Court justices.

The Courier-Journal

Louisville, Ky., May 3, 1972

THE ULTIMATE tragedy of J. Edgar Hoover was not that he was a bad cop, but that he came to symbolize for so many millions of Americans the very dangers that 48 years ago he was appointed to avert.

The young Mr. Hoover, as a junior attorney in the Justice Department, had seen what can happen when crime-fighting is handled by politicians. As Attorney General Harlan Fiske Stone later wrote of the Bureau, to which he had named Mr. Hoover in 1924 with instructions for a total clean-up:

"The organization was lawless, maintaining many activities which were without any authority in federal statutes, and engaging in many practices which were brutal and tyrannical in the extreme."

The rest is familiar. The dedicated, efficient, new director began to reconstruct an agency that became second to none in its professionalism, and which did much to help elevate the quality of local police forces throughout the nation. Even the FBI's occasional tendency to take credit for the work of others could be overlooked during the glory days of the "G-Men" in the lawless 1930s, and the agency's superb performance during the fearsome days of World War II.

But things began to go sour after that. Mr. Hoover increasingly turned his attention to the dangers of Communist subversion (he published four books on the subject), while for better than a decade ignoring appeals that he focus on organized crime and violations of civil rights. And in recent years, although Mr. Hoover's public popularity had slipped somewhat from his better days, his stock in Congress had slumped badly because of growing belief that his yen for political surveillance of all dissidents now extended to Capitol Hill, too.

In the end he had become that riskiest of all dangers to a democracy: the man everyone is afraid to fire. Far in the past were the days of impersonal and unpolitical professionalism, for in recent years Mr. Hoover had become for many Americans a symbol of those police-state repressions (wiretapping, preventive detention, vindictiveness toward critics, unauthorized surveillance, and the rest) that, like Vietnam and in some ways because of it, have done so much to drive deep divisions among the people of this land.

Yet one can't really blame Mr. Hoover for the timidity of presidents or the fact that so many of our people fail to realize how thin the line can be between freedom and enslavement. For nearly five decades this man gave his nation the best that was in him; and it was not his failure alone that he so long outlived his usefulness in office.

So it isn't entirely a rebuke to the memory of Mr. Hoover for any of us to vow that the office he held—like any other identified with power—must in future be laced around with greater precautions against abuse. In a nation of laws, not men, we let the balance tip at our own peril.

The Seattle Times

Seattle, Wash., May 3, 1972

THEY said he was out of touch with the times. After all, didn't he forbid pantsuits on women employees and frown on long sideburns for men?

They said he was an autocrat. He had to be. His agents were under iron-handed discipline more than 30 years, yet it kept the world's most sensitive police agency from becoming politicized.

But the strong leadership style, the occasionally unfortunate public remarks—these were superficial issues that did not get to the heart of John Edgar Hoover's role in American life.

His personal habits and Calvinist view of society — described as those of a Victorian gentleman and reflective of his boyhood ambition to the ministry —were in vivid contrast to his official duties.

Gangsters, kidnapers, Nazis, Communist subversives: These were the stuff of Hoover's official concern. To deal with them, an admirer once wrote, he did those tough and distasteful things that had to be done by an effective F. B. I. in the real world we live in.

Not long before his death Monday night, Hoover remarked: "I have a philosophy. You are honored by your friends and distinguished by your enemies."

True enough. And in the perspective of more than 50 years of dedicated public service, Hoover earned for himself a niche in American history as one of the great men of his era.

No man is irreplaceable. But J. Edgar Hoover's boots will not be wholly filled.

Minneapolis Tribune

Minneapolis, Minn., May 3, 1972

Death has done what no president dared to do: removed J. Edgar Hoover from his lifetime job as director of the Federal Bureau of Investigation. For 48 years and under eight presidents, Mr. Hoover led the nation's most prestigious law-enforcement agency. In many respects, Mr. Hoover was the FBI and the FBI was Mr. Hoover.

Granted, there was increasing criticism of Mr. Hoover and the bureau in recent years. Even presidential candidates have called for the FBI director to step down or be replaced. The FBI was said to have become overzealous in its surveillance of protest groups and less effective in its battle against crime. Mr. Hoover, who was 77 at his death, was said to have become autocratic and vindictive.

Some of the criticism was justified. But none of the critics could deny that Mr. Hoover had established a remarkable record for the bureau and himself after he took it over in 1924, cleaned it of corruption and gave it an international reputation for integrity and professionalism. Incredibly, not a single FBI agent was charged with a crime during his tenure as chief. At the same time, Mr. Hoover kept the bureau out of partisan politics while concentrating on espionage and crime, violence and subversion.

J. Edgar Hoover, for all his faults, was one of the nation's most dedicated public servants. He literally gave his life to that service. His epitaph need say no more.

Wisconsin State Journal

Madison, Wis., May 3, 1972

Death has finally intervened to do what no American President would dare or want to do — remove J. Edgar Hoover, 77, as director of the Federal Bureau of Investigation.

Mr. Hoover, who built the FBI almost from scratch into one of the world's super crime-fighting organizations, won the admiration and esteem of citizens generally. In his lifetime he became one of the most unassailable figures in government.

A grateful nation will recall how Hoover took over a sickly, inept, politics-ridden agency back in 1924 and built it into one of the most effective investigative agencies in the world, with the possible exception of Scotland Yard.

The stern, uncompromising FBI chief and his bureau were largely responsible for ending the era of notorious gangsterism and kidnaping that marked the 1930s.

Later Mr. Hoover was just as relentless when the spread of Russian Communism caused concern following World War II. For his efforts he earned the undying hostility of the Far Left and their journalistic patsies.

Despite all the attacks against the FBI and its able chief, the reputation of the nation's primary domestic investigative agency remains unscathed.

Mr. Hoover's rugged honesty, his unchanging fight against lawlessness in a permissive age, his profound sense of duty, his unquestioned loyalty through a long career, make his monument.

Other men will lead the FBI in the years to come, but J. Edgar Hoover, known as "Mr. FBI," will forever remain a hero to generations of Americans who will recall his superb contributions to law enforcement in this country.

THE SUN

Baltimore, Md., May 5, 1972

President Nixon's designation of L. Patrick Gray 3d, an old personal friend and governmental associate, as acting director of the Federal Bureau of Investigation points up the need for a careful assessment of the current work and the future responsibility of this agency. It has been obvious for some years that the personalized directorship, the all-pervading one-man control, maintained by J. Edgar Hoover should not be continued under a new director.

Mr. Hoover was a power unto himself, holding a special position beyond the usual supervision of presidents, attorneys general and Congress principally because of a general confidence in his personal integrity and professional competence. A weakness in this system became apparent on his sudden death this week: a number of able, younger men who might have been in line for promotion to his office had found other jobs in recent years, and Mr. Nixon had to go outside the FBI, to Mr. Gray, an assistant attorney general, for an acting director.

Mr. Nixon may have been influenced in his designation of Mr. Gray as the acting director by the fact that his nomination of Mr. Kleindienst as Attorney General probably will be debated at some length in the Senate, with vigorous political exchanges between Democrats and Republicans, and by the fact that Mr. Gray was his first choice to become Deputy Attorney General, Mr. Kleindienst's present post. It would have been hard to keep the nomination of a permanent FBI chief out of the political crossfire in the Senate this sum-

mer, and the appointment can wait until after the election.

But more important than this political factor, we would suggest, is the need for the President and Congress to obtain a clear view of the current state of the FBI before a permanent director is appointed. We should remind ourselves once again that this is a government of laws, not of men, that the administration of the great power vested in the federal police chief must be kept subject to the overall supervision of the President and Congress, and hence that the President and Congress must have a closer share in the responsibility for the broad policy to be followed and enforced by the FBI. Mr. Gray should be able in the course of the next several months to give the President and the public an outline of the best way to go about this.

THE ATLANTA CONSTITUTION

Atlanta, Ga., May 5, 1972

It is going to be hard, very hard, to find a man who can fill the shoes of the late FBI Director J. Edgar Hoover.

Even those who were opposed to Hoover's philosophy and some of his policies in recent years admit that he was perhaps the most dedicated, conscientious and effective public servant in American history.

One major reason for Hoover's success was that he kept himself above partisan politics. This was reflected in the fact that he was a friend and confident of almost every American president, whether Democrat or Republican, since the days of Calvin Coolidge.

President Nixon has acted with commendable wisdom in appointing an

acting director of the FBI instead of immediately naming a permanent director. Filling in is Assistant Attorney General Patrick Gray.

This is an election year and almost every move the President makes is open to criticism and debate as being motivated primarily by political consideration. If the President named a permanent FBI director now, we could expect to see that rule in full and perhaps unseemly operation.

Delaying the permanent appointment until after the election insures that the FBI will continue to be what Hoover made it in his 48 years of service as director — a brilliantly efficient and effective and strictly nonpartisan law enforcement institution, probably the best in the world.

Pittsburgh Post-Gazette

Pittsburgh, Pa., May 5, 1972

PRESIDENT Nixon has acted prudently in naming an interim director of the Federal Bureau of Investigation to succeed the late J. Edgar Hoover. The choice of Asst. Atty. Gen. L. Patrick Gray III as acting FBI director does not sit well with Senate Democrats, however, who are not happy over Mr. Gray's accession to power during a period of intense political and social ferment.

Plainly, Mr. Nixon was motivated in his decision by a desire to avoid a protracted confirmation squabble during an election year. A permanent appointment would undoubtedly arouse partisan passions and hobble the effectiveness of the new director. Although the Senate may have profound misgivings at the extreme conservatism of Attorney General Gray, the temporary appointment will per-

mit the candidate elected to the presidency in November to choose his own FBI director.

Meanwhile, a limited tenure for the new FBI head will allow time for a dialogue on the shape and direction of the powerful bureau and what the scope of its authority should be.

In the early years of his stewardship, J. Edgar Hoover molded an agency of admirable efficiency and integrity. Mr. Hoover's increasing involvement in s e n s i t i v e political issues during the latter years of his directorship raised critical questions concerning the FBI's intrusion into areas not properly s u b j e c t to its authority.

The colossal growth of the FBI makes mandatory a review of its aims and methods in a crucial time for imperiled democratic values.

THE BLADE

Toledo, Ohio, May 8, 1972

IF THERE was a single fundamental principle that accounted most for J. Edgar Hoover's legendary success in converting the Federal Bureau of Investigation from a scandal-tainted assemblage of hacks into the world's most proficient law enforcement agency, it was the divorcement of the agency from political influence. Although Mr. Hoover personally held and voiced strong ideological convictions, his dogged resistance to partisan interference with the professional operations of the bureau made it what President Nixon properly called the "eternal monument" to the longtime director.

It seemed at first glance very much in the spirit of preserving this principle of nonpolitical professionalism that the President decided not to name a permanent successor to Mr. Hoover immediately. As the White House press secretary put it, the Chief Executive did not want the appointment, which would require Senate confirmation, to become involved in partisan politics in an election year.

So whom did Mr. Nixon tap to take over the reins of the FBI as acting director until after the November elections? A man who has had no experience at all in professional law enforcement; whose work as a Nixon administration appointee in the Justice Department has been with the civil division rather than in criminal law; whose selection for the FBI assignment thus appears to be attributable primarily to his long friendship with the President. And that association, it seems, has been concerned mostly with various campaign tasks and other partisan functions.

Against such a background, acting director L. Patrick Gray's statement that he will run the FBI with a "clear difference in manner and style" from Mr. Hoover's is not nearly as reassuring as was intended. Indeed, this appointment—cast so much in the crass Mitchell-Kleindienst mold that has been the Nixonian mark on the Justice Department—unavoidably raises the question of how long the FBI may remain the "eternal monument" to the partisan free standards of J. Edgar Hoover's tenure.

DESERET NEWS

Salt Lake City, Utah, May 10, 1972

With the death of Director J. Edgar Hoover, the Federal Bureau of Investigation is almost bound to undergo some fundamental changes.

One of the first policies that ought to go is the long-standing decision against hiring women as special agents.

The FBI does, of course, hire women as secretaries and file clerks but not as special agents on the grounds that the work is "too hazardous" for them.

This attitude is hard to understand, since there are thousands of policewomen and lady detectives all over the country and the Central Intelligence Agency employs a large number of women agents.

Former FBI Agent Bernard F. Conners, now a prominent New York businessman, says the bureau's refusal to hire women agents "inhibits the FBI's law enforcement operations, often making the arrest of women criminals an almost impossible undertaking."

As L. Patrick Gray III takes over as acting director, he should treat the FBI as a law enforcement agency — not an exclusive men's club.

SAXBE, KELLEY RELEASE REPORT ON FBI'S 'COINTELPRO' CAMPAIGN

Attorney General William B. Saxbe and Clarence M. Kelley, director of the Federal Bureau of Investigation released Nov. 18 some details of a 21-page study ordered by Saxbe. A joint FBI-Justice Department effort, the report outlined counter-intelligence operations the FBI conducted from 1965 to 1971 under the codename COINTELPRO. While the report called COINTELPRO "abhorrent in a free society", Kelley defended the operations as having "helped to bring about a favorable change."

The COINTELPRO activities were characterized in the report as sending anonymous or fictitious materials to groups to create internal dissension; leaking of informant-based or non-public information to friendly media sources; use of informants to disrupt a group's activities; informing employers, credit bureaus and creditors of members' activities; informing or contacting businesses and persons with whom members had economic dealings of members' activities; attempting to use religious and civil leaders and organizations in disruptive activities; and informing family or others of radical or immoral activities. The report also singled out over 20 instances that it called "most troubling" or "egregious" examples of COINTELPRO actions. Among them were investigating the love life of a group leader for dissemination to the press and obtaining income tax returns of members of a group.

Some of the organizations on the FBI's list for surveillance were the Southern Leadership Conference (SCLC), the Congress of Racial Equality (CORE), various Ku Klux Klan groups, Students for a Democratic Society (SDS), the Progressive Labor Party, and the Black Panther Party.

The Evening Bulletin

Philadelphia, Pa., November 25, 1974

For the second time in recent months past clandestine operations by U.S. agencies have surfaced to reveal an abuse of federal power that violated individual rights.

Most recently, U.S. Attorney General William B. Saxbe opened the closet door on a now banned Federal Bureau of Investigation program to disrupt organizations ranging from civil rights groups to the Ku Klux Klan.

The FBI employed a variety of "dirty tricks" for 15 years, halting only after files were stolen from its office in Media, Pa. Publication of these files proved that the FBI was investigating persons whose only crime was to dissent, such as a Swarthmore student whose father was a congressman opposed to the Vietnam War.

The FBI also exceeded its authority when it planted informers as agents provocateurs to play major roles in alleged conspiracies like the Harrisburg 7 and the Camden 28, which the Nixon Administration tried to prosecute unsuccessfully.

Similarly, the Internal Revenue Service investigated 99 organizations it labeled as "subversive and militant" at the Nixon Administration's request. But whereas the IRS' responsibility is tax violations, only 12 percent of the organizations and individuals it screened were found to have relevant taxable incomes.

Both these disclosures recall the recent criticism of the CIA, for violating a prohibition against domestic activity by involvement with the White House "plumbers" in the Ellsberg case. There was also its misuse in Chile to destabilize the elected government.

The danger of misusing the power of such agencies, particularly the agencies that act in secret, persists and requires constant vigilance. One safeguard has already been proposed in pending legislation to set up a joint House-Senate committee to police all U.S. intelligence. Introduced in September by two Watergate Committee senators, Howard Baker and Lowell Weicker, it calls for a committee that would monitor both domestic and foreign operations and all agencies including the FBI, CIA, Secret Service and armed forces branches. The bill currently awaits hearings.

All congressmen should take their cue from U.S. Attorney General William B. Saxbe, who called such a committee "one of the greatest safeguards we could have in this country." In addition the IRS, because of its access to confidential personal data, should receive special, regular and tough scrutiny from Congress.

New York Post

New York, N.Y., November 19, 1974

As revealed in the Watergate tapes and elsewhere, the Nixon Administration's conception of domestic affairs often involved a vision of US against THEM—the United States versus various alleged Troublemakers, Harassers, Enemies and Militants.

But the covert deployment of government agents against "subversives" did not begin with the Nixon inauguration. It developed into a matter of routine for the Federal Bureau of Investigation under J. Edgar Hoover years ago; some massive new evidence on that point has just been produced by Attorney General Saxbe.

Starting in 1956, the FBI undertook literally thousands of "counterintelligence" operations against organizations deemed "radical" or "immoral" or "extreme." The activities—defamation of individuals and groups, infiltration, provocations and disruption—are all familiar to the CIA and other espionage agencies around the world. Many Americans had little idea that their own government was using the same dirty tricks at home.

Beyond that, the Internal Revenue Service is also revealed to have conducted regular surveillance of "militant and revolutionary" and "radical" organizations starting early in the Nixon Administration. The targets included the National Urban League and the Congress of Racial Equality along with the Ku Klux Klan, the John Birch Society and the Founding Church of Scientology. The operation continued for more than four years.

The data was yielded by the IRS because Ralph Nader's Tax Reform Research Group filed suit to get it, citing the Freedom of Information Act.

Not long ago, fresh amendments to the Freedom of Information Act were approved by Congress and sent to President Ford. He vetoed them; his explanation is that they tended to threaten national security. That was the same issue raised yesterday by FBI Director Kelley, who defended the secret FBI tactics and demands continued authority to use them.

That joins the issue clearly; it demands searching reevaluation at the White House. What, after all, can be more "disruptive" and "revolutionary" than the doctrine that the government has almost limitless authority to spy on American citizens, interfere with their rights' of association and even provoke lawlessness? Have we learned anything?

Washington Star-News

Washington, D.C., November 20, 1974

It has become increasingly clear that federal investigative agencies have been riding high, wide and handsome—and perhaps illegally in some instances—in pursuit of goals that have more to do with politics than with law enforcement or protection of American citizens. It also is clear that Congress has an obligation to begin riding herd on operations that it finances.

The latest reports that should disturb anyone interested in guarding individual rights and liberties involve a bag of "dirty tricks" performed by the Federal Bureau of Investigation on various organizations, and harassment of politically oriented groups and individuals by the Internal Revenue Service.

There can be little question that the targeting of 99 "ideological, militant, subversive or radical organizations" for special treatment by the IRS was a political operation. The first steps to create the agency's Special Service Staff that carried it out were taken the day after an aide of former President Nixon told a top IRS official in July 1969 that Nixon wanted the agency to "move against leftist organizations."

During the course of four years (the thing was abandoned when Watergate got hot), the SSS compiled files on 2,873 organizations and 8,585 individuals. The result was that most of them were discovered to have no apparent "revenue significance or potential."

The FBI matter goes back much farther than the Nixon administration—to 1956, when the late director J. Edgar Hoover established an operation named "Cointelpro" to investigate and counter subversion by the Communist party. By the 1960s, Hoover expanded the operation to include espionage groups, white hate groups, black extremists, the Social Workers party and the New Left.

The present FBI director, Clarence Kelley, has defended the activities of Cointelpro as being carried out "entirely in good faith and within the bounds of what was expected of (the FBI) by the President, the attorney general, the Congress and the American people." However, a report by the Justice Department said some of the activities "can only be considered abhorrent in a free society."

Undoubtedly, much of the work of Cointelpro was necessary, legitimate and effective. But somewhere along the line Hoover and his aides got the misguided notion that almost any means justified the end; they became confused as to where legitimate law enforcement ended and the trampling of individual rights and freedom began.

Investigating the love life of the late Martin Luther King, Jr., and trying to peddle it to the press to discredit him as a civil rights leader, hardly falls within the category of legitimate law enforcement tactics. Neither does the use of federal agents to disrupt legitimate protest demonstrations. The Justice Department report includes hundreds of instances in which information—both true and false—was distributed surreptitiously by the FBI to discredit individuals or to disrupt the activities of organizations.

One of the disturbing elements is that few people beyond Hoover and his FBI operatives knew about the Cointelpro operation. It is imperative, as Attorney General William Saxbe seemed to be suggesting the other day, that Congress begin exercising much closer oversight of operations for which it provides the legal basis and the financing. It should not be left to high-level bureaucrats, especially in agencies with awesome investigative authority, nor to White House politicians to decide what is or is not good for the people and then to use highly questionable means to excise that which they consider bad.

There also is a lesson for the press in this episode. One of the methods used by the FBI to discredit individuals and disrupt the activities of organizations was to "leak" information about them to newsmen. The news media ought to be on constant guard against being manipulated by government agencies to do their dirty work.

DAYTON DAILY NEWS

Dayton, Ohio, November 19, 1974

The reports on the political actions of the FBI and of the Internal Revenue Service decorate with some details what was already known in general — that the agencies sometimes violated the public's rights and liberties in the name, of course, of protecting those. The worst offender was the FBI. It initiated its own illegal activities. The IRS merely submitted to political misuse by the Nixon administration. It was the lady of frail virtue; the FBI was out hooking.

In his report. Attorney General William Saxbe deplores some of the FBI's activities as "abhorrent in a free society" but pleads that those be seen in perspective. As Mr. Saxbe says, most of the FBI's 15-year counterintelligence program stayed within the bounds of legitimate practices.

This is always a tricky balancing act in a society that is trying to be free and fair. The law-abiding and the politically ordinary majorities have a sacred duty to permit and in fact to protect political dissent, even at the most ragged fringes of social thought, and they are obliged to put up with a fair amount of tumult in the process. But they also have a right and a duty to protect the institutions that are in their care from violence and from extremists' attempts to take criminal advantage of civil liberties.

The FBI would be derelict if it didn't keep close tabs on what is going on in the farthest-out political orbits and failed to act against any violent intentions. But despite Mr. Saxbe's plea, it was the minority of instances in which the FBI acted wrongly that counts for more than the majority of times when it acted appropriately.

The FBI's secret slanders of radical and not-so-radical leaders. the involvement of its own agents in provoking violence (so that it could then denounce an organization as violent) its dirty tricks meant to disrupt and collapse lawful political groups — such misbehavior adds up to a classic example of the homily that a few bad apples spoil the barrel.

The misdeeds tainted evidence and led to mistrials. They destroyed the bureau's credibility with a sizeable minority of the public. They actually alienated some socially concerned persons from mainstream activities. the counterintelligence program becoming something of a self-fulfilling paranoia.

Much of the problem already has corrected itself. Long-time Director J. Edgar Hoover was so entrenched, so nearly divine among public figures and so skilled in bureaucratic one-upmanship that he achieved a license to use and misuse the bureau according to his personal eccentricities. Congress never questioned him. Attorneys general, technically responsible for the FBI. were ignored by him. Even presidents deferred to him.

That is unlikely to occur again. Congress has taken to venturing an occasional growl in its watchdog role. In the apparent forthrightness of his report — compelled from him though it was by a suit filed under the Freedom of Information act — Mr. Saxbe displays obvious contempt for the FBI s lawless games. The report itself. confirming the misdeeds, will be a check against repetitions.

But if indirectly. maybe the most important restraining influence will be that of an older but wised-up public. which is coming to understand that it can be menaced as much by extremism in its protection as by the ambitions of avowed extremists.

Long Island Press

Jamaica, N.Y., November 20, 1974

Despite Watergate, the director of the Federal Bureau of Investigation, Clarence M. Kelley, still thinks dirty tricks, under certain circumstances, are a necessary tool. He wants Congress to enact legislation authorizing the FBI "under emergency situations, to do some things which counteract the effectiveness" of militant groups at both extremes of the political spectrum.

We're delighted that Attorney General William B. Saxbe has steadfastly refused to endorse the proposal for legislation, and has refused to give Mr. Kelley the permission he needs to take the measures he advocates.

The FBI's dirty tricks were launched many years ago by the late J. Edgar Hoover, and were employed against the Communist party, the Socialist Workers party, "black extremist" and "white hate" groups, and the New Left. Mr. Hoover's views of extremism were, of course, debatable; he included such moderate organizations as the Southern Christian Leadership Conference and the Congress on Racial Equality.

Even the accuracy of Mr. Hoover's labels is unimportant. What is important is that an official government agency deliberately violated the laws which protect all citizens—those who agree with the government and those who disagree.

It is no better for the FBI, for whatever reason, to disrupt the activities of "violence-prone groups" or entrap their members, than for the Watergate burglars to break into the Democratic National Committee headquarters, or for the police to break into your home because they think they may find drugs.

As Mr. Saxbe says, the counterintelligence program that Mr. Hoover instituted, and that Mr. Kelley seeks to continue, "is not something that we in a free society should condone." The laws can just as well be enforced within the law.

* * *

Mr. Saxbe says he leans against legislation that would forbid such dirty tricks outright. We'd support such legislation if it was necessary, but we doubt that new laws are needed. The laws are already on the books, starting with the Bill of Rights. What we need is enforcement of them. We also should take under serious advisement. Mr. Saxbe's suggestion for a joint House-Senate committe to monitor the daily operations of the FBI.

The Watergate affair, and such other unfortunate FBI actions as its harassment of columnist Jack Anderson, led to suggestions that the FBI be removed from the Justice Department's political control. That idea has merit, and deserves consideration, but Congress must also insure that the FBI is not free to go its own way, without controls and without assurance that this agency which enforces the law also obeys the law.

The Des Moines Register

Des Moines, Iowa, November 19, 1974

Government sources are admitting what was first denied: J. Edgar Hoover had a secret counter-intelligence unit in the FBI, and the Internal Revenue Service had a special unit keeping tabs on individuals and organizations considered suspect by former President Nixon and his White House aides.

Thanks largely to the Freedom of Information Act, the American people are seeing more clearly the kind of secret police apparatus Hoover was making of the FBI. The FBI ran a counter-intelligence unit for 15 years, apparently without the knowledge of presidents and attorneys general.

Purpose of the unit was to discredit and disrupt organizations Hoover considered subversive. The first official government disclosure of Hoover's dirty tricks corps came last year when Atty. Gen. William Saxbe, under court order, made public a sheaf of FBI memos and other materials related to the operation. Now Saxbe has been given a more complete report from a Justice Department committee headed by Asst. Atty. Gen. Henry Petersen.

It took 13 months for a Ralph Nader group to pry out of the Internal Revenue Service 41 documents pertaining to the Special Service Staff, an intelligence-gathering unit set up in 1969 under pressure from the White House. The unit collected files on more than 11,000 groups and individuals, most of whom had earned the enmity of the Nixon administration.

Under investigation were such diverse organizations as the Black Panthers, the White Knights of the KKK, Students for a Democratic Society, the American Nazi Party, the Minutemen, the John Birch Society, the Unitarian Society, the National Council of Churches and the Welfare Rights Organization.

Existence of the special IRS unit has been suspected for some time. Two years ago, leaders of several mainline Protestant denominations said they had learned the IRS was looking into church involvement in political and racial causes, ostensibly to determine whether there had been violations of the tax-exempt status granted to religious organizations. Then the Watergate investigations let loose a torrent of testimony showing how Nixon administration officials had used the IRS against political enemies.

All of this is cause for dismay, for indignation. Not only were the American people lied to, they were put under suspicion. Institutions they trusted were turned against them.

When told an organization he belonged to was on the IRS list, Prof. David Ozonoff of Massachusetts Institute of Technology replied, "We are very proud." It was the same reply many others had given when they learned they were on the White House "enemies" lists.

Think of it, American citizens announcing boldly they are proud to be enemies of government officials and government agencies. And why not? The American people were treated with contempt by agencies of their government.

Now government officials try to assure the people that this kind of spying is a thing of the past. The government's record of truthfulness being as poor as it is, the people cannot feel safe.

The Seattle Times

Seattle, Wash., November 19, 1974

A JUSTICE Department report resulting from court suits under the Freedom of Information Act says the Federal Bureau of Investigation practiced some "dirty tricks" as part of a counter-intelligence program against extremist groups from 1956 to 1971.

Before the report becomes a rallying point for a new wave of efforts to discredit the F. B. I., the critical findings should be put in perspective from two standpoints.

First, as the report noted, "The overwhelming bulk of the activities carried on under the (counter-intelligence) program were legitimate and proper intelligence and investigative practices and procedures."

Second, the reported "abhorrent practices," such as the establishment of sham organizations and use of fake letters, have no place in the modern F. B. I.

Attorney General Saxbe told law-enforcement officers studying at the F. B. I.'s National Academy recently that "dirty tricks are over at the F. B I."

And by all accounts, Clarence M. Kelley, the thoroughgoing law-enforcement professional who became F. B. I. director in the spring of 1973, has done a remarkable job of restoring to the agency the luster it lost through the Watergate taint of L. Patrick Gray, former acting director.

Although Saxbe and Kelley have eschewed the disruptive tactics practiced against extremist groups of an earlier era, they have not, will not and should not relax their efforts to counter urban-guerrilla terrorism.

Saxbe emphasizes a continuing need for "proper" informational and intelligence-gathering operations when national security is jeopardized.

The vast majority of Americans welcome assurance that their premier national law-enforcement organization is operating "properly," of course.

Even more welcome, however, is Kelley's assurance that "terorism in the United States simply will not be tolerated."

HOUSTON CHRONICLE

Houston, Texas, November 27, 1974

William C. Sullivan, the former assistant director of the Federal Bureau of Investigation, has gone on record as saying the FBI as now structured constitutes a threat to the civil liberties of Americans.

While Sullivan's statement must be viewed with some caution because of his feud with the late FBI director J. Edgar Hoover, the Chronicle believes that fundamentally Sullivan is accurate.

We regret that such a great law enforcement agency as the FBI has been tarnished, but it is better for the agency that any weaknesses be pointed out and for the people to know what has happened in the past.

Sullivan says one of the agency's big problems was that it was sealed off from the outside world and the thinking of others. Issues were black and white, with no grey areas of doubt. And believing themselves in the right, the agency allowed expediency to take precedence over civil liberties. In this atmosphere, it was but a small step to institute questionable techniques and broad electronic surveillance.

Certainly the Chronicle joins Sullivan in fearing the massive electronic surveillance that has been disclosed. Also, we can see from his statement that such surveillance is not just of a recent nature.

One of the most significant things Sullivan said was that presidential use of the FBI to investigate political opponents did not originate with Richard Nixon but goes back as far as President Franklin D. Roosevelt.

Such a perspective, while it does not mean these activities can be condoned, does help point out how distant are the origins from which later transgressions grew.

Although some of the people caught up in the Watergate affair may have been subjected to unfair abuses, the total result of the Watergate scandal will ultimately be good for the nation in that we will have a cleansing of politics in government.

Now, through such things as the Watergate disclosures and the Sullivan statement, matters are being brought to light, and that is a good indicator that such practices will be curbed in the future.

The Register-Republic

Rockford, Ill., November 19, 1974

It is the duty of the Federal Bureau of Investigation to investigate and apprehend those who break federal laws.

But the record of FBI "dirty tricks" — from 1956 to 1971 — is replete with Big Brother bloat and what the FBI itself identifies as "isolated instances of practices that can only be considered abhorrent in a free society."

They include monitoring the "love life" of the late Dr. Martin Luther King for what was clearly intended as blackmail.

There was the "use" of friendly newspapers to print and spread falsehoods — an indictment as much of the acquiescing newspapers as it is of the FBI.

There were campaigns by the FBI to discredit those whose politics did not agree with Hoover's by poisoning the minds of prospective employers and damaging individual credit ratings.

According to the report now released by Atty. Gen. William Saxbe, such campaigns were ordered by Hoover without consulting Justice Department superiors, the White House or Congress.

Some of these campaigns were addressed against "radicals," a designation that could include anyone that Hoover chose to include in that category.

The lawlessness of an agency created to uphold the law is substance enough for revulsion.

But the greater question remains. Who is to ride herd on such flagrant intrusions upon individual privacy?

The disclosures do vindicate one remedy that has been recently imposed, limiting the FBI director's term to 10 years maximum.

But surely, rather than trust to the judgment of future attorneys general, there can be guidelines set down defining the FBI's mode of conduct, its assigned area of responsibility, so that the abuses now disclosed can be preempted before they occur again.

Members of Congress still exist who remember the wrath J. Edgar Hoover once could visit upon them. They should be in the forefront of an effort to assure private American citizens they will not again fall prey to the political whims of federal investigators.

The Chattanooga Times

Chattanooga, Tenn., November 21, 1974

One can appreciate the FBI's problem of combatting groups intent on subverting this country and still remain troubled by the manner in which the agency carried out its tasks, specifically the apparently insufficient legal authority for its actions.

The FBI's highly secret counterintelligence operations, known collectively as "Cointelpro," often used controversial means to disrupt and thereby neutralize domestic political groups such as the Communist Party USA, the Ku Klux Klan and scores of other racial, political and student groups.

It is true, as the report released by Atty. Gen. William Saxbe noted, that "a fair, accurate and comprehensive understanding of the various 'Cointelpro' activities undertaken by the FBI is possible only in the light of the context and climate in which the programs were established."

But it is no less appalling that many of the practices used by the FBI against domestic activist groups — not those generally considered subversive, such as the CPUSA — were carried out under less than clear legal authority, even to the extent that, as the report commented, there is "no indication in Bureau files" that the programs were either approved by or made known to any attorney general or any individual in the Department of Justice.

The seriousness of this aspect of the program — which former FBI Director J. Edgar Hoover began in 1956 and suddenly disbanded 15 years later — is evident in the degree of attention the present director, Clarence Kelley, paid it in making a conflicting statement.

Mr. Kelley emphatically assured the public that Director Hoover "did not conceal from superior authorities (the nation's attorneys general) the fact that the FBI was engaging in neutralizing and disruptive tactics against revolutionary and violence-prone groups."

The apparent discrepancy between the report's comment and Mr. Kelley's statement certainly should be resolved by a congressional investigation.

Some critics have questioned whether the Bureau actually has legal authority to investigate suspected subversive organizations. We would not. But this acceptance of the realistic need for a country to protect itself against enemies who aren't necessarily armed forces must be conditioned on the provisions that appropriate safeguards exist to preclude the Bureau — or some extra-legal group such as Richard Nixon's "plumbers" — from trampling the legitimate constitutional protections of American citizens.

This latter point is where we feel the Bureau, under Mr. Hoover's autocratic rule erred in disrupting the activities of suspected groups that were not at the time involved in criminal activities.

17 FREED IN 'CAMDEN 28' CASE BECAUSE OF USE OF 'PROVOCATEUR'

Seventeen of 28 persons accused in an August 1971 raid on a Camden, N.J. selective service office were acquitted in federal district court May 20 after Judge Clarkson F. Fisher told the jury it could acquit the defendants if it found that the government had exceeded permissible limits in using a "provocateur" in setting up the crime. Defense and prosecuting attorneys concurred in seeking dismissal of all charges against the 10 remaining defendants whose cases had been severed from the current trial. One had pleaded guilty to a misdemeanor.

In his instructions May 17, Fisher said although the defendants admitted breaking into the office and destroying draft files and were predisposed to do so, the jury need not consider the "predisposition of any defendant" if it found the actions of government agents "so fundamentally unfair as to be offensive to the basic standards of decency and shocking to the universal sense of justice."

The key to the case was Robert W. Hardy, a Camden contractor who said the Federal Bureau of Investigation (FBI) had paid him to provide the means to carry out the raid. Testifying for the defense, he said that one of the two FBI agents to whom he had regularly reported told him that "someone in the little White House" in San Clemente, Calif., wanted the FBI to let the crime happen before making arrests, rather than arrest the 28 for conspiracy before the break-in. The defense contended that the reason for waiting was to "create" additional crimes to generate enough publicity to discredit the antiwar movement. Hardy and other defense witnesses said the group had abandoned plans for the raid because of a lack of expertise, but Hardy's intervention with instructions and equipment resurrected the scheme.

THE DAILY OKLAHOMAN
Oklahoma City, Okla., May 22, 1973

FOR the second time in a week persons who admitted in open court breaking the law in actions dealing with official government records have been allowed to go free. In each instance the real question of guilt or innocence was shunted aside by the technical issue of government conduct in the case. In short, the government rather than the defendants was put on trial.

First, it was the dismissal of conspiracy, espionage and theft charges against Daniel Ellsberg and Anthony Russo in the Pentagon papers case. Now 17 war protestors have been found innocent of charges in connection with a 1971 raid on a Camden, N. J., draft board office.

The latter were part of a group arrested in and around the draft board office the night of an anti-war protest operation. They admitted participating in the raid. But they begged off accepting responsibility for their actions by blaming it all on an FBI informer who had infiltrated the group. They claimed they had given up plans for the raid and that the FBI plant revitalized them.

This is similar to the old claim of entrapment often used by defense lawyers, usually in cases involving illegal dope sales. Regardless of the role of any federal agent, however, what they did was against the law. It was just as illegal as the burglary of the Democratic National Committee headquarters in the Watergate office building in Washington, an offense for which s e v e n persons have pleaded guilty or have been convicted.

The Camden defendants were all adults. Presumably they were all intelligent enough to make independent decisions and to know right from wrong. They didn't have to go through with the draft board raid, even if they were egged on by the FBI plant. There is no indication he forced them at gunpoint or by threat to undertake the operation.

The probable fact is that they were proud of their activities at the draft board office, in the manner of most of the anti-war radicals who were dedicated to undermining their government's policy in Vietnam. But the side issue of the extent of governmental participation in the raid was allowed to take precedence over whether the defendants were guilty of conspiracy, breaking and entering and destruction of draft records.

The Star-Ledger
Newark, N.J., May 23, 1973

The acquittal of 17 war protesters of charge stemming from a 1971 raid on a draft board in Camden mercifully marks a close to one of the shabbies episodes in American law enforcement.

With its verdict, a federal court jury gave lega sanction to testimony that U.S. officials, in an ex cess of zeal, to put it charitably, indulged in prac tices that have no place in a free society.

The testimony involved, not for the first time the use of agents provocateurs — governmen agents who incited and actually participated in ille gal acts in order to entrap and convict others.

The agent provocateur in this case, a 33-year old self-employed contractor who served as an FB informer, testified that the raid would not have tak en place "without the FBI and me."

The defendants, who admitted participating i the raid, claimed they had dropped plans for it unti Robert Hardy, the contractor, revitalized them Hardy testified that he used the FBI's money to pa for the burglary tools used to force the illegal entry

In his charge to the jury, Judge Clarkson Fishe put the issue as well as it can be put when he said:

"If you find that the overreaching participatio by government agents or informers in the activitie as you have heard them were so fundamentally ur fair to be an offense to the basic standards of decer cy and shocking to the universal sense of justice then you may acquit any of the defendants to whom this defense applies."

The jury, in acquitting all, obviously deemed applied to all concerned in this matter.

Even if this were an unprecedented and unrelat ed act by government agents, it would be highl deplorable. But it appears to fit a pattern of uncon donable conduct that has been emerging with in creasing frequency.

In the Watergate case and related investiga tions, we have been presented with evidence tha the Central Intelligence Agency gave assistance t two men who perpetrated a common burglary at psychiatrist's office and that, in another instanc the CIA was asked by White House aides to tak part in a coverup of further illegal activities. Happ ly, in the second instance, the CIA refused.

Although it was not part of the legal proceeding it was apparent that the general weariness with th war and the reaction to nation's involvement i what the defense characterized as an "illegal an immoral" conflict strongly influenced the jurors. also was evident in the fact that the acquittal wa the first legal victory for the anti-war movement i the last five years of similar draft-record protes incidents.

Law enforcement officials in America are ent tled to full and complete support from every citizer At the same time, the officials must act in a way t be worthy of that trust. It is quite clear that, in th Camden case, these "basic standards of decency were not met.

The Boston Globe

Boston, Mass., May 22, 1973

The acquittal of 17 antiwar activists in Camden, N.J., is the most dramatic of all of the stunning defeats the Administration has suffered in its effort to silence war protests by putting protesters in prison even when it has to rely on tainted evidence to do so.

Grand juries have continued to be led by Justice Department attorneys into indicting dissenters for their "high crimes." But petit juries have acquitted or courts have dismissed in nearly all cases since the conviction of the so-called Harrisburg Seven for destroying draft records in 1967. The Administration's vindictiveness in that trial and the shabby treatment of two priest-brothers, Fathers Philip and Daniel Berrigan, during their six- and three-year terms of imprisonment, clearly has soured the nation's view of the Administration's heavy-handed effort to have its own way in Indochina no matter what.

Since that guilty verdict, the Administration has been defeated in its fantastic effort to convict the Berrigans and others of "plotting" to kidnap Henry Kissinger and blow up heating mains under government buildings. All five defendants in the mock "conspiracy" have been cleared on appeal. Thirteen Black Panthers have been acquitted in New York, the Soledad brothers were acquitted in California, Black Panther chairman Bobby Seale has been acquitted in New Haven and Huey Newton and nine other "conspirators" were freed in New Bedford. Most important of all, perhaps, at least until the acquittal of the Camden 17 over the weekend, was the dismissal of all charges against Dr. Daniel Ellsberg and Anthony Russo the weekend before that, this one, too, on the ground that the overzealous Administration's case was fatally tainted.

In the Camden case, as in the "plot" to kidnap Mr. Kissinger, the Administration relied on a paid informer and agent provocateur who helped concoct the plot and supplied the expertise and tools. But an even more startling facet of the Camden case is that the defendants, again including two Roman Catholic priests, had admitted that they had indeed broken into the Federal building in Camden in 1971, and they had, as charged, destroyed draft files.

Neither The Globe nor its readers condone burglary. Neither did the presiding judge, Federal District Judge Clarkson S. Fisher, who now joins that select group of judges who grant law enforcement officers no immunity from the laws by which all others are governed. He directed the jury to acquit if it found that the government had overreached propriety by itself participating in the crime for which it had brought others to trial.

If the Administration does not find a valuable lesson in this aspect of the verdict, it may, perhaps, weigh the degree to which the jury was influenced by the defense plea that it nullify the laws against breaking and entering, in this case, on the ground that the illegal and immoral war in Indochina is by far a worse evil. But war or no war, burglary, one would think, is a charge this Administration might hesitate to bring against anyone.

HERALD-JOURNAL

Syracuse, N.Y., May 22, 1973

One thing that keeps nagging at us ever since the acquittal of most of the Camden 28 is the way that the jury apparently agreed with the defense's contention that the defendants ought to go free as they acted "in the national interest."

The Camden 28 broke into a government office and destroyed draft records, according to the charges against them. They maintained it was because they wished to stop an "immoral war."

The men who broke into the Watergate and the office of Daniel Ellsberg's psychiatrist have maintained they were acting "in the national interest." They say they did so as they wished to protect "national security."

We realize the Camden 28 jury announced that the government, by use of an informer, lured the defendants into breaking into the draft offices. But the defendants admitted they planned to do so and apparently were eager enough to take the informer's advice, because they believed it was their patriotic duty.

Haven't the men accused of Watergate and the Ellsberg affair indicated they were adhering to their patriotic duty?

Where's the difference?

The Evening Bulletin

Philadelphia, Pa., May 22, 1973

The verdict exonerating the "Camden 17" of breaking into a draft board office and destroying files amounts to a condemnation of the Federal Government's heavy-handed role in setting up the raid so the participants could be arrested.

The bizarre case adds fuel to the fire of suspicion about the readiness of some officials to exceed the bounds of propriety and, in a pursuit of law enforcement that approaches entrapment, offend a basic sense of decency.

In this case the role of an informer was to report regularly on the break-in planning to the Federal Bureau of Investigation and actually to supply most of the burglary tools along with instructions for carrying out the crime.

During the trial the informer testified that an agent told him "someone in the little 'White House' in San Clemente, Calif., wanted the crime to occur before arrests were made, a disclosure which adds a curious if hearsay dimension to the case, coming at this time.

The Camden 17 were emotionally touched by the Vietnam war, but moral conviction alone could not have stood as a defense, a sort of appeal to higher law. These were intelligent people who broke a reasonable law, however noble their motive.

The hard reality is that no society that aspires to continue in existence can tolerate breaking of laws, whether burglary of a draft board in New Jersey to protest a war, a psychiatrist's office in California to copy a patient's file for so-called security reasons or the Democratic National Committee headquarters in Washington to influence a presidential election.

The difference in the Camden case is that somewhere along the line the culpability of the planners was clouded by the participation of a government agent provocateur—a factor conspicuously missing in the other two break-ins.

ST. LOUIS POST-DISPATCH

St. Louis, Mo., May 22, 1973

By acquitting 17 antiwar defendants charged with breaking into a federal building in Camden, N.J., and destroying draft files, a jury has in effect rebuked the Government for encouraging and helping people to break the law and then prosecuting them for doing so. The defendants in the Camden trial conceded that they had been predisposed to invade a federal building as a protest against the Vietnam war but had abandoned their plan until an FBI informant joined their group, resurrected the plan and provided the leadership, the burglary tools, food, money, transportation and equipment needed to carry out the 1971 raid.

The not guilty verdict was the jurors' response to instructions from the judge that they could acquit if they found that the activities of FBI agents extended to "an intolerable degree of over-reaching Government participation" in the offense and "were so fundamentally unfair as to be offensive to the basic standards of decency and shocking to the universal sense of justice." An acquittal verdict based on these instructions is tantamount to a conviction of the Government for rigging a case. In the light of the finding of Government misconduct, charges should be dismissed against 11 other Camden defendants whose case was severed from that of the acquitted 17.

The profoundly disturbing aspect of the Camden prosecution is that it seems to fall into a pattern of Government attempts to purge antiwar critics by inducing them and aiding them to engage in what turn out to be Government-sponsored protests. Evidence of the similar use of FBI agents provocateur came out in the trial of the "Harrisburg 7" for conspiring to destroy draft files and in the still pending case of a group of Vietnam Veterans Against the War charged last year in Florida with a plot to disrupt the Republican Convention.

Like the prosecution of Daniel Ellsberg, in which White House-hired thugs burglarized his psychiatrist's office to gather information on the defendant, the Camden case and the others reflect a standard of conduct suggesting that the Nixon Administration is ready to use any tactics, however illegal, to suppress people whom it sees as political enemies. It is a standard more in keeping with a totalitarian dictatorship than with a democratic government standing for equal justice under law.

Minneapolis Tribune

Minneapolis, Minn., May 25, 1973

One of the most militant and outspoken members of the Weathermen organization during its peak period of bombing and other violence in late 1969 and early 1970, according to a report by Seymour Hersh of the New York Times, "was an informer and agent provocateur for the FBI."

Hersh, quoting "private and government sources," said that the man in question "has acknowledged participating in bombings and violent demonstrations while living in various underground Weathermen collectives around the country."

Police departments and the FBI say that informers are an essential, if distasteful, part of their business. And the record shows that criminals sometimes are brought to justice as a result of an initial tip passed on in a dark alley or whispered over the telephone by an informer. But an agent provocateur is something else again. By definition, an agent provocateur is a person hired to incite actions that will make others liable to penalty. Such agents have flourished in societies where justice has broken down or has been destroyed. That day has yet to come to the United States.

Grand-jury investigations of Weathermen-connected activities have been convened by the federal government in several cities across the country, including Madison, Wis. Among the first questions that should be asked are: Was the man who acted as an informer hired as such, or did he volunteer his services without pay? If he was hired, was he also hired as an agent provocateur or, in participating so zealously, was he just trying to bolster his credibility with the Weathermen?

If he was hired as an agent provocateur, then the courts and the Congress should move to prevent such practices so contrary to the values of a democratic society.

The Philadelphia Inquirer

Philadelphia, Pa., May 22, 1973

We have mixed feelings about the jury verdict of innocent in the trial of 17 of the "Camden 28" antiwar activists.

The defendants are decent and honorable men and women, members of the "Catholic Resistance," four of them priests, all deeply concerned about the war in Vietnam and determined to strike a blow against it.

But the form their resistance took was deliberately to violate the law. On Aug. 22, 1971, they broke into the Federal building in Camden and tore up draft files. Far from pleading innocent to the charges, they proclaimed their guilt. "I ripped up those files with my hands," declared the Rev. Peter D. Fordi. "They were the instruments of destruction."

★ ★ ★

What the defendants asked of the jury, however, was something that no jury may give in our system of jurisprudence. It was that the jury "ignore the law"; that it make a verdict of guilty on the odious Vietnam war itself; and that it find the defendants innocent on the basis of a higher law which permits law-breaking for a noble cause.

As Federal Judge Clarkson Fisher pointed out in his charge to the jury, the law does not permit "religious or moral convictions as a defense, no matter how noble," no matter how sincerely motivated the defendants may have been.

In this, however, lies the irony, and the tragedy. For by rejecting the philosophic premise of the defendants, the jury in effect found the government guilty of actions which, as Judge Fisher also emphasized in his charge, justified the verdict of acquittal — that is, actions "so fundamentally unfair as to be offensive to the basic standards of decency and shocking to the universal sense of justice."

During the trial, the defendants emphasized that they had given up their plan until the FBI's agent provocateur, Robert W. Hardy, had resurrected it and provided them with the leadership and tools to carry it out. And Mr. Hardy, possibly the first government informer ever called as a witness by the defense rather than the government, admitted as much on the stand. The policy of the agency had been to "make sure the defendants commit as many crimes as possible," and he "provided the aid and strategy they needed."

★ ★ ★

In short, the crime could not have been committed without what Judge Fisher called the "creative activity" of the FBI, and what is so profoundly disturbing is that this is not an isolated incident.

The government indulged in similar "creative activity" is using an informer in the case of the "Harrisburg Seven," which ended in a 10-2 vote of acquittal on charges of conspiring to kidnap Henry Kissinger and blow up heating tunnels in Washington. And in the Watergate revelations and the aborted Pentagon Papers trial, we have seen other "creative activities" that extend to break-ins and beyond.

Thus, while we deplore the behavior of the defendants in deliberately violating the law, we are even more dismayed by the government's own behavior which destroyed the case against them. For when men in high places and others down the line claim they may break the law to defend it, they themselves become "the instruments of destruction" of our law and liberties.

WINSTON-SALEM JOURNAL

Winston-Salem, N.C., May 24, 1973

On the face of it, the jury verdict in a federal trial in Camden, N.J., this week appeared to be a miscarriage of justice.

On trial were 17 antiwar activists for breaking into a draft board office and destroying records of the Selective Service. The facts of the case were never in dispute. The defendants were caught redhanded, and there was a score of FBI agents to testify against them. A plea of innocent could be based only on the self-proclaimed morality of ending the war by destroying draft files. Yet the jury found the defendants innocent on all counts.

It was not sympathy for the defendants that moved most of the jurors, but an instruction from the judge. If the jury found that the government itself had *promoted* the crime for which it was prosecuting, the judge said, then the jury could find the defendants innocent. And that is what the jury found.

Among the group who broke into the draft office was an FBI informer who tipped off the FBI and helped them execute a dramatic capture, complete with television cameramen to record it on film. But the FBI informer the trial established, did much more than inform.

In the pay of the FBI, and with its approval, he joined the defendants and persuaded them to revive an old scheme of attacking a draft board. The FBI undercover man encouraged and planned the raid, provided most of the burglary tools and the expertise, and was in effect the mastermind of the group. "Without me and the FBI," he testified, the draft board raid would not have occurred.

What we have here is not the use of an informer, but an agent provocateur, one paid by the government to incite others to break the law and thereby invite the retaliation of the state. Apparently the Camden case is not the only one in which the FBI promoted such breaking of the law. According to an account in the Sunday Journal and Sentinel, one of the more notorious leaders of the Weathermen, the SDS splinter group, was not a student radical but an agent of the FBI. His mission was not to infiltrate and inform, but to incite others to acts of violence. According to the report he is now before grand juries, testifying against those whose crimes he encouraged and aided.

The judge's ruling in the Camden case sets a much needed precedent. The use of an agent provocateur is a tactic common to governments that fear their own people, and it has no place in a free society. If the FBI has not yet abandoned this abuse of law enforcement, then one hopes the judge's ruling will force it to do so.

The New York Times

New York, N.Y., May 23, 1973

The acquittal of seventeen members of the "Camden 28" and the prosecution's recommendation for dismissal of charges against the remaining eleven defendants is clearly part of a growing revulsion against abuse of governmental power. The anti-war protesters had been arrested in 1971 while breaking into a Federal building and destroying draft records. Since they subsequently admitted their action in court, their acquittal constitutes something of a legal landmark: it was based on the jury's finding that—though the defendants were guilty—their offense was dwarfed by the Government's deliberate use of an *agent provocateur* to assure the commission rather than the prevention of a crime.

The trial showed that Robert W. Hardy, who had acted as informer for the Federal Bureau of Investigation, had in fact provided the tools and the training without which the break-in could not have been accomplished. More important, at the Government's urging, Mr. Hardy actually reactivated the illegal foray after the protesters had all but abandoned it.

Under such circumstances, the Government's game plan could only be interpreted as a deliberate political maneuver to use the protesters as dupes in the Administration's design to discredit foes of its Vietnam policy. Federal District Judge Clarkson S. Fisher, recognizing the danger inherent in such perversion of police power, told the jury that it could acquit the defendants if it concluded that the Government's participation in setting up the crime had gone to lengths "offensive to the basic standards of decency and shocking to the universal sense of justice."

It is precisely such revulsion against governmental scheming and deception that offers hope for a broad-based return to elementary decency. A particularly affirmative sign is the assumption of leadership by the courts in this new drive to restore the balance between the Government's power and the people's rights. The reprimands to the Government, administered so recently by Judge William Matthew Byrne Jr. in the Ellsberg trial and now by Judge Fisher in the case of the Camden 28, are part of the essential process of curbing governmental arrogance.

The Salt Lake Tribune

Salt Lake City, Utah., May 30, 1973

The already snarled subject of police entrapment took another twist recently when 17 defendants in an anti-war demonstration case were found not guilty because a government agent helped encourage their vandalism. The verdict, as sensible as it may be, didn't coincide with an earlier one by the U.S. Supreme Court.

Late last month, the Supreme Court held by a 5-4 split that a defendant can't plead entrapment if he committed a crime he originally planned, even though an undercover policeman later helped lead him to the actual deed. The majority ruling turned on defining how much police "lured" the unsuspecting lawbreaker into the trap. New Jersey Federal District Judge Clarkson S. Fisher took a similar approach, but with different emphasis.

Judge Fisher, presiding over a trial of the so-called "Camden 28," told the jury that if the government had, indeed, "overreached" itself while using an infiltrator to persuade the 28 they should break into a federal building and destroy draft files, a "not guilty" verdict could be returned. That's what the jury concluded.

Understanding the entrapment questions is important since local and federal police obviously rely on the undercover method when it seems necessary. The old "I Was A Communist For The FBI," is being updated to a new book tentatively titled, "The Bombers: I Was A Weatherman For The FBI," written, if preliminary plans jell, by an informer planted with the Weathermen faction.

Early stories identify the man as 25-year old Larry D. Grantwohl, who infiltrated the radical, destructive student group known as Weathermen as an FBI contact. His testimony is currently being used against Weathermen members on trial. And it's claimed he could penetrate the organization because he so effectively preached, planned and carried out random violence.

So who's guilty? The undercover agents who help dream up bombings and riots, or those dumb enough to go along? One or the other or both? Judge Fisher's answer is the most logical and appropriate.

If someone or a group is capable of a crime, encouragement from the government to carry out such actions is uncalled for. And if undercover agents ignore the reasonable limits, possible convictions should be seriously jeopardized.

The legal complications of entrapment are bound to persist. But by emphasizing the policeman's responsibility in resorting to this potentially dangerous practice, courts can exert an essential measure of control.

The Charlotte Observer

Charlotte, N.C., May 22, 1973

A responsible politics of moderation has often been undermined by the violent provocations of the extreme left and the extreme right, sometimes with the two extremes actually helping each other. No one is certain today who burned the German parliament building in 1933 — the Communists, who were blamed by the Nazis, or the Nazis themselves, hoping to create hysterical fear of the Communists.

This comes to mind as each day's news brings evidence that government agents have been deeply involved in episodes of violence and law-breaking on the part of radical groups.

A jury in Camden, N.J., has freed 17 defendants charged with breaking into a federal building and destroying draft files. They were freed even though they admitted the deed. The judge had told the jurors they should acquit the defendants if they found the government had overstepped the bounds of propriety by using an agent to help foment the crime.

The agent, undercover FBI informer Robert W. Hardy, had testified the raid would not have taken place "without the FBI and me." The break-in could not have occurred, others testified, without Hardy's help.

On another front, it was disclosed over the weekend that a leading participant in bombings and violent demonstrations involving the extremist Weatherman group was an FBI informer named Larry D. Grantwohl. He is said to have taken the initiative in promoting violent actions, setting up his cohorts for arrest.

These are only the latest in a series of such revelations.

In the Philip Berrigan case, the government built its prosecution largely upon the word of an informer known to be a habitual liar. It emerged that he was not just an informer in dealing with the Berrigans but also a provocateur, pushing for illegal and violent actions. The jury rejected him; it apparently concluded that the government, not the Berrigan group, was the violent party involved.

The infiltration of extremist groups by FBI informers is not new, of course. FBI informers were so numerous in the Communist Party as it was collapsing a few years ago that the subject was a national joke. They also heavily infiltrated the Ku Klux Klan during its latest heyday and helped bring about the arrest of many Klansmen who had engaged in violence.

There were improprieties in some of those operations, and serious questions of informers' conduct were raised, especially in the case of the Klan. But the latest episodes seem to take the process a dangerous step further. The White House itself evidently has been involved in pressing secret illegal actions against dissenters, some of them hardly extremists, and even encouraging violence.

All of this can be viewed, on one level, as simply an abuse of power in the pursuit of alleged wrongdoers. But there is a deeper political implication. These were actions that helped the cause of national "law-and-order" candidates by fomenting disorders which they, bearing extremist solutions, could make the most of. Those at the top of the hierarchy, who ultimately were responsible for the work of the agent provocateurs, stood to gain politically.

We should recall the example of the Nazi "law-and-order" advocates, who fomented violence and behaved lawlessly while promising to restore order in a frightened Germany. We have not reached that point in the United States but sometimes it seems not so far away.

DURHAM ADMITS BEING FBI INFORMER WHILE IN AMERICAN INDIAN MOVEMENT

Douglas Durham, chief security officer for the American Indian Movement (AIM) during the trial of the leaders of the Wounded Knee occupation, admitted March 12 he had been a paid informant for the Federal Bureau of Investigation. Ken Tilsen, chief counsel for AIM, said the infiltration had constituted an "illegal invasion of the defense." AIM would file motions to have charges dropped against 30 remaining Wounded Knee defendants and to have convictions of nine others set aside, he said.

In an affidavit at the 1974 trial, Justice Department prosecutors had indicated they had no informers in the defense camp. Durham stated, however, "I exercised so much control that you couldn't see Dennis or Russell without going through me. You couldn't contact any other [AIM] chapter without going through me, and if you wanted money you had to see me." Durham, who was paid as much as $1,100 a month by the FBI, said his cover had been broken March 7, when suspicious AIM members confronted him with law enforcement documents establishing his role as an informer.

His first contact with the AIM leadership was as an undercover police operative working as a photographer for an underground newspaper, which assigned him to take pictures of the Indian take-over, Durham said. On returning from Wounded Knee, he was asked by the FBI to infiltrate AIM. A skilled pilot, he was quickly able to get close to Banks, whom he later flew around the country on speaking trips. Subsequently, he became AIM's security office at the trial, Durham said. He told AIM members he was one-fourth Chippewa. Durham said the FBI told him not to report on defense tactics, but to look for signs of foreign involvement, arms caches or plans for other take-overs.

The Des Moines Register

Des Moines, Iowa, March 22, 1975

The actions of the U.S. Department of Justice and Federal Bureau of Investigation in dealing with the American Indian Movement merit a congressional investigation.

Last fall, the eight-month trial of AIM leaders Dennis Banks and Russell Means ended in dismissal of charges when the federal judge charged the FBI with misconduct and the prosecuting attorneys with deceiving the court. The judge said FBI agents gave false testimony and had withheld or given altered documents to the defense.

The AIM leaders were charged in connection with the takeover of Wounded Knee, S.D., in 1973.

Now a former Des Moines policeman who served as AIM's security chief during the trial has announced that he was an FBI informer from the time he joined AIM in Des Moines in 1973. The agent, Douglas Durham, was AIM's chief security officer during the trial of the organization's leaders and had access to the room where defense strategy was discussed.

The issue here is not the use of a paid informer to keep posted on possible illegal activity by a suspect organization, but the possible use of a paid informer to violate the rights of individuals to a fair trial.

The Justice Department does not deny that Durham was an informer. But a department spokesman this week said that no information on defense trial strategy was passed to the FBI or prosecuting attorneys.

Durham had told reporters the previous week that his pay was increased at the time of the trial and he was given a special phone number for reporting defense strategy.

The charges and denials raise questions which merit investigation from outside the department. Congress should seek to get the facts of the Justice Department's handling of Wounded Knee prosecutions.

ST. LOUIS POST-DISPATCH

St. Louis, Mo., March 16, 1975

When leaders of the American Indian Movement were brought to trial for their role in the Wounded Knee incident, federal prosecutors produced a sworn affidavit saying the Government did not have informants in the AIM defense team. That testimony is now inoperative, much to the shame of the Justice Department.

The Federal Bureau of Investigation did have a paid informant who masqueraded as a key aid to the leader of AIM, Dennis Banks. Douglas Durham admitted publicly last week that he became so closely involved with the Indian movement that he often wrote position papers for it, established its national offices and attended secret strategy sessions. Mr. Durham said he even used $1000 provided by the FBI to rent a small plane and secretly fly Mr. Banks to Canada after the occupation of Wounded Knee. During all this time and after, Mr. Durham was on a monthly retainer of $1100 provided by the FBI in exchange for his services as a government spy.

U.S. District Judge Fred J. Nichol dismissed the Wounded Knee case last September after declaring that the prosecutor, the Justice Department and the FBI had engaged in misconduct in attempting to prosecute AIM's two top leaders. Judge Nichol's dismissal was based on unsupported allegations, complained Henry E. Peterson, then Assistant Attorney General. The judge's allegations were that the Government made "errors of judgment and errors of negligence," including the presentation of misleading witnesses and the offering of false testimony.

Now it turns out that Government government also lied in a sworn affidavit regarding infiltration of AIM. Mr. Durham says, in retrospect, he was bothered by his insidious role because he eventually developed an admiration for AIM's dedication to the Indian civil rights struggle. The case should not end here. It is the duty of Senator Frank Church's Select Committee on Intelligence to investigate such outrageous conduct by the FBI and to bring to account those responsible for what amounts to perjury by the Government.

The SENTINEL

Winston-Salem, N.C., April 23, 1975

The U. S. Department of Justice has failed again and again in the last few years to prosecute successfully its targets in "political" trials.

Among the failed cases are the Berrigan brothers' alleged plot to kidnap Henry Kissinger, Daniel Ellsberg's alleged theft of the Pentagon Papers, and numerous other cases brought against anti-war and anti-draft groups, the Black Panthers, and others.

Now to that list must be added the leaders of the American Indian Movement, the group that occupied Wounded Knee, S. D., in early 1973. That occupation was marked by violence and other acts witnessed on national television. Afterward, the government indicted two men, Dennis Banks and Russell Means, for assault on federal officers, larceny, and conspiracy. The evidence was overwhelming, but the government has lost its case forever.

The original trial ended after eight months when a juror became ill, and the government refused to let the trial go on without him. Subsequently it moved to retry Banks and Means, but a federal appeals court ruled that out last week as double jeopardy. Thus Banks and Means will go free (though Means was recently charged with murder in an unrelated barroom incident).

Why the government lost this case is a regrettable story. By the time the juror got sick, federal prosecutors had made such a shambles of their effort that they reportedly feared the 11 jurors remaining were ready to set Banks and Means free.

Throughout the trial, there were instances of government misconduct. So serious were FBI misdeeds in aiding the prosecution that federal Judge Frederick Nichol remarked in court, "It is hard for me to believe that the FBI, which I have revered for so long, has stooped so low."

What brought that comment from the judge was his discovery that the FBI was practically buying the testimony of a witness, by paying him large "relocation" fees and housing him at a plush resort.

Judge Nichol also found that agents suppressed documents showing prosecution testimony to be false. The FBI gave the court misleading information about wiretaps it had placed on the defendants' telephones. And recently it was revealed that the FBI spied on Banks and Means as they conferred in private with their defense attorneys.

A confidant of the defendants was actually an FBI informer working for $1,100 a month. During the trial, the government had denied in court that it had any informer in the defense ranks. Judge Nichol recently faulted the FBI, and not the prosecutors themselves, for misleading him with that denial.

In a study of why it has lost so many "political" cases, the Justice Department said last week that one reason was juries "at least partially composed of people willing to be convinced of government misconduct . . ." In the Wounded Knee case, unfortunately, there was plenty of that.

New York Post

New York, N.Y., March 15, 1975

FBI Director Kelley has recently speculated that current economic conditions may lead to increases in burglary and embezzlement. That may well be true; he could help keep the national crime statistics down by discouraging what can be reasonably termed perjury, fraud and obstruction of justice by his own Bureau.

Douglas Durham says the FBI paid him between $1000 and $1100 a month as an informer at the time he was serving as chief security officer for the American Indian Movement. According to Durham, who now plaintively says he regards AIM as a "concerned organization with high convictions" and grew to respect its leaders, he furnished the FBI secret details on their defense

strategy during the Wounded Knee trial. In that proceeding, the prosecution furnished a false affidavit saying it had no informants.

Kelley voiced his concerns about rising "white collar crime" during an appearance before the House Appropriations subcommittee.

It might give the crime-conscious Director pause for reflection if the committee reduced the appropriation by at least the amount paid Durham. Congress, moreover, has a duty to inquire into the Bureau's extensive funding of spies.

Buying information can often be a delicate matter; in this case the violations of rights and decency alike were flagrant.

Chicago Tribune

Chicago, Ill., March 17, 1975

The FBI, already embarrassed by having been caught with its thumb on the scales of justice during the trial of Dennis Banks and Russell Means on charges arising out of the Wounded Knee episode, has been embarrassed again. Recently American Indian Movement people intercepted a shipment of papers from their trusted colleague, Douglas Durham, to his superiors in the FBI. It turned out that Mr. Durham had been on the FBI payroll and had fed the FBI information from the A. I. M. inner circle—even during Banks' and Means' trial.

Government infiltration of a violent, anti-establishment outfit like A. I. M. should surprise no one. Durham was instructed especially to look for foreign involvement in A. I. M. Every government, including ours, has confidential agents, and would be inviting trouble and neglecting its duty if it did not.

But once the case went to trial, it was a different matter. For defendants in a criminal prosecution to have an unrecognized government agent in their inner circle is offensive to the American legal system as well as to the defendants. Our system requires that people facing criminal charges must be reminded that anything they say to government officials may be held against them. One of a defendant's rights is to be able to tell his advisers from government employes.

The FBI not only kept its man passing out information from the defense camp during a criminal trial; during the trial the government affirmed under oath that it had no informant in the A. I. M. defense team. Perjury becomes the prosecution no more than it does the defense.

Even before revelation of Douglas Durham's dual role, the courts threw out the case against A. I. M. leaders at Wounded Knee and scolded the prosecution. A. I. M. spokesmen now hope that further prosecutions may be clouded by the way the government deployed Mr. Durham.

The lesson here is that a government that wants justice done and guilty lawbreakers convicted needs itself to observe its own rules.

FBI REVEALS COUNTERINTELLIGENCE AGAINST SOCIALIST WORKERS PARTY

The Federal Bureau of Investigation made public over 3,000 pages of internal documents March 18 detailing agency efforts to harass the Socialist Workers Party, a splinter communist party loyal to the ideology of the Leon Trotsky, the Soviet revolutionary. (A civil suit filed under the amended Freedom of Information Act resulted in a federal court order compelling the FBI to release 3,138 pages of documents to the party and its youth affiliate, the Young Socialist Alliance.)

The documents showed that the party had been an object of FBI surveillance since 1944, as well as a target of the agency's counterintelligence program, Cointelpro, whose purpose was to disrupt party activities and harass party members and their families. According to the documents, Cointelpro had involved at 41 separate operations against the party between 1961 and 1971.

Among the activities described by the documents:

■ The arrest and conviction record of the party's candidate for a New York City political office was sent anonymously to the New York Daily News, which later published the information in one of its columns.

■ In 1963 an anonymous letter was sent to a black candidate for mayor of San Francisco, telling him of the presence of party members in his campaign staff.

■ J. Edgar Hoover, director of the FBI until his death in 1972, personally approved dissemination of anonymous leaflets designed to cause dissension among various political factions and parties of the far left.

■ An anonymous phone call alleged that a party-operated print shop was attempting to defraud the State of New York by creating bogus unemployment insurance claims for party members. (A state audit of the print shop's records in 1966 or 1967 produced one violation, a party spokesman said).

Spokesmen for the party said neither the parent organization nor its youth affiliate had been the subject of a federal prosecution since 1945.

The Kansas City Times

Kansas City, March 21, 1975

The Socialist Workers Party is a small, ineffective leftist organization that appears to have been the target of intimidation by the Federal Bureau of Investigation. We have no way of knowing why the FBI decided that this miniscule Marxist group presented so clear and present a danger that it was worth such extraordinary attention. The FBI methods were disturbing and so was the silent, surreptitious way in which the machinery of harassment was put into motion.

Is the supreme law enforcement agency of the nation supposed to send around anonymous letters and pass on gossip with the intention of injuring or destroying reputations because individuals were members of a political group? Does the FBI really have this sort of authority to make charges, judge and punish without benefit of the courts? That is what it amounts to when jobs are threatened and anonymous, defaming letters are written.

Of course the Socialist Workers Party is small and rather pathetic, friendless in this country and with no political significance. It may have a capacity for mischief far beyond its numbers, and possess a potential for harm of which the FBI has knowledge. Certainly only the naive would deny that there are American citizens who would bring down the structure of democratic government while using democratic freedoms for that very purpose.

But the FBI cannot preserve democracy by skirting the Constitution. The Bill of Rights must apply to all, including the Socialist Workers Party, and it must above all be followed by law enforcement agencies. Constitutional rights cannot be suspended when they are inconvenient. No agency, however powerful and with whatever good motives, has the authority to make a judgment and zero in on victims who, by someone's definition, pose a national threat. That is a procedure for the rules of law and the courts.

J. Edgar Hoover may have operated that way. We will not believe that Clarence Kelley does. There is a vast difference between gathering information and using investigative procedures to coerce and punish, and to send out phony letters. The country has had enough of that.

DAYTON DAILY NEWS

Dayton, Ohio, March 20, 1975

To the list of organized crime operations, add the FBI.

Is that too harsh? It has become clear the bureau was involved in widespread, highly organized and thoroughly illegal subversion of a broad array of political, civil rights and antiwar groups. The techniques included abuse of confidential information, personal harassment, misuse of law and violence. It is no longer possible to shrug off the bureau's misdeeds as passing indulgences of the late Director J. Edgar Hoover's occasional political manias.

The lastest revelation from FBI documents: For a decade, the bureau harassed the Socialist Workers party. It maneuvered to get members fired from their jobs, leaked unsavory items about their personal lives to the media, encouraged local police to arrest them for petty offenses, fomented violence at party demonstrations.

In this instance, the campaign not only was unconstitutional. It was nutty. As a political force, the Socialist Workers party ranks with the anti-vivisectionist and temperance parties. It has attracted enthusiasts by the half-dozen, a problem the party now will be able to blame on the FBI's interference.

Even assuming that this was another of the little psychodramas the bureau acted out for Mr. Hoover's political therapy, the emerging evidence of the scope and frequency of such efforts makes it clear that they could not have been undertaken without the serious involvement of some officials in the bureau's command. Officials in decision-making positions at least permitted and accommodated, perhaps additionally encouraged, the FBI's lawlessness.

Those ought to be identified, fired if they have not already left the bureau, prosecuted if their involvement was substantial.

This is no little matter. The FBI's misbehavior is not less serious for having been directed at fringe groups; it is more serious.

It is precisly for such groups that civil liberties are necessary. As a practical matter, there is little need to protect the liberties of ordinary, broadly-based movements; the right to be mainstream is unchallenged. The violation by the government of the political freedom of fringe groups, however, is only another way of saying that Americans have the "right" only to be Democrats or Republicans or indifferent.

Wisconsin ▲ State Journal
Madison, Wis., March 24, 1975

More shocking activity by the Federal Bureau of Investigation has come to light.

Two former FBI agents said the agency carried out illegal kidnapings of a number of persons in the United States it believed to be clandestine foreign agents.

Earlier, FBI documents made public in a court suit show that the agency harassed the Socialist Workers Party for a decade with efforts to have members dismissed from their jobs, leaks to news media of damaging items about their private lives and attempts to foment violence at demonstrations.

In this instance the FBI operated on the home front in the same covert manner that the Central Intelligence Agency has been operating abroad to undermine "unfriendly" political parties and governments.

This kind of activity is uncalled for and dangerous to a free society. It again points up the necessity for a complete review and overhaul of the so-called "intelligence community" in this country.

The Standard-Times
New Bedford, Mass., March 23, 1975

There is a tendency to dust off that once overworked word "dupes" in assaying the current hue and cry from within the United States against two of its pillars of security, the Federal Bureau of Investigation and the Central Intelligence Agency.

A court decision has opened the FBI files on the Socialist Workers party which is suing the FBI for "damages." The files show the agency, under the late J. Edgar Hoover, harassed the party in an effort to undermine its credibility with the public and its influence in domestic affairs.

The tactics used included writing unsigned letters to various organizations, including newspapers and magazines, containing "unsavory" references to persons active in or closely connected to the Socialist Workers party. The reaction to the disclosure in several supposedly influential quarters has been that this is another flagrant example of FBI intrusion into personal rights.

We disagree. The Socialist Workers party has been identified by a former U.S. attorney general (the late Tom Clark) as "a subversive and Communist organization which seeks to alter the form of government of the United States by unconstitutional means." Various U.S. House reports have cited it as a "dissident Communist group."

In April, 1971, Congressman Ichord, D-Mo., told the House that the Committee on Internal Security, of which he was chairman, had found the Socialist Workers party to be a "Communist faction...which advocates the overthrow of the government by force," although of "Trotskyite" and not of official Communist party direction.

It so happens that the FBI, under the Internal Security Act of 1950, is directly charged with "the responsibility...for investigation of espionage, sabotage or subversive acts." Anonymous letters in the course of such action may be dirty business, but much of the FBI's duty is the probing of dirty business. (This newspaper, and we believe most others, do not use anonymous letters, by the way.)

In short, if Mr. Hoover's concept of his job involved harassment of a group like the Socialist Workers party we are not one to find fault. Indeed, we wonder whether some of those complaining now would be so vociferous if the files had concerned the Ku Klux Klan (which, incidentally, Hoover also harassed) instead of an anti-American group constantly parroting its "rights."

The CIA also is still getting a battering, the latest evoked by its multimillion dollar expenditure and subsequent effort in attempting to raise a sunken Soviet submarine off Hawaii. Was the expense worth it, some have intoned? Was there a risk of annoying the Soviet Union if the latter had got wind of the adventure? Has the CIA entirely leveled with us, wonders a freshman congressman?

How irrelevant, how destructive of our own institutions can one get? We have no doubt the effort was worth every penny — from a counterintelligence point of view and, looking ahead, as a development in submarine-raising or submarine-saving that may stand us in priceless stead with regard to our own Navy. Have critics forgotten the 1966 misadventure when an American atomic bomb was lost in the sea off Spain, requiring an agonizing and massive multimillion dollar search of three months to regain it before it could fall into potential hostile hands?

The question of a confrontation (and who is in a position to say any such situation would not have been resolved diplomatically?) really depended on how secret was the expedition. The CIA was able to preserve that secrecy with the cooperation, up to now, of some senators and congressmen and those in the news media who had inkling of it. The actual danger has come with the regrettable action of one newspaper source in Washington in breaking that bond — and perhaps, ruining any chance of completing an enormous intelligence coup.

Security doesn't come cheap, nor at the hands of the inexperienced. But many of the critics of the FBI and CIA seem to feel its a Marquis of Queensbury, open-book game like weight-watching. May we be preserved from the amateurs.

Detroit Free Press
Detroit, Mich., March 21, 1975

AMERICANS engaged in the political process of this country should not be subject to harassment by law enforcement agencies of the federal government.

The FBI and its current director, Clarence M. Kelley, claim the bureau in 1971 halted its activities of harassment and sabotage against unpopular and even radical political groups.

Since he took over the FBI, Mr. Kelley has given us little reason to doubt his word, and the new attorney general, Edward Levi, has made it clear he abhors such tactics and plans to prohibit them.

The latest revelations on how the FBI treated the left-wing Socialist Workers Party show good reasons why such programs should be stopped. Three thousand pages of the FBI's own documents show the bureau's agents systematically tried to sabotage the party's political campaigns and damage the personal and professional reputations of some of its members and leaders.

It is not necessary that one adhere to the programs of the Socialist Workers Party to realize that such tactics could be used against any political organization. Why not right-wing Republicans next? Or members of George Wallace's American Independent Party? Or left-wing Democrats?

If and when the FBI believes that members of any political group are breaking the law, it then has not only a right but a duty to investigate their activities and to bring charges against them if the activities warrant such action.

But the harassment of political groups by the FBI should not be allowed in an open society.

Such repressive measures always have a way of backfiring and even, in some cases, of increasing the influence of those groups subjected to such tactics.

Des Moines Tribune
Des Moines, Iowa., March 20, 1975

The Federal Bureau of Investigation's own documents show that the agency was deeply involved in interfering with political campaigns and individual rights. The FBI has been disclosed at work on such diverse groups as the Socialist Workers party and the Boy Scouts of America. Even the American Legion was not spared the FBI's attentions.

A federal court order forced the FBI to reveal documents involving the Socialist Workers party, which is suing the agency for $27 million, charging that the party's constitutional rights were violated.

The FBI's documents show that its agents mailed anonymous letters aimed at damaging personal and political reputations of Socialist Worker party members.

The tactics grew out of an FBI counterintelligence program (COINTELPRO) against the New Left, black militants, the Ku Klux Klan and foreign espionage agents. The FBI has said that COINTELPRO ended formal operations — which had stretched over the Fifties and Sixties — in April, 1971. Spokesmen for the Socialist Workers party say they have evidence that the FBI still is sabotaging the party.

The FBI was intended to be an investigatory arm of the government, not a political weapon against right, left or middle. In the role of agent provocateur, the FBI undermined the freedoms it was assigned to protect.

The FBI and its role deserve as close public scrutiny as has been ordered for the Central Intelligence Agency.

The SENTINEL
Winston-Salem, N.C., March 21, 1975

Clarence Kelley, the FBI director, said recently that he might order extra - legal tactics to be used again against political fringe groups, if he felt the circumstances warranted such action.

Kelley was referring to a defunct FBI program known as "COINTELPRO," the abbreviation for counter-intelligence program. This effort, halted for unknown reasons in 1971, included FBI actions that could "only be considered abhorrent in a free society," a Justice Department report stated last year. Its targets were political fringe and protest groups that the late J. Edgar Hoover considered beyond the pale of true - blue Americanism.

This week the FBI, under court order, released documents showing a long campaign of harassment, disruption and intimidation of Americans exercising their right to affiliate with the Socialist Workers Party. The group had filed a damage suit against the bureau, claiming the FBI has repeatedly violated its civil liberties.

We would not bid a nickel for the SWP party line, which stems from the old - time working - class theories of Leon Trotsky, the Bolshevik who was exiled, and later murdered by Soviet agents in Mexico City. But as radical groups go, the SWP is harmless. In granting the SWP a restraining order against the FBI last year, federal Judge Thomas P. Griesa told the bureau, "You have been looking at this group for 35 years, and you haven't produced a single solitary crime or incitement to violence in the U. S. by anyone in this organization."

Nonetheless, the FBI's harassment of the SWP bears the marks of a police - state operation. Agents concocted false letters and sent them anonymously to damage individuals connected with it. Even a Boy Scout leader, whose wife was a member, was defamed and seen as a subversive, though the bureau could find nothing amiss in his background.

Yet the man was branded as "a distinct threat to the scouting movement and (he) should be removed or neutralized." And he was, with an agent duly reporting to Hoover that the bureau's clandestine work "reflects the successful application of the disruption program for a worthy cause."

Other spurious letters were used to sow dissension in the ranks of the SWP, and to discredit and harm persons connected with it. As was revealed last year, the FBI even began a subversive file on a teen-age schoolgirl when her letter, addressed to another political group, was received by the SWP through a postal error.

This activity on the FBI's part is far outside the bounds of its mission. That Director Kelley has not renounced the "COINTELPRO" effort entirely raises the question of whether he is the right man to lead the FBI. Political groups like the SWP have been on the ballot for decades, and have gotten nowhere. We have far less to fear from them than from an FBI that distrusts the democratic process, and tramples on the rights of American citizens.

The Courier-Journal
Louisville, Ky., March 25, 1975

LAST FALL, when a Justice Department report lifted the wraps off a dirty tricks operation that the FBI had run against domestic political groups between 1956 and 1971, it was evident that another skeleton had fallen from the agency's bulging closet. But flesh has now been added to the bones of this counter-intelligence program with the court-ordered release of files relating to the FBI war on the Socialist Workers Party.

The intrigue with which the agency went after this organization would be comic except for two factors. One is that some individuals suffered needlessly as a result of this government harassment. The other is that such an illegal use of authority, even against a minor radical organization, has a Kremlin-like ring with disturbing implications for a free society.

The Socialist Workers Party evidently had been the object of intensive investigation for over 30 years, but with no findings warranting prosecution. In the troubled 1960s, however, the FBI went beyond normal surveillance to mount a full-scale, covert effort to disrupt the party's activities. Its methods included tips to news media about unsavory details of the private lives of members who ran for political office, and sending anonymous letters to employers in the hope that members would lose their jobs. Moreover, in most of its in-vestigatory work, the agency seems to have relied for authority on portions of federal laws that had been declared unconstitutional.

Why so much official energy was expended on one small political organization is far from clear. Certainly the party is radical, with origins in the Trotskyite movement that broke away from the mainstream of communism in the 1920s. But its political appeal in this country always has been slim; its membership is a mere 2,500, compared with the orthodox Communist party's claim to 15,000 members. No one seriously thinks it to be a front for any foreign Communist government, nor was it ever linked to the domestic violence of the past decade.

The extent of the FBI operation against this one small party raises the suspicion that the agency is so overstaffed and overfunded that it needs this kind of clandestine activity to keep idle hands at work and to gull Congress at budget time. But far more serious questions arise from the fact that the nation's chief law enforcement agency (led by a man who was collecting private dossiers on congressmen) deliberately and persistently engaged in operations it knew to be illegal. This is the aspect that congressional committees currently investigating abuses in government intelligence-gathering will want to probe.

THE BLADE
Toledo, Ohio, April 5, 1975

CONFIDENTIAL documents stolen from a Federal Bureau of Investigation office in Media, Pa., in 1971 and subsequently made public have led to the unfolding of the FBI's relentless intervention and interference with the activities of the tiny Socialist Workers party. In bringing suit against the Government, the party recently made public an astounding 3,138 pages of documents compiled by the FBI that detailed a campaign of harassment between 1961 and 1971 that trampled individual liberties for no discernible reason.

This strange preoccupation with a political group whose membership at its peak numbered 2,000 and in subsequent decades since 1940 has been around 500 is all the more puzzling since the FBI has never brought a federal suit against it or shown any link between it and any foreign power.

Plainly, the handful of members of this group, and others whose expressed political or social views never were shown to be subversive or in any way endangering freedom in our democracy, had become an obsession with J. Edgar Hoover.

By creating inside his bureau a counterintelligence program (Cointelpro), Mr. Hoover ordered his agents throughout the country to direct disruptive activities and to discredit reputations. A scoutmaster, for example, whose wife was a Socialist Workers party member was drummed out of scouting when Mr. Hoover ignored his agent's "clean" report and informed national Boy Scout headquarters of this man's "subversive background." The civil rights movement and its leaders also came increasingly under the Hoover obsession to persecute if not destroy groups and individuals whose stands he detested. The credit ratings, family relations, and employment status of others were undermined through memos alleging illegal, immoral, radical, and Communist party activities. Anonymous and fictitious letters also raised havoc.

Those excesses on Mr. Hoover's part constituted a horrible waste of the intelligence and skills within the 8,500-man bureau and all the backup staff required to handle the mass of paperwork trivia that each single assignment touched off.

What also is worrisome is the apparent readiness of so many Americans to accept as proper and justifiable the constitutional violations of citizens' rights if they are perpetrated by an otherwise respected body of law enforcement experts such as the FBI. There is a tendency to think that nobody should be concerned about the possibility of government agents investigating him or invading his privacy if he has done nothing wrong. This blind acceptance of authority without challenging propriety or usefulness is as much a threat to our freedoms as are the acts of the Government that violate constitutional protections.

AKRON BEACON JOURNAL

Akron, Ohio, March 18, 1975

ALONG WITH the CIA, the FBI is being boiled in the alphabet soup in Washington, as congressional investigations of the security agencies get under way. Things are already getting mighty hot.

This is the first time the Federal Bureau of Investigation has ever really submitted to having its soiled linen hung out for the public to ogle. Under the long regime of J. Edgar Hoover, the bureau went to incredible lengths to spit-shine its image as the gang that only shot straight.

But, with Mr. Hoover's death, the image cracked and reality started to seep through, revealing signs that this powerful agency had strayed from its authority.

Atty. Gen. Edward H. Levi has confirmed to congressional investigators that Hoover kept secret files on Presidents, high government officials and members of Congress. The dossiers included juicy — but but unsubstantiated — gossip, information about sex and drinking habits and other tidbits which could embarass the high ranking officials.

There is evidence that Presidents Kennedy, Johnson and Nixon misused FBI information, and a strong possibility that Mr. Hoover passed derogatory information on a member of Congress to White House officials.

The latest information to be added to the growing list is the FBI's alleged treatment of the late civil rights leader, the Rev. Martin Luther King Jr. Former FBI men say the bureau tried to silence Rev.

King's criticism of the FBI by mailing to Mrs. King an "unsavory" tape recording made by a secret bug in King's hotel room.

One retired FBI man, Arthur Murtagh, called the effort to "harass" Mr. King second in scope "only to the way they went after Jimmy Hoffa."

To their credit, both Mr. Levi and FBI director Clarence Kelley seem determined to clean up whatever mess is found at the FBI. The first necessary step is to get all the information on wrongdoing on the table. Only then can the Congress determine what must be done to be sure the FBI is under adequate restraint so that it can't abuse its authority and threaten constitutional rights of Americans.

Atty. Gen. Levi has already outlined some steps which sound promising — limiting White House access to FBI files, pulling irrelevant information from existing files, and supporting a law making misuse of FBI files an offense.

Mr. Kelley ordered an internal investigation earlier this year into whether the FBI improperly solicited or misused information on congressmen.

The FBI certainly can't be happy about all of this unfavorable exposure, but the congressional investigation now under way is vital to regain public confidence in the agency. It is important to remember that the price of protecting our individual liberties includes eternal vigilance of agencies such as the FBI which are entrusted with power to protect them.

THE LOUISVILLE TIMES

Louisville, Ky., March 12, 1975

Reports of FBI harassment of the late Dr. Martin Luther King Jr. are among the most disquieting in the long list of recently disclosed abuses by the agency. The mailing of an "unsavory" tape recording of Dr. King to his wife in hopes of breaking up their marriage and reducing Dr. King's effectiveness was a stunt unworthy of an adult human being.

That Dr. and Mrs. King shrugged the tape off is a testimony to their "class" as human beings. The action also speaks volumes—none of them good—about any agency which permits or tolerates such behavior.

Amsterdam News

New York, N.Y., March 15, 1975

Last Sunday, the New York Times quoted a former high official in the Federal Bureau of Investigation as saying that a tape of the proceedings at a party attended by Dr. Martin Luther King Jr. and other Southern Christian Leadership officials was sent to Dr. King's wife. The tape supposedly documented "unsavory" activity.

The late FBI director J. Edgar Hoover personally ordered that the tape be sent in a plain, unmarked package. He didn't want it traced back to the FBI. His precaution is understandable. The act was in violation of the FBI's own regulations, the Federal Communications Act and the Federal Criminal Code.

The former FBI official said further that thousands of FBI hours had been spent on the electronic and physical surveillance of Dr. King. It was J. Edgar Hoover who said Dr. King was "the most notorious Communist in the country." So the late director evidently decided to employ the techniques of the Kremlin to watch him.

This latest revelation is only a tiny portion of the long history of FBI harassment and surveillance of Black leaders. That historical review must be made public once and for all.

The time is long overdue for a thorough investigation of FBI activities by Congressional committees on intelligence. The American people have a right to know the real episodes in the FBI story rather than those they see each week on television.

The SENTINEL

Winston Salem, N.C., March 15, 1975

Two more items in the news of the last week show again how easily secret government agencies may stray into fields where they have no business.

One is the Central Intelligence Agency and the dossier it compiled on a U.S. congresswoman, Mrs. Bella Abzug (D-N.Y.). Mrs. Abzug apparently aroused the CIA's interest back in 1953, when she served as legal counsel for someone called before the House Committee on Un-American Activities.

The CIA has been keeping track of her ever since. It opened mail she wrote on behalf of clients — a violation of lawyer-client privileges — and it monitored her political activity. If Mrs. Abzug gave a speech critical of the Vietnam war, that was duly recorded in the CIA files.

Why an agency set up in 1947 to spy on the Russians is snooping on elected U.S. officials is the unanswered question. The most innocent explanation may be simply that the agency has too much money to spend.

More alarming are new details of how the FBI attempted to smear the reputation of the late Dr. Martin Luther King Jr. A former FBI official told the New York Times that

the campaign waged against Dr. King was second in size "only to the way they (FBI agents) went after Jimmy Hoffa," the convicted Teamster boss.

As part of an attempt to discredit Dr. King as a national leader, the FBI anonymously mailed a tape recording, which it believed compromising, to his wife. That was a clear violation of federal law against using materials gathered in an investigation for purposes other than prosecution. Other agents report that the bureau "routinely" tried to prevent King from being honored by various groups by planting stories, including one that he pocketed money belonging to the Southern Christian Leadership Conference. But despite the FBI's extensive surveillance and wiretapping of Dr. King, the bureau never charged him with any crime. Rather, he was slandered.

Preventing such abuses of government power will take more vigilant oversight of CIA and FBI than Congress or the White House have been willing to undertake in the past. Despite the flurries of interest it has shown lately, Congress appears reluctant to assume the responsibilities.

LEVI TESTIFIES ON HOOVER'S FILES, PRESIDENTS' POLITICAL USE OF FBI

J. Edgar Hoover, director of the Federal Bureau of Investigation until his death in 1972, kept secret files with derogatory information on presidents, congressmen and other prominent persons, Attorney General Edward H. Levi disclosed to a House subcommittee Feb. 27. His testimony—Levi's first as attorney general—also indicated that the FBI had been misused by at least three presidents for political purposes.

Hoover's files, which dated to 1920, contained 164 file folders and jackets, 48 of which concerned "public figures or prominent persons," Levi told the Judiciary Committee's Subcommittee on Civil Rights and Constitutional Rights. Included in the 48 files, Levi said, was information on "presidents, executive branch employes and 17 individuals who were members of Congress." (Two of the men named in the files were still in Congress, Levi added.) One document suggested that derogatory material on a congressman who had attacked Hoover "was improperly disseminated," Levi said without elaboration.

Levi described five instances of "misuse of the resources" of the FBI. He did not name the Presidents who allegedly misused the agency, but Deputy Attorney General Laurence H. Silberman supplied the names to newsman after the hearing. Levi said one instance involved "a check of FBI files on the staff of a campaign opponent." According to Silberman, President Johnson made the request through an aide, Bill Moyers, about Sen. Barry Goldwater, the 1964 Republican candidate.

Chicago Tribune
Chicago, Ill., March 3, 1975

Atty. Gen. Edward H. Levi's disclosures about secret files kept by the late J. Edgar Hoover are appalling—tho not entirely surprising. On balance, tho, they add up to good news, if only because the truth is at last being acknowledged. Mr. Levi's testimony in itself is evidence that the danger represented by these files is ended, and is unlikely [or at least much less likely] to appear again.

In his first appearance before Congress as attorney general, Mr. Levi told a House Judiciary subcommittee Thursday that Mr. Hoover had kept "official and confidential" files of damaging information on at least 48 prominent Americans, including Presidents, executive officials, and 17 or more members of Congress. In at least one case, he said, there was evidence that Mr. Hoover had passed on to the executive branch information discreditable to a congressman who had attacked the director.

In retrospect, all of this may help to explain Mr. Hoover's 48-year grip on his job. To oppose him, it seems, was to put one's reputation in danger.

Mr. Levi's findings knocked a few dents in other halos, as well. He confirmed that Presidents Kennedy, Johnson, and Nixon misused the FBI's files and manpower for political purposes of their own. [An example was later cited by Justice Department spokesmen: In 1967, when a bureau of the Treasury Department was investigating President Johnson's long-time Senate protege Bobby Baker, Mr. Johnson ordered the FBI to check up on the Treasury Department itself; he wanted to know whether any of the officials involved were friends or supporters of Robert F. Kennedy, then attorney general.].

Some members of the civil rights subcommittee were disturbed by one part of Mr. Levi's testimony. He said it was still a general FBI practice to accept and file unsupported charges, including those unrelated to any criminal or national-security investigation, on the ground that they might prove useful some time. The bureau has files on 6.5 million persons; it is not known what proportion of the files consist of unsupported charges.

Mr. Levi did pledge, however, that he will lay down guidelines to prevent misuse of FBI files. We are inclined to rely on his pledge for two reasons.

One is that his frank, detailed testimony about past abuses was the best possible evidence of his good faith in preventing future ones. Another is that Mr. Levi, besides being the right man for this job, is in precisely the right place. He is a trusted intermediary between Congress and the FBI—a kind of buffer who can block unwarranted attacks from either side, while making sure that the best interests of both are served.

If there was ever a time for productive dialog between lawmakers and executives on the duties, powers, and limitations of the FBI, this is the time. And Edward Levi, by virtue of both his office and his attitude, looks like the ideal moderator.

The Courier-Journal
Louisville, Ky., March 5, 1975

ONLY LAST YEAR the nation learned, through revelations about the operations of the Nixon White House before and after Watergate, about the value of having a politically independent FBI director. J. Edgar Hoover, it turned out, had stubbornly resisted attempted White House manipulation. His immediate successor, Nixon-appointee L. Patrick Gray, had been irresponsibly submissive to White House instruction.

Now, through the revelations of newly installed Attorney General Edward Levi, the nation is getting factual support for long-held suspicions that the late Mr. Hoover's independence and entrenched power, developed over four decades as FBI chief, were not unmixed blessings. The same national prestige and bureaucratic shrewdness that enabled him to fend off White House meddling in the operations of his agency made the FBI boss invulnerable to critics in and out of Congress. Yet Mr. Levi has confirmed reports that Mr. Hoover personally kept secret files on public figures, including members of Congress. Moreover, politically advantageous information from these files apparently was transmitted on occasion to former Presidents Johnson and Kennedy, when it suited Mr. Hoover's purposes.

This news doubtless will be dismaying to many Americans who assumed that, whatever shenanigans were going on in Washington, at least J. Edgar Hoover was above reproach. More importantly, it points up the danger of creating conditions — such as a long term in office—under which the director of the FBI can insulate himself from political pressures. If that happens, he can become an untouchable bureaucratic czar, the exact opposite of the eager-to-please Mr. Gray.

From all accounts so far, the current FBI director, Clarence Kelley, has instituted needed reforms and is a man of unquestioned integrity and professionalism. But permanent structural safeguards are needed to protect the FBI from political manipulation and to protect the nation from an autonomous national police chief.

The FBI director is appointed by and can be removed by the President. The appointment must be confirmed by the Senate. Once in power, however, an FBI director with few scruples and a yen for lifelong power has access to information that can be used to blackmail his opponents.

One possible safeguard would be a requirement that the FBI chief be subject to periodic reconfirmation by the Senate, as was once suggested by Senator Robert Byrd of West Virginia. Or perhaps the FBI director should serve a fixed term, say of six years, and not be allowed to succeed himself.

The position, at any rate, is much too sensitive to be allowed to become the lifelong preserve of any man or woman. The chances for abuse are far too great.

ARKANSAS DEMOCRAT
Little Rock, Arkansas, March 4, 1975

They finally found J. Edgar Hoover's own, personal, secret file. If there was much dynamite in it, we haven't heard the boom. But the big question now is, what is to be done with the 3 drawers of 164 files?

We'll bet we aren't the only one to say, burn it. What's tellable has already been told: Presidents Kennedy, Johnson and Nixon asked the FBI to scout their political enemies — which is wrong. We'd guess that Hoover saved these requests as "insurance." They ought to be publicized as an abuse.

But the rest sounds internally administrative or personal. It's these files that Atty. Gen. Edward P. Levi is talking about when he says he can't decide what to do with the stuff. We think Levi wants an order-to-destroy from the President. We think he wants Congress to say what we're saying: Burn the stuff.

No doubt, some would like to see the contents revealed — especially people who hate even Hoover's memory. But even they, in their zeal to prove him a dirty-minded old sensualist, couldn't argue for publication without convicting themselves of wanting to make public what he kept secret.

That's the point about the Hoover file — its secrecy. So far as anybody knows, only Hoover, in his lifetime, saw it. He marked the safe "OC" — official-confidential — but that's inaccurate. The files weren't part of FBI records. They were Hoover's files. Only once, Levi says, did Hoover draw on the files. That was to circulate around the executive department a personal report on a hostile congressman. Otherwise, nothing.

Almost certainly, some of the stuff is lurid and it may make Hoover look bad. But it was Hoover's job to play Johnny-at-the-Rathole. You can quarrel with his private outlook, but chit chat and scandal are both tools of intelligence. In any case, it doesn't necessarily stamp a chief-of-security as an immoralist to gather such details. Hoover's final secret file was his brain box.

And if there are folders on congressmen — well, as somebody said, who the devil are congressmen to be exempt from the security job the FBI does?

Anyway, these yellowed files don't prove that Hoover had anything on anybody. They're not evidence of anything — else Levi wouldn't talk of destroying them.

But the power to destroy, Levi says, can be as bad as the power to compile. We say, balderdash. Forget the power to compile — it was legal. As for the power to destroy, anything else would probably be unlawful, as well as unthinkable.

We think Levi wants suggestions. Ours, we repeat, is destroy the stuff. Considering their private nature, the files have already been seen by too many people, even if they are all authorized. Once the word about the "OC" file got around, Levi naturally had to look. But what he looked at should — consistent with security — be regarded as spent ammunition: Stuff that meant something only to a man now dead.

When all is told that is tellable, the rest is trash. Make a bonfire of it.

New York Post
New York, N.Y., March 1, 1975

Official Washington routinely requests vast sums to spend on improving national defense; a more modest investment might assure protection against a different kind of invasion— the sneak attack on personal privacy. Few deterrents now exist.

The subject has been recently revived by members of a House Judiciary subcommittee on Civil Rights and Constitutional Rights, with special reference to the filing system of the Federal Bureau of Investigation.

Newly-installed Attorney General Edward Levi has now confirmed suspicions dating back many years that the late FBI director J. Edgar Hoover kept scores of gossip-laden files on prominent federal officials. He also confirmed that Presidents Kennedy, Johnson and Nixon encouraged the practice by demanding FBI information for political use. Levi obviously regards that record with distaste. He has advised a Senate investigator that one major intelligence-gathering section of the Department of Justice has been deactivated, and promised to develop "guidelines" for future control of the files.

Are these disclosures and reforms adequate to eliminate the perversion of the FBI record-keeping apparatus? We doubt it. Just the other day, during a special tour of FBI headquarters, Rep. Drinan (D-Mass.) lagged behind his guides for a look at something more interesting: his own file. He then demanded that FBI Director Kelley bring the material to the meeting of the rights subcommittee.

The FBI thereupon issued an angry complaint about Drinan's alleged abuse of "private considerations," Kelley and Levi flatly refused to produce the records and both men subsequently argued that agency files unrelated to any criminal activity—as in Drinan's case—are still legitimate because the data might be useful to the government at some future point.

That is much too slender a rationale for keeping data on a law-abiding American on file at any law enforcement agency anywhere, much less the FBI. The issue is not whether the FBI and Department of Justice have the authority to gather facts. It is how that authority can be held accountable to prevent the abuse of Constitutional protections in which the government has freely indulged in recent years. "Guidelines" in these matters are not simple to draw. But broader citizen access to the files is clearly one valid safeguard.

The Washington Star
Washington, D.C., March 4, 1975

Testimony by Attorney General Edward Levi clearly shows that at least three former presidents used and abused the investigative power of the Federal Bureau of Investigation for political purposes. And the late FBI director, J. Edgar Hoover, not only was a willing accomplice but had some power plays going on his own.

One of the worst White House offenders appears to have been Lyndon Johnson. According to Justice Department officials, Johnson asked the FBI to gather data on Republican presidential candidate Barry Goldwater in 1964, had it wiretap the suite of Martin Luther King Jr. at the 1964 Democratic convention, had it look into Spiro Agnew's long distance telephone calls in 1968, and had it investigate a unit of the Treasury Department in 1965 for being so brash as to poke around in the affairs of his political protege, Bobby Baker.

Levi also told a House Judiciary subcommittee the other day that former Presidents Richard Nixon and John Kennedy, as well as Johnson, ordered the FBI in a "few instances" to report on certain activities of members of Congress who opposed presidential policies.

Hoover, on his own, kept secret files of derogatory information on a number of prominent people, including presidents, members of Congress, federal officials and others who he thought might be out to get him. It is not clear to what extent Hoover used his information as a political lever or to blacken reputations of his enemies, but testimony indicated that in at least one instance derogatory information on a congressman was disseminated to executive branch officials.

There are several points we would like to make about all of this:

Watergate investigators who so diligently dug into misuse of government agencies by the Nixon administration managed, either accidentally or deliberately, to overlook or play down flagrant abuses by previous administrations.

The public should not assume that the FBI is shadowing every congressman and other public official in town. Levi said the private Hoover files uncovered contained some 164 file jackets, of which 48 were on "public figures or prominent persons" and only 17 of which were on congressmen.

Members of Congress should be no more immune than other citizens from scrutiny by law agencies, when that scrutiny has a legitimate purpose.

Finally, the abuse of federal investigative authority, however much or little it was or is, has got to stop.

Congress should make it clear, through legislation if necessary, that the directors of the FBI and other federal agencies are subject to terms in the slammer if they don't stand up and tell presidents, "No!" when they order the misuse of governmental investigative apparatus. And Congress ought to make sure that no director of an investigative agency ever again will be allowed to attain the untouchable position J. Edgar Hoover held.

The Virginian-Pilot

Norfolk, Va., March 2, 1975

While he lived J. Edgar Hoover was sacrosanct, or nearly so. Although he was criticized toward the end, when he overstayed his years as chief of the Federal Bureau of Investigation, he still was popular with the public and he still was given the respect which is paid to power in Washington.

"The Federal Bureau of Investigation, the G-men, and Mr. J. Edgar Hoover form one of the most important elements of the American myth — symbols of perfection in detective methods, wholesome anti-communism, ruthless pursuit of gangsters and spies, and of a dedicated, puritanical but unselfseeking chief above and outside politics; the nation's watchdog and the President's counsellor," the British critic Cyril Connolly once wrote.

That image of J. Edgar Hoover has been somewhat tarnished in the wake of Watergate. We know now that he was not "above and outside politics," and that he connived occasionally at the FBI's involvement in matters political, usually at the instance of someone within the White House.

Appearing before a House Judiciary subcommittee last Thursday Attorney General Edward H. Levi and FBI Director Clarence M. Kelley testified to the abuses and "misuse of the resources" of the FBI occurring under Presidents Kennedy, Johnson, and Nixon. In each instance, the FBI files and/or FBI personnel were put to political uses, such as checking on critics and investigating political rivals' staff workers.

Furthermore, Attorney General Levi confirmed the common rumor that Mr. Hoover kept files with derogatory information about Congressmen and other persons in his own office, and one must suspect that he did not always resist the temptation to put them to what might be described delicately as persuasive uses.

Nevertheless, it is best to keep the matter in perspective. If Mr. Hoover was willing to cater to the baser instincts of Lyndon Johnson and Richard Nixon, if he occasionally titillated listeners in high places with the juicier tidbits about the private lives of public people, the blame must be shared by those that he pandered to.

Certainly the revelations do not dignify Mr. Hoover — though they do show that he was human, after all, beneath his stuffed shirt. It is no secret that he held his job too long or that he became cranky. It is no secret that Lyndon Johnson and Richard Nixon weren't very nice people. Both were by nature secretive and suspicious and, like a lot of old men who've grown used to having power, Mr. Hoover was stubborn and vain. It ought not to be surprising that he sometimes transgressed. It is one of the reasons why he died still in office. Politics ain't beanbag, as Mr. Dooley said.

But the fact that Mr. Levi and Mr. Kelley testified to the abuses is evidence enough that they do not persist. And it is also a fact that the FBI is dependable, effective, and honest. It is free from the corruptions by which lawmen are routinely tempted. Mr. Hoover never permitted the agents to be commercialized (as the astronauts are, for instance) or to be demeaned; he gave them a dignity and pride in their work. If the Bureau has a high reputation, an army of agents has earned it over the years. Give the bedeviled Mr. Hoover his due.

The Morning Star

Rockford, Ill., March 2, 1975

L. Patrick Gray could not bring himself to say it.

William Ruckelshaus fell mute as well.

But a Chicagoan new to the office of United States attorney general, Edward Levi, finally has said from the witness chair what was rumored for years — that the Federal Bureau of Investigation has been repeatedly misused for political snooping and blackmail.

Levi is a distinguished University of Chicago scholar and President Ford's choice for restoring the Department of Justice to a position of trust and respect.

Painful as the process is, Attorney General Levi is moving with dispatch to purge the FBI of its prior taint. The project bodes well for true adherence to law and order, for Levi's own distinguished career, and for the President's administration.

The record establishes that former FBI Director J. Edgar Hoover, who gave the FBI its initial prestige, then leached off it with all the heavy handedness of a cheap and corrupt politician.

In his private suite, Hoover kept tabs on the bedroom antics of public officials — Presidents to Congressmen. And he used the file to dispatch critics, to retain power and to blackmail as the occasion arose.

The same file shows that Presidents, Republican and Democrat, called upon and were given the services of the FBI for their own political advantage.

Thus, Lyndon Baines Johnson used the FBI to pry into Sen. Barry Goldwater's campaign staff and GOP doings. With singular impartiality, Johnson also set the FBI to sniffing after Democrats who might challenge the Johnson Presidency.

So too, Richard Milhous Nixon used the FBI to shadow his Republican critics and challengers.

This intrusion of the executive branch can be curbed, if not eradicated, by law. It remains for Congress to provide that law.

In that regard, one of the nation's laws that needs overhaul is the one that requires the FBI to keep every tidbit fed it, whether it bears on criminality or not, whether it is mere scandal or not. No wonder the dung heap stands so high.

Thanks to Edward Levi, the first shovel has been planted and we can begin digging out from under the accrued mess, revolting as it is.

The Cleveland Press

Cleveland, Ohio, March 4, 1975

There now can be no doubt that J. Edgar Hoover kept — and sometimes misused — secret files on presidents, congressmen and other prominent Americans during his 48 years as director of the FBI.

To those who knew or had reason to fear Hoover over the years, the testimony by Attorney General Edward Levi before a House subcommittee the other day probably came as no surprise.

The revelations should spur the FBI, under Clarence Kelley, and the Justice Department, under Levi, to make sure that such abuses of power are not repeated.

There is no legitimate reason for an FBI director to gather derogatory information on congressmen or others in public life who might disagree with his policies or opinions.

Yet the Levi testimony shows that Hoover kept 164 secret files. Among them were files on 48 prominent Americans, 17 of them congressmen, two of whom are still in office.

In at least one instance, Hoover passed along to "others in the executive branch" derogatory information on a congressman who had criticized him.

There also is evidence that Hoover sometimes gave such information to presidents to use against their political foes.

Perhaps "blackmail" is too strong a word, but such practices are an invasion of privacy and a threat to political dissent.

This is not to say that Hoover was an ineffective FBI director. He simply stayed too long and accumulated too much power.

Nor does it mean that a congressman, or any other public figure, should be exempt from criminal investigation if merited.

What it does mean is that the FBI should stick to law enforcement, avoid partisan politics and leave personal vendettas to somebody else.

The Boston Globe

Boston, Mass., March 3, 1975

The belated cleansing of J. Edgar Hoover's dirty linen ought to have a more salutary consequence than merely fortifying revisionist historians: If bits of information about the late FBI director's excesses have fed the rumor mills in Washington for years, the testimony on Thursday of newly-installed Attorney General Edward H. Levi represented the first official confirmation of the allegations.

Levi divulged that Mr. Hoover accumulated a personal cache of derogatory information about politicians and prominent persons, that in at least one instance he attempted to use the material to discredit a congressman critical of his administration of the FBI, and that he complied with the requests of several past Presidents in conducting investigations for partisan or improper purposes.

As the unsavory details of Mr. Hoover's transgressions become available, they will tarnish the reputation of a controversial American figure who became a kind of folk hero for bringing much needed discipline and professionalism to the FBI during his five decades as its director. But it is far better to remember Mr. Hoover warts and all.

It is regrettable that the sensationalism over Mr. Hoover has overshadowed the more immediate issue involving the voluminous FBI files. Levi disclosed that the agency maintains dossiers on 6.5 million Americans, apart from its records of criminal convictions and arrests.

The House Judiciary Subcommittee on Civil and Constitutional Rights, which summoned the Attorney General as part of an inquiry into the FBI's surveillance powers, ought to demand an accounting of these files. Levi acknowledged that some of them contain raw data, unsubstantiated by the bureau, as well as chaff unrelated to any criminal or national security investigation.

The FBI performs a legitimate function in gathering information as part of an investigation of a specific crime. But it exceeds its authority and violates civil liberties when it amasses data capriciously, as it did in 1973 when it started a file on a 16-year-old high school girl merely because she wrote the Socialist Workers Party as part of a social studies project, to cite but one example.

When an FBI file has no justification other than as an expression of disagreement with a particular political viewpoint, then it works as an intolerable encroachment on free speech. The file that the FBI keeps on Rep. Robert F. Drinan (D-Mass.), an outspoken opponent of the Vietnam war in the 1960s, apparently falls in this category.

Mr. Levi and the present FBI director, Clarence M. Kelly, deserve credit for admitting past abuses in the bureau and promising to frame guidelines to prevent their recurrence. The House subcommittee, on which Rep. Drinan is serving with his usual perseverance, ought to hold the FBI and the Attorney General to their promises.

THE STATES-ITEM

New Orleans, La., March 1, 1975

The truth is out and the groundwork is laid for congressional monitoring of the Federal Bureau of Investigation so that it will not be used as an instrument of political intrigue.

All the reports and rumors about the FBI's abuse of authority were confirmed by newly installed Atty. Gen. Edward H. Levi, Deputy Atty. Gen. Lawrence Silberman and FBI Director Clarence M. Kelley.

Appearing before a House Judiciary Subcommittee, Atty. Gen. Levi said the late Director J. Edgar Hoover filed derogatory information about presidents and congressmen in his office. Deputy Atty. Gen. Silberman said Presidents Lyndon B. Johnson and Richard M. Nixon used the FBI to investigate congressional critics and that Mr. Johnson had used the agency for political work.

Fleshing out the abuse of power, Director Kelley said the FBI under Hoover had given derogatory material to congressmen to use against other congressmen.

Mr. Kelley assured the committee, however, that there has not been one attempt to use the FBI politically in the 19 months he has been director.

Director Kelley's reassurances are comforting, but it is up to Congress to see to it that involvement of the FBI in political intrigue does not occur again. While the onus of overstepping authority cannot be lifted from the FBI, Congress must share the blame for its failure to keep a closer check on FBI operations during Mr. Hoover's authoritarian administration. Periodical congressional review of the agency to establish its degree of political involvement is needed.

The Houston Post

Houston, Texas, March 6, 1975

As the FBI comes under multiple congressional investigations to determine to what extent its immense powers have been abused by its own officialdom or its governmental superiors, questions will undoubtedly be raised about the agency's internal security law enforcement authority. In view of the evidence already put on the record by the Ford administration, we are likely to see recommendations that the bureau's powers be circumscribed.

Last week the House civil and constitutional rights subcommittee opened the first of a series of hearings planned by at least five congressional groups into the bureau's activities. The subcommittee heard testimony by Justice Department officials that the FBI, under the leadership of J. Edgar Hoover, gathered information on political opponents of the last three presidents, either at the request of the chief executives or their aides. Atty. Gen. Edward H. Levi also told the congressmen that Hoover kept files of derogatory information on a number of officials and, on at least one occasion, used them against an opponent.

Any abuse of the FBI's authority, whether by agents or officials of the bureau or by those higher in the executive branch, is deplorable. It undermines public confidence in the agency, damages employe morale and thus hurts the agency's effectiveness. But in examining ways to control misuse of FBI power, Congress must be careful not to cripple the bureau's legitimate counterespionage, national security and law enforcement functions.

This country has evinced an unfortunate tendency in recent years to over-react to mistakes and wrongdoing in high places. We not only want to punish or censure the offending officials, which is proper, but we often call for drastic changes in the institutions of which they are only the temporary custodians. Institutions, lacking the proper counterbalances, can become too powerful. Institutions can become obsolete. They may need to be abolished or altered to fit changing needs and conditions. But we should be extremely cautious about making such changes.

One of the primary responsibilities of the FBI is policing security within the United States. This role expanded greatly during and after World War II, putting the bureau in an increasingly delicate position because the potential for abuse has also vastly increased. But this does not diminish the need for the FBI with all its experience and expertise. Congress should keep this in mind, whatever steps it may take to curb abuses of the authority the agency must have to discharge its responsibilities.

The Evening Bulletin

Philadelphia, Pa., March 5, 1975

The testimony by the new U.S. attorney general, Edward H. Levi, comprises the latest installment of the sensational and apparently unfinished story of abuses by federal agencies.

Mr. Levi's disclosures that the Federal Bureau of Investigation conducted political espionage have confirmed that misuse of the FBI was systematic and not restricted to any single political party or President.

Many of the already disclosed FBI abuses such as harassing of political enemies and of dissidents could be directly traced to the almost unchecked power attained by J. Edgar Hoover, its director from 1924 when it was reorganized until 1972 when he died.

However, the incidents catalogued by Mr. Levi span three Washington administrations. They reveal that three holders of this country's highest office not only condoned Mr. Hoover's tactics of intimidation, but also ordered them used to promote their personal political ambitions. According to the attorney general, Presidents Kennedy and Nixon sought FBI reports on their opponents in Congress while President Johnson ordered the FBI to investigate opposing presidential candidates.

The failure to reveal these incidents in addition to the existence of 164 of Mr. Hoover's private files until three years after the former director's death raise questions about the candor of Mr. Levi's predecessors during that period.

Perhaps the most disturbing aspect of such systematic abuse is that it suggests an attitude that these were not abuses at all, but rather acceptable political tactics and prerogatives of an imperial presidency.

Putting a halt to such dangerous delusions requires increasing congressional check on the agency. This can best be undertaken by the Select Senate and House Committees currently investigating all intelligence agencies.

KELLEY ADMITS FBI BURGLARIES TO OBTAIN U.S. 'SECURITY' DATA

Clarence M. Kelley, director of the Federal Bureau of Investigation, admitted July 14 that the agency had conducted a number of burglaries and break-ins since World War II in order to get "information relative to the security of the nation." Speaking at a news conference to mark the start of his third year in office, Kelley said the break-ins had continued beyond 1966, previously given as the year they had been terminated, but that he himself had not been asked to approve any while serving as FBI director.

He described the number of break-ins he knew about as "not many" and said he did "not note in these activities any gross abuse of authority." They were not, he said, "a corruption of the trust that was placed in us." Kelley indicated that at the request of the Senate Select Committee on Intelligence the agency was compiling materials on past break-ins and would hand them over to Attorney General Edward H. Levi to decide the form and manner in which they should be given to the committee. Regarding the prospect of future FBI break-ins, Kelley added: "If ever anything of this type comes up—and I can't foresee this need—but if ever it did come up and it became a matter of grave concern, a matter that is to be solved only through such activity, I would present it to the attorney general and would be guided by his opinion as to such activity."

THE MILWAUKEE JOURNAL
Milwaukee, Wis., July 15, 1975

In confirming ugly stories about "national security" burglaries by FBI agents, Director Clarence Kelley isn't about to apologize.

Although Kelley says the practice has been halted, he defends past break-ins as legal and in the national interest. Moreover, he does not rule out the tactic in future cases of "grave concern." Rather, he says he would ask the attorney general for guidance and act accordingly.

Where does Atty. Gen. Levi stand? The latest pronouncement of the Justice Department is that a warrantless search, including surreptitious entry, is legal under "proper circumstances when related to foreign espionage or intelligence." This apparently means that if you have any connection with a foreign power you could be in line for an FBI "bag job."

That's chilling. Words such as "foreign intelligence" and "proper circumstances" can all too easily be stretched to cover a wide range of possibilities. Under extreme conditions—such as wartime—a case perhaps can be made for certain kinds of warrantless searches. But what the FBI did for nearly 30 years, and now apparently is willing to do in the future, is menacingly broader in scope.

There are two courses of action. One is in the courts where a clear ruling could be sought. Levi reportedly favors such a step. Although at least one lower court has basically rejected burglaries in national security cases, the Supreme Court has not directly addressed the point.

Another course is legislative. Sen. Church's committee investigating the CIA and other intelligence gathering agencies should dig deeply into the burglary question and recommend legislative safeguards. The nation has a historic commitment to privacy of home and possessions. It is a tradition worthy of fierce defense.

Los Angeles Times
Los Angeles, Calif., July 18, 1975

So many disclosures have surfaced so rapidly that the public may have become inured to still more revelations about improper activities of government intelligence agencies. Yet the admissions and comments Monday by FBI Director Clarence M. Kelley should not be permitted to pass unnoticed:

—The FBI for many years engaged in "national security" burglaries, and, presumably, foreign embassies in Washington were among the targets.

—The FBI still compiles "personal behavior" information on government officials, including members of Congress and prominent private citizens.

In defending the burglaries, Kelley said: "I am convinced that in these matters where there might be some criticism there is an underlying intent to do that which is good for the nation. I have not come across any activities which I would construe as being illegal or being directed toward personal gain or to enhance the personal reputation of anyone."

This analysis, even if accurate—which is doubtful—betrays a misunderstanding of the responsibilities of an agency like the FBI in a democratic society.

A warning some 20 years ago by Supreme Court Justice Felix Frankfurter goes to the heart of the problem. Frankfurter said, "The accretion of dangerous power does not come in a day. It does come, however slowly, from the generative force of unchecked disregard of the restrictions that fence in even the most disinterested assertion of authority."

Of special significance was Kelley's revelation that the FBI continues to collect personal information on congressmen and others who are not under criminal investigation. His explanation was nothing less than astonishing. He said such information, which includes sex and drinking habits, "might very well be helpful to us in later investigations." Of course it might, but that tactic is the very essence of a police state.

The bureau, Kelley said, is drawing guidelines, in cooperation with the Justice Department, to control the collection of "personal behavior" information not related to criminal investigations. No guidelines are necessary, because no American citizen should be the target of such an investigation.

"I have not reviewed files to find out about reporters, congressmen or other public figures," Kelley said, but here again he was wide of the mark. The discretion or lack of it, or the good intention of an FBI director or lack of it, does not meet the issue. Such files should not exist.

After the Senate Select Committee on Intelligence Agencies completes its investigation, Congress must redefine the roles of the FBI, the CIA and other elements of the intelligence community, which includes thousands of employes and which spends $6 billion to $8 billion a year. Their secret operations, and the manpower and billions they command, give them vast power. That power must be brought under firm control.

Some mechanism must be devised that is more effective than the present oversight committees of Congress, which, based on their record, could be more accurately dubbed the "overlook" committees of Congress.

OREGON **Journal**
AN INDEPENDENT NEWSPAPER
Portland, Ore., July 18, 1975

The Charlotte Observer
Charlotte, N.C., July 20, 1975

When is a burglary not a burglary? When it is committed by the Federal Bureau of Investigation, according to FBI Director Clarence Kelley.

Mr. Kelley answered that riddle last week after admitting that FBI agents had been burglarizing offices of various domestic and foreign organizations for 30 years — but not, he said, since he took over as director in 1973. He said some of those burglaries would be "imprudent, in today's context."

Imprudent? They'd be criminal, just as they were when they were conducted. Attorney General Edward Levi quickly set the record straight on that the day after Mr. Kelley's astounding statement. The agents who committed the burglaries, and their superiors who issued the orders, should be sent to prison. That's improbable, to be sure; even Mr. Levi, who knows a crime when he sees one, didn't sound enthusiastic about putting federal law enforcement officers behind bars.

But why not? If persons who swear to uphold the law don't mind breaking it for their own convenience, why should anyone else? If the Nixon years taught us anything, it should be that this country's democratic processes are in grave danger if the most powerful people in government consider themselves above the law.

The Bill of Rights, bolstered by nearly two centuries of legal interpretation, clearly outlaws such vigilante actions. There are established legal procedures for securing the authority to conduct legal searches. Those procedures insure the right of the public to combat crime while protecting individuals from harassment by the government. An FBI agent who flouts the law and becomes a burglar should be treated like any other burglar. Mr. Kelley's contention that FBI burglaries are all right because the FBI has "good intentions" is ludicrous and shocking.

Where do they find these people to direct the FBI? Does the office do something to them? J. Edgar Hoover ran it as a personal fiefdom for decades, using his power to intimidate congressmen, titilate Presidents with risque tapes obtained illegally, conduct illegal searches and smear people he disliked. Then came L. Patrick Gray, who departed in disgrace after admitting he destroyed Watergate evidence. Now comes Mr. Kelley, who thinks burglaries are all right if they're his agency's burglaries.

If the FBI and other government agencies are to regain the public's respect, they must be led by officials who believe the law applies equally to everyone — even to government officials.

In Washington, D. C., Clarence M. Kelley, FBI director, has said that until recent years the FBI had been breaking into foreign embassies "and other places," without warrants in national security cases.

Now, Edward H. Levi, our new U. S. attorney general, is attempting to get a Supreme Court ruling on the legality of "surreptitious entries."

We who live in these United States believe that ours is a country where law and order prevail, even if we have to double bolt our doors and in some cases are wise not to walk the streets at night.

At least we know and the marauders know what the law is and the possible consequences of breaking it. And we know that in most cases we are protected again warrantless search.

We also know that there are among us those who owe allegiance to a foreign power, often who are employes of a foreign embassy, who do not recognize our law.

Under most circumstances, such as the customs search or diplomatic mail pouch searches, they are immune from U. S. law.

How, then, to deal with their activities? At what point and by whose decision are members of organizations such as the FBI entitled to act in a manner contrary to our normal lawful procedure in the name of national security?

In a letter defending the legality of warrantless surveillance, including surreptitious entry, the Justice Department last May said these are justified, "under proper circumstances when related to foreign espionage or intelligence."

FBI Director Clarence Kelley, at a news conference, said, "The FBI has conducted surreptitious entries for national security. We acted in good faith. The actions were reasonable. The impact was to protect the country."

This sounds reasonable. But what are the "proper circumstances" to which the Justice Department refers? Who is to determine what "national security" is? And who is to determine whether or not the FBI acted in the "good faith" of which Kelley speaks?

One of the reasons that the CIA now finds itself in trouble is that someone exercised faulty judgment when deciding questions like these.

Perhaps no one, not even the Supreme Court, from which Attorney General Levi seeks an opinion, can lay down rules to cover all cases.

Guidelines will help but in the final analysis, probably we will have to hope that presidents appoint men to head surveillance agencies who have good judgment and respect at least the rights of citizens who may be the subject of investigation.

The Salt Lake Tribune
Salt Lake City, Utah, July 16, 1975

"Surreptitious entries" is how Director Clarence M. Kelley euphemistically describes the way some Federal Bureau of Investigation agents during the 1960s violated the United States Constitution.

But the breaking into and entering of foreign embassies or the offices of civil rights groups and other domestic organizations was quite all right Mr. Kelley says, because "the intent was a very good one, to protect the country."

Protect the country from what? A relative few civil rights activists, whose primary goal was to gain for every American the same liberties and rights already enjoyed by the then lily-white FBI.

It gets a little tiresome hearing federal bureaucrats condone their violations of the fundamental principles of this country with weak-kneed excuses that their actions, no matter how reprehensible, were done "to protect the country."

In fairness, it must be emphasized the "surreptitious entries" were authorized and carried out during the tenure of Mr. Kelley's predecessor, the late J. Edgar Hoover. And a measure of commendation is due Mr. Kelley for revealing the past practices. The revelations are very much in accord with the new "openness" that has characterized the FBI since Mr. Kelley took over two years ago.

Nevertheless, it is impossible to accept Mr. Kelley's defense of actions that were in direct violation of the Fourth Amendment of the U.S. Constitution. No portion of this nation's basic law grants anyone the right to illegal search and seizure on the basis that it might "protect the country."

The Fourth Amendment does provide for search, but only " . . . upon probable cause, supported by oath or affirmation, and particularly describing the place to be searched, and the persons or things to be seized."

Technically, it might be wrong to describe "surreptitious entries" as "burglaries." A burglary is generally defined as the illegal entry of a premises with intent to commit a felony, most often theft or larceny. While FBI agents of a former day might not be guilty of burglary, they have, as Mr. Kelley quite publicly acknowleged, committed a massive violation of one cardinal principle of this nation. They indulged in illegal searches.

Mr. Kelley asserted, "I do not note in these activities any gross abuse of authority. I do not feel that it was a corruption of the trust that was placed in us." The statement rings hollow. "Surreptitious entries" are a trampling of the rights every American has under the Constitution. And any FBI agent who indulged in them violated the oath of office in which he swore to uphold and defend the Constitution.

Protecting the country is an honorable undertaking, but only if it is done according to the principles spelled out in the Constitution. Those FBI agents who surreptitiously entered the offices of any civil rights group or any other domestic organization were not behaving honorably and they have absolutely corrupted the trust placed in them.

Detroit Free Press

Detroit, Mich., July 16, 1975

THE TRUTH is slowly coming out about the government's massive violations of our civil rights and liberties. The process is gradual but inevitable. Each time it seems that the last abuse has been exposed, some new bombshell explodes.

The latest episode in this lengthy drama came Monday, when FBI Director Clarence M. Kelley confirmed prior reports that FBI agents had committed unauthorized break-ins and burglaries against civil rights groups and other domestic political organizations.

Mr. Kelley admitted that the burglaries—which began at the end of World War II and which continued until at least 1966 and possibly beyond—were never authorized by any court warrants. He sought to defend the burglaries by hoisting the tattered banner of "national security," arguing that the FBI's actions were legal because the intent was "to protect the country."

There is more than a little irony to that rationale. It would seem that if the country needs protecting, it is from government agencies that secretly trample on the basic rights of American citizens.

Mr. Kelley's assertion of the legality of the burglaries raises fundamental legal issues. The language of the Constitution in this area is clear and precise. The Fourth Amendment guarantees "the right of the people to be secure in their persons...against unreasonable searches and seizures." It specifically forbids searches unless authorized by a warrant, issued on the basis of probable cause.

This latest story of FBI misdeeds, like the revelations of CIA and Watergate abuses that preceded it, demonstrates how systematically the government has undermined basic concepts of civil liberties. The nation is getting a long-overdue look at government agencies grown arrogant and self-serving, running amok at the expense of the average citizen.

The process of exposure is sometimes painful and unpleasant, but it's necessary and ultimately healthy. Americans are getting a good look at four decades of unchecked growth in the power of the federal government, and the abuses created by that growth.

There can be no turning away from the harsh realities that have been revealed. The country must begin to control its institutions, rather than the other way around. The government must literally be recaptured from the faceless bureaucrats and arrogant agencies that have come to dominate it.

That is the basic lesson posed by these ongoing revelations of official abuses of power. In the meantime, it would be naive to expect that this latest expose will be the last. We're just beginning to turn over the rock of governmental secrecy, and all kinds of unseemly things are crawling out.

The Wichita Eagle

Wichita, Kans., July 18, 1975

It looks so rational and normal in the movies: Special Agent-Hero cunningly outwits a mass of electronic surveillance gear, delicately moves the combination lock dial this way and that and unerringly selects the right compartment in the strange vault. At that point, having disarmed the alarm system, he may actually pry open a lock — being careful, of course, to leave no fingerprints.

It's all so romantic and exciting on the screen that you want to applaud when he bluffs (or perhaps kills) the alert guard who seems about to prevent his safe getaway.

But when you learn that the FBI actually has — by its present director's admission — some three decades of burglary experience, the news comes as a shock.

That all the break-ins reportedly were committed in the name of national security is only slightly comforting. And the fact that many of the burglaries occurred in foreign embassies can hardly enhance our diplomatic image.

It would, of course, be naive to assume that law enforcement and intelligence agencies could get all their information from cooperative citizens who volunteer it, never spy and never eavesdrop. But just as it's becoming increasingly hard to justify police actions that violate civil rights, we may be in for a stiffening of national conscience as regards those that violate criminal law.

There are, of course, times when ends really do justify the means. And if you don't believe that, listen to the explanation you get from your child the next time you catch him doing something he shouldn't have.

The Register-Republic

Rockford, Ill., July 17, 1975

It is a painful paradox to learn that the nation's No. 1 law enforcing agency — the FBI — may have engaged in as many as 100 burglaries a year between the years of World War II and 1966.

The justification for such action has been labeled "national security."

Some sources said the burglaries were committed at foreign embassies in Washington, aimed at gaining information to permit the National Security Agency to break foreign radio codes.

That cover story is insufficient, however, to cover 100 such break-ins annually.

For that reason, we applaud the decision of Atty. Gen. Edward Levi who has ordered an investigation of the break-ins to determine if any laws were broken and if anyone should be prosecuted.

We can recall the national indignation when former U.N. Ambassador Adlai Stevenson went before that body to disclose how Russians had effectively "bugged" an American embassy by placing a hidden microphone on a statue of the American Eagle.

We professed then to be a nation that respected law and obeyed the law.

We can not condone those who bend those principles.

Des Moines Tribune

Des Moines, Iowa, July 21, 1975

FBI Director Clarence Kelley has confirmed that FBI agents participated in break-ins and burglaries. Such activity had been reported but it had not been officially acknowledged until now.

Kelley said the incidents occurred about the time of World War II and continued until some time after 1966. He said all of the entries were related to foreign intelligence or national security.

The Fourth Amendment to the U.S. Constitution requires a search warrant before anyone's premises can be entered and searched by law officers. The FBI conducted its break-ins without benefit of warrants. Nevertheless, Kelley said there was no "gross abuse of authority." He defended the FBI's actions as legal.

Kelley seems to be echoing the view expressed recently by Atty. Gen. Edward Levi, who said the government has a right to make warrantless "surreptitious entries" in cases of "foreign espionage or intelligence." If Kelley and Levi are so confident about the legality of the break-ins, why doesn't the FBI continue the practice? J. Edgar Hoover evidently doubted the legal basis for searches without warrants when he called them off.

The place to get the legality of a practice settled is in the courts. The Justice Department has an obligation to have its reading of the Fourth Amendment tested in a court case. Until that is done, Americans will have reason to be uneasy about the security of their "persons, houses, papers and effects."

The Fourth Amendment cannot be much of a bulwark against unreasonable searches and seizures so long as the nation's chief law enforcement officer and his top lieutenant proclaim a government right to ignore it.

The Standard-Times
New Bedford, Mass., July 18, 1975

It's a funny thing that happens to the sense of proportion in Washington, D.C., especially among those who view secrecy as synonomous with evil.

Having the Central Intelligence Agency on the griddle, the Potomac warriors now are homing in on the Federal Bureau of Investigation for having conducted "break-ins" and "burglaries."

It seems, according to FBI Director Clarence M. Kelley, the department has engaged in such practices for more than 30 years, although very infrequently since 1966, and, insofar as he knows, not at all in the last two years. In every instance, he said, they related to national securi-ty or foreign intelligence.

"I do not note in these activities any gross abuse of authority," he said. "I do not feel it was a corruption of the trust placed upon us."

Our guess is, a great majority of Americans would agree with the Kelley view, and, indeed, give thanks that "someone down there" was watching over them in these respects. But, we note, some of those questioning Kelley wondered out loud whether he or the Justice Department was going to prosecute the FBI agents involved as criminals.

To what ridiculous extremes will the Washington opinion-givers—abetted, alas, by the media—go in their harassment of the nation's security apparatus? Surely the selectivity of the FBI's break-in activities is attested by the fact that there hasn't been a single recorded complaint by anyone whose premises was entered and/or burgled. The first indication of any such FBI activity came from a retired member of the department this year.

But more, let Congress weigh its own record on the matter of entering a domicile without a warrant. The 1970 District of Columbia Crininal Procedure Act (approved in the House 332-64, in the Senate, 54-33) provides for what is now known as "no-knock" entry.

This sweeping act (which, by the way, materially reduced the Capital's crime rate) provides that police may enter premises without notice (or warrant) if the officer "has probable cause to believe" notice is likely to result in destruction of evidence sought . . . . or where such notice would be a useless gesture.

If these stipulations render legitimate what amounts to a "break-in" in Washington, they are far more applicable in the investigations of the FBI. It is a regrettable truth that routine process would 1) positively assure destruction of evidence and 2) positively be a "useless gesture."

LEDGER-STAR
Norfolk, Va., July 16, 1975

The use of the break-in as a routine national-security tool is every bit as disturbing a practice as the late J. Edgar Hoover finally decided it was when he called a halt in 1966.

But the issue is not black-and-white, and the current FBI director, Clarence M. Kelley, did not treat it that way in his refreshingly candid admissions of a few days ago.

Mr. Kelley said that prior to the 1966 decision the FBI undertook burglaries of unnamed foreign embassies, over a period of 30 years, to secure "information related to the security of the nation." There were a few subsequent to 1966, but none had been proposed to him in his two years as director, he revealed. And if any were proposed in a grave situation he would present the question to the attorney general and be guided accordingly.

Some Americans, undoubtedly, will deplore the leaving of any loophole at all in the no-burglary policy, but the Kelley position takes account of realities which may well have to be coped with in safeguarding the nation.

As with wiretaps and certain other surreptitious implements of counter-intelligence operations, there is great danger in simply conceding blanket authority to the law enforcers to burglarize private premises normally protected by law.

But it isn't impossible to imagine conditions under which a transcendent national urgency involving a foreign threat would justify an entry by agents. The need is to keep any such action severely limited and under the tight control of the highest echelon of government—which is what Director Kelley has indicated.

It is difficult to believe that any sensible citizen would say the FBI nay if it acted tomorrow, via a break-in, to head off a theft of vital secrets by some modern version of Russia's Colonel Abel.

It's a matter of taking extreme protective measures only when the danger is extreme, but not having the hands of the nation's protectors completely tied when that occasion arises.

TULSA DAILY WORLD
Tulsa, Okla., July 16, 1976

DIRECTOR CLARENCE M. KELLEY'S acknowledgement that FBI agents have occasionally broken into foreign embassies and other buildings in the interest of national security is certain to produce screams of outrage.

Frankly, we are more concerned about the Director's statement that the practice had been halted.

Certainly, there is no need for widespread burglary by the FBI or any other security agency. And it is true that a good deal of abuse in the name of "national security" has been revealed in the last two years. But spying has never been exactly a clean and wholesome business. There are certainly extreme circumstances when "breaking and entering" might be condoned.

Today's detente notwithstanding, several great powers now have the capacity to utterly destroy one another.

A dozen years ago, it was learned that Russian nuclear weapons were going into Cuba. Wouldn't it have been worth a break-in at the Cuban embassy to determine the truth of the reports and to learn who would control the weapons?

The idea that we are supposed to play the spy game by gentlemanly rules while the other fellow plays by his own rules doesn't make much sense.

The Birmingham News
Birmingham, Ala., July 21, 1975

If evidence arises that a current practice by a federal agency is illegal, immoral or otherwise abhorrent to the public, then it would be appropriate for Congress to air every detail and legislate a remedy.

But, on the other hand, when bad practices have been discontinued long ago, what point is there in dredging up endless details of the past?

This, in essence, was the question that an irritated Atty. Gen. Edward H. Levi put to the press recently. He said government officials are being turned into "archivists" by a constant demand from the press and members of Congress to hash over practices which have long been discontinued.

The particular question which provoked Levi concerned an admission by FBI Director Clarence M. Kelley that agents under J. Edgar Hoover committed burglaries to obtain national security information. Kelley had said that no such activities have been allowed under his administration.

It is understandable that Levi would be irritated with this obsession with the dead past. The only important thing is what is happening today. If the would-be investigators would get their chronology up to date, the public's interest would be better served.

FBI'S DISPARATE ROLES PRESENTED BY LEVI, KELLEY AT ABA MEETING

The role of the Federal Bureau of Investigation was given disparate interpretations by Attorney General Edward H. Levi and FBI Director Clarence M. Kelley at the American Bar Association meeting in Montreal. Levi Aug. 13 proposed guidelines to curtail some FBI intelligence investigations based on "interests of individuals in privacy." By contrast, Kelley had told the ABA Aug. 9 that the rights of individuals must not be allowed "to transcend the safety and security of others."

The attorney general recalled that "Before 1972, and for a number of prior years, the bureau engaged in special programs directed at domestic groups; for example, it improperly disseminated information from its files to discredit individuals, or arranged for the sending of anonymous letters, or the publication of material intended to create opposition."

Levi recommended abolishing the use of informers to instigate crimes, a "periodic" report from the attorney general to Congress on "preventive action plans" he had authorized the FBI to undertake, restricting domestic intelligence gathering to circumstances that may threaten violence, and wiretapping only in the case of long-range investigations. Information received by the FBI on government officials and private citizens would be destroyed within 90 days if it could not be connected to a criminal act. Levi said the FBI would undertake probes for the White House only upon written request by specific officials.

"We must surrender a small measure of our liberties to preserve the great bulk of them," Kelley said. He recommended no further restrictions on wiretapping because the nation's security demanded special "latitude" to gather foreign intelligence data: "If an individual's rights are violated by a law enforcement officer, remedies are available. But there is no appeal, no remedy for a terrorist's bomb." The FBI director argued that it was a "commendable philosophy" to "present ourselves as sterling examples of people who know no limits in the recognition of human rights," but "what if one of [a foreign nation's] top priorities is the destruction of our democracy?"

THE BLADE
Toledo, Ohio, August 27, 1975

WATERGATE disclosures brought great public disenchantment with the Federal Bureau of Investigation because of its involvement in many operations deemed excessive and "sometimes outrageous," as Attorney General Edward H. Levi put it. As a result, calls for severe restrictions on the FBI have followed. But extreme restrictions could as readily cripple the FBI's effectiveness as the mistrust that currently burdens the agency.

Congress is especially sensitive and consequently in a mood to impose stringent controls because of the agency's gathering and retention of files on congressional members. But much of that was at the behest of the late J. Edgar Hoover who, in his declining years as the bureau's longtime director, unhappily tarnished his own illustrious image and that of the bureau.

For decades the FBI commanded the respect, admiration, and appreciation of the American people. Its reputation for incorruptibility, its professionalism in dealing with crime, its example and assistance for local law enforcement agencies throughout the country have properly earned national pride.

That pride needs restoring. No one understands this better than does Mr. Levi. Hence, in a speech to the American Bar Association's recent convention, he used that fitting platform to disclose proposals to curtail the FBI's domestic intelligence operations—the principal area, in which the bureau strayed too far in its zeal to suppress social protest.

But the attorney general was equally earnest in emphasizing the need for reasonable latitude within the discretion of the Justice Department to insure that legitimate functions continue. Guidelines for accountability rather than handcuffs as retribution for past excesses are sensible appeals. Once it is evident that such restraints are indeed in practice, the public's mistrust will diminish, and the FBI will regain the respect it needs to function properly.

The News and Courier
Charleston, S.C., August 19, 1975

Tighter controls the U.S. attorney general has proposed for domestic intelligence activities of the Federal Bureau of Investigation reflect a line of thought which clashes with that of the FBI director on the matter of individual liberties.

In advocating new guidelines, Atty. Gen. Edward Levi told the American Bar Association, he is seeking to balance legitimate intelligence needs against the interest of individual rights—which he said have been abused by the FBI in the past. In an earlier address at the same bar meeting, FBI Director Clarence Kelley had contended that Americans "must be willing to surrender a small measure of our liberties to preserve the great bulk of them." But to Mr. Levi, it is not a question of giving up individual liberties, but "of fulfilling them."

The difference of opinion pits the theorist, inclined to take the lofty view of what ideally should obtain, and the practicalist, persuaded by experience in law enforcement that in some circumstances individual rights become shelters for those few whose ultimate aims would imperil the liberties of the many.

The ideal society is the totally free society, insofar as exercise of individual liberties is concerned. Trouble arises when those who would breach the law or subvert the government rely on the protection of guaranteed, individual rights to thwart those agencies charged with preserving peace and order.

Frustrations have caused those engaged in enforcing the laws protecting society and government to take a slightly different view of individual rights because they have seen those rights perverted so often. Still, individual liberties are of such high value that it is better, in the long run, to assure blanket protection than to risk creeping infringement on rights of the innocent.

Presumably it is to that end that Atty. Gen. Levi suggested new restrictions on some FBI techniques, periodic reports on investigations and judicial warrants for electronic surveillance.

The Courier-Journal
Louisville, Ky., August 17, 1975

THE SEEMINGLY contradictory statements recently by the nation's top cop and his boss at the Justice Department, concerning FBI abuses of civil liberties, are more than a little confusing. Who, one wonders, is really running the show: FBI Director Clarence Kelley or Attorney General Edward Levi? By law, Mr. Levi is in charge and ultimately responsible for FBI activities and policies, and that seems all for the good.

Mr. Levi, much to his credit, makes no excuses for past FBI illegal activities, including burglaries, unauthorized wiretaps of suspected domestic "subversives," and mail openings. Moreover, he has proposed new guidelines to prevent FBI agents from trampling on the constitutional rights of Americans in their zealous pursuit of radicals they consider dangerous.

Mr. Levi's remarks last week stand in sharp contrast with Director Kelley's earlier warning that "we must be willing to surrender a small measure of our liberties to preserve the great bulk of them." He also suggested that, after the FBI has been purged of past, unsavory practices, the nation should shift its emphasis from "an obsession for restraints" on intelligence agencies to enhancing national security capabilities.

This "obsession" by the news media and congressional investigatory committees doubtless has hurt morale and perhaps has damaged the effectiveness of the FBI and the Central Intelligence Agency. But this is an unavoidable consequence of the necessary job of finding out what went wrong at these agencies and of devising means of curbing future abuses.

While the reforms Mr. Levi proposes may make the FBI's job more difficult and may be accepted only grudgingly by Mr. Kelley, the Attorney General and the FBI Director are in agreement on one point: warrantless wiretaps in the foreign intelligence field should continue. At present, such wiretaps are still legally permissible, since a 1972 Supreme Court ruling against national security wiretaps without court orders exempted wiretaps used to gather foreign intelligence and counterespionage data.

This exemption presumably allows the FBI routinely to tap the phones of foreign embassies and trade and cultural missions without the bother of obtaining warrants. While these wiretaps may produce intelligence of considerable value, neither Mr. Levi nor Mr. Kelley has made a convincing argument why court approval should not be received in advance. Moreover, even foreign intelligence wiretaps may invade the privacy of American citizens who contact foreign embassies to obtain visas or for other legitimate business.

Nevertheless, Mr. Levi's suggestions for ending illegal and unethical FBI activities — including the infiltration of and provocation within domestic organizations — are most welcome. Civil liberties may impede the work of police and spies, but without them a democracy degenerates into tyranny that is not worth protecting.

THE MILWAUKEE JOURNAL
Milwaukee, Wisc., August 21, 1975

One wonders whether FBI Director Clarence Kelley and his boss, Atty. Gen. Edward Levi, have been communicating lately.

Levi has been very open about illegal activities of the FBI in past years. He decries the illegal wiretaps, burglaries, mail opening and infiltration of domestic organizations. And he promises that from now on the FBI will operate within the law. He thinks that the rights of citizens are precious and must be observed.

But Kelley says Americans must "be willing to surrender a small measure of our liberties to preserve the great bulk of them." He deplores what he calls "an obsession for restraints" on intelligence work. And he wants to strengthen what he calls capabilities in the field of national security.

The two seem to be going in opposite directions. Perhaps Kelley should study the Bill of Rights and then have a conference with Levi.

THE NASHVILLE TENNESSEAN
Nashville, Tenn., August 16, 1975

ATTORNEY GENERAL Edward H. Levi outlined to the American Bar Association the proposed new guidelines for the Federal Bureau of Investigation which, if put into effect, would be a major step forward for that agency.

Mr. Levi said the FBI will be sharply limited in its use of informants, wiretaps and other surveillance techniques in domestic subversion cases. And he added that the Justice Department will strictly curb investigations sought by low-level White House officials and keep FBI files free of unsolicited and useless derogatory information about citizens.

The new guidelines have been tentatively endorsed by Mr. Levi but not yet finally adopted by him. They would end the decades-old FBI practice of conducting open-ended, unsupervised probes of private citizens' groups suspected of domestic subversive activity.

Regrettably, Mr. Levi maintained his position that wire-tapping without warrants in the foreign intelligence field is constitutional and that Congress should not require court approval for counterespionage eavesdropping.

The problem with that is, as demonstrated in the past, foreign intelligence operations can be widely defined. The FBI stands accused of engaging in mail openings, promiscuity in using wiretaps and a generally free-wheeling attitude in dealing with espionage.

That brand of thinking is not gone from the FBI, if one can judge from the remarks of Mr. Clarence Kelley, the FBI director, who also spoke in Montreal to the National Conference of Bar Presidents.

Referring to demands that the FBI and other agencies cease wire-tapping without warrants, Mr. Kelley said:

"We must be willing to surrender a small measure of our liberties to preserve the great bulk of them. If we do not...we shall surely finish last in the world arena."

This is the kind of thought-cliche that law enforcement always seems to fall back on when the Supreme Court or Congress moves to insure that due process is not to be lightly regarded.

It might be a lot easier to solve crimes by beating confessions out of someone, just as it might be a lot easier to deal with espionage by copious wiretapping and open-ended probes of citizens.

In a free society and a democracy, and under a Constitution that has stood the nation well these many years, a great many things have to be done the hard way, the prudent way, and in keeping with the rights of citizens. In a police state there are no problems of rights, no sanctity of the individual, and little respect for life itself.

The question is not whether the citizens should surrender some individual liberties in order to protect other freedoms. The question is whether there is the capacity, the will and the determination to deal with threats to freedom on the basis set forth in the Constitution. It has worked and it can continue to do so.

On the whole, Mr. Levi obviously perceives this and it would be to his credit and that of the country if he put his proposed FBI guidelines into effect.

CHICAGO DAILY NEWS

Chicago, Ill., August 18, 1975

A significant difference in emphasis, if not fundamental conviction, appears to have opened up between the Justice Department's new boss, Atty. Gen. Edward H. Levi, and his subordinate, Director Clarence M. Kelley of the Federal Bureau of Investigation. We trust that Levi's views will prevail; they betoken a welcome concern for individual liberty.

Kelley, addressing the American Bar Assn. meeting in Montreal on Aug. 9, said that "Americans must be willing to surrender a small measure of our liberties to preserve the great bulk of them." In a practical sense this is true. But it has ominous emphasis considering that the FBI has been discovered to have trampled on those liberties rather brutally in recent years. What does Kelley regard as "a small measure of our liberties"? An innocent and unsuspecting private citizen whose name has gone secretly onto a list of potential subversives has been put in peril of losing substantial liberty, while the nation has been pushed significantly nearer the condition of police state. Wherever domestic spying is deemed necessary, the public has the duty to require credible justification.

And that was what Levi promised in his talk last Wednesday before the same audience.

Levi came down solidly on the side of liberties. He said the FBI in times past has been "foolish and sometimes outrageous." And he outlined some particular measures his department is proposing to take to eliminate that kind of arrogant trifling with individual liberty.

These proposals include:

• Throwing out within 90 days all files containing unsolicited charges against individuals unless the charges are proved.

• Requiring White House officials to put their requests for FBI surveillance in writing.

• Requiring the attorney general to report "periodically" to Congress on "preventive action plans" in progress.

• Limiting electronic surveillance to "full-scale" investigations.

• Requiring the attorney general's approval for "preventive action," including disseminating information to discredit people. The attorney general would be required to determine that "there is probable cause to believe that violence is imminent and cannot be prevented by arrest."

• Forbidding the FBI to originate "the idea of committing a crime" or to induce others to commit crimes.

These restrictions make sense. If they represent a compromise between what the FBI believes necessary to fulfill its mission and what congressional critics believe detrimental to individual rights, that seems to us exactly what is needed. The dangers the FBI seeks to combat are real. It must have all the freedom that is consistent with a due regard for the nation's basic tenets.

Most encouraging of all is the critical attitude that Levi brings to his job. After Watergate, the nation needed a man to head the Justice Department who could be trusted to run it in behalf of the citizens. That appears to be what Levi has in mind.

The San Diego Union

San Diego, Calif., August 15, 1975

Clarence Kelley, director of the Federal Bureau of Investigation, has stirred yet another national political storm with his recent contention that individual Americans should be willing to surrender a minimum of individual liberties if that is what it takes to meet the threat that foreign espionage poses to the United States of America.

The narrow question that he was addressing is whether intelligence agencies of the United States have the authority to wiretap and conduct other surveillance of enemies without first obtaining a court warrant. All such activity within the United States requires the approval of a judge.

Mr. Kelley believes that Americans "must be willing to surrender a small measure of our liberties to preserve the bulk of them....If we do not, if investigative agencies charged with national security responsibilities are so fettered as to be ineffective, then we shall surely finish last in the world arena."

Mr. Kelley's words predictably fell on fertile political ground in this strange post-Watergate era. Albert E. Jenner, Jr., who was minority counsel during the Watergate hearings, drew what the press described as prolonged applause when he attacked Mr. Kelley with time-worn cliches. Mr. Jenner declared that this is "a government of laws, not men," and went on to talk about surrendering constitutional rights in the name of expediency — indeed to interpret the constitution to support his rhetoric.

We doubt that Mr. Kelley is any less interested than Mr. Jenner in preserving the liberties that Americans have, and certainly he can make a strong historical and logical case for his point of view.

For example, is the threat to the United States Constitution greater from the Soviet Union or the FBI?

Moreover, we doubt that any power in the Constitution is absolute. Individual and institutional liberties already are being infringed upon for the good of the greater society. It can be said that a free press is circumscribed and, properly, by libel and anti-pornography laws. A fair trial is balanced with a free press, not every American can demand a jury trial and a felon loses a host of civil rights.

Indeed, if we read history correctly, The Founding Fathers, particularly those who went on later to be presidents, believed that survival of the nation was essential before its citizens could address individual rights.

Mr. Kelley's assertions go to the heart of many national issues that trouble us today, not only the problems of crime and espionage. Once we establish that the United States must exist as a nation, which is what the FBI director is saying, then a lot of other pieces will begin to fall into place.

St. Petersburg Times

St. Petersburg, Fla., August 12, 1975

FBI Director Clarence Kelley, as a personal Bicentennial project, should dust off the sparkling, brave words of America's early patriots for restudy.

COULD ANYONE grasping the wisdom of those who first labored to found and then struggled to save this nation fall so easily into the trap Kelley did when he told the American Bar Association, "We must be willing to surrender a small measure of our liberties to preserve the great bulk of them."

If Americans are alarmed that a director of the FBI — so powerful and so influential — would promote seriously such an idea, they should be. It is dangerous because it does not sound so dangerous. It seems limited. It seems non-threatening. It seems plausible.

Kelley said there is a threat to our national security, "a real threat to the free exercise of the doctrines of democracy," from foreign espionage agents. To counter that, he proposed that the FBI and law enforcement agencies be able to wiretap without first obtaining a wiretap warrant in the courts. Just a small surrender of a principle.

BUT WHY? Why violate principle when all the FBI needs to wiretap foreign suspects is enough reasonable suspicion of a threat to convince a judge to grant a wiretap warrant? Why tamper? Why chip away at any bulwark of liberty when one chip begins to weaken the whole structure?

Kelley said, "Our national security today is at a very critical juncture." No doubt. The United States has many enemies. But it would be an error to think we might find safety in abandoning even "a small measure" of the principles that make this a great nation. Our early leaders knew that.

Benjamin Franklin must have had in mind some future fearful Clarence Kelley when he said, "Those who would give up essential liberty to purchase a little temporary safety, deserve neither liberty nor safety."

Daniel Webster must have had in mind the fainthearted who might rationalize backing away from the tough job of defending great ideals when he said, "God grants liberty only to those who love it, and are always ready to guard and defend it."

Emerson said, "There is always safety in valor."

And Abraham Lincoln, in soft but stirring words, warned against the recurring temptation to sacrifice what we stand for to achieve safety. The threat, Lincoln said, is not from "monsters" from abroad but from within. "At what point then is the approach of danger to be expected? I answer if it is ever to reach us it must spring up amongst us; it cannot come from abroad. If destruction be our lot, we must ourselves be its author and finisher."

ABRAHAM LINCOLN understood what Clarence Kelley seems not to: That Americans dare not "surrender a small measure of our liberties," for as Lincoln said, "Our reliance is in the love of liberty . . ." So it remains.

Long Island Press

Jamaica, N.Y., August 13, 1975

FBI Director Clarence Kelley does not believe that the FBI should obtain court warrants before conducting wiretaps in national security cases. Permission of the President or the attorney general is enough of a safeguard against abuse, he argues.

Besides, Mr. Kelley adds, a growing threat of espionage by foreign agents in this country can be met only if Americans are willing to surrender some individual liberties. "We must have a certain amount of latitude," he concludes.

Mr. Kelley is wrong. Orders by a president or an attorney general to wiretap without court permission can lead to serious abuses of individual liberties, as former President Nixon and former Attorney General Mitchell demonstrated so ably in the Watergate scandal.

We fail to see how a requirement for a wiretap warrant would hobble the FBI in investigations of national security matters, or anything else. Does Mr. Kelley believe that the federal courts would hesitate to approve a legitimate warrant sought by a president or attorney general?

The FBI director argues further that individual liberties would be adequately protected by congressional oversight. That would be helpful, of course, but what's wrong with judicial oversight, too — just to keep the hands of all three government branches into matters as important as national security and individual liberties?

Des Moines Tribune

Des Moines, Iowa, August 13, 1975

FBI Director Clarence Kelley has warned that the nation may be unable to cope with external threats unless Americans give up some of their freedoms. He told an American Bar Association meeting that "our national security today is at a very critical juncture."

Referring to growing demands for tighter restraints on intelligence gathering by law enforcement agencies, Kelley said that "we must be willing to surrender a small measure of our liberties to preserve the great bulk of them. If we do not — if investigative agencies charged with national security responsibilities are so fettered as to be ineffective — then we shall surely finish last in the world arena."

He was critical of proposals that would prohibit domestic surveillance and require the FBI to get court permission for all wiretapping. Under present practice, the president and attorney general authorize wiretaps for certain national security purposes.

Kelley did not elaborate on his remark about threats to national security. It fits, however, with a renewed effort on the part of some federal officials to keep alive concern about a Communist threat to American survival.

At the same time, though, other federal officials hail the prospect of peaceful coexistence with Communist nations.

Kelley's comment that Americans must be willing to surrender some of their personal rights to save most of them is reminiscent of the explanation of an American colonel who told how his men had destroyed a Vietnamese city in order to save it.

The liberties Kelley may be willing to sacrifice are part of the cherished heritage that has made the United States different from most other nations. Without those liberties, the United States might endure as a collection of people, a geographic entity, but it would no longer be the "land of the free." That is what we should strive to preserve, and that can't be done by chipping away at the Bill of Rights.

The Philadelphia Inquirer

Philadelphia, Pa., August 15, 1975

Conceding that the FBI may have "fallen short of the desired standards" in recognizing the rights of individuals, Director Clarence Kelley has asserted nevertheless that too much concern for individual rights may jeopardize our national security. In an address to the American Bar Association's meeting in Montreal, Mr. Kelley asked rhetorically:

"Do we want the rights of the individual, no matter what be his philosophy or his goals, to transcend the safety and the security of others?"

It is an old question, and part of the answer is that it is the wrong question. Individual rights and national security are not separate concepts, at opposite ends of the pole. Indeed, the men who drafted and promulgated the Constitution of the United States considered them to be part of a single whole.

They identified the safety of the nation with the safety of the individual against the government and with the protection of individual rights—the right to adhere to any philosophy one chooses and to speak one's mind freely, the right of peaceable assembly, the right to be secure in one's home and one's papers, and so on.

And they made no exceptions for "national security."

We defy Mr. Kelley or anyone else to find a single word in the Constitution or in the writings of the men who created it to justify the kind of activities to which the FBI has been compelled to confess—burglaries, unauthorized and illegal wiretaps, mail-opening, spying on and disruption of "dissident" groups, using agent provocateurs to instigate crimes, and damaging the reputations of citizens with anonymous accusations.

Such activities, Mr. Kelley's superior, Attorney General Edward H. Levi, declared in his speech to the ABA, are "foolish and sometimes outrageous," and he disclosed plans to put sharp restrictions on the FBI's behavior in the future.

Mr. Kelley contends that Americans should be "willing to surrender a small measure of our liberties to preserve the great bulk of them."

"I would not have put it that way," replied Mr. Levi, and neither would we. Benjamin Franklin put it the right way. "They that can give up essential liberty to obtain a little temporary safety deserve neither liberty nor safety."

The Wichita Eagle

Wichita, Kans., August 13, 1975

If the workings of the nation's intelligence community are to be considered realistically, the concession will be made that certain unethical, if not unlawful, practices occasionally are necessary.

But FBI Director Clarence Kelley was less than discreet when he told an audience of American Bar Association members in Montreal that Americans must sacrifice a "small measure of our liberties to preserve the great bulk of them" because of growing threats to national security.

Most Americans do not put so little value on their freedoms and liberties, no matter how "small" the measure.

Kelley was equally wrong to express disdain for congressional guidelines, which he sees as interfering with the agency's security functions. Even he admitted the guidelines are being urged because the FBI has been accused of "engaging in mail openings, promiscuity in using wiretaps, committing burglaries and a general disregard for individual rights."

The central problem is reconciling the conduct of intelligence operations with the values of a free democratic society. In theory at least, government secrecy is basically antithetical to democracy and is more characteristic of totalitarianism.

Therefore, any government agency which operates in secrecy employs totalitarian tactics to achieve its goals. Such organizations inevitably violate the ethics of a constitutional democracy and may undermine due process of law which safeguards democratic rights and liberties.

In 1967, Sen. J. William Fulbright, D-Ark., contended that "fighting fire with fire" is both bad morals and bad policy.

"It tends to undermine the very purpose for which it was undertaken," Fulbright said then. "It has not yet, thank God, made us a police state but it has brought us closer to it and, what is even more alarming, to greater public acceptance of certain practices associated with a police state — secret policy making, unchecked executive power, subversion of foreign governments, bugging and spying and wiretapping our own people — than we have ever been in history."

In the eight years since those words were written, the nation has come even closer to this image of a police state.

It remains to be seen what effect the Watergate affair may have on continued public acceptance of such tactics by the intelligence community and what changes the outcome will make in the nation's history.

But, as of now, the proposal that greater congressional control over the FBI be imposed sounds like the best protection possible for every American.

LEDGER-STAR

Norfolk, Va., August 16, 1975

Though he may get clobbered for putting the intelligence and counter-intelligence imperatives in such blunt terms, FBI Director Clarence Kelley deserves some praise for the honesty of his remarks at the annual meeting of the American Bar Association.

And in quite practical terms, too, the country needs to accept the trade-off he perceives as justified: the sacrifice of some individual liberties to preserve the vast bulk of them. This is the balancing struggle familiar to this democracy from its birth.

By extension, moreover, the Kelley case 'or not impairing vital national security functions also applies to the CIA, which is being even more seriously threatened than the FBI by excessive carping and exposure.

In accepting the Kelley trade-off principle, however, a strong condition needs to be made a corollary. And that is the erection of some reasonable safeguards to make sure the latitude of executive decision doesn't expand from the small area of liberty infringement and begin, without public notice, to whittle away at the "great bulk" of American freedoms Mr. Kelley seeks to preserve. The nation must be satisfied, too, that liberties unequivocally guaranteed by the Constitution aren't infringed upon.

Just as an example of the safeguarding process (using one of the very activities the FBI director was discussing), why should "national security" wiretaps be left totally to executive decision? Why not have some system of court authorization? Maintenance of secrecy need not be compromised by the use of such a warrant method, and the extra check would be valuable as well as reassuring to the American people. Is this really—to use Mr. Kelley's word—so "unwise"?

The Washington Star

Washington, D.C., August 14, 1975

Clarence Kelley seems to be gradually acquiring the inflated view of his responsibilities that can lead to the sort of helium-filled conclusions which have become depressingly familiar in recent history. We hope this is not the drift, but his speech to leaders of the American Bar Association in Montreal last weekend left that impression. He appears to be working toward the notion that the survival of the free world depends on the FBI, and hence the bureau must be excused some deviations now and then from the normal restrictions of law upon invasion of personal rights, as related to privacy.

True enough, he was talking about foreign threats as distinguished from the field of domestic law enforcement and inquiry. But as we have seen in recent times, this division may not be distinguished very well when an excess of zeal or patriotic excitement gets mixed up in the investigative processes. We wonder if the FBI director noted that, by coincidence, his speech was given on the first anniversary of Richard Nixon's helicopter departure from this city, after a downfall that was brought about in part by his administration's shocking misuse of investigative agencies, including the FBI.

Of course much of the bureau's wrongdoing preceded Mr. Nixon, stemming in some respects from the overblown zeal of the late Director J. Edgar Hoover. Only recently, Mr. Kelley revealed that the FBI indeed had engaged in break-ins and burglaries, in the Fifties and Sixties, until Mr. Hoover came to believe, as Mr. Kelley recalls, that "possibly in the context of the times this was not a viable procedure." One might construe this to mean that Mr. Hoover decided that the FBI no longer could get away with it.

In any case, the current director has defended his predecessor's dubious doings as being in the service of national security, and in the context of those hectic times. We must assume that his context argument doesn't extend to the private citizen who gains entry in the night with a glass-cutter and pleads that this was done in a context of ultimate desperation, economic or otherwise. This is what's known in most courts as a weak alibi. In fact Mr. Kelley confessed to the lawyers in Montreal that "the FBI has made some mistakes," that in the past some law enforcement methods had "an aura of illegality and unconscionable behavior." But "after a flood of revelation" he has imposed disciplines to assure that the bureau does not engage in shady tactics. And we are inclined to take him at his word, as a man who doesn't intend for his agency to run roughshod over individual liberties as it goes about protecting the national security.

But men are transient, and interpretation of what is in the interest of national security can prove elastic from time to time. Hence, the disquieting part of his thesis was what sounded like an appeal for extra-legal powers for the FBI and other intelligence agencies. He is disturbed by "an obsession for restraints" on intelligence gathering which might cause this country to "finish last in the world arena." He thinks "we must be willing to surrender a small measure of our liberties to preserve the great bulk of them." In some instances, he is saying, against a larger picture of foreign menace which he seems to see, the liberties of the individual should take second place.

The obvious question is, who will set the measure? The degree of danger in such an arrangement depends on who happens to be drawing the definitions at a given time. The "small measure" could grow in a period of tension, the admitted "mistakes" of the past could be repeated or enlarged under some future leadership.

Mr. Kelley's main concern seems to be for continued use of wiretaps without warrants in foreign-intelligence cases; he does not say whether resumption of breakins might be deemed essential. Obtaining federal warrants for such wiretaps doesn't seem to be all that insurmountable a difficulty. But he warns ominously that other, adversary powers in this perilous world are not bound by the same legal restraints that we are.

That's the point of what we're celebrating this year and next; we have something special here, in those hard-won constitutional rights. And we need to be ever more jealous of them. Least of all in this Bicentennial time we ought not even toy with the idea of letting anyone decide which of them can be chipped away because of what are perceived to be extraordinary circumstances. All times are dangerous, and not the least those in which our liberties first were secured.

THE DAILY HERALD

Biloxi, Miss., August 18, 1975

Attorney General Edward Levi says the FBI has come close to infringing on the constitutional rights of Americans.

We don't doubt that for a minute. In fact, recent evidence suggests that Mr. Levi may be guilty of an understatement.

Speaking before the American Bar Association's annual meeting in Montreal, Levi offered safeguards to end the bureau's surveillance of domestic organizations unless they pose violent threats.

"The proposed guidelines would limit domestic intelligence activities to the pursuit of information about activities that may involve the use of force or violence in violation of federal law in specified ways," Levi said.

The guidelines, devised by a committee of six lawyers, have not yet been given final approval by the Justice Department, although the attorney general said they represent current practices.

According to the new safeguards, domestic FBI investigations will be subject to review outside of the bureau and wiretapping is to be restricted to "full scale" investigations of groups which threaten violence.

Levi did not otherwise define what determines if an investigation is "full scale."

If domestic groups pose a violent threat, the FBI is to report directly to the attorney general who is to decide what type preventative action will be taken.

White House requests for special investigations must be made in writing, clearly stating the reasons for the action in an effort to protect the bureau from influence over investigations such as in the Watergate coverup case

In addition, the FBI would destroy unsolicited information it receives "not alleging serious criminal behavior that needs to be investigated by the bureau or reported to other law enforcement agencies" within 90 days.

We believe it is possible for the FBI to remain a strong and efficient police agency without sacrificing the personal liberties guaranteed each citizen or legal resident under the United States Constitution.

The bureau operates within a legal framework and with enough resources that it does not, and should not, have to place itself on the same level as those it seeks to arrest for breaking the law.

BUFFALO EVENING NEWS

Buffalo, N.Y., August 21, 1975

Stuffing a menacing genie back in the protective bottle is never easy. But U. S. Atty. Gen. Edward Levi is making thoughtful progress along those lines. We are referring to his efforts to define, restrict and, occasionally, prohibit the use of investigative techniques in the field of domestic intelligence that were sometimes abused in the past by law-enforcement agencies now under his control as head of the Justice Department.

We like specifically the proposed guidelines drawn up by his department, and disclosed in part by Mr. Levi in Montreal the other day, bearing upon the FBI's domestic intelligence operations. They put certain disreputable tactics—like having FBI informers instigate suspect groups to commit crimes—out of bounds, and they restrict the use of other potentially threatening techniques.

Most important, they lay more directly in the lap of this and future attorneys general the real responsibility for FBI operations in this sensitive area, a responsibility that was more nominal than real during the long and largely unsupervised reign of J. Edgar Hoover. Technically, attorneys general were over the FBI chief, but in practice he enjoyed immensely more influence than they did.

Personalities aside, this was and would be an unhealthy situation. Sound principles of democratic accountability argue compellingly that professional staff people in the federal bureaucracy must be in both law and fact responsible to appointed civilian department heads who, in turn, are directly responsible to the elected President. In this sense, a professionally directed FBI should be accountable to a civilian attorney general much as the military chiefs of staff are to the civilian secretaries and secretary of defense.

The Levi proposals strengthen this concept. They also seem to contradict the thrust of FBI director Clarence Kelley's heedless remark that Americans "must be willing to surrender a small measure of our liberties to preserve the great bulk of them." After Watergate and, apparently, all too many earlier instances of law-breaking by federal agents, the emphasis clearly must be not on a surrender of any but on buttressing protections of all individual liberties.

None of this means we would give the attorney general any kind of blank-check in this area, or that Congress can be relieved of responsibility to tighten the laws governing both FBI and CIA practice and to maintain its own more effective surveillance over their performance. But the attorney general is moving in the right direction, it seems to us, to get that genie back in the bottle.

Democrat Chronicle

Rochester, N.Y., August 19, 1975

A United States Justice Department task force has issued guidelines to prevent the Federal Bureau of Investigation from trampling upon the rights of individuals. The guidelines are not yet final, but seem well-designed to prevent the kind of misjudgments which have blemished the FBI record in the past.

Oversight of the FBI and the establishment of legal guidelines for it seems an appropriate function for the Justice Department to perform. The alternative would be congressional oversight or statutory limitation of FBI activities. While some laws to limit domestic investigation may be needed, there's a danger that political factors might cause them to be needlessly restrictive.

The Washington Post

Washington, D.C., August 19, 1975

ATTORNEY GENERAL Edward H. Levi's speech to the American Bar Association in Montreal last week is an encouraging progress report on his important effort to develop guidelines for future investigative operations by the FBI. Given the range and complexity of this work, it is not surprising that the Justice Department's task force has not found all the answers yet. What is impressive is the department's willingness to address the hard questions of governmental conduct and control in a very sensitive field where conflicts between individual liberties and public protection are inevitable.

For one thing, the Attorney General seems to be contemplating a sharp cutback in domestic intelligence-gathering and FBI intervention in the affairs of dissident groups. Though the guidelines are still incomplete and tentative, Mr. Levi's remarks indicate that he wishes to end the vacuum-cleaner approach to intelligence that has led to the collection and retention of so many files on law-abiding citizens and groups. Under the guidelines, for instance, the FBI would be required to throw away unsolicited derogatory information that does not bear on possible serious criminal conduct. This in itself would be a great departure from present practices, under which the Bureau has been keeping everything that comes in—including nasty letters about public officials—because it might have some future use.

More important, the guidelines would restrict domestic intelligence activities, including electronic surveillance, to the collection of information about activities that may involve the use of force or violence in violation of federal law. The kinds of harassment and manipulation of domestic groups employed in the Cointel program would be even more sharply curtailed. The exact language of the guidelines has not been set, and it will no doubt be intensely debated. But the thrust of these proposals is clearly toward a far more precise, discriminating program of preventing or investigating specific crimes, rather than probing into the business of any person or organization that seems to be, by someone's gauge, radical or obstreperous or vaguely threatening. At the same time, the department is trying to devise new rules for foreign intelligence operations, including wiretapping, break-ins and other activities undertaken for the sake of national security—as properly and narrowly defined. In this acutely sensitive area, Mr. Levi last week seemed somewhat more receptive to congressional and judicial involvement than he has been in the past.

No matter what guidelines may be developed, their success will hinge on establishing and maintaining a more reliable system of oversight and accountability. In the past, many unlawful and questionable FBI operations have been launched on the say-so of one man—whether a White House aide or an agent in the field—and have been perpetuated because senior officials failed to notice and call a halt. As outlined last week, the guidelines would generally call for much closer review of FBI activities by the Attorney General. While this is highly desirable, it will work only to the extent that the Attorney General and his staff carry out their responsibilities. As the records of the Cointel program show, breakdowns of management often occurred not because the FBI failed to report its practices, but because top Justice Department officials did not really read the reports.

AKRON BEACON JOURNAL
Akron, Ohio, August 16, 1975

ALTHOUGH Attorney General Edward H. Levi has come up with some needed housecleaning plans for the Federal Bureau of Investigation, his "Mr. Clean" image seems to be tarnishing around the edges.

Levi told the American Bar Association he'll propose that all FBI files with unsolicited charges about individuals be thrown out after 90 days if the charges can't be substantiated. This is a sound approach to clean up an area of FBI operations that has led to "Big Brother" charges.

Another sensible proposal is that all White House orders to the FBI from now on should be in writing from high-ranking administration officials. This is obviously aimed at preventing the FBI from getting another black eye similar to the one it got during the Watergate mess when it acted in questionable manner on oral orders from Nixon administration officials.

Both proposals are the kind we hoped to see come from Mr. Levi, who stepped into the Justice Department at a time when regard for the FBI was at an all-time low because of charges that the FBI was used for political purposes, and indications that the bureau got involved in cloak-and-dagger scheming to cause rifts in some organizations.

Mr. Levi came into the job talking tough, and it was reassuring. But speaking before the American Bar Association, his tune seems to have changed on some issues. At times he sounded suspiciously like a man who has been captured by the FBI.

For example, Mr. Levi previously had been extremely critical of the bureau when it was disclosed that the FBI in the 1960s regularly tried to cause dissension in the ranks of such groups as the National Association for the Advancement of Colored People.

But now he says such activities are acceptable under "carefully controlled" circumstances.

He hedged on the question of keeping files on the "personal habits" of government officials and Congressmen, which the late FBI director, J. Edgar Hoover, reportedly enjoyed sharing occasionally with a President. Instead of condemning the practice, Mr. Levi now says such details could come in handy "if there is a subsequent attempt at anonymous extortion or other threats."

The attorney general also hedged on how he would control wiretapping.

All of this suggests that while Mr. Levi has been on the right track in cleaning up the FBI, and has come up with some worthwhile guidelines, the Congress should keep a close watch on him. The FBI has awesome powers which, if misused, can threaten individual liberties, and continuing pressure from the Congress can only help Mr. Levi remember that he is there to restore public confidence in the Justice Department and the FBI.

ST. LOUIS POST-DISPATCH
St. Louis, Mo., August 14, 1975

Attorney General Edward Levi deserves a great deal of credit for proposing guidelines for the Federal Bureau of Investigation. While some of the guidelines may be open to criticism, they are the first comprehensive controls suggested by an attorney general.

In general, Mr. Levi suggests that the FBI be required to report full-scale domestic intelligence operations to the attorney general, who could close such investigations when they were not justified. The guidelines would restrict the use of electronic surveillance and prohibit use of informants to instigate crimes. Files containing unsolicited information not alleging serious criminal behavior would be destroyed in 90 days.

Certainly recent disclosures indicate the need for each regulation: the FBI has conducted long and pointless domestic inquiries with no review, it has been charged with using agents of provocation and illegal wire tapping, and its voluminous files involving unsubstantiated political as well as criminal material are an insult to First Amendment rights.

Unfortunately, Mr. Levi may not have an adequate answer for the FBI's past record of trying to discredit left-wing groups and use of disruptive tactics (Cointelpro) which amounted to political meddling outside the agency's charter.

Mr. Levi says the guidelines would allow the FBI to continue certain programs that are aimed at diminishing violence but only if the attorney general found that violence might be imminent and could not be prevented by arrest. In substance, this allows him considerable discretion to go beyond the usual norms of law enforcement. Programs such as Cointelpro should be flatly prohibited.

Under the late J. Edgar Hoover the FBI engaged in free-wheeling activities over which several attorneys general appeared to have little supervision. Hence the guidelines now being drafted by a Justice Department committee are essential as internal controls. They will be internal, however, and the public will not know how they are working unless Congress itself demands the kind of accountability to which the FBI was not subjected in the past.

THE ATLANTA CONSTITUTION
Atlanta, Ga., August 15, 1975

While the FBI has enjoyed and still enjoys a high reputation, like many other federal agencies it has run into severe criticism in the post-Watergate moral revival.

Some of that criticism is deserved. The FBI, our foremost law enforcement agency, is apparently not above breaking the law itself. It has conducted illegal break-ins, illegal wiretapping and other forms of surveillance and has yielded to political pressure in conducting investigations. A former acting director of the agency resigned during the Watergate squabble when it was learned he had destroyed evidence possibly useful in the investigation.

Obviously, this sort of thing can't be allowed to go on unchecked if we are to remain a free society under a constitutional system of law. Attorney General Edward Levi evidently subscribes to that view because he has vowed to crack down on some of the FBI's "Big Brother" operations. He said he is going to propose destroying all files of unsolicited charges concerning individuals, limit electronic surveillance to full scale investigations, and set guidelines for such activities as the infiltration of dissident or suspect organizations. He also wants any White House request or order to the FBI put in writing.

No individual or organization in this country should be considered outside the rule of law. Most especially that rule should apply to our law enforcement agencies.

Newsday
Garden City, N.Y., August 19, 1975

Only one obstacle emerged during attorney-general Edward Levi's confirmation hearings last January: In 1955, he had supervised a bugging project that surreptitiously probed how jurors function behind supposedly closed doors.

Rather than defend that action, Levi called it a mistake and promised to issue firm guidelines on governmental surveillance. Last Wednesday, he announced his proposals in a speech to the American Bar Association. The FBI will be limited sharply in its use of informers, wiretaps, and other domestic surveillance. Investigations sought by low-level White House officials will be severely curbed, and FBI files will be purged of unsolicited derogatory information about individuals if an investigation proves nothing. But Levi insisted—as did FBI Director Clarence Kelley a few days earlier—that wiretaps in foreign intelligence and counterespionage work should not require court approval.

The line between foreign and domestic intelligence is easily blurred, as has been demonstrated repeatedly during the Watergate and CIA investigations. If a wiretap—any wiretap—is desirable or essential for national security, surely the Justice Department should be able to find a judge willing to issue a warrant and able to keep quiet about it. Kelley's argument that Americans "must be willing to surrender a small measure of their liberties to preserve the great bulk of them" is the same argument used by every police state. The fact is that U.S. law makes no distinction between one type of wiretapping and the other.

Levi's guidelines are an excellent start in correcting some of the legal deficiences exposed during the time of Vietnam and Watergate. But in making an exception of foreign intelligence operations, Levi perpetuates one of the most dangerous attitudes of that period—that wherever the law is vague or silent, police are free to act outside the spirit of the Constitution.

The Wiretapping Issue

The Courts

Domestic wiretaps limited. U.S. District Court Judge Warren J. Ferguson ruled in Los Angeles Jan. 11, 1971 that the government could not conduct wiretaps without warrants in domestic cases, even if national security was involved. The ruling, to take effect in 30 days pending an expected appeal by the Justice Department, came in the case of Melvin Carl Smith, 41, a Black Panther convicted in October 1969 on charges of being a felon and possessing firearms.

The government had long claimed the right to eavesdrop without a warrant in national security cases involving foreign subversives. In 1969, in connection with the Chicago conspiracy trial, Attorney General John A. Mitchell had said the government could use wiretaps without prior court approval in cases involving domestic groups if the national security was threatened.

Ferguson said the U.S. Constitution protected domestic political activity, but "the government seems to approach these dissident domestic organizations in the same fashion as it deals with unfriendly foreign powers." He said: "The government cannot act in this manner when only domestic political organizations are involved, even if those organizations espouse views which are inconsistent with our present form of government. To do so is to ride roughshod over numerous political freedoms which have long received constitutional protection."

Keith agrees with Ferguson—A U.S. district court judge in Detroit ruled Jan. 25 that the government could not conduct wiretaps in domestic cases without court warrants on grounds that the national security was involved. The ruling by Judge Damon J. Keith was similar to a Jan. 11 decision by Judge Warren J. Ferguson in Los Angeles.

Keith said transcripts of the illegal wiretaps on Lawrence R. (Pun) Plamondon, 25, accused of conspiracy in the Sept. 29, 1968 bombing of a Central Intelligence Agency building in Ann Arbor must be handed over to the defense. The Justice Department said Jan. 27 that it would appeal the ruling and that Keith had continued the trial date until Feb. 9. In the Los Angeles case, Ferguson had given the government 30 days to appeal.

The Detroit judge said: "An idea which seems to permeate much of the government's argument is that a dissident domestic organization is akin to an unfriendly foreign power that must be dealt with in the same fashion."

He said this argument "strikes at the very constitutional privileges and immunities that are inherent in United States citizenship." Keith challenged the government's right to "determine unilaterally what comes within its own definition of national security." He said that "attempts of domestic organizations to attack and subvert the existing structure of government" were criminal "only where it can be shown that such activity was accomplished through unlawful means."

Plamondon was one of three members of the Ann Arbor-based White Panther party charged in the bomb plot. The other defendants were John A. Sinclair, 29, who was serving a 10-year sentence for possession of marijuana, and John W. Forrest, 21. Their lawyers were two Chicago 7 attorneys, William M. Kunstler and Leonard I. Weinglass, and Hugh M. Davis.

Kleindienst presents government case— Deputy Attorney General Richard G. Kleindienst, in a United Press International interview published Feb. 22, defended the government's claim of the right to conduct wiretaps without court approval in domestic national security cases. The government had appealed Keith's ruling Feb. 5. The U.S. had earlier appealed Ferguson's ruling.

Kleindienst said: "It would be silly to say that an American citizen, because he is an American, could subvert the government by actions of violence and revolution and be immune from, first, identification, and second, prosecution." He said, "The whole question of internal security is not a divisible subject matter. . . . You can't divide subversion into two parts—domestic and foreign."

Among other developments:

■ The U.S. Court of Appeals in Washington, D.C. ruled Feb. 16 that the defendants in the Chicago conspiracy trial were entitled to an immediate hearing on their suit that the Federal Bureau of Investigation illegally wiretapped their phones. The ruling overturned a lower court decision placing an indefinite stay on the Chicago defendants' lawsuit, pending final disposition of the charges against them that arose out of demonstrations at the 1968 Democratic National Convention.

■ The American Bar Association (ABA), at a meeting of its House of Delegates in Chicago Feb. 8, approved electronic surveillance standards for states similar to a 1968 federal statute permitting court-approved wiretaps in criminal cases. The ABA action did not deal with the government's claim that it could conduct wiretaps without court warrants in domestic security cases. ABA delegates rejected three proposed amendments that would have placed tighter restrictions on police wiretapping than provided in the federal statute. Currently 12 states had court warrant procedures to permit police to conduct wiretaps, and the ABA model statute was expected to encourage other states to enact such laws.

■ At the ABA delegates' meeting, Kleindienst said the Administration's use of court-approved wiretaps against organized crime had led to more than 800 arrests and 72 convictions in the past two years. In 1969 and 1970, he said, the Justice Department had obtained 253 court warrants for eavesdropping, 45 of them extensions for taps already approved. Kleindienst said 163 of the surveillance orders had been obtained for use in gambling cases, 58 in narcotics, 21 in loan sharking probes and the rest in various crime syndicate investigations.

Keith's ruling upheld—The U.S. Court of Appeals for the 6th Circuit, ruling in Cincinnati April 8, rejected the Justice Department's contention that the government had a right to conduct wiretaps in "domestic subversion" cases without court warrants. The court's 2-1 ruling upheld federal Judge Damon J. Keith's decision that the government had to disclose information obtained in an illegal wiretap or drop its bomb conspiracy charges against Lawrence Plamondon, leader of the Ann Arbor, Mich.-based White Panthers.

In the first federal appellate court ruling on Attorney General John N. Mitchell's assertion that the government could conduct unwarranted taps in domestic security cases, Judge George C. Edwards Jr. said there was not "one written phrase" in the Constitution to justify the attorney general's claim. Commenting on the government's statement that "the awesome power sought by the attorney general will be used with discretion," Edwards said "obviously, even in very recent days, this has not always been the case." Edwards was joined in his ruling by Judge Harry Phillips.

In a dissent, Judge Paul C. Weick said the President had the sworn duty "to protect and defend the nation from attempts of domestic subversives, as well as foreign enemies, to destroy it by force and violence."

Wiretapping curb eased. The Supreme Court ruled 5–4 April 5 that wiretapping without a warrant was legal with the consent of one of the parties in the tapped conversation. The justices overturned a lower court ruling that banned the use of a wired informer without court authorization.

The majority opinion, delivered by Justice White, said that wiretapping with the consent of one party did not constitute an unreasonable search. The ruling reinstated the narcotics conviction and 25-year sentence of James A. White of Chicago.

Justice Harlan, in a dissent, said unauthorized "third-party bugging" was bound to "undermine that confidence and sense of security in dealing with one another that is characteristic of individual relationships between citizens and society." Justices Douglas, Brennan and Marshall filed separate dissents.

Domestic wiretap appeal set. The Supreme Court agreed June 21 to hear the government's appeal of a lower court ruling against wiretapping of domestic radicals without court approval. The case, which was set for argument in the fall, involved the pending trial of Lawrence R. Plamondon, a member of the White Panther party, who was accused of conspiring to bomb a Central Intelligence Agency office in Ann Arbor, Mich.

U.S. District Court Judge Damon J. Keith, in Detroit, had ordered the Justice Department to turn over wiretap transcripts to Plamondon. The 6th U.S. Circuit Court of Appeals, upholding Keith's ruling, had said there were no constitutional grounds for an exception in "domestic subversion" cases from the need for warrants to wiretap.

Mitchell argument—In a speech before the Virginia Bar Association June 11, John N. Mitchell defended the government's position. He argued that "the threat to our society from so-called 'domestic' subversion is as serious as any threat from abroad" and that if it were possible to separate them, "history has shown greater danger from the domestic variety."

Mitchell said, "never in our history has this country been confronted with so many revolutionary elements deter-

mined to destroy by force the government and the society it stands for." He said radicals being tapped "are idealogically and in many instances directly connected with foreign interests."

Making a distinction between wiretaps for "intelligence" purposes or for prosecution, Mitchell asserted that the Administration and not the courts was in a better position to know if taps should be installed for intelligence. Mitchell said: "The Constitution of the United States cannot possibly be construed as containing provisions inconsistent with its own survival. It is the charter for a viable government system, not a suicide pact."

Wiretap appeal to be reviewed. The Supreme Court said Dec. 14 it would decide if witnesses subpoenaed before grand juries could legally refuse to testify until the government established that the juries' questions were not based on information learned through illegal wiretapping.

The justices agreed to hear the Justice Department's appeal of a U.S. circuit court decision in which civil contempt citations against Sister Jogues Egan and Anne Walsh were dismissed. The two women had been subpoenaed to testify before a grand jury in Harrisburg, Pa. to tell what they knew about the alleged plot to kidnap Henry A. Kissinger.

Sister Egan, 52, was named a co-conspirator but not a defendant in the case. Anne Walsh, 29, was a former nun who had been active in the antiwar movement.

Both had been granted immunity from prosecution and were ordered to testify before the grand jury, which was gathering evidence in connection with federal indictments of the Rev. Philip F. Berrigan and others who had been linked to the alleged plot.

Sister Egan and Miss Walsh were held to be in civil contempt of court after they refused to testify, but the 3rd Circuit U.S. Court of Appeals quashed the citations.

At the center of the case was whether the 1968 Omnibus Crime Control Act gave grand jury witnesses the standing to refuse to testify until the government showed that its questions were not based on information obtained from illegal eavesdropping.

'Harrisburg 7' lose wiretap appeal. The Rev. Philip P. Berrigan and his six colleagues in the Catholic antiwar movement were refused a hearing on their allegations that the government had used electronic surveillance to gather evidence in their case. The U.S. Court of Appeals for the 3rd District in Philadelphia Jan. 7, 1972 refused without comment to order Judge R. Dixon Herman to conduct an immediate hearing on the alleged use of wiretaps.

The seven defendants were scheduled to go on trial in Harrisburg on charges of conspiring to kidnap Presidential adviser Henry Kissinger, bomb Washington, D.C. heating tunnels, and raid draft of-

fices in several states. Besides Berrigan, the defendants were Eqbal Ahmad, Sister Elizabeth McAlister, Rev. Neil R. McLaughlin, Rev. Joseph Wenderoth, Anthony Scoblick, a separated priest, and Scoblick's wife Mary Cain Scoblick, a former nun. All were Catholics except Ahmad, a Pakistani national studying in the U.S.

Berrigan, McAlister sentenced—The Rev. Philip F. Berrigan was sentenced Sept. 5 in U.S. district court in Harrisburg, Pa. to four concurrent two-year terms, and Sister Elizabeth McAlister to a one-year-and-a-day term for smuggling letters at Lewisburg, Pa. federal penitentiary. Immediately after the sentences were read, U.S. attorneys moved to drop all conspiracy charges against the two and their fellow defendants in the "Harrisburg Seven" case, which had ended in a mistrial on the major charges.

In denying the motion for acquittal Aug. 28, Judge Herman said the defense had failed to prove discrimination, and he rejected another defense charge, that illegal wiretaps had "tainted" the government's case, since the transcripts of the tapes, handed over to the defense, contained only "innocuous" and "insignificant" conversations. The defense contended that no prosecution had ever been brought in similar letter-smuggling cases. The Federal Bureau of Prisons had dropped restrictions on the flow of mail in its penitentiaries before the Harrisburg trial had gone to the jury.

Wiretap law held unconstitutional. For the first time in a U.S. court, a judge in Philadelphia ruled June 1, 1972 that the 1968 federal law authorizing law enforcement agencies to wiretap phones under certain circumstances was unconstitutional.

In more than a dozen other cases, federal judges had upheld the law. The Supreme Court had not yet ruled on the constitutionality of the 1968 law.

But Judge Joseph S. Lord 3rd found the law "unconstitutional on its face" because it violated the Constitution's Fourth Amendment protecting citizens against "unreasonable searches and seizures."

At issue in the case was a motion sought by seven defendants in a gambling case to suppress evidence gathered by electronic surveillance.

In granting the defendants' request, Lord wrote: "The privacy of every citizen is in jeopardy if we become a nation which sanctions the indiscriminate use of secret electronic searches by the government."

U.S. Attorney Carl J. Melone said he would consult with the Justice Department before deciding whether to appeal Lord's decision.

In a related development, newly-confirmed Attorney General Richard G. Kleindienst said in a speech to members of the legal profession June 9 that wiretapping "is a legitimate, constitutional means to root out organized crime," asserting that the Administration would continue using it. Speaking to the Philadelphia chapter of the Federal Bar Association, Kleindienst foresaw a continued use of the wiretaps. "This will be done while this President [Nixon] is President and while I am attorney general."

Supreme Court curbs wiretapping. The Supreme Court June 19, 1972 declared unconstitutional the federal government's use of wiretapping and electronic surveillance to monitor domestic radicals without first obtaining court warrants.

Three of President Nixon's four appointees to the bench—Chief Justice Warren Burger, Harry A. Blackmun and Lewis F. Powell Jr.—joined the other justices in an 8-0 decision rejecting the Administration claim that warrants for taps in such cases were unnecessary. The Justice Department had argued that the President's authority to protect the country from internal subversion gave the government the constitutional authority to use wiretaps on "dangerous" radicals without court approval.

The fourth Nixon appointee, Justice William H. Rehnquist, had helped shape that argument while he was a Justice Department official. He did not participate in the ruling.

The court's decision was a major legal setback for the Nixon Administration, which had argued strenuously for its position.

But the court held in an opinion by Powell that "Fourth Amendment freedoms cannot properly be guaranteed if domestic surveillances may be conducted solely within the discretion of the executive branch." The Fourth Amendment protected citizens against "unreasonable searches and seizures."

While the court did not rule on wiretapping without court warrants of agents of foreign nations, the justices held that "national security" wiretapping of domestic radicals who had no foreign ties can be done only with the type of warrants now in use by police investigating organized crime.

In writing the court's opinion, Powell relied heavily upon the threat to free speech he saw in unchecked wiretapping of dissenters by the government.

"History abundantly documents the tendency of government—however benevolent and benign its motives—to view with suspicion those who most fervently dispute its policies."

Powell held that in cases involving domestic radicals as well as in ordinary criminal investigations, the Fourth Amendment protections against unreasonable searches and seizures required court approval for wiretapping.

"Unreviewed executive discretion may yield too readily to pressures to obtain incriminating evidence and overlook potential invasions of privacy and speech."

Free speech, Powell wrote, was at the heart of the matter. He added:

"The price of lawful public dissent must not be a dread of subjection to an unchecked surveillance power. Nor must the fear of unauthorized official eavesdropping deter vigorous citizen dissent and discussion of government action in private conversation."

Aside from the immediate effect of having the government stop its warrantless wiretapping of domestic radicals, the court's decision meant that any defendant in a federal prosecution had the right to see complete transcripts of any conversations monitored through warrantless taps in a domestic case so that his attorney could make certain that no illegally obtained information was being used in the prosecution.

Since 1968, the Justice Department had used wiretaps without warrants in a number of prominent cases, including the prosecution of the Chicago Seven riot-conspiracy defendants and the kidnaping and conspiracy case against the Rev. Philip F. Berrigan and other antiwar activists.

(The Justice Department said following the court's ruling that it would screen all such cases now under way to decide whether to release the wiretap transcripts or drop the prosecutions.)

The court's decision came in a case involving the government's wiretapping of three members of the radical White Panther party who had been accused of plotting to blow up a government building in Detroit. The government had appealed the case to the Supreme Court after a U.S. district court judge ordered the Justice Department to disclose the transcripts of the defendants' conversations which had been obtained through a warrantless wiretap.

Chief Justice Warren E. Burger noted that he concurred only in the court's result. Also concurring in a separate opinion was Justice Byron R. White.

Kleindienst issues order—After learning of the decision, Attorney General Richard G. Kleindienst said June 19 he had "directed the termination of all electronic surveillance in cases involving security that conflict with the court's opinion."

Kleindienst added that henceforth surveillance would be done "only under procedures that comply" with the court's ruling.

Curb set on wiretap evidence—Over the dissent of the four Nixon-appointed justices, the court June 26 held 5-4 that grand jury witnesses had the right to refuse to answer questions gleaned from information overheard on illegal listening devices.

The court's decision sustained the challenge brought by Sister Jogues Egan and Anne Walsh, a former nun, against their convictions for refusing to testify about an alleged plot to kidnap Presidential adviser Henry A. Kissinger.

The government had argued that a ruling in the plaintiffs' favor would slow down the work of grand juries by requiring tedious searching through wiretap transcripts before questioning could begin.

Hoffman, Plamondon charges dropped—In two separate cases, the Justice Department dropped charges July 28 against Yippie leader Abbie Hoffman in Washington and against Lawrence Plamondon and two other White Panther Party leaders in Detroit, rather than disclose transcripts of unauthorized national security wiretaps.

Hoffman had been charged with crossing state lines to participate in a riot, in connection with the 1971 Mayday demonstrations. Plamondon had been charged in a 1968 bombing case that led to the Supreme Court's wiretap decision.

U.S. drops Seale charges—The Justice Department said Sept. 27 it would drop contempt charges against Black Panther leader Bobby Seale imposed by U.S. District Court Judge Julius Hoffman during the "Chicago 7" trial in 1969.

The 7th U.S. Circuit Court of Appeals in Chicago had ordered the charges dropped unless the department turned over to Seale's attorney a transcript of electronically overheard conversations that had been introduced in Hoffman's chambers during the trial. The department had admitted that the conversations, overheard while Seale was in jail, were relevant to the contempt charges.

The conversations had been intercepted by a "national security" wiretap installed without court approval, a practice recently ruled unconstitutional by the Supreme Court. U.S. Attorney James R. Thompson told the appeals court that disclosure of the transcripts "would be inimical to our national security interests."

Douglas says court, LBJ were tapped. Justice William O. Douglas Oct. 15, 1973 charged that the Supreme Court's secret conference room had been "bugged." He said also that when Lyndon Johnson was president he complained that his phone had been tapped.

Douglas' assertion came in a dissenting opinion he wrote for a case in which the court had refused to grant bail to a defendant who claimed her phone had been improperly tapped by the government. He wrote: "I am indeed morally certain that the conference room of this court has been bugged, and President Johnson during his term in the White House asserted to me that even his phone was tapped." Douglas refused to elaborate.

In an interview published in the *New York Times* Oct. 29, Douglas elaborated on his Oct. 15 assertion that the Supreme Court's conference room had been bugged. "I don't know how many times Hughes [Chief Justice Charles Evans Hughes, 1930–41] detected there was a bug. . . . He discovered it was placed there by a D.C. policeman and two court employes. He had the bug removed and discharged the two court employes within the hour."

Wiretap disclosure ordered. U.S. District Court Judge Aubrey E. Robinson Jr. ruled in Washington Jan. 11, 1974 that the Justice Department must reveal the nature and extent of wiretaps and other surveillance of antiwar activists in 1968–69.

The ruling came in a civil suit filed in 1969 under the Omnibus Crime Act of 1968 providing compensation for victims of illegal wiretapping. The suit had been delayed during criminal trials of some of the plaintiffs, including the "Chicago Seven." Other plaintiffs were the War Resisters League, the Catholic Priests Fellowship, the Southern Conference Education Fund and the Black Panther Party.

Judge Robinson rejected Justice Department contentions that the wire taps should be kept secret for national security reasons and refused as "highly irregular" a government request that he examine the information privately.

Weathermen indictments dropped. U.S. District Court Judge Julius J. Hoffman Jan. 3, 1974 dismissed the 1970 indictment of 12 Weathermen charged with conspiring to incite the "days of rage" riots in Chicago in October 1969.

Dismissal had been requested by government attorneys, who said that Supreme Court restraints on wiretapping would have hampered prosecution of the case.

The accused were: William Ayers, Kathy Boudin, Judy Clark, Bernardine Dohrn, Linda Evans, John Jacobs, Jeffrey Jones, Howard Machtinger, Terry Robbins, Mark Rudd, Michael Spiegel and Lawrence Weiss.

Court voids Mitchell wiretap evidence. The Supreme Court ruled unanimously May 13, 1974 that former Attorney General John N. Mitchell failed to meet the requirements of the Organized Crime Control Act of 1968 when he allowed his executive assistant to approve wiretap applications, rather than doing it himself or designating a specific assistant attorney general to act in his place, as required by law.

In ruling that the wiretap requests approved by Mitchell's executive assistant Sol Lindenbaum were illegal, the court upheld the dismissal of a narcotics indictment against Dominic N. Giordano of Baltimore. The ruling was expected to have the same effect in 60 other narcotics and gambling cases involving 626 defendants.

While the full court agreed that evidence from the wiretaps authorized by Lindenbaum was inadmissible, the four Nixon appointees to the court—Chief Justice Warren E. Burger and Justices Harry A. Blackmun, Lewis F. Powell Jr. and William H. Rehnquist—argued in a separate dissent that court-ordered extensions of the Lindenbaum-authorized taps were not improper.

Writing for the court in its unanimous ruling, Justice Byron R. White brushed aside government arguments that the defective procedures were merely technicalities. White said he had traced the history of the provision and found that Congress had included it to make "doubly sure that statutory authority [would] be used with restraint."

In a parallel case, the court upheld by a 5–4 margin the validity of another set of wiretaps affecting 99 cases and 807 defendants. Here, wiretap applications had been authorized by Mitchell but signed by former Assistant Attorney General Will R. Wilson, who had not actually played any part in their preparation. The court majority said it did not "condone" Mitchell's practices, but attributed defects in these wiretap requests to poor bookkeeping practices. Arguing in dissent that the Wilson-signed tap authorizations resulted in tainted evidence were Justices William O. Douglas, William J. Brennan Jr., Potter Stewart and Thurgood Marshall.

Court begins 1974–75 term. The Supreme Court issued its first decisions of the 1974–75 term Oct. 15. It agreed to hear and decide 25 cases, resolved some of the others without further consideration, but rejected a vast majority of the 1,011 appeals, motions and requests before it.

Among the court's major actions:

The court declined to hear a challenge to the President's right to authorize warrantless wiretaps to gather foreign intelligence. The court's refusal to hear the case, which involved the 1964 espionage conviction of Soviet national Igor A. Ivanov, did not signify its approval or disapproval of wiretapping, but had the effect of permitting federal agents to continue the practice. In upholding Ivanov's conviction, the Court of Appeals for the 3rd Circuit had ruled that the evidence obtained from the wiretap was admissible in court if the surveillance had been found to be reasonably related to the exercise of presidential power in the area of foreign affairs.

Three of court's justices, one short of the required number, voted to take jurisdiction. They were William O. Douglas, William J. Brennan Jr. and Potter Stewart. Justice Thurgood Marshall, who served as soliciter general for two years during which the case was pending, did not participate.

Warrantless wiretapping curbed. The U.S. Circuit Court of Appeals for the District of Columbia June 23, 1975 ruled that the executive branch needed court approval before it could wiretap domestic organizations, even if the surveillance were for reasons of national security.

The decision involved a warrantless wiretap placed for 208 days in 1970 and 1971 on the New York City headquarters of the Jewish Defense League, a militant Zionist group whose anti-Soviet activities in the U.S. were creating diplomatic tension between the U.S. and U.S.S.R.

In arguing that the tap had been legal, the federal government had defended the surveillance on the grounds that it "was authorized by the President..., acting through the attorney general in the exercise of his authority relating to foreign affairs, and was deemed essential to protect this nation...against hostile acts of a foreign power and to obtain foreign intelligence information deemed essential to the security of the United States."

The appellate court rejected that reasoning, however, holding that then-Attorney General John N. Mitchell should have obtained court approval of the tap since it was being installed on a domestic organization that was neither an agent of nor acting in collaboration with a foreign government.

While the court did not address the issue of wiretaps on agents of foreign governments, it did state: "Indeed, our analysis would suggest that, absent exigent circumstances, no wiretapping in the area of foreign affairs should be exempt from prior judicial scrutiny, irrespective of the justification for the surveillance or the importance of the information sought."

Justice Department told to heed ruling—President Ford told the Justice Department to heed the June 24 appeals court ruling on wiretaps, it was announced July 1. The Justice Department was considering an appeal of the decision, and the President instructed Attorney General Edward H. Levi to follow the ruling even outside of the District of Columbia while the appeal was pending. Press Secretary Ron Nessen told reporters that Ford was considering legislation requiring a court order for any electronic surveillance.

Wiretaps decline—The number of wiretaps officially sanctioned by state and federal courts in 1974 was down 16% from the year before, the Administrative Office of the U.S. Courts said in its annual wiretapping and electronic surveillance report to Congress May 2. In the 24 jurisdictions where the practice was legal, 728 interceptions were authorized and 694 bugs installed, enabling agents to listen to more than 40,000 persons engaged in 590,000 conversations, the office reported.

Federal court-ordered wiretaps numbered 121 in 1974, down from 130 in 1973. State courts issued 607 wiretap orders, 127 fewer than the previous year. The report also indicated that no federal judge turned down a Justice Department request for a tap. On the state level, only two applications were denied, both in Connecticut.

The cost of federal wiretaps, which had been as high as $2.2 million in 1971, fell to $1.3 million in 1974. Expenditures on the state level were $4.2 million. Average state and federal costs rose to $8,087 per installation, up from $5,632 in 1973.

Warrantless wiretaps up since 1972—The incidence of warrantless wiretapping by the federal government for purposes of national security rose sharply between 1972 and 1974, according to Justice Department statistics made public June 24. The figures, contained in a letter from Attorney General Edward H. Levi to Sen. Edward M. Kennedy (D, Mass.), showed that such wiretaps had averaged 108 for each year between 1969–1972 and then increased to an average of 156 a year during 1973–1974. In addition, Levi's letter said that microphone surveillances, installed without judicial warrant to intercept room conversations, had averaged 20 a year during 1969–1972, but jumped to an average of 41 a year in 1973 and 1974.

Levi in his letter, which Kennedy released without comment, defended national security wiretaps conducted without prior judicial approval. "Based on an examination of the relevant precedents," Levi said, "it is the position of the Justice Department that the executive may conduct electronic surveillance in the interests of national security and foreign intelligence and in the aid of his conduct of the nation's foreign affairs, without obtaining a judicial warrant."

In a related development, the National Wiretap Commission released data June 23 showing that fewer than 2% of the violations of federal wiretapping laws uncovered by telephone company employes resulted in the arrest or federal prosecution of those responsible for the taps. The statistics, compiled for the commission by the Federal Bureau of Investigation and the various operating companies of American Telephone & Telegraph Corp., indicated that 1,457 wiretaps had been discovered on or near company instruments during the 7½-year period ended June 30, 1974. Federal arrests or prosecution followed in 27 of those cases, the commission said.

Congress and the FBI

Senator suspects phone taps. Sen. Joseph M. Montoya (D, N.M.) said March 19, 1971 that he and other senators believed the Justice Department had tapped private telephone lines of congressmen. Montoya did not reveal the basis for the belief. A Justice Department spokesman said March 20 the suspicion was "absolutely false."

In a speech at Colorado's Jefferson-Jackson Day Dinner in Denver, Montoya said the Nixon Administration had encouraged and actively participated in "frightening invasions of citizens' rights and privileges." He said that "even the United States Senate is not immune" and that several senators "have plainly stated they believe their conversations have been monitored."

Montoya also said the Post Office had opened first-class mail without the knowledge of the recipients.

Boggs demands Hoover ouster. Rep. Hale Boggs (D, La.), in a one-minute speech on the House floor April 5, accused the Federal Bureau of Investigation (FBI) of tapping telephones of congressmen. The House majority leader asked that FBI Director J. Edgar Hoover be fired.

Boggs accused the bureau of adopting "the tactics of the Soviet Union and Hitler's Gestapo" and called on Attorney General John N. Mitchell to "have enough courage to demand [Hoover's] resignation." He said: "When the FBI taps the telephones of members of this body and members of the Senate, when the FBI stations agents on college campuses to infiltrate college organizations, . . . then it is time that the present director no longer be the director."

Mitchell issued a statement April 5 in which he "categorically" denied that the FBI had ever tapped a congressman's phone. He accused Boggs of "slanderous falsehoods" and said his charges "reached a new low in political dialogue. He should recant at once and apologize to a great American."

Boggs repeated his charges April 6 and said he would produce evidence "in the near future" to support the allegations. He stated "categorically" that the FBI "had me under surveillance, my personal life." An FBI spokesman denied that Boggs was under surveillance, but he said the bureau would not comment on whether Boggs had been investigated in the past. The spokesman said, "We are not and never have been tapping senators and congressmen."

Mitchell said in an April 6 press release, "Mr. Boggs's statements . . . now confirm the plain fact that his charges . . . have no factual basis whatever." White House Press Secretary Ronald L. Ziegler said April 6, "the President, of course, does not favor the tapping of phones of members of Congress."

Senate Majority Leader Mike Mansfield (Mont.) and Minority Leader Hugh Scott (Pa.) both said April 6 they had received no complaints from their colleagues about suspected FBI phone taps. However, Sen. Joseph M. Montoya (D, N.M.) had said March 19 that several congressmen suspected they had been the subjects of Justice Department wiretaps.

Deputy Attorney General Richard G. Kleindienst said April 7 that Boggs was "either sick or not in possession of his faculties" when he made his charges on the House floor. Kleindienst said he would "welcome an investigation by the responsible members of Congress" of the allegations. "Unless that is done or Mr. Boggs retracts his statements," Kleindienst said, "you have hanging in the air the charge itself—wiretapping the telephones of members of Congress."

Rep. Bella S. Abzug (D, N.Y.) introduced a resolution April 7 calling on the House Judiciary Committee to conduct "a full and complete investigation" of the FBI, including "investigation of the ability of the director." Rep. Charles H. Wilson (D, Calif.) introduced a bill to limit the tenure of the head of the bureau to 10 years and to set a mandatory retirement age of 65. Hoover, 76, had been director of the bureau since 1924.

Rep. Wayne Hays (D, Ohio), chairman of the House Administration Committee, said April 7 he would commission a "reputable firm" to check whether House members' phones were being tapped or their offices bugged. Robert G. Dunphy, the Senate sergeant-at-arms, had said April 6 that he periodically received requests from senators to check their telephone lines. He said he might receive one or two such requests a month and said he knew of no evidence that taps had been found.

Boggs repeats charges—Boggs attempted to back up his case against the FBI in an hour-long House speech April 22. He denounced the "secret police spying and prying" of the FBI and asked President Nixon to appoint an investigatory commission "to go to the core of this cancer and remove it before the poisons spread further."

Boggs said the telephone line in his private home had been tapped in 1970. He said a Chesapeake and Potomac Telephone Co. investigator had determined that his line had been tapped but that the tap had been removed. He said that later, in an official report, the telephone company stated that no taps were discovered. Boggs said he learned subsequently that the company's policy was to deny the existence of a tap if it had been placed by the FBI.

The House majority leader also suggested that an electronic surveillance device had been used at the home of Sen. Charles H. Percy (R, Ill.) and that listening devices had been placed in the offices of former Sen. Wayne Morse of Oregon and Sen. Birch Bayh (D, Ill.). However, Boggs did not directly accuse the FBI of installing the surveillance devices.

Boggs' allegations, warrantless wiretaps discussed—Rep. Clarence J. Hogan (R, Md.), who had formerly worked for the FBI, immediately rebutted Boggs' charges. Hogan said Boggs had offered "innuendoes" but had "failed completely" to substantiate his charges with positive proof.

Attorney General John N. Mitchell said April 23 that Boggs had failed to produce "one iota of proof of the reckless charges" made in his speech and that he was suffering from "a new type of paranoia—called Tappanoia."

Mitchell, who made his remarks to a Kentucky Bar Association meeting in Cincinnati, also defended the Administration's right to use wiretaps against domestic subversives without obtaining court warrants. A federal appeals court in Cincinnati had ruled that such taps could only be installed under court order, and on April 27, the Justice Department announced it was appealing that ruling to the Supreme Court.

Rep. Emanuel Celler (D, N.Y.), chairman of the House Judiciary Committee, in an interview April 25, disputed Mitchell's claim that unwarranted wiretaps were justified "when, in his opinion, the national security is involved." Celler said, "that's a huge umbrella that can cover thousands of actions. . . . Who is to be judge of national security? . . . He is to be the judge? That's not government by law, that's government by personality."

In two rival Law Day speeches, delivered to opposing factions of the District of Columbia Bar Association and the Federal Bar Association in Washington April 27, Assistant Attorney General Robert C. Mardian defended the Administration's security policies and Sen. Harold E. Hughes (D, Iowa) sharply attacked the Administration for fostering "a private climate wherein official spying is the name of the game."

Mardian, invited as the official speaker, told about 100 lawyers and judges that the need for information made government intelligence gathering "an obligation rather than a right or privilege." He said proper information might have prevented the assassination of President Kennedy. He also suggested that miscalculations based on inadequate information might have contributed to the situation in which four Kent State University students were killed by National Guardsmen in May 1970.

Hughes' address was heard by some 300 lawyers who attended a rival Law Day meeting set up by young lawyers who objected to the invitation extended to Mardian, the Justice Department's chief security official. Hughes, considered an unannounced candidate for the Democratic presidential nomination, accused the Nixon Administration of creating a "trend toward repression." He cited "the relentlessly increasing emphasis on wiretapping, bugging, no-knock entry, subpoenaing of private notebooks and tapes from news reporters, increased surveillance by the government of dissident political groups and the attempts by the government to intimidate the communications media."

Nixon justifies wiretapping—At his press conference April 29, President Nixon said there were only one half as many taps today as there were in 1961, 1962 and 1963, Nixon said, and the "hysteria" and "political demagogury" about the FBI tapping telephones "simply doesn't serve the public purpose." He considered as "justified" the taps approved by the attorney general in cases "dealing with those who would use violence or other means to overthrow the government." Such taps, he said, were currently limited to less than 50 at any one time.

"This is not a police state," Nixon declared, and his Administration was "against any kind of repression, any kind of action that infringes on the right of privacy." He was for "that kind of action that is necessary to protect this country from those who would imperil the peace that all the people are entitled to enjoy."

On April 16 Nixon had said, "despite all the talk about surveillance and bugging and the rest, let me say I have been in police states, and the idea that this is a police state is just pure nonsense. And every editorial paper in the country ought to say that."

Nixon said, "I can assure you that there is no question in my mind that Mr. Hoover's statement that no telephone in the Capitol has ever been tapped by the FBI is correct." On the question of telephone taps in national security cases, Nixon said the "high, insofar as those taps are concerned," was in 1961-63 when there were between 90 and 100 taps each year.

Bugging of Dowdy revealed. Documents released by a federal judge April 16 revealed that the FBI had recorded four telephone conversations between Rep. John Dowdy (D, Tex.) and an FBI informant. The documents also showed that agents had escorted the informant to Dowdy's Capitol Hill office where a conversation with the congressman was recorded by a tape machine concealed on the informant's person.

The documents, which appeared to contradict recent statements by Justice Department officials that the FBI did not use electronic surveillance on congressmen or tap their lines, were released by U.S. District Court Judge Roszel C. Thomsen in Baltimore. The FBI actions, connected with a bribe conspiracy charge against Dowdy had been reported in the *New York Times* April 16. Thomsen said he had kept the papers secret at Dowdy's request but said the article in the *Times* "removed the principal reason for keeping them sealed."

According to the court papers, Dowdy's telephone conversations had been monitored at the informer's end of the line, and no listening device was ever placed on the congressman's telephone. FBI agents had wired the informer's telephone and equipped him with a tape recorder on his visit to Dowdy. The activity had been approved in a court warrant and had been undertaken with the knowledge of Attorney General Mitchell and FBI Director Hoover. (The Supreme Court later ruled April 5 that such surveillance, when conducted through an informer, did not need court approval.)

In an interview with a *Washington Post* reporter April 17, Deputy Attorney General Richard G. Kleindienst said the recording of Dowdy's conversations did not constitute "surveillance" as defined by the Justice Department. Kleindienst had been asked to explain the Dowdy incident in light of his statement April 7 that the FBI had not used "electronic surveillance or the tapping of telephones of senators and congressmen" even in criminal investigations.

Kleindienst said April 17 that "surveillance" occurred when neither party to a conversation knew that it was being recorded. He said Dowdy's conversations were recorded with the informer's permission and that this action constituted "consensual conversation" and not "surveillance."

Senate Majority Leader Mike Mansfield (D, Mont.), who had said April 15 that the recent criticism of the FBI and Hoover contained "more noise than substance," said April 17 that the Dowdy incident was "a cause for grave concern." He said the eavesdropping on Dowdy had not been a proper use of FBI powers "even though they acted under a court order."

Sen. Sam J. Ervin Jr. (D, N.C.), whose Subcommittee on Constitutional Rights had been investigating government domestic surveillance, called the FBI conduct in the Dowdy case "reprehensible" April 18, and he said, "I'm not sure it's illegal." He said he would not include FBI activities in his investigation until he saw some evidence of illegality.

However, Ervin said he would order a staff review of the charges in the Dowdy affair.

Hoover barred FBI surveillance on Capitol Hill. An unnamed, former high-ranking FBI official told the *Washington Post* Dec. 30, 1974 that J. Edgar Hoover, the late FBI director, declared the grounds of the U.S. Capitol in Washington "off limits" to FBI agents. Hoover feared criticism from congressmen, who periodically accused him of tapping their telephones and compiling dossiers on their private lives, the official said. Soviet agents quickly learned of the prohibition and scheduled meetings there, the former official added.

Hoover reports FBI phone taps. Federal Bureau of Investigation Director J. Edgar Hoover, in House Appropriations subcommittee testimony released June 8, 1971, said the bureau was conducting 33 telephone taps and four microphone bugging devices in national security cases. In testimony given March 17, Hoover also said the bureau was operating 14 court-approved wiretaps and two bugging devices in organized crime cases.

The Justice Department said June 8 that FBI surveillance had remained stable since Hoover's appearance before the committee. The FBI director had said then that Attorney General John N. Mitchell had authorized all the taps "in the security field" and that the FBI had requested two additional authorizations. He said courts had issued warrants for 12 additional organized crime taps and that the bureau was seeking warrants for 45 more.

Hoover insisted that newspaper reports of FBI wiretapping were "replete with distortions, inaccuracies and outright falsehoods." He cited *Washington Post* articles published Feb. 7 and 8 that quoted former Attorney General Ramsey Clark as saying that FBI taps were double the number Hoover reported to Congress and "one well-informed source" that the number of FBI taps was reduced just before Hoover was to testify before a Congressional committee and resumed afterwards. Hoover also declared, "we have never tapped a telephone of any congressman or any senator since I have been director of the bureau."

Hoover appeared before the subcommittee, chaired by Rep. John J. Rooney (D, N.Y.), to request a fiscal 1972 budget of $318.6 million. He also asked for a $44.2 million increase in the current FBI budget.

Wiretaps cited as valuable. J. Edgar Hoover, director of the Federal Bureau of Investigation, said Jan. 6, 1972 that wiretaps had contributed to what he described as an increase in the conviction of gangsters involved with organized crime.

Hoover said "these devices have been increasingly valuable in penetrating these complex, tightly knit conspiracies involving intricate security precautions, and most of the 1,200 arrests under the

Organized Crime Control Act were made possible by them."

According to Hoover, more than 650 persons linked to organized crime were convicted in 1971, a rise of almost 200 from 1970. He said that much of the gain "should go to court-approved electronic surveillance devices provided for in recent legislation.

Kelley asks widened FBI wiretap powers—Clarence M. Kelley, director of the FBI, said Sept. 21, 1974 that it properly watch revolutionaries who planted bombs. With increased freedom to wiretap, Kelley said, the FBI could effectively watch the groups that he said were responsible for many of the 2,000 bombings annually in the U.S.

Noting that civil libertarians might object to legislation widening FBI electronic surveillance powers, Kelley said the bombers presented a more serious threat to U.S. society than a new wiretapping law. "We are responsible people and are not going to cause people to needlessly lose their rights," he said.

FBI tapped King at 1964 convention. The *Washington Post* reported Jan. 25, 1975 that President Johnson had ordered the FBI to eletronicly bug and wiretap civil rights leaders during the 1964 Democratic national convention in Atlantic City, N.J. The source of its story, the *Post* said, was a Senate Watergate Committee memorandum summarizing a 1973 interview with Leo T. Clark, a former FBI agent, who was a key member of the team that carried out the surveillance.

According to the memorandum, wiretaps were installed in the hotel suite of Martin Luther King Jr., the late civil rights leader, and at an Atlantic City storefront used by civil rights groups. As a result of the wiretaps, the memo said, President Johnson obtained reports on the conversations of then Attorney General Robert F. Kennedy, members of Congress and other key convention delegates.

In the interview, Clark indicated that the stated purpose of the FBI operations was to gather intelligence on potential violence or disruptions. However, Clark acknowledged that Cartha D. DeLoach, assistant to the late FBI Director J. Edgar Hoover, ordered the surveillance kept secret from the Secret Service and the FBI's Newark N.J. office, which normally would have coordinated security at the convention.

Information from the operation, Clark said, was transmitted to President Johnson over a special telephone line that bypassed the White House switchboard. Clark also told the interviewers DeLoach had admitted that Kennedy, as the attorney general, had not been informed of the bugs. But DeLoach, Clark said, indicated Johnson was aware of them.

"'In a DeLoach conversation with the President, Clark heard mention of discussions concerning the seating of delegates or delegations, of vice presidential candidate possibilities, and the identities of congressmen and senators going in and

out of King's quarters,' " the Post quoted the memo as saying.

The *Post* also obtained DeLoach's sworn testimony in 1973 before the Senate Watergate Committee. In the secret testimony DeLoach denied having had a direct line to Johnson or having spoken to him during the convention. Instead, DeLoach said FBI activities focused on one delegate suspected of connections with the Communist Party and on possible violence at the convention.

Sen. Howard H. Baker (R, Tenn.), a member of the Watergate Committee, said on the ABC program "Issues and Answers" Jan. 26 that Clark's information had not been made part of the committee's final report because "it was not involved in the '72 Presidential campaign."

FBI tapped black lawyer. In legal papers filed in the federal district court in Detroit, the FBI admitted monitoring 40 conversations of a black lawyer who was not under criminal investigation, Melvin Wulf, legal director of the American Civil Liberties Union (ACLU), said Feb. 4. The FBI filed the papers, Wulf said, in response to a civil suit by Abdeen M. Jabara, a Detroit attorney.

Jabara had charged the FBI with violating his constitutional rights of free speech and assembly by investigating him although it had no reason to believe he had engaged in criminal activity. The ACLU joined in the suit.

According to Wulf, the bureau's interest in Jabara stemmed from the fact that he represented a group of Arab students in the U.S. Jabara also had advocated changing Israel into a state for Arabs, Jews and Christians.

Since 1972, the FBI papers said, Jabara had been monitored 40 times, during which he spoke to persons who were the targets of 13 separate surveillance operations by the bureau. No taps were placed on his home or office telephones, the papers said.

Tighter wiretap curbs urged. A Senate study released Feb. 16, 1975 recommended tighter controls on national security wiretapping. The study, conducted by panels of the Judiciary Committee and Foreign Relations Committee, concluded that during the Nixon Administration, the White House played a major and "unparalleled" role in initiating and maintaining wiretaps on 14 federal officials and three newsmen; that an attempt was made to hide the wiretaps and to deny their existence; and that some of the targets were followed as well as wiretapped.

The study cited testimony that members of Congress and members of their staffs were wiretapped. It found that agencies other than the Federal Bureau of Investigation had installed taps and said a presidential directive that the attorney general approve all warrantless wiretaps in advance had been ignored at times.

Soviet taps of U.S. phones reported. The *Chicago Tribune* reported June 22 that the Soviet Union had put into effect a massive operation to monitor, record and

identify private phone calls within the U.S. The Soviets had long possessed the technology necessary to intercept microwaves, which were used in the U.S. to transmit 70% of all long distance telephone calls, but had only recently developed the computer technology required to separate the conversations and identify the callers, according to the *Tribune*.

The disclosure, the *Tribune* said, had prompted investigations by the White House and congressional committees to determine how much information was being gathered, how it was used and what, if anything, was being done by U.S. intelligence agencies to stop the monitoring by the KGB, the Soviet security police.

The newspaper indicated that the information had been disclosed in testimony to the Rockefeller commission during its probe of domestic U.S. intelligence but that the testimony had been heavily censored from the commission's final report for reasons of national security.

Kelley opposes wiretap curbs. FBI Director Clarence M. Kelley told the House Civil Liberties Subcommittee June 26, 1975 that congressional proposals to prohibit warrantless wiretapping would have a "crippling impact." According to Kelley, the proposals to base court orders for electronic surveillance on the probability of commission of crimes "would drastically curtail, if not eliminate, the intelligence function of the executive branch of the government." The subcommittee had disclosed that 232 wiretaps and bugs were used in 1974 without court orders, compared to 163 in 1973.

The Press, the NSC, and the FBI

Time **charges wiretaps by FBI.** *Time* magazine charged in its March 5, 1973 issue that the White House ordered over a period of more than two years the Federal Bureau of Investigation (FBI) to tap the telephones of "six or seven" newsmen and a number of White House aides in order to pinpoint a news leak in the executive staff. *Time* attributed the story to "four different sources in the government." It declined, however, to name the sources or the newsmen involved. The magazine said the late J. Edgar Hoover, then director of the FBI, at first balked at using wiretaps, but was ordered by then Attorney General John Mitchell to follow White House orders.

Time said the wiretapping actually kept Hoover in office. Mitchell's deputy Richard Kleindienst, the present attorney general, wanted Hoover to retire, but quickly dropped the issue when Hoover threatened to expose the wiretaps to Congress. *Time* said the taps failed to uncover any leaks.

Kleindienst issued a statement Feb. 26 denying the *Time* magazine charges with regard to both himself and Mitchell.

Taps on Times reporters disclosed—The phones of at least two reporters for the *New York Times* were tapped by members of the Nixon Administration in connection with the Pentagon Papers disclosure, the *Washington Post* reported May 3.

The *Post* cited one highly placed Administration source as saying the wiretapping was supervised by Watergate co-conspirators E. Howard Hunt Jr. and G. Gordon Liddy, and that former Attorney General John N. Mitchell authorized the taps.

The source said the team of wiretappers, supervised by Hunt and Liddy, operated independent of the FBI, the agency normally responsible for electronic surveillance.

According to *Post* sources, the wiretaps followed earlier White House-ordered taps of other reporters, the purpose of which was to discover leaks of information about the strategic arms limitation talks to the news media.

The sources also said the home or office phones of at least 10 White House staffers were tapped in an effort to stem other news leaks.

"In late 1971 or early 1972, it was decided at a Nixon campaign strategy meeting that some members of the same vigilante squad responsible for the Pentagon Papers wiretapping would be used to wiretap the telephones of the Democratic presidential candidates...," the *Post* said.

1969 phone taps reported—The Nixon Administration, concerned over leaks of classified information—especially with regard to the strategic arms limitations talks beginning in 1969—ordered wiretaps placed on the telephones of reporters from three newspapers and at least one government official, the *New York Times* reported May 11.

Times sources said reporters placed under surveillance were William Beecher and Hedrick Smith of the *New York Times*, and Henry Brandon, a Washington-based correspondent for the *Sunday Times* of London. Phones of unidentified reporters for the *Washington Post* also were tapped, the *Times* said.

The government official was Morton H. Halperin, a member of the National Security Council until 1971. The tap on his home phone was revealed in a memo given May 9 by Acting FBI Director William Ruckelshaus to Pentagon Papers trial Judge William M. Byrne.

According to the account supplied by *Times* sources, former Attorney General John N. Mitchell called the late director of the FBI, J. Edgar Hoover, in the spring of 1969, requesting that the taps be placed. Hoover refused to comply without written authorization from Mitchell, who subsequently sent the late FBI chief an unspecified number of forms used to request "national security" wiretaps. The Supreme Court had ruled in 1972 the government needed court orders before it could install wiretaps in national security cases, except where foreign connections were involved.

According to *Times* sources, Mitchell and Assistant Attorney General Richard Kleindienst, sometime after, suggested to Hoover, for reasons that were unclear, that a Congressional committee be allowed to investigate the FBI. Hoover refused consent, saying he might be asked about the wiretap installations.

In September 1971, the Justice Department retrieved the forms.

Ruckelshaus ordered an investigation of the 1969-71 buggings, but had not been able to determine if records still existed, the *Times* said.

Missing FBI wiretap files found. William D. Ruckelshaus, acting director of the Federal Bureau of Investigation disclosed at a May 14, 1973 press conference that missing records of 17 FBI wiretaps placed on newsmen and government officials had been discovered May 11 in a safe in the outer office of former presidential adviser John Ehrlichman.

Ruckelshaus, declining to identify those under surveillance, said he personally retrieved them May 12.

In a related development, the *New York Times* reported May 17 that national security adviser Henry Kissinger, acting under presidential authorization, formally submitted requests for the taps to the late FBI director, J. Edgar Hoover.

Contained in the records was information relating to the wiretap that had been placed on the home telephone of Morton H. Halperin, an adviser to the National Security Council. It was on Halperin's phone that former Pentagon Papers defendant Daniel Ellsberg was overheard by the FBI. Ruckelshaus said the records were discovered an hour after Judge William M. Byrne had dismissed charges against Ellsberg and Anthony J. Russo Jr. Ruckelshaus declined to speculate on the effect the records might have had on the trial if they had been found in time.

Ruckelshaus said the FBI had assumed the records had been destroyed. This was based on two pieces of FBI correspondence, bearing notations in Hoover's handwriting, that indicated former Attorney General John N. Mitchell had so informed the late director. Ruckelshaus noted that Mitchell had previously denied making such a statement.

(Ehrlichman said May 14 he had the records in his safe for more than a year. He said he had "skimmed" them but was unaware they contained any material about Ellsberg. A White House spokesman said May 15 that President Nixon had not known the files were in Ehrlichman's safe.)

Ruckelshaus explained that the FBI had ascertained the records still existed in a May 10 interview in Phoenix, Ariz. with Robert C. Mardian, former assistant attorney general in charge of the now defunct Internal Security Division.

Mardian suggested they might be in the White House, Ruckelshaus explained.

Ruckelshaus said an FBI investigation showed that after the wiretaps had been removed in 1971, the records were placed in the custody of William C. Sullivan, then assistant director of the FBI. Sullivan later contacted Mardian about the records and recommended they be transferred. According to Mardian, the recommendation had been made because Sullivan thought Hoover might use them against the attorney general or the President, Ruckelshaus said.

Sullivan confirmed the sequence of events in an interview published in the *Los Angeles Times* May 14. He said the records were kept in the White House because Hoover was "not of sound mind" in his later years. Sullivan gave the files to Mardian before being forced to retire Oct. 6, 1971, since he felt Hoover "could not be trusted" to keep the files confidential. However, contrary to what Ruckelshaus had said, Sullivan claimed Mitchell ordered the files given to Mardian.

Sullivan, noting that Hoover had ordered the files kept outside the regular FBI filing system, said Justice Department officials, who were aware of the files, became very upset when they learned Sullivan was leaving the FBI.

"They could no longer depend on Hoover. He had been leaking stuff all over the place. He could no longer be trusted. So I was instructed to pass the records to Mardian," Sullivan said.

Hoover, who was concerned about being fired as director, retained the records "to keep Mitchell and others in line," Sullivan continued.

"The fellow was a master blackmailer and he did it with considerable finesse despite the deterioration of his mind," Sullivan said.

Sullivan said neither Mardian nor Mitchell ever specifically told him they did not want Hoover to have the files because they could not trust Hoover. But Sullivan said he could "read between the lines."

W. Mark Felt, acting associate director of the FBI, May 16 criticized Sullivan's statements as "irresponsible." Felt said Hoover, the day before his death, "demonstrated extraordinary acuity in making significant decisions on the investigative work of the bureau."

Nixon authorized wiretaps—The White House May 16 acknowledged that President Nixon personally authorized the use of 17 wiretaps against 13 members of his own Administration and four newsmen.

The New York Times reported May 17 that Henry A. Kissinger, assistant to the President for national security affairs, personally provided the FBI with the names of a number of his aides on the National Security Council (NSC), whom he wanted wiretapped. The *Times* cited Justice Department officials as its source.

The White House, in formally acknowledging the existence of the wire taps, said they were made in 1969 after publication in the *Times* May 9, 1969 of an article by William Beecher disclosing American B-52s were bombing Cambodia.

Kissinger, in an interview with the *Times* May 14, confirmed he had seen summaries of the wiretaps, but he said he had not asked that they be installed nor had he specifically approved them in advance. He also admitted he held one or two conversations with Hoover in 1969 in which he expressed "very great concern" that national security information be fully safeguarded.

The *Washington Post* reported May 18 that specific wiretaps had also been authorized by H. R. Haldeman, Nixon's former chief of staff.

Other former NSC officials whose phones were reported tapped were Anthony Lake, Daniel I. Davidson, and Winston Lord. Lord, a personal aide to Kissinger during the Paris peace talks and during his visits to Peking and Moscow, was on a one-year leave from the NSC.

Kissinger takes responsibility for taps— Henry A. Kissinger, President Nixon's national security adviser, May 29 conceded "his office" supplied names of some of the members of the National Security Council to the Federal Bureau of Investigation beginning in 1969 to wiretap their phones.

Kissinger, branding wiretaps as "a distasteful thing in general," defended them in safeguarding national security.

Kissinger declined to explain what he meant by "his office." "I am responsible for what happens in my office, and I won't give the names of the people who did it," Kissinger said.

He had denied authorizing any wiretaps May 14.

Nixon's comments— The House Judiciary Committee July 18, 1974 released a four-volume 2,090-page record of the evidence accumulated by its staff concerning clandestine activities sponsored by the White House. A 225-page rebuttal by the President's special counsel, James D. St. Clair, accompanied the publication of the evidence.

The mass of evidence suggested that clandestine White House activities originated because of national security concerns but later became overtly political operations. The documents also showed that Nixon and his top aides were aware in March and April 1973 that some of the activities of the White House "plumbers" investigative unit were illegal.

The evidence cited White House concern about leaks of national security information and the highly secret wiretap program that was instituted in 1969 to combat the leaks. In 1970, the evidence indicated, the President was ready to approve implementation of the domestic surveillance plan proposed by White House aide Tom Charles Huston. Nixon rescinded his approval at the last minute because of objections from FBI Director J. Edgar Hoover, who refused to countenance the illegalties of the plan.

In 1971, White House efforts against news leaks took the form of 17 wiretaps against government officials and newsmen, as well as the creation of the

"plumbers." Part of the evidence released was Nixon's assessment of the wiretaps, which he made known to John W. Dean 3rd, his counsel, Feb. 28, 1973. "They never helped. Just gobs and gobs of material: gossip and bullshitting," Nixon said. The evidence pointed out that two of the taps remained in effect even after the two officials in question—unnamed in the report, but widely known to be former National Security Council advisers Morton Halperin and Anthony Lake—had left the Administration and become foreign policy advisers to one of the 1972 Democratic presidential hopefuls.

Tighter wiretap curbs urged. A Senate study released Feb. 16, 1975 recommended tighter controls on national security wiretapping. The study, conducted by panels of the Judiciary Committee and Foreign Relations Committee, concluded that during the Nixon Administration, the White House played a major and "unparalleled" role in initiating and maintaining wiretaps on 14 federal officials and three newsmen; that an attempt was made to hide the wiretaps and to deny their existence; and that some of the targets were followed as well as wiretapped.

The study cited testimony that members of Congress and members of their staffs were wiretapped. It found that agencies other than the Federal Bureau of Investigation had installed taps and said a presidential directive that the attorney general approve all warrantless wiretaps in advance had been ignored at times.

Kissinger

Kissinger confirmation hearings. Henry A. Kissinger's role in the 1969–71 wiretapping of government officials and newsmen became the major question before the Senate Foreign Relations Committee as it opened public confirmation hearings Sept. 7, 1973 on Kissinger's nomination as secretary of state.

Kissinger defended the wiretapping as necessary to stop leaks to the press. He said he had consented to the practice in 1969 on the advice of then Attorney General John N. Mitchell and the late director of the Federal Bureau of Investigation (FBI), J. Edgar Hoover. He disclaimed deep involvement in the operation and said his office's involvement ended by the summer of 1970. Kissinger urged the committee to deal directly with Attorney General Elliot L. Richardson in further pursuit of the matter. In response to a question, he said "there were cases in which the sources of some leaks were discovered and corrective action taken."

Wiretapping report requested— The panel had requested from the Justice Department the FBI report on the wiretap operation. Committee access to the report became a central factor. Committee member Clifford P. Case (R, N.J.) told Kissinger it was "very clear that the committee will not be in the position to act on the nomination until that report has been received." Committee Chairman J. W. Fulbright (D, Ark.) agreed with Case.

Richardson met in closed session with the committee Sept. 10 and provided a memorandum on Kissinger's role in the wiretapping. The panel released the memo, which was based on FBI records. The memo said Kissinger's role "included expressing concern over leaks of sensitive material and when this concern was coupled with that of the President and transmitted to the director of the FBI it led to efforts to stem the leaks, which efforts included some wiretaps of government employes and newsmen." The memo continued, "His role further involved the supplying to the FBI of names of individuals in the government who had access to sensitive information and occasional review of information generated by the program to determine its usefulness."

The committee voted later Sept. 10 14–0 to authorize two of its members, Case and Sen. John J. Sparkman (D, Ala.), to meet with Richardson "to obtain information on Dr. Kissinger's role respecting his initiative, or concurrence in wiretap surveillance."

At the committee's public session later Sept. 10, Kissinger was asked by Sen. Edmund S. Muskie (D, Me.) whether he would continue to approve wiretapping as secretary of state.

"The issue of wiretapping raises the balance between human liberty and the requirements of national security," Kissinger replied, "and I would say that the weight should be on the side of human liberty and that if human liberty is infringed, the demonstration of national security must be overwhelming and that would be my general attitude."

Richardson complied with the committee's action and made the FBI report available to Case and Sparkman Sept. 11. Later, the two senators met with Kissinger and Richardson to discuss it. Sparkman told newsmen there was no data in the report to jeopardize Kissinger's confirmation. Case said the committee's access to the report seemed to remove a major threat to the confirmation.

In a letter requested by Fulbright on the current policy on wiretapping, Richardson said Sept. 12 that wiretaps without court warrant would be used only "in a limited number of cautiously and meticulously reviewed instances" that involved "a genuine national security interest." He listed three criteria to be applied to determine such instances, that the surveillance would be ordered only if it met one of these conditions: "1. To protect the nation against actual or potential attack or other hostile acts of a foreign power; 2. To obtain foreign intelligence information deemed essential to the security of the United States; or 3. To protect national security information against foreign intelligence activities."

Kissinger reported certain of wiretap— Henry A. Kissinger told a former White House associate that he was "virtually certain" his telephone had been tapped at some point since he had joined the Administration in 1969, according to the *New York Times* Nov. 25.

According to the *Times'* source, identified only as a "former White House official," Kissinger remarked on the wiretap shortly before his confirmation as secretary of state Sept. 21. When the former official pursued the remark, the *Times* said, Kissinger replied, "At least you know the plumbers don't work for me." (The plumbers were a special White House force, whose alleged function was to plug leaks of classified information to the press.)

Halperin suit affidavit released. Morton H. Halperin, a former National Security Council (NSC) official, asserted in a sworn statement made public Nov. 27 that three days after NSC member Henry A. Kissinger had orally agreed to limit Halperin's access to sensitive national security data, Halperin's telephone was tapped as part of a White House effort to stop leaks of such information.

The statement was part of an affidavit given by Halperin in connection with his civil suit against Kissinger and others, whom he held responsible for illegal wiretaps that were placed on him for 21 months beginning in May 1969.

In a brief filed in the suit Sept. 30, the Justice Department had acknowledged that the tap continued on Halperin nine months after he had ceased to have any connection with the NSC. In April 1970, Halperin became an unsalaried foreign policy adviser to then presidential aspirant Sen. Edmund S. Muskie (D, Me.).

In its brief, the Justice Department admitted that former Attorney General John N. Mitchell failed to renew the authorization for the tap on Halperin every 90 days, although Justice Department rules required it.

In a related development, the *New York Times,* citing authoritative sources, reported Oct. 15 that a second former NSC official, Anthony Lake, was the object of an Administration wiretap until February, 1971—two months after Lake also became a foreign policy adviser to the Muskie campaign.

*Nixon defendant in Halperin's suit—*Former President Nixon was named a defendant in a civil suit Sept. 30, 1974 by Morton H. Halperin, a former National Security Council (NSC) official, whose home telephone was tapped by the Federal Bureau of Investigation (FBI) between 1969 and 1971. (The pardon granted Nixon Sept. 8 by President Ford did not exempt Nixon from civil liability for his acts as President.)

Halperin, an aide to NSC Director Henry A. Kissinger when the tap was begun May 9, 1969, charged that Nixon had participated in illegal electronic surveillance and that he had helped conceal the record of the operation from the Justice Department.

In a related development, the Senate Foreign Relations Committee Sept. 29 released testimony by FBI agents that former Attorney General John N. Mitchell had not signed the authorization for the Halperin wiretap until three days after it had been installed. The hitherto secret testimony was taken by the committee during its probe of Kissinger's role in the wiretap operations.

Kissinger's role questioned. The House Judiciary Committee continued its closed hearings June 4-6, 1974 to consider evidence gathered by its staff in the impeachment inquiry. The June 6 session considered the Administration's secret domestic surveillance activities, including 17 wiretaps effected in 1969 against government officials and reporters. Much of the wiretap material consisted of summaries of FBI transcripts of recorded conversations, with the names of those subjected to the taps excised.

The wiretap session led to renewed speculation concerning the extent of the role played by Secretary of State Henry A. Kissinger, whether he initiated any of the surveillance or saw or utilized information gleaned from it. At a press conference June 6, Kissinger declared he "did not make a direct recommendation" for such surveillance and he reiterated his Senate testimony that his role had been limited to supplying names of some aides who had access to sensitive material that had been leaked and thus became targets of the surveillance. When he was pressed by reporters for details, Kissinger bristled. "This is a press conference and not a cross-examination," he said, "I do not conduct my office as a conspiracy."

*Kissinger to resign unless charges are cleared—*Secretary of State Kissinger threatened to resign June 11 unless charges that he had participated in "illegal or shady" wiretapping activity were cleared up. The secretary made the remark during an emotional news conference in Salzburg, Austria, during President Nixon's stopover preparatory to his Mideast tour.

Appearing to be hurt and angry, Kissinger, in a shaking voice, complained of "innuendoes" and said he did not believe it was possible to conduct the foreign policy of the nation "under these circumstances when the character and credibility of the secretary of state is at issue." "And if it is not cleared up, I will resign," he declared.

Kissinger's surprise threat to quit his post was prompted by reports from unidentified Congressional sources that Kissinger had a more extensive role in federal wiretapping efforts than he had led senators to believe at his confirmation hearing in 1973.

The reports suggested the following: he had initiated the wiretapping undertaken by the government against 13 federal officials and four newsmen from 1969-71; he had prior knowledge of formation of the White House investigation unit known as the "plumbers" in 1971; the order to end the "national security" wiretaps came from his office; and then-National Security Council (NSC) aide Alexander M. Haig Jr., presumably acting for Kissinger, vetoed at least two, and possibly three, FBI proposals in mid-1969 to terminate one tap, at the home of Morton I. Halperin, because it was unproductive.

Before leaving with the presidential party on the Mideast trip, Kissinger appeared before the Senate Foreign Relations Committee June 7 to defend his credibility on the issue. According to unpublished White House transcripts, circulating to members of the House Judiciary Committee, President Nixon had remarked on Feb. 28, 1973 in a White House talk that Kissinger had asked that the 1969 taps be instituted. Sen. Edmund S. Muskie (D, Me.) asked Kissinger at the hearing June 7 if he originated the recommendation for the wiretapping program. "I did not," Kissinger replied. He said he "had the impression" that the President's comments were "based on a misapprehension."

Kissinger said his role "was in supplying names as part of a program instituted by the President, the attorney general and the director of the Federal Bureau of Investigation (FBI) to protect the national security."

The day before, during a news conference at which he expected to deal primarily with his Mideast diplomacy, Kissinger's role in the wiretapping was again raised. One question was whether he had retained counsel "in preparation for a defense against a possible perjury indictment." Kissinger, stung, retorted he did not conduct his office as a conspiracy.

After Kissinger's Salzburg news conference, Senate Democratic Leader Mike Mansfield (Mont.) disclosed that he had met Kissinger June 8 and "he was in some distress" because of the wiretapping thing "hanging over him." Kissinger had indicated, Mansfield said, "he might have to consider resigning." Mansfield added: "I told him not to even think of it."

At Salzburg, Kissinger reaffirmed his testimony before the Senate that he only provided names of individuals with access to sensitive information in the wiretapping effort from 1969 to 1971. He denied instigating the wiretapping or having prior knowledge of creation of the "plumbers."

"I find wiretapping distasteful," Kissinger said. "I find leaks distasteful, and therefore a choice had to be made. So, in retrospect, this seems to me what my role has been." Because of his concern about "egregious violations" of national security items, or leaks of classified material, he said, he had spoken to the President in 1969 and Nixon had ordered, on the advice of John N. Mitchell, then attorney general, and FBI Director J. Edgar Hoover, "the institution of a system of national security wiretaps." Kissinger said his office supplied the names of persons with access to the security data.

"The fact of the matter is that the wiretaps in question were legal," Kissinger declared. "They followed established procedures."

Kissinger said he had sent a letter to the Senate Foreign Relations Committee requesting a new review of the wiretapping charges. He read parts of the letter: "The innuendoes which now imply that new evidence contradicting my testimony has come to light are without foundation."

Senate panel accepts review—Kissinger's request for a review of his testimony was accepted unanimously June 11 by the Senate Foreign Relations Committee. Chairman J. W. Fulbright (D, Ark.) said the panel would renew its request to the Justice Department to provide it with documents on the original authorization of the wiretaps. The department had declined to provide the data.

There were indications of support for Kissinger and opposition to his resignation from both Democrats and Republicans on the committee.

52 senators express support—A resolution backing Kissinger was introduced in the Senate late June 12, 1974 with early sponsorship of 39 Republicans and Democrats. By June 13, 52 senators had signed the resolution, including Majority Leader Mansfield and Minority Leader Hugh Scott (R, Pa.). The resolution, submitted by Sen. James B. Allen (D, Ala.), said the Senate "holds in high regard Dr. Kissinger and regards him as an outstanding member of this Administration, as a patriotic American in whom it has complete confidence, and whose integrity and veracity are above reproach."

In a Senate speech, Sen. Barry Goldwater (R, Ariz.) urged an end to the "incessant nit-picking" over the wiretapping incident and called for "a determined inquiry" to stop leaks of secret information. It was time to decide "once and for all," he said, "whether it is more important to protect secret information relative to our government or more important to provide more circulation for newspapers, more viewers and listeners to the electronic media, and more money and adulation for people willing to turn against their government."

After his Senate speech June 12, Goldwater accused the *Washington Post* of committing an "act of treason" by publishing secret FBI documents that indicated Kissinger had initiated some of the wiretaps in question. "It's very obvious to me that any information that the government has can be obtained by the *Washington Post* or any other newspaper that wants to pay the price," he said. "This is plain, outright treason, and I won't stand for it."

Benjamin C. Bradlee, executive editor of the *Post*, in a statement later June 12, said: "That's really an outrageous charge. We neither stole the documents nor bought them." "We have a right to look at any information given to us by responsible government officials, whether it's a senator or a president or a bureaucrat," he said. "And we have a responsibility to print all information that is relevant and newsworthy."

Reports on the FBI documents had been published June 12 by the *Post*, the *New York Times* and the *Boston Globe*, along with reports of Kissinger's Salzburg news conference.

According to one document, entitled "Sensitive Coverage Placed at Request of White House" and dated May 12, 1973, specific requests for the wiretaps had come from either Kissinger, then national security adviser, or his aide, Gen. Alexander M. Haig Jr., currently White House chief of staff. The document was addressed to Leonard M. Walters, then assistant director of the FBI, now retired.

The narrative at the beginning of the document read: "The original requests were from either Dr. Henry Kissinger or General Alexander Haig (then Colonel Haig) for wiretap coverage on knowledgeable NSC personnel and certain newsmen who had particular news interest in the SALT talks. The specific requests for this coverage were made to either former Director J. Edgar Hoover or former Assistant to the Director William C. Sullivan (and on one occasion by General Haig to SA Robert Haynes, FBI, White House liaison). Written authorization from the Attorney General of the United States was secured on each wiretap."

Another document, dated May 13, 1973, said "it appears that the project of placing electronic surveillance at the request of the White House had its beginning in a telephone call to Mr. J. Edgar Hoover on May 9, 1969, from Dr. Henry A. Kissinger."

Kissinger was said in the documents to have received 37 FBI summaries of the wiretapped information and to have received the summaries as late as Dec. 28, 1970. An FBI document dated May 31, 1973 was reported to have contained Kissinger's assertion that "what he was learning as a result of the [wiretap] coverage was extremely helpful to him while at the same time very disturbing." The document also said a preliminary estimate of the wiretap operation was that there had been no evidence of federal illegality gleaned from the wiretaps nor any instance that data had been leaked to unauthorized persons.

Ex-NSC aide files new wiretap suit—William Anthony K. Lake, a former staff member of the National Security Council (NSC), filed suit against Kissinger and Nixon June 12, charging that wiretaps were unconstitutionally placed on his home telephone. Lake, who served on Kissinger's NSC staff from June 1969 to June 1970, argued that the wiretap violated his civil liberties, since it was not based on evidence that he had disclosed or was likely to disclose classified information.

Lake's suit, which named other Nixon Administration officials as well as the Chesapeake & Potomac Telephone Co. as defendants, contended that the tap had been placed after he had left the NSC. The tap was ordered, Lake asserted, because he was believed to oppose some Administration policies.

A second wiretap suit by former NSC staff member Richard M. Moose, a Kissinger aide from January to September 1969, was withdrawn June 12, only hours after it had been filed. Moose's attorney, Nathan Levin, said the action came at the request of Sen. Fulbright, who thought it inappropriate for Moose, a consultant to the Senate Foreign Relations Committee, to be involved in such litigation, since the committee had agreed to review Kissinger's role in initiating the wiretaps.

Ruckelshaus backs Kissinger. William D. Ruckelshaus, former acting director of the Federal Bureau of Investigation, supported Secretary of State Henry A. Kissinger June 16 in his account of his wiretapping role in 1969–71. Renewed charges concerning Kissinger's involvement in the government effort to plug security leaks by tapping officials and newsmen during that period had evoked a Kissinger threat to resign unless he was cleared on the issue.

Ruckelshaus, who first investigated the wiretapping effort and report on it a year earlier, said Kissinger's role was "pretty much as he's described it." Appearing on the CBS "Face the Nation" program, Ruckelshaus suggested an explanation of one of the questions involved: whether Kissinger did or did not initiate the wiretaps. "In the sense that he supplied the names, he initiated it," he said. "But his definition of initiation is that it wasn't his idea to tap; he simply complained about the leaks." Ruckelshaus said "in the process of supplying those names it may well have been described in FBI memoranda that this was a request coming from the National Security Council or Mr. Kissinger."

Ruckelshaus agreed there were "some questions" about one aspect of the wiretapping effort, that some persons with "only a peripheral, if any, relationship to national security" were among those tapped.

On Watergate, Ruckelshaus said he expected "more surprises" in the investigation. "There is information that I'm aware of that has not as yet become public," he said.

Government documents relating to the authorization of the wiretaps were being sent to the Senate Foreign Relations Committee, a Justice Department spokesman said June 14. The committee, which had accepted Kissinger's request for a review of the issue, had let it be known the data had been requested but withheld up to this point. The record of the wiretaps was under court control arising from a civil lawsuit brought by one of the tap targets, Morton Halperin. The Justice Department, in announcing it was supplying the committee with material "directly or indirectly" relating to Kissinger's role, said permission for transfer of documents had been authorized by U.S. Judge John L. Smith, presiding judge in the Halperin case. Procedures to safeguard the secrecy of the material were worked out between the committee and the department.

Smith June 19 refused a request from Halperin's counsel to make the wiretap files public, since much of it had already been publicized. Smith said Halperin would not benefit by release of the data.

APPEALS, SUPREME COURT SPLIT ON WIRETAPS WITHOUT WARRANTS

The U.S. Court of Appeals for the 6th Circuit April 8 rejected the Justice Department's contention that the government had a right to conduct wire-taps in "domestic subversion" cases without court warrants. The 2–1 ruling upheld federal Judge Damon J. Keith's Jan. 25 ruling. The Supreme Court had ruled April 5, however, that wiretapping without a warrant was legal with the consent of one of the parties involved.

BUFFALO EVENING NEWS
Buffalo, N.Y. April 28, 1971

The Justice Department now plans to carry to the Supreme Court its contention that the federal government has the right to wiretap in domestic national security cases without first obtaining a customary court warrant. This contention, fervently defended by Atty. Gen. John Mitchell in a recent speech, seems to us a dangerous breach of traditional American civil liberties.

If granted, such warrantless taps on American citizens could lead to virtually unchecked power for the federal executive in this highly ambiguous "national security" area. And even if Mr. Mitchell or President Nixon exercised such sweeping power with the most scrupulous restraint, who could guarantee that some successor wouldn't grievously misuse it later on?

Admittedly, the legal limitations on official wiretapping and eavesdropping are hazy. Their sanction now stems from a loosely drafted 1968 federal statute still untested in the Supreme Court. Mr. Mitchell says he cannot separate threats to national security, whether they result from home-grown or foreign subversives. But one certain distinction is that Americans enjoy the protection of the Bill of Rights. In a 1967 decision, the Supreme Court ruled that wiretaps fell under the Fourth Amendment protections against "unreasonable searches and seizures." In the majority opinion, Justice Potter Stewart wrote:

"Over and over again this Court has emphasized that the mandate of the amendment requires adherence to judicial processes, and that searches conducted outside the judicial process, without prior approval by judge or magistrate, are per se unreasonable under the Fourth Amendment."

His eminently sound reasoning merely insures that police must get a court warrant, which amounts to an independent check against abuse, before installing a tap. Nor have such warrants proved all that difficult to obtain. If the probable cause necessary to do so is lacking, then why should that not cause denial of a warrant with regard to American suspects protected by the Fourth Amendment?

Two lower federal courts have rejected the Mitchell doctrine. We hope the Supreme Court will do the same.

THE LINCOLN STAR
Lincoln, Neb., April 10, 1971

Given the mood of the country, it could be assumed that a majority of Americans would agree that the federal government should use wiretapping to keep tabs on any domestic group thought to constitute a threat to national security. Anything goes in catching the subversives, is the argument.

The Nixon administration claims wide wiretap authority and in the appeal of a Michigan conspiracy case, the Justice Department argued that the President should have just as much authority to order domestic wiretaps when he feels the nation's security is in danger as he does when the danger comes from a foreign government. The 6th U.S. Court of Appeals thought differently, however, in holding that conversations of the defendant were illegally intercepted and that the government's policy violates the Constitution's Fourth Amendment prohibition against unreasonable search and seizure.

What may happen if the government takes the case to the U.S. Supreme Court is another matter. Other bugging cases have been before the court and it is fact that the majority of justices have applied other than "strict construction" of the Constitution in certain instances. In one case, the high court issued a decision permitting agents to send informers into the homes of narcotics suspects with hidden radio transformers and to use the recorded conversations in the prosecutions.

The ruling prompted Justice William O. Douglas to note in dissent that electronic surveillance is "the greatest leveller of human privacy ever known." He asked: "Must everyone live in fear that every word he speaks may be transmitted or recorded and later repeated to the entire world? I can imagine nothing that has a more chilling effect on people speaking their minds and expressing their views on important matters. The advocates of the regime should spend some time in totalitarian countries and learn first-hand the kind of regime they are creating here."

All sorts of things can be imagined in connection with a president's claimed authority to wiretap. There are even charges currently that third parties are listening in on the phones of another domestic group, the United States Congress.

We have no Big Brother complex, but neither can we be assured that everything will always be in good hands, that presidents will never step out of bounds and violate the citizens' constitutional protection in the name of national security.

THE SACRAMENTO BEE
Sacramento, Calif., April 14, 1971

The courts have served notice the Nixon administration has no authority to ignore the Fourth Amendment in the name of expediency, a fact which should have been amply evident to the Justice Department and the President.

The Sixth US Circuit Court of Appeals in Cincinnati upheld the protection of all citizens against unreasonable searches and seizures when it rejected evidence obtained through wiretapping without a court order. The use of electronic surveillance of private citizens has grown alarmingly during the present administration. It is good the court called a halt.

___

At issue was the case of a man accused of involvement in the bombing of a Central Intelligence Agency office in Ann Arbor, Mich., in 1968. Federal wiretaps were used to gather evidence against him, without prior recourse to court orders to determine whether such action was reasonable search.

The appeals court declared it was not, that it violated the Fourth Amendment. If the Fourth Amendment's protection are to have any meaning, they must apply to all — radical or any other citizen. To permit the expediency of internal security to override this constitutional protection would lay every citizen open to government snooping with only the government in the role of judge as to whether the invasion of privacy was legal.

The President has no authority to bypass the courts and order wiretaps on domestic groups suspected of being a threat to the country, the court ruled, and thereby it set down claims by the Nixon administration that in certain cases the safeguards of the Fourth Amendment may be overriden.

___

The court's ruling should constitute an ultimatum to the Justice Department as to the use of wiretapping.

It is not up to the President, as the government argued, to suspend the Constitution whenever he determines it interferes with guarding internal security against certain individuals or groups. If he can arrogate that kind of power to himself, what is to stop him from suspending any or all of the Constitution's protections?

This nation and its institutions are not so fragile they cannot survive without resorting to unconstitutional security methods. The day these become commonplace, the country will be in worse jeopardy than from any subversive factions to which it overreacts.

THE DENVER POST
Denver, Colo., April 11, 1971

SUPREME COURT JUSTICE Louis D. Brandeis once observed that the most comprehensive of rights and the right most valued by civilized men is "the right to be let alone."

In an age of wiretapping and other kinds of electronic eavesdropping—an age of widespread government spying upon pivate and public citizens—the right to be let alone has been placed in increasing jeopardy.

But last week, the U.S. Court of Appeals for the Sixth Circuit in Cincinnati applied the brakes to a widening program of wiretapping by the U.S. Department of Justice.

Atty. Gen. John N. Mitchell had argued that the Justice Department has an inherent power under the Constitution to eavesdrop on "dangerous" groups that Mitchell considers a threat to the government.

The Court declared that it could find no such power in the Constitution and ruled that the kind of wiretapping the Justice Department has been doing without warrants from the court is a constitutional violation.

If the attorney general believes that a group is endangering the government, he has to send one of his men into court to convince a judge of that danger before his department can engage in wiretapping.

He needs a warrant to wiretap in the same way that he needs a warrant to search, and he needs it to eavesdrop on radicals just as he needs it to eavesdrop on persons suspected of non-political crimes.

THE COURT TOOK NOTE of the "historic role of the judiciary to see that in periods of crisis, when the challenge to constitutional freedoms is greatest, the Constitution of the United States remains the supreme law of the land."

We hope the judiciary will continue to perceive and exercise that role. As government intrusion into the privacy of the citizen continues to grow, the courts may offer the only protection that is left short of the voting booth.

The Salt Lake Tribune
Salt Lake City, Utah, April 26, 1971

Should the individual's constitutional right to privacy be entrusted to a judge or the attorney general of the United States?

At what point does the right to privacy give way to what Attorney General John N. Mitchell calls "the right of the public to protect itself?" And when does this right of self protection evolve into suppression of legitimate dissent?

These are among the difficult questions posed by modern surveillance techniques and current patterns of domestic unrest. There are no easy answers because the exact moment at which good turns to evil or evil to good remains elusive.

Mr. Mitchell makes a good case for the surveillance authority he has assumed to tap without court order in domestic security matters. If wire tapping without court order could have prevented one or more of the presidential assassinations who could find fault with the practice? If planting a hidden microphone in the home of a man planning to blow up an office building could frustrate those plans, few would quibble over the niceties of obtaining permission from a judge. These are extreme examples.

Not all wiretapping and electronic surveillance is directed against such patently dangerous operators and this is where the problem arises. Mr. Mitchell or any other attorney general might approve taps and bugs which they honestly believe to be in the best interests of the country. But attorneys general are political appointees, what they see as real danger may be influenced by political belief. They have a personal stake in many of the surveillance requests upon which they must pass.

Judges are not perfect either. Neither are they free of political leanings. But their personal involvement in any given request for wiretapping or bugging is likely to be nil. They are in a better position to weigh a request impartially.

The attorney general implies there are times when taking the trouble to obtain court approval would destroy effectiveness of the ultimate surveillance. He further says the government's agents often need to tap or bug early in an investigation, presumably at a point when they would not already have enough evidence to support a request for court approval. No doubt such situations arise but the fact that they do is not sufficient justification for bypassing court approval.

While we do not doubt the personal integrity of the present attorney general, we believe that the public now, and under attorneys general of the future, would be better served if his claimed surveillance powers were denied. We find it hard to believe that law enforcement will be seriously hindered by going to the courts for permission to tap and bug a citizen only suspected of wrongdoing.

THE KANSAS CITY STAR
Kansas City, Mo., April 24, 1971

When is a wire tap not a wire tap? Apparently, in the eyes of the Justice department, if electronic apparatus is placed on the telephone of a co-operating informant who consents to the surveillance. Whoever turns up on the other end of the line—congressman, private citizen or whatever—is presumed not to be under surveillance and his privacy unviolated.

This hardly seems logical. It could go beyond the ordinary tapping of telephone lines because a degree of entrapment easily might be involved. In defining entrapment Webster's dictionary offers an example of usage: "Brutality, third degree, duress and entrapment are vigorously condemned." The quote is attributed to J. Edgar Hoover, director of the Federal Bureau of Investigation.

By the narrowest of interpretations, we suppose, you could say that the telephone on the other end of the line was not tapped. Other calls would not be heard. But that is an interpretation altogether meaningless in the context of the purpose of the tap.

The trouble with the whole business is that wire tapping, once authorized for whatever good and legal purposes in an individual case, becomes an entity unto itself. If the equipment is available, it is going to be used. Not necessarily by law enforcement agents in an illegal manner, but possibly by politicians and private interests with various motives. Blackmail, coercion and simply the advantage of knowing with other parties unaware of the fact are among those motives. In many instances the value in obtaining information has nothing to do with possible action in the courts.

No one should be so naive as to assume that wire tapping is unfair or unreasonable in matters affecting national security. But that phrase needs to be strictly defined. If anything, electronic surveillance appears to require much stricter rules and more safeguards, not a broadening of its use.

CHICAGO DAILY NEWS
Chicago Ill., April 12, 1971

A federal court of appeals in Cincinnati has pulled the rein on the government's power to tap wires, and we say hooray for the court. With electronic snoopery gaining ground at every turn, the more constraints that can be applied the better.

The astonishing thing about this case, which grew out of a White Panther trial in Detroit, was that Atty. Gen. John Mitchell tossed in a brand new argument. The executive branch, he said, had an "inherent right" to tap wires any time it suspected a domestic organization of being radical or subversive, and could do so without a court order.

No so, said the court. No such right exists under the Constitution, and the Fourth Amendment specifically forbids unreasonable search and seizure. Any wiretapping of domestic organizations must be done under strict court supervision — the same requirement that is imposed in criminal cases.

The Supreme Court will doubtless have the final word on this, but for everybody's peace of mind the "inherent right" argument ought to be buried deep. By Mitchell's way of thinking, the government could snoop on anybody or any group at any time, for who would decide whether a given person or organization was radical or subversive? Could a government run by Republicans decide that all Democrats were subversive, or vice versa? Even granting the best of intentions on the part of the present administration, this is an open-ended doctrine that in the wrong hands could lead to spying without limit. Today the Panthers, tomorrow the Rotary Club.

The appeals court has at least put a temporary block on that road. We hope it stays closed.

The Morning Star

Rockfrod, Ill., April 16, 1971

In the aftermath of two recent court decisions, it is difficult to sense any specific route the courts are taking these days on the controversial practice of "bugging" or wiretapping.

It might be said that the Justice Department won one and lost one within the past week.

The U.S. Supreme Court ruled that informers can legally enter a dope suspect's home without a warrant and record on hidden transmitters evidence to be used against the suspect.

The high court ruling is limited in its effects to government informers only, but there is an implied impetus toward the further use of the bugging tool by law enforcement agencies.

However, a federal court of appeals in Cincinnati ruled that any wiretapping of domestic organizations must be done under strict court supervision — the same requirement that is imposed in criminal cases.

The appeals court rejected the contention of Atty. Gen. Mitchell that the executive branch had an inherent right to tap wires any time it suspected a domestic organization of subversion.

In its ruling, the court cited the Fourth Amendment of the Constitution which specifically forbids unreasonable search and seizure.

Somewhat reluctantly, we have come to accept the premise that wiretapping may be justified under certain circumstances and with court restraints.

But we have decided reservations about the right of government to spy on anyone without a court order. The appeals court decision, which probably will be taken to the Supreme Court, seems to be the proper one.

The Cincinnati Post

Cincinnati, Ohio, April 17, 1971

There is scarcely any issue in American life which has caused more confusion or provoked more indignation in recent months than the question of whether the government has the right to spy on its own citizens.

The question is debated not only in Congress and the courts, but among thoughtful persons who wonder whether the increasing use of wiretaps and hidden microphones is compatible with the privacy protections implicit in the bill of rights.

THE DEEP-SEATED differences of opinion on the subject were demonstrated again recently by two apparently contradictory court decisions in which:

● The U.S. Supreme Court ruled the government has a right to eavesdrop without court permission on a private conversation as long as one of the two parties (usually an agent or informer) has given his consent.

● The U.S. Circuit Court of Appeals in Cincinnati ruled the government has no right to tap a telephone line without court permission, even in cases involving domestic threats to national security.

Thus, the Supreme Court was making it easier to "bug" a conversation while the lower federal court in Cincinnati was making it more difficult.

Wiretapping and other forms of electronic surveillance—properly used —are an indispensable part of modern police work.

In the last two years, for example, federal agents have used 40 wiretaps to arrest 190 drug suspects and seize $14 million worth of heroin, cocaine and LSD.

But in all 40 cases the wiretapping was done only after a judge was convinced such measures were necessary.

Wiretapping or "bugging" without court approval puts too much power in the hands of paid informers and government agencies.

Justice John M. Harlan, in dissenting from the Supreme Court ruling the other day, stated the danger quite clearly.

Americans will be afraid to make "frivolous, impetuous, sacrilegious and defiant" statements even to their friends, he said, if electronic snoopery becomes a common practice.

The argument that wiretapping without a warrant is merited in bomb plots and other security cases doesn't stand up.

Certainly some way can be found for judges to issue swift and secret warrants in such cases.

Without legal constraint, any individual who criticizes government policy, or belongs to a "radical" group, could be considered fair game for a federal wiretap.

As Justice Harlan points out:

"The burden of guarding privacy in a free society should not be on its citizens; it is the government that must justify its need to electronically eavesdrop."

Detroit Free Press

Detroit, Mich., April 12, 1971

APPARENTLY the Justice Department will appeal last Thursday's decision by the 6th U.S. Circuit Court, which limited the department's authority to wiretap in domestic cases involving "national security." An appeal would be healthy. Though the Circuit Court's decision was fair and proper, the question is easily important enough to deserve pronouncement from the Supreme Court itself.

At issue is wiretapping done in the case of Lawrence R. (Pun) Plamondon and two others accused in the 1968 bombing of CIA offices in Ann Arbor. Defense Attorney William M. Kunstler argued that the taps were illegal and that he should therefore be allowed to see their transcripts. U.S. District Judge Damon J. Keith of Detroit agreed.

It is important to note that Judge Keith has hardly declared war on wiretapping. He said that unrestricted tapping might well be proper in subversion cases involving bona fide foreign agents. And he did not say that electronic devices necessarily shouldn't have been used in the Plamondon case.

He said only that in this latter instance the government was obliged to get a judicial warrant before placing the taps, as the 1968 Crime Control Act specifies. That is, the government is required to abide by the same processes in pursuing criminal suspects who are politically radical as in pursuing criminal suspects who are, say, Republicans.

For reasons that remain unclear, the Justice Department is reluctant to go through the relatively simple process of obtaining a warrant. Its spokesmen insist that the President has inherent power to do whatever is necessary against domestic as well as foreign subversive threats to the survival of the government. They say that he also is empowered to determine when the activities of a given domestic group pose such a threat.

This is the nub of the issue. Set aside the question of whether dissident domestic groups should be treated the same as unfriendly foreign powers. Set aside even the question of whether Plamondon's alleged activities represented any real threat to the government.

The administration is really arguing not for one or another answer, but for sweeping power to determine the answers to such questions when and as it pleases. The administration is arguing that it may, using modern investigating tools, fish and search in the private lives of citizens as it thinks necessary, without review and without restraint.

Far less than a legal scholar might conclude that the administration's position does not readily square with plain rights given American citizens under the Constitution. And we would like to see the Supreme Court have a chance to say so.

AKRON BEACON JOURNAL
Akron, Ohio, April 12, 1971

Is it permissible for the government to infringe upon constitutional rights in order to protect itself against subversives?

"No," says the Sixth District Court of Appeals in a 2-to-1 decision rejecting Attorney General John W. Mitchell's contention that federal agents may legally wiretap radical groups without getting court approval.

Judge George C. Edwards Jr., for the majority, held that the Fourth Amendment's prohibition against unreasonable search a n d seizure requires government agents to obtain warrants to listen in on domestic radicals, just as in any other criminal investigation.

We agree with a n d applaud this view even though a judge for whom we n a v e the greatest respect, Paul C. Weick of Akron, dissented.

Judge Weick said that the President has the sworn duty "to protect and defend the nation from attempts of domestic subversives, as well as foreign enemies, to destroy it by force and violence."

He said that the threat to government was as great from domestic enemies as from foreign and that such domestic groups may be aided by foreign powers.

The ticklish problem, it seems to us, is whether a President and his Attorney General might move against persons or groups which express legitimate political dissent under the claim that such dissenters are subversives.

On that score, Judge Edwards cited "the historic role of the judiciary to see that in periods of crisis, when the challenge to constitutional freedom is greatest, the Constitution of the United States remains the supreme law of the land."

Judge Edwards acknowledged that government lawyers had asserted that "the awesome power sought for the Attorney General will always be used with discretion." He said, however, that "even in very recent days this has not always been the case."

The judge was careful to point out that the court was not deciding one way or another as to the President's wiretapping powers where attacks, espionage or sabotage by a foreign power were involved.

The case will undoubtedly be carried to the Supreme Court for final resolution. Just as in the appellate court, learned judges are likely to reach conflicting conclusions.

Protection of our government is important. But so also is protection of "the right of the people to be secure in their persons, houses, papers and e f f e c t s against unreasonable searches and seizures," as stated in the Fourth Amendment.

This guarantee was written by wise men who realized that a government is made up of fallible officials who may sometimes overreach.

Pittsburgh Post-Gazette
Pittsburgh, Pa., April 8, 1971

A DIVIDED Supreme Court has given legal status to the principle that an individual has no inherent right to expect privacy when he talks to another person, since there is always the risk that his confidence will be violated. By a vote of 5 to 4, the high court has ruled that law enforcement officers do not need a warrant when they rig an informer with electronic surveillance devices to trap suspected lawbreakers.

The decision reinstated the narcotics conviction and 25-year sentence of a Chicago narcotics violator and gave major impetus to the practice of electronic surveillance by law enforcement agencies. Justice Byron White reaffirmed the validity of a 1952 Supreme Court ruling which sustained the use of a wired informer without court authorization.

Although a 1967 Supreme Court ruling held that wiretapping and bugging constitute a violation of the Fourth Amendment, Justice White argued that the 1952 decision was still sound law because the use of a microphone hidden on an informer is not the kind of search prohibited by the Fourth Amendment.

One of the four dissenting judges, Justice John M. Harlan, opposed the majority opinion on the ground that the constitutional right to privacy demands that agents secure a search warrant from a court by showing probable cause to believe that a suspect has committed a crime. He asserted that electronic surveillance without authorization would "undermine that confidence and sense of security in dealing with one another that is characteristic of individual relationships between citizens and society."

Justice Harlan wisely admonishes the nation that without the protection of warrants law-abiding citizens as well as criminals are exposed to the treachery of informers. He maintains that widespread "third-party bugging" could destroy that spontaneity of discourse which is the essence of freedom. A society whose right to privacy is being steadily eroded will ignore the warnings of Justice Harlan at its peril.

THE LOUISVILLE TIMES
Louisville, Ky., April 12, 1971

The 6th U.S. Circuit Court of Appeals handed down a welcome decision last week with its 2-1 ruling opposing wiretapping without a court order in "domestic subversion" cases. It was a reaffirmation of individual freedom that should be accepted by the Supreme Court to help calm the nationwide paranoia about wiretapping.

It must be emphasized at the outset that this was not, contrary to what the law-and-order bunch might like to think, another instance of courts coddling criminals. The ruling does not affect the government's ability, under due-process procedures, to get court orders permitting wiretapping as a weapon in fighting a long list of specified crimes. These procedures are spelled out in the Omnibus Crime Act of 1968 and are in use.

Nor did the court suggest the government lacks the power to use wiretaps against foreign subversives.

What Judges George C. Edward and Harry Phillips wisely rejected was the proposition that "the President, acting through the attorney general, may constitutionally authorize the use of electronic surveillance in cases where he has determined that, in order to preserve the national security, the use of such surveillance is reasonable."

In everday language those words, according to Alan Barth of *The Washington Post,* mean: "All power to the President."

Whether this power is inherent to the presidency, as contended by Atty. Gen. Mitchell, is an issue whose merits go far beyond the question of the guilt or innocence of Lawrence Plamondon, minister of defense of the White Panther Party, who is accused of bombing CIA offices in Ann Arbor, Mich., in 1968, He asked U.S. district court in Detroit for permission to search the transcripts of his intercepted conversations to see if the government illegally had obtained any of the evidence against him.

This the district court upheld. The government appealed. There are three similar cases in district courts, two of them involving rulings that agreed with the government position. One other does not. However, they are before other circuit courts which are not bound to follow the 6th Circuit decision.

We simply cannot accept the proposition that the executive branch—regardless of who heads it—should have the sole power to determine when wiretaps are needed. As Judge Edwards noted in his decision, the constitutional division of powers "was designed to require sharing in the administration. . . ."

Further, the threat of domestic subversion is not so immediate as to require such a drastic arrogation of power by the executive. At the very least, the executive should be required to obtain permission of a judicial officer before invading the privacy of any citizen.

THE ROANOKE TIMES
Roanoke, Va., April 12, 1971

The ideologically reshaped U.S. Supreme Court has handed down a pivotal decision that greatly reinforces the federal government's authority to eavesdrop on private citizens of all kinds and of any political persuasion.

On its face, the ruling could be taken as simply a large assist to law and order, especially in the struggle against the illegal drug trade. The case involved a conviction obtained against an alleged narcotics peddler by means of evidence recorded via a radio transmitter hidden on an informer's body. We are repelled by the idea of platoons of wired-up informers circulating within our society, but we find even worse the results of the vicious, d e s t r u c t i v e drug trade; so we could live with this kind of ruling if the tactic seemed essential to controlling drug traffic.

Except for one thing. The really important difference about this decision was that, agreeing with the aims of the U.S. Justice Department, the Supreme Court said that such eavesdropping does not require a prior court order. This is so, the court held, because all that is needed is the consent of one party to the conversation—that is, the informer.

Even this might not disturb us so much, were it not for the fact that the Justice Department seems so intent upon expanding its authority to eavesdrop so as to include electronic surveillance of domestic radicals and militants. As we noted on this page the other day, the department currently is asking a federal court in Chicago to rule that the President or the attorney general may authorize a wiretap without a court order, if either deems it to be in the interest of national security.

That kind of p o w e r obviously goes well beyond conventional keeping of law and order. If the President or attorney general is left to decide for himself what comes under the heading of national security—and in its Chicago brief, the Justice Department declared that criminal prosecution is not the sole end of the surveillance authority it seeks—then no man is safe from electronic snoopery. The net of repression could gather in anyone who espoused politically dissident views that somehow offended a high official's views of what the national security demands. In a different administration, it could even happen that an attorney general would attempt a tap on the conversations of a president he considered ideologically impure.

We do not think we are carrying our argument too far; not when one considers the extent of government surveillance of the public that already is going on. It bids to become much b r o a d e r, with the Supreme Court having handed the Justice Department the right to sit in on private conversations, and the department a s k i n g also for virtually untrammeled authority to extend its domestic spying activities. There would, under this kind of policy, be no checks or balances of the kind we are accustomed to; just reliance on what one witness before Sen. Ervin's hearings pitifully described as the "self-discipline" of the executive branch.

If federal investigators want to eavesdrop on someone, we think they should first have to demonstrate satisfactorily to a court that they have good reason to suspect that person of criminal activity. The 6th circuit court of appeals in Cincinnati has just upheld that concept. But in view of its own ruling in the radio transmitter case, the Supreme Court seems as likely as not to grant the Nixon Administration the sweeping authority it seeks.

This ruling was a turnabout from the principle the court laid down in 1967, when it said that the Constitution protects conversations from electronic monitoring without a court order, if the conversations were intended to be private. The change in viewpoint was made possible by the departure of Chief Justice Warren and Justice Abe Fortas, and their replacement by Chief Justice Burger and Justice Blackmun; their votes made the difference this time.

We have repeatedly said that we do not quarrel with the idea of Mr. Nixon's attempting to reshape the court in a more conservative image. Nor, certainly, do we oppose sane measures to aid law enforcement agents in fighting crime, one of the most pressing problems of our tortured society.

But it does not seem necessary to us that the Justice Department be given the power to set out on fishing expeditions aimed not just at criminals but at political dissidents. If the high court upholds this kind of activity, then it is striking a blow at the First Amendment. And where then will s t r i c t construction have vanished?

The Times-Picayune
New Orleans, La., April 7, 1971

If the United States Supreme Court, under Chief Justice Earl Warren, tied the hands of law enforcement officers with many of its decisions, then it is also true that the court of Chief Justice Warren E. Burger is untying those hands.

The latest incident is this week's 6-3 decision that "bugging" is legal in the fight against narcotics. Federal agents can use informers wired for sound to go into dope suspects' homes, and recorded conversations are usable in p r o s e c u t i o n. No search warrants are necessary.

That this official sanction can be a tool of inestimable value against trafficking in narcotics is readily apparent.

It comes less than two months after a 5-4 decision sharply limiting the effect of the Warren court's 1966 Miranda decision. In that opinion the court held that police could not use statements by suspects who had not been advised of their constitutional rights to remain silent.

The Burger court said in February that prosecutors may use illegally obtained confessions to prove to a jury that a defendant who takes the stand is lying. In other words, this ruling assists juries in sizing up the credibility of defendants.

That the pendulum is swinging back toward the side of strict construction of the Constitution became apparent months ago, and recent decisions have added their verification.

In about a dozen cases this year the court has refrained from judging issues which earlier it had agreed to hear. Back the cases went for further proceedings at a lower level. And the court told lower federal courts to cease "interfering" in state and local criminal prosecutions. This has bearing in Louisiana on anti-pornography efforts.

If there has been an attitude of "what's the use?" in local law enforcement across the nation, the changing stance of the Supreme Court should be a new source of inspiration.

The Washington Post
Times Herald
Washington, D.C., April 8, 1971

The brilliant service rendered by Mr. Justice Harlan's penetrating dissent in the electronic eavesdropping case decided by the Supreme Court on Monday is that it sets forth with perfect clarity the conflicting priorities involved. The choice confronted by the court in a most difficult case entailing a complex of earlier decisions was essentially a choice between liberty and safety, between the protection of privacy and the facilitation of law enforcement. The court concluded that the Fourth Amendment does not require the police to obtain a warrant or court order in advance when they record a conversation broadcast electronically by a microphone concealed on the person of an informer.

The gist of the prevailing view, set forth in an opinion by Mr. Justice White, was that the Constitution affords no protection to a defendant who talks imprudently to a person in whom he mistakenly has confidence and that the situation is not altered by the use of an electronic device to broadcast the conversation to listening police officers. There is an undoubted logic to this reasoning; and there is no doubt that it helps in catching criminals. As Justice White noted, "an electronic recording will many times produce a more reliable rendition of what a defendant has said than will the unaided memory of a police agent."

But when this has been acknowledged, there ought to be consideration also, as Justice Harlan points out, for "the nature of a particular practice and the likely extent of its impact on the individual's sense of security balanced against the utility of the conduct as a technique of law enforcement . . . Were third party bugging a prevalent practice, it might well smother that spontaneity—reflected in frivolous, impetuous, sacrilegious, and defiant discourse—that liberates daily life."

Can anyone seriously doubt, in the light of recent disclosures concerning military surveillance and FBI investigating practices, that snoopers or informers, "wired for sound" would be employed very extensively indeed to root out those expressions of political heterodoxy which officialdom might regard as "disloyal" or as a threat of some sort to national security? Justice Harlan put the proposition with great force. The interest which the court decision fails to protect, he said, "is the expectation of the ordinary citizen, who has never engaged in illegal conduct in his life, that he may carry on his private discourse freely, openly, and spontaneously without measuring his every word against the connotations it might carry when instantaneously heard by others unknown to him and unfamiliar with his situation or analyzed in a cold, formal record played days, months, or years after the conversation."

It seems to us that imposition of a warrant requirement before listening in on conversations to which they are not a party does not impose upon the police a burden too onerous in light of the great values and interests which the warrant was designed to safeguard. A search warrant obtained in advance of such eavesdropping does not provide very much protection to citizens; it is too easily obtained from complaisant or careless judges. But it serves at least to remind the police that vital constitutional rights are involved and, perhaps, to put some restraint upon their intrusions into privacy.

The reach of the Fourth Amendment in forfending such intrusions is, of course, open to conscientious argument. We should suppose that the First Amendment would equally restrain police intrusions of this sort. For such intrusions undoubtedly have a chilling influence on the exercise of First Amendment rights. Citizens are unlikely to speak with the freedom indispensable to the democratic process if they fear that an army of snoopers may be taking down for indefinite preservation every dubious opinion, every extravagance of expression they may utter.

The Hartford Courant
Hartford, Conn., April 7, 1971

The "bugging" decision handed down by the United States Supreme Court this week is a major victory for commonsense and the public weal.

The court has given government agents permission to send informers into the homes of narcotics suspects with hidden radio transmitters and to use the recorded conversations for prosecution.

Moreover, Justice White said. the agent does not need a search warrant since there has been no invasion of the suspect's "constitutionally justifiable expectations of privacy."

Normally, the Justice said, no one has a right to expect that a person with whom he is conversing will not reveal the conversation to the police, "especially one contemplating illegal activities."

To this, Justice Douglas made plaintive dissent. He asked "Must everyone live in fear that every word he speaks may be transmitted or recorded, and later repeated to the entire world?"

The answer is a loud "Yes!" when that everyone is a drug pusher. Drugs are now at the forefront of American crime, and at the root of some of the country's greatest problems. Drug peddlers should not be allowed to forget for a single moment that the law is out to get them. In some countries persons caught trafficking in drugs are taken out and shot. Conversely, in other countries, and no more notably than in the United States, the courts are too often showing as much concern for the rights of criminals as for the protection of the public.

The best way for the person who is chary of his right to privacy and wants to guarantee it, is to keep out of crime in the first place. This simple solution even antedates constitutional guarantees. As for those like Justice Douglas who fear that the law enforcement agencies are going to be turned loose on everybody and everything, let them be reassured. The law has more than its hands full trying to get at criminals without wasting its time snooping for the sake of snooping. And one of the reasons why is exactly that law enforcement is being denied weapons it needs to fight crime. It is high time that the Supreme Court reversed the leniency of the Warren regime to protect the public instead and stop the criminal from laughing up his sleeve.

THE COMMERCIAL APPEAL
Memphis, Tenn., April 7, 1971

THE SWING of the Burger Supreme Court toward crime control and prevention got another push this week with a 6-3 ruling that allows electronic surveillance within the homes or quarters of narcotics suspects.

Justice Byron R. White, writing the majority opinion. used this reasoning: It is not unconstitutional for a police informer to work his way into the confidence of a narcotics suspect. and to witness and hear things which could lead to arrest, trial and conviction. Therefore, it is just as legal for the agent to carry on his person a hidden radio transmitter which can pick up conversations, beam them to an outside tape recorder near enough to pick up the signal, and use this as evidence, all without invading the suspect's "constitutionally justifiable expectations of privacy."

THE DECISION is important in fighting drug abuse, but even more because it indicates a shift toward aiding law enforcement and protecting the law-abiding citizen, by a court which in recent years has been more concerned with the rights of the accused.

Justice White's reference to "justifiable expectations of privacy" is significant.

A couple of years ago a Jaycee club in Washington State set up a secret project to fight drug abuse in a small town. Several club members went underground, posing as buyers of narcotics from out-of-town wholesale pushers. As a result they broke up most of the dope pushing in their town, and led to bigger game in Seattle and San Francisco The addition of the "bug" to such undercover work. as the court saw it. does not alter the constitutionality of sending an informer into a private residence. A criminal never has a guarantee that people he confides in will not inform on him.

The Dallas Morning News
Dallas, Tex., April 9, 1971

Informers, says the Supreme Court, can legally enter a dope suspect's home without a warrant and record on hidden transmitters evidence to be used against them.

It was one of those split decisions that have put some of the old court liberals in the minority in recent months.

Justice William O. Douglas complained that people will live in fear of every word they say. But Justice Byron White, writing for the majority, said a dope suspect has "no constitutionally justifiable expectation of privacy."

If you're talking or contemplating crime, says the majority in effect, you can't normally expect that nobody will go to the police with what's said.

The new weapon should hand law enforcement a broad new field of evidence against pushers, who are the main target of the decision. The Justice Department has been seeking the ruling strenuously over the past two years.

The subject of "bugging" by law enforcement generally has been becoming more and more respectable. The high court ruling is limited in its effects to government informers only, but the impetus toward use of the bugging tool in all law enforcement is strong. The court ruling will help.

The Senate Jurisprudence Committee of the Texas Legislature has approved a bill to legalize wiretapping in Texas and permit use of the evidence in court. Such bugging could not be done without a court order. State law-enforcement officials are strongly for it, but opponents call it an invasion of privacy.

They should ponder Justice White's words about criminal privacy.

Richmond Times-Dispatch
Richmond, Va., April 10, 1971

Since it is entirely legal for one person later to reveal by word of mouth what the other person says by that, as legal if the informer takes along a hidden radio transmitter and reveals what the other person says by that means?

Yes, said the U. S. Supreme Court in an opinion this week.

Four members of the court said they see no difference in principle between (1) an informer's using his own voice to testify as to a conversation, and (2) the informer's use of electronic equipment to transmit the conversation to police. Two other justices filed separate opinions but concurred in the basic decision that an informer can use electronic devices.

"Inescapably," said the prevailing opinion, "one contemplating illegal activities must realize and risk that his companions may be reporting to the police."

From a law enforcement standpoint, the decision is to be hailed. The court told why:

"An electronic recording will many times produce a more reliable rendition of what a defendant has said than will the unaided memory of a police agent. It may also be that with the recording in existence it is less likely that the informant will change his mind, less chance that threat or injury will suppress unfavorable evidence and less chance that cross examination will confound the testimony.

In dissenting opinions, Justices William O. Douglas, John Marshall Harlan and Thurgood Marshall said it violates a person's right to privacy if his remarks made to another person, in what he believes to be a private conversation, are broadcast or are recorded and used against him, unless a court warrant has first been obtained authorizing the use of such devices.

"Must everyone live in fear that every word he speaks may be transmitted or recorded and later repeated to the entire world?" asked Douglas.

And Harlan declared:

"Were third-party bugging a prevalent practice, it might well smother that spontaneity--reflected in frivolous, impetuous, sacrilegious, and defiant discourse--that liberates daily life. Much off-hand exchange is easily forgotten and one may count on the obscurity of his remarks, protected by the very fact of a limited audience, and the likelihood that the listener will either overlook or forget what is said, as well as the listener's inability to reformulate a conversation without having to contend with a documented record."

But the dissenters in this case overlook a fact which a majority of the court often overlooked in deciding criminal cases in recent years—namely, that if the public is to be protected from criminals, law-abiding people necessarily must accept some minimal inconveniences, or even minor abridgements of what they may consider to be their rights. Even free speech, as cherished a principle as it rightly is, is not an absolute constitutional guarantee under every conceivable condition. And neither is the right of privacy, as some may interpret that right.

The Des Moines Register
Des Moines, Iowa, April 12, 1971

The U.S. Supreme Court has moved the nation a notch closer to the day of the "eavesdropped society" with its ruling upholding the legality of snooping by third parties if one party to a conversation consents.

In the case before the court, police put a radio transmitter on a government informer and listened to his conversations with a man suspected of violating the narcotics laws. The police eavesdropped without first obtaining a court order.

The Supreme Court said no court order was necessary, because the overheard conversations could have been relayed to the police anyway. The court declared that transmitting the conversation directly is no different from transmitting notes jotted down by the informer immediately following the conversation.

Anyone who talks to another person realizes that the conversation may be repeated. That is far different, it seems to us, than having one's words recorded without one's knowledge and having this permanent record distributed to others. As Justice John Harlan declared in his dissenting opinion:

"The impact of the practice of third-party bugging must be considered such as to undermine that confidence and sense of security in dealing with one another-that is characteristic of individual relationships between citizens in a free society . . . Words would be measured a good deal more carefully and communication inhibited if one expected his conversations were being transmitted and transcribed. Were third-party bugging a prevalent practice, it might well smother that spontaneity — reflected in frivolous, impetuous, sacrilegious and defiant discourse — that liberates daily life."

The Supreme Court ruling does not just subject lawbreakers to third-party bugging. Justice Harlan points out that "it subjects each and every law-abiding member of society to that risk. . . . Interposition of a warrant requirement is designed not to shield wrongdoers, but to secure a measure of privacy and a sense of personal security throughout our society."

The majority ruling leaves the way clear for anyone's conversations to be broadcast and recorded by police without restriction, so long as one party consents. That represents a dangerous erosion of the right of privacy.

Detroit Free Press
Detroit, Mich., April 7, 1971

OPPONENTS of the Supreme Court's 6-3 decision permitting the use of electronic surveillance under certain circumstances are sure to argue that a little bit of bugging is like a little bit of pregnancy.

Ordinarily, we would be tempted to agree. Bugging is a dirty practice which smacks more of the police state than of an open society. Which is why the FBI is supposed to be restricted to doing its bugging in national security cases and under specific court orders comparable to search warrants.

But under a strict definition of the terms, what the Supreme Court authorized this week does not qualify as electronic surveillance.

By definition, surveillance means watching, or in the case of electronics, listening to, the acts or words of one or more parties by a third party. That is, the conversation of two suspected criminals is tapped by someone who is not a party to the conversation. The deed is done without the knowledge of any of the suspected criminals or parties to the conspiracy. This is the electronic equivalent of no-knock, under which a policeman can invade a private home without a search warrant. And it is for this same reason that the law requires a search warrant for bugging.

But what the Supreme Court approved is the practice of permitting police informers to go into the homes of suspected narcotics agents with hidden transmitters, and to have the recorded conversations used in court.

In this case, one of the parties to the conversation is doing the bugging himself. It is merely a recording of a conversation by one of the parties to it. And, in our opinion, it is no more an invasion of privacy than if the informer told the police and later testified in court to what was said. The major difference is that the record is more accurate, the testimony more credible.

The Fourth Amendment is not stretched, as Justice Byron White argued for the majority, when the court rules that no one has a right to expect that a person with whom he is conversing will not reveal the conversation to the police.

The informer may hardly be a gentleman, and he is certainly not to be trusted, but neither is he a violator of the Constitution.

THE MILWAUKEE JOURNAL
Milwaukee, Wis., April 29, 1971

Atty. Gen. Mitchell has again defended the administration's wire tapping policy, arguing that the government has a right to protect itself from violent attack. Critics continue to take issue with how the administration does it.

Mitchell claims that the quest for national security must take precedence in some cases over an individual's right to privacy. Who determines what is in the interest of national security? Mitchell says that power belongs solely to the president or himself acting as presidential agent. No court checks are needed.

In cases of extreme national emergency or grave danger such as war this might be true. But such conditions certainly do not exist today. Individual freedom, the right to security and privacy are cherished principles. They should not be open to invasion on the arbitrary whim of the executive. Continuing revelations about FBI procedures already raise serious questions in this area.

Encouragement of such policies leads to a police state psychology, anathema to what this nation is all about.

SUPREME COURT BARS WIRETAPPING WITHOUT PREVIOUS COURT APPROVAL

The Supreme Court June 19 declared unconstitutional the federal government's use of wiretapping and electronic surveillance to monitor domestic radicals without first obtaining court warrants. The 8–0 majority included three Nixon appointees to the court—Chief Justice Warren E. Burger, Harry A. Blackmun, and Lewis F. Powell, the author of the opinion. The fourth Nixon appointee, Justice William H. Rehnquist, did not participate in the decision since he had helped to prepare the government's argument while he was a Justice Department official.

The decision was a major legal setback for the administration, which had argued strenuously that the President's authority to protect the country from internal subversion gave the government the constitutional authority to use wiretaps on "dangerous" radicals without court approval. The court did not rule on wiretapping without warrants of agents of foreign nations. Under the court's decision, any defendant in a federal prosecution would have the right to see a complete transcript of any conversations monitored through warrantless taps in a domestic case. The decision came in a case involving the government's wiretapping of three members of the White Panther Party who had been accused of plotting to blow up a government building in Detroit. The government had appealed the case after a U.S. district court judge in Michigan ordered the Justice Department to disclose the transcripts obtained through a warrantless tap.

In another wiretapping decision, a federal judge in Philadelphia ruled June 1 that the 1968 federal law authorizing law enforcement agencies to wiretap phones under certain conditions was unconstitutional as a violation of the Fourth Amendment, protecting citizens against "unreasonable searches and seizures." At issue in the case was a motion sought by seven defendants in a gambling case to suppress evidence gathered by electronic surveillance. In more than a dozen other cases, federal judges had upheld the law.

HERALD-JOURNAL
Syracuse, N.Y., June 22, 1972

The Supreme Court, by an 8 to 0 decision, has declared unconstitutional any wiretapping of suspected domestic subversives without first obtaining court approval.

We believe a warrant from a court should be obtained for any type of wiretapping — subversive or criminal investigations. Without such an order, there definitely is the question of unchecked invasion of privacy and free expression.

Here in Onondaga County court permission must be obtained. We have not heard any law investigator complain that it hinders his work.

The Supreme Court ruling, of course, was immediately hailed by the liberal press as a "stunning setback" against the "dangerous policies" of the Nixon administration.

But we believe Justice Lewis F. Powell Jr., the Nixon court appointee who wrote the opinion, put the future effects in proper perspective without such political hysteria when he wrote:

"Although some added burden will be imposed upon the attorney general, this inconvenience is justified in a free society to protect constitutional values. Nor do we think the government's domestic surveillance powers will be impaired to any significant degree."

The ruling reassures the public that indiscriminate wiretapping cannot occur.

And that is a good thing.

San Francisco Chronicle
San Francisco, Calif., June 21, 1972

BY HIS OPINION in the wiretapping case, Justice Lewis F. Powell Jr. has fortified the reputation for legal breadth and discrimination with which he went onto the Supreme Court. The words ring true and in tune with the deepest traditions of this country when he writes:

"The danger to political dissent is acute where the government attempts to act under so vague a concept as the power to protect 'domestic security.' The price of lawful public dissent must not be in dread of subjection to an unchecked surveillance power."

This adjusts the balance between the government's interest and the citizen's rights, a balance which was seriously altered when the Justice Department in 1968 began asserting the authority of the government to bug people suspected of threatening "domestic security" without a court order.

THE NIXON ADMINISTRATION'S lawyers made a good try, said Justice Powell, but they failed to prove to the Court that the requirement of the Fourth Amendment for a warrant "issued upon probable cause" should or could be bypassed when the law-enforcers were intent on bugging. He said the Federal Safe Streets Act, passed in 1968 under the Johnson Administration, did not authorize eavesdropping without a judge's consent beforehand, as the Government had contended.

Electronic eavesdropping has of course been welcomed and employed by the law enforcement-minded in America for as long as the art has existed. The famous Justice Holmes early recognized it to be a "dirty business," but that did not discourage Yankee ingenuity from inventing and applying ever more sophisticated devices, like tiny television eyes in the wall, or acute sound pickups in the olives of martinis, to the task of spying on suspected malefactors.

IT IS ADMITTED by the Justice Department that 100 unauthorized wiretaps were hooked up last year and more than 50 already this year. If an ample allowance is made for additional State and local wiretapping, the extent of this snoopery begins to come through to the ordinary citizen. It is probable, however, that that citizen is of two minds about the business. He abhors the idea of his own privacy, or that of people he approves of, being invaded at the whim of a government sleuth. But it appears that hardly anyone disapproves of bugging the premises of a suspected foreign espionage agent. As to that practice, the Powell decision made clear the Court was not pronouncing upon it. What the Court did, in its own words, was give reassurance to "the public generally that the indiscriminate wiretapping and bugging of law-abiding citizens cannot occur."

OKLAHOMA CITY TIMES

Oklahoma City, Okla., June 21, 1972

JUST when it appeared the U. S. Supreme Court had swung around to a conservative "law and order" judicial mood, it came up with a ruling that wiretapping in domestic security cases is illegal without court permission. Those who fear the court has turned its back on civil rights progress should have no quarrel with this decision.

Further confounding the critics, the opinion was written by Justice Lewis F. Powell Jr., one of President Nixon's appointees. He said the use of telephone taps and listening devices without first obtaining a warrant is unconstitutional and was not authorized by the 1968 Safe Streets Act. Judicial permission is necessary in order to safeguard privacy and dissent, the justice wrote.

IT is important to note that the high court dealt only with the narrow field of domestic security and then only with cases in which a warrant had not been issued. As Atty. Gen. Richard G. Kleindienst observed, the ruling does not affect the use of electronic surveillance in national security matters.

The opinion said the danger to political dissent is acute where the government attempts to act under so vague a concept as the power to protect domestic security. It added: "The price of lawful public dissent must not be a dread of subjection to an unchecked surveillance power. Nor must the fear of unauthorized official eavesdropping deter vigorous citizen dissent and discussion of government action in private conversation. For private dissent, no less than open public discourse, is essential to our free society."

BUT a question does arise over the definition of "domestic" dissidents, acting either individually or as a group. There may be a narrow shade of difference in some cases whether an organization is strictly a native dissident group or is actually an agent for a foreign power. Sometimes the only way to determine this essential point is to learn the source of its funds. It is known that certain leaders of radical groups that caused so much turmoil on the campuses and in the streets in the latter half of the 1960s owe their allegiance to the international Communist movement.

Wiretapping is only one phase of electronic surveillance, which has grown highly sophisticated with all sorts of exotic devices. Their use by individuals may also constitute invasion of privacy, a point not touched upon yet by the courts.

Chicago, Ill., June 21, 1972

WHEN you see s o m e b o d y fooling around with a delicate piece of machinery he obviously doesn't understand, your impulse is to warn him away from it in a manner he won't forget. The Supreme Court has just performed this service for the Constitution, and we are obliged to it.

In an 8-to-0 decision Monday, the court threw out a contention by the Justice Department that it had the right to order wiretaps without a court's permission. Former Atty. Gen. John N. Mitchell had argued, in essence, that constitutional checks and balances were fine in their place, but surely they didn't have to apply to a trustworthy public servant like him. The court's blunt answer was that this is exactly the point of constitutional safeguards; they mean you don't HAVE to trust in any official's willingness to respect your rights. They are guaranteed, whether he likes it or not.

We hope Atty. Gen. Richard Kleindienst can grasp this basic fact about the Constitution better than his predecessor did.

Little Rock, Ark., June 21, 1972

THE PROLIFERATION of wiretaps has posed a deadly threat to freedom in this country, and it still does. In truth the expanded use of such electronic listening devices has made George Orwell read more and more like a prophet and less and less like a novelist in his book *1984*, the one wherein every citizen's television set is watching *him*, rather than vice versa.

Nevertheless, the United States Supreme Court has finally blown the whistle, as it were, on wiretapping in its most virulent form, which is — or was — FBI wiretapping without even a court order in any case involving "domestic subversion." It was the Nixon administration, of course, which had honed the wiretap rationale down to the claim that the attorney general or his minions might wiretap anyone, any time, whenever there was a (purported) suspicion of such subversion.

There still exists altogether too much authority for wiretaps, under court order, but the FBI can no longer tap any telephone line at its own discretion or whimsy, at least not *legally*. What's needed now may be some stiff criminal penalties for the use of wiretaps not lawfully authorized.

In any event the Supreme Court's decision in this crucial case warrants the closest scrutiny.

THE DECISON was 8-0, reassuringly, although two of the justices were equivo-cal on the fundamental point, Chief Justice Burger declining to join in the majority opinion and Mr. Justice White writing his own flaccid opinion arguing simply that Congress hadn't authorized the kind of wiretapping in dispute. Mr. Justice Rehnquist recused himself because it was he, as an assitant attorney general, who had prepared the outrageous government case in the first place before he was nominated to the high court. Mr. Rehnquist had not previously shown even this much discernment on questions of recusal, and we must be grateful for whatever favors are forthcoming from him.

But if the Chief Justice remained enigmatic about his own reasoning, and if Mr. Rehnquist had to recuse himself, the other two of President Nixon's four appointees to the court responded splendidly to the issue, and indeed, Justice Lewis F. Powell, one of the two most recent appointees, wrote the opinion that stated the question on the basic constitutional ground that it deserved.

Mr. Justice Powell was sent to the Supreme Court in a sort of after-thought during one of President Nixon's recurring confrontations with the Senate, but his credentials are so impeccable that we entertained and have continued holding hopes that he would make a good record. His opinion in the wiretap matter serves to sustain such hopes and good wishes. In his summary he wrote that "* * * the historic judgment * * * is that unreviewed executive discrimination may yield too readily to pressures to obtain incriminating evidence and overlook potential invasions of privacy and protected speech."

If the point was understated, the decision and the reasoning were certainly clear. Inadvertently the new attorney general, Richard Kleindienst, moved at once to punctuate and emphasize the insight of the Powell opinion. This administration has not cared a whit for constitutional restraints on the power of the executive and Mr. Kleindienst announced forthwith plans to take the wiretap matter to Congress to set new legislative standards for such surveillance of "domestic subversives." It is characteristic of this administration that when the Court defines a constitutional point the President goes running to Congress to pass statutory law (as in the busing controversy) purporting to tell the Supreme Court how it should have interpreted the Constitution.

It is often said, politely, that the issue in protecting the constitutional system is not whether a particular administration would abuse executive power but whether some administration off there in the future might. As it happens, with the crowd now holding sway in Washington, theoretical illustrations are not needed; there is altogether too much illustration in the here and now. The Nixon gang is constantly attacking both the rights of the individual and the authority of the other two branches to restrain the executive in the unbridled exercise of power.

The Washington Post
Times Herald

Washington, D.C., June 20, 1972

The decision by the Supreme Court yesterday that the Federal Government cannot constitutionally use electronic surveillance devices in domestic security cases unless it gets judicial permission to do so is a landmark in the long struggle to maintain individual freedom in this country. The effect of it—if the Executive Branch complies with it, and we trust that will happen—should be to reduce substantially the near-paranoiac fears among some citizens that their conversations are being tapped or bugged by the government. Beyond this, the decision is a sharp slap at the Nixon Administration which had baldly attempted to justify as a legitimate exercise in presidential power a practice that had begun years ago and grown steadily more dangerous.

This decision, as far as we can tell, will have no substantial impact on the Executive Branch's legitimate efforts to gain information about those who would engage in acts of political espionage or terrorism. It simply requires the Department of Justice to handle its investigations into those areas as it already handles its investigations into other kinds of crime. What it does rule out is the procedure ardently advocated by this administration under which the Attorney General alone determined when wiretapping and eavesdropping equipment was to be used in domestic security cases. In the future, a judge is to make that determination under traditional standards of the Fourth Amendment. This rule, it should be noted, has not yet been extended to cover investigations into subversive activities by other governments.

It should be said that the procedure defended by the Nixon Administration in this case did not originate with it; what this administration did was give it a much more explicit rationale. For at least 25 years, the Department of Justice through the FBI has carried out electronic surveillance in domestic security cases without court approval. Lying behind these efforts to protect the domestic peace, at least in the beginning, were fears of Communist subversion and espionage. More lately, the fears have expanded to include other kinds of domestic unrest and the phrase "domestic security" seems to have grown in meaning to encompass many kinds of strong dissent against the status quo. The Court seems to have recognized this. In a powerful opinion by Justice Powell, it said:

History abundantly documents the tendency of government—however benevolent and benign its motives—to view with suspicion those who most fervently dispute its policies. Fourth Amendment protections become the more necessary when the targets of official surveillance may be those suspected of unorthodoxy in their political beliefs. The danger to political dissent is acute where the government attempts to act under so vague a concept as the power to protect "domestic security."

Underlying the Court's decision was an explicit rejection of the key argument which the Nixon Administration had used in claiming the right to broad surveillance power. That claim was that the President could not fully discharge his constitutional duty to protect domestic security unless his agents were free to engage in whatever wiretapping and eavesdropping the Attorney General might authorize. To this, Justice Powell replied, "We recognize, as we have before, the constitutional basis of the President's domestic security role, but we think it must be exercised in a manner compatible with the Fourth Amendment."

The Justice turned aside each of the arguments the government had made to support that assertion—that this kind of surveillance was primarily intelligence gathering, not law enforcement, that domestic security matters are too complex for courts to evaluate, and that secrecy would be compromised by requiring warrants in advance. The last two points were brushed aside and to the other, Justice Powell noted that security surveillances are particularly sensitive because, among other things, of "the temptation to utilize such surveillances to oversee political dissent."

Perhaps the most important effect of this decision will come outside of government. The idea that the government is always listening has become widespread in some areas of our society and has something to do, we think, with some of the bitterness loose in the land. Adherence to the spirit of this decision, or whatever minor modifications Congress might be able to make in it, by the Executive Branch would remove one of the grievances which is helping to increase the alienation of some citizens from their government.

Richmond Times-Dispatch
Richmond, Va., June 20, 1972

It was hardly by mere chance that Richmonder Lewis F. Powell Jr. was selected by the Chief Justice to write yesterday's U.S. Supreme Court opinion on wiretapping. Before appointment to the court, Powell had been an outspoken defender of governmental wiretapping, and an article along this line that he wrote for The Times-Dispatch last year was one of the few things cited against him when President Nixon nominated him for the high court.

So when Justice Lewis Powell wrote an opinion declaring that the government cannot tap the wires of suspected domestic subversives without a warrant, certainly no one could say that the writer of the opinion was unsympathetic to the use of wiretapping per se.

Prior to yesterday there was widespread, though not universal, understanding that under the federal wiretapping law and the Constitution:

(1) The government could tap wires in ordinary criminal investigations only after obtaining warrants from federal judges.

(2) In cases in which the national security was endangered by the activities of foreign agents — Soviet spies, for example — wiretaps probably could be instituted without warrants.

But there was an uncertain gray area: the threat to internal security by dissident Americans not acting as agents for any foreign power. Were warrants required in such cases?

In his Times-Dispatch article, Powell wrote that "there may have been a time when a valid distinction existed between external and internal threats" but that "such a distinction is now largely meaningless." He went on to say that "the radical left...is plotting violence and revolution" and that its leaders "visit and collaborate with foreign Communist enemies."

Even before his confirmation by the Senate as a member of the Supreme Court, Powell had said that he did not spell out his views in the article as carefully and accurately as he should have. Yesterday's opinion was certainly not in full accord with the statements quoted above.

In effect, what Justice Powell and other members of the court held was that wiretapping is a valuable and useful law-enforcement tool but that its use must not be unbridled or left solely to the decision of the Justice Department in cases involving internal subversives.

"The price of lawful public dissent must not be a dread of subjection to an unchecked surveillance power," Powell wrote. "Nor must the fear of unauthorized official eavesdropping deter vigorous citizen dissent and discussion of government action in private conversation. For private dissent, no less than open public discourse, is essential to our free society."

It would be easy to misinterpret yesterday's opinion as somehow putting a serious obstacle in the way of legitimate governmental wiretapping. The decision does no such thing. It doesn't say at all that the government shouldn't tap wires in cases involving internal threats; it merely says that before such taps are made, warrants must be obtained. There is no reason whatever to believe that federal judges won't issue warrants in all cases in which the government can show any reasonable cause for suspecting the persons whose conversations are to be monitored.

So nothing in yesterday's opinion should hamper in any meaningful way the government's power to protect us from internal subversives. On the other hand, the opinion gives added protection to the people against eavesdropping which some administration might some day attempt to use to harass or squelch legitimate non-violent dissent. For that reason, the decision represents a fair balancing of the right of society to protect itself, on the one hand, and the right of individual privacy, on the other.

Finally, it should be pointed out that the decision does not reach to the question whether warrants are necessary for wiretaps when the nation's security is threatened by external foes. But we believe it is safe to predict that if this question were put before the court, a majority of the justices would rule that under his inherent constitutional powers, the President has the right to authorize taps without warrants in such cases.

The Salt Lake Tribune

Salt Lake City, Utah, June 24, 1972

Back in 1940 President Roosevelt decided he needed no warrant to tap the telephones of suspected German spies. In 1946 President Truman broadened the assumed presidential authority to include American citizens suspected of foreign espionage.

Twenty-one years later the Supreme Court held that electronic surveillance was subject to Fourth Amendment warrant requirements though it did not deal specifically with so-called national security surveillance.

The following year Congress passed the Safe Streets Act which authorized police to obtain wiretap warrants to investigate a variety of illegal activities. However, the 1968 law specifically stated it would not affect any constitutional authority the President might have to wiretap in national security cases without warrants.

The Nixon administration, faced with rising civil disturbance and under pressure to take positive counteraction, read the 1968 act as permission to tap without warrant in domestic security cases in which no foreign threat was involved. Monday, in an 8-0 decision written by one of the President's latest court appointees, the Supreme Court said the government had overstepped its authority. Warrants, Justice Lewis F. Powell Jr. wrote, are necessary to properly guarantee Fourth Amendment freedoms in domestic surveillance.

As a result of the Monday ruling, defendants in federal prosecutions now have the right to see transcripts of any conversation overheard on a warrantless "domestic security" listening device. Access to transcripts enables their attorneys to determine if the prosecution is using illegally - obtained evidence or information.

The Justice Department, quick to announce it would stop warrantless bugging, must now decide what to do about the cases already prosecuted or about to be. By making transcripts available to the defense the government risks blowing its cover and might prefer to drop charges.

Before he was appointed to the Supreme Court, Justice Powell described the domestic security tapping controversy as a "tempest in a teapot." From the government's side of the argument that is an apt description.

It has never been clear to us why the government objects to obtaining warrants. The process is not a complicated one and we doubt that many judges are disposed to turn down reasonable requests. Reluctance to seek a warrant strikes us as tacit admission that the projected surveillance is more a fishing expedition than legitimate attempt to enforce the law.

Monday's decision will not end electronic eavesdropping and it does not directly affect a President's thus far unchallenged authority to tap without warrant in foreign espionage cases. But the ruling goes far to restore the balance between individual freedom and the government's need to protect itself from subversion.

Further, the wiretapping decision should impress upon hardline "law and order" elements that even in times of great national tension the constitutional niceties must not be taken lightly. Indeed, it is a such times that strict official respect for constitutional guarantees is most essential

The Evening Bulletin

Philadelphia, Pa., June 21, 1972

The U. S. Supreme Court has resolved a major source of tension between constitutional rights and the Executive Branch's duty to protect the Government.

In an 8-to-0 decision, the court held that the Government cannot, without prior court approval, tap the wires of unorthodox domestic political groups or individuals who have no significant connection with a foreign power but are considered by the executive branch to be subversive.

Rejected was the Justice Department's unrealistic contention that executive discretion alone was sufficient to prevent abuses. The historic ruling is a more comfortable guarantee, now requiring the Government to show probable cause that a law is about to be violated.

"History abundantly documents the tendency of government — however benevolent and benign in its motives — to view with suspicion those who most fervently dispute its policies," Justice Lewis F. Powell Jr. said in his written opinion.

The ruling deals with the vague area of domestic security, the definition of which theoretically and, unfortunately, in practice could be stretched to repressive lengths. It does not prevent the Government from using wiretapping against foreign subversives without court approval.

At stake were Fourth Amendment freedoms against unreasonable searches and seizures. The court duly noted the difficulty in expecting the executive branch, which must enforce laws, to act as a neutral magistrate in sensitive matters of political dissent.

Again in his reassuring opinion, Justice Powell stated: "The price of lawful public dissent must not be a dread of subjection to an unchecked surveillance power. Nor must the fear of unauthorized official eavesdropping deter vigorous citizen dissent and discussion of government action in private conversation."

Certainly this decision will gladden liberal dissenters. But at the same time it should hearten those whose conservative attitude toward the Constitution convinces them that an internal erosion of individual rights can, in the long run, be every bit as devastating to this nation as external force.

The Chattanooga Times

Chattanooga, Tenn., June 22, 1972

How strong is the Fourth Amendment's protection against unreasonable invasions of privacy of the forces of government seeking incriminating evidence?

Strong enough, the Supreme Court has said in an opinion given without dissent, to force the government to secure court orders for using secret surveillance devices in all cases except those involving external threats to the national security.

The opinion is a resounding reversal of the Nixon Administration's position that it had the power on its own initiative to use wiretaps and the like for gathering evidence against suspected "internal subversives."

The ruling cannot be blamed on the "liberal Court" whose interpretations the President's appointees were to reverse. Of the four men Mr. Nixon has named to the Court, Mr. Justice Powell wrote the opinion for the Court, Mr. Justice Blackmun concurred, Mr. Chief Justice Burger agreed in the result in the case at hand without necessarily following the constitutional reasoning involved, and Mr. Justice Rehnquist recused himself because of his service in the Justice Department when the policy was set.

At issue was a determination of the extent a 1968 law limited governmental power to use electronic surveillance equipment. Only in national security cases were investigators exempt from getting specific court orders to install the devices. Attorney General John Mitchell assumed the right to broaden that exception to cases involving "internal subversives," or persons suspected of anti-government activity. He apparently took the position he would never be challenged, or that the Supreme Court as reconstituted would uphold the practice.

Mr. Justice Powell demolished the assumption in strong language:

"Fourth Amendment freedoms cannot properly be guaranteed if domestic surveillances may be conducted solely within the discretion of the Executive Branch . . .

"History abundantly documents the tendency of government — however benevolent and benign its motives—to view with suspicion those who most fervently dispute its policies . . .

"The price of lawful public dissent must not be a dread of subjection to an unchecked surveillance power. Nor must the fear of unauthorized official eavesdropping deter vigorous citizen dissent and discussion of government action in private conversation."

Although not a part of the record, official statistics reveal the need for curbing the Nixon Administration's heavy use of electronic eavesdropping—a useful, but nasty, tool of law enforcement which can be a threat to the innocent but unwary conversationalist whose words are recorded in secret.

Official figures show 94 wiretaps were used in 1969 on "domestic security" cases, 113 in 1970 and 100 in 1971.

In 1971, other reports show, 794 court-ordered electronic eavesdrops were installed, a 36 per cent increase over the 583 installed the previous year. The total cost in equipment and manpower was figured at $3.3 million, close to $11,000 for each of the 306 convictions resulting.

While the price per tap runs high in dollars per conviction in approved installations, the Supreme Court's decision has lowered the cost in terms of individual rights for unauthorized uses.

The New York Times
New York, N.Y., June 20, 1972

The Supreme Court has delivered a sharp rebuke to those ideologues of the executive branch who consider the President's "inherent powers" superior to the Constitution. In an 8-to-0 decision the Court has rejected the assertion that the Government has the right, without court orders, to tap the wires of "dangerous" radical groups. Justice Lewis F. Powell Jr., who wrote the opinion, said: "The price of lawful public dissent must not be a dread of subjection to an unchecked surveillance power."

Former Attorney General Mitchell's position that the Republic would be in danger if the Justice Department could not tap wires without court orders has now, fortunately, been completely demolished by this unanimous vote of the "Nixon Court," in which only Justice William H. Rehnquist, who was an advocate of the Government's case while he was in the Justice Department, did not join. The Government claimed that in order to get a court's permission to tap wires, it would have to submit too much concrete evidence. But this fear of disclosure—even to the courts—goes to the heart of the matter: The Constitution means to protect all citizens against vague fishing expeditions by the executive.

It was Mr. Mitchell's view that civil liberties would be safe so long as it was he who had to give personal approval in each instance of electronic surveillance. Fortunately, the Court was not persuaded by a system of constitutional safeguards dependent on the Attorney General's, or even the President's, infallibility or, as Mr. Mitchell put it, on the "self-discipline of the executive branch." Moreover, there has been growing evidence that there is far more domestic spying than has been authorized by the Attorney General.

The Supreme Court understood the historic lesson that a blank check of official powers is the prelude to their abuse. "Vigorous citizen dissent and discussion of Government action in private conversation," Justice Powell warned, must not be deterred by fear that unauthorized Government monitors are listening. Those who argued the Government's case admitted that they were asking for an "awesome power" but pledged to use it with "discretion."

The Supreme Court, ignoring the usual division between "liberal" and "conservative," has now reminded the Government that it is just because its powers are so awesome that their exercise cannot be left to the discretion of men without precise restraint of law, under the Constitution.

Detroit Free Press
Detroit, Mich., June 21, 1972

ALMOST AS gratifying as the Supreme Court's wiretap decision itself is the manner and source of its coming.

The opinion affirming Judge Damon Keith's workmanlike ruling was written by Lewis F. Powell Jr., President Nixon's southern appointee to the U.S. Supreme Court. He spoke in measured phrases reminiscent of an earlier generation of Virginians who helped devise much of our original constitutional structure.

"The price of lawful public dissent must not be a dread of subjection to an unchecked surveillance power," Mr. Justice Powell wrote. "Nor must the fear of unauthorized official eavesdropping deter vigorous citizen dissent and discussion of government action in private conversation. For private dissent, no less than open public discourse, is essential to our free society."

Those charged with investigative and prosecutive functions, he said, "should not be the sole judges of when to utilize constitutionally sensitive means in pursuing their tasks." So he and the unanimous court held that government does not have the right to eavesdrop on those citizens it classes as dangerous without first obtaining a warrant.

The same man who wrote this opinion wrote an article shortly before going on the court in which he dismissed the distinction drawn between domestic and foreign subversives as "largely meaningless." And he had dismissed the complaints against government wiretapping as a "tempest in a teapot."

The contrast between Justice Powell's earlier, offhand comments and his ringing defense of dissent can be attributed in no small measure to the solid legal scholarship of Judge Keith, who made the original finding, and to William Gossett, the Detroit lawyer who presented Judge Keith's position to the Supreme Court. The proof of their persuasiveness is in Mr. Justice Powell's opinion.

Mr. Nixon said he was appointing a conservative court, but in Mr. Justice Powell, at least, he seems to have gotten something more than he bargained for—a true conservative who thinks the highest duty of the Supreme Court is to protect the individual even when to do so frustrates the state.

The country can be grateful to the astute Detroit judge who first flung down the gauntlet to government over "the evil of the uninvited ear" and to the Supreme Court justice who was so thoroughly persuaded by the arguments.

The Cincinnati Post
TIMES ← STAR
Cincinnati, Ohio, June 24, 1972

Newly revived fears that the United States is fast becoming the land of the unauthorized snoop should have been put to rest by the Supreme Court.

The court said it is unconstitutional for the federal government to tap a private telephone conversation without a court order in an attempt to gather evidence against suspected domestic subversives.

SUCH POWER, wrote Justice Lewis F. Powell Jr. in an Ann Arbor, Mich., bombing case, is a clear violation of the Fourth Amendment to the Constitution, which guarantees the right of the people against "unreasonable searches and seizures and requires warrants even when the government has probable cause" for suspicion.

The Nixon Administration had been insisting it had the right to make some warrantless wiretaps under a section of the 1968 crime act.

In fact, says Justice Powell, there is nothing in the act that gives the President, or his attorney general, the right to override normal constitutional restraints, except in cases where foreign espionage may be involved.

Granting the government — any government — the right to tap conversations of its own citizens without the permission of a judge or magistrate is a step toward Big Brotherism and a potential curb on political dissent.

"History abundantly documents the tendency of governments to view with suspicion those who most fervently dispute its policies," Justice Powell points out.

TO ARGUE, as the Justice Department did, that judges really don't understand subversion, or that word will leak out if warrants must be approved, shows a woeful lack of faith in the judicial process.

Justice Powell makes it emphatically clear, however, that court-approved wiretapping, in certain circumstances, is not only justified but absolutely necessary to protect the national interest and cope with organized crime.

That point needs to be asserted and reasserted in the face of foolish efforts to abolish legal wiretapping altogether.

But as long as privacy and free expression are held sacred in this country, the use of the government wiretap must be carefully, and judiciously, circumscribed.

THE PLAIN DEALER
Cleveland, Ohio, June 21, 1972

The government must not wiretap, eavesdrop or plant a "bug" on anyone without first getting a warrant from a judge, the U.S. Supreme Court ruled this week.

We get great satisfaction from this decision. It forbids the witch-hunting plans which arise in the minds of Justice Department people who see subversives under beds and lurking in chimney corners, or going to end-the-war meetings.

Justice Lewis F. Powell Jr., a Richmond (Va.) conservative, wrote the opinion, and there was no dissenter. That added to our satisfaction.

Though President Nixon's appointments to the court are tilting it away from the liberal Earl Warren court direction, this opinion proves that one's right to dissent is still held precious by the present interpreters of the Constitution.

Former Atty. Gen. John N. Mitchell had claimed the right to eavesdrop without the equivalent of a search warrant. His grounds were that some individuals and groups "may pose a danger to national security."

But all too often the Justice Department, the Army or other federal organs have drawn up their own secret lists of suspected subversives. Once listed, any dissenter from "correct thinking" — as defined by some government official — became fair game for the snooper squad.

Justice Powell found the concept of "domestic security" as so used to be too vague. He wrote:

"The price of lawful public dissent must not be the dread of subjection to an unchecked surveillance power. Nor must the fear of unauthorized eavesdropping deter vigorous citizen dissent and discussion of government action in private conversation. For private dissent, no less than open public discourse, is essential to our free society."

The right to criticize one's government in one's own living room, or office, as well as in public, is one of democracy's great advantages over systems in which every telephone or restaurant table may be bugged.

Nosing into people's private lives on filmy rumor or suspicion thankfully has been ruled illegal.

The Birmingham News
Birmingham, Ala., June 21, 1972

THE SAGINAW NEWS
Saginaw, Mich., June 23, 1972

When the U.S. Supreme Court ruled unanimously the other day that the wiretap was not the exclusive privile e of the executive branch of our government to be used against the people it did more than strike a vindicating blow for radical groups.

The court's thinking, we are pleased to say, went far beyond that to the very heart of Constitutional guarantees contained in the Fourth Amendment. Simply ,the highest court applied strict constructionist thinking in arriving at its verdict. The court has deduced that any such practice unilaterally engaged in by the government violates the amendment's fundamental precept—protection of all citizens against unreasonable search and seizure.

Clearly the most important aspect of the court's ruling is that it will serve to put a brake on willynilly tapping of telephones at every suspicious whim of the government through the Justice Department. If this happens to be a setback for the present administration's approach, so be it. The fact is that this peculiar form of snooping has mushroomed in recent years reaching invidious and alarming proportions under the government's broad interpretations of what constitutes its right of surveillance.

That interpretation has been extremely broad under the immediate past tenure of Attorney General John Mitchell. As reported several months ago, Michigan had become the most telephone tapped state in the Union in 1970.

The result, despite government denials, was a chilling effect on many citizens. It did tend to suppress action and movement. Many did become overly careful of what they said, who they were seen with, what groups they might affiliate with"Thus a blow has

been struck for the right to protest and the right of dissent quite aside from whatever it is that constitutes radicalism.

In clearest possible terms the court has seen the danger to domestic freedom in unbridled government wiretapping. The message is that from now on no such practice may be engaged in without court order—and that the request had better be backed with some very solid, very valid reasons.

It should be understood, of course, that the Supreme·Court ruling addressed itself solely to the question of domestic wiretaps in relation to matters of national security. Yet the ruling, by implication, could have far-reaching effect.

In upholding the findingsof U.S. District Judge Damon Keith in the Lawrence (Pun) Plamondon White Panther case, it may clarify a host of other questions. It was Keith who said that the government had used an unauthorized wire tap on Panther headquarters. It was Keith who said that the defendant had the right to see and hear any evidence so obtained in a case against hiu. And it was Keith who said the government had that wiretap right only in national security cases involving foreign groups or persons.

The high court's ruling can be seen no other way than as a landmark decision striking a mighty blow for the right of privacy and the right to assemble and dissent.

Justice Lewis F. Powell, one of Mr. Nixon's most recent appointees to the high court summed up nicely when he wrote that Fourth Amendment freedoms "cannot be properly guaranteed if domestic security surveillances may be conducted solely within the discretion of the executive branch." That says a great deal in a very few words.

The 1968 federal wiretapping law, a part of the Omnibus Crime Bill, contains provisions which Congress intended as safeguards for the rights of citizens against unreasonable violations of privacy. But the intent of the law was to permit law enforcement agencies to use reasonable electronic surveillance against criminal and subversive activities.

The subject of wiretapping has always been controversial. Now two new chapters in the controversy have been opened by the U.S. Supreme Court in a decision handed down Monday, and by a U.S. District Court decision last week. The two courts were ruling in very different circumstances, but in both instances the question of constitutional guarantees of the First and Fourth Amendments were involved.

In the earlier instance. U.S. District Judge Joseph S. Lord ruled at Philadelphia that the wiretapping law is unconstitutional. Judge Lord held that "the protections afforded the citizens against unreasonable governmental intrusion are largely illusory."

Monday the Supreme Court's unanimous decision was that it is unconstitutional for government security agencies to wiretap "domestic subversives" without first obtaining court-approved search warrants.

The Supreme Court examined the wiretap constitutionality in the light of conflict between the inherent power of the President to protect the national security and citizen freedoms guaranteed in the First and Fourth Amendments.

In writing the Supreme Court opinion, Justice Lewis Powell wrote: "The price of lawful dissent must not be a dread subjection to an unchecked surveillance power. Nor must the fear of unauthorized official eavesdropping deter vigorous citizen dissent and discussion of government action in private conversation. For private dissent, no less than open public dscourse, is essential to our own free society."

As a result of the Supreme Court decision, the FBI and other security agencies must, along with other enforcement bodies, now apply to a federal magistrate, presenting evidence that the government has "probable cause" to believe the person or group to be wiretapped poses a threat to national security.

We believe the Supreme Court has ruled wisely. We would not favor indiscriminate or unreasonable use of wiretapping. The process of obtaining a search warrant does not seem to be an unreasonable hinderance to agencies charged with maintaining the security of the nation.

Given the proper safeguards, a wiretap law can be a very effective tool of investigation without subjecting the citizen to unreasonable intrusions. If the safeguards in the present law are inadequate, then Congress should amend the law so as to meet constitutional requirements.

THE BLADE
Toledo, Ohio, June 24, 1972

WHEN THE U.S. Supreme Court announced a year ago that it would hear a case involving wiretaps without court warrants against "domestic subversives," it simultaneously handed down an opinion in another case stating that those who seek exemption from the warrant requirement bear the burden of showing that the need is imperative. This coincidence was interpreted as an unusual advance hint that the Nixon administration would not have an easy time persuading the justices that the Government should be free to "bug" homefront radicals without bothering to get judicial approval.

Intended or not, the hint turned out to have been prophetic indeed. The court has unequivocally rejected the concept developed by former Attorney General John Mitchell and embraced with, if possible, even more zeal by his successor, Richard Kleindienst. They contended that there is no essential difference between a threat to national security from outside and one from within; thus the attorney general, under delegation of presidential authority, can exercise the same sweeping discretion in dealing with domestic subversives that he has been allowed in practice and by the 1968 wiretapping law to use against alien saboteurs.

That the court's decision is a stern rebuff to the Administration is emphasized in several ways. For one thing, it is a unanimous judgment, with only Justice William Rehnquist abstaining because of his role in the case when he was a Mitchell assistant. That means, obviously, that even Mr. Nixon's own "strict constructionist" appointees concurred in rejecting the Government's position. More significantly still, the major opinion was written by Justice Lewis Powell, who has in the past forthrightly supported official use of electronic surveillance and specifically endorsed the provisions for it in the 1968 anti-crime law.

His decision did not alter his viewpoint in either regard. Rather, Justice Powell focused on the point that the protection of "domestic security" is too vague a notion to justify granting unchecked official power. There is too great a danger that the label of "subversive threat" might be applied against any and all political dissent, private or public. Neither the Constitution's Fourth Amendment prohibition against unreasonable searches and seizures nor the surveillance authority of the 1968 statute sanctions such unbridled discretion on the part of a government official, the justice said. The "time-tested means" of judicial warrants are required to guard against improper use of wiretaps or bugs in such situations.

The opinion was, we think, a conservative one in the best sense of the word: a wisely discerning balance between the right of society to protection against threats to its existence and good order and the right of citizens to protection against intrusive and abusive law enforcement. Or, put another way, the right of a free society to protection against seeing basic liberties eroded in the name of keeping it safe.

ARKANSAS DEMOCRAT
Little Rock, Ark., June 8, 1972

A federal judge in Philadelphia ruled last week that wiretaps were unconstitutional, throwing out the conviction of some gambling czars who had been nailed by FBI agents listening to their telephone conversations.

Americans have a fundamental right to privacy, the judge said. He's right, of course. But Americans also have a fundamental right to be protected against their enemies by their government. There's the dilemma, and the judge didn't do much to solve it with his idealistic ruling.

It's our opinion that wiretaps ought to be allowed only under two broad conditions: The first is that the need for it be justified. Under the part of the 1968 Omnibus Crime Control and Safe Street Act that the judge set aside, this was provided. Each wiretap had to be approved by the Attorney General, and subsequently a federal judge had to agree and issue a warrant. Putting the onus on the attorney general is important because, unlike a judge, he is within reach of the people's representatives since he has to be approved by the Senate.

Second, the use of wiretaps ought to be limited to federal officers and in cases involving national security or organized crime. Certainly no one would argue about national security and it has been demonstrated time and time again that gambling, narcotics smuggling and bribery of public officials (the staples of organized crime) are almost impossible to prove without wiretaps. Last year 816 taps were authorized, resulting in the arrest of 1,120 racketeers who, in the words of the acting head of the FBI, probably would not have been caught any other way.

Unfortunately, 20 states (not, happily, including Arkansas) also have wiretap laws, and these are dangerous. Prosecutors, law enforcement officers and even some judges are elected in states, and the temptation to use wiretaps for political reasons is too great to be resisted universally. Anyway, if the feds can keep track of the Mafia and saboteurs, the real menaces can be controlled.

In passing the 1968 law, the Congress not only did not remove the states' wiretap authority but it made it easier for them to exercise it. Also, it greatly increased the number of offenses that wiretaps c o u l d be used to investigate — robbery, rioting, obstructing criminal investigations, theft from interstate shipments, bankruptcy frauds, etc. President Nixon criticized these additions, but he signed the bill because he definitely wanted the use of wiretaps in his administration's crackdown on organized crime.

For this reason, the Department of Justice undoubtedly will appeal the district court's decision. Hopefully, the court would uphold the use of wiretaps (it has in the past) in combating organized crime. But we wish either it or the Congress would remove the states' authority in this area and restrict the use of wiretaps to those serious offenses where information can be obtained virtually in no other way.

The Houston Post
Houston, Tex., June 9, 1972

Wiretapping, like clothing fashions, has been going in and out of style in almost annual variations since the passage of the Federal Communications Act in 1934. A Philadelphia federal judge now says it is out this year.

Various forms of electronic eavesdropping by federal, state and local officials have been both attacked and defended under the Constitution's Fourth Amendment, which guarantees privacy against illegal search and intrusion. Some judges have held that a phone tap under a court order is as legal as a search warrant, while others have ruled it is an invasion of privacy under any circumstance.

The wiretapping practice proliferated during t h e World War II years when federal agents were given free hands and open ears in ferreting out subversives. The practice grew and spread to local law enforcement agencies until President Lyndon Johnson put the clamps on electronic bugging in 1965.

Then came the Omnibus Crime Control and Safe Streets Act of 1968, which decreed that wiretapping was in again. The Philadelphia judge now says this is unconstitutional. He apparently agrees with Justice Oliver Wendell Holmes, who called wiretapping "a dirty business," and with former Atty. Gen. Ramsey Clark, who called it ineffective and a poor substitute for sound police work.

It is time to resolve the issue permanently by outlawing wiretapping through strict interpretation of the Constitution, thus insuring that a citizen will not be subject to legal bugging during periodic plagues of electronic locusts.

The Philadelphia Inquirer
Philadelphia, Pa., June 12, 1972

If anything is certain in this world, it is that the government will appeal the ruling by Chief Judge Joseph S. Lord 3d of the U. S. District Court in Philadelphia declaring that the wiretap law passed by Congress in 1968 is "unconstitutional on its face."

Beyond that, certainty ends. Four days later, a Federal court in St. Louis upheld the legality of the wiretap law.

We cannot know how the Supreme Court will rule in the matter. If it follows its own precedents, though, we think it should uphold Judge Lord, and we hope it will. For as the Court declared in a 1967 case cited by Judge Lord:

"We cannot forgive the requirements of the Fourth Amendment in the name of law enforcement. This is no formality that we require today but a fundamental rule that has long been recognized as basic to the privacy of every home in America. . . . Few threats to liberty exist which are greater than that posed by the use of eavesdropping devices."

Judge Lord's ruling came in a case involving seven defendants charged with operating a $10 million betting ring. The judge threw out the evidence against them on the ground that the statute violates the Fourth Amendment's prohibition against "unreasonable searches and seizures."

So the central question involved is what constitutes "unreasonable." Judge Lord holds that it is unreasonable to permit continuous searches for months on end.

He holds it unreasonable to put so much discretion in the hands of the police and too little control in the courts.

And, breaking new ground, he holds it unreasonable that, since "the secret search is such an extraordinary procedure under the Fourth Amendment," the law does not require postsearch notice to all those whose conversations have been overheard by the government.

Plainly, the question is not merely a matter of semantics but of substance— the substance of the individual liberty which the men who framed our Constitution intended to protect against government tyranny.

The Justice Department claims that electronic surveillance, the volume of which rose last year by 37 percent, is an effective tool in the fight against crime. There are serious doubts on that score.

Last year, authorities eavesdropped more than 73,000 times in the Philadelphia area, but the result was only 758 arrests, and only 52 convictions, mostly for gambling offenses.

It might also be an effective tool for the police if they could search citizens' homes without warrants, as often as they liked, and never inform the citizens whose homes had been searched. We doubt, however, that anyone would seriously argue in favor of giving the police such a tool. Yet wiretapping, under the 1968 law, is precisely that kind of tool. The Founding Fathers never dreamed of it, but the document they wrote guards against it.

SUPREME COURT RULES AGAINST MITCHELL'S WIRETAP EVIDENCE

The Supreme Court ruled unanimously May 13 that former Attorney General John N. Mitchell failed to meet the requirements of the Organized Crime Control Act of 1968 when he allowed his executive assistant to approve wiretap applications, rather than doing it himself or designating a specific assistant attorney general to act in his place, as required by law. In ruling that the wiretap requests approved by Mitchell's executive assistant Sol Lindenbaum were illegal, the court upheld the dismissal of a narcotics indictment against Dominic N. Giordano of Baltimore. The ruling was expected to have the same effect in 60 other narcotics and gambling cases involving 626 defendants.

While the full court agreed that evidence from the wiretaps authorized by Lindenbaum was inadmissable, the four Nixon appointees to the court—Chief Justice Warren E. Burger and Justices Harry A. Blackmun, Lewis F. Powell Jr. and William H. Rehnquist—argued in a separate dissent that court-ordered extensions of the Lindenbaum-authorized taps were not improper. Writing for the court in its unanimous ruling, Justice Byron R. White brushed aside government arguments that the defective procedures were merely technicalities. White said he had traced the history of the provison and found that Congress had included it to make "doubly sure that statutory authority [would] be used with restraint."

In a parallel case, the court upheld by a 5–4 margin the validity of another set of wiretaps affecting 99 cases and 807 defendants. Here, wiretap applications had been authorized by Mitchell but signed by former Assistant Attorney General Will R. Wilson, who had not actually played any part in their preparation. The court majority said it did not "condone" Mitchell's practices, but attributed defects in these wiretap requests to poor bookkeeping practices. Justices William O. Douglas, William J. Brennan Jr., Potter Stewart and Thurgood Marshall dissented.

OKLAHOMA CITY TIMES

Oklahoma City, Okla., May 15, 1974

SEEING CRIMINAL CASES thrown out of court on technicalities has been a maddening experience for the lay public. Most people want individual rights protected. What angers them is for criminal suspects to escape justice for a reason having nothing to do with guilt or innocence.

Now the U. S. Supreme Court, which has thrown so many roadblocks in the pursuit of justice and the fight against crime, has done it again. It has invalidated wiretap evidence in hundreds of organized crime and narcotics cases on the flimsiest of technicalities.

THE COURT ruled that former Atty. Gen. John N. Mitchell did not follow the Omnibus Crime Control and Safe Streets Act in requesting wiretapping permission. He allowed many of the requests to be signed by his executive assistant. The law specifies the attorney general himself or a specially designated assistant attorney general must approve the requests.

Yet the taps in question were authorized in each instance by a federal judge. If the matter of who actually signed the request was so important, why wasn't the wiretap permission denied right there?

WASHING OUT criminal cases against 600 or more defendants does a disservice to the nation. The damage to the welfare of the people is far more serious than any infringement on individual rights where only the technicality of who signed a piece of paper is involved.

Constantly the public reads of suspects being freed because of technical defects in the arrest procedure. Just this week the alleged confession of a Tulsan charged with possession of cocaine with intent to distribute was ruled illegal because a narcotics agent took the statement unaware the man had already asked for an attorney.

A CALIFORNIA appellate judge wrote recently that the courts, in the search for perfection in legal procedure, have allowed the idea of punishing the guilty become secondary.

The frustrated public can only hope that in the wiretap cases some remedy can be found short of dropping prosecution completely.

Washington Star-News

Washington, D.C., May 20, 1974

It should be obvious to everyone by now that John Mitchell was not very careful in the way he supervised intelligence-gathering operations, be they in the political or the legal realm.

Partly because of his slipshod (or worse) management of the 1972 Republican presidential campaign, the Nixon administration is in tatters and may ultimately fall as a result of an investigation set in motion by an illegal break-in and bugging of the Democratic party's headquarters. Whether Mitchell actually approved the illegal operation is a matter still in dispute, but the fact is that it was carried out by underlings in a campaign that was in his charge.

Now it turns out that the former attorney general — the "Big Enchilada" of the Watergate tape transcripts — handled wiretap operations at the Justice Department in such a manner that cases against some 600 criminal defendants are on shaky grounds and many of the accused may go free. The Supreme Court ruled last week that Mitchell did not follow the prescribed legal procedure in placing wiretaps on the individuals.

The pity of it is that the ruling could free a good many members of organized crime — narcotics traffickers and the like — who ought to be behind bars. Not many of the individuals have come to trial yet, so there is not going to be a mass exodus from prison walls. But it means that prosecutors are going to have a harder time convicting the defendants and they probably will have to drop some cases in which evidence other than that obtained by the illegal wiretaps is insufficient.

What happened was that Mitchell didn't follow the letter of a 1968 law that says wiretap orders must be approved by the attorney general or by a designated assistant attorney general. Mitchell didn't designate an assistant attorney general to approve them but rather let his office assistant sign the orders in his absence. The court ruling may seem to be splitting hairs but the law is the law and the attorney general, above all, ought to be cognizant and careful of his responsibility. The Supreme Court pointed out in its unanimous opinion that the intent of Congress was to "centralize and limit" the authority to issue wiretap orders and did not intend that the attorney general should delegate his authority at will.

The Constitution guarantees the right of individuals against unreasonable search and seizure, and laws designed to safeguard this protection should not be treated in cavalier fashion. It appears that the "Big Enchilada," a vigorous exponent of law and order, was long on order but rather short on the law. It is unfortunate that the guilty sometimes go free in order for officials to be reminded of the law and of their own responsibilities.

HERALD EXAMINER
Los Angeles, Calif., May 20, 1974

The recent Supreme Court decision invalidating a number of anticrime wiretaps is disheartening to citizens aware of the grave extent of crime rampant throughout America.

For all its pedantic, legalistic "reasoning," the court decision is another grave setback for anticrime forces, and yet another victory for the criminal element our legal system too often coddles and protects.

Once again, "proper procedure" takes priority over arguments of criminality. Emphasis shifts once again from concerns of guilt or innocence to small-minded technicalities over how evidence was obtained.

In a nutshell, because former Attorney General John Mitchell failed to designate a specific member of his staff to act in his behalf in requesting wiretap authority from the courts, most or all of 626 criminal suspects will be returned to the streets without their deserved trial.

Administration reasoning that the attorney general should have wide latitude in delegating authority among his staff members fell on deaf ears in the High Court. Nitpicking justices followed a narrow interpretation of the applicable law, but violated the spirit of the law in the process.

Months of effort and great expense will be flushed into the sewer labeled "due process," as hundreds, perhaps thousands, of degenerate criminals celebrate yet another major victory over law and morality.

The American judicial system has long been a laughing stock to educated English barristers and other European adherents of law, and weak court decisions such as this can only generate greater discredit to this nation and the cause of justice.

The Des Moines Register
Des Moines, Iowa, May 20, 1974

The federal government is faced with nullification of hundreds of criminal convictions because of the cavalier way John Mitchell handled his responsibilities for wiretapping during his years as attorney general.

The federal wiretap law requires "the attorney general or any assistant attorney general specially designated by the attorney general" to approve wiretap applications before federal judges can issue wiretap orders. Asst. Atty. Gen. Will Wilson had been named by Mitchell as the other Justice Department official authorized to pass on wiretap requests submitted by federal law enforcement agencies.

When a U.S. attorney in Maryland decided to wiretap Dominic Giordano, suspect in a narcotics case, he submitted to a federal judge a letter purportedly signed by Wilson approving the request. Giordano's lawyers discovered when they challenged the wiretap procedure that Wilson had not reviewed or approved the request, even though his name was signed to a letter stating that he did.

Instead, the wiretap request had been reviewed by Mitchell's executive assistant, who put Mitchell's initials on it. The assistant said he acted because Mitchell was out of town and the assistant concluded from "his knowledge of the attorney general's actions on previous cases that he would approve the request if submitted to him."

The form bearing Mitchell's initials then went to Wilson's office. Someone there noted Mitchell's "approval" and drafted a letter to the judge and put Wilson's name on it.

Wiretap advocates frequently cite the "safeguards" in the federal wiretap law. One of the safeguards is supposed to be close scrutiny of each wiretap request by a high Justice Department official. The Giordano case has revealed how illusory this safeguard is. Instead of being scrutinized carefully by the responsible official, the wiretap requests were passed on by an assistant who guessed that his superior would approve.

★ ★ ★

The letter with Wilson's name on it perpetrated a fraud upon the court. The judge was assured that Wilson had studied the wiretap request when he had not reviewed it. The procedure followed in the Giordano case apparently was used in many other cases.

Mitchell was such a zealous advocate of wiretapping that it probably would have made no difference if he personally had reviewed each case. Former Asst. Atty. Gen. William Ruckelshaus told a congressional committee last week that Mitchell approved wiretaps for alleged "national security" reasons that had "had very little if any relationship to national security." Ruckelshaus said results of the taps showed no evidence that they were proper or added to national security.

The federal wiretap law has more loopholes than safeguards. Mitchell and Wilson were merely careless. They could have rubber-stamped the wiretap requests and gotten away with it.

The Houston Post
Houston, Tex., May 23, 1974

The unanimous decision of the Supreme Court to void evidence gained by illegally authorized wiretaps involving hundreds of defendants is reassurance that there is still strong concern for the public's right to privacy. Undoubtedly, the ruling will be criticized by some as an action showing leniency toward criminal activity. At issue, however, is a law designed to protect the rights of millions of Americans from overzealousness and unwarranted surveillance by investigators.

Even if the cases against all 626 defendants affected are dismissed as a result of the decision, it is more important that a basic principle of freedom has been protected from an inroad that could grow. When Congress passed the Omnibus Crime Control Act of 1968, the wording made it clear that this danger was recognized. The avowed purpose of one section of the act was to minimize government intrusion on personal privacy by keeping tight control over wiretapping and by limiting those officials who could authorize electronic surveillance.

The loose procedure under which the wiretaps were authorized by the Department of Justice while John Mitchell was attorney general left open the possibility of routine approval of requests. Instead of designating an assistant attorney general to approve or deny requests in his absence, as the law requires, Mitchell allowed his executive assistant to perform that function. In another instance, the high court determined that the Justice Department told judges that wiretap authorizations had been handled by then Assistant Atty. Gen. Will Wilson who actually had nothing to do with them. Although there was no apparent intent of deception, it demonstrated a lack of serious consideration of each application and of Congress' intent to centralize and limit the authority. These deviations from the letter of the law were described in Justice Department appeals as "harmless errors" and "minor and technical departures." But, fortunately, the Supreme Court took the position that provisions of a law involving the constitutional rights of every citizen must not be taken so lightly.

Eavesdropping on telephone conversations involves not only the target persons but all those on the other end of the line. Depending on the length of the surveillance, conversations of dozens of persons having no connection with criminal activity may be recorded and placed on file with the potential for harming their reputations. For such reasons strong arguments against legalization of any form of wiretapping have been voiced for several years.

Unless the restrictions attached to allowable interceptions of conversations are strictly adhered to, law enforcement could lose a valuable tool. The Supreme Court has acted to keep under control a crime-fighting mechanism designed to protect the public but one that could turn against it if allowed to get out of hand.

Richmond Times-Dispatch
Richmond, Va.
May 22, 1974

It seems there is no end to the embarrassment and disappointment which the Nixon administration is inflicting upon those who put it into office.

One of the latest developments is a U. S. Supreme Court ruling which presumably will throw out hundreds of federal criminal convictions because of the improper manner in which former Atty. Gen. John N. Mitchell administered the wiretap law.

The 1968 statute clearly states that "the attorney general or any assistant attorney general specially designated by the attorney general" may authorize applications to federal judges for permission to intercept oral or written communications of criminal suspects.

Yet despite this clear provision governing wiretap authorization, the Supreme Court found that in at least 60 cases involving 626 defendants, applications to the courts were authorized by the attorney general's executive assistant, who had no power to do so.

This newspaper, along with other believers in strong law enforcement, has consistently supported moves that permit wiretapping under properly controlled conditions. We supported passage of the 1968 law because it seeks to allow wiretapping while at the same time providing sufficient safeguards to prevent its misuse.

There was nothing sinister in the Justice Department's failure to follow the law to the letter in the cases now at issue; almost certainly the wiretap requests authorized by the executive assistant would have been authorized by the attorney general or an assistant attorney general designated by him if the cases had been brought to them. As the government argued before the Supreme Court, the executive assistant's handling of the requests was simply an administrative convenience which was harmless from the standpoint of infringing anyone's rights.

Nevertheless, Attorney General Mitchell should have scrupulously followed the letter of the law, especially since the whole subject of wiretapping is such a sensitive and controversial one.

Instead, Mr. Mitchell and his aides took a shortcut, and, as a result, hundreds of persons convicted on drug and other charges may go free. It is another deep disappointment to those Americans who helped put into office what they believed would be a strict law-and-order administration.

The Birmingham News
Birmingham, Ala., May 16, 1974

Viewing the decision strictly in terms of legal purity, the U. S. Supreme Court probably had no choice other than to come down on the side of the challengers in ruling this week on federal wiretap cases.

While there was no question that the Justice Department was in technical violation of the Omnibus Crime Control Act of 1968 in its method of authorizing wiretaps, it is deplorable that the substance of the government's case against the appellant was not a factor in the decision.

The court's unanimous decision hinged on an interpretation of the law which requires authorization by the U. S. attorney general or a "specially designated" assistant attorney general before a wiretap is approved. In the cases under review, the authorizations were issued by Atty. Gen. John Mitchell's executive assistant, Sol Lindenbaum.

The technical error on the part of the Justice Department was simply that Lindenbaum was not "specially designated."

Most fair-minded persons would agree that the Justice Department was right in claiming that at worst it had committed only "harmless error." They will be hard put to understand why the simple lack of a "designation" would be sufficient cause to throw out a conviction which has cost the taxpayers untold amounts.

The consequence of the decision is that more than 1,400 cases — primarily involving narcotics and gambling charges — may be voided.

These cases were worked up by a variety of law enforcement agencies over long periods of time and at a cost of millions of dollars of taxpayers' money. As a result of the decision even those of unquestioned guilt will go free to prey again on the public.

Despite the technical error, it is clear that the public interest has once again been sacrificed for legal niceties.

The Salt Lake Tribune
Salt Lake City, Utah, May 15, 1974

It was a mere technicality, a matter of the wrong person signing an application for permission to wiretap criminal suspects. Those charged as a result of the wiretaps were found guilty. Why quibble over who signed what?

It's a familiar argument by persons who want crime stopped at any price. It's a line often trotted out by critics of the courts who think "soft headed judges" are "coddling criminals." And it's a dangerous belief that the U.S. Supreme Court was recognized as such Monday.

The court, in a unanimous decision, ruled that a group of narcotics sellers had been illegally convicted in 1970 because the Department of Justice presented evidence against them which was obtained with invalid wiretap orders. The decision affects some 600 other offenders convicted with similarly invalid evidence.

The 1968 Omnibus Crime Control Act authorized wiretapping over the objection of President Johnson. Partly to counter Mr. Johnson's complaints and that of other critics, Congress agreed that the government could only place a tap after obtaining the express approval of the attorney general or a designated assistant attorney general.

But former Atty. Gen. John N. Mitchell either didn't read or understand the then new law or, as now seems possible in the light of Watergate revelations, didn't feel bound by it. The government argued before the Supreme Court that Mr. Mitchell had broad power to delegate his authority, broad enough that the attorney general's executive assistant—not mentioned in the law—could sign wiretap applications.

The question of who signed the wiretap applications might seem a small thing, especially in view of the probable guilt of those ultimately convicted. But it is vital to the concept of the rule of law. And it should be another stern lesson to over-zealous investigators and prosecutors that circumventing the law as written can be a costly shortcut.

If laws are to have any meaning, those who enforce them must follow both the spirit and the letter right down to the last comma. A man such as Mr. Mitchell, who at that time was a symbol of a new "law and order" administration, had a greater than ever responsibility to play by the rules.

The provision that only the attorney general or his designated assistant could sign applications for wiretapping was written specifically to prevent the very thing which the former attorney general tolerated. Not to uphold the law now, even if it means setting hundreds of convicted persons free, would be to invite further, perhaps more serious, abuses in the future.

The Philadelphia Inquirer

Philadelphia, Pa., May 18, 1974

If, in the Omnibus Crime Control and Safe Streets Act of 1968, Congress had intended to authorize flunkies in the Department of Justice to seek court approval for legal wiretaps, Congress would have said so.

Congress, however, did not say so. As Justice Byron White pointed out in behalf of a 9-0 majority of the U. S. Supreme Court in the Giordano case, Congress did not take a casual attitude toward intrusions on the privacy of American citizens.

It insisted that there might be restraints in this sensitive area. Thus, under the 1968 law, permission to wiretap a suspect must be obtained from a judge in regular criminal cases, but first the U. S. attorney seeking such permission must have the approval of the "Attorney General, or any assistant attorney general specially designated by the Attorney General."

Is that procedure so difficult to follow? Well, the "law and order," "strict constructionist" former Attorney General, John N. Mitchell, seems to have found it so. Loosely construing the law, he delegated his authority to an underling, his executive assistant, and did not even bother to do so in writing.

As a result, the Supreme Court has ruled that several persons, including the aforementioned Nicholas Giordano, were convicted illegally of selling narcotics. And as a result of this decision, the convictions of or the cases against upwards of 600 other persons will be upset.

It should be emphasized that it's not the Supreme Court which is "letting criminals go free." The onus for that is upon the former attorney general, with his casual attitude toward the law and his duties as chief law enforcement officer of the nation.

And these cases, we might add, involve "legal" wiretapping, not the illegal wiretapping toward which the administration's approach has been not merely casual but cavalier.

Thus, the concern is not with "mere technicalities" but with the essence of law itself. The basic question, as in the larger matter which has come to be known as Watergate, is whether government officials follow the law or may flout it for their own convenience. The Supreme Court has given the only answer it could, and unanimously.

SAN JOSE NEWS

San Jose, Calf., May 15, 1974

Wiretapping is an important law enforcement tool and one that is easily abused. That is why it is important that the procedures and safeguards surrounding use of the "bug"—electronic surveillance — be carefully defined and scrupulously followed.

The U. S. Supreme Court this week ruled illegal a whole batch of wiretaps from the 1969-70 period. The wrong Justice Department official authorized the bugging.

The government argued that at worst it committed only "harmless error." In the unanimous opinion of the Court, however, the technicalities were important ones.

The tragic part of this story is that 1,430 people arrested on the basis of this tainted wiretap information probably will go free whether or not they are guilty. Some are narcotics pushers. In addition, many thousands of hours of police work are wasted.

The villain, however, is not the Court. The villain is bureaucratic bungling in the Justice Department.

THE ATLANTA CONSTITUTION

Atlanta, Ga., May 15, 1974

Legal wiretapping is a necessary evil in the U.S. But it must be legal, or there must be no wiretapping.

That's the essence of this week's Supreme Court ruling that said the Department of Justice under former Atty. Gen. John Mitchell performed hundreds of wiretaps in violation of federal law. The ruling is one of those difficult ones that must be supported because its immediate bad effects are far outweighed by its long-range effects.

The ruling probably means acquittal for defendants involved in about 600 narcotics and gambling cases because wiretap evidence against them was obtained in the way ruled to be illegal—and the fact that those people may escape immediate prosecution is very bad.

But the civil rights of all Americans must be protected, and the government must not be allowed to use illegal means to gather evidence against anyone. It might just be possible criminals today. But tomorrow it could spread to anyone.

That wouldn't happen in the U.S.A., you say? Probably not, but how do you know it wouldn't? Do you want to chance it?

The Supreme Court did not rule out wiretaps. It just said—and very rightly—that they must be authorized according to strict legal standards set down in 1968 by Congress—and this is what the Department of Justice under Mitchell did not do.

The law says that applications to a federal judge for use of wiretaps must be directly approved by the attorney general or a specified assistant attorney general named by the attorney general. But under Mitchell, his executive assistant routinely approved wiretaps applications—and the high court ruled 9-0 that that was illegal.

Some folks will say that the Supreme Court is protecting criminals. But that's not really the case. It's for sure that crime is a super-major problem in this nation, and the government must take all necessary—but legal — steps to control it. It must not, however, commit a crime to solve a crime.

The Supreme Court ruling does not protect criminals, but it does protect you and me from Big Brother going too far. And there are precious few things more important than that.

Wisconsin State Journal

Madison, Wis., May 21, 1974

Wiretapping and other forms of electronic surveillance are two-edged swords in the constant struggle of a free nation to enforce its laws while providing maximum freedom for its citizens.

Law enforcement agencies see such techniques as vital to the performance of their jobs. They must recognize the danger, however, of the misuse of such powerful and potentially tyrannical tools.

The U. S. Supreme Court, therefore, is to be commended for its decision last week that the U.S. justice Dept. consistently violated the law in its procedures for obtaining wiretap.

The decision was based on an interpretation of the Omnibus Crime Control Act of 1968 which contains specific provisions for obtaining wiretap orders. The Justice Dept., the Court ruled, bypassed those provisions.

The action will probably kill narcotics and gambling prosecutions involving humdreds of persons which have been pending in courts throughout the country awaiting the determination by the high court.

It is unfortunate that many guilty persons may escape prosecution because of what many may regard as a technicality.

The technicality, however, is a vital one, absolutely essential to the freedom of every American.

The Supreme Court rightly said, in effect, that regardless of motives, regardless of righteousness of cause, regardless of short-term expediencies in enforcing democratically passed laws, the government must follow the letter and spirit of the laws which safeguard all of our rights.

The unanimous decision of the Court is probably part of a post-Watergate backlash against the always dangerous contention that the ends can somehow justify the means.

Errors and missteps are inevitable in any endeavor but as long as our system can continue to prove itself by righting those errors and missteps before irreparable harm is done, the democratic experiment will continue to be successful.

The Afro American

Baltimore, Md., May 18, 1974

For years there has been a steady cackling from the "law and order" pundits about how lenient judges were sabotaging the efforts of policemen and other citizens to put criminals behind bars and keep them there.

Now we have the spectacle of hundreds of criminals being cleared of convictions because former "law and order" Attorney General John Mitchell failed to live up to legal requirements regarding wiretaps.

Congress required that Mr. Mitchell or his designated deputy would have to approve wiretap requests to make them legal.

Mitchell always seemed to have felt the law was what he said it was, thus he allowed someone else to do the wiretap approvals. Mitchell had lost by 8 to 0 a Supreme Court test on the question of his getting wiretaps without going through what he considered red tape. The courts considered it safeguards.

Thus it was clear that Mr. Mitchell could not turn the authority of requesting wiretaps from federal judges to a subordinate other than the one required by law.

Lower level prosecutors took every precaution to meet lawful requirements in seeking wiretaps needed to trap smooth-operating criminals. Then the Washington bosses who felt they were above the law gummed up the works.

It is a real travesty of justice when something like this occurs. Not only are a lot of criminals going to beat convictions but some of them may be able to win suits against the government. Ironically, the normally loudmouthed "law and order" pundits are as quiet as thieves at work.

Post-Tribune
Guarding Your Interests Daily

Gary, Ind., May 18, 1974

We would regret any interruption — even temporary — of the federal government's recent drive against organized crime and racketeering.

Still, progress along those lines, desirable as it is, should not be made at the risk of losing individual liberties.

On that basis, we have to go along with the Supreme Court's decision early this week invalidating wire tappings in such cases — and possibly in others — made in violations of strict guidelines earlier set up.

What the court held was that former Atty. Gen. John Mitchell ignored requirements of the Omnibus Crime Control and Safe Streets Act in delegating authority for wire tapping approval to his executive assistant.

That may appear nit picking to some since the law provided that either the attorney general or a specially designated assistant attorney general would have to give such approval.

However, the dangers of wiretapping have been made plainer by developments in the Watergate case.

When the Justice Department overlooks specifics of a law involving so basic a right as that of privacy, it seems time to call a halt.

If any major malefactors go free as a consequence we will regret it.

Nevertheless, basic liberties are more important than temporary "law and order" gains.

Minneapolis Tribune

Minneapolis, Minn., May 17, 1974

The U. S. Supreme Court this week threw out the convictions of a group of narcotics sellers on grounds that the Justice Department had gathered evidence against them with improperly obtained wiretap orders. The decision is likely to free not only the narcotics sellers whose cases were involved in the appeal to the high court, but also other offenders — a total of about 600 in all — whose convictions were obtained with the same kind of tainted evidence.

"It's just too bad," one federal prosecutor said — predictably — in response. "Someone up there must like them." But while that kind of response might be predictable, it is also wrong. The court's reasoning, far from being the kind of legalistic sophistry so often blamed for "setting the guilty free," was instead based on a principle that should be clear to anyone who believes in law and order (a category that certainly should include federal prosecutors). The principle is simply this: Law and order works both ways — on those who enforce the law as well as on those who break it. If those whose duty and responsibility it is to uphold the law break it in pursuit of that goal, they become in that respect like the lawbreakers who are their quarry.

The Supreme Court demonstrated in this decision not that it likes lawbreakers, but rather that it likes — and respects — the rules of a democratic society. Neither law-enforcement agencies nor lawbreakers may ignore those rules with impunity. It is too bad that 600 convictions may have to be thrown out to bring that lesson home to the Justice Department.

THE DALLAS TIMES HERALD

Dallas, Tex., May 17, 1974

FORMER ATTY. Gen. John N. Mitchell did a signal disservice to law enforcement with his failure to follow the dictates of the law governing electronic survelliance.

Either through negligence in familiarizing himself with the provision in the 1968 Omnibus Crime Control Act regulating federal wiretapping or through sheer carelessness, Mitchell did not fully comply with the provision in many cases. The result, reports the Department of Justice, is that wiretap evidence in some 600 cases will be inadmissible in court. Many of these cases will now be untriable while others will be considerably weakened.

All of the cases involve serious offenses, such as narcotics violations and organized crime.

The law was carefully drawn to provide necessary safeguards against abuse of the use of electronic surveillance by federal law enforcement officials. It provides that requests for wiretaps must be signed by the attorney general or an assistant attorney general designated by him. The requests then must be approved by a federal judge.

Mitchell, however, allowed his executive assistant to sign many requests for permission to use electronic surveillance, requests which were subsequently granted by federal judges. The U.S. Supreme Court in a unanimous decision held that this was a clear violation of the federal law and that evidence obtained from those wiretaps is inadmissible in court.

Mitchell's failure to comply with the law is most unfortunate in two respects. Many organized crime figures and narcotics traffickers who otherwise might have been convicted will now be free to continue their nefarious activities. And the argument, which we have long supported, that electronic surveillance under carefully controlled conditions is legitimate law enforcement too, will be weakened.

The Topeka Daily Capital

Topeka, Kans., May 16, 1974

Because the U.S. Supreme Court found another uncrossed "t" and another undotted "i," federal charges against 628 defendants, including many being prosecuted for alleged organized crime and narcotics offenses, have been invalidated.

The court said evidence gathered against these defendants was not admissible because it has been obtained by improper wiretaps. They had been authorized by the attorney general's executive assistant rather than by an assistant attorney general as specified by the Omnibus Crime Control and Safe Streets Act.

The "illegal" wiretaps occurred during the tenure of John N. Mitchell and it is probable that procedures now follow the law to the letter regarding wiretaps.

By a narrow, 5-4, decision the court did manage to salvage 807 cases where wiretaps had been authorized by Mitchell, himself, or irregularly by an assistant attorney general, Will Wilson.

It is less than amusing to find the nation's highest court requiring all law enforcement officials to play by a strict set of rules while the criminals they seek have no rules and hide behind the traditional right of privacy.

The Supreme Court's ruling came on appeals by defendants being prosecuted for narcotics deals, one allegedly was one of the biggest heroin dealers in New Jersey.

Surely the court, in its reputed wisdom, can exercise better judgment than to nullify on a technicality the diligent and otherwise effective efforts of countless law enforcement officers.

The nine justices of our highest court do well to guard the privacy of individuals, but there must be a way this can be done without also putting roadblocks in the paths of law enforcement officers. After all, each wiretap was approved by a federal judge before it was installed and activated.

To free probable criminals on technicalities is nitpicking.

The Detroit News

Detroit, Mich., May 15, 1974

Of all people, the U.S. attorney general should know the law and follow it to the letter. Former Atty. Gen. John Mitchell didn't know the law on wiretaps; or, if he did, he shrugged off its technicalities. Consequently, hundreds of convicted or suspected narcotics peddlers probably will go scot free.

Echoing Judge Cornelia Kennedy's opinion in Detroit's Anchor Bar case, the U.S. Supreme Court ruled this week that the Justice Department failed to follow procedures outlined in the Omnibus Crime Control Act of 1968. Under that act, only the attorney general or a designated assistant attorney general may approve a request for a wiretap.

Three years ago, a task force of FBI agents and local police arrested 151 Michigan residents thought to be involving in illegal gambling operations. The task force used the federal wiretap authority to monitor activities at the Anchor Bar, considered to be the headquarters of the operations.

When the case went to court, the government admitted that an executive aide, rather than the attorney general or a designated assistant, had signed wiretap applications. Judge Kennedy ruled against use of wiretap evidence illegally gathered.

Although this week's ruling by the Supreme Court was delivered in another case and involved but a few defendants, it could affect the Anchor Bar defendants along with an estimated 1,500 suspected narcotics dealers, gamblers and racketeers throughout the nation.

This is a high price for the country to pay for legal hair-splitting in the courts. Realistically, an application signed by an aide of the attorney general reflects the authority of the attorney general and should be acceptable. Certainly the technical violation is not serious enough to justify releasing hundreds of suspects.

The point is, however, that courts are prone to split hairs in this fashion; therefore the Justice Department cannot afford to take anything for granted. It must do its homework on the law and follow the law as closely as possible. John Mitchell's Justice Department did not do so.

As far as previous cases are concerned, the damage has apparently been done. Looking toward the future, Congress should consider enlarging the circle of Justice Department officials authorized to exercise the attorney general's wiretap authority. Until that happens, we assume that the current attorney general will take the wiretap law, every comma of it, seriously.

THE ROANOKE TIMES

Roacnoke, Va., May 17, 1974

Federal courts have frequently been accused of taking the handcuffs off criminals and putting them on the police, and many people will view the U.S. Supreme Court's recent decision on wiretaps in just that light. The court ruled that authorities had illegally obtained evidence via wiretap in a case involving a narcotics defendant—just one case, but the findings can be extended to scores of others, invalidating evidence similarly obtained against more than 600 defendants. If enough other evidence is not available, they will go free.

Before railing at the high court, law-and-order people should consider the reason for this decision. It is an eminently strict construction of the law involved, the 1968 Safe Streets Act. Contrary to what some civil libertarians preferred, that act gave approval of law to electronic snooping—as long as each application to a federal judge ior a wiretap is authorized by the U.S. attorney general or any assistant attorney general he specifically designates.

That seems simple enough. But with a carelessness for due procedure that seems to have been almost habit with this administration, then Atty. Gen. John Mitchell ignored the act's clear wording and for some two years, allowed his executive assistant—not an assistant attorney general—to make the wiretap authorizations.

"To us," said the nine Supreme Court jurists (four appointed by President Nixon), "it appears wholly at odds with the scheme and history of the act to construe (it) to permit the Attorney General to delegate his authority at will, whether it be to his executive assistant or to any officer in the department other than an Assistant Attorney General."

The Nixon administration never had a very high opinion of Congress, so perhaps it is not strange that the Attorney General felt he could ignore its stated wishes in the law. He had long contended that he or the President could authorize a wiretap in a domestic security matter without going through a judge, but the court has struck him down on that too. So Mr. Mitchell liked wiretaps; he just didn't care for dotting all the i's and crossing the t's. But that's what the law requires. In this case it wasn't a court that took the handcuffs off hundreds of accused criminals; it was John Mitchell.

Long Island Press

Jamaica, N.Y., May 16, 1974

The Supreme Court has struck a blow for government by law, not by men who twist the law to their own convenience.

In a 9-to-0 decision, the court ruled that the Justice Department, under former Atty. Gen. John D. Mitchell, used improper procedures in approving wiretaps. The 1968 Omnibus Crime Control Act was very specific that wiretap applications must be approved by Mr. Mitchell or a specially designated assistant attorney general. Instead, Mr. Mitchell permitted his executive assistant to approve the applications.

To some law-and-order advocates, the difference may seem minor, hardly enough to void 60 serious criminal cases, involving 625 defendants. In fact, the difference is significant.

The legislation was very specific, with good cause. Congress did not want wiretap authority to be used indiscriminately; thus it carefully restricted the number of officials who could request it.

This is the second unanimous verdict against different aspects of Mr. Mitchell's wiretapping orders. We hope the message is clear — that law-and-order is more than a slogan. The law must apply equally to those entrusted to enforce it as well as those who break it if we are to have order.

APPEALS COURT ORDERS WARRANTS FOR WIRETAPPING OF U.S. GROUPS

The U.S. Circuit Court of Appeals for the District of Columbia June 23 ruled that the executive branch needed court approval before it could wiretap domestic organizations, even if the surveillance were for reasons of national security. The decision involved a warrantless wiretap placed for 208 days in 1970 and 1971 on the New York City headquarters of the Jewish Defense League, a militant Zionist group whose anti-Soviet activities in the U.S. were creating diplomatic tension between the U.S. and U.S.S.R.

In arguing that the tap had been legal, the federal government had defended the surveillance on the grounds that it "was authorized by the President..., acting through the attorney general in the exercise of his authority relating to foreign affairs, and was deemed essential to protect this nation ... against hostile acts of a foreign power and to obtain foreign intelligence information deemed essential to the security of the United States." The appellate court rejected that reasoning, holding that the then-Attorney General, John N. Mitchell, should have obtained court approval of the tap since it was being installed on a domestic organization that was neither an agent of nor acting in collaboration with a foreign government. While the court did not address the issue of wiretaps on agents of foreign governments, it did state: "Indeed, our analysis would suggest that, absent exigent circumstances, no wiretapping in the area of foreign affairs should be exempt from prior judicial scrutiny, irrespective of the justification for the surveillance or the importance of the information sought."

The incidence of warrantless wiretapping by the federal government for purposes of national security rose sharply between 1972 and 1974, according to Justice Department statistics made public June 24. The figures, contained in a letter from Attorney General Edward H. Levi to Sen. Edward M. Kennedy (D, Mass.), showed that such wiretaps had averaged 108 for each year between 1969–1972 and then increased to an average of 156 a year during 1973–1974. In addition, Levi's letter said that microphone surveillances, installed without judicial warrant to intercept room conversations, had averaged 20 a year during 1969–1972, but jumped to an average of 41 a year in 1973 and 1974. Levi in his letter, which Kennedy released without comment, defended national security wiretaps conducted without prior judicial approval. "Based on an examination of the relevant precedents," Levi said, "it is the position of the Justice Department that the executive may conduct electronic surveillance in the interests of national security and foreign intelligence and in the aid of his conduct of the nation's foreign affairs, without obtaining a judicial warrant."

Des Moines Tribune
Des Moines, Iowa, June 30, 1975

A federal appeals court has moved to curb the government's wiretapping authority by ruling that law enforcement agencies must get warrants before wiretapping organizations without direct connections to foreign governments.

The case stemmed from an order by former Atty. Gen. John Mitchell authorizing the FBI to put wiretaps on the New York headquarters of the Jewish Defense League (JDL) late in 1970. The organization used peaceful and violent demonstrations to protest the Soviet Union's restrictive emigration policy on Jews.

An affidavit by Mitchell indicated that the Soviet Union had objected to the league's activities. Mitchell said the wiretapping was "authorized by the President of the United States . . . in the exercise of his authority relating to the nation's foreign affairs and was deemed essential to protect this nation and its citizens against hostile acts of a foreign power and to obtain foreign intelligence information deemed essential. . . ."

When 16 league members sued Mitchell and nine FBI agents, Federal Judge John H. Pratt threw the case out of court at the government's request. He saw the league's actions as a threat to continued peaceful relations between this country and the Soviet Union.

A majority of the Circuit Court of Appeals in Washington declared that government use of wiretaps without warrants violated the Fourth Amendment prohibition against unreasonable search and seizure.

The ruling said that "a warrant must be obtained before a wiretap is installed on a domestic organization that is neither the agent nor acting in collaboration with a foreign power." The opinion added that a presidential claim of national security would not be sufficient ground to sidestep the requirement for judicial approval of the wiretapping.

The court stated its view in an aside that "no wiretapping in the area of foreign affairs should be exempt from prior judicial scrutiny, irrespective of the justification for the surveillance or the importance of the information sought." But it has not decided a specific case of wiretapping of an organization with foreign connections involving a threat to the national security.

"Many of the JDL activities which antagonized the Soviet government were clearly protected exercises of First Amendment rights," the appeals court declared. "Indeed, there is no evidence that more than a small percentage of the thousands of JDL members engaged in criminal activity. Yet the actions of that minority have formed the basis for intrusive surveillance that lasted over seven months and that resulted in seizure of the contents of the conversations of innumerable innocent individuals."

It is bad enough when government agencies claim authority to spy on American citizens and to keep secret files on their political activities. It is worse when such assaults on constitutional rights are begun in response to complaints from foreign governments, in this case the Soviet Union.

Congress has refused to curb warrantless wiretapping in "national security" cases. Proposals to require court orders for all electronic surveillance have run into the argument that the nation's safety would be imperiled if the government could not wiretap at will. The circuit court ruling is notice to Congress that if it won't act to protect constitutional rights, the courts will.

The New York Times

New York, N.Y., June 28, 1975

The United States Court of Appeals for the District of Columbia took a major step in shoring up the principle of constitutional government when it decided there were limits on Federal authority to install "national security" wiretaps.

Since the beginning of World War II, the executive branch has asserted that the constitutional limit on unreasonable searches and seizures did not apply to electronic surveillance designed to protect the national security. Over the years, the concept of national security, which grew out of such concrete images as the threats posed by Nazi saboteurs, has been distorted to the point where it was used to justify such diverse intrusions as the burglary of a psychiatrist's office, the bugging of a civil rights leader's hotel room and the tapping of the telephones of journalists and high officials without court order.

The Government has argued that to require prior court approval of national security taps would stretch the guarantees of the Fourth Amendment too broadly and that the efficiency of national security enterprises would be impeded by such a constitutional limitation. Since the Supreme Court has up to now avoided the issue and the Court of Appeals for the District of Columbia is the highest court to deal with it, the decision is of enormous importance.

The Court of Appeals did not dispose of the entire question. It merely decided that the Government is required by the Constitution to obtain a warrant prior to placing a national security wiretap on the phone of a domestic group which is *not* dealing with a foreign power. Although the court went on to say that its analysis "would suggest that absent exigent circumstances, no wiretapping in the area of foreign affairs should be exempt from prior judicial scrutiny," it did not extend the principle that far because the facts of the case did not require it to do so.

The decision as it stands reasserts the judiciary's authority and responsibility to interpret the Constitution even where the Executive claims a national security reason for its action. It also slows the snowballing tendency of Government recklessly to assert power in delicate areas of individual privacy and freedom.

The Philadelphia Inquirer

Philadelphia, Pa., July 6, 1975

It used to be a well-established principle that government officials, however exalted their station, could not flout the Constitution in order to protect it. Somewhere along the line that principle itself has been flouted.

During the Nixon Administration, Attorney General John N. Mitchell advanced the theory that the government could tap the telephones of citizens, without a court order, for "national security" reasons, and officials did so with enthusiasm. They also, following the orders of the President, bugged and burglarized and otherwise subverted individual rights and liberties, all for "national security."

Sad to say, Attorney General Edward H. Levi still upholds the curious principle of his predecessor several times removed—curious in the light of what the Founding Fathers clearly intended when they wrote the Fourth Amendment prohibition against "unreasonable searches and seizures."

Several weeks ago, in a letter filed in connection with the appeal of John D. Ehrlichman and three other persons from their conviction in the 1971 break-in of the office of Daniel Ellsberg's psychiatrist, the Justice Department declared that "it is and has long been the department's view that warrantless searches involving physical entries into private premises are justified . . . when related to foreign espionage or intelligence."

Now, in another letter, to Sen. Edward Kennedy, chairman of a Judiciary subcommittee looking into warrantless surveillance, Mr. Levi reported that the government installed 148 "national security" taps last year—more than in any of the previous five years. He also reiterated the Mitchell position that "the executive may conduct electronic surveillance in the interests of national security and foreign intelligence, and in the aid of his conduct of the nation's foreign affairs, without obtaining a judicial warrant."

Mr. Levi is thus asserting claims to very broad authority indeed for the executive branch — authority for which we find no ground in our copy of the Constitution.

As a matter of fact, the letter to Sen. Kennedy came one day after an eight-member federal Court of Appeals for the District of Columbia took quite a different view. In a case involving a fringe group called the Jewish Defense League, the court held it unconstitutional to install taps without court orders on domestic organizations unconnected to foreign powers. It went on to suggest that "no wiretapping in the area of foreign affairs should be exempt from prior judicial scrutiny, irrespective of the justification for the surveillance or the importance of the information sought."

The courts rarely if ever turn down a legitimate request for a tap, but the obligation of going to the courts is a necessary check on the executive.

And after the recent history of abuses by the Executive Branch, we do not see how anyone can be satisfied to trust it with the kind of unrestrained authority Mr. Levi asserts.

The Founding Fathers did not make an exception for "national security." When they declared that "no warrants shall issue but upon probable cause, supported by oath or affirmation, and particularly described the place to be searched, and the persons or things to be seized," they did not intend that prohibition to be evaded by issuing no warrants at all.

The Charlotte Observer

Charlotte, N.C., June 25, 1975

The Nixon Administration showed the country just how willy-nilly the government could be in applying the term "national security" to cover its sins. The wiretapping of government officials, newsmen and other private citizens proceeded at an alarming pace, sometimes for no real purpose except to serve the narrow interest of politicians intent upon protecting themselves.

But the Nixon Administration did not invent that practice; it simply extended it.

Now the courts are moving in to reestablish Americans' protections against such Big Brother practices. A ruling Monday by the U.S. Court of Appeals in Washington, which seems likely to stand when it reaches the Supreme Court, adds significantly to those protections.

Three years ago the Supreme Court ruled that the government must obtain court warrants before wiretapping domestic groups or individuals in the name of national security. The ruling, however, did not deal with domestic wiretapping in cases in which the government alleged that the tap was to prevent foreign threats to American security. That decision went a long way toward preventing the government from arbitrarily tapping its domestic political enemies.

The ruling Monday by the Court of Appeals went a step further. The court said warrants must be obtained for domestic tapping even if it ostensibly is for purposes related to intelligence-gathering for foreign policy purposes. In other words, the government must obtain a court warrant to tap a church, a club or an individual simply on grounds that it may learn something helpful in dealing with foreign threats.

Clearly Americans need that protection. It does not terminate the government's privilege of wiretapping lines within the country when the justification is to listen in on foreign groups or suspected foreign agents — a matter that the Supreme Court has not dealt with conclusively.

Do these two rulings — the one Monday and the one three years ago — badly interfere with the government's role in protecting national security? We think not. The government still may go to judges and, upon showing cause behind closed doors, obtain warrants for wiretapping even when no foreign agents or groups are directly involved. Even that could endanger the rights of innocent people, since many judges would readily accept the government's statement of its justification.

Electronic invasions of privacy are an increasing threat to private citizens because advanced technology makes many sophisticated forms of intrusion possible. Thus it is more important than ever for the courts to tightly define what is constitutionally acceptable — not only in the case of wiretapping but also in the case of eavesdropping of various kinds.

Those legal definitions have been too slow in coming. We hope the Supreme Court will move soon to deal with them as clearly and as extensively as possible.

San Jose Mercury
San Jose, Calif., June 25, 1975

The doctrine that the Executive branch of the federal government can use the cloak of "national security" to cover illegal acts was dealt another deserved blow in court this week.

The United States Court of Appeals in Washington ruled that the government may not tap the telephones of domestic organizations without a properly issued judicial warrant. At issue was the 1970-71 case of the Jewish Defense League and its protests against the emigration policy of the Soviet Union.

The JDL, a militant organization, employed methods ranging from peaceful demonstrations to bombings to protest Moscow's refusal to permit Jews to emigrate to Israel. The JDL's actions were a sore embarrassment to the Nixon administration which was pressing for detente with the U.S.S.R. at the time, and the Justice Department, under then Atty Gen. John N. Mitchell decided to keep the JDL under surveillance—including a tap on the organization's telephones.

Inasmuch as the Department did so without obtaining a warrant, its actions were unconstitutional, the Court of Appeals ruled on Monday.

Earlier a federal district court had dismissed the JDL's suit against Mitchell and nine special Federal Bureau of Investigation agents on the ground that the organization's actions threatened the continued peaceful relations between the and Soviet Union and the United States and hence were covered by the "national security" cloak.

In rejecting this reasoning, Appeals Judge J. Skelly Wright observed for the majority:

"We hold today only that a warrant must be obtained before a wiretap is installed on a domestic organization that is neither the agent of nor acting in collaboration with a foreign power, even if the surveillance is installed under presidential directive in the name of foreign intelligence gathering for protection of the national security.

"We do not reach this conclusion lightly or without sensitivity to the import or the controversiality of the problem of national security wiretapping. But the Constitution compels us to do no less."

That, of course, is the crux of the matter. Wiretapping, even in national security cases, must be conducted with respect for the American citizen's constitutionally guaranteed freedoms. When any agency of government departs from this standard it invites the sort of judicial rebuke delivered by the Court of Appeals this week.

The Cincinnati Post
Cincinnati, Ohio, May 5, 1975

Investigations of Watergate and the FBI and CIA have disclosed abuses of "national security" wiretaps and understandably have brought moves for reform.

A number of bills in Congress would limit the President's power to order wiretaps in foreign-intelligence cases. They would force him to seek prior approval in federal court.

After a long silence, Attorney General Edward H. Levi has come out against the restrictive bills. Though we have long had a uneasy feeling about wiretapping, we tend to agree with him.

LEVI ARGUES THAT the bills would severely restrict "the executive's ability both to guard against the intelligence activities of foreign powers and to obtain foreign intelligence information essential to the security of this nation."

That is a nice way of saying that if counterintelligence work must pass through the leaky atmosphere of federal courthouses, it will be much harder to track down spies and to keep tabs on what foreign powers are up to in this country.

If the President keeps the power to order wiretaps in security matters, what insurance is there that he will not bug newsmen, White House aides and politicians, as did the Nixon and earlier administrations?

WE SUGGEST THAT Congress let the President keep his present authority, but pass a law clearly making it a crime to order or participate in warrantless wiretaps when national security is not involved.

Such a law would not handicap counterintelligence. But any president tempted to wiretap for personal reasons would know that he risks abuse-of-power charges and the FBI employe who installed the tap would face a prison term.

THE CHRISTIAN SCIENCE MONITOR
Boston, Mass., June 25, 1975

Several United States court decisions this week have continued the prevailing trend toward protecting the rights of Americans — and thus challenging them to act under these rights in ways to enhance their society rather than injure it. The issues range from the secretly tapped telephone to the public display of nudity. The quality and security of American life will be affected as much by how officials and the public conduct themselves under the rulings as by the rulings per se.

If government men had not conducted themselves unscrupulously in the use of warrantless "national security" wiretaps, there would have been less urgency for the kind of decision now handed down by the U.S. Court of Appeals in Washington. The Supreme Court had ruled against warrantless wiretaps for "national security" reasons involving only domestic organizations, but it deliberately did not rule on instances involving foreign countries. The Court of Appeals now says that the executive branch must obtain a warrant for wiretapping purely domestic organizations even when foreign threats to national security are involved. It goes on to suggest that, except under "exigent circumstances," there should be no foreign-affairs wiretapping "exempt from prior judicial scrutiny." It is certainly in this spirit that government officials ought to conduct themselves in the future if rights are to be protected in fact as well as in legal theory.

Meanwhile, the Supreme Court itself this week left standing a lower-court decision striking down a city zoning ordinance against multiple-dwelling apartments. The ordinance had been judged a discriminatory attempt to exclude blacks.

This is one kind of case that need not have gone to the Supreme Court — if citizens and communities were acting on their own in the spirit of cooperation and human concern. The day of discriminatory housing ordinances is past. Communities need to take the steps to open their portals rather than close them.

Another situation that needs solving at the local level, and is often solved there, has to do with cooperation in maintaining constitutional freedom of speech while having regard for the sensitivities of those who don't want themselves or their children exposed to indecency.

The Supreme Court ruled against a local ordinance that made it a criminal offense for drive-in theaters to show movies with nude scenes that could be seen from outside the theater grounds. We have to agree with Chief Justice Burger's dissenting view that it is "absurd to suggest" that such a law "operates to suppress expression of ideas." Yet civil libertarians could argue for avoiding the risk of nibbling away at free speech in other areas by holding to a firm line even in what appears superficial realms.

Surely the answer is for citizens and organizations to work together within communities for a mutual upholding of the standards of those communities. It should not have to take laws for a theater to exercise the community responsibility not to force dubious films on the attentions of those who do not want to pay to see them. Even if a constitutional law could be written for such a purpose, American society would be better enhanced by growth toward self-generating standards of public display.

HE BLADE

Toledo, Ohio, June 27, 1975

IT is disconcerting, to say the least, to see that federal wiretaps without court warrants were employed even more in 1974 than they were during the years of the Nixon administration with its psychotic fixation on combatting alleged domestic subversion.

Attorney General Edward Levi has revealed that 148 persons were subjects of warrantless wiretaps last year in the investigation of what the Justice Department called national security cases. That total represents a steady growth in such surveillance over the past five years, and the attorney general reports that already this year there have been as many as 91 such wiretaps in operation at one time.

Although the trend is disturbing, this is not to say that wiretapping per se is necessarily either unjustified or illegal. As an important tool of law enforcement, it can be immensely useful in ferreting out and prosecuting criminals. There is, however, a significant difference between wiretaps duly authorized beforehand by courts of law and those used without warrants, based solely on the discretion of the Justice Department.

That distinction was clearly spelled out in the Crime Control Act of 1968 and subsequently upheld unanimously by the U.S. Supreme Court — that warrantless wiretapping is acceptable only when the national security is threatened by criminal activity that can be linked to subversive elements outside the nation's borders. To include alleged domestic subversion in that category, the court said, would be to unduly endanger citizens' rights.

In view of the cavalier manner in which wiretapping was carried on under the direction of former Attorney General John Mitchell, it is further unsettling to hear Mr. Levi cite precedent as justification for warrantless wiretaps. The weakness of that argument was underlined by a U.S. Court of Appeals ruling, only the day before the attorney general's statement, that wiretapping of the Jewish Defense League in 1970 and 1971 without a warrant was unconstitutional.

In fairness to Mr. Levi, there has been no indication yet that the Justice Department under his supervision has followed that example; but the numbers simply do not look good. In light of the abuse of wiretapping authority in recent years, one would think the department naturally would be inclined to use that power more selectively and lean over backward to insure compliance with the laws governing its use. Certainly, if there is doubt about a particular case, it would make more sense to request a warrant before ordering a wiretap than to face a long and expensive legal action after the fact.

Rather than try to justify the increased use of warrantless wiretapping in the name of national security, the department would be far better advised to emulate the FBI's recently adopted policy of reducing the number of wiretaps in the prosecution of organized crime in the nation.

ST. LOUIS POST-DISPATCH

St. Louis, Mo., June 27, 1975

Senator Church's Committee on Intelligence Activities is investigating reports that the National Security Agency, which intercepts electronic communications of foreign nations, has also been monitoring telephone calls of American citizens. Not only the Russians pose a threat to the right of privacy. Indeed, the National Wire Tap Commission is presently holding hearings that reflect the awesome buildup of both official and private electronic spying in this country.

At the federal level, Attorney General Levi says he has power to authorize wire taps, without court warrants, against domestic groups planning unlawful activity against a foreign country. The Justice Department clings to this view of its arbitrary power despite court decisions requiring warrants for espionage against domestic groups. Just the other day an eight-man panel of the U.S. Court of Appeals in Washington held, in a case involving the Jewish Defense League, that a warrant must be obtained to eavesdrop on any domestic organization that is not the agent of a foreign power.

Meanwhile the Wire Tap Commission reports that police in Missouri, Illinois and 17 other states have bought surveillance equipment they are not authorized to have. That is because federal law permits police to own bugging equipment only if state law permits it, and Missouri and the others lack such laws.

With law enforcement agencies engaged in such dubious activities, it is no wonder that private illegal use of electronic surveillance is spreading. Mr. Levi reports 806 federal wire taps without warrants between 1969 and 1974 and a higher total of all wire taps, 1,148, last year than in any of the previous five years. But that is barely the top of the iceberg, considering activities by local police and the totally unreported private operations.

The commission itself consulted 115 private investigating agencies and found that 42 either engaged in electronic surveillance or referred callers to agencies that did. Manufacturers of surveillance equipment told the commission that loopholes in the 1968 Omnibus Crime Control Act permit illegal sales and purchases. As an example, infinity transmitters once sold as an intercept device could be bought only for legal purposes; now they are advertised as alarm systems on the open market.

The Bell System finds up to 250 wire-tap devices on its lines every year (13 were found in the St. Louis area over a seven-year period), but nobody knows how many have been removed. The Justice Department has received about 4000 complaints of wire tapping since 1968, but has convicted fewer than half the 158 persons it has taken to court. Critics say the FBI is not enthusiastic about investigating illegal wire tapping by police. In any case surveillance technology has been developed to a point where evidence of its illegal use is not easy to find.

In substance, Congress opened a can of worms by legalizing wire tapping in 1968, and official abuse of electronic surveillance predictably has encouraged private misuse. And what protection do the people have? At least they have the right to expect law enforcement agencies to be more diligent in prosecuting illegal spying. Certainly they should expect the same agencies to respect the law themselves, and that means obtaining court orders.

BUFFALO EVENING NEWS

Buffalo, N.Y., July 7, 1975

A White House spokesman says President Ford will consider legislative proposals to require a court order for any electronic eavesdropping. That's a fine idea, too long delayed, and in the meantime we hope the President will instruct the Justice Department to follow that enlightened course in its current wiretapping and bugging practices.

Such a change in this important civil liberties area would clarify a lingering muddle of sticky federal law and practice — a muddle where accumulating court rulings now allow electronic surveillance without the usual judicial review in some special cases and not in others.

The sobering experiences of Watergate, as well as the revelations of indefensible taps in the Kennedy administration against the Rev. Martin Luther King and in the Johnson administration against political foes in 1968, warn plainly about the dangers of ambiguity and drift concerning standards for such surveillance.

Thus Congress should close the loopholes and clarify the foggy language in the 1968 wiretap law. But the President should not wait for that to set an example by closing the worst existing loophole, which concerns the warrantless use of federal bugs and taps in an all-too-vaguely defined area of national security.

Here, we can see no reason why there should not be some form of judicial review of ANY such eavesdropping on an American citizen. Even where discretion is a security imperative, there is no reason a reasonably safeguarded court warrant cannot be required; the government, after all, can always find a judge whose discretion it would trust as much as it would that of the FBI agent it assigns to do the tapping. The lone exception that occurs to us might involve surveillance of foreign embassies or agents where considerations of diplomatic immunity and the concept of reciprocity in our treatment of the nationals of certain hostile foreign powers come prominently into play.

BOGGS DEMANDS HOOVER RESIGN, CITES FBI'S VIOLATION OF RIGHTS

In a hard-hitting speech on the House floor April 5, House Majority Leader Hale Boggs charged the Federal Bureau of Investigation with tapping the telephones of congressmen and called for the ouster of FBI Director J. Edgar Hoover. Accusing the FBI of adopting "the tactics of the Soviet Union and Hitler's Gestapo," the Louisiana Democrat declared: "I ask that Mr. Mitchell, the attorney general of the United States, have the courage to ask for the resignation of this man."

Mitchell immediately issued a statement "categorically" denying that the FBI had ever tapped any congressman's phone. He accused Boggs of "slanderous falsehoods" and said his charges "reached a new low in political dialogue. He should recant at once and apologize to a great American." The following day, however, Boggs reiterated his charges against Hoover by stating—also "categorically"—that the FBI had had him under surveillance and that he would produce evidence "in the near future." He repeated his attack on Hoover, saying "the country cannot survive under a man who in his declining years has violated the Bill of Rights of the United States."

Deputy Attorney General Richard Kleindienst joined the acrimonious dispute a day later. He called Boggs either "sick or not in possession of his faculties" when he made his accusations against Hoover and the FBI. Kleindienst also said he would "welcome an investigation by the responsible members of Congress."

St. Louis Globe-Democrat
St. Louis, Mo., April 7, 1971

J. Edgar Hoover is one of those misunderstood Americans who frequently serve as lightning rods for the unwarranted criticisms of this nation's Cassandras.

Despite his brilliant administration of the sprawling Federal Bureau of Investigation and his almost superhuman efforts to protect the United States from the enemies within, Hoover repeatedly has been the target of irresponsible attacks by those on the left.

More recently, the FBI director has become a pawn in the game played by Democrats who seek to further their political prospects. With only vague generalities to buttress their arguments, the Democrats have asserted that the handling of bureau affairs has been unsatisfactory and warrants Hoover's replacement.

The latest entry in this game is House majority leader Hale Boggs. He lashed out at the bureau for what he claimed was its use of telephone taps on Congressmen and of undercover agents on college campuses.

Not unexpectedly, Boggs offered no documentation to back up his inflammatory statements. No congressional victims were listed, nor were college campuses specified. It was just a provocative charge which, of course, received generous coverage in the liberal news media.

Isn't it time to blow the whistle on these insidious tactics? Isn't it time to demand immediate documentation or an immediate apology? Isn't it time for the media to discriminate between reasonable complaints and puffed-up nonsense?

A great American is under siege, and the situation demands that patriotic citizens stand up on his behalf.

Minneapolis Tribune
Minneapolis, Minn., April 7, 1971

Hale Boggs of Louisiana is no radical. The 57-year-old House majority leader is a solid member of the congressional establishment, a man who was Sam Rayburn's protege and who supported President Johnson's Vietnam policy. It came as a surprise, therefore, when Boggs this week became the first Democratic congressional leader publicly to demand the resignation of FBI Director J. Edgar Hoover. Rising unexpectedly near the beginning of a House session, Boggs accused Hoover and his agency of tapping the telephones of members of Congress — a charge that was also made last month by Sen. Joseph Montoya, D-N.M.—and of using "the tactics of the Soviet Union and Hitler's Gestapo." He challenged Atty. Gen. Mitchell to "have the courage to ask for the resignation of this man."

The incident provided a major indication of how far disenchantment with Hoover's autocratic operation of the FBI and its disregard for civil liberties has spread into the previously sycophantic congressional establishment. Other prominent Democrats, including two presidential contenders, Sens. Muskie of Maine and McGovern of South Dakota, have also rushed in where even many liberals have heretofore feared to tread, and have demanded Hoover's resignation.

Boggs's references to the tactics of the Soviet Union and of the Gestapo are frighteningly well-based in fact. Too many instances have come to light in which FBI agents infiltrated groups and investigated individuals whose only offense was peaceful political dissent. Most recently, records stolen from the FBI office in Media, Pa., documented the agency's use of harassment and intimidation as weapons. Constant surveillance of members of peace groups, the records said, is useful even when it produces no information, for it builds fear and paranoia in those who are watched and, as a result, limits their activity.

Americans have always considered that fear of the secret agent, of who might be listening, of the knock on the door in the night, is something faced by those who live in a police state. It could never happen in the free, democratic United States. But this country is moving toward being a police state when a federal investigative agency takes the position that intimidation is a useful and proper tool; when members of Congress commonly believe, as one of Montoya's aides said, that many of their telephones are tapped by the agency; when the agency's head considers himself to be above controls and criticism.

Americans should not forget Hoover's significant contributions to his country, but they should also not let gratitude for the good the 76-year-old director has done stand in the way of their recognizing the dangers represented by some recent developments in the agency he runs. If Boggs can succeed in convincing the public of the validity of his charges, he will have contributed to a political climate in which more members of Congress will demand FBI reforms. Part of any such reform program should be the selection of a new FBI director.

THE MILWAUKEE JOURNAL
Milwaukee, Wis., April 11, 1971

J. Edgar Hoover, director of the Federal Bureau of Investigation, long lived in glorified isolation, immune to criticism. Newly elected presidents made it a first order of business to assure the nation that Hoover would continue in office. But in the last five months Hoover, now 76, has been criticized for his judgment, veracity, methods, dictatorial manner and attacks on those he considers enemies. The demand for his retirement is snowballing, even from longtime supporters.

House Majority Leader Hale Boggs has now charged that the FBI tapped phones of congressmen. Atty. Gen. Mitchell has denied the charge. Deputy Atty. Gen. Kleindienst responded that Boggs must have been "either sick or . . . not in possession of his faculties."

That is only the latest controversy. Recently an FBI office was robbed of files, which have been doled out by the thieves to newspapers and congressmen. The files show that, on Hoover's orders, the FBI has been keeping universities and students and professors under surveillance. It has been snooping on young blacks and so-called left wing groups with paid informers. Agents were told to keep pushing student groups until they got the idea that there was a G-man "behind every mailbox."

An FBI agent wrote of strengths and weaknesses of the FBI to a professor he had studied under. He decided not to send the letter, tore it up and threw it in his wastebasket. The letter was pasted back together and given to Hoover, who fired the agent "with prejudice," which has prevented the man from getting other work. Ten agents wrote to Sen. McGovern (D.-S. D.) complaining that Hoover was "stifling" the FBI. McGovern demanded an investigation. He immediately got a letter from 21 agents calling him an irresponsible, reprehensible opportunist.

Hoover, in a Time magazine interview, angered Puerto Ricans and Mexicans when he said that they "don't shoot straight, but if they come at you with a knife, watch out." He angered blacks by tapping the phones of the late Martin Luther King and then alleging that King was guilty of moral turpitude.

In an article in the Encyclopaedia Britannica, Hoover wrote that all FBI agents "must be graduates of an accredited law school . . . or must have graduated from an accredited four year college with a major in accounting and have three years personal experience in that field." The FBI recently admitted that only 22.3% of its agents are lawyers and only 9.1% accountants.

Hoover went before a Senate subcommittee and named a group that he charged had plotted to kidnap Henry Kissinger, President Nixon's foreign policy adviser, and blow up Capitol heating tunnels. The Justice Department issued a press release on the testimony. No formal accusations had been made. Later the FBI charged the Berrigan brothers, Catholic priests, and others with the plot and then started an intensive effort to find proof of the charges. There is said to be fear in the Justice Department that Hoover's statement may destroy any possible case against the Berrigans, to the great embarrassment of the administration.

Many Americans have long felt the FBI needs new leadership. And it is time for Congress to take a careful look at the FBI.

ST. LOUIS POST-DISPATCH
St. Louis, Mo., April 7, 1971

Citizens who have concluded from J. Edgar Hoover's 46-year reign over the FBI that Mr. Hoover might just go on forever are now entitled to some doubts. At the age of 76, the "chief" seems to be in for hard times.

The most concrete evidence for doubt about Mr. Hoover's perpetuity is the latest demand that he resign. It does not come from some liberal do-gooder or even a subversive. It comes from the House Majority Leader, Representative Hale Boggs of Louisiana. Mr. Boggs has not so far been accused of trying to subvert either the nation or the FBI, though perhaps his time will come.

This Southern Congressman accuses the FBI of tapping the telephones of Congressmen, of putting agents on college campuses and of "adopting the tactics of Hitler's Gestapo or the Soviet Union." Since there is nothing new about FBI agents on campuses, what bothers Mr. Boggs must be the notion that Mr. Hoover's men checked out members of Congress.

Attorney General John Mitchell angrily denies the Boggs charge, and says the FBI never tapped congressional telephones. The trouble is, nobody outside the FBI can be absolutely sure of that; Mr. Mitchell's experience with wiretapping is a great deal shorter than Mr. Hoover's. And we recall that Mr. Mitchell conceded that "inadvertent" electronic surveillance was involved in the fraud cases against a lobbyist and an aid of former Speaker John McCormack. Who conducted that bit of eavesdropping?

Mr. Hoover's operation is under fire from other sources and for other reasons, too. Representative Parren J. Mitchell of Maryland recently accused the FBI of improper surveillance of "individuals, peace groups, black student groups" or any organization whose name included words like Freedom, Afro or Black.

Senator George McGovern of South Dakota challenged Mr. Hoover's vindictive firing "with prejudice" of an FBI agent who had criticized the chief in private. Representative William R. Anderson of Tennessee, who had commanded the submarine Nautilus, criticized Mr. Hoover for accusing one of the Berrigan brothers before the latter was even indicted.

Then there is the matter of the purloined files. These documents taken from FBI records at Media, Pa., indicated activities ranging from the ridiculous to the dangerous. The FBI had spied on a Boy Scout leader who had inquired about taking some Scouts on a trip to Russia. The FBI had, indeed, kept close watch on colleges, professors, black and peace groups and even individuals not cited as belonging to any organization under surveillance.

The worst shocker in the purloined files was official notice to FBI agents to increase interviews with dissenters "for plenty of reasons chief of which are it will enhance the paranoia endemic in these circles and will further serve to get the point across there is an FBI agent behind every mailbox."

The point that is gotten across to us is that the FBI is not acting as an investigating agency but as an intimidating agency. For there is a vast difference between investigating crime and throwing a scare into dissenters so that, undoubtedly, they will cease their dissent. That is the work of a political police.

When the Federal Bureau of Investigation has come to this point, it seems unlikely that even the resignation of its aging director would entirely reverse the trend. What is needed also is a serious congressional study of the bureau as a preliminary check on its almost unlimited power to invade the political affairs of citizens. After that the nation should demand that the FBI be placed back on is track, which is law enforcement. Attacking dissent is truly outside the law.

The Evening Bulletin

Philadelphia, Pa., April 9, 1971

The long tenure and advanced age of the FBI's famous and widely revered director, J. Edgar Hoover, has posed an increasingly painful administrative dilemma.

How long should a vital agency be dominated by any one man, no matter how capable?

Even admirers of Mr. Hoover might privately have hoped that some time since he would have bowed to time and gracefully stepped down, resting on a proud record. Even his critics, appraising the full record, might regret that, after so long a time, the storm clouds should be gathering over him.

The resolution of this problem—always a delicate personnel matter with raucous political overtones—has been compounded by two developments.

Information disclosed in the files stolen from the FBI's Media office has raised questions as to whether the activities of the federal investigative agency have exceeded proper bounds in a democratic society. And now the waters have been additionally roiled by the categorical accusation—as categorically denied—that the FBI has tapped congressmen's telephones.

If the latter charge were true, of course, Mr. Hoover should be instantly dismissed. House Majority Leader Hale Boggs (D-La), who made the charge, should produce his proof promptly or tender a full apology to the FBI director. If he does not do either, he will stand branded of demagogy.

In the meantime, Mr. Boggs has not helped his position by first accusing Mr. Hoover of using "the tactics of the Soviet Union and Hitler's Gestapo" then clearly retreating by paying homage to him as a "dedicated and able public servant" and "a man whose fairness and patriotism are unquestionable."

A "fair man" using Gestapo tactics? How absurd.

Beyond this intemperance, there is the curious feature that Mr. Boggs has not been supported by others in the congressional Democratic leadership in his charges of wiretapping. Nor, for that matter, has there been so far any rush of congressmen to support his charges. But it is due Mr. Hoover and it is due Congress that the charge either be supported or withdrawn.

What could happen, however, is simply that the murky controversy that has arisen over administration of the FBI will be deepened. It may be more difficult to get the needed examination of certain features of FBI operations. It will certainly be more difficult for the 76-year-old Mr. Hoover to retire, gracefully, now—as he should be encouraged to do—under the kind of attack Mr. Boggs has made, so far without proof.

From any viewpoint, this is an unfortunate business. As normal procedures, the command at the FBI should be changed from time to time. And in these abnormal times, the whole apparatus of domestic intelligence clearly should be subjected to tighter controls and review.

CHICAGO DAILY NEWS

Chicago, Ill., April 9, 1971

In demanding the resignation of J. Edgar Hoover as chief of the Federal Bureau of Investigation, House Democratic leader Hale Boggs showed far more daring than most politicians have. For Hoover is the most feared man in Washington, and the best equipped to wreak vengance. Surveillance is the peculiar and comprehensive function of the FBI. Hoover uses it according to his own personal view of the requirements of security. In that exercise, not even the President of the United States has dared to put a checkrein on him.

Just now the issue is whether Hoover has tapped the telephones of several opposition congressmen, with Boggs, Sen. Birch Bayh of Indiana and others contending that he has, and Hoover's "boss," Atty. Gen. John Mitchell, declaring "categorically" that he has not. It's hard to prove one way or the other. But what is incontrovertible is that the man who became director of the FBI in the administration of Calvin Coolidge and who deserves credit for building it into one of the world's great law enforcement organizations has become a petulant dictator whose bureau desperately needs a new boss.

The view of professional lawmen to this effect is supported by the evidence. At various times — as in the cases of Martin Luther King and the Berrigan brothers — he has released character-damning evidence against people without the courtesy of any legal proceeding where they could defend themselves. He has been notorious for running the FBI like a private domain, sidetracking bright, younger men who could possibly compete for his job and eliminating those — like Special Agent Jack Shaw — who dared criticize him, even in a private letter.

Those who criticize Hoover encounter the passionate resistance usually reserved for critics of the flag or motherhood; it's far safer to pick flaws in the President of the United States.

And yet this 76-year-old curmudgeon is just not the same man who stamped out kidnapers, bank robbers and gangsters in the 1930s and so ably supported the war effort in the '40s by containing subversive elements.

Hoover's arrogance, especially his glowering suspicion that any who even mildly disagree with him must be enemies of the state, is an increasingly divisive force in the government and the society. His arrogance grows more rigid with the passing months, and the damage to the FBI is increasingly obvious.

With his growing tendency to interfere in areas remote from his duties (such as his campaign against the consular treaty with Russia), Hoover has become an increasing embarrassment to the President, who must ardently wish the old man would step down gracefully. But there is no sign of that, so we urge Mr. Nixon to use his leverage as firmly as necessary to persuade Hoover to lay down the duties he holds six years beyond regulation retirement age, and let the FBI move into the 1970s.

Long Island Press

Jamaica, N.Y., April 8, 1971

House Democratic Leader Hale Boggs has made a very serious charge against the Federal Bureau of Investigation and its director, J. Edgar Hoover. He says the bureau has been tapping the phones of members of Congress, and that several of them have given him detailed information "confirming my own experience." Rep. Boggs wants Mr. Hoover to resign.

What sets this apart from similar accusations in the past — including charges that some governors as well as congressmen were under federal, including Army, surveillance — is that it comes from a moderate man who holds a powerful office, commands respect, is not known for shooting off his mouth, and whose patriotism cannot be questioned.

Rep. Boggs overstated his case in comparing FBI activities "with the Soviet Union and Hitler's Gestapo." But he is not alone in his fear and anger. Some congressmen agree with him, includ Sen. Joseph M. Montoya (D-N.M). Others susp their phones have been tapped but have no pro Last December a survey of congressmen disclos that 25 per cent believed their phones were tapp or their offices bugged.

The seriousness of this charge, and the storm has raised, require that the matter be brought a head — in the open — as quickly as possib Congress should heed the advice of Deputy At Gen. Richard Kleindienst who yesterday urg "responsible members" of Congress to investig "the whole operation of the FBI so that this ma can be settled once and for all." There must be the slightest doubt about the nation's high legislative body being free of police harassment.

KGB, SOVIET INTELLIGENCE, MONITORS TELEPHONE CONVERSATIONS WITHIN U.S.

The *Chicago Tribune* reported June 22 that the Soviet Union had put into effect a massive operation to monitor, record and identify private phone calls within the U.S. The Soviets had long possessed the technology necessary to intercept microwaves, which were used in the U.S. to transmit 70% of all long distance telephone calls, but had only recently developed the computer technology required to separate the conversations and identify the callers, the *Tribune* said.

The disclosure, according to the *Tribune,* had prompted investigations by the White House and congressional committees to determine how much information was being gathered, how it was used and what, if anything, was being done by U.S. intelligence agencies to stop the monitoring by the KGB, the Soviet security police.

The newspaper indicated that the information had been disclosed in testimony to the Rockefeller commission during its probe of domestic U.S. intelligence, but that the testimony had been heavily censored from the commission's final report for reasons of national security.

The San Diego Union

San Diego, Calif., March 27, 1975

The Rockefeller Investigation Commission's investigation of the Central Intelligence Agency has learned that the most intensive spying on citizens of the United States of America is done for the Russian intelligence agency, the KGB.

The reminder introduces a discordant quality in the present inquiries into the activities of the U.S. intelligence agencies. The Soviets are in the intelligence game for keeps and the KGB is vastly larger than the CIA and FBI put together.

Russia's spies haven't come in from the cold war yet. We must be careful to assure that they are not the principal beneficiaries of efforts to police our own intelligence agencies.

San Jose Mercury

San Jose, Calf., June 25, 1975

So long as the United States must exist in a world where spying is the rule rather than the exception, Americans must have adequate intelligence and counter-intelligence agencies of their own.

If anybody needed an argument in favor of retaining the Central Intelligence Agency and similar arms of government intact, the story about massive Soviet monitoring of American telephone calls should provide it.

THE MILWAUKEE JOURNAL

Millwaukee, Wis., June 24, 1975

Nothing is simple these days, not even spying. Take the latest revelations about the Russian KGB. The KGB, it turns out, has been monitoring hundreds of thousands of US phone conversations, all in the hope of gleaning US secrets.

How do we know that the Russians were doing this? Elementary, my dear Watson. It turns out that the National Security Agency (NSA) was monitoring the KGB to see what it was learning from us.

With a little imagination it is not difficult to complicate this situation even further. It is quite possible to believe that the FBI may have been monitoring the NSA to find out what the NSA was finding out about the KGB. And, of course, there is the further possibility that the CIA was snooping on the FBI to discover what the FBI knew about what the NSA knew about the KGB.

A simple phone call between US agencies requesting to know what each was doing could save snooping and countersnooping. But that call probably would have been monitored by the KGB. . . .

ARGUS-LEADER

Sioux Falls, S.D., June 24, 1975

News note from Washington: The Senate Intelligence committee plans to question FBI and CIA officials about Soviet capabilities of monitoring long distance telephone calls within the United States, according to an informed source.

The Rockefeller Commission report on the Central Intelligence Agency mentioned the Communists' ability to intercept U.S. phone calls. Long distance phone calls (presumably those transmitted by microwave) were monitored and recorded by Russian satellites and antennas atop the Soviet embassy in Washington.

The Rockefeller Commission report said "Communist countries. . . .appear to have developed electronic collection of intelligence to an extraordinary degree of technology and sophistication for use in the United States and elsewhere through the world."

Chairman Frank Church said his committee would look into the problem of penetration by the KGB (the Soviet Spy agency) and "the necessary protection we need to invoke." Presumably the revelations in the Rockefeller Commission report are not news to the top levels of the United States government. Telephone calls of President Gerald Ford and key defense personnel would be scrambled. Other precautions would be taken.

The Russians will get a lot of American yak-yak along with any intelligence tidbits they may pick up from eavesdropping on long distance calls. Their surveillance could yield business, trade and other information essential to an analysis of American capabilities and knowhow.

The Russians' capability and their use of such data should give anyone who advocates abolition of the Central Intelligence Agency some second thoughts. The British cracked the German's code in World War II and read Adolf Hitler's radio messages even before some of his generals did. Americans broke the Japanese code before Pearl Harbor, and managed to keep the secret despite a wartime slip.

Anyone who thinks the Russians or other world powers won't try to read our secrets is mistaken. Meantime, may the yak-yak of thousands of ordinary American social and business calls overload the Russian computers!

Springfield Republican
Springfield, Mass., June 29, 1975

Detente between the United States and Soviet Union has hardly been strengthened by the revelation that Russian intelligence has engaged in extensive eavesdropping of telephone calls by American government leaders.

According to sources in the Federal Bureau of Investigation, the Soviets are capable of monitoring even some of the calls of the President of the United States. This is no doubt a distressing development.

This revelation comes at a time when the Central Intelligence Agency has been subjected to extensive scrutiny for its own activities. Needless to say, the disclosure of the Russian eavesdropping capabilities must not serve as an excuse for the CIA to engage in similar activities in the U.S., as has been alleged.

According to the FBI source, the Soviet intelligence apparatus and secret police known as the KGB "has tremendous resources to carry out programs like this." It is believed that the Soviet Union has extremely sophisticated electronic equipment to monitor private telephone conversations in the U.S. and elsewhere in the world.

What this means is that — aside from governmental caution in transmitting sensitive information — the FBI must embark on a legitimate program of domestic counterintelligence without violations of civil liberties.

According to the Rockefeller Commission's report on abuses by the CIA, the Russian capability to monitor American telephone calls raises "the real specter that selected American users of telephones are potentially subject to blackmail that can seriously affect their actions, or even lead in some cases to recruitment as espionage agents."

The Standard-Times
New Bedford, Mass., June 27, 1975

One of the principal complaints made against the Central Intelligence Agency was that it engaged in intercepting telephone conversations to and from the United States.

The thundering allegations of "wiretapping" and "eavesdropping" could be heard all over Washington. And when the Rockefeller commission confirmed the existence of such CIA activity many a smug "We told you so" emanated from the anti-intelligence partisans.

Ah, but now a new twist. It seems the commission also uncovered the fact (well known to the CIA) that the Soviet Union has been eavesdropping on domestic and foreign telephone calls of many Americans, including government and business leaders and members of Congress. One source quoted by the Knight News Service estimated the total as "hundreds of thousands, even millions of telephone conversations."

Informed of this, a senator told Knight, "We were being spied on by the Russians and our own intelligence agencies knew about it and didn't tell us." And he wondered why "the flow" was not stopped "immediately" by the intelligence services.

Of course the only reason the U.S. intelligence apparatus was able to know the Russians were engaging in this activity was by counterintelligence — in effect, eavesdropping on the Soviet eavesdropping — quite a feat in itself.

Indeed, this achievement was hinted at in the commission's report: "Monitoring of foreign conversations is an important aspect of modern intelligence collection. Several new systems developed by the agency (the CIA) for use overseas have been tested in the United States. In the process of this testing, private communications, presumably between U.S. citizens, have sometimes been overheard."

It would seem, then, that the CIA domestic activity in eavesdropping produced an ability to monitor the Soviet Union's far greater activity in the same field.

This CIA breakthrough was a notable service to national security, a knowhow still apparently eluding the Soviet.

But the CIA cannot win. First it was pilloried for telephone intercepts. Now a senator complains (and the Church committee of the Senate is going to look into the matter) that his calls may have been tapped by the Russians but that U.S. intelligence didn't tell him, when the fact is, the only way U.S. intelligence could detect the intercept was through its own experiments in tapping.

The anti-intelligence coterie must be getting high marks in Moscow.

The Philadelphia Inquirer
Philadelphia, Pa., June 30, 1975

A spokesman for Vice President Rockefeller has denied the report that the Commission on Central Intelligence Agency Activities "censored" references to the Soviet capacity to intercept and record telephone conversations within the U. S. among government officials, military leaders and private citizens. The spokesman concedes, though, that the commission did seek "the advice of experts on classification as to certain sensitive matters" and that a few passages had been "rephrased."

Well, on that question we shall have to suspend judgment for the time being, but we are puzzled by a couple of other aspects of the situation.

Apparently, the Russians had developed the ability to intercept microwave telephone transmissions, by means of antenna such as those positioned on the roof of the Soviet embassy in Washington. It may be noted by the way that the U. S.—and perhaps the CIA can be thanked for this —had also developed the capacity to listen in on Soviet officials calling each other in their limousines.

In any case, the U. S. Government, or at least someone in the U. S. Government, had known about the Soviet capability for some time. But the U. S. Government kept this top secret until the Rockefeller Commission alluded to it in its report.

The commission observed: "Americans have a right to be uneasy if not seriously disturbed at the real possibility that their personal and business activities . . . could be recorded and analyzed by agents of foreign powers."

Now we are uneasy, indeed seriously disturbed, at the failure of the U. S. Government to apprise the American people of this long ago.

Obviously, the object couldn't have been to deprive the Russians of information as to what they themselves were doing. Was it, then, to keep them from knowing that we knew what they were doing? But if so, why? What useful purpose could be served by their government's knowing, and our government's knowing, but the American people's not knowing of what the Rockefeller Commission called "the real specter" of potential blackmail? If it was to deceive the Russians with phony information, that is too high a price to pay.

A White House official says that members of Congress "undoubtedly must be among those that were overheard" by the Russians. That raises the question of whether the Russians knew what they are doing. We don't mean to be facetious about a serious matter, but it does strike us that Soviet agents must be wasting thousands of man hours tuning in to a tremendous amount of conversations that aren't worth hearing at all.

Watergate: The Security Agencies' Politization Revealed

The Break-in

Democratic headquarters raided. Five men were seized at gunpoint at 2 a.m. June 17, 1972 in the headquarters of the Democratic National Committee in Washington. Alerted by a security guard, police apprehended five men, along with cameras and electronic surveillance equipment in their possession, after file drawers in the headquarters had been opened and ceiling panels removed near the office of Democratic National Chairman Lawrence F. O'Brien.

Those arrested and charged with second-degree burglary were: Bernard L. Barker, alias Frank Carter; James W. McCord, alias Edward Martin; Frank Angelo Fiorini, alias Edward Hamilton; Eugenio L. Martinez, alias Gene Valdes; Raul Godoy, alias V. R. Gonzales. All but McCord were from Miami and all of them were reported to have had links at one time or another with the Central Intelligence Agency.

McCord, who had retired from the CIA in 1970 after 19 years with the agency, currently was employed as a security agent by both the Republican National Committee and the Committee for the Re-Election of the President.

Barker, apparently the leader of the raid, reportedly played some role for the CIA in the abortive invasion of Cuba in 1961 and had met in Miami in early June with E. Howard Hunt, the CIA official in charge of the invasion. Hunt recently was a consultant to Charles W. Colson, special counsel to President Nixon and other high White House officials. The White House confirmed this June 19 and said Hunt had ended his consulting work March 29.

Nixon's campaign manager, John N. Mitchell, said June 18 that none of those involved in the raid were "operating either on our behalf or with our consent." O'Brien called June 18 for an FBI investigation. A full-scale investigation by the FBI was announced by the Justice Department June 19.

At a news conference June 20, O'Brien called the raid a "blatant act of political espionage" and announced the party was filing a $1 million civil lawsuit against the Committee to Re-Elect the President and the raiders on charges of invasion of privacy and violation of civil rights of the Democrats.

Citing the "potential involvement" of Colson, O'Brien said there was 'a developing clear line to the White House."

Mitchell responded later June 20 with a statement deploring the raid and denouncing the Democratic lawsuit as "demagoguery" by O'Brien. White House Press Secretary Ronald L. Ziegler said June 20 Colson had "assured me that he has in no way been involved in this matter."

Gray upholds Administration probe— L. Patrick Gray 3rd, acting director of the Federal Bureau of Investigation, upheld the practice of the Nixon Administration itself investigating the Watergate case, involving former Administration aides and a Republican committee. Anyone who wrote that the Administration could not investigate itself, he said Oct. 2, was "really leveling a general indictment against all public officials."

He had taken the Watergate probe "under my own wing," Gray said, and "there's not been one single bit of pressure put on me or any of my special agents" concerning the probe.

Gray also discounted the possibility of presidential involvement in the Watergate incident. "It strains the credulity that the President of the United States— if he had a mind to—could have done a con job on the whole American people," he said.

Ex-FBI agent delivered information. A former agent for the Federal Bureau of Investigation disclosed Oct. 5 that he had delivered information obtained by espionage from the Democratic headquarters at the Watergate building in Washington to an official at the Nixon campaign office. In an interview published in the *Los Angeles Times*, the ex-FBI agent, Alfred C. Baldwin 3rd, said he had monitored telephone and other conversations at Watergate for three weeks while employed by the Committee to Re-elect the President, working from a room in a motor lodge across from Watergate.

Baldwin said the official to whom he delivered the information was not one of those indicted in the Watergate headquarters raid. Baldwin revealed that he, himself, was a member of the raid crew. He was not indicted after agreeing to cooperate with the Justice Depart-

ment. He was a key witness for the government in the case.

The *Washington Post* reported Oct. 6 that Baldwin had informed the FBI that memorandums describing the intercepted Democratic conversations were sent to members of the White House staff and Nixon campaign staff.

The *Post* reported Oct. 10 that the Watergate raid was but part of a larger espionage and sabotage effort against the Democrats on behalf of the Nixon re-election effort. The newspaper quoted federal investigators as describing the intelligence operation by the Nixon campaign organization as "unprecedented in scope and intensity." The story reported attempts to disrupt campaigns of Democratic candidates for president. One such effort, according to the story, involved a letter used in the New Hampshire primary against Sen. Edmund S. Muskie (Me.). He was accused in it of having condoned use of the epithet "Canucks" in reference to Americans with French-Canadian backgrounds. *Post* reporter Marilyn Berger reported that White House aide Ken W. Clawson, deputy director of communications for the executive branch, had told her Sept. 25 he had written the letter, which had been ascribed at the time to a Paul Morrison of Deerfield Beach, Fla. Attempts to locate such a person had failed. The *Post* also reported that Clawson later denied authorship of the letter.

The *Post* article also related an account from three attorneys that they had been offered, and rejected, proposals to work as agents provocateurs on behalf of the Nixon campaign. The *Post* report said the FBI had information that at least 50 undercover Nixon operatives were at work throughout the country in an attempt to disrupt and spy on Democratic campaigns.

The Gray Nomination

Opposition to Gray nomination. L. Patrick Gray 3rd, 56, acting director of the Federal Bureau of Investigation since the death of J. Edgar Hoover in May 1972, was nominated to be permanent FBI director, the White House announced Feb. 17, 1973.

The nomination encountered serious opposition at hearings held by the Senate

Judiciary Committee. Gray's most vocal opponent in the committee, Sen. Robert C. Byrd (D, W. Va.), charged Feb. 19 that Gray, a long time political associate of President Nixon, had been "openly partisan" during the 1972 presidential election.

Gray replied Feb. 28: "I am not a partisan guy. . . . If I am unable to persevere in this determination for any reason—if my loyalties to the nation's elected leadership, to the Constitution and to my job ever come into conflict—I will resign at once and return to my beloved law firm in southeastern Connecticut."

But a White House memorandum to Gray, provided to the committee by the FBI, contradicted Gray's earlier testimony, according to the *New York Times* March 5.

The note, written on White House stationery by Patrick E. O'Donnell, a presidential assistant, asked Gray's "participation as a key speaker" at a meeting of the City Club of Cleveland Aug. 11, 1972.

"With Ohio being crucially vital to our hopes in November, we would hope you will assign this forum some priority in planning your schedule," O'Donnell wrote.

The speaking invitation was the subject of an FBI memorandum prepared June 16, 1972 which was intended for internal FBI use. (The document was based on information provided by the Cleveland FBI office.)

The paper described the club as having "no political connections"; however, the FBI cautioned that the membership was comprised of "liberals" who engaged in "discussing controversial subjects and it is entirely possible that some embarrassing questions would be put to Mr. Gray which might prove embarrassing to him and the bureau."

But, the FBI document added, "these are the type of people we should be contacting in an effort to 'convert them'."

In testimony Feb. 28, Gray asserted that the decision to appear before the group had been entirely his own and denied that it was intended as a political contribution to the Nixon campaign. The Cleveland speech emphasized the recent decline in crime and criticized those who feared an erosion of civil liberties. His purpose in making the talk, Gray declared, was to carry the "FBI's message to the people."

Asked about the O'Donnell memo at his press conference March 2, the President said, "If there was anything indicating that during the campaign that we were trying to enlist him in that [involving Gray in political activities], it certainly didn't have my support and would not have it now."

Nixon also responded indirectly to a charge Feb. 23 by Sen. William Proxmire (D, Wis.) that the President had used "the device of the temporary appointment to put his man in this job without Senate approval."

"I said I was not going to send his [Gray's] name last year because I felt that we should wait until we got past the political campaign so that the Senate could consider it in a nonpolitical and nonpartisan atmosphere, and the Senate is now doing that," Nixon declared.

Proxmire cited a letter from Comptroller General Elmer B. Staats that Gray's service as acting FBI director after June 3, 1972 had been illegal because positions in the executive branch requiring Senate confirmation could be filled temporarily "for not more than 30 days."

Proxmire called on Gray "to stand aside at once" but Justice Department officials said Feb. 23 there was "no question of Pat Gray stepping down."

FBI gathered data for the GOP—*Time* magazine, in its Nov. 6, 1972 issue, disclosed that, at the request of Presidential Assistant John D. Ehrlichman, a letter signed by Acting Director of the Federal Bureau of Investigation L. Patrick Gray 3rd. was sent to 21 FBI field offices soliciting information from local agents on the issue of criminal justice in order "to give the President maximum support during campaign trips over the next several weeks."

The directive, teletyped Sept. 8 to offices in 14 states, sought a list of local "criminal justice problems such as the Fort Worth Five that we should flag for the President" and "a list of events relating to the criminal justice area that would be good for John Ehrlichman to consider doing."

Time, whose sources of information were within the FBI, noted that while the White House request did not break any law, it "was in violation of the FBI's nonpartisan tradition."

The FBI sources did not indicate what information was relayed to Gray by the Sept. 11 deadline.

Ehrlichman admitted Oct. 30 that he had requested political aid from the Justice Department, which he said must remain "responsive to the political system," but criticized an unnamed Justice Department official, and by implication the FBI, for passing along the request and then acting on it.

Ehrlichman said, "It isn't going to happen again," stressing that a nonpolitical role for the agency was necessary to maintain its "total credibility and objectivity."

Ehrlichman said similar requests had been sent to other Cabinet departments.

Gray announced Oct. 27 that he was suspending the routine collection of information on Congressional and gubernatorial candidates, which Gray said had been going on since 1950 "as part of the Congressional relations program of the FBI."

The directives authorizing the data collection by agents had specifically excluded inquiries at credit bureaus or newspaper morgues and limited the search to "public source material readily available to you and data from your files."

White House got Watergate files
Another basis of Byrd's opposition to the Gray appointment was the charge that the FBI had supplied the White House and the Nixon campaign committee with information gathered in its investigation of the Watergate breakin.

Gray acknowledged Feb. 28 that extensive records of the FBI probe had been made available to the White House and claimed that the late FBI director, J. Edgar Hoover, had provided other Administrations with progress reports of important investigations.

(Gray coupled the disclosure with a promise to open the FBI files on the Watergate breakin to any senator.)

Gray said he based his decision on advice from his legal staff after John W. Dean 3rd, a presidential counsel conducting a separate White House inquiry into the Watergate breakin, "asked us to give him what we had to date." The request was made in August 1972, according to Gray.

Gray said he had provided Attorney General Richard G. Kleindienst with the report and added, "I have every reason to believe that it then went to the White House."

Dean also got a copy of the "Dita Beard memorandum," Gray disclosed March 6. The memo, allegedly written by the International Telephone & Telegraph Corp. (ITT) lobbyist, established a connection between the settlement of an antitrust suit pending against ITT by the government and ITT's contribution to the 1972 GOP presidential campaign. The document figured prominently in Attorney General Kleindienst's confirmation battle in 1972.

The original Beard memorandum, obtained by columnist Jack Anderson and turned over to the Senate Judiciary Committee which asked the FBI to examine the paper, was also examined by ITT. The firm presented scientific evidence to the committee disputing the document's authenticity.

"I do not know how it [the paper] got into the hands of ITT or its experts," Gray said March 7. He added that after Dean returned the document to him, Gray turned it over to the Judiciary Committee.

Gray also revealed March 6 that White House special counsel Charles W. Colson had told FBI agents in August 1972 about a trip he had authorized in August 1972 for E. Howard Hunt. Hunt had visited Beard in Denver where she was recuperating from a heart ailment suffered during the height of the controversy. After his visit, Beard disavowed the memorandum and ITT presented evidence disputing its veracity.

The disclosure was made during the FBI's Watergate investigation, in which Colson and Hunt were implicated. The FBI made no further effort to learn the purpose of Hunt's trip, Gray said, because "there was no involvement of the ITT case with the Watergate bugging."

It was also revealed that Dean ordered Hunt's office safe emptied June 28, 1972, three days after he had been arrested for the Watergate breakin. The papers were not turned over to the FBI until a week after the safe had been opened.

When asked about the time lag between the two events, Gray said, "I see nothing irregular about it. The President's got a rather substantial interest as to what might be in those papers."

Gray also revealed Feb. 28 that FBI agents had questioned Donald H. Segretti in June 1972 regarding his involvement in alleged political espionage activities.

The *Washington Post* had reported Oct. 15, 1972 that Segretti had been shown FBI documents by White House aides to prepare him for grand jury testimony. Gray told the committee he had checked those reports with Dean, who had denied them, but no further effort had been made to determine if the White House had made improper use of the files.

Gray added March 7 that agents had questioned a former presidential assistant, Dwight Chapin, March 5 and that he also denied having given the FBI reports to Segretti.

Information supplied the committee by Gray March 7 indicated that Nixon's personal lawyer, Herbert W. Kalmbach, had paid Segretti between $30,000 and $40,000 in GOP funds from Sept. 1, 1971 until March 15, 1972.

According to Gray, Kalmbach claimed that he was only a "disbursing agent" with no knowledge of Segretti's use of the money or how he obtained his instructions from the party. Kalmbach admitted he kept no financial records of the salary and expense money paid Segretti.

Kalmbach, who was Nixon's principal fund raiser during 1971 until the appointment of Maurice Stans, said the money was drawn from funds collected before April 7, 1972 when the source and purpose of campaign finances were made public according to requirements of the new federal election law.

Kalmbach told the FBI that Chapin had "informed" him that Segretti was about to be discharged from the Army and that "he may be of service to the Republican party."

Gray told the committee March 7 that Dean received FBI reports of interviews with Segretti as well as accounts of FBI interviews with Alfred C. Baldwin, who had admitted tapping Democratic party telephones. Dean received information on the "nature" and "substance" of Baldwin's eavesdropping, Gray said.

A 12-page summary of the FBI investigation on the Watergate affair, dated July 21, 1972, was submitted to the Senate committee March 5. The report charged that attorneys for the Committee to Re-elect the President had hampered FBI efforts to question GOP campaign officials.

Gray told the panel March 6 that an unspecified number of Nixon campaign officials had sought and obtained FBI interviews which were conducted when GOP lawyers were not present. Dean received reports of those interviews as well.

Dean, "in his official capacity as counsel to the President," demanded and was allowed to be present during the FBI's questioning of all White House personnel, despite his vociferous objections, Gray claimed. Had he objected, no White House interviews would have been permitted, Gray added.

As Gray was speaking before the Senate committee March 6, White House Press Secretary Ronald L. Ziegler told reporters that Dean sat in on the interviews of only those White House staff members who had requested his presence.

Gray testified March 1 that John Mitchell, Nixon's former campaign manager, prevented the FBI from questioning his wife on a matter related to the Watergate probe. The questions were not pursued, Gray said, because "this man was a former attorney general of the United States and I think we would have accorded that courtesy to any person in a position like that."

Gray amended those remarks March 7, saying that after the initial rebuff, Mitchell had offered to allow his wife to "come to Washington for an interview, if our agent thought it was necessary." The agent "stated that he did not," according to Gray.

The FBI was also unable to interview a top campaign official, Robert C. Mardian, about the destruction of campaign finance records and did not talk with presidential assistant H. R. Haldeman, whose staff members had been linked to political espionage charges, Gray disclosed March 1. However, another White House aide, John Ehrlichman, had been questioned.

More testimony on Gray—Testimony opposing Gray's confirmation was given the committee by columnist Jack Anderson March 9 and United Auto Workers counsel Stephen I. Schlossberg March 12. Anderson said it was "immeasurably wrong to put a man in charge of the FBI whose prime interest is pleasing the President." He also said he had proof that the FBI had files on persons who "opposed the policies of the men in the White House" and on persons "because they apparently had exotic sex lives or, in an astounding number of cases, simply because they were black."

Schlossberg cited for contrast Gray's attacks on labor leaders for opposition to the Administration's wage freeze and Gray's "presumption of regularity," as Gray had phrased it before the committee, concerning White House and Nixon campaign aides and Watergate involvement.

Gray resigns FBI post. L. Patrick Gray 3rd announced his resignation as acting director of the Federal Bureau of Investigation April 27. Environmental Protection Agency Administrator William D. Ruckelshaus was named later that day as his temporary successor.

Gray said he was resigning, effective immediately, "as a consequence" of reports he had burned files removed from the office safe of E. Howard Hunt Jr., a confessed Watergate conspirator who had worked as a White House consultant.

"Serious allegations concerning certain acts of my own during the ongoing Watergate investigation are now a matter of public record," Gray said, and his resignation was "required to preserve in both image and fact the reputation, the integrity and the effectiveness" of the FBI. He said the agency "has been in no way involved in any of those personal acts or judgments that may now be called into question" and "deserves the full trust of the American people: That is bedrock and must always remain so."

Ruckelshaus accepted the FBI appointment in a caretaker capacity until a permanent director was found. He said he expected to serve only a few months.

Ruckelshaus said he had requested and received assurance from the President that "no matter who is involved [in Watergate] there would be no sparing of anyone." Nixon made clear to him, he said, "he wants me to operate the FBI in as vigorous and honest a way as I possibly could."

The reports of Gray's connection with the Watergate case originated with the *New York Daily News* late April 26 and were confirmed by the *New York Times* and other newspapers the next morning.

According to the *Times*, the Hunt files were handed to Gray at a White House meeting June 28, 1972 with John D. Ehrlichman, assistant to the President for domestic affairs, and John W. Dean 3rd, counsel to the President. The story, attributed to Sen. Lowell P. Weicker Jr. (R, Conn.), a close friend of Gray, reported that Dean had cautioned the files "should never see the light of day."

While he could not swear that either Dean or Ehrlichman "ordered" destruction of the papers, Gray was said to have remembered Dean describing the files as "political dynamite" but not dealing with the Watergate bugging. Gray accepted receipt of the files according to the account and then, after Dean left, had a discussion with Ehrlichman about Watergate probe news leaks, the original purpose of his White House appointment. Gray reportedly took the Hunt files home, where they remained until July 3 when he took them to FBI headquarters, tore them up without looking at them and put them in his FBI "burn bag," a container whose contents were destroyed at the end of each day.

Gray recently had discovered, according to the account, that just prior to his arrival in Ehrlichman's office Ehrlichman had asked Dean why it was necessary to hand the files over to the FBI. He was alleged to have said, "You drive over the [Potomac River] bridge every night, why don't you throw them over?"

Ehrlichman statement—In a statement issued late April 26 in response to the story, Ehrlichman confirmed that "Mr. Gray received some of the contents of the Hunt safe at my office from Mr. Dean in June 1972." He had assumed "up until

April 15" that Gray still had the papers. Ehrlichman said Dean had described the material, which was sealed, as "sensitive" and "not in any way related to the Watergate case." Ehrlichman said, "I do not know the nature of the contents" and never instructed Gray on "what should be done with the contents."

On April 15, Ehrlichman said, he "learned certain new facts concerning the disposition of the contents of the Hunt safe" and "promptly reported my findings to the President." The information was relayed to the Justice Department and had been "under investigation" since then.

The *New York Times* reported April 27 that Gray was told April 16 by Assistant Attorney General Henry E. Petersen, in charge of the federal Watergate investigation, that Dean had informed him of the meeting on the Hunt files and that Gray could be questioned by the grand jury about it. In testimony before the Judiciary Committee March 7, Gray had said Dean had been questioned about Hunt's material and he [Gray] was "unalterably convinced" there had been no effort at concealment.

Illegal Activities Alleged

Vast Administration plot since 1969. The *Washington Post* reported May 17, 1973 that since 1969 the Nixon Administration had engaged in a wide pattern of illegal and quasi-legal activities against radical leaders, students, demonstrators, news reporters, Democratic candidates for president and vice president, the Congress and Nixon Administration officials suspected of leaking information to the press.

Reporters Carl Bernstein and Bob Woodward quoted "highly placed sources in the executive branch" who said that although most of the clandestine operations were political in nature, they were conducted by the Federal Bureau of Investigation, the Secret Service and special teams working for the White House and the Justice Department under the guise of "national security."

"Watergate was a natural action that came from long existing circumstances. It grew out of an atmosphere. This way of life was not new. There have been fairly broad [illegal and quasi-legal] activities from the beginning of the Administration. I didn't know where 'national security' ended and political espionage started," one source said.

The *Post* named former presidential chief of staff H. R. Haldeman, former Attorney General and Nixon campaign director John N. Mitchell, former domestic affairs adviser John D. Ehrlichman, former White House counsel John W. Dean 3rd and former Assistant Attorney General Robert C. Mardian as the officials who supervised covert activities.

According to the *Post,* seven high Administration officials cited Haldeman and former White House special counsel Charles W. Colson as the prime movers behind the espionage operations conducted during the 1972 presidential campaign.

"It was a campaign that went astray and lost its sense of fair play. Secrecy and an obsession with the covert became part of nearly every action," a highly placed former Administration official said.

Known instances of illegal and quasi-legal activities:

■ Information was gathered by the Secret Service on the private life of at least one Democratic presidential candidate. On two occasions, the Administration considered leaking some of the reports to the press. Colson admitted receiving such information about one prominent Democrat, but denied that the information originated with Secret Service agents.

(The *New York Times* had reported Nov. 2, 1972 that Secret Service agents were providing the White House with confidential information regarding meetings held by Sen. George McGovern (D, S.D.) and potential financial backers.)

■ The medical records of Sen. Thomas Eagleton (D, Mo.), McGovern's running mate for a brief period, were obtained by Ehrlichman several weeks before the information regarding Eagleton's treatment for nervous exhaustion was leaked to the press.

Former Attorney General Ramsey Clark said the records were in FBI files. According to *Post* sources, Mardian, who had left the Justice Department to become political coordinator of the Nixon campaign, gave the FBI files to the White House.

■ Paid provocateurs were used to foment violence at antiwar demonstrations during Nixon's first term of office and also during the 1972 presidential campaign.

A former assistant to Colson, William Rhatican, told reporters that campaign money was used to finance Vietnam veterans in support of Nixon. A Veterans Administration official, Mel Stevens, was assigned to Colson's office to organize a pro-Nixon veterans' group using government money but having the appearance of a voluntary organization. Rhatican also said he was "sure" Colson used campaign funds to send telegrams of support to the White House following presidential adviser Henry Kissinger's "peace is at hand" speech Oct. 26, 1972.

■ Clandestine activities against persons considered opponents of the Administration were conducted by "suicide squads," which if apprehended in illegal activities would be disavowed by the FBI and the White House.

■ Paid "vigilante squads" were hired by the White House and Justice Department to conduct wiretapping and other forms of political espionage and to infiltrate radical groups for purposes of provocation.

Convicted Watergate conspirators E. Howard Hunt Jr. and G. Gordon Liddy supervised the squads, made up of former FBI and Central Intelligence Agency (CIA) operatives.

The transfer of these activities from the White House to the Committee to Re-elect the President in late 1971 and early 1972 was arranged by Haldeman and Mitchell and was part of an elaborate plan to extend the "dirty tricks" operations to the 1972 campaign, the *Post* reported.

■ Frederic V. Malek, formerly in charge of recruiting personnel for the Nixon Administration and a deputy campaign manager, and presently deputy director of the Office of Management and Budget, established an information network in nearly 50 states to report on the McGovern campaign.

"Viola Smith" was the code-named contact at the Nixon re-election committee for the "McGovern Watch" spies. The re-election committee also provided the agents with forms marked confidential which contained space for details about staff changes, speeches and polls in the McGovern campaign. The *Post* based its information on a memo entitled, "Intelligence on Future Appearances of Mc-Govern and Shriver," which Malek admitted writing although he denied its intent was espionage.

DeVan L. Shumway, Nixon re-election committee spokesman, also admitted that on orders from deputy campaign director Jeb Stuart Magruder, he had asked two reporters to provide him with McGovern's campaign schedule. (The reporters rejected the proposal.)

One Democratic presidential contender sought legal advice after determining that he and his family were under surveillance, an activity which a former Nixon campaign official acknowledged he had authorized.

Mardian supervised two spies in the McGovern campaign who reported directly to him. Other Nixon campaign aides, on loan from the Republican National Committee, regularly posed as newsmen to obtain routine data on McGovern.

■ Colson organized a group of 30 Nixon supporters to "attack" news correspondents through use of write-in, telephone and telegraph campaigns, according to Tom Girard, a former Nixon committee press aide.

Another instance of covert activity directed against newsmen was the 1971 investigation of Columbia Broadcasting System correspondent Daniel Schorr. Haldeman personally ordered the FBI probe, the *Post* reported.

Probe of newsman disputed—Press Secretary Ronald Ziegler admitted Nov. 11, 1971 that the White House had ordered an FBI investigation of Columbia Broadcasting System correspondent Daniel Schorr, but denied that the probe was related to criticism of Schorr's reporting by President Nixon and Administration aides. Ziegler and Frederic V. Malek, White House personnel aide, said Schorr had been under consideration in August for an unspecified federal job, which occasioned the investigation.

Schorr said Nov. 10 that he had never been told of any job offer, even when he questioned Malek about the probe in October.

Ziegler said the FBI investigation had been started in accord with a "tightly administered procedure," which he said he was unable to explain, with Malek's knowledge. Malek said, however, that the investigation had been "kicked off" by an assistant without his knowledge.

Schorr had been criticized by Nixon, Ziegler and Charles W. Colson, a Presidential aide, for his coverage of the antiballistic missile program, federal aid to parochial schools and Nixon's new economic program.

Ervin on FBI probes—Sen. Sam J. Ervin Jr. said Feb. 1, 1972 he would introduce legislation to bar Federal Bureau of Investigation probes of an individual except in criminal cases.

Ervin made the announcement at a hearing of his Constitutional Rights Subcommittee at which CBS newsman Daniel Schorr testified on his own investigation by the agency. The Administration had said the Schorr probe was related to a job he was to be offered, but the newsman testified that he was first contacted by FBI agents one day after being called to the White House to hear criticism of one of his television reports.

Ervin said Jan. 31 that the Administration had refused his request that it permit the officials involved to testify, and charged that conflicting accounts of the supposed job had been given by different Administration spokesmen.

Details of 1970 plan revealed. White House plans in 1970 to launch a massive counter-insurgency plan against the Black Panthers, Arab extremists, antiwar radicals, and Soviet espionage agents were revealed by the *New York Times* May 24, 1973. Sources said the late director of the Federal Bureau of Investigation, J. Edgar Hoover, refused to go along with the project because President Nixon would not give him written authorization for use of FBI personnel for illegal wiretaps and illegal breaking-and-entering operations.

(Prior to Nixon's May 22 speech, the *Times* had reported May 21 the White House had established in 1970 a secret intelligence unit—Intelligence Evaluation Committee—operating out of the Justice Department, whose purpose was to collect and evaluate information about antiwar and radical groups and then pass it on to former White House counsel John W. Dean 3rd and John J. Caulfield, then an aide to Dean.)

The plan was outlined in a secret report that was among the documents taken from the White House by former presidential counsel John W. Dean 3rd.

According to a *Times* source who worked on the report in 1970, "the facts we had available in this country then showed that we were faced with one of the most serious domestic crises that we've had. One of our greatest problems was that the informed public didn't understand it."

Another official who worked on the report told the *Times* the most serious issue facing the Nixon Administration in mid-1970 was the "black problem." The source said there was suspicion that the Black Panthers were being covertly financed by certain Caribbean countries and certain nations in North Africa, of

which one was strongly suspected to be Algeria.

There was further fear that the "vigilante police action [killing]" against Chicago Black Panther Fred Hampton in 1969 had brought many moderate blacks over to the side of the Panthers, whom the official called "thugs and murderers."

Hoover's decision in 1966 to limit domestic intelligence operations severely hampered the FBI's ability to penetrate the Panthers and other radical groups, the source said.

A second source of concern among Administration officials was the possibility of Arab sabotage of the Middle East talks that were scheduled to be held at the United Nations in 1970.

Another project that was "wiped out" by Hoover was one involving the analysis of handwriting of immigrants to the U.S., to determine if they had attended Soviet schools and thus, were potential spies.

In a related development, the *Washington Post* reported May 24 that Hoover's decision in 1966 to end internal security operations might have been an internal FBI matter and might have escaped the attention of the Johnson Administration.

Neither Nicholas deB. Katzenbach, attorney general in 1966, nor his successor, Ramsey Clark, could recall any action in 1966 that would explain the discontinuation, the *Post* said. Katzenbach noted that a directive in 1965 from President Johnson had banned all wiretapping except in national security and foreign intelligence cases; but Katzenbach said the FBI would not have been hamstrung because there were specific loopholes in the order, the *Post* reported.

Intelligence unit being phased out—The super-secret Intelligence Evaluation Committee set up by the Nixon Administration in 1970 to evaluate intelligence concerning internal security was being quietly abolished by the Justice Department, it was reported June 1.

Henry E. Petersen, chief of the Justice Department's criminal division, had prepared an order dismantling it. The *Washington Post* said Petersen's criminal division unknowingly inherited the committee when former Attorney General Richard Kleindienst abolished the department's Internal Security Division, of which the committee was a part. Petersen was not aware of the committee until told by the Senate panel investigating Watergate a few days before President Nixon revealed its existence in his May 22 speech on Watergate, the *Post* reported.

Petersen then inquired into the committee's operations and found they offered nothing practical. A survey by Petersen among other intelligence agencies indicated they simply did not care what happened to the committee, the *Post* reported.

The *Post* and the *New York Times* cited sources who said the committee had served only as a clearinghouse for intelligence gathered by other agencies and that it had never been an operational agency actively seeking primary intelligence.

CIA disputed radicals' foreign ties—The White House was told by the Central Intelligence Agency (CIA) in 1969 and 1970 that there was no substantial evidence to support Administration suspicions that the Black Panthers and other radical groups were being financed by foreign nations, the *New York Times* reported May 25.

However, the White House refused to believe the agency's evaluations and sent 35 Federal Bureau of Investigation agents abroad to intelligence posts in 20 different countries, an act that enraged then CIA director Richard Helms, the *Times'* sources said.

The *Times* quoted one CIA analyst who worked on the studies as recalling: "We tried to show that the radical movements were home grown, indigenous responses to perceived grievances and problems that had been growing for years. We said the radicals were clean and that we couldn't find anything. But all it turned out to be was another nail in Helms' coffin." Helms was replaced as CIA director late in 1972.

Another CIA source said the White House had a preoccupation with foreign influence on domestic radicals: "When kids went abroad there were those in the White House who were convinced they were meeting with Communists and coming back with dope."

The CIA studied three distinct areas in 1969–70, the source said.

One was student patterns in Europe, North Africa, and South America to determine connections between activities there and in the U.S. No illegal actions were uncovered.

A second area of study was Arab students in the U.S. and their connections with the Arab bloc nations. Nothing substantial was found.

The third main study area concerned Algerian support for the Black Panthers. "Every intelligence agency said we think it's an interesting hypothesis but, by and large, the judgment of the intelligence community in 1970 was that there was no significant Algerian support for the domestic operations of blacks. History supports the judgment completely," the source said, pointing out that the Panthers were ousted from Algeria in March.

Times sources said the net result of the CIA evaluations was a loss of confidence in the agency by the President.

Nixon knew of illegalities of 1970 plan. President Nixon in 1970 approved a plan for expanded intelligence gathering operations with the knowledge that certain aspects of it were clearly illegal, the *New York Times* reported June 7.

In his May 22 statement on the Watergate affair, President Nixon had acknowledged establishment of an interagency committee for better intelligence operations. However, he said, the committee was scrapped after Federal Bureau of Investigation Director J. Edgar Hoover voiced opposition.

According to the *Times*, the plan approved by Nixon involved "serious risks" to his Administration if revealed. As a result the program was approved by him through presidential Chief of Staff H. R. Haldeman after Tom Charles Huston, then a staff assistant to Nixon, told Haldeman: "We don't want the President linked to this thing with his signature on paper . . . [because] all hell would break loose if this thing leaked out."

The *Times* obtained three memoranda written by Huston: one dealt with recommendations to the President by the Interagency Committee on Intelligence; a second recommended means to overcome Hoover's opposition; and the third was a presidential directive, written by Huston, that the plans be implemented.

These memoranda were among the documents given to Watergate Judge John J. Sirica by former White House Counsel John W. Dean 3rd.

The memo of recommendations contained among its proposals suggestions for relaxation of restrictions on the "surreptitious entry of facilities occupied by subversive elements." "This technique would be particularly helpful if used against the Weathermen and Black Panthers." "Use of this technique is clearly illegal: it amounts to burglary. It is highly risky and could result in great embarrassment if exposed."

Another committee proposal was that "present restrictions on covert [mail] coverage should be relaxed on selected targets of priority foreign intelligence and internal security interest. . . . Covert coverage is illegal and there are serious risks involved. However, the advantages to be derived from its use outweigh the risks."

"Covert coverage" involved the opening and examination of mail before delivery.

The Huston memo noted that Hoover opposed even the legal monitoring of mail, which involved recording sender and addressee without breaking any seals. Hoover's concern was said to stem from opposition by "civil liberty people."

Other recommendations by the committee as reflected in the Huston memo:

■ Permission for the National Security Agency (NSA) to monitor "the communications of U.S. citizens using international facilities. [telephone and telegraph circuits.]"

■ "Intensification of coverage of individuals and groups in the U.S. who pose a major threat to internal security." The memo said in connection with this that everyone on the committee except Hoover felt that "existing coverage is grossly inadequate." The Hoover statement that the FBI would not stand in the way of any other agency seeking approval for electronic surveillance was "gratuitous," as only the FBI possessed the necessary capability, the memo said.

■ An increase in the number of campus operatives to "forestall widespread" violence. Huston called campuses "the battleground of the revolutionary protest movement." The memo noted the FBI's refusal to employ campus intelligence sources younger than 21 years old for fear of risk of exposure. Committee consensus—with Hoover objecting—was that

risk of exposure was minimal and that it was a price to be paid for effective campus coverage.

The second Huston memo dealt with ways to overcome Hoover's objections to the intelligence plan. He said Hoover's objections were twofold: current operations were satisfactory and "no one has any business commenting on procedures he [Hoover] has established for the collection of intelligence by the FBI." According to Huston, Hoover stood alone among committee members in his objections, which the presidential aide labeled "inconsistent and frivolous—most express concern about possible embarrassment to the intelligence community (i.e. Hoover) from public disclosure of clandestine operations."

Huston offered several suggestions to the President as means of overcoming Hoover's opposition. The President should call Hoover into his office for a "stroking session," in which the President would explain his decision to Hoover, thank him for his past cooperation, and indicate he was counting on Hoover for continuing help. Afterwards, the entire committee should be called in and an official photo, to be autographed by the President, should be taken. Later an official memorandum outlining the plan should be distributed to those involved.

Huston concluded that he was certain that Hoover would accede to Nixon's wishes, and the President should not be reluctant to override the director. "Mr. Hoover is set in his ways and can be as bull-headed as hell, but he is a loyal trooper. Twenty years ago he would never have raised the kind of objections he has here, but he's getting old and worried about his legend. . . . he'll respond to direction by the President."

On July 15, 1970 Huston sent the third memo to Hoover, Central Intelligence Agency (CIA) Director Richard Helms, Defense Intelligence Agency (DIA) Director Gen. Donald V. Bennett, and NSA Director Adm. Noel Gayler, informing them that the President had carefully studied the committee's recommendations and agreed to their full implementation.

The *Times* reported that when Hoover received this memo "he went through the roof." Hoover had assumed that when the President saw a number of footnotes he had attached to the original recommendations, in which he voiced his objections, the President would not approve the plan.

A *Times* source who participated in the report's preparation said Hoover made no principled objections to the plan; instead his opposition stemmed from the issue of "whether he was going to be able to run the FBI any way he wanted to run it."

President Nixon rescinded his approval of the plan July 28, 1970, five days after Hoover received the memo approving it.

According to the *Times*, Huston made one more attempt to get his plan past Hoover by composing another memorandum which he sent Aug. 5, 1970. The plan was not revived.

Break-ins against radicals reported. *Newsweek* magazine reported in its June 11 issue that investigators for the Senate select committee probing Watergate were looking into allegations that certain aspects of the 1970 intelligence gathering plan were operational before the birth of the White House "plumbers" group in the summer of 1971.

Newsweek said illegal methods—including burglary and unauthorized wiretaps—were used to stop sensitive leaks, to monitor the domestic left, and gather information for prosecution cases against radicals. Senate investigators were told by high Administration officials that burglaries were committed in connection with the Seattle Seven, the Chicago Weathermen, the Detroit Thirteen and the Berrigan cases. Senate investigators were also reported to be studying charges that Administration operatives buglarized the offices of the Brookings Institution in Washington seeking information on Morton Halperin, a former member of the National Security Council and a friend of Pentagon Papers trial defendant Daniel Ellsberg. *Time* magazine June 11 said the Brookings Institution burglary was never carried out.

(The case against the Seattle Seven involved destruction of federal property in a 1970 demonstration in Seattle. The Weathermen case stemmed from four days of battles between police and demonstrators in Chicago in 1969. The Detroit Thirteen were accused of plotting a bombing campaign at a Flint, Mich. meeting in 1968. The Berrigan case involved charges that the Rev. Philip Berrigan and six others conspired to kidnap White House Foreign Affairs Adviser Henry A. Kissinger.

Senate investigators told *Newsweek* they were not sure what Administration figures had been responsible for the burglaries.

In a related development, the *New York Times* reported June 2 that the FBI was looking into the possibility that the 1970 intelligence plan had been put into operation. The FBI investigation was said to be focusing on four break-ins in 1971 and 1972 at the offices and residences of Chilean diplomats in New York City.

The *Times* June 6 revealed two previously unreported wiretaps that had been authorized by former presidential Domestic Affairs Adviser John D. Ehrlichman. One was placed in 1969 against syndicated columnist Joseph Kraft and the other against an unnamed White House official.

White House investigators John J. Caulfield and Anthony T. Ulasewicz, former New York City policemen hired by Ehrlichman, besides placing the taps, were reported to have looked into the background of Rep. Mario Biaggi (D, N.Y.) for possible Mafia ties. Biaggi had criticized as "insulting to Italian-Americans" a 1969 Nixon crime message calling for an attack on organized crime.

Caulfield and Ulasewicz also were ordered to check the accuracy of reports about the massacre at Mylai.

The *Times* called Caulfield and Ulasewicz the precursors to the White House plumbers group.

In a related matter, the Justice Department May 31 admitted the FBI had wiretapped the phone of a prominent radical lawyer 23 times between 1955 and 1970. The lawyer was identified as Arthur Kinoy, an associate of William Kunstler, who worked for the defense in the Chicago Seven trial.

"At the time I was handling the Chicago Seven appeals, the government was listening to my phone conversations. It was the most outrageous invasion of privacy ever admitted to," Kinoy said.

A 1969 break-in by FBI agents at the offices of the underground newspaper, the *Washington Free Press,* was disclosed by the *New York Times* June 1. Aiding the FBI were members of the Army's 116th Military Intelligence Detachment, the *Times* said. The raid took place just before the Nixon inauguration, when there was concern about a series of planned counter-inaugural activities. The FBI June 1 admitted entering without a search warrant, but a spokesman claimed agents had been given a key by the building landlord.

Weathermen case dropped—Detroit District Court Judge Damon J. Keith Oct. 15 granted a government request to dismiss conspiracy charges against 15 Weathermen indicted in 1970 for plotting a bombing and terrorism campaign.

In a motion to dismiss, U.S. Attorney Ralph B. Guy Jr. said the government could not comply with Keith's order to reveal whether "espionage techniques" had been used in obtaining evidence without compromising "foreign intelligence information deemed essential to the security of the United States."

Defense attorneys said after the dismissal that a hearing into the sources of government evidence would have revealed illegal acts such as wiretaps and burglary and that an Administration plan for domestic intelligence gathering had actually been put into effect.

In presenting his motion, Guy said sworn statements denying illegal conduct in the case by the government had been obtained from the White House, the Central Intelligence Agency, the Federal Bureau of Investigation and other intelligence agencies. Nevertheless, Guy said, the government had chosen to request dismissal.

Guy acknowledged that communications involving one of the uncaptured defendants had been intercepted by a government agency, but that the circumstances of the interception were so secret that the government did not want to reveal them even in the judge's chambers.

Only six of the accused had surrendered or been captured: Robert G. Burlingham, Russell T. Neufeld, Mark Real, Dianne Marie Donghi, Linda Evans and Jane Spielman. The remainder, including Weathermen leaders Mark Rudd and Bernadine Dohrn, had disappeared.

Pentagon Papers Case

CIA involved in burglary. The Central Intelligence Agency admitted that its former deputy director, at the request of the White House, gave assistance to convicted Watergate conspirators E. Howard Hunt Jr. and G. Gordon Liddy as they were planning the break-in at the office of Daniel Ellsberg's former psychiatrist Lewis J. Fielding in Los Angeles.

The 1947 statute creating the CIA said in part that the agency should "have no police, subpoena, law enforcement powers or internal security functions."

The CIA involvement was disclosed in testimony given by Hunt May 2, 1973 to the Washington grand jury investigating the Watergate break-in.

The *New York Times* reported May 7 that Gen. Robert E. Cushman Jr., present commandant of the Marine Corps and then deputy director of the CIA, gave aid to Liddy and Hunt in the form of false identification papers, disguises, a tape recorder, and a miniature camera. This aid, the *Times* said, came at the request of John D. Ehrlichman, who had been ordered by President Nixon to head an investigation into a series of national security leaks in 1971. Cushman was also chief military adviser to Vice President Nixon from 1957 to 1961.

In testimony May 9 before the Senate Appropriations subcommittee on CIA operations, CIA director James R. Schlesinger admitted the agency had been "insufficiently cautious" in providing materials for the break-in. He denied that the CIA was aware that Liddy and Hunt had decided to break into Fielding's office. Schlesinger noted that aid to Hunt and Liddy had been discontinued one week before the Los Angeles break-in occurred because Cushman was becoming "increasingly concerned" over Hunt's repeated requests for assistance. The agency chief also said that former director Richard Helms had personally ordered CIA officers to assist in the preparation of a personality profile of Ellsberg.

In his grand jury testimony May 2, Hunt told how he and Liddy had been hired by White House aides Egil Krogh Jr. and David Young to investigate leaks of the Pentagon Papers. One offshoot of this was the question of the prosecutability of Daniel Ellsberg, a topic that led to the suggestion of a "bag job" (break-in) at the office of Ellsberg's former psychiatrist in Los Angeles. Hunt said the Federal Bureau of Investigation and the Secret Service were ruled out of the operation because Liddy felt neither was equipped for the task.

A decision was then made to use himself and Liddy, Hunt said. He and Liddy flew to Los Angeles Aug. 25, 1971, where they reconnoitered the office of Dr. Fielding. One of their devices was a camera fitted into a tobacco pouch.

Hunt said the camera had been supplied by a technical services representative of the CIA at a "safe house" on Massachusetts Avenue in Washington, "the same one we used when we were given disguises and other physical equipment." Hunt added that Krogh told him where to make contacts with the CIA.

After he and Liddy returned from their first trip to Washington, they submitted a report to Krogh through Young, recommending that the operation continue, Hunt stated.

At this point Hunt traveled to Miami, where he recruited three men to aid in the mission. They were Bernard L. Barker, Eugenio Rolando Martinez, both later convicted for the Watergate break-in, and Felipe de Diego, who reportedly assaulted Ellsberg on the steps of the Capitol May 2, 1972 while he spoke at a rally.

On Labor Day weekend in 1971 the five met in Los Angeles. Two of the Miami men had a cleaning woman Sept. 3 let them into the office of Fielding. Disguised as delivery men, they left a suitcase containing a camera in the office. Later that night, while Liddy remained nearby and Hunt watched Fielding at his home, either two or three of the Miami operatives broke into the office, and searched for files on Ellsberg.

Hunt said the men were unable to find any material with Ellsberg's name on it. (Fielding earlier submitted an affadavit to Pentagon Papers trial Judge William M. Byrne, in which he stated that files on Ellsberg had been present in his office.)

Hunt and Liddy then returned to Washington, where they reported their lack of results to Krogh, Hunt testified.

Hunt denied he had spoken to Ehrlichman about the burglary and that Ehrlichman told him not to do it again.

The role of the CIA in the Los Angeles burglary was further detailed in four Justice Department memos made public by Pentagon Papers trial defendants Ellsberg and Anthony J. Russo Jr. May 8.

One memo dated Dec. 4, 1972 told of secret meetings of an unnamed CIA agent, "Mr. Blank," with Hunt and Liddy, at which they were given documents and disguises, as well as the tobacco pouch camera. It also said Hunt called "Mr. Blank" Aug. 26, 1971 and asked "Mr. Blank" to meet him at Dulles Airport outside Washington at 6 a.m. the following morning because he had film that had to be developed by that afternoon.

A second undated memorandum told of a July 22, 1971 meeting between Hunt and Cushman, at which time Hunt asked for CIA aid. Cushman said he would look into the matter and get in touch with Hunt at his White House office.

Subsequently Cushman complied with Hunt's requests until the day the CIA received the film that was to be developed. On that day the "Mr. Blank" instructed CIA technical personnel not to comply with further Hunt requests because they had gone beyond the original understanding. More important, they appeared to involve the CIA in domestic clandestine operations. The unnamed agent reported his findings to Cushman, who then called the White House to inform the "appropriate individual" that there would be no more CIA aid.

The testimony given by CIA Director Schlesinger May 9 amplified these facts. He said Ehrlichman had originally requested CIA aid, and Ehrlichman was telephoned by Cushman Aug. 21 and told no more CIA assistance would be forthcoming. Schlesinger's recall of Aug. 21 as the date of the Cushman call to Ehrlichman was in conflict with the date of Aug. 27, as given in the Justice Department memo.

In other testimony, Schlesinger said CIA officials gave former Acting FBI Director L. Patrick Gray 3rd an account by letter July 5 and 7, 1972 of the CIA involvement with Hunt in the Ellsberg case, which they repeated in a July 28, 1972 meeting. Attorney General Richard Kleindienst and Assistant Attorney General Henry E. Petersen reviewed the report in October 1972, Schlesinger added. Chief Watergate prosecutor Earl Silbert was also briefed on the incident during the same period, Schlesinger said.

FBI tap on Ellsberg revealed. Evidence of wiretaps on telephone calls made by Pentagon Papers trial defendant Daniel Ellsberg in late 1969 or early 1970 was disclosed in a memorandum sent May 9 by Acting FBI Director William D. Ruckelshaus to presiding Judge William M. Byrne.

The Ruckelshaus memo said "that an FBI employe recalls that in late 1969 or early 1970 Mr. Ellsberg had been overheard talking from an electronic surveillance of Dr. Morton Halperin's residence." The memo also said a search of FBI records had failed to disclose the existence of such wiretaps. Halperin, a defense consultant and witness in the trial, headed the study group that compiled the Pentagon Papers.

Judge Byrne immediately suspended court proceedings and asked the government to produce all its logs and other records concerning the taps. He ordered both sides to prepare arguments as to why charges against Daniel Ellsberg and Anthony J. Russo Jr. should not be dismissed because of the disclosure of the wiretaps and the fact that records concerning them had disappeared.

Disclosure of the wiretaps raised the question of whether the government's case might be tainted.

The government contended May 10 it had "testimonial evidence" that the electronic surveillance of Halperin's home that picked up any Ellsberg conversation had been "authorized by the attorney general in accordance with national security procedures." At the same time it conceded "the records, however, have not been found."

Meanwhile the court May 11 had several defense motions before it:

■ A motion to dismiss the case because the burglary of Ellsberg's psychiatrist's office and other alleged government misconduct so seriously compromised the rights of Ellsberg and Russo, their connection with actual evidence need not be shown.

■ A motion to throw the case out as a sanction against the prosecution for withholding exculpatory evidence from the court and the defense.

■ A motion for a directed acquittal on the grounds that the government failed to produce sufficient evidence to convict Russo and Ellsberg. Defense attorneys were to argue this before Byrne decided whether to dismiss the case.

■ A motion to dismiss part of the indictments, including the conspiracy and theft charges, on the grounds they involved the unconstitutional use of the relevant statutes.

■ A motion for extensive hearings on whether the evidence in the case had been tainted by the burglary of the office of Daniel Ellsberg's former psychiatrist and other aspects of an independent White House investigation of the case.

Judge Byrne May 4 rejected a defense motion for dismissal based on the fact that he had been compromised by meetings he had with John D. Ehrlichman, former adviser to President Nixon.

Left unresolved was a defense contention that the case against Ellsberg and Russo involved "discriminatory prosecution" for acts regularly committed by government officials, namely the disclosure of classified material. Byrne said this matter should be taken up in a post-trial hearing.

In other trial developments, the prosecution May 4 gave the court a file on Ellsberg that had been compiled by E. Howard Hunt Jr. The file, which had been in the possession of the Justice Department for 10 months, contained a 28-page chronology of Ellsberg's life, including notations of private phone calls and visits he had made to two psychiatrists. The Justice Department had no explanation for its earlier failure to disclose the file.

Four Justice Department officials submitted affadavits May 9 to Judge Byrne in which they swore they had not become aware of the burglary of the office of Ellsberg's former psychiatrist until April 16, 1972. They were Assistant Attorney General Henry E. Petersen; Kevin T. Maroney, a deputy assistant attorney general; John L. Martin, another Justice Department lawyer; and David R. Nissen, chief prosecutor in the Pentagon Papers case.

Charges against Ellsberg, Russo dismissed. Government charges of espionage, theft and conspiracy against Pentagon Papers trial defendants Daniel Ellsberg and Anthony J. Russo Jr. were dismissed by presiding Judge William M. Byrne in Los Angeles May 11. Byrne worded the dismissal so as to preclude retrial.

In granting the dismissal, Byrne was highly critical of government conduct during the case. "Bizarre events have incurably infected the prosecution of this case," he said. "The totality of the circumstances . . . offend 'a sense of justice,'" he added. [See text p. 299]

Citing government misconduct as the reason for the dismissal, Byrne said that after two weeks of extraordinary disclosures beginning April 26, the government had raised more questions than it had answers for.

Of greatest significance was not the disclosure of a wiretap on phone conversations of Ellsberg, but that the government had lost the records pertaining to the tap. "There is no way . . . [anybody] can test what effect these interceptions may have had on the government's case. . . ."

The dismissal also resulted from the break-in at the office of Ellsberg's psychiatrist, which Byrne took care to note had been abetted by the Central Intelligence Agency "presumably acting beyond its statutory authority."

Noting that the CIA had provided the White House with two psychological profiles of Daniel Ellsberg, Byrne reasoned he could not be sure that other material gathered by the special White House unit did not exist.

Byrne chastised the government for causing delays by not speedily producing exculpatory evidence it possessed. Stating that these delays had already compromised the defendants' right to a speedy trial, Byrne said "no investigation is likely to provide satisfactory answers where improper government conduct has been shielded so long from public view and where the government advises the court that pertinent files and records are missing or destroyed."

A poll of the trial jurors, taken by the Associated Press after the dismissal, showed seven leaned toward acquittal. In interviews after the dismissal, the jurors were nearly unanimous in their high regard for Byrne.

The defendants were jubilant after the dismissal. "This was the right way to end it," Ellsberg said outside the court. "It should have been ended. It was the government that cheated the jury out the right to hear the evidence," he said.

Ellsberg added, "The trial isn't over until that bombing is over in Cambodia.

"Don't we have the right not to be tried under Nazi law? This Administration has been very straight about where it is. It is up to us to tell them what it means to be an American.

"If facts prove to be what they appear to be, the President has led a conspiracy, not only against Tony [Russo] and me, but against the American public."

Ellsberg said he intended to bring suit against the government to recover $900,-000 spent by the defense. He indicated the defense still faced a $50,000-$75,000 deficit. Government expenses were put at more than twice those of the defense.

Russo commented May 12 that the trial's conclusion was "not as clear-cut as we wanted to see," but he added, "We were unable to let the trial go to the jury. We were forced to take every action we could for dismissal. I think it was a victory, not just for Dan and me, but for millions of people."

Cushman, Helms explain CIA role. The former director and deputy director of the Central Intelligence Agency appeared before Congressional panels investigating the role played by the agency in the burglary of the office of the former psychiatrist of former Pentagon Papers trial defendant Daniel Ellsberg.

Former deputy director of the CIA and current Commandant of the Marine Corps Gen. Robert E. Cushman Jr. May 11 admitted giving aid to E. Howard Hunt Jr. at the request of former presidential adviser John D. Ehrlichman, who had been asked by President Nixon to head an investigation into security leaks that eventually led to the break-in in Los Angeles. Cushman said that when Ehrlichman asked for assistance, he assumed Ehrlichman was speaking on Nixon's behalf.

Cushman also revealed that the former director of the CIA, Richard Helms, agreed to give agency assistance after being informed of a July 22, 1971 meeting between Hunt and Cushman, during which specific requests were made by Hunt. However, Cushman denied knowing what the aid was for, claiming that Hunt would only say it was for the welfare of the nation.

Cushman testified before and submitted affadavits to the House Armed Services special subcommittee on intelligence, the Senate Armed Services committee, and the Senate Appropriations subcommittee on intelligence operations.

Helms, the current ambassador to Iran, appeared before the Senate Appropriations subcommittee May 16, where he admitted granting a 1971 White House request for a "personality assessment" of Ellsberg. Although he said he did not feel the request was proper, he agreed because it came from the White House, Helms reportedly said.

CIA psychiatrists had told the same subcommittee May 10 the Ellsberg profile was the only one ever done on an American citizen by the agency.

Ellsberg urges anti-secrecy laws—Appearing before a Senate subcommittee on government secrecy May 16, former Pentagon Papers trial defendant Daniel Ellsberg urged Congress to pass laws sharply curtailing the power of the executive branch to impose secrecy in government.

Ellsberg charged that J. Fred Buzhardt, appointed May 10 as special counsel to the President on Watergate matters, may have been "culpable" on perjury charges when he testified at the Pentagon Papers trial in January he had no knowledge of a Pentagon study asserting that Ellsberg's disclosure of one of the Pentagon Paper volumes had done no harm to the national security.

Ellsberg warned the panel composed of three Senate subcommittees that data classified above top secret and available only to the highest officials could become "a magic potion that turns ordinary human beings into arrogant, contemptuous menaces to democracy."

Ellsberg said he told President Nixon's national security adviser, Henry Kissinger, in 1968: "Security corrupts just as power corrupts. . . . the first impact will be that you will feel like a fool. You have written articles and rubbed shoulders for decades with people who had these clearances. But . . . after a week or so of having four star generals bring you special pouches and briefcases . . . you will forget that once you were a fool and remember only that everyone else is a fool who does not have that information."

Ellsberg cited a Kissinger meeting with reporters in June 1971, in which Kissinger denied having read the Pentagon Papers until they had been published by the *New York Times*. "That was a lie," Ellsberg charged. He said Kissinger had told him in 1969 he had read the Pentagon Papers.

In other testimony, Ellsberg charged that government secrecy had become so pervasive there were 20 classifications above top secret.

Text of Judge Byrne's Ruling May 11 in Ellsberg Case

This ruling is based upon the motion in that scope that Mr. [Leonard] Boudin has just stated. It is not based solely on the wiretap, nor is it based solely on the break-in and the information that has been presented over the last several days.

Commencing on April 26, the government has made an extraordinary series of disclosures regarding the conduct of several governmental agencies regarding the defendants in this case.

It is my responsibility to assess the effect of this conduct upon the rights of the defendants. My responsibility relates solely and only to this case, to the rights of the defendants and their opportunities for a fair trial with due process of law.

As the record makes clear, I have attempted to require the government and to allow the defendants to develop all relevant information regarding these highly unusual disclosures. Much information has been developed, but new information has produced new questions, and there remain more questions than answers.

The disclosures made by the government demonstrate that governmental agencies have taken an unprecedented series of actions with respect to these defendants.

After the original indictment, at a time when the government's rights to investigate the defendants are narrowly circumscribed, White House officials established a special unit to investigate one of the defendants in this case.

The special unit apparently operated with the approval of the FBI, the agency officially charged with the investigation of this case.

We may have been given only a glimpse of what this special unit did regarding this case, but what we know is more than disquieting. The special unit came to Los Angeles and surveyed the vicinity of the offices of the psychiatrist of one of the defendants.

After reporting to a White House assistant and apparently receiving specific authorization, the special unit then planned and executed the break-in of the psychiatrist's office in search of the records of one of the defendants.

From the information received, including the last document filed today, it is difficult to determine what, if anything, was obtained from the psychiatrist's office by way of photographs.

The Central Intelligence Agency, presumably acting beyond its statutory authority, and at the request of the White House, had provided disguises, photographic equipment and other paraphernalia for covert operations.

The government's disclosure also revealed that the special unit requested and obtained from the CIA two psychological profiles of one of the defendants.

Of more serious consequences is that the defendants and the court do not know the other activities in which the special unit may have been engaged and what has happened to the results of these endeavors.

They do not know whether other material gathered by the special unit was destroyed, and though I have inquired of the government several times in this regard, no answer has been forthcoming.

Though some governmental officials were aware of the illegal activities of this unit directed at the defendants, and thus at this case, the court nor the defendants nor, apparently, the prosecution itself was ever aware of these facts until Mr. [Earl J.] Silbert's memorandum, and then not for some 10 days after it had been written.

These recent events compounded the record already pervaded by incidents threatening the defendants' right to a speedy and fair trial. The government has time and again failed to make timely productions of exculpatory information in its possession, requiring delays and disruptions in the trial.

Within the last 48 hours, after both sides had rested their case, the government revealed interception by electronic surveillance of one or more conversations of defendant [Daniel] Ellsberg. The government can only state and does only state that the interception or interceptions took place.

Indeed, the government frankly admits that it does not know how many such interceptions took place, or when they took place or between whom they occurred or what was said. We only know that the conversation was overheard during a period of the conspiracy as charged in the indictment.

Of greatest significance is the fact that the government does not know what has happened to the authorizations for the surveillance, nor what has happened to the tapes nor to the logs nor any other records pertaining to the overheard conversations.

This lack of records appears to be present not only in the Justice Department, but in the Federal Bureau of Investigation, from the response forwarded by Mr. Petersen yesterday that the records of both the FBI and the Justice Department appear to have been missing.

The matter is somewhat compounded also by the fact that the documents had been missing since the period of July to October of 1971.

The FBI reports that, while the files did once exist regarding this surveillance, they now apparently have been removed from both the Justice Department and the FBI. As I state it, it is reported by the FBI that the records have been missing since mid-1971.

There is no way the defendants or the court or, indeed, the government itself can test what effect these interceptions may have had on the government's case here against either or both of the defendants.

A continuation of the government's investigation is no solution with reference to this case. The delays already encountered threaten to compromise the defendants' rights, and it is the defendants' rights and the effect on this case that is paramount and each passing day indicates that the investigation is further from completion as the jury waits.

Moreover, no investigation is likely to provide satisfactory answers where improper government conduct has been shielded so long from public view and where the government advises the court that pertinent files and records are missing or destroyed.

My duties and obligations relate to this case and what must be done to protect the right to a fair trial.

The charges against these defendants raise serious factual and legal issues that I would certainly prefer to have litigated to completion. However, as I just mentioned at the opening of this session, the defendants have the right to raise these issues when they desire. They desire to raise them now, and it is my obligation and duty to rule on them now.

However, while I would prefer to have them litigated, the conduct of the government has placed the case in such a posture that it precludes the fair, dispassionate resolution of these issues by a jury.

In considering the alternatives before me, I have carefully weighed the granting of a mistrial, without taking any further action. The defendants have opposed such a course of action, asserting their rights, if the case is to proceed, to have the matter tried before this jury. I have concluded that a mistrial alone would not be fair.

Under all the circumstances, I believe that the defendants should not have to run the risk, present under existing authorities, that they might be tried again before a different jury.

The totality of the circumstances of this case, which I have only briefly sketched, offend "a sense of justice." The bizarre events have incurably infected the prosecution of this case.

I believe the authority to dismiss this case in these circumstances is fully supported by pertinent case authorities, including United States v. Eastern District, United States v. Coplon, United States v. Apex Distributing, United States v. Heath, Rochin v. California and Rules 12, 16 (g) and 48 of the Federal Rules of Criminal Procedure.

I have decided to declare a mistrial and grant the motion to dismiss.

I am of the opinion, in the present status of the case, that the only remedy available that would assure due process and a fair administration of justice is that this trial be terminated and the defendants' motion for dismissal be granted and the jury discharged.

The order of dismissal will be entered; the jurors will be advised of the dismissal, and the case is terminated.

Thank you very much, gentlemen, for your efforts.

CIA Involvement

Attempt to blame CIA alleged. The *New York Times* reported May 9, 1973 charges by convicted Watergate conspirator James W. McCord Jr. that he had been pressured twice prior to his trial to ascribe the Watergate break-in to the Central Intelligence Agency. The charges were said to have been made by McCord in a memorandum submitted to federal and Senate probers and also made available to the *Times.* McCord reported in it being told by his attorney, Gerald Alch, (1) that his personnel records at the CIA could be altered, if needed, to show he had been restored to active duty since his retirement in 1970, and (2) that James R. Schlesinger, the newly designated CIA director, could be subpoenaed to testify at the trial "and would go along with it."

His refusal to accept the plan, McCord said, aborted it and incurred the anger of fellow conspirator E. Howard Hunt Jr.

By the time of his trial, the memorandum said, McCord "was completely convinced that the White House was behind the idea and ploy which had been presented and that the White House was turning ruthless and would do whatever was politically expedient at any one particular point in time to accomplish its own ends."

The memorandum also alleged a White House attempt to dominate the CIA and referred to a similar effort at political control by the White House at the Federal Bureau of Investigation.

CIA involvement was sought. High Administration officials sought to involve the Central Intelligence Agency in the Watergate affair, according to testimony presented to the Senate Armed Services Committee. The committee was inquiring into the CIA's involvement in domestic undercover work, which was barred under the 1947 National Security Act.

The hearings were closed, but Sen. Stuart Symington (D, Mo.), the committee's acting chairman, reported after the first session May 14 that "there were other matters besides the Ellsberg case in which the White House tried to get the CIA involved."

On the basis of testimony by Lt. Gen. Vernon A. Walters, deputy director of the CIA, Symington reported that the White House aides involved in the apparent attempt to compromise the CIA were ex-White House aides H.R. Haldeman, John D. Ehrlichman and John W. Dean 3rd.

"Ehrlichman, and Haldeman—particularly Haldeman," Symington said, "were up to their ears in this, along with Dean, in trying to involve the CIA in this whole Watergate mess."

In releasing a summary of Walters' testimony May 15, Symington said "it is very clear to me that there was an attempt to unload major responsibility for the Watergate bugging and cover-up on the CIA." According to the summary:

■ Dean asked Walters 10 days after the Watergate break-in (in June 1972) if the CIA could provide bail or pay the salaries for the men apprehended there. Walters refused and declared he would rather resign than implicate the agency in such a scheme.

■ As recently as January or February, Dean sought to obtain CIA assistance in retrieving from the Federal Bureau of Investigation (FBI) "some materials" obtained from the CIA for use in the break-in at the office of Pentagon Papers defendant Daniel Ellsberg's psychiatrist.

■ Haldeman and Ehrlichman intervened in an attempt to have the CIA press the FBI to call off its probe in 1972 into Nixon campaign funds that had been routed or "laundered" to prevent tracing through a Mexican bank and, at one point, through several of the Watergate defendants. The CIA's approach to the FBI would be made on the ground that national security was involved and pursuit of the probe would compromise certain CIA activities and resources in Mexico. Walters met with Acting FBI Director L. Patrick Gray 3rd several times. The first time he related to Gray that senior White House aides had told him pursuit of the probe would compromise certain CIA activities and resources in Mexico.

After Gray later said he would need a written statement to that effect—that CIA assets would be endangered—before the FBI inquiry could be ended, Walters, apparently on word from then-CIA Director Richard M. Helms, informed Gray the CIA activity actually was not in jeopardy by the FBI probe.

Helms, currently ambassador to Iran, testified May 16 before a Senate Appropriations subcommittee, which was examining the same issue. Chairman John L. McClellan (D, Ark.) said afterward that Helms had expressed concern about the White House overtures to the CIA for domestic activity, which he considered improper, but said he had never conveyed his concern to President Nixon.

"He did not feel at that time that he should go to the President about it," McClellan reported. "He did not want the CIA involved."

According to McClellan, Helms confirmed Walters' testimony and defended his own statements at his confirmation hearings on the ambassadorship that the CIA had never been involved in Watergate. "He [Helms] did not relate these events to the Watergate" at the time, McClellan said.

More testimony was released May 17, as Helms and Walters returned before the Armed Services panel. Walters said he told Gray in their meeting in early July 1972 he considered the attempts "to cover this up or to implicate the CIA or FBI would be detrimental to their integrity" and he was "quite prepared to resign on this issue."

Gray "shared my views" and "he, too, was prepared to resign on this issue," Walters said. He also recounted a conversation with Gray in a second meeting a week later: "I said that I had told Dean that the best solution would be to fire

those responsible. Gray said he had made the same recommendation."

Symington said May 17 all the recent witnesses had "stated that they did not know whether the President" knew about White House efforts to implicate the CIA in Watergate. "But it's hard for me to visualize that the President knew nothing about this," Symington commented.

Gray says he alerted Nixon—According to sources within the Senate Watergate committee, which interrogated former Acting FBI Director Gray May 10 (the testimony was leaked May 11), Gray testified President Nixon telephoned him about another matter July 6, 1972. Gray took the opportunity to express concern about White House interference in the Watergate probe and to caution the President that he was being "wounded" by men around him "using the FBI and CIA." According to Gray, Nixon responded that Gray should continue to press his investigation.

The July 6 date was the same day Walters visited Gray to inform him the FBI probe would not jeopardize CIA activity. In that visit, Walters identified, as he had not in his previous talk with Gray, the White House aides who were pressing for an end to the FBI probe—Ehrlichman and Haldeman.

According to some accounts of Gray's testimony, he also reported arranging a meeting with CIA Director Helms about possible CIA complications, but received a call from Ehrlichman that firmly suggested he cancel it because of the security aspect. The call reportedly was made June 28, 1972, the day Gray received in Ehrlichman's office files, which he said he burned, from one of the Watergate defendants. Gray was said by the sources to have revised, in his May 10 testimony, his account of the time and place he burned the files. Instead of having done it in his office five days after receiving them, he said he kept them until Christmas at his home, where he then incinerated them.

Gray's reported testimony May 10 that he had also called Nixon's campaign chairman, Clark MacGregor, July 6, 1972 to express concern about the obstacles to his probe, was confirmed May 12 by MacGregor, who said he was in California at the time, which was about 2 a.m. in Washington. He said Gray had seemed "agitated, concerned" and "wondered if I recognized how serious Watergate was." MacGregor reported being aware of the seriousness of the crimes involved in the break-in and said Gray did not bring the subject up again.

Nixon's name invoked in cover-up. The deputy director of the Central Intelligence Agency (CIA) was told by former White House chief of staff H. R. Haldeman "it is the President's wish" that he ask L. Patrick Gray 3rd, former acting director of the Federal Bureau of Investigation, to halt his agency's investigation into the laundering of campaign funds through a bank in Mexico City.

This information was contained in one of 11 memoranda written by Deputy CIA

Director Vernon A. Walters and given to the Senate Foreign Relations Committee. It was made public May 21 by committee member Sen. Stuart Symington (D, Mo.)

One "memorandum of conversation" written by Walters related to a meeting he had with Haldeman, former presidential aide John D. Ehrlichman, and former CIA Director Richard Helms June 23, 1972, six days after the Watergate break-in. Within an hour of the meeting, an appointment for Walters with Gray had been set up.

Haldeman issued a statement May 21: "I can flatly say the President was not involved in any cover-up of anything at any time."

Another Walters memorandum revealed that Gray told Nixon during a telephone conversation that the Watergate case could not be covered up and that the President should get rid of those who were involved.

According to the memorandum dated July 13, 1972, Nixon had called Gray to congratulate him on the handling of an attempted hijacking. "Toward the end of the conversation, the President asked him [Gray] if he had talked to me [Walters] about the case. Gray replied that he had. The President then asked him what his recommendation was in this case. Gray had replied that the case could not be covered up and it would lead quite high and he felt the President should get rid of the people that were involved. Any attempt to involve the FBI or the CIA in this case could only prove a mortal wound and would achieve nothing."

"The President then said, 'Then I should get rid of whoever is involved, no matter how high up?' Gray replied that was his recommendation.

"The President then asked what I [Walters] thought, and Gray said my views were the same as his. The President took it well and thanked him."

The memorandum continued that Gray then called former White House counsel John W. Dean 3rd and informed him of his conversation with the President. Dean responded, "Okay," the memorandum said.

According to Symington, the committee had obtained two sets of documents that purported to deal with Administration plans during the summer of 1970 to commit burglary and engage in other illegal activities to gather intelligence about some U.S. citizens. Symington said the plans were never carried out.

Helms, who also appeared before the committee May 21, substantiated the Walters memoranda and added that during the June 23, 1972 meeting Haldeman had said "the opposition" was "capitalizing" on the Watergate case.

Asked why he hadn't gone directly to the President about the attempted cover-up, Helms replied that his "total preoccupation" was in keeping the CIA uninvolved in the matter.

Helms was asked by Sen. Charles Percy (R, Ill.) whether his refusal to go along with any cover-up played a role in his departure from the CIA. Informed sources claimed that Helms had been

summarily fired by President Nixon after the 1972 elections, the Washington Post reported May 22.

Helms responded, "I honestly don't know." He added that the President had at no time mentioned Watergate to him.

Nixon did not ask CIA about Watergate —President Nixon at no time called the Central Intelligence Agency after the Watergate break-in to directly determine the role the agency might have had in the burglary, Deputy CIA Director Walters told a Senate panel May 23.

(President Nixon said in his May 22 statement on Watergate that within a few days of the break-in, "I was advised that there was a possibility of CIA involvement in some way." He said that since former CIA personnel were involved in the burglary, he feared that some covert CIA operations might be exposed. Nixon did not say who "advised" him of CIA involvement.)

Walters, appearing before the Senate Appropriations intelligence operations subcommittee, said Nixon spoke to him on the phone several weeks after the Watergate break-in; but it was about an unrelated matter.

In other May 23 testimony before the intelligence operations subcommittee chaired by Sen. John L. McClellan (D, Ark.), CIA Director James R. Schlesinger denied having been approached by Nixon regarding CIA involvement in Watergate.

White House Involvement, Secret Probe Conceded

Nixon explains White House role. In a statement released May 22, 1973 President Nixon conceded the probable involvement of some of his closest aides in concealing some aspects of the Watergate affair and acknowledged that he had ordered limitations on the investigation because of national security considerations "of crucial importance" unrelated to Watergate.

He reiterated, however, his own lack of prior knowledge of the burglary and the attempted cover-up while acknowledging that aides might have "gone beyond" his directives to protect "national security operations in order to cover up any involvement they or certain others might have had in Watergate."

In a summary accompanying the statement, Nixon made the following replies to specific allegations against White House activities:

"1) I had no prior knowledge of the Watergate operation.

2) I took no part in, nor was I aware of, any subsequent efforts that may have been made to cover up Watergate.

3) At no time did I authorize any offer of executive clemency to the Watergate defendants, nor did I know of any such offer.

4) I did not know, until the time of my own investigation, of any effort to provide the Watergate defendants with funds.

5) At no time did I attempt, or did I authorize others to attempt, to implicate the CIA in the Watergate matter.

6) It was not until the time of my own

investigation that I learned of the break-in at the office of [Pentagon Papers case defendant Daniel] Ellsberg's psychiatrist, and I specifically authorized the furnishing of this information to Judge [William M.] Byrne.

7) I neither authorized nor encouraged subordinates to engage in illegal or improper campaign tactics."

The President said that in 1970 he was concerned about increasing political disruption connected with antiwar protests and decided a better intelligence operation was needed. He appointed the late J. Edgar Hoover, director of the Federal Bureau of Investigation, as head of a committee to prepare suggestions. On June 25 1970, Nixon said, the committee recommended resumption of "certain intelligence operations that had been suspended in 1966," among them the "authorization for surreptitious entry—breaking and entering, in effect"—in specific situations related to national security.

He said Hoover opposed the plan and it was never put into effect. "It was this unused plan and related documents that [his former counsel] John Dean removed from the White House and placed in a safe deposit box," Nixon added.

Further efforts to improve intelligence operations were made in December 1970 with the formation of the Intelligence Evaluation Committee, for which he said he had authorized no illegal activity, nor did he have knowledge of any.

Nixon said he had "wanted justice done in regard to Watergate" but he had not wanted the investigation to "impinge adversely upon the national security area." He noted that, shortly after the break-in, he was informed that the CIA might have been involved and that he instructed H. R. Haldeman and John Ehrlichman to "insure that the investigation of the break-in not expose either an unrelated covert operation of the CIA or the activities of the White House investigations unit."

Nixon also declared his intention to remain in office, saying "I will not abandon my responsibilities. I will continue to do the job I was elected to do."

At a news briefing after the release of the statement, Presidential counsel Leonard Garment, Press Secretary Ronald L. Ziegler and special counsel J. Fred Buzhardt Jr. attempted to reconcile the statement with earlier Nixon comments on the Watergate case.

Asked specifically whether Nixon had ordered a restriction on the FBI investigation of the "laundering" of funds through Mexican banks, Garment replied, "No, there is nothing that I have ascertained . . . in these weeks of investigations that would suggest that at all."

Both Buzhardt and Garment declined to expand on Nixon's recollection of being told that the CIA might have been involved in the Watergate break-in, despite several questions as to who had given Nixon the information.

Text of President's May 22 Statement on Watergate Affair

Allegations surrounding the Watergate affair have so escalated that I feel a further statement from the President is required at this time.

A climate of sensationalism has developed in which even second- or third-hand hearsay charges are headlined as fact and repeated as fact.

Important national security operations which themselves had no connection with Watergate have become entangled in the case.

As a result, some national security information has already been made public through court orders, through the subpoenaing of documents and through testimony witnesses have given in judicial and Congressional proceedings. Other sensitive documents are now threatened with disclosure; continued silence about those operations would compromise rather than protect them, and would also serve to perpetuate a grossly distorted view—which recent partial disclosures have given—of the nature and purpose of those operations.

The purpose of this statement is threefold:

■ First, to set forth the facts about my own relationship to the Watergate matter.

■ Second, to place in some perspective some of the more sensational—and inaccurate—of the charges that have filled the headlines in recent days, and also some of the matters that are currently being discussed in Senate testimony and elsewhere.

■ Third, to draw the distinction between national security operations and the Watergate case. To put the other matters in perspective, it will be necessary to describe the national security operations first.

In citing these national security matters it is not my intention to place a national security "cover" on Watergate, but rather to separate them out from Watergate—and at the same time to explain the context in which certain actions took place that were later misconstrued or misused.

Long before the Watergate break-in, three important national security operations took place which have subsequently become entangled in the Watergate case.

■ The first operation, begun in 1969, was a program of wiretaps. All were legal, under the authorities then existing. They were undertaken to find and stop serious national security leaks.

■ The second operation was a reassessment, which I ordered in 1970, of the adequacy of internal security measures. This resulted in a plan and a directive to strengthen our intelligence operations. They were protested by Mr. Hoover, and as a result of his protest they were not put into effect.

■ The third operation was the establishment, in 1971, of a special investigations unit in the White House. Its primary mission was to plug leaks of vital security information. I also directed this group to prepare an accurate history of certain crucial national security matters which occurred under prior Administrations, on which the government's records were incomplete.

Here is the background of these three security operations initiated by my Administration.

By mid-1969, my Administration had begun a number of highly sensitive foreign policy initiatives. They were aimed at ending the war in Vietnam, achieving a settlement in the Middle East, limiting nuclear arms, and establishing new relationships among the great powers. These involved highly secret diplomacy. They were closely interrelated. Leaks of secret information about any one could endanger all.

Exactly that happened. News accounts appeared in 1969, which were obviously based on leaks—some of them extensive and detailed—by people having access to the most highly classified security materials.

There was no way to carry forward these diplomatic initiatives unless further leaks could be prevented. This required finding the source of the leaks.

In order to do this, a special program of wiretaps was instituted in mid-1969 and terminated in February 1971. Fewer than 20 taps, of varying duration, were involved. They produced important leads that made it possible to tighten the security of highly sensitive materials.

I authorized this entire program. Each individual tap was undertaken in accordance with procedures legal at the time and in accord with long-standing precedent.

The persons who were subject to these wiretaps were determined through coordination among the director of the FBI, my assistant for national security affairs, and the attorney general. Those wiretapped were selected on the basis of access to the information leaked, material in security files, and evidence that developed as the inquiry proceeded.

Information thus obtained was made available to senior officials responsible for national security matters in order to curtail further leaks.

In the spring and summer of 1970, another security problem reached critical proportions. In March a wave of bombings and explosions struck college campuses and cities. There were 400 bomb threats in one 24-hour period in New York City. Rioting and violence on college campuses reached a new peak after the Cambodian operation and the tragedies at Kent State and Jackson State. The 1969-70 school year brought nearly 1,800 campus demonstrations, and nearly 250 cases of arson on campus. Many colleges closed. Gun battles between guerrilla-style groups and police were taking place. Some of the disruptive activities were receiving foreign support.

Complicating the task of maintaining security was the fact that, in 1966, certain types of undercover FBI operations that had been conducted for many years had been suspended. This also had substantially impaired our ability to collect foreign intelligence information. At the same time, the relationships between the FBI and other intelligence agencies had been deteriorating. By May, 1970, FBI Director Hoover shut off his agency's liaison with the CIA altogether.

On June 5, 1970, I met with the director of the FBI, (Mr. Hoover), the director of the Central Intelligence Agency (Mr. Richard Helms), the director of the Defense Intelligence Agency (Gen. Donald V. Bennett) and the director of the National Security Agency (Adm. Noel Gayler). We discussed the urgent need for better intelligence operations. I appointed Director Hoover as chairman of an inter-agency committee to prepare recommendations.

On June 25, the committee submitted a report which included specific options for expanded intelligence operations, and on July 23 the agencies were notified by memorandum of the options approved. After reconsideration, however, prompted by the opposition of Director Hoover, the agencies were notified five days later, on July 28, that the approval had been rescinded. The options initially approved had included resumption of certain intelligence operations which had been suspended in 1966. These in turn had included authorization for surreptitious entry—breaking and entering, in effect—on specified categories of targets in specified situations related to national security.

Because the approval was withdrawn before it had been implemented, the net result was that the plan for expanded intelligence activities never went into effect.

The documents spelling out this 1970 plan are extremely sensitive. They include—and are based upon—assessments of certain foreign intelligence capabilities and procedures, which of course must remain secret. It was this unused plan and related documents that John Dean removed from the White House and placed in a safe deposit box, giving the keys to Judge Sirica. The same plan, still unused, is being headlined today.

Coordination among our intelligence agencies continued to fall short of our national security needs. In July, 1970, having earlier discontinued the FBI's liaison with the CIA, Director Hoover ended the FBI's normal liaison with all other agencies except the White House. To help remedy this, an Intelligence Evaluation Committee was created in December, 1970. Its members included representatives of the White House, CIA, FBI, NSA, the Departments of Justice, Treasury, and Defense, and Secret Service.

The Intelligence Evaluation Committee and its staff were instructed to improve coordination among the intelligence community and to prepare evaluations and estimates of domestic intelligence. I understand that its activities are now under investigation. I did not authorize nor do I have any knowledge of any illegal activity by this committee. If it went beyond its charter and did engage in any illegal activities, it was totally without my knowledge or authority.

On Sunday, June 13, 1971, The New York Times published the first installment of what came to be known as "the Pentagon Papers." Not until a few hours before publication did any responsible government official know that they had been stolen. Most officials did not know they existed. No senior official of the government had read them or knew with certainty what they contained.

All the government knew, at first, was that the papers comprised 47 volumes and some 7,000 pages, which had been taken from the most sensitive files of the Departments of State and Defense and the CIA, covering military and diplomatic moves in a war that was still going on.

Moreover, a majority of the documents published with the first three installments in The Times had not

been included in the 47-volume study—raising serious questions about what and how much else might have been taken.

There was every reason to believe this was a security leak of unprecedented proportions.

It created a situation in which the ability of the government to carry on foreign relations even in the best of circumstances could have been severely compromised. Other governments no longer knew whether they could deal with the United States in confidence. Against the background of the delicate negotiations the United States was then involved in on a number of fronts—with regard to Vietnam, China, the Middle East, nuclear arms limitations, U.S.-Soviet relations, and others—in which the utmost degree of confidentiality was vital, it posed a threat so grave as to require extraordinary actions.

Therefore during the week following the Pentagon papers publication, I approved the creation of a special investigations unit within the White House—which later came to be known as the "plumbers." This was a small group at the White House whose principal purpose was to stop security leaks and to investigate other sensitive security matters. I looked to John Ehrlichman for the supervision of this group.

Egil Krogh, Mr. Ehrlichman's assistant, was put in charge. David Young was added to this unit, as were E. Howard Hunt and G. Gordon Liddy.

The unit operated under extremely tight security rules. Its existence and functions were known only to a very few persons at the White House. These included messrs. Haldeman, Ehrlichman and Dean.

At about the time the unit was created, Daniel Ellsberg was identified as the person who had given the Pentagon papers to The New York Times. I told Mr. Krogh that as a matter of first priority, the unit should find out all it could about Mr. Ellsberg's associates and his motives. Because of the extreme gravity of the situation, and not then knowing what additional national secrets Mr. Ellsberg might disclose, I did impress upon Mr. Krogh the vital importance to the national security of his assignment. I did not authorize and had no knowledge of any illegal means to be used to achieve this goal.

However, because of the emphasis I put on the crucial importance of protecting the national security, I can understand how highly motivated individuals could have felt justified in engaging in specific activities that I would have disapproved had they been brought to my attention.

Consequently, as President, I must and do assume responsibility for such actions despite the fact that I, at no time approved or had knowledge of them.

I also assigned the unit a number of other investigatory matters, dealing in part with compiling an accurate record of events related to the Vietnam war, on which the government's records were inadequate (many previous records having been removed with the change of Administrations) and which bore directly on the negotiations then in progress. Additional assignments included tracing down other national security leaks, including one that seriously compromised the United States negotiating position in the SALT talks.

The work of the unit tapered off around the end of 1971. The nature of its work was such that it involved matters that, from a national security standpoint, were highly sensitive then and remain so today.

These intelligence activities had no connection with the break-in of the Democratic headquarters, or the aftermath.

I considered it my responsibility to see that the Watergate investigation did not impinge adversely upon the national security area. For example, on April 18th, 1973, when I learned that Mr. Hunt, a former member of the special investigations unit at the White House, was to be questioned by the U.S. attorney, I directed Assistant Attorney General Petersen to pursue every issue involving Watergate but to confine his investigation to Watergate and related matters and to stay out of national security matters. Subsequently, on April 25, 1973, Attorney General Kleindienst informed me that because the government had clear evidence that Mr. Hunt was involved in the break-in of the office of the psychiatrist who had treated Mr. Ellsberg, he, the attorney general, believed that despite the fact that no evidence had been obtained from Hunt's acts, a report should nevertheless be made to the court trying the Ellsberg case. I concurred, and directed that the information be transmitted to Judge Byrne immediately.

The burglary and bugging of the Democratic National Committee headquarters came as a complete surprise to me. I had no inkling that any such illegal activities had been planned by persons associated with my campaign; if I had known, I would not have permitted it. My immediate reaction was that those guilty should be brought to justice and, with the five burglars themselves already in custody, I assumed that they would be. Within a few days, however, I was advised that there was a possibility of CIA involvement in some way.

It did seem to me possible that, because of the involvement of former CIA personnel, and because of some of their apparent associations, the investigation could lead to the uncovering of covert CIA operations totally unrelated to the Watergate break-in.

In addition, by this time, the name of Mr. Hunt had surfaced in connection with Watergate, and I was alerted to the fact that he had previously been a member of the special investigations unit in the White House. Therefore, I was also concerned that the Watergate investigation might well lead to an inquiry into the activities of the special investigations unit itself.

In this area, I felt it was important to avoid disclosure of the details of the national security matters with which the group was concerned. I knew that once the existence of the group became known, it would lead inexorably to a discussion of these matters, some of which remain, even today, highly sensitive.

I wanted justice done with regard to Watergate; but in the scale of national priorities with which I had to deal—and not at that time having any idea of the extent of political abuse which Watergate reflected—I also had to be deeply concerned with insuring that neither the covert operations of the CIA nor the operations of the special investigations unit should be compromised. Therefore, I instructed Mr. Haldeman and Mr. Ehrlichman to insure that the investigation of the break-in not expose either an unrelated covert operation of the CIA or the activities of the White House investigations unit—and to see that this was personally coordinated between General Walters, the deputy director of the CIA, and Mr. Gray of the FBI. It was certainly not my intent, nor my wish, that the investigation of the Watergate break-in or of related acts be impeded in any way.

On July 6, 1972, I telephoned the acting director of the FBI, L. Patrick Gray, to congratulate him on his successful handling of the hijacking of a Pacific Southwest Airlines plane the previous day. During the conversation Mr. Gray discussed with me the progress of the Watergate investigation, and I asked him whether he had talked with General Walters. Mr. Gray said that he had, and that General Walters had assured him that the CIA was not involved. In the discussion, Mr. Gray suggested that the matter of Watergate might lead higher. I told him to press ahead with his investigation.

It now seems that later, through whatever complex of individual motives and possible misunderstandings, there were apparently wide-ranging efforts to limit the investigation or to conceal the possible involvement of members of the Administration and the campaign committee.

I was not aware of any such efforts at the time. Neither, until after I began my own investigation, was I aware of any fund-raising for defendants convicted at the break-in at Democratic headquarters, much less authorize any such fund-raising. Nor did I authorize any offer of executive clemency for any of the defendants.

In the weeks and months that followed Watergate, I asked for, and received, repeated assurances that Mr. Dean's own investigation (which included reviewing files and sitting in on FBI interviews with White House personnel) had cleared everyone then employed by the White House of involvement.

In summary, then:

(1) I had no prior knowledge of the Watergate bugging operation, or of any illegal surveillance activities for political purposes.

(2) Long prior to the 1972 campaign, I did set in motion certain internal security measures, including legal wiretaps, which I felt were necessary from a national security standpoint and, in the climate then prevailing, also necessary from a domestic security standpoint.

(3) People who had been involved in the national security operations later, without my knowledge or approval, undertook illegal activities in the political campaign of 1972.

(4) Elements of the early post-Watergate reports led me to suspect, incorrectly, that the CIA had been in some way involved. They also led me to surmise, correctly, that since persons originally recruited for covert national security activities had participated in Watergate, an unrestricted investigation of Watergate might lead to and expose those covert national security operations.

(5) I sought to prevent the exposure of these covert national security activities, while encouraging those conducting the investigation to pursue their inquiry into the Watergate itself. I so instructed my staff, the attorney general and the acting director of the FBI.

(6) I also specifically instructed Mr. Haldeman and Mr. Ehrlichman to insure that the FBI would not carry its investigation into areas that might compromise these covert national security activities or those of the CIA.

(7) At no time did I authorize or know about any offer of executive clemency for the Watergate defendants. Neither did I know, until the time of my own investigation, of any efforts to provide them with funds.

With hindsight, it is apparent that I should have given more heed to the warning signals I received along the way about a Watergate cover-up and less to the reassurances. With hindsight, several other things also become clear:

- With respect to campaign practices, and also with respect to campaign finances, it should now be obvious that no campaign in history has ever been subjected to the kind of intensive and searching inquiry that has been focused on the campaign waged in my behalf in 1972.

It is clear that unethical, as well as illegal, activities took place in the course of that campaign.

None of these took place with my specific approval or knowledge. To the extent that I may in any way have contributed to the climate in which they took place, I did not intend to; to the extent that I failed to prevent them, I should have been more vigilant.

It was to help insure against any repetition of this in the future that last week I proposed the establishment of a top-level, bipartisan, independent commission to recommend a comprehensive reform of campaign laws and practices. Given the priority I believe it deserves, such reform should be possible before the next Congressional elections in 1974.

- It now appears that there were persons who may have gone beyond my directives, and sought to expand on my efforts to protect the national security operations in order to cover up any involvement they or certain others might have had in Watergate. The extent to which this is true, and who may have participated and to what degree, are questions that it would not be proper to address here. The proper forum for settling these matters is in the courts.

- To the extent that I have been able to determine what probably happened in the tangled course of this affair, on the basis of my own recollections and of the conflicting accounts and evidence that I have seen, it would appear that one factor at work was that at critical points various people, each with his own perspective and his own responsibilities, saw the same situation with different eyes and heard the same words with different ears. What might have seemed insignificant to one seemed significant to another; what one saw in terms of public responsibility, another saw in terms of political opportunity; and mixed through it all, I am sure, was a concern on the part of many that the Watergate scandal should not be allowed to get in the way of what the Administration sought to achieve.

The truth about Watergate should be brought out in an orderly way, recognizing that the safeguards of judicial procedure are designed to find the truth, not to hide the truth. With his selection of Archibald Cox—who served both President Kennedy and President Johnson as solicitor general—as the special supervisory prosecutor for matters related to the case, Attorney General-designate Richardson has demonstrated his own determination to see the truth brought out. In this effort he has my full support.

Considering the number of persons involved in this case whose testimony might be subject to a claim of executive privilege, I recognize that a clear definition of that claim has become central to the effort to arrive at the truth.

Accordingly, executive privilege will not be invoked as to any testimony concerning possible criminal conduct or discussions of possible criminal conduct, in the matters presently under investigation, including the Watergate affair and the alleged cover-up.

I want to emphasize that this statement is limited to my own recollections of what I said and did relating to security and to the Watergate. I have specifically avoided any attempt to explain what other parties may have said and done. My own information on those other matters is fragmentary, and to some extent contradictory. Additional information may be forthcoming of which I am unaware. It is also my understanding that the information which has been conveyed to me has also become available to those prosecuting these matters. Under such circumstances, it would be prejudicial and unfair of me to render my opinions on the activities of others; those judgments must be left to the judicial process, our best hope for achieving the just result that we all seek.

As more information is developed, I have no doubt that more questions will be raised. To the extent that I am able, I shall also seek to set forth the facts as known to me with respect to those questions.

Further CIA Involvement

Ehrlichman says Nixon knew of inquiry. A John D. Ehrlichman, President Nixon's former chief domestic affairs adviser, told a Senate panel that President Nixon knew six days after the Watergate break-in that the Federal Bureau of Investigation was conducting an investigation into "Mexican aspects" of the case.

Ehrlichman, appearing before the Senate Appropriations Committee's Subcommittee on Intelligence Operations May 30, 1973 said Nixon told him and B White House chief of staff H. R. Haldeman to instruct the Central Intelligence Agency to tell the FBI to go slow in its investigation so as not to expose covert intelligence operations in Mexico.

Ehrlichman said Deputy CIA Director Vernon A. Walters at that meeting was unable to unequivocally say CIA operations would not be exposed.

Exactly what the President knew about the "Mexican aspects" referred to by C Ehrlichman—which subcommittee members took to mean the laundering of $89,-000 of Nixon campaign funds through a Mexican bank—was left unclear.

Sen. John L. McClellan (D, Ark.), subcommittee chairman, in recapitulating Ehrlichman's closed-door testimony for reporters, said the President was specifically aware of the FBI investigation centering on the funds channeled through a Mexican bank that were ultimately used D to finance operations of the Nixon reelection committee and the Watergate break-in.

Afterwards, Ehrlichman told newsmen he did not know whether the President was aware of the nature of the transaction of the funds.

McClellan also revealed that former CIA Director Richard Helms told former Acting FBI Director L. Patrick Gray 3rd June 22, 1972 that the CIA was not implicated E in the Watergate break-in and that no covert operations would be compromised by an FBI investigation.

(It had been revealed earlier that Haldeman, in a June 23, 1972 meeting with Ehrlichman, Helms and Deputy CIA Director Walters, had told Walters to inform Gray that covert CIA operations in Mexico might be jeopardized by FBI investigators. According to additional information revealed by Rep. Lucien Nedzi (D, Mich.) May 30, Helms told F Haldeman at the June 23 meeting what he had told Gray the day before. Nedzi's Armed Services Subcommittee on Intelligence was also investigating the CIA.)

Ehrlichman told reporters after Walters met with Gray (June 23) that Walters told the White House the CIA would not be imperiled by an FBI investigation. But, Ehrlichman continued, the President did not believe Walters, although he did authorize Gray to conduct a full G investigation.

"The President told me then that he still personally believed and feared that the FBI investigation might harm the agency [CIA]."

"He [Nixon] said he believed the CIA would be making a mistake if it pretended

A an investigation would not disclose some of its current operations. He said he hoped the general and other CIA management were not covering up for their subordinates," Ehrlichman said.

"The President said substantially: a man makes a grave mistake in covering up for subordinates. That was President Truman's error in the [Alger] Hiss case when he instructed the FBI not to cooperate," Ehrlichman said.

B *Haldeman denies cover-up try*—H. R. Haldeman, former chief of staff to President Nixon, appeared before the McClellan subcommittee May 31. His testimony paralleled Ehrlichman's remarks the day before, contradicted the CIA, and left the subcommittee's members dissatisfied.

Haldeman denied "categorically" that he had engaged in any attempt to cover-up the Watergate break-in. He disputed Deputy CIA Director Walters' version of the June 23, 1972 White House meeting which dealt with the question of covert CIA operations in Mexico that might have been compromised by an FBI investigation.

C However, he acknowledged that CIA Director Helms in the June 23 meeting "assured us that there was no CIA involvement in the Watergate and also that he had no concern from the CIA's viewpoint regarding any possible connections of Watergate personnel with the Bay of Pigs."

D Haldeman said the June 23 meeting was ordered by the President as a result of a report by former White House Counsel John W. Dean 3rd that "the FBI had requested guidance regarding some aspects" of the Watergate case that might concern the CIA.

Haldeman said after reading Dean's report he suggested Nixon call the meeting. At the meeting "Gen. Walters was asked to meet with [L. Patrick] Gray of the FBI to insure that any unrelated covert operations of the CIA or any unrelated national security activities which had been previously undertaken by some of the Watergate principals, not be compromised in the process of the Watergate investigation and the attendant publicity and political furor. This was done with no intent or desire to impede or cover up any aspect of the Watergate investigation itself. Any other actions taken or suggestions made by others were without my knowledge and without the knowledge of the President. I believe all my actions were proper, in accord with the President's instructions and clearly in the national interest."

E Sen. John O. Pastore (D, R.I.) was dissatisfied with Haldeman's testimony and complained of "glaring inconsistencies" between the testimony of Haldeman and Ehrlichman and the testimony of CIA officials Walters and former Deputy Director Robert E. Cushman.

G Pastore said Haldeman had not made it clear how the FBI investigation could have been related to the abortive CIA-sponsored invasion of Cuba in 1962, even though some of the Watergate conspira-

tors had been involved in both. He said the Watergate-Bay of Pigs connection seemed "a little farfetched."

McClellan said he was unable to understand why Haldeman and Ehrlichman had not gone directly to Helms about CIA operations that might be endangered.

He said Haldeman's answers to questions regarding the June 22, 1972 conversation between Helms and Gray "were somewhat vague" and "not entirely satisfactory."

"It seemed to me that if the purpose of it [the June 23 meeting] was to find out of any CIA involvement or any adverse results to it by reason of continuation of this investigation, they had Helms there and they could have asked him directly."

Ehrlichman denies call to Cushman— Some of Ehrlichman's testimony before the McClellan subcommittee resulted in a contradiction with what had been said earlier by former CIA Deputy Director Cushman.

Cushman had said May 11 in a sworn statement and in testimony before House and Senate panels investigating the role of the CIA in the break-in of the office of the former psychiatrist of former Pentagon Papers trial defendant Daniel Ellsberg Sept. 3-4, 1971: "About 7 July 1971 Mr. John Ehrlichman of the White House called me and stated that Howard Hunt was a bona fide employee, a consultant on security matters, and that Hunt would come to see me and request assistance which Mr. Ehrlichman requested that I give."

Ehrlichman said May 30, "I can flatly say that I do not have even the faintest recollection of having done so. I can say with assurance that any call to the CIA is the kind of call that I usually have little or no difficulty remembering."

Ehrlichman admitted receiving a call from Cushman in August 1971 requesting that CIA aid to Hunt be ended. Ehrlichman said he readily agreed when he learned Hunt claimed to be working for the White House.

In a prepared statement for the McClellan subcommittee which was made public, Ehrlichman said he did not learn of the burglary of Ellsberg's psychiatrist's office until about a week after it occurred. He said he had not told the President of the break-in and that the President had learned of it "relatively recently."

In response to the Ehrlichman denial, Cushman told a news conference at Marine Corps headquarters near Washington May 31 "a painstaking" search of CIA records "turned up" minutes of a daily CIA staff meeting for July 8, 1971. Cushman said he had mentioned at the meeting a conversation with Ehrlichman the day before about giving aid to E. Howard Hunt.

According to Cushman, the initial conversation with Ehrlichman went along the lines of "Here's Mr. Hunt; he works for us; he'll be around to see you."

Cushman said there was nothing improper about Ehrlichman's call, as Ehrlichman had said nothing about what Hunt wanted.

Cushman indicated he had given the minutes of the CIA staff meeting to the "necessary Congressional committees."

CIA memos dispute security issue. Central Intelligency Agency memoranda released by the Senate Appropriations Committee's Subcommittee on Intelligence Operations June 3 showed that key White House officials were not worried about danger to national security by Federal Bureau of Investigation probes of the Watergate break-in. Rather, they were concerned over the massive political implications of a public airing of the scandal.

The memos, written for the most part by Deputy CIA Director Vernon A. Walters, recollected a series of meetings in June–July 1972 that he held with former presidential aides H. R. Haldeman, John D. Ehrlichman, and John W. Dean 3rd as well as former Acting FBI Director L. Patrick Gray 3rd, in which the ramifications of Watergate were discussed.

In a memo dated June 28, 1972, Walters described a White House meeting held five days before, attended by Walters, Haldeman, Ehrlichman, and then CIA Director Richard Helms.

At the meeting Walters was asked by Haldeman to talk to Gray and suggest that, since five suspects had already been arrested, the FBI not push its inquiries into Watergate, especially in Mexico. This was done over Helms' assurances that the CIA was not implicated in the affair. Helms even noted he had spoken to Gray the day before about this issue.

Haldeman's reasoning was that the FBI investigation could lead to a "lot of important people" and that "the whole affair was getting embarrassing and it was the President's wish that Walters call on Gray." (In a cover note submitted by Walters along with the documents, the Haldeman statement, "it is the President's wish," was disclaimed. Walters said the "thought was implicit in my mind. I did not, however, correct the memo since it was for my use only."

In another memorandum dated June 28, 1972, Walters detailed the Haldeman-instigated meeting with Gray. As per Haldeman's request, Walters warned Gray that continued FBI investigation into Mexican aspects of Watergate "could trespass" on covert CIA operations and that it would be best if it tapered off. Gray, noting "this was a most awkward matter to come up during an election year," said he would see what could be done.

Other Walters memoranda dealt with private meetings he had with Dean June 26 and 28, 1972. At the first meeting, Walters rejected a request by Dean that the CIA provide bail and salaries for the Watergate conspirators, warning that such news would be quickly leaked and "the scandal would be 10 times greater."

The second meeting was similar, with Walters again warning Dean that CIA involvement in Watergate was too risky. "Intervention such as he [Dean] suggested could transform it [Watergate] into a high megaton hydrogen bomb. . . . Direct intervention by the agency would be electorally mortal if it became known and chances of keeping it secret until the election were almost nil," the memo said.

Further Walters memoranda told of a July 6, 1972 meeting with Gray following a phone conversation between the men the previous evening, in which Gray said he would need written authorization to curb the FBI investigation.

At the July 6 meeting, Walters recounted what was said at the June 23 White House meeting, although he did not mention Haldeman and Ehrlichman by name. Walters also told Gray how he had rejected Dean's requests for CIA help in a cover-up.

Gray in turn related to Walters that he had warned then-Attorney General Richard Kleindienst and Haldeman and Ehrlichman the FBI investigation would have to continue. Gray told the latter two he would prefer to resign but that it would raise questions that would be injurious to the President.

"He [Gray] did not see why he or I should jeopardize the integrity of our organizations to protect some mid-level White House figures who had acted imprudently. . . . He felt it important that the President should be protected from his would-be-protectors."

At a July 12, 1972 meeting between Gray and Walters, Gray said he had been pressured by key officials (he did not name them) to force Harold H. Titus Jr., U.S. attorney for the District of Columbia, to stop his efforts at subpoenaing the financial records of the Republican re-election committee. Gray said he had declined to help. Gray also related to Walters a conversation—reported earlier—he had had with the President.

Other information in the memoranda: Dean told Walters in their June 26, 1972 meeting that Dean suspected that Bernard L. Barker, later convicted for the Watergate break-in, "had been involved in a clandestine entry into the Chilean embassy" in Washington. Walters replied that none of the Watergate suspects had been on the CIA payroll for at least two years.

One memorandum written by CIA Director James R. Schlesinger, dated Feb. 9, 1973, indicated he had received a phone call from Dean, who expressed concern about a pending Senate Foreign Relations Committee investigation into International Telephone and Telegraph (ITT) in connection with the "Chilean problem." Dean warned that the "investigation could be rather explosive." Schlesinger noted he did not share Dean's concern since the CIA was in no way involved.

IRS

Political pressure on IRS confirmed. Former Internal Revenue Service (IRS) Commissioner Randolph W. Thrower revealed a 1970 Administration plan to launch an IRS investigation of radical organizations and individuals in a *Washington Post* report June 27, 1973. Thrower resigned his post in January 1971 after he had successfully resisted White House pressure on him to hire John J. Caulfield, implicated in the Watergate cover-up, and G. Gordon Liddy, convicted Watergate conspirator, to direct the investigations.

The Administration's "strong pressure" to hire Caulfield and Liddy was relayed repeatedly to him by Charls E. Walker, then undersecretary of the Treasury, from a person "high in the White House," Thrower said. (An unidentified *Washington Post* source Robert Greene, a *Newsday* reporter, was Nixon's chief domestic affairs adviser, issued the order.)

Thrower said he rejected the bid to name Caulfield as director of the Bureau of Alcohol, Tobacco and Firearms in August-September 1970. A suggestion that Liddy be named to the same post was rejected in October 1970, Thrower said.

(After leaving the White House in March 1972, Caulfield worked for the Committee to Re-elect the President for two months and then joined the staff of the bureau's enforcement division. He was named acting assistant director for enforcement July 1, 1972, a post he resigned May 24, 1973.)

Caulfield's name was again mentioned in December 1970 when the Administration asked that he be named director of the enforcement division of the bureau. (Authority for the bureau, at that time under the IRS, was shifted to the Treasury Department.)

Also in December 1970, Thrower said, the White House pressured him to make the bureau's enforcement division "a personal police force" reporting directly to him as part of a crackdown on "subversive organizations allegedly engaged in acts of terrorism." Although he resisted this suggestion, Thrower admitted acquiescing in a White House plan to set up an IRS unit, the Special Service Group, to conduct tax audits on radical groups and individuals. Thrower insisted that both right and left wing extremist groups were investigated.

As other witnesses before the Watergate hearings had testified, Thrower said political conditions in the country, as perceived by the Nixon Administration, justified these special measures.

"You've got to go back to the atmosphere that existed at that time in early 1970. There was great concern in the country about the use of explosives and firearms by subversive groups. [The Special Service Group] was set up partly in response to the wave of subversive bombings that was just reaching its peak then," Thrower declared.

One of the memos submitted June 27 to the Senate Watergate hearings by former White House counsel Dean revealed Administration displeasure with Thrower's efforts to balk the politicization of the IRS. The memo, written by Dean based on "material provided to me by Caulfield," outlined a plan to make "the IRS politically responsive to the White House." Although the memo was written after Thrower had left the IRS, Dean termed Thrower "a total captive of the Democratic assistant commissioners. In the end, he was actively fighting both Treasury and the White House," according to the memo.

"In brief, the lack of key Republican bureaucrats at high levels precludes the initiation of policies which would be proper and politically advantageous. Practically every effort to proceed in sensitive areas is met with resistance, delay and the threat of derogatory exposure," Dean wrote.

A Thrower report, dated Sept. 19, 1970, submitted to the Watergate hearings by Dean, to Tom Charles Huston, a member of the Special Service Group, stated that data on 1,025 organizations and 4,300 individuals had been completed. "Enforcement action" on 26 groups and 43 persons had resulted, Thrower said.

Dean also revealed that a politically motivated IRS audit of the tax returns of Robert Greene, a Newsday reporter, was requested by Caulfield. Greene had headed a team of reporters investigating President Nixon's friend, Charles G. Rebozo.

Dean tells of Nixon's plans to use IRS. The Senate Select Committee on Presidential Campaign Activities resumed its televised hearings on Watergate June 25–29, 1973. The week's only witness was former presidential counsel John W. Dean 3rd. The June 27 session was highlighted by the release of the list of the Administration's political "enemies" and Dean's testimony that the White House had tried to "politicize" the Internal Revenue Service. Among the documents Dean submitted in evidence were lists "several inches thick" of Nixon's "political enemies."

The "Opponents List and Political Enemies Project" turned over to the Senate committee, Dean said, was compiled beginning in 1971 by various Administration officials and was frequently updated.

In one of the documents, written by Dean Aug. 16, 1971, intended to accompany the undated master list of opponents, Dean suggested ways in which "we can use the available federal machinery to screw our political enemies." Methods proposed included Administration manipulation of "grant availability, federal contracts, litigation, prosecution, etc."

Dean testified that the memo was sent to then-White House Chief of Staff H. R. Haldeman and John D. Ehrlichman, then the President's adviser for domestic affairs, for approval. Dean said he did not know if the plan became operational; however, subsequent memos, also submitted to the committee, indicated that the plan was adopted.

Although Dean later recommended that the Administration utilize Internal Revenue Service (IRS) audits to harass political enemies, other documents which were provided to the committee showed that the White House had been unable to win IRS cooperation. An undated memo, submitted by Dean, identified "the problem: Lack of guts and effort. The Republican appointees appear afraid and unwilling to do anything with the IRS that would be politically helpful. For example: We have been unable to crack down on the multitude of tax exempt foundations that feed left-wing political causes. We have been unable to obtain information in the possession of IRS regarding our political enemies. We have been unable to stimulate audits of persons who would be audited. Walters [IRS Commissioner Johnnie M.] should be told that discreet political action and investigations are a firm requirement and responsibility on his part."

In the August 1971 memo, Dean wrote: "I feel it is important that we keep our targets limited for several reasons: (1) A low visibility of the project is imperative; (2) It will be easier to accomplish something real if we don't overexpand our efforts; and (3) We can learn more about how to operate such an activity if we start small and build."

The master list of political enemies was prepared by the office of then White House counsel Charles W. Colson, Dean said. A condensed list of 20 prime political enemies slated for reprisals was also produced by Colson's office, according to Dean. Others named by Dean who had direct input in the lists were former White House aide Lyn Nofziger and Haldeman aide Gordon Strachan.

The larger list, divided in categories, included 10 Democratic senators, all 12 black House members, more than 50 newspaper and television reporters, prominent businessmen and labor leaders, and entertainers. Another list included large and small contributors to Sen. Edmund S. Muskie's (D, Me) presidential campaign.

2nd 'enemies' list revealed—The Joint Committee on Internal Revenue Taxation disclosed in a report Dec. 20 that the White House gave the Internal Revenue Service (IRS) in September 1972 a list of 575 persons "to see what type of information could be developed concerning the people on the list." The report was based on testimony from Johnnie Walters, then IRS commissioner, who said he received the list from former White House counsel John W. Dean 3rd as an intermediary for former Nixon aide John D. Ehrlichman.

Walters told the panel he apprised Treasury Secretary George P. Shultz of the matter and was directed to "do nothing" about it. The panel's own investigation concluded that there was "no evidence" that the IRS had acted on the matter and that, in fact, there was evidence some persons on the list should have received closer scrutiny by the IRS.

The list, composed primarily of contributors to Sen. George McGovern's Democratic presidential campaign and of McGovern staffers, was separate from the first White House "enemies" list previously disclosed by Dean to the Senate Watergate committee.

Colson sought IRS aid. Charles W. Colson, then President Nixon's special counsel, directed other White House aides to ask the Internal Revenue Service (IRS) for the names of contributors to the National Council of Senior Citizens, a Washington lobbying group which Colson described as an "outfit giving us trouble," according to a court document filed Aug. 2.

According to Roy Kinsey, a former aide to White House Counsel John W. Dean 3rd, Colson also ordered inquiries into the possibility of withdrawing tax exempt status from two other organizations regarded by the Nixon Administration as "political enemies"—Common Cause and Vietnam Veterans Against the War.

Kinsey's statements were contained in a deposition in connection with a lawsuit brought by the Center for Corporate Responsibility. The center claimed that it had been the target of political reprisals by the IRS, which had revoked its tax exempt status.

Colson's instructions to Dean were passed to him, Kinsey said. His contact at the IRS on "sensitive" matters was Roger V. Barth, deputy chief counsel, according to Kinsey.

He was unable to obtain information on the senior citizens group, Kinsey reported. He did not reveal what action was taken against the Vietnam veterans but he said the Common Cause issue was not pursued because the group had obtained only a limited tax exempt status.

IRS to disband activists study unit—The IRS announced Aug. 9 that it was dismantling a special division that had studied liberal and radical organizations for possible violations of tax laws. The group was created in August 1969 as a result of Senate investigations of extremist groups, according to Donald C. Alexander, IRS commissioner.

Testimony before the Senate Watergate committee had linked the IRS unit to planned White House reprisals against political enemies.

Alexander said that since 1972 the IRS unit had been limited to investigations of "tax rebels," which he defined as those "tax-resistance organizations and those individuals who publicly advocate noncompliance with the tax laws."

Political use of IRS detailed. Sen. Lowell P. Weicker Jr. (R, Conn.), a member of the Senate Watergate Committee, accused the Internal Revenue Service April 8, 1974 of acting as a "public lending library" for White House efforts to aid political friends and harass political enemies.

Appearing at a joint hearing of Senate Judiciary Subcommittees on Constitutional Rights and Administrative Practice and Procedure, and the Foreign Relations Subcommittee on Surveillance, Weicker disclosed a collection of documents, gathered by the Watergate Committee, showing politically motivated tax audits, undercover White House investigations and military spying on civilians.

One 1969 IRS memo describing the creation of a special activists "study unit" advised that the unit's function of examining tax returns of "ideological, militant, subversive, radical or other" organizations must not become publicly known, since disclosure "might embarrass the Administration." The unit was abolished in August 1973 after, according to Weicker, assembling tax data on about 10,000 persons.

According to the documents, former presidential counsel John W. Dean 3rd and former White House and Treasury Department official John J. Caulfield—both involved in the Watergate coverup—were central characters in political use of the IRS.

A 1971 set of Dean-Caulfield memos suggested that the Administration was interested in helping evanglist Billy Graham and actor John Wayne, both supporters of President Nixon, with their tax problems. One memo referred to a "backdoor" copy of an audit on Graham and promised similar material on Wayne. Dean was later supplied with audit histories of several entertainment figures "whose economic condition is similar to that of John Wayne."

Another 1971 series of memos from Caufield to Dean outlined possible measures to conduct "discreet" audits on Emile DeAntonio, producer of "Millhouse: A White Comedy," a film satirizing Nixon, and on the film's distributors. Caulfield also referred to the release of derogatory Federal Bureau of Investigation data on DeAntonio.

Council to study IRS policies. The Administrative Conference of the United States announced May 16, 1974 it would undertake a study of the operations of the Internal Revenue Service. The study was to cover confidentiality of taxpayer data, collection and settlement procedures, civil penalties, processing of citizen complaints and selection of returns for audit.

The conference, an independent federal agency, was set up to identify the causes of inefficiency, delay and unfairness in the administrative proceedings of all federal agencies.

Some of these areas had come under question May 15 by the Tax Reform Research Group, a Ralph Nader organization. Of the more than two million delinquent taxpayer accounts for fiscal 1972, the group said, about one million led to seizure of assets, 500,000 to payment in full and the remainder were handled by other methods. "Who took advantage of the arrangements?" it asked. "Do the poor, the minorities, the foreign born get installment plans, abatements and so on in proportion to the number of delinquent accounts they represented, or were the arrangements more often made for wealthier, better educated taxpayers?"

The Nader group was critical of a recent General Accounting Office (GAO) study of a sampling of randomly selected delinquent accounts for the 1972 year. The study concluded that the IRS procedures had been applied with consistency. The Nader group considered the study "inadequate."

Evidence on IRS misuse released. The House Judiciary Committee July 16, 1974 released evidence collected in its impeachment inquiry concerning possible White House attempts to misuse the Internal Revenue Service for political gain. The committee previously released eight other volumes of evidence on the Watergate affair.

The ninth volume detailed repeated attempts by the White House, some successful, to gain confidential tax information on individuals from the IRS and to use its tax-return audits to hurt political enemies and protect friends of the President.

Among the evidence was testimony from both of the Nixon Administration's first two commissioners of Internal Revenue that they had offered their resignations in protest against what they considered improper White House pressures and actions. One of them, Randolph W. Thrower, did resign in January 1971 after he tried without success to see Nixon to warn him, as Thrower put it in an affidavit, "that any suggestion of introduction of political influence into the IRS would be very damaging to him and his administration, as well as to the revenue system and the general public interest."

Thrower's successor, Johnnie Walters, testified that former White House counsel John W. Dean 3rd gave him a list in September 1972 of 490 supporters of the Democratic presidential nominee, Sen. George McGovern (D, S.D.), and asked the service to inspect their taxes. Walters said he advised Dean "that compliance with the request would be disastrous for the IRS and for the administration."

Walters said he also had intense pressure from Nixon aide John D. Ehrlichman in the summer of 1972 to create a tax problem for Lawrence F. O'Brien, then Democratic national chairman. O'Brien had been audited and his return closed, Walters said, but Ehrlichman continued to press for action, with some of the requests relayed through then-Treasury Secretary George P. Shultz. Walters said he told Ehrlichman over the telephone, with Shultz on an extension, that the IRS file on O'Brien's return was closed. Ehrlichman was said to have replied angrily, "I'm goddamn tired of your foot-dragging tactics." Walters said he then had told Shultz "that he could have my job any time he wanted it."

The committee included in its data Ehrlichman's statement at a closed hearing of the Senate Watergate committee, that IRS personnel "down in the woodwork" had "75 well-selected reasons why they shouldn't audit him [O'Brien], and they weren't having any of the same reasons with regard to Republicans at that time, and I thought there was a little unevenhandedness." "I wanted them to turn up something and send him to jail before the election," Ehrlichman told the Senate committee, "and unfortunately it didn't materialize."

The IRS did pass along to the White House a report requested in March 1970 by Clark Mollenhoff, then White House special counsel, on the taxes of Gerald Wallace, brother of Gov. George C. Wallace (D, Ala.). Mollenhoff's affidavit said he sought the report only after Nixon aide H. R. Haldeman assured him "the report was to be obtained at the request of the President." Mollenhoff delivered the report to Haldeman, he said, but later was accused by Haldeman, among others, of being the source of a "leak" of derogatory material from the report to columnist Jack Anderson.

Anderson's column, apparently based on the leaked report, appeared three weeks before the Alabama gubernatorial primary in 1970. Mollenhoff asserted in the affidavit that the leak came from "the highest White House level." (Anderson said he had been shown the report by the late Murray Chotiner, a long-time political adviser to Nixon.)

Confidential information from the IRS was obtained on several occasions by Dean, according to the evidence. In September 1971 Dean received data on an IRS audit of evangelist Billy Graham, a friend of Nixon's, which he relayed to Haldeman with a note, "Can we do anything to help?" Haldeman's answer was, "No, it's already covered." In October 1971 Dean obtained a copy of a tax audit of actor John Wayne, a supporter of Nixon. The evidence included Dean's testimony at a closed hearing of the Senate Watergate committee that Nixon requested that tax audits "be turned off on friends of his."

Other evidence indicated Nixon's desire to have the IRS harass left-wing organizations. "Nearly 18 months ago, the President indicated a desire for IRS to move against leftist organizations taking advantage of tax shelters," White House aide Tom Huston wrote Haldeman in September 1970. Huston added he had pressed the IRS on the issue "to no avail."

Nixon's interest in pressing for probes of his political opponents was indicated in a transcript of a Sept. 15, 1972 White House tape. According to the text, Haldeman told the President that Dean was "moving ruthlessly on the investigation of McGovern people, Kennedy stuff, and all that too . . . and Dean's working the thing through IRS. . . ."

The latter part of the tape was missing from the evidence because of presidential defiance of a committee subpoena. The section had been turned over to U.S. Judge John Sirica but was in litigation on the issue of executive privilege.

Dean had told the Senate Watergate committee that the conversation turned eventually to "use of the Internal Revenue Service to attack our enemies." Dean said he cited the White House lack of "clout" at the IRS because of Democratic holdovers in the agency and "the President seemed somewhat annoyed and said that the Democratic administrations had used this tool well, and after the election we would get people in these agencies who would be responsive to White House requirements."

Dean told Nixon on March 13, 1973, according to another transcript, that "we have a couple of sources" at the IRS and "we can get right in and get what we need."

One of the sources was revealed in the committee's evidence to be Vernon D. Acree, assistant commissioner of Internal Revenue, who was promoted in April 1972 to be commissioner of customs.

Contrasting IRS investigations—The committee's report pointed out the disparity in treatment accorded Nixon's friend Charles 'Bebe' Rebozo and Lawrence O'Brien, the former Democratic national chairman, both of whom were the subjects of investigations by the Internal Revenue Service. During the course of the IRS investigation of the Hughes organization that turned up the $100,000 campaign gift to Rebozo, it was revealed that O'Brien's public relations firm had been paid a "substantial" sum by Hughes Tool Co. in 1970.

The report said that the committee took testimony from IRS officials, who said that O'Brien's tax returns were audited and, except for a small deficiency, they were found in order. In late 1971 or early 1972 top IRS officials decided that with the election approaching, it would be wise to postpone until after the election investigations that were "politically sensitive." Because of this policy, the report said, the IRS did not interview Rebozo or F. Donald Nixon until six months after the election. In contrast, "the IRS . . . did succumb to pressures from the Administration and interviewed O'Brien before the 1972 election," the report stated.

In addition, the committee recounted testimony by Ehrlichman that "I wanted them [IRS] to turn up something and send [O'Brien] to jail before the election and unfortunately it didn't materialize." Ehrlichman similarly testified to what he told then-IRS Commissioner Johnnie Walters about what he (Ehrlichman) thought about the audit, ". . . it was my first crack at [Walters] . . . this was the first chance I had to tell the commissioner what a crappy job he had done. . . ."

IRS watched 'subversives.' The National Council of Churches and the Urban League were on the list of potentially subversive organizations the Internal Revenue Service kept under tax surveillance in 1969–73, according to Tax Reform Research Group Nov. 17, 1974. The group, a Washington-based affiliate of Ralph Nader's Public Citizen, obtained the list as part of IRS data released to it in a Freedom of Information Act case.

According to the data, the IRS set up a

special group, eventually named the Special Services Staff (SSS), July 2, 1969, one day after a White House aide, Tom Charles Huston, informed the IRS that President Nixon wanted the agency "to move against leftist organizations." The SSS was to monitor tax records and keep watch over "ideological, militant, subversive, radical and similar type organizations," the documents revealed.

Files were collected on 2,873 organizations and 8,585 individuals before the SSS was dismantled in August 1973. A final report said 78% of these were found to have "no apparent revenue significance or potential." The other 22% of the files were said to have been preserved. No serious tax cheating was reported discovered by the operation, which produced about $100,000 in additional tax revenues.

Congressional Investigations

CIA destroyed its Watergate tapes. The Central Intelligence Agency destroyed tape recordings related to the Watergate break-in one day after it had acknowledged receipt of a letter from Senate Majority Leader Mike Mansfield (D, Mont.) asking the CIA to save any Watergate evidence it might have, National Broadcasting Co. (NBC) News reported Jan. 31, 1974.

William E. Colby, director of the CIA, Jan. 29 had admitted the destruction of all but one of its tapes from the Watergate period. A tape recording of the June 22, 1971 conversation between E. Howard Hunt Jr., then a White House investigator, and Marine Gen. Robert B. Cushman Jr., then deputy director of the CIA, had "survived normal procedures of destruction because it was put into a separate drawer somehow," Colby said. All other tapes had been destroyed periodically "when the storage space got too full," Colby added.

According to NBC, Mansfield had sent requests to various federal agencies asking them to save any material pertinent to Watergate. A receipt in Mansfield's office files showed that a high-ranking CIA official had signed for the letter Jan. 17, 1973. CIA tapes were destroyed the following day, NBC reported.

Presidential power assailed. A panel of experts in public administration reported to the Senate Watergate Committee March 20 that many of the abuses associated with the Watergate scandals could be traced to a "centralization of power in the presidency," under which "the prevailing view is that the whole government should be run from the White House."

The report, by a 12-member panel from the National Academy of Public Administration, had been commissioned by the Senate committee in preparation for the final report on its investigations.

While noting that many of the problems in the federal government had begun in earlier administrations, the report stated that Watergate was an "aberration" and culmination of "converging trends" which

had seriously damaged the image of the public service.

The report said the "most alarming" of the Watergate disclosures had been the misuse of law enforcement and intelligence agencies against supposed "enemies" and the increasingly "partisan climate" in the Justice Department. The panel urged that Congress give "special attention and oversight" to the Federal Bureau of Investigation, the Central Intelligence Agency and the Internal Revenue Service. The panel also urged Congress to prohibit the White House from conducting "intelligence activities."

The Justice Department should be "divorced from politics," the report said, and the attorney general "should be precluded from advising the President in the latter's political or personal capacity."

CIA's involvement in Watergate found. A report by the Watergate Committee's minority staff on the Central Intelligence Agency's involvement in the Watergate scandal was made public July 2. The 43-page document had been prepared under the direction of Sen. Howard H. Baker Jr. (R, Tenn.), the committee's vice chairman.

While the preparers of the report expressly refrained from drawing conclusions, they did reveal, among other things, that the CIA had used a Washington public relations firm as a "cover" for agents outside the U.S., that the agency had destroyed its own records despite a request by Senate majority leader Mike Mansfield (D, Mont.) to keep them intact, that a CIA agent might have functioned as a domestic operative in violation of the agency's charter, that there were unanswered questions about the agency's fore-knowledge of the 1971 break-in at Daniel Ellsberg's psychiatrist's office, and that a CIA employe fought within the agency against withholding data from the Watergate committee. In addition, the report detailed instances in which the CIA attempted to frustrate committee investigators by refusing to make its employes available as witnesses and by ignoring, resisting or refusing requests for documents and other materials.

■ The report said that the public relations firm of Robert R. Mullen & Co. had employed convicted Watergate conspirator E. Howard Hunt Jr., a retired CIA operative, at the time of the burglary of the Watergate headquarters of the Democratic National Committee. Mullen, the report said, was serving as a cover for two CIA agents stationed abroad, and employed retired CIA agents.

Robert F. Bennett, head of Mullen, in the weeks following the Watergate break-in, "was supplying information to the CIA about many aspects of the Watergate incident and was at that time serving as liaison between Hunt and [Watergate conspirator G. Gordon] Liddy, [and] there is no indication that these facts were disclosed to the FBI, the report said.

■ The report also dealt with the CIA's knowledge of the Sept. 3, 1971 break-in at the Los Angeles offices of Daniel Ells-

berg's psychiatrist, Dr. Lewis J. Fielding. At the request of John Ehrlichman, the CIA had supplied a camera to Hunt, who used it to take photographs near Fielding's office. According to the report, the CIA developed the negatives, realized they were "casing" photographs, and terminated its assistance to Hunt. In testimony, however, agency officials said that aid to Hunt had been discontinued because of his escalating demands for agency assistance.

The report contradicted the CIA's claims that it had no contact with Hunt after Aug. 31, 1971. "Recent testimony and secret documents indicate that Hunt had extensive contact with the CIA after" Aug. 31, 1971, that he had a "large role" in the preparation of a CIA psychological profile of Ellsberg completed in November 1971, and that Hunt had other contacts with the CIA.

The report said the committee asked to see the memorandums of the psychiatrist, but the CIA refused.

■ The report expressed concern at the activities of CIA operative Lee R. Pennington, who assisted the wife of Watergate burglar James W. McCord Jr.—a former CIA employe—in destroying papers at her home shortly after the Watergate break-in. There was an effort by agency officials, the report noted, to keep from the FBI, the Watergate committee and other Congressional committees information about Pennington's visit.

Subsequently, when FBI agents asked about "Mr. Pennington," the CIA furnished information about a former employe with a similar name—the wrong Mr. Pennington. In January 1974, the agency's former director of security attempted to exclude material on the Pennington visit from a CIA Watergate file made available to the Watergate and other Congressional committees. Only when a lower echelon security officer protested did the agency reverse itself, the report said. The Pennington material was provided, and the chief of security was reportedly forced to retire.

"The Pennington matter," the report said, apparently "was extremely sensitive . . . because Pennington may have been a domestic agent" in violation of the agency's charter, which forbade intelligence activities in the U.S. However, the report did not make clear what domestic activities might have been involved, although it did contain a passing reference to a CIA file on syndicated columnist Jack Anderson.

In discussions with a CIA psychiatrist who aided them in preparation of the profile, the report said, Hunt and Liddy stated that they wanted to "try Ellsberg in public, render him the 'object of pity as a broken man' and be able to refer to Ellsberg's 'Oedipal complex.'" The psychiatrist, "extremely concerned about Hunt's presence and remarks," ignored Hunt's requests that he not reveal Hunt's activities to anyone else in the CIA and voiced his apprehension to his superiors.

Nixon's misuse of CIA, FBI, IRS charged.
The Senate Select Committee on Presidential Campaign Activities, known as "the Watergate Committee" or "the Ervin Committee," released the final report July 13, 1974 on its investigation of the Watergate and other scandals related to the 1972 presidential campaign. It recommended the following reforms of the CIA, FBI, and IRS:

The Committee recommends that the appropriate Congressional oversight committees should more closely supervise the operations and internal regulations of the intelligence and law enforcement "community." In particular, these committees should continually examine the relations between federal law enforcement and intelligence agencies and the White House, and promptly determine if any revision of law is necessary relating to the jurisdiction or activities of these agencies.

From its beginning, the Central Intelligence Agency has been prohibited from performing police and internal security functions within the United States....

Notwithstanding this clear and long-standing prohibition, the select committee found that the White House sought and achieved CIA aid for the Plumbers and unsuccessfully sought to involve the CIA in the Watergate cover-up....

As for law enforcement agencies, testimony of the former acting director of the Federal Bureau of Investigation, Patrick Gray, as well as evidence received by the Committee of efforts by the White House to interfere with the IRS, indicate that similar oversight functions should be strengthened with regard to the FBI, and IRS and similar agencies.

House committee votes for impeachment.
The House Judiciary Committee recessed July 30 after approving three articles of impeachment. President Nixon was charged with obstruction of justice in connection with the Watergate scandal, abuse of presidential powers and attempting to impede the impeachment process by defying committtee subpoenas for evidence. The first and second articles specified his misuse of the investigative agencies:

Judiciary Committee's Articles of Impeachment

Article I *(Approved 27-11)*
In his conduct of the office of President of the United States, Richard M. Nixon, in violation of his constitutional oath faithfully to execute the office of President of the United States and, to the best of his ability, preserve, protect, and defend the Constitution of the United States, and in violation of his constitutional duty to take care that the laws be faithfully executed, has prevented, obstructed, and impeded the administration of justice, in that:

On June 17, 1972, and prior thereto, agents of the Committee for the Re-election of the President:

Committed unlawful entry of the headquarters of the Democratic National Committee in Washington, District of Columbia, for the purpose of securing political intelligence. Subsequent thereto, Richard M. Nixon, using the powers of his high office, engaged personally and through his subordinates and agents in a course of conduct or plan designed to delay, impede, and obstruct the investigation of such unlawful entry; to cover up, conceal and protect those responsible; and to conceal the existence and scope of other unlawful covert activities.

The means used to implement this course of conduct or plan have included one or more of the following:

1. Making or causing to be made false or misleading statements to lawfully authorized investigative officers and employes of the United States.

2. Withholding relevant and material evidence or information from lawfully authorized investigative officers and employes of the United States.

3. Approving, condoning, acquiescing in, and counseling witnesses with respect to the giving of false or misleading statements to lawfully authorized investigative officers and employes of the United States and false or misleading testimony in duly instituted judicial and Congressional proceedings.

4. Interfering or endeavoring to interfere with the conduct of investigations by the Department of Justice of the United States, the Federal Bureau of Investigation, the office of Watergate Special Prosecution Force, and Congressional committees.

5. Approving, condoning and acquiescing in the surreptitious payment of substantial sums of money for the purpose of obtaining the silence or influencing the testimony of witnesses, potential witnesses or individuals who participated in such illegal entry and other illegal activities.

6. Endeavoring to misuse the Central Intelligence Agency, an agency of the United States.

7. Disseminating information received from officers of the Department of Justice of the United States to subjects of investigations conducted by lawfully authorized investigative officers and employes of the United States, for the purpose of aiding and assisting such subjects in their attempts to avoid criminal liability.

8. Making false or misleading public statements for the purpose of deceiving the people of the United States into believing that a thorough and complete investigation had been conducted with respect to allegations of misconduct on the part of personnel of the executive branch of the United States and personnel of the Committee for the Re-election of the President, and that there was no involvement of such personnel in such misconduct: or

9. Endeavoring to cause prospective defendants, and individuals duly tried and convicted, to expect favored treatment and consideration in return for their silence or false testimony, or rewarding individuals for their silence or false testimony.

In all of this, Richard M. Nixon has acted in a manner contrary to his trust as President and subversive of constitutional government, to the great prejudice of the cause of law and justice and to the manifest injury of the people of the United States.

Wherefore Richard M. Nixon, by such conduct, warrants impeachment and trial, and removal from office.

Article II *(Approved 28-10)*
Using the powers of the office of President of the United States, Richard M. Nixon, in violation of his constitutional oath faithfully to execute the office of President of the United States, and to the best of his ability preserve, protect and defend the Constitution of the United States, and in disregard of his constitutional duty to take care that the laws be faithfully executed, has repeatedly engaged in conduct violating the constitutional rights of citizens, impairing the due and proper administration of justice in the conduct of lawful inquiries, of contravening the law of governing agencies of the executive branch and the purposes of these agencies.

This conduct has included one or more of the following:

1. He has, acting personally and through his subordinates and agents, endeavored to obtain from the Internal Revenue Service in violation of the constitutional rights of citizens, confidential information contained in income tax returns for purposes not authorized by law; and to cause, in violation of the constitutional rights of citizens, income tax audits or other income tax investigations to be initiated or conducted in a discriminatory manner.

2. He misused the Federal Bureau of Investigation, the Secret Service and other executive personnel in violation or disregard of the constitutional rights of citizens by directing or authorizing such agencies or personnel to conduct or continue electronic surveillance or other investigations for purposes unrelated to national security, the enforcement of laws or any other lawful function of his office.

He did direct, authorize or permit the use of information obtained thereby for purposes unrelated to national security, the enforcement of laws or any other lawful function of his office. And he did direct the concealment of certain records made by the Federal Bureau of Investigation of electronic surveillance.

3. He has, acting personally and through his subordinates and agents, in violation or disregard of the constitutional rights of citizens, authorized and permitted to be maintained a secret investigative unit within the office of the President, financed in part with money derived from campaign contributions which unlawfully utilized the resources of the Central Intelligence Agency, engaged in covert and unlawful activities, and attempted to prejudice the constitutional right of an accused to a fair trial.

4. He has failed to take care that the laws were faithfully executed by failing to act when he knew or had reason to know that his close subordinates endeavored to impede and frustrate lawful inquiries by duly constituted executive, judicial and legislative entities concerning the unlawful entry into the headquarters of the Democratic National Committee and the cover-up thereof and concerning other unlawful activities including those relating to the confirmation of Richard Kleindienst as Attorney General of the United States, the electronic surveillance of private citizens, the break-in into the offices of Dr. Lewis Fielding and the campaign financing practices of the Committee to Re-Elect the President.

5. In disregard of the rule of law he knowingly misused the executive power by interfering with agencies of the executive branch including the Federal Bureau of Investigation, the Criminal Division and the office of Watergate special prosecution force of the Department of Justice, and the Central Intelligence Agency, in violation of his duty to take care that the laws be faithfully executed.

In all of this Richard M. Nixon has acted in a manner contrary to his trust as President and subversive of constitutional government to the great prejudice of the cause of law and justice and to the manifest injury of the people of the United States.

Wherefore, Richard M. Nixon by such conduct warrants impeachment and trial and removal from office.

House accepts impeachment report—The
House Judiciary Committee's report on its impeachment inquiry of President Nixon was accepted by the House Aug. 20 by a vote of 412–3. The report was submitted to the House by Committee Chairman Peter W. Rodino Jr. (D, N.J.). House Democratic Leader Thomas P. O'Neill Jr. (Mass.) offered a resolution stating that the House "accepts the report," commending the committee for its "conscientious and capable" effort and calling the inquiry "full and complete."

House Republican Leader John J. Rhodes (Ariz.) took the necessary parliamentary step of demanding a second and the resolution was voted without debate. The three votes against it were cast by Reps. Earl F. Landgrebe (R, Ind.), G. V. Montgomery (D, Miss.) and Otto E. Passman (D, La.).

The report thus became part of the official House record. It was published Aug. 22 as House Report 93-1305 and as Part II of the *Congressional Record.*

The committee's 528-page report contained the evidence, which it considered "clear and convincing," on which the committee recommended impeachment of Nixon under three articles on the grounds that he had obstructed justice in the Watergate case, abused his presidential powers for his personal and political benefit and defied Congressional demands for information for its impeachment probe. The report also contained personal statements by all the committee members except chairman Rodino.

The majority and minority opinions were expressed on each article after the listing of evidence.

On Article I, a finding that Nixon participated in a criminal conspiracy to cover up the Watergate burglary, there was a unanimous recommendation of impeachment. The committee had approved the article July 27 during its inquiry by a vote of 27–11. However, on Aug. 5, four days before he resigned, Nixon had released new evidence and the 11 Republicans who voted against the article reversed their stands.

This new evidence was cited by the 11 in their "minority views" of the committee's report. "We know," they said, "that it has been said, and perhaps some will continue to say, that Richard Nixon was 'hounded from office' by his political opponents and media critics. We feel constrained to point out, however, that it was Richard Nixon who impeded the FBI's investigation of the Watergate affair by wrongfully attempting to implicate the Central Intelligence Agency; it was Richard Nixon who created and preserved the evidence of that transgression and who, knowing that it had been subpoenaed by this committee and the special prosecutor, concealed its terrible import, even from his own counsel, until he could do so no longer. And it was a unanimous Supreme Court of the United States, which in an opinion authorized by the Chief Justice whom he appointed, ordered Richard Nixon to surrender that evidence to the special prosecutor, to further the ends of justice. The tragedy that finally engulfed Richard Nixon had many facets. One was the very self-inflicted nature of the harm. It is striking that such an able, experienced and perceptive man, whose ability to grasp the global implications of events little noticed by others may well have been unsurpassed by any of his predecessors, should fail to comprehend the damage that accrued daily to himself, his Administration and to the nation, as day after day, month after month, he imprisoned the truth about his role in the Watergate coverup so long and so tightly within the solitude of his Oval Office that it could not be unleashed without destroying his Presidency."

The majority's report on Article I cited 36 specific items against the President that it said formed "a pattern of undisputed acts" that "cannot otherwise be rationally explained" except as part of a conspiracy to obstruct justice.

"President Nixon's action," the majority said, "resulted in manifest injury to the confidence of the nation and great prejudice to the cause of law and justice, and was subversive of constitutional government. His actions were contrary to his trust as President and unmindful of the solemn duties of his high office. It was this serious violation of Richard M. Nixon's constitutional obligations as President, and not the fact that violations of federal criminal statutes occurred, that lies at the heart of Article I."

All in all, President Nixon's conduct, the majority concluded, "posed a threat to our democratic republic."

On Article II, concerning abuse of presidential power and violation of the oath of office to execute the nation's laws, the report reaffirmed the committee's 28–10 vote for adoption on July 29. The minority of 10 Republicans said they did "deplore in strongest terms the aspects of presidential wrongdoing to which the article is addressed." But they found the article vague and a "catch-all repository for miscellaneous and unrelated Presidential offenses." "It is a far-reaching and dangerous proposition," they said, "that conduct which is in violation of no known law but which is considered by a temporary majority of Congress to be 'improper' because undertaken for 'political' purposes can constitute grounds for impeachment."

The majority view on Article II cited allegations against Nixon of attempted misuse of the Internal Revenue Service, the Federal Bureau of Investigation and other agencies. It concluded that Nixon had "repeatedly used his authority as President to violate the Constitution and the law of the land. In so doing, he violated the obligation that every citizen has to live under the law. But he did more, for it is the duty of the President not merely to live by the law but to see that law faithfully applied. Richard M. Nixon repeatedly and willfully failed to perform that duty. He failed to perform it by authorizing and directing actions that violated the rights of citizens and that interfered with the functioning of executive agencies. And he failed to perform it by condoning and ratifying, rather than acting to stop, actions by his subordinates interfering with the enforcement of the laws."

Blocking of investigation admitted. The presidential statement and tape transcripts that triggered the intense pressure leading to Nixon's resignation August 9, 1974 had been released August 5. They effectively constituted a confession to obstruction of justice—the charge contained in the first article of impeachment voted by the House Judiciary Committee.

The transcripts [See below] covered three meetings with H. R. Haldeman, then White House chief of staff, on June 23, 1972, six days after the Watergate break-in. Informed that the Federal Bureau of Investigation's probe of the break-in was pointing to officials in his re-election campaign, Nixon instructed Haldeman to tell the FBI, "Don't go any further into this case period!"

While Nixon's earlier statements on the Watergate case attributed his concern over the FBI's investigations to national security problems and possible conflicts with the Central Intelligence Agency, the latest transcripts—and Nixon's own statement about them—finally indicated that political considerations had played a major role.

According to the transcripts, Nixon told Haldeman to base the curtailment of FBI activities on possible reopening of questions about the CIA's role in the abortive 1961 "Bay of Pigs" invasion of Cuba (some of the Watergate burglary conspirators had been involved in the CIA operation). Haldeman assured Nixon that the CIA ploy would give L. Patrick Gray, then acting FBI director, sufficient justification to drop the investigation of the "laundering" (through a Mexican lawyer and bank) of the campaign funds used to finance the Watergate operation.

Nixon then told Haldeman that Gray should be instructed—through CIA Director Richard Helms and Deputy Director Vernon A. Walters—to curtail the investigation.

In the written statement announcing release of the transcripts, Nixon referred to other transcripts released earlier (April 29–30), which he said then would "tell it all" concerning his role in Watergate and the cover-up.

But in early May, he continued, he had begun a "preliminary review" of some of the 64 conversations subpoenaed by Watergate special prosecutor Leon Jaworski, including two from June 23, 1972. Nixon said he recognized that the tapes "presented potential problems," but he "did not inform my staff or my counsel of it, or those arguing my case, nor did I amend my submission to the Judiciary Committee. . . ." As a result, those arguing and judging his case were proceeding with "information that was incomplete and in some respects erroneous. This was a serious act of omission for which I take full responsibility and which I deeply regret."

Nixon stated that since the July 24 Supreme Court order that the tapes be surrendered for the Watergate prosecution, he and his counsel had reviewed and analyzed many of the tapes, a process which "made it clear that portions of the tapes of these June 23 conversations are at variance with certain of my previous statements."

These included, Nixon said, the statement of May 22, 1973, in which he recalled that he had been concerned that the FBI's investigation of Watergate might expose "unrelated covert activities" of the CIA or "sensitive national security matters" involving the special White House investigative unit known as the "plumbers." He thus ordered that the FBI "coordinate" its investigation with the CIA. The May 22 statement, he said, was based on his "recollection at the time"—some 11 months after the break in—"plus documentary materials and relevant public testimony of those involved."

In his latest statement, however, Nixon acknowledged that the June 23 tapes showed he had discussed the "political aspects of the situation" at the time he gave the instructions, and that he was "aware of the advantages this course of action would have with respect to limiting possible public exposure of involvement by persons connected with the re-election committee."

Nixon said his review of additional tapes had not revealed other "major inconsistencies with what I have previously submitted," and that he had no reason to believe that there would be others.

Acknowledging that a House vote of impeachment was "virtually a foregone conclusion," Nixon addressed two points of caution to the potential Senate trial: first, as to "what actually happened" as a result of his instructions concerning the FBI, Nixon said Walters had informed Gray that the CIA would not be "compromised" by the FBI's probe. When Gray had expressed concern about "improper attempts to limit his investigation, as the record shows, I told him to press ahead vigorously with his investigation—which he did."

Nixon also urged that "the evidence be

looked at in its entirety, and the events be looked at in perspective." Whatever his mistakes in handling Watergate, Nixon continued, "the basic truth remains that when all the facts were brought to my attention I insisted on a full investigation and prosecution of those guilty." Nixon concluded that the full record "does not justify the extreme step of impeachment and removal of a President."

The transcripts: June 23, 1972

First Meeting: the President and Haldeman in the Oval Office, joined briefly by Press Secretary Ziegler, 10:04–11:39 a.m.

Haldeman turned quickly to the ominous implications of the FBI's investigation of the Watergate break-in:

H. Now, on the investigation, you know the Democratic break-in thing, we're back in the problem area because the FBI is not under control, because Gray doesn't exactly know how to control it and they have—their investigation is now leading into some productive areas—because they've been able to trace the money—not through the money itself—but through the bank sources—the banker. And, and it goes in some directions we don't want it to go. Ah, also there have been some things—like an informant came in off the street to the FBI in Miami who was a photographer or has a friend who is a photographer who developed some films through this guy Barker and the films had pictures of Democratic National Committee letterhead documents and things. So it's things like that that are filtering in. Mitchell came up with yesterday, and John Dean analyzed very carefully last night and concludes, concurs now with Mitchell's recommendation that the only way to solve this, and we're set up beautifully to do it, ah, in that and that—the only network that paid any attention to it last night was NBC—they did a massive story on the Cuban thing.

P. That's right.

H. That the way to handle this now is for us to have Walters call Pat Gray and just say, "stay to hell out of this—this is ah, business here we don't want you to go any further on it." That's not an unusual development, and ah, that would take care of it.

P. What about Pat Gray—you mean Pat Gray doesn't want to?

H. Pat does want to. He doesn't know how to, and he doesn't have, he doesn't have any basis for doing it. Given this, he will then have the basis. He'll call Mark Felt in, and the two of them—and Mark Felt wants to cooperate because he's ambitious—

P. Yeah.

H. He'll call him in and say, "we've got the signal from across the river to put the hold on this." And that will fit rather well because the FBI agents who are working the case, at this point, feel that's what it is.

P. This is CIA? They've traced the money? Who'd they trace it to?

H. Well they've traced it to a name, but they haven't gotten to the guy yet.

P. Would it be somebody here?

H. Ken Dahlberg.

P. Who the hell is Ken Dahlberg?

H. He gave $25,000 in Minnesota and, ah, the check went directly to this guy Barker.

P. It isn't from the committee though, from Stans?

H. Yeah. It is. It's directly traceable and there's some more through some Texas people that went to the Mexican bank which can also be traced to the Mexican bank—They'll get their names today.—and (pause)

P. Well, I mean, there's no way—I'm just thinking if they don't cooperate, what do they say? That they were approached by the Cubans. That's what Dahlberg has to say, the Texans too, that they—

H. Well, if they will. But then we're relying on more and more people all the time. That's the problem and they'll stop if we could take this other route.

P. All right.

H. And you seem to think the thing to do is get them to stop?

P. Right, fine.

H. They say the only way to do that is from White House instructions. And it's got to be to Helms and to—ah, what's his name—? Walters.

P. Walters.

H. And the proposal would be that Ehrlichman and I call them in, and say, ah—

P. All right, fine. How do you call him in—I mean you just—well, we protected Helms from one hell of a lot of things.

H. That's what Ehrlichman says.

P. Of course, this Hunt, that will uncover a lot of things. You open that scab there's a hell of a lot of things and we just feel that it would be very detrimental to have this thing go any further. This involves these Cubans, Hunt and a lot of hanky-panky that we have nothing to do with ourselves. Well what the hell, did Mitchell know about this?

H. I think so. I don't think he knew the details, but I think he knew.

P. He didn't know how it was going to be handled though—with Dahlberg and the Texans and so forth? Well who was the asshole that did? Is it Liddy? Is that the fellow? He must be a little nuts.

H. He is.

P. I mean he just isn't well screwed on is he? Is that the problem?

H. No, but he was under pressure, apparently, to get more information, and as he got more pressure, he pushed the people harder to move harder—

P. Pressure from Mitchell?

H. Apparently.

P. Oh, Mitchell. Mitchell was at the point (unintelligible).

H. Yea.

P. All right, fine, I understand it all. We won't second-guess Mitchell and the rest. Thank God it wasn't Colson.

H. The FBI interviewed Colson yesterday. They determined that would be a good thing to do. To have him take an interrogation, which he did, and that—the FBI guys working the case concluded that there were one or two possibilities—one, that this is a White House—they don't think that there is anything at the election committee—they think it was either a White House operation and they had some obscure reasons for it—nonpolitical, or it was a Cuban and the CIA. And after their interrogation of Colson yesterday, they concluded it was not the White House, but are now convinced it is a CIA thing, so the CIA turnoff would—

P. Well, not sure of their analysis, I'm not going to get that involved. I'm (unintelligible).

H. No, sir, we don't want you to.

P. You call them in.

H. Good deal.

P. Play it tough. That's the way they play it and that's the way we are going to play it.

H. O.K.

P. When I saw that news summary, I questioned whether it's a bunch of crap, I thought, er, well it's good to have them off us awhile, because when they start bugging us, which they have, our little boys will not know how to handle it. I hope they will though.

H. You never know.

P. Good. . . .

After discussion of unrelated subjects, Nixon returned to the FBI-CIA problem, instructing Haldeman:

"When you get in (unintelligible) people, say, 'Look, the problem is that this will open the whole, the whole Bay of Pigs thing, and the President just feels that ah, without going into the details—don't, don't lie to them to the extent to say no involvement, but just say this is a comedy of errors, without getting into it, the President believes that it is going to open the whole Bay of Pigs thing up again. And, ah, because these people are plugging for (unintelligible) and that they should call the FBI in and (unintelligible) don't go any further into this case period!"

Second meeting: The President and Haldeman in the Oval Office, 1:04–1:13 p.m.

The transcript in its entirety:

P. O.K., just postpone (scratching noises) (unintelligible) just say (unintelligible) very bad to have this fellow Hunt, ah, he knows too damned much, if he was involved—you happen to know that? If it gets out that this is all involved, the Cuba thing it would be a fiasco. It would make the CIA look bad, it's going to make Hunt look bad, and it is likely to blow the whole Bay of Pigs thing which we think would be very unfortunate—both for the CIA, and for the country, at this time, and for American foreign policy. Just tell him to lay off. Don't you?

H. Yep. That's the basis to do it on. Just leave it at that.

P. I don't know if he'll get any ideas for doing it because our concern political (unintelligible). Helms is not one to (unintelligible)—I would just say, lookit, because of the Hunt involvement, whole cover basically this

H. Yep. Good move.

P. Well, they've got some pretty good ideas on this Meany thing. Shultz did a good paper. I read it all (voices fade).

Third meeting: the President and Haldeman in the Executive Office Building office, joined by Ziegler, 2:20–2:45 p.m.

Haldeman reported on FBI and CIA reactions to White House directives about the Watergate investigations:

H. Well, it was kind of interest. Walters made the point and I didn't mention Hunt, I just said that the thing was leading into directions that were going to create potential problems because they were exploring leads that led back into areas that would be harmful to the CIA and harmful to the government (unintelligible). . . .

H. (Unintelligible) I think Helms did to (unintelligible) said, I've had no—

P. God (unintelligible)

H. Gray called and said, yesterday, and said that he thought—

P. Who did? Gray?

H. Gray called Helms and said I think we've run right into the middle of a CIA covert operation.

P. Gray said that?

H. Yeah. And (unintelligible) said nothing we've done at this point and ah (unintelligible) says well it sure looks to me like it is (unintelligible) and ah, that was the end of that conversation (unintelligible) the problem is it tracks back to the Bay of Pigs and it tracks back to some other the leads run out to people who had no involvement in this, except by contacts and connection, but it gets to areas that are liable to be raised? The whole problem (unintelligible) Hunt. So at that point he kind of got the picture. He said, he said we'll be very happy to be helpful (unintelligible) handle anything you want. I would like to know the reason for being helpful, and I made it clear to him he hasn't going to get explicit (unintelligible) generality, and he said fine. And Walters (unintelligible). Walters is going to make a call to Gray. That's the way we put it and that's the way it was left.

P. How does that work though, how, they've got to (unintelligible) somebody from the Miami bank.

H. (Unintelligible). The point John makes—the bureau is going on this because they don't know what they are uncovering (unintelligible) continue to pursue it. They don't need to because they already have their case as far as the charges against these men (unintelligible) and ah, as they pursue it (unintelligible) exactly, but we didn't in any way say we (unintelligible). One thing Helms did raise. He said, Gray—he asked Gray why they thought they had run into a CIA thing and Gray said because of the characters involved and the amount of money involved, a lot of dough. (unintelligible) and ah, (unintelligible).

P. (unintelligible)

H. Well, I think they will.

P. If it runs (unintelligible) what the hell who knows (unintelligible) contributed CIA.

H. Ya, it's money CIA gets money (unintelligible) I mean their money moves in a lot of different ways, too. . . .

The Watergate Trial

Prosecution ties defendants to cover-up. Jurors in the Watergate cover-up trial heard testimony Nov. 11, 1974 that former President Nixon told H.R. Haldeman, his chief aide and a trial defendant, to direct officials of the Central Intelligence Agency to tell the head of the Federal Bureau of Investigation to curtail his investigation into the June 17, 1972 break-in at the Watergate headquarters of the Democratic National Committee.

The testimony followed a week-long

break in the Watergate special prosecutor's presentation of evidence that the five trial defendants had sought to obstruct government investigation of the break-in. The previous week had been consumed by arguments concerning admissibility of 26 White House tape recordings as evidence. After hearing testimony from two Secret Service agents involved in the design, installation and operation of the secret recording system, as well as testimony from Alexander P. Butterfield, a former presidential aide who verified the tapes' authenticity, presiding Judge John J. Sirica ruled Nov. 7 that he would allow the tapes' admission as evidence.

Vernon A. Walters, deputy director of the CIA, and L. Patrick Gray 3rd, former acting director of the FBI, appeared as witnesses Nov. 11. Both testified in conjunction with the playing of tape recordings of three Nixon-Haldeman meetings on June 23, 1972. (Nixon resigned the Presidency Aug. 9, four days after he released transcripts of these recordings.)

According to the first tape, which was played to establish chain of command, Haldeman entered the President's office the morning of June 23, 1972. The FBI investigation of the break-in was "not under control," Haldeman told Nixon. Haldeman recommended, "the way to handle this is for us now to have Walters call Pat Gray and just say, 'stay the hell out of this ... this is the CIA.'" Haldeman said that he and John D. Ehrlichman, Nixon's chief domestic policy adviser and a cover-up trial defendant, would call in CIA officials and enlist their aid.

Nixon voiced his approval of the plan, adding "When you get these people in, say, 'look, the problem is that this will open the whole Bay of Pigs thing'.... Don't lie to them to the extent to say no involvement, but just say, this is a comedy of errors, without getting into it, the President believes this is going to open the whole Bay of Pigs thing up again. And, ah,

because these people are plugging for, for keeps, and that they should call in the FBI and say that we wish for the country, don't go any further into this case, period."

Walters testified that he and Richard Helms, then director of the CIA, were asked to meet Haldeman and Ehrlichman at the White House sometime that morning.

When Walters and Helms arrived, Haldeman was again meeting with the President. According to the tape of this meeting, Nixon urged his chief of staff to invoke the Bay of Pigs affair and then emphasized, "I don't want them to get any ideas we're doing it because our concern is political."

Walters testified that he and Helms met with the White House aides in Ehrlichman's office. Haldeman, who did the talking, said the Watergate incident was making "a lot of noise," and it "might get worse" if the Democrats exploited it, Walters testified. According to Walters, Helms responded that the CIA had nothing to do with the Watergate break-in and that he had already told Gray. But Haldeman replied, Walters said, "'It is the President's wish that Mr. Walters go to the FBI,'" and tell Gray that pursuit of the FBI's investigation might "'uncover some assets or covert operations of the CIA.'" Walters said he made an appointment to see Gray later that day.

In his meeting with Gray, Walters testified, he told the FBI official that he "had just come from the White House" with instructions to inform Gray "that further pursuit of the investigation could expose or touch on CIA cover operations in Mexico."

In conjunction with what Walters said, the prosecution played the tape of the third Watergate-related meeting between Nixon and Haldeman. Haldeman, reporting back to the President, said, "Well

it's no problem. [I] had the two of them in ... I just said that ... we're gonna create some very major potential problems because they were exploring leads that led back to areas [where] it will be harmful to the CIA, harmful to the government.... Helms kind of got the picture." Nixon suggested that the money found on the Watergate burglars might still pose a problem but he added, "we'll cross that bridge later."

Gray testified that at the request of Walters, he held up the FBI's investigation for two weeks before he (Gray) finally concluded that he needed a formal, written request from the CIA. Consequently, he convened a meeting with Walters July 6, 1972, Gray said. However, Gray said, at the July 6 meeting Walters balked at putting anything in writing and then admitted there was no CIA connection to Watergate. Gray recalled Walters saying, "I'm not going to let those kids at the White House kick me around."

A Watergate Postscript

Colby concedes CIA lag on Watergate. CIA Director William E. Colby said Oct. 15, 1975 that "we didn't fall all over ourselves rushing to the policemen," in response to an allegation by Seymour M. Hersh who claimed that the CIA "could have blown the whistle at any time" about Watergate. (Hersh had written about the illegal domestic spying of the CIA for the *New York Times*.)

Hersh and Colby were in Williamsburg, Va. to participate in a panel discussion at the Associated Press Managing Editors conference. Colby said that the CIA felt in June 1972 that its involvement in giving assistance to E. Howard Hunt Jr. might become sensationalized if it had told the prosecutors earlier about the Watergate break-in.

FORMER CIA MEN CAUGHT IN RAID ON DEMOCRATIC NATIONAL OFFICES

Five men were arrested at 2 a.m. June 17 while engaged in an apparent espionage raid on the headquarters of the Democratic National Committee in the Watergate Hotel in Washington, D.C. The raiders, who were in possession of electronic eavesdropping devices and photographic equipment when captured, included James W. McCord Jr., a former Central Intelligence Agency employee currently working as a security agent for the Republican National Committee and the Committee for the Re-Election of the President. Also arrested were Bernard L. Barker, the group's alleged leader, Frank Angelo Fiorini, Eugenio L. Martinez and Virgilio R. Gonzales. All reportedly had CIA links in the past and had been involved in anti-Castro activities in Florida.

John N. Mitchell, President Nixon's campaign manager, denied June 18 that any of those involved in the raid were "operating either on our behalf or with our consent." Republican National Committee Chairman Sen. Robert J. Dole (Kans.) echoed Mitchell's position. Democratic National Chairman Lawrence F. O'Brien called for a full-scale FBI investigation into the incident and termed the raid a "blatant act of political espionage." O'Brien announced that the Democrats were filing a $1 million civil suit against the Committee to Re-Elect the President for its alleged involvement in the raid. The Justice Department disclosed June 19 that the FBI had begun an investigation of the affair.

ST. LOUIS POST-DISPATCH

St. Louis, Mo., June 20, 1972

The abortive raid on the headquarters of the Democratic National Committee by five men with burglary tools and sophisticated eavesdropping devices and photographic equipment has profoundly disturbing implications for the integrity of the country's political processes. Even if we accept at face value the expressions of dismay and disapproval by John N. Mitchell, chairman of the Committee for the Re-election of the President, and Senator Robert J. Dole, chairman of the Republican National Committee, the fact that the raid occurred indicates that there is a market for political data gathered by the grossest kind of invasion of privacy. The natural inference that someone is prepared to pay for and use campaign material garnered at the highest level by such despicable methods suggests how unrestricted political surveillance has become a fact of life in the nation.

While the housebreaking at Democratic headquarters would be unsettling enough as an independent unauthorized entrepreneurial venture, the unrefuted circumstantial evidence leads to the suspicion that it was more than that. Since James W. McCord, one of the raiders, is employed as a security agent by the Republican National Committee and the Committee for the Re-election of the President, the suspicion arises that he was working for his employers in this enterprise. Both Messrs. Mitchell and Dole must have known of and valued Mr. McCord's eavesdropping specialty when they hired him. It may be surmised too that the former employment by the CIA of Mr. McCord and of Bernard L. Barker, the reputed leader of the group, did not go unappreciated. Mr. Barker also is reported to have important Republican Party links in Florida.

In the light of this background and in view of the Nixon Administration's support for wiretapping and eavesdropping, even without court orders in alleged domestic security cases, the whole episode has a distasteful aura which cannot be dispelled by bland and unelaborated disclaimers from top Republican strategists.

A thorough FBI investigation, which has been promised, is fully warranted. But since that agency has itself engaged in illegal wiretapping and since it had been politicized by the late director J. Edgar Hoover and is now headed by a Nixon appointee, even its report on the raid cannot be anticipated with complete confidence. Yet considering the possibly damning ramifications of this case and the difficulties of getting to the bottom of them, it must be recognized that no matter how nonpartisan the FBI's investigation may be, the agency's report may be incomplete. Time will show whether a further inquiry seems to be called for in order establish confidence that this form of contemptible political activity will not be tolerated.

ARKANSAS DEMOCRAT
Little Rock, Ark., June 22, 1972

We won't dwell on the comic-opera aspects of the weird case in which several bumbling would-be wire-tappers — one with high-level Republican connections — apparently plotted to bug the offices of the National Democratic Committee. Suffice it to say that poor Larry O'Brien, who has longsuffered in silence as the Nixon Administration gilded its record, seems to have gone giddy over the thing. Having finally found something (anything!) to gibe the GOP with, he's thrown dignity and restraint to the wind. Ergo, the million-dollar lawsuit against the Committee for the Re-election of the President, in whose hire one of said bumblers seems to have been. The suit seems an improbable solution, if the only feasible one that's yet appeared, to the ponderable question of how the Democrats can ever get the party out of hock. The unanswered question, in that rationale, remains: Why a mere million, which would hardly pay the interest on the party's staggering debts?

Our concern, rather, is that the serious aspects in this case not be obscured by the absurdities. A minor question is why the subdued, almost apathetic response by the administration. We can't believe it actually had anything to do with the bizarre scheme — sitting as it is in the political catbird seat, with nothing to gain in such an escapade (What could it possibly hope to overhear?) and everything to lose. But rather than firmly and unequivocally dissociating the administration from the thing, Ron Ziegler, the President's mouthpiece, persists in trying to trivialize it. It's understandable that he would want to play it down, lest it blow up into an issue the Democrats can get their teeth into; but the fact remains that the incident is anything but trivial. And ignoring it won't make it go away.

By the sheerest coincidence, it was a Nixon appointee to the Supreme Court — Justice Lewis F. Powell — who pointed up the seriousness of this case. In a court opinion on an unrelated case — delivered ironically on the same day that the alleged wiretap plotters were arrested — Mr. Justice Powell wrote:

"The price of lawful public dissent must not be a dread of subjection to the unchecked surveillance power. Nor must the fear of unauthorized official eavesdropping deter vigorous citizen dissent and discussion of government action in private conversation. For private dissent, no less than open public discourse, is essential to our free society."

No evidence has yet appeared that the attempted eavesdropping in this case was either authorized or official. But the implications — and the gleeful insinuations by O'Brien & Co. — of official involvement, official sanction, or at the least official indulgence, not only reflect badly on the administration. They also raise serious questions in the public mind that merit more than the "routine" investigation the FBI has promised and more concern than the pooh-poohing the government has given the matter so far.

The Des Moines Register

Des Moines, Iowa, June 28, 1972

Democratic National Chairman Lawrence O'Brien has asked the President to have the attorney general name a special prosecutor "of unimpeachable integrity and national reputation" to investigate the attempted bugging of Democratic national headquarters.

Democrats are trying to make political capital out of the arrest of five men caught apparently in the act of planting electronic bugs in the party's national offices. One of the five was in charge of security for the committee to re-elect Nixon. Two of the men carried address books with the name of a former White House consultant. Democrats filed a $1 million civil suit against the five men and the Commitee to Re-elect the President.

The attempt of the Democrats to get political mileage out of the incident paradoxically makes the suggestion that a special prosecutor be named a good one. If for any reason the men are not successfully prosecuted, or their motives are not revealed, there is certain to be widespread suspicion of a political cover-up. One would not have to be a partisan Democrat to share in that suspicion when the heads of the FBI, the Justice Department and the committee being sued by the Democrats are all political associates.

The one thing worse than attempted illegal political espionage would be a whitewash of the attempt. Even the appearance of less-than-vigorous prosecution and full disclosure would be severely damaging.

If the White House has nothing embarrassing to hide, it ought to welcome the suggestion for the appointment of a special prosecutor. The public, as well as the Democratic Party, is entitled to assurance that this politically explosive case will be dealt with in a non-partisan manner.

The TENNESSEAN

Nashville, Tenn., June 21, 1972

AS A PLOT for the television series "Mission Impossible," it would have been entertaining but as an actual mission into the offices of the Democratic National Committee, the five-man breakin raises ugly questions about the political process and about the administration in power.

* * *

One of the five men who staged the breakin was, when arrested, the security coordinator for the Committee to Re-Elect the President, the chief campaign agency for Mr. Nixon which is headed by Mr. John Mitchell, the former attorney general.

The man, Mr. James W. McCord Jr., also did work for the Republican National Committee, according to Chairman Robert Dole, who has severed relations with him.

Mr. Mitchell, who was technically Mr. McCord's boss, said the man had other clients which his committee didn't know about. He threw in an ambiguous statement about security problems of his own committee and finally said "we will not permit or condone" such activities.

For a man charged with the re-election of Mr. Nixon, Mr. Mitchell seems singularly uninformed about a great many things. He knew nothing about the problems of selecting San Diego as the first GOP convention site and had no idea that ITT was offering a financial commitment—so his testimony in the ITT case indicated.

Who would hire a security coordinator without knowing something of his other clients and relationships? That would be the first breach of internal security. Admittedly, Mr. Mitchell may not have hired him, but somebody did. And therein lies deep suspicions which are buttressed by the fact that this has been a government hag-ridden by its own fears and uncertainties.

Nothing else can explain its love for wire-tapping, the Army's surveillance of peace groups, the Agnew attacks on the media, the subpoenaing of reporters' notes, the raucous cries against a "treasonable" opposition, the desperate wrigglings in the face of the "Anderson papers," the sly, but persistent urging that "fat cat" contributors to the campaign fund give massively before the law making such contributions public went into effect, and the chortling plans of the Committee to Re-Elect the President to us all and any weapons to meet its goal.

Whether the breakin at the Democratic headquarters was part of that philosophy isn't known. But Democratic National Chairman Lawrence O'Brien has announced a one million dollar damage suit against the Committee to Re-elect the President and the five men accused of breaking and entering.

He has cited civil rights laws protecting voting rights, charges invasion of privacy and violations of the 1968 Safe Streets Acts forbidding wiretapping by private parties.

* * *

"As far as I am personally concerned," said Mr. O'Brien, "there is certainly in every sense a clear line (in this incident) to the Committee to Re-elect the President . . ." How plainly that clear line will be revealed depends, ironically, on the FBI and the Justice Department, whose old boss is now chairman of the Committee to Re-elect the President.

THE LOUISVILLE TIMES

Louisville, Ky., June 21, 1972

As opera bouffe, the bungled burglary of the Democratic party's national offices would be a bust. Its music is atonal; its story is pure Art Buchwald and its cast is even more inept than the Marx Brothers ever pretended to be in their zaniest moment.

Its revelations about the state of American political morality are even more fascinating than the inevitable speculation as to the culprits' motives. For it is hard to believe that any skilled political operative would be stupid enough to hire so rank a band of amateurs.

According to one report from Washington, wiretapping equipment of the type seized went out "with high-button shoes." Among the bugging devices were transmitters powered by flashlight batteries and microphones the size of half-dollars. One wiretap expert was incredulous when the equipment was described; another found it shocking that five men were involved.

"If they follow the usual route, they hire only one man . . .," was his comment. Another belittled the idea of bringing in outsiders rather than hiring "local, top talent. . . . They know the field, they have the contacts."

But had the plot succeeded, what would have happened to the information? Would a politician turn it down? It is doubtful. All he would demand is that he never know how it was obtained. It is the same dodge that is used in collecting campaign funds. Political morality has it that the candidate is not tainted by illegally collected money if he is unaware of the source. That, of course, is pure hokum

So, the issue is not who hired the burglars because—at least to our way of thinking—no one could be quite that stupid. The relevant question is who would have used the illegally obtained information. And, we think, no politician could truthfully say he would have turned his back on it if he thought he could benefit through its use.

The upshot is another blow at the credibility of our political system and all the FBI probes will not erase that, the FBI's own credibility being what it is today. Most of the damage naturally falls to the Republicans because it was their employe who got caught.

The general public probably won't hold that against the GOP, though. Some of the party's big contributors might, however. They probably are Scotch enough to think that the party has better things to do with their money than to pay a loser like J. W. McCord Jr. $14,000 a year for services as "security coordinator."

THE DENVER POST

Denver, Colo., June 20, 1972

SURVEYING WHAT IS KNOWN so far about the bizarre attempted burglary and bugging of the Democratic National Committee headquarters in Washington, our impression is that it is the Republicans. who need a better security system.

One of the five men arrested during the break-in at Democratic headquarters was employed at the Committee for the Re-election of the President, Nixon's main campaign committee, as a security expert. He was hired, according to Committee Chairman John N. Mitchell, Nixon's former attorney general, "to assist with the installation of our security system."

But this guy may not be around much longer. Anyway, he probably was hired to assure the President's campaign committee of security against opponents such as Democrats and nosy newspapermen.

And that, obviously, is not the Republicans' real problem.

What they need is a security system to protect them against some of their friends and supporters.

For instance, another of the men caught in the Democrats' headquarters is a Miamian who is reputedly an important Republican party wheel in Florida. He is also reported to have been one of the top CIA planners of the spectacularly bungled Bay of Pigs invasion of Cuba in 1961.

With helpers of that caliber, the GOP clearly needs all the security protection it can get.

What puzzles us right now, though, is why Larry O'Brien, the Democratic national chairman, is demanding a full investigation of this whole idiotic caper.

Admittedly, it is only human for O'Brien to be curious as to who gave the five burglary suspects the $6,500 in crisp new bills found on them and in their hotel rooms. He might be smarter, though, to smooth the whole thing over, if that would keep the Republicans from finding out who was responsible for this odd affair.

FOR WHOEVER FINANCED this caper either has far more money than brains—in which case he can be expected to foul the Republicans up again in some way—or else he is secretly the Democrats' best friend.

After all, no admitted Democrat could have dreamed up a more attention-getting way to impugn the intelligence and integrity of the main GOP campaign organization. So why would O'Brien want to cramp this character's imaginative style?

THE RICHMOND NEWS LEADER

Richmond, Va., June 22, 1972

As they demonstrate daily, the Democrats are becoming increasingly desperate for ammunition—any ammunition—with which to assault President Nixon. So when an employee of the President's re-election organization reportedly was discovered, hand thrust deep into a cookie jar and body wrapped in bugging equipment at the Democratic National Headquarters in the Watergate complex, candidates and other party leaders could barely restrain their well-orchestrated cries of horror and outrage.

Larry O'Brien, the Johnson hangover and Democratic National Chairman, set the tone by exclaiming that the "bugging incident . . . raised the ugliest questions about the integrity of the political process that I have encountered in a quarter century. No mere statement of innocence by Mr. Nixon's campaign (staff) will dispel these questions." Senators Humphrey, Muskie, and McGovern chimed in with suitably ominous pronouncements, all intended to imply that if the police had arrived sooner on the scene, they might have found Richard Nixon at the wheel of the getaway car.

It is predictable election-year Mickey Mouse, of course, but surely the Democrats are pushing our sense of humor too far. When George Wallace was gunned down, we watched—in slow motion, no less—as a man stepped up to the Governor, pulled the trigger five times, then was beaten to the ground and carted off. Yet despite the TV coverage, Arthur Bremer still rates an "alleged" before every reference to his being a "would-be assassin." President Nixon, who was not filmed at the Watergate nor sneaking over the White House fence, finds himself tried and convicted in absentia, while hordes of hopeful Democrats scout around for an appropriate length of rope.

What makes the Democrats' performance even more shameful is the easy availability of an alternative explanation for the incident. Mike Mansfield, hardly a Nixon-lover, read beyond the headlines and discounted the possibility of Republican double-dealing: Mansfield apparently noted that the Nixon employee arrested in the alleged raid, as well as four other men from Miami captured with him, all have long histories of involvement with the CIA and the Cuban liberation

movement. Whatever they hoped to gain—perhaps proof that the Democratic platform will support recognition of Red Cuba—probably had more to do with personal politics and politics within the Cuban exile community in Miami, than with national politics and the re-election of President Nixon.

Presumably we will know the right answers before long, as scoop-happy reporters from the Washington Post and the New York Times try to tie everything to the White House. Whether we will accept the answers remains a separate matter particularly if the Democrats insist on parading more puffed-up outrage. After all, the ITT "affair" proved absolutely nothing, showed absolutely no wrongdoing, and resulted in not one indictment, let alone one conviction. Yet the average American continues to conceive of the ITT sideshow as a replay of Teapot Dome. The raid on the Democratic National Committee Headquarters will share the same fate, unless we all—including Democratic leaders—bone up on our civics books and remember the injunction about "innocent until proven guilty."

Chicago Tribune

Chicago, Ill., June 22, 1972

You'd think Santa Claus had come six months early, the way Chairman Larry O'Brien of the Democratic National Committee is carrying on—and in a sense, this is just what has happened. Only this Santa came in the form of several men; they didn't come down the chimney of Democratic headquarters, they sneaked in a door; and when they were caught at 2:30 a. m. they weren't carrying gifts, they were carrying eavesdropping equipment. Best of all, from Mr. O'Brien's point of view, some of them were linked indirectly to the White House.

There is nothing the Democrats need more, at the moment, than a good, lively

issue. The war and the economy are rapidly losing their appeal as issues, and it looks as if the Democratic Party is going to find itself with an unplanned candidate, in the form of Sen. McGovern, whom many of the party regulars look upon with something less than enthusiasm. The bugging attempt came at the perfect moment, and Mr. O'Brien deliberated for a full 15 seconds [as Republican Chairman Bob Dole put it] before leaping upon it as proof of Republican "gutter politics." He has even filed a $1 million damage suit against the Committee for the Reelection of the President, a Republican campaign group with which one of the alleged eavesdroppers was linked.

The bugging scheme is a deplorable example of stupidity and contempt for the law, especially at a time when the Supreme Court has just ruled that the government itself cannot resort to eavesdropping, even in cases affecting the domestic security, without court approval. It is hard to believe that it had the participation, approval, or knowledge of any official Republican organization, let alone the White House. More likely it was the brainchild of a few individuals who may have hoped to make points for themselves by picking up Democratic secrets and passing them along.

Whatever the facts, they should be determined as soon as possible so as to prove—or disprove—Mr. O'Brien's pointed insinuations. He can feel safe filing the suit because he knows it probably won't come to trial before the election and can then be conveniently forgotten. If his charge that the Republican Party is officially involved proves true, then so will his charge of gutter politics. But in this country [except in the Democratic National Committee] people are generally considered innocent until proved guilty; and lacking further evidence, it is Mr. O'Brien who is guilty of gutter politics and of charging guilt by association.

The Charlotte Observer

Charlotte, N.C., June 24, 1972

The mere thought of a Republican National Committee employe's being nabbed inside Democratic National Committee headquarters wearing rubber surgical gloves and armed to the teeth with photographic equipment and electronic listening devices was enough to move one to laughter. But now the laughter is being replaced by grim speculation.

Democratic Chairman Lawrence O'Brien has filed a $1 million suit against the Committee for the Reelection of the President, naming this influential group as co-conspirators in a plot to "bug" Democratic headquarters. Mr. O'Brien's action will probably be dismissed by some as no more than a political maneuver. To some extent it is that. The Democrats have a decided interest in prolonging this embarrassment to the GOP and the President's committee.

But seeking answers is also very much in the public interest — if only to dispel the ugly questions raised by the intrigue that placed five men inside Democratic headquarters early last Saturday morning.

One of those arrested — James W. McCord — is a former CIA agent who has worked recently as a "security specialist" for the Republican National Committee and the Committee for the Reelection of the President. Mr. McCord was hired several months ago by former Atty. Gen. John Mitchell (who is the President's campaign chairman) and occupied an office in Republican headquarters.

The man who apparently led the midnight raid was Bernard Barker, who also worked closely with the CIA and who apparently helped plan the 1961 Bay of Pigs operation. The other men also have been active in anti-Cuban activities.

Some of the questions raised in this case are obvious. Who engaged these five men and for what reason? Or did they act on their own? Police found about $6,500 in new, consecutively numbered bills (mostly $100 bills) on their persons and in their hotel room. Where did this money come from? And what did they hope to find in the Democrats' files and confidential reports? What information did they expect to get from "bugging" Democratic communications? And what of the indications of ties to the President's reelection committee?

Police investigations turned up a notebook with some intriguing entries. It contained the name and home telephone number of E. Howard Hunt Jr., a former CIA agent who has been working as a consultant to White House special counsel Charles W. Colson. It also contained the notations "W. H." and "W. House." Among the possessions of one of the arrested men was a personal check from Mr. Hunt in the amount of $6.

The common bonds between the suspects and Mr. Hunt may well be their backgrounds in the CIA rather than their current employment. (Mr. Hunt was a CIA agent for 21 years, until resigning in 1970.) But that raises still more questions, perhaps more ominous ones than those related to Republican-Democratic politics.

Now four more men are being sought in connection with this and possibly other "buggings" and burglaries. And an obscure 800-member organization of right-wing, anti-Castro Cubans is coming into the picture. Was it involved? Did it seek only to discredit the Democrats and thus help assure a Republican victory? Or did it have even more dangerous objectives?

There are other questions. Where has the FBI been? Perhaps in some way it led police to make the arrests. Yet it appears possible that a large band of rightwing extremists, ambitious enough to attempt to turn national events through use of a private spy system, has been operating dangerously close to some of its objectives. And does the CIA still have contact with these people? The spectre of a secret rightwing group with close ties to the government's own giant spying apparatuses should be disturbing to anyone concerned about freedom.

We hope this episode will not now be dismissed as mere election-year maneuvering, embarrassing, perhaps, but of no great consequence. Every aspect of the case should be seriously pursued. Much more than political partisanship is involved.

THE ARIZONA REPUBLIC

Phoenix, Ariz., June 24, 1972

Sen. Barry Goldwater is understandably amused by the inflated rhetoric and $1 million suit against Republican officials by high-ranking Democrats because some people connected with the campaign to re-elect President Nixon were caught either installing or removing wiretap equipment designed to eavesdrop on business conducted at Democratic National Committee headquarters in Washington.

Senator Goldwater would be the last person to condone such political espionage. But his amusement obtains from his own experience as a presidential candidate eight years ago, when Moira O'Conner, a pretty 23 - year - old Democratic spy, boarded his campaign train as a "reporter," and used her good looks and cover as a journalist to collect juicy tid-bits for the Democrats.

Miss O'Conner, who openly admitted connections with the Democratic National Committee, was paid by California Democratic strategist Richard Tuck to spy on the Goldwater campaign operation and publish an anti-Goldwater newspaper based on information she collected before she was discovered by the senator's associates.

The Democrats also tried in 1964 to fake an espionage attempt and blame the Republicans by informing the press that Louis Flax, night teletype operator in Washington for the Democrats' nationwide communications network, was being paid large sums of money by the GOP to furnish them with copies of Democratic teletype transmissions.

A trap was arranged by the Democrats, and reporters and photographers were on hand to witness a supposed clandestine meeting between Flax and his Republican contact, at which he was to be paid for his regular delivery.

When Flax arrived with the material, pre - screened by the Democrats, it was openly accepted by Republican National Committee executive director John Grenier in his office — hardly unusual under the circumstances. But there was no pay-off — indeed Grenier refused to pay for the information — and no proof that any prior arrangement existed between Flax and the Republicans to steal Democratic secrets.

Senator Goldwater knows as well as any political strategist, however, that intelligence gathering is a standard part of professional political operations. Undoubtedly, there are times when such surreptitious activities are conducted unlawfully. And they are often done without the knowledge or sanction of party leaders or those running campaign operations.

There is still much that we do not know about the alleged wiretapping of Democratic National Committee headquarters by James McCord, security chief for the Committee to Re-elect the President, and others. Former Atty. Gen. John Mitchell, head of the President's re-election campaign, has firmly denied that McCord was acting in the committee's behalf, and there is no reason to believe otherwise.

There is, however, a considerable difference in the way Democrats and the press have reacted to this latest political spy story. When Senator Goldwater and the Republicans were victims of beautiful spies and James Bond tactics of the Democrats, the stories were featured as light asides in an otherwise heated, issue-oriented campaign year.

But now that the Democratic campaign sanctuary has supposedly been breached by GOP functionaries — one of them a former CIA agent — a hue and cry against treachery and reprehensible political tactics has been echoed and re-echoed by the Democrats at the expense of President Nixon and his supporters.

For the Democrats, it is an obvious attempt to get some publicity and sympathy when their political fortunes are at an all-time low. And so far as press critics are concerned, Senator Goldwater probably put things into perspective when he said that the Republicans are likely being blamed only because their spies are not "well-stacked."

GRAY'S NOMINATION AS FBI CHIEF CHALLENGED IN SENATE HEARINGS

The Senate Judiciary Committee held hearings in late February and March on the nomination of L. Patrick Gray 3rd, acting director of the Federal Bureau of Investigation, as permanent director.

On Feb. 19 Sen. Robert C. Byrd (D, W. Va.) charged that Gray, a long time political associate of President Nixon, had been "openly partisan" during the 1972 presidential election. A White House memorandum addressed to Gray asking his "participation as a key speaker" at a Cleveland gathering in August 1972 because Ohio was "vital to our hopes in November" was disclosed in hearings Feb. 28. Gray denied, however, that his attendance at the gathering was politically motivated, saying it was solely for the purpose of carrying the "FBI's message to the people." That same day, Gray admitted under Byrd's questioning that extensive records of the FBI probe of the Watergate affair had been supplied to the White House. Gray said John W. Dean 3rd, a presidential counsel conducting a separate White House inquiry into Watergate, had asked for and received all Watergate data beginning in August 1972. Gray defended the action saying the bureau had provided other Administrations with progress reports of important investigations. Gray also testified that Dean had been granted permission to be present when the FBI conducted investigative interviews with White House personnel. The committee also elicited testimony which tended to substantiate charges that the FBI had been less than thorough in its investigation of the Watergate affair.

The Detroit News
Detroit, Mich., March 15, 1973

Rarely has a committee of the U.S. Senate played a more brazen and ruthless game of politics than the Judiciary Committee is now playing with L. Patrick Gray III, President Nixon's nominee for the post of FBI director.

As acting head of the FBI, Gray has already demonstrated his ability to run the FBI in an effective and efficient manner. It is safe to say that if he were the appointee of a Democratic president, the Democrats on the Judiciary Committee would be singing his praises instead of trying to wash him down the political drain.

Ironically, Gray's nomination stands in jeopardy because he has displayed a wide measure of candor, the alleged lack of which drew so much criticism from liberals against the late J. Edgar Hoover. Hoover's detractors said he was too independent, too aloof, too reluctant to communicate desired information.

Even Sen. Edward Kennedy admits that in his dealings with the committee, Gray has been "responsive." Gray could merely have told the committee, with regard to the Watergate investigation: "This is a matter of highly confidential FBI information, and I cannot talk about it." Instead, he provided detailed information, some of which reflects none too well on people connected with the administration which nominated him.

As a reward for his patient and honest cooperation, Gray hears that he may not be confirmed unless President Nixon allows White House Counsel John W. Dean to testify about the Watergate investigation. Thus, some members of the Judiciary Committee hold Gray hostage in order to get the President to retreat on the issue of executive privilege.

This is politics at its shabbiest. Incidentally, President Nixon sought to avoid a political hassle over the FBI nomination when he appointed Gray last year as an acting, rather than permanent, official. That action assured the next president (It turned out to be Mr. Nixon, but could have been a Democrat, Sen. George McGovern) the opportunity to name his own director.

Such gestures mean nothing, however, to politicians with the smell of blood in their nostrils. Sen. John Tunney, for example, won't relent to the point of accepting an informal conference, rather than a formal committee hearing, with John Dean. The defeat of President Nixon on the issue of executive privilege must be abject and complete.

It is unfortunate that Gray may become a casualty in this conflict between Senate and President, but Mr. Nixon should stick by his guns. He should offer to let Dean talk with the committee under certain prearranged guidelines satisfactory to the White House, but should not retreat on the well-founded principle of executive privilege.

The New York Times
New York, N.Y., March 11, 1973

In his first statement after appointment as acting director of the Federal Bureau of Investigation last May, L. Patrick Gray 3d said President Nixon had instructed him to operate the F.B.I. in a totally nonpolitical way. Not long after that virtuous declaration Mr. Gray delivered speeches which could only have had the effect of supporting Mr. Nixon's re-election campaign.

Now it develops that a memorandum by a Presidential adviser had explicitly urged Mr. Gray to come to the aid of the party by way of one such appearance. Although the President insisted the other day that any campaign role for Mr. Gray "certainly didn't have any support and would not have it now," others in the White House clearly took a more permissive attitude toward nonpartisan purity. So apparently did Mr. Gray himself.

At issue are the independence and integrity of the F.B.I. as well as the capacity and will of its director to act as a shield against any political penetration of the bureau's activities. A number of pertinent questions on this score have been raised — and not persuasively answered—during the current hearings before the Senate Judiciary Committee.

Uneasiness over Mr. Gray's qualifications for a post that requires a granitelike disregard of the special claims of the powerful and influential was heightened by the "courtesies" the director extended in canceling an interrogation of Mrs. Martha Mitchell at her husband's request. This was no routine consideration of a man's concern for his wife; it was a special concession to John N. Mitchell because he had been Mr. Nixon's Attorney General as well as his campaign manager. The resulting impression that Mr. Gray is overawed by the mighty is not lessened by his subsequent testimony that Mr. Mitchell later agreed to let his wife be interviewed if the F.B.I. considered it necessary.

An even more serious question about Mr. Gray's grasp of the importance of F.B.I. independence has been raised by his acquiescence in the presence of John W. Dean 3d, a Presidential counsel, when the bureau's agents interviewed members of the White House staff about the Watergate affair. Mr. Gray testified that he acceded to this procedure with utmost reluctance and only because he feared that the White House might otherwise bar such questioning altogether. But such capitulations merely illustrate the extent to which the agency's independence had already been compromised.

Equally disconcerting is Mr. Gray's view that Mr. Dean's role could be excused because the presence of legal counsel "happens more frequently in today's world." Mr. Dean clearly was not acting as counsel for the persons under interrogation but as an interested listener, to use a kind phrase, from the White House. It would be naive to suggest that such a presence might not have inhibited the testimony or that Mr. Dean's knowledge of what was told to the F.B.I., if relayed to high-ranking Republicans implicated in the affair, might not have given them a signal advantage in any subsequent investigation.

In any event, something larger is at stake than the possibility that Mr. Gray's actions may inadvertently have further muddied the messy trail to the truth about Watergate. Mr. Gray relaxed the rules concerning the confidentiality of F.B.I. files when White House aides breathed down his neck. By now offering members of Congress similar access to such files, Mr. Gray has underscored the risk that each political indiscretion will serve as an excuse for the next.

The crucial question to be answered by the Senate is whether Mr. Gray can stand firmly enough against political pressures whether from the White House or Capitol Hill, to avoid politicizing the F.B.I. Not only would political intrusion be a serious blow to public faith in Federal law-enforcement; it could ultimately pose a threat to political liberty.

The Boston Globe

Boston, Mass., March 10, 1973

White House press secretary Ronald Ziegler has expressed outrage (real or feigned, it is hard to tell) because the Senate Judiciary Committee has looked so closely into FBI files disclosing how tenderly the FBI treated former Attorney General John N. Mitchell and other White House personages and friends of the President in its investigation of who did what in the Watergate wiretapping and burglary conspiracy to sabotage and disrupt the Democratic presidential primaries and the final campaign.

Mr. Ziegler piously deplores the Senate Judiciary Committee's hearing on the confirmation of Acting FBI Director L. Patrick Gray 3rd, appointed as Director by Mr. Nixon: "We hope the Judiciary Committee would reconsider the problem concerning unevaluated raw data from FBI files."

This is all well and good. The American Civil Liberties Union also deplores the way in which unevaluated raw data can damage the reputation of innocent persons. So does The Globe. In this instance, however, one wishes the White House would be less concerned with comfortable ethical problems and more concerned than it is with hard facts to which Mr. Gray has sworn.

Mr. Gray has sworn, for instance, that Herbert W. Kalmbach, Mr. Nixon's California lawyer, admitted that he paid $30,000 or $40,00 to another California friend of the President, Donald H. Segretti, for unspecified "services." He said this had been done at the direction of Dwight L. Chapin, long time intimate of the President and at that time the President's appointments secretary. Mr. Chapin since has left the White House and now is employed in private industry at $70,000 a year. But his post was right outside Mr. Nixon's office last August when Mr. Nixon stated "categorically . . . no one presently employed at the White House was involved in the Watergate burglary, directly or indirectly."

Mr. Ziegler now has "no comment" on this. Nor will he comment on the Kalmbach-Chapin-Segretti connection although it is commonly understood that Mr. Segretti was one of the brains behind the sabotage and espionage for which seven minor Re-election Committee agents are now awaiting sentence.

Mr. Ziegler had no comment when he was asked if White House chief of staff H. R. Haldeman was aware that Mr. Chapin had disbursed funds to Mr. Segretti—presumably out of the mysterious cash box which was always replenished out of a fund that has been described as not less than $700,000 and probably more.

Mr. Gray has testified that he sees no impropriety in supplying FBI files to White House Counsel John W. Dean 3d, files which thereafter were used in coaching Mr. Segretti on what he should say as a grand jury witness. It is an interesting view of propriety.

Mr. Ziegler's irritation at newsmen's efforts to be set straight on the White House position is understandable enough. A press secretary would of course want the newsmen to forget the whole thing. But "no comment" does not suffice as an answer to vital questions in which the integrity of the White House itself is involved. Mr. Ziegler should be reminded that "No comment" can be interpreted as reluctant affirmation.

One of many questions raised by Mr. Gray's testimony concerns Mr. Gray himself. This is as to whether Mr. Gray, who has testified that the White House arranged a speaking schedule for him in last November's campaign, should be confirmed as the head of the FBI, up to now politically independent as a secret police agency has to be.

He will probably be confirmed. The question is as to whether he should be. His testimony clearly points to an intimate and intolerable political partnership with the White House. The integrity of the FBI cannot survive political taint of any kind whatsoever. Mr. Gray appears to have painted partisan politics all over the institution he has been appointed to head.

THE CHRISTIAN SCIENCE MONITO[R]

Boston, Mass., March 9, 1973

It is now clear that L. Patrick Gray III, although acting director of the FBI at the time, did do things during the recent political campaign which no FBI chief should have done. However, in our opinion what he did should not disqualify him from confirmation by the Senate — which we assume will take place in due time. Indeed, we incline to think that he will make a safer and better FBI chief for having made a mistake.

Whether he knew at the time that he was doing something improper is not certain. He made one speech in Cleveland during the campaign at the instigation of the White House, and he allowed White House representatives to read his file of documents on the Watergate affair. Both were helpful to the Republican cause. The director of the FBI has no business taking part in partisan politics at any time in any way. President Nixon agrees with us, that the job should be "nonpartisan." Mr. Gray should have known better — in both instances.

But it is a fair guess that Mr. Gray is both sadder and wiser now and understands, as perhaps he didn't before, that he is supposed to keep out of partisan politics. Also, he is vulnerable on this subject and therefore can be expected to be careful to avoid finding himself another time in a similar mistake.

Presidents are required by the Constitution to retire after eight years in that office. A similar time limit might well be placed on the directorship of the FBI. They should never be political. But they should not be indispensable. Perhaps the term ought to be something like 10 years — so it would not overlap with a single presidency.

We urge Mr. Gray to profit by his mistakes and ensure that the position he is apparently about to succeed to remains above partisanship and party politics.

The San Diego Union

San Diego, Calif., March 13, 1973

In 1968 at the twilight of the career of the late J. Edgar Hoover as director of the Federal Bureau of Investigation, Congress ruled that his successor would require confirmation of the Senate. The decision made sense. Mr. Hoover was a hallmark of unimpeachable integrity, literally a public servant whose shoes could never be filled. However, advice of the Senate could assist in finding someone who approached his stature.

Those who have watched the last two weeks of hearings by the Senate Judiciary Committee on the qualifications of L. Patrick Gray III to become the permanent FBI director must have wondered on at least several occasions whether Congress made the right decision five years ago.

True, members of the committee have the responsibility to ask hard, penetrating questions. However, they also have the duty to protect the integrity and good name of the FBI. Indeed, we believe that most committee members would agree that however important it is to get to the bottom of the so-called Watergate affair, the protection of the FBI is transcendent.

Unfortunately the hearings over Mr. Gray's qualifications appear to be sliding toward a Greek chorus that could harm the FBI. It does this important organization no good to have outsiders inspect its raw files—something that Mr. Hoover would not even let presidents do. Nor does it build public confidence to have the likes of columnist Jack Anderson testify. Have we already forgotten the role of Anderson in defaming Sen. Tom Eagleton by printing false information?

So far the principal unsubstantiated accusations against Mr. Gray appear to be that he is politicizing the FBI. Some of the senators definitely appear to be doing so.

The Charleston Gazette
Charleston, W.Va., March 14, 1973

West Virginia's Sen. Robert C. Byrd, the Democratic whip and a member of the committee examining Gray's credentials to be permanent director, summed up his opposition well when he said:

"Personally, I feel that Gray has been too politically active. In any other case such as that for a Cabinet post, it would not bother me too much. But I don't believe the head of the FBI should be a political person. The politicalization of the FBI is tantamount to setting up an American gestapo."

Placing a man of such inclinations in the position of FBI director would be particularly dangerous in view of presidential tendencies to head the Justice Department, of which the FBI is an arm, with political appointees. Under President Truman, J. Howard McGrath was moved from Democratic national chairman to attorney general. President Eisenhower appointed his campaign manager, Herbert Brownell, to that post. President Kennedy gave it to his brother Robert, his chief political adviser. President Nixon's first choice was his campaign manager, John N. Mitchell, and Mitchell's successor, Richard G. Kleindienst, has shown he's not above playing politics with justice. Indeed, over the last 25 years, only President Johnson to his credit gave professional attention to the office with his appointment of Ramsey Clark.

Certainly the Justice Department itself over the last four years has been deeply involved in politics, ever ready to protect the politically favored and to spy upon those looked upon as political enemies. To add to this an FBI director willing to play the political game — for the President, for the Congress, or for anyone—would be going too far.

Sen. Byrd has stated clearly that he will not vote for the confirmation of Gray. But we have not yet heard from West Virginia's senior senator, Jennings Randolph.

We're well aware of Sen. Randolph's long standing policy of voting to confirm presidential appointees on the ground that the president has the right and the responsibility to make such appointments. We appreciate Randolph's position up to a point — the point being that there is little reason for having the confirmation process if the Senate is to apply automatically the rubber stamp of approval, no matter who or what is involved.

Clearly, especially in the present situation, the new FBI director should be a man of impeccable qualifications who would be acceptable not only to President Nixon but to the next president if he be a Democrat. Otherwise we can expect to see a change of director with every new president — the politicizing of a federal agency whose independence should be kept sacred. Surely Sen. Randolph can perceive the dangers of Gray's confirmation.

To put it mildly, the Federal Bureau of Investigation has not been the same since L. Patrick Gray III took over as acting director 10 months ago.

From Gray's own testimony before the Senate Judiciary Committee, and from other evidence, one is led to the conclusion that the once-independent FBI has become immersed in politics and seems more interested in feeding information to the White House about the Watergate affair than in getting to the bottom of that shabby business.

It is hardly to be expected, for example, that the director of the FBI would trot off to Cleveland to make a political speech — as Gray did last year — at the request of a White House underling with the admonition that "Ohio is important to us." And it is hardly the measure of a non-political director to permit White House counsel John W. Dean III to sit in on all interviews with White House staffers, which Gray said he did against his better judgment because "if we want the interview, we take it the best way we can get it."

We do not think Gray is an evil man; indeed, he has made some admirable moves to update the bureau. But there is every reason to believe he is pliable, especially when the pressure of presidential politics is applied.

THE ROANOKE TIMES
Roanoke, Va., March 22, 1973

Several days ago the editors of The Roanoke Times received a letter from L. Patrick Gray III, acting director of the Federal Bureau of Investigation. The letter thanked the newspaper for its editorial, published Feb. 23, praising Mr. Gray's tenure at the FBI and supporting his appointment as permanent director.

The letter was reminiscent of the ways of J. Edgar Hoover. Over the years, the late director of the FBI never failed to write appreciatively to editors of any publication that ran an article or comment praising Mr. Hoover's agency. Mr. Gray, like his legendary predecessor, recognizes the value of good public relations; and he has, as we observed earlier, done a lot as acting director to clear out cobwebs that accumulated during Mr. Hoover's later years.

Unfortunately, it has become evident in recent weeks that Mr. Gray does not also recognize, as did Mr. Hoover, the immense value to the bureau of remaining totally above politics. If he does recognize it, perhaps he simply has not been allowed to follow the rigid standard of independence J. Edgar Hoover set down for himself and the bureau back in the 1920s. Since Pat Gray's ascendancy to the Hoover chair, the White House has proceeded on the assumption that the FBI was just another functionary, an agency that could be commanded to jump to White House whim.

Thus, it had Mr. Gray make thinly veiled political speeches for President Nixon's re-election; it asked the FBI to feed to campaign officials any political tidbits that might be useful; it stationed its man to look over the FBI's shoulder while the Watergate bugging case was being investigated, and even insisted the director violate confidences for the White House's benefit.

Through all this, Mr. Gray was anxious to please. He went along with what was wanted of him and the bureau. He bowed and scraped when a former Attorney General declined to have his wife interviewed. He went on an "assumption of regularity" about what people in the White House were doing regarding the Watergate investigation.

He was even eager to please the Senate, which must confirm him, but there his effort boomeranged. He told the senators incriminating things about people like Herbert Kalmbach, the President's personal lawyer, and the White House—acting through the Justice Department—told him to shut up. Since then, Mr. Gray has been a courteous clam. All sensitive questions will be handled higher up.

It is impossible to imagine J. Edgar Hoover or his beloved FBI in such a situation. Mr. Gray remains a decent, well-meaning and capable man who has instituted some needed procedural reforms at the bureau. But he is not his own man; he is Mr. Nixon's, for that is what the White House insists on. It is a bad precedent for the FBI, and as the man who embodies that unhealthy change, L. Patrick Gray III should be rejected by the Senate as permanent FBI director.

FORT WORTH STAR-TELEGRAM
Fort Worth, Tex., March 15, 1973

President Nixon and the Senate Judiciary Committee appear to be headed into an unpleasant situation if not an outright confrontation over Mr. Nixon's nomination of L. Patrick Gray as permanent director of the FBI.

Gray has been acting director of the bureau since the death of J. Edgar Hoover.

His nomination as permanent successor to Hoover presently is being scrutinized by the judiciary committee. Some members of the committee, at least, have expressed the view that they aren't getting enough factual information to enable them to make an intelligent decision on whether or not to confirm the president's appointment.

Specifically, committee members have voted to invite White House counsel John W. Dean III to appear before them for questioning about an investigation he conducted for the President of the bugging of Democratic headquarters at the Watergate complex in Washington last June.

President Nixon, invoking executive privilege, has said he will not allow Dean to appear before the Senate panel for questioning.

In his own testimony before the Senate committee, Mr. Gray has indicated he and Mr. Dean had extensive communication about the Watergate investigation and the FBI's role in it.

The Senators have heard in much detail Mr. Gray's version of the affair. Now they want Mr. Dean's version.

Sen. Robert Byrd, D-W. Va., a committee member and assistant Democratic leader of the Senate, said flatly that if Mr. Nixon is unwilling to let Dean appear then the President should withdraw Gray's nomination.

Mr. Nixon, in declining to allow Dean to appear, invoked the traditional "executive privilege" under which presidents prevent members of their staffs from making formal appearances before congressional committees.

The President did say, however, he would continue to "provide all necessary and relevant information through informal contacts between my present staff and committees of the Congress in ways which preserve intact the constitutional separation of the branches" of government.

Certainly, years of experience in use of the executive privilege have proven the value, and in some cases, the urgent necessity of the practice. Obviously, if he is to do an effective job, the president must be accorded the right to communicate privately with his advisors and staff members.

At the same time though, as with all rights and privileges, it is one that can be abused if not responsibly and judiciously used.

Because of the suspicions and doubts generated by the Watergate episode — and the FBI's role in investigating it — it seems entirely reasonable that the Senators are entitled to receive all factual and pertinent information about Mr. Gray's role in the affair.

Members of the Senate, like the President, have certain constitutional duties, and one of them is to pass judgment on and confirm appointments made by the president. It is difficult to imagine how they can discharge this duty in the public interest if they are denied information on which to base a decision.

In order to clear the air President Nixon ought to offer a compelling reason why Mr. Dean and other executive staff members with knowledge of the situation are not being allowed to appear before the committee or he ought to send them to testify.

That does not mean Mr. Nixon should surrender forever the executive privilege but rather that he should lend the full weight of his office to clarifying the situation with facts.

WORCESTER TELEGRAM.

Worcester, Mass., March 20, 1973

President Nixon's suggestion that the Supreme Court should make a "definitive decision" on the question of executive privilege is a clever political ploy. There is not much chance that the Supreme Court wants to get involved in the sort of political crossfire now going on between the President and the Congress.

President Nixon likes to put the dispute on the lofty level of high constitutional issues. And, indeed, executive privilege does have important constitutional implications. Presidents as far back as George Washington have refused to allow Congress to get its hands on delicate information dealing with important domestic and foreign policies.

But Nixon's concern is not with matters of state policy. He is fighting a congressional attempt to pry into the open some sordid political dealings connected with his own re-election campaign. The Watergate Affair is the most dramatic of these episodes, but there are others that, if let out, would not add to the luster of the President's party.

We can hardly blame the President for wanting to keep these things under the rug. It might be awkward in the extreme if the roles played by some of his highest confidantes were exposed.

But Nixon is making a mistake if he thinks the American people are going to buy his talk about constitutional issues. The issue here is not the interest of the country, but the interest of the Administration that happens to be in the White House.

The Courier-Journal

Louisville, Ky., March 21, 1973

PRESIDENT NIXON'S arguments for invoking executive privilege may very well protect White House counsel John Dean from having to testify in the Senate inquiry into the FBI's role in the Watergate inquiry. But the over-all effect on presidential credibility of that political espionage "caper" continues to be the best argument for both the White House and the Committee to Re-Elect the President to make full disclosures of their shady-looking roles in last year's election.

Instead, Mr. Nixon appears willing to sacrifice FBI chief L. Patrick Gray III, while blaming senators for making the FBI directorship "hostage" to a political inquiry on the Watergate crimes. And the Attorney General has ordered Mr. Gray to withdraw what seemed at the time a good-faith, belief-inspiring offer to open an FBI file for senators' eyes only — in a manner that reminded Mr. Nixon himself (as he told the nation last week in his news conference) of J. Edgar Hoover's tactic in the late 1940s of showing "raw" FBI documents to then-decidedly-junior Congressman Nixon.

Now, listening to the President's justifications, one has the sense of panic hiding behind seeming candor—the same intuition that Mr. Nixon told biographer Earl Mazo he had felt on the opening day of the Hiss inquiry.

What's curious is that the President wavers between having one case for executive privilege and having three or four. The person who gives a bundle of reasons for his action may be found to have no single, legitimate reason. Is it (1) the argument that the President's aides must remain anonymous, or (2) the sanctuary of lawyer and client confidentiality, or (3) the assertion that the White House has told Congress all it needs to know, or will do so, in writing, on its own terms.

Without cross-examination

The first argument for executive privilege might, in itself, be good enough to maintain Mr. Nixon's case, as it happens. Who can say what the Supreme Court would decide in this field of constitutional law? There are few cases. More often than not, Congress has conceded to the Chief Executive his right to employ assistants with that "passion for anonymity" FDR sought as a touchstone of faithful service. However the second argument he advanced has put the President on dangerous ground. If Mr. Dean cannot testify because of the confidential lawyer-client relationship, then is one expected to believe that the entire White House staff employs Mr. Dean out of choice? That the "house lawyer" for the presidential mansion moonlights by caring for a staff that instinctively turns to him when in trouble? As for the third item in Mr. Nixon's brief, Senator Sam Ervin disposed of it by noting that it's "impossible to cross-examine a written answer." If the dealings between Congress and the White House counsel are to be in writing, and restricted, as the President said, to "pertinent" questions on the FBI and Watergate, then the Senate might as well close up its investigatory shop. Mr. Dean could define the issues, re-phrase the question and veer off on a self-serving course of his own choosing.

It could be, as the Republican members of the Judiciary Committee are arguing, that there's less to the Gray-Watergate-Dean matter than meets the eye. The same committee agreed last year to question Peter Flanigan on his dealings with Attorney General Kleindienst, despite White House bluster about executive privilege. It could also be that President Nixon has been ill-served by Cabinet cronies and by a presidential aide, Mr. Dean, who meddled in an FBI investigation, leaked the FBI's secret files to Republican Party leaders — not in government service — and recommended officials who recruited others for espionage and sabotage of the rival political party.

If Mr. Dean were to appear before the Judiciary Committee, and refuse to say anything, he would not compromise Mr. Gray's testimony — which, as Senator Bayh has noted, was frank and full, even if a little demeaning of the FBI as an institution. If Mr. Dean were to stand in contempt of Congress for that act, then the President could get the Supreme Court ruling he appears to want.

But the President shouldn't at the same time tell the people how open and forthcoming his administration is. The case is too intricate to be very good. Behind all this is a lawyer (and, as he reminds us now and then, Mr. Nixon *is* a lawyer) who isn't willing to reveal all he knows.

The New York Times

New York, N.Y., March 20, 1973

A growing number of Republican Senators no longer share the Administration's apparent hope that public apathy will allow President Nixon to ride out the Watergate storm by pretending that the affair does not really concern him. No amount of public apathy could justify Mr. Nixon's posture of disengagement; but the Administration can no longer claim that only the news media are interested in the Watergate "caper."

It has long since become evident that the Watergate scandal was no "caper." After hearing the testimony by James W. McCord Jr., Senator Marlow W. Cook, Republican of Kentucky, said he now believed that some of the Administration's "underlings" had "really thought that it might be necessary to rig a Federal election."

Tampering with the election process of the United States is no laughing matter. However, Senator Cook may be in error when he suggests that the effort to rig the election was masterminded at the "underling" level.

Underlings were caught in the act of political espionage. Underlings were brought to trial. Underlings apparently were persuaded, like good spies, to remain silent and take the rap—until Mr. McCord broke ranks. But the evidence is now overwhelming that the underlings were not just a gang of overzealous Nixon supporters acting on their own. The very term—underlings—implies that these men acted under instructions from more powerful quarters. It is perfectly clear that their money and their orders came from command posts very close to the center of the Administration.

John W. Dean 3d, the President's legal counsel, has been charged by L. Patrick Gray, the acting director of the F.B.I., of lying when he denied knowing that E. Howard Hunt, one of the convicted Watergate conspirators, had operated from an office inside the White House. Yet, the same Mr. Dean still heads the "investigation" of the Watergate affair ordered by the President. The same Mr. Dean also took to himself the right to sit in on the F.B.I. interrogation of witnesses to the Watergate case. And the same Mr. Dean continues to enjoy the President's personal protection, labeled "executive privilege," that keeps him immune from Senatorial questioning.

The President's personal lawyer, Herbert W. Kalmbach, has told the F.B.I. that he paid substantial amounts of money to Donald Segretti, another "underling" alleged to have been involved in the political espionage. Mr. Segretti, in turn, came recommended from inside the White House by Dwight L. Chapin, then the President's appointments secretary.

The money allocated to these extraordinary activities that were characterized by Senator Cook as efforts to "rig" the election came out of accounts, safes and suitcases under the direct jurisdiction of the two top campaign managers, John N. Mitchell and Maurice Stans, both former Cabinet officers and the President's close personal and political associates.

Thus the web of the conspiracy was evidently spun by men who were the President's surrogates. The fact that it has not been charged that the President had personal knowledge of these crimes, plotted and committed in the cause of his re-election, is no longer particularly relevant. They were plotted and financed at a level of power for which the President must assume personal responsibility.

It would be a high watermark of hypocrisy for Mr. Nixon, who has made himself a spokesman for "law and order," to pretend that lawlessness within the high ranks of his Administration is of no direct concern to him personally as well as to the Office of the President.

Senate Republican Leader Hugh Scott, one of Mr. Nixon's loyal supporters, yesterday expressed his concern over these "developments which taint the political process." Senator Charles Mathias Jr., Republican of Maryland, demands a restoration of confidence. When those who have undermined that confidence are so close to the Presidency, it is clearly up to the President to take personal charge of the process of full disclosure. Nothing less can re-establish faith in the Administration and in the integrity of Government.

GRAY ASKS NIXON TO WITHDRAW HIS NOMINATION AS FBI CHIEF

The nomination of L. Patrick Gray 3rd to become director of the Federal Bureau of Investigation was withdrawn April 5. Gray disclosed he had asked President Nixon to withdraw his nomination, and a spokesman at the Western White House at San Clemente, Calif. said the President had "regretfully agreed." Gray had been acting FBI director since the death of J. Edgar Hoover in May 1972. [See pp. 392–399]

The nomination had become enmeshed in the Watergate political espionage controversy. The Senate Judiciary Committee, in its hearings on Gray's confirmation, had explored the connection between Gray and John W. Dean 3rd, counsel to the President, who had been linked to the Watergate defendants. After Dean's refusal to testify, the committee sought to broaden the inquiry and delay decision on the nomination. The panel held a surprise session April 5 to consider a motion to kill the nomination by indefinitely postponing confirmation, but adjourned without taking action. A few hours later, Gray announced his withdrawal, saying the FBI should have "permanent leadership at the earliest possible time."

The President's announcement observed that, "in view of the action of the Senate Judiciary Committee" it was "obvious that Mr. Gray's nomination will not be confirmed by the Senate." Therefore it was being withdrawn, he said, "in fairness to Mr. Gray, and out of my overriding concern for the effective conduct of the vitally important business of the FBI." The President referred to Dean's controversial role in his statement. Because he asked Dean to conduct a thorough investigation of "alleged involvement in the Watergate episode," he said, Gray was asked to make FBI reports available to Dean and "his compliance with this completely proper and necessary request . . . exposed Mr. Gray to totally unfair innuendo and suspicion and thereby seriously tarnished his fine record as acting director and promising future at the bureau."

THE ARIZONA REPUBLIC

Phoenix, Ariz., April 8, 1973

The Eastern establishment has made Pat Gray walk the plank.

At Gray's r e q u e s t, President Nixon has withdrawn his appointment as director of the Federal Bureau of Investigation.

Of course, all's fair in politics. But abrasive, repetitive attacks on Nixon a p p o i n t e e s, the use of smear and innuendo to force the rejection of his nominees — these tactics can only increase the difficulty every president has in getting good men to accept high position in the federal government.

One charge against Gray was that he had shown a congressional committee some raw files containing material collected by the FBI. Oddly enough, Gray's predecessor, J. Edgar Hoover, was frequently condemned because he wouldn't s h o w congressional committees the files they wanted to see.

Another charge against Gray was that he indicated some support for President Nixon. Again it is odd to note that the charge was brought largely by those who criticized Hoover for being too independent.

Pat Gray's full name is L. Patrick Gray III. He follows the path of G. Harrold Carswell and Clement F. Haynsworth Jr., both of whom were Nixon nominees for the S u p r e m e Court, in being forced to bow out.

It would be facetious to say all three appointments were scuttled because they put the initial at the beginning of their names instead of in the middle, or because they remembered their ancestors with designations at the end of their names.

But that would be just about as good an excuse as any given by the senators who fought these appointments.

The real reason is politics.

The Standard-Times

New Bedford, Mass.
April 9, 1973

Now that Senate Democrats have succeeded in torpedoing the nomination of L. Patrick Gray III to be director of the FBI, the question is whether any other nominee will be able to win confirmation.

Having had their taste of blood, the Democrats are unlikely to pay much attention to Gray's parting comment that "the FBI, a great and unique American institution of vital service to the president and the American people, is entitled to permanent leadership at the earliest possible time."

What sank Gray's hopes were his admissions to the Senate Judiciary Committee that he had given White House counsel John W. Dean III access to raw FBI files on the Watergate investigation and had made pro-Nixon comments in at least one speech during the 1972 presidential campaign.

The major criticism centered on the Watergate investigation which the Democrats are still pursuing, in large part for political advantage. Yet on this issue it appears Gray merely obeyed the order of the President himself, as transmitted through his counsel, Dean.

Yet what is any future nominee to reply, when he is asked whether he will obey the orders of the President and the attorney general, his bosses, and whether he will provide them with information they request? Presumably, if he replies affirmatively, he will be denied confirmation just as Gray was.

That being the case, Gray possibly could stay on as acting FBI director for the last 45 months of Mr. Nixon's term because it is unlikely Mr. Nixon will nominate anyone who would announce in advance he wouldn't obey the President.

Whether matters will reach such ridiculous heights is problematical, however. Gray, after all, is the victim of the confrontation between the President and the Democratic Congress over the Watergate case and the broader issue of the executive privilege claimed by Mr. Nixon for his administrative aides.

As The News has said before, the White House staff has bungled the handling of the Watergate case and thus in part is responsible for the fate that befell L. Patrick Gray, who was torpedoed by the Democrats, not because he lied but because he told the truth as he knew it.

Ironically, it was the Republicans who back in 1968 persuaded Congress to make appointment of future FBI directors subject to Senate confirmation in order to protect the post from politics. What has happened is just the opposite. The FBI has been thrust deep into politics with the help of those who claimed they wanted to save it from that fate.

The Washington Post

Times Herald

Washington, D.C., April 11, 1973

Having spearheaded the effort to turn back President Nixon's nomination of L. Patrick Gray III to be director of the FBI, Sen. Robert Byrd (D-W. Va) has turned his attention to quite serious issues of the governance of the bureau, which flow both from J. Edgar Hoover's 48-year tenure in the director's chair and from the Gray hearings. Senator Byrd has introduced a bill which he hopes will improve the bureau and take it out of politics. The central purposes of the bill are to take the bureau out of the Department of Justice and make it an independent agency and to limit the director's term in office to seven years. Sen. Henry Jackson (D-Wash.) is introducing a bill which would give the director a 15-year term with no possibility of reappointment and require that the nominee have at least 10 years experience in the FBI.

There can be little doubt that the issues which these two measures seek to address are extraordinarily important. The dangers of politicizing the FBI or even giving the appearance of doing so have been graphically demonstrated in the last few weeks. It is not simply the distribution of John Ehrlichman's request for information which would be useful in the campaign to FBI field offices last year or even the appearance that Mr. Gray acted at least like a quasi surrogate for the President in the campaign. Those things are bad enough. More to the point is the nightmarish position of a few employees of the Committee for the Reelection of the President who, wanting to discuss matters involved in an FBI investigation freely and out of the presence of their superiors, arrange to do so and then find that their information has made a full circuit right back to the people whose intervention they sought to avoid in the first place. Finally, of course, there is the sad story of Mr. Hoover's ossifying political views and concurrently ossifying control over the FBI in his later years.

Although these two bills attack very real problems, we are not, at least at this juncture, persuaded that the remedies proposed are either appropriate or wise. The establishment of the bureau as an independent agency, while attractive at first blush, might create more problems than it solves. In a very real and substantial sense, the FBI serves as the investigative arm of the federal criminal process. As such, it is imperative that it have the closest and most cooperative relationship with the lawyers who are trying to develop cases and who ultimately will have to try them. During the last years of Mr. Hoover's tenure, that relationship was either nonexistent or constricted and carried out with the greatest difficulty by lawyers within the Justice Department for, although Mr. Hoover was nominally the Attorney General's subordinate, he and the bureau were in a very real sense independent. Sen. Byrd's bill would simply perpetuate that problem.

We have already addressed the fixed term proposals in this space. Sen. Jackson's 15-year idea with the requirement that candidates be drawn from people who had put in at least 10 years in the bureau seems to us unduly restrictive of the President's freedom to choose the best person available, no matter what he or she might be engaged in at the time of the vacancy. Moreover, the trouble with a fixed term, whether it be 7 years or 15 or something in between, is that it would prevent the President from firing a person who had turned out to be his or some past President's mistake. Despite the perils of politicization, we think the system can be made to work if the President and his Attorney General are convinced that the Congress actually wants and is prepared to work to achieve a truly non-political and highly professional FBI.

And that, it seems to us, is the healthiest aspect of the Byrd and the Jackson proposals. For Sen. Byrd said some very important things when discussing his reasons for introducing his bill. He said that there was a real need to take a careful look at the FBI after Mr. Hoover's long rule, that he did not want the directorship to become a patronage plum and, most importantly, that he considered his bill a stimulus to congressional oversight and study of this whole matter. That last is the nub of it. If Congress can mount serious and sustained oversight on the problems of the governance of the bureau, all of these problems will be manageable. If it cannot, no gimmicks like fixed terms for the director will work. In providing a stimulus to active congressional participation in the management of the FBI, Sen. Byrd and Sen. Jackson have performed a useful public service.

The Detroit News

Detroit, Mich., April 9, 1973

And so L. Patrick Gray 3d is out as a candidate for permanent head of the FBI, thanks largely to a political power play, his own candor and perhaps a touch of naivete.

Certainly, Gray made mistakes since he took over as acting director after J. Edgar Hoover's death almost a year ago.

He really should have known better than to go off making partisan political speeches on President Nixon's behalf. And Gray's handling of some aspects of the Watergate bugging investigation left something to be desired.

His giving FBI reports to White House counsel John Dean 3d, who has been accused of involvement in the Watergate affair, seems particularly naive . . . but perhaps only through hindsight.

The fact remains Gray was caught in a political tug-of-war between the President who nominated him and the Senate, who had to confirm him.

Since President Nixon has refused to let aides such as Dean testify, Gray was the only man the Senate Judiciary Committee could use to reopen Watergate and reopen it they did — with a vengeance.

Gray was frank — painfully frank in his replies to the committee's days of interrogation and this undoubtedly led to his downfall. Because he answered questions so honestly — and revealingly — the White House turned cool on his nomination and withdrew its support . . . all the while voicing its wholehearted endorsement.

It's ironic that some of the same senators decrying Gray's "involvement" are the same senators who so bemoaned J. Edgar Hoover's aloofness from everyone.

The most important thing now is to find a permanent FBI head, one in whom the Congress, the President — and the country — can have complete confidence.

DAYTON DAILY NEWS

Dayton, Ohio, April 8, 1973

President Nixon typically hymned Acting FBI Director Patrick Gray toward oblivion, as he has others of his failed nominees, with a denunciation of the senators who were repelled by the proposition to confirm. The President said Mr. Gray was a victim of "totally unfair innuendo and suspicion."

Like blazes he was. Mr. Gray was a victim of his and the President's acts, as forthrightly (to give Mr. Gray his due) testified to by the acting FBI director in his hearings before a Senate committee. The fact is that Mr. Gray at the President's behest, unable to resist invitations to impropriety, used the FBI as a partisan political agency.

Whatever his failings — and they were several in his later years —, the late and so-far-only FBI Director J. Edgar Hoover kept the bureau out of politics, a bedrock integrity the public interest demands. Mr.

Gray, however, stumped for Mr. Nixon's re-election, used FBI agents as campaign researchers and played ball with White House staff members assigned to damage-limiting the Watergate crimes.

Those are not matters of innuendo and suspicion. Mr. Gray swore to them. Like depressingly many of Mr. Nixon's nominees for the judiciary, Mr. Gray turned out to be a man habituated to the short-term rewards of acquiescence.

President Nixon can do better by the FBI now that he has had his way with Mr. Gray and has got him out of the way. He can look beyond his anteroom of political hacks for a person of irreducible integrity, one with germane qualifications and with some appreciation of the necessary subtleties of modern law enforcement. The Senate would be charmed.

St. Louis Globe-Democrat

St. Louis, Mo., April 7, 1973

L. Patrick Gray III should have been confirmed as director of the FBI. He would have been a worthy successor to the late J. Edgar Hoover.

He simply was a victim of the deadly crossfire between the Senate Judiciary Committee and the White House.

Certain members of the committee charged Gray had made a grave error by showing FBI reports on the Watergate investigation to John W. Dean III, counsel to the President.

The point that was not emphasized during the lengthy hearings is that Dean also was investigating the possible role of White House staff members in the Watergate incident. There was every good reason why Gray should provide Dean, as the representative of the President, reports on the FBI findings to aid Dean in his investigation.

President Nixon also failed to back up Gray as might have been expected. In our opinion, Mr. Nixon should have ordered every member of his staff to cooperate fully with the Judiciary Committee rather than try to claim executive privilege. Since none of Mr. Nixon's policies were involved in this issue, there was no valid case for executive privilege.

If full cooperation had been given to the committee, we are confident that Gray would have been confirmed because the complete picture would have shown he (1) was guilty of no wrongdoing in the Watergate probe; (2) conducted a thorough investigation, (3) is well qualified for the post of FBI director.

It is tragic that a man who has served his country with distinction as a submarine captain and as acting director of the FBI should be used for bayonet practice in the battle between the Judiciary Committee and the White House.

The nation is the loser as well as Gray in this sordid affair. He deserves high praise for his conduct before the committee and his courage under the most difficult and unfair circumstances.

Chicago Tribune

Chicago, Ill., April 9, 1973

Seven men have pleaded or been found guilty of complicity in the Watergate affair; but the first to be formally penalized for it, ironically, is the acting head of the FBI, L. Patrick Gray III, who had nothing to do with the ill-fated invasion of Democratic headquarters.

At Mr. Gray's request, President Nixon has withdrawn his nomination as director of the FBI.

Mr. Gray found himself in the impossible position of having tried to investigate a crime which his bosses in the White House did not want investigated, at least not too thoroly, and of then trying to explain his actions to a Senate committee which was ostensibly considering his confirmation but seemed really more interested in tying the White House to Watergate.

From the moment he found himself in this arena, Mr. Gray was almost a sure loser. If he had sung [or rather kept quiet] to the White House tune, he would have queered himself with the senators. If he had sung the song the senators wanted to hear, he would have angered the White House and the job he sought wouldn't have been worth much to him. As matters turned out, he offended both sides, and under the circumstances this is probably to his credit.

Mr. Nixon blames Mr. Gray's troubles on his compliance with a White House request for secret FBI reports on the Watergate investigation. "This completely proper and necessary request," the President said Thursday, "exposed Mr. Gray to totally unfair innuendo and suspicion and thereby seriously tarnished his fine record."

Since the request for the reports was from John Dean, the Presidential assistant who has himself been named as a participant in the planning of Watergate, the propriety and necessity of the request come out somewhat blurry. But no matter how you look at it, Mr. Gray's real problems stem not from unfair innuendoes by the senators or the public, but from the White House itself.

If the White House was right in asking for the secret data, and it is hard to deny it that right, then it was wrong in not cooperating with the investigation. If Mr. Gray was right in everything he did, then it was cowardly of the White House to abandon him just because he was having trouble with the senators. If the suspicions aroused by Mr. Gray's action or inaction were unfair, the White House could have cleared him by seeing that all the facts were made public.

The longer the uncertainties persist, the more suspicions are going to be aroused and the more people may be spattered unfairly with the Watergate mud. Federal Judge John J. Sirica has shown a commendable determination to get to the bottom of the whole thing, and he deserves the cooperation of everyone, including the President.

DAILY ❏ NEWS

New York, N.Y., April 7, 1973

Three liberal Senators, Birch Bayh (D-Ind.), John Tunney (D-Calif.) and Teddy Kennedy, must be hugging themselves with glee now that L. Patrick Gray 3d has been forced to withdraw from nomination as head of the FBI.

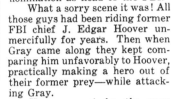

L. Patrick Gray

What a sorry scene it was! All those guys had been riding former FBI chief J. Edgar Hoover unmercifully for years. Then when Gray came along they kept comparing him unfavorably to Hoover, practically making a hero out of their former prey—while attacking Gray.

He may not be the man Hoover was, but he was capable, tough and strong on law and order. He did all right in the 11 months he was acting FBI boss. He moved younger men up the ladder, hired women agents and relaxed some of Hoover's rigid rules.

The FBI as an institution has come through all the hearings unscathed and with continued public confidence. That is a tribute to Gray's ability and leadership.

The big mistake Gray made was in acting too eager for the job. He talked too much and too rashly to the Senate Judiciary Committee, and he never should have shown those raw FBI files to Presidential counsel John Dean. Dean should never have asked for them. He needed only a summary. For that mistake President Nixon should censure Dean.

Any nominee to head the FBI was likely to be attacked as political in the wake of the Presidential election, even if he wore wings and had a halo. That's why it might be a good idea to stagger the director's term by making it 7, 9, or 11 years to keep it out of Presidential year political vendettas.

The President should act quickly on a successor. The man should be experienced, non-political and respected. Then if those high binder Senators will hang up their political bullwhips for a while and vote his confirmation, the FBI can get on with the important work it has to do for the country.

The Pittsburgh Press

Pittsburgh, Pa., April 8, 1973

With the Gray nomination wisely withdrawn, President Nixon now has the opportunity to appoint an FBI director with qualifications the U. S. Senate cannot question.

This means nominating a man who is neither a close friend nor a political ally of the President. He should be a strong administrator with a keen knowledge of the law.

The nomination of acting Director L. Patrick Gray III was in trouble from the start because Mr. Gray, for all his energy and candor, was a Nixon crony and political partisan.

In the Watergate investigation last summer, he chose to turn over confidential Watergate files to White House lawyer John W. Dean III on the questionable theory that because Mr. Dean was the President's man he had a right to such information.

Unwittingly or not, Mr. Gray made a series of what sounded like pro-Nixon speeches last summer and fall, and FBI agents (mistakenly, the White House says) were asked to gather background material for the presidential campaign.

It should have been no surprise, then, that the more the Watergate case began to unravel, the slimmer were Mr. Gray's chances of being confirmed by a Democratic-controlled Senate.

His request that the President withdraw his name was the only sensible course Mr. Gray could take. Even if he had been confirmed, his credibility — and the credibility of the FBI — would have been damaged.

Speculation now is that Mr. Nixon will act promptly, perhaps within a day or two, to submit a new nominee in Mr. Gray's place. Certainly a long delay would be unwarranted.

For the FBI has been operating without a permanent director since last May. That's long enough for any organization — and particularly for an organization that depends on leadership and esprit de corps.

It isn't necessary for the President to pick a police chief, or a prosecuting attorney, or a judge or even an old FBI hand for the job.

What matters most is that the President nominate the best man available.

THE DENVER POST
Denver, Colo., April 1, 1973

A WEEK AFTER President Nixon's re-election last November, The Denver Post called upon him "to take his own strong steps to root out—even to the very doors of his office—any and all persons whose presence brings the slightest taint of wrongdoing to his administration."

At that time, we were convinced we had supported an honest man for re-election to the presidency. We believed it likely that the charges of corruption in high places, aired during the campaign, were mostly the product of political animus.

LIKE MOST AMERICANS, we were greatly impressed by the skill with which President Nixon had managed our withdrawal from Vietnam, and diplomatic relations with Communist China, Russia and North Vietnam.

But we feared that the President's leadership at home would be compromised unless he moved energetically to disprove the charges of corruption raised against various levels of his administration—including persons in the White House itself.

After all, there were two very serious general charges tarnishing the good name of the Nixon administration in November: 1) that administration members had engaged in corrupt and downright criminal behavior; and 2) that the administration had used the power of the White House and cabinet-level agencies to cover up this corruption.

IN SOME RESPECTS, we regard the second charge as more damaging to the reputation, not only of the Nixon administration but of the whole federal government, than the first. And we felt it imperative that the Nixon administration open up the records, expose all the questioned dealings to full public inspection and either prove it had nothing to hide or else bring any wrongdoers to full and exact justice.

Nothing of this sort has happened yet. And nearly five months passed before the President began, late last week, to talk as if he might begin to do soon what a decent respect for public opinion should have required of him last November.

In the intervening months the charges of scandal have multiplied and widened—and involved persons ever closer to the President himself. Perjury has been alleged in the Watergate federal district court trial, and the integrity of the FBI investigative process in that case has been impugned—not to mention the integrity of John Dean, the presidential aide who meddled in that FBI investigation.

And as of this writing, the President had not yet opened the records, had not yet cooperated in turning the full light of publicity on the various affairs and those involved.

Instead he had kept quiet, refused to let Dean and other aides testify before Senate investigators, and triggered a campaign of abuse against the newspapers and reporters who have done the most to investigate the Watergate.

IN SUM, ALTHOUGH HE has said—through an intermediary, not directly—that the White House has nothing to hide, he most certainly has not proved it. He has, in fact, acted like a man trying to hide whatever can be hidden.

So we are disturbed, and we have to wonder. We are no longer willing to accept on faith that this is a basically honest administration. We wonder when the President will drive out those who are tarnishing his administration.

And what we are wondering, many another American who supported President Nixon for re-election must be wondering too.

Only last Friday did the first signs of cooperation emerge from the White House — and those very small and vague signs. A presidential spokesman said the White House, while still unwilling to let staff members such as Dean testify under oath before an open congressional hearing, would be willing to work out some compromise- perhaps an appearance before an informal, closed committee hearing.

The spokesman added that if a grand jury called any White House staff member to testify, the President would require him to do so. This is not much of a concession. The President does not have the power to keep a White House staffer from answering a grand jury summons.

So what the President is offering is too little, and rather late. At the very least, he should order his aides to cooperate fully in any and all investigations of the scandals now imputed to them. And let any guilty heads roll where they may.

The good of the nation requires no less.

THE MILWAUKEE JOURNAL
Milwaukee, Wis., April 3, 1973

The White House, all along, has attempted to brazen out the Watergate scandal and put it to sleep before it infects the whole administration. That's a lost cause; the mess won't wash. Instead of lying down quietly, Watergate is now well on the way to striking home. It has gone too far to be turned back now by mere pious denials and arrogant cover-ups.

The essential quest is to learn which Republican bigwigs, how high up in President Nixon's official family — whether with or without his own foreknowledge—conceived and financed a criminal conspiracy against the Democratic Party last summer. The plot surfaced when a seven man gang, including some with White House and Nixon campaign ties, were nabbed in the act of burglarizing and bugging Democratic National Headquarters in Washington's Watergate complex.

The seven have been convicted, but they were small potatoes. Who put them up to it and promised to protect them? Who pressured five of them to plead guilty and not pass the blame in self-defense? Who knew about the plot beforehand? Who put the campaign funds into it?

* * *

The continued search for these vital answers has raised other messy national issues. It has fouled up Nixon's nomination of his henchman L. Patrick Gray to be permanent director of the FBI, since the FBI's own integrity has been compromised. It is leading to a thunderous showdown over Nixon's abuse of "executive privilege"—extending the White House rule of secrecy even to a purely criminal investigation, unrelated to national policy making.

This has imperiled — in many minds already destroyed — the credibility of the Nixon administration itself. More and more by the week, it is appearing unprincipled, unscrupulous. The seasoned Washington journalist Joseph Kraft recently termed the Watergate affair "a political bomb that could blow the Nixon administration apart."

Not least alarming to the American public should be Nixon's attempt, now clearly shown up, to "politicize" the FBI through Gray, to turn the nation's powerful police arm into a submissive tool of the White House for partisan political purposes. Among other indications of this, Acting Director Gray let the president's chief counsel John Dean, with obviously chilling effect, sit in on FBI interviews about Watergate with White House aides. As one comfort at least, the Gray nomination is apparently a dead duck in the Senate.

* * *

It is not unusual for administrations to be embarrassed by misdeeds of persons close to the president, with or without his condonation. What counts is how a president responds. For months, Nixon has taken the route of Warren G. Harding, who responded with an excess of loyalty when cronies betrayed his trust. Nixon has obstructed investigation, withheld information from Congress, expressed undimmed faith in the purity of everyone associated with him.

But the bipartisan pressure is becoming too great. The president now at least indicates that his aides will be ready to testify before a federal grand jury and that some compromise is possible regarding appearances before congressional investigators. This is the direction in which Nixon must move in full good faith, otherwise the drizzle now spattering mud on the White House roof will soon become a deluge.

New York Post
New York, N.Y., April 7, 1973

Two serious obligations continue to confront the Senate following the Nixon Administration's decision to withdraw the nomination of L. Patrick Gray as permanent—rather than "acting"—director of the FBI.

The two responsibilities are (1) assuring that the next FBI director will be professionally competent and non-political and (2) unearthing the full story of the Watergate scandal. These tasks have become somewhat entangled at recent Senate hearings but that is not the legislators' fault. The confusion was inevitable in the circumstances.

Simply stated, the Nixon Administration has sought to install a compliant loyalist at the head of the FBI but has been obliged to withdraw his name because his total fealty to the White House —as demonstrated by his supine agreement to turn over Watergate data to an involved White House aide and to accept political speechmaking assignments — became painfully vulnerable. In a sense Gray was victimized by the pressures of the Administration; his worst deeds were performed on request from those to whom he owed his appointment. But that hardly offered promise of independence in office.

It is, of course, possible that the White House will be chastened by this reversal, seek out and nominate a more impressive candidate and, in addition, drop the "executive privilege" evasion and arrange for White House aides to answer Senate questions.

But that is speculative. White House counsel John Dean, whose veracity Gray publicly questioned, is still balking at an appearance; no substantive signs of change are in sight and it will be recalled that the Administration's record on "second nominees" is not highly encouraging. When the Haynsworth nomination for the Supreme Court did not find favor, for instance, the next suggestion was Carswell. It remains for the Senate to protect the public by diligently exercising its "advise and consent" function.

Certainly recent events have dramatically confirmed the importance of the FBI director's post, and the need for an appointee whose credentials are beyond suspicion on any level. Gray's exit will be a poor triumph for his opponents if they passively accept a mediocre substitute.

'IMPROPER GOVERNMENT CONDUCT' CITED IN PENTAGON PAPERS CASE

Government charges of espionage, theft and conspiracy against Daniel Ellsberg and Anthony J. Russo in the Pentagon Papers case were dismissed by Judge William R. Byrne in Los Angeles May 11 because of "improper government conduct." Judge Byrne's ruling, which precluded a retrial, was based on: (1) the government's inability to produce records of wiretaps made on phone conversations involving Ellsberg in 1969 and 1970, evidence of which was disclosed May 9 in a memorandum from acting FBI director William Ruckelshaus to Byrne; (2) evidence that a break-in had taken place at the office of Ellsberg's former psychiatrist by a special White House unit, whose other activities might never be known, operating independently of the FBI and with the apparent unlawful assistance of the CIA; and (3) government delays in producing exculpatory evidence it possessed, which, Byrne said, had compromised the defendant's right to a speedy trial.

The Evening Star and The Washington Daily News

Washington, D.C., May 8, 1973

On and on come the ugly revelations, the almost daily disclosures of how this nation's political and judicial processes have been manipulated and corrupted. Now we learn that the Central Intelligence Agency shares heavily in the responsibility for the Ellsberg case, which if not directly related to Watergate nevertheless helped set the stage for it and is indisputably part of the same poisonous syndrome.

Start with the premise that, for its own purposes, the CIA had no interest in digging up damaging information on Daniel Ellsberg and his role in leaking the Pentagon papers in June, 1971. But the White House surely did. And someone at the White House, possibly John Ehrlichman, induced someone high at CIA, probably General Robert E. Cushman, to authorize the use of the agency's clandestine services in the burglary of the office of Ellsberg's psychiatrist. That happened in September, 1971, while Richard Helms was still head of CIA and two months before General Cushman left his post as deputy director of the agency to become commandant of the Marine Corps. Meanwhile, and just as disturbing, the head of CIA's psychological assessment unit was directed (by whom?) to cooperate with the White House in working up a psychological profile of Ellsberg.

At this point, the CIA-Ellsberg episode is subject to any number of interpretations. Loose threads and unanswered questions are everywhere. Yet even an interpretation most favorable to the agency leads to conclusions that are devastating.

The CIA, in brief, has been used and compromised and discredited in somewhat the same way that the FBI, under Patrick Gray, was used and compromised and discredited in the

Watergate investigation. Perhaps it was the guiltier of the two. For the CIA lent its offices to the perpetration of a shoddy crime, to the trampling of civil liberties and to a domestic surveillance operation that by law it had no business conducting even indirectly.

It is difficult to believe that Helms, a canny and professional man, would have known all this beforehand and consented to such an improbable venture as the Hunt-Liddy burglary of the psychiatrist's office. Of course, anything is possible, as the nation has learned with relentless regularity the last few weeks.

General Cushman, even if his implication in the affair can be partially explained as unthinking, has a great deal to answer for. He is, to be sure, a distinguished military officer. He is also a longtime friend and supporter of the President's. Those two things need not have been incompatible. But in this case, apparently, they were. In the anything-goes pattern of Watergate, an otherwise decent man appears to have blocked off conscience and good judgment, and gone along with whatever the White House requested.

At first the Watergate scandal was said to be the work of a few ideological zealots. Lately, it has been fashionable to lay the blame on men close to the President with a super-loyal, ad-agency turn of mind. But the web of Watergate-Ellsberg spreads much farther than that. In the FBI, in Justice, now in the CIA, it involves men and vital institutions the American public should have had every reason to trust, but now do not. Aside from the diminished stature of the presidency itself, that is what is hardest to take.

CHICAGO Sun-Times

Chicago, Ill., May 3, 1973

The text of a Federal Bureau of Investigation interview with John D. Ehrlichman, formerly one of President Nixon's two most intimate and trusted advisers, clearly reveals a complacent and unpardonable acceptance of a criminal act. If the FBI report is accurate and complete, Ehrlichman may also be guilty of misprision of a felony, withholding evidence, obstruction of justice and criminal conspiracy.

Ehrlichman told the FBI that, pursuant to a directive from Mr. Nixon, he organized a 1971 inquiry into the Pentagon papers case and that he enlisted the services of two men later convicted in the Watergate bugging trial — E. Howard Hunt Jr. and G. Gordon Liddy. Hunt and Liddy apparently took it upon themselves to burglarize the office of a psychiatrist then treating a defendant in the Pentagon papers case, Daniel Ellsberg. The FBI report revealed that when he was told of the burglary, Ehrlichman said, mildly, that he "did not agree with this method of investigation" and that he merely told Hunt and Liddy "not to do this again." Nowhere in the FBI report is there any hint that Ehrlichman even considered reporting his knowledge of this felony to the appropriate authorities or even that he disciplined anyone. Clearly, Ehrlichman was so deeply trapped in the miasma of chicanery that he was paralyzed. He was committed to persons who, like himself, regarded themselves as part of an imperial regime, immune from both criminal laws and basic standards of human conduct.

This is the same man who, in resigning his White House job, told Mr. Nixon that "the appearance of honesty and integrity is every bit as important to such a position as the fact of one's honesty and integrity." This is the same man Mr. Nixon on Monday night called one of the "finest public servants it has been my privilege to know" and whom Mr. Nixon defended against any hint of wrongdoing and allowed to remain on the payroll.

There can be no confidence in any investigation of the Watergate scandal conducted by persons associated, however innocently, with this arrogant and institutionalized hypocrisy. The Senate has adopted a resolution calling for the appointment of a special, independent prosecutor. We repeat our endorsement of this appointment. The resolution has wide, bipartisan support, and if Mr. Nixon wants a showdown over this matter, he is entitled to one. In light of the threat posed by this historic scandal on the office of the Presidency, the appointment of a special prosecutor may be the only — not simply the best — course of action.

THE STATES-ITEM
New Orleans, La., May 12, 1973

Revelations that the Central Intelligence Agency provided disguises and equipment used by a Nixon Administration operative in the break-in of Daniel Ellsberg's psychiatrist's office should be of great concern to the American people.

The information is particularly alarming because the people probably know less about the operation of the CIA, and have less control over it, than any other agency of government.

It is for this reason that there is in the CIA the potential for the kind of "secret police" operation that we deplore in totalitarian nations.

The dangers and the power of such an agency were fully understood when it was established. That is why the 1947 law under which the CIA was organized specifically bars the CIA from conducting covert operations inside the United States.

The CIA was intended to be an independent arm of government. Certainly it was not meant to be used as a partisan political tool of the administration in power. That, however, was the way the agency was used in the Ellsberg case, and the direction came from an authority in the White House.

Specifically, according to memorandum submitted by the CIA in the Pentagon Papers trial of Mr. Ellsberg, the agency equipped E. Howard Hunt Jr. with false identification papers, disguises, business cards and recording equipment. Mr. Hunt was later convicted for the Watergate break-in.

When the CIA decided to stop cooperating with Mr. Hunt, Gen. Robert E. Cushman, then deputy director of the CIA and now commandant of the Marine Corps, called a so-far unnamed White House official to inform him of the decision.

It is frightening to speculate on the ultimate consequences of a shadowy organization such as the CIA used at cross purposes with the people it was established to protect.

THE RICHMOND NEWS LEADER
Richmond, Va., May 14, 1973

So instead of being convicted and sent off to cool his hot ideological theories in a federal penitentiary, Daniel Ellsberg is to become the newest patron saint of the New Left. The dismissal of charges against him will be translated into an exoneration of all the irresponsible things he has said and continues to say, such as: The White House uses "Mafia tactics;" President Nixon masterminded a "conspiracy to deprive us of our civil liberties;" and the "country is run by criminals." One need only contemplate those crackpot statements to confirm that Daniel Ellsberg is on an ideological trip.

Yet it cannot be denied that a seemingly endless string of governmental buffooneries is the fundamental reason that Daniel Ellsberg is not on his way to the federal penitentiary. Governmental wiretaps on Ellsberg's telephone, the undercover White House investigation of his activities, the ransacking of his psychiatrist's files — all those things served to lead the judge to the ineluctable conclusion that the government was not leveling with the court. And this is but the latest example — for whatever reason — of the evident inability of the federal government to lock up for long the darlings of the New Left. Perhaps this ruling will mark the expiration of the statute of limitations on the government's incompetences, stupidities, and deceptions in such prosecutions.

The skunking of the government, however, should not be permitted to undermine the essential validity of the charges against Ellsberg. The charges against Ellsberg were charges of espionage, conspiracy, and theft. The defense sought — successfully — to cloud the major point through extraneity. The major point is that Daniel Ellsberg stole classified government documents. At the very least, and notwithstanding his pretentious justifications, he is an admitted thief. Whether he is guilty of espionage is debateable. But for the sake of argument let us assume that Ellsberg was engaged in espionage; let us also assume that the Nixon administration was engaged in espionage, albeit of a different sort, to keep itself informed about what Ellsberg was up to. Surely the espionage of Ellsberg should not be defended while the espionage of the Nixon administration is condemned.

The prospect now is that Ellsberg will be trotted across the pages of *The New York Times*, and before college audiences, which will pay him assiduous court. In self-congratulatory tones, he will verbally bump and grind before the bulging eyes of the media — mouthing his tired old non-sequiturs. He will tell the public about all the fascists in the Nixon administration, and, sadly, the public will listen, because these days there is nothing quite so safe to fall upon as the Nixon administration. But before cynically concluding that the Nixon administration is vile and Ellsberg is pure, it is important to reflect on a crucial fact: Sympathy for what Ellsberg did is sufficiently widespread that a majority of the jurors in the Ellsberg case have said that on the substantive issues, they would have voted for...acquittal.

St. Louis Globe-Democrat
St. Louis, Mo., May 3, 1973

Resigned presidential aide John D. Ehrlichman is reported to have told the FBI that President Nixon in 1971 designated him to make an independent investigation of the Pentagon Papers case.

The President certainly had good reason to do this.

But from what Ehrlichman is quoted as having told the FBI, the former top aide apparently went off the deep end in carrying out Mr. Nixon's request.

The two men chosen by Ehrlichman to conduct the probe, G. Gordon Liddy and E. Howard Hunt, were said to have broken into the office of Daniel Ellsberg's psychiatrist looking for information about Ellsberg's "psychological profile."

Ehrlichman told the FBI that he didn't learn of the burglary until after it happened and then told Hunt and Liddy "not to do this again."

If this interview represents the facts in the case, Ehrlichman acted improperly in several of ways.

First, he obviously failed to define the limits of the investigation and failed to properly supervise the two men who later became key figures in the Watergate scandal.

Secondly, his "don't do it again" response upon learning of the break-in was totally inadequate. At that point he should have fired both Liddy and Hunt and preferred charges against them. Instead they apparently remained on the payroll and continued their nefarious work.

This provides a prime example of how power, if not properly harnessed, can be flagrantly abused. Liddy and Hunt apparently thought they were the CIA, the FBI and Ehrlichman's secret agents, all wrapped up into one.

The penalty for such arrogance and stupidity is, of course, enormous. Liddy and Hunt, caught on their mission into Watergate with five others, now have been convicted for that break-in. Their exploits and the failures of those who were supposed to be keeping an eye on these "investigators" have now come back to haunt and plague President Nixon.

THE TENNESSEAN
Nashville, Tenn., May 3, 1973

THE WHITE House's role in burglarizing Mr. Daniel Ellsberg's psychiatric records and injecting itself into Mr. Ellsberg's trial on charges of stealing the Pentagon Papers is one of the most shocking aspects in the series of scandals now rocking the Nixon administration.

Mr. John D. Ehrlichman, who resigned as adviser to the President Monday, told the FBI last Friday that Mr. Nixon designated him in 1971 to make an independent investigation into the leak of the Pentagon Papers.

Mr. Ehrlichman said Gordon Liddy and Howard Hunt — later convicted in the Watergate break-in — were sent to make an "indepth investigation of Ellsberg to determine his habits, mental attitudes, motives, etc." In the course of their investigation, Liddy and Hunt — who seem to have been the administration's steady break-in artists — broke into the office of Mr. Ellsberg's psychiatrist and rifled Mr. Ellsberg's medical records.

Mr. Ehrlichman told the FBI he did not know about the burglary until after it occurred and that when he heard about it he instructed Liddy and Hunt "not to do this again." But apparently Mr. Ehrlichman's warning was not taken seriously, for a few months later — as members of the Nixon re-election campaign team — these break-in experts were involved in the burglarizing of the Democratic campaign headquarters at the Watergate Apartments in Washington.

This is the gist of the burglarizing of Mr. Ellsberg's private medical records. But it is not the end of the story of the administration's apparent attempt to influence the outcome of the Ellsberg trial.

In the middle of the trial, on April 5, the presiding judge was called to the western White House at San Clemente by Mr. Ehrlichman for discussion of his possible appointment as head of the FBI. Judge Byrne himself confirmed this yesterday but, to his credit, rejected the offer of the FBI post until the trial was over. Judge Byrne also deserves great credit for seeing that the facts of the break-in at the psychiatrist's office were dug out and made public.

Mr. Ellsberg and his lawyers have interpreted the job offer to Judge Byrne as an attempt by the Nixon administration to influence the outcome of the trial and see that Mr. Ellsberg was convicted for embarrassing the administration by making public the Pentagon Papers. It is difficult to see how the situation can be interpreted in any other way.

The disclosures in the Watergate and Ellsberg cases all but destroys the Nixon administration's credibility as an administration concerned about law and order and justice. An administration that fails to prosecute break-ins and concealment of evidence by its members, which attempts to interfere with the processes of justice, and sees nothing wrong with spying on the personal records of private citizens it wants to see punished for political reasons, has no claim to being a defender of law and order.

Mr. Ehrlichman told his story to the FBI last Friday. Three days later he resigned as Mr. Nixon's aide. That night Mr. Nixon went on television and expressed confidence in Mr. Ehrlichman, saying there was no implication of wrongdoing on his aide's part.

It seems incredible that a President who heads the most extensive intelligence-gathering agencies in the world didn't know one of his top aides was spilling the beans about administration complicity in criminal activity.

But the alternative to this is to believe that President Nixon did know what Mr. Ehrlichman was saying and could see nothing wrong in what his aide had done — or failed to do to uphold the law.

In either case, the Nixon administration's pretensions of concern for law and order in the nation are revealed as a monumental hoax on the American people.

Long Island Press

New York, N.Y., May 13, 1973

The judge's decision to throw out the Pentagon Papers case against Dr. Daniel Ellsberg and Anthony Russo was a foregone conclusion.

The government clearly violated the defendants' rights in many ways. It withheld evidence, it authorized the invasion of Dr. Ellsberg's psychiatrist's office, it tapped telephone conversations, it offered the presiding judge the directorship of the FBI while the trial was in progress.

As Judge Matt Byrne said in declaring a mistrial and acting to prevent a retrial, "The conduct of the government has placed the case in such a posture that it precludes the fair, dispassionate resolution of these issues by a jury."

The judge deserves the gratitude of the defendants, but even more, of the American people. In refusing to discuss the FBI job offer made by John Ehrlichmann, the ousted presidential aide, he properly put the integrity of the judiciary above self. And in demanding the answers to the covert activities of the government, he exposed the shameful lengths to which the administration was willing to go in its efforts to get a conviction.

The only regrettable aspect is that the judge's action precluded a jury decision on the case itself, and the larger issue of government secrecy. Most of the jurors said after the charges had been dismissed that they were leaning toward acquittal of Dr. Ellsberg and Mr. Russo. It is easy to see why.

From the evidence we saw, there was no real reason for keeping the Pentagon Papers secret. Rather, it appeared to be another instance of government trying to hide its embarrassments from public view under the abused label of national security.

Because the jury could not rule on the merits, the government remains free to pursue its secretive policies. We hope, though, that the public exposure of the abuses of governmental secrecy will lead to reform — by the administration itself and by the Congress.

The Philadelphia Inquirer

Philadelphia, Pa., May 15, 1973

"Government agencies have taken an unprecedented series of actions against these defendants."

So declared Federal Judge William Matthew Byrne Jr. as he dismissed all charges against Dr. Daniel Ellsberg and Anthony J. Russo Jr., and so ended the Pentagon Papers trial, nearly two years after the defendants were indicted on charges of espionage, theft and conspiracy, for copying and revealing the classified Defense Department study of the origins of America's involvement in Vietnam.

The issues raised at the trial, however, are by no means resolved. In its bizarre denouement, the trial became inextricably linked to what we generally refer to as the Watergate affair, which perhaps ought better to be referred to as the Watergate attitude. Consider some of the "unprecedented" actions taken by men working for the U. S. Government, as a result of which Judge Byrne threw out the case as hopelessly "tainted."

It has been disclosed that the Beverly Hills office of Dr. Ellsberg's psychiatrist had been broken into in an effort to obtain his "psychiatric profile," and that this burglary, about a year before the Watergate break-in at Democratic headquarters, had been committed by a team led by none other than G. Gordon Liddy Jr., and E. Howard Hunt Jr., convicted leaders of the Watergate conspiracy.

It has been disclosed that the Central Intelligence Agency supplied Hunt with disguises and other espionage equipment, notwithstanding the law forbidding the CIA to be involved in domestic undercover activities.

It has been disclosed that this was done on the request of John D. Ehrlichman, Mr. Nixon's former domestic chief of staff, who himself has acknowledged that he learned of the Beverly Hills burglary but did not report it — he just told its perpetrators not to do it again.

It has been disclosed that even before Ellsberg revealed the Pentagon Papers, the FBI had been intercepting his phone conversations, but the records mysteriously vanished until, as Acting FBI Director William Ruckelshaus informed a news conference yesterday, they turned up in — of all places — a safe in Mr. Ehrlichman's White House office, along with 16 other files involving wiretaps of government officials and newsmen.

Judge Byrne himself has disclosed that, as the trial was coming to its end, Mr. Ehrlichman personally discussed with him the possibility of his becoming the next director of the FBI.

In the beginning, the government had brought the defendants before the bar of justice for allegedly violating "national security." In the end, it is the government itself which is found guilty of violating national security in the deepest sense, through an extraordinary pattern of interference by the executive branch into the processes of justice and individual rights.

The legal question of the government's right to withhold information as against the public's right to know have not been settled. But if the Pentagon Papers case has had any beneficial effect, it is in the demonstration of what the obsession with secrecy can lead to.

The Watergate attitude is that for the sake of "law and order" the government itself may break the law — that the end justifies the means. This is not the traditional American attitude toward the governance of a free society.

The Virginian-Pilot

Norfolk, Va., May 14, 1973

The Pentagon Papers trial turned into "Watergate West" in the last two weeks. The disclosures of the Government's gross misconduct in the prosecution of Daniel Ellsberg and Anthony Russo Jr. were so sensational that Judge W. Matt Byrne Jr. was compelled to free the defendants.

The "extraordinary series of disclosures regarding the conduct of several government agencies," to borrow Judge Byrne's quaint understatement, started with the burglary of the office of Dr. Ellsberg's psychiatrist by an espionage squad working under White House orders.

The Central Intelligence Agency had a hand in the operation — that is against the law, too. Not only was defendant Ellsberg the subject of systematic wiretapping, the evidence of the wiretaps was concealed from the court and from the defense, which is entitled to it legally. The Federal Bureau of Investigation seems to have destroyed the record of the wiretaps, a fact that was revealed only last week. The Government had maintained for the past year that there were no wiretaps. And the action that most offends one's sense of justice and fair play was the arrant attempt to bribe Judge Byrne by dangling an offer of the directorship of the FBI before him during the progress of the trial. That happened in March, when the scandal was starting to smell strongly. Judge Byrne declined to discuss the job, quite properly. A flintier judge might have declared a mistrial right there.

"The bizarre events have incurably infected the prosecution of this case," Judge Byrne summed up. So saying, he declared a mistrial and dismissed the indictment against defendants Ellsberg and Russo for conspiracy, espionage, and theft. That is the end of the Pentagon Papers trial, with the question of the defendants' guilt in the papers' publication unresolved. Under the circumstances most will be satisfied with the Scotch verdict.

The defendants, meanwhile, are threatening to sue Mr. Nixon and others for "conspiracy to deprive us of our civil liberties," which would be in keeping with the reversal of roles in trial.

If the American people hadn't been conditioned by now to the notion that agents acting for the President of the United States were involved in burglary, bugging, bribery, destruction of evidence, obstruction of justice, perjury, and anything else necessary to law 'n' order, Nixon style, the story would be unbelievable. As it is, it's just part of the larger story of Watergate, which has brought the indictment of former Attorney General John Mitchell, his replacement's resignation, the sacking of the acting director of the FBI, the besmirching of the FBI, the CIA, the Presidency, and dozens of individual reputations thus far. And who knows what's to come next?

The Topeka Daily Capital

Topeka, Kans., May 10, 1973

Americans are being treated to one of those anomalies that occurs often these days in our search for fairness in court trials.

Daniel Ellsberg and Anthony Russo are being tried in federal district court in Los Angeles on charges of stealing the so-called Pentagon Papers and jeopardizing U.S. security.

These are the papers marked "Top Secret" which were given to numerous newspapers and published in part before court actions begun by the Justice and Defense departments "sanitized them."

There is no question that the papers were marked "Top Secret" and were stolen by Ellsberg and Russo, but here comes the quirk that keeps bobbing up in court trails:

Because it turns out that an illegal attempt was made to obtain the psychiatric report on Ellsberg by burglarizing his doctor's office, Ellsberg and Russo are seeking dismissal of the charges.

Their attorneys are contending that the evidence against the two may have been tainted by the illegal acts by federally paid agents. Since the burglars failed to find and copy Ellsberg's psychiatric report, Judge Matthew Byrne, presiding at the trial, must determine whether the defense attorney's point is valid.

Meanwhile in this comedy of errors, it turns out that Judge Byrne was sounded out by a Nixon aide on the possibility of his selection as head of the Federal Bureau of Investigation.

Perhaps it was never intended to engender a friendlier attitude by the judge toward the prosecutors, but the thought has occurred to too many persons for it to be ignored.

Two wrongs don't make a right — and neither do three!

The Charlotte Observer

Charlotte, N. C., May 15, 1973

It is regrettable that the Pentagon Papers trial ended without resolving the basic issue: To what extent can the government classify information without infringing on the people's right of know? In the charges brought against Dr. Daniel Ellsberg and Anthony Russo, the government sought to extend its control over information to an unprecedented degree. Whether the jury would have defeated this power grab with a verdict of not guilty is not known.

However, the conduct of the government concerning this case, as well as testimony given, shows that the government already has too much power and uses classification without a proper regard for the people's right to know.

Of course, Judge Matthew Byrne had little choice but to dismiss the case. The trial had become contaminated by a string of bizarre revelations, including the burglary of Dr. Ellsberg's psychiatrist's office at the instigation of the White House and with the CIA's help. In fact, the 89-day trial ended last week with evidence that the Administration's misconduct far exceeded that charged to the defendants.

But what can be said about the evidence offered during the trial?

A central contention of the Administration was that the release of the Pentagon's Vietnam war study to the press harmed the national security. Thus, the defendants were charged with espionage even though they never dealt with a foreign power. On this point, many expert witnesses testified pro and con. Generally, these experts disagreed, but from what they said several conclusions can be drawn.

One is that "national security" is an imprecise and elastic concept used to cover a broad range of activities and information. Also, those who happen to be in power define the term more rigidly than those who are not. The primary reason those in power take this rigid view is because they want to control what information about their deeds the public sees. And so "national security" is often nothing more than a rug under which bureaucrats sweep their misdeeds and mistakes.

There is evidence that the jury realized this. According to reports, a majority of the jurors favored acquittal when the case was dismissed.

Yet the Administration persists in trying to abridge the people's right to know. President Nixon has proposed an official secrets act that would make the unauthorized release of public documents and their publication a crime. The United States has never had such a law. The classification of documents is done by executive order.

Given what the public now knows about the Pentagon Papers trial and the Watergate scandal, the power sought in such an official secrets act would seem to strike against democracy itself.

The Courier-Journal

Louisville, Ky., May 15, 1973

BECAUSE THE Pentagon Papers trial was politically inspired in the first place, there is a certain justice in the fact that the political overspill from the Watergate flood forced its premature end. Indeed, the disclosures of recent weeks seemed to minimize the chance that the case would ever get to the jury. The whole trial had become so politically tainted that it was both legally correct and morally right for the judge to dismiss the charges.

Unfortunately, the dismissal also means that the trial has ended without a clear court decision on the constitutional issues underlying the criminal charges. Central to both the indictment and the defense was the issue of circumstances under which the federal government may withhold important information from the American people, and the question of whether an individual is justified in seeking to make public information which he considers to be improperly withheld.

A roundabout allegation

Daniel Ellsberg and Anthony Russo were charged with conspiracy, espionage and theft. The theft concerned not governmental property in the physical sense, since the papers they Xeroxed were, in fact, private and personal copies of the Pentagon study lawfully in the possession of various government officials. Instead, they were charged with stealing the information contained in those papers, a charge that is not only unprecedented but that, if upheld, could have opened the door to government claims to "ownership" of all kinds of information that always have been considered to be in the public domain.

The espionage charge was equally frightening. No current military secrets were involved, nor were Ellsberg and Russo passing this information to foreign agents. Their first intent was to inform Congress, which at that time knew little of the origins of the Vietnam war as documented in the Pentagon Papers. When Congress showed no interest—surprising though that may seem today—the papers were later made available to the press. As defense testimony at the trial showed, the subsequent publication of parts of the studies gave nothing away to our enemies that they didn't already know.

Both the Soviet Union and the North Vietnamese apparently were better informed on the beginnings of U.S. involvement in Vietnam than were either the Congress or the American people.

If the government had been able to make either of these charges stick—and the conspiracy charge was a backstop designed to catch the defendants if the other two failed—the consequences could have been enormous. The Executive's power to classify and thus conceal information that it didn't want revealed would have been strengthened, and the right of the American people to know what their government is doing in their name would have been seriously curtailed. A jury acquittal still would have failed to answer all the constitutional questions involved, but it would at least have headed us in the right direction. For now, we are left unsure whether, if the government had not engaged in such incredible improprieties as burglarizing a psychiatrist's office and dangling the FBI directorship before the judge, the prosecution might have won.

Of course, it's still possible, though unlikely, that Judge Byrne's dismissal will be appealed. And a Boston grand jury is still investigating the circumstances surrounding Mr. Ellsberg's transfer of the text of the papers to *The New York Times* and other newspapers. But even if there are to be no more Pentagon Papers trials, the debate over the Ellsberg case is likely to go on until the basic issues that it raised have been settled.

Nor will the political misconduct that came to light in the closing weeks of the trial be soon forgotten. When a government drags its people into a miserable, drawn-out war because of a long series of miscalculations and misjudgments, and then tries to prevent the people from finding out its mistakes, the nation inevitably suffers. But when the government stoops to burglary and wiretapping to harrass and prosecute those who dare to expose its weaknesses, the country is indeed in danger. Both strands were woven into the Pentagon Papers trial. And though it wasn't the landmark case that many had hoped for, this whole affair helps open the way for a new look at the relationship between government and people.

NIXON CONCEDES AIDES' ROLE IN COVER-UP

President Nixon May 22 conceded the probable involvement of some of his closest aides in concealing some aspects of the Watergate affair and acknowledged that he had ordered limitations on the investigation because of national security considerations "of crucial importance" unrelated to Watergate. He reiterated, however, his own lack of prior knowledge of the burglary and the attempted cover-up while acknowledging that aides might have "gone beyond" his directives to protect "national security operations in order to cover up any involvement they or certain others might have had in Watergate."

In a summary accompanying his statement, Nixon made the following replies to specific allegations against White House activities:

"1) I had no prior knowledge of the Watergate operation; 2) I took no part in, nor was I aware of, any subsequent efforts that may have been made to cover up Watergate; 3) At no time did I authorize any offer of executive clemency of the Watergate defendants, nor did I know of any such offer; 4) I did not know, until the time of my own investigation, of any effort to provide the Watergate defendants with funds; 5) At no time did I attempt, or did I authorize others to attempt, to implicate the CIA in the Watergate matter; 6) It was not until the time of my own investigation that I learned of the break-in at the office of [Pentagon Papers case defendant Daniel] Ellsberg's psychiatrist, and I specifically authorized the furnishing of this information to Judge [William M.] Byrne. 7) I neither authorized nor encouraged subordinates to engage in illegal or improper campaign tactics."

Nixon also declared his intention to remain in office, saying "I will not abandon my responsibilities. I will continue to do the job I was elected to do."

In his statement, Nixon sought to separate secret investigations begun earlier in his term from the Watergate case. He told of a "special program of wiretaps" set up in 1969 to prevent leaks of secret information important to his foreign policy initiatives. He said there were "fewer than 20 taps" and they were ended in February 1971. (The New York Times reported May 17 that Henry A. Kissinger, assistant to the President for national security affairs, personally provided the FBI with the names of a number of his aides on the National Security Council (NSC) whom he wanted wiretapped. Kissinger confirmed the report May 29.) The President said that in 1970 he was concerned about increasing political disruption connected with antiwar protests and decided a better intelligence operation was needed. He appointed the late FBI director J. Edgar Hoover to head a committee to prepare suggestions. On June 25, 1970, Nixon said, the committee recommended resumption of "certain intelligence operations that had been suspended in 1966," among them the "authorization for surreptitious entry—breaking and entering, in effect"—in specific situations related to national security. He said Hoover opposed the plan and it was never put into effect. "It was this unused plan and related documents that John Dean removed from the White House and placed in a safe deposit box," Nixon added.

Further efforts to improve intelligence operations were made in December 1970 with the formation of the Intelligence Evaluation Committee, for which he said he had authorized no illegal activity, nor did he have knowledge of any. After the New York Times began publishing the Pentagon Papers in June 1971, Nixon said, he approved the formation of a special investigations unit in the White House to "stop security leaks." The unit, known as the "plumbers," was directed by Egil Krogh Jr. and included convicted Watergate conspirators E. Howard Hunt and G. Gordon Liddy. Nixon recalled that he had impressed upon Krogh the importance of protecting the national security and said this might explain how "highly motivated individuals could have felt justified in engaging in specific activities" he would have disapproved had he known of them. "Consequently," Nixon said, "I must and do assume responsibility for such actions, despite the fact that I at no time approved or had knowledge of them."

Nixon said he had "wanted justice done in regard to Watergate" but he had not wanted the investigation to "impinge adversely upon the national security area." He noted that, shortly after the break-in, he was informed that the CIA might have been involved and that he instructed H. R. Haldeman, John Ehrlichman and Assistant Attorney General Henry E. Petersen to "insure that the investigation of the break-in not expose either an unrelated covert operation of the CIA or the activities of the White House investigations unit." The President reiterated that in the months following the Watergate incident, he was given repeated assurances that the White House staff had been cleared of involvement. But with hindsight, Nixon conceded, it was apparent that "I should have given more heed to the warning signals I received along the way . . . and less to the reassurances."

President Nixon would not give oral or written testimony to the grand jury or the Senate select committee investigating the Watergate case, White House Press Secretary Ronald L. Ziegler said May 29. "It would be Constitutionally inappropriate," he said. "It would do violence to the separation of powers."

President Nixon May 24 affirmed the government's right to secrecy in national security matters and denounced "those who steal secrets and publish them in the newspapers," a reference to Daniel Ellsberg's release of the Pentagon Papers. The President's remarks came at a State Department gathering of 600 former prisoners of war.

The Des Moines Register
Des Moines, Iowa, May 24, 1973

President Nixon fell back to a familiar line of defense in his statement on the Watergate affair. This is the line that where vital national secrets are concerned extraordinary methods of restricting individual freedom are justifiable.

When the Watergate burglary-bugging first came to light in the press, the White House position was that this was just newspaper sensationalism. After the burglars came to trial and were convicted, the defense was that the President was so busy in the important work of foreign. affairs—Vietnam, China, Russia—he couldn't know what was going on in the lower reaches of his campaign organization.

This was the line in his speech of 'Apr. 30. The evidence had piled so high and the contamination was obviously so widespread in the administration, Nixon could not ignore it. But he said he knew nothing about it in advance. He praised his top staff men in the White House and the attorney general as dedicated public servants, while accepting their resignations because of the cloud of suspicion and their association with people involved in the Watergate matter.

Now Nixon returns to his long career of fighting the battle of national security through exposing spies, subversives and weak links in the secrecy system. He is not the only national leader who has been obsessed with secrecy in the last quarter century. Indeed, the nation as a whole has been obsessed with fear of subversion and the loss of secrets to foreign powers.

The beauty of this line of defense is that you don't have to tell what the secrets are. Thus the public cannot judge their importance and whether the cover-up was justified.

So now Nixon is telling us that he got worried about leaks of "vital" information to the press and directed a probe to find the culprits by means of a special set of wiretaps. He also says that he suspected the CIA was involved in Watergate. So he ordered the FBI, the Department of Justice and his own staff not to carry their investigations of the Watergate burglary "into areas that might expose covert national security activities."

This is a revealing statement, because it shows the President was more concerned about possible loss of foreign affairs secrets than he was about possible corruption of the American political process. It reflects the fetish about secrecy which has been a national disease for many years.

Nixon's alarm about the release of the Pentagon Papers moved him to authorize extreme measure to find the leaks. But nothing in the Pentagon Papers has been shown to have a significant bearing on national security. The stuff was all ancient history; what the Papers did reveal was the deception and reckless decision-making of earlier administrations concerning Indochina.

★ ★ ★

There undoubtedly are some secrets that ought to be secrets. But if they leak out, the American government is not justified in violating the Constitution and violating the laws on burglary to spot the leaks. The relative values of the Nixon administration in this matter of national security are un-American.

They are more like the values of the Communists or Fascists in placing a narrowly defined security above liberty.

The end does NOT justify the means in this country.

President Nixon has come close to admitting his own complicity in covering up the Watergate scandal. Instead of handing out whitewash and refusing to explain anything, he has for the first time attempted a rational, factual explanation.

But he did not come very far toward a clean exposure. He did not mention the facts that two of his former Cabinet members have been indicted. He did not comment on the Senate investigation, except to speak of "inaccurate charges that have filled the headlines and are currently being discussed in Senate testimony and elsewhere." He still apparently cannot face up to complete openness on Watergate, and he is resorting to the oldest dodge in politics—"classified information, vital to national security."

The whole business is still so murky that the Senate investigation must go on until the muddy bottom of this mess is fully revealed.

The Washington Post
Washington, D.C., May 24, 1973

On Tuesday the President suddenly issued (via Mr. Ziegler) a document of several thousand words seeking to clarify his role in the Watergate crime and cover-up and in the related squalors that have come to public attention. It is interesting—and it is also heartbreaking. For appalling as many of the revelations have been that have come to us through the press, the courts and the Ervin Committee hearings, none has provided so damning an indictment of the Nixon presidency as does Mr. Nixon's own attempt to defend it. The President's lengthy statement is—by turn—pathetic, unconvincing, confused. What emerges, however, is all too clear. If you take Mr. Nixon's explanations at face value, there emerges the picture of a kind of incompetence bordering on the criminally negligent, a failure of authority and responsibility and plain sense that all but defies belief.

Three years ago, Mr. Nixon tells us, in the face of what he regarded as grave security threats, he set up an interagency committee to work out — among other things—some "options for expanded intelligence operations." One "option" which was approved was described by the President as follows:

"authorization for surreptitious entry—breaking and entering, in effect—on specified categories of targets in specified situations related to national security."

But, the President tells us, he could not get the Director of the FBI, J. Edgar Hoover, to go along with this burglary business or the rest of the plan. So approval of the "option" was rescinded. And Mr. Nixon, a while later, set up an Intelligence Evaluation Committee (whose activities he says he now understands to be "under investigation") and—a while after that—a special White House investigative group called the "plumbers" whose number included such sterling fellows as G. Gordon Liddy and E. Howard Hunt. The President assures us that if any of the above was up to any hanky panky (such as, for example, the kind approved and then disapproved at Mr. Hoover's insistence a while before), he didn't authorize it or know about it.

Well, what *did* he know about? And what *did* he think he authorized? A President sets up what are essentially domestic spying groups. They don't have their headquarters in Vienna or Prague: one group is ensconced in White House offices. Its minions come to work there every day—or at least when they are not out exercising an "option" somewhere. Did Mr. Nixon not understand that he had created a para-police unit that, *at the very least,* required strict supervision by him? And if the work of these groups, indeed their very creation and existence, had been mandated—as Mr. Nixon would have us believe—by extreme and momentous national security threats, are we to believe that the President more or less ignored their activities after he had set them up? According to Mr. Nixon, we are. That is what we mean when we say the President's statement constituted a worse indictment of his performance than has been made by any of the other evidence being invoked against him.

But that is not all. There is the question specifically of his response to the news of the Watergate break-in and the connection of plumbers Liddy and Hunt with it. Mr. Nixon was "alerted" that Howard Hunt had been part of the White House domestic spying squad. So when Mr. Hunt's name "surfaced" in connection with the crime, Mr. Nixon feared—he explains—that the investigation "might well lead to an inquiry into the activities of the Special Investigations Unit [plumbers] itself." And he also suspected that there might be a CIA connection—in fact, he was "advised" of such a possibility. So what does he do? Does he get in touch with CIA Director Helms and find out if there is such a connection? Does he inquire into exactly what the CIA might be doing in this area which clearly lies outside its statutory mandate? Does he rattle the china around at the White House or over at the re-election committee and demand to find out what is really going on? Not by his own account. Rather, Mr. Nixon tells us, he tried to get the investigators charged with bringing the Watergate criminals to book to tailor their investigation so as not to bring these other things out in the open. And now, finally, almost a year later, the President informs us that his information remains "fragmentary and to some extent contradictory."

Almost from the beginning of the current flood of Watergate disclosures, the public has been faced with a dreadful choice so far as the President's own role is concerned—namely, a choice between an assumption of staggering incompetence on the one hand and dissembling and complicity on the other. None of the President's statements has resolved the dilemma. Each has only raised the stakes, made either the folly or the knavery seem 10 times worse. And this is what Mr. Nixon's Tuesday declaration did too. Where it differed from the President's earlier public statements was in its special protective stress on national security. This deserves a special word.

Presidents of the United States, over the past couple of decades have been granted by the people considerable license to invoke national security needs as a justification for all manner of activities that otherwise would not be permitted and which certainly would not be permitted to go on in secrecy. This is an enormous trust, and from time to time, our Presidents have abused it. You could argue—and many people do—that President Johnson abused it in the course of escalating the American Vietnam involvement. But nobody argues that he abused it for small or personal or political reasons: the dissembling was undertaken, he believed, to fulfill a genuine, if unpopular, national security imperative abroad. Whether he was right or wrong, that is a distinction of some importance. For what we must reluctantly suspect now is not just that Mr. Nixon's campaign and government appointees abused the prerogatives of White House power, but that the President himself is invoking the sacred and serious national security claim frivolously and to ends for which it was never intended. Trust me, the President says. With every effort of his own to maintain such trust, he makes it harder.

The Boston Globe

Boston, Mass., May 27, 1973

In his May 22 acknowledgement of "unethical as well as illegal activities" in his re-election campaign, President Nixon touched briefly on the possibility that he himself "may have contributed to the climate in which they took place."

He denied any such intent. But the truth is that Mr. Nixon did indeed create the climate. It is a climate of fear, hyperbole, innuendo and coercion on which he has thrived politically for almost three decades.

In the beginning, it was the fear of communism that was implanted with carefully-worded suggestions that all of his political opponents were so tainted. In his presidency, the steady drumfire has been that the national security somehow is in grave jeopardy and can be restored only if Mr. Nixon and the men around him are permitted the freest possible exercise of the presidential will.

Thus, the end of national security was served in the 1968 campaign's aftermath, as Mr. Nixon saw it, through the means of "authorization for surreptitiuos entry — breaking and entering, in effect — on specified categories of targets."

It is served by supplying tools, plans, and leadership to dissident groups, as most recently, in the case of the Camden, N.J., war protesters and others before that.

It is served, at least as Mr. Nixon sees it, by bombing Cambodia, and, conversely, it was "threatened" by dissenters during Mr. Nixon's four years of war in Vietnam.

It is served, or so we are told, by the illegal impoundment of funds authorized by Congress for specific purposes. Is it then served or threatened by the constant denigration of Congress as "irresponsible" when it asserts its own constitutional will?

The climate the President has created is one in which civil rights go down the drain one after another, all somehow in the interest of national security — preventive detention, no-knock raids on private homes in the dead of night, sweep-street arrests, the bugging of private telephones, the misuse of grand juries to entrap dissenters, the suppression of evidence that might acquit in criminal cases. The nation is asked to suffer all of these invasions of traditional freedoms guaranteed by the Bill Rights lest the nation teeter on its foundations. Security is "threatened" by those who protest these lawless invasions.

The unwary could be led to believe that the Bill of Rights is itself a threat to the national security.

In his Watergate statement last week, Mr. Nixon referred to "national security" 24 times. And where he did not see the "national security" endangered, it was "internal security" or "domestic security" that somehow was at the brink despite the vigilance of intelligence and secret police agencies which the President himself listed in another part of his statement — the FBI, the CIA, the National Security Agency, the Secret Service, intelligence agencies of the Defense Department (and other departments the President did not list) as well as the Intelligence Evaluation Committee in the White House.

National security has become a code word. A President can invoke it at will, without either explanation or consultation.

One wonders, however, how the national security could really be threatened were a national election permitted to run its unimpeded course. By exposing the unlawful impediments?

The security of the nation can of course be imperiled. The bombs that fell on Pearl Harbor are proof enough. But how secure is a nation which becomes either inured to or bored by the repeated cry of "wolf?" How secure is it when "the national security" is invoked to permit or to conceal the lawless acts of those sworn to enforce the laws?

Detroit Free Press

Detroit, Mich., May 24, 1973

NATIONAL SECURITY is a good patriotic issue, one that everybody is for and the one President Nixon has chosen to cloud the real issue of his own questionable handling of the Watergate case.

Mr. Nixon's lengthy statement Tuesday in which he admitted for the first time that there was a high level cover-up of the break-in and bugging of Democratic national headquarters may well have been true—from his point of view.

But the President's point of view is now at least as questionable as his ability to choose honest aides.

And a platoon of plumbers, hopefully not from the White House, may be needed to plug the leaks in Mr. Nixon's statement.

The President said, for example, that "Elements of the early post-Watergate reports led me to suspect, incorrectly, that the CIA had been in some way involved." If we believe that statement, and there is no reason we should not, then Mr. Nixon must explain why heads did not roll at the CIA, or at least why the suspected CIA involvement was not thoroughly investigated.

The CIA cannot, by law, involve itself in covert domestic activity. What could be more covert than a late-night burglary? What could be more domestic than the Washington, D.C., headquarters of the nation's majority political party?

Mr. Nixon also said he "specifically instructed Mr. Haldeman and Mr. Ehrlichman to insure that the FBI would not carry its investigation into areas that might compromise these covert national security activities or those of the CIA."

Why the distrust of the FBI, whose agents have security clearance? Was the President really concerned about national security or did he fear that FBI agents would discover that the CIA was being used illegally for political purposes?

Secrecy is, of course, sometimes required for national security. No one doubts that. But it is too often used as a face-saving device. Make a mistake? Classify it top secret and nobody will ever know you made it.

The Pentagon Papers, cited in Mr. Nixon's statement as "a security leak of unprecedented proportions," did not hurt the United States, but they did embarrass some former government officials. Most of the information was already known.

Now, in the name of national security, Mr. Nixon admits wiretapping and says burglary ("surreptitious entry") would have been given official approval except for opposition by J. Edgar Hoover.

Unchecked, national security can obviously lead to police state tactics. The law, of course, provides a check, but some of Mr. Nixon's chosen henchmen considered themselves above the law.

So Mr. Nixon now says he thought he was covering up for illegal activities of the CIA and not illegal activities of his re-election committee. He has more explaining to do.

St. Louis Globe-Democrat

St. Louis, Mo., May 24, 1973

President Nixon's second statement on the Watergate affair and the events that preceded it have now put the episode in the proper perspective.

Mr. Nixon explained that internal domestic violence and attempts to undermine the government compelled him to create new intelligence-gathering units to protect the government and the American people.

These new security teams did identify subversive elements and succeeded in plugging leaks that were undermining foreign policy. But, unfortunately, they apparently also went on to commit certain illegal and stupid acts such as breaking into the Democratic national headquarters. Mr. Nixon categorically said he had no knowledge of the Watergate incident or the attempted cover-up.

☆ ☆ ☆

The President said that he did instruct his top aides to make certain that the investigation did not interfere with or reveal activities of the Special Investigations Unit, covert operations of the CIA or other matters affecting national security. There was no attempt to cover-up in connection with Watergate, the President said, but rather a move to separate national security operations from the Watergate probe.

In our opinion President Nixon was completely justified in creating new special investigative units in response to the bombings, police killings, riots and leaks of sensitive, secret information that obviously were aimed at frustrating United States foreign policy.

In fact, when the President's actions are viewed in the context of the FBI sharply reducing its undercover operations and cutting off liaison with the CIA, as it reportedly did in 1970, Mr. Nixon would have been derelict if he hadn't created new intelligence units to meet the alarming internal threat.

For these were not simply "dirty tricks" radicals and subversives were playing on the Nixon Administration. The operatives of anti-Nixon forces infiltrated the Defense Department and other agencies and then began leaking sensitive information.

On one occasion in 1969 one of their number leaked the plan for the bombing of major North Vietnamese base areas in Cambodia. The purpose of the leak obviously was intended to wreck the project and force Prince Sihanouk to join the Communists.

There were other leaks on Israel, North Vietnamese operations, Korea and secret U.S. position papers on the SALT talks with the Russians — all aimed at undermining Nixon foreign policy.

There also was a reported plot by an anti-war group to kidnap presidential adviser Henry Kissinger and blow up government installations. In May, 1971, tens of thousands of anti-war militants marched on Washington with the avowed purpose of bringing the government to a halt. Much violence ensued and the government very nearly was brought to a halt.

Then came Daniel Ellsberg and the Pentagon Papers. Ellsberg lifted the papers from volumes of "sensitive files of the Departments of State and Defense and the CIA, covering military and diplomatic moves in a war that was still going on."

President Nixon said he ordered one of the intelligence units to find out all it could about "Mr. Ellsberg's associates and his activities" but didn't authorize any illegal actions.

As revealed in court, two agents of this intelligence unit subsequently broke into Ellsberg's psychiatrist's office and this illegal action was largely responsible for the Ellsberg case being thrown out of court.

In this same context, Watergate could have been another stupid overreaction by highly-motivated men who somehow thought they were acting in the best interests of their government. This, of course, does not excuse Watergate or exonerate those who broke the law, or remove the need to take whatever steps are necessary to see that such an invasion of the political process never happens again.

But the American people should bear in mind what preceded Watergate. It didn't happen in a vacuum. It possibly was an unfortunate by-product of the President attempts to cope with some of the most vicious assaults that have been made against the government in modern times.

THE DENVER POST

Denver, Colo., May 27, 1973

IN RESPONSE to the Watergate scandal, President Nixon issued last week one of the most remarkable documents in the history of the American presidency.

"I should have given more heed to the warning signals . . . I should have been more vigilant . . . ," the President said. "Because of the emphasis I put on the crucial importance of protecting the national security, I can understand how highly motivated individuals could have felt justified in engaging in specific activities that I would have disapproved .'.'."

As no president has done before him, Mr. Nixon has described some of the secret national security operations of his administration. He has acknowledged that he authorized a series of wiretaps, that he approved — and then disapproved — a plan for illegal breaking and entering, and that he ordered subordinates to try to limit the scope of the Watergate investigation so that national security operations would not come to light.

THE PRESIDENTIAL STATEMENT suggested that for a period of time after the Watergate breakin the President's contacts with the CIA were not good enough to enable him to know whether the CIA was involved in the breakin or not.

This is surely one of the most chilling implications of the statement. If the President of the United States does not know what the CIA is up to—or can't find out instantly—then who does? If outside supervision of the CIA is that lax, then the agency poses intolerable dangers to our democratic society.

The presidential statement also indicat-ed that for another period of time the President allowed the late J. Edgar Hoover to shut off FBI contacts with the CIA and all other agencies of government except the White House. The power Hoover was allowed by the President to wield, in advanced age and ill health, can only be described as awesome.

IT WAS NO ACCIDENT that the President's new attempt at a full statement on Watergate, 11 months after the breakin, should focus on national security and security agents. For it appears that the FBI, the CIA and the whole "intelligence community" of the United States really lie at the heart of the President's and the nation's problem over Watergate.

The cast of characters being paraded before the Senate Watergate investigating committee contains men who bug telephones, forge documents, use aliases, invent cover stories, take calls in telephone booths, get paid in $100 bills and generally behave in the conspiratorial manner of characters in spy movies.

IN AN OBSESSIVE CONCERN with security, the President's aides brought such men into the high councils both of the government and of the Committee to Reelect the President. They tended to share with these men a conspiratorial view of the national political scene and to approve their operating tactics.

James McCord has referred in his Senate testimony to a book on the training of CIA agents which describes their obligation to lie and deny the CIA's role in an operation, if they are caught at it.

If that is the obligation, is it too much to speculate that McCord himself, after 18 years in the CIA, may still feel bound by it? If the Watergate breakin had, in fact, been a CIA operation, would not McCord have testified, exactly as he has testified, that the CIA had no part in it?

How can the government or the country believe McCord or any other man who has been trained to lie in matters involving the CIA? What guarantee is there that the President himself will be told the truth by the CIA or the FBI or any other part of the "intelligence community"?

THE DANGER OF ALLOWING these agencies to operate outside of reasonable scrutiny and the checks and controls that apply to the rest of the governmental system is impossible to overstate.

Mr. Nixon has suggested in his statement that his effort to restrict the Watergate investigation was justified by the need to protect the work of these agencies, and of certain White House security operations to plug leaks of vital secrets. But it is these agencies and security operations themselves, and their use for political and other purposes by the White House aides, that need investigating most and raise the most serious questions.

Eleven months after Watergate, the President's use of "national security" as an explanation for protecting some part of the fathomless Watergate morass from scrutiny is not satisfying. The whole matter must be looked into further and new and tighter restrictions on the intelligence agencies must come out of it. A decade of national policy dominated by the security "spooks" and their games is enough.

The Evening Star and The Washington Daily News

Washington, D.C., May 22, 1973

In his long statement on Watergate released yesterday, President Nixon assures us that he had no prior knowledge of the bugging operation, that he took no part in—and indeed was unaware of—any cover-up, that he neither authorized nor knew of any offer of executive clemency to the conspirators, that he did not know until his own investigation revealed it of any effort to fund the Watergate defendants or to break into the office of Daniel Ellsberg's psychiatrist, that at no time did he attempt—nor did he authorize others to attempt — to implicate the Central Intelligence Agency, and that he neither authorized nor encouraged his subordinates to engage in illegal or improper campaign tactics.

Mr. Nixon would have us believe that, in actions he may have taken as regards Watergate, he was motivated by nothing but concern for the national security.

It may be so. But there are a few matters which still confuse us and upon which we would welcome further presidential elucidation. For example, Mr. Nixon admits that the White House Special Investigations Unit ("The Plumbers") was set up in June, 1971, with his approval. He describes it as "a small group" under John Ehrlichman, consisting of Egil Krogh, David Young, E. Howard Hunt and G Gordon Liddy, a unit known only to "a very few persons at the White House."

Mr. Nixon says the task of The Plumbers was two-fold: to stop security leaks and to "investigate other sensitive security matters." We can understand the group's first function. But we find it a trifle hard to understand also is stricken with concern "that the Watergate investigation might well lead to an inquiry into the activities of the Special Investigations Unit itself."

When he is worried that the CIA may be involved, does Mr. Nixon ask Richard Helms, then director of the agency, if this is the case? He does not. He instructs Haldeman and Ehrlichman to see that Acting FBI Director L. Patrick Gray and the Deputy CIA director, General Vernon Walters, "coordinate" their activities so that nobody's covert operations are exposed. Why was Helms by-passed and then shipped off to Iran? We'd like to know. And when Walters told Gray that CIA had no operation which could be compromised by the FBI's investigation (in Mexico in this instance) and Gray told Mr. Nixon that on July 6, did not the President smell at least a small laundered mouse?

And why was Mr. Nixon so concerned about the inquiry leading to The Plumbers? National security matters, so he says. And that, presumably, is why he told Assistant Attorney General Petersen to treat his investigation of Watergate virtually as if it were only a common case of breaking and entering, and "to stay out of national security matters." But could the President not have realized that, no matter how pure his motives, instructions of that nature to Petersen could only result in so severely limiting the investigation as to make it virtually worthless? For by his own definition, anything and everything a White House-based group like The Plumbers did could have a national security construction placed on it.

Mr. Nixon declares in his statement that "it is not my intention to place a national security 'cover' on Watergate." We are relieved to hear that, because a close reading of his statement could lead someone who had not totally suspended his critical faculties to believe that that is precisely what Mr. Nixon is trying to do. We are equally relieved to hear that "executive privilege will not be invoked as to any testimony concerning possible criminal conduct or discussions of possible criminal conduct" when men like Haldeman, Ehrlichman and former attorney general John Mitchell testify under oath, and we trust that this will be the case concerning their conversations with the President.

In concluding his statement, Mr. Nixon declares that "as more information is developed, I have no doubt that more questions will be raised." In our view, Mr. Nixon's statement itself raises so many questions and provides so few credible answers that we are sure that he will soon once again find time from "his larger duties" to inform our doubts and dispel our fears.

The Birmingham News

Birmingham, Ala., May 20, 1973

Incredibly, presidential advisor Henry A. Kissinger has become "tainted" with the illegal Watergate espionage because he initiated wiretaps to close security leaks in the National Security Council staff of sensitive foreign policy issues.

Suddenly, a wiretap is a wiretap. It makes no difference if the surveillance is legal and duly authorized by the appropriate authorities. In the climate created in the aftermath of Watergate, logical distinctions become blurred.

Certainly the government has a responsibility to protect its innermost foreign policy secrets; otherwise, it could not negotiate with other governments or protect the interests of its citizens. Kissinger was absolutely correct in saying that "it was my duty" to protect the confidentiality of national security information.

Way down in a story by Peter Lisagor of the Chicago Daily News Service last week was the following clarifying sentence: "The wiretaps of Kissinger staff members had nothing to do with Watergate or the political espionage and sabotage later charged to members of the committee to re-elect President Nixon and the implicated top White House assistants."

Then comes the tarbrush: "However, because of the supercharged environment here, Kissinger's association with the wiretaps put on his staff to safeguard against leaks of information relating to sensitive foreign policy issues was seen as *damaging his own hitherto spotless image.*

"It was seen by many experienced observers as another example of the byzantine atmosphere in the White House in which the prevailing mistrust and suspicion *led to the disarray of Watergate.*"

If the security surveillance which occurred in 1969 had nothing to do with Watergate, and it did not, then why should Kissinger's "spotless image" be damaged? And how can the problem of security leaks be seen by "experienced observers" as leading to the "disarray of Watergate?"

If this is an example of the thinking being done by "experienced observers," heaven knows where this sort of logic will lead them.

The National Security Council leaks and subsequent attempts to plug them, of course, had absolutely nothing to do with the campaign and absolutely nothing to do with the Watergate espionage.

If in some eyes officials in the highest inner circles of national security have their "images" damaged by attempting to protect vital information, then the perception of the observer is out of focus.

The nation must guard against an outbreak of hysterical overreaction to the Watergate incident. Let's keep some perspective.

Wiretapping does not fit neatly into one category. The right of privacy should not be a cloak behind which spies, criminals or leakers of government secrets may hide with impunity.

Where wiretapping is done through legal channels, the right of a citizen against a frivolous invasion of privacy by federal or local investigating agencies is protected. Furthermore, wiretapping can be a valuable tool in bringing lawbreakers to justice or protecting the security of the nation.

Certainly the citizen or a political party should be protected against an illegal or unauthorized invasion of privacy by wiretapping. Seven individuals already have been convicted of the Watergate espionage and hearing and grand jury proceedings are probing into responsibility for the illegal acts at a higher level.

But the indignation over Watergate is no excuse to drag others, such as Kissinger, into a vague and generalized hullabaloo about wiretapping.

The Watergate controversy could end up as a repeat of the McCarthism of the Fifties or the Salem Witch Trials of early Massachusetts if it is allowed to get out of hand.

Judging from some of the press reports, professional journalistic restraint needs to be reaffirmed.

The New York Times

New York, N.Y., May 27, 1973

In a lengthy public statement and again in a speech to former prisoners of war, President Nixon has retreated into a fortress called "national security" as his ultimate defense shelter against the storms of Watergate. The tapping of telephones, the illegal break-ins and burglaries, the creation of a secret police staff operating outside the supervision of Congress or any duly authorized Federal agency, the collection and disbursal of huge sums of cash for undercover activities, and the obstruction of an F.B.I. investigation are all justified because foreign agents and domestic radicals threatened the security of the nation. It is an extraordinary argument which has enjoyed repeated use in recent decades. It is time that argument received careful examination.

What is first of all apparent is that this concern with national security is far out of proportion to any real danger. Secrecy becomes synonymous with security and then becomes an end in itself. Few citizens dispute that military plans are necessarily secret and that certain discussions by a President and his advisers concerning relations with foreign countries are best kept confidential. But the crucial element in whether diplomatic negotiations succeed or fail is how the parties appraise the objective realities of their own situation. No position paper or secret conversation is going to affect decisively how another nation perceives its interests.

As the inner history of the Nixon Administration becomes better known because of the Watergate revelations, it is astonishing to learn how concern with imagined dangers to national security persisted in the absence of evidence. Thus, Mr. Nixon and his associates took office in 1969 with the uneasy conviction that there were financial and espionage links between Black Panthers, student radicals and other dissenters in this country and hostile foreign governments. The Central Intelligence Agency was ordered to investigate such possible relationships. According to reports last week, the C.I.A. not once but twice submitted lengthy reports showing that no evidence supported these suspicions.

* * *

Instead of being reassured, President Nixon turned to the Federal Bureau of Investigation and agreed to the opening of F.B.I. offices in twenty foreign countries, duplicating the C.I.A.'s work but still finding no evidence. Not satisfied, the President approved a far-reaching plan in 1970 to mount a campaign of spying, wiretapping and burglaries against domestic radicals.

When J. Edgar Hoover of the F.B.I. refused to carry out the plan unless he received the President's written authorization, Mr. Nixon rescinded the plan. He next turned to a "special investigative unit" set up in the White House without public knowledge but paid for by public funds to do undercover work. It is this unit which burglarized the files of Daniel Ellsberg's psychiatrist.

If fears about national security were excessive to begin with and persisted in defiance of the evidence, the efforts to validate those suspicions first paralleled and then fused with sleazy undercover work by the Administration against its political opponents. Thus, from the spring of 1969, John D. Ehrlichman, one of the President's senior aides, had two former New York policemen on his staff—one on the public payroll and one on the payroll of Mr. Nixon's private attorney—to gather incriminating or embarrassing information about leading figures in the Democratic party. As the 1972 campaign approached, these ex-policemen were joined in their political undercover work by members of that "special investigative unit" which had been protecting the national security by plugging "leaks" to newspapers and shadowing radicals and peace movement leaders.

* * *

The final irony is that when the bungled burglary at the Watergate endangered the secrecy of these multiple operations, President Nixon and his aides did not hesitate to involve and compromise the F.B.I. and the C.I.A.— the two principal legal agencies established to protect national security—in order to cover their own tracks.

At last Thursday's hearing of the Ervin committee, Senator Herman Talmadge of Georgia asked Bernard L. Barker, one of the convicted Watergate burglars: "How did you think you could liberate Cuba by participating in a burglary in Washington, D. C.?"

A similar question might be asked of President Nixon and his senior White House aides: "How did you think you could make the United States more secure against its foreign enemies by adopting here at home the police state methods of those enemies?"

The only valid answer—but one not found in Mr. Nixon's statements and speeches of recent weeks—is that security is found elsewhere than in private detectives and wiretaps or in ever deeper secrecy. Those are the methods and the favored atmosphere of tyrants who fear the truth and fear their own citizens.

Free men and women find true security in the justice of their laws, in the subordination of police power to an independent judiciary, in the honesty and candor of their elected and appointed public servants, and finally in the freely offered devotion of each citizen to the republic. Total security is the fantasy of a child. Free nations live by the vigorous self-confidence of men and women who understand their own interests and ideals and are prepared to defend them. There is no other security.

Des Moines Tribune

Des Moines, Iowa, May 31, 1973

The White House has announced that President Nixon will refuse to answer questions of Watergate investigators, judicial and legislative. The closed-mouth policy applies to sworn testimony, informal statements and written responses to written questions.

The President is invoking a double standard in connection with probes of the Watergate scandal. He declared on Apr. 18, "All members of the White House staff will appear voluntarily when requested by the (Ervin) committee. They will testify under oath and they will answer fully all proper questions. . . . The judicial process is moving ahead as it should; and I shall aid it in all appropriate ways. . . . All government employes and especially White House staff employes are expected to fully cooperate in this matter."

The President thus wants everyone else in government to submit to questioning about Watergate, but he refuses to do so himself.

The President evidently intends to reveal his version of events as he has in the past, through broadcasts and issued statements. The President's efforts to date have failed to satisfy the public that it has been told the full story. The inability to question the President has left unanswered questions and lingering suspicion. Polls following the President's statements denying involvement in wrongdoing show a majority of Americans believe he was involved in the attempted Watergate cover-up.

The President claims that responding to questions about Watergate from probers "would do violence to the separation of powers." There may be a question whether a President can be compelled to answer questions from representatives of the legislative or judicial branches of government. But there is no issue of separation of powers involved in responding to questions of newsmen. The President's statements about Watergate thus far have been of a self-serving nature, without opportunity to pin him down or obtain clarification.

An effort to force the President to testify might do "violence" to the separation of powers, as the President claims, but there is no constitutional bar to the President volunteering the information he has. Under the circumstances, he ought to be eager to share his knowledge about Watergate with congressional committees, the courts and the public.

The invoking of "separation of powers" to block testimony is reminiscent of the invoking of "executive privilege" to prevent John Dean, then White House counsel, from being questioned under oath. The use of an ill-defined constitutional technicality to maintain a cloak of secrecy around White House involvement in Watergate provoked widespread public suspicion that the White House had something to hide. The suspicion subsequently proved justified.

The President is courting the same suspicion with his separation of powers argument. Until the President is willing to impose on himself the same obligation to give testimony he has imposed on others, that suspicion will not go away.

THE BLADE

Toledo, Ohio, May 26, 1973

THE unfolding of the Watergate scandal has yielded an abundance of exposures on how able and willing the Nixon White House was to use and abuse its power in the achievement of its ends. Now, in what seems almost like a mere footnote in the appalling scope of the whole sordid story, the testimony of Richard Helms has provided a significant glimpse into the means of dealing with resistance to that power and obstacles to those ends.

Mr. Helms told the Senate Foreign Relations Committee that he did not really want to step down from the directorship of the Central Intelligence Agency early this year. Indeed, he said he would have preferred to stay on in the job specifically because he believed he could be more successful than any newcomer in fending off attempts to involve the CIA in the Watergate cover-up. Instead, Mr. Helms was sent off to become ambassador to Iran, an assignment that he told the committee he neither sought nor particularly wanted.

That version of the CIA change of command stands in sharp contrast to the cover story provided for the announcement of his resignation last winter. The White House said then that Mr. Helms wanted to abide by a CIA policy of retirement at age 60. And the President's press secretary talked to newsmen of Mr. Nixon's praise for the outgoing director's dedicated service and the total satisfaction of the White House with his performance.

Nevertheless, it now turns out that Mr. Helms had in fact been repeatedly instrumental in resisting efforts from the Executive Mansion to ensnarl the CIA in the Watergate web. As far back as last June 23—six days after the arrest of five burglars in Democratic headquarters — presidential chief of staff H. R. Haldeman was asking Mr. Helms' deputy to discourage an FBI investigation into at least one aspect of the nefarious affair. And Mr. Helms in turn—although pointedly bypassed in the contact between the White House and his agency—instructed his aid not to comply lest the CIA risk being besmirched and finished "as an American institution."

That may sound strange, perhaps even laughable, to those citizens in whose view the intelligence agency already was tainted with sinister repute. But Mr. Helms was legally, morally, responsibly, and pragmatically right, of course—and it is another of Watergate's many ironies that the CIA appears to stand as one of the few agencies of the U.S. Government able to keep itself relatively clean and aloof from the corrupting pressures of the White House. And, by peculiar coincidence, after thus standing his ground against the schemes of that crew, Mr. Helms found himself summarily exiled to a distant outpost where, it apparently was thought, he could no longer get in the way.

THE DALLAS TIMES HERALD

Dallas, Tex., May 31, 1973

NOW, IN THE latest of the headline blasts at the White House, comes the charge from the usual "sources close to the Watergate investigation," that the government has used secret agents to spy on American radicals.

Question:

So what's wrong with that? Is it totally wrong for the U.S. government to establish certain surveillance over dangerous internal threats? Are we supposed to ignore revolutionary radicals who throw real bombs, kill people and destroy property?

To leave the impresssion with the American public that a huge, evil Gestapo was planned for the United States is carrying this uncontrolled Watergate fever a bit too far. This is not a nation of dictators and thugs putting the screws on the people; running us indoors in fear behind shuttered windows and wondering when the midnight knock on the door will come. That belongs to someone else.

In fact, the Watergate headline hunters of the East should soon come to realize that the rest of the country is weary of the whole thing as a daily fare. It wants to go on to other things — like where are they going to get a tank full of fuel for their car for the family vacation.

This latest story primly reports that the late J. Edgar Hoover vetoed the White House plan for spying on domestic radical groups, but that it was later implemented through an interdepartmental undercover team. Understandably, Mr. Hoover balked at the plan for a new security arm because of his intense pride in his FBI.

It is irony, indeed, when the same elements who fought to shove Hoover out of office now put the white hat on him for opposing this dastardly scheme.

Does anyone recall, in this current sweep of political hysteria aimed at the presidency, that a group called The Weathermen had a game plan to bomb postoffices, banks, public buildings, college science laboratories, etc.? And that they actually pulled off some bombings?

Does anyone recall that the feared violent wing of the Students for a Democratic Society (SDS) planned mad disruption? That it was driven underground and that FBI, and other agents, still seek some of them after raw acts of violence that killed the innocent and did untold property damage?

To call domestic protective measures "a cover for secret police operations" in this pell-mell rush for more Watergate lineage, is putting things out of focus.

Watergate conspirators, whoever they may be, should be handled by grand juries and courts. But to keep traveling these anonymous by-roads through hearsay and supposition is damaging this country.

The Des Moines Register

Des Moines, Iowa, May 25, 1973

John Caulfield, a former White House aide, has admitted that as a White House emissary he urged James McCord to plead guilty and remain silent about Watergate in return for aid to his family, eventual rehabilitation and a promise of executive clemency. Caulfield thus confirmed in essential detail McCord's shocking account of White House participation in an effort to buy silence and obstruct justice.

McCord's story about the CIA, however, was denied totally by his former attorney, Gordon Alch.

One of the more significant aspects of McCord's account is his description of White House efforts to blame the Watergate break-in on the Central Intelligence Agency (CIA). According to McCord, this angered him and he threatened that "every tree in the forest will fall" if the efforts persisted.

McCord's testimony contrasts sharply with the President's latest statement on the Watergate issue. According to the President, he "instructed Mr. Halde-man and Mr. Ehrlichman to ensure that the investigation of the break-in not expose either an unrelated covert operation of the CIA or the activities of the White House investigations unit." Any successful effort to fix the blame for Watergate on the CIA would have had just the opposite effect. Instead of deflecting attention from the CIA, the move would have made it all but certain that a searching public inquiry would be undertaken of the intelligence agency.

This is but one of many contradictions and loose ends that remain to be resolved and tied down by the Ervin committee. Meanwhile, Americans have reason to be grateful to McCord for his rejection of the White House overtures and for his eventual decision to contact the judge presiding at the Watergate trial and tell his story.

The story is painful for Americans to hear, but it is far less painful than if those responsible in the White House had succeeded in their scheme to subvert justice.

SEN. WEICKER ACCUSES WHITE HOUSE OF USING IRS AS 'LENDING LIBRARY'

Sen. Lowell P. Weicker Jr. (R, Conn.), a member of the Senate Watergate Committee, accused the Internal Revenue Service (IRS) April 8 of acting as a "public lending library" for White House efforts to aid political friends and harass political enemies. Appearing at a joint hearing of two Senate sub-committees, Weicker disclosed a collection of documents, gathered by the Watergate Committee, showing politically motivated tax audits, undercover White House investigations and military spying on civilians. One 1969 IRS memo describing the creation of a special activists "study unit" advised that the unit's function of examining tax returns of "ideological, militant, subversive, radical or other" organizations must not become publicly known, since disclosure "might embarrass the Administration." The unit was abolished in August 1973 after, according to Weicker, assembling tax data on about 10,000 persons.

The Salt Lake Tribune
Salt Lake City, Utah
April 10, 1974

Evidence mounts that advisers and staff-men surrounding President Nixon's first White House term participated in an alarming amount of political freewheeling. The latest such disclosure concerns tax information acquired from the Internal Revenue Service.

Ostensibly, detailed data from individual federal tax returns is confidential. No one, presumably not even the President, is afforded access to anyone else's IRS files. Now, however, material uncovered by Sen. Lowell P. Weicker, R-Conn., indicates this protective shield has been breached.

In testimony before a joint session of three Senate subcommittees investigating covert government intelligence-gathering, Sen. Weiker produced memos to the White House containing specific deficiency totals from particular IRS records. Personalities mentioned ranged from California Gov. Ronald Reagan to film actors John Wayne, Jerry Lewis, Peter Lawford and entertainer Sammy Davis Jr. Their exact income tax deficiencies for years during the early and mid-1960s were revealed to White House staffers, including John W. Dean III. The purpose is fuzzy, although Sen. Weicker maintains it was with the idea of either helping or harrassing persons or groups involved.

The senator alleges the practice fits a pattern of using federal agencies to reward friends but mostly punish foes of the administration. As substantiation he provided other documents showing Dean, then a special White House counsel, discussed, in mid-1971, an IRS investigation and a half-million dollar cut-off in federal contracts as a way of disciplining the Brookings Institution, a research organization that had produced reports uncomplimentary of administration programs. Also, Dean and other White House personnel were shown seriously considering ways of encouraging antitrust actions against the Los Angeles Times. It's a dreary picture.

First, it's distressing to learn that IRS officials actually cooperated in these obviously improper activities. And the present IRS commissioner, Donald C. Alexander, acknowledged last weekend that "certain sensitive case reports...were apparently forwarded to the White House." He felt strongly enough about it to add that he refused subsequent requests after he became commissioner and that the indiscretion isn't likely to recur. It shouldn't if the IRS expects to retain public confidence essential for efficient tax collection work.

Secondly, but more distasteful, is the continuing discovery that people at the presidential level were receptive to manipulating federal agencies as a help for friends or a weapon against enemies. That's old ward-heeler politics that has no place in White House responsibilities.

Evidently, few schemes of retribution—those against Brookings and the Los Angeles Times— were ever carried out. Fortunately, almost all the original "whiz kids" are gone from the White House. If anything is gained from their excesses, it's relearning that the nation's institutions are vulnerably fragile and utmost care must be taken when entrusting them to ambitious but inexperienced hands.

Newsday
Long Island, N.Y., April 14, 1974

After disclosure of the White House "enemies list" during the Senate Watergate hearings it became fashionable in some circles to joke about being on the list, or not being on it. Fresh documentation presented last week by Senator Lowell P. Weicker (R-Conn.) makes it clear—if anyone missed the point— that the administration's passion for spying on enemies real or imagined was no joke at all.

Appearing before a joint Senate subcommittee hearing on government surveillance, Weicker produced a sheaf of memos showing that from its first days in office the Nixon administration used federal agencies to compile dossiers on its critics. Most notably, the Service set up a secret intelligence unit in 1969 to study ways of using tax laws against "ideological, militant, subversive, radical or other" organizations. In all, the IRS unit gathered secret files on 10,000 individuals and organizations before it was disbanded— shortly after the enemies list came to light last summer.

Weicker also offered evidence of at least 54 investigations conducted by White House undercover agents in quest of what he called "political dirt" on prominent Democrats, especially Senator Edward Kennedy. Newsday itself, the senator revealed, drew the attention of administration gumshoes when it was preparing a series of articles on President Nixon's relationship with Charles G. (Bebe) Rebozo. The White House seemed determined to prove the series was the result of a Kennedy-inspired conspiracy against the President.

"... A climate of excessive concern over the political impact of demonstrators ... an insatiable appetite for political intelligence," said John Dean in describing the atmosphere of the White House to the Watergate committee. That description gains added weight in the light of the latest deposition by Senator Weicker. The sheer amount of time and energy devoted to spying, to building barricades, to plotting vengeance; the willingness to use every available resource of government to squelch opposition—some may still joke about it, but is anyone still laughing?

The Courier-Journal

Louisville, Ky., April 13, 1974

THE MILLIONS of Americans who are making their annual accounting to the Internal Revenue Service (IRS) this month doubtless expect that their income tax returns are confidential documents—open to scrutiny only by the tax collector and unavailable to anyone else in government who may be "gathering intelligence" or seeking to advance the cause of a political party. And all those citizens who wish to be politically active, express opinions, attend rock festivals, join civic clubs, go to wild parties, or even indulge in a few indiscretions *should* be able to feel free to do so without worrying that they may arouse the curiosity or wrath of Big Brother.

Some of that confidence was certainly eroded last summer when witnesses before the Senate Watergate committee testified that the IRS and other agencies had been used, or rather misused, for political purposes, and that White House "investigators" had been actively engaged in digging up dirt about political "enemies." For instance, John Dean III, who at one time bore the title of counsel to the President, discussed the administration's interest in manipulating federal agencies to "screw" those suspected of posing a threat to President Nixon. And Tony Ulasewicz, the genial New York cop turned White House agent, explained how he compiled intelligence reports about the personal lives of politicians and other citizens.

Documents released this week by Senator Weicker of Connecticut, a member of the Watergate committee, indicate the extent to which the administration was prepared to abuse its power in order to stifle dissent and "screw" those who opposed it. The Weicker disclosures show how the President politicized the federal apparatus to advance his own political fortunes and to attack his opponents.

Coming simultaneously with evidence that the IRS audit of President Nixon's tax returns last year was a quickie "whitewash," plus a disturbing *Wall Street Journal* report this week on how the IRS has skirted the law in seizing the property of people only suspected of dealing in illicit drugs, the case for a full-fledged investigation of this agency is strong. Attorney General Saxbe has said the Justice Department is considering such a probe: *The Christian Science Monitor*, endorsing the idea, says a thorough investigation would not merely show how much reform is needed, but "might help Justice's Watergate-damaged reputation," too.

An arm of White House

Though IRS is supposed to be a model of integrity, Senator Weicker's documents suggest the incredible extent to which the agency, as he put it, had become a "public lending library for the White House." A special task force collected intelligence information from the tax returns filed by activist organizations, groups with "extremist views," and many categories of individuals, including those who go to rock festivals and foster civil rights activity among servicemen. Memos presented by Senator Weicker to Senate subcommittees investigating government surveillance indicated that the White House attempted to intervene with the IRS on behalf of such friends as Billy Graham and John Wayne and to cause trouble for the producer of a film considered uncomplimentary to the President.

Somehow it seems unlikely that Governor Reagan of California and Senator Kennedy of Massachusetts were letting their hair down at the same "wild" Hollywood party. Yet that is the sort of thing that agent Ulasewicz was looking into, along with the sex life of presidential nephew Donald Nixon, the private lives of Senators Humphrey and Muskie, and the activities of the Young Republicans National Federation.

A totalitarian notion

Other documents propose ways of silencing the Brookings Institution, a "think tank" that sometimes comes up with ideas unacceptable to the President. The Watergate committee is also looking into another White House memo that discusses the possibility of a "penetration"—the most exquisite euphemism yet for a crime committed by White House operatives—of Potomac Associates, a small foundation interested in public affairs.

The surveillance of citizens and organizations engaged in perfectly legitimate and legal activities is taken for granted in a totalitarian system but should be totally foreign to a democratic one. When the first national administration of the post-Nixon era takes on the difficult responsibility of restoring some measure of trust between President and public, one of its most important tasks will be to convince the American people that governmental power exists to serve them, not to control and harass them.

The TENNESSEAN

Nashville, Tenn., April 12, 1974

AS REPUGNANT as the White House "enemies lists" were to American ideals of civil liberties, the additional evidence released by Connecticut Sen. Lowell P. Weicker shows that the lists were only the tip of a very ugly iceberg.

* * *

By making public memoranda and other documentary evidence, Mr. Weicker has revealed that this administration — or at least high-ranking members of it — was capable of using the powers of the executive branch in illegitimate ways to harass and damage political and ideological opponents. The main instrument of this warped scheme was to have been the Internal Revenue Service, but tax trouble was not all the White House had in mind for its "enemies."

Senator Weicker said retired New York City policeman Anthony Ulasewicz conducted some 54 undercover investigations designed to dig up dirt on Democrats and others out of favor with the administration. In one case three attempts to link a senator with improper behavior were launched, according to the memos.

The memos reveal the White House at least talked about Army spying on a "Democrats for McGovern" group in Germany, considered taking punitive antitrust action against the Los Angeles Times and discussed the possibility of granting special treatment to a Florida businessman who at that time was in prison.

Almost from the beginning of this administration the IRS was seen as a valuable political tool to "control" opponents and to gather damaging information on activist groups. A special intelligence task force was created in 1969 — and not disbanded until 1973—to find ways to use the tax laws to attack groups the White House didn't like. The documents reveal the force compiled dossiers on 10,000 taxpayers.

A memo signed by a Mr. D.O. Virdin strongly indicates that the IRS was well aware that it was operating at least on the fringes of the law:

"We do not want the news media to be alerted to what we are attempting to do or how we are operating because disclosure of such information might embarrass the administration..."

Perhaps most embarrassing to the administration would have been the knowledge that critical newsmen ranked high on the target lists of such former White House aides as Mr. John W. Dean III and Mr. John Caulfield. The investigating reporters of Newsday, a Long Island paper, were considered for an audit because they were writing a story about Mr. Charles Rebozo, the President's friend.

The political use of IRS clout apparently cut both ways. Memos passed from Messrs. Dean and Caulfield showed an interest in "friends" such as evangelist Billy Graham and actor John Wayne. Both deny that the White House helped them out of tax problems, but their tax files — which were supposed to be confidential — were discussed in the White House, along with those of California Governor Ronald Reagan and actors Sammy Davis Jr. and Frank Sinatra.

If the new evidence made public by Mr. Weicker fails to arouse the public, it could be an indication that such bombshells have become routine in the course of the so-called Watergate probe. The police-state mentality of members of this administration is no longer in doubt. The only real questions are how far up the ladder such activites were condoned and how many American citizens were hurt by such tactics.

* * *

The public owes Senator Weicker a debt for insisting that the memos and documents be given over to the public. As tedious as the process may be, the public has learned that it will be through the determination of concerned congressional leaders and the independent prosecutors that the entire iceberg of White House abuses will be uncovered.

THE SAGINAW NEWS

Saginaw, Mich., April 10, 1974

The news from Washington, like endless waves beating against the shore, brings each day developments more dismaying than the ones that have gone before, each challenging somebody to stand up and say or do the things that prove it isn't so.

Unfortunately, there is no way to say it simply isn't so. Each new development calls for a new and thorough-going investigation.

And so it it now with testimony delivered by a Republican senator before three Senate subcommittees delving into the depths of political spying activities. The latest nagging question is whether the Nixon administration used and abused the Internal Revenue Service and whether indeed the IRS has engaged willingly or under pressure in activities far beyond its lawful realm.

In substance the testimony read into the record says that from 1969 through August of last year the administration had an IRS task force at work protecting the income tax interests of those taken to be friends of the White House and working deliberately to dig up any dirt possible against its critics — some taken to be "enemies."

Sen. Lowell P. Weice Weicker Jr., the Republican from Connecticut and the man who is pointing the finger, may be standing on political quicksand — or he may be on firm ground. Either way, the allegations set forth by Weicker, one of the more outspoken members of the Senate Watergate Committee, are serious and far-ranging so much so that there is no way they can be quietly dismissed.

During the course of the Watergate investigation the nation was exposed to the existence of a so-called "enemies" list set up for special IRS attention. So that part of Sen. Weicker's testimony hardly comes as any shock.

But the Connecticut senator, who was often astounded by some of the things he heard during the Watergate hearings, apparently had his interest aroused. What he has now spread out before the inquiring committees expands to new dimensions material that heretofore had raised serious enough questions.

Weicker is adding new names — a litany of high-ranking government figures and entertainers — telling of new invasions of privacy and adding to the list of government agencies which, he says, were involved in spying and data-gathering. In addition to the IRS, these include the Pentagon, hardly a surprise, and the Commerce , Department — somewhat more so.

Everybody is entitled to know just how good the information is that is being supplied by Sen. Weicker to the committees.

But the sources are interesting. Aides to the senator say the information comes directly from testimony given by Anthony Ulasewicz, since identified as an undercover agent and operative active on behalf of the White House and during the 1972 re-election campaign; from the White House files of John Caulfield, the man to whom Ulasewicz answered; from White House memos relating to the use of the IRS and from memos covering military spying activities on political groups.

At the least, the substance of some of what Weicker has read into the record ought to arouse intense interest with those committees. Reading from an IRS memo dealing with the establishment of task force, Weicker quoted as follows:

"We do not want the news media to be alerted to what we are attempting to do or how we are operating because disclosure of such information might embarrass the administration...."

This is the kind of sickness that has invaded the highest echelons of government and it is the kind of sickness that has created the larger sickness of disgust, doubt and disillusionment that is sweeping the country.

Sen. Weicker has opened a new can of worms. Its contents are not pretty. If true, they are frightening. What they suggest is the active estbalishment within the federal government of an illegal and unauthorized task force to spy on anybody who fit a private definition and, as well, the subversion of the IRS, among other agencies, from lawful purpose. It suggests the rawest abuse of power through the use of confidential information to intimidate.

Sen. Weicker's can of worms can't be closed now. The public again has the right to know if Weicker is correct or overstating it when he says key White House aides had lending library access to individual tax records.

DAYTON DAILY NEWS

Dayton, Ohio., April 10, 1974

Sen. Lowell Weicker's latest report on domestic spying by the Nixon administration served mainly to recall the central, now half-forgotten horrors of the original Watergate scandals and to amplify them with some additional details. Sen. Weicker, a Republican member of the Watergate committee, made the report to three Senate subcommittees t h a t are studying the political misuse of government agencies by the President.

Weicker

The senator revealed that a secret task force was set up in the Internal Revenue service within months of Mr. Nixon's inauguration and that, by the time it was disbanded last year, the task force had compiled files on 10,000 taxpayers. The apparent purposes were to permit harassment, at least, of Mr. Nixon's political "enemies" and to aid the protection of his political friends.

Sen. Weicker also revealed that Anthony Ulasewicz, who told the Watergate committee last summer that he had been hired to dig up dirt on leading Democrats, had conducted 50 separate investigations of more than a dozen senators and other political figures. The private detective's snooping apparently was wider than his public testimony to the Watergate committee had implied.

None of this is quite new, but the extent of it is. Had it all become public at once, a year ago, say, the public shock would have been strong, but it has been one of the worst disservices to the country that the Watergate scandal has calloused Americans to the abuses of their rights and their political processes. Citizens have become almost accustomed to reports of some new outrage against their institutions by Mr. Nixon's operatives.

Sen. Weicker said of the political misuse of IRS and of the resort to politics-by-gumshoe that "obviously something smells." That is true, and bad enough, but it would be worse if we were to let ourselves get so used to the odor that we would rather live with it than bother to root out its cause.

Washington Star-News
Washington, D.C., April 16, 1974

The very foundation of the American tax system—the faith of the taxpayers in the basic fairness of the system and in the confidentiality of their tax returns—is being shaken by a seemingly endless stream of abuses in the Watergate White House.

Some of the latest examples were revealed in a stack of documents handed to three Senate subcommittees by Lowell Weicker, a member of the Senate Watergate Committee. The documents, which were collected during the course of the Watergate investigation and included White House memoranda, showed that former members of the Nixon administration had no compunction about using agencies of the government, particularly the Internal Revenue Service, to do in political enemies and help their friends.

One of the most reprehensible activities was the alleged use of IRS files to compile dossiers on political opponents, which led Weicker to observe that IRS was "acting like a public lending library for the White House." According to Weicker, a special team collected files on some 10,000 taxpayers between mid-1969 and last August when the team was disbanded. A memorandum describing creation of the team said that it would examine the tax records of "ideological, militant, subversive, radical or other" organizations. The memo warned that this activity should be kept from the news media because it "might embarrass the administration."

Other memoranda discussed the use of IRS muscle to harass and damage the producers of "Millhouse," an anti-Nixon film. An IRS probe of the Brookings Institution was discussed as a means of dealing with anything it might be doing adverse to the administration. On the other hand, another set of memos indicated that the administration was interested in helping its friends with their tax problems.

These are not isolated examples. They fit a pattern of tax law abuse and callous disregard of taxpayers' rights. There was, for instance, the disclosure of a memo suggesting that President Nixon wanted his staff to examine the tax returns of former presidents so he could learn what deductions they took.

There was the executive order to allow the Department of Agriculture to examine the returns of 3 million farmers, an order that finally was rescinded when it came to the attention of Congress and drew heavy criticism.

All this, and who knows what else still to be revealed, is piled upon the most publicized finagling of all involving the President's own tax return. After using every tax dodge that could be found to reduce his own taxes and after getting one clean bill of health from IRS, it was belatedly discovered that he really owed more than $400,000 in back taxes.

The American tax system depends on voluntary compliance by the citizens. If the abuses that have been brought to light erode the faith of the taxpayers in the system, that may be the most damaging legacy of Watergate.

CHICAGO DAILY NEWS
Chicago, Ill., April 10, 1974

Sen. Lowell P. Weicker's disclosures of White House snooping into the income tax returns of political enemies early in the Nixon administration should be viewed in the context of the Watergate affair.

Weicker offered documentary evidence showing that within a few months after Mr. Nixon became President in 1969 the White House had set up a secret task force inside the Internal Revenue Service. Before it was disbanded in August, 1973, the task force had gathered a bulging file of 12,000 classified documents concerning 10,000 citizens.

A July, 1969, memo stated that the group would examine tax records of "ideological, militant, subversive, radical or other" organizations. It added that "we do not want the news media to be alerted to what we are attempting to do nor how we are operating because the disclosure of such information might embarrass the administration" or hinder official inquiries.

One subject of such an inquiry was a team of investigative reporters for a Long Island newspaper that had written of Mr. Nixon's relationship with Florida financier C. G. (Bebe) Rebozo. Another concerned a motion picture producer who had made a film critical of President Nixon. Others concerned prominent entertainers, some friends of Mr. Nixon who presumably were to be helped, and some outspoken foes. Many of those in whom the White House expressed interest were audited by IRS, some of them repeatedly.

Weicker charged that the IRS had been used again and again to harass political opponents of the President and said it constituted "a perversion of the American constitutional system."

It seems that way to us.

It also strikes us that the new disclosures by the Connecticut Republican and member of the Senate Watergate Committee help to explain a great deal about Watergate.

For the basic philosophy behind the Watergate break-in was present in the White House in 1969. This was—as it has remained—an attitude of dour distrust in which the motives and in fact the patriotism of all who were not 100 per cent for the administration were suspect. It was also an attitude that the protection of the administration, its tenure and its policies must be absolutely justified by any means whatsoever.

A President who built his personal team upon that credo could hardly have been either astonished or outraged to learn that the Plumbers had bugged the Democratic Party headquarters at Watergate.

THE ANN ARBOR NEWS
Ann Arbor, Mich., April 12, 1974

THE Internal Revenue Service, which saves its biggest noise for this time of year, has been tabbed by Sen. Lowell Weicker Jr. of Connecticut as an agency working in concert with the White House to gather data on potential "enemies."

Weicker's revelations cause chagrin but not surprise. In the Washington of Watergate, the FBI was politicized, too. News that the independent IRS until recently was prepared to audit the taxes of anyone attending a rock concert or burning his draft card somehow loses its shock value.

Still, outrage at this latest invasion of privacy by government ought to reach the halls of Congress, where every effort should be made to cleanse the IRS. Taxpayers need to be assured that they are not only taxed fairly, but also that their signed returns are kept private and out of the hands of mischief makers.

Pressure from the White House is an awesome thing, something the IRS was not up to resist when the occasion demanded. But in letting itself become politicized, the IRS has undermined its standing with the nation's taxpayers. Paying taxes is not a pleasant chore to begin with, and now the knowledge that the IRS helped to play tricks on people enrages all over again.

The Miami Herald

Miami, Fla., April 10, 1974

EVEN the hardened skeptic who can find little if anything sacred must be shocked by Sen. Lowell Weicker's testimony before a Senate hearing on government spying.

The Internal Revenue Service, said the Connecticut Republican, has furnished or has been compelled to furnish the White House with confidential files on thousands of taxpayers, including some of prominence. In most cases they were either " "enemies" or "friends" of the Nixon administration.

The IRS collects taxes on a scale matched by no other agency in the world. Internal revenues account for the largest share of national governmental revenues of all the major economies. This year it will take in about $120 billion in personal income taxes alone.

This is a mammoth operation, as old as the Republic and just as long regarded as sacrosanct in its confidentiality. But Sen. Weicker, citing documents uncovered in the Watergate investigation, charges that the IRS "was acting like a public lending library for the White House."

Since the President — any President — is nominally the head of all agencies, the IRS must do his bidding. The implication is plain that IRS files have been used to punish political enemies and reward political friends. This is an abuse of power of the most serious sort for it is an abuse of the privacy of an individual in a free and open society.

The late Lyndon Johnson was similarly criticized for delving into FBI reports, a practice which seemed to be a sort of White House recreation. LBJ was furnished juicy items from raw files and read them to his cronies with much merriment.

That indiscretion may be a precedent but it does not excuse President Nixon from using tax information for political purposes. As Sen. Weicker puts it, "Clearly this is not material that should be in the hands of anyone but the taxpayer and the IRS."

If the present regulations on confidentially are either too loose or too vague, Congress should tighten them and spell them out in positive terms. The surest way to destroy the tax structure of the United States and the efficiency of its highly praised machinery is to cause it to lose the confidence of Americans who think, unlike Hemingway's hero, that some things are sacred, after all.

New York Post

New York, N.Y. April 9, 1974

I am not going to discuss the President's income taxes. I think that's a personal matter.

—*White House Deputy Press Secretary Warren, Sept. 12, 1973.*

* * *

Three months later, the President was still declaiming on the right to financial privacy. Making public a quantity of documentary information, including tax figures, he observed that he was acting "even though both American law and tradition protect the privacy of the papers I am releasing today . . ."

Yet, up until a few weeks before Warren's expressions of dismay about inquiries on the President's taxes, the Internal Revenue Service, at the direction of the Nixon Administration, was sheltering a political espionage operation which was routinely given access to American citizens' tax returns.

That is the contemporary history described at length yesterday, after a special investigation, by Sen. Weicker (R-Conn.) of the Senate Watergate Committee, who reported that the "intelligence" unit accumulated secret files on some 10,000 persons, incorporating 12,000 classified records, before it was disbanded late in the summer of 1973.

If the exposure had come in the days before Watergate, political subversion of the federal tax agency—and of military intelligence—on the scale described by Sen. Weicker might have kindled immediate public outrage, dominated the news pages for weeks and developed irresistible momentum for reform. It is a measure of the extent to which news of political, moral and financial debasement has become daily stuff that the story will seem only another unsurprising chapter. But that does not minimize the importance of the Senate's investigations, nor does it justify failure to restore the integrity of the IRS — an agency which routinely appeals to the honesty of the taxpayer.

THE MILWAUKEE JOURNAL

Milwaukee, Wisc., April 22, 1974

The time has come for a long, hard look at the Internal Revenue Service, a crucial agency whose reputation for integrity and effectiveness has fallen under a darkening cloud.

A limited congressional inquiry last year into accusations that the Nixon administration had used the IRS to harass foes and help friends found no pattern of abuse. Meanwhile, a newly appointed IRS commissioner, Donald Alexander, has pledged to move the agency to new peaks of honorable performance. However, allegations of bad practice keep coming.

Sen. Weicker (R-Conn.) has offered a sheaf of documents indicating that the Nixon administration was more successful in politicizing the IRS than previously supposed. One of the most reprehensible activities was the alleged use of IRS files to compile dossiers on troublesome political activists. Weicker charges that the IRS acted as a "lending library for the White House." If Weicker is not exaggerating, the chilling conclusion is that the IRS, for at least a time, became a kind of strike force against political dissent in America.

The IRS is also taking heat on other fronts. Its initial bungling of President Nixon's tax returns has not been adequately explained. Indeed, that shabby episode gives added weight to charges that the IRS is failing to deal effectively with an increasing incidence of tax avoidance and evasion. At the same time, there is a persistent lament that ordinary taxpayers are often unfairly treated, that they are not adequately advised of their rights at the outset of tax disputes or are victimized by an informal "quota" system that rewards agents for harshness. Then, too, certain IRS tactics have raised civil liberty issues, as when the agency snooped into telephone records of newsmen.

Commissioner Alexander appears to be laboring mightily to halt erosion of public confidence. He fully realizes that widespread cynicism could have a ruinous effect on our system of voluntary tax assessment, which is the envy of many nations. But Alexander cannot give the IRS what it now needs most — a comprehensive outside audit. That is the task of Congress and it should be made a high priority without delay.

Post-Tribune

Guarding Your Interests Daily

Gary, Ind., April 16, 1974

At this time of the year, it is popular for the Internal Revenue Service to be unpopular, so we ought to be charitable in weighing accusations that the IRS has been acting improperly.

But Sen. Lowell Weicker's charges that the agency was used to control the Nixon administration's political and ideological opponents are too serious to brush off as just more anti-Nixon sentiment.

Some memos produced by Weicker during a Senate sub-committee hearing indicate the activity was at least questionable and frightening. The White House, for example, was supplied specific comparison tax audit information on such entertainers as Frank Sinatra, Lucille Ball and Sammy Davis, Jr.

One IRS memo about the special intelligence task force discussed ways the tax laws could be used to attack what were described as "activist, ideological, radical, militant or subversive groups."

Citizens can draw their own conclusions about the meaning of that, and about the meaning of this portion of the memo:

"We do not want the news media to be alerted to what we are attempting to do or how we are operating because disclosure of such information might embarrass the administration . . ."

Our conclusion is that the evidence suggests an abuse of power and invasion of privacy. Whether that will embarrass this administration or not is questionable. But it is wrong.

THE COMMERCIAL APPEAL

Memphis, Tenn., April 10, 1974

IN A SPIN-OFF from the Senate Watergate investigations of last year, Sen. Lowell P. Weicker Jr. (R-Conn.) has given another Senate committee information on how the Nixon administration got frequent access to confidential Internal Revenue Service files on political friends and foes of President Nixon.

A thick stack of documents he presented Monday to the Judiciary subcommittee on constitutional rights, which like the Watergate committee is headed by Sen. Sam J. Ervin (D-N.C.), provides a lengthy recital of alleged White House improprieties in prying into the private affairs of individuals and organizations.

It shows among other things that an administration task force set up in mid-1969 to gather tax information on "activist organizations" collected files on about 10,000 taxpayers before the unit was disbanded last August. It caused Weicker to observe that "the IRS was acting like a public lending library for the White House."

Those investigations reached out in all sorts of strange directions.

They involved White House scrutiny of IRS audits of the tax returns of Billy Graham, the evangelist friend of the President, and of actor John Wayne as well as the suggestion that the White House initiate "discreet IRS audits" on the producer of a film that lampooned the President and "a comedian named Dixon who was doing imitations of the President." There also were investigations to determine whether there were any "scandals or skeletons" in the backgrounds of Sen. Edmund Muskie (D-Maine) and Sen. Hubert H. Humphrey (D-Minn.).

ALL THIS may strike citizens as just more of what they already have heard about so much in the last year or so. But though it is, that is no reason for discounting it or ignoring it. The very fact that the information keeps pouring out of these investigations should be enough to shock thinking citizens again and again.

It reflects the philosophy of the administration in the White House which rode roughshod, firm in the belief that it and it alone knew what what was good for the nation and determined to use any means to get its way and crush its critics at all levels.

It demonstrates that this has been an administration which while putting the greatest emphasis on the need for confidentiality for the presidency was willing and eager to destroy the confidentiality of its citizens.

There are times when citizens' affairs must be scrutinized by government. Lacking that ability, the government would not be able to prosecute tax law violators or get the needed information on suspected criminals in other fields. But there are proper ways of going about getting such information. They involve due process.

What the White House staff was about did not involve such due process. The charges growing out of these investigations are that those staff members were searching for information to use as political rather than legal weapons. Both their purposes and their methods were wrong. It was a misuse rather than a proper use of governmental agencies.

THIS WAS, in short, a form of "big brotherism" which cannot be tolerated.

It may not be possible to legislate against such abuse beyond what already has been legislated. But the revelations can serve as a warning to be on guard even more in the future against such abuses.

Detroit Free Press

Detroit, Mich., April 10, 1974

AS APRIL 15 rolls around once again, and as millions of Americans face the annual federal income tax deadline, the country needs assurances from Congress that integrity is being restored to the Internal Revenue Service.

The new revelations produced Monday by Sen. Lowell P. Weicker Jr., R-Conn., not only show further abuses of power by President Nixon's White House, but also clearly demonstrate the need for restoring public confidence in the IRS.

By releasing a small mountain of documents and memos, Mr. Weicker has clearly proved that the president's agents in the White House were eager to destroy the sanctity of individual tax returns to gain political power or to help the president's friends.

The documents show that the White House, as early as 1969, created a secret unit of government to collect tax information from IRS files on so-called "activist organizations." The unit was not disbanded until last August, and by that time had amassed files on 10,000 individuals. The information was not sought to aid in collecting taxes from those singled out; the IRS itself enforces the tax laws, or is supposed to. The data was designed to aid the White House in harassing those it saw as political enemies.

The thrust of this effort was clear in an early government memo uncovered during the Watergate hearings, in which one official cautioned, "We do not want the news media to be alerted to what we are attempting to do or how we are operating because disclosure of such information might embarrass the administration."

The White House, Sen. Weicker showed, displayed an unusual interest in gaining from the IRS details of the tax problems of such people as Billy Graham, John Wayne, Frank Sinatra, Sammy Davis Jr., Fred MacMurray, Peter Lawford, Jerry Lewis, Richard Boone, Lucille Ball and Ronald Reagan. Some were clearly political friends of the president.

Coming on top of the way the IRS initially glossed over Mr. Nixon's own returns, these disclosures of abuse of power add further weight to the need to clean up the IRS.

Public confidence is not enhanced by the fact that the IRS official who congratulated Mr. Nixon on those tax returns for which the president is now under scrutiny for possible fraud won a promotion out of the episode.

American taxpayers must know that they are all being treated fairly by the nation's tax collectors, and that the privacy of their returns is not being abused so that they can be harassed by the government. Congress should take whatever steps are needed to reinstate those protections in our tax system.

NIXON'S MISUSE OF IRS CHARGED BY HOUSE JUDICIARY COMMITTEE

The House Judiciary Committee July 16 released evidence collected in its impeachment inquiry concerning possible White House attempts to misuse the Internal Revenue Service for political gain. The ninth volume of evidence on the Watergate affair detailed repeated attempts by the White House, some successful, to gain confidential tax information on individuals from the IRS. Among the evidence was testimony from both of the Nixon Administration's first two commissioners of Internal Revenue who had offered their resignations in protest against what they considered improper White House pressures. John Ehrlichman had said before the Senate Watergate Committee that IRS personnel did not cooperate with information on Lawrence F. O'Brien, then Democratic national chairman: "I wanted them to turn up something and send him to jail before the election." Other evidence indicated Nixon's desire to have the IRS harass left-wing organizations.

THE SUN
Baltimore, Md., August 2, 1974

One of the strengths of our political system is that we are quite literally a nation of taxpayers; reluctant taxpayers, in many instances, but compliant taxpayers to an extent unknown in any other country on earth. This American trait, which is based on a sense of fairness, has been under stress because of growing inequities in our tax system—inequities the administration has utterly failed to correct. Now it has been further affronted by evidence that Mr. Nixon and his top aides manipulated the Internal Revenue Service for their own seedy purposes.

How did they do this? Well, there is testimony that the White House (a) goaded the IRS into auditing the political returns of "enemies;" (b) intervened to protect political "friends" whose tax returns were being audited; (c) planted its agents in supposedly civil service posts in the tax agency ("We have a couple of sources over there that I can get to," John W. Dean 3d once remarked to an approving President); and promoted private rulings to help friendly corporations in litigation involving tax questions. Such "abuses" of the IRS were rightly found grounds for impeachment by the House Judiciary Committee.

It is well that the Internal Revenue Service is taking steps to clean house. IRS Commissioner Donald C. Alexander has informed Congress he will confine reports involving "sensitive" persons to his own agency. These reports will not be given to the White House, as has been the casual practice in recent years, unless they are requested in writing by the President or one of his authorized assistants. In addition, the IRS will make public its so-called "letter rulings" to prevent the kind of secrecy and coverup seen in the ITT case.

These steps by Commissioner Alexander are right on target so far as they go. But Congress should consider legislation that would abolish entirely the routine practice of writing special reports on prominent or politically sensitive persons. This kind of operation is contrary to the concept that all taxpayers should be treated equally. In addition, Congress might want more tightly written legislation specifying procedures under which the President and his top aides should be granted tax information on individuals and corporations.

No matter what administrative changes the IRS undertakes, it will not recover easily from the President's failure to set a good example in the matter of his own tax returns. Mr. Nixon's loopholing and finagling will not soon be forgotten by the multitude of compliant taxpayers whose honesty is the bedrock of a workable revenue system. If Americans are to keep paying their taxes as diligently as they have in the past, the public will need assurance that the IRS is free of politics and that tax reform will promote greater fairness and equity.

The Charlotte Observer
Charlotte, N.C., July 19, 1974

The Nixon Administration's effort to turn the Internal Revenue Service into a weapon against "enemies" of the President is one of the most frightening of the many abuses of power documented by the House Judiciary Committee in its impeachment inquiry.

No other agency in government knows as much about the lives of most Americans as the Internal Revenue Service. It knows how we taxpayers earn our money and how we spend much of it. Without any evidence of wrongdoing, its agents have the the power to make detailed audits to determine the accuracy of our tax returns—audits that cost us time and money and require us to reveal even more details about our most intimate business and personal activities.

The potential for misuse of such information was so obvious that Congress wrote laws requiring the IRS to keep it secret and establishing criminal punishment for anyone who violates that secrecy.

Yet according to massive evidence gathered by the House Judiciary Committee, key officials of the Nixon Administration — with the knowledge of the President himself — broke these laws and attempted to use the IRS to help the supporters and hurt the opponents of the Administration. Two IRS commissioners who were appointed by Mr. Nixon — Randolph Thrower of Georgia and Johnny Walters of South Carolina, both Republicans — resigned in protest against the repeated efforts to turn IRS accountants into political hatchet men.

Whether President Nixon initiated such criminal attempts to pervert the Internal Revenue Service is unimportant. According to tapes and witnesses, he knew what John Ehrlichman—that fine public servant — and others were up to, and he made no effort to stop it. Indeed, the record enables only the most naive reader to believe that this was not a Nixon project.

The evidence that the Nixon Administration broke the law at will and subverted the IRS, the CIA, the FBI, the Justice Department and other institutions of government in its lust for power has become mountainous.

But as Sen. Lowell Weicker, the Connecticut Republican, observed, for a time the nation was moving quickly toward tyranny. "Several years ago," he said, "many Americans were willing to silently tolerate illegal government activity against militants, terrorists or subversives as an expeditious way to circumvent precise processes of our justice system. Though quick, it also proved to be only a short step to using such illegal tactics against any dissenting Americans. The result was that we almost lost America. Not to subversives, terrorists or extremists of the streets but to subversives, terrorists and extremists of the White House."

The House of Representatives does not need to look further to determine whether there is ample reason to approve articles of impeachment against Mr. Nixon. It needs only to determine which of numerous impeachable offenses to charge him with and how to state the charges. The Nixon subversion of the IRS is one of the strongest cases against him developed so far.

Washington Star-News

Washington, D.C., July 18, 1974

An incredible misuse of the Internal Revenue Service by the White House has been laid bare in a report just released by the House Judiciary Committee. Whether any illegality on the part of the President and his men is involved is a matter for the Congress and the courts to decide. But President Nixon can hardly plead that he wasn't aware of what was going on There are indications, in fact, that he encouraged it.

A previously released Watergate tape revealed the President's thinking with regard to using government agencies against political enemies. In a September 15, 1972, conversation with John Dean, during which the President specifically threatened to turn the FBI and Justice Department loose on his enemies, Mr. Nixon said: "I want the most comprehensive notes on all those who tried to do us in they are asking for it and they are going to get it. "

It is apparent from the Judiciary Committee's report that political enemies were in fact "getting it" on the IRS front long before that conversation took place. A former aide said the White House leaked confidential information to a columnist in April 1970 about tax problems of George Wallace's brother, obviously with the aim of damaging the Alabama governor politically. In September 1970, a White House aide wrote a report about IRS investigations of tax-exempt organizations that apparently were involved in political activities the White House didn't like. Political enemies lists were put together by various aides and high White House officials gave orders to run them through the IRS tax wringer Dean said that on the other hand, Mr Nixon asked that the IRS be turned off on friends of his.

The producer of an anti-Nixon film was another target. Mr. Nixon's domestic policy chief, John Ehrlichman, pressured IRS to investigate Democratic National Chairman Lawrence O'Brien, hoping to put him in jail before the 1972 election. The White House was said to have inspired an anonymous letter to put in motion a tax investigation of a New York reporter who had written an article considered unfavorable to Mr. Nixon's friend, Bebe Rebozo. Dean asked IRS to investigate 575 supporters of Democratic presidential candidate George McGovern.

The abuse was so blatant that two IRS commissioners — Johnnie Walters and Randolph Thrower—threatened to resign in protest. That Mr. Nixon was aware of at least some of the activity is evident in the September 15 conversation, when Haldeman informed him that Dean was "moving ruthlessly on the investigation of the McGovern people" and that Dean was working the list "through the IRS."

There seems to be some question as to whether an "enemies-list" operation such as that alleged against the White House is covered by the criminal laws. If it isn't covered, the Congress ought to correct that oversight forthwith.

Whether or not criminal or impeachable behavior is involved, the abuse of public trust, the misuse of power, and the lack of moral principle on the part of men in the White House are evident on the face of it.

The Houston Post

Houston, Tex., July 25, 1974

What would happen to our freedoms if the Internal Revenue Service stood ready to pounce on everyone whose only mistake was that of supporting the losing presidential candidate? The White House attempt to use the IRS to get at Democratic political figures and to gain consideration for special White House friends is one of the most distressing aspects of the whole complex known as Watergate. But it is an aspect the administration does not deny: John Ehrlichman testified before the Senate Watergate committee that, in demanding an IRS investigation of Democratic National Chairman Lawrence F. O'Brien, "I wanted them to turn up something and send him to jail before the election.

Under federal law, and under our American concept of supporting our government through taxation, the IRS must be held safe from any political pressures or from any executive department misuse. Every American must feel secure in the knowledge that however burdensome his taxes may seem, his tax return is private business between him and the IRS. And every American must feel secure in the knowledge that he may support the candidate of his choice without fear that political pressure will be brought to bear on the IRS to harass him.

The White House seemed not to understand this. Two IRS commissioners have testified under oath about repeated pressures from the White House so strong that both commissioners offered to resign rather than comply. Randolph W. Thrower, who resigned in 1971, said he tried to see the President to express his "concern about White House attitudes toward the IRS," but was refused an appointment by H. R. Haldeman on the grounds that "the President did not like such conferences."

Johnnie M. Walters, who succeeded Thrower, has testified about Ehrlichman's insistance that the IRS seek some major error in the tax returns of O'Brien. When Walters refused to pursue the matter beyond the point of an interview, Ehrlichman said, "I'm . . . tired of your foot-dragging tactics." And Ehrlichman himself told the Senate Watergate committee that he was convinced the IRS was deliberately delaying the audit on O'Brien's returns because the IRS "down in the woodwork" was sympathetic to Democrats.

When John Dean asked the commissioner to investigate a list of staff workers and contributors to Sen. George McGovern's campaign, Walters replied that "compliance with the request would be disastrous for the IRS and for the administration and would make the Watergate affair look like a Sunday school picnic." It is inspiring that two IRS commissioners fought the pressures and resigned rather than comply. But defeated by the top office, White House aides then by-passed the commissioners to get information they wanted from lesser staff members.

This is, in the word of Walters, "disastrous." Congress must pass legislation making any breach of the IRS confidential files a felony and placing a punishment so heavy that no one would ever again dare to try to suborn the Internal Revenue Service. If Congress did no more than enact such legislation now, if Congress would build an impenetrable wall around the IRS, the entire session would have been worthwhile.

Los Angeles Times

Los Angeles, Calif., July 18, 1974

The power of government in a modern state is awesome. A minor functionary, backed by the machinery of government, can inflict irreparable harm on a citizen through the misuse of authority. The official who stands at the pinnacle of government in a democratic society can, by abuse of power, threaten the very existence of democratic government.

We have not reached this juncture in the United States—yet. How close we may have come to the brink appears now, fortunately, to be a matter for future historians to decide.

But we have been badly wounded by the calculated assault on the democratic process and our democratic institutions, an assault that can be generally characterized under the rubric of Watergate. The wound has been one of the spirit, and the effect, intangible as it may appear to be, is real because it has to do with the confidence of people in the fairness of government.

So many disclosures, so many charges and countercharges have emanated from Washington in the past two years that they inevitably have begun to generate a miasma of confusion. But the report issued Tuesday by the House Judiciary Committee cannot be misunderstood.

It revealed in stark form, and with supporting evidence, that President Nixon attempted to corrupt the independence of the Internal Revenue Service by converting it into a political club against political opponents whom the White House described as political "enemies." Much that followed was certain to result from an attitude that is the antithesis of the best traditions of this nation. A large part of the evidence released by the committee had been published, but the report's detailed presentation provides for the first time a comprehensive review of the concerted effort by the Administration to misuse the IRS.

The presentation is damning.

Two former IRS commissioners tried to block White House access, but were only partly successful.

John W. Dean III, the President's counsel, told him on one occasion that "I don't have to fool around with Johnnie Walters (then IRS commissioner) or anybody; we can get right in and get what we need."

John D. Ehrlichman, former White House domestic adviser, tried to force the IRS to discover something wrong with the tax returns of Lawrence F. O'Brien, Democratic national chairman.

Commissioner Walters reports that Dean requested an IRS investigation of Sen. George S. McGovern's staff and campaign contributors.

Such disclosures represent more than political skulduggery. They represent a contempt for democracy and a willingness to sacrifice democracy to retain power.

The revelations, and others, confront the American people with a judgment, a judgment that has been thrust upon them and must be made.

The Courier-Journal

Louisville, Ky., July 23, 1974

THE CONFIRMATION, in evidence made public by the House Judiciary Committee, that the President's first two commissioners of internal revenue resigned rather than permit the IRS to be prostituted by politicians, draws an instructive contrast with more recent comments by other Nixon appointees.

For example, there's the Commerce Secretary who last week said a recession isn't a recession, despite two consecutive declines in the U.S. gross national product. There's the Attorney General who says he hasn't had the time to draw conclusions about the House committee's inquiry into impeachment issues. And there's the Vice President who, after listening at last to proffered White House tape recordings, hardly pauses a beat before drawing what seems to be an intuitive conclusion about Mr. Nixon's absolute innocence.

All of which indicates that a new breed of men, with stronger stomachs, has replaced the types who held office earlier in the Nixon administration. Relations between the White House and IRS chiefs were strained from the very start of the first term. The first appointee, Randolph Thrower, twice had to threaten to quit to head off attempts to put Jack Caulfield and G. Gordon Liddy, both later to emerge as key figures in the Watergate revelations, in charge of the IRS' Alcohol, Tobacco and Firearms Division.

Unfortunately, for him, Mr. Thrower was restrained in the conduct of his battles with the White House. As a career tax lawyer, he was so conscious of the political neutrality demanded of the IRS chief that he went to the White House to complain about a 1970 news "leak" about the tax affairs of Governor George Wallace's brother, Gerald. The irony of that episode, which upset Mr. Thrower the more because the leak so clearly occurred in H. R. Haldeman's office, was that Jack Anderson was the newsman used by the White House to embarrass a political opponent.

What finally drove Mr. Thrower to resign, in January 1971, was the fact that White House aides would not grant him a personal interview with Mr. Nixon to discuss the threat to the IRS of the White House conduct. Told by appointments secretary Dwight Chapin that the President knew how he felt and didn't want to see him, Mr. Thrower resigned.

His successor, Atlanta lawyer Johnnie M. Walters, suffered equally grave insults from White House muscle men. One key issue was the effort by John Ehrlichman to get Lawrence O'Brien prosecuted on tax charges during the 1972 campaign. In that episode, Mr

Ehrlichman accused Mr. Walters, profanely, of "foot-dragging" on the politically sensitive investigation.

Later, John Dean's direct effort to procure investigations of George McGovern's staff and campaign contributors agitated Commissioner Walters. Here Mr. Walters had the support of former Treasury Secretary George Shultz for filing away the White House demands. But Mr. Dean persisted, during September 1972, in forcing requests for tax action on the IRS. The whole affair is intimately related in a portion of the key September 15, 1972, tape-recorded Oval Office conversation among Messrs. Nixon, Haldeman and Dean, concerning which the Judiciary Committee reported that it, too, had run into some footdragging.

Although IRS Commissioner Walters reported that he had succeeded in suppressing demands for audits of 490 "enemies" of the Nixon administration—the Colson-Dean list—there is some question about that. Probably because of the White House penetration of the lower echelons of the IRS, outside studies indicate that 27 per cent of those on the "enemies" list were audited—a rate twice the norm for the entire population and high, perhaps, even for people with generally large incomes.

These are matters that should be looked into by the Joint Committee on Internal Revenue Taxation and by the legislative committees in each house with authority over tax affairs. Does every questioned tax return get the same treatment at IRS? Would further investigation into Bebe Rebozo's handling of campaign funds, his safe-deposit boxes and gifts of gems to Mrs. Nixon stand up under straightforward scrutiny? When the President's closest confidante switches funds (some of them donated for campaign purposes) among three accounts in two banks in one day, the matter shouldn't be left hanging.

The Internal Revenue Service required a long time to recover from the Truman-era bribery scandals. IRS insulation from political interference and misuse is of utmost importance to the American system of taxation. People pay their taxes out of respect for the integrity of that system, as well as out of fear of prosecution. In this respect, the Nixon administration has been more than a disaster for a few office-holders. It has posed a real threat to the workability of the U.S. tax system.

The Des Moines Register

Des Moines, Iowa, July 18, 1974

The House Judiciary Committee staff report on the misuse of the Internal Revenue Service by the Nixon White House contains nothing not previously disclosed. But it adds up to a damaging account of ruthless efforts to "get" political enemies through tax information supposedly secret.

Nixon's staff apparently looked upon the machinery of the federal government as their own property to use as they saw fit for gaining and holding political power and enhancing the power of their chief. As with the FBI and the CIA, the IRS was pressed to provide intelligence and to harass people the White House considered enemies.

The IRS head officials resisted this pressure in a number of instances. Former Commissioner Randolph Thrower refused to accept John Caulfield, one of the White House men, in a top IRS post, because he thought Caulfield was not qualified. Thrower threatened to resign if Caulfield were appointed.

Thrower also sought a meeting with the President to state his concern about the introduction of political influence into the IRS. He said this would be very damaging to the President and his administration. He was brushed off by the White House, but his prediction turned out to be accurate.

Johnnie Walters, a later IRS commissioner, also balked at doing some of the dirty work John Ehrlichman and John Dean wanted him to do. Dean wanted him to investigate a list of staff members of the George McGovern campaign and contributors to the campaign. Walters refused and was backed up by George Shultz, secretary of the Treasury.

The fact that the traditions and respect for law in the IRS were upheld in many instances does not shake the feeling that the tax agency was corrupted to some degree. There is no doubt whatsoever that the men around President Nixon, with the obvious acquiescence if not the urging of the President, were

willing to abuse their positions for personal and political advantage. It is a shocking thing, and by the standards laid down by the chief authors of the Constitution is ground for an impeachment trial.

Much emphasis has been placed so far in the impeachment inquiry on obstruction of justice concerning the Watergate break-in. That is a criminal offense and important as a consideration in impeachment of the President. But in terms of subversion of the American governmental system, the misuse of the intelligence, police and tax agencies of the government is far worse.

HOUSE JUDICIARY GROUP APPROVES THREE ARTICLES OF IMPEACHMENT

The House Judiciary Committee recessed July 30 after approving three articles of impeachment charging President Nixon with obstruction of justice in connection with the Watergate scandal, abuse of presidential powers and attempting to impede the impeachment process by defying committee subpoenas for evidence.

The second article, offered by Rep. William L. Hungate (D, Mo.), was approved July 29 by a 28–10 vote.

Personally and through his subordinates and agents, Nixon attempted to use the Internal Revenue Service to initiate tax audits or obtain confidential tax data for political purposes. He initiated a series of secret wiretaps under the guise of "national security" and misused the results of the tapes. He authorized and permitted to be maintained in the White House a secret, privately financed investigative unit which engaged in "covert and unlawful activities." He "knowingly misused the executive power by interfering" with the lawful activities of the Federal Bureau of Investigation, the Central Intelligence Agency, the Justice Department, and the Watergate special prosecutor's office.

CHICAGO DAILY NEWS
Chicago, Ill., July 31, 1974

The second article of impeachment, approved by the House Judiciary Committee by a 28-to-10 vote, contains the heart of the case against President Nixon. A great deal of the evidence amassed against the President has to do with relatively petty matters suggesting avarice or arrogance or vindictiveness in the conduct of the office. There is nothing petty about the abuses of power charged here.

The article charges that he tried to use the Internal Revenue Service both as a source of confidential information to use against foes, and as a bludgeon to harass political enemies. It charges he similarly misused the FBI, Central Intelligence Agency and Secret Service, trying to utilize their investigative skills and equipment for ends wholly contrary to their lawful missions. It charges that he used his power illegally to try to impede lawful investigations and to hide unlawful activities.

It was evidence regarding this particular set of actions that persuaded so staunch a Republican as Illinois' Robert McClory to come over and cast his vote for impeachment — and properly so. These actions meddled perilously with the foundations of government.

For the government of this republic operates on the basis of the faith of the citizens — faith that it will function fairly and honorably to provide equal justice before the law. If the power vested in a government agency can be perverted to a stealthy, vengeful attack on a private citizen, then every American stands in jeopardy of such oppression, and the door is open to the beginning of a police state.

The evidence before the committee indicates that the abuses urged upon the agencies in the President's name and with the President's consent were grave enough to cause the proprietors of those agencies to rise up in dismay and indignation. J. Edgar Hoover simply refused to go along. And a parade of attorneys general filed in and out of the Justice Department's head office as Mr. Nixon kept seeking a man with a conscience flexible enough to do his bidding.

"Power tends to corrupt," wrote Lord Acton; "absolute power corrupts absolutely." He might well have been writing about an administration that has now seen the vice president, four Cabinet members, the President's two top aides and a score of other White House functionaries convicted or indicted for various acts of corruption.

On the basis of all of this the Congress is amply warranted in turning to the man at the top in seeking a common denominator, a central explanation for all that has occurred to the shame of the nation and the detriment of decent, orderly government.

Certainly Richard Nixon is not the proprietor of John Connally's conscience, nor Spiro Agnew's nor John Mitchell's nor even John Ehrlichman's or H.R. Haldeman's. But just as certainly, an ordinary sense of rectitude in the Oval Office would have set a vastly different moral standard for the executive branch. The tragic shortfall of that fundamental quality is the burden of the Judiciary Committee's second article of impeachment.

The New York Times
New York, N.Y., July 19, 1974

Watergate, President Nixon stated in a recent interview, is "the broadest but the thinnest scandal in American history, because what was it about?"

The President was commenting on the comparison with Teapot Dome, pointing out that while in that famous oil-lease scandal of the nineteen-twenties large sums of money were involved (the Secretary of the Interior was convicted of accepting a bribe), none of the high officials accused of criminal conduct in the Nixon Administration had received any financial benefit from their actions.

Even on the assumption that that statement is true, it is revealing that Mr. Nixon evidently conceives of the betrayal of public trust—whether it be Teapot Dome or Watergate—primarily in monetary terms. Irrespective of the money involved, Teapot Dome represented an unconscionable sellout of property belonging to the American people; Watergate, a sellout of their constitutional rights. Of the two, Watergate was incomparably the more serious threat to this Republic.

"What is Watergate about?" asks the President. Is it possible that at this late date he still really does not know? Can he really be so uncomprehending that he considers it, to use his word, a mere "blip"? In his consistent evasion of his responsibilities to Congress, to the courts and to the American electorate—and in his sleazy efforts to escape all personal blame for the degradation of the White House during the last five and a half years, Richard M. Nixon has finally reached the nadir of moral obtuseness in asking this cynical question.

• • •

What, indeed, is Watergate all about?

Watergate is about a President of the United States who has repeatedly shown contempt for Congress and the courts; who has established a new and imperial doctrine of "executive privilege"; who has subverted the Constitution by his disregard of powers reserved to the Congress; who has flouted the constitutional injunction to "take care that the laws be faithfully executed" and who is deeply suspect of obstruction of justice as well; whose minions dared to trifle both with the electoral process and also with some of the most sensitive agencies of the United States Government; whose close associates and subordinates—for whose actions he is ultimately responsible—have been convicted of crimes against the people of the United States; who himself has already been named as a co-conspirator; who has connived in misuse of campaign funds; who has cut corners on his own income tax returns; whose careful excision of relevant material in supplying transcripts to the public suggests a sense of ethics more fitting to a slippery political fixer than to the President of the United States.

This is what Watergate is all about; and this is why the Judiciary Committee of the House of Representatives now has the clear duty of considering whether articles of impeachment should be presented to the House against Richard M. Nixon—based on the entire spectrum of evidence covering alleged violations of constitutional and statutory law, and, in a broader and more fundamental sense, of the duties and obligations of the Chief Executive to the people of these United States.

ST. LOUIS POST-DISPATCH

St. Louis, Mo., July 30, 1974

Had the framers of the Constitution been able to witness the debate yesterday in the House Judiciary Committee over the second article of impeachment against President Nixon they would have been immediately at home with the premise which underlay the specific charges, namely, that a Chief Executive can and should be removed for the gross abuse of his office. Indeed, more than any other danger, the framers feared the possibility that a president might abuse his great power and so they provided impeachment and conviction — not criminal prosecution — as the remedy for executive wrongdoing.

The charges against Mr. Nixon, proposed by Representative Hungate of Missouri and approved with minor modifications last night by a vote of 28-to-10, all relate to acts that are uniquely presidential offenses. Mr. Nixon is accused under Article II of misusing the Internal Revenue Service against his political opponents, of misusing the Federal Bureau of Investigation and the Secret Service, of authorizing the clandestine plumbers unit, of misusing his executive power to interfere with federal agencies such as the FBI and the office of the Watergate prosecutor and of failing to take care to faithfully execute the law in regard to the Watergate cover-up. In the narrow sense, these are not criminal acts such as treason or bribery, but they are undisputably high crimes against the American government.

The framers of the Constitution could not foresee wire-tapping or the harassment of tax audits, but they could foresee that a president might misuse his authority and have to be removed from office for it. To James Madison, "The limitation of the period of his service was not a sufficient security." And they could see, also, that a president might abuse his office through the acts of his agents. Representative Donohue of Massachusetts did not forget last night that Madison said, too, that a president should be made "responsible for their conduct, and subject . . . to impeachment himself, if he suffers them to perpetrate with impunity high crimes or misdemeanors against the United States, or neglects to superintend their conduct, so as to check their excesses."

Though they lived in the eighteenth century, the framers were scarcely unaware of the lust for power and the mortal harm it could do the Republic if allowed to go unchecked in government. (Indeed, the long list of grievances against George III is described in the Declaration of Independence as a "Train of Abuses and Usurpations.") "The Executive," declared Edmund Randolph of Virginia, "will have great opportunities of abusing his power." And his fellow Virginian George Mason asked, "Shall any man be above justice? Above all, shall that man be above it who can commit the most extensive injustices?" The answer, clearly, was No, and the guarantee against excesses by the Chief Magistrate was the impeachment clause, which James Monroe called "the main spring of the great machine of government."

Representative Wiggins of California, a Nixon loyalist, argued yesterday that the charges "failed to state an impeachable offense under the Constitution." But not to call Mr. Nixon to account for the offenses alleged in Article II is, in effect, to say that henceforth presidents are to be allowed to pervert federal agencies for their own partisan or personal ends and to impede justice when and where they choose. The framers would have recoiled in horror at such a notion.

In a very real sense, the impeachment process has turned into a re-examination of the principles of government which the framers of the Constitution put forth. In adopting Article II last night, the members of the Judiciary Committee kept faith with their forefathers who represented their states and their people 187 years ago.

Arkansas Gazette.

Little Rock, Ark., July 31, 1974

The House Judiciary Committee on Monday night voted out a second article of impeachment by a margin of 28-to-10 after a kind of replay of the general tenor and tone of the arguments that preceded the 27-to-11 vote for the first article on Saturday night. The second vote thus was a net pick up of one vote for the pro-impeachment forces — and that of another Republican at that, Representative Robert McClory of Illinois. Indeed, McClory was a prime mover in the drafting of the second article, to which he attached a degree of over-riding seriousness that *he* at least said he had been unable to find in Article I, which he opposed for that reason.

We will agree with Congressman McClory that Article II, taken in the main, no doubt does raise even more serious charges against the President than were raised in Article I — though in a sense Article II is supplementary as well as complementary to the earlier article — but we must say also that, in our judgment, either article by itself would justify the President's impeachment and conviction, and that there was never any danger that the deeply serious men who make up the bi-partisan majority on the Committee that would ever vote an article of impeachment that was not serious in the extreme. It is a serious business.

It is a serious business, and the men who make up the minority on the Committee who still oppose impeachment are serious men, too. But while, as we have said, the Monday night arguments in a sense were a re-run of the Saturday night arguments, it appeared to us at least that the defense arguments put forward by people like Charles W. Sandman and David W. Dennis had, if anything, grown even thinner and shriller. Not to say, more desperate.

The majority members, on the other hand, seemed even more deliberate and restrained, more secure in the confidence that they have the confidence of the American people, gracefully yielding up big chunks of their own time to the anti-impeachment speakers to dilate on such themes as "The Russians Are Coming" (they are, but they are only after the wheat) and the notion that if a President should be made accountable for the wrongdoings of more than a score of his top-level aides who have been indicted or worse, then future Presidents will have to be held accountable if some junior filing clerk lifts something out of petty cash in some bureaucratic warren that not only is unknown to the President but unknown to anyone else other than its occupants. There was almost nothing said from the pro-impeachment side that we haven't all known — or been able to know if we wanted to — for quite some time now. But, just for one example, it was refreshing to hear again, in rebuttal to the "he-didn't-know-what-was-going-on" argument, the words of Alexander Butterfield telling of the fussy personal attention to minute detail that Mr. Nixon always gave even to White House social gatherings, seating arrangements, menus, wine cards, selection of entertainers and even the musical numbers performed. This has not yet been picked up by Mr. Sandman and converted into an "explanation" of *why* Nixon did not know what Ehrlichman, Haldeman and the others were up to, but the defense's show isn't over yet.

What Article II does is to underpin the case for impeaching the President on the basis of the record of a systematic abuse of the powers of his office in a wide variety of areas, all of it adding up, again, to the violation of his sworn oath of office under the Constitution.

At one time in the Judiciary Committee's earlier deliberations, it was reported that the Committee, for the sake of narrowing the focus of the impeachment vote when it came, might pass over the many instances in which the President has sought to use the most sensitive agencies of government for private political ends, many times successfully — a pattern of abuses involving the IRS, the FBI, the CIA and others. In the end this very critical example of misuse of the powers of the presidency constituted a major part of the substance of the impeachment article voted upon Monday night. In some cases, the heads of the agencies thus leaned upon, would not go along, or, having gone along for a time, finally refused to go along any further. Such an example was Johnnie M. Walters, the former IRS Commissioner, whom we recently singled out for praise in these columns for that reason, and who on Monday night was rightly praised by his fellow South Carolinian, James R. Mann, for the same reason. The CIA, too, finally refused to go along any more, and the then Director, Richard Helms, was shipped to Turkey for his trouble, just as Walters, as we saw, was not long left for his office, either. Hoover. Though possibly for the wrong reasons, J. Edgar Hoover finally refused to go along, too, a fateful act that led directly to the forming of the extra-constitutional clandestine group known as the "Plumbers", most of whose active members are now in jail or recently were there. It was heavily stressed by the pro-impeachment side in Monday night's arguments that the Plumbers were not only without legitimacy as an investigative arm of government, but that there were paid out of private rather than out of public funds — out of campaign funds, actually, a point that we have made time and time again over the months.

★   ★   ★

BEFORE Richard Nixon ever took office for his first term, this newspaper warned formally that all of us had better batten down the hatches, for the real assault to come would be upon the Constitution, the Bill of Rights especially. No special prescience was required to say this, but, sure enough, it all came to pass in fairly short order, reaching a kind of crescendo in the long months of buildup during which the President who didn't know what was going on was trying to anticipate and finesse — by any means — any remote possibility that someone somehow might prevent "the Re-election of the President."

It was the extremes to which this vow to stay in office at any cost were carried that led us to where we are now, that lie at the heart of the second article of impeachment that the House Committee now has settled upon and that make it imperative that the man responsible be removed from office constitutionally for his failure to behave constitutionally as President.

DAYTON DAILY NEWS
Dayton, Ohio., July 18, 1974

Among the abuses of power for which President Nixon must be impeached is his political subversion of independent federal agencies. Even the FBI and CIA sometimes were driven to doing the White House's political dirty work. The most sustained of the White House's subversive efforts, however, apparently were reserved for the Internal Revenue service, according to evidence released by the House Judiciary committee.

The pressure to use tax audits to harass Mr. Nixon's political "enemies" — and to skip some audits in order to reward his political allies — became so great that one former IRS commissioner, to his lasting credit, threatened to resign and publicly denounce the misuse of IRS unless the pressure stopped.

Even so, the White House attempted at different times to put the Watergate burglary planner G. Gordon Liddy and the top administration political spy John Caulfield in charge of an IRS enforcement division. And despite the efforts of at least two IRS commissioners to ward off the White House's illegal demands, Mr. Nixon's aides still managed occasionally to get and to misuse tax information about individuals.

In at least one documented instance — others are suspected — the White House, which supposedly hates leaks as a matter of principle, leaked damaging tax information to the press about the relative of a potential political opponent. There is a law, a very clear one, against such acts.

That President Nixon knew about and approved the subversion of IRS is not in serious doubt. He was present at a couple of meetings during which his aides discussed plans for misusing IRS in clearly illegal ways. And further evidence apparently exists. The White House is fighting in the courts to withhold the tape recording of a conversation in which, according to testimony by former counsel John Dean, Mr. Nixon specifically stated his determination to make IRS responsive to his political orders.

One of the tragedies of Mr. Nixon's misbehavior as President is the damage he has done to public institutions that were generally respected by overwhelming majorities of Americans. IRS and the FBI, as two examples, apparently managed to withstand most of, and the worst of, Mr. Nixon's attempts to convert them into political arms of his personal rule, but their reputations have been undermined.

Mr. Nixon's misuses of the presidency have degraded the once-healthy skepticism that Americans always have had toward government as a general proposition and toward its agencies in particular into a doubting near-cynicism. Not only has he inspired that attitude. Worse, he has made it reasonable.

The Miami Herald
Miami, Fla., July 30, 1974

IMPEACHMENT is, by nature, a political process, as Alexander Hamilton wrote in the Federalist Papers. Yet the adoption of the first article of impeachment by the House Judiciary Committee against Richard Nixon is politics of a different hue. So, to be sure, is the pursuit of the second article.

Hamilton warned against politicization of the process. "A well-constituted court for the trial of impeachment," he maintained, "is an object not more to be desired than difficult to obtain in a government wholly elected."

Yet the House committee has shown great forebearance in not indulging in politics of the ordinary sort.

The vote on the first article cut across party lines, regional sentiments and ideological differences. The nearly three-to-one majority brought into league conservatives and liberals, Southerners and Northerners, Republicans and Democrats.

The same is evident in the second article, which diverges in largest part from Watergate to the misuse of power "in order corruptly to impede the due and proper administration of justice."

In a sense it is a far more serious issue than Watergate, which first struck the public as a prank not untypical of partisan politics.

The record is clear that the FBI, the CIA and the IRS were manipulated by the White House for its own ends. Most serious to the average citizen, perhaps, is the meddling with the Internal Revenue Service, which must be impartial and aloof (and should be made so by law giving it independent status) if it is to administer the tax laws fairly.

The very administration whose bitter-end advocates love to misquote Lord Acton who said that "all power **tends** to corrupt, and absolute power corrupts absolutely" clearly used the clout of respected federal agencies to punish its enemies and intimidate its critics.

After the first two, it is possible that there will be three more articles of impeachment. It is important that the Judiciary Committee expedite its deliberations, for the government of the country is stalled at dead center and Congress, which has left major legislation unattended, is as preoccupied as the White House with impeachment.

The way to do this, of course, is the way it has been done since the beginning. With sobriety and not a little majesty the Judiciary Committee has gone about its tasks in a sincere, if troubled, manner which has impressed the American people. It can do no less in the days ahead.

The SENTINEL
Winston-Salem, N.C., July 24, 1974

The proposed articles of impeachment that counsel John Doar has put before the Judiciary Committee get to the heart of the matter before the House. They summarize in broad form what has been learned over the past two years, and documented again during the committee's months of inquiry.

In brief, these are the charges that Doar makes:

—Watergate cover-up. Mr. Nixon "has made it his policy to cover up and conceal responsibility for the burglary, the identity of other participants, and the existence of and scope of related unlawful covert activities."

—Ellsberg burglary. The burglary "was part of a pattern of massive and persistent abuse of power for political purposes, involving unlawful and unconstitutional invasion of the rights and privacy of individual citizens." Included are the misuse of the CIA, the FBI, the Internal Revenue Service, and illegal wiretapping.

—House subpoenas. By rejecting Judiciary Committee subpoenas, Mr. Nixon leaves the House no recourse but to impeach him. Failure to comply kept the committee from fully investigating allegations of "condoning of false testimony" before the Senate, and the bribery charge in the 1971 milk decision. "The assumption is justified that had they (tapes and documents) been exculpatory of Richard M. Nixon, he would have produced them," Doar wrote.

—Income taxes. Mr. Nixon's tax returns "constituted a fraud upon the United States" because of the deception involved in deductions for his personal papers. Only the fact that Mr. Nixon was President kept the IRS from the "normal use of the criminal process."

These articles are hardly the sort that one would present before a "kangaroo court," as Ronald Ziegler, speaking for Mr. Nixon, charged last Friday. On the contrary, they are exhaustively detailed and supported, and the less well-documented allegations have been pruned away.

Mr. Nixon's defenders now are making a last stand, not on the evidence, but on the enormity of the impeachment decision. The question they raise is whether the "best interests" of the country would be served if impeachment proceeded.

The answer to that is that halting impeachment now would serve the *worst* interests of the country. Everyone recognizes the drastic nature of impeachment and trial in the Senate. But allowing a President to continue in office unchallenged, after being accused of these many offenses against law and the Constitution, would be an unconditional surrender of principles that have guided the United States for nearly two centuries. There is an overwhelming case for the House to direct the Senate to hold a full trial on Mr. Nixon's fate. Appeals for the "good of the country" cannot blink that fact away.

The Washington Post

Washington, D.C., July 21, 1974

He has endeavored to use the Executive power vested in him by the Constitution to obtain confidential information from executive agencies that could be used for his personal political advantage. —From the proposed articles of impeachment recommended by Special Counsel John M. Doar to the House Judiciary Committee.

LAST WEEK, the House Judiciary Committee released its extensive study of efforts by the Nixon White House to politicize the Internal Revenue Service and use its confidential files for political ends. The study revealed, among other things, that damaging material on Alabama Gov. George C. Wallace and his brother was acquired from the IRS under a pretext of legality and then released to columnist Jack Anderson by Mr. Nixon's mentor, the late Murray Chotiner, who was a White House aide at the time. The material was released three weeks before a primary in which Nixon campaign money had been slipped to Mr. Wallace's opponent. In addition, Lawrence F. O'Brien, while he was campaign manager for George McGovern, was the subject of intense White House interest, brought to bear through the IRS. When the IRS failed to provide any damaging information, John Ehrlichman complained of its "foot dragging" in such a way as to suggest that the IRS could surely have come up with something if it worked hard enough at it. On at least two occasions, according to the testimony of John W. Dean III, President Nixon himself discussed the use of the IRS in such a manner as to suggest that it was his view also that the IRS should be used to punish his enemies. And we have it from Mr. Dean and others that the highest councils of the White House also thought the IRS should be helpful to Nixon friends.

Traditionally, the IRS has sought to be a non-political agency for the very sound reason that it deals in the personal details of all our lives. If it can be manipulated for political purposes, then grave damage to individuals is bound to result. To their credit, two commissioners of the IRS refused to go along with the heavy-handed tactics of the White House. Nonetheless, damage was done to the IRS's integrity because White House agents were able to develop other sources of information. As Dean boasted to the President, "We have a couple of sources over there that I can go to. I don't have to fool around with Johnnie Walters (then the IRS commissioner) or anybody, we can get right in and get what we need."

It is possible to infer from Mr. Dean's testimony with respect to his meeting with the President on Sept. 15, 1972, that those White House agents who tampered with the IRS did so with Mr. Nixon's acquiescence, if not at his instruction. The Nixon-Dean meeting of March 13, 1973, during which Mr. Dean assured the President he could obtain the information he needed while bypassing Commissioner Walters, also includes a question from the President to Dean: "Do you need any IRS (unintelligible) stuff?"

One of the fundamental principles on which our government is founded is that equal justice under law is a guarantee made to *every* citizen—whether he is a member of the President's party or of no party, whether he gives money to the opposition or doesn't, or whether he even votes at all. Some aspects of this commitment to equal justice are written down, either in the Constitution, in the laws or in decisions of the courts. But others are assumed.

And this assumption that the agencies of government which have peculiar powers over the behavior of each of us as citizens—the police power, the taxing power—will not be abused for political purposes is a fundamental part of the people's confidence in their government. That Mr. Nixon should have trifled with the source of this confidence and done so for the most frivolous and self-interested of reasons—and that he should have done so not just once but repeatedly— seems to us, as it apparently does to both the majority and minority counsels of the Judiciary Committee, sufficiently grave to qualify as yet another component of an article of impeachment against the President.

Before the disclosures relating to Watergate were made, most citizens felt that a President of the United States would hardly be likely to turn to a political aide and ask, "Do you need any IRS stuff?" People expected our government to be above using the agencies within its awesome power to defame or harass individuals for being politically different.

That is why there is in the IRS disclosures a touch of chill that is sobering indeed. By one means or another, this administration will pass into history, but it will not have done so before it has drastically altered our common conception of the meaning of the founders' faith in the idea of equality before the law. It is possible the Congress will legislate away the dangers of abuse of the IRS by the President's agents and the abuse of other agencies and powers. What the Congress can never legislate is an atmosphere of trust on the part of the governed about their government. Only by means of the impeachment process now under way can members of the Congress indicate to the public that the standards to which the Nixon administration sank do not reflect their concept of what is acceptable —or even tolerable.

LEDGER-STAR

Norfolk, Va., July 31, 1974

One of the arguments for impeachment of President Nixon which has loomed large in recent days is used in the adjacent column by James Reston, of The New York Times. This involves some most questionable logic, and could be unwontedly influential to the extent that it may tip the scales among Americans (including congressmen) who find solid evidence, pro or con, hard to come by.

The argument is this: that not to impeach the President would somehow condone the scandalous array of conduct exposed in his administration. Mr. Reston makes the point by saying that Congress has as one choice the "precedent of excusing his (Mr. Nixon's) record."

★　★　★　★

However, to tell the Congress that Mr. Nixon will be "excused" if he is not impeached and/or convicted, is to abandon the needed sense of balance in weighing the provability of the various things charged to him and in weighing the gravity of such actions as are provable. For removal-by-impeachment of a president is and ought to be only an extreme, last-resort device. His offense or offenses should be of the worst possible order, and surely proof should be beyond all challenge. If Mr. Nixon is actually guilty, the abuse-of-power article adopted by the Judiciary Committee Monday night, with its allegations of misuse of the IRS, would involve the degree of gravity we have in mind.

Anything less than matters of that degree (and provable) does not call for impeachment, but this is not to say that something short of truly impeachable behavior is approved or treated lightly if Mr. Nixon isn't ousted.

★　★　★　★

It could turn out that the present inconclusiveness of the evidence against Mr. Nixon will be dispelled, that the (provable) wrongdoing by him and the hurt to the nation will be found to be of dire dimensions. And if that should be the case, impeachment and conviction would of course become amply justified, assuming that Mr. Nixon didn't resign beforehand.

But that should be the requirement. And not some fear of condoning the demonstrated shabbiness of the White House operation and the cynical attitudes Mr. Nixon's words have revealed. These things won't be — haven't been and aren't being — "excused" by the American people or their representatives in Congress. For Mr. Nixon will have to live with an ugly blot on his performance. If something worse is adduced from solid evidence, he ought to be removed. But in any event the blot will remain, along with the ravages of the long ordeal he has, with considerable justice, experienced and along, too, with the knowledge of the nation's condemnation.

And as to the temptation for future chief executives to engage in similar conduct, it is absurd to imagine any one of them, whether Mr. Nixon is acquitted or not, inviting the shame this President is bearing.

TAX REFORM PANEL ISSUES REPORT ON IRS SURVEILLANCE OF 99 GROUPS

The Internal Revenue Service (IRS) kept 99 organizations under surveillance from July 1969 to August 1973, according to the 41 documents released to the Tax Reform Research Group, a Washington-based affiliate of Public Citizen, headed by Ralph Nader. The data was first requested 13 months before being released Nov. 8. Included in the list of potentially subversive organizations were the National Council of Churches and the Urban League.

According to the data, the IRS set up a special group, eventually named the Special Services Staff (SSS), July 2, 1969, one day after a White House aide, Tom Charles Huston, informed the IRS that President Nixon wanted the agency "to move against leftist organizations." The SSS was to monitor tax records and keep watch over "ideological, militant, subversive, radical and similar type organizations," the documents revealed. Files were collected on 2,873 organizations and 8,585 individuals before the SSS was dismantled in August 1973. A final report said 78% of these were found to have "no apparent revenue significance or potential." The other 22% of the files were said to have been preserved. No serious tax cheating was reported discovered by the operation, which produced about $100,000 in additional tax revenues.

The Hartford Courant

Hartford, Conn., November 26, 1974

It's not that we need any more depressing news, after Watergate, about how our government has sometimes worked against us. But within the last few days there were reports that both the Internal Revenue Service and the Federal Bureau of Investigation had gone beyond the bounds of the functions of government agencies in a democracy, and had continued those subversions of freedom until the operations were made public.

Acting on word from a Nixon Administration White House aide that Mr. Nixon wanted to move against leftist organizations, the IRS set up a group that eventually completed a list of 99 "ideological, militant, subversive and radical organizations." The list included the National Council of Churches, the Urban League, and Americans for Democratic Action. On the way to compiling it, the IRS group investigated 2,873 organizations and 8,585 persons.

Documents from the White House and the IRS showed that the investigations were primarily based on "getting" the organizations. Three years after the group began its investigations, 51 cases of tax delinquency were found, and $56,000 was collected from settlement of those cases, or slightly more than $1,000 per case, on the average. The IRS documents on the tax investigations were made public by Ralph Nader's Tax Reform Research Group, which obtained the papers after filing a lawsuit under the Freedom of Information Act. Since the IRS lists and documents were released, the IRS has refused to provide information concerning the disposition of the files that were found to contain no tax violations.

The special IRS group was dismantled in August, 1973, by the present Internal Revenue Commissioner, Donald C. Alexander, after details of the IRS activities were made public during the Watergate hearings.

The activities of the FBI went back 20 years, and involved disruptions of suspected subversive organizations by the use of FBI-backed opposition organizations — some of them set up by federal agents — by anonymous letters and derogatory information leaked to the press and public. The tactics, which apparently were known in part to some Presidents, Justice Department officials and some Congressmen, have been denounced by Attorney General William B. Saxbe, who commented that they "are not something that we in a free society should condone." He added that such governmental programs could develop again. "You could have Watergate happen again," he said. "You could have all these things happen again if the people in Congress aren't interested."

It should be remembered that some Congressmen, some Presidents and justice officials knew about the FBI tactics to disrupt allegedly subversive groups with the FBI's own sham organizations, and by derogatory leaks and anonymous smear letters.

What, then, stopped the FBI from continuing those tactics? They were stopped because the documents were made public following the burglary of an FBI field office. It was the fear of public criticism that halted the operations.

All of which is another lesson in the need for open government, for freedom of information, and for making certain that the right of the people to know is not only respected, but honored by all who hold positions of public trust.

The Louisville Times

Louisville, Ky., November 22, 1974

An anonymous federal bureaucrat probably deserves some of the credit for the lopsided vote in Congress this week to override President Ford's veto of amendments to the Freedom of Information Act.

On the day before the House vote, an official at the Internal Revenue Service released documents describing the history and activities of the agency's Special Services Staff. The SSS, as it was called, was set up after President Nixon decided that the nation's tax collector should be used to punish his enemies and advance his administration's political fortunes.

The public has a right to know what the IRS is up to, particularly when it deviates from its assigned mission of collecting income taxes and enforcing tax laws. But consumer advocate Ralph Nader's Tax Reform Research Group spent 13 months trying to pry loose the information on the agency's role as a political support group for the White House.

Congress thus had before it a classic example of why American citizens needed a stronger law to help them keep track of what the federal government is up to. Under the Freedom of Information Act passed in 1966, federal agencies could delay the release of information for months, just as the IRS did.

One of the newly enacted amendments requires a final response within 40 working days at most. After that, a citizen or group can ask a court to force an agency to honor a request for official documents.

The material obtained by the Nader group confirms numerous reports that the IRS singled out many activist organizations, along with 8,000 individuals, for investigation on purely political grounds. The special task force was purportedly looking for violations of the tax laws. But there is considerable evidence that its real purpose was to harass or embarrass Mr. Nixon's opponents.

Although the John Birch Society and the American Nazi party were among the groups investigated, the chief targets of the Special Services Staff were liberal, minority rights or "leftist" organizations. Some, including the Americans for Democratic Action, the Congress of Racial Equality, and the National Council of Churches, could even be considered strongholds of the establishment.

The most unattractive example of the administration's attempt to corrupt a supposedly nonpartisan agency was the investigation of national Democratic chairman Lawrence O'Brien. Former presidential aide John D. Ehrlichman allegedly told the IRS to have Mr. O'Brien jailed on a tax charge before the 1972 election. It was only because two IRS commissioners had the gumption to stand up to White House pressure that attacks on Mr. O'Brien and other ideological "enemies" did not proceed.

Taxpayers who render a substantial portion of their paychecks unto the IRS every week deserve a full accounting of this scandalous behavior and an explanation of what is being done to prevent similar abuses of governmental power in the future. They should also be able to gain access to information about the activities of other federal agencies in a reasonable amount of time.

The amendments that President Ford made the mistake of vetoing should make it much easier for citizens seeking information about their government to overcome the bureaucracy's instinct for delay and secrecy.

THE SUN

Baltimore, Md., November 19, 1974

As the Senate Watergate hearings and the House impeachment hearings clearly demonstrated, President Nixon and his chief aides improperly if not illegally abused their powers by using the Internal Revenue Service to harass political "enemies." Now as the result of a lawsuit filed under the Freedom of Information Act, the public has been given a new look into what was going on in the Internal Revenue Service during the period in which that Special Services Staff was active.

We learn from the new documents that the organization was set up in 1969 immediately after the White House requested it. We learn that in many cases investigations continued even when it was obvious that the groups involved were insolvent. We learn that the organization considered the following groups, among others, to meet the definition "subversive . . . militant . . . revolutionary":

The Urban League, the Unitarian Society, Americans for Democratic Action, the Congress on Racial Equality, Fund for the Republic, Welfare Rights Organization. You get the drift. Liberal organizations whose member's politics were likely to be anti-Nixon. The Ku Klux Klan and the John Birch Society were on the list, too. Considering what we have learned about Richard Nixon and the kind of people he surrounded himself with, one can be excused for wondering if those groups were just added in for cover.

The new revelations about the IRS go beyond just further evidence of Nixonian police state mentality and morality. This practice of harassing one's political enemies with the IRS was in full operation for about two years while the IRS Commissioner was a man who opposed President Nixon's requests to do things that would, as he put it, turn the IRS into a "personal police force." That was Commissioner Randolph Thrower. He was referring to Nixon's insistence that a couple of suspicious characters be added to the IRS executive staff. Thrower eventually quit as the pressure from the White House escalated. But now we see that IRS was behaving more than somewhat like a political police force even then.

What this suggests to us is that the public is not sufficiently protected against abuses of IRS procedures. The new commissioner, Donald Alexander, has informed Congress of new regulations that would end the abuses outlined above—we think. But regulations and other administrative actions aren't always the best tools for ending practices of this sort. Congress ought to take a look at the basic law covering what IRS investigators can and can't do. Americans pay their taxes grudgingly—but they pay them. No country in the world has a better record of voluntary compliance with tax laws. But how long would that last if Americans came to believe the IRS was not an instrument for raising revenues, but an instrument of political repression?

THE TENNESSEAN

Nashville, Tenn., November 22, 1974

THE LIST of organizations spied on by the Internal Revenue Service during the Nixon Administration has been released, the result of a lawsuit filed against IRS, and the list of names reads like a social history of the 60s.

There's SNCC and SSOC and CORE...the Urban League, the SDS, the Black Panthers, the Unitarian Society and the National Student Association...and HAR-YOU (the controversial OEO-funded project in Harlem), Hope Development Inc. and the National Welfare Rights Organization...Americans for Democratic Action, the Nazis and the Revolutionary Action Movement.

It all began with a list of 22 extremist organizations, listed as likely candidates for the collection of back taxes. But court documents tell how the so-called "Special Service Staff" quickly expanded into an intelligence operation that collected files on 11,458 individuals and groups. No wonder that the Nixon people were paranoid!

When a much shorter "enemies list" compiled by the White House was first disclosed, IRS commissioner Donald Alexander and other spokesmen denied that the tax collecting machinery had ever been bent to "harass" citizens, despite pressure from the White House.

Mr. Alexander attempted to cover up the true nature of the special, secret unit by maintaining it had been set up only to investigate tax protestors.

But two memos tell part of the story. One, dated July 29, 1969, said the Special Service Staff was collecting information from the FBI, the Defense Department (with its own domestic intelligence operation) and IRS' own files, as well as "any other federal agency having information."

By October, the unit had discovered that many of the organizations were insolvent. But the spying went on anyway; the unit turned to individuals whose names it apparently obtained through studying the activist organizations.

It is still not known what IRS did with the 11,458 files. Some of those persons on the original "enemies list" said they had been audited, and some organizations have since lost their tax exempt status.

The files may have been run through the busy paper shredders by now. In any event, the militants and the pacifists, the pro-blacks and the pro-whites, all the wide gamut of groups on the list of 99, might agree on at least one thing: they have a right to know what the IRS has on them.

It seems clear that Mr. Alexander has to go. He himself has said that the IRS' job is to collect taxes, not to collect data on its fellow citizens. His firing is necessary, however, not so much as a matter of philosophy but because he lied.

THE INDIANAPOLIS NEWS

Indianapolis, Ind., November 20, 1974

Few Federal agencies have easier access to personal information about citizens than the IRS. The Internal Revenue Service, using citizen-provided data to verify deductions, can glean a person's religious, political and fraternal affiliations, as well as the details of his business dealings.

This detailed accounting is necessary for the process of collecting income taxes from citizens. But newly released documents indicate a secret intelligence gathering arm of the IRS has collected files on thousands of individuals and groups for dubious purposes.

The intelligence gathering unit, called the Special Service Staff, was reportedly set up as a direct result of White House influence in the summer of 1969. At that time, 22 organizations identified by a Senate committee as probable tax-law violators, were to be investigated. But, by the time the Special Service Staff was disbanded at the peak of the Watergate investigation, it had collected files on 11,458 individuals and organizations.

The exact correlation between these files and the subjects' tax status is still unknown. Even as the unit was being disbanded last year, IRS commissioner Donald C. Alexander was apparently still trying to conceal its activities by saying it had been formed to investigate tax protestors and citizens refusing to pay income tax. One of the organizations supposedly included in this category is the Ford Foundation, not at the top of the Nixon administration popularity list.

The prospect of the Special Service Staff being disbanded is a heartening one, but an uneasy question remains.

The IRS refuses to reveal what has become of the top-secret files. If this investigative detail is indeed defunct, what happened to its files?

THE COMMERCIAL APPEAL
Memphis, Tenn., November 19, 1974

THE FIRST SOLID evidence that the Internal Revenue Service had been systematically misused came in the Senate Watergate hearings. The final report of the Watergate committee, issued last July 12, pointed to the IRS as "a preferred target of the (Nixon) White House staff in its attempts to politicize independent agencies."

Of particular concern has been a secret Special Service Staff in the IRS. Donald C. Alexander, current IRS commissioner, has persisted in the public denial that this unit was set up in 1969 at the direct insistence of the Nixon inner circle.

A memo brought to the surface through a Freedom of Information Act suit filed by the Ralph Nader Tax Reform Research Group makes a lie of all those denials.

Documents also indicate Alexander's attempts to hide the true nature of the secret unit even as it was being disbanded last year.

That leaves the administration of President Gerald Ford in the sticky position of having an IRS chief whose credibility and integrity are thoroughly deflated.

IT MAY BE that the secret investigations for political purposes cooked up by an outcast administration are a thing of the past. It does not make what happened less scary, or obnoxious or unethical.

All of us know that our privacy is stripped by the information we put into our tax returns, but we trust the IRS to protect that privacy from other nosy bureaucrats and politicians. Only in cases of criminal investigation are IRS files supposed to be available to others in government.

But the Big Brother hand that reached into the IRS from the White House for blatant political purposes is now a matter of record. And, having denied that this was so, Alexander has no business continuing as commissioner. His polite resignation would be the best way to end this episode. If he is not so moved, the responsibility for showing him the door will rest on the President.

The Boston Globe
Boston, Mass., November 23, 1974

Evidence of Watergate misdeeds, like a loose strand on a sweater, continues to unravel, each rip leading only to larger rips. Even as the Watergate cover-up trial produces more evidence, fresh information about the Internal Revenue Service has been surfacing.

Disclosures over the past two years have documented attempts of the Nixon Administration to usurp the IRS for partisan advantage. A 1972 White House request, submitted by counsel John W. Dean 3d, sought tax audits of 490 "enemies," most of them supporters of Democratic presidential candidate George S. McGovern.

Also, according to Watergate testimony, Mr. Nixon tried to halt IRS action against his supporters, while seeking damaging, confidential information as a club against his opponents. The pressures for illegal operations reportedly forced one IRS commissioner, Randolph W. Thrower, from office and led his successor, Johnnie Walters, to threaten resignation.

If the IRS successfully resisted the pressures in some regards, it yielded in others. In 1970 H. R. Haldeman, Mr. Nixon's major domo, obtained a detrimental IRS memo, eventually leaked to the press, on the tax status of Gerald Wallace, brother of the Alabama governor. White House intervention apparently prompted a special audit of the tax returns of Lawrence O'Brien, then Democratic national chairman.

It has been common knowledge in Washington since 1972 that the Nixon Administration established in the IRS a unit somewhat akin to the plumbers in the White House. The IRS surveillance team apparently refrained from break-ins, but it did collect dossiers on 2873 organizations and 8585 individuals.

Now documents made public by Ralph Nader's Tax Reform Research Group have shown that the IRS sleuths investigated 99 organizations supposedly "ideological, militant, subversive and radical." But the list includes some organizations, like the Americans for Democratic Action and the National Council of Churches, that are hardly more militant or subversive than the Campfire Girls.

One IRS report, also released to Nader's group after it filed a lawsuit under the Freedom of Information Act, concluded that 78 percent of the files collected by the Activist Organization Committee, as the IRS unit originally was called, had no bearing on collection of revenues or on any proper endeavor of the agency.

Bluntly put, Mr. Nixon's corruption of the IRS for personal aggrandizement belongs only in the kind of totalitarian governments against which the former President liked to inveigh. Let government agencies operate at the illicit whim of the President, and the democracy stands in peril.

Regrettably, Congress earlier this year spurned a reform that would have barred the President and his aides from access to IRS files. IRS Commissioner Donald C. Alexander, who endorsed the reform, now has advanced a further proposal. Alexander would insulate the IRS from possible presidential abuse by instituting a five-year term for the commissioner. He now serves at the pleasure of the President.

The proposal has merit. The Watergate events have demonstrated the fragility of the IRS, as now constituted. Congress and the American people will have no one to thank but themselves if they do nothing about it.

Los Angeles Times
Los Angeles, Calif., November 21, 1974

Three observations can be made about the newly revealed and now disbanded secret intelligence operation of the Internal Revenue Service:

—The Nixon administration corrupted the IRS and converted it into a political weapon to harass opponents of the administration or individuals and organizations that the administration assumed were "enemies."

—The present IRS commissioner, Donald C. Alexander, and other IRS spokesmen who denied that the agency succumbed to political pressure, lied to the American people.

—A lawsuit, filed under the Freedom of Information Act, was required to pry the truth from the IRS.

Even now the IRS is refusing to disclose what has become of the top-secret files compiled by the Special Service Staff, set up within the IRS in the summer of 1969 as a result of direct White House influence.

By the time the SSS (do those initials have a reminiscent ring?) was abolished, the intelligence unit had collected files on 11,458 individuals and groups. Who and what are they? Most have not yet been identified, but the organizations include such nationally known groups as Americans for Democratic Action, the National Student Assn., the Urban League and the Unitarian Society.

The list started, as such lists always do, with a few organizations on the extreme left or right, but it quickly expanded to cover a broad political spectrum and, through no coincidence, nearly all the targets were identified with left-of-center social and political causes. One document shows that the SSS sought at least some information about that well-known revolutionary outfit called the Ford Foundation.

Even at the time the SSS was being dismantled last year in the middle of the Watergate scandal, Commissioner Alexander—in the finest government tradition of suppressing the truth—said the unit had been established to investigate tax protesters and persons who refused to pay income taxes.

This from a man who heads an agency that, if used as a political instrument, can ruin an administration's opponents with punitive actions and can reward its supporters with benign interpretations of tax laws.

Robert M. Brandon, director of Ralph Nader's Tax Reform Research Group, which dislodged the incriminating documents, mildly observed that they "show that the IRS went far afield of its mandate to collect taxes and enforce the nation's tax laws."

So it did, and more than that: The IRS crossed the line that separates a democracy from an authoritarian government.

Chicago Sun-Times

Chicago, Ill., November 19, 1974

It has been disclosed that an Internal Revenue Service snoop group identified during the Watergate investigation regarded even the National Urban League and the National Council of Churches as among the country's "ideological, militant, subversive and radical organizations."

In other words, they were among the more than 2,800 organizations and more than 8,500 individuals who were on a Nixon administration enemy list. Thus they were targets of covert investigations by special IRS sleuths. Files upon them apparently still are in various offices of the IRS.

These latest ugly disclosures prompt a number of observations.

For one, it is obvious that the stain of Watergate isn't going to be easily scrubbed away from American government. So long as there is one spite-inspired file or document in existence, there is the danger of damage to the reputation and livelihood of innocent persons.

For another, we wonder why IRS chief Donald C. Alexander disbanded the special unit after assuming office last year while continuing to dissemble about what its duties and effects had been. A clear statement from him on the matter is in order.

Finally, it must be noted that the surveillance list became available at last only because consumer advocate Ralph Nader's Tax Reform Research Group filed suit against the IRS under the Freedom of Information Act.

There is much that still is secret about what the IRS did and collected under its special mandate — granted in 1969 a day after a Nixon aide told IRS officials the President wanted it to move against "leftist" organizations. But what is known is known because the Freedom of Information Act grants the public some limited access to material that otherwise would be hidden from it by fearful bureaucrats.

The act will be even better if Congress overrides President Ford's veto of strengthening amendments. We urge the override. We also urge a continuing effort by Nader, Congress and the courts to find out how deeply into private lives the cancer of politically inspired snooping has spread.

The Evening Gazette

Worcester, Mass., November 29, 1974

When the secret Special Service Staff was set up inside the Internal Revenue Service in 1969, it was instructed to investigate a list of 22 extreme left-and right-wing organizations that had been identified by a U.S. Senate committee as likely candidates for the collection of back taxes.

But under the prodding of a White House determined to use the IRS as a retaliatory weapon against its political "enemies," the Special Service Staff soon expanded its activities. By the time it was disbanded last year in the midst of the Watergate scandal, the undercover group had assembled files on 11,458 organizations and individuals.

That much has been learned from hitherto secret IRS documents made public as a result of a Freedom of Information Act lawsuit filed by Ralph Nader's Citizens' Tax Reform Research Group. Previously, IRS Commissioner Donald C. Alexander tried to conceal the activities of his Special Service Staff by claiming that it was established solely to investigate tax protesters and people who refused to pay income tax.

Certa. IRS must maintain files on taxpayers, both individual and corporate.

Certainly it must investigate either persons or organizations it has good reason to suspect of evading their fair share of taxes.

But those activities must be at least as open and subject to public scrutiny and control as those of any other agency charged with enforcing the law.

Just as the IRS can call in any taxpayer it suspects of cheating for a complete audit, so must the public be able to call the IRS to account.

The Freedom of Information Act is the wedge the public has long needed to pry open the files and see what the IRS — and a lot of other government agencies — have been up to.

The News American

Baltimore, Md., November 22, 1974

ONE of the scariest stories to emerge in the aftermath of the Watergate scandals was this week's detailed documentation of how the Internal Revenue Service, bowing to orders from the Nixon White House, for three years kept special tabs on 99 organizations believed hostile to the administration.

The grimness of the story far exceeds its added proof of power abuse by men suspicious to the point of paranoia. The scary part is that the IRS could and did take part in what amounted to a potential political vengeance apparatus — and neither congress nor the public had any way of knowing it.

According to the newly-disclosed evidence, the IRS was instructed to give special attention to the tax returns of groups described as "ideological, militant, subversive and radical." The purpose, obviously, was to concentrate information in an agency whose authority could be used as an intimidating club.

Like the notorious "enemies" list compiled by the Nixon White House, the list of 99 organizations in the tax surveillance program had its ridiculous aspects. Included in the bunch of little-known and mostly negligible radical groups were many wholly respectable racial and religious bodies — some of them actually being subsidized by federal funds.

The clandestine operation was idiotic to the point of lunacy. Its massive drive resulted in uncovering only a handful of delinquencies and the collection of assessments involved amounted almost literally to peanuts. None of which, however, detracts from the alarming and sinister aspects of the operation.

Almost every organization and citizen, regardless of the size of individual tax bills, exists in fear of the IRS and its periodic special audits. It is an agency whose integrity and independence must never again be subverted for political purposes. Hopefully, that lesson now has been learned.

The Morning Star

Rockford, Ill., November 21, 1974

Yet another sordid mess of the Nixon White House days comes into the public limelight.

Will there be no end to these shocking disclosures of mismanagement from the very top?

This time, it is the Internal Revenue Service (IRS) which is involved.

Documents just released suggest that under a Nixon directive the IRS went well beyond its mandate to collect taxes and help see that federal tax laws were enforced.

Ralph Nader's Tax Reform Research Group — rather than the Watergate investigators — brought the latest events to light.

After more than a year of formal requests and a recent court action, IRS released its investigative documents on more than 11,000 individuals and organizations suspected of being "ideological, militant, subversive and radical."

Even the long-delayed IRS release contained 99 blanked-out organization names. Acting under the Freedom of Information Act, Nader's group sprung loose the complete data.

It was then revealed that among the 99 groups not originally identified by IRS agents were the National Council of Churches, the John Birch Society, and the Urban League.

IRS concluded after halting its investigatory project that only 22 per cent of all individuals and groups investigated were worth following up for tax purposes.

The special investigation unit operated from July, 1969, until late 1973.

What happened in the IRS probe is simply another example of the brutal vindictiveness of the Nixon administration.

Index

This index includes references to information in the news digest and in the editorials. Index entries referring to the news digest can be identified by a marginal letter identification, e.g. 31C3, page 31, section C, column 3. Editorial references have no identification other than the page number, e.g. 18, page 18. In both cases the date of the event is given when possible, e.g. 9-8-75, September 8, 1975.